A Review of the Events of 1989

The 1990 World Book Year Book

The Annual Supplement to The World Book Encyclopedia

World Book, Inc.

a Scott Fetzer company

Chicago London Sydney Toronto

Printed in the United States of America.
ISBN 0-7166-0490-6
ISSN 0084-1439
Library of Congress Catalog Card Number: 62-4818

Staff

Publisher
William H. Nault

Editor in Chief
Robert O. Zeleny

Executive Editor
A. Richard Harmet

Editorial
Managing Editor
Wayne Wille

Associate Editor
Sara Dreyfuss

Senior Editors
David L. Dreier
Robin Goldman
Jinger Hoop
Mary A. Krier
Barbara A. Mayes
Jay Myers
Rod Such

Contributing Editors
Joan Stephenson
Darlene R. Stille

Senior Indexer
Claire Bolton

Staff Indexer
David Pofelski

Statistical Editor
Tom Klonoski

Editorial Assistant
Ethel Matthews

Art
Art Director
Alfred de Simone

Senior Artist, Year Book
Nikki Conner

Senior Artists
Melanie J. Lawson
Lucy Smith

Contributing Artist
Brenda Tropinski

Photographs
Photography Director
John S. Marshall

Senior Photographs Editor
Sandra M. Dyrlund

Photographs Editor
Geralyn Swietek

Product Production
Executive Director
Peter Mollman

Director of Manufacturing
Henry Koval

Manufacturing, Manager
Sandra Van den Broucke

Pre-Press Services
Jerry Stack, Director
Barbara Podczerwinski
Madelyn Underwood

Proofreaders
Anne Dillon
Marguerite Hoye
Daniel Marotta

Research Services
Director
Mary Norton

Researcher
Karen McCormack

Library Services
Bruce McGregor, Head

Cartographic Services
H. George Stoll, Head
Wayne K. Pichler

Contents

See page 16.

See page 71.

See page 96.

4

A tear-out page of cross-reference tabs for insertion in *The
World Book Encyclopedia* appears after page 544.

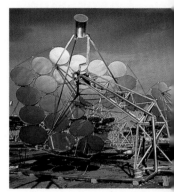

See page 119.

See page 277.

See page 545.

Contributors

Contributors not listed on these pages are members of *The World Book Year Book* editorial staff.

Acorn, Linda R., B.A.; Assistant Editor, American Correctional Association. [Prison]

Alexander, David T., B.Sc., M.A.; Executive Director, Numismatic Literary Guild. [Coin collecting]

Alexiou, Arthur G., B.S.E.E., M.S.E.E.; Assistant Secretary, Committee on Climatic Changes and Ocean. [Ocean]

Andrews, Peter J., B.A., M.S.; free-lance writer; biochemist. [Chemistry]

Apseloff, Marilyn Fain, B.A., M.A.; Associate Professor of English, Kent State University. [Literature for children]

Barber, Peggy, B.A., M.L.S.; Associate Executive Director for Communications, American Library Association. [Library]

Barnhart, Robert K., B.A.; Editor in Chief, Clarence L. Barnhart, Inc. Coeditor, *The World Book Dictionary.* [Dictionary Supplement: Essay]

Bednarski, P. J., Entertainment Media Business Reporter, *Chicago Sun-Times.* [Television]

Bessman, Jim, free-lance writer. [Popular music]

Blackadar, Alfred K., A.B., Ph.D.; Professor Emeritus, The Pennsylvania State University. [Weather]

Boag, Charles, M.A.; columnist and writer, *The Bulletin* magazine, Australia. [Australia]

Bourne, Eric, columnist, foreign affairs, *The Christian Science Monitor.* [Eastern European country articles]

Bradsher, Henry S., A.B., B.J.; foreign affairs analyst. [Asia and Asian country articles]

Brett, Carlton E., B.A., M.A., Ph.D.; Associate Professor of Geological Sciences, University of Rochester. [Paleontology]

Brodsky, Arthur R., B.A., M.S.J.; Senior Editor, *Communications Daily.* [Communications]

Brown, Les, B.A.; Publisher, *Television Business International* magazine. [Special Report: New Choices for TV Viewers]

Campbell, Geoffrey A., B.J.; staff reporter, *The Bond Buyer.* [Civil rights]

Campbell, Linda P., B.A., M.S.L.; national legal affairs correspondent, *Chicago Tribune.* [Civil rights]

Campbell, Robert, B.A., M.S.J., M. Arch.; architecture critic, *The Boston Globe.* [Architecture]

Campion, Owen F., A.B.; Associate Publisher, *Our Sunday Visitor* magazine. [Religion; Roman Catholic Church]

Cardinale, Diane P., B.A.; Assistant Communications Director, Toy Manufacturers of America. [Toys and games]

Commins, Stephen K., B.A., M.Div., Ph.D.; President, Immaculate Heart College Center. [World Book Supplement: Tanzania]

Cormier, Frank, B.S.J., M.S.J.; former White House Correspondent, Associated Press. [U.S. government articles]

Cormier, Margot, B.A., M.A.; free-lance writer. [U.S. government articles]

Cromie, William J., B.S., M.S.; science/medical writer, Harvard University. [Space exploration]

Dalziel, Ian W. D., B.S., Ph.D.; Professor of Geological Sciences, University of Texas at Austin. [Special Report: The Last Unspoiled Continent]

Davidson, Roger H., B.A., Ph.D.; Professor of Government and Politics, University of Maryland. [Congress of the United States (Close-Up)]

DeFrank, Thomas M., B.A., M.A.; White House correspondent, *Newsweek* magazine. [Armed forces]

Dent, Thomas H., B.S.; Executive Director, The Cat Fanciers' Association, Inc. [Cat]

Dirda, Michael, B.A., M.A., Ph.D.; writer and editor, *The Washington Post Book World.* [Poetry]

Dugas, Christine, B.S., M.A.; Marketing and Retailing Reporter, *New York Newsday.* [Advertising]

Ellis, Gavin, Features Editor, *New Zealand Herald.* [New Zealand]

Elsasser, Glen R., B.A., M.S.; correspondent, *Chicago Tribune.* [Supreme Court of the United States]

Evans, Sandra, B.S.J.; staff writer, *The Washington Post.* [Washington, D.C.]

Fanning, Odom, A.B.; free-lance science writer. [Consumerism; Safety]

Farr, David M. L., M.A., D.Phil.; Professor Emeritus, Carleton University, Ottawa. [Canada; Canadian province articles; Mulroney, Brian; Sauvé, Jeanne M.]

Fisher, Robert W., B.A., M.A.; Senior Economist/Editor, U.S. Bureau of Labor Statistics. [Labor]

Fitchett, Joseph, B.A., M.A.; Political Correspondent, *International Herald Tribune.* [Europe and Western European country articles]

Fitzgerald, Mark, B.A.; Midwest Editor, *Editor & Publisher* magazine. [Newspaper]

Galvan, Manuel P., B.A.; Editorial Board member, *Chicago Tribune.* [World Book Supplement: Hispanic Americans]

Gatty, Bob, editor, Periodicals News Service. [Food]

Goldman, Marshall I., B.S., M.A., Ph.D.; Professor of Economics, Wellesley College; Associate Director, Russian Research Center, Harvard University. [Special Report: Opening a Closed Society]

Goldner, Nancy, B.A.; dance critic, *The Philadelphia Inquirer.* [Dancing]

Gordon, Arnold L., Ph.D.; Professor, Columbia University. [World Book Supplement; Ocean]

Gubser, Peter, B.A., M.A., D.Phil; President, American Near East Refugee Aid. [World Book Supplement: Jordan]

Harakas, Stanley Samuel, B.A., B.D., Th.D.; Archbishop Iakovos Professor of Orthodox Theology, Holy Cross Greek Orthodox School of Theology. [Eastern Orthodox Churches]

Haverstock, Nathan A., A.B.; Affiliate Scholar, Oberlin College. [Latin America and Latin-American country articles]

Hawkins, William J., Senior Editor, *Popular Mechanics* magazine. [Special Report: Tuning in Tomorrow]

Heartney, Eleanor, M.A.; free-lance art critic. [Art]

Herreid, Clyde Freeman, A.B., M.Sc., Ph.D.; Distinguished Professor of Biology, State University of New York at Buffalo. [Zoology]

Higgins, James V., B.A.; auto industry reporter, *The Detroit News.* [Automobile]

Hillgren, Sonja, B.J., M.A.; Washington Correspondent, Knight-Ridder Newspapers. [Farm and farming]

Holden, Constance, B.A.; Senior Staff Writer, *Science* magazine. [Special Report: Double Features]

Hunzeker, Jeanne M., D.S.W.; Professor and Associate Dean, Southern University at New Orleans. [Child welfare]

Ifill, Gwen, B.A.; reporter, *The Washington Post.* [Special Report: No Place to Call Home]

Inder, Stuart, former Editor and Publisher, *Pacific Islands Year Book.* [Pacific Islands]

6

Jacobi, Peter P., B.S.J., M.S.J.; Professor of Journalism, Indiana University. **[Classical music]**

Johanson, Donald C., B.S., M.A., Ph.D.; Director, Institute of Human Origins. **[Anthropology]**

Karey, Gerald, B.A., M.A.; Bureau Chief, *Platt's Oilgram News.* **[Environmental pollution (Close-Up)]**

King, Elliot W., Editor, *The Optical and Magnetic Report* magazine. **[Computer]**

Kisor, Henry, B.A., M.S.J.; Book Editor, *Chicago Sun-Times.* **[Literature]**

Knapp, Elaine Stuart, B.A.; Director, Information Products, Council of State Governments. **[State government]**

Knight, Paul G., B.S., M.S.; Instructor, Producer-WPSX/TV, The Pennsylvania State University. **[Weather]**

Kolgraf, Ronald, B.A., M.A.; Publisher, *Adweek* magazine. **[Manufacturing]**

Larsen, Paul A., P.E., B.S., Ch.E.; member: American Philatelic Society; Collectors Club of Chicago; Fellow, Royal Philatelic Society, London; past President, British Caribbean Philatelic Study Group. **[Stamp collecting]**

Lawrence, Al, B.A., M.A., M.Ed.; Executive Director, United States Chess Federation. **[Chess]**

Lawrence, Richard, B.E.E.; International Economics Correspondent, *The Journal of Commerce.* **[International trade]**

Leff, Donna Rosene, B.S.J., M.S.J., M.P.P., Ph.D.; Associate Professor of Journalism and Urban Affairs, Northwestern University. **[City]**

Levi, Charles S., M.A.H.L.; Rabbi, Lakeside Congregation for Reform Judaism. **[Jews and Judaism]**

Levine, Martin, former Editor, *Consumer Electronics Monthly* magazine; free-lance electronics writer. **[Electronics]**

Lewis, David C., M.D.; Director, Center for Alcohol and Addiction Studies, Brown University. **[Drug abuse]**

Liebenow, Beverly B., B.A.; author and free-lance writer. **[Africa and African country articles]**

Liebenow, J. Gus, B.A., M.A., Ph.D.; Rudy Professor of Political Science and African Studies, Indiana University. **[Africa and African country articles]**

Litsky, Frank, B.S.; sportswriter, *The New York Times.* **[Sports articles]**

Maki, John M., B.A., M.A., Ph.D.; Professor Emeritus, University of Massachusetts. **[Japan]**

Maran, Stephen P., B.S., M.A., Ph.D.; Senior Staff Scientist, National Aeronautics and Space Administration-Goddard Space Flight Center. **[Astronomy]**

March, Robert H., Ph.D.; Professor of Physics, University of Wisconsin. **[Physics; Special Report: The Coming Energy Squeeze]**

Marty, Martin E., Ph.D.; Fairfax M. Cone Distinguished Service Professor, University of Chicago. **[Protestantism]**

Mather, Ian J., B.A., M.A.; Defence Correspondent, *The Observer,* London. **[Great Britain; Ireland; Northern Ireland]**

Maugh, Thomas H., II, Ph.D.; science writer, *Los Angeles Times.* **[Biology]**

McCarron, John F., B.S.J., M.S.J.; urban affairs writer, *Chicago Tribune.* **[Chicago]**

McGinley, Laurie, B.S.J.; reporter, *The Wall Street Journal.* **[Aviation; Railroad]**

McGraw, Bill, City-County Bureau Chief, *Detroit Free Press.* **[Detroit]**

Merina, Victor, A.A., B.A., M.S.; staff writer, *Los Angeles Times.* **[Los Angeles]**

Moores, Eldridge M., B.S., Ph.D.; Professor and Chair, Department of Geology, University of California at Davis. **[Geology]**

Moritz, Owen, B.A.; Urban Affairs Editor, New York *Daily News.* **[New York City]**

Morris, Bernadine, B.A., M.A.; Chief Fashion Writer, *The New York Times.* **[Fashion]**

Newcomb, Eldon H., A.B., A.M., Ph.D.; Folke Skoog Professor, Department of Botany, University of Wisconsin-Madison. **[Botany]**

Nguyen, J. Tuyet, B.A.; United Nations Correspondent, United Press International. **[United Nations]**

Petersen, Clarence G., B.A.; feature writer, *Chicago Tribune.* **[Television (Close-Up)]**

Platiel, Rudy, reporter, *The Globe and Mail,* Toronto. **[Indian, American]**

Priestaf, Iris, B.A., M.A., Ph.D.; Geographer and Vice President, David Keith Todd Consulting Engineers. **[Water]**

Raloff, Janet, B.S.J., M.S.J.; Environment/Policy Editor, *Science News* magazine. **[Environmental pollution]**

Reinken, Charles, B.B.A., M.A.; Associate Editor, *The Houston Post.* **[Houston]**

Roccaforte, Sharon, B.A.; Director, Information Service, Magazine Publishers of America. **[Magazine]**

Scanlan, Larry, B.A.; free-lance editor, Ontario. **[Canadian literature]**

Shapiro, Howard S., B.S.; Editor, *Weekend Magazine, The Philadelphia Inquirer.* **[Philadelphia]**

Shewey, Don, B.F.A.; Arts Editor, *7 Days* magazine. **[Theater]**

Siegel, Kenneth L., A.B., D.D.S.; dentist. **[Dentistry]**

Smerk, George M., B.S., M.B.A., D.B.A.; Professor of Transportation, School of Business, Indiana University. **[Transit]**

Spencer, William, A.B., A.M., Ph.D.; writer; former Professor of History, Florida State University. **[Middle East and Middle Eastern country articles; North Africa country articles]**

Stein, David Lewis, B.A., M.A.; author; journalist, *The Toronto Star.* **[Toronto]**

Swanton, Donald W., B.S., M.S., Ph.D., M.B.A.; Chairman, Department of Finance, Roosevelt University. **[Bank; Economics; Stocks and bonds]**

Toch, Thomas, B.A.; free-lance journalist. **[Education]**

Trotter, Robert J., B.S.; Contributing Editor, *Psychology Today* magazine. **[Psychology]**

Tuchman, Janice Lyn, B.S., M.S.J.; Managing Senior Editor, *Engineering News-Record.* **[Building and construction]**

Vesley, Roberta, A.B., M.L.S.; Library Director, American Kennel Club. **[Dog]**

Voorhies, Barbara, B.S., Ph.D.; Professor of Anthropology, University of California at Santa Barbara. **[Archaeology]**

Walter, Eugene J., Jr., B.A.; Director of Publications and Editor in Chief, New York Zoological Society. **[Conservation; Zoos; Special Report: Saving Our Big Birds]**

Windeyer, Kendal, President, Windeyer Associates, Montreal, Canada. **[Montreal]**

Woods, Michael, B.S.; Science Editor. *The Toledo Blade.* **[Industry articles and health articles]**

Wuntch, Philip, B.A.; film critic, *Dallas Morning News.* **[Deaths (Close-Up); Motion pictures]**

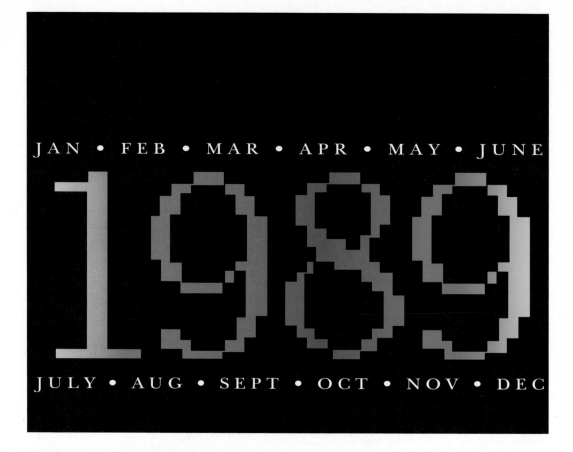

JAN • FEB • MAR • APR • MAY • JUNE

JULY • AUG • SEPT • OCT • NOV • DEC

The Year in Brief

A short essay captures the spirit of 1989,
and a month-by-month listing highlights
some of the year's significant events.

Chopping away in November
at the Berlin Wall. ▶

Hundreds of thousands
of protesters pack
Wenceslas Square in
Prague, Czechoslovakia,
during one of the many
antigovernment demon-
strations in late 1989
that won the Czechoslo-
vaks new freedoms.

The world watched with a mixture of amazement, joy, relief—
and some apprehension—as the Iron Curtain began to fall apart
in 1989. Hungary and Poland, Communist nations in January,
were well on their way to becoming multiparty democracies by
October. East Germany, scrambling to stem the tide of its citizens fleeing to the West, introduced limited democratic reforms
and then—in one surprising week in November—started to dismantle the Berlin Wall. Television cameras relayed the scene
throughout the world as Berliners celebrated throughout days
and nights at the wall. Some used chisels or picks to chip away
pieces of the hated barrier, for almost 30 years the symbol of the
separation between East and West.

Signs of change also appeared in two of the hardest of the
hard-line Communist nations. Bulgaria's long-time leader, Todor
Zhivkov, stepped down, and the new Communist Party leader
pledged to speed reforms. In the face of widespread demonstrations, Czechoslovakia's party leader also resigned, and the country's parliament repealed clauses in the Constitution giving the
Communist Party a guaranteed "leading role" in the government
and establishing Marxism-Leninism as the state ideology.

Eastern Europe's move toward democracy was so unexpected
and so rapid that no one could judge how the political and economic changes it brings will affect not only the East, but also the
West. Nor was there the certainty that the reforms would be
permanent. Indeed, China's Communist government responded
to its citizens' call for democratic reforms with a brutal crackdown in June that left hundreds, perhaps thousands, dead. One
thing was certain, however: The events of 1989 were cause for
hope—and they brought East and West closer than at any other
time in the past 40 years.   *The Editors*

A jubilant Tadeusz Mazowiecki waves to supporters after his August election as Poland's first non-Communist prime minister since the end of World War II.

Happy Berliners party at—and on—the Berlin Wall in November after East Germany opens the hated barrier that divided the city for 28 years.

January						
1	2	3	4	5	6	7
8	9	10	11	12	13	14
15	16	17	18	19	20	21
22	23	24	25	26	27	28
29	30	31				

2　Prime Minister Ranasinghe Premadasa takes office as president of Sri Lanka.

4　United States Navy fighter planes shoot down two Libyan fighter jets over the Mediterranean Sea.

7　Japan's Emperor Hirohito dies, and Crown Prince Akihito assumes the throne.

10　Cuban soldiers begin to withdraw from Angola under a peace agreement signed in December 1988.

Harris Trust and Savings Bank of Chicago agrees to provide $14 million in back pay to women and minority employees in the largest such settlement obtained by the federal government from a single employer.

11　President of the United States Ronald Reagan delivers his farewell address to the nation.

The National Collegiate Athletic Association (NCAA) approves a new rule called Proposition 42 that ends athletic scholarships to freshmen who do not meet minimum academic standards.

12　President-elect George Bush completes his Cabinet, naming retired Admiral James D. Watkins as secretary of energy. Bush also picks former Secretary of Education William J. Bennett to head the new Office of National Drug Control Policy.

13　Bernhard H. Goetz is sentenced to one year in jail and fined $5,000 for illegal gun possession in the 1984 shooting of four young men he said were trying to rob him on a New York City subway train.

15　Thirty-five European nations pledge in Vienna, Austria, to strengthen human-rights safeguards and improve East-West trade.

16　The fatal shooting of a black motorcyclist by a Hispanic policeman in Miami, Fla., triggers two nights of arson, looting, and violence in the city's mostly black Overtown and Liberty City neighborhoods.

17　A gunman identified as Patrick E. Purdy shoots five children to death at a Stockton, Calif., elementary school before killing himself.

18　The U.S. Republican National Committee elects Lee Atwater as its chairman.

19　Ante Marković, a Croatian reformer, is appointed Federal Executive Council President (premier) of Yugoslavia, succeeding Branko Mikulić.

20　George Bush takes office as the 41st President of the United States.

22　The San Francisco 49ers win football's Super Bowl XXIII, defeating the Cincinnati Bengals 20-16.

23　A powerful earthquake in the Soviet republic of Tajikistan kills about 275 people.

23-24　Armed civilian leftists attack and briefly hold an Argentine army base near Buenos Aires.

24　Convicted killer Ted Bundy, who had confessed to more than 20 murders, is executed in Florida's electric chair.

30　New York City lawyer Joel B. Steinberg is found guilty of manslaughter in the beating death of Lisa Steinberg, a 6-year-old child he was raising. He is sentenced on March 24 to 8⅓ to 25 years in prison.

Canada's Prime Minister Brian Mulroney shuffles his cabinet, appointing 6 new ministers and changing the responsibilities of 19 others.

▲

Wide receiver Jerry Rice of the San Francisco 49ers celebrates his game-winning touchdown in Super Bowl XXIII on January 22. The 49ers defeated the Cincinnati Bengals 20 to 16.

▲ Cars ignited by rioters burn on a Miami, Fla., street after racial conflict prompted by a shooting on January 16 erupts into violence.

◀ Hours after being sworn in as President of the United States, George Bush dances with his wife, Barbara, at an Inaugural Ball on January 20.

13

February						
			1	2	3	4
5	6	7	8	9	10	11
12	13	14	15	16	17	18
19	20	21	22	23	24	25
26	27	28				

2 Carlos Andrés Pérez takes office as president of Venezuela.

Japan's Prime Minister Noboru Takeshita meets with President Bush in Washington, D.C., the first foreign leader to do so since the new President took office.

3 Paraguay's long-time dictator President Alfredo Stroessner is ousted in a military coup led by General Andrés Rodríguez Pedotti.

6 The Polish government and leaders of the Solidarity union hold their first formal meeting since the government tried to crush the union in 1981.

7 Congress votes to reject a proposed 51 per cent pay raise for its members, federal judges, and certain other high-level officials.

9 The socialist party of Jamaica's former Prime Minister Michael Manley wins parliamentary elections. Manley is sworn in as prime minister on February 13.

10 The Democratic National Committee elects Ronald H. Brown, a Washington, D.C., lawyer, as its chairman, making him the first black to head a major American political party.

Bush meets with Prime Minister Mulroney in Ottawa, Canada, and pledges legislation to reduce acid rain.

11 Barbara C. Harris becomes the first woman bishop of the Anglican Communion, which includes the Episcopal Church in the United States.

14 Union Carbide Corporation agrees to pay $470-million to compensate victims of the 1984 poison-gas catastrophe in Bhopal, India.

Iran's supreme leader, Ayatollah Ruhollah Khomeini, orders Muslims to kill Salman Rushdie, author of *The Satanic Verses,* a novel Khomeini calls blasphemous.

15 Soviet troops complete their withdrawal from Afghanistan as called for under a United Nations-negotiated agreement signed in 1988.

Sri Lanka's ruling United National Party wins 125 of 225 seats in the nation's first parliamentary elections since 1977, after a violence-marred campaign in which more than 1,000 people were killed.

19 South African police raid the home of antiapartheid leader Winnie Mandela and arrest four of her bodyguards, two of whom are later charged with the murder of a 14-year-old boy.

20 The ruling New Democratic Party narrowly wins reelection in Canada's Yukon Territory, taking nine seats in the territorial legislature to the Progressive Conservatives' seven.

23-27 President Bush travels to Japan, China, and South Korea, attending the funeral of Emperor Hirohito and meeting with Chinese leader Deng Xiaoping and South Korean President Roh Tae Woo.

24 Hirohito's funeral in Tokyo draws leaders from over 160 nations and 27 international organizations.

26 A report on TV's "60 Minutes" charges that apples sprayed with the growth-regulating agent Alar (daminozide) may cause cancer in children, leading many schools to remove apples from their cafeterias.

27 Riots break out over price hikes in Venezuela. About 300 people die in the disturbances, which last until March 1.

14

◀ Soviet army troops complete their pullout from Afghanistan on February 15 under the terms of a 1988 treaty.

An imperial guard escorts the bier of Japan's Emperor Hirohito at his February 24 funeral. The emperor died of cancer on January 7.
▼

March						
			1	2	3	4
5	6	7	8	9	10	11
12	13	14	15	16	17	18
19	20	21	22	23	24	25
26	27	28	29	30	31	

3 Former National Security Adviser Robert C. Mc-Farlane is given two years' probation and fined $20,000 for misleading Congress about the Iran-contra affair.

4 Eastern Airlines' machinists and baggage workers, supported by pilots and flight attendants, walk off the job to protest pay cuts. The airline files for bankruptcy protection on March 9.

Time Incorporated and Warner Communications Incorporated announce that they will merge to form the world's largest communications company, to be called Time Warner Incorporated.

9 The Senate votes 53 to 47 to reject former Senator John G. Tower as secretary of defense. The next day, Bush nominates Representative Richard B. Cheney (R., Wyo.) to the post. Cheney is confirmed and sworn in on March 17.

13-17 The U.S. Food and Drug Administration orders Chilean fruit detained at U.S. ports after finding traces of cyanide in two grapes from Chile.

13-18 The space shuttle *Discovery* launches a tracking and data-relay satellite and conducts a battery of scientific experiments.

15 Israel hands over to Egypt the seaside resort of Taba, ending a seven-year territorial dispute.

16 The Soviet Communist Party Central Committee approves agricultural reforms that give Soviet farmers the right to lease state-owned land for life.

19 Alfredo Cristiani Burkard of the right wing National Republican Alliance is elected president of El Salvador. He takes office on June 1.

21 Congress passes a revised bill to protect the jobs of "whistle blowers"—federal employees who expose government waste or fraud. Bush signs the bill into law on April 10.

22 Pete Rozelle, National Football League (NFL) commissioner since 1960, announces that he will step down when a replacement is found.

A. Brian Peckford resigns as premier of Newfoundland, Canada, and is succeeded by Thomas Rideout.

23 Chemists at the University of Utah in Salt Lake City claim that they have produced controlled nuclear fusion at room temperature, a process that would lead to a safe, clean source of nuclear energy.

23-28 Constitutional changes reducing the self-government of Yugoslavia's Kosovo province trigger six days of ethnic riots among the province's Albanian minority. At least 29 people are killed.

24 The tanker *Exxon Valdez* hits a submerged reef in Prince William Sound, Alaska, and spills an estimated 240,000 barrels of oil into the Pacific Ocean, the worst tanker spill in U.S. history.

26 The Soviet Union holds its first-ever multicandidate elections. Voters reject several top Communist Party officials and elect numerous independent-minded candidates.

29 *Rain Man,* a drama about love between two brothers, wins Academy Awards for best picture, best director, best screenplay, and best actor (for Dustin Hoffman).

▲
Workers attempt to clean an oil-covered Alaskan beach after the tanker *Exxon Valdez* ran aground on March 24 in Prince William Sound. It caused the worst oil spill ever in U.S. waters.

Dustin Hoffman, left, portrays an ▶ autistic man and Tom Cruise plays his brother in the movie *Rain Man,* which won several Academy Awards on March 29.

April						
						1
2	**3**	**4**	**5**	**6**	**7**	**8**
9	**10**	**11**	**12**	**13**	**14**	**15**
16	**17**	**18**	**19**	**20**	**21**	**22**
23	**24**	**25**	**26**	**27**	**28**	**29**
30						

1 **Fighting erupts** between Namibian security forces and black nationalist guerrillas on the day a cease-fire is supposed to begin. Nearly 300 people are killed by April 6.

Sportscaster Bill White takes office as president of baseball's National League, becoming the first black to head a major professional sports league.

2 **A failed coup** in Haiti leads to a standoff between mutinous troops and the government, which does not regain full control until April 10.

3 **The University of Michigan wins** the NCAA men's basketball championship, defeating Seton Hall University 80-79 in overtime.

4 **Richard M. Daley is elected** mayor of Chicago, winning the office held by his father, Richard J. Daley, from 1955 to 1976.

5 **The Polish government** and the Solidarity labor union, outlawed since 1982, sign an agreement restoring Solidarity to legal status and providing for democratic elections in June 1989.

Miners in Virginia and West Virginia go on strike against Pittston Coal Group Incorporated after working 14 months without a contract. By late June, sympathy strikes have idled some 40,000 miners in 10 states.

9 **More than 300,000 demonstrators march** in Washington, D.C., to support legal abortion, the largest women's rights demonstration in U.S. history.

A dispute over grazing rights triggers rioting along the border between the African nations of Senegal and Mauritania in which more than 400 people are killed.

A clash between nationalist demonstrators and government troops causes at least 19 deaths in the Soviet republic of Georgia.

15 **The death of ousted Chinese leader Hu Yaobang** triggers student protests demanding democratic reforms.

Ninety-five fans die as a surging crowd tries to push into a packed soccer stadium in Sheffield, England.

17 **The House Committee** on Standards of Official Conduct charges Speaker of the House James C. Wright, Jr., with violating ethics rules by evading limits on outside income and accepting improper gifts. Wright denies any wrongdoing.

19 **An explosion and fire** on the battleship U.S.S. *Iowa* kills 47 sailors.

20 **The Liberal Party wins** a provincial election in Newfoundland, Canada. Liberal leader Clyde K. Wells takes office as premier on May 5.

24 **Jordan's Prime Minister Zaid Rifa'i resigns** in the wake of riots that began April 18 over government-imposed price hikes. Former armed forces commander Zayd Bin Shakir succeeds Rifa'i on April 27.

25 **Japan's Prime Minister Takeshita** announces that he will resign "to take responsibility" for a stock-trading scandal.

28 **Pope John Paul II begins** a nine-day trip to Africa, during which he visits Madagascar, Zambia, Malawi, and the French island territory of Reunion.

▲
On April 15, 95 soccer fans are crushed to death in an overcrowded stadium in Sheffield, England.

May						
	1	2	3	4	5	6
7	8	9	10	11	12	13
14	15	16	17	18	19	20
21	22	23	24	25	26	27
28	29	30	31			

1 Paraguay's General Rodríguez, who seized power in a February coup, wins by a landslide in a presidential election marked by charges of fraud.

2 The coalition government of Netherlands Prime Minister Ruud Lubbers collapses in a dispute over a pollution cleanup plan.

3 Canada's former Prime Minister John N. Turner announces his resignation as Liberal Party leader.

4 Former White House aide Oliver L. North is found guilty of three criminal charges—obstructing a congressional inquiry, destroying documents, and accepting an illegal gratuity—but is acquitted of nine other charges against him in the Iran-contra case.

The space shuttle *Atlantis* lifts off from Cape Canaveral, Fla., and launches the *Magellan* Venus probe. The shuttle lands at Edwards Air Force Base in California on May 8.

10 Panama's government voids the country's May 7 presidential election, charging foreign interference. Government-organized paramilitary squads attack and beat opposition supporters, who have claimed victory.

11 President Bush orders nearly 1,900 additional U.S. troops to Panama to protect Americans there.

14 Carlos Saúl Menem, political heir of former dictator Juan Perón, sweeps to victory in Argentina's presidential election. Menem takes office on July 8.

15-25 A strike by Los Angeles schoolteachers wins more administrative control and a 24 per cent pay increase over three years.

15-18 Soviet leader Mikhail S. Gorbachev visits China for the first summit between the Communist superpowers since 1959. On May 16, the two nations renew normal relations after 30 years of hostility.

17 More than 1 million Chinese students, teachers, and workers march through Beijing to demand greater democracy in the largest antigovernment protest since the Communists came to power in China in 1949.

19 The Dow Jones Industrial Average (the Dow) closes above 2,500 for the first time since the October 1987 stock market crash, ending the day at 2,501.10.

Italy's Prime Minister Ciriaco De Mita resigns.

20 China imposes martial law on Beijing to quiet student protests.

25 The Calgary Flames win hockey's Stanley Cup, defeating the Montreal Canadiens four games to two.

26 Representative Tony Coelho of California, the third-ranking House Democratic leader, resigns, saying he wants to spare his party and his family from a House investigation of his finances.

29 Argentina declares a nationwide state of siege to combat food riots and looting set off by inflation.

Kremlin rebel Boris N. Yeltsin gains a seat in the Supreme Soviet after a member withdraws in his favor.

The ruling Liberal Party of Prince Edward Island, Canada, wins a decisive victory in provincial elections.

30 The North Atlantic Treaty Organization (NATO) agrees to talks with the Soviet Union on a reduction of short-range nuclear weapons in Europe.

31 Wright announces his resignation as Speaker of the House after a yearlong ethics investigation.

Speaker of the House James C. Wright, Jr. ▶ (D., Tex.) announces his resignation on May 31 after months of ethics investigations.

Guillermo Ford, a candidate for Panama's vice presidency (far right), flees club-wielding members of a government-sponsored paramilitary force. Ford was attending a rally protesting the government's decision to nullify the May 7 presidential elections, which he and other opposition candidates appeared to win.

▼

June						
				1	2	3
4	5	6	7	8	9	10
11	12	13	14	15	16	17
18	19	20	21	22	23	24
25	26	27	28	29	30	

A Chinese protester seeks cover ▶ after government troops open fire on student-led demonstrators in Beijing's Tiananmen Square on June 4.

1-10 Pope John Paul II visits Norway, Iceland, Finland, Denmark, and Sweden.

2 Japan's Foreign Minister Sosuke Uno succeeds Takeshita as prime minister.

3 Fighting breaks out in the Soviet republic of Uzbek between ethnic Uzbeks and a Turkish minority, causing more than 100 deaths by June 15.

Ayatollah Ruhollah Khomeini, Iran's supreme leader, dies.

4 Chinese troops open fire on prodemocracy demonstrators occupying Beijing's Tiananmen Square, killing at least 700 and possibly 2,000 or more.

A gas pipeline explodes near the Soviet Union's Trans-Siberian Railroad, wrecking two passing trains and causing an estimated 460 deaths.

Jerome Robbins' Broadway, an anthology of hits from past Broadway musicals, wins six Tony Awards.

4, 18 In Poland's first election since 1947 involving opposition candidates, the independent Solidarity movement wins 99 of 100 Senate seats and all of the 161 lower house seats it was allowed to contest.

6 The U.S. House of Representatives elects Thomas S. Foley (D., Wash.) to succeed Wright as Speaker.

13 The Detroit Pistons win the National Basketball Association championship, beating the Los Angeles Lakers in four straight games.

Bush vetoes a minimum-wage bill passed by Congress on May 17, saying the proposed increase to $4.55 an hour was excessive and would cost young people jobs. An effort to override the veto fails the next day.

14 A Titan 4, the largest and most powerful unmanned rocket in the U.S. space fleet, blasts off from Cape Canaveral and launches a military satellite.

15 The Fianna Fáil party of Ireland's Prime Minister Charles Haughey falls short of a majority in parliamentary elections.

18 Greece's Prime Minister Andreas Papandreou and his Panhellenic Socialist Movement (PASOK) lose control of Parliament in elections. Papandreou resigns the next day.

21 The U.S. Supreme Court rules that burning the American flag as a political protest is protected by the First Amendment.

23 The film *Batman* opens and quickly sets box-office records, earning more than $40 million its first weekend.

23-24 Three shipping accidents within a 12-hour period create oil spills in Rhode Island, Delaware, and Texas.

24 China's Communist Party ousts reformist General Secretary Zhao Ziyang and replaces him with hard-liner Jiang Zemin.

26 The U.S. Supreme Court rules that states may execute murderers as young as 16 or those who are mentally retarded.

27 A federal appeals court overturns the February 1988 conviction of former White House political director Lyn Nofziger for illegal lobbying.

30 A military coup ousts the civilian government of Sudan's Prime Minister Al-Sadiq Al-Mahdi.

Distraught Iranians mourn the June 3 death of their supreme leader, the Ayatollah Ruhollah Khomeini.
▼

22

Michael Keaton as Batman, left, ▶
confronts Jack Nicholson as The
Joker in the summer movie blockbuster *Batman*.

July						
						1
2	3	4	5	6	7	8
9	10	11	12	13	14	15
16	17	18	19	20	21	22
23	24	25	26	27	28	29
30	31					

Soviet coal miners go on strike in July to demand more ▶ autonomy, higher pay, and better working conditions.

1   Greece's Communists and conservatives form a short-term coalition government to investigate the country's financial scandals. Conservative Tzannis Tzannetakis takes office as prime minister the next day and resigns on October 7.
3   The Supreme Court of the United States upholds the right to an abortion but gives the states new authority to restrict the procedure.
5   South African State President Pieter Willem Botha and imprisoned antiapartheid leader Nelson R. Mandela meet face to face for the first time.
Oliver North is fined $150,000, given a three-year suspended prison sentence and two years probation, and ordered to provide 1,200 hours of community service for his crimes in the Iran-contra affair.
6   A Palestinian grabs the steering wheel of an Israeli commuter bus and sends it hurtling into a ravine near Jerusalem, killing 16 passengers.
9   Tennis players Steffi Graf and Boris Becker of West Germany win singles titles at Wimbledon.
9-12   President Bush visits Poland and Hungary before traveling to Paris for an economic summit.
10   Siberian coal miners demanding better living conditions and less bureaucracy begin a strike that develops into the worst Soviet labor unrest since the 1920's, involving about 300,000 miners.
11   Legendary British actor Laurence Olivier dies.
12   Ireland's Prime Minister Haughey is reelected after his Fianna Fáil party forms a coalition with a small conservative party.
14   Parades, fireworks, and dancing in the streets mark the 200th anniversary of the French Revolution.
14-16   Leaders of Canada, France, Great Britain, Italy, Japan, the United States, and West Germany hold an economic summit in Paris.
17   The B-2 Stealth bomber, designed to evade enemy radar, makes its maiden flight.
19   A United Airlines jetliner crashes while trying to make an emergency landing in Sioux City, Iowa, killing 112 of the 296 people aboard.
Poland's National Assembly elects General Wojciech Jaruzelski to the new, powerful post of president.
21   The Dow closes above 2,600 for the first time since the 1987 crash, ending the day at 2,607.36.
23   Japan's ruling Liberal Democratic Party, hurt by sex and influence-peddling scandals, suffers its worst election setback in 34 years, losing control of the upper house of parliament. Prime Minister Uno says he will resign to take responsibility for the loss.
Giulio Andreotti takes office as Italy's prime minister.
28   Iranian voters overwhelmingly elect parliamentary speaker Ali Akbar Hashemi Rafsanjani to the presidency and endorse constitutional changes that increase the power of his office.
31   Muslim extremists in Lebanon say they have hanged a U.S. hostage, Marine Lieutenant Colonel William R. Higgins, in retaliation for Israel's July 28 kidnapping of a Hezbollah leader.

France celebrates the bicentennial of the French Revolution with fireworks at the Arc de Triomphe on July 14.
▼

August						
		1	**2**	**3**	**4**	**5**
6	**7**	**8**	**9**	**10**	**11**	**12**
13	**14**	**15**	**16**	**17**	**18**	**19**
20	**21**	**22**	**23**	**24**	**25**	**26**
27	**28**	**29**	**30**	**31**		

2 Canada's Consumer and Corporate Affairs Minister Bernard Valcourt steps down after being convicted of drunken driving.

5 Congress passes a $166-billion bailout, the largest in U.S. history, that provides funds to close and merge failing savings and loan institutions and overhauls regulation of the industry. Bush signs the bill into law on August 9.

Jaime Paz Zamora, a former Marxist, is elected president of Bolivia and takes office the next day.

7 A plane carrying U.S. Representative Mickey Leland (D., Tex.) and 15 other people crashes on a tour of refugee camps in Ethiopia, killing all aboard.

The presidents of five Central American countries agree that the U.S.-backed *contra* rebels fighting the government of Nicaragua should be disbanded and evicted from their bases in Honduras by December 5.

8 New Zealand Prime Minister David R. Lange resigns for health reasons and is succeeded by Deputy Prime Minister Geoffrey W. R. Palmer.

8-13 The space shuttle *Columbia* carries out a secret military mission and launches a spy satellite.

9 Toshiki Kaifu, a former education minister, becomes prime minister of Japan, replacing Uno.

10 Bush nominates U.S. Army General Colin L. Powell as chairman of the Joint Chiefs of Staff. He is the first black to hold the highest U.S. military post.

14 Botha resigns as president of South Africa, complaining of lack of support from his Cabinet. Education Minister Frederick Willem de Klerk becomes acting president the next day.

19 Poland's President Jaruzelski names Solidarity official Tadeusz Mazowiecki as Poland's first non-Communist prime minister since 1945.

19-21 Colombian authorities arrest more than 11,000 suspected drug traffickers in response to the murder of a judge, a provincial police chief, and a presidential candidate who campaigned against drug lords.

22 Nolan Ryan of the Texas Rangers becomes the first pitcher in baseball to get 5,000 strikeouts.

23 As many as 1 million people in Estonia, Latvia, and Lithuania link hands in a human chain to protest 50 years of Soviet rule.

24 Colombia's cocaine traffickers declare "total and absolute war" against the government and begin a series of bombings and arson attacks.

The *Voyager 2* spacecraft makes its closest approach to Neptune, coming within 3,000 miles (4,800 kilometers) of the planet.

Cincinnati Reds Manager Pete Rose is banished for life from baseball for gambling, though he denies betting on baseball games.

The Dow reaches a record high for the first time since the 1987 crash, ending the day at 2,734.64.

27 A Delta rocket owned by the McDonnell Douglas Corporation launches a television satellite. It is the first time that a privately owned rocket orbits a payload.

31 Libya and Chad end a 15-year conflict by agreeing to let the World Court decide ownership of the Aozou Strip, a region occupied by Libya since 1973.

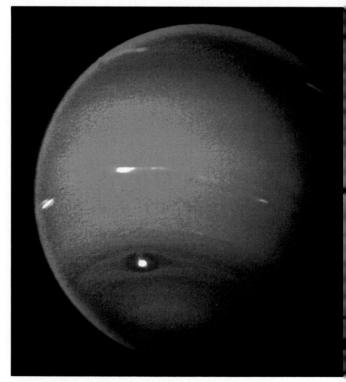

▲
A false-color photograph of Neptune is transmitted to Earth from the unmanned space probe *Voyager 2* in August.

Protesting 50 years of Soviet ▶ rule, up to 1 million citizens of the Soviet republics of Estonia, Latvia, and Lithuania join hands on August 23.

September						
					1	**2**
3	**4**	**5**	**6**	**7**	**8**	**9**
10	**11**	**12**	**13**	**14**	**15**	**16**
17	**18**	**19**	**20**	**21**	**22**	**23**
24	**25**	**26**	**27**	**28**	**29**	**30**

Bound for the West, excited East Germans ▶ display their passports. After Hungary opened its border with Austria on September 11, thousands of East German refugees in Hungary were able to travel to the West.

1   Commissioner of Baseball A. Bartlett Giamatti dies of a heart attack. On September 13, club owners elect Francis T. (Fay) Vincent, Jr., to succeed him.

2-3   Violence and looting break out among college students at a fraternity festival in Virginia Beach, Va.

5   Bush, in his first national televised address from the Oval Office, proposes a $7.9-billion program to combat illegal drugs.

6   The centrist Christian Democratic Party of Netherlands Prime Minister Lubbers retains all 54 of its seats in parliamentary elections. Lubbers forms a new center-left coalition government on November 7.

South Africa's governing National Party suffers its worst electoral setback since 1948, losing 30 seats in the House of Assembly but holding on to a majority.

7   The Ethiopian government and Eritrean rebels meet for peace talks in Atlanta, Ga., with former U.S. President Jimmy Carter as intermediary, in an effort to end a civil war that began in 1961.

8   Former President Reagan undergoes surgery to remove fluid on his brain. He makes a quick recovery.

10-11   Norway's ruling Labor Party suffers its worst election setback since 1945, losing eight seats in parliamentary elections.

11   Hungary opens its border with Austria. By the end of the month, more than 24,000 East Germans who had been waiting in Hungary leave for the West.

17-22   Hurricane Hugo, the most powerful hurricane in a decade, rakes the Caribbean and the Southeastern United States, causing at least 71 deaths and an estimated $8 billion in damage.

19   The Roman Catholic Church calls for removal of a convent near the former Nazi death camp at Auschwitz, Poland. Many Jewish groups had found the convent's presence there offensive.

A French jetliner explodes in midair over Niger, killing all 171 people aboard. Islamic Jihad, a Muslim extremist group, claims responsibility for the blast.

22   An explosion at a music school for British military recruits in Deal, England, kills 10 people. The Irish Republican Army claims responsibility.

23   A cease-fire in Lebanon halts fierce fighting that had taken more than 900 lives since March.

25   Quebec, Canada, voters reelect the ruling Liberal Party with a large majority.

26   Vietnam says it has completed its withdrawal from Cambodia (formerly Kampuchea) after an 11-year occupation.

27-28   Bush brings together the governors of the 50 U.S. states for an "education summit" at the University of Virginia in Charlottesville.

28   Braniff Incorporated files for bankruptcy for the second time since 1982.

29   Drug agents confiscate 21.4 short tons (19.4 metric tons) of cocaine and more than $12 million in cash at a Los Angeles warehouse in the biggest narcotics seizure on record.

30   Nearly 7,000 East Germans in Prague, Czechoslovakia, are allowed to leave for the West after coming from East Germany on special refugee trains.

Federal agents guard some 20 tons of cocaine—worth at least $2 billion—seized in Los Angeles on September 29 in the largest drug bust on record.
▼

Wrecked boats near Charleston, S.C., mark the path of Hurricane Hugo, which blasted the Caribbean and Southeastern United States in September.

▼

October						
1	2	3	4	5	6	7
8	9	10	11	12	13	14
15	16	17	18	19	20	21
22	23	24	25	26	27	28
29	30	31				

3   Panama's General Manuel Antonio Noriega Morena foils an attempt by junior officers to overthrow him.

4   More than 55,000 machinists go on strike against the Boeing Company. They return to work on November 22 after winning higher pay.

5   The Dalai Lama, Tibet's exiled political and spiritual leader, wins the 1989 Nobel Peace Prize.

A jury in Charlotte, N.C., convicts televangelist Jim Bakker of fraud and conspiracy. He is sentenced on October 24 to 45 years in prison and fined $500,000.

6   Canada's Prime Minister Mulroney nominates Ramon J. Hnatyshyn to succeed Jeanne M. Sauvé as governor general when her term expires in 1990.

7   Hungary's Communist party, the Hungarian Socialist Workers' Party, votes to reorganize as a party of social democrats called the Hungarian Socialist Party.

9   The Dow closes at a record high of 2,791.41.

12   The U.S. Congress passes a bill that makes it a crime to knowingly mutilate, deface, burn, or trample the American flag. Bush lets the bill become law without his signature on October 28.

13   Norwegian Prime Minister Gro Harlem Brundtland, whose Labor Party lost September elections, resigns. Conservative leader Jan P. Syse, heading a center-right coalition, succeeds her on October 16.

The Dow plummets 190.58 points, its biggest one-day drop since the 508.00 plunge on Oct. 19, 1987.

15   Hockey star Wayne Gretzky of the Los Angeles Kings becomes the leading scorer in National Hockey League history, surpassing Gordie Howe's record of 1,850 career *points* (goals plus assists).

17   A deadly earthquake jolts northern California, killing at least 62 people and causing an estimated $7-billion in damage.

18   The space shuttle *Atlantis* launches the plutonium-powered *Galileo* space probe, over the objections of antinuclear activists, on a planned six-year journey to Jupiter.

Hungary's National Assembly approves constitutional changes restoring multiparty democracy. On October 23, Hungary declares itself an independent republic.

East German leader Erich Honecker resigns and is succeeded by Egon Krenz.

20   The U.S. Senate convicts federal Judge Alcee L. Hastings of Florida of perjury and conspiracy to obtain a bribe, removing him from office.

A federal jury in New York City convicts Representative Robert Garcia (D., N.Y.) and his wife, Jane Lee Garcia, of extortion and conspiracy.

25   Congress fails to override Bush's veto of a bill that would have restored federal funding—banned since 1981—of abortions for poor women whose pregnancies result from rape or incest.

26   NFL owners elect lawyer Paul J. Tagliabue to succeed Pete Rozelle as commissioner.

28   The Oakland Athletics win the World Series, beating the San Francisco Giants in four games.

31   Turkey's legislature elects Prime Minister Turgut Özal as president, succeeding Kenan Evren.

▲
Californians carry on rescue operations at a freeway that collapsed when a devastating earthquake hit the state on October 17.

Pitcher Dave Stewart of the ▶ Oakland Athletics hurls his team to a World Series win in October. The Athletics defeated the San Francisco Giants in four straight games.

November						
			1	2	3	4
5	6	7	8	9	10	11
12	13	14	15	16	17	18
19	20	21	22	23	24	25
26	27	28	29	30		

1 Nicaraguan President Daniel Ortega ends a cease-fire with U.S.-backed contra rebels that had been in effect since April 1988.

3 The U.S. Senate convicts District Judge Walter L. Nixon, Jr., of lying under oath to a federal grand jury and removes him from office.

7 David N. Dinkins is elected the first black mayor of New York City, and L. Douglas Wilder wins the governorship of Virginia, becoming the first elected black governor in U.S. history.

East Germany's cabinet resigns in response to huge antigovernment protests and an exodus of East Germans to the West. The next day, the Communist party dismisses its policymaking body, the Politburo, and appoints a smaller Politburo with some reform-minded members.

8 Congress passes legislation raising the minimum wage from $3.35 an hour to $4.25 an hour by April 1991. Bush signs the bill on November 17.

9 East Germany opens the Berlin Wall and the rest of its border with the West, allowing its citizens to travel freely for the first time since the wall was erected in 1961.

10 Todor Zhivkov resigns as Bulgaria's Communist Party leader and is replaced by Foreign Minister Petur Toshev Mladenov.

15 Lech Walesa, leader of Poland's Solidarity movement, addresses a joint session of Congress on his first visit to the United States.

15-16 Tornadoes rake the Eastern United States, killing at least 31 people, including 18 in Huntsville, Ala., and 9 schoolchildren in Newburgh, N.Y.

16 Uniformed men kill six priests, a housekeeper, and her daughter at a Roman Catholic university in San Salvador, El Salvador.

The U.S. House of Representatives passes an ethics and pay bill banning honorariums and increasing lawmakers' salaries to $125,000 by 1991. The next day, the Senate gives itself a smaller increase, to $98,400, but votes to continue accepting honorariums.

21 Namibia's Constituent Assembly, chosen in elections November 7 to 11, begins to draft a constitution for an independent Namibia, due in 1990.

22 Congress repeals the Medicare Catastrophic Coverage Act of 1988 because of senior citizens' complaints about the financing of the program.

The space shuttle *Discovery* lifts off from Cape Canaveral after dark. The shuttle lands on November 27 after completing a secret military mission.

A remote-controlled bomb kills Lebanon's President René Moawad, elected on November 5, and 23 other people. Lebanon's parliament elects Elias Hrawi to succeed Moawad on November 24.

24 Czechoslovakia's Communist Party leaders, including General Secretary Miloš Jakeš, resign after a week of demonstrations demanding free elections and other reforms. Karel Urbanek replaces Jakeš.

29 Rajiv Gandhi resigns as prime minister of India after elections in which his Congress-I Party loses about half of its 415 seats.

▲

Poland's Solidarity leader Lech Walesa flashes the victory sign at his November 15 appearance before the United States Congress, where he spoke about the needs of his newly democratic nation.

Germans throng to the Berlin Wall ▶ after the East German government opened the wall—permitting free travel to the West—on November 9.

32

◀ The space shuttle *Discovery* lifts off from Cape Canaveral, Fla., on November 22 to conduct a secret military mission.

December						
					1	2
3	4	5	6	7	8	9
10	11	12	13	14	15	16
17	18	19	20	21	22	23
24	25	26	27	28	29	30
31						

1   Philippine rebels begin a coup attempt against President Corazon C. Aquino, bombing the presidential compound and seizing several military installations in Manila. They abandon their attempt by December 9.
Soviet President Gorbachev, in a meeting with Pope John Paul II, pledges greater religious freedom for Soviet citizens.
2   The *Solar Maximum Mission* research satellite, launched in 1980, crashes back to earth.
V. P. Singh takes office as prime minister of India.
Taiwan's ruling party, the Kuomintang, suffers its worst election setback in its 40 years in power, winning only about 53 per cent of the popular vote.
2-3   Bush and Gorbachev hold informal shipboard talks at Malta.
3   East Germany's entire Communist party leadership, including Secretary General Egon Krenz, resigns. Krenz also resigns as Council of State chairman on December 6 and is replaced by Manfred Gerlach, the first non-Communist to hold that post.
4   Jordan's Prime Minister Zayd Bin Shakir resigns and is succeeded by Mudar Badran.
6   A gunman, later identified as Marc Lepine, kills 14 women and wounds 13 other people at the University of Montreal, then kills himself, in the worst mass murder in Canadian history.
7   A Miami, Fla., jury convicts police officer William Lozano of manslaughter in the January 16 deaths of a black motorcyclist and his passenger.
Czechoslovakia's Premier Ladislav Adamec resigns. Deputy Premier Marián Čalfa succeeds him on December 10.
Lithuania becomes the first Soviet republic in history to abolish the Communist Party's monopoly on power.
9   East Germany's Communist party elects Gregor Gysi, a reformist, to replace Krenz as party leader.
10   Czechoslovak President Gustáv Husák swears in a new cabinet with a non-Communist majority and resigns immediately afterward.
11   The International Trans-Antarctica Expedition, a group of six explorers from six nations, reaches the South Pole traveling by ski and dog sled.
12   Hotelier Leona Helmsley is sentenced to four years in prison and fined $7.2 million for tax evasion.
14   Patricio Aylwin Azócar, a Christian Democrat, wins Chile's first presidential election since 1970.
16-18   Mail bombings kill a federal judge in Birmingham, Ala., and a lawyer in Savannah, Ga.
17   Fernando Collor de Mello, a centrist, wins Brazil's first direct presidential election since 1960.
20   The United States invades Panama and installs a new government headed by President Guillermo Endara.
22   Romanians oust long-time President Nicolae Ceauşescu, who is convicted of crimes against the nation and executed on December 25.
29   Czechoslovakia's Federal Assembly elects dissident playwright Vaclav Havel as president.

▲
President George Bush waves at reporters before a shipboard meeting with Soviet leader Mikhail S. Gorbachev in Malta on December 2 and 3.

▲
Pope John Paul II gives
Gorbachev a mosaic of Jesus
Christ on the Soviet leader's
first visit to the Vatican,
on December 1.

◀ Government troops in Manila
repel a coup attempt against
Philippine President Aquino
from December 1 through 9.

35

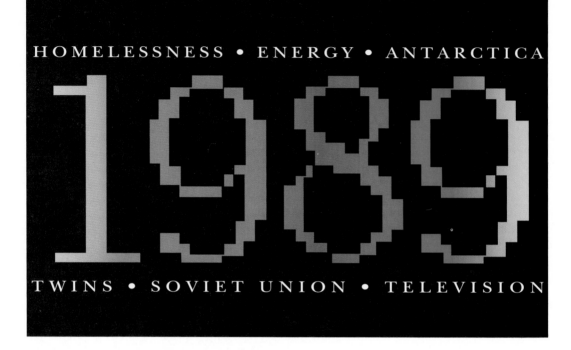

HOMELESSNESS • ENERGY • ANTARCTICA

1989

TWINS • SOVIET UNION • TELEVISION

Special Reports

Six articles and a three-part feature give in-depth treatment to subjects of current importance and lasting interest.

By Eugene J. Walter, Jr.

Saving Our Big Birds

North America has come perilously close
to losing its most majestic birds. But
with a little help from scientists, some of
them are making a comeback.

Glossary

Endangered species: A species that requires immediate protection because its numbers are so small that its extinction is likely.

Fledgling: A young bird that is ready to leave the nest.

Hacking: A technique used to introduce birds into the wild.

Nestling: A bird too young to leave the nest.

Radiotelemetry: A technique in which tiny radio transmitters are attached to animals so their movements can be tracked.

Threatened species: A species whose numbers are more abundant than those of an endangered species but who still runs a serious risk of extinction.

The author:
Eugene J. Walter, Jr., is editor in chief of *Wildlife Conservation* magazine and director of publications at the New York Zoological Society in New York City.

Early morning sun sparkles the surface of a river winding through the Maryland countryside near Chesapeake Bay. High above the river's bank, yellow eyes peer from under the frowning brow of a big, white-headed bird. A ripple in the river catches the bald eagle's attention. It springs from its perch and streaks downward. Just above the water's surface, it brakes its plunge and thrusts its talons underwater. The bird pumps its wings—they span nearly 7 feet (2 meters)—and rises, gripping a helpless, writhing carp.

The feathered hunter flies to a towering pine tree nearby. Sitting in the uppermost branches is a large, twisted nest of tree limbs, twigs, and assorted forest litter. There, the eagle's mate waits with two fuzzy white chicks. The male deposits their fish breakfast and then lifts away toward the river.

The female eagle rips the fish into chunks for her youngsters. She and her mate will spend many years by the bay, raising chicks. Yet only a few years ago, bald eagles—the national bird of the United States—had all but vanished from most states.

Hundreds of miles south, the sun warms billows of mist rising from a marshy peninsula on the Texas coast along the Gulf of Mexico. Two whooping cranes—the tallest birds in North America—stride through the shallows, poking their heads underwater to probe for blue crabs, their favorite food. Occasionally, they stretch upward to their full 5 feet (1.5 meters), peering about anxiously before resuming their search for food. The cranes are feathered in snow-white except for a few black accents, with crimson patches of skin on their heads.

As the sun climbs higher, the whoopers lift their heads and bugle a harsh call that carries for miles across the tidal flats. Extending black-tipped wings a full 7 feet (2 meters), they take off, spiraling upward, their long legs trailing behind. This pair will journey north 2,500 miles (4,000 kilometers) to a Canadian wilderness where groves of pine and spruce mingle with lakes and marshes. The pair will mate and build a nest amid the bulrushes. Their offspring—usually a single chick—will learn to fly within three months. When cold weather sets in, the family will return to Texas. The ability of the chick to survive is critical; few of these majestic whooping cranes survive today.

Far from the cranes' winter home in Texas, an enormous black bird with a featherless, orange-red head perches atop a cliff near the southern California coast. Stretching immense wings, a California condor suns itself.

After a few minutes, the condor folds its wings. It hops to the cliff's edge, and, as it launches into the air, its wings reach out 9½ feet (2.9 meters) and begin flapping. Soon they catch an updraft, which lifts the bird high above the forested valley.

The condor continues gliding, riding air currents that take it almost 8 miles (13 kilometers) without pumping its wings. The feathers near the tips of its wings spread apart like fingers, creating a hissing whistle. This giant bird is shopping for a meal—a

On the endangered list

Only an estimated 220 whooping cranes, *below,* remain in the United States. The outlook for the California condor, *bottom,* is even worse. Just 32 of these birds survive—and only in zoos. After near-extinction, bald eagles, *page 39,* seem to be making a comeback. Experts estimate that more than 50,000 eagles live in the United States and Canada.

freshly killed deer or a stillborn calf. It dips, tracing a wide arc over the pines, but sights nothing promising. It soars over a jagged mountain ridge and out of sight.

Tragically, this scene is merely a memory. California condors—the largest land birds in North America—no longer glide freely through the air. Only 32 remain in the world, in just two zoos. None live in the wild.

Bald eagles, whooping cranes, and California condors are very different in appearance and habits, but they have much in common. Each species exists only in North America, and they are our largest native birds. They also are among the most endangered of North America's vanishing wildlife. And they share the same cause of endangerment—people.

People are directly responsible for the extinction of many wild animals. Some species are hunted until they are extinct. Others are killed off when people destroy their natural habitat to make way for cities and industry. Human beings have also polluted the environment, which has reduced the numbers of many animals.

Nothing can be done about the species that are gone forever. But to help protect the animals that do remain, scientists at the U.S. Fish and Wildlife Service (USFWS) in Washington, D.C., classify those facing possible extinction as either *endangered* or *threatened*. An endangered species is one that requires immediate protection because its numbers are so small that its extinction is likely. A threatened species is usually more abundant, but it still runs a serious risk of extinction.

These three big birds share some biological traits that make them especially vulnerable. One is that they are slow to reproduce. It can take from five to seven years for them to reach sexual maturity. The longer it takes a bird to reach maturity, the greater the risk that it may die before it can reproduce.

Another trait common to these birds is their small number of offspring. Once they mate, they usually lay only one or two eggs at a time—and not always every year. The California condor is the slowest to reproduce. It takes five years or more for a condor to reach breeding age, and then females lay only a single egg. Because a chick depends on its parents for 18 months or longer, a condor pair rears only one offspring every other year. Of these, only about 50 per cent survive. In contrast, an American robin is ready to mate less than a year after it hatches. It nests two or three times a year and lays four eggs each time. The robin's rate of reproduction considerably outpaces that of the condor.

Thousands of years ago, condors flew along the Pacific Coast and across what are now Nevada, Arizona, New Mexico, Texas, and Florida. By the 1800's, their range was limited to the Pacific Coast, and their population was probably fewer than 500.

It was not until 1937 that steps were taken to protect the condor's habitat in California. That year, the Sisquoc Condor Sanctuary was set aside in Los Padres National Forest. More land was added as the Sespe Condor Sanctuary in 1947. California law granted special protection to condors in 1953, and the bird was placed on the first federal endangered species list in 1967. Yet the condors' decline continued. A 1978 survey showed that their population had dwindled to just 25 to 35 birds.

The rapid rise in human population on the West Coast put condors in jeopardy. Initially, the heaviest toll was taken by people hunting them just for sport. Museums also bear part of the responsibility: At least 177 condors and 71 condor eggs were taken for displays. Later, overhead electric power lines aggravated their decline, as many condors died after colliding with the lines.

Diet has also been a big part of the condors' problems. Condors are *carnivores* (meat-eaters). Instead of hunting live prey, they scavenge over vast areas for the bodies of dead animals. According to James W. Wiley, head of the USFWS's condor research program, it appears that lead bullets, which the birds ingested by eating animals killed by hunters, was the real cause of their falling population. Condors, more than other birds, seem susceptible to lead poisoning.

With the species in severe decline, the American Ornithologists' Union, a nonprofit group in Washington, D.C., and the National Audubon Society, a private conservation organization in New York City, appointed a panel of independent experts to review the situation in 1978. The committee recommended more research in the wild, primarily by *radiotelemetry*, a technique in which tiny radio transmitters are attached to the birds so their movements can be tracked. The panel also urged breeding the birds in captivity. The Audubon Society and the USFWS formed a rescue coalition with government agencies, academic institutions, and the zoos in San Diego and Los Angeles.

The recovery program was to begin in 1980, but several local environmental groups protested that capturing condors posed a grave threat to the birds' survival. They insisted that more work be done to protect the condors' habitat. The recovery group argued that such efforts would be futile without more information about the birds. The California Department of Fish and Game issued a permit for the recovery program, and in May 1980, USFWS agents began catching condors and attaching radios to their wings. Only one month later, a condor *nestling* (a bird too young to leave the nest) died, apparently from stress, as researchers were measuring it to gather data on growth rates. The state withdrew its permit, and the opposition renewed its campaign to halt the program. The rescue effort eventually resumed in 1982, and in two years, radio transmitters had yielded more information about condor habits and nesting sites than had been gathered in the preceding 40 years. Armed with this data, the rescue group began removing a few nestlings from the wild to create a captive-breeding flock.

The USFWS also decided to begin removing eggs from California condor nests for captive hatching. The first two eggs were removed in 1983 and flown to the San Diego Zoo, where they were put in an incubator. On March 30, a zookeeper helped a California condor chick emerge from its shell—the first one ever hatched in captivity. A second chick hatched five days later.

Although progress was being made, it was not fast enough. The number of condors in the wild was down to six by 1985. "It looked like there was no hope if the birds were left in the wild," the USWFS's Wiley recalled. "It seemed the only reasonable thing was to bring them in. Most people realize it was the best way, but a few still resisted." The roundup began, and the last condor was captured in 1987.

Since the zoo program began, 13 condors have hatched from eggs collected from the wild, nearly double the number that would have been expected from condors breeding without human aid. Most important, mature birds have been mating, and the first chick bred in captivity hatched in 1988. Four more hatched in 1989, bringing the world population to 32.

The world's remaining California condors are not on public display. They live at the San Diego Wild Animal Park and the Los Angeles Zoo, in enormous aviaries—collectively known as "The Condorminium"—which provide space for them to fly.

While the California condor rescue effort was going on, scientists were also studying Andean condors, the California birds' closest relatives. These South American birds are also endangered, but there are still thousands of them in the wild. In 1989, the condor recovery team began to release Andean condors into the California countryside normally inhabited by the state's native species. The female nestlings—bred in U.S. zoos and at the USFWS's Patuxent Wildlife Research Center in Maryland—were released by a technique known as *hacking*. This calls for chicks to be placed in a cage called a *hacking box*, which sits on a tower or cliff ledge. The box is roomy enough for the birds to exercise their growing wings. Unseen by the birds, a keeper drops food to them down a chute. Once the youngsters become *fledglings* (young birds ready to leave the nest), the door to the box is opened, and they can come and go as they please. The keepers supply the birds with food until they are able to fend for themselves. Biologists are using Andean condors as models to see how California condors may react when they are released. If the Andean condor release is successful, biologists plan to use hacking to return California condors to the wild.

Looking toward a time when a breeding population of condors has been reestablished in California, the recovery committee is considering areas outside the state as possible habitats. High on

Where the birds are

California condors, whooping cranes, and bald eagles were once a familiar sight in many parts of North America. But destruction of their natural habitat and diminishing flocks have reduced their range. The map below shows their approximate range in 1989.

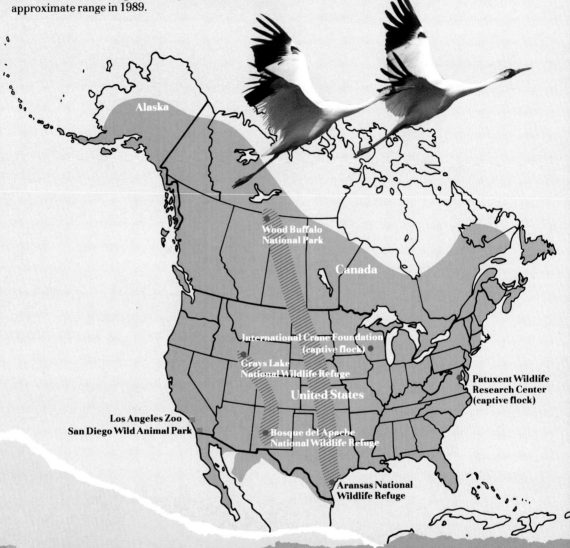

Alaska

Wood Buffalo
National Park

Canada

International Crane Foundation
(captive flock)

Grays Lake
National Wildlife Refuge

United States

Patuxent Wildlife
Research Center
(captive flock)

Los Angeles Zoo
San Diego Wild Animal Park

Bosque del Apache
National Wildlife Refuge

Aransas National
Wildlife Refuge

	California condors	The last remaining California condors live in two zoos; none are in the wild.
	Whooping cranes	There are two migrating whooper flocks and two captive— or nonmigrating—flocks. One migrating flock flies twice a year between Canada and the Gulf of Mexico. The other travels between Idaho and New Mexico.
	Bald eagles	Bald eagles live as far north as Alaska and as far south as northern Mexico, but most make their homes in Canada and Alaska.

Big, vulnerable birds

California condors, bald eagles, and whooping cranes are easy to tell apart. But these big birds do share some traits that make them vulnerable to extinction. They need large, undisturbed habitats in which to live. They also reproduce slowly, hatching few offspring.

California condors are the largest land birds in North America. Their wingspan can reach more than 9 feet (2.7 meters). Their huge wings enabled condors in the wild to soar for long distances in search of dead animals to eat. These birds reproduce very slowly, laying only one egg every two years. Condors that lived in the wild would lay eggs between boulders or in a cave, *right.*

The whooping crane is the tallest bird in North America, reaching a height of 5 feet (1.5 meters). These birds have a loud, buglelike call that can be heard for miles. Whoopers make their nests of plants found in marshes and other wet, open areas. These birds mate for life. Before mating, a pair of whoopers will perform a complex courtship dance in which they leap into the air, bills pointed upward and wings flapping, *far right.*

The bald eagle is the national bird of the United States. This bird can have a wingspan of 8 feet (2.4 meters) or longer. Bald eagles build nests called *eyries* or *aeries* on cliffs or in trees near the water, *above.* Some eyries are huge, as much as 10 feet (3 meters) across and 20 feet (6 meters) deep. Bald eagles mate for life. To make or renew their bond, a pair performs a courtship display in which they fly high into the air, clasp talons, and somersault downward, separating and flying off seconds before they would crash into the ground.

the list of potential homes is the Grand Canyon National Park in Arizona. But before condors fly over the Grand Canyon, they must first soar over California. Wiley believes that, barring an unforeseen disaster, it will happen by 1994.

A species represented by little more than 200 individuals is hardly secure. Yet for the estimated 220 whooping cranes in North America in mid-1990, this figure represents abundance. In 1942, the world population totaled only 22 birds.

Whoopers once ranged from the Arctic Sea to Mexico and from Utah to New Jersey and Florida. By the mid-1800's, however, their breeding range had been restricted to the upper Midwest and north into Canada. Scientists estimate there were only about 500 to 700 cranes in 1870. By 1890, the species had virtually disappeared from its U.S. breeding grounds.

Human activities caused the quick decline of whoopers. The biggest drop in population, which occurred between 1880 and 1900, was primarily due to hunters and museum collectors. The Migratory Bird Treaty, signed by the United States and Canada in 1916, halted this problem, but a more serious threat to the cranes was already underway. As more people moved west, the cranes' habitat was destroyed. Farmers drained wetlands and burned prairies. Electric power lines went up, and countless migrating cranes died because of collisions with them.

Concerned about the cranes' plunge toward extinction, USFWS officials in 1937 established the Aransas National Wildlife Refuge on the Texas coast near Corpus Christi. The refuge is a reedy marshland laced with ponds, sand bars, and mudflats. The waters teem with blue crabs, clams, crayfish, fish, frogs, and other species on which whooping cranes feed.

No sooner was Aransas established than new threats arose. In 1940, when the crane population was down to about 20, the U.S. Army Corps of Engineers decided to extend the Gulf Intracoastal Waterway—an inland water route along the Gulf of Mexico—by dredging a channel along the edge of the refuge. Not only did the channel reduce precious crane territory but it also introduced a steady parade of boats and barges that destroyed the isolation cranes favor. During the same year, oil and gas drilling also began inside the refuge.

The National Audubon Society took an interest in the whooping cranes' plight in the 1940's and began a long-term research project on their behavior and habitat. That study furnished much of the biological information used in whooper protection today. But for a long time, one key element was missing from the study. Although the cranes migrated north in spring, their destination and the site of their nesting ground was a mystery. Finally in 1954, a Canadian pilot spotted the cranes. A follow-up investigation found the birds' nesting grounds in Canada's Wood Buffalo National Park on the Alberta-Northwest Territories border.

By the early 1960's, the crane population had increased to about 30 to 40 birds. Conservationists realized, however, that staving off extinction would require a big increase in the birds' numbers, and that was unlikely to occur naturally. Raymond Erickson, director of the Patuxent Wildlife Research Center, decided that a captive-breeding program was in order. Erickson theorized that because whooping cranes usually lay two eggs but rarely raise more than one chick, it should be possible to remove one egg from their nests without causing any harm. That egg could be incubated artificially, and chicks could be used to start a captive-breeding flock. Biologists first tested this theory on nonendangered sandhill cranes, and concluded that the approach was sound. In 1967, researchers began removing eggs from whooper nests in Canada and flying them to Patuxent. By 1974, they had transferred 50 eggs. Several more have been since added to the thriving captive flock.

The USFWS scientists were eager to establish a second wild flock. Wildlife biologist Roderick C. Drewien of the University of Idaho in Moscow had been studying sandhill cranes at Grays Lake National Wildlife Refuge near Pocatello, Ida. He believed the sandhills could serve as foster parents to whoopers because eggs of the two species are similar in appearance. He removed sandhill eggs from nests and substituted whooping crane eggs, hoping the sandhills would hatch and rear whooper chicks. They did. And the maturing whoopers migrated with their "parents" to wintering grounds in New Mexico.

Between 1975 and 1988, 288 whooper eggs were transferred from Canada and Patuxent to sandhill nests at Grays Lake. The eggs hatched, but most of the young birds did not survive. Many died from collisions with power lines. Others succumbed to disease. By 1989, the number of fostered whoopers was only 13.

But the biggest disappointment at Grays Lake has been the absence of reproduction. None of the fostered birds have produced an egg. Some scientists think that there are not enough birds for mating. Others wonder if the sandhill parents fail to provide role models for whooper sexual behavior.

The normal mating behavior of whooping cranes begins when a male stakes out a territory and then waits for a female. When one shows up, the pair perform an intricate courtship ballet before mating. Leaping several feet into the air with heads thrown back and wings spread, they alight softly and bounce upward again. Repeatedly, they bow to each other. According to James C. Lewis, the USFWS's national whooping crane coordinator, an effort to mate whoopers in May 1989 did not work. A captive-bred female was put in an area next to the territory of a wild male raised by foster parents. The pair courted and mated. But they did not nest or produce an egg, and the male left. A second male showed up, but the outcome was the same.

Warding off extinction

A whooping crane, identified by its snow-white feathers, flies amid a flock of sandhill cranes, *right.* To increase the number of whoopers, scientists place whooper eggs in the nests of sandhill cranes, who hatch and raise the chicks as their own.

Young bald eagles perch on a hacking box high among the trees on Horn Island, Mississippi, *left.* A hacking box is used to introduce captive-bred birds into the wild. Unseen by the birds, keepers place food in the box until the chicks are old enough to fend for themselves.

Captive breeding has increased the number of California condors. A condor chick hatched in a zoo is fed by a keeper whose hand is covered by a puppet resembling an adult condor, *right.* The puppet prevents the chick from identifying with human beings.

Meanwhile, the Texas-Canada flock has continued to grow. As of June 1989, it numbered 152 to 157 birds. Although their Canadian nesting grounds are secure, there are many perils along the 2,500-mile (4,000-kilometer) migration route the whoopers fly twice a year. And their Texas habitat seems to be perpetually under siege. Fifty years of boat and barge traffic along the Intracoastal Waterway, coupled with the high winds that occur naturally in the area, have eroded acres of crane habitat. The barges transport petroleum products and toxic chemicals, so a spill within the refuge is a constant threat. So far, pollution seems to have had little impact on the whoopers, but the potential for catastrophe is high.

In spite of such threats, the outlook for whooping cranes looks promising. In late 1989, the USFWS decided to send 22 of the 57 whoopers in the Patuxent flock to the International Crane Foundation in Baraboo, Wis., to ensure that disease or some other problem does not wipe out the entire captive flock. As for creating new wild flocks, Lewis and his colleagues will try to establish nonmigratory groups in the early 1990's. The birds will be hatched in captivity and then taken to the wild and conditioned to stay within a certain area to reduce their possible contact with people. The long-range goal is 40 nesting pairs in the Canada-Texas population plus 25 nesting pairs at two other locations. If that is achieved, the whooping crane's classification will be upgraded from endangered to threatened.

Compared with whooping cranes and California condors, bald eagles are thriving. Some 20,000 to 30,000 live in Alaska, and there are probably as many in Canada. But throughout the rest of the United States, bald eagles are classified as endangered, except in Oregon, Washington, Minnesota, Wisconsin, and Michigan, where they are classified as threatened.

In the 1960's, the bald eagle seemed well on its way to disappearing from most of the country. At one time, the birds lived almost everywhere in North America—from just south of the Arctic tundra in Canada and Alaska to Mexico, and from the Atlantic Ocean to the Pacific.

These birds of prey began to decline in the early 1900's because of habitat loss. Bald eagles favor forested areas near shorelines rich in fish and waterfowl, the top items in their diet. Not only were forests cut to accommodate expanding human population, but land adjacent to oceans, rivers, and lakes became sites for houses, hotels, resorts, recreational boating, and industry. Unlike many birds that learn to live with human beings, bald eagles cannot tolerate people.

Habitat disturbance and hunting caused a slow, steady decline in the number of bald eagles, but in 1947, their population began to plummet quickly. One of the first to recognize the problem was Charles Broley, a stockbroker who had retired to Florida, where there was a large population of bald eagles. A dedicated bird watcher and conservationist, Broley had kept track of newly hatched eaglets every year since 1939. In 1946, 56 nests on which he kept records produced 103 chicks. But in 1957, only 7 of those nests had chicks—a mere 8 eaglets. The same pattern appeared in other eagle-nesting areas. A National Audubon Society survey in the early 1960's found only 400 nesting pairs in the lower 48 states, where once there had been several thousand.

Broley linked the sudden drop in population to a toxic insecticide called DDT. Several years of studies by various conservation groups and government agencies confirmed Broley's suspicion: DDT was the culprit. DDT had been widely used in agriculture and forestry since the 1940's. The poison entered underground water supplies and flowed into rivers and streams, where it contaminated the fish and waterfowl on which eagles feed.

In a few cases, eagles died after eating a contaminated fish or bird. But the real threat lay in how DDT interfered with the eagles' reproduction by disrupting their ability to process the cal-

Facing extinction

The U.S. Fish and Wildlife Service in Washington, D.C., has classified more than 200 of the world's bird species as endangered. Below are some endangered birds that are native to Canada and the United States.

Masked bobwhite	Light-footed clapper rail
California condor	Yuma clapper rail
Mississippi sandhill crane	San Clemente loggerhead shrike
Whooping crane	Cape Sable seaside sparrow
Eskimo curlew	Dusky seaside sparrow
Bald eagle	Florida grasshopper sparrow
American peregrine falcon	Wood stork
Northern aplomado falcon	California least tern
Peregrine falcon	Least tern
Aleutian Canada goose	Roseate tern
Everglade snail kite	Black-capped vireo
Thick-billed parrot	Least Bell's vireo
Brown pelican	Bachman's warbler
Piping plover	Kirtland's warbler
Attwater's greater prairie-chicken	Ivory-billed woodpecker
California clapper rail	Red-cockaded woodpecker

Attwater's greater prairie-chicken

Brown pelican

cium that is essential to eggs. Many poisoned birds nested but did not produce any eggs. Others laid eggs with shells so thin they broke easily. Eggs that did not break often held dead embryos. In 1972, the U.S. Environmental Protection Agency banned almost all uses of DDT. Soon, bald eagles began to recover—on their own and with the help of wildlife officials.

Beginning in the early 1970's, researchers tried different ways to reintroduce bald eagles to their former habitats. But the only method that has worked is hacking. The scientists place hacking boxes in a suitable eagle habitat and release eaglets into the boxes. Food is provided as long as is necessary. Instinct eventually takes over, and the birds catch their own food.

Since the 1970's, the bald eagle population has grown dramatically. In 1989, the USFWS counted 2,000 nesting pairs in the lower 48 states. Along Chesapeake Bay, the eagle population has swelled from fewer than 60 nests in 1970 to 200 nests. The birds have become so plentiful in Florida that they are being shipped to other Southern states. In 1973, there were only 314 pairs of nesting birds in the Midwest. In 1989, state officials counted 372 in Minnesota alone, and another 326 in Wisconsin.

The National Wildlife Federation, an organization based in Washington, D.C., that promotes wildlife conservation, has monitored the bald eagle population for several years. According to Maurice LeFranc, director of the federation's Institute for Wildlife Research, DDT is no longer a problem. But bald eagles still face other threats. Many are poisoned by lead pellets they ingest when eating animals shot by hunters. And, like most large birds, many eagles are killed in collisions with power lines.

Yet in terms of species survival, these problems are relatively minor. LeFranc points out that it is the loss of eagle habitat that is the big problem right now. "The bald eagle is on its way to recovery if we give it space," he notes. The Wildlife Federation, along with other agencies, is campaigning to persuade farmers and real estate developers to adopt land-management practices that will save some space for eagles.

North America's biggest birds may well survive. As we enter the 1990's, the signs appear promising. But the danger of losing these birds forever is not yet past, and we must remain committed to helping them endure. As American naturalist William Beebe wrote nearly 100 years ago, "The beauty and genius of a work of art may be reconceived, though its first material expression be destroyed . . . but when the last individual of a race of living things breathes no more, another heaven and another earth must pass before such a one can be again."

For further reading:

Patent, Dorothy H. *The Whooping Crane: A Comeback Story.* Clarion Bks., 1988.

Official World Wildlife Fund Guide to Endangered Species of North America. Ed. by John Matthews and David Lowe. Beacham Pub., 1989.

By Marshall I. Goldman

Opening a Closed Society

Mikhail S. Gorbachev's wide-ranging reforms have made the Soviet Union a vastly different place—with tremendous repercussions for the entire world.

For years, the mere mention of the Soviet Union in the United States and other Western countries conjured the image of a tightly regimented state—a single-party Communist system with only one candidate in each election, no open political debate, and strict control of the press. As for the economy, the Soviet state owned all the means of production—the farms, the factories, and the stores. Decisions about what to produce, how much to produce, and at what price to sell it were normally made by central planners in Moscow, the capital.

Then, in March 1985, Mikhail S. Gorbachev became the general secretary of the Communist Party Central Committee—the top post in the Soviet Union. It would be wishful thinking to argue that since Gorbachev's rise to power everything in the Soviet Union has changed. The Communist Party is still the only officially authorized party, and political debate is limited. But because of Gorbachev's policies of democratization, *glasnost* (open criticism), and *perestroika* (economic reform and restructuring), the Soviet Union is fast becoming a different society.

This was dramatically illustrated on March 26, 1989, when the Soviet Union had its first openly contested elections since the October Revolution of 1917 brought the Bolsheviks (later called Communists) to power. In elections for Gorbachev's newly created Congress of People's Deputies, more than one candidate competed for most of the 2,250 seats. This was a radical departure from past voting practices where only one officially spon-

Opposite page: Standing before a statue of V. I. Lenin, the leader of the Russian Revolution, Mikhail S. Gorbachev opens the first session of the Congress of People's Deputies, a new governing body chosen in 1989 in the first free elections in the Soviet Union's history.

Glossary

Glasnost: A policy of open and public discussion of issues, accompanied by the open flow of information in print and broadcast media.

Nomenklatura: The ruling Soviet elite who enjoy many special privileges such as exclusive stores and country homes not available to average citizens.

Perestroika: The name given to a series of sweeping economic reforms instituted by Soviet leader Mikhail S. Gorbachev, aimed at reducing central planning and restructuring the economy.

Russianization: Russian dominance in language and government in republics where other ethnic groups are a majority.

The author:
Marshall I. Goldman is professor of economics at Wellesley College in Massachusetts and associate director of the Russian Research Center at Harvard University in Cambridge, Mass.

sored name appeared on the ballot. Equally important, the elections were by secret ballot. Given this protection, Soviet citizens as often as not voted against the candidate officially sponsored by the Communist Party. Even more striking, in more than 200 cases the officially sponsored party candidates were defeated even though they had no opponent. Soviet voters simply voted no to them, and the candidates lost. As a result, once powerful party officials in the important cities of Moscow, Leningrad, Kiev, and Minsk were publicly humiliated.

Less dramatic but equally radical was the economic restructuring taking place under Gorbachev's policy of perestroika. When Gorbachev came to power, the Soviet Union was one of the world's great military powers, but its economy was second class and in danger of becoming third class. The Soviet Union simply had not kept up with the rapid advances in technology that have become so important in today's industrial world. The profound changes taking place in the Soviet Union today can be traced directly to the economic decline Gorbachev inherited when he assumed the top leadership post.

The economy was in such difficulty that despite the Soviet Union's vast land area, the nation was having trouble feeding itself. The main difficulty was a lack of motivation among the peasants, who do not own the land they work. In the late 1920's and early 1930's, Soviet leader Joseph Stalin confiscated all the country's private farms and combined them into thousands of large collective or state farms.

Since the mid-1930's, peasants have been permitted to grow their own produce on small private plots. They have also received a fixed income, regardless of how hard they work on collective or state-owned farms. Not surprisingly, the peasants' choice has been to concentrate their efforts on their private gardens. As a result, the 3 per cent of cropland set aside for private farming yields about 30 per cent of the Soviet harvest. But the failure to produce bigger crops on the 48,000 state and collective farms has forced the Soviet Union to import as much as 15 per cent of the food it consumes.

The situation in Soviet industry was not much better when Gorbachev assumed power. Although the Soviet Union is the world's second-largest producer of manufactured goods after the United States, its industrial strength is weakened by enormous waste of raw materials. Soviet manufactured goods tend to be technologically backward and poor in quality, so few countries outside the Soviet bloc want to purchase them.

Not only Soviet trading partners but also Soviet consumers were being poorly served. Food rationing, especially of meat and dairy products, occurred in many parts of the nation. Consumers took it for granted that they would stand in long lines to buy such ordinary products as shoes or matches. Few people in the Soviet

The economic reforms begun by Soviet leader Gorbachev were a direct result of a failing economy, as evidenced by frequent long lines to buy scarce food items in Moscow. A scarcity of soap, along with other grievances, sparked a strike by coal miners in July 1989 that involved up to 300,000 miners and developed into the worst Soviet labor dispute since the 1920's.

Union went hungry, but there were not supposed to be such severe shortages almost 70 years after the revolution.

Gorbachev concluded that much of the Soviet Union's problem was due to its system of central planning and tight state control over the economy. That may have been a useful strategy early in the Soviet Union's economic development, but in an age of rapidly advancing technology and rapidly changing consumer tastes, central planning had become the problem, not the solution. Central planning was too slow a process to respond to technological change or consumer demand. So Gorbachev began to call for economic reforms aimed at reducing centralized control.

Gorbachev first called for better work discipline and more intense effort, especially in the machine tool industry. Discipline was lax, and productivity was low, in part because of poor morale. Workers found that shortages were so common that they had little to buy with their money despite adequate wages.

Upheaval in the Soviet empire

Since Mikhail S. Gorbachev came to power in 1985, the non-Russian republics of the Soviet Union and most of the countries of Eastern Europe have experienced unprecedented turmoil. The pace of change seems to quicken with each passing year.

Union of Soviet
Socialist Republics

Facts about the Union of Soviet Socialist Republics

Capital: Moscow.

Official language: Russian.

Area: The Soviet Union is the largest country in the world in area, covering more than half of Europe and nearly two-fifths of Asia.

Population: With an estimated 289,280,000 people in 1989, the Soviet Union was the world's third-largest country in population.

The progress of perestroika, the growth of glasnost

March 1985: Mikhail S. Gorbachev becomes general secretary of the Communist Party of the Soviet Union, at age 54 the youngest Soviet leader since Joseph Stalin.

April 1985: Gorbachev announces a campaign to end corruption in government.

October 1985: Gorbachev announces a new economic program that calls for *perestroika*—"the structural reorganization of the economy." As part of the program, he orders 11 separate ministries combined into a single ministry to oversee the machine tool industry.

August 1986: The Soviet government authorizes a plan allowing foreign companies to set up joint business ventures in the Soviet Union for the first time since the 1920's.

December 1986: Soviet dissident and physicist Andrei D. Sakharov is released from nearly seven years of exile in the city of Gorki.

June 1987: Gorbachev announces details of his plans for perestroika, calling for state enterprises to be more independent from central control and authorizing private businesses run by families and individuals.

December 1987: Gorbachev and U.S. President Ronald Reagan sign the Intermediate-Range Nuclear Forces Treaty, eliminating intermediate-range nuclear missiles.

February 1988: Thirty-two people are killed in riots in the Soviet republic of Azerbaijan after protests in Armenia over the Nagorno-Karabakh Autonomous Region, an area in Azerbaijan that Armenians want to annex.

March 1988: During a visit to Yugoslavia, Gorbachev declares a policy of nonintervention in Eastern Europe, declaring that those countries have the right to develop in their own way.

May 1988: Soviet troops begin to withdraw from Afghanistan, which they had occupied since 1979.

December 1988: At the United Nations, Gorbachev announces unilateral reductions in Soviet armed forces, including the withdrawal of 50,000 troops from Eastern

Map Legend

- Russian S.F.S.R.
- Other republics of the U.S.S.R.
- Other Warsaw Pact countries

Atlantic Ocean

North Sea

Norway

Sweden

Finland

Russian Soviet Federative Socialist Republic

Mongolia

Denmark

Tallinn • Leningrad

Estonian S.S.R.

Riga

Latvian S.S.R.

• Moscow

U. S. S. R.

China

Lithuanian S.S.R.

• Vilnius

K a z a k h   S . S . R .

Alma-Ata •

West Berlin East Berlin

• Minsk

East Germany

Warsaw •

Poland

Byelorussian S.S.R.

• Frunze

Kirghiz S.S.R.

West Germany

Prague •

Czechoslovakia

• Kiev

Ukrainian S.S.R.

Aral Sea

Tashkent •

Austria

• Budapest

Hungary

Moldavian S.S.R.

• Kishinev

Uzbek S.S.R.

Tajik S.S.R.

• Dushanbe

Romania

Yugoslavia

Bucharest •

Caspian Sea

Turkmen S.S.R.

Italy

Sofia •

Bulgaria

B l a c k   S e a

Georgian S.S.R.

Tbilisi •

Baku •

Ashkhabad •

Albania

Azerbaijan S.S.R.

Afghanistan

Greece

Yerevan •

Nagorno-Karabakh

Armenian S.S.R.

Mediterranean Sea

T u r k e y

I r a n

Pakistan

Cyprus

Syria

Lebanon

I r a q

0   500 Miles

0   500 Kilometers

Europe and a troop reduction of 500,000 by 1991.

February 1989: Soviet troops complete their withdrawal from Afghanistan.

March 1989: Gorbachev unveils a new farm policy under which farmers can lease land and equipment for the first time since the 1920's.

March 1989: A ban on the works of exiled Soviet writer Alexander Solzhenitsyn is lifted.

March 1989: The Soviet Union holds its first free, multicandidate elections. Voters reject several leading Communist Party officials and elect numerous dissident candidates, including Sakharov and Kremlin rebel Boris N. Yeltsin.

April 1989: Soviet troops kill at least 19 people demonstrating for independence in Tbilisi, capital of the Soviet republic of Georgia.

May 1989: Gorbachev visits China for the first Sino-Soviet summit since 1959, and thousands of Chinese students and workers occupy Tiananmen Square in Beijing, calling for democratic reforms.

July 1989: Coal miners, demanding better living conditions and less bureaucracy, go on strike in Siberia and the Ukraine and win some demands.

August 1989: As many as 1 million Estonians, Latvians, and Lithuanians link hands, forming a human chain in a demonstration for independence from Soviet rule.

December 1989: After meeting with Gorbachev in Malta, U.S. President George Bush says, "We stand at the threshold of a brand-new era of U.S.-Soviet relations."

December 1989: Lithuania becomes the first Soviet republic to proclaim the abolition of the Communist Party's monopoly on power.

Therefore, they had little incentive to work harder. Gorbachev's initial strategy also involved consolidating the ministries that controlled industry. Where previously there was a separate ministry for virtually every type of industry in the Soviet Union, he merged several ministries into one.

By 1986, Gorbachev came to realize that he would have to move in a different direction. Specifically, he decided to modify the system of central planning under which government bureaucrats told factory managers what to produce, how to distribute their finished products, and where to get the materials needed to make those products. The Soviet government issued a decree ordering state-owned enterprises to find their own customers and suppliers for about 30 per cent of what they produce.

At the same time, managers of state enterprises were told to determine for themselves how many workers to hire. Previously, central planners in Moscow had dictated the size of the work force and the wages to be paid. Factory managers were also warned not to expect any more *subsidies* (support payments) from the state. If a factory could not operate at a profit and no other solution could be found, the factory would be declared bankrupt and sold off or closed down, thereby eliminating unprofitable plants that drained the state's resources.

Reducing central planning was only part of Gorbachev's game plan. Simultaneously, he ordered the legalization of private and cooperative businesses, which had been banned by Stalin in the late 1920's. Gorbachev wanted private initiative because he thought that such businesses would provide competition for state enterprises and thereby serve to prevent undue price increases. In the past, price hikes often went unchecked. Prices were set by the Ministry of Prices in Moscow, which usually approved an increase if a state enterprise showed that it had to absorb higher costs of supplies and materials. Managers, therefore, had little incentive to hold down costs because a price increase meant higher sales figures and higher sales figures often meant larger bonuses for them. By generating competition from private businesses, Gorbachev presumed that the market forces of supply and demand would serve to hold down excessive markups. Gorbachev also hoped that the private and cooperative sector would respond rapidly to consumer demand and fill shortages. These new businesses could produce the goods and provide the services that the central planners had neglected.

In addition, the Soviet government reversed the decrees of the 1920's that prevented joint business ventures with foreign partners. These decrees isolated the Soviet Union from the world economy and took away the opportunity to develop profitable businesses. Under the initial reforms, foreigners could own 49 per cent of such businesses, but as of 1989, they were permitted to hold a majority share. These economic reforms also allowed

Whether perestroika will succeed or fail remains to be seen. Produce is plentiful at free markets, where peasants sell food grown on private plots, but food shortages are still severe and the Soviet Union has to import 15 per cent of the food it consumes. In industry, some factory managers have reportedly been reluctant to take advantage of perestroika's freedoms and so continue to rely on central planners in Moscow.

To combat bureaucratic resistance to perestroika, Gorbachev introduced the policies of glasnost and democratization, leading to the first free elections in the Soviet Union. The March 1989 elections for the Congress of People's Deputies resulted in the unusual spectacle of multicandidate races, with television reporters interviewing supporters of various office seekers.

joint ventures to produce goods within the Soviet Union itself and to hire Soviet workers and use Soviet raw materials.

While these initiatives were all steps in the right direction, few of them have had the desired impact. Most Soviet state enterprises did not seek out their own customers as they were free to do but continued to defer to the ministries in Moscow for orders. As a result, consumer goods have remained in short supply. Farm produce also has remained scarce. The peasants have been reluctant to show much initiative and start their own farms, as provided under the agricultural reforms. They remember what happened to their grandparents who had their land confiscated in the 1920's. Then, successful peasants, known as *kulaks,* were sent off to exile in prison labor camps when they protested the confiscation of their land. Millions lost their lives, mostly due to starvation.

The reforms allowing for the establishment of private and co-operative businesses, however, have had some success. Although there are still relatively few cooperatives and private busi-nesses—14,000 cooperatives involving the work of 150,000 peo-ple as of April 1988—their numbers are increasing. They have responded to profit opportunities and now sell goods, such as blue jeans and T-shirts, or provide services, such as restaurants and taxis, that previously were in short supply. Unfortunately, these businesses frequently charge high prices, and as a result there have been constant complaints of profiteering and specula-tion. As yet, the competition that was expected to develop has not been effective enough to bring down prices.

All this has caused serious confusion among the Soviet people, who aren't sure what to think of Gorbachev's economic reforms. Although industrial production continues to grow, the rate of growth has slowed. Even more serious, the combined tonnage of all the crops harvested in 1988 fell by 15 per cent. Consumer goods and food supplies appeared to be in shorter supply than at any time since 1947. Things got so bad during the summer of 1989 that a shortage of soap helped spark a nationwide coal miners' strike. Spiraling prices also became a serious problem.

Because of the difficulties economic reforms faced, Gorbachev introduced the policies of glasnost and democratization. The So-viet leader realized that people had become cynical and distrust-ful due to the failure of past attempts at economic reform and the clumsy propaganda efforts that tried to disguise those fail-ures. The Soviet media reported nothing but praise for what most Soviet citizens regarded as a rotting and corrupt system. Moreover, even though official propaganda claimed that the So-viet Union was a benevolent socialist community in which the fruits of their labor belonged to the workers and peasants, peo-ple knew that the official version did not correspond to reality. Instead, the benefits of the system were diverted primarily to party leaders, who had access to special shops with abundant goods and who had villas and other privileges set aside for them.

In an effort to win workers' support, Gorbachev decided to shake up the ruling Soviet leadership, known as the *nomenkla-tura,* by exposing corruption and privilege. Initially, Gorbachev thought that he could accomplish this with the policy of glasnost. If Soviet citizens and newspapers complained openly about cor-ruption and poor performance, Gorbachev assumed, the bureau-crats would become more responsive to those complaints and correct them. What happened, however, was that the critics found themselves the victims of retaliation. Typically, workers who criticized factory managers lost their jobs.

By September 1986, Gorbachev realized that something was needed to give such "whistle-blowers" the power to challenge the nomenklatura. For that reason, he announced the policy of democratization. Henceforth, there would be real elections with more than one candidate and secret ballots.

Uncertain as to just how real these promises of openness and freedom of choice really were, Soviet citizens moved cautiously at first. Gradually, however, more and more revelations began to appear in the Soviet press and on Soviet television. Newspapers and broadcasts were once strictly censored and boring, but under glasnost many of them became exciting and interesting. *Moscow News*, a newspaper that had once been nothing more than an outlet for government press releases, and *Ogonek (Little Flame)*, formerly one of the least outspoken magazines in the world, found themselves in the forefront of the reform movement. Each issue was filled with calls for radical reform and revelations about shortcomings of past and present Soviet policy.

Initially, the focus was on Stalin and his crimes in ruthlessly suppressing dissent. Articles began to appear about mass graves filled with ordinary citizens who were killed by Stalin's secret police. But later, even the revered leader of the October Revolution—V. I. Lenin—came in for criticism.

Critical reporting about current events also began to appear. The press began to publish revealing articles about the Soviet role in the civil war in Afghanistan, which had previously gone unreported. Soviet citizens had been led to believe that Soviet troops had a noncombat role in Afghanistan building homes and aiding the people, but Soviet television now began showing actual battle scenes involving Soviet troops. As for the economy, reporters began to acknowledge the existence of poverty, homelessness, and pollution in the Soviet Union, as well as the growing shortages and rationing that confronted the ordinary citizen. Some of the more daring reporters described how senior party officials were able to avoid such inconveniences by shopping in the special stores open exclusively to the party elite.

As bold as such reporting was, there were still areas that were considered too sensitive. Criticism of members of the Politburo—the powerful policymaking body of the Communist Party's Central Committee—or their wives was off-limits. So was publication of the amount of the military budget and such ordinary things as the size of the money supply or the foreign debt. If the reform process continues, this information may yet become public. But in 1989, the glasnost and democratization process seemed to be taking some steps back. For example, anyone who wanted to stage a demonstration had to apply for a permit, and a new law was passed making it a crime to conduct "anti-Soviet" activities. A similar law was enacted banning strikes in some industries and instituting a *cooling-off* (no-strike) period before there can be a strike in other industries. These steps were a clear throwback to the pre-Gorbachev era.

This retreat was in part a response to the wave of strikes and

protests among workers and minority ethnic groups that in 1989 swept several of the 15 republics that make up the Union of Soviet Socialist Republics. The republics are based on nationality groups. Ethnic Russians make up 52 per cent of the nation's population and are concentrated in the Russian Soviet Federative Socialist Republic, the largest republic, which includes Moscow. But in republics where other nationality groups are a majority, Russians often hold leading political and economic positions and the Russian language is dominant.

Glasnost and democratization gave these ethnic republics an outlet to express their long-repressed resentment toward Russian control, and they responded by demonstrating for greater independence from Moscow and more respect for their separate languages and cultures. Ethnic Armenians in the Armenian Soviet Socialist Republic (S.S.R.) began this process when they called for the return of the Nagorno-Karabakh Autonomous Region, an area in the Azerbaijan S.S.R. where 75 per cent of the people are Armenian. This dispute inflamed a long-standing conflict between Armenians, who are mostly Christian, and Azerbaijanis, most of whom are Muslim. Finally, some Armenians even

Gorbachev's reforms awakened resentment against Russian control that had for years been smoldering in several Soviet republics. In Lithuania, hundreds of thousands demonstrated for the Baltic state's independence, waving the flag of the independent republic of Lithuania that existed between the two world wars.

Gorbachev's Impact on Eastern Europe

Nowhere has the impact of Soviet leader Mikhail S. Gorbachev's reforms been greater than in Eastern Europe. In a dramatic event that would have been impossible before glasnost and perestroika, East German authorities in November 1989 opened the Berlin Wall. Since it was built in 1961 to hold East Germans in and West German influence out, this wall was the very symbol of the Iron Curtain and the Cold War.

The breaching of the wall was the climax of the liberalization process that Gorbachev helped spark in early 1989. One after another, the Communist governments in Eastern Europe found themselves faced with mass demonstrations, often involving half a million people. In some cases, the initial protests were put down violently by the authorities. This repression only served, however, to generate larger crowds.

As the gatherings became more insistent, Communist party authorities tried to save themselves by retiring older leaders and replacing them with younger but still fervent members of the party. But once change was underway, it became nearly impossible to stay ahead of the latest demands. The Communists' concessions were almost always a case of too little, too late.

In this new environment, calls for change in leadership within the Communist parties' ranks were followed by demands for free elections, which, in turn, prompted the formation of meaningful non-Communist parties. Ultimately, in the case of Poland, the Communist Party candidates were defeated, and on August 24, Tadeusz Mazowiecki was elected as the first non-Communist prime minister in Poland since the 1940's.

One after another, similar shifts rippled through Poland's neighbors. Hungarian authorities approved free elections in October 1989. In the same month, the long-time leaders of Bulgaria and the German Democratic Republic (GDR or East Germany) were removed. In November, the same type of ouster happened in Czechoslovakia.

The last remaining holdout was Romania under the long-time leadership of Nicolae Ceauşescu. In December, Ceauşescu too was toppled from power. He and his wife, Elena, were convicted by a military court of crimes against the nation and were put to death.

There is little doubt that the catalyst for all this upheaval was Gorbachev and his policies of reform. Under previous Soviet leaders, unrest or efforts at East European accommodation with the West were met with brutal repression. Soviet troops suppressed a Hungarian uprising in 1956 and Czechoslovakia's "Prague Spring" reform movement of 1968.

In the early 1980's, Soviet leader Leonid I. Brezhnev came close to sending in Soviet troops when Polish labor leaders in the Solidarity movement seemed to be taking control from the Communist leadership. In that era, the "Brezhnev Doctrine" proclaimed the notion of limited sovereignty for Eastern Europe, and the Soviet Union acted as a brake on economic and political liberalization there.

But as Gorbachev began to focus on the revitalization of political and economic life within the Soviet Union, by example and by explicit instruction, he signaled the people of Eastern Europe that similar reforms not only would be

A young boy sitting atop the Berlin Wall in November 1989 symbolizes the end of barriers separating the East and the West.

possible there but also would be highly desirable. Under Gorbachev, the Soviet Union became the accelerator for change, not the brake.

Naturally not all Communist leaders within the region were eager to relinquish their power and their privileges. Membership in the Communist party, especially in the upper echelons of the hierarchy, brought with it wealth and special treatment.

Moreover, although we refer to Eastern Europe as if it were a single entity, uniform throughout, each Communist party had a different makeup, reflecting each country's varied nationality groups. In the pre-Communist era, many of the Eastern European nations had gone to war with one another because of these differences. As long as the Soviet Union insisted on compliance with orthodox Marxist ideology and compulsory membership in the Warsaw Pact—the military alliance it dominated—these countries managed to live alongside one another in forced harmony. As the grip of Communist rule has weakened, however, there have been signs of rising tensions among members of the bloc. The Hungarians have begun to complain about the treatment of those with Hungarian backgrounds in Romania, and the Poles have criticized East German claims to what became Polish territory following World War II.

Questions also exist about the future of the Communist parties in the region. As in Poland, once free elections have been approved, the various Communist parties are likely to end up as minority parties. In Hungary, Communist party officials abolished the Communist party itself and created a Socialist party in its place. But, in a reflection of popular disenchantment, only 30,000 of the 720,000 members of the old Communist party agreed to continue as members of the new Socialist party.

Euphoria over the political changes sweeping the area is not enough, however, to offset Eastern Europe's serious economic problems. The countries of Eastern Europe are racked by inflation, labor unrest, shortages of consumer goods, and adverse balances of payment.

Thus, while Gorbachev's reforms have opened up possibilities that were previously unthinkable, they have also engendered much economic and political uncertainty. The big unknown is whether any of the East European countries will be able to free themselves from the straitjacket of their centrally planned economic systems. While the new political freedoms will generate additional willingness on the part of the people to make sacrifices for the future of their countries, the economic problems they face are so grave that the prospects are not encouraging.   [M.I.G.]

began to call for secession from the Soviet Union itself.

Similar unrest has spread to the republics of Estonia, Lithuania, and Latvia, which border the Baltic Sea, and to the Georgian S.S.R., where almost daily protests occurred. Some of these protests, as in Georgia, have become violent, and in April 1989, at least 19 people were killed in Tbilisi, the Georgian capital, when Soviet troops broke up a peaceful demonstration. The ethnic regions, including the Ukraine and Byelorussia, resent the Russianization of their languages, cultures, and economies. They complain that too many decisions affecting their day-to-day lives have been made in Moscow, with no allowance for local needs or regard for ethnic sensitivity.

This pent-up resentment was apparent in the March 26 elections for the Congress of People's Deputies. These elections became the first test of Gorbachev's policy of democratization. Given a choice and secret ballots, the people voted against the official party candidates and for candidates who were protesting the privileges of party officials and the lack of real economic improvement. In the republics, candidates advocating more independence from Moscow and an end to control by Russians won a majority of the seats being contested.

However mixed the reactions may be to Gorbachev's efforts at home, in the outside world there is widespread applause for his initiatives, particularly in international relations. Some observers even speculate that the Cold War, the hostility that has characterized Soviet relations with the West since the late 1940's, may be at an end. It seems hard to remember that as recently as 1983, negotiators for the Soviet Union walked out of arms control discussions in Geneva, Switzerland, to protest U.S. plans to install medium-range Pershing missiles in Western Europe. Once Gorbachev came to power, the arms control talks reconvened, leading to an Intermediate-Range Nuclear Forces Treaty (INF) in 1987 that eliminated medium-range nuclear weapons. In 1989, all remaining Soviet troops were removed from Afghanistan. In addition, Gorbachev announced that the Soviet Union will reduce its troop

Despite Gorbachev's uncertain popularity in the Soviet Union, he has been an unqualified success abroad, drawing crowds of well-wishers, as in Czechoslovakia, *above*, and in dozens of other countries.

strength by 500,000 and its military budget by 14 per cent. He also pledged to remove 50,000 Soviet troops from Eastern Europe, which also underwent radical change in 1989.

At the same time, Gorbachev has embarked on a series of visits to world capitals in an effort to reduce tension so that he can in turn divert resources from the Soviet military to civilian industry. That need, more than anything else, has explained his numerous trips to Western Europe, where he has generally received a hero's welcome. That also has explained his five summit meetings with U.S. President Ronald Reagan, and his May 1989 visit to China. The two Communist nations have had tense relations since an open dispute over Communist doctrine led to a border clash in 1969.

With tensions relaxed, Gorbachev has also called for an increase in economic ties to the capitalist world. He wants more trade, more loans, and membership in international organizations such as the General Agreement on Tariffs and Trade, which aims to promote trade among its more than 90 members. If successful, these efforts would aid the rehabilitation of the Soviet economy and enhance its ability to respond to the needs of the Soviet people.

Observers of the Soviet Union wonder what Gorbachev will come up with next. At the same time, they wonder how long the Soviet military will continue to support his efforts. There is reason to suspect that Gorbachev may have gone beyond what many in the Soviet military regard as prudent. Several Soviet generals have expressed their concern that the Cold War has not ended and that the United States in particular has not made concessions to match those the Soviet Union has made. They worry that the United States will gain military superiority.

The Western reaction to Soviet arms control initiatives is far from unanimous. Some Western observers, though relatively few in number, worry that the initiatives are a trick by the Soviet Union to deceive the West. Others worry that if Gorbachev succeeds, the Soviet Union will become even more of a military threat than it is now because it will be able to produce the advanced technology that it presently lacks. They believe that if the Soviet Union falls behind in technology, its military effectiveness inevitably will become obsolete. Therefore, if perestroika succeeds, the danger to the West may increase.

A growing number of other observers, especially in Western Europe but many in the United States as well, fear the opposite. They worry that because Gorbachev has encountered so many difficulties with his economic reforms, his term of office may be cut short. How long, they wonder, will the Soviet people tolerate a decline in their standard of living and the spread of rationing for such basic products as sugar, meat, and dairy products? The March 1989 election showed that the Soviet people were unhappy with the present situation. Some observers questioned whether Gorbachev himself would have won if he had run for a contested seat, rather than the assured seats that he and 99 other party officials had reserved for themselves.

These observers believe that if perestroika succeeds, the Soviet Union will not necessarily become a more threatening rival. As they see it, perestroika will succeed only if glasnost and democratization also succeed. But that would mean greater popular influence over the allocation of the nation's resources, which would likely lead to a greater reduction in military expenditures and more spending on housing and consumer needs.

Western government leaders worry about how to respond to Gorbachev. Some fear that failure to react quickly to his foreign policy initiatives may help weaken Gorbachev at home, but others argue that Gorbachev's successes or failures will be determined by developments within the Soviet Union and not by the actions of Western leaders.

One troubling question concerns what might happen if Western leaders make concessions to Gorbachev and then he is removed from office: Will his successors honor commitments made under Gorbachev's government? His experiment is a bold one; in effect, he is trying to transform the Soviet economic and political system. Considering how this transformation may affect the world economy and prospects for world peace, it seems clear that not only the Soviet people but also the people of the entire world have a stake in what Gorbachev is trying to do.

For further reading:

Goldman, Marshall I. *Gorbachev's Challenge: Economic Reform in the Age of High Technology.* Norton, 1987.

Gregory, Paul, and Stuart, Robert. *Soviet Communism: Structure and Performance.* Harper & Row, 1989.

Taubman, William and Jane A. *Moscow Spring.* Summit Bks., 1989.

Television: The Changing Picture

In 1989, television broadcasting in the United States observed its 50th anniversary, a milestone that came as changes were sweeping the industry. In the following three-part special section, *The World Book Year Book* examines the American TV business and also takes a look at Canadian and European television and the coming technology.

The simple sets and black-and-white camera of a 1949
studio drama, *opposite page,* are a far cry from the
sophisticated color equipment and slick production
techniques of "The Cosby Show," *above,* one of the
most popular television programs of the 1980's.

By Les Brown

New Choices
for TV Viewers

The three big U.S. television networks—ABC, CBS, and NBC—long ruled the roost, but those days are over. The networks must now fight for viewers with a host of high-tech competitors.

The great American pastime of television watching isn't what it used to be. In particular, people in the United States aren't tuning in to network shows the way they once did. The networks still get plenty of viewers, but a larger and larger share of the television audience is looking elsewhere for its entertainment. In big cities, small towns, and rural areas alike, the TV times are changing. Households across the nation are being wired for cable TV, and satellite receiving dishes are sprouting in backyards like giant mushrooms. The tiniest hamlets have a video rental shop. All these developments have contributed to an abundance of TV options undreamed of 20 years ago.

The futuristic TV technology that is now becoming so common began to arrive in the mid-1970's, and with it came the realization that the next decade would bring swift and dramatic change to the television industry. Soon, the three great networks—American Broadcasting Companies (ABC), CBS Inc., and the National Broadcasting Company (NBC)—found that they were losing their hammer lock on the American TV audience as viewers were at last able to make some real choices. Videocassette recorders (VCR's) enabled people to watch motion pictures, concerts, and other entertainment at whatever time they wished. And cable and satellite TV brought dozens of new channels into U.S. households. As these developments gathered force through the 1980's, no prophetic vision was required to predict that the television industry was about to be rocked by an earthquake.

Fifty years of growth and evolution

Remarkably, the new age of television dawned virtually on the 50th anniversary of the industry. The first regularly scheduled telecasts in the United States were begun by NBC in 1939, and it was not a promising beginning for the new medium. In a public demonstration at the New York World's Fair that year, television —a chunky set with a screen 8 inches (20 centimeters) high— drew large crowds but was largely dismissed as an electronic marvel with a dubious future. A number of "experts" declared that television transmissions were too expensive to compete with radio, that the channel frequencies were too few in number, and that television sets were too complicated for most people to operate.

Television might have proved the naysayers wrong sooner, but U.S. involvement in World War II from 1941 to 1945 stopped the medium's development for the duration. Immediately after the war, however, there was no question that television had arrived. Owning a TV set became part of the postwar American dream, and the prosperity of the 1950's helped that dream along.

Television modeled itself on radio. The new medium snapped up radio's program forms, its economic structure, its executives, stars, and advertisers. And soon enough, its audiences as well.

As in prewar radio, TV programs were presented by single sponsors—advertisers who paid all the costs of producing and airing the show. This arrangement gave advertisers considerable control over program content. In addition, companies often became strongly linked in the public mind with the shows they sponsored. To this day, many people associate comedian Milton Berle with the Texaco oil company. Berle's Tuesday night program, "The Texaco Star Theater," which debuted in 1948 and ran until 1956, was television's first genuine mass-audience hit. Berle went on the air just as TV sets were dropping in price and becoming a fixture in middle-class homes. He is credited with helping television overtake radio in mass appeal.

Three networks dominate the industry

Initially, there were four TV networks—NBC, CBS, ABC, and DuMont. The DuMont network was founded by Allen B. DuMont, one of the inventors of television. But it was the smallest of the four entrants, and because there was scarcely enough television advertising at the time to support three networks, it went out of business in 1955. ABC struggled for survival for the next 10 years as the third network in what was often characterized as a two-and-a-half network economy.

Searching for new ways to compete, ABC in the mid-1960's introduced participating advertising, a system in which spot commercials are placed in a program like advertising pages in a magazine. The economic realities of broadcasting at that time— climbing production costs, the expense of airing "blockbuster" movies, and the dwindling number of companies that could af-

The author:
Les Brown is the publisher of *Television Business International* magazine and the author of several books on television.

The beginning
At the 1939 World's
Fair in New York City,
where television made
its broadcasting debut,
visitors to the RCA Cor-
poration (the NBC net-
work) pavilion view a
bulky TV set with a
glass cabinet. The entry
of the United States into
World War II in 1941
suspended further de-
velopment of TV for
about four years.

ford to underwrite the entire cost of programs—prompted CBS
and NBC to also adopt this form of advertising. Spot commercials took direct program control away from advertisers and
handed it over to the networks. Moreover, participating advertising enabled many more companies than before to buy commercial time on national telecasts, resulting in larger profits for
the networks with each passing year.

By the 1970's, the three networks were on an equal footing in
the competition for viewers and advertising dollars. And they
ruled the TV industry. The Big Three networks held such domin-
ion over the airwaves that all other TV broadcasters combined—
independent commercial stations and public television affiliates
—could muster barely 10 per cent of the *prime-time* (evening)
viewership. The demand for network commercial spots so exceeded the supply that the networks were able to raise their ad
rates—the amount they charged advertisers—by 10 per cent or
more each year. In the 1970's, network television became a fail-
ureproof business; even programs that flopped made money. The
networks got to be such money machines that NBC sank into
third place in the competition for program ratings—the number
of viewers on which advertising rates are based—and still
posted record profits.

But the richer and more powerful the networks grew, the
more they were resented. The federal government became so
concerned about the networks' domination of the TV industry
that it began looking for ways to limit their power and open the
airwaves to greater competition. In the early 1970's, the Federal
Communications Commission (FCC), which regulates broadcast-

ing, adopted several new measures aimed at reining in the networks. The financial-interest and syndication rule, for example, barred the networks from demanding an ownership stake in the programs they put on the air and thereby forced them out of the profitable business of selling their own reruns to local stations.

Cable and satellites create new competitors

Just when network television was at its peak of power, the marriage of two previously separate technologies—video cable and satellite communications—made it possible to deliver programs coast to coast in a new and more economical way. Before the satellite connection, a typical cable operation was simply a tall antenna that brought in programs—mostly network programs—in areas of poor reception and relayed them by wire to subscribers' homes. In 1975, Home Box Office (HBO), a pay-television service, began feeding its line-up of programs by satellite to cable-TV systems in the United States. By reaching homes throughout the country, HBO became, in effect, a new national network. The only cable systems that could receive it, however, were those with satellite-dish antennas. Within a year, most of the larger systems had such antennas, and by 1980 they were part of any cable company's standard equipment. By the early 1980's, virtually every cable system in the United States offered

By the late 1940's, TV was in high gear and was dominated by three major networks—NBC, CBS, and, to a lesser extent, ABC. Programs were presented by single sponsors. Many long-time TV viewers still associate comedian Milton Berle, *opposite page, top,* with the Texaco oil company. The Texaco Quartet, *right,* opened and closed Berle's weekly show, "The Texaco Star Theater," which ran from 1948 to 1956.

76

The 1950's

Famous shows of the 1950's included "I Love Lucy," starring comedian Lucille Ball, *below;* "Gunsmoke," with James Arness and Amanda Blake, *below right,* a hugely successful Western that began in 1955 and ran until 1975; and "The Mickey Mouse Club," featuring "mousketeer" Annette Funicello, *bottom.*

The 1960's

"The Ed Sullivan Show," which began in 1948 and became TV's most durable variety program, produced one of the decade's most memorable entertainment moments in 1964 when Sullivan introduced the British rock group the Beatles, *right.* Westerns remained popular in the 1960's, and "Bonanza," *below,* became a smash hit. TV also brought reality closer in the '60's, giving viewers a front-row seat in the Vietnam War, *bottom,* and thrilling the world with live pictures of the first moon landing in July 1969, *below right.*

subscribers 10 or more channels of satellite-relayed programming. (People with their own receiving dishes could pick up satellite broadcasts directly.)

Still, the ability of satellite networks to reach audiences was slight compared to that of ABC, CBS, and NBC. By 1980, cable was available to only about 20 per cent of the nation's households, and most of those were in rural and suburban areas. The major cities remained unwired for cable. Wiring urban areas was difficult and costly, and it was further complicated by local governments, which required cable companies to compete for exclusive franchises. It appeared that the largest cities might not have cable in the foreseeable future, and possibly not until the next century. Without access to urban audiences, cable services had no chance of challenging the great broadcast networks.

As it turned out, public demand brought cable to the cities far sooner than anyone had expected. The demand was not for the technology itself, but for the variety of programs cable offered—channels devoted to news, sports, movies, music, public affairs, arts, and ethnic programming.

Today we remember the 1970's as the last decade in which television was under the absolute dominance of the networks. Through the 1980's, the networks continued to be the great department stores on the main street of television, but, increasingly, the trendy new boutiques along the side streets were picking up business.

Network officials put on a happy face

Executives of the Big Three refused to acknowledge the extent of the threat posed by the growing competition. Typical of their short-sighted outlook was a booklet entitled *The Road to 1990*,

In the 1960's, as in the preceding decade, television was dominated by the three big networks. Already, however, changes were in progress that would eventually transform the industry. Workers installing the wiring for cable-TV systems, *left*, became an increasingly common sight as the '60's drew to a close.

The 1970's

In the 1970's, network comedy shows such as "Saturday Night Live," *right,* and "All in the Family," *below right,* pushed back the boundaries of acceptable TV humor, while miniseries—starting with 1977's highly popular *Roots, below*— allowed time for greater dramatic detail. "Monday Night Football," *bottom,* showed that sports could attract large nighttime audiences.

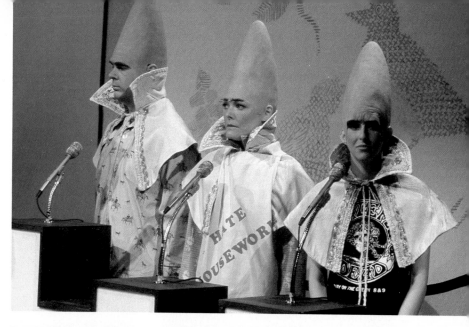

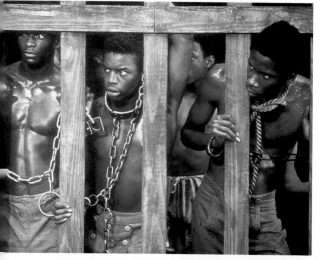

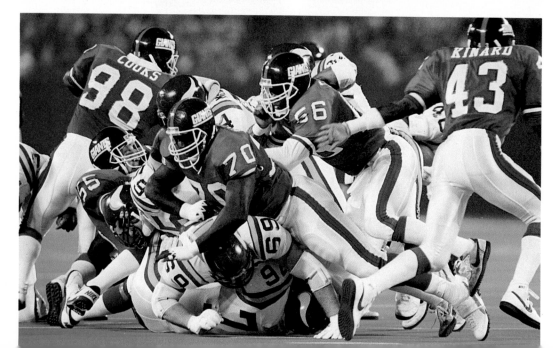

published by CBS in 1984. Largely an exercise in wishful thinking, the brochure was intended to assure advertisers, investors,
and other interested parties that the networks would continue to
be the driving force in television in the 1990's. CBS conceded
that cable program services, then numbering 30, might reduce
the networks' audience share somewhat, but at most by 15 per
cent. And it predicted that with the cable companies' specialized
programming and relatively small audiences, "it is unlikely that
all 30 services will survive."

By 1986, just two years after the booklet came out, the number
of cable channels had grown to 54. In addition, there were five
"superstations" beaming programs across the United States by
satellite, and an ever-increasing number of independent UHF
(ultrahigh-frequency) stations. By this time, also, VCR's—
introduced more than 10 years earlier—had become another
important variable in the TV equation, and thousands of video
rental shops were opening from coast to coast. There was no denying any longer that the networks' day in the sun was drawing
to an end.

In 1986, just as profits were beginning to slide, all three TV
networks were sold to new owners. Capital Cities Communications, Incorporated, bought ABC; the General Electric Company
bought NBC and its parent company, the RCA Corporation; and
CBS effectively went to businessman Laurence A. Tisch, whose
stockholdings fell just a trace short of constituting a legal buyout.
In every case, the new managements were composed of hard-
nosed executives who had little reverence for the history and
traditions of the companies they bought. Concerned solely with
profitability, they proceeded immediately to slash operating
costs by firing hundreds of employees and cutting executive priv-

Videocassette recorders
(VCR's) were intro-
duced in the 1970's,
allowing viewers for the
first time to tape shows
and watch them at their
leisure—and to zip
through commercials.
Perhaps more signifi-
cantly, VCR owners
could now ignore regu-
lar programming alto-
gether and instead
watch prerecorded
tapes of movies, con-
certs, and other video
offerings.

81

The 1980's

The 1980's marked the end of the networks' near-monopoly on the TV industry. Large video-rental stores, *above,* opened by the thousands, and the expansion of cable systems in large cities gave satellite broadcasters access to audiences that the networks had previously had almost completely to themselves.

ileges and other nonessential expenditures. Almost overnight, the glamour and fun went out of network television as it struggled to meet the cold realities of the "bottom line."

Over the next two years, some 3,500 network staff members lost their jobs. The news divisions were hit hardest by the personnel cuts, in part because—being "in-house" operations—theirs was the only programming whose costs the network managers could control. But the new owners also reasoned that since local TV stations make money on their news departments, there was no reason why the networks should be *losing* money on news. As a result of all this belt-tightening, the networks were back on a profitable track but at nowhere near the levels of the past.

Trying to win back viewers

The shakeup at the Big Three did nothing, however, to stop the erosion of network viewership. By late 1989, the networks' share of the prime-time audience had slipped to about 64 per cent, down from 90 per cent just 10 years before. Meanwhile, more than half of U.S. households—some 52 million in all—had been wired for cable.

The networks were by now ready to try just about anything to bring back the good times. In their desperation, they ventured into a practice that ended up backfiring on them: sensationalistic programming, also dubbed "tabloid TV" because of its similarity to the crime, sex, and weird goings-on formula of many tabloid newspapers.

In making a foray into tabloid TV, the Big Three were largely following the lead of yet another competitor—the Fox Broadcasting Company, launched by Australian-American media tycoon Rupert Murdoch in 1986. Fox became the first new regular broadcast network—as opposed to a satellite-cable network—to last more than a year or two since the failure of DuMont more than 30 years earlier.

Most analysts wrote Fox off as a reckless and doomed undertaking. Murdoch, however, had conceived a clever strategy for his network. His plan was to offer programs that appealed particularly to younger viewers, to produce the shows for less money than the networks paid, to establish just one night a week of programming each year, and to introduce new series in the summer—opposite network reruns. The strategy worked. Television critics, having little else to write about in the summer, gave the Fox line-up considerable attention, while interest among young people spread through word-of-mouth.

But Fox succeeded mostly by taking the low road. Its programs included such titillating shows as "A Current Affair," "America's

Explosive growth of VCR's and cable TV

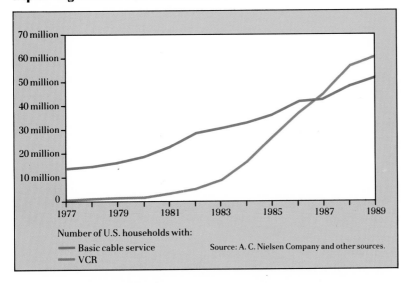

Number of U.S. households with:

— Basic cable service   Source: A. C. Nielsen Company and other sources.
— VCR

The networks' declining audience

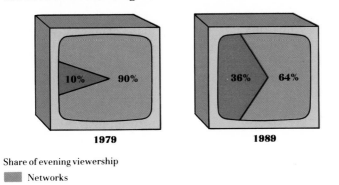

Share of evening viewership

■ Networks
■ Other options   Source: A. C. Nielsen Company.

The number of VCR's and cable-TV hookups in U.S. households increased tremendously in the 1980's. In mid-1989, some 52 million American homes were wired for cable, up from about 13 million in 1977. The increase in VCR's during the same period was even more dramatic. More than 60 million American households owned VCR's by mid-1989, compared with a mere 240,000 in 1977. As options for television viewers have proliferated, the networks' share of the TV audience has declined significantly. The networks were attracting only about 64 per cent of the evening viewership in 1989, a drop of 26 percentage points from 1979.

Most Wanted," and "The Reporters," all of which tended to blur the line between fact and fiction by mixing reenactments of crimes and other events with actual news footage.

Soon, tabloid TV—its harshest critics called it "trash TV"—was all over the dial, including on the major networks. ABC, for example, presented a made-for-television movie in which a mentally disturbed man sets fire to his son, and NBC checked in with a special on devil worship. That program, hosted by free-lance reporter Geraldo Rivera, attracted the largest audience of any two-hour documentary in network history.

Many viewers, though, were disturbed by the new trend. When citizens' groups began threatening to boycott companies supporting lurid shows, a number of major advertisers headed for cover. The brunt of the backlash was directed against the Big Three, even though they had been minor offenders compared with the Fox network. When they chose their schedules for the 1989-1990 season, the chastened networks opted for safer programs that would not scare off advertisers.

Another contender: pay-per-view

There seems to be no end to competitors for the TV viewer's attention. As the 1990's approached, another new technology—pay-per-view (PPV)—was coming on strong.

With PPV, cable subscribers can elect to receive a special program, sporting event, or movie by paying an "admission price." The charge, which may range from about $5 for a movie to $50 for a blockbuster event such as a heavyweight championship boxing match, is added to the monthly cable bill.

The key to PPV is technology that makes each program "addressable"—that is, capable of being delivered only to the homes that request it. In some areas, subscribers must order PPV shows by phone a few hours, or even several days, in advance, but newer systems allow for on-the-spot "impulse buying." The push of a few buttons on a remote-control unit sends a program order to a central computer, which delivers the show to the subscriber's TV set within minutes, or at a specified time.

In 1989, about 10 per cent of cable-wired households were hooked into PPV systems. According to some projections, that figure will grow to nearly 40 per cent by 1995. Few TV industry insiders think that PPV will contribute significantly to the erosion of the networks' national viewing audience. PPV *could* damage the Big Three, though, by obtaining the rights to many popular events that might otherwise have been presented on network broadcasts.

The fickle viewers: zipping, zapping, grazing

A more immediate problem for the networks, and for commercial television as a whole, is the changing nature of the viewer. Once upon a time, most TV watchers tuned their sets to a single channel for the duration of a show. Advertising spots were allowed to play, though they might be ignored. Then came the handheld remote-control tuner, which permitted viewers to "graze" over program offerings and "zap" commercials by switching channels. According to a 1988 study by a TV-research company, 16 per cent of the prime-time audience, and 23 per cent of the weekend sports audience, engages in channel hopping when commercials come on.

The viewers' exercise of power is even greater with programs taped by VCR for watching at a more convenient time. When playing the tape, the viewer can zip through commercials by pressing the fast-forward button on the VCR remote-control unit. In 1989, some 65 per cent of U.S. households owned VCR's.

Zipping, zapping, and grazing have raised concerns in the advertising industry about whether TV is losing its effectiveness as a vehicle for reaching consumers. Some large advertisers—the Campbell Soup Company, for one—have cut back their investments in television spots and switched to print ads or direct-mail marketing.

The outlook for the 1990's

More change is assured for the television industry in the decade to come. One question that remains to be settled is how most TV programs will eventually be delivered to the home. Cable systems may prove to be just as vulnerable as the networks have been. Many industry watchers predict that direct-broadcast satellite technology (DBS)—transmitting TV signals directly to home antennas—will emerge as the biggest threat to cable. Right now, satellite signals can be received only with huge—and expensive—receiving dishes, but that is expected to change. Within a few years, it should be possible to pick up satellite beams with a small antenna mounted on the roof or even hung out a window. DBS may well become the TV technology of the 1990's.

But then again, maybe not. The ultimate winner in this contest might be . . . the telephone company. The federal government is currently debating whether to allow local phone companies to compete with cable-TV systems for the delivery of program services and information. Cable systems in most municipalities are effectively monopolies; competing cable installations could perhaps be built, but in most cases economics or politics (or both) prevent it. Telephone technology, however, is essentially the same as cable, the chief difference being the size of the wire. Telephone companies are now rebuilding their systems with *fiber-optic cable*—glass or plastic wire that transmits information with pulses of laser light rather than electricity. Fiber optics has the capacity to provide both telephone and cable-TV service and, in fact, could make everyone's television a window on the world. Wherever optical telephone lines go—banks, stores, museums, libraries—it would be possible, with the installation of video equipment, to provide a link with home TV screens.

As satellite-cable broadcasters consolidate into a relative handful of powerful national operators, and as local cable systems continue to raise subscriber rates, the argument to let the telephone companies into the TV business is gaining force. If the phone systems get the go-ahead from Congress and the courts, the cable television industry will be dealt a blow similar to that felt by broadcast television in the 1980's—the trauma of real competition.

The federal government is also considering another question: whether to allow the three major networks to share in the ownership of the programs they broadcast. Under the restriction imposed by the FCC in the 1970's, the networks may commission series of programs from production companies but only under a leasing arrangement. They may present each episode of a series twice but are barred from earning any profits from later sales of the programs. Network executives argue that this system is unfair in today's highly competitive TV market. In reply, the production companies contend that if the networks were allowed back into program ownership, they would once again control the TV industry.

Whatever happens, it is unlikely that the Big Three will ever again dominate television as they once did. But with good management and some luck, they could find renewed strength and continue to be a major factor in the industry for a long time to come. Already, ABC and NBC have hedged their bets by purchasing large shares of several national cable program services, so the networks are far from down for the count.

However the free-for-all in the U.S. television industry finally turns out, one thing is certain: American viewers will have an incredible spectrum of video offerings available to them. There may in fact be so many channels, carrying such a wide variety of programming, that the choices will become a bit overwhelming. Indeed, some Americans may discover a hankering for those good old days when the three networks presented a fixed menu of shows that nearly everyone watched and that served, for better or worse, as a shared national experience. Even now, it is a memory to cherish if only because, like the heydays of national radio and the Hollywood studio system, we will not see its like again. On TV screens across the land, the future has arrived.

For further reading:

Abramson, Albert. *The History of Television.* McFarland & Company, 1987.
Television Technology in Transition. Ed. by Jeffrey Friedman. Society of Motion Picture and Television Engineers, 1988.

By David L. Dreier

Fast-Forward in Europe

As trade barriers fall, Europe's TV industry is being transformed almost overnight. Canadian TV, as always, has a major headache: U.S. television.

The new freewheeling video age is not confined to the United States, nor could it be. There is no stopping the relentless advance of television technology, and the TV industries of nations around the world are being forced to adjust. Some of the greatest changes are taking place in Europe, where satellite broadcasting has been the apparent impetus for a television revolution that is now sweeping Great Britain and the Continent. But technology is only half the story in Europe; a history-making revamp of the region's economic system is also at work. With the 12 nations of the European Community (EC, or Common Market) poised to merge into a "United States of Europe" in 1992, laws that had protected national television networks from competition are being tossed aside. In this spirit of deregulation, new commercial channels are being created by the score.

The boom in European television has had a ripple effect. TV production companies throughout Europe, and as far away as Australia and Canada, have flourished to meet the growing demand for programming. For the Canadians, however, the good times are tempered by a problem of long standing: how to compete with the giant U.S. television industry so close by.

Nothing bridges geographical boundaries quite so effectively as a communications satellite. Satellites are thus a touchy issue in Europe, where many traditionalists now see the cultural identity of their nations threatened by unwanted programming and commercials raining from the sky. Whether they like it or not, that assault will continue. Several satellite networks beaming programs to virtually the whole of Western Europe were created in the 1980's, though as of mid-1989 none of them had yet posted a profit.

Realists in Europe have long since concluded that invasion by

"La Roue de la Fortune," *above,* is the French version of "Wheel of Fortune," one of the most popular game shows in the United States. Many Europeans—especially in France—dislike the pervasive influence of U.S. television on the European TV industry and are seeking to diminish it. In late 1989, the European Community adopted voluntary TV quotas for its member countries, calling for at least 50 per cent of programming to be produced in Europe. With the expansion of cable and satellite TV systems in Great Britain, *right,* and on the Continent, the demand for programming—whatever the country of origin—has soared.

satellite is inevitable and there is no sense wringing one's hands over it. They have pushed for opening up the TV industry throughout Europe to allow unrestricted competition with relatively few restraints on advertising. While that stance has carried the day, it was more than a bit radical, given the nature of European television. For decades, most European countries had only state-run networks providing government-produced programs with little or no advertising. But by the late 1980's, just about every Western European country (Sweden being the notable exception) had begun opening its airwaves to commercial television.

"Big Four" establishing dominance

The arguments in favor of free enterprise are also economic. Why allow satellite broadcasters based in other countries to make all the money, the reasoning goes, when the business people at home might be making some of it. By all indications, though, most of the money will be made by four communications tycoons who appear well on their way to dominating European television. The four are Silvio Berlusconi, reputed to be one of the richest men in Italy; Leo Kirch of West Germany; Robert Maxwell, a Czechoslovak-born Briton; and Rupert Murdoch, an Australian-American whose television enterprises also include the Fox network in the United States.

Although the Big Four are usually portrayed as archrivals, they actually cooperate to a large degree. In Great Britain, for example, Maxwell and Murdoch both own part of Premiere, a movie channel. In 1989, the four were in the process of developing several joint ventures aimed at solidifying their grip on the industry. One of their goals, being urged on them by advertisers, is to establish a "stratified broadcasting system" presenting both national and continentwide programming. Such a system would enable them to broadcast some programs in the native language of individual countries and to beam other programs by satellite to a wide area in just one language. The latter programming would most likely include music shows, sports events, and other presentations that do not rely heavily on language.

A skyrocketing demand for programming

The new channels sprouting throughout Europe have created a superheated market for programs. American movies and dramatic series such as "Dallas" and "Dynasty" have always done well in Europe, and now the demand for them is greater than ever. European stations and networks bought about $1 billion worth of American programming in 1989, triple the amount they purchased just four years earlier.

Many Europeans, however, would like to see fewer shows from the United States, not more. Again, the issue is often national identity. The French, in particular, long concerned about the influence of Hollywood entertainment on French culture,

The author:
David L. Dreier is a senior editor of *The World Book Year Book.*

have stepped up their resistance to the influx of American programs. Other opponents include European actors, producers, and scriptwriters, who support quotas on the purchase of imported programs as a means of stimulating employment at home.

Because it is vastly cheaper, European programmers usually prefer buying American fare to mounting original productions. Still, Europe has produced a great deal of programming during the current boom, and a large community of independent production companies has emerged and is thriving in the shadow of the four TV titans. But raising the money for ambitious TV programs, the kinds that can compete successfully with glossy American shows, has been difficult for the independents. To finance such ventures, they have found it necessary to join with other producers in multinational partnerships. Such arrangements, known as coproductions, are expected to become more common as the TV barriers between European nationals continue to fall.

Looking forward to 1992

The increasingly frenetic activity in European TV is largely in anticipation of the economic unification slated for completion in 1992. Under the new system, the Common Market countries (Belgium, Denmark, France, Great Britain, Greece, Ireland, Italy, Luxembourg, the Netherlands, Portugal, Spain, and West Germany) will harmonize their trade policies and permit the free movement of goods across national boundaries. The economic federation will constitute a market of some 325 million customers—and television viewers—almost one-third more than in the United States. That is an audience that advertisers are dying to reach.

As part of the preparations for 1992, EC ministers spent most of 1989 working on a body of rules to govern the television industry within the Common Market. The rules, aimed at creating "television without frontiers," will eliminate laws that had sheltered national networks from outside competition and will establish regulations for TV advertising.

The issue of quotas for programs produced outside the Common Market—namely those from the United States—was the most hotly debated item on the agenda. France and Italy and the European creative community were strongly in favor of such limits, while U.S. television interests were just as strongly opposed. In October, the ministers adopted a compromise plan: European broadcasters will be urged, though not required, to devote at least 50 per cent of their air time to shows produced in Europe. But even that halfway measure was roundly criticized by U.S. television executives and trade officials, who said that the restrictions, despite being nonbinding, are a form of economic protectionism.

To a great extent, though, the question was becoming academic long before the EC ministers cast their votes. The Europeans realized that whatever quotas they imposed, U.S. producers would get around them by blurring the origin of their programs through various kinds of coproduction agreements.

Coproductions: U.S. option, Canadian necessity

The coproduction of programs is becoming an increasingly common way of doing business for both European and U.S. television companies. For United States producers, coproduction represents more than just a means of evading import quotas; it is also an opportunity to tap into new segments of the expanding world market for TV. Some U.S. producers are talking up the idea of developing "bicontinental programs"—shows that would be produced by a partnership on both sides of the Atlantic Ocean and released simultaneously in Europe and the United States. In the meantime, some European partnerships are starting to produce their shows in English, often with at least one American star, in the hope of selling them in the U.S. market. For distribution on the Continent, the programs are dubbed into the languages of the countries where they are shown.

Although coproduction is just now becoming a major factor in U.S. and European television, it has long been a way of life for producers in Canada. The Canadian TV industry has always been in a somewhat precarious position simply because of its nearness to the United States. Virtually every network and satellite show broadcast to U.S. homes is also received in Canada, and about half of all Canadian households also receive U.S. programs on cable. To cope with this deluge of programming, Canada has had to develop mechanisms to support domestic TV production. Through government grants and contracts with Canada's national television network, Canadian producers can usually raise about two-thirds of needed financing at home. For the other third, they must look elsewhere, usually to Europe.

For the French-speaking province of Quebec, France has been the main source of coproduction financing. Riding high in the current European TV boom, the French television industry has given a generous helping hand to its French-Canadian counterpart. But the relationship benefits both sides; French producers look on Quebec as a market for their programs. The economics of television production has, in fact, brought the entire French-speaking world closer together.

Of course, TV is bringing *all* parts of the world closer together. Today, we can speak in terms of an international television community, and the United States is becoming a full member of that community, not only joining in production partnerships but also opening itself up to a wider variety of foreign programs. And such programs are certain to increase in number in coming years. Some may be from Canada, and even from Japan and Australia, but most are likely to originate in Europe. One way or another, the revolution in European television is bound to affect what Americans see on their TV sets in the 1990's and beyond.

By William J. Hawkins

Tuning in Tomorrow

In the near future, we will watch TV programs on huge screens that hang flat on the wall, with better images, better sound—and perhaps 3-D.

As you enter your home media room, soft music soothes your ears and a swirl of colored light dances on the wall in front of you. You sink into an easy chair and press a button on your remote control. The music becomes even softer and the room lights slowly dim. Soon the room is pitch-black and silent.

Suddenly, the wall bursts with pictures—vivid, dazzling pictures, alive with color and detail and filling your entire field of vision. Thunderous chords strike your ears from all sides. In seconds, you are immersed in a sea of sight and sound.

Welcome to the television of the future—but not the distant future. Electronics experts predict that within the next few years you will view such high-definition television (HDTV) images on wall-sized screens in your home.

The HDTV picture will be comparable in quality to an image produced by a 35-millimeter slide. The HDTV picture also will be wider than today's TV image. The present-day picture has 4 inches (10 centimeters) of width for each 3 inches (7.6 centimeters) of depth—a 4:3 ratio. The HDTV image will have a ratio of 16:9, approximately the same as that of a screen in a motion-picture theater.

The sound that accompanies the HDTV image will be as good as what today's best compact discs can deliver—and much more realistic, because the conventional stereophonic TV system now used will be replaced by multiple-channel digital audio. Add to all this both visual and auditory 3-D effects as well as *interactive*

viewing (in which, for example, you will be able to control the plot of a mystery show), and you begin to "get the picture" of tomorrow's TV.

The technology behind the picture

The TV image you see on your present television set is "painted" on the inside of the picture tube a line at a time by a beam of electrons that scans from left to right and from top to bottom. What seems to be a moving picture is actually many still ones—each called a frame—created by about 525 scan lines.

Because scan lines convey picture information, the more lines there are, the more detail in the image. Future HDTV sets will likely use well over 1,000 lines, with each line carrying nearly twice as much picture information as today. As a result, the picture could be blown up to the size of a theater screen with no perceptible loss in visual quality.

Government approval needed

But before HDTV becomes a reality, a regulatory obstacle must be overcome. An HDTV picture requires about five times as much video information as does a conventional TV image. This is too much data for the technique presently used to broadcast pictures to our homes. Fortunately, developing a new technique to handle the additional information has turned out to be a relatively minor problem in electronics. In fact, researchers at companies throughout the United States, Europe, and Japan have developed several HDTV transmission techniques. Only one, however, can be chosen as a standard for the United States.

A high-definition television (HDTV) picture, *above,* contains much more detail than a conventional picture, *above left.* A number of companies and research organizations in the United States, Europe, and Japan are working on HDTV systems, and the U.S. Federal Communications Commission expects to select a standard for American television by 1992.

The author:
William J. Hawkins is Senior Electronics Editor of *Popular Science* magazine.

93

Otherwise, if every broadcaster used a different HDTV system, you might need a separate TV set for every channel.

At the end of 1989, the Federal Communications Commission (FCC)—the agency that regulates television and radio broadcasting in the United States—was studying HDTV proposals from about two dozen companies and planned to pick one by 1992. The commission had already ruled that whatever system it chooses must work with today's TV sets. That is, an HDTV broadcast will have to produce a conventional image on a present-day set.

New kinds of screens

Once the FCC selects a standard, it will likely take at least three years for HDTV sets to become available. What will they be like? Expensive—costing about $5,000 to start—and big. To

The television of the not-so-distant future will hang flat on the wall like a painting, as shown in the simulation at *right.* Tomorrow's TV images may be three-dimensional. Some researchers are investigating a laser technology called *holography, below,* in an attempt to develop a revolutionary form of 3-D television. Holographic TV pictures would seem to float in midair and could be viewed from various angles.

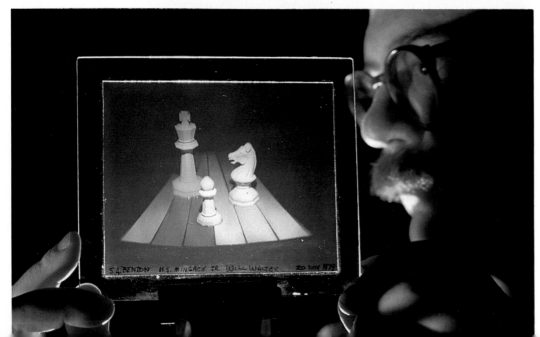

display the enhanced picture quality in a way that can be fully appreciated, the screen must measure at least 32 inches (81 centimeters) diagonally.

Furthermore, as screen size increases, an essential piece of TV hardware—the conventional glass picture tube—will become increasingly cumbersome. Such a tube would be too large and heavy to display the wall-sized images that experts foresee. Designers are already at work on new imaging devices. One device is made up of hundreds of glass picture tubes—each 2 inches (5 centimeters) deep—that are arranged side by side. The tubes are interlocked electronically so that the image seems to be displayed on a single gigantic screen.

Other designs for wall screens use liquid crystal displays (LCD's)—devices like those in a pocket-TV. In fact, one such design is a single, huge panel of LCD's. In another device, a small LCD panel plays the role of the film in a conventional movie projector. A beam of light passes through this panel and is projected onto a large screen that reflects light like a movie screen.

New kinds of viewing

Hardware and software producers are teaming up to take advantage of the capabilities of these future sets. One result of this teamwork will be interactive television. By pressing a button, you will be able, for example, to change the way a story ends. Or instead of merely watching a game show, you will play along at home. To provide interactive viewing, TV sets will accept *multiple video tracks*, each a broadcast of a slightly different version of a show. When you press the button, the TV will switch tracks.

Other designers are using a two-track system, but for an entirely different reason. This system displays two slightly different images that alternate in rapid succession. When the viewer puts on a pair of special glasses, the flat TV image gains a remarkable quality—3-D.

The 3-D effect is a result of precise timing. The glasses contain liquid-crystal lenses that can either allow light to pass through—as if they were made of glass—or block the light. The lenses "blink" on and off alternately as the display switches back and forth between the two images. The left eye sees a slightly offset version of what the right eye sees, and the brain combines the two flat images into one 3-D picture.

Engineers are already readying production timetables for tomorrow's HDTV, wall-screen television, interactive viewing, and 3-D TV. And beyond tomorrow? Experiments have begun on holographic television—a system that will require no screen at all. Instead, 3-D images will be projected via laser light into your media room. One day, thanks to the magnificent illusion of holographic TV, you may "walk around the stage" in the middle of a play. Or you may watch game-show contestants compete—while they are seated on your couch.

Impossible? Sit back and relax. The show is about to begin.

By Gwen Ifill

No Place to Call Home

Homelessness strikes all types of people—male and female, young and old. And their troubles go beyond simply finding a place to live.

If you live in an American city, or even in a smaller town, you've probably seen the homeless. By day, they wander the streets, carrying a lifetime's possessions in a few shopping bags. By night, they sleep on park benches, over heating grates, or in transit stations, where they work to stave off hunger, cold, and attack. Some manage to get beds in overnight shelters, where they can turn their attention to keeping their few possessions from the hands of the stranger in the next bunk. For these people, a shower, a telephone number, or a private room are luxuries.

Once, people who slept on the streets were considered victims only of their own inability to rise to the American dream. Segregated on skid rows and away from the mainstream, these outcasts were easily ignored. When they were noticed, they were seen as the blameworthy exceptions to the rule: too lazy, too shiftless, or too morally weak to keep a roof over their heads.

But social scientists, community leaders, and the general public have come to realize that homelessness now goes far beyond this stereotype. Today's homeless are both male and female, urban and rural, young and old. They include not only the unemployed and unemployable but also the working poor.

In most cases, the troubles of homeless individuals go far beyond simply finding a place to live. Homelessness is intertwined with a score of other social ills—including poverty, unemployment, alcoholism, drug abuse, poor health, illiteracy, crime, and mental illness. And like these problems, homelessness is neither easily explained nor easily remedied.

Preceding pages: "Bag ladies," such as this homeless woman in New York City, have long been a familiar sight in urban streets and alleys. But in the last decade, homeless people have become common even in suburban or rural areas.

No one knows exactly how many Americans lack a permanent residence—simply because the homeless are almost impossible to count. By definition, they have no addresses and no telephones. They move frequently, often crowding in temporarily with friends or relatives. And some—such as illegal immigrants, runaways, or criminals—work hard not to be found.

Estimates range widely. The U.S. Department of Housing and Urban Development (HUD) weighs in at the low end of the scale with its estimate that 250,000 to 300,000 Americans are without homes. HUD based this figure on the numbers of people who use homeless shelters and soup kitchens. The Urban Institute, a nonpartisan Washington, D.C.-based think tank, placed the number twice as high—at close to 600,000—after surveying soup kitchens and shelters in 20 cities in 1988.

But independent advocacy groups, especially the Washington, D.C.-based National Coalition for the Homeless, put the count at about 3 million. The coalition—an umbrella organization for homelessness groups nationwide—says its figure is so high because other estimates miss people who don't use shelters.

In hope of clearing up some of the confusion, the Census Bureau will take an unprecedented head count in 1990. From 6 p.m. March 20 to 4 a.m. the following morning, census workers will fan out into the nation's streets, alleys, doorways, and shelters. In addition to counting the homeless people they find, the workers will record each person's sex, race, and age, based on interviews or observation. But census officials concede that even this painstaking count will probably be imprecise.

The number of the homeless is only the first of many unanswered questions. Equally disputed is who the homeless are.

Cities have always had homeless residents, and at their core have always been the people who lack the physical ability, the mental skills, or the simple desire to work. The Great Depression of the 1930's temporarily swelled the ranks of the homeless to include not only the unemployable, but also the unemployed—including many transient laborers and their families.

Homelessness declined with the later prosperity of the 1940's through the 1970's, and the small homeless population nearly

The author:
Gwen Ifill reports on housing issues for *The Washington* (D.C.) *Post.*

The first line of attack on the problem of homelessness is simply to provide for basic needs: a place to stay and food to eat. A woman cleans lice from her daughter's hair, *above,* in their makeshift quarters at a Los Angeles campground for homeless people. Homeless people in Washington, D.C., line up for a free Thanksgiving dinner, *left,* at a soup kitchen in Lafayette Square.

Barracks-style facilities, such as this New York City shelter for men, *above,* can provide a temporary place to sleep for people without homes. But many homeless people, such as this St. Louis, Mo., man, *right,* end up sleeping in public places—either because they choose not to use the shelters or because there isn't enough room.

disappeared, relegated to skid-row flophouses. From this time comes the stereotyped picture of the homeless person—a single man smelling of cheap wine and days without a shower.

In the 1980's, however, various factors combined to create a changing homeless population that defies generalizations. Studies show that although many of the homeless are still single men, as many as half the total are single women or families with children. These people typify what University of Massachusetts sociologist Peter H. Rossi calls "the new homeless."

The U.S. Conference of Mayors, in an annual 27-city study, has documented this change. Single men, the survey showed, made up 49 per cent of the 1988 homeless population—down from 60 per cent in 1985. Families with children accounted for 34 per cent—up from 27 per cent in three years. The proportion of single women, 13 per cent in 1988, stayed roughly the same. Twenty-three per cent of the 1988 total were employed.

A 1989 U.S. Department of Education report estimated that 220,000 school-aged children are homeless; 30 per cent of them do not attend school at all. Many studies cite children under age 18 as the fastest-growing segment of the homeless population.

Another significant homeless group consists of unaccompanied teen-agers—typically runaways. These young people make up 5

per cent of the total homeless population, and up to 10 per cent in some cities, according to the mayors' study. An article in the Sept. 8, 1989, issue of *The Journal of the American Medical Association* cited studies numbering homeless runaway boys and girls anywhere between 519,000 and 2 million.

In some cities—Cleveland and Seattle are two—more than 40 per cent of the homeless abuse alcohol or drugs, the mayors' survey found. Other studies estimate that up to 38 per cent of the homeless are alcoholic, up to 25 per cent abuse drugs, and up to 24 per cent are convicted felons or former prisoners.

In a few cities, including Boston and Denver, more than 30 per cent of the unhoused were severely mentally ill, the mayors' study found. This tallies with several other studies, which agree that about a third of today's homeless adults are mentally ill.

In fact, many analysts attribute much of the increase in homelessness to *deinstitutionalization*, a policy that encouraged the release of mental patients from public institutions during the 1960's and 1970's. The number of patients in state mental hospitals dropped from more than 550,000 in the 1950's to fewer than 150,000 today. But the community-based programs that were supposed to help the newly released were never fully funded. Without jobs, money, and supervision, critics charge, many former mental patients were unable to manage living in society and ended up on the streets—followed by other people who would once have been placed in institutions.

Whether or not deinstitutionalization played a major role in today's homelessness, it is only one of the three most often cited contributing factors. By far, the most common cause is poverty. It seems simplistic to say that poverty creates homelessness, but no discussion of the issue can ignore the one factor that cuts across all lines of race, age, and ability. People without shelter are generally those who don't have the money to pay for it.

Perhaps half of all homeless individuals are unemployable—and thus poor—because they are alcoholics, drug abusers, elderly, or mentally or physically impaired. In other cases, however, a homeless person's poverty reflects larger economic trends. In some cities, the loss of one large business has left many families without sufficient income for rent. In rural areas, downturns in the agricultural economy have forced farms into foreclosure, leaving farmers to seek employment elsewhere, often without success. And demand for unskilled labor has declined nationwide, leaving untrained workers without jobs.

Meanwhile, widespread cuts in federal welfare and social service spending—including funds for dependent children, food stamps, and health care as well as housing—have made some poor people even poorer. Analysts point out that the current rise in homelessness barely hints at the potential problem. According to an August 1989 report from the American Affordable Housing Institute, a research center at Rutgers University in New Brunswick, N.J., some 4 million to 14 million poor families hover only a paycheck away from homelessness. "In a mild recession, homelessness in America is likely to double and triple almost overnight," the report says.

The other major factor contributing to homelessness is a dramatic drop in the availability of low-cost housing. As sociologist Rossi points out in his book, *Without Shelter: Homelessness in the 1980's*, the early 1980's saw "a severe shortage of housing that poor households could afford without bearing excessive rent burdens."

The federal housing budget, which pays for subsidized housing, dropped by three-fourths during the Administration of President Ronald Reagan—from $30.2 billion in 1981 to $7.3 billion in 1987. Other economic developments, including the expiration of federal incentives designed in the 1960's to encourage low-rent housing, have led landlords to convert existing low-income units into more-profitable luxury apartments, offices, or condominiums. These trends, along with the destruction or deterioration of many buildings, have contributed to a steady pinch in the supply of housing that rents for 40 per cent or less of poverty-level incomes, as charted by HUD's annual housing surveys.

To passers-by, these men in New York City's Bowery neighborhood, *below,* seem to typify the old stereotype of the homeless as shiftless or alcoholic. And indeed, about half of all homeless people are on the streets because of mental illness, alcoholism, drug addiction, or other problems that separate them from the social mainstream. A social worker, *right,* speaks with a mentally ill homeless man in New York City's Central Park.

Poverty and a lack of housing combine into a formula for homelessness. A decade ago, a person or family evicted from one apartment for nonpayment of rent might simply have moved to another. Today, when vacancy rates in major cities average only 1 to 2 per cent, other inexpensive apartments are rarely available—and eviction often means homelessness.

"Today's homeless are the first victims of a nationwide housing crisis," says Maria Foscarinis of the Washington-based National Law Center on Homelessness and Poverty. "Middle-income families can no longer afford to buy homes. Lower-income families pay dangerously high proportions of their income in rent. And the most vulnerable—the poorest, the weakest, the oldest, and the youngest—join the ranks of the homeless."

Even as the problem of homelessness has grown and changed, so has public opinion. The news media have paid particular attention to the stories of homeless families and homeless working people, and many individuals can't help noticing greater numbers of street people—including women and children—in their own cities and towns. Fifty-one per cent of the 1,533 people responding to a January 1989 *New York Times*/CBS News poll said they had seen homelessness firsthand, compared with 36 per cent in 1986. Sixty-five per cent said they would approve of in-

The "new homeless" population of the 1980's includes women and children— such as this Midwestern family, *right,*— forced onto the streets by poverty and a shortage of low-cost housing. An Atlanta, Ga., volunteer group called the Mad Housers, *below,* attacked the housing shortage by helping homeless people build plywood huts on government land.

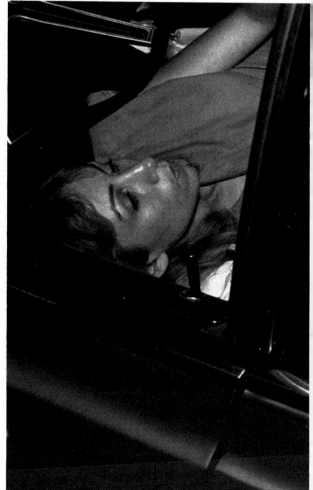

creased federal spending for the homeless, and 49 per cent were willing to pay higher taxes to make that possible.

"A lot of people thought this homeless thing was a short-term phenomenon," says Representative Bruce F. Vento (D., Minn.), the sponsor of a housing bill before Congress in 1989. "What is becoming evident is it is becoming a permanent issue."

In the states, cities, and counties that have struggled against homelessness, the first line of defense is usually to provide shelter. In Washington, D.C., New York City, and other large urban areas, old hotels have been turned into shelters for families who have nowhere else to go. But even suburbs and rural areas are having to find—or build—places to house the homeless.

Shelters, intended as temporary places to sleep, often become an institution in themselves, as homeless people grow to depend on them for extended periods. This tendency has drawn criticism of the shelter system. In a June 1989 press conference, Jonathan Kozol, author of *Rachel and Her Children: Homeless Families in America*, called shelters "the biggest permanent poorhouse in the world." Kozol, who often writes on social issues, predicted "housing riots" if the federal government does not institute new programs to construct permanent housing.

But the government is funding less, not more, housing for the

poor. The National Task Force on Housing—a group of housing-industry experts established by Congress—reported that more than 1 million federally subsidized units of low-income housing were built from 1976 to 1982—an average of nearly 170,000 each year. In 1988, only 23,000 units were built.

Current government strategies take a different approach. The centerpiece of the federal effort is the 1987 Stewart B. McKinney Homeless Assistance Act, the first comprehensive attempt to link federal agencies in a single assault on the problem. As envisioned by McKinney, a Republican congressman from Connecticut who died in 1987, the measure was to make the best use of government resources to bring housing and other help to those who most need it. The act provides for emergency food and shelter programs, grants to health-care facilities for the homeless, job training, and adult literacy programs. The law also encourages a return to single-room-occupancy hotels as a housing alternative for homeless individuals. It even allows for local organizations to use government funds to rent mobile homes or recreational vehicles for shelters.

But many of these plans have been stalled. In its first three years, the measure received only about 70 per cent of the funds authorized for it. In 1989, President George Bush fulfilled a campaign promise by proposing full funding of $746 million for the McKinney Act in the 1990 budget. Still, congressional hearings have turned up numerous complaints about the program's administration. And in a 1988 lawsuit, the National Coalition for the Homeless charged the government with failing to act on a provision of the law that calls for turning underused government buildings into shelters. A court order in September 1988 set deadlines for HUD to identify suitable sites.

Other proposed legislation focuses specifically on housing. The $2-billion Permanent Housing for Homeless Americans Act, if approved, would open up 140,000 housing units a year by increasing funding for existing programs. Another bill before Congress, the National Affordable Housing Act, would provide more housing aid not only for the homeless but also for such groups as the elderly and the handicapped.

Local governments are also seeking solutions. For example, in 1989 the city of Chicago increased its 15-cent per pack tax on cigarettes by 1 cent. The extra $1.8 million the measure is expected to bring in has been earmarked for shelter programs.

But local officials, including leaders of the U.S. Conference of Mayors, have complained that cities, counties, and towns can do too little too late. Waiting lists for public housing were closed in 17 of the 27 cities in the mayors' survey.

"We're already far in the hole. It's kind of like trying to tread water with your hands and your feet tied behind your back," says Phil Jille, the coordinator of homeless programs for Westchester County, New York. That prosperous county saw its budget for homeless programs rise from $1 million to $64 million in just the six years from 1983 to 1989. "Making a dent in homelessness means building permanent, affordable housing," Jille says. "You can't rely on the private sector."

Still, some private-sector groups have taken up the cause. For example, the American Institute of Architects has involved its members in designing shelters and single-room-occupancy hotels. And the American Bar Association has offered free legal help to homeless assistance groups and individuals.

President Bush and Jack F. Kemp, the secretary of HUD, have argued for greater involvement on the part of private and nonprofit community groups, charities, and churches. A HUD survey found that in 1988, 9 out of 10 shelters were operated by such groups, which relied on 80,000 volunteers nationwide—four times the number of five years before. But the volunteers themselves are often quoted in the media as saying their efforts are merely "Band-Aids" on a major wound.

Public officials continue to debate just who is ultimately responsible for solving the problem of homelessness. But all those concerned agree that a solution must be found. "If the good news is that public awareness has increased, the bad news is that homelessness has become a problem we are confronted with in every city, in every season," Senator Albert A. Gore, Jr. (D., Tenn.) said at a March 1989 press conference.

Even as officials recognize the importance of helping the homeless, they also acknowledge that the presence of homeless people can itself be a problem or an embarrassment. In early 1989, Detroit Mayor Coleman A. Young vetoed a city ordinance that would have opened municipal buildings—including the Civic Center—to the homeless at night. Young said the proposal would cost too much, undercut existing programs for the homeless, and hamper the city's ability to attract conventions.

Miami, Fla., police drew nationwide attention—and much criticism—for arresting homeless people for sleeping, eating, bathing, and congregating in public in advance of the January 1989 Orange Bowl football game. And in New York City, San Francisco, and Los Angeles, city officials are coping with an embarrassing form of homeless protest: tent cities and shantytowns erected in conspicuous areas.

It's obvious that a problem with no single cause also has no single solution. To keep people off the street for the long term, the programs that help them must not only offer shelter but also address a complicated network of social ills and economic concerns. Whatever the roots of the crisis—mental illness, housing shortages, alcohol or drug abuse, tight job markets, or tighter government budgets—finding a solution will present a formidable challenge for individuals and government at all levels.

By Robert H. March

The Coming Energy Squeeze

Fossil fuels, fission, or fusion? Rising demands, dwindling supplies of conventional fuels, and environmental damage will soon force us to make better use of energy sources and develop new ones.

What do the words *energy crisis* mean to you? If you're like many Americans, the term may have an almost nostalgic ring. It could bring to mind sitting in long lines at gasoline stations, listening on your car radio to the Watergate hearings. Or maybe you read about the gasoline shortages of the mid-1970's in a history book. But two incidents in March 1989 reminded us that the energy crisis did not go away with the gas lines or fade into the history books.

One of these events was an oil spill in Alaska, when the supertanker *Exxon Valdez* hit a reef in Prince William Sound and began to pour more than 240,000 barrels of crude oil into the water. The second was a press conference at the University of Utah in Salt Lake City, at which two chemists claimed to have produced *nuclear fusion*, the combining of atomic nuclei, in a glass jar on a tabletop at room temperature.

The oil spill, which killed about 35,000 birds and 1,000 otters, provided a grim reminder of the environmental price we sometimes pay for depending on a fuel such as oil. Oil and other so-called *fossil fuels*—chiefly coal and natural gas—can exact a tremendous price in the form of air pollution, acid rain, and, in all likelihood, an enhancement of a natural phenomenon called the *greenhouse effect*. This phenomenon could warm the earth's atmosphere rapidly, causing frequent drought in some of today's best food-producing areas and a flooding of seaports. In addition, the world's supply of fossil fuels eventually will run out.

The Utah announcement reminded us of the decades of disappointment that have marked scientists' efforts to find an acceptable nuclear alternative to fossil fuels, and it suddenly raised hopes of an almost limitless source of safe, clean, low-cost energy. Present-day nuclear power plants generate electricity from the *fission* (splitting) of uranium or plutonium nuclei. Unfortunately, the nuclei left over after this process are highly radioactive, so the plants must have extremely sturdy structures and complicated machinery to prevent radioactive substances from escaping into the environment—expensive safeguards that have not always worked. And even if all fission plants worked perfectly, a way would still have to be found to safely dispose of their "used" fuel and other radioactive materials.

Nuclear fusion involves much less radioactivity, so for more than 40 years, the United States, the Soviet Union, and other countries have spent billions of dollars trying to develop a practical fusion device to generate electricity. Fusion produces the heat and light of the sun and stars—and the explosive force of the hydrogen bomb. To attempt to harness fusion, researchers have built huge, complex machines that heat swarms of nuclei and electrons to incredibly high temperatures, generate immense magnetic fields, and produce laser beams with awesome power.

The low-temperature approach, however, had remained virtually unexplored until the Utah chemists performed their experiments. Because of the novelty of this approach, and because it requires only a small, simple device, the Utah announcement seemed almost too good to be true.

Most scientists now believe that this announcement raised false hopes. Nevertheless, it still serves to remind us of the awesome potential of fusion, if and when we ever tame it.

Our bounty of power

Power (the rate at which energy is consumed) is measured in units called *watts* and *kilowatts* (1,000 watts). The human race currently consumes energy at a rate of 10 billion kilowatts (kW). That represents more than 2 kW of power for each of the 5 billion men, women, and children on earth. The individual 2-kilowatt share is the same as the power consumed by twenty 100-watt light bulbs.

Not all of us share equally in this bounty of power, however. In the United States, for example, the rate per person is 11 kW, while in India it is about 0.2 kW. The Indian figure is probably close to the world average at the time of the American Revolutionary War (1775-1783). So, while the global consumption of energy has grown tremendously in about 200 years, India still has a long way to go. And so does the remainder of the Third World. As developing countries acquire more factories, farm machinery, and transportation facilities, their rate of energy use per person will increase rapidly. Furthermore, the population of

The author:
Robert H. March is a professor of physics at the University of Wisconsin in Madison.

the Third World is growing so quickly that it may double by the year 2020. So the total amount of energy consumed in developing countries is bound to soar.

Problems with the bounty

More than 91 per cent of the world's energy comes from burning the fossil fuels, so called because like fossils, they developed from the remains of prehistoric plants and animals. Another 6 per cent of global energy comes from burning fuels that are constantly being renewed, mainly wood and animal wastes. The remaining 3 per cent comes from such sources as hydroelectric dams, nuclear power plants, and solar devices.

Some forms of burning have specific problems associated with them. Much of the world's coal and fuel oil, for example, is rich in sulfur. Burning the sulfur produces sulfur dioxide, which goes up the smokestack. In the atmosphere, sulfur dioxide combines with raindrops to form sulfuric acid. Furthermore, when coal or oil burns at high temperatures, nitrogen and oxygen in the air can combine, leading to the formation of nitric acid. Sulfuric and nitric acids in acid rain threaten forests and lakes from New England to central Europe.

Incomplete burning of gasoline and diesel fuel in the engines of automobiles and trucks is the main source of the ugly brown smog that hangs over many of the world's cities and threatens the health of their inhabitants. And although wood is a renewable energy source, in general it is being used up faster than it is being replaced.

Even the cleanest fossil fuel produces carbon dioxide (CO_2) gas when it burns. A build-up of CO_2 in the atmosphere may enhance the greenhouse effect. Carbon dioxide in the atmosphere operates as a one-way "gatekeeper" for energy. It allows sunlight to warm the earth, but prevents heat from escaping back into space. This trapping of heat is called the greenhouse effect, because it is similar to the way in which the walls of a greenhouse keep the structure warm.

Over the last century, the amount of CO_2 in the atmosphere has increased by about 20 per cent. During this time, the world's average temperature has risen only about 0.9 of a Fahrenheit degree (0.5 of a Celsius degree). The consumption of fossil fuels is accelerating, however. To make matters worse, the destruction of tropical rain forests—often by more burning (which also, of course, adds CO_2 to the atmosphere)—is decreasing the global rate of *photosynthesis*, in which green plants remove CO_2 from the air and return oxygen.

Most scientists agree that an increase in atmospheric CO_2 enhances the greenhouse effect, but many disagree concerning how long we have before we begin to see serious environmental consequences such as droughts and flooding. Pessimists give us a decade or two, while optimists hope for a century. It takes heavy investment and many years of effort to harness new sources of

Glossary

Deuterium: A form of hydrogen that is twice as heavy as ordinary hydrogen.

Electrode: An electric terminal.

Electrolytic cell: A chemical device that uses electricity to split molecules.

Fossil fuel: Coal, natural gas, oil, or any other fuel that developed from the remains of prehistoric plants and animals.

Greenhouse effect: A process in which certain atmospheric gases allow sunlight to warm the earth but prevent heat from escaping back into space.

Kilowatt (kW): A unit of power equal to 1,000 watts.

Nuclear fission: The splitting of an atomic nucleus.

Nuclear fusion: The joining of atomic nuclei.

energy, so regardless of who is correct, we should begin to move in that direction as quickly as possible.

This brings us to the last 3 per cent of our energy supply, the part that does not come from combustion. Any solution to the energy crisis must elevate this sector to a dominant role.

The largest current single component of this sector—hydroelectric power—will soon reach the limit of its potential. Most of the best sites for power dams have already been developed. Many people view the second largest component—nuclear fission—as too risky, and the remaining sources either have too little potential or are too expensive as presently developed.

Power from nuclear fission

Only two decades ago, nuclear fission looked like the best choice for the future. Today, that future is clouded. The problem with fission power is—and always will be—radioactivity. In a fission reactor, about 7 per cent of the energy due to fission is not released immediately, but remains in the form of radioactive nuclei in the fuel. This energy is released later as nuclear radiation, most of it in a matter of days. Enough radioactivity remains, however, to cause problems for tens of thousands of years.

"Used" nuclear fuel is so radioactive that it must be kept out of the environment at all costs. After "used" fuel is removed from a reactor, it is stored underwater at the power plant for many years until it cools enough to ship. Next, it is reduced to a *sludge* (mudlike mass) and stored in underground holding tanks for decades. In the United States, current plans call for reducing the wastes to solid blocks that resemble glass or rock, to lock the radioactive substances into solid structures. Finally, the glass or rock is to be buried.

There are special requirements for this entombment. Water could still dissolve parts of the solids and carry them away, so the solids must be buried in a place that can never be reached by ground water—the source of most drinking water.

Nuclear burial grounds seem a terrible burden to leave to future generations. Given the huge stockpile of wastes already on hand, however, we have no choice but to create them. France has shown that with careful central planning and training, it is possible for a nation to generate most of its electric power from nuclear fission with reasonable safety.

The solar alternative

To many thoughtful people, the risks of nuclear power outweigh the gains—despite the good safety record. When asked what they would put in its place, most point to the sun.

At first glance, solar energy is an inviting prospect. Every day, the sun delivers to our planet 20,000 times as much energy as we use. There are two problems with solar energy, however—there is not always enough of it where and when it is needed, and it is not very concentrated.

Putting the squeeze on today's energy sources

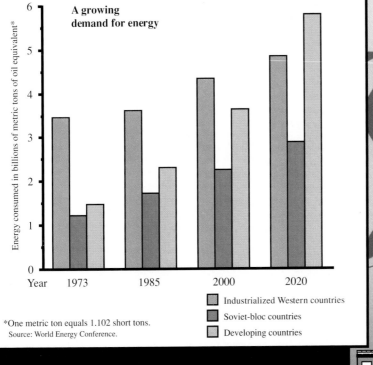

A growing demand for energy

Energy consumed in billions of metric tons of oil equivalent*

6
5
4
3
2
1
0

Year   1973   1985   2000   2020

■ Industrialized Western countries
■ Soviet-bloc countries
■ Developing countries

*One metric ton equals 1.102 short tons.
Source: World Energy Conference.

The industrialized Western nations consume much more energy than do either the Soviet-bloc states or the developing countries, *above*, with industrial applications drawing the most power, *right*. Energy demand in the West and in the Soviet bloc will likely continue to grow steadily. The developing countries, however, have a huge and growing population, so even a slow industrial build-up will cause their energy demand to sky-rocket, putting a tight squeeze on global supplies of fuel.

Energy use in the West

43% Industrial

35% Residential and commercial

22% Transportation

Source: U.S. Department of Energy.

A growing demand for fossil fuels

More than 91 per cent of the world's energy comes from the burning of fossil fuels—chiefly coal, *right,* oil, and natural gas, *below.* The use of these fuels will likely grow to meet a rising demand, *bottom.*

Energy experts predict that the consumption of fossil fuels throughout the world will continue to rise sharply in coming decades. A shift away from oil that began during the energy crisis of the 1970's will likely continue, with coal becoming the dominant fuel by 2020.

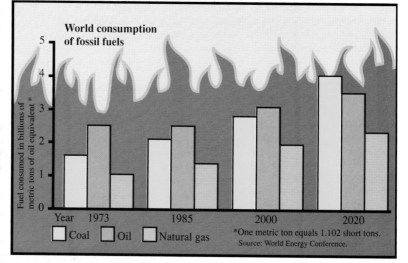

World consumption of fossil fuels

Fuel consumed in billions of metric tons of oil equivalent *

Year 1973   1985   2000   2020

☐ Coal   ☐ Oil   ☐ Natural gas

*One metric ton equals 1.102 short tons.
Source: World Energy Conference.

Fossil fuels: dwindling and damaging

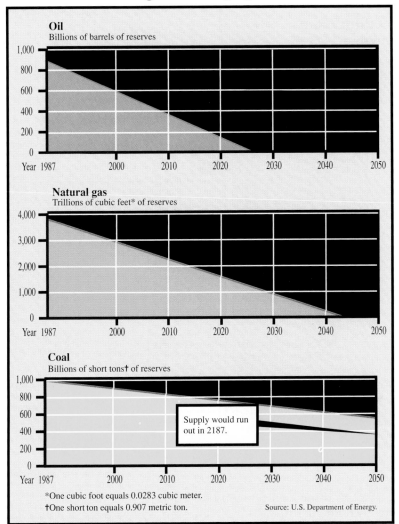

Oil
Billions of barrels of reserves

1,000
800
600
400
200
0
Year 1987 2000 2010 2020 2030 2040 2050

Natural gas
Trillions of cubic feet* of reserves

4,000
3,000
2,000
1,000
0
Year 1987 2000 2010 2020 2030 2040 2050

Coal
Billions of short tons† of reserves

1,000
800
600
400
200
0
Year 1987 2000 2010 2020 2030 2040 2050

Supply would run
out in 2187.

*One cubic foot equals 0.0283 cubic meter.
†One short ton equals 0.907 metric ton.

Source: U.S. Department of Energy.

Continued burning at today's rates would exhaust the world's oil and gas current reserves by 2050, *left,* but leave plenty of coal. The abundance of coal and the fact that new reserves of all fossil fuels are found each year would seem to indicate that worries about supplies are unwarranted. Demand is rising sharply, however, so reserves likely will dwindle much more rapidly than shown.

Environmental problems resulting from a heavy reliance on fossil fuels include air pollution, *below,* acid rain, and, in all likelihood, an enhancement of a natural phenomenon called the greenhouse effect—causing frequent drought in some of the world's best food-producing areas.

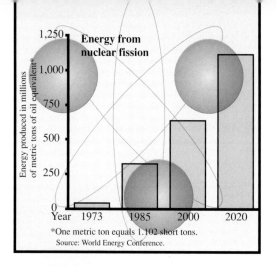

*One metric ton equals 1.102 short tons.
Source: World Energy Conference.

Nuclear fission: freedom from fossil fuels—at a price

The use of nuclear fission as an energy source avoids the pollution and supply drawbacks associated with fossil fuels but introduces a staggering environmental problem—radioactivity.

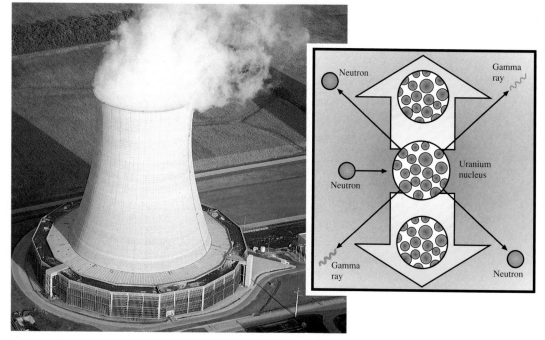

Nuclear fission begins when a neutron bombards a heavy nucleus such as that of a uranium atom, *inset above*. The nucleus splits into two highly energetic fragments, emits gamma rays, and releases neutrons, which can split other uranium nuclei. In a reactor, *above*, this process repeats itself over and over, releasing energy that is converted to electricity. The use of fission will likely continue to grow, *top*.

Each year, enough sunlight falls on the roof of a typical U.S. family home to provide for all of its energy needs, even if only 25 per cent of the energy in the sunlight were converted into a usable form such as electricity. But with low doses of sunlight in the winter months and none at all at night, much of the energy collected during summer days would have to be stored. At present, there is no cost-effective way to store it.

Even if there were such a way, however, there would not be a worthwhile amount of solar energy to store. In the middle of the brightest day, the concentration of sunlight is so low that it is cheaper to buy gas for heating and electricity for lighting than it is to generate energy from sunlight at home.

The devices called *solar cells* that convert sunlight to electricity cost 5 to 10 times as much as a nuclear power plant per kilowatt of power, when both the cells and the plant are producing as much power as they can. Furthermore, over the course of a year, a nuclear plant can average about 60 per cent of its maximum power, while at most locations it would be unusual for a solar cell to average 15 per cent.

Research is underway to develop cheaper devices that can convert sunlight to usable amounts of electricity. If this succeeds, solar power could provide a significant fraction of our electricity, but in the foreseeable future it is not likely to meet all our needs.

Power from wind, water, and rocks

People in a few favored locations can obtain usable amounts of energy from winds, tides, or *geothermal heat* (energy contained in underground rocks and fluids). In California, for example, there are more than 15,000 wind turbines, with a combined output of 1.5 million kW, enough electricity to meet the needs of 750,000 households. But wind power is practical only in areas that have strong, steady winds.

The only location in which tidal energy can be tapped economically is a bay that is penetrated by high tides and which can be closed off by a dam. During high tide, the bay fills with water. During low tide, the ocean level drops below the level of the water stored behind the dam. The stored water is then released. As the water falls, it drives turbines that generate electricity. The first tidal power plant was built in 1966 on the Rance River near

A prototype nuclear burial ground represents one price that must be paid for the use of fission as an energy source. The radioactivity of uranium fuel poses such a health risk that even "used" fuel must be kept out of the environment—in this case, by placing the fuel in cylindrical casks, burying these containers in a deep tunnel, and sealing them.

St.-Malo, France, to produce 544 million kilowatt-hours of electricity each year.

Geothermal energy is relatively cheap only when sources of intense heat are available at the surface of the earth or at shallow enough levels to make it practical to drill down to the sources. So far, Italy, Japan, the Philippines, the United States, and other nations have built about 130 geothermal power plants with a combined capacity of 3 million kW.

In addition, several countries use geothermal heat directly to heat buildings. Water from hot springs, for example, heats all the buildings in Reykjavík, the capital and largest city of Iceland.

An experimental technique known as Ocean Thermal Energy Conversion uses the difference in temperature between warm surface water and cool, deep water to drive turbines. In the United States, coastal waters of the Gulf of Mexico and off southern California may be the only locations with sufficient differences in water temperatures to make this type of power available at an affordable cost.

As a result of all these limitations, the winds, the tides, and geothermal and ocean heat are unlikely to provide more than a few per cent of the world's energy needs in the foreseeable future. So it is no wonder that the world's industrialized nations have invested billions of dollars over the last 35 years in the quest for fusion energy.

Power from nuclear fusion

The most promising fuel for fusion reactions is deuterium, an *isotope* (form) of hydrogen that is twice as heavy as ordinary hydrogen. Only 1 hydrogen atom in 7,000 is a deuterium atom, but a 1-million-kW electric power plant—equivalent to the largest fossil fuel or fission plant now in service—would consume less than 28 ounces (800 grams) of deuterium each day. Scientists estimate that there is enough deuterium in the world's oceans to provide all our current energy needs for several million years, at the end of which sea level will have dropped only about 1 foot (0.3 meter). And this would not end the use of controlled fusion as an energy source. Deuterium is not the only fuel suitable for fusion; it is merely easiest to use.

All experimental fusion devices have the same goal—to bring nuclei close enough together to fuse. For two nuclei to fuse, they need not actually touch, but they must come extremely close. A usable amount of fusion would occur in deuterium fuel if its nuclei came within 5 billionths of a millimeter of each other. It is difficult to get nuclei this close because particles with like charges repel one another. Nuclei have positive electric charges, and their mutual electrical repulsion tends to keep them apart.

At temperatures and pressures normally encountered on earth, nuclei hardly ever get close enough to fuse. In a hydrogen molecule, for example, the nuclei of the two atoms that make up the molecule stay 76 billionths of a millimeter apart. But the

Renewable sources: a steadily growing contribution

Energy supplied by renewable sources, mainly water power, will likely continue to rise, *right*. Solar devices, *below*, have tremendous potential but will likely remain too costly to achieve much growth.

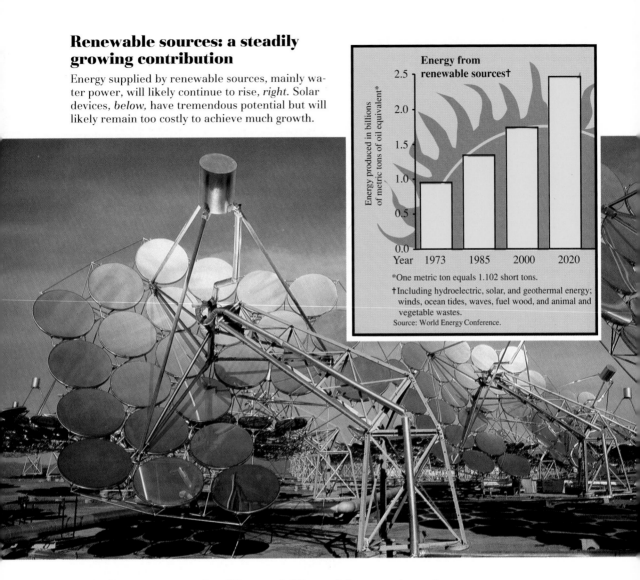

Energy from renewable sources†

Energy produced in billions of metric tons of oil equivalent*

| Year | 1973 | 1985 | 2000 | 2020 |

*One metric ton equals 1.102 short tons.

†Including hydroelectric, solar, and geothermal energy; winds, ocean tides, waves, fuel wood, and animal and vegetable wastes.
Source: World Energy Conference.

core of a star can reach millions or billions of degrees. At such temperatures, atoms move so swiftly that nuclei approach to within 1 billionth of a millimeter of one another.

There is no way to maintain such temperatures in a fusion device for more than an instant. These temperatures are high enough to turn any solid structure into vapor. Rather, scientists hope to achieve ultrahigh temperatures for an instant, producing many brief pulses of fusion energy. The walls of the reactor would then remain at a much lower temperature than the burning fuel. The deuterium in a reactor must not touch the walls, however. Nuclei that touched walls would instantly become too cool to fuse. In fact, the problem of confining nuclei so that they do not touch reactor walls is one of the main challenges of fusion research.

There are two approaches to this problem—*magnetic confinement* and *inertial confinement*. Magnetic confinement makes use

Nuclear fusion: after decades of research, still "promising"

In one fusion reaction, *below,* a tremendous amount of heat energy forces deuterium nuclei to combine to form a helium nucleus and emit a neutron with even more heat energy. Scientists have tried for decades to harness such reactions by building large devices such as a multiple-beam laser, *bottom,* to fuse large numbers of nuclei. In March 1989, however, chemists at the University of Utah, *right,* claimed that they had fused deuterium at room temperature in jarlike devices. But by year-end, there was no persuasive evidence to back this claim.

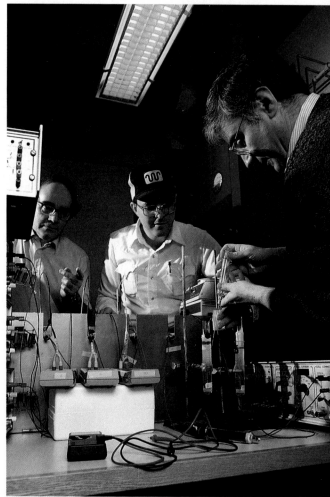

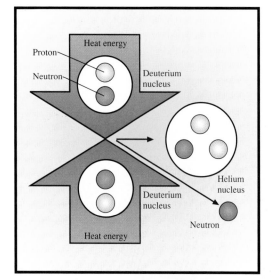

Heat energy

Proton

Neutron

Deuterium nucleus

Deuterium nucleus

Helium nucleus

Neutron

Heat energy

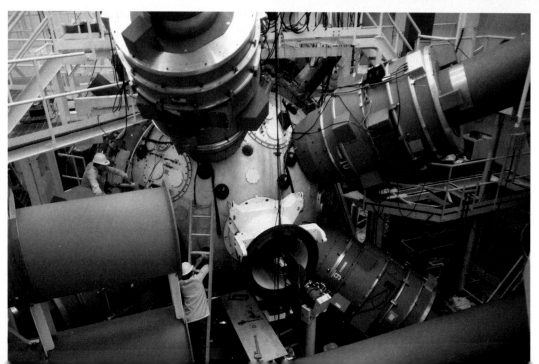

of the fact that the deuterium fuel is electrically charged. At high temperatures, hydrogen atoms come apart, producing a state of matter called a *plasma*, consisting of positively charged nuclei and negatively charged electrons. These particles can be manipulated by magnetic fields generated by huge and expensive machines. The goal of magnetic confinement is to lock the plasma in a "magnetic bottle" that pushes the plasma away from the walls of the container. Unfortunately, a plasma cannot be bottled up for long, because moving electrons create magnetic fields that disrupt the fields generated by the machine.

At present, the mightiest fusion machine is a $300-million magnetic-confinement device, the Tokamak Fusion Test Reactor in Princeton, N.J. In three years of operation, this machine has approached—but never reached—*scientific breakeven*, the point at which the reactor produces as much energy as it takes to heat it.

Inertial confinement is a newer approach in which converging beams of laser light or subatomic particles heat and compress a pellet of solid hydrogen. This is how a hydrogen bomb works, with a nuclear fission device supplying radiation that compresses the fusion fuel. A fusion reactor working on this principle would produce repeated miniature nuclear explosions, each with the energy equivalent of a few pounds of high explosive rather than millions of tons. At present, inertial confinement devices are much further from scientific breakeven than are the magnetic confinement machines.

At the beginning of the fusion effort in about 1950, optimists predicted scientific breakeven within five years. Today they are making the same estimate, which prompted one pessimist to remark that "fusion is the energy source of the future, and always will be."

Even if researchers achieved breakeven, there would still be some problems. Fusion reactions generate neutrons, which are a nightmare for machine designers. As neutrons fly through matter, they knock atoms out of place, weakening any solid material—so they would weaken reactor walls, which therefore eventually would have to be replaced. But some neutrons are absorbed by nuclei of various materials that then become radioactive, so the "used" walls would be somewhat radioactive. Thus, although fusion reactors would create less of a waste disposal problem than do fission reactors, this problem would still be a serious one.

"Cold fusion" claimed

In March 1989, chemists Martin Fleischmann of the University of Southampton in England and B. Stanley Pons of the University of Utah startled the world by claiming that they had produced fusion at room temperature. The two chemists said that fusion had occurred in a simple, common chemical apparatus called an *electrolytic cell*. This device had two *electrodes* (electric terminals). The negative terminal was made of the metal palladium, and the positive terminal was platinum. The researchers mounted the electrodes in a glass vessel containing *heavy water*, whose molecules contain oxygen and the deuterium isotope of hydrogen.

When the scientists connected the electrolytic cell to a source of electricity, water molecules split up into positively charged hydrogen atoms and negatively charged oxygen atoms. Because unlike charges attract, hydrogen atoms flowed to the negative electrode and oxygen atoms headed for the positive electrode.

In cells using common electrode materials such as carbon, the hydrogen and oxygen atoms bubble to the water's surface as gases. A palladium electrode attracts hydrogen so strongly, however, that the electrode can store a great deal of hydrogen in the spaces between its palladium atoms. Fleischmann and Pons had reasoned that once enough hydrogen atoms had been taken up by the palladium, they might be packed close enough to produce fusion.

The two chemists reported that, after a few weeks of operation, their cell began to produce much more heat than the electric current could have provided. Furthermore, they claimed to have detected neutrons, though at a rate 1 billion times smaller than expected if the heat had been produced by the common fusion reactions. (There are fusion reactions that emit no neutrons, but under normal conditions they are far less likely to occur than are the reactions that do emit neutrons.)

Hundreds of scientists rushed to conduct electrolytic-cell experiments to check the results reported by Fleischmann and Pons. A few researchers claimed—like the Utah chemists—that their experiments produced more heat than could have been provided by the electric current supplied to the electrolytic cells. Other scientists observed neutrons. The vast majority, however, saw no evidence for fusion at all. Efforts to check Fleischmann and Pons's results were complicated by the fact that the two chemists released few details because the University of Utah wanted to guard the patent rights to their discovery.

The muon approach

Even if the Utah chemists' results turn out to be incorrect, their work has encouraged scientists to reexamine other approaches to fusion. One approach employs unstable atomic particles called *muons*, which are similar to electrons but 200 times heavier; and deuterium molecules, which are made up of two deuterium nuclei and two electrons in orbit about the nuclei. Scientists create muons in the laboratory and then guide them into a chamber containing deuterium molecules. A muon tends to replace one of the electrons in a deuterium molecule. When this happens, the molecule shrinks to $1/200$ of its normal size and the two nuclei fuse. The muon then usually replaces an electron of another deuterium molecule, and fusion again takes place.

In almost all cases, however, after a few repetitions of fusion reactions, the muon disintegrates or goes into orbit around one of the fusion products such as a helium nucleus. Unfortunately, the fusions caused by the muon do not generate enough energy to make up for the energy used to create the particle. Scientists hope to find a way to minimize the absorption of muons by fusion products.

But neither the muon approach nor any of the others—magnetic confinement, inertial confinement, or "cold" fusion—promises to provide abundant fusion energy in the near future. There are many things we can do to buy more time to search for new energy sources, however. The most important of these is to conserve the sources that we already have.

A not-so-glamorous solution

Although the energy crisis of the 1970's forced Americans to conserve fuels, the United States still uses much more energy than it really needs, partly because until recently its own domestic reserves were cheap and plentiful. Western Europe and Japan, not so favored by nature, have managed to match the U.S. standard of living while using about half as much energy per inhabitant. A well-planned effort to improve the energy efficiency of transportation, industry, and home heating and cooling systems could help the U.S. economy by reducing energy imports and the cost of manufacturing, while minimizing damage to the environment. Much of this is happening already. New factories and homes, for example, are much more energy-efficient than the ones they are replacing.

On the supply side, a multifaceted approach will have to do. Although energy from the sun, wind, tides, and volcanoes may never be the final answer, these sources can supply an increasing share of our energy needs. And as supplies of fossil fuels begin to run out, their price is bound to rise, favoring energy sources such as solar cells that now seem too expensive. Even at present rates of consumption, petroleum supplies may be exhausted early in the next century, natural gas in midcentury, and coal by 2200.

So even though science has no instant solutions to our energy problems, it does give us ways to manage the continuing energy crisis while reducing the stress on our environment. This "nickel-and-dime" approach may not have the glamour of a scientific breakthrough, but it can work.

For further reading:
Ashley, Steven. "New Life for Solar?" *Popular Science*, May 1989.
Gibbons, John H., and others. "Strategies for Energy Use." *Scientific American*, September 1989.
Heppenheimer, T. A. *The Man-Made Sun: The Quest for Fusion Power.* Little, Brown, 1984.

By Ian W. D. Dalziel

The Last Unspoiled Continent

Antarctica is the coldest, windiest, harshest place on earth. But the teeming life in its icy waters and its value as an international scientific outpost make it worth protecting.

It was a perfect summer day in Antarctica. The temperature was well above freezing, and the sea glistened calmly in the sunshine. Although the date was Jan. 21, 1989, it was midsummer. Antarctica lies south of the equator—in fact, it is the southernmost continent on earth—so its seasons are opposite those in the Northern Hemisphere.

I rode with 22 other professional geologists in two inflatable boats, all of us dressed in red parka-like life jackets and yellow oilskin pants. We steered our boats in a zigzag course around the islands off the Antarctic Peninsula. From time to time, we stopped and, using the gear we had brought with us—cameras, hammers, magnifying glasses—studied the area's granite rocks to gather data about the mountain formations of Antarctica. As we worked, pelicanlike cormorants flew overhead as if checking up on us. Chinstrap penguins fished nearby in the crystal-clear water.

I have spent every Antarctic summer since 1968 doing geologic research on the frozen continent, but this was the first such trip for 20 of my colleagues. In the course of their work, these international experts had explored many parts of the world—from the Rocky Mountains to the Himalaya. Yet despite the sights they had seen, they were enthralled with the unspoiled landscape before us. All were struck by the Antarctic's dramatic interplay of rock, ice, and sea.

One week later, a shipping accident blemished this spotless landscape. The *Bahía Paraíso*, an Argentine ship carrying supplies and tourists, ran aground off Anvers Island and capsized, leaking several thousand gallons of diesel fuel into the ocean. It was Antarctica's first oil spill. Within weeks, the fuel had killed hundreds, perhaps thousands, of penguins and other birds. Because oil spills in cold climates are slow to break down into harmless chemicals, the fuel may continue damaging Antarctica's wildlife for years.

The *Bahía Paraíso* spill came at a time of changing attitudes toward the future of the frozen continent. Long the domain only of explorers, sealers, whalers, and scientists, Antarctica is now the topic of newspaper articles and prime-time television shows. Diplomats discuss the continent's future at meetings of the United Nations. Greenpeace and other environmental groups sound warnings about the possibility that our planet's last unspoiled continent may be permanently violated. Conservationists see threats to Antarctica's unique environment in mineral exploitation, fishing, tourism, and even scientific projects.

Adding to these concerns is the widespread belief that the Antarctic Treaty will expire in 1991. For 30 years, this international agreement has prohibited the use of Antarctica as a military outpost and encouraged cooperation among scientists working there. Actually, the treaty does not expire in 1991, though it may be subject to review. Nevertheless, concern about the future of Antarctica remains.

The author:
Ian W. D. Dalziel, shown here in the Pensacola Mountains in Antarctica, is senior research scientist and professor of geological sciences at the University of Texas, Austin.

A land of harsh extremes

At first examination, Antarctica seems hardly the place to arouse so much interest. If you were to travel there, you would probably be struck by its almost unbelievable desolation. This is the coldest place on earth, with temperatures that rise above freezing only along the coasts during the brief southern summer. Covered with a thick cap of ice and compressed snow that reaches depths of nearly 3 miles (4.8 kilometers), Antarctica is the highest of the earth's continents. In some places, a person can become light-headed from the scarcity of oxygen even when standing on level ground. The interior of the continent is also extremely dry—drier even than the Sahara. The land, especially along the coasts, is swept by bitterly cold winds that often reach hurricane strength.

Stormy seas isolate the frozen continent from the other southern continents—Africa, Australia, and South America. Unimpeded by land masses and driven by the rotation of the earth, a strong ocean current called the Circumpolar Current flows continuously clockwise around Antarctica within the Southern Ocean (sometimes called the Antarctic Ocean). The Circumpolar Current prevents warmer waters from reaching Antarctica and moderating its climate.

Although wildlife is plentiful along Antarctica's coasts, survival in the frigid interior is difficult not only for human visitors but

First oil spill
The *Bahía Paraíso,* a ship carrying supplies and tourists, ran aground off the Antarctic Peninsula on Jan. 28, 1989. All aboard were rescued, but as the ship capsized, it spilled thousands of gallons of diesel fuel.

127

also for animals and plants. Shrouded in near total darkness for eight months of the year, the continent supports few plants other than mosses and lichens. The largest land animal is a wingless fly less than ½ inch (12 millimeters) long.

In short, a more forbidding place cannot be found on earth. It is no wonder that British explorer Captain James Cook, the first person to sail around Antarctica, said in 1775, "I make bold to declare that the world will derive no benefit from it."

A natural "laboratory" for scientists

Cook was mistaken. Humanity has found a way to derive a great deal of benefit from Antarctica—by taking advantage of the continent's unique features that make it a superb site for scientific research. Today, Antarctica is dotted with more than 50 research stations. Scientists from more than 20 nations are engaged in scores of research projects in atmospheric science, biology, geology, and other disciplines.

The very fact that Antarctica is the only continent too inhospitable to be widely colonized means that it is the most unspoiled

The bottom of the world
Antarctica is the southernmost continent, *below*. Important geographical features of the continent, *bottom,* are shown on a false-color image made from a compilation of satellite photographs.

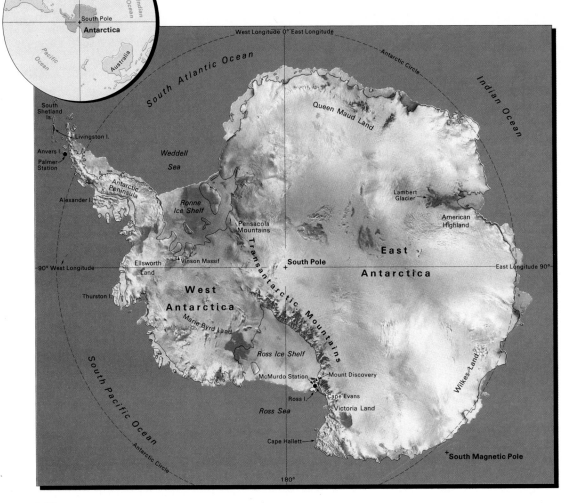

environment left on earth. As such, it has great value as a standard for assessing environmental changes around the globe. The Antarctic icecap is a unique source of information on former atmospheric conditions because it contains bubbles of air trapped tens of thousands and even hundreds of thousands of years ago. Using special drilling equipment, scientists can remove samples of ancient ice—and hence, ancient air—for study. This helps us learn about the climate of earth thousands of years ago. Such information is useful in determining whether the climate is beginning to warm because of increased air pollution—a phenomenon called the *greenhouse effect*.

Because Antarctica lies close to the *south magnetic pole*, the southern point indicated by compass needles, and has extremely cold and dry climatic conditions, it excels as a base to study atmospheric phenomena caused by radiation coming from the sun or space. For example, the Antarctic sky glows in the long winter night with displays of light called *auroras*. The continent has also been a superb site for observation of the stars in the southern sky, including Supernova 1987A, a rare exploding star detected in February 1987.

Then, too, Antarctica is a treasure trove of meteorites. These chunks of stone or metal that fall to earth from space are much easier to find in Antarctica than in other parts of the world. Meteorites that land on the icecap are soon covered by snow but are eventually brought to the surface again as ice slowly flows from the interior of the continent toward the coasts. More than one-third of all the meteorites found on earth—including fragments of the moon, and possibly even Mars—have been discovered in Antarctica.

Plentiful wildlife

Biologists can find much to study in Antarctica, if for no other reason than that the continent is home to most of the world's penguins. Penguin species range from the stately emperor penguins of the southern Ross Sea to the quiet gentoo and the small, aggressive chinstrap penguins of the northern Antarctic Peninsula and offshore islands. All of these flightless birds waddle awkwardly on land but use their flippers to swim gracefully in the sea.

More than 40 other kinds of birds, including the albatross, giant petrel, and tiny tern, migrate to the southernmost continent in the summer. Most of these flying birds make their nests on land and seek food at sea. Many whale species also spend the summer in the Southern Ocean. Some species, including blue whales and humpback whales, feed on krill, shrimplike sea creatures that reproduce rapidly and attain vast numbers during the days of 24-hour sunshine.

Biologists trying to understand how Antarctic organisms have adapted to their harsh environment have made valuable discoveries. They have learned, for example, that some Antarctic fish produce a natural antifreeze that keeps them alive and unfrozen even though the water they swim in is filled with ice. The interior of the continent provides a natural laboratory for the study of how plants and animals manage to survive in the most extreme conditions.

Scientists who study weather are keenly interested in Antarctica because the region is a driving force in the world's climate patterns. The icy continent cools warm air in the atmosphere, creating storms that spiral across the Southern Hemisphere. In a similar fashion, the frigid waters and strong currents of the Southern Ocean influence oceanic circulation and weather far north of Antarctica.

Atmospheric scientists also use Antarctica as a base to study the effects of air pollution. It was here that researchers discovered the much-publicized "ozone hole," a thinning of the protective ozone layer in earth's upper atmosphere. The thinning is probably caused by chemicals known as *chlorofluorocarbons* or *CFC's*.

Antarctica has great value to geologists, of course. It rests upon one of the seven major plates that make up earth's crust. These plates, which carry the continents upon them, are in slow, continuous motion. Any study of the interactions between them—which can help scientists predict earthquakes, for example—must involve Antarctica. One of the aims of my own geologic research in Antarctica is to understand the motion of these plates. Another focus of my research is the geologic history of the continent. This type of research provides us with information about how the entire planet has changed during the course of millions of years.

Finally, aside from its scientific importance, Antarctica is of symbolic importance to all of us. For 30 years, through politically difficult and unstable times, international efforts have kept this land at the bottom of the earth peaceful. The continent can be seen as a laboratory for cooperation among nations.

Threats to the last unspoiled continent?

This peaceful cooperation would not have existed had the Antarctic Treaty not been drafted in 1959 by 12 nations, including Australia, Great Britain, the United States, and the Soviet Union. The treaty was signed and went into force in 1961. Twenty-six other nations agreed to abide by the treaty after it was signed, more than half of them doing so in the 1980's, as the continent's potential value became clearer.

The thrust of this treaty is to encourage peaceful scientific cooperation in Antarctica, but it has other important provisions. Before the document was drafted, seven nations claimed ownership of parts of Antarctica. The treaty effectively suspended new claims and the acceptance of existing ones. It also prohibited countries from testing nuclear weapons in Antarctica or disposing of radioactive waste there.

Like nowhere else

● Antarctica holds the record for the lowest temperature ever recorded on earth: −128.6°F. (−89.2°C), several degrees below the temperature of dry ice.

● Antarctica is the windiest continent, with gusts of 120 miles (190 kilometers) per hour often measured at the coasts. Winds of 74 miles (119 kilometers) per hour are considered hurricane force.

● The interior of Antarctica receives only about 2 inches (5 centimeters) of snowfall per year. Death Valley, Calif., has approximately the same amount of annual precipitation.

● Antarctica's ice sheets flow from the interior of the continent to the coasts. The movement is generally very slow, but in some places, the ice travels as much as 9 feet (3 meters) per day.

● Fossils found in Antarctica indicate that millions of years ago, the continent was an ice-free, tree-covered place inhabited by mammals, huge birds, and dinosaurs.

● The thick icecap that covers most of Antarctica is so heavy that it pushes the underlying land mass below sea level and slightly flattens the earth's curvature.

● The geographic South Pole—near the center of Antarctica, where all lines of longitude meet—is not the point compasses indicate as south. This place, known as the magnetic south pole, moves a few miles every year and in the late 1980's was in the Southern Ocean.

● The largest iceberg sighted in recent history broke off Antarctica's Ross Ice Shelf in 1987. It was twice the size of Rhode Island.

What of the widespread belief that this important treaty will expire in 1991, 30 years after its ratification? Many newspaper and magazine articles state this as fact. It's a reflection of popular interest in Antarctica that cabdrivers in cities as far apart as London and Cape Town, South Africa, have brought up this date when I mention that I work in Antarctica.

But it is not true that the pact will end in 1991. The actual wording of the Antarctic Treaty is only that a conference "to review the operation of the Treaty" may be held after 1991 if any of the parties involved requests one. The treaty has already been modified 164 times since 1961, so another review would hardly be unusual. Nevertheless, the 30-year-review clause does provide some uncertainty, as do a number of other recent developments concerning the continent.

Environmental issues are by far the most important concern. One problem is the ozone hole, which has appeared during the southern spring every year since the late 1970's. In September 1989, scientists again detected an especially drastic thinning of

Antarctic wildlife

Most of the continent's plants and animals live along the coasts, where conditions are less extreme than in the interior. A group of Adélie penguins strut at Cape Evans, *above.* A crab-eater seal—which despite its clumsy appearance can move across land almost as quickly as a person can run—basks on Livingston Island, *opposite page.*

the ozone layer above Antarctica. Researchers were surprised at the rapid growth of the hole, which could eventually become far larger than the entire continent. Because the ozone layer protects living things from harmful solar radiation, biologists worry about how the hole may affect the Antarctic's wildlife and indeed eventually human beings.

Environmentalists are equally concerned about how the frozen continent might be harmed by the greenhouse effect. The huge Antarctic icecap contains $7\frac{1}{4}$ million cubic miles (30 million cubic kilometers) of ice and snow—70 per cent of earth's fresh water. If the world's climate were to warm even slightly, the icecap might begin to melt. This would raise sea levels and in the process drastically alter coastlines and flood coastal cities.

Even scientific research itself is sometimes cited as an environmental problem. In August 1988, the Environmental Defense Fund, a group based in New York City, charged that U.S. scientific bases in Antarctica were polluting the continent's fragile environment. The group claimed, for example, that sewage from the McMurdo Station on Ross Island had at one time been dumped untreated into the ocean.

Such charges are often described as an environmentalist-versus-scientist confrontation, but the issue is more complicated

Scientific outpost

About 20 nations have established permanent research stations in Antarctica. The
largest is the United States McMurdo Station on Ross Island, *above.* During the
Antarctic summer, well over 1,000 people
work at this bustling facility, engaged in
projects such as measuring atmospheric
levels of ozone using special weather bal-
loons, *right.* Geologists from a New
Zealand research station take rock samples from one of Antarctica's windswept,
ice-free valleys, *below.*

than that. Opinions have changed among scientists working in Antarctica, as they have elsewhere in the world, as to what practices are environmentally acceptable. As the Environmental Defense Fund charged, research teams of several nations often dumped waste into the ocean, burned it, or merely left it at the site of a project in the early years of scientific research on the continent.

Today, however, scientists have begun to closely examine the environmental impact of their research. Many organizations that fund scientific projects—such as the Division of Polar Programs of the U.S. National Science Foundation in Washington, D.C.— now ensure that funded research programs allow for proper disposal of waste and equipment.

Science and conservation go hand in hand much of the time. Results of scientific experimentation are needed to design and carry out sound conservation and management practices. But at other times, there is a conflict between the desire to preserve an environment and scientists' needs to use it for their research. Biologists seeking to learn all they can about a penguin species may need to kill and dissect a few of the birds—a practice some conservationists find objectionable. Geologists using sound waves to chart the structure of the sea floor in the Southern Ocean sometimes need to set off explosions that may kill a limited number of aquatic animals.

Coming: Antarctic mining camps?

Conservationists are also concerned about the possibility of mineral exploitation in Antarctica. In June 1988, 20 of the nations abiding by the Antarctic Treaty met in Wellington, New Zealand, to draw up the Convention for the Regulation of Antarctic Mineral Resource Activities. That document set forth rules for how companies may prospect for, and eventually exploit, Antarctica's petroleum and mineral resources. In August 1989, Australia and France withdrew their support for the convention, making it unlikely to receive immediate ratification.

The mineral convention is still highly controversial. Some people view it as a diplomatic triumph, in that it established regulations for the development of Antarctica's mineral resources even before any important deposits had been discovered. But many environmentalists see the convention as a disturbing encouragement of the continent's exploitation.

Is the Antarctic likely to become an oil drilling and mining center in addition to a scientific outpost? A look at its geologic history is necessary to provide a better understanding of this question. About 175 million years ago, Antarctica was united with Africa, Australia, India, New Zealand, and South America in a vast continent geologists call Gondwanaland. Through time, the continents drifted away from one another, but their former connection has led to dreams of untapped mineral resources beneath Antarctica's ice.

The South American, African, and Australian parts of what was once Gondwanaland are rich in gold, diamonds, iron ore, copper, and other important minerals. Substantial oil fields have been discovered off southern Australia and in southernmost South America. Because the Antarctic's Ross Sea and Weddell Sea are similar geologic environments, they too may contain reserves of petroleum.

Given the expense of overcoming the formidable natural problems, however, I do not expect to see Antarctic mineral resources exploited any time soon. Studies of the continent have so far yielded only two minor indications of significant petroleum, coal, and iron ore deposits, and smaller amounts of copper and other minerals. Even if larger deposits were to be detected, imagine the difficulty of drilling in the Antarctic's stormy seas filled with icebergs far larger than their Arctic equivalents. The price of oil is now so low that nothing less than a gigantic oil field in Antarctica would attract the interest of oil companies.

As to mining, the mineral deposits in developing nations will probably be exploited long before it becomes economically feasible to open mines in Antarctica. Here again, the difficulty of the project would often outweigh the possible gain. Heavy machinery, laborers, food, and supplies would have to be shipped to Antarctica from elsewhere before mining could begin. Shipping costs would require that raw ore be refined on the ice-laden continent, necessitating even more laborers, fuel, and supplies. To find a more expensive place to establish a mine and refinery, one would have to go to the moon.

Fishing and tourism

Another continuing concern about Antarctica's future is that fishing off the coast may disrupt the food web of the Southern Ocean. Despite the fact that only about 100 species of fish are found in Antarctic waters, compared with the more than 20,000 kinds of fish in the warmer waters of the world, commercial fishing has become common in the Southern Ocean. Fleets of a dozen or more deep-sea vessels from Japan, Poland, South Korea, and the Soviet Union can often be seen seeking krill and fish off the northern Antarctic Peninsula during the summer. Clearly, these nations find that it pays to fish in Antarctic waters, and their activities will doubtless continue.

Fishing is, however, already governed by another set of regulations drawn up by the signers of the Antarctic Treaty—the Convention on the Conservation of Antarctic Marine Living Resources, which sets limits on the amount of fish that can be harvested. And commercial whaling, long a matter of grave concern to environmentalists but now monitored by the International Whaling Commission, has all but ceased.

If change has come to Antarctica, it arrived on a chartered tourist ship. When I went to Palmer Station, the U.S. base on

Civilization encroaches

Antarctica is no longer completely unspoiled. Human activity has led to pollution; penguins, *left,* pick their way through a garbage dump near a research station. Tourism has also come to Antarctica as thousands of travelers head south every year in search of adventure. A group of vacationers, *below,* land in the Antarctic Peninsula shortly before their ship, the *Bahía Paraíso,* runs aground.

Anvers Island, in January 1989, I learned that nearly 1,000 tourists had visited the base during the preceding three weeks. Since the late 1960's, tour operators have offered vacationers the opportunity to fly over the continent or explore the coastline by ship. In 1984, operators began to sell overland trips as well. Adventurous tourists can climb Vinson Massif, the highest peak on the continent, or ski to the South Pole.

Access to the continent by tourists, mountaineers, and boaters has become routine—and sometimes understandably frustrates scientists who have their work disrupted by visits to bases where their laboratories are housed. For this reason, individual nations have begun to restrict the number of tourists given permission to visit their stations, and policies will probably become more strict as more vacationers head for the Antarctic. Nevertheless, tourism seems to have ended Antarctica's days as purely a "continent for science."

Opposite page: Dwarfed by the immensity of the icecap, geologists work on a rock outcropping on Thurston Island.

Antarctica tomorrow

Tourism and scientific research will undoubtedly continue to coexist in Antarctica. None of the nations of the world can afford to waste money on research programs in Antarctica that could be accomplished at lower cost in less remote regions, however. For this reason, fewer projects may be undertaken, and scientists from various nations may increasingly cooperate as they seek to solve scientific problems of mutual concern at the lowest possible cost.

The pictures of planet earth taken by astronauts made many people aware of Antarctica for the first time as a true continent rather than merely a name or an irregular line across the bottom of a map of the world. It is in this global context that Antarctica is of vital interest to us all. As I set out for another season of field work in the interior of the continent, it is my fervent wish that Antarctica will remain a peaceful spot where the best type of international interaction takes place. I'm confident that the many different interests active in Antarctic planning will reach agreements that will enable my children, their children, and their grandchildren to visit the continent and experience its beauty as I have, while learning still more about its importance to planet earth.

For further reading:

Beck, Peter J. *The International Politics of Antarctica.* St. Martin's Press, 1986.

Fifield, Richard. *International Research in the Antarctic.* Oxford Univ. Press, 1987.

Parfit, Michael. *South Light: A Journey to the Last Continent.* Macmillan Pubs., 1985.

Pyne, Stephen J. *Ice: A Journey to Antarctica.* Ballantine Bks., 1988.

Reader's Digest Editors. *Antarctica: Great Stories from the Frozen Continent.* Random House, 1985.

By Constance Holden

Double Features

Studies of twins are yielding new clues about how heredity influences our beliefs, our interests, and our behavior.

The similarities in the lives of Jim Lewis and Jim Springer, identical twins raised apart since infancy, range from the seemingly coincidental to the outright bizarre. Both married and divorced women named Linda and then married women named Betty. One twin named his first son James Alan; the other named his James Allan. Both had a dog named Toy, drove the same model blue Chevrolet, smoked the same brand of cigarette, and vacationed at the same beach in Florida. As students, both liked math and hated spelling. Both enjoyed woodworking and built a white wooden bench around a tree in the backyard. Both had law-enforcement training and worked part-time as a deputy sheriff. The twins also had identical blood pressure and suffered from migraine headaches. Both bit their fingernails to the quick.

The similarities shared by the two men, known as the "Jim twins," are particularly striking considering that the two were

separated when they were only 4 weeks old and adopted by different families. (Their adoptive families independently named the boys Jim.) Although each of the two had known since childhood that he had a twin brother, they were not reunited until they were 39 years old.

Jerry Levey and Mark Newman, like the Jim twins, are identical twins separated at birth. Volunteer fire fighters, they were reunited at age 31 after a co-worker of Newman's saw Levey at a fire fighters' convention, was struck by the resemblance between the two men, and arranged a meeting. Like the Jim twins, Levey and Newman are amazingly alike. Both are bachelors who wear droopy mustaches and aviator-style eyeglasses. They enjoy the same pastimes and have the odd habit, when drinking beer, of stretching the little finger across the bottom of the can.

Intriguing similarities such as these are only part of the fascination twins hold for most people. Many scientists share this fascination—and with good reason. For more than 100 years, twins have served as a natural laboratory for studying the relative influence of heredity (genes) and environment (upbringing and surroundings) on physical and mental disorders. In the past 20 years, however, the focus of twin studies has expanded to include personality. The findings, which challenge long-held theories about the dominance of environmental influences, suggest that heredity is at least as strong an influence as environment on many of our beliefs and interests and much of our behavior.

Twins are the most common type of multiple birth, occurring about once in every 89 births. There are about 2.4 million sets of twins in the United States, with some 33,000 more sets born every year.

A mysterious condition known as the "vanishing twin syndrome," however, suggests that many more of us than the statistics indicate start out as twins. Sometimes, tests early in pregnancy will reveal two fetuses. In later tests, only one fetus appears. In most cases, the mother's body, for reasons still unknown, has absorbed one of the fetuses. In other cases, one twin is absorbed or enveloped by its sibling. One of the most dramatic examples of vanishing-twin syndrome involved a gas-station attendant who experienced blinding headaches. During exploratory brain surgery, doctors discovered a mass of embryonic hair, skin, and bone. Apparently, the man had enveloped his twin while still in the womb.

The author:
Constance Holden is senior staff writer for *Science* magazine.

Two-way split

Twins owe their physical similarities to the genes they have in common. Each human cell has many hundreds of thousands of genes, the basic unit of heredity, grouped on 23 pairs of threadlike structures called *chromosomes*. Each parent supplies half a child's chromosomes.

The types of twins differ in the number of genes they have in common. Twins are either identical—known as *monozygotic*—

One egg or two

Twins are either identical or fraternal, depending on
whether they develop from one egg or two.

Identical twins, also
known as monozygotic
twins, result when a
fertilized egg splits in
two. This split produces
two people of the same
sex who have 100 per
cent of the same genetic
material. Despite their
shared genes, however,
no identical twins are
ever totally alike.

Fraternal twins, also
known as dizygotic
twins, result when a
woman releases two
eggs at about the same
time and these are
fertilized by different
sperm. Fraternal twins,
who can be of the same
or the opposite sex, are
genetically no more alike
than ordinary siblings.

or fraternal—known as *dizygotic*. Identical twins result when a
fertilized egg splits in two. This split, which occurs at random,
produces two people—always of the same sex—who have 100
per cent of the same genetic material. About one-third of all
twins are identical.

Despite their shared genes, no identical twins are ever totally
alike. For example, such twins do not have exactly the same fingerprints, though their fingerprint patterns are usually similar.
With many identical twins, one twin is taller and more robust
than the other. This difference in size and strength may result
from a condition called *twin transfusion syndrome* in which one

Jim Springer, at left in the photograph on the right, and Jim Lewis, identical twins separated at birth, discovered striking parallels in their lives when reunited at age 39. One parallel was their interest in woodworking in their basement workshops.

twin gets more than his or her share of the blood supply in the womb. In extreme cases, the short-changed twin may die before birth.

Even twins with remarkable similarities are different in many ways. The Jim twins, for example, wear their hair differently. In addition, one twin is much better at expressing himself aloud, while the other is a better writer.

Fraternal twins result when a woman releases two eggs at about the same time and these are fertilized by different sperm. Fraternal twins, who can be of the same or opposite sex, are genetically no more alike than ordinary siblings. All siblings share, on average, 50 per cent of the same genetic material. But some fraternal twins may look nearly identical if they happen to share a high proportion of the same genes. The tendency to have fraternal twins—actually the tendency for a woman to release two eggs at a time during ovulation—may run in families.

The rate at which identical twins are born is the same world-wide. The rate of fraternal twinning, however, is another story. Black women have twice as many fraternal twins, proportion-ately, as do white women. White women, in turn, have twice as many fraternal twins, proportionately, as do Oriental women. Scientists aren't sure why such variations exist. One theory is that there may be racial differences in the level of the female hormone that triggers the release of eggs from the ovary.

Another self

Twins, especially identical twins, often seem to share a special bond. Having a twin is probably the closest anyone can come to having a soul mate. Indeed, all types of twins, with the exception of male-female fraternal twins, are far less likely to marry than the general population, possibly because the close relationship with their same-sex twin satisfies their need for companionship.

Although the existence of a psychological connection between twins has never been proved scientifically, stories about this spe-cial closeness abound. Twins have reported sensing when the other is in trouble. There have been many reported cases where one twin felt pain in a particular part of the body only to dis-cover that his or her twin had suffered an injury there. People whose identical twin died at birth often feel they have a missing half. Even twins raised apart and unaware of the other's exist-ence have reported such feelings.

Sometimes, the closeness between twins causes problems. About 40 per cent of twin toddlers develop a common language, largely unintelligible to others. Usually, twins discard this special language by age 5 or 6. Those who fail to do so, however, often have learning problems and difficulties dealing with others.

Sometimes the closeness between twins can be destructive, if they fail to develop separate personalities. For example, the Chaplin twins of Great Britain move, walk, and talk in unison. The twins, who live in a hospital for the mentally handicapped, cannot tolerate the slightest difference between them, such as wearing different colored gloves, or bear to be separated.

Simply being a twin can increase the risk of some difficulties. Although twins make up only 1 per cent of all births, they ac-count for 11 per cent of all newborn deaths, mainly because of low birth weight.

Heredity versus environment

To scientists, the similarities between twins make for more than interesting tales. Twins are providing researchers with a way to probe one of the deepest mysteries of human nature—how heredity and environment interact in shaping personality.

The assumption underlying these studies is that if two people share the same genetic makeup, the differences between them must be the result of environmental influences. Such influences include everything that happens to us from conception onward, ranging from the supply of nutrients in the womb to parental care and education to illness and accidents. On the other hand, similarities between identical twins raised apart, whose environments are presumably no more similar than those of any two people selected at random, suggest strong genetic influences. Studies of twins reared apart provide scientists with the opportunity to examine how environment interacts with two versions of the same person. In this way, they provide new insights into how we all come to be what we are.

Probing similarities and differences

The most intensive and best-known twin study in the United States is being conducted at the University of Minnesota's Center for Twin and Adoption Research in Minneapolis. The study, directed by psychologist and behavioral geneticist Thomas J. Bouchard, Jr., was launched in 1979. (*Behavioral genetics* is the science of separating out the contributions of genes and environment to human behavior.) At the center, researchers conduct extensive comparisons of groups of twins—both identical and fraternal—separated at birth and raised apart, or reared together.

Over the years, Bouchard's research team has studied 63 pairs of identical twins and 36 pairs of fraternal twins separated at birth and many more pairs of twins brought up together. In addition to psychologists and psychiatrists, the team includes heart specialists, allergists, ophthalmologists, dentists, geneticists, and even a *chronobiologist* (a scientist who studies biological cycles and rhythms, such as those of sleeping and waking and of body temperature).

Twins evaluated at the center undergo a battery of physical and psychological tests lasting six days. In addition to taking a detailed medical history from each subject, the researchers conduct a thorough medical examination that includes tests of heart and lung function, an analysis of the twins' disease-fighting immune systems, and measurements of their brain-wave activity.

In-depth psychological examinations, which include 15,000 written questions, cover everything from upbringing and beliefs to food tastes and television viewing habits. The twins take more than 20 tests that measure various aspects of intellectual ability, including skill with numbers, mechanical aptitude, and memory. The researchers also observe the way the twins walk, talk, and dress; their gestures; and their sense of humor.

The similarities between identical twins raised apart revealed by this probing have amazed the researchers. Daphne and Barbara from Great Britain were both constant gigglers. Both women were tight with money and studiously avoided stress, to the point of refusing to state their opinion on noncontroversial subjects. Irene and Jeannette, also from Britain, compulsively counted everything they saw, such as the wheels on trucks, and even counted themselves to sleep. Both disliked escalators.

Oscar Stöhr and Jack Yufe, raised in different environments, may provide the most dramatic example of similarity between twins despite radically different backgrounds. Stöhr, reared in Germany by his grandmother, was a Roman Catholic and member of a Nazi youth organization during World War II. Yufe was raised as a Jew by his father in Trinidad and Israel. When the two men were reunited at age 47, they wore identical wire-rimmed glasses and sported similar mustaches. They both liked spicy foods and sweet liqueurs. They also shared several odd habits: They flushed the toilet not only after but also *before* using it; they stored rubber bands on their wrists; and they thought it was funny to sneeze on a crowded elevator to startle their fellow passengers.

The power of heredity

From the wealth of information provided by all the twins they have studied, the Minnesota researchers have drawn some startling conclusions about the influence of genes. For example, the researchers discovered not only that identical twins tend to develop the same diseases but also that they tend to develop them at the same time. This is true for diseases caused by defective genes, such as cystic fibrosis and hemophilia. But it is also true for diseases whose development is more closely linked to such environmental factors as poor diet or smoking.

Identical twins evaluated in Minnesota have developed high blood pressure, stroke, glaucoma, epilepsy, and childhood leukemia, among other diseases, within a short time of each other. Levey and Newman both developed hernias at age 10. The Jim twins each began getting migraine headaches at age 18. Identical twins also tend to fight off illness equally well.

Over the years, the question of whether intelligence is determined more by heredity or by environment has been the most controversial aspect of the debate over nature versus nurture. The research at Minnesota supports other twin research in finding that intelligence is the most genetically determined of all behavioral traits. On a battery of intelligence tests, identical twins raised together scored about .86. (To measure similarity, the researchers use an index that ranges from 0 to 1, with 0 indicating no similarity and 1 indicating complete similarity.) A score of .86 is similar to the score that one individual gets by taking the tests at two different times. Fraternal twins who grow up together score about .72—a score much higher than the .47 for ordinary siblings. More remarkably, identical twins raised apart score about .75.

Scientists have been conducting personality research using twins for a shorter time than they have been doing intelligence research. In addition, personality is more variable and harder to measure than intelligence. But here, too, the Minnesota

Twin testing

At the University of Minnesota's Center for Twin and Adoption Research, twins undergo a battery of physical and psychological tests lasting for six days.

Researchers at the twin center, *above* and *left,* wire a set of twins to a polygraph to measure their physiological responses to various stimuli.

A set of twins at the University of Minnesota answer some of the 15,000 written questions included in the psychological examination. The questions explore in detail the twins' family histories, values, interests, and tastes in everything from food to music.

Nature versus nurture		Degree to which inherited
Personality trait		
Social potency	Is masterful and forceful; likes to be the center of attention.	61%
Traditionalism	Follows rules; respects authority; believes in high moral standards.	60%
Stress reaction	Feels vulnerable and sensitive; worries and is easily upset.	55%
Absorption	Has a vivid imagination; easily becomes lost in thought.	55%
Alienation	Feels mistreated and exploited; thinks "the world is out to get me."	55%
Well-being	Is cheerful, optimistic, and confident.	54%
Harm avoidance	Avoids risks and dangers; takes the safe route even if boring.	51%
Aggression	Is physically aggressive and vindictive; is "out to get the world."	48%
Achievement	Works hard; is a perfectionist.	46%
Control	Is cautious, rational, and sensible; prefers to plan carefully.	43%
Social closeness	Comfortable with emotional intimacy; turns to others for help.	33%

Source: Minnesota Center for Twin and Adoption Research.

research, as well as many studies elsewhere, suggests that heredity plays an important role. In fact, to their surprise, the Minnesota scientists have found genetic influences no matter which characteristic they were testing. "Every conceivable trait we've looked at seems to have some genetic influence," Bouchard said. "It doesn't seem to matter what it is."

To determine the strength of this influence, the Minnesota researchers use a test called a Multidimensional Personality Questionnaire, developed by staff psychologist Auke Tellegen. The test covers 11 key personality traits, including zest for life, social closeness, pessimism, and even conservatism. According to the Minnesota researchers, identical twins exhibit striking similarities in all these traits. In 7 of the 11 characteristics, the scientists reported, heredity is more influential than environment.

The scores, reported as percentages, do not indicate that a trait is, say, 60 per cent genetic and 40 per cent environmental for any particular individual. The proportions can vary widely from person to person, and are averages for the group tested.

For example, the test results suggest that heredity accounts for about 60 per cent of social potency, a characteristic that includes leadership ability and being masterful and forceful. In other words, 60 per cent of the differences in leadership ability among people can be attributed to their genes. Other traits strongly influenced by heredity, according to the Minnesota researchers, are cheerfulness and optimism, a capacity for imaginative experiences, vulnerability to stress, and a desire to avoid risks. Genes even seem to have a small but significant effect on whether people are satisfied with their job.

Surprisingly, a trait called traditionalism is also strongly influenced by genetics, the researchers report. This trait is defined as a willingness to follow rules, a respect for authority, and a belief in high moral standards. The strong genetic element of this trait suggests that heredity may help determine political beliefs.

Fascinating facts about twins

Twins are the most common type of multiple birth, occurring in about 1 in every 89 births.

Among blacks and Native Americans, twins account for 1.7 per cent of all live births; among whites, 1 per cent; and among Asians, 0.5 per cent.

Siamese twins occur in about 1 in every 50,000 births. More properly called *conjoined twins,* Siamese twins are identical twins who result when a fertilized egg does not split completely. The name "Siamese twins" originated with conjoined twins named Chang and Eng, who were born in Siam (now Thailand) in 1811. The twins, who were joined at the chest by a thick band of tissue, toured the world as part of P. T. Barnum's traveling circus. The twins later settled in North Carolina, married sisters, became farmers, and, between them, fathered 22 children. They died within a few hours of each other in 1874 at age 62.

The number of multiple births in the United States reached a 30-year high in 1985—21 per 1,000 live births. That figure was 13 per cent higher than the number in 1980. More than 97 per cent of these births were of twins.

The tendency to give birth to fraternal twins—actually the tendency for a woman to release two eggs at a time during ovulation—may run in families.

About one-third of twins are identical twins. Among identical twins, about 1 pair of twins in 600 are mirror images of each other. Mirror-image twins have opposite fingerprint and hair-growth patterns, with those of one twin swirling clockwise and those of the other, counterclockwise. One twin is right-handed; the other, left-handed. In rare cases, mirror-image twins may have their internal organs on opposite sides of their bodies.

The greatest number of twins ever born to one woman is 16. The woman, the wife of a Russian peasant named Vassily, gave birth to the eight sets of twins—each set consisting of a girl and boy—between about 1725 and 1765. During that period, the woman also had 7 sets of triplets and 4 sets of quadruplets.

Advice columnists Abigail Van Buren, *left*, and Ann Landers

Olympic skiers Phil Mahre, *right*, and Steve Mahre

Some famous twins

★ Anthony Shaffer and Peter Shaffer—British playwrights; their plays include *Sleuth* (1970), written by Anthony, and *Amadeus* (1979), by Peter

★ Robin Gibb and Maurice Gibb—British pop musicians who, with their brother Barry, formed the Bee Gees

★ Mario Andretti and Aldo Andretti—Italian-born race car drivers

★ Tom Van Arsdale and Dick Van Arsdale—former professional basketball players

★ Auguste Piccard and Jean Piccard—Swiss scientists

Legendary rock star Elvis Presley had a twin, Jesse, who was stillborn.

The longest known interval in the birth of twins was 37 days. Mrs. Danny Berg of Rome delivered the first twin, a girl named Diana, on Dec. 23, 1987. The second twin, another girl named Monica, was born by Caesarean section on Jan. 30, 1988.

The oldest recorded twins were Eli and John Phipps, born in Virginia in 1803. When Eli died in 1911, the twins were 108 years old.

The lightest surviving twins on record were Mary and Margaret Stimson, born in 1931 in Great Britain. They weighed 1 pound (0.45 kilogram) and 1 pound 3 ounces (0.54 kilogram), respectively.

The record for the heaviest twins ever born belongs to the twins born to Mrs. J. P. Haskins of Fort Smith, Ark., in 1924. One twin weighed 14 pounds (6.4 kilograms); the other, 13 pounds 12 ounces (6.2 kilograms).

Other twin studies done elsewhere have reported similar findings. For example, in a study of 573 sets of twins in Great Britain, psychologist J. Philippe Rushton of the University of Western Ontario in London, Canada, found that heredity accounts for at least 60 per cent of differences in *altruism* (a desire to help others) and aggressiveness.

Some researchers, in fact, believe that virtually all personality traits are significantly affected by our genes. The exception, according to developmental psychologist Robert Plomin of Pennsylvania State University in College Station, may be a characteristic he calls "niceness." In research with nearly 700 Swedish twins published in 1989, Plomin found that being trusting, sympathetic, and cooperative is heavily influenced by environment, especially environment in early childhood.

According to the Minnesota researchers, other personality traits little affected by heredity—and thus, strongly influenced by environment—include achievement (a capacity for hard work); control (a tendency to be cautious and sensible and to plan carefully); and social closeness (being comfortable with emotional intimacy).

Twin studies have also revealed that genetics plays a significant role in a variety of psychological and behavioral disorders, including schizophrenia, manic depression, suicide, and alcoholism. Genetics may even play a role in phobias. For example, Daphne and Barbara, the giggling twins from Britain, were both timid about swimming in the ocean but had independently hit on the same way of dealing with the problem—by backing into the water.

Perhaps the most intriguing similarities between twins revealed by the Minnesota research have been those of personal taste and style, characteristics thought to be highly influenced by family environment. "It's probably the feature of the study that's grabbed us the most," Bouchard said.

When Oscar Stöhr and Jack Yufe showed up at the twin center, for example, they were wearing identical blue shirts with epaulets on the shoulders. Mark Newman and Jerry Levey each wore keys dangling from their belt on the right side. Twin sisters who had never met before appeared at the center each wearing seven rings.

Despite heredity, differences persist

Bouchard has found that identical twins raised together sometimes score the same *less* often than identical twins reared apart. He explains this finding as an example of what is known as the differentiation phenomenon. According to this theory, identical twins raised together may try to set themselves apart—consciously or subconsciously—by cultivating differences in behavior.

Even behavioral geneticists who believe that heredity exerts a powerful influence on behavior stress that behavior is the result of the interaction of past experience and present environment as well as genes. Genes do not establish that a person will be aggressive or interested in helping others. Rather, genes determine a range of possibilities. Genes may also establish predispositions, or susceptibilities, which then require an environmental trigger to develop or become apparent. For example, twins may inherit the same predisposition to heart disease. But the twin who lives a stressful life and smokes two packs of cigarettes daily has a greater chance of developing heart disease than the twin who takes life more in stride and does not smoke. In the same way, people who inherit musical talent may never develop that talent if they lack the opportunity—or desire—to take music lessons.

The ways in which genes influence behavior are still poorly understood. No one has identified a "personality" gene. Genes make proteins, and scientists have not yet traced the complex pathway between those proteins and behavioral traits. And many scientists, particularly social scientists, question whether the influence of heredity is as strong as that exerted by environment. These scientists point out that twin studies of personality are too recent and have involved too few people to draw sweeping conclusions about human nature. They also argue that these studies have discounted the effects of "twinness"—that is, wearing the same clothes and being treated alike by parents—that could make twins appear to be more alike than they really are. And the scientists note that while many twins raised apart display amazing similarities, others are quite different.

Many scientists also question whether personality traits, such as cheerfulness and leadership ability, exist as independent aspects of personality or whether they are actually responses to environmental influences. Finally, these scientists say twin researchers do not take into account the possibility that the two sets of adoptive parents of twins raised apart may be similar to each other. As a result, similarities attributed to genes could actually be the result of environmental likenesses. Twin researchers say, however, that the greatest value in their studies is not explaining how genes control our lives but in revealing how environment and genetics interact in complex ways to produce what we describe as human nature.

For further reading:
Abbe, Kathryn McLaughlin, and Gill, Frances McLaughlin. *Twins on Twins.* Crown, 1980.
Cassill, Kay. *Twins: Nature's Amazing Mystery.* Atheneum, 1982.
Theroux, Rosemary T., and Tingley, J. F. *The Care of Twin Children: A Common-Sense Guide for Parents.* 2nd ed. Center for Study of Multiple Births, 1984.

BERLIN WALL • EARTHQUAKE • OIL SPILLS

1989

BATMAN • WORLD SERIES • SHUTTLE

The Year on File

Contributors to **The World Book Year Book** report on the major developments of 1989. The contributors' names appear at the end of the articles they have written, and a complete roster of contributors, listing their professional affiliations and the articles they have written, is on pages 6 and 7.

Articles in this section are arranged alphabetically by subject matter. In most cases, the article titles are the same as those of the articles in **The World Book Encyclopedia** that they update. The numerous cross-references guide the reader to a subject or information that may be in some other article or that may appear under an alternative title. "See" and "See also" cross-references appear within and at the end of articles to direct the reader to related information elsewhere in **The Year Book**. "In **World Book,** see" references point the reader to articles in the encyclopedia that provide background information to the year's events reported in **The Year Book.**

See page 311 ▶

Advertising

Advertising. Many United States television advertisers found themselves in hot water in 1989 for airing their commercials during controversial programs. In March, for example, McDonald's Corporation, Procter & Gamble Company, and Mitsubishi Motors Corporation withdrew advertising from Fox Broadcasting Company's series "Married . . . With Children," after a Michigan woman wrote the companies to complain about the sexual content of the programs. Other companies pulled their commercials from such shows as "Nightingales," "Tattinger's," and "HeartBeat" because religious groups and other organizations as well as individual viewers said they were offended by the programs.

And in April, PepsiCo Incorporated shelved a TV commercial featuring rock singer Madonna after threats of boycotts from religious groups. The flap had nothing to do with the contents of the ad, which aired only twice in the United States. Rather, the controversy focused on Madonna's music video "Like a Prayer," which some groups found sacrilegious.

Health claim. Cereal makers continued during the year to seek ways to promote health benefits of their products. Quaker Oats Company in June launched a major ad campaign for its new Quaker Oat Bran cold cereal. One TV spot claimed that the product fights cholesterol "when part of a fat-modified, high-fiber diet. With something as important as your heart, trust the oat bran expert."

Later in 1989, the attorney general of Texas sued Quaker for deceptive advertising in the campaign. In an unusual move, the company countersued. Quaker's complaint alleged in part that the attorney general's suit placed an undue burden on the company's advertising and business practices.

Not her father's Oldsmobile. Automakers in 1989 sought out hip celebrities to help give more youthful, contemporary images to their cars. Former Beatle Ringo Starr, for example, appeared with his daughter, Lee, in a commercial for Oldsmobile that was a humorous take-off of the Beatles' 1964 movie *A Hard Day's Night.*

Not his father's ad campaign. One of the longest running and most successful ad campaigns in history ended in the fall of 1989. That campaign had made Wisk brand laundry detergent known for 22 years as the brand that ends "ring around the collar." Ironically, the son of the man who had been responsible for the original campaign created the new theme for Wisk: "Tsk, tsk, tsk! Wisk Wisk Wisk." J. J. Jordan, copywriter for the advertising agency J. Walter Thompson, credited his father's work by adding the words "Ring around the collar was just the beginning" to the new ad.

Unusual campaigns. Soft drink giants PepsiCo and Coca-Cola Company flexed their marketing muscle during the January 1989 Super Bowl—one of the major television events of the year for advertisers. Coke

Former Speaker of the House Thomas P. (Tip) O'Neill pops up out of a suitcase in a 1989 TV commercial for a chain of motels.

sponsored a three-dimensional half-time show—the first live 3-D television broadcast. Not to be outdone, PepsiCo sponsored a pregame talent show featuring one player from each National Football League team.

Although advertisers usually count on TV programs to deliver viewers for their commercials, CBS Inc. decided to turn to an advertiser to help boost its viewer ratings. In the fall of 1989, CBS kicked off a major promotional tie-in with K Mart Corporation, a discount retailer. CBS viewers could win more than $6 million in prizes by collecting game cards that were distributed in K Mart Sunday newspaper inserts, then watching for the winning numbers to be announced during the network's shows that aired from 8 to 9 p.m. The National Broadcasting Company (NBC) later teamed up with Sears, Roebuck and Company in a similar tie-in.

Advertising agencies continued to attract almost as much attention as their creative products in 1989. In March, Saatchi & Saatchi PLC, the London-based international advertising and consulting empire built by brothers Maurice and Charles Saatchi, ran into trouble. The company announced that for the first time in its 19-year history it expected profits to decline in 1989. So serious were the firm's problems that Maurice Saatchi said he would consider selling the company's nonadvertising businesses.

While the Saatchis were struggling with their financial woes, a man who once was the finance director of Saatchi & Saatchi was attempting to build an advertising company that would rival that of his former employers. Martin Sorrell, the chief executive of London-based WPP Group PLC, in May 1989 succeeded in his hostile take-over of one of the most venerable New York City agencies, the Ogilvy Group. In 1987, Sorrell had stunned the advertising world with the first hostile take-over of a major New York advertising agency, J. Walter Thompson.

Higher spending predicted. In June 1989, Robert J. Coen, senior vice president and director of forecasting for McCann-Erickson Incorporated, an advertising agency based in New York City, predicted that spending on advertising in the United States would rise 6.9 per cent in 1989. He said spending on national advertising was more robust than local advertising, which was affected by sluggishness in retail sales.

Coen noted also that, continuing a trend of recent years, spending on advertising in other countries generally was growing at a faster pace than in the United States. He predicted that the biggest gainers in 1989 would be Spain, Australia, and the Netherlands.

Philip Morris Companies, Incorporated, became the first firm to surpass the $2-billion mark in yearly advertising and promotional spending in the United States, according to an annual study published by *Advertising Age* magazine. Philip Morris, which was the largest U.S. advertiser in 1987, was tops again in 1988, with $2.06 billion budgeted for advertising and promotion. Christine Dugas

In *World Book,* see **Advertising.**

Afghanistan. The Soviet Union, which invaded Afghanistan in 1979, completed its withdrawal from that country on Feb. 15, 1989. Soviet officials said that despite the war's high cost—$75 billion, 14,143 killed, and 35,000 wounded—the invasion had failed to eliminate guerrilla resistance to the Communist regime in Kabul. In October, Soviet Foreign Minister Eduard A. Shevardnadze said that the invasion had violated both Soviet law and "international norms of behavior." Resistance leaders estimated Afghan deaths at more than 1 million and said more than half the country's people were refugees abroad or were living in Afghanistan away from their homes.

Kabul rally. Both Soviet and Western officials expected the regime headed by Najibullah—who uses only one name—to collapse soon after the Soviets left. On February 23, the leaders of the seven main guerrilla groups based in Peshawar, Pakistan, formed an "interim government" to take power. Najibullah rallied his forces, however. By the end of 1989, the conflict showed no sign of resolution.

Siege of Jalalabad. Resistance forces on March 5 attacked Jalalabad, a major Afghan city 40 miles (65 kilometers) from the Pakistani border. By July, however, the effort had bogged down. One reason was the murder of 79 Afghan soldiers who had surrendered to a guerrilla group. This incident stiffened the resistance of Najibullah's forces.

Internal discord also weakened the guerrillas. A number of rebel commanders refused to join the battle because they felt the interim government did not fairly represent all Afghan interests.

Some guerrilla groups then concentrated their efforts on a smaller town, Khowst, also near Pakistan. But other guerrilla bands refused to send troops.

Guerrilla weakness. The most dramatic example of guerrilla infighting was the murder on July 9 of 30 key members of the Council of the North, the main guerrilla group in northeastern Afghanistan. The men were killed by rebels loyal to Gulbuddin Hekmatyar, the leader of an Islamic fundamentalist group. In response, the United States cut off arms deliveries to Hekmatyar's group.

Government changes. In February, Mohammad Hassan Sharq, a non-Communist, resigned as prime minister and was replaced by Soltan Ali Keshtmand. A Communist, Keshtmand had earlier served in that post. Western observers attributed the change to the failure of Sharq to attract other non-Communists who would broaden support for the regime.

Soviet economic and military aid sustained the Kabul regime. Western diplomats said the Soviet Union ran the largest airlift in its history to supply Kabul, which was surrounded by rebels. They estimated that $1.5 billion in weapons, plus food and other supplies, were delivered in the first six months after the Soviet withdrawal. Henry S. Bradsher

See also **Asia** (Facts in brief table). In *World Book,* see **Afghanistan.**

Africa

The victory of the South West Africa People's Organization (SWAPO) in elections supervised by the United Nations (UN) in mid-November brought independence from South Africa one step closer for the people of Namibia. It signaled, moreover, the end of a historic era. With South Africa scheduled to surrender the last vestiges of its control over Namibia in early 1990, the final curtain will ring down on 400 years of European colonial rule in Africa.

The achievement of Namibian independence comes after 40 years of pressure within the UN, 23 years of guerrilla warfare on the part of SWAPO, and the patient negotiations of the United States, which in 1988 got South Africa, Angola, and Cuba to agree on a formula for peace in southwestern Africa. Namibia was the first focus of that pact.

The second part of the 1988 agreement sought to end a civil war that had been going on in Angola since 1975, a conflict that was complicated by the intermittent invasion of southern Angola by South African troops in search of SWAPO guerrillas. The withdrawal in 1988 of all South African forces from Angola was matched in 1989 by the start of a phased withdrawal, to end in 1991, of an estimated 50,000 Cuban troops who had been supporting the regular Angolan army. Also as part of that pact, the African National Congress (ANC), the largest South African black rebel group, shut down its training bases in southern Angola early in 1989.

The one unresolved issue in the 1988 accord was the role that the major rebel group in Angola—the National Union for the Total Independence of Angola (UNITA)—would play in Angolan society and politics once a lasting peace has been achieved. Under prodding from eight African heads of state as well as from the United States and other non-African powers, the Angolan government and UNITA met in June 1989 in Zaire and agreed to a cease-fire and negotiations. Although neither objective was immediately achieved, at year's end UNITA and the government of Angolan President José Eduardo dos Santos had started serious peace discussions.

The prospects for peace elsewhere. Taking the cue from Namibia and Angola, other African leaders and Western diplomats managed to persuade representatives of the Mozambican government to meet in Nairobi, Kenya, in August with the leaders of the Mozambique National Resistance (Renamo). Renamo, the most violent guerrilla organization in Africa, had carried out a systematic campaign of terror and destruction in Mozambique for more than a decade and

Marchers in Katutura, Namibia, in mid-1989 celebrate the prospect of independence from South Africa —and demand no further interference.

Facts in brief on African political units

Country	Population	Government	Monetary unit*	Exports†	Foreign trade (million U.S.$) Imports†
Algeria	25,174,000	President Chadli Bendjedid; Prime Minister Mouloud Hamrouche	dinar (8.18 = $1)	8,186	7,029
Angola	10,000,000	President José Eduardo dos Santos	kwanza (29.9 = $1)	1,840	682
Benin	4,737,000	President Mathieu Kérékou	CFA franc (304 = $1)	167	288
Botswana	1,283,000	President Quett K. J. Masire	pula (1.93 = $1)	653	535
Burkina Faso (Upper Volta)	8,996,000	Popular Front President, Head of State, & Head of Government Blaise Compaoré	CFA franc (304 = $1)	83	405
Burundi	5,450,000	President Pierre Buyoya	franc (155 = $1)	129	205
Cameroon	11,236,000	President Paul Biya	CFA franc (304 = $1)	924	1,271
Cape Verde	378,000	President Aristides Pereira; Prime Minister Pedro Pires	escudo (77.8 = $1)	4	110
Central African Republic	2,911,000	President André-Dieudonne Kolingba	CFA franc (304 = $1)	131	252
Chad	5,674,000	President Hissein Habré	CFA franc (304 = $1)	111	366
Comoros	518,000	President Haribou Chebani	CFA franc (304 = $1)	23	42
Congo	2,183,000	President Denis Sassou-Nguesso; Prime Minister Alphonse Poaty-Souchlaty	CFA franc (304 = $1)	673	528
Djibouti	337,000	President Hassan Gouled Aptidon; Prime Minister Barkat Gourad Hamadou	franc (178 = $1)	13	225
Egypt	53,522,000	President Hosni Mubarak; Prime Minister Atef Sedky	pound (1.10 = $1)	4,352	16,226
Equatorial Guinea	411,000	President Obiang Nguema Mbasogo; Prime Minister Cristino Seriche Bioko	CFA franc (304 = $1)	17	41
Ethiopia	48,630,000	President Mengistu Haile-Mariam; Acting Prime Minister Hailu Yimenu	birr (2.07 = $1)	358	1,102
Gabon	1,172,000	President Omar Bongo; Prime Minister Léon Mébiame	CFA franc (304 = $1)	1,271	866
Gambia	820,000	President Sir Dawda Kairaba Jawara	dalasi (7.66 = $1)	35	100
Ghana	15,020,000	Provisional National Defense Council Chairman Jerry John Rawlings	cedi (300 = $1)	909	919
Guinea	6,871,000	President Lansana Conté	franc (440 = $1)	538	511
Guinea-Bissau	985,000	President João Bernardo Vieira	peso (650 = $1)	9	57
Ivory Coast	12,053,000	President Félix Houphouët-Boigny	CFA franc (304 = $1)	3,110	2,241
Kenya	25,081,000	President Daniel T. arap Moi	shilling (21.9 = $1)	961	1,756
Lesotho	1,757,000	King Moshoeshoe II; Military Council Chairman Justin M. Lekhanya	loti (2.60 = $1)	25	343
Liberia	2,552,000	President Samuel K. Doe	dollar (1 = $1)	382	308
Libya	4,356,000	Leader of the Revolution Muammar Muhammed al-Qadhafi; General People's Committee Secretary (Prime Minister) Umar Mustafa al-Muntasir	dinar (0.30 = $1)	5,000	4,500

*Exchange rates as of Dec. 1, 1989, or latest available data. †Latest available data.

Country	Population	Government	Monetary unit*	Exports†	Foreign trade (million U.S.$) Imports†
Madagascar	11,969,000	President Didier Ratsiraka; Prime Minister Victor Ramahatra	franc (1,360 = $1)	332	302
Malawi	8,198,000	President H. Kamuzu Banda	kwacha (2.77 = $1)	295	412
Mali	8,278,000	President Moussa Traoré	CFA franc (304 = $1)	260	493
Mauritania	2,021,000	President Maaouiya Ould Sid Ahmed Taya	ouguiya (87.2 = $1)	428	382
Mauritius	1,105,000	Governor General Sir Veerasamy Ringadoo; Prime Minister Aneerood Jugnauth	rupee (15.3 = $1)	901	1,013
Morocco	25,169,000	King Hassan II; Prime Minister Azzedine Laraki	dirham (8.31 = $1)	3,603	4,772
Mozambique	15,627,000	President Joaquím Alberto Chissano; Prime Minister Mário da Graça Machungo	metical (821 = $1)	77	377
Namibia (South West Africa)	1,874,000	Administrator-General Louis Pienaar	rand (2.60 = $1)	878	652
Niger	7,905,000	Supreme Military Council President Ali Saibou; Prime Minister Oumarou Mamane	CFA franc (304 = $1)	209	345
Nigeria	112,765,000	President Ibrahim Babangida	naira (7.48 = $1)	7,383	3,917
Rwanda	7,222,000	President Juvénal Habyarimana	franc (79.7 = $1)	101	368
São Tomé and Principe	123,000	President Manuel Pinto da Costa	dobra (107 = $1)	10	3
Senegal	7,360,000	President Abdou Diouf	CFA franc (304 = $1)	606	1,023
Seychelles	71,000	President France Albert René	rupee (5.61 = $1)	22	114
Sierra Leone	4,146,000	President Joseph Momoh	leone (63 = $1)	110	152
Somalia	7,106,000	President Mohamed Siad Barre; Prime Minister Mohamed Ali Samantar	shilling (410 = $1)	85	280
South Africa	36,696,000	State President Frederick Willem de Klerk	rand (3.91 = $1)	13,060	17,355
Sudan	23,797,000	National Revolutionary Council Chairman Umar Hasan Ahmad al-Bashir	pound (4.5 = $1)	333	961
Swaziland	779,000	King Mswati III; Prime Minister Obed Mfanyana Dlamini	lilangeni (2.60 = $1)	311	353
Tanzania	25,955,000	President Ali Hassan Mwinyi; Prime Minister Joseph S. Warioba	shilling (155 = $1)	282	850
Togo	3,451,000	President Gnassingbé Eyadéma	CFA franc (304 = $1)	242	487
Tunisia	8,095,000	President Zine El-Abidine Ben Ali; Prime Minister Hamed Karoui	dinar (0.94 = $1)	2,395	3,688
Uganda	17,593,000	President Yoweri Museveni; Prime Minister Samson Kisekka	shilling (371 = $1)	588	241
Zaire	35,330,000	President Mobutu Sese Seko; Prime Minister Kengo wa Dondo	zaire (445 = $1)	970	756
Zambia	8,459,000	President Kenneth David Kaunda; Prime Minister Malimba Masheke	kwacha (19.2 = $1)	1,141	835
Zimbabwe	9,700,000	President Robert Mugabe	dollar (2.28 = $1)	1,419	1,046

had forced an estimated 1.5 million Mozambicans to seek refuge in neighboring countries. The Nairobi peace meetings—the first between the two parties—laid the framework for future negotiations.

Peace also seemed possible in Somalia and Ethiopia, as the 1988 truce in their war over ownership of Ethiopia's Ogaden region continued to hold. More importantly, two civil wars that have plagued Ethiopia for years—in the areas of Eritrea and Tigre—at last moved to the negotiating table. Recent military successes of the Eritrean and Tigrean liberation fronts, as well as pressure from the Soviet Union—Ethiopia's primary supporter—persuaded the government of President Mengistu Haile-Mariam to reverse its previous stance against negotiating with the rebels.

In Somalia, however, a conflict between the government of President Mohamed Siad Barre and a northern-based rebel group, the Somali National Movement (SNM), continued unabated. Seeking to escape those hostilities, an estimated 1 million people have fled across the border to Ethiopia or moved to other parts of Somalia.

Border disputes. The arbitrary political boundaries drawn by the European colonial powers continued to cause strained relations between African nations in 1989. In a few cases, border disputes were resolved in a friendly way. In September, for instance, Mozambique and Tanzania settled a border disagreement peacefully, as did Zaire and Zambia.

But at least one territorial dispute—between Mauritania and Senegal—resulted in bloodshed. An argument over grazing rights in a contested border area on April 9 turned violent, with killing, looting, and property damage. By the end of the month, the conflict had spread to distant areas in both countries, and more than 400 people had died. In August, the two nations severed diplomatic relations.

Of historic note, 1989 witnessed the demise of a rare attempt by two African nations to merge. In September, Senegal and Gambia ended an eight-year effort to create a Senegambia Confederation.

The military and politics. Coups and attempted military interventions continued to undermine the stability of governments throughout Africa during 1989. On June 30, the government of Prime Minister Al-Sadiq Al-Mahdi of Sudan was toppled by junior officers under the command of Lieutenant General Umar Hasan Ahmad al-Bashir. The Al-Mahdi government had been unable to end a rebellion in southern Sudan that had resumed six years earlier or to deal with official corruption and a slumping economy.

Military regimes themselves are vulnerable to coups, as was demonstrated in Ethiopia in mid-May when President Mengistu, a former army officer, had to return hurriedly from a state visit to East Germany to put down a revolt by senior military officers in Addis Ababa and Asmara. The officers had been angered by political meddling in their conduct of the seemingly endless civil wars in Eritrea and Tigre.

Other failed coups against either civilian or military regimes were reported in Chad in April, Madagascar in July, and in Liberia and Burkina Faso on two occasions each. All the coup attempts were quickly suppressed. In March, the democratically elected prime minister of Mauritius, Sir Aneerood Jugnauth, escaped an assassination attempt.

Comoros President Ahmed Abdallah Abderemane was assassinated on November 26. On December 15, French troops took control of Comoros and expelled a group of European mercenaries who had installed Abdallah in 1978 and held much power since.

Civilian rule. The return to civilian rule following a military intervention has been a difficult process for many African nations. Military regimes have often created their own political parties and taken other steps to perpetuate their hold on power. That is not always the case, however. Ghana's military leader, Jerry John Rawlings, moved his nation steadily away from military domination in 1989 by creating a series of popularly elected district councils.

But only in Nigeria was the military leadership systematically preparing for a return to civilian rule. Under a constitution prepared by a civilian assembly and presented to President Ibrahim Babangida in April, elections will lead to the restoration of civilian government in 1992. Two broad-based national parties will put up candidates for state and local elections in 1990 and a presidential election in 1991.

South African elections. Frederick Willem de Klerk, a long-time figure in South African politics, was elected South Africa's state president in September. He had been acting state president since mid-August, taking over for Pieter Willem Botha. Botha, president since 1984, resigned because of poor health. De Klerk promised to work for a new era of equitable race relations in South Africa.

De Klerk's ruling National Party retained its majority in the all-white chamber of Parliament in the September elections but lost seats to the right wing Conservative Party and the more liberal Democratic Party. De Klerk has stated his willingness to dismantle *apartheid* (racial separation), and during the year he ordered the release of several imprisoned leaders of the banned African National Congress, the major black rebel group in South Africa, and permitted several anti-apartheid rallies to take place.

Other political developments. One-party presidential elections took place in Madagascar in March, Equatorial Guinea in June, and Benin in August. Madagascar did, however, allow multiparty competition in June parliamentary elections. Nonetheless, the governing party stayed firmly in control, winning 120 out of 137 seats. Somalia announced plans in August to rewrite its Constitution so as to permit opposition parties to challenge the ruling Somalia Revolutionary Socialist Party.

Elsewhere in Africa, the concept of multiparty competition was on the decline in 1989. President Omar

Refugees from the civil war in Somalia—one of several conflicts raging in Africa—receive food handouts at a relief camp in Ethiopia in mid-1989.

Bongo of Gabon announced in August that the government had rejected the possibility of party competition on the grounds that it would be disruptive to national unity. In Ivory Coast, the emergence of a potential challenger to President Félix Houphouët-Boigny led to the rival's arrest; he was convicted and sentenced to 20 years in prison. The elections for local councils in Ghana were held on a nonpartisan basis because President Rawlings—though moving away from military rule—rejects the idea of multiparty competition.

But the concept of the single-party state was challenged in Zimbabwe, where President Robert Mugabe has sought to consolidate the monopoly of the Zimbabwe African National Union-Patriotic Front (ZANU-PF). In May, Edgar Z. Tekere, a founder of ZANU-PF and once its secretary general before his expulsion from the party in 1988, announced the formation of the Zimbabwe Unity Movement. He hoped to capitalize on discontent over government corruption, unemployment, and the lack of economic growth.

The political role of university students was demonstrated throughout Africa in 1989. During the year, there were student riots and boycotts in Botswana, Ethiopia, Mauritania, Nigeria, and Zaire. The students' grievances ranged from inadequate college financial aid and housing to political issues such as governmental corruption and ideology. In each case, the government resorted to force in breaking the strike or boy-cott, and universities with the most unrest were closed for extended periods.

Religion remained at the heart of political conflict in many areas of the continent. The rebellion in southern Sudan is based in large measure on the reluctance of Christians and followers of traditional religions to have Islamic law applied to them.

In Somalia, despite the acceptance of Islam by both the government and the general population, religious leaders were in the forefront of those criticizing the government of President Siad Barre for its political and economic policies. The government's jailing of four religious leaders on July 13 led to protests the following day. Cracking down violently, government troops indiscriminately fired on worshipers as they left their mosques in the capital city of Mogadishu, leaving 450 dead.

Famine continued to be a major problem in the eastern half of the continent in 1989. Natural disasters, including flooding in southern Sudan and the beginnings of another drought in Ethiopia, were major factors in the food shortages. Most of the starvation in those and other countries, however, was war-related. Military activities disrupted agriculture and prevented donated food shipments from reaching their intended recipients.

The debt problem. Sub-Saharan Africa's foreign debt in 1989 exceeded $125 billion. The debt load of several countries was a serious obstacle to them in se-

163

Agriculture

curing loans, investment capital, and foreign grants. Belgium, France, Spain, West Germany, and other European governments canceled sizable portions of the debts owed them by African countries in 1989 in order to stimulate those nations' development.

A majority of African nations have come to accept the strict conditions laid down by the UN's International Monetary Fund (IMF) for the awarding of loans and the rescheduling of interest payments on existing debt. The IMF requirements include reducing government spending and employment, devaluing inflated national currencies, removing cumbersome import restrictions, selling inefficient government-owned businesses, and introducing free-market principles.

Zambia, Benin, and other countries that had previously refused to adopt those measures were compelled to do so in 1989 in the face of severe economic crises. But a number of African leaders complained about the consequences of the IMF conditions. Debt repayment, these leaders argued, took too high a priority over education, health, transportation, and other elements of national development. The unpopular belt-tightening aspects of the IMF requirements led to riots in Nigeria and elsewhere in 1989.   J. Gus Liebenow and Beverly B. Liebenow

See also the various African country articles. In the World Book Supplement section, see **Tanzania.** In *World Book,* see **Africa.**

Agriculture. See Farm and farming.

AIDS. The drug AZT (zidovudine) showed new promise in 1989 as a treatment for AIDS. Researchers at the National Institutes of Health (NIH) in Bethesda, Md., reported in August that AZT may help many of the 1½ million Americans who are infected with the human immunodeficiency virus (HIV), which causes AIDS. Two NIH studies showed that AZT, the only drug licensed for AIDS treatment, can slow the disease's progression. Until the studies, AZT had been used to treat only the most severely ill patients.

The first study, released on August 3, concluded that AZT can delay the onset of AIDS in people who have only early signs of immune system damage. A second study, issued on August 17, found that the drug also can delay the onset of AIDS in people infected with HIV who have no symptoms. Health officials hailed the discoveries as landmarks in the battle against AIDS. They urged homosexuals, intravenous drug abusers, and other high-risk people to be tested for HIV infection so treatment can begin early.

AZT dosage. Researchers at the University of Miami in Florida on July 13 reported that smaller doses of AZT may be just as effective in treating AIDS as the large doses used in the past. The researchers said the finding could extend AZT's benefits to thousands of patients who cannot tolerate the side effects associated with full doses of the drug.

Vaccine hope. An experimental AIDS vaccine has successfully boosted the immune systems of 14 volun-

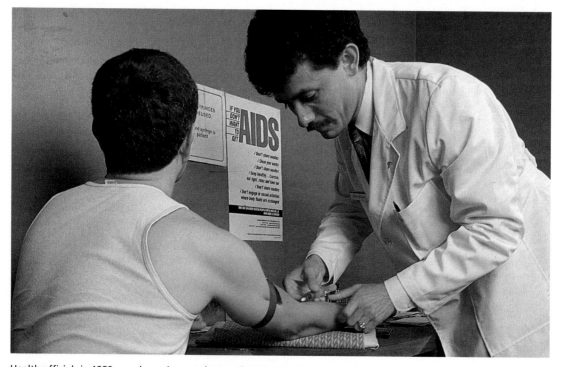

Health officials in 1989 urged people to undergo voluntary testing for the AIDS virus so they could receive therapy as soon as possible.

164

teer AIDS patients, researchers reported on October 16. The vaccine, called VaxSyn HIV-1 AIDS, is one of two vaccines undergoing tests. Scientists at the Walter Reed Army Institute of Research in Bethesda said preliminary findings indicate that the vaccine may prevent the development of AIDS in people with early signs of HIV infection. The developers of the vaccine said the next step will be to determine if the vaccine's effect on the immune system postpones or stops symptoms of AIDS.

Disease on campus. On May 22, the first study of AIDS infection on college campuses in the United States reported that 2 out of every 1,000 students show signs of HIV infection. The American College Health Association, which conducted the study, took blood samples from 16,861 students at 19 campuses. The study noted that the rate of infection among college students, though lower than the national average, "should cause real concern."

AIDS cases. By Nov. 30, 1989, the U.S. Centers for Disease Control in Atlanta, Ga., reported 115,158 cases of AIDS and 68,441 AIDS deaths in the United States since the disease was first identified in 1981. The World Health Organization on May 8, 1989, predicted that more than 5 million new AIDS cases would be reported by the year 2000.   Michael Woods

In *World Book,* see **AIDS.**

Air Force. See **Armed forces.**

Air pollution. See **Environmental pollution.**

Akihito (1933-   ), crown prince of Japan, became emperor on Jan. 7, 1989, immediately after the death of his father, Emperor Hirohito. The Japanese government chose the name *Heisei,* which means *peace and concord,* for Akihito's reign. He will be known as the *Heisei Emperor.* See **Japan.**

Akihito was born in Tokyo on Dec. 12, 1933. The circumstances of his life reflect the changes in Japan's political structure after World War II (1939-1945). Before the war, members of the Japanese imperial family were considered divinities, and the crown prince's early life was sheltered and restricted. Akihito was 11 when the Japanese surrender ended the war. Soon afterward, Hirohito renounced all claims to divinity, and the Japanese people accepted a new constitution that stripped political power from the emperor to establish a democratic form of government.

Akihito's life then became more open to outside influences. He studied under an American tutor and traveled to England and several other Western countries. In 1959, he broke with tradition by marrying Michiko Shoda, a bride of his own choice who was also a commoner.

In private life, Akihito is a scholar devoted to marine biology. He and his wife have three children, two of whom have been educated at Oxford University in England.   Jinger Hoop

Alabama. See **State government.**

Alaska. See **State government.**

Albania, a rigidly Communist state, in 1989 strengthened its economic ties with most major Western European countries, yet remained hostile toward the Soviet Union's policy of *perestroika* (economic and social restructuring) and the even more radical changes taking place in Hungary, Poland, East Germany, Czechoslovakia, Bulgaria, and Romania. Albania's leadership acknowledged an urgent need to modernize the state's planning and management structure—in ways "suited to Albanian conditions"—to overcome obstacles to further economic development. And both economists and politicians took a pragmatic view toward the future of trading links with the European Community (EC), an organization of 12 Western European states, as the EC prepared to launch a "single market" economy in 1992.

The economy of Albania continued to lag in 1989 in sectors vital to the country's export business, notably mining and agriculture. The central authorities in the agricultural sector granted some local independence to state and cooperative farms, encouraged material incentives for farm groups, and funded substantial imports of farm machinery. These moves, however, had no meaningful impact in 1989. Because of drought and obsolescent equipment, food imports in 1989 cost the country $70 million in Western currency resources—twice the amount spent in 1988.

A constant propaganda theme of the government was "the need for higher technology to help us in world markets." Albania did not contemplate any form of affiliation with the EC or the European Free Trade Association (EFTA), an organization of six Western European states. Members of the EC and EFTA already buy 20 per cent of Albania's exports. Albanian economists revealed, however, that formal studies were already underway to determine how to meet problems that Albania will face as the Western market becomes more closely integrated.

Albania and Italy in November signed an agreement to increase their cooperation in agricultural, industrial, and technical matters. The accord also calls for Albania to take part in a regional effort to clean up the Adriatic Sea.

Cultural challenges. Meeting with Communist Party ideologues in April, leading Albanian writers strongly challenged the party's—and therefore the state's—restrictive dogma concerning the arts. The year also saw a vigorous boost in the teaching of English, French, and German and in the translation of Western books.

In August, Mother Teresa made an unprecedented visit to Albania. That Roman Catholic missionary to India's poor is of Albanian descent and was born in what is now southern Yugoslavia.

Albania's official ban on religion continued in 1989. Observers noted, however, that "private belief" was acknowledged with tolerance.   Eric Bourne

See also **Europe** (Facts in brief table). In *World Book,* see **Albania.**

Alberta. Alberta's Progressive Conservative (PC) Party, in power since 1971, won its sixth consecutive majority in an election on March 20, 1989. The party captured 59 seats in the Legislative Assembly—only 2 fewer than it held before the election—but its share of the popular vote fell from 51 per cent to 44 per cent. The New Democratic Party, which held fast at 16 seats, kept its place as the official opposition, while the third-place Liberals doubled their share of seats from 4 to 8.

Although the PC's won the election, PC leader Donald R. Getty, premier since 1985, suffered a surprising loss in his Edmonton district. Because a premier is also expected to hold a seat in the provincial legislature, another party member stepped down, allowing Getty to run for—and win—a seat in a May 9 special election in the farming community of Stettler.

In July 1989, Getty promised compensation to investors in the bankrupt Principal group of trust companies, which collapsed in 1987. About 67,000 investors were expected to recover 75 per cent of their investment through the sale of Principal's assets plus a government payout of up to $85 million Canadian ($71-million U.S.). Employment and Career Development Minister Constance Osterman, formerly responsible for regulating financial institutions, was dropped from the cabinet after an inquiry found her actions "misguided."   David M. L. Farr

See also **Canada.** In *World Book,* see **Alberta.**

Algeria. The process of political and economic reform, dubbed the "second Algerian revolution," continued in 1989 as the government of President Chadli Bendjedid worked to transform the country from a one-party socialist state into a multiparty democracy. Since 1962, when Algeria won its independence from France, the ruling National Liberation Front (FLN), Algeria's only legal political party, has controlled nearly all aspects of Algerian life.

Bendjedid initiated the reform process in October 1988 after riots broke out in Algiers, the capital, and other Algerian cities. Triggered by economic austerity measures, the riots quickly became protests against government corruption and the FLN's heavy-handed political control.

Constitutional referendum. On Feb. 23, 1989, Algerian voters overwhelmingly approved a new Constitution. Although not expressly permitting the formation of opposition political parties, the document grants Algerians the "right to create associations of a political character."

Some 20 groups representing various political and regional interests quickly applied for recognition by the government. Of that number, five parties were granted permission to participate in municipal elections scheduled for December. At the same time, the FLN leadership attempted to revitalize the party and counter charges of elitism by launching a major drive to recruit new members.

Government shakeup. On September 9, Bendjedid, impatient with the government's slow progress in carrying out the reforms, dismissed Prime Minister Kasdi Merbah and appointed Mouloud Hamrouche, a presidential aide, to the position. Bendjedid also appointed a new cabinet.

Regional relations. Algeria played a key role in the formation in February of the Arab Maghreb Union (AMU), a five-member North African common market. Made up of Algeria, Morocco, Libya, Mauritania, and Tunisia, the AMU was organized to increase trade within the region by eliminating trade barriers. The treaty establishing the AMU also created a number of councils to promote regional economic development and political cooperation.

Western Sahara. Improved relations between Bendjedid and Morocco's King Hassan II as well as the Algerian government's concern with internal reforms effectively ended Algerian support for the Polisario Front guerrillas in Western Sahara. Since 1972, the guerrillas have been fighting for the independence of the region, which is controlled by Morocco. Algeria began reclaiming arms from the Polisario Front in March after Morocco ratified a 1972 border treaty. A large section of the border between the two countries had been disputed since Algeria became independent in 1962.   William Spencer

See also **Africa** (Facts in brief table). In *World Book,* see **Algeria.**

Angola. The 1988 regional peace pact involving Angola, South Africa, and Cuba reached a new phase in January 1989 as the first 3,000 Cuban troops—of an estimated 50,000—were withdrawn from Angola. The staged withdrawal, which South Africa had insisted on before it would agree to grant neighboring Namibia its independence, is to take place over a 27-month period. Also as part of the settlement, the African National Congress—the main South African black rebel group—closed its military training bases in Angola.

Ending the civil war. The main unresolved issue in the peace accord was the future of the National Union for the Total Independence of Angola (UNITA), an Angolan rebel force that for 14 years has been engaged in a civil war with the governing Popular Movement for the Liberation of Angola (MPLA). Although the guerrillas control a third of Angola, President José Eduardo dos Santos has long opposed granting UNITA a legitimate role in governing the country.

Eight African heads of state engaged in delicate negotiations with UNITA and the MPLA in early 1989. Those diplomatic efforts led on June 22 to peace talks at Gbadolite in Zaire, where Dos Santos and UNITA's leader, Jonas Savimbi, met for the first time and agreed to a cease-fire. The Gbadolite meetings set the stage for the creation of a government of national unity and reconciliation under the leadership of the MPLA. Questions of political beliefs, electoral procedures, and other details were to be worked out. The

Cuban soldiers, scheduled to return home from Angola as Cuba phases
out its military presence there, mix with the populace in Luanda in January.

agreement almost fell apart, however, when Dos Santos claimed that Savimbi had agreed at Gbadolite to go into temporary "retirement."

In July and August, each side accused the other of violating the cease-fire, and Cuba threatened to delay the departure of its troops. Only with prodding from the eight African heads of state and from the United States and South African governments—UNITA's primary supporters—did the parties agree in October to resume discussions, to be mediated by President Mobutu Sese Seko of Zaire.

The economy. In anticipation of Angola's admission on July 20 to the International Monetary Fund (IMF)—an agency of the United Nations—the MPLA hastened its move away from socialism and toward a free-market economy. State monopolies gave way to private enterprise in manufacturing, farming, ranching, transportation, tourism, and the retail trade. In May, the government introduced an economic plan aimed at attracting foreign investment, and shortly after that it announced a drastic two-stage devaluation of the kwanza, its national unit of currency. With the civil war seemingly at an end, the government also invited companies in the United States and other Western countries to explore in Angola for oil and minerals.　　J. Gus Liebenow and Beverly B. Liebenow

See also **Africa** (Facts in brief table). In *World Book,* see **Angola.**

Animal. See **Cat; Conservation; Dog; Zoology; Zoos.**

Anthropology. Evidence that hominids lived in Europe about 2.5 million years ago, much earlier than most anthropologists believe, aroused spirited debate at a conference in Paris in April 1989. (Hominids are modern human beings and our closest human and prehuman ancestors.) The evidence—stone objects identified as tools—was presented by archaeologist Eugène Bonifay of the National Center for Scientific Research in Marseille, France.

Most anthropologists believe that hominids arrived in Europe from Africa about 1 million to 1.5 million years ago. The oldest known stone tools from Europe—discovered by Bonifay at Soleihac in southeastern France—have been determined to be about 930,000 years old.

Bonifay's newest find consists of four stone objects found at Saint-Eble in south-central France. Bonifay has dated the discoveries to 2.5 million years ago by means of animal fossils of that age found with them and by potassium-argon dating of volcanic rock that overlay the objects.

Anthropologists at the conference debated whether the objects are human artifacts or natural objects. One difficulty in identifying extremely ancient tools is that the older the tools are, the cruder they are and the more they resemble naturally broken stones. Some archaeologists pointed out that geologic processes, such as volcanic explosions, can fracture stones, causing them to look like human artifacts. But most scien-

"Look . . . Java Man's invented something!"

tists at the conference agreed with Bonifay that the objects are tools.

The scientists, however, expressed considerable skepticism about Bonifay's date for the tools. One reason is that no human fossils older than about 500,000 years have been found in Europe.

If the tools really are 2.5 million years old, anthropologists would have to revise their theories about which hominid arrived first in Europe. Most anthropologists now believe that the first human species to migrate out of Africa was *Homo erectus*, which evolved about 1.6 million years ago and appeared in Europe about 1 million years ago. If the migration occurred earlier, the Saint-Eble toolmaker probably was *Homo habilis*, a species from which *Homo erectus* evolved. The oldest known *Homo habilis* fossils are about 2 million years old.

Speech for Neanderthals? A 60,000-year-old fossil bone found in Israel suggests that Neanderthals may have been as capable of speech as modern human beings. The discovery of the fossils was reported by a team of scientists led by anatomist Baruch Arensburg of Tel Aviv University in Israel. Neanderthals, an early form of *Homo sapiens*, became extinct about 35,000 years ago.

Anthropologists have long debated whether Neanderthals had a language. Because the vocal tract consists of soft tissue that does not fossilize, anthropologists have had little direct evidence on which to base their theories. As a result, they have turned to indirect evidence. For example, they have used fossil skulls to reconstruct Neanderthals' *larynx* (voice box). Scientists have also made casts of the inner surface of Neanderthal skulls. Because the brain presses against the skull, it leaves an impression of its structure, including areas associated with speech.

The fossil bone found in Israel is a *hyoid*, a small U-shaped bone that, in modern human beings, is found just below the lower jaw and is instrumental in producing human speech. According to the researchers, the fossil, the only Neanderthal hyoid ever found, is virtually identical to the hyoid in modern human beings. On this basis, the researchers concluded that Neanderthals could speak.

Native American remains. Several scientific institutions agreed in 1989 to return skeletal remains of Native Americans in their collections to tribes for reburial. In September, the Smithsonian Institution in Washington, D.C., announced it would return the remains in its Native American collection, which contains an estimated 18,000 human bones, in cases where there is a "preponderance of evidence" linking the remains to a particular tribe.

In some cases, the Smithsonian has records clearly identifying the remains. In other cases, scientists will be able to establish tribal identity by examining the remains and accompanying *funerary objects* (beads, weapons, and clothing buried with bodies). Native

Americans pledged not to request remains that scientists are unable to link with a particular tribe.

Native Americans applauded the decision, saying it would help make up for the disrespect they contend anthropologists have shown for their religious beliefs by digging up the bones of their ancestors.

In June, Stanford University in California agreed to give its collection of Native American remains to the Ohlone-Costanoan tribe of northern California. But anthropologist Bert Gerow, who found the remains—which are from a few hundred to a few thousand years old—contested the decision. He argued that most of the bones were found at a site occupied by other Indian groups for most of that period. He contended that because the bones have not been clearly identified as those of Ohlone-Costanoan ancestors, the tribe has no right to them.

Many other anthropologists were also dismayed by the decisions to return the remains. They argued that the remains could provide information needed to reconstruct Native Americans' history. They also contended that because most of the remains have not been studied thoroughly, their reburial would be a tragic loss to science. Robert McCormick Adams, secretary of the Smithsonian, however, argued that the religious feelings of Native Americans outweigh the demands of science.   Donald C. Johanson

In *World Book,* see **Anthropology; Indian, American.**

Archaeology. Excavations at construction sites in London in 1989 uncovered the remains of two theaters considered to be the birthplace of English drama. In October, archaeologists from the Museum of London found the remains of two walls and several foundation ditches from the Globe Theatre, which was partly owned by the great Elizabethan playwright William Shakespeare and which premiered many of his greatest plays. Earlier, in March, museum archaeologists unearthed the remains of the Rose Theatre, where Shakespeare is believed to have appeared as a young actor and where his earliest works were probably staged.

The Globe, built in 1599, burned in 1613 and was rebuilt in 1614. The theater, which presented Shakespeare's *Hamlet, Othello,* and *King Lear,* was demolished in 1643. At the site, archaeologists also found a large pile of crushed hazelnut shells. They speculated that Elizabethan theatergoers may have snacked on nuts during performances.

The Rose Theatre was constructed in 1587 and remodeled once before being demolished in 1600. All of Christopher Marlowe's plays, as well as Ben Jonson's works, were staged there.

From the remains, archaeologists have determined that the Rose probably had 14 sides and was a timber-frame structure of galleries that may have been three stories high. Some theater patrons sat on benches in these galleries, while others stood in an open yard be-

An archaeologist brushes a 3,300-year-old statue of Hathor, the ancient Egyptian goddess of the sky, unearthed in Luxor, Egypt, in January.

Archaeologists excavate the remains of the Rose Theatre, found in
London in March. William Shakespeare appeared there as a young actor.

fore the stage. The galleries and stage were roofed,
probably with thatch.

Archaeologists discovered that the Rose was smaller
than theater historians had believed. Originally, its
capacity was approximately 2,000 people. After remodeling, it may have accommodated 2,425 people.
The Globe appears to have been about half again as
big as the Rose.

The War of the Rose. The discovery of the remains of the Rose triggered a battle between the corporation that owned the property, which wanted to
proceed with plans to erect an office building on the
site, and preservationists, who wanted the site protected as a historic monument. British courts and the
British government refused to halt construction. But
Imry Merchant Developers, the owner, bowing to public pressure, announced it would erect the office building on concrete stilts. The company argued that the
stilts would preserve the theater remains and allow
the public access to the site. Preservationists, however,
continued to oppose the plan.

Hanson PLC, the international conglomerate that
owns the site where the Globe was found, planned to
ask the British government to list the site as a protected public monument.

Luxor statues. In one of the most important discoveries in Egypt in the past 50 years, Egyptian archaeologists in 1989 uncovered 20 statues representing
gods and ancient royalty beneath a courtyard of a

temple near Luxor. The temple was constructed more
than 3,300 years ago within the ancient city of Thebes,
across the Nile River from the Valley of the Kings,
where ancient Egyptian royalty were buried.

The archaeologists found the statues in two groups,
one buried beneath the other. The first group lay only
3 feet (1 meter) below the courtyard's surface.

The first group of statues included images of the
pharaoh Amenhotep III, who ruled between 1397 and
1360 B.C., and his principal wife, Tiy. Amenhotep III,
whose statue is more than 8 feet (240 centimeters)
tall, was the most famous ruler of Dynasty XVIII. With
Dynasty XVIII, Egypt entered a period of its history
called the New Kingdom, when it became the world's
strongest power. Also found were a statue of pharaoh
Horemheb, the last ruler of that dynasty, and two
statues of gods. One of the statues represents Hathor,
the ancient Egyptian goddess of the sky.

Archaeologists found the second group of statues
buried deeper beneath the courtyard. These statues
included representations of some of Egypt's best-
known rulers and gods. One of the statues, a cobra
made of white granite, probably represents Mertsager, the goddess of silence. According to ancient
Egyptian beliefs, Mertsager's job was to keep secret
the location of the ancient royal tombs.

Bronze-Age tin mines. Ancient mines at Kestel in
the Taurus Mountains of south-central Turkey may be
the long-sought source of tin used by metalworkers in

the eastern Mediterranean to make bronze during the late Bronze Age. During the Bronze Age, bronze, an alloy of copper and tin, was widely used for weapons and tools. This period, which occurred at different times in different places, began in southwestern Asia about 4,000 B.C.

A team of United States and Turkish archaeologists found stone mining tools scattered on a hillside near the open pit mines and shaft entrances, which are mainly collapsed. They believe the tools were used to construct the shafts and tunnels. Ceramics unearthed with the tools range in age from 1,500 to 6,000 years, which suggests that the mine operated over a long period. Charcoal in deposits inside the mine was radiocarbon-dated to the early Bronze Age, confirming the age of the mine.

The discovery of the mine suggests that the metals trade in Southwestern Asia was more complex than archaeologists have believed. In the absence of tin mines in the region, archaeologists had assumed that the metal came from more distant sources, perhaps as far away as what are now Great Britain and Nigeria. This view was supported by information on the metals trade in ancient Assyrian texts. The find at Kestel indicates that the metalworkers of the region also had local sources of tin.   Barbara Voorhies

In *World Book,* see **Archaeology; Bronze Age; Egypt, Ancient; Shakespeare, William** (The Elizabethan theater).

Architecture news was dominated in 1989 by I. M. Pei, a Chinese-born New Yorker who is perhaps the dean of American architects. In March, the vast Louvre art museum in Paris—once a royal palace—reopened after being completely redone by Pei. Its new entrance, a 71-foot (21.6-meter) pyramid of glass and stainless steel, became a hit with the French. They called it "Le Pyramide" and quickly made it, like the 100-year-old Eiffel Tower, a symbol of the city.

In September, Pei's Morton H. Meyerson Symphony Center in Dallas opened to acclaim. And the name of his firm changed in 1989 from I. M. Pei & Partners to Pei Cobb Freed & Partners, recognizing the contributions of Henry N. Cobb and James Ingo Freed and perhaps signaling the intention of the 72-year-old Pei to retire.

Notable buildings of 1989, in addition to those by Pei, included two college art centers and a civil rights memorial. British architect James Stirling designed the Cornell University Center for the Performing Arts in Ithaca, N.Y., which opened in April. The center, a cluster of theaters and art studios, stands on the edge of a deep gorge. The architect designed the buildings to resemble, without copying, the Renaissance architecture of Italy.

Wexner Center for the Visual Arts at Ohio State University in Columbus, a long-awaited and highly experimental building by Peter Eisenman of New York City and Richard Trott of Columbus, opened in November.

White-painted steel scaffolding runs the length of the building and serves as a walkway between the center's four exhibition galleries, film theater, and other facilities.

Maya Ying Lin, who designed the Vietnam Veterans Memorial in Washington, D.C., created an equally simple Civil Rights Memorial in Montgomery, Ala. The memorial, dedicated in November, consists of a bowl-shaped table of black granite with a curved wall behind it. It lists the names of 40 people killed in the civil rights movement of the 1950's and 1960's.

Competitions—events in which more than one architect submits a design, with the winner picked by judges—were important in 1989. Many major competitions of the year took place in the Washington, D.C., area. Freed of Pei Cobb Freed & Partners won out over six rivals with a design to complete the Federal Triangle, a block of government office buildings on Pennsylvania Avenue. Construction was due to begin early in 1990. Edward Larrabee Barnes of New York City won a competition for a federal judiciary building near Washington's Union Station. And the young architectural team of Marian Weiss and Michael Manfredi defeated more than 130 other entrants with a design for a Memorial to Women in Military Service for America at the entrance to Arlington National Cemetery in nearby Arlington, Va.

Notable exhibitions of 1989 were few. In the spring, the Museum of Modern Art in New York City showed work by two young architects working in that city, Argentine-born Emilio Ambasz and American Steven Holl. Both men have completed only a few buildings but have created many designs that influence other architects.

In the summer, the Walker Art Center in Minneapolis, Minn., showed the work of Morphosis, an architectural firm based in Santa Monica, Calif. The firm's young partners, Michael Rotondi and Thom Mayne, favor glittery, sharp-edged, rather risky-looking architecture.

Prince Charles of Great Britain, who made headlines in 1984 when he denounced a modern extension to London's National Gallery as "a monstrous carbuncle," continued to make news in 1989. In September, Doubleday published the prince's book *A Vision of Britain: A Personal View of Architecture*, and Charles opened an exhibit on the same theme at London's Victoria and Albert Museum. Both the book and the exhibit were seen as attacks on modern architecture and as pleas for a return to older values.

The prince, in the spring, announced a master plan for 3,000 new homes, shops, offices, and schools in four model villages on 400 acres (160 hectares) he owns near Dorchester. Luxembourg-born architect Leon Krier will design the villages. Krier advocates low, compact towns with homes, workplaces, and other necessities all within walking distance, as opposed to scattered modern cities of skyscrapers and freeways.

Architect I. M. Pei used sleek glass walls for two 1989 buildings, an entrance to the Louvre in Paris, *above,* and a symphony hall in Dallas, *below.*

Controversy dogged architecture as always, much of it in New York City. A new scheme there for Columbus Circle, designed by Skidmore, Owings & Merrill of Chicago, struggled toward approval. A citizens' suit had succeeded in defeating an early, grander proposal by Israeli-born Canadian architect Moshe Safdie.

A blocky design by Princeton, N.J., architect Michael Graves for an addition to the Whitney Museum of American Art in New York City met with little more favor than two earlier proposals by the same architect. Critics felt that all three designs detracted from the Whitney's original building, a stark 1966 design.

An even more controversial proposal, for a cluster of four fat office towers in Times Square by the New York City firm of John Burgee Architects with Philip Johnson, made news in August 1989. The architects unexpectedly changed their buildings from sedate granite and limestone to jazzy neon and colored glass.

In addition, there was concern about a proposal to double the size of a building regarded by many as the best example of American architecture since the 1940's. This is the Kimbell Art Museum in Fort Worth, Tex., designed by the late Louis Kahn in the 1960's and completed in 1972. The architect for the expansion, Romaldo Giurgola of New York City, plans to duplicate Kahn's famous skylit vaults in his new addition, but some critics argued that so fine a building should not be changed at all.   Robert Campbell

In *World Book,* see **Architecture.**

Argentina. Carlos Saúl Menem, leader of the populist Justicialist Party, was sworn in for a six-year term as president of Argentina on July 8, 1989. It marked the first time in 61 years that one elected civilian president of Argentina transferred power to another of a different party. To ease the transition, outgoing President Raúl Alfonsín resigned five months early. Argentina's deepening economic woes were beyond the help of his lame-duck administration.

In Menem's inaugural speech, the 59-year-old president, the political heir of the populist dictator Juan Perón and the Perónist movement, candidly acknowledged that Argentina "is broke." Menem inherited a $60-billion foreign debt, an inflation rate exceeding 100 per cent a month, a political atmosphere poisoned by recriminations, and an unhappy military. Among the most obvious targets of recrimination were wealthy Argentines, who have invested an estimated $50 billion abroad during recent years of economic chaos at home. Among those demanding restitution were Argentine workers, the mainstay of the Justicialist Party, who have tried to scrape by on wages that have a purchasing power of less than $50 a month.

Concessions to military. To win support from the nation's powerful armed forces, President Menem on July 12 named General Isidro Cáceres as chief of staff of the army. The appointment was looked on favorably by dissident officers, who had mounted three abortive rebellions during Alfonsín's administration.

To forestall such threats to his own government, Menem issued a sweeping pardon on October 7 of officers prosecuted or jailed for human-rights abuses committed from 1976 to 1983. Then, some 10,000 Argentines "disappeared," and thousands more were tortured and jailed without trial. The pardons were bitterly criticized by human-rights groups, who called the action a "sham of justice." Among the 277 military men and civilians pardoned were 16 generals, 2 admirals, and a former president, General Leopoldo Galtieri, who was jailed for his mismanagement of the 1982 war with Great Britain over the Falkland Islands. Argentina lost the war.

Foreign relations. At the United Nations (UN) in New York City on September 25, Menem repeated Argentina's claims of sovereignty over the Falklands, but his administration also began talks with Britain in October, aimed at restoring full diplomatic relations. Menem also met with President George Bush and officials of various international financial agencies. Before he left the United States, the International Monetary Fund, an agency of the UN, announced that it would make $1.5 billion in credit available to Argentina—a step expected to help the country resolve its differences with creditors.   Nathan A. Haverstock

See also **Latin America** (Facts in brief table); **Menem, Carlos Saúl. In** *World Book,* see **Argentina.**

Arizona. See State government.

Arkansas. See State government.

Armed forces. The United States invaded Panama on Dec. 20, 1989, in its largest combat operation since the Vietnam War (1957-1975) and installed a new government headed by Guillermo Endara, who had appeared to win presidential elections in May. United States President George Bush ordered the action to overthrow the dictatorship of General Manuel Antonio Noriega Morena. Bush said the invasion was necessary to protect the 35,000 Americans living in Panama.

The attack, dubbed "Operation Just Cause," involved Air Force, Army, Marine, and Navy personnel. The approximately 12,000 troops already stationed in Panama were reinforced with about 12,000 rangers, paratroopers, and other soldiers mobilized from Fort Bragg, N.C.; Fort Lewis, Wash.; Fort Ord, Calif.; Fort Polk, La.; and Fort Stewart, Ga. The combined troops were organized in five task forces, each with its own military objectives. The Air Force's secret F-117 Stealth fighter was used in combat for the first time during the operation, with apparent success.

American forces quickly took control of the headquarters of the Panamanian Defense Forces. They secured Panama City's airport and the Panama Canal. United States troops took more than 3,700 prisoners, including Noriega, who surrendered on Jan. 3, 1990. At least 23 U.S. soldiers were killed in the fighting, and some 320 were wounded. See **Panama.**

Arms control. After several years of unsuccessful negotiations, the United States and the Soviet Union

A submarine-launched Trident II missile spirals out of control during the missile's first test firing near Cape Canaveral, Fla., on March 21.

appeared to be making significant progress toward greatly reducing their arsenals of strategic nuclear weapons. Both sides predicted that a strategic arms reduction treaty (START) could be achieved within one year, and Bush and Soviet leader Mikhail S. Gorbachev met in December and agreed to hold a formal summit in 1990.

After meeting with U.S. Secretary of State James A. Baker III in Wyoming in September, Soviet Foreign Minister Eduard A. Shevardnadze announced that his country was prepared to conclude a START agreement even if the United States would not limit its development of the space-based missile defense system known as the Strategic Defense Initiative (SDI), or Star Wars. Meanwhile, by May 31, more than 1,000 inter-mediate-range nuclear weapons had been destroyed under the terms of a treaty signed in 1987 that calls for the elimination of all such weapons from U.S. and Soviet inventories.

The superpowers also seemed poised to reach an accord on sharp reductions in chemical weapons. Bush told the United Nations in September that the United States would destroy 80 per cent of its chemical munitions if the Soviet Union agreed to reduce its stockpile to the same level. Bush also pledged to destroy all U.S. chemical weapons within 10 years if a treaty were reached banning all such weapons worldwide. The Soviets endorsed the proposal.

Strategic forces. Congressional and scientific critics continued to argue that the SDI was too expensive and not likely to work. For the fourth consecutive year, Congress insisted on sizable cutbacks in SDI development funds. United States Secretary of Defense Richard B. Cheney acknowledged in March that the program had been oversold during the previous Administration. Pentagon officials said they were studying a new defensive system dubbed Brilliant Pebbles that would place thousands of small interceptor missiles in space instead of clusters of multiple-missile satellites.

The development and testing of several strategic weapons programs were also delayed in 1989. A series of technical problems set back until July the first flight of the B-2—nicknamed the Stealth bomber because it is designed to evade enemy radar. Escalating cost estimates for the plane infuriated critics in Congress. The Air Force claimed that building 132 B-2 bombers would cost $70 billion and estimated the total program cost at nearly $100 billion. But defense experts alleged that the costs were certain to go higher—perhaps up to $1 billion per plane. The Pentagon's former procurement director recommended in May that the B-2 program be scrapped because of exorbitant costs and poor quality.

In April, Bush ended an extended policy debate over the use of land-based strategic missiles by ordering both the deployment of existing MX missiles and the development of the Midgetman missile. But in May, the first test firing of the Midgetman failed when the missile veered off course and had to be destroyed shortly after its launching. Similarly, the Navy's Trident II submarine-launched missile failed in two out of three undersea test firings in 1989.

Technical problems continued to dog the B-1B strategic bomber as well. A government report released in February said that correcting the bomber's defects could cost $400 million per plane. The Air Force grounded its entire fleet of 97 bombers in March for safety inspections after a movable wing on one plane went out of control and punctured a fuel tank. It was the third time in 18 months that the fleet had been grounded. Inspectors subsequently found that 70 of the 97 planes were leaking lubricants into the wings.

Conventional forces. Bush unveiled a plan to significantly cut back American troop strength in Western Europe at a meeting of the North Atlantic Treaty Organization (NATO) on May 29. Bush called for U.S. troops to be reduced by 20 per cent to about 275,000, provided the Soviet Union agreed to the same ceiling for its troops in Eastern Europe. Bush also proposed that NATO and Warsaw Pact nations reduce their conventional weapons in Europe.

Development proceeded on a variety of conventional weapons systems, including an advanced tactical fighter plane, a nonnuclear cruise missile, the SSN-21 Seawolf-class attack submarine, an experimental jet fighter, a new family of armored vehicles, and a laser pistol. The first of the DDG-51 Burke-class nuclear destroyers was launched in September.

Smoke pours from a gun turret on the battleship U.S.S. *Iowa* after a shipboard explosion kills 47 sailors on April 19.

Drug wars. After years of reluctance, the U.S. military significantly expanded its involvement in efforts to reduce the flow of illegal drugs into the United States. The Pentagon increased its technical support to antidrug operations in several countries, particularly Colombia, Bolivia, and Peru. As part of a $65-million emergency aid package, the U.S. military in August provided Colombian armed forces with helicopters, aircraft, boats, small arms, medical equipment, and military advisers. The military was also expected to assume a larger role in detecting and preventing drug trafficking along U.S. borders.

Iowa **tragedy.** On April 19, 47 sailors were killed when a gun turret exploded on the 47-year-old U.S.S. *Iowa* during a training exercise in the Atlantic Ocean. The accident rekindled debate over the wisdom of recommissioning the *Iowa* and three sister ships as part of the defense build-up begun in 1980; critics claimed that battleships were obsolete.

A Navy board of inquiry concluded on September 7 that Gunner's Mate Clayton M. Hartwig, who died in the explosion, was "most likely" responsible for the tragedy. The board said that Hartwig, the gun captain at the time of the blast, probably placed an igniting device between powder bags in the gun, causing the explosion. Officials conceded, however, that they had not discovered a motive for Hartwig's alleged actions or undeniable evidence to support their conclusion. A congressional subcommittee launched an investiga-

The B-2 bomber, called the Stealth because it was designed to evade enemy radar, makes its maiden flight over California in July.

tion into the board's findings. In October, the chairman of the committee reported that laboratory tests conducted by the Federal Bureau of Investigation (FBI) failed to turn up any evidence of sabotage.

The board of inquiry also found that some crew members in the gun turret were not fully trained for their jobs and were improperly supervised. Superiors gave the *Iowa*'s captain and three other crew members light administrative punishment in October after determining that their dereliction of duty "did not cause or contribute to the explosion in any way."

Safety check. In October and November, a number of unrelated accidents involving Navy personnel and equipment resulted in 10 deaths and more than 40 injuries. As a result, the Navy ordered an unprecedented 48-hour suspension of operations on November 15 and 16 to review safety procedures.

Personnel developments. United States military troop strength stood at 2,124,654 on November 30, a decrease of 5,784 from the previous year. In late 1988, the Army failed to meet its recruitment quotas for the first time in eight years, and the Navy reached its goal only by canceling enlistment delays for some recruits. The shortages were attributed to a lower unemployment rate, the declining population of young Americans, and budget constraints.

Base closings. Congress declined to block plans for a major military base reduction on April 18, clearing the way for the Pentagon to begin closing 91 facilities.

The closings were to begin no later than Sept. 30, 1991, and would be completed by Sept. 30, 1995. The shutdown had been devised in 1988 as a means to reduce Pentagon spending, though critics charged that the plan would not produce the projected savings of $5.6 billion over 20 years.

Defense budget. President Ronald Reagan's final budget for the Department of Defense was submitted to Congress on Jan. 9, 1989. For the 1990 fiscal year beginning Oct. 1, 1989, the Administration asked for $305.6 billion in spending authority, an increase of $6.1 billion from the previous year and a 2.1 per cent rise after inflation. The total request for national defense, which includes the Energy Department's nuclear-weapons programs, was $315.2 billion. The budget was widely viewed as unrealistic, and Bush reluctantly agreed to a $10-billion cut in defense spending mandated by congressional budget committees. On April 25, Cheney announced that the cut would require "very, very painful" reductions in troop strength and weapons programs.

The Pentagon announced plans to reform its scandal-ridden procurement system in July. The plans called for saving $30 billion over five years by reducing waste and mismanagement, streamlining operations, eliminating some jobs, toughening ethics rules, and reducing the number of Pentagon consultants.

Appointments. The Senate rejected Bush's nomination of former Senator John G. Tower (R., Tex.) as secretary of defense on March 9, after a bitter three-month debate. Opponents had charged that Tower's personal conduct rendered him unfit for the job. His defenders argued that Tower's personal life was irrelevant, that many of the charges against him were unfounded, and that he was a victim of partisan politics.

Immediately after Tower was rejected, Bush nominated Cheney, a popular Republican representative from Wyoming. The Senate unanimously confirmed Cheney on March 17. See **Cheney, Richard B.**

The entire civilian leadership structure of the Pentagon changed hands after Bush took office. Deputy Defense Secretary William H. Taft IV was replaced by Donald J. Atwood, Jr., vice chairman of the General Motors Corporation. Michael P. W. Stone was appointed secretary of the Army, H. Lawrence Garrett III was named secretary of the Navy, and Donald B. Rice became secretary of the Air Force.

Admiral William J. Crowe, Jr., retired as chairman of the Joint Chiefs of Staff on September 30. He was replaced by General Colin L. Powell, the commander of Army combat forces in the continental United States. At 52, Powell became the youngest chairman of the Joint Chiefs in history and the first black to serve in the country's top military post. See **Powell, Colin Luther.**   Thomas M. DeFrank

In *World Book,* see the articles on the branches of the armed forces.

Army. See **Armed forces.**

Art. A series of controversies brought art into the news in 1989. In March, Richard Serra's sculpture *Tilted Arc,* a 120-foot (36.6-meter) curved wall of rusted steel, was removed from New York City's Federal Plaza. Since 1981—when the $175,000 piece was commissioned under a federal program that pays for art in or near public buildings—people who worked nearby campaigned for its removal, calling it an eyesore and an obstruction. Serra maintained that the site was integral to the artwork and that moving the sculpture would ruin it. Serra withdrew his last court challenge March 15, and the sculpture was removed that night.

A controversial exhibit in Chicago received national attention in March 1989. "Dread" Scott Tyler, a student at the School of the Art Institute of Chicago, spread a United States flag on the gallery floor as part of a show of student work. Tyler's display—titled *What Is the Proper Way to Display a U.S. Flag?*—also included photographs of flag-draped coffins and a ledger in which viewers could write comments. Local politicians and veterans' groups, charging that the display desecrated the flag, staged protests that closed the exhibit for a week. A Cook County, Illinois, circuit court judge ruled that the display was legal, but the Illinois state legislature voted to cut the school's state funding from $65,000 to a symbolic $1. The episode added fuel to arguments over flag display that occupied Congress later in 1989. See **Congress of the U.S.**

The National Endowment for the Arts (NEA), a federal agency that provides government grants for art, came under fire from Congress in 1989 over the propriety of two NEA-funded projects. The first case involved a photograph by Andres Serrano, who received $15,000 in NEA funds through the Southeastern Center for Contemporary Art in Winston-Salem, N.C. The photograph showed a crucifix submerged in the artist's urine. The second controversial project was a traveling exhibition of photographs by Robert Mapplethorpe, sponsored by the Institute for Contemporary Art in Philadelphia and funded with $30,000 from the NEA. The show included some explicit images of men performing homosexual acts.

On July 12, the U.S. House of Representatives voted to cut the NEA's 1990 funding by $45,000, the sum of the two grants. A Senate attempt to prohibit federal funding for offensive art, defined in sweeping terms in a proposal by Senator Jesse Helms (R., N.C.), was rejected by the House. The final bill, passed October 7, denies federal funds to art that falls under an older legal definition of obscenity.

Even as Congress debated the exhibition's propriety, the Mapplethorpe show created problems for the Corcoran Gallery of Art in Washington, D.C. The show had appeared earlier in Philadelphia and Chicago without arousing local protest, but in June, Corcoran director Christina Orr-Cahall canceled the show's scheduled Washington appearance, which would have coincided with Congress's July review of the NEA budget. Orr-Cahall feared that a local display of the controversial show at that time might be turned into a political issue by legislators already displeased with Mapplethorpe's work.

Instead of defusing the issue, however, the cancellation created more turmoil. The Washington (D.C.) Project for the Arts quickly arranged to hang the show, and 700 protesters demonstrated at the Corcoran on June 30, the day the exhibition was to have opened there. The Corcoran was forced to cancel two other planned shows when the invited artists declined to participate in protest of the Mapplethorpe decision. In September, the Mapplethorpe show's curator, Jane Livingston, announced her resignation. Several days later, Orr-Cahall made a formal apology to the art world for canceling the Mapplethorpe show. In December, Orr-Cahall also resigned.

The new curbs on the NEA were not officially to go into effect until 1990, but they received their first test in early November 1989, when the endowment withdrew a $10,000 grant supporting a New York City art show on AIDS titled "Witnesses: Against Our Vanishing." John E. Frohnmayer, head of the NEA, said he based his decision not on the content of the artworks —some of which depicted homosexual acts—but on the show's catalog, which included an essay criticizing specific political and religious leaders for their positions on AIDS. The action drew angry responses from the arts community, capped by composer Leonard

A student's art exhibit, which features a flag spread on the floor, *left,* prompts protests outside the Art Institute of Chicago in March, *right.*

Bernstein's refusal to accept a National Medal of Arts, a presidential award, reportedly in protest over the NEA's action. On November 16, Frohnmayer reversed his decision and restored the grant, under the condition that it not be applied to publication of the catalog. He also expressed his intent to work to remove the new restrictions.

Lawsuits. In June 1989, the Supreme Court ruled on a copyright case involving an artwork. The work, a sculpture of a homeless family, was commissioned in 1985 by the Community for Creative Non-Violence, an advocacy organization for the homeless in Washington, D.C. Sculptor James Earl Reid donated his services and was reimbursed for materials. When the organization began reproducing the work on calendars and cards to raise funds, Reid sued for copyright infringement. The court ruled in Reid's favor, declaring that free-lance artists retain ownership of copyright on commissioned works. The ruling was expected to have widespread effects on publishers, advertising agencies, and other businesses that rely heavily on free-lance art, music, and writing.

In August 1989, a U.S. federal judge in Indianapolis ruled that a set of Byzantine mosaics dating from the A.D. 500's, which had been stolen in 1974 from a church in Cyprus and purchased in 1988 by an Indiana art dealer, must be returned to the original owners. The ruling, which stresses that art buyers are responsible for knowing whether a seller legally owns art of-

fered for sale, was expected to affect museums' and dealers' acquisitions policies.

Retrospective exhibitions. "Andy Warhol: A Retrospective," the first major Warhol show since 1971, surveyed the artist's work from the early pop-art paintings to the Last Supper scenes he created just before his death in 1987. It opened at the Museum of Modern Art in New York City from Feb. 6 to May 2, 1989, and traveled to Chicago, London, and West Germany in 1989. Additional stops were scheduled for 1990 in Italy and France.

The Hirshhorn Museum in Washington, D.C., marked the 80th birthday of British painter Francis Bacon with a retrospective. The show—the first U.S. exhibition of Bacon's work since 1975—appeared at the Hirshhorn from Oct. 12, 1989, to Jan. 7, 1990, and was to travel to Los Angeles and New York in 1990.

Historical shows of 1989 included "Picasso and Braque: Pioneering Cubism," a collection of more than 350 paintings, collages, and constructions from the 1907-1914 collaborations between Pablo Picasso and Georges Braque. The show was at the Museum of Modern Art from Sept. 24, 1989, to Jan. 16, 1990.

A comprehensive display of work by Canaletto, a Venetian painter of the 1700's, hung from Nov. 2, 1989, to Jan. 21, 1990, at the Metropolitan Museum of Art in New York City. The show featured many of the artist's celebrated scene paintings of Venice and London, as well as 50 books and prints. The Metropolitan also opened a show of works by Spanish baroque painter Diego Velázquez from Oct. 3, 1989, to Jan. 7, 1990, in collaboration with the Prado museum in Madrid, Spain.

The first major U.S. exhibit of paintings by Frans Hals, a Dutch portraitist of the 1600's, appeared from Oct. 1 through Dec. 31, 1989, at the National Gallery of Art in Washington, D.C., with 1990 stops scheduled for England and the Netherlands. The National Gallery also sponsored a show of early work by postimpressionist Paul Cézanne from Jan. 23 to April 30, 1989.

International shows. The most important international group show of 1989 was "Magicians of the Earth," from May 18 to Aug. 14, 1989, at two Paris locations, the Pompidou Center and the Grand Hall at La Villette. Billed as an effort to move beyond the European and American focus of most international shows, the exhibition involved more than 100 artists— half from Europe and the United States, and half from such countries as the Philippines, South Africa, Tibet, Haiti, and Zaire. Works ranged from Western-world photography and video to Australian Aboriginal sand paintings and African ceremonial masks.

The Louvre, Paris' national museum, officially reopened on March 30, 1989, after six years of renovations. The centerpiece of the remodeling was architect I. M. Pei's much-debated glass-and-steel pyramid, which now forms the entryway to the Louvre's refurbished galleries. Additional gallery space is scheduled

Picasso's self-portrait *Yo Picasso* (1901), which was auctioned in May for $47.85 million, held the price record for Picasso's works only until November.

to open in 1993, making the Louvre the largest museum in the world.

Auctions continued to set—and overturn— records for high prices in 1989. At the New York City auction house of Sotheby's, a May 9 sale of impressionist and modern art brought in a record total of $204.8 million. On November 14, Christie's New York auction house topped that by selling $232.4 million in artwork. The Christie's sale included Edouard Manet's *Rue Mosnier, Paris, Decorated with Flags on June 30, 1878,* which sold for $26.4 million, more than twice the price for any other Manet work. Sotheby's regained the single-sale record the next day, bringing $269.5 million for 71 impressionist and modern works.

Sotheby's May sales set records for many artists, notably Picasso, whose 1901 self-portrait *Yo Picasso* brought $47.85 million—the second-highest price ever paid for an artwork at auction. That record held only until November 30, when Picasso's *Pierette's Wedding* sold in Paris for $48.9 million.

Other notable records included Andy Warhol's *Shot Red Marilyn* (1964), which sold on May 3 at Christie's for $4.07 million, the top price for any Warhol work. On May 31 at Christie's, *The Halberdier,* a portrait by the Florentine Renaissance painter Jacopo Pontormo, sold for $35.2 million, tripling the previous record price for an Old Master painting.   Eleanor Heartney

In *World Book,* see **Art and the arts; Painting; Sculpture.**

Asia. The two largest wars in Asia changed from international conflicts to bitter civil wars in 1989, and the sad plight of Asian refugees failed to improve. Nevertheless, most Asian nations enjoyed peace as well as economic progress, which slowly improved living standards.

The Soviet Union completed the withdrawal of its army from Afghanistan on February 15. For nine years, the Soviets had unsuccessfully tried to destroy Muslim guerrilla resistance to Afghanistan's Communist government. After the Soviet withdrawal, the Afghan regime denied that it was Communist, but it failed to win wider support among the people. The Soviets airlifted supplies to aid the government, while anti-Communist nations equipped the guerrillas. Despite international efforts to bring peace, neither side was prepared to compromise.

Vietnam said it had withdrawn the last of its troops from Cambodia (formerly Kampuchea) on September 26. Almost 11 years earlier, Vietnam invaded Cambodia to drive out Cambodia's murderous Communist regime—the Khmer Rouge—and set up a friendly Communist government.

Even before the Vietnamese troops left Cambodia, Khmer Rouge guerrillas, supplied with weapons made in China, threatened to resume a powerful role in Cambodian affairs. This frustrated Southeast Asian and Western nations that supported smaller, militarily less effective non-Communist forces also fighting the

Fulfilling a 1988 agreement to end the Soviet occupation of Afghanistan,
Soviet troops cross the Afghan border and return home in February 1989.

regime set up by Vietnam. International diplomacy
failed to find a compromise in Cambodia, and the
fighting grew more savage throughout 1989.

Refugees from these wars remained stranded in
nearby nations. In 1989, more than 3 million Afghan
refugees were living in camps in Pakistan, and more
than 2 million Afghans were in Iran. Some 325,000
Cambodians lived in camps along the Thai border,
from which the Khmer Rouge forced many of them to
transport ammunition into combat areas.

In addition, a continuing flow of refugees from
Vietnam troubled Asia and the rest of the world. The
Vietnamese refugees are known as *boat people* because most escaped their impoverished country by undertaking risky voyages on small, overcrowded fishing

boats. In the late 1970's—when many boat people
fled Vietnam's Communists—the United States, Canada, Australia, France, and other countries saw the
boat people as political refugees and took them in.
But many nations believe that refugees leaving Vietnam in the late 1980's were fleeing poverty rather
than political repression. Few nations were willing to
make room for such economic migrants.

Hong Kong—which in 1988 began screening refugees to determine whether they were fleeing economic hardship or political repression—sent 75 boat
people back to Vietnam on March 3, 1989. On March
13, six Southeast Asian nations announced that they
would also begin such screening and would not help
economic migrants resettle abroad.

A United Nations conference in Geneva, Switzerland, on June 13 and 14 discussed attempting to get the economic migrants to return home. Vietnam's foreign minister and officials from other nations rejected the idea of forced repatriation, and the conference failed to come up with any alternative.

Hong Kong and the British government responsible for the colony wanted to force the 57,000 boat people encamped there to return to Vietnam because no other country would take them. Although Hong Kong's present prosperity was built with the cheap labor of Chinese refugees and the colony now has a labor shortage, officials said the Vietnamese did not fit in. Hong Kong put the boat people into virtual prison camps on short rations, and both riots and cholera epidemics broke out. The British colonial government in December began sending refugees home by force.

Nothing stemmed the flow of refugees during 1989. By the end of August, when seasonal changes reduced boat traffic, 61,345 boat people had landed outside Vietnam, the highest number since 1981. Uncounted others died before reaching land, some at the hands of Thai pirates, others at sea after authorities in Thailand and Malaysia pushed their boats from shore.

Hong Kong residents became increasingly worried about China's scheduled 1997 take-over of the British colony, despite a 1984 agreement between Great Britain and China that allows Hong Kong to keep its own laws after the take-over. On June 4, 1989, the Chinese government killed hundreds, possibly thousands, of student demonstrators in Beijing and later fired Hong Kong officials of Chinese-owned media that had supported the students.

These events intensified apprehensions that China would not carry out its promises to respect Hong Kong's separate character. Some 42,000 of the colony's best-educated and most successful residents left during 1989 to resettle abroad, and many more tried to emigrate. The British government angered Hong Kong residents by refusing to allow more than a few to settle in Britain.

India's neighbors found the nation, South Asia's largest, difficult to deal with in 1989. Some countries, such as Bangladesh, complained that India refused to let the four-year-old South Asian Association for Regional Cooperation handle disputes involving India. India insisted that each dispute could be handled bilaterally, which meant that India's neighbors could not join forces to exert pressure.

Bangladesh also accused India of supporting guerrillas fighting the Bangladeshi government. Sri Lankan officials found India reluctant to withdraw army troops stationed in their country. The Indian government did complete a withdrawal of troops from Maldives, however. The last of these 1,600 Indian soldiers —who rescued the Maldives government from an attack by mercenaries in late 1988—left the island nation on Nov. 3, 1989.

Nepal suffered from a partial trade blockade by India in 1989. A landlocked nation whose routes to world commerce lie through India, Nepal had made separate treaties with India covering transit rights and trade. When the treaties expired on March 23, India sought to combine them. Nepal, arguing that transit is an international right separate from any trade arrangement, resisted what it saw as India's effort to force it to reduce ties with its only other neighbor, China, and do India's bidding. In response, India closed 19 of 21 border crossing points and imposed tariffs of up to 150 per cent on the few goods that did cross the border.

This created severe shortages in Nepal. Baby food, coal, medicines, and other items became scarce, and prices rose 30 to 40 per cent. Construction slowed as the cement and brick industries virtually closed for lack of coal. To replace the fuel, Nepal cut more firewood, speeding the deforestation of the Himalaya and thus contributing to future flooding. Already one of the world's poorest nations—where some 40 per cent of the population of 19 million are malnourished—Nepal saw its economic growth stop.

Although cultivating an image of itself as a valiant little country resisting a big bully, Nepal itself came under fire. Asia Watch Committee, a human-rights organization based in Washington, D.C., said in September that King Birendra Bir Bikram Shah Dev ran a repressive regime that did not tolerate dissent or criticism of the monarchy, and that the torture of prisoners was widespread. The report noted, however, that technically illegal political parties were allowed to operate openly and that Nepal's legal system served as a partial check on the regime.

Soviets leave Mongolia. The Soviet Union announced that on May 15 it began the first stage of a two-year withdrawal of 50,000 troops from Mongolia—75 per cent of the total stationed there. This stage ended on October 5. The troops had begun to arrive in Mongolia in 1966, at a time of growing hostility between the Soviet Union and China, Mongolia's only other neighbor. The withdrawal came as the Soviet Union and China reestablished diplomatic relations. Many of the 50,000 Soviet civilians working in Mongolia to develop its economy also left in 1989, as Mongolia—long dependent on Soviet aid and trade—diversified its foreign contacts.

United States military bases in the Philippines continued to be a source of controversy as the 1991 renewal date for the agreement allowing them there approached. In a surprise move, Singapore on August 4 offered to provide facilities for U.S. armed forces. Singapore officials explained that many nations in Southeast Asia had prospered because the U.S. presence guaranteed the region's stability and that other countries should share the burden of hosting American forces. United States technical teams surveyed Singapore's facilities, and officials discussed the possibility of using bases there.

Facts in brief on Asian countries

Country	Population	Government	Monetary unit*	Exports†	Foreign trade (million U.S.$) Imports†
Afghanistan	15,885,000	President & People's Democratic Party General Secretary Najibullah; Council of Ministers Chairman Soltan Ali Keshtmand	afghani (55 = $1)	564	942
Australia	16,365,000	Governor General Bill Hayden; Prime Minister Robert Hawke	dollar (1.28 = $1)	32,734	33,245
Bangladesh	116,000,000	President Hussain Mohammad Ershad; Prime Minister Qazi Zafar Ahmed	taka (33 = $1)	1,347	2,729
Bhutan	1,513,000	King Jigme Singye Wangchuck	Indian (rupee (17 = $1) & ngultrum (17 = $1)	15	69
Brunei	277,000	Sultan Sir Hassanal Bolkiah	dollar (1.95 = $1)	1,747	653
Burma (Myanmar)	41,279,000	State Law and Order Restoration Council Chairman Saw Maung	kyat (5.35 = $1)	138	244
Cambodia (Kampuchea)	6,993,000	People's Revolutionary Party Secretary General & Council of State President Heng Samrin (Coalition government: President Norodom Sihanouk; Vice President Khieu Samphan; Prime Minister Son Sann)	riel (150 = $1)	3	28
China	1,100,258,000	Communist Party General Secretary Jiang Zemin; Premier Li Peng; President Yang Shangkun	yuan (3.72 = $1)	47,530	55,254
India	853,532,000	President Ramaswamy Iyer Venkataraman; Prime Minister V. P. Singh	rupee (17 = $1)	11,596	16,754
Indonesia	180,594,000	President Suharto; Vice President Sudharmono	rupiah (1,790 = $1)	17,136	12,370
Iran	56,800,000	Leader of the Islamic Revolution Ayatollah Ali Hoseini Khamenei; President Ali Akbar Hashemi Rafsanjani	rial (71.6 = $1)	20,247	18,296
Japan	123,749,000	Emperor Akihito; Prime Minister Toshiki Kaifu	yen (143 = $1)	264,959	187,343
Korea, North	22,965,000	President Kim Il-sŏng; Premier Yon Hyong-muk	won (0.97 = $1)	1,700	2,000
Korea, South	43,650,000	President Roh Tae Woo; Prime Minister Kang Young Hoon	won (673 = $1)	60,696	51,811
Laos	4,070,000	Acting President Phoumi Vongvichit; Council of Ministers Chairman Kaysone Phomvihan	kip (583 = $1)	12	48
Malaysia	17,344,000	Paramount Ruler Azlan Muhibbuddin Shah ibni Sultan Yusof Izzudin; Prime Minister Mahathir bin Mohamad	ringgit (2.71 = $1)	20,771	16,585
Maldives	215,000	President Maumoon Abdul Gayoom	rufiyaa (9.37 = $1)	25	64
Mongolia	2,185,000	People's Great Hural Presidium Chairman Jambyn Batmonh; Council of Ministers Chairman Dumaagiyn Sodnom	tughrik (3.36 = $1)	no statistics available	
Nepal	19,157,000	King Birendra Bir Bikram Shah Dev; Prime Minister Marich Man Singh Shrestha	rupee (24 = $1)	194	688
New Zealand	3,402,000	Governor General Sir Paul Reeves; Prime Minister Geoffrey Palmer	dollar (1.69 = $1)	8,806	7,305
Pakistan	113,163,000	President Ghulam Ishaq Khan; Prime Minister Benazir Bhutto	rupee (21.3 = $1)	4,497	6,590
Papua New Guinea	3,824,000	Governor General (vacant); Prime Minister Rabbie Namaliu	kina (0.86 = $1)	1,399	1,200
Philippines	62,446,000	President Corazon C. Aquino	peso (22.1 = $1)	7,035	8,731
Singapore	2,704,000	President Wee Kim Wee; Prime Minister Lee Kuan Yew	dollar (1.95 = $1)	39,305	43,862
Sri Lanka	16,779,000	President Ranasinghe Premadasa; Prime Minister D. B. Wijetunge	rupee (39.5 = $1)	1,466	2,227
Taiwan	20,454,000	President Li Teng-hui; Premier Li Huan	dollar (26.1 = $1)	39,800	24,200
Thailand	55,760,000	King Bhumibol Adulyadej; Prime Minister Chatchai Chunhawan	baht (25.8 = $1)	15,384	18,559
Union of Soviet Socialist Republics	288,239,000	Communist Party General Secretary & Executive President Mikhail S. Gorbachev; Council of Ministers Chairman Nikolay I. Ryzhkov	ruble (0.62 = $1)	110,559	107,229
Vietnam	67,084,000	Communist Party General Secretary Nguyen Van Linh; Council of State Chairman Vo Chi Cong; Council of Ministers Chairman Do Muoi	dong (4,500 = $1)	785	1,590

*Exchange rates as of Dec. 1, 1989, or latest available data. †Latest available data.

Chinese Premier Li Peng and Soviet leader Mikhail S. Gorbachev toast
their nations' renewed relations during Gorbachev's May trip to China.

Singapore's neighbors, Indonesia and Malaysia, initially reacted against its offer, but Malaysian Prime Minister Mahathir bin Mohamad eventually spoke out in favor of the continued American military presence in the Philippines. It was the first time a nation other than Singapore expressed such approval.

Economic growth. Generally good weather in 1989 enabled Asia's farmers to feed the region's growing population. International experts warned, however, that Asia did not have enough land and water to continue increasing food production, and that agricultural improvements were unlikely to keep pace with population growth. Rapid logging of Asia's tropical timberlands left wide areas of wastelands.

Asian programs to reduce population growth had little effect, even in countries such as China where the government enforced them rigorously. In other nations, such as the Philippines, rapidly growing populations caused major problems, but officials virtually ignored the need for population control.

Despite this, industrialization improved standards of living in Taiwan, Thailand, and elsewhere. But in such nations as India and Pakistan, the modernized industrial sector of the economy gave little benefit to rural areas, and people continued to move from overcrowded farmlands to equally overcrowded cities, where appalling slums expanded.   Henry S. Bradsher

See also the various Asian country articles. In **World Book,** see **Asia.**

Astronomy. In a historic year for solar system exploration, the interplanetary probes *Voyager 2* and *Phobos 2* visited Neptune and Mars, respectively, in 1989. Observers on the ground unmasked a gigantic comet that had long passed for an asteroid. And exploring beyond the solar system, astronomers found strong evidence for the existence of the long-sought *brown dwarfs*— objects intermediate between stars and planets.

New findings about Neptune. *Voyager 2*, a spacecraft launched by the National Aeronautics and Space Administration (NASA) in 1977, flew past the distant planet Neptune on Aug. 25, 1989, coming within about 3,000 miles (4,800 kilometers) of Neptune's cloud tops. It was the last planetary encounter in a long journey that took *Voyager 2* to Jupiter in 1979, Saturn in 1981, and Uranus in 1986.

Voyager 2's television cameras revealed that Neptune has four rings encircling the planet. Previously, astronomers had suspected that Neptune's rings, if any, were only arcs, not complete circles. *Voyager 2* found six new moons, making a total of eight known moons around Neptune.

Neptune receives only 5 per cent as much energy from the sun as Jupiter because it is about 2.3 billion miles (3.7 billion kilometers) farther from the sun. But *Voyager 2* found that Neptune's weather patterns are remarkably similar to Jupiter's. A huge hurricanelike formation, dubbed the Great Dark Spot, was found on

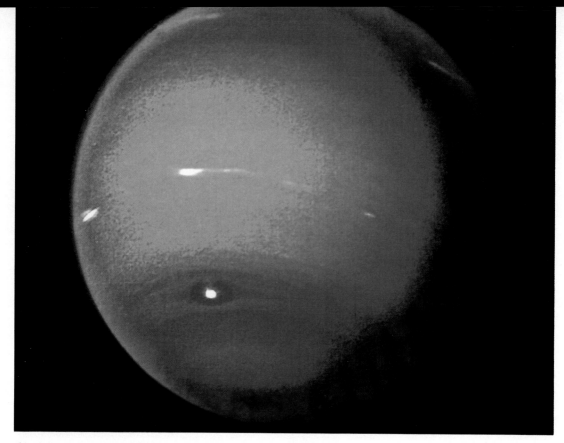

The planet Neptune's blue atmosphere reveals white cloud systems and a red haze in this image returned by the *Voyager 2* spacecraft in August.

Neptune, at the same latitude (22° south) that Jupiter's Great Red Spot is situated on that planet, and with proportionately the same size as the Great Red Spot. Winds rushing at up to 730 miles (1,170 kilometers) per hour were found on Neptune, comparable to the fast winds on Jupiter. Apparently, the amount of solar energy received is not crucial for determining weather conditions on a gaseous planet, because Neptune is so similar to Jupiter, yet receives so much less energy from the sun.

After sweeping past Neptune, *Voyager 2* continued on to the planet's largest moon, Triton. Images returned from Triton produced the greatest surprise of all: volcanic eruptions, probably driven by frozen nitrogen and perhaps also by frozen methane. Triton is now the third known body in the solar system where volcanic activity is underway. The others are Earth and Io, a large moon of Jupiter. Volcanism may also be at work on Venus, but investigators cannot confirm it.

Mission to Mars. The Soviet Union's *Phobos* mission, a pair of spacecraft launched in July 1988, suffered problems yet attained some success. The probes were intended to study Mars and to deposit small lander craft on Phobos, one of the planet's two moons.

Due to a ground controller error, contact was lost with *Phobos 1* in August 1988. *Phobos 2* went into orbit around Mars on Jan. 29, 1989. For a period of seven weeks, *Phobos 2* explored the Martian environment, obtaining valuable data. Then, it was steered

into an orbit close to Phobos, where it arrived on March 21. After taking a series of photographs of the moon, *Phobos 2* was about to be maneuvered to within 50 yards (46 meters) of its namesake to analyze the composition of the moon's surface. But bad news came again on March 27: Contact was lost with the robot spacecraft, and its mission ended.

A comet, not an asteroid. Ever since 1977, when the distant object Chiron was discovered, astronomers have puzzled over its nature. Most experts guessed that it was a large *asteroid* (a rocky object sometimes called a minor planet) because it appeared as a sharp point of light on telescopic photographs, as asteroids do. Nearly all known asteroids, however, are located in the *asteroid belt*, a region lying between the orbits of Mars and Jupiter, and they have elliptical orbits that are nearly circular. By contrast, Chiron has an extremely elongated elliptical orbit around the sun and is located far from the asteroid belt. When it was discovered, Chiron orbited the sun at a distance of about 17.8 astronomical units (AU). One AU equals the distance from Earth to the sun, about 93 million miles (150 million kilometers). Chiron was thus about twice as far from the sun as Saturn is.

Chiron has come closer to the sun in recent years, and in 1988, astronomers observed it brighten abruptly on at least two occasions. Such brightenings are uncharacteristic of asteroids, but some comets do brighten dramatically as they get closer to the sun.

Heat from the sun causes the outer layer of a comet's icy nucleus to evaporate, which in turn forms a bright *coma* (atmosphere) around the nucleus.

In 1989, observers set out to seek evidence that a coma might be forming around Chiron. On April 10, they found it. Astronomers Karen J. Meech of the University of Hawaii at Honolulu and Michael J. S. Belton of the National Optical Astronomy Observatories in Tucson, Ariz., used an electronic camera and the 4-meter (157-inch) Mayall telescope at Kitt Peak National Observatory near Tucson to record a dim coma extending from Chiron. The coma presumably consists of microscopic dust or ice grains, and gas. Chiron, accordingly, has been reclassified as a comet.

With a diameter of as much as 250 miles (400 kilometers), Chiron's nucleus dwarfs that of Halley's Comet, which has a diameter of 9 miles (14 kilometers). But Chiron will never be as bright as Halley because it will never get close enough to the sun for the sun to heat its nucleus sufficiently.

Brown dwarfs. Astronomers continued to search for brown dwarfs in 1989. Brown dwarfs are hypothetical objects that are believed to form in the breakup and condensation of interstellar gas and dust clouds, just as stars do. But brown dwarfs have less mass than stars. Because the estimated masses of brown dwarfs are so small, the pressure of overlying layers is not enough to make the central regions sufficiently hot to ignite steady nuclear burning of hydrogen, the hallmark of true stars, such as the sun.

What appears to be the best evidence yet for the existence of brown dwarfs was announced in June by astronomer William J. Forrest of the University of Rochester in New York and co-workers from other institutions. The Forrest team used a new, highly sensitive infrared camera to photograph regions around a group of relatively young stars called the Taurus star-forming association. The young stars in Taurus are only about 1 million years old. Our sun, on the other hand, is about 4.5 billion years old. The astronomers looked in the regions around these young stars because they thought that if brown dwarfs formed at the same time, they would still be detectable at such an early age. Brown dwarfs cool and fade rapidly, making them less likely to be detectable in regions around older stars.

Of 20 candidate objects found in Forrest's infrared photographs, as many as 9 may be brown dwarfs, judging from their temperature, color, and brightness. Another astronomer, Burton F. Jones of the Lick Observatory in Santa Cruz, Calif., found evidence that a few of the objects are moving through space at the same speed and in the same direction as stars that are known to be part of the Taurus star-forming association. This seemed to rule out the possibility that these objects are extremely distant stars that shine dimly in infrared photographs. Stephen P. Maran

See also **Space exploration.** In *World Book,* see **Astronomy; Neptune.**

Australia. Prime Minister Robert Hawke and his Labor Party continued to dominate the political scene in 1989. The opposing National and Liberal parties, on the other hand, were in disarray for most of the year, thanks to changes in leadership. In May, both parties chose new leaders. Andrew Peacock replaced John Howard as Liberal Party leader. Howard, who was hurt by a lackluster public image and an immigration policy perceived as anti-Asian, had replaced Peacock as Liberal leader in 1985. The National Party exchanged its long-time leader Ian Sinclair for Charles Blunt.

Aviation woes. Hawke's Labor government, however, did have its share of problems. Disrupted airline service dogged Australia's tourist industry for much of 1989. On April 13, air traffic controllers, protesting low pay and poor working conditions at the Sydney Airport, refused to work overtime or to fill in for sick colleagues. This forced the temporary shut-down of the airport several times during the year.

Local air travel came to a halt on August 24, when all of the country's domestic pilots resigned in a pay dispute. The pilots wanted pay raises of almost 30 per cent. Airlines hired new staff on individual contracts, but flights were still far from normal by year-end.

Flight first. Qantas Airways Limited on August 17 set a new record for long-distance travel when one of its 747-400 jetliners flew nonstop from Sydney to London. The plane flew a total of 11,100 miles (17,900 kilometers) in just over 20 hours.

Environment. Public concern over the destruction of forests and water pollution grew in 1989. In January, the federal government approved logging in national forests in New South Wales, igniting a battle between loggers and environmentalists.

In the same month, the news media in Sydney launched a campaign against beach pollution in New South Wales. For years, authorities had allowed the dumping of *screened* sewage directly into the ocean near public beaches. (Screened sewage is passed through a coarse sieve that does not remove microscopic contaminants.) In response to the campaign, the state's Liberal government levied an $80-a-year "environment tax" on residents to help pay for an improved sewage system. At year-end, the government pledged $6 billion over 20 years for the treatment. (Unless otherwise noted, monetary amounts in this article are in Australian dollars; $A 1 = U.S. 78 cents as of Dec. 1, 1989.)

On July 20, the Hawke government announced a $320-million environmental program. The program included a number of proposals, such as the planting of 1 billion trees over the next 10 years. The program did not impress environmentalists, however, who said that it sidestepped major issues, such as uranium mining.

Science focus. In May, Prime Minister Hawke announced the creation of the Science Council, a new government organization to handle scientific issues, such as the environment. Hawke also named Ralph O.

Passengers experience the novelty of traveling in military transport planes during strikes that grounded Australia's civilian jetliners in 1989.

Slatyer, who headed the Research School of Biological Sciences at the Australian National University in Canberra, to the new government post of chief scientist.

Economy. Australia's economic growth slowed somewhat in 1989. Inflation remained steady during the year at just under 8 per cent. The Australian dollar, after reaching a high of $A 1 = U.S. 89 cents in February, was at about U.S. 78 cents in December.

The economy was plagued by a burgeoning trade deficit and rising interest rates. The trade deficit, which stood at $1.5 billion in January, reached a record $2.58 billion by August. In July, home-loan interest rates hit 18 per cent, further reducing consumer confidence in the economy. The situation prompted Moody's Investors Services, Incorporated, an international credit-rating firm based in New York City, to describe Australia's economy as "borderline." During the year, Moody's lowered the nation's credit rating.

On August 15, Treasurer Paul J. Keating issued his budget report for the 1989-1990 fiscal year. Keating reported that the country would end the fiscal year with a record budget surplus of $9.1 billion. The government planned to use the surplus to help reduce the country's debt.

State news. In Queensland, hopes for reform—directed especially at gerrymandered electoral districts that give one party an unfair advantage in elections—were stifled in 1989 by upheaval in the ruling National Party. In September, the National Party replaced the

state's Premier Michael J. Ahern, who supported reform, with Russell Cooper, the former minister for police. But in December elections, the National Party lost to the Labor Party, and Wayne Goss was named premier.

On November 29, the Australian Capital Territory was granted self-rule. The territory is the seat of Australia's federal government, which is located in the city of Canberra. Previously, it had been administered by the federal government. The territory's first elections, held on March 4, resulted in a ruling coalition of Labor and minority parties. This coalition was replaced in December by a Liberal coalition.

Elections in Tasmania on May 13 resulted in loss of support for the state's conservative Liberal Party, but no clear majority for any other party. The Liberal Party lost support, in part because of its backing of a proposed woodchip mill in Wesley Vale, a project unpopular with environmentalists.

On June 29, Tasmania's premier and Liberal Party leader Robin T. Gray lost a vote of confidence in the legislature and announced his resignation. (A vote of confidence is taken to measure support in the legislature for the government's policies.) A coalition formed by the Labor Party and Green Independents assumed control of the government and chose Labor leader Michael Field as the state's new premier.

Bond's troubles. Brewing and media tycoon Alan Bond suffered setbacks in 1989. His newly built Bond

University, which opened in Queensland during the year, struggled to attract students. In April, the Australian Broadcasting Tribunal (ABT) challenged Bond's "moral judgment" to retain licenses for his six television and nine radio stations. Debt forced Bond to put his main television station—Channel 9—up for sale by the end of the year.

Race relations. To offset racism—and to capitalize on the opposition's lack of a stand on the issue—Prime Minister Hawke on July 26 announced a $60-million program to promote "multiculturalism" in Australia. Hawke said the program was designed to create "a more tolerant, more fair and more prosperous Australia."

In September, an 11-year battle over the ownership of Katherine Gorge National Park in the Northern Territory ended when the federal government returned the land to the Aborigines, the people who were Australia's original inhabitants. The Aborigines said they would lease some of the land back to the government so it could continue as a national park, renamed Nitmiluk Katherine Gorge National Park.

Quake hits. On December 28, an earthquake hit New South Wales, killing 12 people in Newcastle. It was one of the strongest quakes ever to hit Australia and the first to claim lives. Property damage was estimated at $1.5 billion.   Charles Boag

See also **Asia** (Facts in brief table). In *World Book*, see **Australia**.

Austria struggled in 1989 with its unique problems as a neutral nation located between Western and Eastern Europe—hoping to emerge as a partner of both Europes and a bridge between them. Austria applied on July 17 to join the European Community (EC or Common Market, a group of Western European states). Foreign Minister Alois Mock acknowledged, however, that negotiations with the EC could start in earnest only after the EC emerged as a single market—a development scheduled for 1992. Austria's business and political leaders were anxious about being left out of the EC, which takes two-thirds of Austria's exports and provides 70 per cent of its imports.

The main obstacle to joining the EC was Austria's neutral status. Admitting a neutral state might thwart the EC's ambition to move toward political unity. The Soviet Union had expressed objections to Austria's membership in the EC, despite reassurances provided by Chancellor Franz Vranitzky in December 1988 that Austria could function in the EC without violating its neutrality. Austrian diplomats hoped that economic and political reforms occurring in Poland and especially in Hungary would convince governments of EC states that they should establish closer ties with Eastern European countries, thus minimizing Austria's difficulties.

Relations with Hungary improved in 1989. A semiofficial black market developed during the year in Vienna, Austria's capital, enabling Soviets and other

A hearse carries the coffin of Zita, the last empress of Austria, through the center of Vienna on April 1.   Zita died at the age of 96.

Automobile

Eastern Europeans to barter for Western goods to take home via the Danube River, which flows through Austria and Hungary. In May, Hungary dismantled the barbed wire fence along its border with Austria. And on September 10, Hungary announced that it would no longer prevent East Germans in Hungary from fleeing to West Germany via Austria. The announcement triggered a mass exodus. Between September 11 and 14 alone, more than 13,000 East Germans passed through Austria.

On May 13, Hungary yielded to pressure from reformers and environmentalist groups and decided to halt work on a hydroelectric dam on the Danube. Austria responded by seeking compensation for its investments in the dam and the loss of electric power it had been promised. The two countries proceeded, however, with plans for an Austro-Hungarian world's fair in 1995 in Vienna and Budapest to symbolize the renewal of ties between Europe's "two halves."

A far-right political party, the Freedom Party, surged into national prominence in March 1989 by winning up to 15 per cent of the vote in local elections that saw its leader, Jörg Haider, elected governor of Carinthia Province. Haider, who took control of the Freedom Party in 1986, said his principal aim was to combat corruption in government, but critics said that the party had neo-Nazi roots.   Joseph Fitchett

See also **Europe** (Facts in brief table). In *World Book,* see **Austria.**

Automobile. Falling sales and rising competition made 1989 a difficult year for the United States automobile industry. But car lovers enjoyed the introduction of some of the most appealing cars in decades.

Overcapacity. The industry's top problem worldwide was excess production capacity. The rise of Asian automakers in the 1970's and 1980's had led to an overabundance of auto plants, capable of producing far greater numbers of vehicles than could ever be sold. A study by General Motors Corporation (GM) predicted that in the early 1990's, the auto industry worldwide would have the ability each year to produce 6 million vehicles more than it could find buyers for. This would create "life-and-death combat between companies," according to a GM official.

Big Three losses. The cost of idling factories was one reason the Big Three domestic firms—GM, Ford Motor Company, and Chrysler Corporation—suffered financial losses in their North American automotive operations during the third quarter of 1989. Worldwide earnings remained strong from booming sales in Europe and strong performance by the companies' nonautomotive businesses in finance, aerospace, and other fields.

Sales. In addition to driving up internal costs, excess capacity pushed competition in the U.S. market to its most intense level since the end of World War II in 1945. Virtually all automakers offered large cash rebates and other price incentives to buyers in 1989.

Americans bought 14.8 million new cars and trucks in 1989, down 6 per cent from 15.8 million in 1988 and off 9 per cent from the 1986 record of 16.3 million. Although a few auto executives warned that a recession was at hand, most economists and industry officials predicted a milder sales slowdown.

The 1989 sales were shared among increasing numbers of automakers. According to GM, 18 companies were selling 198 automobile models in the United States in 1976. In 1989, 33 companies sold 490 models. Only three of those companies had U.S. headquarters, but many had North American production facilities.

Transplants — foreign-owned auto plants in the United States and Canada—continued to boom. Every major Japanese automaker except Daihatsu was involved in North American car or truck production by the end of 1989, and total transplant production capacity was expected to reach 2.5 million units in the early 1990's.

In April, Japan's Toyota Motor Corporation announced a $200-million investment for production of pickup trucks at its Fremont, Calif., plant. Also in April, South Korean automaker Hyundai Motor Company began producing Sonata sedans in Bromont, Canada. Fuji Heavy Industries and Isuzu Motors, both of Japan, began producing Isuzu pickup trucks and Subaru passenger sedans at a jointly owned assembly plant in Lafayette, Ind. In September, CAMI Automotive, a joint venture between GM and Japan's Suzuki Motor Company, began shipping cars and sport-utility trucks from its Ingersoll, Canada, plant. Japanese automaker Honda Motor Company in November began producing Civic subcompacts at its second U.S. assembly plant, located in East Liberty, Ohio.

Asian automakers also began to move toward using American facilities to produce major components as well as for assembly of vehicles. Honda, Toyota, Nissan Motor Company, and Mazda Motor Corporation announced investment in production of such items as engines, transmissions, axles, and braking systems. They also made commitments to boost purchases of parts and services from U.S. suppliers.

It was widely assumed that Japanese automakers' American plants would merely supplement imports of Japanese-made vehicles. But the weaker U.S. dollar decreased profits from vehicles or parts imported from Japan, while quality and efficiency gains by the Big Three domestic firms made them stronger competitors. As a result, shipments of completed vehicles from Japan to the United States declined. In October, Japanese car shipments to the United States dropped 22 per cent and truck exports were off 32 per cent.

Plant closings among the Big Three firms continued in 1989. Domestic automakers responded to competition from transplants with more shutdowns. GM announced plans to close its plants in Framingham, Mass.; Lakewood, Ga.; and Van Nuys, Calif. Chrysler said it will close its Jefferson Avenue assembly plant in Detroit. As part of ongoing efforts to reduce costs,

Chrysler in July cut U.S. salaried employment by 2,300, and GM said it will eliminate as many as 5,000 salaried positions per year during the early 1990's through attrition, in addition to its 30 per cent cut in salaried staff since 1986.

Joint ventures. The firms also renewed their efficiency drives, making huge investments in new products and increasing participation in cost-saving joint ventures with other automakers. Chrysler and French automaker Renault announced plans to develop a Jeep sport-utility truck for sale throughout the world in the 1990's. Ford bought British luxury carmaker Jaguar Cars outright for $2.5 billion in an attempt to enter higher-priced and more profitable vehicle ranges.

GM and Chrysler broke tradition when they announced in October 1989 that they would team up to build automotive transmissions and four-wheel-drive components. Previously, Big Three automakers had entered joint ventures only with foreign-based partners. The deal was hailed as a sign of a new era in cooperation among the Big Three, but no other such combinations were on the immediate horizon.

New models. Automakers in 1989 introduced several significant new vehicles. Outstanding among these were Japan's first V-8-powered luxury sedans. Lexus, Toyota's new high-priced division, and Infiniti, Nissan's luxury line, went on sale in September and October and received enthusiastic response from car critics and the public. The Lexus LS 400 and Infiniti Q45, which sold in the $35,000 to $40,000 range, offered quality, comfort, equipment, and performance equal to BMW and Mercedes sports sedans priced several thousand dollars higher, according to some automotive experts.

Their impact on the luxury market was immediate. BMW, Audi, and Jaguar cut prices on their top-level performance sedans to bring them closer to Lexus and Infiniti prices, and Mercedes-Benz added equipment to its 1990 models without equivalent price increases. Other Japanese automakers announced plans to enter the luxury market, which promised to become a competitive battleground in the 1990's.

Most of the year's important new vehicles fell into the family car category, however. The most daring were the GM minivans—the Chevrolet Lumina APV (all-purpose vehicle), Pontiac Trans Sport, and Oldsmobile Silhouette. With plastic body panels on a steel subframe and sharply sloping snouts, these vehicles broke new ground in styling as well as technology. Honda's totally redesigned 1990 Accord and Nissan's all-new Stanza were important Japanese entries in the family sedan market, along with GM's new line-up of four-door family sedans—Chevrolet Lumina, Pontiac Grand Prix, Oldsmobile Supreme, and Buick Regal. In contrast, Mazda created a furor at midyear with the introduction of its Miata roadster, a two-seat convertible taking its theme from British sports cars of the 1950's and 1960's.   James V. Higgins

In *World Book,* see **Automobile.**

Automobile racing. Emerson Fittipaldi of Brazil won the 1989 Indianapolis 500, the most glamorous United States automobile race, and Alain Prost of France won the World Drivers Championship. After the season, both switched teams. Fittipaldi wanted stronger mechanical and financial support, and Prost could not get along with his teammate, Ayrton Senna of Brazil, who was also his major rival.

Indianapolis 500. The prequalification favorites for the Indy 500 were Rick Mears of Bakersfield, Calif., and Danny Sullivan of Louisville, Ky. Both drove Penske PC-18's with Chevrolet engines for Roger Penske's team. On May 14, when the four-lap qualifying began, Mears won the pole position and set Indianapolis records of 224.254 miles per hour (mph), or 360.902 kilometers per hour (kph), for one lap and 223.885 mph (360.308 kph) for four laps. But on May 28, after 113 laps of the 200-lap race, Mears and Sullivan had dropped out.

The race was decided on the 199th lap. Fittipaldi and Al Unser, Jr., of Albuquerque, N. Mex., entered the third of the four turns side by side. Fittipaldi's car appeared to come up from the inside, and his right front wheel touched Unser's left rear wheel. Unser's car spun into the outside wall, and Unser, though uninjured, was out of the race. Both drivers said the contact was unintentional. The 42-year-old Fittipaldi went on to win in his Penske PC-18 with a 2.65-liter turbocharged Chevrolet engine. His purse of $1,001,604 was an Indianapolis record.

Other CART races. The Indianapolis 500 was one of the 15 races (14 in the United States and 1 in Canada) in the Championship Auto Racing Teams (CART) series for Indianapolis-type cars. These open-cockpit, open-wheel cars are similar to but heavier than those in the World Drivers Championship series.

Fittipaldi won five races and the series title, and his prize money of $2,146,078 made him the first Indianapolis-car driver to exceed $2 million in one year. When the season ended, Fittipaldi and his sponsor joined the Penske team for 1990.

Formula One. The World Drivers Championship was contested in a series of 16 Grand Prix races—10 in Europe and 1 each in the United States, Canada, Mexico, Brazil, Australia, and Japan. In 1988, driving McLaren-Hondas, Senna won 8 races and Prost 7, and Senna became the world champion. In 1989, using new V-10 engines with 650 horsepower, Senna won 6 races and Prost won 4. Owing to his more consistent finishes, however, Prost led in the points competition for the championship.

Senna had to win the last two races to retain the title. In the next-to-last race on October 22 in Suzuka, Japan, Prost was leading when Senna tried to pass him in a tight turn. They collided, and Prost was out of the race. Senna got a push start from track marshals and finished first, but he was disqualified for taking a shortcut. Senna appealed to the International Auto Sports Federation. The federation rejected the appeal,

Emerson Fittipaldi of Brazil takes the lead as Al Unser, Jr., hits the wall after their wheels touched on the next-to-last lap of the Indy 500 in May.

fined Senna $100,000, and suspended his license for six months.

Thus, Prost became the world champion. Prost disliked Senna so much that he left the McLaren team after the season and signed with Ferrari.

Other races. The National Association for Stock Car Auto Racing conducted 29 races worth $18 million for stock cars modified for racing. Rusty Wallace of Fenton, Mo., in a Pontiac, won 6 races; the points title (4,176 to 4,164 for Dale Earnhardt of Kannapolis, N.C.); and $2,237,950 in prize money and bonuses. Darrell Waltrip of Franklin, Tenn., in a Chevrolet, won 6 races, including the Daytona 500 on February 19 in Daytona Beach, Fla.

The International Motor Sports Association ran 15 races for GTP sports cars. Geoff Brabham of Australia, in a Nissan, won his second straight series title. Drivers of Mercedes sports cars finished first and second in the major international endurance race, the 24 Hours of Le Mans held on June 10 and 11 in France.

The National Hot Rod Association's 19 races were worth $18 million. In the fastest cars, those in the top-fuel class, Joe Amato of Old Forge, Pa., set a speed record of 290.32 mph (467.22 kph) on September 17 in Reading, Pa. Gary Ormsby of Roseville, Calif., set the fastest elapsed time for the quarter-mile (4.919 seconds) on October 8 in Ennis, Tex. Ormsby won 8 races and kept the championship.   Frank Litsky

In *World Book,* see **Automobile racing.**

Aviation. The United States airline industry was rocked in 1989 by a string of fatal accidents, continued fears about terrorism, and, on the financial side, a wave of take-over efforts.

On February 24, a gaping hole opened up in the fuselage of a United Airlines jet flying over Hawaii. Nine people were sucked out and died, though the pilot managed to land the plane safely in Honolulu.

On July 19, a United Airlines DC-10 jet crashed just short of the runway at the airport in Sioux City, Iowa, while attempting an emergency landing. The accident killed 112 of the 296 people aboard. Investigators said that the plane's tail engine exploded and shards of metal severed the hydraulic system, which is needed to maneuver the plane. A crack in the engine's fan assembly caused the engine to explode.

The crash in Iowa prompted the U.S. Federal Aviation Administration (FAA) to order airlines to conduct ultrasonic inspections—tests using high-frequency sound waves—on engines similar to those on the United plane. In addition, the McDonnell Douglas Corporation, manufacturer of the plane, announced safety improvements in the hydraulic systems of its DC-10 and MD-11 jets to prevent similar accidents.

On September 20, the crew of a USAir flight aborted a take-off at La Guardia Airport in New York City, and the plane crashed into the East River. Two people were killed in the accident. According to newspaper reports, both the pilot and copilot had little experience flying the type of plane that crashed, a 737 jetliner.

Two congressmen die. Two members of Congress were killed in separate plane crashes within a week in 1989. On August 13, U.S. aerial search teams in Ethiopia found the wreckage of a plane in which Representative Mickey Leland (D., Tex.) and 15 other people died on August 7 while on a trip to inspect a refugee camp in Sudan. On the same day Leland's plane was discovered, Representative Larkin I. Smith (R., Miss.) died in a light-plane crash in his home state.

Other accidents. A number of major crashes occurred in other countries during the year. One of the worst happened on September 19, when a French jet carrying 171 people exploded in flight over Niger. Among those killed was Bonnie Pugh, wife of Robert L. Pugh, the U.S. ambassador to Chad. Islamic Jihad, a Muslim extremist group, claimed responsibility. On February 8, a charter plane operated by Independent Air Holdings, a Tennessee company, crashed in the Azores, a group of islands 800 miles (1,300 kilometers) off the coast of Portugal. The crash killed 137 Italian passengers and 7 U.S. crew members.

Safety. In May, the FAA proposed sweeping modifications for older Boeing jets and in September extended the order to older McDonnell Douglas planes. Both actions stemmed from an April 1988 accident in which a 19-year-old Aloha Airlines jet lost the top part of its fuselage in flight. On May 23, 1989, the National Transportation Safety Board blamed the accident on Aloha's maintenance program, which failed to detect cracks caused by metal fatigue.

Security. The FAA took a number of steps to strengthen security on U.S. airlines in the aftermath of the explosion and crash of a Pan American World Airways jet in Lockerbie, Scotland, in December 1988. Investigators believe that the crash was caused by a bomb disguised as a radio-cassette recorder.

On March 14, 1989, the FAA ordered foreign airlines flying into the United States to submit security plans for review. On September 5, it directed U.S. carriers to install costly new bomb-detection devices at 40 airports in the United States and other countries that were designated as being at high risk for terrorist attacks. The FAA on September 20 proposed fining Pan Am $630,000 for alleged security lapses on six flights, including the one that crashed at Lockerbie.

Take-overs. The take-over frenzy rampant among U.S. companies reached the airline industry. The activity made some members of Congress nervous and prompted efforts to pass legislation that would require leveraged buy-outs in the industry to receive approval by the U.S. Department of Transportation prior to completion. In a leveraged buy-out, an individual or group buys all the outstanding shares of stock of a company by borrowing heavily against the acquired company's assets, such as—in the case of an airline—its airplanes and hangars.

New York City tycoon Donald J. Trump announces on May 24 that the Eastern Airlines shuttle he bought will take off in June as the Trump Shuttle.

Investigators inspect a United Airlines jet that lost a door in midair over Hawaii on February 24, sending nine passengers to their death.

On June 19, NWA Incorporated, the parent company of Northwest Airlines, agreed to be purchased for $3.65 billion by a group of investors headed by Alfred A. Checchi of Los Angeles. KLM Royal Dutch Airlines provided a large part of the money for the leveraged buy-out. The deal did not sit well with the federal government, however. Transportation Secretary Samuel K. Skinner voiced concern that the buy-out potentially violated a United States law that limits foreign investment in a U.S. airline to 25 per cent of total voting rights and prohibits foreign control of a U.S. carrier. Under pressure from Skinner, the Checchi group agreed in September to reduce KLM's investment.

Other take-over bids also had a rocky road. On September 14, the board of directors of UAL Corporation, the parent company of United Airlines, approved a $6.75-billion offer from a group led by United pilots and management and backed by money from British Airways PLC. On October 14, however, United Airlines management said it was having trouble getting banks to lend it enough money for the purchase. In another take-over bid, New York City tycoon Donald J. Trump on October 4 offered $7.54 billion for AMR Corporation, the parent company of American Airlines. He withdrew the offer 12 days later.

Bankruptcies and strikes. Eastern Airlines, a unit of Texas Air Corporation, filed for bankruptcy on March 9, five days after the airline's pilots and flight attendants walked off the job to support a machinists' strike. In May, a federal bankruptcy judge approved the $365-million sale of Eastern's shuttle service, which links New York City with Boston and Washington, D.C., to Trump. The Trump Shuttle began operating on June 8. Eastern pilots and flight attendants abandoned their strike on November 22 and 23, respectively, leaving only the machinists to continue their walkout.

Burdened by debt, Braniff Incorporated filed for bankruptcy on September 28. It was the second time the airline filed for bankruptcy since 1982. On October 4, more than 55,000 machinists went on strike against the Boeing Company, the world's biggest airplane manufacturer. The workers said that the company was offering inadequate wages and benefits, despite soaring profits. On November 22, the machinists returned to work after agreeing on a new contract that would improve pay and medical benefits.

No smoking. On November 14, Congress gave final approval to legislation that permanently bans smoking on all domestic airline routes within the continental United States and on flights of less than six hours to Alaska and Hawaii.

FAA news. On June 30, James B. Busey IV, the former chief of U.S. naval forces in Europe, was sworn in as FAA administrator. Busey replaced T. Allan McArtor, who resigned in February.   Laurie McGinley

In *World Book,* see **Aviation.**

Awards and prizes presented in 1989 included the following:

Arts awards

Academy of Motion Picture Arts and Sciences. "Oscar" Awards: Best Picture, *Rain Man.* **Best Actor,** Dustin Hoffman, *Rain Man.* **Best Actress,** Jodie Foster, *The Accused.* **Best Supporting Actor,** Kevin Kline, *A Fish Called Wanda.* **Best Supporting Actress,** Geena Davis, *The Accidental Tourist.* **Best Director,** Barry Levinson, *Rain Man.* **Best Original Screenplay,** Ronald Bass and Barry Morrow, *Rain Man.* **Best Screenplay Adaptation,** Christopher Hampton, *Dangerous Liaisons.* **Best Cinematography,** Peter Biziou, *Mississippi Burning.* **Best Film Editing,** Arthur Schmidt, *Who Framed Roger Rabbit.* **Best Original Score,** Dave Grusin, *The Milagro Beanfield War.* **Best Original Song,** Carly Simon, "Let the River Run" from *Working Girl.* **Best Foreign-Language Film,** *Pelle the Conqueror* (Denmark). See **Foster, Jodie; Hoffman, Dustin.**

American Academy and Institute of Arts and Letters. Gold Medal for Fiction, Polish-born author Isaac Bashevis Singer. **Gold Medal for Sculpture,** American sculptor Louise Bourgeois. **Arnold W. Brunner Memorial Prize in Architecture,** British architect Richard Rogers. **Award for Distinguished Service to the Arts,** Vartan Gregorian, president of Brown University and former president of the New York Public Library.

American Dance Festival. Samuel H. Scripps-American Dance Festival Award, American modern dance pioneers Doris Humphrey, José Limón, and Charles Weidman (all posthumous).

American Film Institute. Life Achievement Award, British director Sir David Lean.

American Institute of Architects. Gold Medal, Joseph Esherick. **Honor Awards,** Beyer Blinder Belle, New York City, for restoration of an aqueduct spanning the Upper Delaware River at Lackawaxen, Pa., designed in 1847 by John A. Roebling; Clark & Menefee Architects, Charleston, S.C., for a farmhouse near that city; Derthick, Henley & Wilkerson and Koetter, Kim & Associates, Boston, for a downtown park and public recreation area in Chattanooga, Tenn.; Chad Floyd, Essex, Conn., for a pier and pavilion in Watkins Glen, N.Y.; Hammond Beeby and Babka Incorporated, Chicago, for a private residence in Wilmette, Ill.; Hartman-Cox Architects, Washington, D.C., for enlargement of the Folger Shakespeare Library in that city; Steven Holl Architects, New York City, for a vacation home on Martha's Vineyard, Massachusetts; Eric Owen Moss, Culver City, Calif., for an office building at the University of California at Irvine; Perkins & Will, Chicago, for the Desert View Elementary School in Sunland Park, N. Mex.; Scogin Elam and Bray Architects, Atlanta, Ga., for a library in Jonesboro, Ga.; Tilton + Lewis Associates Incorporated, Chicago, for restoration of the Meyer May House, a 1909 Frank Lloyd Wright design in Grand Rapids, Mich.; Tod Williams Billie Tsien and Associates, New York City, for an indoor swimming pool added to a house on Long Island, New York.

American Music Awards. Pop/Rock Awards: Female Vocalist, Whitney Houston. **Male Vocalist,** George Michael. **Duo or Group,** Gloria Estefan & Miami Sound Machine. **Single,** "Sweet Child o' Mine," Guns N' Roses. **Album,** *Dirty Dancing.* **Favorite New Artist,** Tracy Chapman.

Soul Music/Rhythm and Blues Awards: Female Vocalist, Whitney Houston. **Male Vocalist,** George Michael. **Duo or Group,** Gladys Knight and the Pips. **Single,** "Nice 'n' Slow," Freddie Jackson. **Album,** *Faith,* George Michael. **Favorite New Artist,** Al B. Sure!

Country Music Awards: Female Vocalist, Reba McEntire. **Male Vocalist,** Randy Travis. **Duo or Group,** Alabama. **Single,** "I Told You So," Randy Travis. **Album,** *Always & Forever,* Randy Travis. **Favorite New Artist,** Patty Loveless.

Heavy Metal Awards: Favorite Artist, Def Leppard. **Favorite Album,** *Hysteria,* Def Leppard.

Rap Music Awards: Favorite Artist, D. J. Jazzy Jeff and The Fresh Prince. **Favorite Album,** *He's the D.J., I'm the Rapper,* D. J. Jazzy Jeff and The Fresh Prince.

Cannes International Film Festival. Golden Palm Grand Prize, *sex, lies, and videotape* (United States). **Special Jury Prize,** *Too Beautiful for You* (France) and *New Cinema Paradise* (Italy). **Jury Prize,** *Jesus of Montreal* (Canada). **Best Actor,** James Spader, *sex, lies, and videotape.* **Best Actress,** Meryl Streep, *A Cry in the Dark.* **Best Director,** Emir Kusturica, *Time of the Gypsies.* **Best Artistic Contribution,** Jim Jarmusch, *Mystery Train.*

Hyatt Foundation. Pritzker Architecture Prize, Frank O. Gehry (United States).

John F. Kennedy Center for the Performing Arts. Honors, singer Harry Belafonte, French-born actress Claudette Colbert, Russian-born dancer Alexandra Danilova, actress Mary Martin, and composer William Schuman.

MacDowell Colony. Edward MacDowell Medal, filmmaker Stan Brakhage.

National Academy of Recording Arts and Sciences. Grammy Awards: Record of the Year, "Don't Worry, Be Happy," Bobby McFerrin. **Album of the Year,** *Faith,* George Michael. **Song of the Year,** "Don't Worry, Be Happy," Bobby McFerrin, songwriter. **Best New Artist,** Tracy Chapman.

Pop Awards: Pop Vocal Performance, Female, "Fast Car," Tracy Chapman. **Pop Vocal Performance, Male,** "Don't Worry, Be Happy," Bobby McFerrin. **Pop Vocal Performance by a Duo or Group,** *Brasil,* Manhattan Transfer. **Pop Instrumental Performance,** *Close-Up,* David Sanborn.

Rock Awards: Rock Vocal Performance, Female, *Tina Live in Europe,* Tina Turner. **Rock Vocal Performance, Male,** "Simply Irresistible," Robert Palmer. **Rock Vocal Performance by a Duo or Group,** *Desire,* U2. **Rock Instrumental Performance,** *Blues for Salvador,* Carlos Santana. **Hard Rock/Metal Performance,** *Crest of a Knave,* Jethro Tull.

Rhythm and Blues Awards: Rhythm and Blues Vocal Performance, Female, "Giving You the Best That I Got," Anita Baker. **Rhythm and Blues Vocal Performance, Male,** *Introducing the Hardline According to Terence Trent D'Arby,* Terence Trent D'Arby. **Rhythm and Blues Vocal Performance by a Duo or Group,** "Love Overboard," Gladys Knight and the Pips. **Rhythm and Blues Instrumental Performance,** "Light Years," Chick Corea. **Rhythm and Blues Song,** "Giving You the Best That I Got," Anita Baker, Skip Scarborough, and Randy Holland, songwriters. **Rap Performance,** "Parents Just Don't Understand," D. J. Jazzy Jeff and The Fresh Prince.

Country Awards: Country Vocal Performance, Female, "Hold Me," K. T. Oslin. **Country Vocal Performance, Male,** *Old 8 x 10,* Randy Travis. **Country Vocal Performance, Duo or Group,** "Give a Little Love," The Judds. **Country Vocal Collaboration,** *Crying,* Roy Orbison and k. d. lang. **Country Instrumental Performance,** "Sugarfoot Rag," Asleep at the Wheel. **Country Song,** "Hold Me," K. T. Oslin, songwriter. **Bluegrass Recording,** *Southern Flavor,* Bill Monroe.

Video Awards: Performance Music Video, "Where the Streets Have No Name," U2. **Concept Music Video,** "I'm Fat," Weird Al Yankovic.

Jazz Awards: Jazz Fusion Performance, *Politics,* Yellowjackets. **Jazz Vocal Performance, Female,** *Look What I Got!,* Betty Carter. **Jazz Vocal Performance, Male,** "Brothers," Bobby McFerrin. **Jazz Vocal Performance, Duo or Group,** "Spread Love," Take 6. **Jazz Instrumental Performance, Solo,** *Don't Try This at Home,* Michael Brecker. **Jazz Instrumental Performance, Group,** *Blues for Coltrane: A Tribute to John Coltrane,* McCoy Tyner, Pharoah Sanders, David Murray, Cecil McBee, and Roy Haynes. **Jazz Instrumental Performance, Big Band,** *Bud & Bird,* Gil Evans and the Monday Night Orchestra.

Classical Awards: Album, *Verdi: Requiem and Operatic Choruses,* Robert Shaw conducting the Atlanta Symphony Orchestra and Chorus. **Performance by a Soloist with Orchestra,** *Mozart: Piano Concerto No. 23 in A,* Vladimir Horowitz with Carlo Maria Giulini conducting the La Scala Opera Orches-

Folk singer-songwriter Tracy Chapman won three Grammy awards in February, including best new artist and best pop vocal performance by a female.

tra. **Performance by a Soloist Without Orchestra,** *Albeníz: Iberia; Navarra; Suite Espagnola,* Alicia de Larrocha. **Orchestra Recording,** *Rorem: String Symphony; Sunday Morning; Eagles,* Robert Shaw conducting the Atlanta Symphony Orchestra. **Opera Recording,** *Wagner: Lohengrin,* Sir Georg Solti conducting the Vienna State Opera Choir and Vienna Philharmonic. **Choral Performance,** *Verdi: Requiem and Operatic Choruses,* Robert Shaw conducting the Atlanta Symphony Chorus and Orchestra.

National Academy of Television Arts and Sciences. Emmy Awards, Comedy: Best Series, "Cheers." **Lead Actor,** Richard Mulligan, "Empty Nest." **Lead Actress,** Candice Bergen, "Murphy Brown." **Supporting Actor,** Woody Harrelson, "Cheers." **Supporting Actress,** Rhea Perlman, "Cheers."

Drama Awards: Best Series, "L.A. Law." **Lead Actor,** Carroll O'Connor, "In the Heat of the Night." **Lead Actress,** Dana Delany, "China Beach." **Supporting Actor,** Larry Drake, "L.A. Law." **Supporting Actress,** Melanie Mayron, "thirtysomething."

Other Awards: Drama or Comedy Special, *Day One* and *Roe vs. Wade.* **Miniseries,** *War and Remembrance.* **Variety, Music, or Comedy Program,** "The Tracey Ullman Show." **Lead Actor in a Miniseries or Special,** James Woods, *My Name Is Bill W.* **Lead Actress in a Miniseries or Special,** Holly Hunter, *Roe vs. Wade.* **Supporting Actor in a Miniseries or Special,** Derek Jacobi, *The Tenth Man.* **Supporting Actress in a Miniseries or Special,** Colleen Dewhurst, *Those She Left Behind.*

New York Drama Critics Circle Awards. Best New Play, *The Heidi Chronicles,* Wendy Wasserstein. **Best New Foreign Play,** *Aristocrats,* Brian Friel. **Special Citation,** *Largely New York,* Bill Irwin.

Antoinette Perry (Tony) Awards. Drama Awards: Best Play, *The Heidi Chronicles.* **Leading Actor,** Philip Bosco, *Lend Me a Tenor.* **Leading Actress,** Pauline Collins, *Shirley Valentine.* **Featured Actor,** Boyd Gaines, *The Heidi Chronicles.*

Featured Actress, Christine Baranski, *Rumors.* **Direction,** Jerry Zaks, *Lend Me a Tenor.*

Musical Awards: Best Musical, *Jerome Robbins' Broadway.* **Leading Actor,** Jason Alexander, *Jerome Robbins' Broadway.* **Leading Actress,** Ruth Brown, *Black and Blue.* **Featured Actor,** Scott Wise, *Jerome Robbins' Broadway.* **Featured Actress,** Debbie Shapiro, *Jerome Robbins' Broadway.* **Direction,** Jerome Robbins, *Jerome Robbins' Broadway.* **Choreography,** Cholly Atkins, Henry LeTang, Frankie Manning, and Fayard Nicholas, *Black and Blue.*

Best Revival of a Play or Musical, *Our Town,* Lincoln Center Theater. **Lighting Design,** Jennifer Tipton, *Jerome Robbins' Broadway.* **Costume Design,** Héctor Orezzoli and Claudio Segovia, *Black and Blue.* **Scenic Design,** Santo Loquasto, *Cafe Crown.*

United States government. National Medal of Arts, preservationist Leopold Adler; Dayton Hudson Corporation, Minneapolis, Minn., for corporate sponsorship of the arts; dancer and choreographer Katherine Dunham; photographer Alfred Eisenstaedt; museum director Martin Friedman; Leigh Gerdine, president of Webster University, St. Louis, Mo.; jazz trumpeter Dizzy Gillespie; sculptor Walker Kirtland Hancock; Russian-born pianist Vladimir Horowitz (posthumous); Polish poet Czeslaw Milosz; painter Robert Motherwell; writer John Updike.

Journalism awards

American Society of Magazine Editors. National Magazine Awards: General Excellence, Circulation over 1 Million, *Sports Illustrated;* **Circulation of 400,000 to 1 Million,** *Vanity Fair;* **Circulation of 100,000 to 400,000,** *American Heritage;* **Circulation Under 100,000,** *The Sciences.* **Personal Service Journalism,** *Good Housekeeping.* **Special Interest Reporting,** *Condé Nast Traveler.* **Reporting,** *The New Yorker.* **Public Interest Journalism,** *California.* **Design,** *Rolling Stone.*

Photography, *National Geographic Magazine.* **Essays and Criticism,** *Harper's.* **Fiction,** *The New Yorker.* **Feature Writing,** *Esquire.* **Single-Topic Issue,** *Hippocrates.*

Long Island University. George Polk Memorial Awards: National Reporting, Keith Schneider, *The New York Times,* for articles about safety problems in nuclear weapons production. **Local Reporting,** David Gomez and Patricia Guthrie, *The Albuquerque* (N. Mex.) *Tribune,* for a six-part series on alcoholism among Indians in Gallup, N. Mex. **Foreign Reporting,** John Kifner, *The New York Times,* for his articles on the Palestinian uprising. **Financial Reporting,** *National Thrift News* for its coverage of the savings and loan industry. **Economic Reporting,** Donald L. Barlett and James B. Steele, *The Philadelphia Inquirer,* for their investigation of special tax breaks in the Tax Reform Act of 1986. **Environmental Reporting,** Mary Bishop, *Roanoke* (Va.) *Times and World-News,* for her series on Virginia's unlicensed pesticide industry. **Cultural Reporting,** Lawrence Wechsler for *Shapinsky's Karma, Boggs's Bills,* essays about the relationship between the arts and economics. **Photojournalism,** Mary Ellen Mark for photographs of street children in Seattle. **Local Television Reporting,** KING-TV, Seattle, for a series on race relations in that city. **Network Television Reporting,** Brian Ross, correspondent, and Ira Silverman, producer, National Broadcasting Company (NBC) News, for reports on banks that launder cash for drug dealers. **Radio Reporting,** Patricia Neighmond, National Public Radio, for a two-year series on an AIDS patient.

The Society of Professional Journalists, Sigma Delta Chi. Sigma Delta Chi Distinguished Service Awards, Newspaper Awards: **General Reporting, Circulation More than 100,000,** Gary Thatcher, *The Christian Science Monitor,* for a series on chemical and biological weapons. **General Reporting, Circulation Less than 100,000,** Peggy O'Crowley, *News Tribune,* Perth Amboy and Woodbridge, N.J., for a series describing a crisis in the Perth Amboy school system. **Editorial Writing,** Church Green, Fred Brown, and Jack Cox, *The Denver Post,* for editorials that helped unseat a district attorney in northeastern Colorado. **Washington Correspondence,** James O'Shea, *Chicago Tribune,* for his coverage of the crisis in the savings and loan industry. **Foreign Correspondence,** Douglas Farah, *The Washington* (D.C.) *Post,* for his articles about death squads in El Salvador. **News Photography,** Joe Cavaretta, *The Albuquerque Tribune,* for photographs exploring the problem of alcoholism among Indian residents of Gallup, N. Mex. **Editorial Cartooning,** Jack Higgins, *Chicago Sun-Times.* **Public Service in Newspaper Journalism, Circulation More than 100,000,** *The Philadelphia Inquirer* for an investigation of the special tax breaks included in the Tax Reform Act of 1986. **Public Service in Newspaper Journalism, Circulation Less than 100,000,** *The Anchorage* (Alaska) *Daily News* for its investigation of the impact of alcohol on Alaska's Native Americans.

Magazine Awards: Magazine Reporting, Jacqueline E. Sharkey for an article in *Common Cause* exploring charges that the Administration of President Ronald Reagan overlooked the involvement in drug trafficking by Central American officials who supported the *contra* rebels in Nicaragua. **Public Service in Magazine Journalism,** *Atlanta* (Ga.) *Magazine* for an article exploring why some teen-agers succeed and others fail in high school.

Radio Awards: Radio Spot-News Reporting, KRRI-FM, Boulder City, Nev., for reporting on an explosion at a rocket fuel plant in Las Vegas, Nev. **Public Service in Radio Journalism,** KNX-AM, Los Angeles, for its reporting on the California automobile insurance crisis. **Editorializing on Radio,** G. Donald Gale, vice president of KSL Radio, Salt Lake City, Utah, for editorials about three initiatives on Utah's November 1988 ballot, all of which were defeated by the voters.

Television Awards: Television Spot-News Reporting, WTHR-TV, Indianapolis, for coverage of a fire at a historic landmark theater in that city. **Public Service in Television Journalism, Stations in the Top 50 Markets,** American Broadcasting Companies, Incorporated (ABC) News for *Nightline in*

the *Holy Land: Town Meeting,* a broadcast that brought Jewish and Arab panelists together in Jerusalem, Israel. **Public Service in Television Journalism, Small-Market Stations,** WBRZ-TV, Baton Rouge, La., for its coverage of evangelist Jimmy Swaggart and his involvement in a sex scandal. **Editorializing on Television,** John Beatty, Paul Sands, and Ed Quinn, KGTV, San Diego, for editorials on various issues.

Research About Journalism: Thomas B. Littlewood for *Coals of Fire: The Alton Telegraph Libel Case.*

University of Georgia. George Foster Peabody Broadcasting Awards, WHAS Radio News, Louisville, Ky., for *A Matter of Time: The Crisis in Kentucky Corrections;* WBUR-FM Radio, Boston, for *Speaking for Everyman: Ian McKellen Celebrates Shakespeare's Birthday;* KMOX Radio, St. Louis, Mo., for *Hate Crime: America's Cancer,* an exploration of ethnic intimidation; National Public Radio for *Cowboys on Everest,* an account of an American team's effort to climb Mount Everest; British Broadcasting Corporation (BBC) World Service for Africa for *Nothing Political/Mandela at 70,* about South African civil rights leader Nelson R. Mandela; KTAR Radio, Phoenix, for *The Impeachment of Evan Mecham;* WPLG-TV, Miami, Fla., for *Caution: Precious Cargo,* a report on unsafe school buses; MacNeil/Lehrer Productions for the 1988 election coverage on "The MacNeil/Lehrer NewsHour"; Frontline, Boston, for *Frontline: The Choice,* a background report on the 1988 presidential candidates; CBS News for *Abortion Battle* and *On Runaway Street,* two programs from the series "48 Hours"; KCBS-TV, Los Angeles, for *MCA and the Mob,* an investigative report on organized crime and the entertainment industry; CBS Entertainment and Telecom Entertainment, in association with Yorkshire Television, for *The Attic: The Hiding of Anne Frank;* BBC and WNET/13, New York City, for *The Singing Detective;* NBC-TV for *The Murder of Mary Phagan;* ABC Television and the Bedford Falls Company in association with MGM/UA Television for "thirtysomething"; Children's Television Workshop for *3-2-1 Contact Extra: I Have AIDS, A Teen-Ager's Story;* South Carolina Educational Television Network and the Mosaic Group, Incorporated, for *Children's Express NEWSMAGAZINE: Campaign '88;* The Christian Science Monitor Reports for *Islam in Turmoil;* WTTW, Chicago, in association with Chloe Productions Incorporated for *. . . And the Pursuit of Happiness,* a look at the new wave of American immigrants; Home Box Office (HBO) for *Dear America: Letters Home from Vietnam;* HBO in association with Pro Image Productions for *Suzi's Story,* an account of a woman's struggle against AIDS; WBRZ-TV, Baton Rouge, La., for *The Best Insurance Commissioner Money Can Buy,* an investigative report on a Louisiana official; Turner Network Television for *The Making of a Legend: Gone with the Wind;* CBS News for *Mr. Snow Goes to Washington* on "60 Minutes"; WJLA-TV, Washington, D.C., for "The Radon Watch Campaign"; Public Affairs Television for "Bill Moyers' World of Ideas"; publisher Walter Annenberg for his "philanthropic role in support of the educational uses of radio and television"; Don Hewitt, CBS News, for "exceptional contributions to television news"; Jim McKay, ABC-TV sports commentator.

Literature awards

Academy of American Poets. Lamont Poetry Selection, *Crime Against Nature,* Minnie Bruce Pratt. **Walt Whitman Award,** *The Game of Statues,* Martha Hollander. **Harold Morton Landon Translation Award,** *Five Plays* by Heinrich von Kleist, translated by Martin Greenberg.

American Academy of Arts and Sciences. Emerson-Thoreau Medal, writer Norman Mailer.

American Library Association. Newbery Medal, *Joyful Noise: Poems for Two Voices,* Paul Fleischman. **Caldecott Medal,** *Song and Dance Man,* Stephen Gammell, illustrator.

Association of American Publishers. National Book Awards: Fiction , *Spartina,* John Casey. **Nonfiction,** *From Beirut to Jerusalem,* Thomas L. Friedman. **Medal for Distinguished Contribution to American Letters,** former Librarian of Congress Daniel J. Boorstin.

Awards and prizes

Booker Prize, *The Remains of the Day,* Kazuo Ishiguro.

Canada Council. Governor General's Literary Awards, English-Language: Fiction, *Nights Below Station Street,* David Adams Richards. **Poetry,** *Furious,* Erin Mouré. **Drama,** *Nothing Sacred,* George F. Walker. **Nonfiction,** *In the Sleep Room,* Anne Collins. **Translation,** *Second Chance,* English translation by Philip Stratford of Diane Hébert's *Un Second Souffle.* **Children's Literature (Text),** *The Third Magic,* Welwyn Wilton Katz. **Children's Literature (Illustration),** *Amos's Sweater,* illustrated by Kim LaFave.

French-Language: Fiction, *Le Silence ou le Parfait Bonheur,* Jacques Folch-Ribas. **Poetry,** *Papiers d'épidémie,* Marcel Labine. **Drama,** *Le Chien,* Jean Marc Dalpé. **Nonfiction,** *Écrire dans la maison du père,* Patricia Smart. **Translation,** *Nucléus,* French edition by Didier Holtzwarth of Robert Bothwell's *Nucleus.* **Children's Literature (Text),** *Cassiopée ou L'Été polonais,* Michèle Marineau. **Children's Literature (Illustration),** *Les Jeux de Pic-mots,* illustrated by Philippe Béha.

Canadian Library Association. Book of the Year for Children Award, *Easy Avenue,* Brian Doyle. **Amelia Frances Howard-Gibbon Illustrator's Award,** *Amos's Sweater,* illustrated by Kim LaFave.

Columbia University. Bancroft Prizes in American History, *Reconstruction: America's Unfinished Revolution, 1863-1877,* Eric Foner; and *Inventing the People: The Rise of Popular Sovereignty in England and America,* Edmund S. Morgan.

Ingersoll Foundation. Ingersoll Prizes: T. S. Eliot Award for Creative Writing, novelist George Garrett. **Richard M. Weaver Award for Scholarly Letters,** sociobiologist Edward O. Wilson.

National Book Critics Circle. National Book Critics Circle Awards, Fiction, *The Middleman and Other Stories,* Bharati Mukherjee. **General Nonfiction,** *Parting the Waters: America in the King Years, 1954-63,* Taylor Branch. **Biography/Autobiography,** *Oscar Wilde,* Richard Ellmann. **Poetry,** *The One Day,* Donald Hall. **Criticism,** *Works and Lives:*

The Anthropologist as Author, Clifford Geertz. **Citation for Excellence in Reviewing,** William Logan, free-lance critic.

PEN American Center. Faulkner Award, *Dusk and Other Stories,* James Salter.

Royal Society of Canada. Chaveau Medal, John M. Robson, University of Toronto. **Jason A. Hannah Medal,** *The Secret Plague: Venereal Disease in Canada 1838-1939,* Jay Cassel. **Innis-Gérin Medal,** Albert Faucher, Laval University, Ste.-Foy. **Lorne Pierce Medal,** Maurice Lemire, Laval University.

Whitbread Book of the Year Award, *The Comforts of Madness,* Paul Sayer.

Nobel Prizes. See **Nobel Prizes.**

Public service awards

American Institute for Public Service. Jefferson Awards, Marc Buoniconti, cofounder of the Miami Project, a center for research on spinal cord injuries; David Cain, founder of the Children's Organ Transplant Association; Leo Cherne, chairman of the International Rescue Committee, a voluntary agency to aid international refugees; Kimi Gray, president of the Kenilworth-Parkside Management Corporation Board, a group of low-income people who became owners of the public housing project where they lived in Washington, D.C.; Clara J. Johansen, a pilot who carries donated blood between Fergus Falls and St. Paul, Minn.; Stephen P. Klinker, an Austin, Tex., dentist who founded an organization to provide free medical and dental services to the needy in Honduras; Julia Middleton, founder of a community center for underprivileged children in San Francisco; Paul H. Nitze, head of the U.S. delegation to the Intermediate-Range Nuclear Forces negotiations with the Soviet Union; and Brent Wyatt, for his work with the mentally retarded in Greenville, S.C.

American Philosophical Society. Benjamin Franklin Award, Paul Mellon, president and chairman of the National Gallery of Art.

"The Tracey Ullman Show," starring Ullman, right, in September won the Fox network's first Emmys, including the award for best variety, music, or comedy show.

Franklin and Eleanor Roosevelt Institute. Freedom Medal, Justice William J. Brennan, Supreme Court of the United States. **Freedom of Speech Medal,** Walter Cronkite, retired CBS News anchor. **Freedom from Want Medal,** Dorothy Height, president of the National Council of Negro Women. **Freedom from Fear Medal,** former Senator J. William Fulbright (D., Ark.), founder of the Fulbright Scholarships. **Freedom of Worship Medal,** Raphael Lemkin (posthumous), for his efforts to combat genocide.

National Association for the Advancement of Colored People. Spingarn Medal, civil rights leader Jesse L. Jackson.

Alexander Onassis Foundation. Onassis Prize, former Senator J. William Fulbright (D., Ark.) for establishing the Fulbright Scholarships, an international exchange program.

Templeton Foundation. John M. Templeton Prize for Progress in Religion, Lord MacLeod of Fuinary (George MacLeod), Scottish clergyman who founded an interfaith center called the Iona Community; and West German physicist and philosopher Carl Friedrich von Weizsäcker, who explored the links between physics and theology.

United States government. Presidential Medal of Freedom, comedian Lucille Ball (posthumous); former Secretary of the Treasury C. Douglas Dillon; aviation pioneer James H. Doolittle; diplomat George F. Kennan; Mike Mansfield, former U.S. ambassador to Japan; Senator Claude D. Pepper (D., Fla.); Secretary of State George P. Shultz; former Senator Margaret Chase Smith (R., Me.); Polish Solidarity leader Lech Walesa.

Pulitzer Prizes

Journalism. Public Service, *The Anchorage* (Alaska) *Daily News* for articles about alcoholism among Alaska's Native Americans. **General News Reporting,** *The Louisville* (Ky.) *Courier-Journal* for its coverage of a 1988 school-bus crash that killed 27 people. **National Reporting,** Donald L. Barlett and James B. Steele, *The Philadelphia Inquirer,* for articles on the special tax breaks in the Tax Reform Act of 1986. **Investigative Reporting,** Bill Dedman, *The Atlanta* (Ga.) *Journal and Constitution,* for his investigation of racial discrimination by lending institutions in that city. **Explanatory Journalism,** David Hanners, William Snyder, and Karen Blessen, *The Dallas Morning News,* for detailing how the federal government investigated a 1986 airline crash. **Specialized Reporting,** Edward Humes, *The Orange County* (California) *Register,* for reporting on the Southern California military establishment. **International Reporting,** Glenn Frankel, *The Washington Post,* for his coverage of the Palestinian uprising, and Bill Keller, *The New York Times,* for his articles on the Soviet Union. **Feature Writing,** David Zucchino, *The Philadelphia Inquirer,* for a series of articles depicting the lives of black people in South Africa. **Commentary,** Clarence Page, *Chicago Tribune,* for his columns, many of them on black issues. **Criticism,** Michael Skube, *The* (Raleigh, N.C.) *News and Observer,* for his book reviews. **Editorial Writing,** Lois Wille, *Chicago Tribune,* for editorials on Chicago and Illinois politics. **Editorial Cartooning,** Jack Higgins, *Chicago Sun-Times,* for political cartoons. **Spot News Photography,** Ron Olshwanger, St. Louis, Mo., for a photograph of a fire fighter giving mouth-to-mouth resuscitation to a child. **Feature Photography,** Manny Crisostomo, *Detroit Free Press,* for photographs depicting student life in a Detroit high school.

Letters. Biography, *Oscar Wilde,* Richard Ellmann. **Fiction,** *Breathing Lessons,* Anne Tyler. **General Nonfiction,** *A Bright Shining Lie: John Paul Vann and America in Vietnam,* Neil Sheehan. **History,** *Parting the Waters: America in the King Years, 1954-63,* Taylor Branch, and *Battle Cry of Freedom: The Civil War Era,* James M. McPherson. **Drama,** *The Heidi Chronicles,* Wendy Wasserstein. **Poetry,** *New and Collected Poems,* Richard Wilbur.

Music. Music Award, *Whispers Out of Time,* Roger Reynolds.

Science and technology awards

Columbia University. Louisa Gross Horwitz Prize. Edwin G. Krebs, Howard Hughes Medical Institute and University of Washington School of Medicine, Seattle; Alfred G. Gilman, University of Texas Southwestern Medical Center, Dallas.

Gairdner Foundation. Gairdner Foundation International Awards, Mark M. Davis, Stanford University School of Medicine, California; Jean-Marie Ghuysen, University of Liège, Belgium; Louis M. Kunkel, Children's Hospital, Boston; Lloyd D. MacLean, McGill University, Montreal, Canada; Tak Mak, Ontario Cancer Institute, Toronto, Canada; Erwin Neher, Max Planck Institute for Biophysical Chemistry, Göttingen-Nikolausberg, West Germany; Bert Sakmann, Heidelberg University, West Germany; Ronald G. Worton, Hospital for Sick Children, Toronto.

Albert and Mary Lasker Foundation. Albert Lasker Basic Medical Research Award, Michael J. Berridge, Cambridge University, England; Alfred G. Gilman, University of Texas Southwestern Medical Center; Edwin G. Krebs, Howard Hughes Medical Institute and University of Washington School of Medicine; Yasutomi Nishizuka, Kobe University School of Medicine, Japan. **Albert Lasker Clinical Medical Research Award,** Étienne-Émile Baulieu, University of Paris School of Medicine. **Albert Lasker Public Service Award,** Lewis Thomas, Cornell University Medical College, Ithaca, N.Y.

Royal Society of Canada. Sir William Dawson Medal, Henry G. Thode, McMaster University, Hamilton. **Thomas W. Eadie Medal,** Ashok K. Vijh, Hydro-Québec Institute of Research, Varennes. **McLaughlin Medal,** Samuel Solomon, McGill University. **Willet G. Miller Medal,** William H. Mathews, University of British Columbia, Vancouver. **Rutherford Medal in Chemistry,** Peter Hackett, National Research Council, Ottawa. **Rutherford Medal in Physics,** Nathan Isgur, University of Toronto. **Henry Marshall Tory Medal,** Boris P. Stoicheff, University of Toronto.

United States government. National Medal of Science, Arnold O. Beckman, Beckman Instruments, Incorporated, Irvine, Calif.; Richard B. Bernstein, University of California at Los Angeles; Melvin Calvin, University of California at Berkeley; Harry G. Drickamer, University of Illinois, Urbana; Katherine Esau, University of California at Santa Barbara; Herbert E. Grier, AVX Corporation, Great Neck, N.Y.; Viktor Hamburger, Washington University, St. Louis, Mo.; Samuel Karlin, Stanford University, California; Philip Leder, Harvard Medical School, Boston; Joshua Lederberg, Rockefeller University, New York City; Saunders MacLane, University of Chicago; Harden M. McConnell, Stanford; Rudolph A. Marcus, California Institute of Technology (Caltech), Pasadena; Eugene N. Parker, University of Chicago; Robert P. Sharp, Caltech; Donald C. Spencer, Princeton University, New Jersey; Roger W. Sperry, Caltech; Henry M. Stommel, Woods Hole Oceanographic Institution, Massachusetts; Harland G. Wood, Case Western Reserve University, Cleveland.

National Medal of Technology, Herbert W. Boyer, University of California at San Francisco; Stanley N. Cohen, Stanford; Robert R. Everett and Jay W. Forrester, Massachusetts Institute of Technology, Cambridge; Helen T. Edwards, Richard A. Lundy, J. Ritchie Orr, and Alvin V. Tollestrup, Fermi National Accelerator Laboratory, Batavia, Ill.

University of Southern California. Tyler Prize for Environmental Achievement, Paul J. Crutzen, Max Planck Institute for Chemistry, Mainz, West Germany, atmospheric chemist who contributed to the theory of nuclear winter; and Edward O. Goldberg, Scripps Institution of Oceanography, San Diego, oceanographer who pioneered in ocean pollution research.

Wolf Foundation. Wolf Foundation Prize, Alberto Calderon, University of Chicago; John Milnor, Princeton University, N.J. Sara Dreyfuss

Bahamas. See West Indies.
Bahrain. See Middle East.

Baker, James Addison, III

Baker, James Addison, III (1930-   ), became United States secretary of state on Jan. 25, 1989. Baker, a skilled negotiator and political strategist, had managed Vice President George Bush's successful 1988 presidential campaign. The post at the State Department was Baker's third high-ranking position since 1981. He served as chief of staff and secretary of the treasury under President Ronald Reagan.

Baker was born on April 28, 1930, in Houston. After graduating from Princeton University in New Jersey in 1952, he served in the U.S. Marine Corps. In 1957, he received a law degree from the University of Texas School of Law in Austin and joined a corporate law firm in Houston.

Baker directed Bush's 1970 bid for the U.S. Senate and in 1976 served as chairman of President Gerald R. Ford's bid for a new term in the White House. Although both campaigns failed, they established Baker's reputation as a talented political organizer.

In 1980, Baker directed Bush's run for the Republican presidential nomination. After Bush withdrew from the race, Baker guided Reagan's successful campaign for the White House. Reagan made Baker his chief of staff in 1981. In 1985, Baker switched jobs with Treasury Secretary Donald T. Regan.

Baker married his second wife, the former Susan Garrett, in 1973. They have eight children, including seven from previous marriages.   Barbara A. Mayes

Ballet. See **Dancing.**

Bangladeshis survey floodwaters during 1989's summertime monsoon season, which was less destructive than those of 1987 and 1988.

Bangladesh. On July 6, 1989, Prime Minister Moudud Ahmed introduced into Parliament a constitutional amendment limiting a president to two elected five-year terms and making the vice presidency an elective instead of an appointive office. Parliament passed the amendment on July 10, and President Hussain Mohammad Ershad issued a decree putting it into effect on October 1. The new amendment permits Ershad to call a presidential election before his term ends in 1991. On Aug. 12, 1989, Ershad dismissed Nurul Islam as vice president and gave the post to Moudud Ahmed. He also promoted Zafar Ahmed, a deputy prime minister, to prime minister.

Tumultuous politics. Ershad's Jatiya Dal (National Party) suffered some defections in 1989, and political rivalries contributed to student fighting that temporarily closed the campus of Dhaka University in the capital. The Awami League and the Bangladesh Nationalist Party, the two main opposition parties, also feuded. On April 2, Hasina Wajed, head of the Awami League, charged that former President Ziaur Rahman (known as Zia) had been a ringleader in the 1975 murder of her father, Sheik Mujibur Rahman, the nation's first prime minister. A spokesman for Zia's widow, Khaleda Zia, who is head of the Bangladesh Nationalist Party, countered by charging that Wajed was behind Zia's 1981 assassination.

Ethnic conflict. In the Chittagong Hill Tracts of southeastern Bangladesh, a 14-year-old conflict continued as Buddhist and Hindu ethnic groups rebelled against the intrusion of ethnic Bengali settlers, who are Muslim. The settlers had the support of the army, which observers accused of massacring rebels or driving them into adjacent India. Leaders of the rebel guerrilla army said that India had secretly supplied the guerrillas for more than a decade.

In an effort to end the conflict, Parliament on March 1 passed legislation to establish three local government councils with power over land transfers. Although most council seats were to be reserved for members of the Hindu and Buddhist majority, rebel leaders said the proposal was inadequate unless all Bengali settlers were ousted. Despite a boycott of the June 25 council elections, the government installed council chairmen on July 2.

Natural disasters. In 1989, the nation built embankments around low-lying areas in and near Dhaka that had been submerged by record floods in 1988. Although the monsoon flooding in 1989 was not destructive, the years of natural disasters slowed economic progress. As Bangladesh neared the end of its third five-year economic development plan, unemployment was far higher than expected, and private and government investment was much lower. In April, foreign countries promised Bangladesh $2.2 billion in aid for 1990.   Henry S. Bradsher

See also **Asia** (Facts in brief table). In *World Book,* see **Bangladesh.**

Bank. In 1989, the United States economy, along with most countries' economies in the rest of the world, continued the expansion begun in late 1982. The news was not all good for the banking industry, however. In the United States, 206 banks failed in 1989, and savings and loan associations (S&L's) faced grave troubles.

Money supply. Most economists believe that a nation's money supply has an important short-term influence on its economy and long-term influence on its inflation rate. One definition of the U.S. money supply, $M1$, is the amount of currency in circulation and in checking accounts. At the beginning of 1989, M1 was $790.5 billion. It slowly fell to $783.1 billion by the end of April, then plunged to $768 billion by the third week of June. M1 increased to more than $780-billion by mid-September and finished the year at $802.4 billion. The unusual decline in the spring was the result of a drop in checking-account deposits between March and June. During this time period, certificates of deposit (CD's) and other short-term savings accounts paid at least 4 percentage points more interest than interest-bearing checking accounts.

Since the late 1970's, economists have preferred to use a broader definition of the money supply, M2. M2 represents M1 plus the amount of money in short-term CD's, money-market deposit accounts, and money-market mutual funds. (Money-market accounts are like checking accounts, in that some checks can be written on them, but they generally pay higher interest than interest-bearing checking accounts.) M2 began the year at $3,069.5 billion and rose slowly to $3,072.1 billion by the end of May. In the summer, the U.S. central bank—the Federal Reserve System, or the Fed—began increasing reserves in the U.S. banking system. As reserves increased, M2 rose, finishing the year at $3,227.1 billion.

The money-supply growth rate, which was only 0.3 per cent during the first five months of the year, increased to 7.3 per cent for the next five. An increase in the money-supply growth rate will generally increase the inflation rate and the growth rate of the overall economy within two years. A more immediate, though temporary, effect of an increased money-supply growth rate is a drop in interest rates. When the Fed increases the money supply by making more reserves available to banks, banks become more willing to make new loans, and they lower their short-term interest rates. Later, as the inflation rate rises, interest rates will also rise. Critics of the Fed had been calling for a faster money-supply growth rate and lower interest rates since May 1988.

Interest rates. Banks loan one another money, often for only one day, so that money is available for loan to the best possible borrowers. The interest rate banks charge each other for these very short-term loans is called the *federal funds rate*. When 1989 began, the federal funds rate was 9.1 per cent. It quickly rose and hovered at about 9.8 per cent until the end

Earl Engleman, *The Wall Street Journal*; permission Cartoon Features Syndicate

"The banking industry is in worse shape than I thought."

of May. The rate fell to 9.0 per cent by the end of July, then held steady through September and October. It fell to 8.0 per cent by year-end.

The rate banks pay for 90-day CD's, normally about the same as the federal funds rate, began the year at 9.2 per cent. In mid-March, the rate peaked at 10.2 per cent; then it fell to the year's low, 8.4 per cent in early August. The rate stayed just under 9 per cent through September before falling to 8.4 per cent again in mid-October. At the end of the year, it was 8.1 per cent.

The prime rate, the interest rate banks charge to their best corporate customers, determines the rate of many consumer loans. In January, the prime rate was 10.5 per cent, and it rose 1 percentage point by early March. It held steady until June, when it fell to 11.0 per cent, and then decreased to 10.5 per cent in August, where it stayed until the end of the year.

S&L woes. Banks faced serious troubles in the 1980's—a slump in the oil industry and the Third World debt crisis, for example—but banks as a whole did fairly well in 1989. S&L's, on the other hand faced much more difficult times.

The S&L problems began in the late 1970's, when the need to pay high interest rates to depositors made old, low-rate mortgages a losing proposition. Raising interest rates on new mortgages was not enough to make some S&L's profitable. By passing the Deregulation Act of 1980, Congress gave S&L's the power to make commercial and personal loans in addition to mortgages. While some S&L's did very well in these new, and in some cases high-risk, areas of business, many failed. In addition, the Federal Home Loan Bank Board reported in January 1989 that fraud had become widespread in the S&L industry.

The Federal Savings and Loan Insurance Corporation (FSLIC), which insured deposits in S&L's for up to $100,000 per account, merged failing S&L's with healthy ones when possible and paid off insured depositors when necessary. By the end of 1988, FSLIC reserves—which were collected by charging S&L's 75 cents per year for every $1,000 in deposits—were dangerously low. By June 1989, the FSLIC itself became insolvent, facing at least $100 billion in expected payouts with less than $10 billion in reserves.

S&L bailout. On Aug. 9, 1989, President George Bush signed into law a bill that completely changed the way S&L's do business. The new law, which provided for the biggest federal rescue in history, dissolved the FSLIC and placed S&L's under the Federal Deposit Insurance Corporation (FDIC). It formed the Resolution Trust Corporation (RTC) and gave it $50-billion to buy and sell off the assets of failed S&L's. S&L premiums for deposit insurance doubled to $1.50 per $1,000 in deposits, and their *capital requirements* —the percentage of an S&L's assets that must be raised from its stockholders as cash—increased to 1.5 per cent by 1990 and 3 per cent by 1994.

S&L's that found themselves unable to meet these new requirements would have to sell assets or go out of business. When the bailout bill was signed into law, an estimated 750 S&L's were already in this category, and paying off insured depositors would cost the FDIC at least $160 billion. To make these S&L's more attractive candidates for private buyers, the new law gave commercial banks the right for the first time to buy S&L's with no strings attached and to merge them with branch offices. The remaining S&L's must generate at least 70 per cent of their assets from mortgages, and they may not buy stock or junk bonds to finance real-estate purchases unless they can meet even stiffer capital requirements.

Critics saw the new law as a way to make taxpayers foot the bill for federal regulators' neglect of an industry protected by influence peddling and plagued by fraud. Indeed, the law does not solve the basic problem that led to the collapse of the FSLIC: All S&L's, whether well or poorly managed, pay the same insurance premiums. This means that if an S&L gets into trouble, its managers will be tempted to make risky loans, because if these high-rate loans pay off, they will provide enough money to compensate for the bad loans. If the high-risk loans default, on the other hand, the deposit insurance agency, not the S&L, must pay off depositors. In this way, federal insurance encourages S&L's to increase their likelihood of failure if they get into trouble.   Donald W. Swanton

In **World Book,** see **Bank.**

Barr, Roseanne (1952-   ), charmed television audiences in 1989 with her portrayal of a sharp-tongued working mother in ABC's "Roseanne." Debuting in October 1988, the situation comedy vied with "The Cosby Show" for the top A. C. Nielsen ranking. Off the set, Barr had a stormy relationship with the show's creator, who left the sitcom in January 1989, giving Barr creative control of the series.

Born on Nov. 3, 1952, to Jewish parents in predominantly Mormon Salt Lake City, Utah, Barr was raised within both the Jewish and Mormon faiths. Her teenage years were troubled, and at 17, she spent eight months in a mental institution. The next year, Barr, a high school dropout, left Utah for Colorado, where she married Bill Pentland, later a co-writer on her show.

The couple had three children, and Barr was a homemaker until 1981, when she began working as a cocktail waitress. According to Barr, her customers enjoyed her cutting wit so much that they encouraged her to become a stand-up comedian. She began appearing in Denver comedy clubs, then polished her act by touring clubs in the Southwest. In 1985, Barr moved to Los Angeles and was soon booked to appear on "The Tonight Show" and network and cable TV comedy specials.

In 1989, Barr costarred in her first motion picture, *She-Devil.* She filed for divorce in July. Her autobiography, *Roseanne: My Life as a Woman,* was published in the fall.   Jinger Hoop

Baseball. It was a sad year for baseball in 1989. First, Pete Rose, a revered hero, was accused of betting on games, including those of the Cincinnati Reds, the team he managed. In the end, he agreed on August 24 to be banned from baseball for life. Then, on September 1, eight days after that agreement, A. Bartlett Giamatti, the commissioner who had handled Rose's case, suffered a heart attack and died at age 51. He had been baseball commissioner only five months.

A month later came a World Series between the Oakland Athletics and the San Francisco Giants that was interrupted for 10 days after a strong earthquake struck the San Francisco Bay area, killing at least 62 people. The A's went on to sweep the series.

Pete Rose. On April 1, 1989, Giamatti, the National League president and a former president of Yale University, succeeded Peter V. Ueberroth as baseball commissioner. Giamatti was succeeded as National League president by Bill White, a broadcaster and former player, who became the first black to head a major professional sports league (see **White, Bill**).

Giamatti's first task as commissioner was to investigate reports that Rose had bet on baseball games in violation of major league rules. Rose, 48, was baseball's all-time leader in hits (4,256) and games played (3,562). Since 1984, he had managed the Reds, the team he played for during most of his career.

After a six-month investigation, John Dowd, the special counsel appointed by Giamatti, named nine

Final standings in major league baseball

American League

Eastern Division

	W.	L.	Pct.	G.B.
Toronto Blue Jays	89	73	.549	
Baltimore Orioles	87	75	.537	2
Boston Red Sox	83	79	.512	6
Milwaukee Brewers	81	81	.500	8
New York Yankees	74	87	.460	14½
Cleveland Indians	73	89	.451	16
Detroit Tigers	59	103	.364	30

Western Division

	W.	L.	Pct.	G.B.
Oakland Athletics	99	63	.611	
Kansas City Royals	92	70	.568	7
California Angels	91	71	.562	8
Texas Rangers	83	79	.512	16
Minnesota Twins	80	82	.494	19
Seattle Mariners	73	89	.451	26
Chicago White Sox	69	92	.429	29½

American League champions—Oakland Athletics (defeated Toronto Blue Jays, 4 games to 1)
World Series champions—Oakland Athletics (4 games to 0)

Offensive leaders

Batting average—Kirby Puckett, Minnesota	.339
Runs scored—Wade Boggs, Boston, and Rickey Henderson, Oakland (tie)	113
Home runs—Fred McGriff, Toronto	36
Runs batted in—Ruben Sierra, Texas	119
Hits—Kirby Puckett, Minnesota	215
Stolen bases—Rickey Henderson, Oakland	77
Slugging percentage—Ruben Sierra, Texas	.543

Leading pitchers

Games won—Bret Saberhagen, Kansas City	23
Win average (15 decisions or more)—Bret Saberhagen, Kansas City (23-6)	.793
Earned run average (162 or more innings)—Bret Saberhagen, Kansas City	2.16
Strikeouts—Nolan Ryan, Texas	301
Saves—Jeff Russell, Texas	38
Shutouts—Bert Blyleven, California	5

Awards*

Most Valuable Player—Robin Yount, Milwaukee
Cy Young—Bret Saberhagen, Kansas City
Rookie of the Year—Gregg Olson, Baltimore
Manager of the Year—Frank Robinson, Baltimore

National League

Eastern Division

	W.	L.	Pct.	G.B.
Chicago Cubs	93	69	.574	
New York Mets	87	75	.537	6
St. Louis Cardinals	86	76	.531	7
Montreal Expos	81	81	.500	12
Pittsburgh Pirates	74	88	.457	19
Philadelphia Phillies	67	95	.414	26

Western Division

	W.	L.	Pct.	G.B.
San Francisco Giants	92	70	.568	
San Diego Padres	89	73	.549	3
Houston Astros	86	76	.531	6
Los Angeles Dodgers	77	83	.481	14
Cincinnati Reds	75	87	.463	17
Atlanta Braves	63	97	.394	28

National League champions—San Francisco Giants (defeated Chicago Cubs, 4 games to 1)

Offensive leaders

Batting average—Tony Gwynn, San Diego	.336
Runs scored—Will Clark, San Francisco; Howard Johnson, New York; and Ryne Sandberg, Chicago (tie)	104
Home runs—Kevin Mitchell, San Francisco	47
Runs batted in—Kevin Mitchell, San Francisco	125
Hits—Tony Gwynn, San Diego	203
Stolen bases—Vince Coleman, St. Louis	65
Slugging percentage—Kevin Mitchell, San Francisco	.635

Leading pitchers

Games won—Mike Scott, Houston	20
Win average (15 decisions or more)—Sid Fernandez, New York (14-5), and Scott Garrelts, San Francisco (14-5) (tie)	.737
Earned run average (162 innings or more)—Scott Garrelts, San Francisco	2.28
Strikeouts—José DeLeon, St. Louis	201
Saves—Mark Davis, San Diego	44
Shutouts—Tim Belcher, Los Angeles	8

Awards*

Most Valuable Player—Kevin Mitchell, San Francisco
Cy Young—Mark Davis, San Diego
Rookie of the Year—Jerome Walton, Chicago
Manager of the Year—Don Zimmer, Chicago

*Selected by Baseball Writers Association of America.

---

people who had implicated Rose in betting on major league games, though never against his own team. Giamatti wanted to give Rose a hearing before rendering a decision. Rose said Giamatti was not impartial and fought in an Ohio court and then a federal court to prevent the hearing.

The resolution came without a hearing. Rose admitted consorting with felons and betting on sports events, but not baseball. He agreed not to pursue the matter in court, and he was assured that Giamatti would not find him guilty of betting on baseball.Rose accepted a lifetime ban from baseball, with the right to apply for reinstatement in a year.

Finances. In January, three weeks after Ueberroth had negotiated a four-year, $1.1-billion network-television contract with CBS Inc., he concluded a four-year, $400-million cable-TV agreement with ESPN. Both contracts take effect in 1990.

Ueberroth said the 26 major league teams earned $100 million in 1988. In 1989, the Seattle Mariners were sold for $77 million, the most ever paid for an American League team.

Players were earning big money, too. After the season, pitcher Mark Langston signed with the California Angels for $16 million over five years, pitcher Mark Davis with the Kansas City Royals for $13 million over four years, outfielder Rickey Henderson with Oakland for $12 million over four years, outfielder Kirby Puckett with the Minnesota Twins for $9 million over three years, and outfielder Joe Carter with the San Diego

Baseball

Padres for $9 million, also to be paid over a period of three years.

Regular season. The division winners were Oakland by seven games in the American League West, the Toronto Blue Jays by two games in the American League East, San Francisco by three games in the National League West, and the surprising Chicago Cubs by six games in the National League East.

Oakland added pitcher Mike Moore before the season as a free agent and outfielder Rickey Henderson during the season in a trade. The A's overcame injuries that sidelined outfielder José Canseco, shortstop Walt Weiss, and relief pitcher Dennis Eckersley.

When Toronto started the season with a 13-24 record, manager Jimy Williams was fired and replaced by Cito Gaston. On the last weekend of the season, Toronto clinched the division title by winning two of three games from the second-place Baltimore Orioles.

In the American League championship series, Oakland defeated Toronto, 4 games to 1. Henderson stole eight bases in eight attempts, reached base 14 times in 23 at bats, and was voted the series' Most Valuable Player.

In the National League, San Francisco's third- and fourth-place hitters—first baseman Will Clark and outfielder Kevin Mitchell—combined for 70 home runs and 236 runs batted in. Scott Garrelts was moved from relief pitcher to starter, and he led National League starters with a 2.28 earned-run average.

The Cubs, fourth in their division in 1988, were not expected to improve significantly in 1989, but they had two talented rookie outfielders—Dwight Smith and Jerome Walton. Both became Rookie of the Year candidates, and the Cubs moved into first place on August 7 and stayed there.

In the play-offs, San Francisco whipped the Cubs, 4 games to 1. Clark, with 13 hits, a .650 batting average, and eight runs batted in, was voted the Most Valuable Player. After the season, Walton was voted Rookie of the Year; Smith was second.

World Series. In the 1988 series, the Dodgers beat the Athletics in five games. This time, Oakland, again managed by Tony LaRussa, was favored because of its strong pitching. It won the first two games, 5-0 and 5-1, behind the pitching of Dave Stewart and Moore.

On October 17, only 27 minutes before the third game was scheduled to start, a killer earthquake shook San Francisco's packed Candlestick Park and the surrounding area. In the park, there were no injuries and damage was minimal.

The series was suspended. As Francis T. (Fay) Vincent, Jr., who had succeeded Giamatti as commissioner, said, "Our modest little sporting event is unimportant now." With the approval of local authorities, the games were resumed on October 27, and Oakland won that night, 13-7, and the next, 9-6.

Stewart, who won two games and allowed only three runs in 16 innings, was named the Most Valu-

Texas Ranger pitcher Nolan Ryan becomes the first pitcher to record 5,000 career strikeouts, fanning Oakland's Rickey Henderson on August 22.

able Player. Henderson, who had six hits in 15 at bats for a .400 average in the league play-offs, had 9 for 19 for an average of .474 in the World Series.

The stars. Nolan Ryan, at 42 the oldest pitcher in the major leagues, signed as a free agent with the Texas Rangers and in August became the first pitcher to reach 5,000 career strikeouts. Early in the season, pitcher Steve Carlton, second in all-time strikeouts with 4,136, retired at 44; and third baseman Mike Schmidt, seventh in all-time home runs with 548, retired at 39.

Outfielder Tony Gwynn of the San Diego Padres (.336) overtook Clark (.333) on the final day and won his third straight National League batting title. Third baseman Wade Boggs of Boston (.330), seeking his fifth straight American League title, finished third, as Puckett won with .339.

Hall of Fame. The baseball writers elected catcher Johnny Bench, who hit 389 home runs in 17 years, all with Cincinnati, and outfielder Carl Yastrzemski, who hit 452 in 23 years, all with Boston. Both players were on the ballot for the first time. The veterans committee elected second baseman Red Schoendienst, who played 19 years in the major leagues, 14 of them with the St. Louis Cardinals, and Al Barlick, a National League umpire for 28 years. Barlick became only the fifth umpire elected to the National Baseball Hall of Fame.   Frank Litsky

In *World Book,* see **Baseball.**

Basketball. The University of Michigan won the 1989 championship tournament of the National Collegiate Athletic Association (NCAA), the first team to take the title under an interim coach. The Detroit Pistons dethroned the Los Angeles Lakers in four straight games and won the National Basketball Association (NBA) championship, the first in their 41-year history as a professional team.

College. The preseason polls established Duke University as the best team in the United States, and Duke did have a good season. In the Associated Press's postseason poll of sportswriters and broadcasters, however, Arizona (27-3) was ranked first, Georgetown (26-4) second, Illinois (27-4) third, and Oklahoma (28-5) fourth.

Those teams were seeded first in the four regional competitions of the NCAA tournament, which began on March 16. Among the 64 teams in the tournament were Michigan (24-7), ranked 10th nationally, and Seton Hall (26-6), ranked 11th. Kansas, the 1988 national champion, could not defend its title because the NCAA had banned it from the tournament and had placed it on probation for recruiting violations.

In May, following the tournament, the NCAA placed the University of Kentucky's basketball program on probation for three years because of recruiting and academic violations. The NCAA also took the unusual step of banning a single Kentucky player, Eric Manuel, from further NCAA competition because he had "committed academic fraud by cheating" on a college-entrance examination, the NCAA said. Probation meant that Kentucky would be ineligible for postseason competition in 1990 and 1991. The number of basketball scholarships it could offer in those years was also reduced.

NCAA tournament. Three of the four tournament favorites were eliminated early. Georgetown barely won its opening game, 50-49, against a Princeton team seeded last in its regional. A week later, Duke eliminated Georgetown, 85-77. Arizona lost to the University of Nevada, Las Vegas, 68-67, and Oklahoma was defeated by Virginia, 86-80.

The teams that advanced to the Final Four in Seattle were Duke (for the third time in four years), Illinois,

National Basketball Association standings

Eastern Conference

Atlantic Division	W.	L.	Pct.	G.B.
New York Knicks	52	30	.634	
Philadelphia 76ers	46	36	.561	6
Boston Celtics	42	40	.512	10
Washington Bullets	40	42	.488	12
New Jersey Nets	26	56	.317	26
Charlotte Hornets	20	62	.244	32

Central Division				
Detroit Pistons	63	19	.768	
Cleveland Cavaliers	57	25	.695	6
Atlanta Hawks	52	30	.634	11
Milwaukee Bucks	49	33	.598	14
Chicago Bulls	47	35	.573	16
Indiana Pacers	28	54	.341	35

Western Conference

Midwest Division				
Utah Jazz	51	31	.622	
Houston Rockets	45	37	.549	6
Denver Nuggets	44	38	.537	7
Dallas Mavericks	38	44	.463	13
San Antonio Spurs	21	61	.256	30
Miami Heat	15	67	.183	36

Pacific Division				
Los Angeles Lakers	57	25	.695	
Phoenix Suns	55	27	.671	2
Seattle SuperSonics	47	35	.573	10
Golden State Warriors	43	39	.524	14
Portland Trail Blazers	39	43	.476	18
Sacramento Kings	27	55	.329	30
Los Angeles Clippers	21	61	.256	36

NBA champions—Detroit Pistons (defeated Los Angeles Lakers, 4 games to 0)

Individual leaders

Scoring	G.	F.G.	F.T.	Pts.	Avg.
Michael Jordan, Chicago	81	966	674	2,633	32.5
Karl Malone, Utah	80	809	703	2,326	29.1
Dale Ellis, Seattle	82	857	377	2,253	27.5
Clyde Drexler, Portland	78	829	438	2,123	27.2
Chris Mullin, Golden State	82	830	493	2,176	26.5
Alex English, Denver	82	924	325	2,175	26.5
Dominique Wilkins, Atlanta	80	814	442	2,099	26.2
Charles Barkley, Philadelphia	79	700	602	2,037	25.8
Tom Chambers, Phoenix	81	774	509	2,085	25.7
Akeem Olajuwon, Houston	82	790	454	2,034	24.8

Rebounding	G.	Tot.	Avg.
Akeem Olajuwon, Houston	82	1,105	13.5
Charles Barkley, Philadelphia	79	986	12.5
Robert Parish, Boston	80	996	12.5
Moses Malone, Atlanta	81	956	11.8
Karl Malone, Utah	80	853	10.7

203

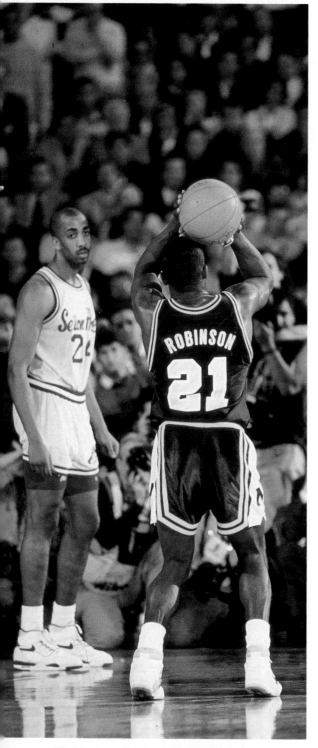

With three seconds left in overtime, Rumeal Robinson sets for the free throw that won the NCAA tournament for Michigan, 80-79, in April.

Michigan, and Seton Hall. In the semifinals on April 1, Michigan upset Big Ten rival Illinois, 83-81, when Sean Higgins grabbed a rebound and scored with time running out. Seton Hall rallied from an 18-point deficit to upset Duke, 95-78.

The final on April 3 matched two unlikely teams. Less than 48 hours before Michigan's first tournament game, coach Bill Frieder announced he would leave Michigan after the tournament to coach Arizona State. Instead, an angry Bo Schembechler, the Michigan athletic director, told Frieder to leave immediately and named assistant coach Steve Fisher as interim head coach.

Seton Hall had no such coaching problem. In fact, after the tournament, its coach, P. J. Carlesimo, turned down a much higher-paying coaching job at Kentucky. Seton Hall's immediate problem was maintaining momentum. Before the season, the Big East coaches had picked Seton Hall to finish seventh in the nine-team conference. Instead, Seton Hall finished second to Georgetown.

The exciting NCAA final matched Michigan's explosive offense against Seton Hall's clawing defense. Michigan won, 80-79, in overtime on Rumeal Robinson's two free throws with three seconds left. Glen Rice of Michigan scored 31 points in the final. His 184 points for six tournament games broke the NCAA scoring record of 177 points in five games set in 1965 by Bill Bradley of Princeton, now a United States senator. Rice was voted the Most Valuable Player of the Final Four. Later, Fisher was named head coach.

Honors. Hank Gathers, a junior at Loyola Marymount in Los Angeles, led the nation's major colleges in scoring (averaging 32.7 points per game) and rebounding (13.7 per game). Danny Ferry of Duke, Sean Elliott of Arizona, and Stacey King of Oklahoma were named Player of the Year in various polls.

Among the players cited on All-America teams were Ferry, Elliott, King, Pervis Ellison of Louisville, Mookie Blaylock of Oklahoma, Sherman Douglas of Syracuse, and freshman Chris Jackson of Louisiana State. The first players taken in the NBA draft were Ellison, Ferry, and Elliott, in that order. Ferry passed up the NBA and played in Italy in 1989.

Women. In the regular season, Auburn (28-1) was undefeated until it lost to Tennessee. At season's end, Tennessee was ranked first in the nation and Auburn second. Center Clarissa Davis of Texas was named Player of the Year.

Tennessee and Auburn led 48 teams into the NCAA championship tournament, held from March 15 to April 2, and both advanced to the final in Tacoma, Wash. Tennessee, coached by Pat Summitt, won, 76-60, for its second title in three years. Forward Bridgette Gordon led Tennessee with 27 points and 11 rebounds and was named the tournament's Most Valuable Player.

Professional. The NBA, like the colleges, attracted record crowds. For the first time, college game attend-

The 1988-1989
college basketball season

College tournament champions

NCAA (Men) Division I: Michigan
           Division II: North Carolina Central
           Division III: University of Wisconsin at Whitewater

NCAA (Women) Division I: Tennessee
           Division II: Delta State (Miss.)
           Division III: Elizabethtown (Pa.)

NAIA (Men): St. Mary's (Texas)
     (Women): Southern Nazarene (Okla.)

NIT: (Men): St. John's (N.Y.)
     (Women): Oregon

Junior College (Men): Northeastern Oklahoma A&M
           (Women): Central Arizona

College champions

Conference	School
American South	New Orleans (regular season) Louisiana Tech (tournament)
Atlantic Coast	North Carolina State (regular season) North Carolina (tournament)
Atlantic Ten	West Virginia (regular season) Rutgers (tournament)
Big East	Georgetown*
Big Eight	Oklahoma (regular season) Missouri (tournament)
Big Sky	Boise State—Idaho (tie; regular season) Idaho (tournament)
Big South	Coastal Carolina (regular season) North Carolina-Asheville (tournament)
Big Ten	Indiana
Big West	Nevada-Las Vegas*
Colonial A.A.	Richmond (regular season) George Mason (tournament)
East Coast	Bucknell*
ECAC North Atlantic	Siena*
Ivy League	Princeton
Metro Athletic	Florida State (regular season) Louisville (tournament)
Metro Atlantic	La Salle*
Mid-American	Ball State*
Mid-Continent	Southwest Missouri State
Mid-Eastern	South Carolina State*
Midwestern	Evansville (regular season) Xavier (tournament)
Missouri Valley	Creighton*
Northeast	Robert Morris*
Ohio Valley	Middle Tennessee State*
Pacific Ten	Arizona*
Southeastern	Florida (regular season) Alabama (tournament)
Southern	Tennessee-Chattanooga (regular season) East Tennessee State (tournament)
Southland	North Texas (regular season) McNeese State (tournament)
Southwest	Arkansas*
Southwestern	Southern-Baton Rouge— Texas Southern—Grambling State (tie; regular season) Southern-Baton Rouge (tournament)
Sun Belt	South Alabama*
Trans America	Georgia Southern (regular season) Arkansas-Little Rock (tournament)
West Coast	St. Mary's (regular season) Loyola-Marymount (tournament)
Western	Colorado State (regular season) Texas-El Paso (tournament)

*Regular season and conference tournament champions.

ance exceeded 33 million and NBA attendance 15 million. The NBA was helped by the addition of the Charlotte (N.C.) Hornets and the Miami Heat; both teams attracted virtual sellout crowds at home.

In October, the Denver Nuggets were sold for $54 million to Bertram M. Lee and Peter C. B. Bynoe of Chicago. They became the first blacks to own a significant share of a major American professional sports franchise.

In the NBA's regular season from November 1988 to April 1989, the 25 teams played 82 games each. The division winners were the Pistons (63-19) by six games, the Lakers (57-25) by two games, the New York Knicks (52-30) by six games, and the Utah Jazz (51-31) by six games. The Phoenix Suns made a remarkable turnabout, improving their record of 28-54 the previous season to 55-27. Phoenix led the league in scoring with 118.6 points per game, and its coach, Cotton Fitzsimmons, was voted Coach of the Year.

Play-offs. The Lakers had won five NBA championships in the 1980's and were trying for their third straight. They won their last five games of the regular season, and in the play-offs, they rolled up an 11-0 record in eliminating the Portland Trail Blazers, the Seattle SuperSonics, and Phoenix.

Detroit, a physical team coached by Chuck Daly, did almost as well. In the 16-team play-offs, the Pistons eliminated the Boston Celtics (3-0), the Milwaukee Bucks (4-0), and the Chicago Bulls (4-2).

The Pistons-Lakers championship series started on June 6 and ended on June 13 as the Pistons won in four straight games. Hamstring injuries kept one Lakers guard, Byron Scott, out of the finals and severely limited the other, Earvin (Magic) Johnson. Joe Dumars, a Pistons guard known for defense, averaged 27.3 points per game in the championship series and was voted its Most Valuable Player.

Stars. In the previous season, Michael Jordan, Chicago's shooting guard, led the league in scoring, averaging 35 points per game. This time, Jordan was switched to point guard for part of the season but led again with an average of 32.5.

Johnson, the Lakers' point guard, was voted Most Valuable Player. Jordan was second in the voting and Karl Malone, Utah's power forward, third. They were also voted to the all-star team along with Charles Barkley, the Philadelphia 76ers power forward, and Akeem Olajuwon, the Houston Rockets center.

There were two notable absences from the all-star game in Larry Bird of the Celtics and Johnson of the Lakers. Bird played six games before he underwent surgery to remove bone spurs from both heels, and he did not play again during the season. Johnson, out with a hamstring injury, was replaced by Kareem Abdul-Jabbar, who was playing his last season. After 20 seasons, Abdul-Jabbar retired at age 42 as the NBA's all-time leader in scoring, seasons played, games played, and many other categories.   Frank Litsky

In *World Book,* see **Basketball.**

Belgium

Belgium completed the creation of a federal system of government on Jan. 9, 1989, to accommodate its two major ethnic groups—the Walloons, who speak French, and the Flemings, whose language is Dutch. Since 1980, the central government has been transferring power to three economic regions—Wallonia in the south, Flanders in the north, and the capital, Brussels, which is bilingual. The central government is to remain responsible to Parliament, with each region run by its own executive branch of government.

The 1989 laws transferred nearly one-third of government spending to regional budgets, mainly for education. The measures also created a constitutional court to rule on problems of power transfer.

Social and cultural antagonism between Walloons and Flemings had sharpened in the 1980's because of growing economic disparities between the two communities. Wallonia built its wealth on coal mines and steel mills. But now Wallonia is part of Europe's "rust belt," whose heavy industry has been outmatched by competition from newly industrialized countries—such as South Korea—which have more modern equipment and cheaper labor. As Wallonia's industrial base eroded, so did its tax base; and so Walloons began to look to Flanders as a source of tax revenue.

Flanders, with a more diversified economy, has been relatively immune to foreign competition, so its tax base has remained intact. Flanders was willing to let some of its tax revenues go to Wallonia, provided Flanders obtained fuller political and cultural independence and Belgium as a whole distanced itself from the influence of neighboring France.

Rightists, Greens gain. The separatist challenge to moderate political leadership was evident in results of June 15 elections for members of the European Parliament, the legislative branch of the European Community (EC or Common Market). The ultranationalist Vlaams Blok Flemish Party won 5 per cent of the vote, an unprecedentedly strong showing for an extreme right wing faction. *Green* (environmentalist) parties won 14 per cent of the vote, a record high.

The kidnapping of former Prime Minister Paul Vanden Boeynants on January 14 stunned Belgium. He had been convicted of tax fraud and forgery in 1986 and was under investigation in 1989 for misappropriation of state funds. The kidnappers released him on the night of February 13-14, reportedly after his family paid a ransom of nearly $1 million.

Tension with Zaire, a former Belgian colony in Africa, grew due to Belgian press stories of corruption in the government of Zaire's President Mobutu Sese Seko. Zaire threatened to break diplomatic ties, but tensions eased in August when Belgium offered to cancel part of Zaire's debt.   Joseph Fitchett

See also **Europe** (Facts in brief table). In *World Book,* see **Belgium.**
Belize. See **Latin America.**
Benin. See **Africa.**
Bhutan. See **Asia.**

Biology. Researchers made great strides in 1989 in locating genetic defects that cause diseases. *Genes—* components of cells that carry the coded instructions for all inherited traits—can influence a person's vulnerability to certain diseases.

Researchers from the University of Michigan in Ann Arbor and the Hospital for Sick Children in Toronto, Canada, reported in August that they had discovered the defect that causes most cases of *cystic fibrosis,* a disease that occurs chiefly among whites. About 1 in every 20 white Americans carries the gene for cystic fibrosis, and about 1 in every 2,000 white children is born with the disease.

Cystic fibrosis, which is marked by a build-up of mucus in the lungs, leads to breathing problems, trouble with digestion, and frequent bacterial infections. Nearly all victims die before age 30. Researchers hope that knowledge about the gene will lead to new therapies for the disease. Identification of the gene also makes it possible to detect carriers of the disease and to diagnose the disease in a fetus before birth. Scientists are working to refine such genetic tests for widespread use.

In July, researchers at Trinity College in Dublin, Ireland, and at the University of Texas Health Science Center in Houston announced that they had narrowed down the location of a gene that causes one form of *retinitis pigmentosa.* This eye disease, often associated with diabetes, has blinded about 1½ million people worldwide, including 100,000 in the United States. Researchers hope that the eventual identification of the gene and the biochemical workings of the disease will help in developing a treatment.

Gene transfer in human beings. The first authorized experiment to use *genetic engineering*—the scientific alteration of genetic material—in human subjects began in May 1989. Researchers at the National Institutes of Health in Bethesda, Md., injected genetically engineered cells into patients suffering from *malignant melanoma,* a potentially fatal skin cancer. The volunteers were undergoing a cancer treatment in which they received white blood cells treated with a protein that enhances the cells' cancer-fighting ability.

The gene experiment involved adding an altered gene as a passenger in the treated white blood cells. The gene—which should have no effect on the cancer—served as a marker on the treated cells, enabling scientists to track them in the body. By monitoring the cells' progress, the scientists hope to learn more about how the cancer treatment works.

In September, the researchers reported that the added genes were performing as expected, without harm to the patients. The scientists hope eventually to use the same technique to introduce altered genes that will help in actively treating disease.

Genetically engineered drug. In June 1989, the U.S. Food and Drug Administration approved the sale of a genetically engineered drug called *epoetin* (EPO), making it the sixth such drug approved for use in hu-

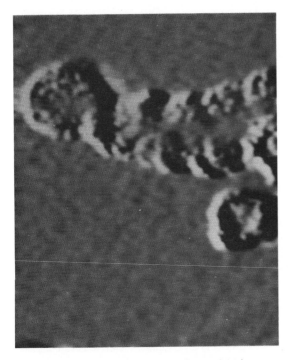

An advanced type of microscope in 1989 produced the first image of DNA—the molecule that carries the genetic code—in its natural state.

ers hope eventually to use them to prevent such diseases as diabetes and arthritis.

Antibodies for medical use are most commonly made in special cell cultures that produce specific antibodies. But the cell lines are difficult to prepare and expensive to maintain. The Scripps researchers predicted that the new method would greatly reduce the cost of antibodies used in therapy.

Mouse house burns. Biological research projects throughout the world were disrupted in May 1989 when a fire killed 500,000 mice at the Jackson Laboratory in Bar Harbor, Me. The laboratory, one of the world's leading suppliers of research mice, sells more than 2 million specially bred animals annually to 6,500 researchers in 33 countries.

The nonprofit laboratory maintains about 1,700 strains of mice, many of which are available nowhere else. The mice are bred for special characteristics—such as vulnerability to certain illnesses—for use in studies of such conditions as cancer, diabetes, and obesity. An experiment's validity often depends on using many mice of the same particular strain.

Breeding stock of all the strains was saved from the blaze, but Jackson officials estimate it will take two years to repair and repopulate the facility. In November, Congress appropriated $15 million to assist with rebuilding.   Thomas H. Maugh II

See also **Health and disease; Medicine.** In *World Book*, see **Biology; Genetic engineering; Genetics.**

man beings. The drug is manufactured with genetic engineering techniques to duplicate the structure of *erythropoietin*, a hormone normally produced in small quantities in the kidneys that stimulates the bone marrow to make red blood cells. The drug is used to treat *anemia*, a shortage of red blood cells.

The initial approval was for use by people with chronic kidney failure. Many of these people must undergo regular *dialysis*, a mechanical process that removes toxic wastes from the body. Dialysis also destroys red blood cells, however, often causing anemia. In addition, kidney failure itself can decrease the body's natural erythropoietin production and lead to anemia. Anemia can be treated with blood transfusions, but repeated transfusions may cause disease or lead to a harmful build-up of iron in the body.

Also in June, the FDA allowed use of EPO by AIDS patients. Nearly half of these patients are anemic because of the disease itself or because they take the medication AZT (zidovudine), which impairs red blood cell production.

Antibodies in plants. In November, researchers at the Scripps Clinic in La Jolla, Calif., announced that they had discovered an inexpensive way to make animal antibodies in plants. *Antibodies* are protein molecules created by the body's immune system to fight specific foreign chemicals, viruses, and bacteria in the bloodstream. Specially prepared antibodies are used to treat cancer and other diseases, and many research-

Boating. The United States, which won the America's Cup on the water in 1988, lost it in court in March 1989 to New Zealand, then regained it in court in September.

The America's Cup is the most important competition in yachting. Its rules were established by the century-old Deed of Gift and are interpreted by the New York State Supreme Court. In 1987, the United States regained the cup from Australia, after losing it in 1983. New Zealand then quickly issued a challenge for 1988, not in the traditional sloops of the 12-Meter Class but in a much larger monohull.

When the San Diego Yacht Club, which held the cup, was ordered by the New York court to accept the challenge, it refused to build a 132-foot (40-meter) monohull, as the New Zealanders did. Instead, San Diego built a faster, high-tech 60-foot (18-meter) *catamaran* (twin-hulled yacht) and trounced New Zealand in two consecutive races.

New Zealand then asked the New York court to disqualify the Americans for breaching the spirit of the rules. On March 28, 1989, the court agreed and awarded the cup to New Zealand. On September 19, however, a New York appeals court overturned that decision and restored the cup to the United States.

Speed records. In 1854, a clipper ship named *Flying Cloud* sailed from New York City around Cape Horn to San Francisco in 89 days 8 hours. That was the record for a sailing vessel until February 1989, when

Bolivia

Thursday's Child, a 60-foot (18-meter) ocean racer skippered by Warren Luhrs, completed the trip in 81 days 20 hours. Then, in May, *Great American*, a *trimaran* (three-hulled boat) skippered by George Kolesnikovs of Niagara Falls, Canada, lowered the record to 76 days 23 hours.

The transatlantic record for powerboats was broken by Tom Gentry of Honolulu, Hawaii, in a $6-million, 110-foot (34-meter), three-engine speedboat named *Gentry Eagle*. He drove from New York to England in 62 hours 57 minutes, averaging 55 miles per hour (mph), or 89 kilometers per hour (kph), and breaking the record by more than 17 hours.

Powerboats. Charles Marks of Potomac, Md., won the U.S. offshore championship in a series of eight races from April to October. He won six of the first seven races in *Eric's Reality*, a $750,000, 48-foot (15-meter) Cougar catamaran powered by four turbocharged engines generating 3,800 horsepower. The boat reached speeds of 130 mph (210 kph).

Unlimited hydroplanes competed in 10 races from May to September in sleek, aerodynamically designed boats that exceeded 180 mph (290 kph) on straightaways. *Miss Budweiser* dominated the series for the fourth consecutive year, though its driver, Jim Kropfield of Cincinnati, Ohio, was fired in midseason by the owner, Bernie Little. His replacement was Tom D'Eath of Fair Haven, Mich.   Frank Litsky

In *World Book*, see **Boating; Sailing.**

Bolivia. On Aug. 6, 1989, Jaime Paz Zamora of the Movement of the Revolutionary Left was sworn in as Bolivia's president. It was the first time in 25 years that an elected government succeeded another elected government that had completed its term.

Because none of the contenders for the presidency won a majority of the votes in elections on May 7, the victory of Paz Zamora, who placed third, was decided by Bolivia's Congress. Former President Hugo Banzer Suárez, who came in second in the balloting, threw his congressional support to Paz Zamora, assuring his election. Paz Zamora had been jailed under General Banzer's military regime in the 1970's for his Marxist-Leninist politics. Paz Zamora has since become a social democrat. As president, he formed a national unity government with Banzer's conservative National Democratic Action Party.

Paz Zamora continued to battle the production of coca, the raw material for the drug cocaine, which has come to account for more than one-fifth of Bolivia's total agricultural output. He also continued to exert pressure on the United States and other wealthy nations to provide more than $600 million in aid for a program of rural road construction and electrification, meant to make it profitable for farmers to grow legal crops.   Nathan A. Haverstock

In *World Book*, see **Bolivia.**

Books. See **Canadian literature; Literature; Literature for children.**

Botany. Botanists have long known that some plants generate large amounts of heat from their flowers. On the day they bloom, these *thermogenic* flowers can warm themselves to as much as 25°F. (14°C) above air temperature. One known function of this hot flash is to release odors—often foul to human beings—that attract insects to pollinate the flowers. Now, research reported in 1989 by botanist Ilya Raskin and two co-workers at the Du Pont Company in Wilmington, Del., has shed more light on the heat.

Raskin studied the voodoo lily, a Southeast Asian flower related to the skunk cabbage plant of the Eastern United States. In earlier studies, the Du Pont scientists, together with Bastiaan J. D. Meeuse of the University of Washington in Seattle, had isolated the chemical compound that switches on the heating mechanism. In 1989, they reported that after the initial burst of heat at blooming, which lures insects deep into the flower, the lily produces a second, milder heat wave that stimulates the insects trapped inside the floral chamber to become active. This helps the insects spread pollen within the flower. After the blossom withers, releasing the insects, they may then carry some of the pollen to other voodoo lilies as well. The process is considered a remarkable example of the development of an elaborate means to ensure insect pollination.

Beware the bunya-bunya tree. In August 1989, police cordoned off three large bidwilli bunya-bunya trees growing on the campus of Pierce College in Woodland Hills, Calif., to protect shade lovers from being hit by falling seed pods. In warm weather, the trees drop bristly pods the size of bowling balls, filled with sap and seeds and weighing 5 pounds (2.3 kilograms), from as high as 80 feet (24 meters).

A new nitrogen-fixer. Although many plants draw nitrogen—a necessary nutrient—from the soil, some plants are able to grow in nitrogen-poor soil with the help of special bacteria. These bacteria take nitrogen gas from the air and convert, or "fix," it into a form the plant can use. In turn, these helpful bacteria depend on the host plant for food and energy.

Early in 1989, scientists at Cornell University's Boyce Thompson Institute for Plant Research in Ithaca, N.Y., reported that they had discovered a novel nitrogen-fixing bacterium. The new bacterium, named *Photorhizobium thompsonum*, not only fixes nitrogen gas but also makes its own food, using sunlight through a process called *photosynthesis*, which normally is found in plants and some marine bacteria.

The researchers said that the new bacterium is particularly efficient in helping plant growth because it does not draw energy from its host plant for itself. The scientists hope that further research may enable them to develop nitrogen-fixing methods for crop plants that normally require nitrogen-rich, fertilized soil.   Eldon H. Newcomb

In *World Book*, see **Botany.**

Botswana. See **Africa.**

Bowling. Mike Aulby of Indianapolis and Robin Romeo of Van Nuys, Calif., broke the single-season earnings records in bowling in 1989. Aulby, a 29-year-old left-hander, won $298,237 on the Professional Bowlers Association (PBA) tour for men. The 31-year-old Romeo earned $113,750 in Ladies Pro Bowlers Tour (LPBT) competition.

Men. Aulby; Pete Weber of St. Louis, Mo.; and Del Ballard, Jr., of Richardson, Tex., won the three major PBA tournaments. Aulby captured the richest tournament in the sport, the $500,000 United States Open, held from March 26 to April 1 in Edmond, Okla. He was the last qualifier for the 24-man match play, then went on to defeat Jim Penach of Richmond Heights, Ohio, 195-178, in the last game of the stepladder finals. First prize was worth $100,000.

For the year, Aulby won five tournaments, including the American Bowling Congress (ABC) Masters. Amleto Monacelli of Venezuela won four, and Randy Petersen of Santa Maria, Calif., and Ballard three each. Ballard's victories included the $250,000 Firestone Tournament of Champions, held from April 18 to 22 in Fairlawn, Ohio.

Recovering from personal problems, Weber won the PBA National Championship, held from March 12 to 18 in Toledo, Ohio. Weber thus became only the third bowler to win the PBA's three major events, having won the 1987 Tournament of Champions and the 1988 United States Open. In the final of the national,

he turned back Dave Ferraro of Kingston, N.Y., 221-216, and two weeks later he surpassed $1 million in career earnings.

Weber had been fighting alcohol and drug problems for five years. In August 1988, he was suspended for six months by Joseph R. Antenora, the PBA commissioner, for continued detrimental conduct on the tour. On the recommendation of Weber's rehabilitation counselors, Antenora reinstated him five weeks early after Weber had missed 11 tournaments.

The highest scores of 1989 were bowled in a scratch double league in Union, N.J., by Tom Jordan, a welder and part-time professional from Paterson, N.J. On March 7, the 22-year-old left-hander rolled successive games of 300, 299, 300, and 299. He made 23 straight strikes, then missed the 10 pin, made 23 more strikes, . then missed the 7 pin. He set records of 899 for three games and 1,198 for four games.

Women. While the men's tour embraced 36 tournaments worth more than $5 million, the women competed in 26 tournaments worth one-fourth of the men's purses. Still, in 1988, the women's tour had surpassed $1 million in purses for the first time, and it continued to grow in 1989.

Robin Romeo won five tournaments, and Cheryl Daniels of Detroit took four. Romeo was winner of the $200,000 United States Open, which was held from May 4 to 10 in Addison, Ill.   Frank Litsky

In *World Book*, see **Bowling.**

Bowling alleys in 1989 helped keep young children out of the gutter as many alleys began to install inflated bumper guards to keep the ball in the lane.

Boxing

Boxing. In 1989, at age 22, Mike Tyson continued to rule the heavyweight ranks with an iron fist. He decimated all the contenders he faced, and the only one he avoided was Evander Holyfield, the number-one-ranked contender. Don King, the promoter who lined up bouts for Tyson, wanted to wait until 1990 for a Tyson-Holyfield fight to build public interest. Also, Holyfield did not seem ready for Tyson.

Tyson's opponents in 1989 did not last long. On February 25 in Las Vegas, Nev., Tyson stopped Frank Bruno of England in five rounds. On July 21 in Atlantic City, N.J., he stopped Carl (the Truth) Williams at 1 minute 33 seconds of the first round. Tyson was scheduled to fight again in November, but he developed pleurisy and the bout was canceled. Tyson was recognized as the world heavyweight champion by the sport's three major governing bodies—the World Boxing Council (WBC), the World Boxing Association (WBA), and the International Boxing Federation (IBF). Tyson was also earning money—$3 million for fighting Bruno and $4 million for Williams.

In 1988, Holyfield abandoned the cruiserweight division, put on weight, and fought as a heavyweight. On March 11, 1989, in Las Vegas, he stopped Michael Dokes, a former WBA heavyweight champion, in 10 rounds. On November 4 in Atlantic City, he took many punches before stopping Alex Stewart in eight rounds.

Leonard-Durán. In 1981, when Sugar Ray Leonard was a welterweight and Roberto Durán of Panama was an overblown lightweight, they staged two memorable fights. In June 1981, Durán outpointed Leonard and took his welterweight title. In November of that year, Leonard regained the title when Durán said, "No más, no más" (Spanish for "No more, no more") and quit in the eighth round.

In the years since, both fighters put on weight, fought, retired, fought again, and retired again. In 1989, when Leonard was 33 and Durán 38, their paths crossed again.

On February 24 in Atlantic City, Durán took a split decision from the favored Iran Barkley and won Barkley's WBC middleweight title. On June 12 in Las Vegas, Leonard fought another old foe, Thomas Hearns, for Leonard's WBC supermiddleweight title. Leonard was knocked down twice but escaped with his title in a 12-round draw.

Although Leonard did not look good in that fight, he earned $13 million and a chance for another large purse. That came when he fought Durán on December 7 in Las Vegas for Leonard's title. Leonard easily won in a unanimous decision as a sluggish Durán landed only 14 per cent of his punches.

Amateur. Eric Griffin of Houston won the gold medal in the 48-kilogram (106-pound) class in the world championships held from September 17 to 30 in Moscow. Of the 12 gold medals, the Soviet Union won 5 and Cuba 4.   Frank Litsky

In *World Book*, see **Boxing; Tyson, Mike.**

World champion boxers

World Boxing Association

Division	Champion	Country	Date won
Heavyweight	Mike Tyson	U.S.A.	1987
Junior heavyweight	Evander Holyfield	U.S.A.	1986
	vacant		
	Taoufik Belbouli	France	April '89
	vacant		
	Robert Daniels	U.S.A.	Nov. '89
Light heavyweight	Virgil Hill	U.S.A.	1987
Super middleweight	Fulgencio Obelmejias	Venezuela	1988
	Baek In-chul	South Korea	June '89
Middleweight	Sumbu Kalambay	Italy	1987
	vacant		
	Mike McCallum	Jamaica	May '89
Junior middleweight	Julian Jackson	U.S. Virgin Islands	1987
Welterweight	vacant		
	Mark Breland	U.S.A.	Feb. '89
Junior welterweight	Juan Martin Coggi	Argentina	1987
Lightweight	Julio César Chávez	Mexico	1987
	vacant		
	Edwin Rosario	Puerto Rico	July '89
Junior lightweight	Brian Mitchell	South Africa	1986
Featherweight	Antonio Esparragoza	Venezuela	1987
Junior featherweight	Juan José Estrada	Mexico	1988
	Jesus Salud	U.S.A.	Dec. '89
Bantamweight	Moon Sung-kil	South Korea	1988
	Khaokor Galaxy	Thailand	July '89
	Luisito Espinosa	Philippines	Oct. '89
Junior bantamweight	Khaosai Galaxy	Thailand	1984
Flyweight	Fidel Bassa	Colombia	1987
	Jesus Rojas	Venezuela	Dec. '89
Junior flyweight	Myung-Woo Yuh	South Korea	1985
Minimumweight	Leo Gamez	Venezuela	1988
	vacant		
	Kim Bong-jun	South Korea	April '89

World Boxing Council

Division	Champion	Country	Date won
Heavyweight	Mike Tyson	U.S.A.	1986
Cruiserweight	vacant		
	Carlos de León	Puerto Rico	May '89
Light heavyweight	vacant		
	Dennis Andries	Great Britain	Feb. '89
	Jeff Harding	Australia	June '89
Super middleweight	Sugar Ray Leonard	U.S.A.	1988
Middleweight	Iran Barkley	U.S.A.	1988
	Roberto Durán	Panama	Feb. '89
Super welterweight	Donald Curry	U.S.A.	1988
	René Jacquot	France	Feb. '89
	John Mugabi	Uganda	July '89
Welterweight	Lloyd Honeyghan	Great Britain	1988
	Marlon Starling	U.S.A.	Feb. '89
Super lightweight	Roger Mayweather	U.S.A.	1987
	Julio César Chávez	Mexico	May '89
Lightweight	Julio César Chávez	Mexico	1988
	vacant		
	Pernell Whitaker	U.S.A.	Aug. '89
Super featherweight	Azumah Nelson	Ghana	1988
Featherweight	Jeff Fenech	Australia	1988
Super bantamweight	Daniel Zaragoza	Mexico	1988
Bantamweight	Raul Perez	Mexico	1988
Super flyweight	Gilberto Roman	Mexico	1988
	Nana Konadu	Ghana	Nov. '89
Flyweight	Kim Yong-gang	South Korea	1988
	Sot Chitalada	Thailand	June '89
Light flyweight	German Torres	Mexico	1988
	Lee Yol-woo	South Korea	March '89
	Humberto Gonzales	Mexico	June '89
Strawweight	Napa Kaitwanchai	Thailand	1988
	Choi Jeum-hwan	South Korea	Nov. '89

Brazil. The first direct presidential election in Brazil since 1960 drew a massive turnout on Nov. 15, 1989, of voters who faced a choice from among 22 candidates. As expected, none of the candidates won a majority, and a runoff between the top two vote-getters was required. In that election on December 17, Fernando Collor de Mello of the National Reconstruction Party defeated Luis Inácio Lula da Silva of the Workers Party to claim the presidency.

In the November 15 election, Collor, a center-right candidate, had led the field with 30 per cent of the vote. He had been the front-runner much of the year. Endowed with movie-star looks, Collor benefited greatly from the open backing of the Rêde Globo television network, which gave his campaign generous air time in a country where 94 per cent of the people regularly watch television.

In fact, television's influence was so powerful that when Silvio Santos, one of Brazil's most popular TV show hosts, announced his presidential candidacy in early November, he was immediately ranked by the polls ahead of Collor. Santos' campaign was short-lived, however. The Superior Electoral Tribunal declared him ineligible for the office on November 9 because Brazilian law prevents directors of state enterprises from running for the presidency. Santos held a directorship of a state concession—a television network.

The campaign. The December 17 runoff featured youthful candidates—in a country where 16-year-olds were able to vote for the first time and half of Brazil's 82 million voters were under 35 years of age. Collor was only 40 years old. His opponent, da Silva, was 44 years of age.

A former governor of the small and impoverished state of Alagoas, Collor campaigned on a platform of encouraging foreign investment to recharge Brazil's flagging economy. He also advocated foreign assistance to preserve the Amazon rain forest.

To attract TV coverage, Collor became a "hunter of maharajahs," a reference to civil servants who collect big paychecks for doing little. In so doing, he was able to capitalize on the popularity of a television series called "Savior of the Nation." This prime-time soap opera, avidly watched by some 50 million people, portrays the Brazilian Congress as a place where the nation's business takes a distant second to womanizing and putting friends and relatives on the federal payroll. Angry real-life lawmakers sought unsuccessfully to bar film crews from shooting footage for the show in their chambers.

Collor had little trouble in documenting the real-life excesses played up by the TV series. He revealed that a state legislator in Paraíba earned $99,888 per year—$10,000 more than a United States senator—in a state where the per-capita income is about $500 a year.

Bounced check. With inflation and speculation raging in Brazil's troubled economy, a $29-million bad check written to a brokerage firm by a prominent

Kaiapo Indians march in Altamira, Brazil, in February to protest the proposed construction of dams they say threaten the Amazon rain forest.

trader caused a crash on June 9 in the country's financial markets.

The bad check was written by Naji Roberto Nahas, a Brazilian who is known in the United States for his role in a scheme in the 1970's to corner the world's silver market. In 1986, Nahas agreed to pay a fine of $250,000 to settle charges stemming from the scheme, which also involved brothers Herbert, Lamar, and Nelson Bunker Hunt of Texas. The bounced check made the financial markets jittery, and the result was a 67 per cent drop in the value of stocks traded in Rio de Janeiro between June 9 and June 19 and a 61 per cent drop in the market index in São Paulo during the same period.

Violent crime became so commonplace in Rio de Janeiro, Brazil's second-largest city, in 1989 that only a record toll of 37 homicides in a day captured much attention. In a single month, 528 murders were reported in Rio, which has a population of more than 5 million, compared with a monthly average of about 166 homicides in New York City with a population of more than 7 million.

In May, a monument designed by famed architect Oscar Niemeyer was bombed only hours after it had been dedicated. The monument was a memorial to three steelworkers who were killed by soldiers during a strike in November 1988.   Nathan A. Haverstock

See also **Latin America** (Facts in brief table). In *World Book,* see **Brazil.**

British Columbia. The popularity of Premier William N. Vander Zalm showed a decline in 1989 when his Social Credit Party failed to win four seats in the Legislative Assembly in *by-elections* (special elections to fill vacant seats). The most serious defeat was on September 20 in the district of Cariboo where, after four visits by the premier and promises of large government expenditures, Social Credit lost a seat it had controlled since 1952. On the same day, Vander Zalm was forced to dismiss from his Cabinet a minister charged with misusing funds. On October 3, four Social Credit legislators resigned from the party caucus to sit in the Assembly as independents.

Public service unions, frustrated by government cost-cutting, took to the picket lines. In June 1989, nurses staged a 13-day strike that affected 80 of the province's 144 health facilities. Union members rejected a settlement in July, but on August 18 a mediator granted the 17,500 nurses a two-year contract with a wage increase of almost 21 per cent.

An 18-day strike by unionized fishing crews and shore workers, which started on July 21, threatened to ruin the province's important salmon fishery. But after the August settlement, the largest salmon run in 75 years brought an influx of fishing boats to the Fraser River and windfall profits to fishing crews and shore workers.   David M. L. Farr

In *World Book,* see **British Columbia.**
Brunei. See Asia.

Building and construction. The most closely watched construction project of 1989 was the English Channel tunnel, the first fixed link between Great Britain and France. The 31-mile (50-kilometer) tunnel, which will carry electric trains between Dover, England, and Calais, France, will be underwater for 23.5 miles (37.8 kilometers), making it the longest underwater tunnel in the world.

The project has been plagued by problems and delays. Early mechanical difficulties put tunneling behind schedule. Then, in October 1989, deep financial troubles appeared. Eurotunnel—an association of banks and construction companies that owns and operates the venture—revealed that it was short $1.6 billion in the funds needed to complete the work. Costs were believed to have escalated by more than $3.2 billion over the 1987 estimate of $7.8 billion. The funding gap left Eurotunnel in trouble because of a strict loan agreement with its lending banks. Still, work continued to progress toward the planned June 1993 completion date.

Notable achievements. In July 1989, workers topped out the 46,000-seat Florida Suncoast Dome, a multipurpose arena in St. Petersburg, Fla. The 688-foot (210-meter) dome, which spans an area of more than two football fields, is made from a web of steel cables and posts called a *cable truss,* which supports a fabric roof installed in huge wedge-shaped panels. Although the cable truss weighs just 8 pounds per square foot (39 kilograms per square meter), it is strong enough to support 60 short tons (54 metric tons) of audio equipment on a frame above a stage.

The 58-story building at Two Union Square in Seattle, which was completed in July, set a record for the highest-strength concrete ever used in a building. Its central services core is braced by steel-pipe columns filled with concrete that has a strength of 19,000 pounds per square inch (1,330 kilograms per square centimeter). That broke a concrete-strength record of 14,000 pounds per square inch (980 kilograms per square centimeter).

In Dallas, the Morton H. Meyerson Symphony Center opened in September. Famed Chinese-born architect I. M. Pei modeled the concert hall after the great old halls of Europe, with modifications to handle the greater variety of music performed today. Reverberation chambers up to 60 feet (18 meters) deep are arranged around the auditorium's upper level. Doors on the chambers can be moved to adjust the reverberation. The lobbies are enveloped in curving glass curtain walls that form geometric shapes.

The largest church in the world was completed in 1989. The Basilica of Our Lady of Peace in Ivory Coast's new capital city of Yamoussoukro seats 7,000 worshipers and accommodates another 11,000 standing. Its dome resembles the dome over St. Peter's in Rome, but is more than twice as large: 295 feet (90 meters) in diameter, rising 518 feet (158 meters) high. Some 1,500 workers—all African except for 36 European engineers and site supervisors—worked to ready the church for consecration by the pope early in 1990.

Disasters. Two major disasters affected buildings and construction late in 1989. Hurricane Hugo slammed into the Southeastern United States in September, and an earthquake hit the San Francisco Bay area in October. See **Disasters; Weather.**

The *swing span* (a part of a bridge that swings aside to allow ships to pass) of the Ben Sawyer Bridge in Charleston, S.C., was among the structures mangled by Hugo. The 246-foot (75-meter) span, which carries U.S. Route 17 over the Intracoastal Waterway between Mount Pleasant and Sullivan's Island, reportedly broke its restraints and pivoted two or three times before stopping, tilting toward the water at a 30-degree angle. An emergency contract was let to temporarily realign and then repair the span.

But Hugo's greatest effect on the construction industry may be as a test to South Carolina's Beachfront Management Act of 1988, which limits rebuilding on vulnerable oceanfront property. About 65 per cent of the buildings along a 120-mile (190-kilometer) stretch of shoreline were destroyed. Property owners, eager to rebuild, are challenging the law.

Damage estimates from Hugo mounted to more than $5½ billion in the United States alone. But the California earthquake took an even higher toll—more than $7 billion in property loss and scores of deaths. Most of the earthquake-caused deaths occurred when a 1-mile (1.6-kilometer) section of the upper deck of Interstate 880 in Oakland collapsed. A section of the upper deck of the San Francisco-Oakland Bay Bridge also fell, sending cars plummeting to the lower deck. Officials launched an investigation of the California Department of Transportation's program to strengthen its older structures against earthquakes.

Many buildings collapsed in Santa Cruz, and a bayside San Francisco residential area called the Marina was devastated, probably due to liquefaction of soft soil beneath it. Engineers were pleased to find, however, that many high-rise buildings rode out the quake successfully. Most of the buildings were designed to comply with building codes that required them to be resistant to seismic forces. But geologists predict much stronger earthquakes throughout California in the next 20 to 50 years.

Accidents and mistakes. A major construction accident occurred in August when an overpass crossing the Baltimore-Washington Parkway in Laurel, Md., collapsed as workers were pouring concrete. Nine workers and five motorists were hurt. Investigators began focusing on the design and construction of the structure's temporary supports.

A prominent building in Chicago will have its troubled face corrected, Amoco Corporation officials announced in March. Amoco will spend more than $60-million to replace the 43,000 Italian marble panels on its 80-story headquarters. The panels had been sagging, and stainless-steel straps were installed in 1988

Toronto's SkyDome stadium opened for its first baseball game in June 1989. Its retractable roof can be rolled into place in 20 minutes.

to keep them from crashing to the ground. Amoco engineers believe that the panels were too thin to withstand Chicago's extreme temperature variations.

Markets. New construction contract awards in the United States for the first nine months of 1989 (excluding residential work) reached $126.3 billion, down 1 per cent from the same period in 1988, according to construction economists at McGraw-Hill Incorporated, a leading source of construction-industry data. The heavy construction and highway sector signed $37.5-billion in new contracts during the first nine months of 1989, down 3 per cent from the same period in 1988. The sector showed gains in sewerage and waterworks contracts, but these were outweighed by losses in airport and utility work.

Contracts for nonresidential buildings totaled $69-billion in the first nine months of 1989, up 2 per cent from 1988. A downturn of 6 per cent in factory construction and 4 per cent in office buildings was balanced by growth in new contracts for stores, government buildings, educational facilities, hospitals, and medical centers.

A National Association of Home Builders report in September 1989 estimated single-family housing starts for the year at 1,005,000, down from 1,080,000 in 1988. The association estimated multifamily housing starts at 375,000, a decrease from 407,000 in 1988.   Janice Lyn Tuchman

In *World Book*, see **Building construction; Tunnel.**

Bulgaria

Bulgaria changed leaders and lost a tremendous number of its citizens in 1989. At a meeting of the Communist Party Central Committee on November 10, Todor Zhivkov resigned as general secretary of the party and chairman of the State Council, the top government post. Zhivkov, 78, had ruled since 1954.

Foreign Minister Petur T. Mladenov, 53, succeeded Zhivkov as party chief. On November 16, Mladenov removed three close allies of Zhivkov from the 10-member Politburo (the party's executive board) and dropped seven others from major positions in the party. The next day, the National Assembly (parliament), meeting for the first time since Zhivkov resigned, elected Mladenov chairman of the State Council. Zhivkov fell from power because he and his hardline associates had stubbornly refused to yield to mounting public pressure for the kind of drastic political and economic change that had already swept through much of Eastern Europe.

Crowd pressures regime. On November 18, about 50,000 people gathered in Sofia for a rally that was approved by the government but organized by dissident groups. A resolution drafted by the organizers included political demands such as freedom of the press, elimination of the secret police, access to police files on individuals, and release of political prisoners.

The Central Committee on December 8 fired 4 additional members of the Politburo, leaving the Politburo with only 3 of the 10 individuals who were members when Zhivkov was in power. The Central Committee also dismissed 28 others from leading positions in the party.

The National Assembly decided on December 14 that it could not repeal the Communist monopoly on power for another month. A crowd of up to 50,000 waiting outside the parliamentary building jeered and whistled when the decision was announced. On December 27, the Politburo agreed to open talks with opposition groups on Jan. 3, 1990.

Mass emigration. By late summer 1989, about one-third of Bulgaria's ethnic Turks—people of Turkish ancestry—had immigrated to Turkey. The human tide ended in August, when Turkey began to demand Turkish visas as a condition of entry, then closed its rail link with Bulgaria.

The ethnic Turks left mainly because in late 1984 Bulgaria had begun to carry out an old plan for their complete assimilation. The plan involved compulsory changes to Slavic names and curbs on Turkish schools, language, and religious practice.

The ethnic Turks had been forbidden to leave Bulgaria, but on May 23, 1989, Zhivkov called on Turkey to accept all "Bulgarian Muslims." What had been a trickle of illegal emigration became a flood of legal emigration. On December 29, the new government ended the assimilation program.   Eric Bourne

See also **Europe** (Facts in brief table). In *World Book,* see **Bulgaria.**

Burkina Faso. See Africa.

Burma. The civil unrest that began in 1988 continued in 1989. In 1988, rioters and demonstrators called for an end to the 26-year dictatorial rule of General Ne Win, who officially retired in July 1988. Burma continued to be racked by agitation, and the army seized power on Sept. 18, 1988, and created the ruling State Law-and-Order Restoration Council. The council promised to hold democratic elections in 1990, but a government journal said in June 1989 that the elections would be only one step toward ending military rule.

On June 21, 1989, soldiers fired on demonstrators commemorating the anniversary of the start of the agitation. This sparked more rallies against the regime. Many were led by Aung San Suu Kyi, head of the main opposition party, the National League for Democracy. Suu Kyi accused the council of blocking progress toward free elections and claimed that Ne Win controlled the council from behind the scenes.

On July 20, the government charged Suu Kyi and her party deputy with trying to "destroy the armed forces and revive anarchy." The two were put under house arrest. The government then granted a general amnesty, freeing 17,657 criminals—apparently to clear jail room for thousands of activists from the National League and other opposition political parties, who were rounded up. In October, courts began to give long prison sentences to some activists.

The United States Department of State said on September 13 that it had "credible, first-hand reports that instances of torture, beatings, and mistreatment are commonplace" for political prisoners in Burma and that "deaths have resulted." Burma's chief of intelligence then accused U.S. Ambassador Burton Levin—who had publicly sided with the regime's opponents—of supporting a right wing conspiracy.

Communist Party splinters. The army's main justification for its domination since 1962 was that the government was threatened by Communists. But in March and April 1989, members of the Communist Party of Burma—most of whom belong to ethnic minorities and live near the Chinese border—rebelled against their aging leaders. After the Communist leaders fled into China, the party splintered along ethnic lines. These factions became hardly distinguishable from Burma's many other minority ethnic groups, who for four decades had conducted occasional guerrilla warfare against domination by the Burmese majority.

Other developments. Burma's economy—which Ne Win's long rule reduced from moderate prosperity to virtual collapse—staggered badly in 1989. The annual inflation rate was estimated at 30 to 40 per cent.

Burma changed its name to the Union of Myanmar (pronounced *mee ahn MAH*) in June 1989. Officials also changed the name of Rangoon, the capital, to Yangon (pronounced *yahn KOH*).   Henry S. Bradsher

See also **Asia** (Facts in brief table). In *World Book,* see **Burma.**

Burundi. See Africa.

Bus. See Transit.

Bush, George Herbert Walker (1924-   ), took the oath as 41st President of the United States on Jan. 20, 1989. Declaring that "a new breeze is blowing," he promised to seek a "new engagement" with the Democratic-controlled Congress and to continue "the new closeness" with the Soviet Union.

Bush moved into the White House with a vague agenda and seemingly only one inflexible goal—to get through his first year with "no new taxes," a promise made many times during his 1988 campaign. Once in office, Bush showed caution, a willingness to compromise, and a knack for proposing broad new programs with only shoestring financing. By midsummer, he enjoyed approval ratings, as measured by national polls, that eclipsed those of his predecessor, Ronald Reagan.

Obviously, Bush did some things right. He was friendly and accessible and was actively engaged in the day-to-day affairs of government, which Reagan often seemed to avoid. Bush also tried to bring Republicans and Democrats together on issues and energetically wooed members of Congress. He reached agreement with Congress on the issue of aid to the *contra* guerrillas opposing Nicaragua's Sandinista government, and he won enactment of a plan to rescue the savings and loan industry (see **Bank**). The President made his boldest move in late December, when he sent units of the Army, Air Force, Navy, and Marines to Panama to oust the brutal regime of General Manuel Antonio Noriega Morena. That operation resulted in a new government for the Central American nation.

U.S.-Soviet relations. Bush's caution was most evident in his dealings with the Soviet Union and its venturesome leader, Mikhail S. Gorbachev. While the Soviet president made headlines with bold pronouncements, Bush remained silent for much of the year, excusing himself by citing a continuing review of U.S. foreign policy. Meanwhile, some of his key national security assistants, including Secretary of Defense Richard B. Cheney, expressed misgivings about Gorbachev's ability to retain power, fearing he might be succeeded by figures hostile to U.S. interests.

On May 12, Bush began making a series of foreign-policy talks that offered few surprises. Although he called for a new relationship with the Soviet Union, he suggested that Gorbachev's sincerity needed "testing."

Brussels summit meeting. The new Administration did not come to grips with East-West issues until confronted with a crisis that threatened to divide the allies of the North Atlantic Treaty Organization (NATO). Time was a major factor because Bush was to attend a late-May summit in Brussels, Belgium.

The dispute involved principally the United States and West Germany. The West German government, facing political pressures at home, was resisting the modernization of short-range U.S. nuclear missiles

With his wife, Barbara, looking on, President-elect Bush takes the oath of office from U.S. Chief Justice William H. Rehnquist on January 20.

Bush donned his old college baseball mitt to throw out the first ball in the Baltimore Orioles' opening-day game against the Boston Red Sox on April 3.

based in Germany and was urging Bush to negotiate with Gorbachev on removal of the weapons. Bush said he was willing to postpone modernization but would not consider removing the missiles or reducing their number, arguing that NATO—in that case—would have nothing with which to offset the big advantage in conventional military forces held by the Warsaw Pact nations of Eastern Europe.

Ironically, Gorbachev made another of his bold moves on May 23 that gave Bush the opportunity to resolve his dispute with the West Germans. To the surprise of many, Gorbachev embraced a March NATO proposal to establish parity in weapons and troops between its forces and those of the Warsaw Pact. Gorbachev accepted the exact NATO proposals for reductions of tanks and suggested that each side be limited to 1 million troops.

Against this backdrop, Bush developed a policy that he unveiled in Brussels on May 29. He called for a ceiling of 275,000 on troops stationed in Europe by each of the two superpowers, and he further proposed that talks on cutbacks in conventional arms and forces be completed within 6 to 12 months. To the West Germans, Bush said the negotiations would embrace a "partial" reduction of short-range nuclear missiles—enough to end his argument with Bonn.

Bush was back in Europe for 10 days in July, attending an economic summit in Paris and visiting Poland and Hungary, where the forces of Communism

appeared to be in full retreat. Because of budget restraints at home, he offered Poland's new non-Communist government only $115 million in aid—a sum that many in Congress, including Republicans, derided as too little. Bush said three months later that he would seek an extra $200 million.

The Malta summit. Bush met with Gorbachev at shipboard talks in early December at the island nation of Malta in the Mediterranean Sea. Although they reached no formal agreements, they said the United States and the Soviet Union were embarked on a new era of cooperation. They expressed hope that a U.S.-Soviet arms treaty greatly reducing the number of long-range nuclear missiles in the two superpowers' arsenals would be signed in 1990, and they said they would work to cut conventional forces in Europe.

Hostage crisis. The captors of American hostages in Lebanon announced that they had hanged one of them on July 31, 1989, in retaliation for Israel's kidnapping in southern Lebanon of Sheik Abdul-Karim Obeid, a reputed terrorist leader. The murdered hostage was Marine Lieutenant Colonel William R. Higgins, assigned to United Nations forces in Lebanon. The hostage-takers threatened to hang a second American, Joseph J. Cicippio, if Israel did not free its prisoner. Bush responded by moving U.S. naval vessels to the eastern Mediterranean. Faced with the possibility of armed retaliation, Cicippio's captors spared his life, and, for a time, negotiators made attempts to arrange a broad exchange of Mideast hostages and prisoners, but nothing came of those efforts.

Invasion of Panama. On December 20, Bush ordered military action in Panama to overthrow Manuel Noriega and—he said—to protect the lives of the approximately 35,000 Americans living there. At least 12,000 U.S. military personnel were already stationed in Panama. To those, Bush sent reinforcements of about 12,000, including 3,100 paratroopers. Noriega eluded capture for two weeks but finally surrendered on Jan. 3, 1990. He was flown to the United States to face drug-trafficking charges.

Although most Americans seemed supportive of the operation, many, including some members of Congress, asked why Bush had not acted as decisively in October 1989 when a group of Panamanian military officers tried to oust Noriega. During that uprising, Noriega was held briefly by the rebels and could have been taken into U.S. custody. See **Panama.**

In contrast with Panama, another Central American trouble spot—Nicaragua—caused Bush few problems in 1989. In March, he made a bargain with Congress regarding the Nicaraguan contras. He agreed not to seek a resumption of military aid to the contras until at least February 1990, the month for which the Sandinistas had scheduled free elections. The accord gave four congressional committees power of approval over humanitarian aid to the rebels.

Bush and China. Bush was criticized following the June 4 massacre of Chinese prodemocracy students in

On a visit to China in February, the President waves to crowds outside the entrance to the Forbidden City in Beijing's Tiananmen Square.

Beijing's Tiananmen Square. Even many Republicans faulted Bush for showing a lack of emotion in condemning the killings and for not imposing strict economic sanctions against the Chinese government.

In early December, two senior Administration officials, National Security Adviser Brent Scowcroft and Deputy Secretary of State Lawrence S. Eagleburger, made a secretive trip to Beijing, supposedly to brief Chinese leaders on the Malta summit. After they returned, the White House said it might authorize the sale of three communications satellites to China. Congressional Democrats protested the trip loudly. On December 18, the White House admitted that Scowcroft and Eagleburger also visited Beijing in July, just about a month after the brutal crackdown.

Personal finances, health. On April 12, Bush and his wife, Barbara, revealed that they paid $62,106 in federal income taxes on a 1988 income of $287,171. They contributed $12,468 to charity.

Also on April 12, Mrs. Bush was treated at Washington, D.C.'s Walter Reed Army Medical Center for Graves' disease, a thyroid disorder that causes weight loss and eye irritation. The President had a checkup in May and was pronounced "in extremely sound physical condition."   Frank Cormier and Margot Cormier

See also **Cabinet, United States; Congress of the United States; United States, Government of the.** In *World Book,* see **Bush, George Herbert Walker.**
Business. See **Bank; Economics; Manufacturing.**

Cabinet, United States. On March 9, 1989, the Senate voted 53 to 47 to reject former Senator John G. Tower (R., Tex.) as secretary of defense. Tower, who had been accused of drinking, sexual misconduct, and conflicts of interest, was the first Cabinet nominee to be denied Senate confirmation since 1959.

On March 10, President George Bush named Representative Richard B. Cheney (R., Wyo.) as his new nominee for the defense post. Cheney was confirmed by a vote of 92 to 0 on March 17. By that time, the Senate had given overwhelming approval to all the other Cabinet appointees named by Bush in 1988. They were Edward J. Derwinski (veterans affairs); Elizabeth H. Dole (labor); Jack F. Kemp (housing and urban development); Manuel Lujan, Jr. (interior); Robert A. Mosbacher (commerce); Samuel K. Skinner (transportation); Louis W. Sullivan (health and human services); and Clayton K. Yeutter (agriculture).

Tower vote a rebuff to Bush. The Senate's rejection of Tower was a personal defeat for Bush, who had lobbied hard for the four-term senator. The final vote was highly partisan. Fifty-two Democrats and 1 Republican voted against Tower, while 44 Republicans and 3 Democrats voted for him.

Tower himself labored to win the favor of the Senate. Although he asserted that he had "never been an alcoholic or dependent on alcohol," he made an unusual public pledge that if he were confirmed he would refrain from drinking for his entire term as sec-

California

retary. Tower was also accused of "womanizing," but little clear-cut testimony was presented at the confirmation hearings about that aspect of Tower's behavior. With regard to the conflict-of-interest charges, Tower promised that his past work as a consultant to several weapons contractors would not influence his performance as secretary of defense.

Other appointments. President Bush on January 12 named William J. Bennett, secretary of education from 1985 to 1988 in the Administration of President Ronald Reagan, to head his antidrug program. Later in the month, the President announced that Bennett would not be a member of the Cabinet. Bush said that decision resulted from his desire to limit the size of the Cabinet and did not diminish Bennett's role.

Bennett, who was confirmed by a vote of 97 to 2 on March 8, heads the Office of National Drug Control Policy, established by Congress in 1988 as part of major antidrug legislation. The bill stipulated that the so-called drug czar would have Cabinet rank. Bush's failure to abide by that provision prompted criticism from some members of Congress, who questioned the President's commitment to the drug war.

Also on January 12, Bush named James D. Watkins, a retired Navy admiral, as secretary of energy. He was confirmed, 99 to 0, on March 1.   David L. Dreier

See also biographies of the various Cabinet members. In *World Book,* see **Cabinet.**

California. See **Los Angeles; State government.**

Cambodia plunged into civil war in September 1989 after Vietnam announced that it had withdrawn all its troops stationed there. (On April 30, the nation resumed use of the name Cambodia after calling itself Kampuchea for several years.)

The Vietnamese had invaded Cambodia in late 1978 to end the rule of the Khmer Rouge, whose Communist regime killed more than 1 million Cambodians in a reign of terror that began in 1975. The Vietnamese installed a new Communist government, which in 1989 was headed by a former Khmer Rouge official, Prime Minister Hun Sen. The Vietnamese withdrawal followed unsuccessful international efforts to negotiate a political end to fighting between Hun Sen's regime and a coalition headed by Norodom Sihanouk. Sihanouk's loose coalition included the Khmer Rouge and two non-Communist guerrilla organizations.

A meeting of all sides in Jakarta, Indonesia, from February 16 through 21 failed to arrange a settlement because of a disagreement over how to hold elections. On April 5, Vietnam—which had vowed to withdraw from Cambodia by the end of 1990—moved up the date for the pullout to stimulate the factions to work out a settlement. Sihanouk met Hun Sen in Paris on July 24 but found no compromise. A conference including the Cambodian factions, 19 other nations, and the United Nations secretary-general then met in Paris from July 30 to August 30. It too failed to find a solution and was suspended.

Vietnamese troops—who had occupied Cambodia since 1978—leave the nation during a pullout said to be completed by the end of September.

The lack of a political settlement spurred several nations to refuse to undertake international supervision of the Vietnamese withdrawal. Without such supervision, observers found it difficult to make an accurate estimate of the extent of the pullout.

Vietnam said that the last 26,000 troops of an occupation force that had once numbered 200,000 had left Cambodia by September 26. But Son Sann, leader of a non-Communist faction, claimed that Vietnam left 30,000 soldiers concealed in Hun Sen's army, and that 100,000 armed Vietnamese lived as civilians in Cambodia.

Civil war. With the Vietnamese apparently gone and no political settlement in sight, the Khmer Rouge and the non-Communist guerrillas launched separate offensives against Hun Sen's forces. A Vietnamese general estimated that the Khmer Rouge guerrillas in Cambodia numbered 17,000 and that at least 10,000 more guerrillas—8,000 of them Sihanouk's troops— were fighting the Cambodian regime. By late October, the Khmer Rouge were reported to have taken a western district capital, Pailin. On December 10, a Cambodian editor said Hun Sen was considering dismantling his Cabinet and allowing the United Nations to supervise national elections in which the Khmer Rouge would play a part.   Henry S. Bradsher

See also **Asia** (Facts in brief table). In *World Book,* see **Kampuchea.**

Cameroon. See **Africa.**

Canada. Prime Minister Brian Mulroney's Progressive Conservative (PC) government, reelected in November 1988, saw only a slight reduction in its majority in the House of Commons during 1989. A judicial recount turned an Ontario seat over to the Liberals in January. In March, a special election to fill a vacancy caused by the death of a PC member in Alberta was won by a member of the Reform Party. This new party expressed Western Canada's dissatisfaction with national economic and linguistic policies, which it claimed favored Central Canada. In May, a PC member resigned his seat after being convicted of fraud. And a Liberal member from Quebec died in November.

These changes left the 295-seat Commons with 167 PC members and 82 Liberals. The New Democratic Party (NDP) held 43 seats, and the Reform Party held 1. Two seats were vacant.

The leaders of the two principal opposition parties both resigned in 1989. John N. Turner, chosen in 1984 to lead the Liberals, had suffered two election defeats by Mulroney. In May, Turner announced his retirement from politics, to be effective at an undisclosed time before the selection of a new leader in June 1990. Edward Broadbent, who had led the NDP since 1975, resigned his post in March. His party seemed frozen in popular support, which had hovered around 20 per cent for many years. Broadbent's successor, Audrey McLaughlin, was chosen at a December convention as the first woman leader of a major party.

Sweeping tax changes dominated political discussion in 1989. The changes, outlined by the Mulroney government in 1987, included a reduction in personal income taxes and the introduction of a retail sales tax on a wide range of goods and services. The income tax changes, which reduced the number of levels of tax, were approved in 1988 and took effect on Jan. 1, 1989. The proposed sales tax was delayed to enable the federal government to hammer out an agreement with the 10 provinces on the form of a national sales tax. The new tax would combine existing provincial sales taxes with a long-established federal tax on manufactured products.

Discussions on the sales tax ended in April when a meeting between federal Finance Minister Michael H. Wilson and his provincial counterparts broke up without agreement. The primary problem was the great variation in existing provincial tax rates; these ranged from no sales tax at all in Alberta to 12 per cent in Newfoundland. The provinces, confined by the constitution to raise revenue only through direct taxation, resented the federal government's entrance into this area. The federal authority, under the constitution, has unlimited taxing power.

Wilson announced in the House of Commons on April 24 that the federal government had broken off discussions with the provinces and would establish a national sales tax on its own. He provided details of the new tax in his budget message three days later.

Canadian Prime Minister Brian Mulroney and United States President George Bush met in Canada in February 1989 to discuss acid rain.

Federal spending in Canada

Estimated budget for fiscal 1989-1990*

Ministry (includes the department and all agencies for which a minister reports to Parliament): **Millions of dollars†**

Agriculture	2,371
Atlantic Canada Opportunities Agency	379
Communications	
Canadian Broadcasting Corporation	965
Canadian Film Development Corporation	146
Other	704
Consumer and corporate affairs	183
Employment and immigration	4,963
Energy, mines, and resources	
Atomic Energy of Canada Limited	126
Other	1,238
Environment	871
External affairs	3,308
Finance	47,067
Fisheries and oceans	720
Forestry	207
Governor general	9
Indian affairs and Northern development	3,339
Industry, science, and technology	
Canada Post Corporation	185
Regional industrial expansion	1,197
Other	1,237
Justice	582
Labour	218
National defence	11,359
National health and welfare	32,117
National revenue	1,478
Parliament	258
Privy Council	94
Public works	
Canada Mortgage and Housing Corporation	1,800
Other	1,288
Secretary of state	3,759
Solicitor general	
Royal Canadian Mounted Police	1,056
Other	1,046
Supply and services	598
Transport	3,098
Treasury Board	1,001
Veterans affairs	1,712
Western economic diversification	287
Total	**130,966**

*April 1, 1989, to March 31, 1990.
†Canadian dollars; $1= 85 U.S cents as of Dec. 1, 1989.

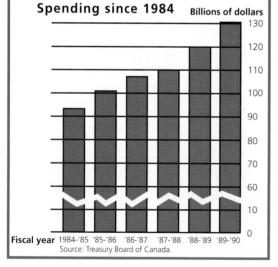

Spending since 1984   Billions of dollars

Fiscal year 1984-'85 '85-'86 '86-'87 '87-'88 '88-'89 '89-'90
Source: Treasury Board of Canada.

The proposed goods and services tax (GST)—a value-added tax similar to that used in England, New Zealand, and a number of other countries—would be imposed at every stage of production. Wilson announced a rate of 9 per cent for the new tax but promised that it would not be collected on basic groceries or prescription drugs and medical devices. Services such as rent, health and dental services, day care, legal aid, and education would also be tax-exempt.

Motions to implement the GST, introduced in the House of Commons on September 25, brought a barrage of criticism. Opponents claimed the tax would have an immediate inflationary impact on the economy, perhaps raising prices by 2 or 3 per cent. They also argued that it would impose an impossible burden on small businesses, which would have to cope with the collection of separate federal and provincial taxes, and that it would require a large number of officials to handle collection. Finally, critics charged, a tax on consumption would lay a heavy burden on poor people.

In succeeding months—as an all-party parliamentary committee toured the country soliciting views on the GST—the government pressed ahead with plans for the new tax. It argued that the GST was essential for sound financial management and the maintenance of vital public services, that it would improve Canada's economic output, and that it would help relieve the country's public debt. And in December, Wilson countered some criticisms by announcing measures that would reduce the GST's rate to 7 per cent.

Unemployment insurance. Another important measure on the government's economic agenda was a bill to revise the unemployment insurance system. The new system, proposed in April 1989, would reallocate about $1.3 billion Canadian ($1.1 billion U.S.)—10 per cent of the total budget for unemployment benefits—to such programs as job training and parental leave. Overall, benefits would be harder to obtain and harder to keep, though a sliding scale would provide a longer period of benefits in areas with a high jobless rate. The changes were passed to the Senate for approval in December. The government hoped to implement the changes early in 1990.

The budget. Finance Minister Wilson's budget was released in a swirl of controversy on April 26, 1989. The budget was scheduled to be presented in Parliament on April 27, but a summary of the document was leaked to an Ottawa television station, which broadcast it a day early. Wilson immediately called a late-night press conference to announce the main points of the budget.

Although there was no evidence that anyone had profited from the budget leak, the opposition parties demanded that Wilson take responsibility for the breach of secrecy and resign his post. When the minister read the full budget to the Commons the next day, opposition members left the chamber in protest. Investigation of the leak later led to charges against five

A taxi driver protests the government's proposed goods and services tax (GST) in an October 1989 demonstration in Ottawa, Canada.

men for possession of stolen goods and theft from the government printing plant.

The furor diverted attention from important changes in both the revenue and expenditure sides of the budget. Tax increases and spending cuts were prompted by Wilson's concern over the growing public debt, which reached $320 billion Canadian ($269-billion U.S.) on April 1. Interest charges on this debt stand as the government's largest single expenditure, costing more than health care, family allowances, old age security, and social assistance programs combined. Wilson promised to cut $5 billion ($4.2 billion U.S.) from the growth expected in the deficit for 1989-1990. About two-thirds of this reduction was to be achieved by raising taxes, with the remainder to come from cuts in government spending.

The manufacturers' sales tax (to be eliminated when the GST comes into effect) was raised from 12 to 13.5 per cent on a wide range of manufactured goods. Income taxes for large companies and high-income individuals were increased. The government withdrew all payments for unemployment insurance, leaving employees and employers to bear all costs in higher premiums. The budget also took an unprecedented step to modify the principle of universality in Canada's social security programs (which decrees that all Canadians are entitled to the same benefits): High-income earners receiving family allowances and old age pensions were to repay them in a new tax.

The most spectacular reduction in spending was Wilson's announcement that a plan to build a fleet of nuclear-powered submarines would not be carried forward. Plans for other new defense equipment—long-range patrol aircraft and tanks and other tracked vehicles—were either postponed or scaled down. Fourteen military bases were to be closed or reduced in operation.

Official development assistance (foreign aid) was to be reduced, as were transfers of funds to the provinces for postsecondary education and health care. Federal financial support for more child-care capability, announced in 1987, was postponed indefinitely. But tax assistance was to be provided for 1.4 million families with preschool children. For fiscal year 1989-1990, the government expected revenues of $112.4-billion ($94.4 billion U.S.) and expenditures of $142.9-billion ($120 billion U.S.) , leaving a deficit of $30.5-billion ($25.6 billion U.S.).

Rail cutback. In October 1989, the Mulroney government announced a massive cutback in passenger railroad services across the country provided by the heavily subsidized Via Rail. The cuts were forced by a budget provision to reduce the government's railway subsidy by $500 million ($420 million U.S.) over the next five years.

Beginning in January 1990, 18 of 38 railway lines would be eliminated, resulting in the loss of 4 million passengers, or 60 per cent of the current ridership. It was possible that some of the lines affected by the cutbacks—such as the scenic route through the Canadian Rockies, which was destined to be reduced to one train a week during the summer only—would be augmented by private operations.

Constitutional accord. Looming in the background of the legislative program was an important constitutional problem: the ratification of the Meech Lake Accord. The agreement, fashioned by Prime Minister Mulroney and the 10 provincial premiers in June 1987 at Meech Lake, north of Ottawa, was designed to bring Quebec under the provisions of Canada's 1982 constitution. Quebec had originally rejected the constitution, fearing that it would not protect the province's French-Canadian character. To take effect, the Meech Lake Accord must be approved by the federal Parliament and the legislatures of all 10 provinces by June 1990.

As 1989 began, only Manitoba and New Brunswick had failed to pass supporting legislation. They referred the Meech Lake document to legislative committees, each of which submitted reports in late October recommending changes. In addition, Newfoundland, whose PC government was replaced by a Liberal one in May, began voicing second thoughts about Meech Lake. Quebec maintained that any changes in the accord would destroy it. The fate of the accord, and the consequences of rejection for federal-provincial relations in Canada, were undecided as the year ended.

The Ministry of Canada*

Brian Mulroney—prime minister
Charles Joseph Clark—secretary of state for external affairs
John Carnell Crosbie—minister for international trade
Donald Frank Mazankowski—deputy prime minister; president of the Queen's Privy Council for Canada; minister of agriculture
Elmer MacIntosh MacKay—minister of public works; minister for the purposes of the Atlantic Canada Opportunities Agency Act
Arthur Jacob Epp—minister of energy, mines, and resources
Robert R. de Cotret—president of the Treasury Board
Henry Perrin Beatty—minister of national health and welfare
Michael Holcombe Wilson—minister of finance
Harvie Andre—minister of regional industrial expansion; minister of state for science and technology; acting minister of consumer and corporate affairs
Otto John Jelinek—minister of national revenue
Thomas Edward Siddon—minister of fisheries and oceans
Charles James Mayer—minister of state (grains and oilseeds); minister of Western economic diversification
William Hunter McKnight—minister of national defence
Benoît Bouchard—minister of transport
Marcel Masse—minister of communications
Barbara Jean McDougall—minister of employment and immigration
Gerald Stairs Merrithew—minister of veterans affairs
Monique Vézina—minister of state (employment and immigration); minister of state (seniors)
Frank Oberle—minister of state (forestry)
Lowell Murray—leader of the government in the Senate; minister of state (federal-provincial relations)
Paul Wyatt Dick—minister of supply and services
Pierre H. Cadieux—minister of Indian affairs and Northern development
Jean J. Charest—minister of state (youth); minister of state (fitness and amateur sport); deputy leader of the government in the House of Commons
Thomas Hockin—minister of state (small businesses and tourism)
Monique Landry—minister for external relations
Gerry Weiner—minister of state (multiculturalism and citizenship); secretary of state of Canada
Douglas Grinslade Lewis—minister of justice and attorney general of Canada; leader of the government in the House of Commons
Pierre Blais—minister of state (agriculture); solicitor general of Canada
Lucien Bouchard—minister of the environment
John Horton McDermid—minister of state (privatization and regulatory affairs)
Shirley Martin—minister of state (transport)
Kim Campbell—minister of state (Indian affairs and Northern development)
Mary Collins—associate minister of national defence
Jean Corbeil—minister of labour
Gilles Loiselle—minister of state (finance)
Alan Redway—minister of state (housing)
William Charles Winegard—minister of state (science and technology)
*As of Dec. 31, 1989.

Premiers of Canadian provinces

Province	Premier
Alberta	Donald R. Getty
British Columbia	William N. Vander Zalm
Manitoba	Gary A. Filmon
New Brunswick	Frank J. McKenna
Newfoundland	Clyde K. Wells
Nova Scotia	John Buchanan
Ontario	David Peterson
Prince Edward Island	Joseph A. Ghiz
Quebec	Robert Bourassa
Saskatchewan	Grant Devine

Government leaders of territories

Northwest Territories	Nick Sibbeston
Yukon Territory	Tony Penikett

Cabinet changes. Mulroney shuffled his cabinet on January 30, paring it from 40 to 39 members and replacing 6 ministers who had lost their seats in the November 1988 election. Nineteen ministers exchanged portfolios. The most powerful members of the cabinet were left untouched: Charles Joseph (Joe) Clark in external affairs, Wilson in finance, John C. Crosbie in international trade, and Barbara J. McDougall in employment and immigration. Donald F. Mazankowski remained as deputy prime minister and was also made responsible for agriculture.

Ramon J. Hnatyshyn, a former minister from Saskatchewan who was defeated in the 1988 election, was appointed governor general, representing Canada's head of state, Queen Elizabeth II. He was to take office early in 1990, succeeding Jeanne M. Sauvé.

The economy. Canada's economic growth slackened during 1989. Sales abroad were sluggish, and October brought Canada's first merchandise trade deficit in 13$\frac{1}{2}$ years. The setback stemmed from a rise in the value of the Canadian dollar, which climbed to U.S. 86 cents in December. The real gross domestic product (GDP)—the total value, adjusted for inflation, of all goods and services produced within the country—rose only 1.3 per cent in the second quarter, giving a seasonally adjusted annual rate of $643.7 billion ($540.7 billion U.S.). The summer months saw employment growth, but the number of jobs decreased in September. In November, unemployment stood at 7.6 per cent.

The consumer price index, which had shown a worrying rise earlier in the year, subsided to a moderate 5.2 per cent in November. The Bank of Canada maintained high interest rates in order to restrain inflation, though its actions came under sharp attack from the provinces and consumer groups. The bank's rate, which fixes terms for commercial borrowing, dropped only slightly, from a high of 12.62 per cent in May to 12.44 per cent in December.

Mass murder. The worst mass murder in Canada's history occurred on Dec. 6, 1989, when a lone gunman killed 14 women, mostly students, at the engineering school of the University of Montreal. He also injured 13 other students before killing himself.

The gunman, 25-year-old Marc Lepine, separated women from men in classrooms and hallways before shooting the women with a high-powered hunting rifle. He left a letter stating that he had committed the acts to oppose feminism.

Fish fights. One fishing dispute moved toward settlement in 1989, while another continued to arouse strong feeling on Canada's Atlantic Coast. The first concerned France's territorial claims around its tiny island possessions St.-Pierre and Miquelon, which lie near the southern coast of Newfoundland. The rich fishing waters are used by both French and Canadian fishing crews. On March 31, the government announced that the long-standing disagreement would be sent to arbitration by an international tribunal.

In return for agreeing to arbitration on the issue, France was given greater access to cod in the disputed waters while the arbitration was underway. This concession was fiercely protested by the government of Newfoundland and by fish companies and workers in the province, who insisted that it would add to the problem of overfishing in Canada's Atlantic waters.

Overfishing was the basis of a dispute with members of the European Community over the amount of cod taken from the waters beyond Canada's exclusive fishing zone, which extends 200 nautical miles (370 kilometers) from Canada's shore. Fishing by foreign fleets—mostly Spanish and Portuguese—was alleged by Canada to have seriously depleted inshore stocks.

In response to scientific studies, Canada cut its own quotas for cod by 12 per cent for 1989. The cut would be borne by Canadian offshore trawlers, leaving inshore fishing crews free to continue their traditional occupation. Countries of the European Community, however, refused in September to accept restrictions—applying beyond Canada's economic zone—proposed by the Northwest Atlantic Fisheries Organization, an international body representing fishing nations. Canada planned to appeal directly to European goverments through diplomatic channels, telling them that the North Atlantic resources were being critically depleted.

International relations. Prime Minister Mulroney attended the economic summit of the leading industrial powers in Paris in July 1989. In late October, he met in Kuala Lumpur, Malaysia, with the other 48 heads of government of the Commonwealth countries. (The Commonwealth is an association that includes Great Britain plus Canada and other nations that were once British colonies.) He joined the other leaders in agreeing that economic pressure should be intensified toward South Africa until that country begins to dismantle *apartheid* (racial segregation). Mulroney clashed with Prime Minister Margaret Thatcher of Britain, who took the view that economic sanctions were not capable of moving South Africa but would only cause hardship for the country's majority black population.

Mulroney and United States President George Bush met several times to discuss environmental and trade matters. Bush flew to Ottawa on February 10—his first trip to a foreign country as President—for four hours of discussion with the Canadian prime minister. The two met again on May 3 when Mulroney was in Washington, D.C., to open a new Canadian Embassy. Mulroney pressed for a Canada-U.S. treaty setting out objectives in the campaign to reduce environmentally dangerous acid rain. He urged Bush to accept the goal of a 50 per cent reduction in trans-border acid rain pollution by 1994. Bush refrained from a commitment, saying he first wanted to see his Administration's legislation on acid rain through Congress.

At an October meeting of foreign ministers in Costa Rica, Canada announced that it would join the Organ-

Canada, provinces, and territories population estimates

	1989
Alberta	2,429,200
British Columbia	3,055,600
Manitoba	1,084,200
New Brunswick	718,500
Newfoundland	570,000
Northwest Territories	53,400
Nova Scotia	886,800
Ontario	9,569,500
Prince Edward Island	130,200
Quebec	6,688,700
Saskatchewan	1,007,000
Yukon Territory	25,400
Canada	**26,218,500**

City and metropolitan population estimates

	Metropolitan area 1987 estimate	City 1986 census
Toronto, Ont.	3,501,600	612,289
Montreal, Que.	2,942,700	1,015,420
Vancouver, B.C.	1,412,700	431,147
Ottawa-Hull	833,100	
Ottawa, Ont.		300,763
Hull, Ont.		58,722
Edmonton, Alta.	788,400	573,982
Calgary, Alta.	677,400	636,104
Winnipeg, Man.	631,100	594,551
Quebec, Que.	607,400	164,580
Hamilton, Ont.	566,900	306,728
London, Ont.	347,500	269,140
St. Catharines-Niagara	346,900	
St. Catharines, Ont.		123,455
Niagara Falls, Ont.		72,107
Kitchener, Ont.	316,900	150,604
Halifax, N.S.	300,000	113,577
Victoria, B.C.	260,400	66,303
Windsor, Ont.	256,700	193,111
Oshawa, Ont.	210,400	123,651
Saskatoon, Sask.	204,000	177,641
Regina, Sask.	189,400	175,064
St. John's, Nfld.	162,200	96,216
Chicoutimi-Jonquière	159,800	
Chicoutimi, Que.		61,083
Jonquière, Que.		58,467
Sudbury, Ont.	147,500	88,717
Sherbrooke, Ont.	132,200	74,438
Trois-Rivières, Que.	130,600	50,122
Thunder Bay, Ont.	123,100	112,272
Saint John, N.B.	122,000	76,381

ization of American States, a regional organization of 32 nations in the Western Hemisphere. Canada had long hesitated over membership, which had been seen as exposing Canada to pressures from the United States or Latin-American countries that might limit Canada's diplomatic freedom.

Facts in brief. Population: 26,218,500. Government: Governor General Jeanne M. Sauvé; Prime Minister Brian Mulroney. Monetary unit: dollar. Value of foreign trade: exports, $121,462,342,000; imports, $116,238,614,000.   David M. L. Farr

See also the Canadian provinces articles; **Canadian literature; McLachlin, Beverley M.; Montreal; Mulroney, Brian; Sauvé, Jeanne M.; Toronto; Wells, Clyde K.** In *World Book,* see **Canada.**

Canadian literature. Despite the almost 6,000 Canadian books published in 1989, fears persisted about foreign domination of the Canadian book industry. Most publishing firms operating in Canada were Canadian-controlled; only about 15 per cent were foreign-controlled firms. But the profit picture greatly favored the latter: More than three-fourths of the revenue from English-language books sold in Canada went to foreign interests.

Fiction. The year 1989 marked the return of Mordecai Richler, after a 10-year absence, with *Solomon Gursky Was Here*, an ambitious novel that ranges over one man's several lives. Sandra Birdsell's *The Missing Child*, perhaps the finest first novel of the year, explored the power of traumatic childhood memories to shape the present. Memory's tricks were also the theme of Janette Turner Hospital's *Charades*, her most sophisticated novel to date.

Eric McCormack's *The Paradise Motel*, another first novel, was inspired by one of the author's macabre short stories. And several poets turned to fiction: Paulette Jiles wrote *Song to the Rising Sun*, and Marilyn Bowering offered *To All Appearances a Lady*.

The family and human relationships were the focus of four novels: Jane Rule's *After the Fire*, Joan Barfoot's *Family News*, Guy Vanderhaeghe's *Homesick*, and Michel Tremblay's *The Heart Laid Bare*. Other notable novels included Heather Robertson's *Igor: A Novel of Intrigue*, the third in a trilogy that portrayed in fiction the life of former Prime Minister Mackenzie King; Antonine Maillet's *On the Eighth Day*; H. R. Percy's *An Innocent Bystander*; Bharati Mukherjee's *Jasmine*; and Susan Swan's *The Last of the Golden Girls*.

Canadian authors continued to favor the short story. *The Orange Fish*, by Carol Shields, depicted ordinary characters locked in an extraordinary game of survival. Cynthia Holz, an expatriate from the United States, made her debut with an impressive short-story collection called *Home Again*. W. O. Mitchell's *According to Jake and the Kid* was inspired by a celebrated Canadian radio series written in the 1950's by the colorful prairie author. Among other short-story collections were W. P. Kinsella's *The Miss Hobbema Pageant*, Dorothy Livesay's *The Glass House and Other Stories*, and Katherine Govier's *Before and After*.

Biographies and memoirs. Among prominent biographies were Philip Marchand's *Marshall McLuhan: The Medium and the Messenger*, which examined the life of the world's leading analyst of communication and culture; Roy MacGregor's *Chief: The Fearless Vision of Billy Diamond*, about the colorful Cree Indian politician and entrepreneur; and John Ayre's *Northrop Frye: A Biography*, about the Canadian literary scholar. Joan Givner's *Mazo de la Roche: The Hidden Life* chronicled the life of a renowned but intensely private author of the 1920's and 1930's who invented details of her past.

Much anticipated but generating mixed reviews was the posthumous publication of *Dance on the Earth*, the memoirs of author Margaret Laurence. A companion to that volume was Don Bailey's *Memories of Margaret: My Friendship with Margaret Laurence*.

Among the best memoirs of the year were *Wordstruck*, in which broadcaster Robert MacNeil described growing up in Nova Scotia, and R. A. D. Ford's *Our Man in Moscow: A Diplomat's Reflection on the Soviet Union*. Ford, who is also a poet, served 21 years as a Canadian diplomat in the Soviet Union.

Essays and criticism. In *Metropolitan Mutations: The Architecture of Emerging Public Spaces*, edited by Detlef Mertins, architects and urban planners assessed the creative and not-so-creative use of space in Canadian cities. One of the richest collections of essays was Rudy Wiebe's *Playing Dead: A Contemplation Concerning the Arctic*, which argued that Canadians should look to the North for their true identity, and not to the sunny South.

History and politics. With *The House Is Not a Home*, former Deputy Prime Minister Erik Nielsen caused a national stir when he heaped abuse on his Progressive Conservative colleagues. On a similar theme was Stevie Cameron's *Ottawa Inside Out: Power, Prestige and Scandal in the Nation's Capital*.

John English's *Shadow of Heaven: The Life of Lester Pearson, Volume 1, 1897-1948* profiled the life of the former prime minister. Cameron Smith's *Unfinished Journey: The Lewis Family* charted the history of a prominent family in Canadian politics. Harold Horwood's *Joey: The Life and Political Times of Joey Smallwood* told the story of the premier who brought Newfoundland into Canada's confederation.

The year 1989 was the 75th anniversary of the outbreak of World War I and the 50th anniversary of the beginning of World War II. J. L. Granatstein and Desmond Morton reconsidered Canada's role in those wars in two books: *Marching to Armageddon: Canadians and the Great War, 1914-1919*, and *A Nation Forged in Fire: Canadians and the Second World War, 1939-1945*. James Bacque claimed in his controversial book *Other Losses* that hundreds of thousands of German prisoners died in postwar prison camps due to neglect by their American and French captors. George Woodcock, one of Canada's most prolific authors, took a personal look at Canadian history in the 1800's in *The Century That Made Us*.

Business and finance. Robert Campeau, the real estate wizard who made aggressive forays into the United States market before his fortunes suddenly dipped, was the focus of *Campeau: The Building of an Empire*, by Michael Babad and Catherine Mulroney. Ian Brown's *Free Wheeling: The Feuds, Broods and Outrageous Fortunes of the Billes Family and Canada's Favourite Company* looked at a Canadian institution—the Canadian Tire franchise—and the family that founded the hardware empire.

Perhaps typical of a growing Canadian infatuation with nature was *Leopard in the Afternoon: An African Tenting Safari* by Christopher Ondaatje. The tycoon-turned-publisher, who is the brother of author Michael Ondaatje, wrote of his voyage of self-discovery on the Serengeti Plain in Tanzania, Africa.

Awards. The 1988 Governor General's Literary Awards for books in English went to David Adams Richards for *Nights Below Station Street* (fiction), Erin Mouré for *Furious* (poetry), Anne Collins for *In the Sleep Room* (nonfiction), George F. Walker for *Nothing Sacred* (drama), Welwyn Wilton Katz for *The Third Magic* (children's literature—text), and Kim LaFave for *Amos's Sweater* (children's literature—illustration). The awards for French-language books went to Jacques Folch-Ribas for *Le Silence ou le Parfait Bonheur* (fiction), Marcel Labine for *Papiers d'épidémie* (poetry), Patricia Smart for *Écrire dans la maison du père* (nonfiction), Jean Marc Dalpé for *Le Chien* (drama), Michèle Marineau for *Cassiopée ou l'Été polonais* (children's literature—text), and Philippe Béha for *Les Jeux de Pic-mots* (children's literature—illustration).

Philip Stratford won the Canada Council translation prize for *Second Chance*, his English translation of Diane Hébert's *Un Second Souffle*, and Didier Holtzwarth won for *Nucléus*, his French translation of Robert Bothwell's *Nucleus*. Joseph Kertes received the Stephen Leacock Memorial Award for humor for his first novel, *Winter Tulips*.   Larry Scanlan

In *World Book*, see **Canadian literature.**
Cape Verde. See Africa.

Cat. The cat continued to be the most popular pet in the United States in 1989, according to estimates by the Market Research Corporation of America. The firm reported that cats were kept as pets in more than 27 million U.S. households in 1989. The total number of pet cats in the nation was 57.5 million, according to the corporation.

The Persian was the most popular breed registered by The Cat Fanciers' Association (CFA), and Persians won top awards in 1989. The CFA's National Best Cat for 1989 was Grand Champion Toshika's Summer Delight, a black Persian female owned by Penny and Gary Nordman of Elkhart, Ind. The award-winning cat was bred by the Nordmans, John Philpot of Flemington, N.J., and Susan Philpot of Lexington, Ky.

The National Best Kitten for 1989 was also a Persian —Grand Champion Capodicapi Fruit Loops of Khaszar, a calico female. The kitten was bred and owned by Jill Marie Spero of New York City and Wayne McTighe of Manotick, Canada.

The National Best Alter for 1989 was Grand Premier Grand Champion Scottish Ear I Be, a Scottish fold with a white-and-brown tabby coat. The cat's breeders were Gay and Marvin Turner of Benicia, Calif., and Nancy Abbott of Ballwin, Mo. Robin Maring of Jackson, Mich., was the owner.   Thomas H. Dent

In *World Book*, see **Cat.**
Central African Republic. See Africa.
Chad. See Africa.

Chemistry. A chemical process that cleans the exhaust of coal-fired electric power plants and helps pay for itself at the same time seems almost too good to be true. But in September 1989, chemist Shih-Ger Chang of Lawrence Berkeley Laboratory (LBL) in Berkeley, Calif., announced the successful demonstration of such a process in the laboratory. Chang used a small-scale model of a *scrubber*, which mixes chemicals with the exhaust before the exhaust goes up the smokestack.

The LBL process enables conventional sulfur dioxide scrubbers, already used on 190 coal-fired plants in the United States, to clean up nitrogen oxides also. The cost of the operation is about half the cost of the standard method of cleaning up nitrogen oxide—a technique involving *catalysts* (substances that cause chemical reactions while themselves remaining unchanged).

In the LBL process, a series of chemical reactions remove 90 per cent of the sulfur dioxide and up to 100 per cent of the nitrogen oxides, compounds that lead to smog and acid rain. Reactions convert these compounds into valuable commercial chemicals—phosphate compounds, which are used to make fertilizers; and gypsum, employed as a construction material. LBL and the Bechtel Power Corporation of San Francisco are jointly testing a full-scale scrubber in the laboratory.

Fusion in a test tube? Two chemists shocked the scientific community in March 1989 when they announced that they had created a fusion reaction in a tabletop device. B. Stanley Pons of the University of Utah and Martin Fleischmann of the University of Southampton, England, said that they had operated the device successfully for 100 hours and that it gave off four times as much energy as they put into it.

A fusion reaction joins atomic nuclei and releases a tremendous amount of energy. Fusion provides the energy of the sun and the other stars. In an effort to harness this powerful process for useful energy, physicists have built massive machines aimed at reproducing the extreme temperatures and pressures that bring about fusion in the sun.

The two chemists claimed that they had success with a device you could hold in your hand. If so—and there are many doubters—this breakthrough holds tremendous promise for an inexpensive, nonpolluting, and almost limitless source of energy.

The core of the device was an electrode made of the metal palladium. The researchers placed this electrode in a vessel containing deuterium oxide—heavy water with hydrogen atoms that have double the normal mass. With platinum as the other electrode, the scientists ran electricity through the system, breaking up heavy-water molecules into oxygen and deuterium atoms. The chemists detected a tremendous burst of heat that they claim was too large to have been produced by chemical reactions. They theorized that deuterium atoms were drawn inside the palladium elec-

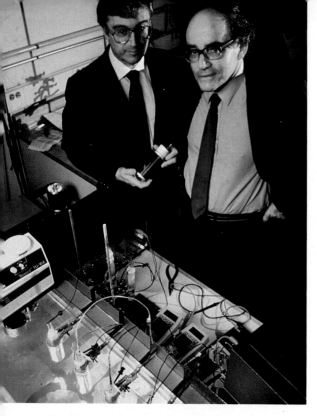

Chemists B. Stanley Pons, left, and Martin Fleischmann display jarlike cells in which they say they produced controlled nuclear fusion.

Diamond chips. A group of physicists and chemists reported in February 1989 that they had coated silicon crystals with diamond in a way that could make it possible to produce smaller, faster, and sturdier computer chips and other microelectronic devices. A diamond is a crystal made up almost entirely of carbon. Physicists J. Lee Robertson and Simon C. Moss of the University of Houston, together with collaborators from Soreq Nuclear Research Center in Yavne, Israel, used a technique called *ion-beam epitaxy* to coat the crystals. They bombarded crystals of silicon—of which today's chips are made—with carbon atoms at high energies. The beam penetrated the silicon crystal slightly and built up a diamond layer one or two atoms thick. The silicon and carbon crystal structures were in alignment, a necessary condition for use as chips. An earlier method called *chemical vapor deposition* can join carbon and silicon, but not with the crystal structures in alignment.

Chip makers are interested in diamond coatings because the manufacturers have advanced the technology of silicon chips about as far as they can. Diamond is an excellent conductor of heat—even better than copper—and a good electrical insulator. In addition, it has optical properties that could become valuable as laser light takes over many tasks presently performed by electricity in computers and communications devices.   Peter J. Andrews

In *World Book,* see **Chemistry.**

trode and packed together so tightly that they fused, releasing heat.

A number of other scientists have offered alternative explanations of the Utah results, many of the researchers attributing the results to error. By year's end, intense efforts to duplicate the experiment at many research centers failed to generate either excess heat or other evidence that would support the fusion claim. Still, other laboratories have reported data that support the Utah claim. In the Special Reports section, see **The Coming Energy Squeeze.**

Cocaine stopper. Psychologist Nancy K. Mello and her colleagues at Harvard Medical School-McLean Hospital in Belmont, Mass., reported in August 1989 that buprenorphine, a drug already used to treat heroin addicts, may help to reduce a craving for cocaine as well. The scientists worked with rhesus monkeys that had been taking cocaine each day for more than six months. The monkeys obtained the cocaine by pressing a button at certain times of day. During the experiment with buprenorphine, some of the monkeys received regular doses of that drug and were given the same opportunity to press the button. Those animals decreased their use of cocaine by more than 90 per cent after 30 days. Buprenorphine is especially promising because it has already been shown to be safe and effective for heroin addicts, bringing it closer to approval by the United States Food and Drug Administration than are other experimental drugs.

Cheney, Richard Bruce (1941-   ), was sworn in as United States secretary of defense on March 21, 1989. President George Bush nominated Cheney for the Cabinet post after his first secretary-designate, former Senator John G. Tower (R., Tex.), was rejected by the Senate amid charges of personal misconduct. Cheney, a well-respected Republican representative from Wyoming, was confirmed without opposition though he had little expertise in defense matters.

Born in Lincoln, Nebr., on Jan. 30, 1941, Cheney moved with his family to Casper, Wyo., in 1954. He received bachelor's and master's degrees in political science from the University of Wyoming in Laramie in 1965 and 1966, respectively.

Cheney entered government service in 1969, working as a minor federal official until 1973, when he left public service briefly to work for an investment company. In 1974, he served as a member of President Gerald R. Ford's transition team. The next year, he was named White House chief of staff, a position he held until the end of Ford's term in January 1977.

In 1978, Cheney sought and won a seat in the U.S. House of Representatives. He was reelected five times. While a member of Congress, Cheney served on the House intelligence committee, and in December 1988 he was elected House Republican whip.

Cheney's wife, Lynne, is chairperson of the National Endowment for the Humanities. The couple have two daughters.   Jinger Hoop

Chess. Elimination matches to determine who will challenge world champion Gary Kasparov of the Soviet Union continued in 1989. Three matches took place in February. Soviet Artur Yusupov eliminated Canadian Kevin Spraggett in Quebec City, Canada. Former world champion Anatoly Karpov of the Soviet Union defeated Icelander Johann Hjartarson in Seattle. And Jan Timman of the Netherlands defeated Hungarian Lajos Portisch in Antwerp, Belgium.

In London in October, Karpov eliminated Yusupov and Timman defeated Jonathan Speelman of London. The winner of a Karpov-Timman match is scheduled to meet Kasparov in a match in Lyon, France, in October 1990.

The Soviet Union won the 1989 World Team Championship, held in Lucerne, Switzerland, from October 27 to November 9. This contest takes place every two years among the top national teams.

U.S. championship. Yasser Seirawan, 29, of Seattle; Roman Dzindzichashvili, 45, of Astoria, N.Y.; and Stuart Rachels, 20, of Birmingham, Ala., won the 1989 U.S. Championship, held in Long Beach, Calif., from November 8 to December 3. In July, Alexey Rudolph of Los Angeles won the 1989 women's championship at Converse College in Spartanburg, S.C. Rudolph thus qualified for the next in a series of matches to determine a challenger for women's world champion Maya Chiburdanidze of the Soviet Union.

Other tournaments. Soviet player Mikhail Gurevich won the World Open in Philadelphia on July 4, topping a field of more than 1,100. Lev Alburt of New York City led a field of more than 600 to win the U.S. Open in Chicago on August 13.

John Fedorowicz of New York City won the New York International Tournament on March 28. After the tournament, it was announced that 14-year-old Soviet star Gata Kamsky and his father were seeking political asylum in the United States.

Younger players. Benjamin Finegold, 20, an American studying in Brussels, Belgium, and Alex Sherzer, 18, of Fallston, Md., became U.S. junior co-champions on July 16 in Washington, D.C. Playing in Murray, Ky., on July 30, Andrew Serotta, 19, of Lansdale, Pa., won the U.S. Junior Open for the third year.

A record-breaking 2,501 school players competed in national team chess championships traditionally held throughout the United States each spring. In April, Dalton School of New York City won its third consecutive elementary school team championship, in matches played in Tempe, Ariz. Playing from May 12 to 14 in Peoria, Ill., Woodrow Wilson Junior High School of Terre Haute, Ind., became champion of the eighth grade and below. Two New York City teams, Dalton School and Horace Mann School, were co-champions of the ninth grade and below. Woodrow Wilson School of Portland, Ore., won the national high school championship tournament held on May 6 and 7 in Knoxville, Tenn.   Al Lawrence

In *World Book,* see **Chess.**

Chicago. Richard M. Daley, a Democrat, was elected mayor of Chicago in a special election on April 4, 1989. Daley received 56 per cent of the vote compared with 3 per cent for Republican Edward R. Vrdolyak and 41 per cent for Alderman Timothy C. Evans, the third-party choice of most of the city's black voters. Daley had won the Democratic primary on February 28 by defeating incumbent Eugene Sawyer, who was named acting mayor by the City Council following the death of Mayor Harold Washington on Nov. 25, 1987. See **Daley, Richard M.**

After taking office later in April 1989, Daley—the son of Richard J. Daley, the legendary politician who was Chicago's mayor for 21 years until his death in 1976—moved quickly to defuse racial bitterness. He retained the city's black superintendent of police and named several blacks and Hispanics to cabinet-level posts. Nevertheless, many black leaders vowed to unseat Daley in the regular election scheduled for early 1991.

Budget and taxes. In December, the City Council approved a $3-billion municipal budget for 1990 that provided a slight rollback in property taxes but also a new 95 cents-a-month tax on telephone lines. The property tax relief was passed after many property owners protested loudly about huge increases in tax bills earlier in the year.

School reform. On October 11 and 12, more than 300,000 voters elected representatives to local councils formed to oversee the city's 540 public schools. The new council members included parents, teachers, and community residents. Mandated in 1988 by the state legislature, the councils were given the power to hire and fire principals, develop educational plans, and approve school budgets.

On October 16, the Board of Education announced the hiring of Ted D. Kimbrough, formerly schools chief in Compton, Calif., to replace Manfred Byrd as superintendent of schools. The need for reform was underscored later in the month with the release of a report showing that students in 31 of the city's 64 high schools scored, on the average, in the bottom 1 per cent on national college entrance tests.

The economy. On June 26, Sears, Roebuck and Company, the city's largest private employer, announced plans to move its 6,000-employee Merchandise Group to offices it will build in suburban Hoffman Estates. The announcement of the move ended a bidding war that saw Illinois and several other states offer tax reductions and other incentives to attract the new Sears office complex. Illinois won with $61 million worth of promised site improvements and direct aid. By year's end, several of the city's other major employers were asking for taxpayer help in expanding their operations.

The city's manufacturing sector continued its comeback during the year, thanks to the booster effect that the dollar's decreased value relative to foreign currencies has had on United States exports. But business

In a shower of confetti, Chicago's mayor-elect, Richard M. Daley—son of long-time Mayor Richard J. Daley—celebrates his election on April 4.

leaders expressed growing concern over the take-over by out-of-town conglomerates of old-line Chicago firms such as Marshall Field & Company and Montgomery Ward & Company.

Trader abuses exposed. The city's booming *futures* trading markets, already under criticism for their role in the stock market crash of October 1987, were again jolted on Aug. 2, 1989, when a federal grand jury indicted 46 futures traders for cheating their customers. Futures are contracts for the purchase or sale of commodities or securities on a given date at a set price.

For two years, undercover federal agents had worked in the trading pits of the Chicago Board of Trade and Chicago Mercantile Exchange, where they allegedly discovered order-rigging, tax evasion, and systematic overcharging of customers. By year's end, at least 14 brokers had agreed to cooperate with prosecutors, and more indictments were expected.

Civil liberties. During a three-week period in February and March, thousands of demonstrators gathered daily outside the Art Institute of Chicago to protest a student art exhibit that included an American flag placed on a floor where it could be stepped on by viewers. In response to the outcry, the Illinois state legislature in June passed a law of doubtful constitutionality, making it illegal to display the United States flag on a floor.   John F. McCarron

See also **City.** In *World Book,* see **Chicago.**

Child welfare. Congress in 1989 moved closer to expanding federal aid for child care in the United States. The Senate on June 23 and the House of Representatives on October 5 passed bills that would provide tax credits for parents and grants to the states to help pay for day-care programs. At year-end, however, the House and Senate had not reconciled differences between their two bills.

Children with AIDS. The problem of children and adolescents with AIDS continued to confront the child welfare system in 1989. Numerous children and teenagers who either had AIDS or whose parents had died from AIDS were in foster care.

AIDS is a fatal disease that affects the body's disease-fighting immune system. The virus that causes AIDS is most commonly spread by intimate sexual contact or by sharing hypodermic needles or syringes. Most children with AIDS contract the disease at birth from mothers already infected with the AIDS virus. According to Surgeon General of the United States C. Everett Koop, nearly 65 per cent of babies born to infected mothers will contract AIDS.

The federal Centers for Disease Control in Atlanta, Ga., reported in January 1989 that the number of children in the United States infected with AIDS had quadrupled in 18 months. In June 1987, there were more than 240 children under 12 years old suffering from AIDS. In January 1989, pediatric AIDS patients numbered 1,393.

Focus on education. Child-welfare experts in the United States welcomed a new national focus on education in 1989. Better education, they agreed, would enhance children's chances of being prepared to take a place in the competitive world of the future.

On September 27 and 28, President George Bush called together the governors of the 50 U.S. states for an "education summit," held at the University of Virginia in Charlottesville. The President and the governors agreed to develop a national agenda for educational reform.

One focus of the national agenda involved enhancement of preschool and kindergarten programs such as Head Start and other services for that age group. Another of the agenda's goals was to promote greater parental involvement in education for all school-aged children.

Although a detailed plan for educational reform had not been formulated by year-end, it appeared that no new federal funding would be available. The governors did request, however, that they be given greater flexibility in how they may use the federal money they did receive—7 per cent of the funds spent on public school education in the United States. The remaining funds came from state and local school districts.　Jeanne M. Hunzeker

See also **Education.** In *World Book,* see **Child welfare.**

Children's books. See **Literature for children.**

Chile. Chileans thronged to the polls on Dec. 14, 1989, to choose a civilian leader in the first free presidential elections since 1970. The winner was Patricio Aylwin Azócar, 71, of the Christian Democratic Party, standardbearer of a coalition of 17 political factions.

Aylwin scored a convincing victory over two other opponents, winning about 55.5 per cent of the vote, or more than enough to avoid a run-off election. His nearest opponent, former Finance Minister Hernan Buchi, won only 29 per cent of the vote.

Aylwin was scheduled to take office on March 11, 1990, under the terms of a Constitution that was approved in 1980. That document, drafted under the military dictatorship of President Augusto Pinochet Ugarte, prevents the new president from replacing Pinochet as commander in chief of the armed services until 1998. Aylwin's impressive majority in the elections, however, may give him the political leverage needed to force Pinochet's early retirement.

During 1989, Pinochet made it clear that he sought to retain his command in order to block any attempt to prosecute military officers for human-rights violations during the 1973 coup that ousted the government of Marxist President Salvador Allende Gossens. Some 700 supporters of the Allende government were killed, and thousands of others were tortured.

Letelier killing. The past continued to haunt Pinochet. In January 1989, a retired Chilean diplomat charged that high-level Chilean officials had identified

Chilean President Augusto Pinochet Ugarte samples grapes after the U.S. Food and Drug Administration found two cyanide-tainted Chilean grapes in March.

the former head of Chilean intelligence, General Juan Manuel Contreras, as the person who ordered the 1976 murder in Washington, D.C., of Orlando Letelier, Chile's foreign minister under Allende. Letelier and a co-worker at the Institute for Policy Studies, Ronni Moffitt, were killed in a car bomb explosion. That a political assassination could occur in the United States capital stunned the diplomatic community there.

Political killings continued in 1989. In September, Jacar Neghme, 29, a leader of a moderate faction of the Leftist Revolutionary Movement (MIR), was gunned down by suspected rightists. A banned political organization, MIR had split into three groups, and Neghme's faction had pledged its support to Aylwin. Neghme's father, a Socialist, had been executed by firing squad during the Pinochet-led coup.

Contaminated grapes. On March 2, 1989, following an anonymous telephone call to the United States Embassy in Santiago, Chile's capital, U.S. authorities began examining imports of Chilean fruit for poison. On March 12, traces of cyanide were found on two grapes from a batch of Chilean grapes that had been shipped to the Philadelphia docks. An estimated $50-million to $75 million worth of Chilean fruit was then destroyed, and stores temporarily removed Chilean fruit from their shelves. Chilean exporters and U.S. importers lost about $240 million.　Nathan A. Haverstock

See also **Latin America** (Facts in brief table). In *World Book,* see **Chile.**

China

China suffered from political turmoil and economic recession in 1989. A continuing struggle over political direction exploded on June 4, when government troops killed hundreds of student demonstrators calling for democratic reforms. This marked an important turn within the Communist Party from making reforms to more rigidly controlling the government and nation. As conservatives gained influence, Deng Xiaoping—China's dominant, reform-minded leader for a decade—resigned his official posts.

Economic troubles intensified a controversy within the party leadership in early 1989. In the first four months of the year, prices were 27 per cent higher than in the same period in 1988. Unemployment increased, and the gap widened between people who benefited from China's economic reform program and those who were left out. Arguing that greater economic freedom and competition was the best way to overcome these problems, Party General Secretary Zhao Ziyang supported political reforms to loosen the party's grip on the economy. Opposing him was Premier Li Peng, who advocated continued state control of the economy, with the party firmly guiding the government.

China's legislature, the National People's Congress, adopted an austerity program backed by Li at its annual session from March 20 through April 4. Although the delegates followed party orders as expected, they showed discontent over corruption within the government and the special privileges accorded to the children of top officials.

Discontent erupted into a full-blown protest movement upon the death of Hu Yaobang on April 15. A liberal follower of Deng, Hu had become party general secretary in 1980. In January 1987—after student supporters of Hu held large demonstrations to call for a more democratic government—Deng forced Hu to resign in order to placate conservative party leaders. The demonstrations had undermined Deng's political plans for reform and unleashed a law-and-order backlash by conservatives. Nevertheless, Deng wielded enough power to replace Hu with Zhao, another supporter of reforms.

Students mourning Hu's death gathered in Shanghai and Beijing, the capital, chanting, "Long live democracy." On April 18, 1989, some 2,000 Beijing students rallied in Tiananmen Square, a huge open area in the center of Beijing next to the former imperial residence, the Forbidden City. The students demanded freedom of the press and the repudiation of the government's earlier campaigns against liberalization. By April 21, some 100,000 protesters had gathered in the square. Many refused the government's orders to leave after memorial services for Hu were held on April 22. They boycotted their classes and demanded a dialogue with government leaders.

The Communist Party newspaper *People's Daily* on April 26 called the student movement an illegal "planned conspiracy which, in essence, aims at negating the leadership of the party and the socialist system." Angered, the protesters intensified their demonstrations. On May 13, about 2,000 students began a hunger strike in the square, which was now filled with hundreds of thousands of students and other citizens. Intellectuals and students in other cities supported the demonstrators.

Zhao, whose liberal policies had student backing, asked the hunger strikers to leave the square on May 17. They refused, and about 1 million of their supporters demonstrated there later that day and the next. On May 19, a tearful Zhao visited the students and indicated that he was losing a political struggle over how to deal with their protest. Indeed, Zhao appeared to have been defeated by early May 20, when Li and President Yang Shangkun, an 82-year-old general, announced that they had imposed martial law and deployed troops to end the demonstrations.

But Beijing residents blocked the passage of army troops—in some cases lying down in front of armored vehicles—and the student occupation of Tiananmen Square continued. On May 23, someone in the square splashed paint on a huge portrait of Mao Zedong, Communist China's founder, which hung at the entrance to the Forbidden City. On May 30, students erected a large statue of the "Goddess of Democracy," a version of the Statue of Liberty. The statue faced a replacement portrait of Mao, symbolically challenging the party dictatorship he created.

Massacre at Tiananmen Square. By now, the protest was beginning to flag as fatigue, illness, and unsanitary conditions affected the students. On the night of June 3, only about 5,000 remained in the square. Shortly after midnight, some of the 100,000 soldiers ordered to Beijing began to march toward the square. They fired into crowds of unarmed civilians who tried to block their way and crushed people under tanks and armored cars. By 5:15 a.m. on June 4, troops had entered the square. They shot at students and set fire to their tents. Many of the students who fled the square were met by soldiers' gunfire in nearby streets. At 7:40 a.m., the government announced that the army had suppressed a "rebellion" in the square. Occasional shootings of defiant civilians continued for several more days as the troops established control.

The true death toll was unknown because the government tried to hide the number of people who died during the incident. After making contradictory statements, officials finally said that 10 soldiers and 36 students had been killed. Western journalists who tried to reconstruct the confusing events reported that between 400 and 800 people had died, with most estimates around 700. Amnesty International, a London-based human-rights organization, concluded

Chinese protesters, *right,* gather around a "Goddess of Democracy" statue erected in Beijing's Tiananmen Square in late May.

230

Demonstrators hit the dirt after troops open fire in Tiananmen Square on June 4. At least 700, and possibly 2,000 or more, were killed.

that at least 1,300 civilians were killed between June 3 and 9, with 1,000 of them in Beijing and 300 in Chengdu, a southern city in which demonstrators had also sought democracy. A Chinese Red Cross official reportedly said that 2,600 people were killed in Beijing but later denied having given a figure.

After the massacre, repression began with a nationwide hunt for students accused of "inciting and organizing counterrevolutionary activities." Amnesty International estimated that tens of thousands of people had been arrested by late August. The organization reported that scores had been executed, most of them secretly, following more than a dozen publicized executions in June. By August, 8 of the 21 student leaders on the government's most-wanted list had been arrested, but some escaped abroad.

Escapees and exiles from around the world met in Paris on September 22 through 24 and organized the Federation for Democracy in China. The 150 delegates agreed to work to bring China a multiparty political system, free enterprise, and expanded human rights. They elected Yan Jiaqi, a former Communist Party official and close associate of Zhao, president of the federation. The Chinese government denounced the exiles as traitors trying to destroy Communism.

Security officials tightened controls within China, reinvigorating the street committee system for observing the actions of ordinary citizens. Most college graduates were told to work in a village or factory before

doing graduate study, and the number of students allowed to enroll abroad was slashed.

Zhao ousted. The Communist Party's Central Committee met June 23 and 24 and ousted Zhao from the general secretary's job and his other party positions. A press campaign against him charged that he had encouraged the demonstrators, opposed martial law, damaged the economy, and hampered the fight against corruption. Most observers saw the campaign as the conservatives' attempt to weaken the authority of Zhao's sponsor, Deng.

Leading the conservatives were Yang and two elderly advocates of rigid central economic planning— Chen Yun and Peng Zhen. Daily affairs were left in the hands of men who also had doubts about the policies of liberalization, led by Li Peng, his deputy Yao Yilin, and security chief Qiao Shi.

The man named to replace Zhao as party general secretary was Jiang Zemin. Jiang had been a moderate economic reformer but political hard-liner as mayor and party boss of Shanghai. He lacked a personal power base and the experience usually associated with party leadership. On October 10, however, *People's Daily* called him "the core of the third-generation collective leadership." This implied that Deng had accepted Jiang as his successor. See **Jiang Zemin.**

Deng resigns. In weakening health, his reforms being reversed, the 85-year-old Deng was losing his ability to control the succession. On November 9,

A lone protester holds his ground against oncoming tanks the day after the Tiananmen Square crackdown. Friends reportedly pulled him to safety.

Deng relinquished his last party job and base of power, chairmanship of the party's Central Military Commission. Jiang succeeded him, possibly in Deng's attempt to strengthen Jiang's authority. But the new party chief's future was left in doubt. Five previous designated successors to Mao and then to Deng had lost power in bitter personal fights over policy.

Foreign reaction to China's suppression of the prodemocracy movement was strongly critical. United States President George Bush came under fire in the United States for canceling some sanctions imposed against China. Although Bush said he had banned high-level government exchanges between the two nations, U.S. officials made a diplomatic visit to China in December and Bush revealed they had also met there secretly with Chinese officials in July.

The economic consequences of the crackdown were severe. Tourism, which had earned China $2.2-billion in 1988, declined sharply. The foreign investment that China needed to modernize its industries also dried up as investors became wary.

By autumn, the economy was sliding into recession. Factories operated at well below capacity, partly because of frequent power cuts. Hotels emptied, retail sales fell, and crowds of jobseekers thronged cities. Facing these problems, Chinese leaders fell back on tighter economic controls. They drew up a plan for cuts in investment, consumption, and private economic activity, all of which had grown under Deng.

Tibetan troubles. Anti-Chinese demonstrators gathered in Lhasa, the capital of Tibet, on March 5, to mark the 30th anniversary of a nationalist uprising in which 87,000 Tibetans were killed and Tibet's spiritual leader, the Dalai Lama, fled into exile in India. The 1989 demonstrations were the fourth occasion in 18 months when Chinese police fired on Tibetan crowds. The government said that 16 people were killed, but unofficial reports said the death toll was 30 or more. Tibetan exiles charged that more than 800 Tibetans were later executed.

The Dalai Lama's efforts to negotiate with Chinese authorities for Tibet's autonomy broke down, but on October 5, he was named to receive the Nobel Peace Prize for his nonviolent struggle against Chinese domination. China denounced the award, which reportedly was intended partly as recognition of the Tiananmen demonstrators.

Gorbachev visit. After 30 years of animosity, China and the Soviet Union reestablished normal relations when Soviet leader Mikhail S. Gorbachev visited China from May 15 to 18. Chinese-Soviet economic ties expanded but remained small compared with China's trade with Japan and the West. Henry S. Bradsher

See **Asia** (Facts in brief table). In **World Book,** see **China.**

Churches. See **Eastern Orthodox Churches; Jews and Judaism; Protestantism; Religion; Roman Catholic Church.**

A fire set by arsonists burns in Miami, Fla., in January during riots after a Hispanic police officer killed a black motorcyclist.

City. Many cities in the United States in 1989 continued to be plagued by illegal drugs and crime, and several were hit by violent natural disasters. Cities also continued to struggle with shrinking federal support for housing and development. Yet in spite of these problems, U.S. cities responded with optimism, rehabilitating buildings and experimenting with creative solutions to urban problems.

Development. Shoppers in Columbus, Ohio, gained new places to spend their money in August 1989 with the opening of City Center in the downtown area. Chicago's Marshall Field & Company joined Lazarus, an Ohio retailer, as anchor stores in the new mall.

The city of Indianapolis began construction on its own downtown project in March 1989—a $1-billion enclosed complex of housing, hotels, stores, and office buildings linked by overhead walkways and underground tunnels. City leaders hoped the new complex would revive Indianapolis' flagging downtown retail trade.

The city of Pittsburgh, Pa., which has been recycling land abandoned by steel companies, began construction of a 48-acre (19-hectare) center for high-technology businesses in late 1989. The development, called the Pittsburgh Technology Center, is being built on the former site of the Jones & Laughlin steelworks. It is a project of the city, the county, private developers, and two universities.

A similar group of city, county, university, and private developers joined forces in Memphis, but in a cultural—rather than retail—enterprise. The group is backing the construction of a $55-million pyramid on the bank of the Wolf River. Work on the pyramid's foundation began in January 1989. The pyramid is to honor the ancient Egyptian city of Memphis. When completed, it will stand 321 feet (98 meters) tall and will house an arena, an Egyptian artifacts museum, and an American music museum.

After nine years of construction, Dallas' new 2,066-seat symphony hall opened on Sept. 8, 1989. Designed by Chinese-born architect I. M. Pei, the limestone and glass building stands on 3 acres (1.2 hectares) of land at the edge of the city's downtown area. It cost $106-million to build. See **Architecture.**

Housing. A survey of the 25 largest cities in the United States revealed in March 1989 that people living in Boston spend a greater proportion of their incomes on rent than residents in other cities. The survey, conducted by Sound Advice, a California-based research firm, found that the median monthly rent in Boston, $586 in 1988, was 21.3 per cent of the city's median family income. Houston had the lowest rents, according to the survey. Houston residents paid an average of $346 a month—or about 13 per cent of their median household income—for rent in 1988.

An experiment aimed at enticing people to move into a run-down section of Minneapolis, Minn., began in August 1989 with the sale of 21 new, low-priced houses in the Hawthorne neighborhood. The city's redevelopment agency provided the 3.5 acres (1.4 hectares) for the homes at a cost of $1. The city also granted the developer $500,000 if the houses were sold for an average of $75,000, about $50,000 less than a comparable suburban home.

Public housing officials continued in 1989 to ponder the future of their troublesome high-rise buildings. In Newark, N.J., on August 17, a federal court decided to stop the city from tearing down 39 of its 46 high-rise public housing buildings. But the decision allowed the city to demolish 8 of the most run-down buildings in 1990 if it agreed to replace some of the demolished apartments with town houses and to refurbish some of the existing units.

Homelessness. An annual survey released in January 1989 by the U.S. Conference of Mayors found that requests for emergency shelter rose by an average of 13 per cent in 1988 among the 27 cities studied. That included an 18 per cent average increase in requests for shelter by homeless families. City officials estimated that they were unable to fulfill 19 per cent of the requests overall; for families, 23 per cent of the requests went unmet. In the Special Reports section, see **No Place to Call Home.**

Miami riot. A Hispanic police officer in Miami, Fla., shot a black motorcyclist on Jan. 16, 1989, touching off a wave of violence in the city's mostly black Overtown section. The motorcyclist was killed at the scene, and his passenger died later of injuries caused in the crash. Angry black residents said the shooting was only one of several incidents of police brutality in their community. The police officer, who said he acted in self-defense, was convicted of manslaughter on December 7.

Natural disasters. Nature played havoc with some of the most beautiful cities in the United States in 1989. A powerful earthquake rumbled through northern California on October 17, killing 62 people and injuring 3,000 others. Estimates placed the cost of the damage statewide at more than $7 billion.

In San Francisco, where 1,100 housing units were left uninhabitable, the worst property damage occurred in the picturesque Marina district near Fisherman's Wharf. By November, the city's shops, restaurants, and tourist attractions were suffering from lost business. Lingering anxiety over the earthquake's economic impact may have contributed to the narrow defeat on November 7 of a referendum calling for a new baseball stadium to be built for the San Francisco Giants.

Across the San Francisco Bay in Oakland, 42 people were killed when the quake caused the collapse of a 1-mile (1.6-kilometer) section of the Nimitz Freeway (Interstate 880). The road leads to the San Francisco-Oakland Bay Bridge, which connects the two cities. A section of the bridge itself also collapsed, killing two people. The bridge was reopened in a month, but its

50 largest cities in the world

Rank	City	Population
1.	Mexico City	10,061,000
2.	Seoul, South Korea	9,645,932
3.	Tokyo	8,353,674
4.	Moscow	8,275,000
5.	Bombay, India	8,227,332
6.	New York City	7,352,700
7.	São Paulo, Brazil	7,033,529
8.	Shanghai	6,880,000
9.	London	6,767,500
10.	Jakarta, Indonesia	6,503,449
11.	Cairo, Egypt	6,052,836
12.	Beijing	5,760,000
13.	Teheran, Iran	5,734,199
14.	Hong Kong	5,659,000
15.	Istanbul, Turkey	5,475,982
16.	Tianjin, China	5,300,000
17.	Karachi, Pakistan	5,208,170
18.	Bangkok, Thailand	5,153,902
19.	Rio de Janeiro, Brazil	5,093,232
20.	Delhi, India	4,884,234
21.	Leningrad, Soviet Union	4,295,000
22.	Santiago, Chile	4,225,299
23.	Lima, Peru	4,164,597
24.	Shenyang, China	4,130,000
25.	Bogotá, Colombia	3,982,941
26.	Pusan, South Korea	3,516,807
27.	Ho Chi Minh City, Vietnam	3,419,978
28.	Los Angeles	3,352,700
29.	Wuhan, China	3,340,000
30.	Calcutta, India	3,305,006
31.	Madras, India	3,276,622
32.	Guangzhou, China	3,220,000
33.	Madrid, Spain	3,188,297
34.	Berlin (East and West), East and West Germany	3,062,979
35.	Yokohama, Japan	2,992,644
36.	Sydney, Australia	2,989,070
37.	Chicago	2,977,500
38.	Baghdad, Iraq	2,969,000
39.	Lahore, Pakistan	2,952,689
40.	Alexandria, Egypt	2,917,327
41.	Buenos Aires, Argentina	2,908,001
42.	Rome	2,830,569
43.	Chongqing, China	2,730,000
44.	Melbourne, Australia	2,645,484
45.	Pyongyang, North Korea	2,639,448
46.	Osaka, Japan	2,636,260
47.	Harbin, China	2,590,000
48.	Hanoi, Vietnam	2,570,905
49.	Chengdu, China	2,540,000
50.	Bangalore, India	2,476,355

Sources: 1988 Bureau of the Census estimates for cities of the United States; censuses or government estimates for cities of other countries.

50 largest cities in the United States

Rank	City	Population*	Per cent change in population since 1980	Unemployment rate†	Mayor‡
1.	New York City	7,352,700	+4.0	5.0%	David N. Dinkins (D, 1/94)
2.	Los Angeles	3,352,700	+12.9	5.0	Thomas Bradley (NP, 6/93)
3.	Chicago	2,977,500	−0.9	5.4	Richard M. Daley (D, 5/91)
4.	Houston	1,698,100	+6.5	6.3	Kathryn J. Whitmire (NP, 1/92)
5.	Philadelphia	1,647,000	−2.4	4.0	W. Wilson Goode (D, 1/92)
6.	San Diego	1,070,300	+22.2	4.3	Maureen F. O'Connor (D, 6/92)
7.	Detroit	1,035,900	−13.9	7.6	Coleman A. Young (D, 1/94)
8.	Dallas	987,400	+9.1	5.8	Annette G. Strauss (NP, 5/91)
9.	San Antonio	941,200	+19.8	7.9	Lila Cockrell (NP, 4/91)
10.	Phoenix	923,800	+17.0	4.5	Terry Goddard (D, 12/91)
11.	Baltimore	751,400	−4.5	4.8	Kurt L. Schmoke (D, 12/91)
12.	San Jose	738,400	+17.3	4.3	Thomas McEnery (D, 12/90)
13.	San Francisco	731,600	+7.8	3.7	Art Agnos (NP, 1/92)
14.	Indianapolis	727,100	+3.8	2.8	William H. Hudnut III (R, 12/91)
15.	Memphis	645,200	−0.2	5.3	Richard C. Hackett (I, 12/91)
16.	Jacksonville	635,400	+17.5	6.2	Thomas L. Hazouri (D, 7/91)
17.	Washington, D.C.	617,000	−3.4	3.0	Marion S. Barry, Jr. (D, 1/91)
18.	Milwaukee	599,400	−5.8	4.4	John O. Norquist (D, 4/92)
19.	Boston	577,800	+2.6	3.4	Raymond L. Flynn (D, 1/92)
20.	Columbus, Ohio	569,600	+0.8	5.0	Dana G. Rinehart (R, 1/92)
21.	New Orleans	531,700	−4.3	8.6	Sidney J. Barthelemy (D, 5/90)
22.	Cleveland	521,400	−9.1	5.0	Michael R. White (D, 1/94)
23.	El Paso	511,000	+20.2	10.9	Suzanne S. Azar (NP, 6/91)
24.	Seattle	502,200	+1.7	4.4	Norman B. Rice (NP, 1/94)
25.	Denver	492,200	−0.1	6.3	Federico Peña (D, 6/91)
26.	Nashville, Tenn.	481,400	+5.7	4.2	William H. Boner (D, 9/91)
27.	Austin, Tex.	464,700	+34.3	5.9	Lee Cooke (NP, 5/91)
28.	Kansas City, Mo.	439,000	−2.0	5.5	Richard L. Berkley (NP, 4/91)
29.	Oklahoma City	434,400	+7.5	4.6	Ronald J. Norik (D, 4/91)
30.	Fort Worth, Tex.	426,600	+10.8	5.9	Bob Bolen (NP, 5/91)
31.	Atlanta, Ga.	420,200	−1.1	5.7	Maynard H. Jackson (D, 1/94)
32.	Portland, Ore.	418,500	+13.7	4.3	J. E. (Bud) Clark (NP, 12/92)
33.	Long Beach, Calif.	415,000	+14.8	5.0	Ernie Kell (D, 7/90)
34.	St. Louis, Mo.	403,700	−10.8	5.5	Vincent C. Schoemehl, Jr. (D, 4/93)
35.	Tucson, Ariz.	385,700	+16.7	4.8	Thomas J. Volgy (D, 12/91)
36.	Albuquerque, N. Mex.	378,500	+13.9	6.0	Luis Saavedra (NP, 11/93)
37.	Honolulu, Hawaii	376,100	+2.2	2.7	Frank F. Fasi (R, 1/93)
38.	Pittsburgh, Pa.	375,200	−11.5	4.7	Sophie Masloff (D, 11/93)
39.	Miami, Fla.	371,100	+7.0	6.7	Xavier L. Suarez (NP, 11/91)
40.	Cincinnati, Ohio	370,500	−3.9	5.0	Charles J. Luken (D, 11/91)
41.	Tulsa, Okla.	368,300	+2.0	5.8	Rodger A. Randle (D, 5/90)
42.	Charlotte, N.C.	367,900	+16.6	3.6	Sue Myrick (R, 11/91)
43.	Virginia Beach, Va.	365,300	+39.3	4.3	Meyera E. Oberndorf (NP, 7/92)
44.	Oakland, Calif.	356,900	+5.2	4.8	Lionel J. Wilson (D, 12/90)
45.	Omaha, Nebr.	353,200	+12.4	4.1	P. J. Morgan (NP, 6/93)
46.	Minneapolis, Minn.	344,700	−7.1	4.4	Donald M. Fraser (D, 1/94)
47.	Toledo, Ohio	340,800	−3.9	6.1	John McHugh (D, 12/91)
48.	Sacramento, Calif.	338,200	+22.6	5.3	Anne Rudin (NP, 12/91)
49.	Newark, N.J.	313,800	−4.7	4.5	Sharpe James (D, 7/90)
50.	Buffalo, N.Y.	313,600	−12.4	5.5	James D. Griffin (D, 12/93)

*1988 estimates (source: U.S. Bureau of the Census).
†June 1989 figures for metropolitan areas (source: U.S. Bureau of Labor Statistics).
‡The letters in parentheses represent the mayor's party, with D meaning Democrat, R Republican, I independent, and NP nonpartisan. The date is when the term of office ends (source: mayors' offices).

temporary closing meant Oakland's 356,000 residents could reach San Francisco only by lengthy detours. As a result, Oakland's downtown experienced an unexpected surge of business.

Optimism prevailed in historic Charleston, S.C., after Hurricane Hugo slammed into the heart of the city on September 21. The storm uprooted trees and destroyed many buildings, though most of the city's oldest homes—built in the 1700's—survived. By December, the city had processed $36.8 million in building permits to restore damaged properties.

Violent crime continued to be a major concern for United States cities in 1989. An upsurge in drug- and gang-related shootings boosted murder rates in many urban areas. At least seven cities—Charlotte, N.C.; Kansas City, Mo.; Milwaukee; New Haven, Conn.; New Orleans; Philadelphia; and Washington, D.C.—broke their previous records for the most homicides in a year. In Milwaukee, 115 people had been murdered by late December, compared with 86 for all of 1988. In Atlanta, Ga., 242 people were killed in 1989, compared with 219 the previous year.

Elections. Blacks, Hispanics, and women have been elected mayors in 15 of the nation's 20 largest cities, a number of them in 1989. On November 7, voters in New York City, Seattle, and New Haven, Conn., elected black mayors for the first time. In New York City, voters elected Democrat David N. Dinkins, president of the borough (district) of Manhattan, to succeed Edward I. Koch, who had been mayor since 1977 (see **Dinkins, David N.**). Democrat Norman B. Rice, a City Council member, was elected mayor of Seattle, and in New Haven, voters elected John C. Daniels, a Democratic state senator, as their mayor.

In Pittsburgh on November 7, Democrat Sophie Masloff became the city's first elected woman mayor. In December 1988, Masloff, then president of the City Council, had become acting mayor following the death of Mayor Richard S. Caliguiri.

In other 1989 elections, Mayor Vincent C. Schoemehl, Jr., of St. Louis, Mo., was reelected in April, and former Atlanta Mayor Maynard H. Jackson was returned to office in October. In November, incumbents Coleman A. Young of Detroit, Kathryn J. Whitmire of Houston, Donald M. Fraser of Minneapolis, and Xavier L. Suarez of Miami, Fla., were reelected. In Ohio, state Senator Michael R. White was elected Cleveland's second black mayor. The city's first black mayor, Carl Stokes, left office in 1971.

On April 4, Chicago voters elected Cook County State's Attorney Richard M. Daley to fill the final two years of the term of Mayor Harold Washington, who died in 1987. Daley succeeded Acting Mayor Eugene Sawyer. See **Daley, Richard M.**

Mayoral power. Voters in Kansas City, Mo., on April 4 rejected an amendment to the city charter that would have increased the power of the mayor at the expense of City Council members. Residents of predominantly black wards in the inner city voted 8 to 1

against the change, which would have diminished minority representation on the City Council.

Referendums. Denver voters on May 16 voted overwhelmingly to construct what will be the world's largest airport. In Seattle, residents on May 16 adopted an initiative to limit the number of downtown buildings and to restrict their height to between 35 and 40 stories. In June, voters in Sacramento, Calif., became the first in the United States to order the shut-down of an operating nuclear plant. Voters in San Francisco in November narrowly rejected an ordinance that would have granted unmarried couples employed by the city the right to register as domestic partners. The measure would have given a partner the right to funeral leave on the death of the other partner and to visit a hospitalized partner.

Move over, Detroit. San Diego replaced Detroit as the sixth-largest city in the United States, according to the U.S. Bureau of the Census in November. The population of another California city—San Jose—grew enough to move ahead of San Francisco and Indianapolis as the nation's 12th-largest city. New York City held its position as the largest city in the United States, followed by Los Angeles and Chicago. The last time the bureau had estimated city populations was in 1986.   Donna Rosene Leff

See also **Chicago; Detroit; Elections; Houston; Los Angeles; New York City; Philadelphia.** In *World Book,* see **City.**

Civil rights. Among the most important developments in United States civil rights law during 1989 was a series of rulings by the Supreme Court of the United States on race and sex discrimination, mainly in the workplace. In *Richmond v. Croson,* announced on January 23, the justices made it more difficult for cities and states to justify minority set-aside programs. Such programs channel a certain percentage of municipal contract work to companies owned by women, blacks, or Hispanics. The court struck down a set-aside plan in Richmond, Va., that allocated 30 per cent of that city's construction contracts to minority-owned firms, ruling that the plan violated the constitutional rights of white male contractors. As a result, similar programs in other cities were revised or dropped.

Another ruling, on June 12, gave white men more latitude to file reverse-discrimination lawsuits against their employers. In *Martin v. Wilks,* the justices said that fire fighters in Birmingham, Ala., could challenge a 1981 court-approved affirmative-action settlement designed to increase the number of blacks hired and promoted by the fire department. Also on June 12, the court, in *Lorance v. AT&T Technologies,* said workers relying on the Civil Rights Act of 1964 must challenge seniority systems that allegedly discriminate against women or minority groups within 300 days of the adoption of the system. The ruling means that employees cannot challenge plans adopted long before they were hired or plans whose discriminatory effects

Hundreds gathered in Philadelphia, Miss., in June to mark the 25th anniversary of the murder there of three civil rights workers.

are not evident until years after the plans have been established.

In *Wards Cove Packing Company v. Atonio*, a case involving workers at Alaskan salmon canneries, the court on June 5 limited employees' ability to use statistics to show that their employers violated Title VII of the 1964 civil rights act. Title VII prohibits job discrimination based on race, sex, religion, or national origin.

Another ruling, in *Patterson v. McLean Credit Union*, announced on June 15, narrowed the scope of an 1866 civil rights law guaranteeing blacks the same rights as those of whites to make and enforce contracts, including those covering employment. The law, strengthened by a 1976 Supreme Court decision, had been commonly used in cases involving private acts of racial discrimination. In the 1989 case of a North Carolina woman, the court said the law does not cover racial harassment and other discriminatory working conditions, only discrimination in hiring.

On Nov. 20, 1989, the National Association for the Advancement of Colored People (NAACP) Legal Defense and Educational Fund reported that at least 96 job discrimination claims were dismissed in 4½ months because of the *Patterson* decision. At least 35,000 civil rights demonstrators protested the rulings with an August 26 silent march past the Supreme Court Building and the United States Capitol in Washington, D.C.

In contrast to the string of rulings against workers, the court on May 1 said employers violate Title VII's antidiscrimination provisions when they stereotype workers because of their sex. The case, *Price Waterhouse v. Hopkins*, involved a former accounting firm manager who claimed she was not promoted because the firm's partners considered her too aggressive and unfeminine.

Civil rights chiefs. The post of chief enforcer of the government's civil rights policies remained vacant in 1989. In April, President George Bush nominated Detroit lawyer William C. Lucas, a former sheriff, to be assistant attorney general for civil rights in the Department of Justice. The Senate Judiciary Committee, however, rejected the nomination on August 1 on the grounds that Lucas lacked experience for the job.

On October 18, the White House announced that Bush had accepted the resignation of William Barclay Allen as chairman of the U.S. Commission on Civil Rights. Allen had come under criticism during 1989 for a number of controversial actions. Earlier in October, the other members of the commission had voted to disassociate themselves from a speech titled "Blacks, Animals, and Homosexuals: Who Is a Minority?" that Allen had given in California.

Flag burning. The Supreme Court ignited a firestorm of national debate shortly before Independence Day by declaring that laws cannot stop political protesters from burning the American flag. The June 21 ruling struck down a Texas law and a 1967 federal statute that banned public flag burning. Many observers hailed the ruling as a key victory for freedom of speech. But Congress passed a new flag-burning law on Oct. 12, 1989. Under the new statute, a person who "knowingly mutilates, defaces, physically defiles, burns, maintains on the floor or ground or tramples upon" a U.S. flag could be sentenced to prison for up to one year and fined up to $100,000.

Voting rights. Black Americans scored a major victory in a special election on June 20 when Mississippi voters elected five black trial court judges, the most in state history. The elections resulted from a 1988 federal court ruling ordering the state to redraw various judicial district boundaries because they violated the Voting Rights Act of 1965. The act prohibits states and cities from drawing voting districts in a way that diminishes the voting power of minority groups. Similar lawsuits challenging the election of judges were pending in Louisiana, Texas, Alabama, Georgia, Illinois, Arkansas, and Ohio.

Racial violence. An increase in the number of "hate crimes," attacks motivated by racial bias, attracted nationwide attention in 1989. One of the most widely publicized incidents occurred on August 23 in Bensonhurst, a predominantly Italian neighborhood in the Brooklyn section of New York City. A 16-year-old black youth seeking to buy a used car was shot to death when he and three friends were attacked by about 30 white men. The whites reportedly objected to blacks being invited to a party in the area and attacked the first group of blacks they saw. Six men were charged with a variety of crimes, including murder. Authorities suspected a racial motive in another widely publicized crime, a series of mail bombings in the South in late December (see **Crime**).

Civil rights memorial. The first memorial to people killed in the United States civil rights movement was dedicated in Montgomery, Ala., on November 5. The memorial is engraved with the names of 40 people who died in the struggle for racial equality, including Martin Luther King, Jr. It was designed by Maya Ying Lin, who also created the Vietnam Veterans Memorial in Washington, D.C.

Drug testing. The Supreme Court on March 21 issued its first ruling on mandatory drug testing, upholding drug- and alcohol-testing programs for U.S. Customs Service employees and railway workers. The justices said the government can require testing of employees in sensitive law-enforcement positions or jobs involving public safety.

Homosexual rights. Massachusetts on November 15 became the second state to recognize civil rights protections for homosexuals when Governor Michael S. Dukakis signed a law that bans discrimination in employment, housing, public accommodations, credit, and insurance based on a person's sexual orientation. The only other such law in the United States was adopted by Wisconsin in 1982.

International report. Amnesty International, a human-rights organization based in London, reported human-rights violations in 133 countries in its 1989 annual report. The group reported that tens of thousands of men, women, and children were killed in 1988 by their governments. Among the countries cited for large-scale killings were Burma (Myanmar), China, El Salvador, Iraq, and the Philippines. According to the report, more than half of the world's governments tortured or mistreated prisoners.

Amnesty International, which opposes the death penalty in all circumstances, reported that 11 prisoners in the United States were executed in 1988 and that an unprecedented 2,182 prisoners in 34 states remained on death row.

Israel criticized. The U.S. Department of State severely criticized Israel for "a substantial increase in human rights violations" in the occupied territories in 1988 in its annual report on human-rights policies around the world. The report, issued in February 1989, said that Israeli troops had caused "many avoidable deaths and injuries" by firing on Palestinian protesters in the Gaza Strip and West Bank.

The Soviet Union in March agreed to accept the jurisdiction of the International Court of Justice, an organ of the United Nations, in disputes involving five international human-rights agreements. It was the first time the Soviets had agreed to binding arbitration in disputes concerning the pacts, which cover genocide, slavery, women's rights, racism, and torture.   Linda P. Campbell and Geoffrey A. Campbell

In *World Book,* see **Civil rights.**

Classical music. Past and future made the biggest news in classical music in 1989. Retirement and resignation were the catalysts of change. So was the desire of musical institutions to look ahead to the 1990's.

In January, the Chicago Symphony announced that Daniel Barenboim would succeed Sir Georg Solti, who planned to step down as music director in 1991. Barenboim had been fired only weeks earlier from his position as artistic and music director of the new Opera de la Bastille in Paris. The dismissal followed months of quarreling between Barenboim and the president of the board that oversees the opera. Selected to replace Barenboim was the promising but little-known Myung-Whun Chung, the 36-year-old Korean-born music director of an orchestra in Saarbrücken, West Germany.

In April 1989, Herbert von Karajan resigned as conductor of the Berlin Philharmonic Orchestra, a post he had held for 34 years. Karajan died on July 16. The prestigious Berlin post went to Claudio Abbado, music director of the Vienna State Opera.

In April, André Previn resigned abruptly as music director of the Los Angeles Philharmonic orchestra following a dispute with the orchestra's general manager over artistic control. Previn was replaced by Esa-Pekka Salonen, the Finnish-born music director of the Swedish Radio Orchestra.

Looking ahead. New York City's Metropolitan Opera commissioned minimalist composer Philip Glass to create for 1992 an opera commemorating the 500th anniversary of Christopher Columbus' landing in the New World. Six cultural institutions in Europe and the United States announced their joint commissioning of a new opera by John Adams, creator of *Nixon in China*. The new opera will be based on the 1985 hijacking by terrorists of the Italian cruise ship *Achille Lauro*, during which an American was murdered. The work will premiere in Brussels, Belgium, in 1991.

The Lyric Opera of Chicago announced a program called "Toward the 21st Century." It will include productions of 3 new operas by U.S. composers (the first, a work by William Bolcom), 7 additional American operas judged by the company as the most important of the 1900's, and 10 European classics of that period.

Both Dallas and Tokyo looked toward the future by opening new concert halls in 1989. The inauguration in September of the Morton H. Meyerson Symphony Center featured a gala by the Dallas Symphony Orchestra. That same month, Richard Wagner's *Tannhäuser*, performed by the Bayreuth Festival Theatre, was the bill of fare at the unveiling of Orchard Hall, the centerpiece of Tokyo's new cultural center.

Financial woes. The New York City Opera lost most of its autumn season because of a contract dispute with orchestra musicians. A settlement in November, however, saved the spring 1990 schedule.

In August, members of the Detroit Symphony Orchestra voted to accept a 10 per cent pay cut to keep their orchestra alive. Also that month, the orchestra

returned to a renovated Orchestra Hall, which it had left for bigger quarters 50 years earlier. The members of the bankrupt Denver Symphony Orchestra reorganized to form the Colorado Symphony and opened their first season in November.

Anderson tribute. In August, an array of musical artists gathered in Danbury, Conn., to mark the 50th anniversary of a memorable event in the civil rights struggle: the refusal by the Daughters of the American Revolution to allow contralto Marian Anderson, who is black, to perform at Constitution Hall in Washington, D.C. The action brought instant fame to Anderson, who sang instead before 75,000 people at the Lincoln Memorial. Anderson, 87, was present to accept the homage of friends and fans.

Other notes. The Texaco-Metropolitan Opera Radio Network celebrated its 50th anniversary season in December. Australian opera star Dame Joan Sutherland sang her farewell stage performance in the United States in November in the Dallas Opera production of Franz Lehár's *The Merry Widow*. Sutherland began her U.S. career in Dallas in 1960. For American pianist Van Cliburn, an 11-year absence from the concert stage ended in June when he joined the Philadelphia Orchestra for performances of piano concertos by Franz Liszt and Peter Ilich Tchaikovsky. Pianist-conductor Vladimir Ashkenazy in November gave his first concerts in the Soviet Union since he immigrated to the West 26 years ago.

Music played a crucial role in festivities held in July to celebrate the 200th anniversary of the French Revolution. Jessye Norman—costumed in red, white, and blue—sang "La Marseillaise," France's national anthem, at a huge parade-fireworks-stage extravaganza. The Opera de la Bastille was christened by a concert of arias from French operas and programs by four youth orchestras from the Soviet Union, China, West Germany, and Indiana University in Bloomington.

The National Symphony under conductor Mstislav Rostropovich introduced in January a cantata written in about 1960 by Russian composer Dmitri Shostakovich. Called *Rayok*, it satirizes Soviet dictator Joseph Stalin and his policies on music.

Symphony premieres. United States orchestras were busy playing new works in 1989. Some offered concertos for instruments written for only infrequently. Two examples were Ellen Taafe Zwilich's Concerto for Trombone and Orchestra, premiered by the Chicago Symphony, and Joseph Turrin's Trumpet Concerto, introduced by the New York Philharmonic.

Jacob Druckman's *Brangle*, performed by the Chicago Symphony, made enjoyable use of the glockenspiel and vibraphone. Percussion was the focus also of Dennis Eberhard's *The Bells of Elsinore*, commissioned by the Cleveland Orchestra.

More traditional music was not shunned. Public response seemed enthusiastic when the Cincinnati (Ohio) Symphony Orchestra, for instance, offered Joel Hoffman's Violin Concerto—modeled, Hoffman said, on the music of Germany's Ludwig van Beethoven.

The Oklahoma City (Okla.) Orchestra on April 22, the 100th anniversary of the beginning of Oklahoma's land rush, premiered Samuel Adler's *Beyond the Land*. Other premieres included Adler's *Choose Life* and Philip Glass's *Itaipu* (Atlanta, Ga.); Steven Stucky's *Son et lumière* (Baltimore); *Corona* by Robert Erickson (Los Angeles); *With Music Strong* by Lukas Foss (Milwaukee); Stanley Wolfe's Violin Concerto and Roger Kellaway's *Songs of Ascent* (New York City); and Alberto Ginastera's *Popol Vuh* and Joan Tower's *Island Prelude* (St. Louis, Mo.).

Opera premieres. The flow of new operas continued as well. Among the stage creations inspired by literature were Edward Thomas' *Desire Under the Elms*, based on Eugene O'Neill's play of that name (January, New York City); *Charlotte's Web*, drawn from the popular E. B. White tale (February, Wilmington, Del.); and *Doktor Faustus* by Giacomo Manzoni, based on the works of Christopher Marlowe and Thomas Mann (May, Milan, Italy). Encouraging to music observers was the premiere in September of a new opera in Grand Forks, N. Dak., *Sakakawea: The Woman with Many Names* by Thomas Peterson.

The Cleveland Opera Theater premiered *Holy Blood and Crescent Moon* by Stewart Copeland, drummer for the now-disbanded rock group The Police, in October. The performances sold out, but the opera received mostly negative reaction from the press.

The opera company in Barcelona, Spain, anticipated the anniversary of Columbus' first voyage by staging *Cristóbal Colón*. Composed by Leonardo Balada, a Pittsburgh-based musician born in Barcelona, the opera employs flashbacks to political and personal crises as the explorer sails to the New World. The music, according to critics, is more successful in its orchestration than its vocal lines. But with tenor José Carreras as Columbus and soprano Montserrat Caballé as Queen Isabella, the opera had the benefit of star power.

The Houston Grand Opera turned to Great Britain's Sir Michael Tippett for a new work. He responded at age 84 with his fifth opera, *New Year*, which debuted in October. An allegory about psychology, human interaction, and the future, Tippett gave the opera, according to *USA Today*, a blend of "rap music, reggae, and Balinese music with English modernism," all in a "dazzling and integrated synthesis."

Other opera premieres included Hugo Weisgall's *Will You Marry Me* (March, New York City); Kenton Coe's *Rachel* (April, Knoxville, Tenn.); William Schuman's *A Question of Taste* (June, Cooperstown, N.Y.); and Anthony Davis' *Under the Double Moon* (June, St. Louis).   Peter P. Jacobi

In *World Book,* see **Classical music; Opera.**

Clothing. See Fashion.

Loge, the fire god, at right, makes his entrance during a new production of Richard Wagner's *Ring* cycle at New York City's Metropolitan Opera.

Coal. In a long-term forecast for the United States coal industry issued on March 1, 1989, the National Coal Association (NCA) predicted that production will exceed 1 billion short tons (900 million metric tons) per year by 1995. According to the NCA, an industry organization based in Washington, D.C., coal production will rise at an annual rate of 1.5 per cent per year to 1.1 billion short tons (1 billion metric tons) by the year 2000.

The U.S. Department of Energy (DOE) on Sept. 25, 1989, reported that U.S. coal production during the first half of 1989 totaled 485.9 million short tons (441 million metric tons), 6 per cent more than during the same period in 1988. Coal exports increased by about 22 per cent to 49.9 million short tons (45.3 million metric tons), and coal prices declined slightly.

Cheaper methanol. An experimental process that uses coal to produce large quantities of methanol is three times faster than existing processes using coal, according to a DOE report issued in April. Methanol is a type of alcohol that can be used as an automobile fuel and for other purposes. DOE officials estimated that the new process could produce fuel-grade methanol for about 40 cents per gallon (11 cents per liter)—about 20 per cent less than the cost of similar systems currently in use.   Michael Woods

See also **Energy supply; Environmental pollution; Mining.** In the Special Reports section, see **The Coming Energy Squeeze.** In *World Book,* see **Coal.**

Coin collecting. The United States Congress in 1989 commissioned a set of commemorative coins honoring Congress's 200th anniversary. The first few coins were minted at the Capitol in Washington, D.C., on June 14—Flag Day—with coin presses transported from the Philadelphia mint.

The commemorative coins included a $5 gold piece, a silver dollar, and a *clad* (layered base metals) half dollar. The gold piece, which depicts the Capitol dome and the gilded eagle of the Old Senate Chamber, was priced at $200 for the uncirculated coin and $215 for the proof coin. The silver dollar, picturing the statue of Freedom atop the Capitol dome and the *mace* (symbol of authority) of the House of Representatives, was priced at $26 in uncirculated and $29 in proof. And the half dollar, showing the head of Freedom and the Capitol facade, was $6 uncirculated, $8 proof.

In October, the U.S. Mint released the designs for a Dwight D. Eisenhower commemorative silver dollar that will be produced in 1990. Meanwhile, many coin collectors debated whether any modern U.S. commemorative coins are worth the price. That controversy heated up in March 1989, when the business publication *Barron's* came out with a highly critical article asserting that commemorative coins are overpriced and a poor investment.

Coins from other countries. Great Britain celebrated the 500th anniversary of the gold sovereign—a coin worth 1 pound, or less than $2—with a design depicting a seated Queen Elizabeth II and the Tudor rose. Canada in 1989 added platinum and silver coins to its series of Maple Leaf coinage. Each coin contains 1 troy ounce (31.1 grams) of the precious metal.

Quarters without mint marks. An unknown number of 1989 quarters emerged from the Philadelphia mint early in the year without a "P" mint mark stamped on them. Coin experts said the error was caused when grease clogged the indented "P" on the die from which the coins were struck. Such "filled die" errors have little value to most collectors.

Record sale prices. An 1804 silver dollar—considered the finest of the 15 known to exist—sold for $990,000 at an auction in Chicago in July. That figure was the highest price ever paid for a single coin at an auction. Although stamped 1804, the silver dollars were actually minted in the 1830's and 1850's for collectors.

In a private sale in September, an unidentified buyer paid $1,350,000 for a proof specimen of a so-called Humbert $20 territorial gold piece. That price was a record for a U.S. coin. Humbert gold pieces were minted from 1851 to 1853 by Augustus Humbert, an official of the U.S. Assay Office.

Gold and silver prices fell in 1989. Gold sold for $414 per troy ounce on January 1 and $403 at year-end. Silver prices fell from $6.10 to $5.18 per troy ounce during the year.   David T. Alexander

In *World Book,* see **Coin collecting.**

Colombia. Senator Luís Carlos Galán, a leading presidential candidate in elections scheduled for 1990, was fatally wounded on Aug. 18, 1989, by suspected drug traffickers. An outspoken foe of Colombia's powerful cocaine cartels, Galán was gunned down at a campaign rally in a suburb of Bogotá, the capital.

In response to his murder, Colombia's President Virgilio Barco Vargas declared all-out war on drug trafficking. He announced that drug traffickers facing criminal charges in the United States would be extradited without delay, bypassing Colombian courts. Under death threats from the cartels, the Colombian Supreme Court in 1987 had effectively ended an extradition treaty between the United States and Colombia. Since 1981, about 220 judges and court employees have been slain in connection with drug-related cases.

Colombia's army and police moved vigorously in late August and early September 1989, raiding the homes and ranches of suspected drug dealers. In accord with emergency measures declared by Barco Vargas, they seized nearly 1,000 buildings and farms—all said to belong to drug operatives. More than 11,000 people were arrested, but the raids netted few of the top drug dealers facing extradition. One exception was Eduardo Martínez Romero, who was extradited in early September in connection with a $1.2-billion money-laundering operation. Several middle-level drug operatives were extradited in October and November. In December, José Gonzalo Rodríguez Gacha,

A memorial ceremony in August marks the grave of Luis Carlos Galán, a Colombian presidential candidate who was slain by suspected drug dealers.

the number-two leader of the Medellín cocaine cartel, died in a shoot-out with the police.

Counterattack. The drug lords struck back quickly with a stepped-up campaign of murder and bombing. They issued a communiqué declaring war "on the government, on the industrial and political oligarchy," on journalists, judges, and "all those who have persecuted and attacked us." The communiqué was signed by a group calling itself the Extraditables.

The campaign of retaliation targeted newspaper offices, police and court officials, and politicians. Two plainclothes police officers who belonged to the unit that held Martínez Romero in custody prior to his extradition were murdered on September 15.

Colombia's drug kingpins take in an estimated $4-billion annually in supplying about 80 per cent of the cocaine consumed in the United States and Europe. By contrast, Colombia's most important legal export, coffee, produces about $1.5 billion annually.

Seeking legitimacy. The ultimate aim of the drug cartels is to secure legitimacy for those who have made fortunes from the narcotics trade. In August, according to the ruling Liberal Party, the cartels secretly financed the formation of a new political party—the National Restoration Movement—aligned with the far right.   Nathan A. Haverstock

See also **Latin America** (Facts in brief table). In *World Book,* see **Colombia.**

Colorado. See **State government.**

Communications. The United States communications industry assumed more of a global presence in 1989 than ever before, as the American Telephone and Telegraph Company (AT&T) and regional holding companies (RHC's) looked for new opportunities to expand. (Seven RHC's, regional telephone companies sometimes referred to as the "Baby Bells," were formed on Jan. 1, 1984, when AT&T broke up.) All of the RHC's hoped to gain a foothold in other countries—particularly in Europe—before the European Community (EC) forms a unified market in 1992. Some believe that such a unified market may exclude non-EC businesses.

AT&T on June 5, 1989, agreed to a complicated joint manufacturing venture, buying 20 per cent of Italtel S.p.A., a telecommunications equipment manufacturer that is a subsidiary of the government-run Italian telephone company Società Finanziaria Telefonica (STET). At the same time, STET bought a 20 per cent share in AT&T's network systems group. The deal will allow AT&T to take part in a planned $25-billion upgrade of the Italian telephone network.

Five RHC's—American Information Technologies Corporation (Ameritech), Bell Atlantic Corporation, NYNEX Corporation, Pacific Telesis Group, and U S West Incorporated—were each part of groups that bid for a contract to build and operate a new nationwide cellular telephone system in West Germany. The system would compete with one run by a govern-

Communications

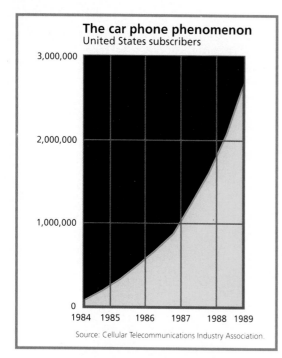

The car phone phenomenon
United States subscribers

Source: Cellular Telecommunications Industry Association.

Cellular communication, which provides car telephone service through radio transmitters linking areas called *cells,* has grown rapidly in the 1980's.

ment-controlled corporation. Three RHC's—Pacific Telesis, U S West, and BellSouth Corporation—and GTE Corporation also bid for a nationwide "personal communications system" to be built in England. The system would use a network of radio transmitters and antennas attached to tall buildings to enable customers to make and receive telephone calls on small, handheld devices.

Media merger. Three hours after a three-justice panel of the Delaware Supreme Court removed a final legal stumbling block, Time Incorporated on July 24 acquired Warner Communications Incorporated. The merger created one of the largest information and entertainment companies in the world, with an annual revenue of more than $10 billion from film and other programming, magazines, books, and cable TV.

The merger had been stalled by attempts by Paramount Communications Incorporated and some Time shareholders to block the transaction. Paramount, which had made a hostile take-over bid for Time, had argued before the Delaware Chancery Court that Time's corporate directors had an obligation to seek the highest short-term stock price for the company. But the court's ruling, upheld by the three-judge panel, supported the contention of Time's board that directors have the right to make business-strategy decisions without requiring a shareholder vote on such decisions. After the ruling, Paramount said it would end its $12.2-billion bid for Time and would not make

an offer for the combined Time Warner Incorporated.

New FCC chairman. Dennis R. Patrick, a strong supporter of deregulation during his two years as chairman of the Federal Communications Commission, resigned on April 5, 1989. Patrick's main accomplishment as chairman was the institution of a new regulatory system for AT&T, which sets the prices AT&T can charge for its services. The old system determined how much money AT&T could earn on its investments. The Senate on August 4 confirmed Alfred C. Sikes, head of the Department of Commerce's National Telecommunications and Information Administration, as the new chairman.

Telephone pornography ruling. In a case affecting "dial-a-porn"—sexually explicit recorded messages provided by special telephone services—the Supreme Court of the United States on June 23 struck down part of a 1988 law banning such services. The law, enacted as a result of concern that children would be exposed to pornography, had banned both obscene and indecent telephone messages for commercial purposes.

The court upheld the part of the 1988 law banning obscene messages. But it ruled that the Constitution's guarantee of free speech protects messages that are merely indecent, not obscene.   Arthur R. Brodsky

In the Special Reports section, see **Television: The Changing Picture.** In *World Book,* see **Communication. Comoros.** See Africa.

Computer sales throughout the world increased by less than 10 per cent in 1989, compared with a hefty 17 per cent rise in 1988. Sales of the large, high-powered machines known as *mainframe computers* climbed in 1989 by only 4 per cent. Sales of personal computers (PC's), however, continued to increase at a rate of 15 to 20 per cent.

Also during the year, manufacturers began to use a new design for attaching special circuit boards to PC's, and International Business Machines Corporation (IBM) announced new hardware and software for business computing—and was sharply challenged in the mainframe field. Two important laptop computers appeared—one extremely versatile and the other extremely inexpensive.

Reasons for the slump. Industry analysts cited three major reasons for the sales slowdown. First, manufacturers introduced new products more rapidly than customers could absorb even the old ones. Second, software developers could not write new programs quickly enough to take full advantage of new hardware before another generation of hardware appeared. And third, it proved difficult to sustain double-digit growth, even in a total market of $188-billion, especially when each year saw new equipment that was smaller, more powerful, and less expensive than the year before.

Alternative architecture. The most highly anticipated development in PC's was the fall debut of ma-

''Now that is a *real* word processor!''

chines incorporating a new *architecture* (design) for attaching circuit cards that perform specialized tasks. In September 1988, a consortium of nine PC manufacturers had announced the new design, called *extended industry standard architecture* (EISA), as an alternative to the Micro Channel Architecture (MCA) used by IBM.

The main difference between MCA and EISA is that circuit cards built for older IBM AT-type computers can be used on machines with EISA but not on computers with MCA. IBM has patented MCA technology, and other companies must license it to be allowed to incorporate it into their hardware.

Office automation. IBM on May 16 turned up the heat in the branch of business computing known as office automation, unveiling OfficeVision software. OfficeVision is part of IBM's Systems Application Architecture (SAA) software—which enables customers to connect databases and business-applications software running on computers that had previously been incompatible. SAA can tie IBM mainframe computers, AS/400 minicomputers, and PS/2 PC's into a single network.

Digital introduces mainframe. Digital Equipment Corporation of Maynard, Mass., on October 24 announced its first line of mainframe computers, called VAX 9000. This announcement was a direct challenge to IBM, which commands about 70 per cent of the mainframe market. Digital said that it would

begin shipping the new machines in the spring of 1990. The company priced the computers at $1.2 million to $3.9 million, much lower than IBM machines with comparable power.

New laptops. Apple Computer, Incorporated, of Cupertino, Calif., on September 20 introduced a long-awaited product, a Macintosh laptop computer. Called the Portable, the new machine has the same graphic capabilities as desktop Macs, according to Apple, and can run all standard Macintosh software. The Portable sold for $5,799.

At the other end of the price spectrum, Atari Corporation of Sunnyvale, Calif., began shipping Portfolio, the smallest, lightest, least expensive laptop yet. The 1-pound (450-gram), pocket-sized computer sold for $399. The Portfolio is IBM-compatible and comes with built-in word processing and a spreadsheet program.

Bleak bottom lines. Sun Microsystems of Mountain View, Calif., shocked the computer industry in June by posting its first quarterly loss ever. The company blamed its problems on a faulty computer system and production snafus. Sun makes *workstations*, computers that are more powerful than PC's but not as powerful as minicomputers. Ashton-Tate of Torrance, Calif., publisher of the most popular database software programs for PC's, also announced in June that it would report a quarterly loss.   Elliot King

See also **Electronics.** In *World Book,* see **Computer. Congo.** See **Africa.**

Congress of the United States.

The 101st Congress, controlled by the Democrats, did little more than it had to in 1989. The Senate got off to its slowest start in years, and the House of Representatives endured months of uncertainty and upheaval as it wrestled with ethical questions that ended the careers of two top Democrats and threatened others in both parties.

Still, essential government business was carried out before Congress adjourned on November 22. Money was appropriated. The savings and loan (S&L) industry was bailed out to the tune of $100 billion-plus. The minimum wage was hiked. A new antidrug program was enacted, and smoking on most domestic airline flights was banned. Aid was extended to Poland. "Whistle blowers" who expose government corruption and mismanagement were protected. And the national debt limit was boosted from $2.8 trillion to $3.1 trillion in November, just hours before the Treasury otherwise would have defaulted for the first time in history.

Wright, Coelho resign. Speaker of the House James C. Wright, Jr., (D., Tex.) resigned from the House on June 6 after being accused by his peers of violating House rules through financial dealings with a wealthy constituent and seeking to sidestep a House limit on *honorariums* (payments for speeches). Wright was the first Speaker ever forced from office in midterm because of ethical questions.

Wright's departure, climaxing a year of investigations into his financial affairs, had been widely expected. More startling, because it came as a surprise, was a decision by House Democratic Whip Tony Coelho of California to resign from the House on June 15 and thus spare himself an ethics inquiry involving a 1986 investment in "junk" bonds.

As a result of the Wright and Coelho resignations, House Democrats had to elect new leaders. Wright, who had been Speaker since 1987, was succeeded by Thomas S. Foley of Washington, a House member for 25 years who had been majority leader under Wright. To succeed Foley as majority leader, House Democrats on June 14 elected Representative Richard A. Gephardt of Missouri. Elected party whip to succeed Coelho was Representative William H. Gray III of Pennsylvania, a Baptist clergyman and former chairman of the Budget Committee.

The Senate also had a new majority leader in 1989—George J. Mitchell, a Maine Democrat, who was elected in late 1988 to succeed Robert C. Byrd of West Virginia. Byrd gave up the post after 11 years to chair the Appropriations Committee.

The ethics accusations against Wright were raised in February 1988 by House Republican Whip Newt Gingrich of Georgia; he filed formal charges with the ethics committee—known formally as the Committee on Standards of Official Conduct—three months later. Wright insisted he had not violated

The newly elected Speaker of the House, Thomas S. Foley (D., Wash.), left, accepts the gavel from Minority Leader Robert H. Michel (R., Ill.) in June.

Members of the United States Senate

The Senate of the second session of the 101st Congress consisted of 55 Democrats and 45 Republicans when it convened in January 1990. Senators shown starting their term in 1989 were elected for the first time in the Nov. 8, 1988, elections. Others shown ending their current terms in 1995 were reelected to the Senate in the 1988 balloting. The second date in each listing shows when the senator's term expires.

State	Term	State	Term	State	Term
Alabama		**Louisiana**		**Ohio**	
Howell T. Heflin, D.	1979-1991	J. Bennett Johnston, Jr., D.	1972-1991	John H. Glenn, Jr., D.	1974-1993
Richard C. Shelby, D.	1987-1993	John B. Breaux, D.	1987-1993	Howard M. Metzenbaum, D.	1976-1995
Alaska		**Maine**		**Oklahoma**	
Theodore F. Stevens, R.	1968-1991	William S. Cohen, R.	1979-1991	David L. Boren, D.	1979-1991
Frank H. Murkowski, R.	1981-1993	George J. Mitchell, D.	1980-1995	Don Nickles, R.	1981-1993
Arizona		**Maryland**		**Oregon**	
Dennis DeConcini, D.	1977-1995	Paul S. Sarbanes, D.	1977-1995	Mark O. Hatfield, R.	1967-1991
John McCain III, R.	1987-1993	Barbara A. Mikulski, D.	1987-1993	Bob Packwood, R.	1969-1993
Arkansas		**Massachusetts**		**Pennsylvania**	
Dale Bumpers, D.	1975-1993	Edward M. Kennedy, D.	1962-1995	John Heinz, R.	1977-1995
David H. Pryor, D.	1979-1991	John F. Kerry, D.	1985-1991	Arlen Specter, R.	1981-1993
California		**Michigan**		**Rhode Island**	
Alan Cranston, D.	1969-1993	Donald W. Riegle, Jr., D.	1976-1995	Claiborne Pell, D.	1961-1991
Pete Wilson, R.	1983-1995	Carl Levin, D.	1979-1991	John H. Chafee, R.	1976-1995
Colorado		**Minnesota**		**South Carolina**	
William L. Armstrong, R.	1979-1991	David F. Durenberger, R.	1978-1995	Strom Thurmond, R.	1956-1991
Timothy E. Wirth, D.	1987-1993	Rudy Boschwitz, R.	1978-1991	Ernest F. Hollings, D.	1966-1993
Connecticut		**Mississippi**		**South Dakota**	
Christopher J. Dodd, D.	1981-1993	Thad Cochran, R.	1978-1991	Larry Pressler, R.	1979-1991
Joseph Lieberman, D.	1989-1995	Trent Lott, R.	1989-1995	Thomas A. Daschle, D.	1987-1993
Delaware		**Missouri**		**Tennessee**	
William V. Roth, Jr., R.	1971-1995	John C. Danforth, R.	1976-1995	James Sasser, D.	1977-1995
Joseph R. Biden, Jr., D.	1973-1991	Christopher S. (Kit) Bond, R.	1987-1993	Albert A. Gore, Jr., D.	1985-1991
Florida		**Montana**		**Texas**	
Bob Graham, D.	1987-1993	Max Baucus, D.	1978-1991	Lloyd M. Bentsen, Jr., D.	1971-1995
Connie Mack III, R.	1989-1995	Conrad Burns, R.	1989-1995	Phil Gramm, R.	1985-1991
Georgia		**Nebraska**		**Utah**	
Sam Nunn, D.	1972-1991	J. James Exon, D.	1979-1991	Edwin Jacob Garn, R.	1974-1993
Wyche Fowler, Jr., D.	1987-1993	Robert Kerrey, D.	1989-1995	Orrin G. Hatch, R.	1977-1995
Hawaii		**Nevada**		**Vermont**	
Daniel K. Inouye, D.	1963-1993	Harry M. Reid, D.	1987-1993	Patrick J. Leahy, D.	1975-1993
Spark M. Matsunaga, D.	1977-1995	Richard H. Bryan, D.	1989-1995	James M. Jeffords, R.	1989-1995
Idaho		**New Hampshire**		**Virginia**	
James A. McClure, R.	1973-1991	Gordon J. Humphrey, R.	1979-1991	John W. Warner, R.	1979-1991
Steven D. Symms, R.	1981-1993	Warren B. Rudman, R.	1980-1993	Charles S. Robb, D.	1989-1995
Illinois		**New Jersey**		**Washington**	
Alan J. Dixon, D.	1981-1993	Bill Bradley, D.	1979-1991	Brock Adams, D.	1987-1993
Paul Simon, D.	1985-1991	Frank R. Lautenberg, D.	1982-1995	Slade Gorton, R.	1989-1995
Indiana		**New Mexico**		**West Virginia**	
Richard G. Lugar, R.	1977-1995	Pete V. Domenici, R.	1973-1991	Robert C. Byrd, D.	1959-1995
Dan R. Coats, R.*	1989-1991	Jeff Bingaman, D.	1983-1995	John D. Rockefeller IV, D.	1985-1991
Iowa		**New York**		**Wisconsin**	
Charles E. Grassley, R.	1981-1993	Daniel P. Moynihan, D.	1977-1995	Robert W. Kasten, Jr., R.	1981-1993
Tom Harkin, D.	1985-1991	Alfonse M. D'Amato, R.	1981-1993	Herbert Kohl, D.	1989-1995
Kansas		**North Carolina**		**Wyoming**	
Robert J. Dole, R.	1969-1993	Jesse A. Helms, R.	1973-1991	Malcolm Wallop, R.	1977-1995
Nancy Landon Kassebaum, R.	1978-1991	Terry Sanford, D.	1986-1993	Alan K. Simpson, R.	1979-1991
Kentucky		**North Dakota**			
Wendell H. Ford, D.	1974-1993	Quentin N. Burdick, D.	1960-1995		
Mitch McConnell, R.	1985-1991	Kent Conrad, D.	1987-1993		

*Coats was appointed by Indiana Governor Robert D. Orr to fill the Senate seat vacated by Dan Quayle, elected Vice President.

Members of the United States House of Representatives

The House of Representatives of the second session of the 101st Congress consisted of 257 Democrats and 176 Republicans with two vacancies (not including representatives from American Samoa, the District of Columbia, Guam, Puerto Rico, and the Virgin Islands), when it convened in January 1990, compared with 259 Democrats and 174 Republicans with two vacancies when the first session convened. This table shows congressional district, legislator, and party affiliation. Asterisk (*) denotes those who served in the 100th Congress; dagger (†) denotes "at large."

Alabama
1. H. L. Callahan, R.*
2. William L. Dickinson, R.*
3. Glen Browder, D.
4. Tom Bevill, D.*
5. Ronnie G. Flippo, D.*
6. Ben Erdreich, D.*
7. Claude Harris, D.*

Alaska
†Donald E. Young, R.*

Arizona
1. John J. Rhodes III, R.*
2. Morris K. Udall, D.*
3. Bob Stump, R.*
4. Jon L. Kyl, R.*
5. Jim Kolbe, R.*

Arkansas
1. Bill Alexander, D.*
2. Tommy F. Robinson, R.*
3. John P. Hammerschmidt, R.*
4. Beryl F. Anthony, Jr., D.*

California
1. Douglas H. Bosco, D.*
2. Wally Herger, R.*
3. Robert T. Matsui, D.*
4. Vic Fazio, D.*
5. Nancy Pelosi, D.*
6. Barbara Boxer, D.*
7. George E. Miller, D.*
8. Ronald V. Dellums, D.*
9. Fortney H. (Pete) Stark, D.*
10. Don Edwards, D.*
11. Tom Lantos, D.*
12. Tom J. Campbell, R.
13. Norman Y. Mineta, D.*
14. Norman D. Shumway, R.*
15. Gary A. Condit, D.
16. Leon E. Panetta, D.*
17. Charles Pashayan, Jr., R.*
18. Richard H. Lehman, D.*
19. Robert J. Lagomarsino, R.*
20. William M. Thomas, R.*
21. Elton Gallegly, R.*
22. Carlos J. Moorhead, R.*
23. Anthony C. Beilenson, D.*
24. Henry A. Waxman, D.*
25. Edward R. Roybal, D.*
26. Howard L. Berman, D.*
27. Mel Levine, D.*
28. Julian C. Dixon, D.*
29. Augustus F. (Gus) Hawkins, D.*
30. Matthew G. Martínez, D.*
31. Mervyn M. Dymally, D.*
32. Glenn M. Anderson, D.*
33. David Dreier, R.*
34. Esteban E. Torres, D.*
35. Jerry Lewis, R.*
36. George E. Brown, Jr., D.*
37. Alfred A. McCandless, R.*
38. Robert K. Dornan, R.*
39. William E. Dannemeyer, R.*
40. C. Christopher Cox, R.
41. William D. Lowery, R.*
42. Dana Rohrabacher, R.
43. Ronald C. Packard, R.*
44. Jim Bates, D.*
45. Duncan L. Hunter, R.*

Colorado
1. Patricia Schroeder, D.*
2. David E. Skaggs, D.*
3. Ben Nighthorse Campbell, D.*
4. Hank Brown, R.*
5. Joel Hefley, R.*
6. Daniel Schaefer, R.*

Connecticut
1. Barbara B. Kennelly, D.*
2. Samuel Gejdenson, D.*
3. Bruce A. Morrison, D.*
4. Christopher Shays, R.*
5. John G. Rowland, R.*
6. Nancy L. Johnson, R.*

Deleware
†Thomas R. Carper, D.*

Florida
1. Earl Hutto, D.*
2. Bill Grant, R.*
3. Charles E. Bennett, D.*
4. Craig T. James, R.
5. Bill McCollum, R.*
6. Cifford B. Stearns, R.
7. Sam M. Gibbons, D.*
8. C. W. Bill Young, R.*
9. Michael Bilirakis, R.*
10. Andy Ireland, R.*
11. Bill Nelson, D.*
12. Thomas F. Lewis, R.*
13. Porter J. Goss, R.
14. Harry A. Johnston II, D.
15. E. Clay Shaw, Jr., R.*
16. Lawrence J. Smith, D.*
17. William Lehman, D.*
18. Ileana Ros-Lehtinen, R.
19. Dante B. Fascell, D.*

Georgia
1. Lindsay Thomas, D.*
2. Charles F. Hatcher, D.*
3. Richard B. Ray, D.*
4. Ben Jones, D.
5. John Lewis, D.*
6. Newt Gingrich, R.*
7. George Darden, D.*
8. J. Roy Rowland, D.*
9. Edgar L. Jenkins, D.*
10. Doug Barnard, Jr., D.*

Hawaii
1. Patricia F. Saiki, R.*
2. Daniel K. Akaka, D.*

Idaho
1. Larry E. Craig, R.*
2. Richard H. Stallings, D.*

Illinois
1. Charles A. Hayes, D.*
2. Gus Savage, D.*
3. Marty Russo, D.*
4. George Sangmeister, D.
5. William O. Lipinski, D.*
6. Henry J. Hyde, R.*
7. Cardiss Collins, D.*
8. Dan Rostenkowski, D.*
9. Sidney R. Yates, D.*
10. John Edward Porter, R.*
11. Frank Annunzio, D.*
12. Philip M. Crane, R.*
13. Harris W. Fawell, R.*
14. J. Dennis Hastert, R.*
15. Edward R. Madigan, R.*
16. Lynn M. Martin, R.*
17. Lane A. Evans, D.*
18. Robert H. Michel, R.*
19. Terry L. Bruce, D.*
20. Richard J. Durbin, D.*
21. Jerry F. Costello, D.*
22. Glenn Poshard, D.

Indiana
1. Peter J. Visclosky, D.*
2. Philip R. Sharp, D.*
3. John Patrick Hiler, R.*
4. Jill Long, D.
5. James Jontz, D.*
6. Danny L. Burton, R.*
7. John T. Myers, R.*
8. Frank McCloskey, D.*
9. Lee H. Hamilton, D.*
10. Andrew Jacobs, Jr., D.*

Iowa
1. Jim Leach, R.*
2. Thomas J. Tauke, R.*
3. David R. Nagle, D.*
4. Neal Smith, D.*
5. Jim Ross Lightfoot, R.*
6. Fred Grandy, R.*

Kansas
1. Pat Roberts, R.*
2. James C. Slattery, D.*
3. Jan Meyers, R.*
4. Dan Glickman, D.*
5. Bob Whittaker, R.*

Kentucky
1. Carroll Hubbard, Jr., D.*
2. William H. Natcher, D.*
3. Romano L. Mazzoli, D.*
4. Jim Bunning, R.*
5. Harold (Hal) Rogers, R.*
6. Larry J. Hopkins, R.*
7. Carl C. (Chris) Perkins, D.*

Louisiana
1. Robert L. Livingston, Jr., R.*
2. Corrinne C. (Lindy) Boggs, D.*
3. W. J. (Billy) Tauzin, D.*
4. Jim McCrery, R.*
5. Thomas J. (Jerry) Huckaby, D.*
6. Richard Hugh Baker, R.*
7. James A. (Jimmy) Hayes, D.*
8. Clyde C. Holloway, R.*

Maine
1. Joseph E. Brennan, D.*
2. Olympia J. Snowe, R.*

Maryland
1. Roy P. Dyson, D.*
2. Helen Delich Bentley, R.*
3. Benjamin L. Cardin, D.*
4. Thomas McMillen, D.*
5. Steny H. Hoyer, D.*
6. Beverly B. Byron, D.*
7. Kweisi Mfume, D.*
8. Constance A. Morella, R.*

Massachusetts
1. Silvio O. Conte, R.*
2. Richard E. Neal, D.
3. Joseph D. Early, D.*
4. Barney Frank, D.*
5. Chester G. Atkins, D.*
6. Nicholas Mavroules, D.*
7. Edward J. Markey, D.*
8. Joseph P. Kennedy II, D.*
9. John Joseph Moakley, D.*
10. Gerry E. Studds, D.*
11. Brian J. Donnelly, D.*

Michigan
1. John Conyers, Jr., D.*
2. Carl D. Pursell, R.*
3. Howard E. Wolpe, D.*
4. Frederick S. Upton, R.*
5. Paul B. Henry, R.*
6. Bob Carr, D.*
7. Dale E. Kildee, D.*
8. Bob Traxler, D.*
9. Guy Vander Jagt, R.*
10. Bill Schuette, R.*
11. Robert W. Davis, R.*
12. David E. Bonior, D.*
13. George W. Crockett, Jr., D.*
14. Dennis M. Hertel, D.*
15. William D. Ford, D.*
16. John D. Dingell, D.*
17. Sander M. Levin, D.*
18. William S. Broomfield, R.*

Minnesota
1. Timothy J. Penny, D.*
2. Vin Weber, R.*
3. Bill Frenzel, R.*
4. Bruce F. Vento, D.*
5. Martin O. Sabo, D.*
6. Gerry Sikorski, D.*
7. Arlan Stangeland, R.*
8. James L. Oberstar, D.*

Mississippi
1. Jamie L. Whitten, D.*
2. Mike Espy, D.*
3. G. V. (Sonny) Montgomery, D.*
4. Mike Parker, D.
5. Gene Taylor, D.

Missouri
1. William L. (Bill) Clay, D.*
2. Jack Buechner, R.*
3. Richard A. Gephardt, D.*
4. Ike Skelton, D.*
5. Alan D. Wheat, D.*
6. E. Thomas Coleman, R.*
7. Mel Hancock, R.
8. Bill Emerson, R.*
9. Harold L. Volkmer, D.*

Montana
1. Pat Williams, D.*
2. Ron Marlenee, R.*

Nebraska
1. Doug Bereuter, R.*
2. Peter Hoagland, D.
3. Virginia Smith, R.*

Nevada
1. James H. Bilbray, D.*
2. Barbara F. Vucanovich, R.*

New Hampshire
1. Robert C. Smith, R.*
2. Charles C. Douglass III, R.

New Jersey
1. James J. Florio, D.*‡
2. William J. Hughes, D.*
3. Frank Pallone, Jr., D.
4. Christopher H. Smith, R.*
5. Marge Roukema, R.*
6. Bernard J. Dwyer, D.*
7. Matthew J. Rinaldo, R.*
8. Robert A. Roe, D.*
9. Robert G. Torricelli, D.*
10. Donald M. Payne, D.
11. Dean A. Gallo, R.*
12. Jim Courter, R.*
13. H. James Saxton, R.*
14. Frank J. Guarini, D.*

New Mexico
1. Steven H. Schiff, R.
2. Joe Skeen, R.*
3. William B. Richardson, D.*

New York
1. George J. Hochbrueckner, D.*
2. Thomas J. Downey, D.*
3. Robert J. Mrazek, D.*
4. Norman F. Lent, R.*
5. Raymond J. McGrath, R.*
6. Floyd H. Flake, D.*
7. Gary L. Ackerman, D.*
8. James H. Scheuer, D.*
9. Thomas J. Manton, D.*
10. Charles E. Schumer, D.*
11. Edolphus Towns, D.*
12. Major R. Owens, D.*
13. Stephen J. Solarz, D.*
14. Guy V. Molinari, R.*

15. Bill Green, R.*
16. Charles B. Rangel, D.*
17. Ted Weiss, D.*
18. vacant
19. Eliot L. Engel, D.
20. Nita M. Lowey, D.
21. Hamilton Fish, Jr., R.*
22. Benjamin A. Gilman, R.*
23. Michael R. McNulty, D.
24. Gerald B. Solomon, R.*
25. Sherwood L. Boehlert, R.*
26. David O'B. Martin, R.*
27. James T. Walsh, R.
28. Matthew F. McHugh, D.*
29. Frank Horton, R.*
30. Louise M. Slaughter, D.
31. William Paxon, R.
32. John J. LaFalce, D.*
33. Henry J. Nowak, D.*
34. Amory Houghton, Jr., R.*

North Carolina
1. Walter B. Jones, D.*
2. Tim Valentine, D.*
3. H. Martin Lancaster, D.*
4. David E. Price, D.*
5. Stephen L. Neal, D.*
6. Howard Coble, R.*
7. Charlie Rose, D.*
8. W. G. (Bill) Hefner, D.*
9. J. Alex McMillan III, R.*
10. Cass Ballenger, R.*
11. James McClure Clark, D.*

North Dakota
†Byron L. Dorgan, D.*

Ohio
1. Thomas A. Luken, D.*
2. Willis D. Gradison, Jr., R.*
3. Tony P. Hall, D.*
4. Michael G. Oxley, R.*
5. Paul E. Gillmor, R.
6. Bob McEwen, R.*
7. Michael DeWine, R.*
8. Donald E. (Buz) Lukens, R.*
9. Marcy Kaptur, D.*
10. Clarence E. Miller, R.*
11. Dennis E. Eckart, D.*
12. John R. Kasich, R.*
13. Donald J. Pease, D.*
14. Thomas C. Sawyer, D.*
15. Chalmers P. Wylie, R.*
16. Ralph Regula, R.*
17. James A. Traficant, Jr., D.*
18. Douglas Applegate, D.*
19. Edward F. Feighan, D.*
20. Mary Rose Oakar, D.*
21. Louis Stokes, D.*

Oklahoma
1. James M. Inhofe, R.*
2. Mike Synar, D.*
3. Wesley W. Watkins, D.*
4. Dave McCurdy, D.*
5. Mickey Edwards, R.*
6. Glenn English, D.*

Oregon
1. Les AuCoin, D.*
2. Robert F. Smith, R.*
3. Ron Wyden, D.*

4. Peter A. DeFazio, D.*
5. Denny Smith, R.*

Pennsylvania
1. Thomas M. Foglietta, D.*
2. William H. (Bill) Gray III, D.*
3. Robert A. Borski, Jr., D.*
4. Joseph P. Kolter, D.*
5. Richard T. Schulze, R.*
6. Gus Yatron, D.*
7. W. Curtis Weldon, R.*
8. Peter H. Kostmayer, D.*
9. E. G. (Bud) Shuster, R.*
10. Joseph M. McDade, R.*
11. Paul E. Kanjorski, D.*
12. John P. Murtha, D.*
13. Lawrence Coughlin, R.*
14. William J. Coyne, D.*
15. Don Ritter, R.*
16. Robert S. Walker, R.*
17. George W. Gekas, R.*
18. Doug Walgren, D.*
19. Wiliam F. Goodling, R.*
20. Joseph M. Gaydos, D.*
21. Thomas J. Ridge, R.*
22. Austin J. Murphy, D.*
23. William F. Clinger, Jr., R.*

Rhode Island
1. Ronald K. Machtley, R.
2. Claudine Schneider, R.*

South Carolina
1. Arthur Ravenel, Jr., R.*
2. Floyd Spence, R.*
3. Butler Derrick, D.*
4. Elizabeth J. Patterson, D.*
5. John M. Spratt, Jr., D.*
6. Robert M. (Robin) Tallon, D.*

South Dakota
†Tim Johnson, D.*

Tennessee
1. James H. Quillen, R.*
2. John J. Duncan, Jr., R.*
3. Marilyn Lloyd, D.*
4. James H. Cooper, D.*
5. Bob Clement, D.*
6. Bart Gordon, D.*
7. Donald K. Sundquist, R.*
8. John S. Tanner, D.
9. Harold E. Ford, D.*

Texas
1. Jim Chapman, D.*
2. Charles Wilson, D.*
3. Steve Bartlett, R.*
4. Ralph M. Hall, D.*
5. John W. Bryant, D.*
6. Joe Barton, R.*
7. Bill Archer, R.*
8. Jack Fields, R.*
9. Jack Brooks, D.*
10. J. J. (Jake) Pickle, D.*
11. J. Marvin Leath, D.*
12. Preston P. (Pete) Geren, D.
13. Bill Sarpalius, D.
14. Greg Laughlin, D.
15. Eligio (Kika) de la Garza, D.*
16. Ronald D. Coleman, D.*
17. Charles W. Stenholm, D.*

18. Craig A. Washington, D.
19. Larry Combest, R.*
20. Henry B. Gonzalez, D.*
21. Lamar S. Smith, R.*
22. Tom DeLay, R.*
23. Albert G. Bustamante, D.*
24. Martin Frost, D.*
25. Michael A. Andrews, D.*
26. Richard K. Armey, R.*
27. Solomon P. Ortiz, D.*

Utah
1. James V. Hansen, R.*
2. Wayne Owens, D.*
3. Howard C. Nielson, R.*

Vermont
†Peter P. Smith, R.

Virginia
1. Herbert H. Bateman, R.*
2. Owen B. Pickett, D.*
3. Thomas J. (Tom) Bliley, Jr., R.*
4. Norman Sisisky, D.*
5. Lewis F. Payne, Jr., D.*
6. James R. Olin, D.*
7. D. French Slaughter, Jr., R.*
8. Stanford E. (Stan) Parris, R.*
9. Frederick C. Boucher, D.*
10. Frank R. Wolf, R.*

Washington
1. John R. Miller, R.*
2. Al Swift, D.*
3. Jolene Unsoeld, D.
4. Sid Morrison, R.*
5. Thomas S. Foley, D.*
6. Norman D. Dicks, D.*
7. Jim McDermott, D.
8. Rod Chandler, R.*

West Virginia
1. Alan B. Mollohan, D.*
2. Harley O. Staggers, Jr., D.*
3. Robert E. Wise, Jr., D.*
4. Nick J. Rahall II, D.*

Wisconsin
1. Les Aspin, D.*
2. Robert W. Kastenmeier, D.*
3. Steven Gunderson, R.*
4. Gerald D. Kleczka, D.*
5. Jim Moody, D.*
6. Thomas E. Petri, R.*
7. David R. Obey, D.*
8. Toby Roth, R.*
9. F. James Sensenbrenner, Jr., R.*

Wyoming
†Craig Thomas, R.

Nonvoting representatives
American Samoa
Eni F. H. Faleomavaega, D.

District of Columbia
Walter E. Fauntroy, D.*

Guam
Ben Blaz, R.*

Puerto Rico
Jaime B. Fuster, D.*

Virgin Islands
Ron de Lugo, D.*

‡Florio was scheduled to resign his seat to take office as governor of New Jersey on Jan. 16, 1990.

Congress of the United States

House rules and said he welcomed an inquiry. On April 17, 1989, the ethics committee unanimously accused Wright of violating the rules on 69 occasions.

The committee's chairman, Representative Julian C. Dixon (D., Calif.), said bulk sales of Wright's book, *Reflections of a Public Man*, were "an overall scheme to evade" House limits on outside income. He said the Speaker also improperly accepted $145,000 in gifts from a businessman friend, George A. Mallick, in the form of a salary for Wright's wife, free and reduced-rate housing, and use of a Cadillac.

The ethics merry-go-round continues. Gingrich faced ethics accusations of his own in 1989. Those charges were unresolved at year-end, as was another, unrelated question: how far the House ethics committee would go in looking into allegations of sexual misconduct by House members.

Gingrich, a fiercely conservative partisan, was elected minority whip on March 22 to succeed Richard B. Cheney, who resigned his Wyoming House seat to become secretary of defense. The new Republican whip said he wanted to make ethics a major issue in the 1990 elections.

Gingrich's troubles, which began in late March 1989, resulted from questions about a sum of money—a total of $105,000—that he raised from 21 political supporters to promote a 1984 book of his own, *Window of Opportunity*. In April 1989, Representative Bill Alexander (D., Ark.) filed formal charges against Gingrich, who promised to cooperate with an ethics committee inquiry. On October 25, Alexander filed additional charges, alleging that Gingrich broke numerous House rules and federal laws relating to his personal finances and the use of campaign funds.

Sexual misconduct. A prominent House liberal, Representative Barney Frank (D., Mass.), became an ethics committee subject after admitting on August 25 that in 1985 he privately hired a male prostitute with a criminal record as a personal aide and housekeeper at his Washington, D.C., apartment. Frank, an acknowledged homosexual, said he fired the aide 18 months later after learning that the man had used the apartment for prostitution.

Three other House members also were subjects of inquiries involving allegations of sexual and official misconduct. They were Donald E. (Buz) Lukens (R., Ohio), sentenced on June 30 to 30 days in jail after being convicted in his home state of having sex with a 16-year-old girl; Gus Savage (D., Ill.), who denied accusations of sexually assaulting a Peace Corps volunteer during a trip to Africa; and Jim Bates (D., Calif.), accused of sexually harassing women on his staff. On October 18, the committee sent Bates a "letter of reproval"—the mildest form of official punishment.

New York congressman convicted. Representative Robert Garcia (D., N.Y.), was convicted on October 20, along with his wife, Jane Lee Garcia, of extorting more than $170,000 in payoffs from the Wedtech Corporation, a defense contractor in the South Bronx, an

area of New York City. On Jan. 2, 1990, he announced that he would resign on January 7. Garcia was the second congressman brought down in an investigation of Wedtech; Representative Mario Biaggi (D., N.Y.), a House member for 20 years, resigned in 1988 after being convicted of illegally obtaining federal contracts for the company.

In the Senate, the Select Committee on Ethics voted to investigate five members who intervened with banking regulators on behalf of Charles H. Keating, Jr., a central figure in a mammoth S&L scandal that the George Bush Administration inherited from the Administration of President Ronald Reagan. The five, who apparently accepted about $1.3 million in campaign contributions from Keating and his associates, denied wrongdoing. They were Senators John McCain III (R., Ariz.); Dennis DeConcini (D., Ariz.); Alan Cranston (D., Calif.); Donald W. Riegle, Jr., (D., Mich.); and John H. Glenn, Jr., (D., Ohio). The Senate committee was also making a separate investigation of a book-publishing deal involving Senator David F. Durenberger (R., Minn.).

Needing to rescue the stricken S&L industry, Treasury Secretary Nicholas F. Brady aroused public protests in January by suggesting that customers of banks and S&L's help finance the rescue by paying a fee on their deposits. Bush finally silenced the outcry on February 6 by proposing a bailout plan that did not involve deposit fees. It did, however, involve many billions of the taxpayers' dollars.

On August 5, Congress gave final approval to compromise legislation expected to cost between $100-billion and $240 billion over the next decade. The measure, signed by Bush on August 9, rewrote the rules under which the S&L industry operates and initially provided $50 billion to quickly shut down hundreds of insolvent institutions. The vote was 201 to 175 in the House and 17 to 7 in the Senate.

Pay hike. Congress had more trouble approving money for itself, and much of the blame for that was dumped on Speaker Wright. In fact, Wright's handling—or mishandling—of a proposed 50 per cent congressional pay raise was thought by many to be a significant factor in his downfall.

On January 5, shortly before leaving office, President Reagan approved pay hikes for Congress, federal judges, and other top officials, to take effect unless rejected by both the Senate and House by February 8. Reagan said that even his proposal for a 50 per cent congressional pay raise, to $135,000 a year from $89,500, would not make up for the loss to inflation over the years. Congress had received just one raise—a 16 per cent increase in 1987—since 1969.

The Senate voted 95 to 5 on February 2 to reject the pay package and thus avoid the possible wrath of constituents. Wright, however—following a script arranged in advance—announced that he would not schedule a vote in the House before the February 8 deadline, meaning that the raises would go into ef-

The First Congress: Democracy at Work

The First Congress of the United States met in New York City on March 4, 1789, heralded by roaring cannons and ringing church bells. The gathering was a momentous one. This was to be one of the first real tests of the U.S. Constitution, which had been drawn up during the Constitutional Convention in 1787.

Only a handful of lawmakers, however, were present on that March day. The rest were still making their way to New York City, a bustling port of 29,000 people and the temporary capital of the United States. The congressmen traveled by horseback, wagon, stagecoach, and ship. Some were delayed by bad roads and ice-clogged rivers, others by storms and even a shipwreck. Not until the first week in April did *quorums*—majorities in both the House of Representatives and the Senate—arrive to conduct business.

President-elect George Washington took even longer to make it to New York City. The barge he rode did not reach the city until the end of April. The trip from his home in Mount Vernon, Va., had turned into a triumphal procession, with crowds and celebrations following his journey. He was sworn in on April 30 before thousands of assembled citizens on a balcony outside Federal Hall. At last the new government was in place.

While waiting for the others to arrive, Virginia Representative James Madison worried that only a few of the new lawmakers would "share in the drudgery of business." Yet the First Congress compiled a record that remains awe-inspiring even after 200 years. They adopted rules and pro-

cedures for lawmaking. They assisted Madison in the drafting of the Bill of Rights. They set down laws establishing a court system as well as three executive departments—war, treasury, and foreign affairs (later called the State Department). Before adjourning in March 1791, the First Congress enacted commercial laws, created a central bank, and called for a nationwide census. In a fateful political bargain—arranged by Alexander Hamilton and others—Southern lawmakers accepted the provision that the national government repay the Revolutionary War debt in exchange for relocating the capital to the banks of the Potomac River in 1800.

Looking back at the First Congress, one is struck by its small size. The Senate had only 26 members—2 members for each of the 13 original states. The House of Representatives, with membership based on population, had just 65 members. The first census, in 1790, counted fewer than 4 million people in the United States. That meant 1 representative for every 35,000 people.

Two hundred years later, the 100 members of the Senate represent states ranging in population from 500,000 to more than 27 million people. The House of Representatives has 435 voting members from the 50 states and 5 nonvoting members from the District of Columbia and the U.S. territories of Puerto Rico, Guam, the Virgin Islands, and American Samoa. Each represents about 565,000 citizens.

The Congress of 1789 was also very different in makeup from the Congress of 1989. No women or blacks were among those lawmakers who first met in New York City. Today, however, women, blacks, and people of many different ethnic backgrounds serve in Congress.

Congress's workload—once small in volume—has grown to gigantic proportions. The First Congress passed 118 laws, an incredible number for that time. In contrast, the 100th Congress (1987-1988) passed 761 measures out of more than 11,000 that were introduced.

As Congress has grown, so has the activity that surrounds it. Instead of the handful of clerks who served the First Congress, more than 24,000 workers are involved in congressional matters. Once Congress was a part-time institution; lawmakers stayed in boarding houses in the capital and returned home as often as possible. Today, Congress is virtually a full-time institution, and Capitol Hill, the section of Washington, D.C., in which the Capitol is located, is busy year-round.

Although the size of Congress and its workload may have changed over the years, one thing has remained the same. Americans today can still voice their wide-ranging concerns to their senators and representatives—and expect Congress to listen and to act.   Roger H. Davidson

A fife and drum corps marches through Congress on March 2 to celebrate the 200th anniversary of the First Congress of 1789.

Ileana Ros-Lehtinen, a Florida Republican, was elected to the U.S. House of Representatives in August. She is the first Cuban-American in Congress.

fect. But the Speaker later bowed to public pressure and permitted a vote on February 7. The House rejected the pay boost, 380 to 48, even though most members desperately wanted one, and many were bitter at Wright for abandoning the script that would have raised salaries and would have left him taking the heat.

The pay issue festered for months until a bipartisan agreement in November led to a split pay scale for Senate and House. On November 16, the House voted 252 to 174 to boost pay for itself, federal judges, and top bureaucrats by up to 40 per cent by the end of 1991. House salaries of $89,500 would rise in two steps to just under $125,000. In return for the pay hike, House members would, beginning in 1991, be barred from keeping honorariums for speaking appearances. The legislation also made extensive changes in other ethics rules. But the Senate a day later refused to give up honorariums, voting instead, 56 to 43, to accept a 10 per cent pay hike, to $98,400. The House agreed to those changes, which apply only to the Senate.

Minimum wage. Another pay battle centered around a March 2 Bush proposal to raise the minimum wage for the first time in eight years. On May 11, the House voted 247 to 172 to raise the hourly minimum wage from $3.35 to $4.55 by 1991. The Senate followed suit May 17 by a vote of 63 to 37. Bush vetoed the bill on June 13, terming $4.55 "excessive" and decrying the absence of an Administration proposal for a lower training wage for new employees during their first six months on the job. The House fell 34 votes short of overriding the veto a day later.

On October 31, the White House and congressional Democrats agreed on a compromise that would boost the minimum wage to $3.80 in April 1990 and to $4.25 a year later. In addition, employers could pay workers age 16 to 19 a lower training wage of $3.35 for up to three months. The training wage would expire in 1993 unless renewed by Congress. The House approved the compromise, 382 to 37, on November 1 and the Senate acted, 89 to 8, on November 8. Bush signed the measure on November 17.

Defending the flag. A storm was triggered in Congress on June 21, when the Supreme Court of the United States—reviewing a Texas law—ruled 5 to 4 that burning the American flag was a form of free speech protected under the Bill of Rights. There were immediate cries of outrage in congressional chambers, and the next day the Senate passed a resolution, 97 to 3, denouncing the decision. On June 27, Bush called for a constitutional amendment to protect the flag.

In time, those opposed to making the first change ever in the Bill of Rights advocated legislation as an alternative to amending the Constitution. On October 5, the Senate passed, 91 to 9, a bill designed to circumvent the Supreme Court's ruling and restore criminal penalties for burning the flag. The House passed the legislation, 371 to 43, on October 12, and Bush allowed it to become law without his signature.

Abortion funding. The heated issue of federal funding for abortions for poor women who become pregnant because of rape or incest set Bush and Congress at odds with each other in 1989. The House, after voting eight years straight against such legislation, reversed itself on October 11 by a 216 to 206 vote, and the Senate passed a spending bill that included the abortion provision on October 19 by a 67 to 31 margin. Bush vetoed the bill two days later, and the House upheld the veto on October 25.

Protecting whistle blowers. Five years of efforts to protect federal workers who expose fraud and abuse reached success on April 10 when Bush signed the Whistleblower Protection Act of 1989. The bill had won unanimous congressional approval.

Combating the drug problem. Bush made his first television address to the nation on September 5 to unveil an antidrug program. He termed it a $7.9-billion program, but it actually added only $717 million to spending already planned. Although the program did not violate Bush's "no new taxes" campaign pledge of 1988, his proposals would require increases in state spending that could lead to higher taxes at that level.   Frank Cormier and Margot Cormier

See also **Foley, Thomas S.; United States, Government of the.** In *World Book,* see **Congress of the United States.**

Connecticut. See State government.

Conservation. Conservationists from many countries in 1989 mounted what is probably the largest, most intensive campaign ever to preserve a single species—the African elephant. In 1979, there were more than 1.2 million elephants, but in 1989, the population was down at least to 750,000, with some estimates as low as 300,000. Poachers killed most of the elephants to obtain their ivory tusks.

Ivory wars. In Kenya alone, the elephant population plummeted from about 65,000 in 1970 to about 17,000 in 1989. The loss of these distinctive animals threatens a tourist industry worth more than $400 million annually. Kenya's President Daniel T. arap Moi in February ordered an all-out war against poachers, instructing soldiers to shoot them on sight. Nevertheless, poachers—most of them from neighboring Somalia—killed more than 50 elephants in and near Kenya's Tsavo National Park within about one week.

In May, Kenya, Tanzania, and other African nations urged a worldwide ban on ivory. On June 5, the United States announced a temporary ban on the importation of all ivory. Four days later, the 12-nation European Community followed suit with a similar moratorium. Japan, which buys about 40 per cent of the ivory on the world market, ordered a limited ban on June 16. The bans deprived Hong Kong, where much of the world's ivory is carved, of markets for its ivory products, and it banned raw ivory imports on June 16 as well.

Conservationists hoped that African countries would support the pleas for a ban at a July meeting in Botswana of the African countries that participate in the Convention on International Trade in Endangered Species (CITES). But Zimbabwe, South Africa, and Botswana—which earn substantial income by culling their large elephant populations and selling tusks—declined.

In October, representatives of 103 nations at a CITES meeting in Switzerland voted overwhelmingly to ban international trade in ivory after Jan. 18, 1990. Botswana, Zimbabwe, and Mozambique indicated that they would file reservations, which under CITES rules would allow them to continue to export ivory if buyers could be found. All of the countries that participate in CITES will be prohibited from accepting ivory, however.

Bear poaching. Poachers threaten many species, including some in North America. In January 1989, federal and state wildlife officials arrested 10 people for slaughtering 400 black bears in the Northeastern United States in order to obtain the animals' gallbladders. The organs are sold in Asia, where they are prized as sexual stimulants and as curatives. As Asian bear populations have been depleted, poaching rings have sprung up in several areas of the United States.

Endangered rain forests. The destruction of the Amazon rain forest, particularly in Brazil, continued to worry environmentalists throughout the world. Brazilians have been burning large areas of the rain forest to clear land for farming and ranching. A delegation of U.S. senators visited Brazil in January to discuss a program in which some of Brazil's foreign debt would be forgiven if Brazil preserved large tracts of its rain forest. Brazilian President José Sarney Costa rejected the proposal, condemning it as foreign interference.

Conservationists found some hope in September, when calculations based on satellite photographs showed that forest burning declined in 1988. Heavy rains during the annual dry season were responsible for most of the decrease, but the Brazilian government also played a role. Officials suspended the practice of giving subsidies to landowners who cleared land and ranched it, and cracked down on illegal settlers in the Amazon region.

Deadly nets. Environmentalists, along with U.S. and Canadian commercial fishing crews, were disappointed by a tentative agreement in June 1989 between the United States and Japan. The nations agreed to monitor but not prohibit Japan's use of huge fishing nets, called drift nets, in the North Pacific. Taiwan and South Korea also deploy the nets, some of which are 35 miles (56 kilometers) long. Each year, the nets catch and kill thousands of dolphins and hundreds of thousands of sea birds. The North American fishing crews also complain that the nets snare millions of salmon and steelhead trout in North American waters, violating international treaties. A report in September revealed that Italian and Spanish fishing

Elephant tusks confiscated from poachers by the Kenyan government are burned in July as a symbol of Kenya's resolve to stop the ivory trade.

boats use similar big nets in the Mediterranean Sea.

A similar conflict erupted within the United States when shrimpers defied new regulations requiring *turtle excluder devices* (TED's) on their shrimp nets. TED's provide escape hatches for turtles, thousands of which drown each year because they become entangled in nets. The shrimpers complained that TED's were too expensive and that they let a large part of their catch escape along with the turtles. On July 24, U.S. Secretary of Commerce Robert A. Mosbacher temporarily suspended the regulations. Several conservation groups brought lawsuits, however, and on September 5, the Commerce Department reinstituted the order requiring TED's.

Endangered species. In February, the U.S. General Accounting Office (GAO) accused the Fish and Wildlife Service (FWS) of altering data that would have placed the spotted owl on the endangered species list. (The GAO is an independent agency in the government's legislative branch that examines the operations of most federal agencies.) The timber industry has strongly opposed such a listing, because it would halt logging in the Pacific Northwest's mature forests— the bird's principal remaining habitat. In April, the FWS reversed its decision and proposed the spotted owl as an endangered species. If finalized, the designation will protect 1.5 million acres (600,000 hectares) of old-growth forest. But, on May 19, a federal district judge in Oregon dismissed a lawsuit brought by con-

servationists to prevent logging in western Oregon forests.

On June 25, loggers, environmentalists, and politicians produced a tentative agreement to protect the oldest trees—and the spotted owls—while permitting timber harvest in large areas of the Northwest. On July 26, the Senate voted to permit cutting 4 billion board feet (9.4 million cubic meters) of old-growth timber during 1990 and 1991, a decision that appeared to protect spotted owls but also allowed far more logging than conservationists proposed.

A study reported in July by researchers at Cornell University in Ithaca, N.Y., stated that the populations of seven species of birds found in the United States are declining rapidly. The researchers urged that the spotted owl be added to the endangered species list along with the Harris's hawk, Henslow's sparrow, loggerhead shrike, seaside sparrow, snowy plover, and vermilion flycatcher. The population of each species has dwindled as habitats have been destroyed.

The California condor population grew significantly in April and May, when four chicks hatched and survived at the Los Angeles Zoo and the San Diego Wild Animal Park. In the Special Reports section, see **Saving Our Big Birds.**

The black-footed ferret, which was on the verge of extinction in 1986, has flourished in a captive-breeding regime. In spring 1989, 67 of 76 newborn ferrets survived, increasing the species' total population to 124. Wildlife managers hope to begin releasing ferrets into the wild in 1991.

The designation of the desert tortoise as an endangered species halted the construction of housing developments in the Las Vegas, Nev., area in August. The FWS declared the turtle endangered because an outbreak of disease is severely reducing its population. Now that the turtle is considered endangered, developers cannot erect new buildings in its habitat; nor can they move the tortoises elsewhere.

Other developments. In March, the U.S. Environmental Protection Agency announced that it would review the proposal for the Two Forks Dam in the South Platte River near Denver. The review blocked construction for the foreseeable future. Colorado officials consider the dam essential to provide water for Denver's future development. Environmentalists lobbied against the project because the dam would flood a scenic area rich in wildlife and useful for recreation. They also asserted that the region's needs for water could be met in other ways.

The U.S. Department of the Interior announced the creation of the 30,000-acre (12,000-hectare) Florida National Wildlife Refuge on June 19. The department made the designation primarily to protect the Florida panther, a type of cougar believed to number only 30 to 50.   Eugene J. Walter, Jr.

See also **Environmental pollution; Ocean.** In *World Book,* see **Conservation.**

Consumerism. Consumer prices in the United States rose at an annual rate of 4.6 per cent for the 12 months ending on Nov. 30, 1989, up 0.2 of a percentage point from 1988, as determined by the Consumer Price Index (CPI). The CPI, the standard measure of the cost of goods and services, is compiled by the Bureau of Labor Statistics of the U.S. Department of Labor.

All 99 categories of consumer prices rose for the year. Increases included fuel oil, up 9.9 per cent, and food, up 5 per cent.

A monthly rise of 0.4 per cent in the CPI for urban wage earners in September, which ends the government's fiscal year, triggered an automatic 4.7 per cent cost-of-living increase in 1990 benefits for about 48.1 million Americans. They included 38.9 million social security recipients, civil service workers, military veterans, and railroad retirees.

Consumer fraud. The federal district court in Chicago reached an agreement in April with BankCard Travel Club, its two parent companies, and two corporate officers, under which they agreed to pay up to $2.5 million in compensation to consumers. A complaint filed by the Federal Trade Commission (FTC) in November 1987 had alleged that the defendants failed to honor cancellation requests and improperly charged annual membership fees to consumers' credit cards. The consent orders—which are for settlement purposes only and do not constitute an admission of a law violation—have the force of law.

The FTC also announced in May 1989 that $1.98 million in refunds had been sent to consumers who bought Alaskan oil and gas leases from two *telemarketers* (firms that solicit business by telephone). The refunds were part of a settlement of FTC charges, originally filed in 1984, against Alaska Land Leasing, Incorporated, Federal Lease Filing Corporation, and several individuals. They allegedly persuaded consumers to invest millions of dollars in almost worthless mineral leases. Refunds ranging from $300 to $3,000, representing about 20 per cent of the consumers' investments, went to approximately 1,500 customers.

Mail fraud. A couple allegedly involved in a mail fraud scheme involving time-share vacation properties were brought to trial during 1989. Federal authorities believe that David and Annette DeFusco—under their own names and a variety of aliases—sent out more than enough mailings to have reached each of the nation's 90 million households between 1985 and 1989. The DeFuscos' mailings "guaranteed" large prizes—often a new, expensive BMW automobile or $10,000 worth of gold bullion—to recipients who had only to visit a resort development to claim their prizes. People who responded were pressured to purchase condominiums and generally received such inexpensive gifts as hamburger grills and bathtub bubble-making devices—but never an automobile, gold bullion, or other expensive items.

On October 6, David DeFusco, 34, pleaded guilty in federal district court in Beaumont, Tex., to mail fraud and conspiracy for his role in the time-share resort property case. The related federal charges against Annette DeFusco, 28, were dropped.

On October 20, both DeFuscos pleaded guilty in federal district court in Alexandria, Va., to bankruptcy fraud and money laundering. The U.S. attorney there described how the DeFuscos had used a variety of names, written several million dollars in bad checks, and created phantom corporations to hide profits from their many companies. Meanwhile, they lived a lavish life style at successive homes in Virginia, Texas, and California and enjoyed such luxuries as a $95,000 Rolls-Royce car. Prosecutors said that claims against them for unpaid bills exceeded $2.5 million.

David DeFusco faced a maximum of 20 years in prison but would likely serve 70 to 87 months, then be paroled. Annette DeFusco also faced a maximum of 20 years but would likely serve 41 to 51 months. Sentencing was set for Jan. 12, 1990. David DeFusco's Texas plea carried a maximum sentence of 10 years. A federal judge was to decide if he would serve the sentences concurrently or consecutively.

The American Resort and Residential Development Association, a trade group, deplored the DeFuscos' activities. The association said it represents a majority of the 1,100 owners of time-share developments in the United States.   Odom Fanning

In *World Book,* see **Consumerism.**
Costa Rica. See **Latin America.**

Courts

Courts. In what was probably 1989's most controversial legal decision, a Tennessee judge ruled on September 21 that a human life begins the moment that an egg and sperm cell join together. Although the case pertained solely to who should get custody of several frozen embryos, the judge's ruling that the embryos were unborn children rather than mere clusters of cells set what may be an important precedent, according to legal scholars. Some experts said the decision, if upheld on appeal, would likely strengthen the hand of abortion opponents.

The ruling, by Circuit Court Judge W. Dale Young, was part of a divorce proceeding between a Knoxville couple, Junior Lewis Davis and Mary Sue Davis. In 1980, the couple went to a Knoxville fertility clinic, where Junior Davis' sperm was used to fertilize nine of his wife's egg cells. The fertilized eggs were allowed to divide into embryos of four to eight cells each before being frozen. Two of the embryos were unsuccessfully implanted in Mrs. Davis' womb; the remaining seven were still frozen at the clinic in early 1989 when the Davises filed for divorce.

Mary Sue Davis asked the court for custody of the embryos, saying that they represented her best chance for becoming a mother. Junior Davis countered that the state had no right to force him to become a father. He argued that the embryos should not be used and should be considered part of the joint property of the marriage.

In ruling for the wife, Judge Young treated the case, in effect, as a child-custody dispute rather than a property settlement. "From fertilization, the cells of a human embryo are differentiated, unique, and specialized to the highest degree of distinction," the judge ruled. Thus, he said, "life begins at conception."

Steinberg convicted. On January 30, a New York City jury returned a verdict of first-degree manslaughter against Joel B. Steinberg in the death of 6-year-old Lisa Steinberg, a child he had unofficially adopted. He was acquitted of the more serious charge of murder. Steinberg's highly publicized trial, which began in October 1988, focused the nation's attention on the problems of domestic violence and child abuse.

The jury concluded that Steinberg, a disbarred New York City lawyer, struck Lisa in the head several times with his fist on the evening of Nov. 1, 1987. The girl died several days later from a severe brain injury.

The most dramatic testimony was given by Steinberg's long-time companion, Hedda Nussbaum, who was on the stand for seven days. Nussbaum, her face puffy and disfigured, recounted that Steinberg had beaten and brutalized her for more than 10 years. She said Steinberg had been hitting and mistreating Lisa for several months before she died. On the night that Steinberg struck the fatal blows, Nussbaum said, she and he left the girl lying unconscious for 12 hours before summoning medical help.

Steinberg and Nussbaum both were charged in the case initially. The charges against Nussbaum were

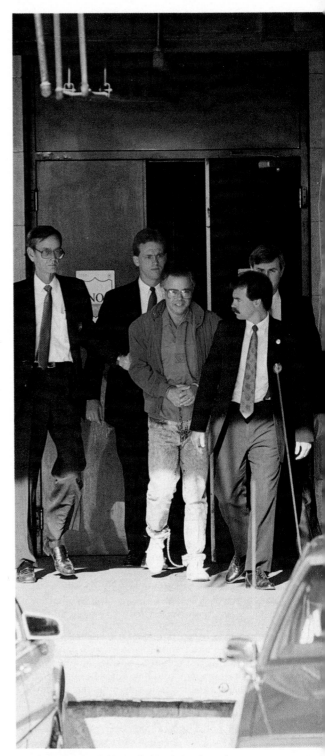

TV evangelist Jim Bakker is led in chains from the federal courthouse in Charlotte, N.C., on October 24 after being sentenced to 45 years in prison for fraud.

dropped after the prosecution decided she had been too severely beaten by Steinberg to have inflicted the fatal wounds on Lisa.

On March 24, Steinberg was given the maximum sentence of 8⅓ to 25 years in prison.

Downfall of a "queen." On August 30, a federal jury in New York City convicted Leona Helmsley, the president of Helmsley Hotels, Incorporated, of 33 counts of income tax evasion, conspiracy, filing false tax returns, and mail fraud. Helmsley, described as the "queen" of the hotels in advertising, was acquitted of the most serious charges against her, conspiring to extort kickbacks from contractors and suppliers.

Two of Helmsley's former employees who were accused of aiding her tax-evasion schemes were co-defendants in the trial and were also found guilty. Helmsley's husband, 80-year-old Harry B. Helmsley, had originally been named in the indictment, but he was later declared mentally unfit to stand trial.

The three defendants were charged with fraudulently billing several million dollars worth of the Helmsleys' personal expenses to the hotel chain and other Helmsley enterprises. The expenditures were deducted as business expenses on the companies' tax returns. On December 12, Helmsley was sentenced to four years in prison and fined $7.1 million.

Stiff sentence for Bakker. Television evangelist Jim Bakker, the former head of the PTL ministry, was convicted of 24 counts of fraud and conspiracy in federal court in Charlotte, N.C., on October 5. On October 24, Judge Robert Potter sentenced Bakker to 45 years in prison and fined him $500,000.

Bakker was accused of defrauding his followers by selling them "lifetime partnerships" in his Heritage USA Christian retreat and theme park in Fort Mill, S.C. For a $1,000 donation, contributors were promised a vacation at Heritage USA every year for life. At the trial, it came out that Bakker used most of the $158-million from contributors for purposes other than constructing the lodging needed to accommodate all the lifetime subscribers.

Wall Street conspirator crashes. Corporate raider Paul A. Bilzerian was convicted in federal court in New York City on June 9 of securities fraud and conspiracy. The verdict was the first major conviction stemming from a three-year government probe of illegal activities in the U.S. stock market. Bilzerian was charged with making illegal securities transactions that netted him millions of dollars.

"Night Stalker" suspect found guilty. On September 20, a Los Angeles jury convicted Richard Ramirez, a 29-year-old drifter from Texas, of 13 murders and 30 other crimes. Ramirez was accused of being the "Night Stalker" who terrorized Southern California in 1985. On November 7, he was sentenced to death.

LaRouche gets 15 years. Lyndon H. LaRouche, Jr., leader of a right wing political group who was convicted of fraud and conspiracy in December 1988, was sentenced on Jan. 27, 1989, to 15 years in federal prison. LaRouche, a three-time independent presidential candidate, was found guilty of cheating supporters out of $30 million.

Conviction in school bus wreck. A jury in Carrollton, Ky., on December 21 found an Owen County man, Larry W. Mahoney, guilty of manslaughter in connection with a 1988 highway collision that killed 27 people. Mahoney had admitted that he was drunk on May 14, 1988, as he drove his pickup truck in the wrong lane on Interstate 71 near Carrollton and hit a school bus. The resulting explosion and fire killed 24 youths and 3 adults, making the wreck the worst drunken-driving accident in U.S. history.

Guilty verdict for Miami cop. William Lozano, a Miami, Fla., police officer on trial for the killing of two men on a motorcycle in January, was found guilty of manslaughter on December 7. A six-member jury rejected Lozano's argument that he fired because the motorcycle—being chased by a police patrol car—was about to run him down. He fired a single shot, killing the driver of the motorcycle. The other rider was injured when the bike crashed and died the next day. Both of the dead men were black; Lozano is Hispanic. The deaths triggered three days of rioting. The verdict was denounced by many Miami-area Hispanics and police officers.   David L. Dreier

See also **Crime; Iran-contra affair; Supreme Court of the United States.** In *World Book,* see **Court; Law.**

Crime. A number of crimes involving semiautomatic firearms in 1989 brought new calls in the United States for limits on the sale and possession of such weapons. A semiautomatic weapon such as an AK-47 assault rifle fires a round each time the trigger is squeezed. The federal government already bans imports of fully automatic weapons, which fire bullets continuously as long as the trigger is squeezed until the supply is exhausted.

School shooting rampage. A man wearing combat fatigues on January 17 opened fire with an AK-47 at children in the schoolyard of Cleveland Elementary School in Stockton, Calif. Five children, all refugees from Southeast Asia, were killed, and 29 other children and one teacher were wounded before the gunman killed himself. The assailant, Patrick E. Purdy, whose age was variously reported as 24, 26, or 27, was a former pupil at the school. Police said they knew no motive for the shootings; however, Purdy reportedly resented the influx of immigrants from Southeast Asia and the success they had attained.

Purdy, armed with two handguns and a Chinese-made AK-47 (an inexpensive copy of a Soviet design), parked his car near the school and set the vehicle on fire as a diversion before entering the school grounds. According to a spokesman for the Stockton Police Department, the gunman, also known as Patrick West, had an "extensive criminal history," including arrests on weapons and narcotics charges. Police officials re-

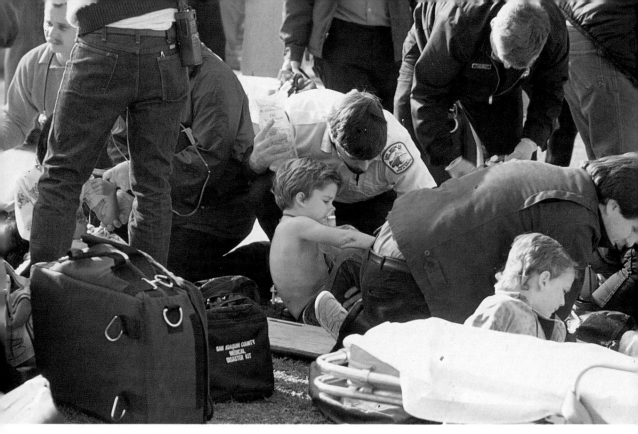

Paramedics treat wounded schoolchildren in Stockton, Calif., after a
gunman opened fire with an assault rifle, killing five, in January.

ported that Purdy had apparently lied about his name
and criminal background on the federal form required
for the purchase of the rifle.

Assault rifle ban. The Stockton killings touched
off a national debate about semiautomatic assault
rifles and prompted efforts by several city and state
legislatures to ban their sale and possession. On March
14, the Administration of President George Bush
banned imports of about 80 per cent of semiautomatic weapons shipped to the United States pending
the results of a study on whether such weapons had
legitimate sporting uses. On April 5, 24 additional
models were added to the list of illegal weapons, widening the ban to include virtually all assault rifle imports. About 75 per cent of the semiautomatic assault
weapons available in the United States are domesti-
cally produced, according to the U.S. Bureau of Alcohol, Tobacco and Firearms.

Printing plant slayings. A gunman armed with an
AK-47 and several other weapons on September 14
killed 8 people and wounded 15 others in a Louisville,
Ky., printing plant where he once worked. The assailant, Joseph T. Wesbecker, 47, then killed himself.

According to police, Wesbecker had worked as a
pressman at the Standard Gravure Corporation printing plant but had been put on permanent disability
leave in 1988 and had been under treatment for
manic-depressive illness. Plant workers said that Wesbecker told them he was "looking for bosses," but

that when he failed to find any, he began randomly
shooting people.

The incident prompted renewed calls for further
restrictions on the sale of automatic weapons. But
President Bush said on September 15 that the shootings had not changed his opposition to further federal
curbs on semiautomatic weapons.

Montreal murders. The largest mass murder in
Canada's history took place on Dec. 6, 1989, when a
gunman entered the University of Montreal engineering building, killing 14 people and injuring 13 others
before shooting himself. Gunman Marc Lepine used a
.223-caliber Sturm-Ruger semiautomatic hunting rifle,
which he had bought legally in Montreal. The incident
prompted calls for tightening Canada's already strict
gun-control laws.

President unveils anticrime plan. On May 15,
President Bush announced a $1.2-billion federal anti-
crime program to "take back the streets" from criminals. Key elements of the plan included tougher penalties for crimes involving guns; banning the import,
sale, manufacture, or transfer of semiautomatic
weapon magazines that carry more than 15 rounds of
ammunition; a permanent ban on some imported
semiautomatic weapons; spending more than $1 bil-
lion for prison construction; and hiring new federal
law enforcement personnel.

Central Park rape. A 28-year-old Wall Street investment banker, jogging in New York City's Central

Park on the evening of April 19, was attacked by a group of about a dozen youths. According to police, the woman was savagely beaten by the youths and raped by at least four of them. The victim was found several hours later and taken to a local hospital, where she remained in a coma until May 3. She returned to work on a limited basis in November.

Police said the attack was part of a crime spree carried out by a loosely organized group of up to 30 teen-agers. Some of the youths brought in for questioning described their actions—random attacks on at least nine people in a two-hour period in Central Park—as "wilding," a term new to the police. Eight suspects aged 14 to 17 were arraigned on April 23 on charges of rape, assault, and attempted murder. A ninth youth was charged with participating in an attack on a male jogger.

Chicago commodities scandal. The U.S. Department of Justice on August 2 announced the indictment of 46 futures traders at the Chicago Board of Trade and the Chicago Mercantile Exchange, accusing them of defrauding customers by stealing and skimming clients' profits. The indictments were the result of a two-year investigation by agents of the Federal Bureau of Investigation (FBI). The agents, who had received special training in commodities trading, infiltrated trading floors and secretly recorded hundreds of conversations between commodity traders, gathering evidence of illegal trading practices.

Wall Street crime. In a record Wall Street criminal settlement, investment brokers Drexel Burnham Lambert Incorporated on September 11 pleaded guilty to six counts of fraud and paid more than $500 million in fines and restitution. On March 29, a federal grand jury had charged the company and the firm's chief junk-bond specialist, Michael R. Milken, with racketeering and securities fraud. The charges cited nearly 100 violations of securities laws, including the manipulation of stock prices and rigging of corporate takeovers. On April 7, Milken pleaded innocent, and a trial in his case was still pending at year-end.

Record cocaine seizure. Drug agents seized 21.4 short tons (19.4 metric tons) of cocaine and more than $12 million in cash on September 29 in a raid in a warehouse complex in Sylmar, a suburb of Los Angeles. The seizure was the largest narcotics haul on record. As of October 1, six suspects, including a former Mexican customs inspector, had been arrested in connection with the case.

Crime rates up. Violent crime and personal theft rose in 1988 for the second straight year, the U.S. Department of Justice reported on Oct. 29, 1989. According to the department's National Crime Survey, the number of these offenses increased 3.1 per cent in 1988. The survey measured personal and household offenses, including crimes not reported to law-enforcement officials, by interviewing people 12 years old or older at their residences. The 1988 survey included interviews of 101,000 people in 50,000 homes.

Mail bombs. A federal judge in Birmingham, Ala., and a Savannah, Ga., lawyer were killed in December 1989 by pipe bombs sent through the mail. Two more bombs—one found in a federal court building in Atlanta, Ga., and the other in the headquarters of the National Association for the Advancement of Colored People in Jacksonville, Fla.—were disarmed.

Investigators cited racial hatred as a likely motive for the attacks. But FBI officials stressed that their investigation was open-ended and that no possibilities, including activities related to drug trafficking, had been ruled out.

The slain federal judge, Robert S. Vance, sat on the bench of the United States Court of Appeals for the 11th Circuit, a court that heard cases relating to desegregation and the Georgia Ku Klux Klan. Robert E. Robinson, the slain lawyer, was one of three blacks on the Savannah City Council. He had been active in civil rights and had handled a number of employment discrimination cases in his law practice.

A few days after the two fatal attacks, a Maryland county circuit court judge, known for strict sentencing in drug cases and for outspoken views favoring gun control, was injured by a pipe bomb. But a federal agent said that the device differed substantially from the bombs used in the other attacks, and the police said they had no clear motive or suspects in the attack.　Joan Stephenson

In **World Book,** see **Crime.**

Cristiani Burkard, Alfredo (1947-　), was elected president of El Salvador on March 19, 1989. Cristiani—the candidate of the right wing National Republican Alliance, known as ARENA—took office on June 1. See **El Salvador.**

Born on Nov. 22, 1947, Cristiani was the son of a wealthy coffee grower. He attended the American School in San Salvador, the capital, and then graduated from Georgetown University in Washington, D.C., with a bachelor's degree in business administration.

Returning to El Salvador after graduation, Cristiani married Margarita Llach. He became president of Seguros y Inversiones, a financial company owned by his wife's family.

Cristiani became head of ARENA following the 1984 presidential elections, in which his party lost to the Christian Democrats. After that defeat, Cristiani helped ARENA try to shed its image as the sponsor of death squads responsible for political assassinations. He sought better relations between ARENA and the U.S. government and put forward moderate political positions during the 1989 election campaign. But critics charged that Cristiani was merely a "pretty" face for an organization that continued to be involved in terrorism.

Cristiani is an avid sportsman. He is a former national squash champion and also once held the national motocross title.　Rod Such

Cuba

Cuba. It was a difficult and perplexing year for Cuban President Fidel Castro, who has ruled Cuba for 30 years, becoming Latin America's longest-ruling leader in 1989. Castro found himself out of step with the reforms taking place in the Soviet Union, Cuba's closest ally. He also discovered that some of his oldest and most trusted collaborators were involved in international drug trafficking, as United States intelligence agencies had charged and Castro had denied for a long time.

In January, the first contingent of some 50,000 Cuban troops withdrew from far-off Angola, where they had been helping Angola's Communist regime fight rebel forces backed by South Africa. In accord with a treaty signed in December 1988, Cuban forces were to be completely withdrawn by July 1991.

On April 2, 1989, Soviet President Mikhail S. Gorbachev, architect of the reforms known as *perestroika* (economic restructuring) and *glasnost* (open criticism), began a three-day visit to Cuba, the first by a top Soviet leader since 1974. Castro dismissed any suggestion that Cuba was ready for Soviet-style reforms: "Perestroika is another man's wife," the bearded Cuban leader quipped. "I don't want to get involved." Still another sign of differences over the reforms came in August, when Cuba banned two Soviet publications—*Moscow News* and *Sputnik*—"for justifying bourgeois democracy."

Human-rights violations also remained a problem in Cuba. During Gorbachev's visit, Hiram Abi Cobas, acting head of the Human Rights Party of Cuba, was arrested and sentenced to three months in jail for trying to organize a demonstration. He was released on probation because of a heart condition.

In August, Cobas was arrested again, along with Elizardo Sánchez, the head of the Cuban Commission for Human Rights and National Reconciliation, and Hubert Jerez, the president of the José Martí Commission on Human Rights. The arrests followed a meeting between the three human-rights activists and foreign journalists. In November, Sánchez was sentenced to two years in prison.

Tourism. During the year, Cuban officials laid out plans for reviving the nation's tourism industry, which in pre-Castro days was the bulwark of the island's economy. Cuban officials signed a contract with an international hotel chain based in Spain to set up hotel schools in government-designated tourist areas. Castro himself, who has long criticized tourism as demeaning and the cause of prostitution, predicted that Cuba could earn more than $500 million a year from tourism, a threefold increase that would make it Cuba's leading business.

Executions. On July 13, the Castro regime announced that a firing squad had executed four officers convicted by a special military tribunal of conspiring to ship tons of cocaine and marijuana to the United States. It was Cuba's biggest scandal since Castro seized power in 1959.

The four officers were General Arnaldo T. Ochoa Sánchez, a highly decorated soldier who had commanded troops in Ethiopia and Angola; the general's aide, Captain Jorge Martinez Valdez; Colonel Antonio de la Guardia, chief of a special smuggling section established by Castro to circumvent the trade embargo imposed by the United States; and Major Amado Padrón Trujillo, who had set up the system for illicitly shipping cocaine from Colombia via Cuba to U.S. markets. Ten other defendants convicted of lesser offenses were sent to jail.

Some U.S. officials theorized that Castro was using the drug scandal to purge the armed forces of disloyal officers and ensure that his brother Raúl, Cuba's defense minister, would eventually be his successor. Others speculated that Castro was determined to mete out harsh punishment to those involved in drugs at a time when corruption within the highest levels of his government was said to be rampant.

TV broadcast. The Voice of America was scheduled to begin beaming television broadcasts to Cuba in December. The broadcasts from Florida were to be bounced off a balloon floating high above the Florida Keys. It was hoped that the broadcasts would become as popular as those of Radio Martí, the U.S.-sponsored radio station based in Florida.　　Nathan A. Haverstock

See also **Latin America** (Facts in brief table). In *World Book,* see **Cuba.**

Cyprus. See **Middle East.**

Czechoslovakia set the stage for drastic political change in 1989. For the first 10 months of the year, the nation's Communist government resisted the wave of reform sweeping through Eastern Europe. Opponents of the regime held demonstrations in Prague's Wenceslas Square, but apparently to little avail.

On November 17, the government angered the Czechoslovak public by breaking up a student demonstration in the square and beating protesters. Student leaders and heads of other opposition groups met in a Prague theater on November 19, forming an umbrella organization called Civic Forum. Hundreds of thousands of demonstrators jammed Wenceslas Square that afternoon and for days thereafter, calling for an end to the Communist monopoly on political power.

The Communist Party yielded to public pressure on November 24, dismissing several members of its policy-making body, the Presidium, including hard-line party chief Miloš Jakeš. Karel Urbanek, who was relatively moderate, replaced Jakeš as party leader. The party yielded further on November 27, agreeing to hold talks with Civic Forum and calling for the creation of a broad-based coalition government. And on November 29, the Federal Assembly (parliament) deleted from the Constitution articles establishing the "leading role" of the Communist Party and requiring that all education be based on Marxist-Leninist teachings.

Communist domination ended in early December. Prime Minister Ladislav Adamec tried to hold the

Demonstrators and police face off in Prague, Czechoslovakia, on January 16, in the first of many antigovernment demonstrations during the year.

line on December 3, announcing a coalition Cabinet made up of 16 Communists and 5 non-Communists. Civic Forum rejected this coalition, however, and protesters returned to Wenceslas Square. Adamec resigned on December 7.

On December 10, President Gustáv Husák, a hardline Communist, swore in the country's first government since 1948 that was not dominated by the Communist Party. The new Cabinet was made up of 10 Communists, 7 ministers with no affiliation, and 2 from each of two small parties that had been closely allied with the Communists. The new prime minister, Marian Calfa, a Communist, said that his government's main job would be "to prepare for free, democratic elections" in 1990. After swearing in the new government, Husák resigned. On Dec. 20, 1989, Adamec replaced Urbanek as Communist Party head.

Reformers elected. On December 28, the Federal Assembly elected Alexander Dubček as its chairman. As Communist Party chief in 1968, Dubček had led a sweeping reform movement. Invading forces from the Soviet Union and other Soviet-bloc countries crushed that movement in August 1968 and Dubček was dismissed in 1969.

On Dec. 29, 1989, the Assembly elected Vaclav Havel president of Czechoslovakia. Havel was a playwright and the leader of Civic Forum.   Eric Bourne

See also **Europe** (Facts in brief table). In *World Book,* see **Czechoslovakia.**

Daley, Richard Michael (1942-   ), state's attorney for Cook County, Illinois, since 1980, was sworn in as mayor of Chicago on April 24, 1989. Daley won a special election on April 4 to fill the final two years of the term of Mayor Harold Washington, who died in 1987. Daley beat out Eugene Sawyer, the city's acting mayor, in a Democratic primary held in February. With his victory, Daley followed in the footsteps of his father, Richard J. Daley, probably Chicago's most politically powerful mayor, who served from 1955 until his death in 1976.

In the April 1989 election, Daley easily defeated his closest opponent, Alderman Timothy C. Evans, who ran as an independent. Although Daley and Evans avoided the race issue during the campaign, the vote split along racial lines. Daley, who is white, carried the white and Hispanic vote. Evans, who is black, received the support of black voters. Before the election, Daley vowed to reach out to all of the city's racial and ethnic groups.

Daley was born in Chicago on April 24, 1942. He received a law degree from DePaul University in Chicago in 1968.

His political career began in 1972, when he was elected an Illinois senator, a position he held until he was elected Cook County state's attorney. As state's attorney, he fought illegal drugs and gangs.

Daley married Margaret Corbett in 1972. The couple have three children.   Mary A. Krier

Dancing

Mikhail Baryshnikov, artistic director of the American Ballet Theatre (ABT) since 1980, quit his job twice in 1989. On June 21, he announced that he would step down in August 1990, at the end of the ABT's 50th anniversary season. He said that he wanted to pursue other interests, among them acting. In March 1989, the Soviet-born ballet star had made his Broadway debut in *Metamorphosis*, a dramatic adaptation of a story by Czech writer Franz Kafka, and had been nominated for a Tony Award.

On September 28, however, Baryshnikov quit the ABT abruptly after the company's board of trustees refused to overrule a management decision to remove his personal assistant. Baryshnikov said the board's action infringed on his rights as artistic director.

Baryshnikov's action was expected to have little bearing on the ABT's daily activities during the 1989-1990 season because the company's repertory had already been set. Baryshnikov had not planned to spend much time with the troupe in any case. Nevertheless, his sudden departure left the ABT without an artistic head.

Mixed reviews. Controversy over repertory surrounded the ABT in 1989. All of the company's major new productions received mixed notices. Baryshnikov's eccentric restaging of *Swan Lake* had much new choreography and reinstated many passages of the original score by Peter Ilich Tchaikovsky that had been cut in later versions. Baryshnikov also reinterpreted the narrative by changing the traditional black swan of Act III into a white swan. Critics appreciated Baryshnikov's musical scholarship, but most found his tinkering with the well-known story silly and his new choreography banal.

Modern accent. The three new works created for the ABT by Twyla Tharp, whom Baryshnikov had appointed as artistic associate in 1988, were not nearly as successful as ballets she had previously choreographed for the company. The three pieces were *Quartet*, set to a score by minimalist composer Terry Riley; *The Bum's Rush*, set to music by jazz pianist Dick Hyman; and *Everlast*, set to songs by musical-comedy composer Jerome Kern.

The range of these works was remarkably wide, but each piece was flawed. Moreover, many observers questioned the wisdom of giving so prominent a place in a classical ballet troupe to a choreographer whose background was primarily in modern dance.

The New York City Ballet also lost significant players in 1989. On November 1, Lincoln Kirstein retired as general director of the company and president of the affiliated School of American Ballet. Kirstein and George Balanchine, the Russian-born choreographer whom Kirstein brought to the United States in 1933, founded the School of American Ballet

The Paul Taylor Dance Company performs in Taylor's *Minikin Fair,* a satire of ballet, which premiered in New York City in April.

in 1934 and a succession of companies that eventually became the City Ballet.

On November 5, Jerome Robbins announced his resignation as codirector as of Jan. 1, 1990. Like Baryshnikov, he wished to pursue other interests. Robbins had joined City Ballet in 1949 and had choreographed many pieces for the company.

Two of City Ballet's senior ballerinas also retired in 1989. On June 4, Patricia McBride was honored by a farewell performance in which she danced many of the ballets created for her during her 30 years with the troupe. On November 26, Suzanne Farrell per-

formed with the company for the last time, in Balanchine's *Vienna Waltzes*. In June, she had created a new role in *Echo*, choreographed by Peter Martins, the company's artistic codirector. This ballet was most notable for bringing Farrell back to the stage after a long layoff due to hip surgery.

Kirov Ballet. Earlier in 1989, Farrell embarked on a new career as a ballet mistress when she staged Balanchine's *Scotch Symphony* for Leningrad's Kirov Ballet. The Soviet troupe also performed his *Theme and Variations*, staged by Francia Russell, coartistic director of the Pacific Northwest Ballet in Seattle. The two productions were the first performances by a major Soviet dance company of works by Balanchine, a former Kirov member.

These ballets proved to be the most exciting aspect of the Kirov's tour of North America during the summer. Although Balanchine was a direct heir of the Kirov tradition, the technique he developed in the West outpaced Russian developments. Could the Soviets master the art of their native son? The answer, most critics said, was yes. Although the Kirov's three-month tour was a financial success, critics in the United States found Soviet modern choreography outdated and looked in vain for dancers as dazzling as former Kirov artists Natalia Makarova, Rudolf Nureyev, and Baryshnikov.

Stranded. High drama, though of a different sort, was provided by another Soviet troupe, the Donetsk Ballet from the Ukraine. This small, little-known

Dancing

Members of the Kirov Ballet from Leningrad in the Soviet Union perform the North American premiere of *Le Corsaire* in New York City in July.

troupe was set to tour small cities across the United States beginning in January but was stranded in Baltimore when the tour's producers suddenly withdrew support. Their reason was the failure of the group to come with guest stars from other Soviet companies, as had been promised.

The Donetsk Ballet was soon rescued by various art patrons who provided them with food and hotel lodgings in Baltimore. An arts management group in New York City then arranged a substitute tour, which opened in New York City in February.

Americans in Paris. In honor of the bicentennial of the French Revolution, both the Alvin Ailey American Dance Theater and the San Francisco Ballet performed in Paris. (Ailey, who formed his company in 1958, died on Dec. 1, 1989. On December 20, dancer and choreographer Judith Jamison was named director of the Ailey company.) Also as part of a Franco-American exchange, eight dance groups from France performed in July at the American Dance Festival in Durham, N.C., and at the Jacob's Pillow Dance Festival in Lee, Mass.

Nureyev resigns. Nureyev resigned as dance director of the Paris Opéra Ballet in November in a dispute with the company's management. He was to continue as the troupe's "premiere choreographer."

Mark Morris. United States-born choreographer Mark Morris, whose dance company is based at the Théâtre de la Monnaie, the opera house in Brussels, Belgium, returned to the United States in June. The

reason was the U.S. premiere of Morris' *Dido and Aeneas* in Boston. Morris upheld his reputation for controversy by performing the roles of Queen Dido and the witch himself. This titillating bit of casting aside, Morris' choreography was deemed masterful by many and a fascinating experiment by all.

Lackluster year. With the exception of the Morris work, it was not a distinguished year for U.S. choreographers. Martha Graham premiered *American Document*, her 179th work, on October 4, opening night of her troupe's three-week season at City Center. *American Document* is based on a work the 95-year-old choreographer made in 1938, with some new choreography and music. Not even the appearance of Baryshnikov, who danced on opening night only, added sharpness to what was considered a confused, rambling dance.

Merce Cunningham presented two new abstract works in September 1989 in Berkeley, Calif. Paul Taylor was in a comic mood, creating the whimsical *Minikin Fair* for his troupe's April season at City Center and *The Sorcerer's Sofa* for an engagement at the John F. Kennedy Center for the Performing Arts in Washington, D.C., the first week of November. The Joffrey Ballet's one premiere of the year also took place there on October 10. *The Pantages and the Palace Present Two-a-Day* by Gerald Arpino, the Joffrey's artistic director, is a tribute to vaudeville.   Nancy Goldner

In *World Book,* see **Ballet; Dancing.**

De Klerk, Frederick Willem (1936-   ), head of South Africa's ruling National Party (NP), was elected state president on Sept. 14, 1989. De Klerk had been acting president since August 15, a day after he and other Cabinet members persuaded State President Pieter Willem Botha to resign. Botha, who had been president since 1984, suffered a stroke in January 1989. Since then, many critics felt, his leadership style had become increasingly ineffective. See **South Africa.**

De Klerk was born on March 18, 1936, in Johannesburg. His father was a senator in the national Parliament and later a Cabinet minister.

De Klerk attended Potchefstroom University in South Africa, graduating in 1958, and he earned a law degree with honors there in 1961. He then practiced law in Vereeniging, near Johannesburg.

In 1972, de Klerk was elected to Parliament, representing the NP. From 1978 to 1989, he held a number of Cabinet positions in the government of Prime Minister (later State President) Botha. De Klerk became NP leader in February 1989—again, succeeding Botha.

Upon assuming the presidency in 1989, de Klerk promised to keep South Africa moving toward a system of government in which the nation's black majority—who have long been excluded from political participation—will be fully represented. He faces strong opposition from many South African whites, however.   David L. Dreier

Deaths in 1989 included those listed below, who were Americans unless otherwise indicated. An asterisk (*) indicates that a biography of the person can be found in *The World Book Encyclopedia.*

Abdallah Abderemane, Ahmed (1919-Nov. 26), president of the Indian Ocean nation of Comoros since 1978.
Adachi, Ken (1928-Feb. 10), Canadian literary critic; longtime contributor to *The World Book Year Book.*
Adamson, George (1906-Aug. 20), British conservationist who worked with his wife, Joy, in Kenya, teaching lions born in captivity to live in the wild. Joy Adamson described their work in *Born Free* (1960) and other books.
Ahidjo, Ahmadou (1924-Nov. 30), president of the African nation of Cameroon from 1960 to 1982.
*****Ailey, Alvin** (1931-Dec. 1), dancer, choreographer, and founder of the Alvin Ailey American Dance Theater.
Allison, Fran (1907-June 13), human co-star of puppets Kukla and Ollie on television's "Kukla, Fran and Ollie."
Allott, Gordon L. (1907-Jan. 17), Republican senator from Colorado from 1955 to 1973.
Alsop, Joseph (1910-Aug. 28), influential conservative political columnist.
Anderson, Forrest H. (1913-July 20), Democratic governor of Montana from 1969 to 1973.
Anderson, Robert B. (1910-Aug. 14), U.S. secretary of the treasury from 1957 to 1961.
Andrews, Harry (1911-March 6), British character actor noted for gruff military roles.
Armour, Richard (1906-Feb. 28), whimsical poet.
Ashmore, Robert T. (1904-Oct. 4), Democratic representative from South Carolina from 1953 to 1969.
Ayer, A. J. (Sir Alfred Ayer) (1910-June 27), British philosopher, knighted in 1970.
Backus, Jim (1913-July 3), actor best known as the voice of Mr. Magoo in cartoons and as the millionaire on TV's "Gilligan's Island." See **Motion pictures (Close-Up).**
Ball, Lucille (1911-April 26), red-haired star of the "I Love Lucy" TV series of the 1950's. See **Television (Close-Up).**
Bari, Lynn (Marjorie Schuyler Fisher) (1913-Nov. 20), husky-voiced actress who played roles in nearly 50 films.
Barrett, Edward W. (1910-Oct. 23), dean of the Columbia Graduate School of Journalism in New York City from 1956 to 1968; founder of *The Columbia Journalism Review.*
Barthelme, Donald (1931-July 23), short-story writer and novelist.
Bavier, Frances (1903?-Dec. 6), actress who played Aunt Bee on "The Andy Griffith Show" and "Mayberry, R.F.D."
Beach, Donn (1908?-June 7), restaurateur who founded the chain of Don the Beachcomber restaurants and invented more than 80 mixed drinks, including the mai tai.
*****Beadle, George W.** (1903-June 9), geneticist who shared the 1958 Nobel Prize in physiology or medicine.
Bechtel, Stephen D. (1900-March 14), president from 1936 to 1960 of Bechtel Corporation, one of the world's largest construction companies.
Beck, Charles (1910?-Nov. 22), creator of the Captain Marvel comic book series.
*****Beckett, Samuel Barclay** (1906-Dec 22), Irish-born author who won the 1969 Nobel Prize for literature.
Beckman, Brad (1964-Dec. 18), tight end for professional football's Atlanta Falcons.
Bentsen, Lloyd M., Sr. (1893?-Jan. 17), real estate developer; father of Senator Lloyd M. Bentsen, Jr. (D., Tex.).
*****Berlin, Irving (Israel Baline)** (1888-Sept. 22), Russian-born songwriter whose best-known hits include "God Bless America," "Blue Skies," and "White Christmas."
Berry, Ricky (1964-Aug. 14), forward for basketball's Sacramento Kings; their top draft pick in 1988.
Blackman, Raymond V. B. (1910-May 17), British military author and journalist; editor of *Jane's Fighting Ships* from 1949 to 1973.

Hirohito, long-reigning emperor of Japan

Vladimir Horowitz, piano virtuoso

Gilda Radner, "Saturday Night Live" star

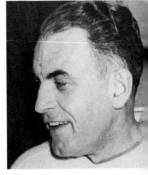

Joe Primeau, Canadian hockey star

Blaik, Red (Earl H. Blaik) (1897-May 6), head football coach at the U.S. Military Academy in West Point, N.Y., from 1941 to 1958.
Blaize, Herbert A. (1918-Dec. 19), prime minister of the Caribbean nation of Grenada since 1984.
Blake, Amanda (Beverly Louise Neill) (1929-Aug. 16), actress who played Kitty on TV's "Gunsmoke."
Blanc, Mel (Melvin Jerome Blanc) (1908-July 10), the voice of Bugs Bunny, Porky Pig, and hundreds of other cartoon characters. See **Motion pictures (Close-Up).**
Blue, Robert D. (1898-Dec. 14), Republican governor of Iowa from 1945 to 1949.
Bolger, William F. (1923-Aug. 21), postmaster general of the United States from 1978 to 1984.
Bond, James (1900-Feb. 14), leading ornithologist whose name was borrowed by British author Ian Fleming for his fictional secret agent.
Booth, Olive (1891-Dec. 13), British leader of the Salvation Army; last surviving granddaughter of founder William Booth.
Brico, Antonia (1902-Aug. 3), Dutch-born symphony conductor who was the subject of the 1974 documentary *Antonia: Portrait of a Conductor.*
Brittain, Donald (1928-July 21), leading Canadian documentary filmmaker.
Browne, Dik (Richard A. Browne) (1917-June 4), creator of the "Hägar the Horrible" comic strip.
Bruce, Louis R., Jr. (1906-May 20), Native American leader who served as commissioner of the U.S. Bureau of Indian Affairs from 1969 to 1973.

Deaths

Burns, Jethro (Kenneth C. Burns) (1920-Feb. 4), mandolin player in the country-music duo Homer and Jethro.

Busch, August A., Jr. (1899-Sept. 29), former president of Anheuser-Busch, Incorporated, the world's largest brewing company, and of the St. Louis Cardinals baseball team.

Calhoun, Lee (1933-June 21), gold medalist in the 110-meter hurdles at the 1956 and 1960 Olympic Games.

Campi, Lou (1905-Aug. 31), Italian-born stonemason who won the first Professional Bowlers Association tournament in 1959; member of American Bowling Congress Hall of Fame.

Case, George W. (1915-Jan. 23), outfielder for the Washington Senators from 1937 to 1945; six-time American League leader in stolen bases.

Cassavetes, John (1929-Feb. 3), actor, director, and screenwriter who received Academy Award nominations in all three categories.

Cavallaro, Carmen (1917-Oct. 12), big-band era pianist, bandleader, and composer.

*****Ceauşescu, Nicolae (1918-Dec. 25)**, long-time dictator of Romania.

Chapman, Graham (1940?-Oct. 4), British physician and actor; a founding member of the comedy group Monty Python's Flying Circus.

Chappell, William V., Jr. (1922-March 30), Democratic representative from Florida from 1969 to 1989.

Chatwin, Bruce (1940-Jan. 17), British travel writer and novelist.

Clarke, T. E. B. (Thomas Ernest Bennett Clarke) (1907-Feb. 11), British screenwriter who won an Oscar for *The Lavender Hill Mob* (1951).

Claude D. Pepper, champion of the aged

Daphne du Maurier, author of *Rebecca*

Huey P. Newton, Black Panther leader

Irving Berlin, prolific songwriter

Cobb, Arnett (1918-March 24), jazz saxophonist.

Collins, James M. (1916-July 21), Republican representative from Texas from 1968 to 1983.

Conlan, Jocko (John B. Conlan) (1899-April 16), National League umpire and member of the National Baseball Hall of Fame.

Constable, William Henry Archibald (1906-Aug. 21), Australian painter and theatrical designer.

Cotter, John M. (1904-Aug. 28), founder of the True Value hardware chain.

Cotton, Norris (1900-Feb. 24), Republican representative from New Hampshire from 1947 to 1954 and senator from that state from 1954 to 1975.

Coulouris, George (1903-April 25), British actor who specialized in villainous roles.

Cowley, Malcolm (1898-March 27), writer and literary critic.

Crook of Carshalton, Lord (Reginald D. Crook) (1901-March 10), British diplomat.

Curtis, Laurence (1893-July 11), Republican representative from Massachusetts from 1953 to 1963.

Cyrankiewicz, Józef (1911-Jan. 20), prime minister of Poland from 1947 to 1952 and from 1954 to 1970.

Daché, Lilly (1892?-Dec. 31), French-born hat designer.

*****Dali, Salvador (1904-Jan. 23)**, Spanish surrealist painter.

*****Davis, Bette (Ruth Elizabeth Davis) (1908-Oct. 6)**, actress known for playing strong-willed women in a film career that spanned more than 55 years.

Davis, Victor (1964?-Nov. 13), Canadian swimming star who won a gold medal at the 1984 Olympic Games.

Davison, William E. (1906-Nov. 14), jazz cornetist known as "Wild Bill" Davison.

De Kooning, Elaine (1920-Feb. 1), painter whose style united realism and abstract expressionism; wife of Dutch-born artist Willem de Kooning.

DeGaetani, Jan (1933-Sept. 15), concert singer.

Dempsey, John N. (1915-July 16), Irish-born Democratic governor of Connecticut from 1961 to 1971.

Diori, Hamani (1916-April 23), Niger's first president, from 1960 to 1974.

*****Du Maurier, Daphne (1907-April 19)**, British novelist best known for the mystery *Rebecca* (1938).

Eldridge, Roy (1911-Feb. 26), one of the great innovators of the jazz trumpet.

Elwyn-Jones, Lord (Frederick Elwyn-Jones) (1909-Dec. 4), British prosecutor at the Nuremberg war-crimes trials in the 1940's; made a life peer in 1974.

Erteszek, Olga (1916?-Sept. 15), Polish-born clothing designer and founder of the Olga Company, a lingerie firm.

Evans, Maurice (1901-March 12), British-born classical actor who played the warlock father on TV's "Bewitched."

Fain, Sammy (Samuel Feinberg) (1902-Dec. 6), Academy Award winning composer who wrote "I'll Be Seeing You" (1938) and "Love Is a Many-Splendored Thing" (1955).

Farley, Walter (1915-Oct. 16), author of *The Black Stallion* (1941) and its sequels, novels popular with young readers.

Farrally, Betty (1915-April 9), British-born Canadian ballet dancer; cofounder of the Royal Winnipeg Ballet.

Festinger, Leon (1919-Feb. 11), psychologist who developed the theory of *cognitive dissonance,* a state of agitation that occurs when two simultaneously held thoughts or beliefs are inconsistent.

Field, Ron (1934-Feb. 6), choreographer who won Tony Awards for his dances in *Cabaret* in 1967 and for his choreography and directing in *Applause* in 1970.

Fitzgerald, Pegeen (Margaret Worrall) (1910-Jan. 30), star of a radio talk show with her husband, Edward.

*****Flahiff, George Bernard Cardinal (1905-Aug. 22)**, retired Roman Catholic archbishop of Winnipeg, Canada; made a cardinal in 1969.

Fools Crow, Frank (1890?-Nov. 27), Sioux Indian spiritual leader who traveled as a young man with Buffalo Bill Cody's Wild West show.

Franz Josef II (1906-Nov. 13), prince of the tiny European country of Liechtenstein since 1938.

Fraze, Ermal Cleon (1913?-Oct. 26), engineer who invented the pull-tab opener used on aluminum beer and soda cans.

French, Victor (1934-June 15), bearded co-star of TV's "Little House on the Prairie" and "Highway to Heaven."

Furillo, Carl A. (1922-Jan. 21), hard-hitting outfielder for the Brooklyn (later Los Angeles) Dodgers from 1946 to 1960.

Gann, Paul (1912-Sept. 11), coauthor of California's Proposition 13 tax-cutting measure.

Giamatti, A. Bartlett (1938-Sept. 1), commissioner of baseball and former president of Yale University.

Goldman, Eric F. (1915-Feb. 19), historian who served as an adviser to President Lyndon B. Johnson.

Gomez, Lefty (Vernon Louis Gomez) (1909-Feb. 17), pitcher for the New York Yankees from 1930 to 1943; member of the National Baseball Hall of Fame.

Gould, Beatrice Blackmar (1898-Jan. 30), coeditor of the *Ladies Home Journal* magazine with her husband, Bruce, from 1935 to 1967.

Green, Richard R. (1936-May 10), educator who in 1988 became the first black chancellor of New York City's public schools.

Griggs, S. David (1939-June 17), astronaut who flew as a mission specialist on the space shuttle *Discovery* in 1985.

*****Gromyko, Andrei Andreyevich** (1909-July 2), foreign minister of the Soviet Union from 1957 to 1985.

Grundig, Max (1908-Dec. 8), founder of the West German electronics company Grundig A.G.

Harding of Petherton, Lord (Allan F. Harding) (1896-Jan. 20), commander of the British division known as the Desert Rats at the Battle of El Alamein in Egypt in 1942.

Harrington, Michael (1928-July 31), political scientist whose 1962 book *The Other America* helped inspire the U.S. government's War on Poverty.

Hart, Harvey (1928-Nov. 21), Canadian filmmaker and director who won a Golden Globe Award for *East of Eden,* a TV miniseries.

Harvey, Doug (1924-Dec.26), Canadian hockey star who, while with the Montreal Canadiens, won the Norris Trophy as the National Hockey League's top defenseman seven times from 1955 to 1962; member of the Hockey Hall of Fame.

Hassenfeld, Stephen D. (1942-June 25), chairman and chief executive of Hasbro Industries Incorporated toy company.

Haynsworth, Clement F., Jr. (1912-Nov. 22), judge whose nomination to the U.S. Supreme Court by President Richard M. Nixon was rejected by the Senate in 1969.

Hays, Wayne L. (1911-Feb. 10), Democratic congressman from Ohio from 1949 until he resigned in 1976 after admitting a sexual relationship with staff member Elizabeth Ray.

Helm, Buck (1931-Nov. 18), longshoreman who survived for 90 hours trapped in the wreckage of a freeway that collapsed in the October 17 California earthquake.

Heywood, Eddie (1915-Jan. 2), jazz pianist who composed the 1950's hit "Canadian Sunset."

Hicks, Sir John (1904-May 20), British economist who won the Nobel Prize in economics in 1972.

Higgins, William Richard (1945-reported killed on July 31), U.S. Marine lieutenant colonel attached to a United Nations (UN) peacekeeping force in Lebanon; a hostage since February 1988.

Hill of Luton, Lord (Charles Hill) (1904-Aug. 22), British physician who broadcast health advice as the "Radio Doctor" of the British Broadcasting Corporation (BBC) during the 1940's; later a member of Parliament and BBC chairman.

*****Hirohito** (1901-Jan. 7), emperor of Japan since 1926.

Hirsch, John (1930-Aug. 1), Hungarian-born Canadian theater director; artistic director of the Stratford Festival from 1980 to 1985.

Hoffman, Abbie (Abbott Hoffman) (1936-April 12), antiwar protester who helped found the radical Yippie movement of the 1960's.

Bette Davis, legendary motion-picture actress

A. Bartlett Giamatti, baseball commissioner

Ayatollah Ruhollah Khomeini, Iran's supreme leader

Salvador Dali, flamboyant artist

*****Horowitz, Vladimir** (1904-Nov. 5), Russian-born virtuoso who was one of the world's greatest concert pianists.

Hoving, Walter (1897-Nov. 27), head of Tiffany & Company jewelers from 1955 to 1980.

*****Hu Yaobang** (1915-April 15), general secretary of China's Communist Party from 1981 to 1987.

Huggins, Nathan I. (1927-Dec. 5), historian and educator who was a leader in Afro-American studies.

Hunt, John E. (1908-Sept. 22), Republican representative from New Jersey from 1967 to 1975.

Ibarruri Gómez, Dolores (1895-Nov. 12), Spanish Communist who, under the name La Pasionaria (The Passionflower), crusaded against fascism during Spain's Civil War (1936-1939).

Ignatieff, George (1913-Aug. 10), Russian-born Canadian diplomat who served as Canada's ambassador to the UN from 1966 to 1969.

James, C. L. R. (Cyril Lionel Robert James) (1901-May 31), Trinidadian-born British historian.

Johnson, Judy (William Julius Johnson) (1899-June 15), Negro League third baseman elected to the National Baseball Hall of Fame.

Jorgensen, Christine (George Jorgensen, Jr.) (1926-May 3), former U.S. Army clerk who in 1952 underwent the first sex-change surgery to become a woman.

Jurriens, Henny (1949-April 9), Dutch-born Canadian ballet dancer; artistic director of the Royal Winnipeg Ballet.

*****Kádár, János** (1912-July 6), leader of Hungary from 1956 to 1988 as general secretary of the Communist party.

*****Karajan, Herbert von** (1908-July 16), Austrian symphony and opera conductor.

Lord of Stage and Screen

Laurence Olivier, often hailed as the greatest actor of his generation, died in his sleep at the age of 82 on July 11, 1989, at his home south of London. His death ended an acting and directing career that embraced stage, screen, and television.

Olivier performed his many roles—onstage and off—with equal mastery. Even as he codirected London's Old Vic Theatre with Sir Ralph Richardson, he directed and starred in the first successful motion-picture versions of Shakespeare. Acclaimed as a classical actor on the English stage, he became a matinee idol in Hollywood. His dedication helped him fight cancer, pneumonia, stage fright, suicidal depression, and, finally, a painful and debilitating muscular disease.

Olivier was born on May 22, 1907, in Dorking, southwest of London. His father, a stern Anglican clergyman, nevertheless encouraged his frail son to pursue an acting career. Olivier's first success was in Noel Coward's sophisticated comedy *Private Lives* in 1930 in London.

Olivier's stage reputation grew with such classic roles as Romeo, Richard III, and Oedipus. In the 1940's, he began directing as well as acting, and in 1963 he became the founding director of Britain's National Theatre. He allied himself with New Wave British playwrights known for their savage realism. One of those "angry young men," John Osborne, created a character whom Olivier immortalized on stage and screen: the vaudevillian Archie Rice in *The Entertainer*.

In his screen career, Olivier's combination of good looks and talent brought him 10 Academy

Laurence Olivier directed and starred in a 1948 film version of *Hamlet*. The now-classic movie won him an Oscar as best actor.

Award nominations, a 1948 Oscar (for his acting in *Hamlet*), 3 Emmys for television acting, and, in 1979, a special Oscar for his life's work. In 1970, he became Lord Olivier of Brighton, the first actor in British history to be made a life peer.

Olivier's relationship with the film industry was rocky from the start. In 1939, he accepted the role of the tormented Heathcliff in *Wuthering Heights* believing that his frequent co-star Vivien Leigh would be cast as the female lead—a role she was denied. During filming, Olivier quarreled with producer Samuel Goldwyn, who called him "Oliver" and criticized his acting as too stagy. But Olivier's vengeful Heathcliff became a classic, lauded again when the film was reissued in 1989.

Olivier was cast in another brooding, lordly role as Maxim de Winter in Alfred Hitchcock's *Rebecca* (1940). The same year, his air of aloofness made him a proper Darcy opposite Greer Garson's Elizabeth in *Pride and Prejudice*.

In a widely publicized affair, Olivier and Leigh divorced their first spouses and wed in 1940. Although they frequently co-starred on stage, they made only one more film together, *That Hamilton Woman* (1941), in which Olivier played Horatio Nelson opposite Leigh's Lady Hamilton.

Ambivalent about Hollywood, Olivier worked through London studios during the late 1940's, when he revolutionized the screen treatment of Shakespeare. His *Henry V* (1944) combined stage and screen techniques with an imaginative use of color. But he filmed his strongly Freudian *Hamlet* (1948) in morose, sensual black and white. Olivier produced, directed, and starred in both films.

Olivier returned to Hollywood films in 1952 as a restaurant maître d' in *Carrie*. Director Elia Kazan wrote of watching Olivier practice for hours at folding a napkin. "The audience may not know," Olivier said, "but I'll know."

Carrie flopped, however, returning Olivier to dubious box-office standing in the United States. His screen version of *Richard III* (1955) did not achieve the success of *Henry V* and *Hamlet*.

The fading of his leading-man looks in the 1960's freed Olivier to concentrate on character acting. After a series of films that culminated with the highly successful *Sleuth* (1972), he announced he was taking roles primarily for money. His career hit bottom in 1982 with his cardboard performance as Douglas MacArthur in *Inchon*. But even during this commercial phase, Olivier did memorable work in such films as *Marathon Man* (1976) and *The Boys from Brazil* (1978).

In one of his last films, *Clash of the Titans* (1981), he brought the god Zeus to life with the words, "It is my wish. It is my command." He pronounced "command" with the nonchalant emphasis of a true deity. To the public, Lord Larry had come to represent just that.   Philip Wuntch

Kee, James (1917-March 11), Democratic representative from Virginia from 1965 to 1973.

Keevil, Norman Bell (1910-Oct. 9), Canadian geophysicist and mining executive; founder of Teck Corporation, one of Canada's leading mining companies.

Kelly, Dan (1936-Feb. 10), announcer for the St. Louis Blues hockey team; member of the broadcast wing of the Hockey Hall of Fame.

Keogh, Eugene J. (1907-May 26), Democratic congressman from New York from 1937 to 1967; principal sponsor of the pension-plan legislation that bears his name.

*Khomeini, Ruhollah (1900?-June 3), Islamic religious authority who became Iran's supreme ruler in 1979.

Kimbrough, Emily (1899-Feb. 11), coauthor, with Cornelia Otis Skinner, of *Our Hearts Were Young and Gay* (1942), a book of reminiscences of Europe in the 1920's.

Kirkwood, James (1924-April 21), novelist, actor, and playwright who won both a Tony Award and a Pulitzer Prize in 1976 for coauthoring *A Chorus Line.*

Knudson, George (1937-Jan. 24), Canada's outstanding professional golfer of the 1960's.

Koontz, Elizabeth D. (1919-Jan. 6), first black president of the National Education Association, the largest organization of U.S. teachers.

Laing, R. D. (Ronald David Laing) (1927-Aug. 23), British psychiatrist who pioneered new treatment for schizophrenia.

Laroche, Guy (1921-Feb. 17), French fashion designer.

Leland, Mickey (George T. Leland) (1944-Aug. 7), Democratic representative from Texas since 1979.

Leone, Sergio (1929-April 30), Italian motion-picture director best known for such Westerns as *A Fistful of Dollars* (1964) and *For a Few Dollars More* (1965).

Lichine, Alexis (1913-June 1), Russian-born French wine expert who founded Alexis Lichine & Company.

Lillie, Beatrice (Lady Peel) (1894-Jan. 20), Canadian-born British stage comedian.

Little, Royal B. (1896-Jan. 12), founder and former chairman of Textron Incorporated.

Lord, John Wesley (1902-Oct. 8), former bishop of the United Methodist Church; a leader in the civil rights and antiwar movements of the 1960's.

*Lorenz, Konrad Z. (1903-Feb. 27), Austrian naturalist who shared the Nobel Prize for physiology or medicine in 1973 for his studies of animal behavior.

Loveless, Herschel C. (1911-May 4), Democratic governor of Iowa from 1957 to 1961.

Lucas, Wingate H. (1908-May 26), Democratic representative from Texas from 1947 to 1955.

Magnuson, Warren G. (1905-May 20), Democratic representative from Washington state from 1937 to 1944 and senator from that state from 1944 to 1981.

Maguire, John J. (1904-July 6), Roman Catholic archbishop; long-time aide to Francis Cardinal Spellman of New York City.

Mahoney, Jock (Jacques O'Mahoney) (1919-Dec. 14), former stuntman who starred in TV's "Yancy Derringer."

Mangano, Silvana (1930-Dec. 16), Italian actress whose first starring role was in *Bitter Rice* (1949).

*Manning, Timothy Cardinal (1909-June 23), Roman Catholic archbishop of Los Angeles.

Mapplethorpe, Robert (1946-March 9), photographer known for his dramatic black-and-white pictures.

*Marcos, Ferdinand E. (1917-Sept. 28), president of the Philippines from 1965 to 1986.

Martin, Billy (Alfred Manuel Martin) (1928-Dec. 25), five-time manager of baseball's New York Yankees.

Martonmere, Lord (John R. Robinson) (1907-May 3), Conservative member of the British House of Commons from 1931 to 1964 and governor general of Bermuda from 1964 to 1972.

Mason, Ford S. (1893-Aug. 16), founder of the Ford Gum & Machine Company, which installed penny gumball machines in stores throughout the United States.

Andrei A. Gromyko,
Soviet foreign minister

Abbie Hoffman,
1960's radical

Georges Simenon, creator
of Inspector Maigret

Mel Blanc, man
of many voices

Matuszak, John D. (1950-June 17), defensive lineman for the Oakland Raiders who became an actor after retiring from football in 1981.

*McCarthy, Mary (1912-Oct. 25), author and critic whose best-known novel was *The Group* (1963).

McGee, Dean A. (1904-Sept. 15), pioneer in the offshore oil drilling industry; president, chairman of the board, and chief executive officer of Kerr-McGee Corporation.

McMahon, Gregory (1915-June 27), Republican representative from New York from 1947 to 1949.

McMillan, Kenneth (1932-Jan. 8), burly character actor who played the boss on the 1970's TV series "Rhoda."

Meillon, John (1934-Aug. 11), Australian actor who played Paul Hogan's sidekick in the "*Crocodile*" *Dundee* movies.

Milanov, Zinka (1906-May 30), Yugoslav-born opera singer.

Miller, Fishbait (William M. Miller) (1909-Sept. 12), folksy doorkeeper of the U.S. House of Representatives from 1949 to 1953 and from 1955 to 1974.

Mills, Herbert (1912-April 12), member of the smooth-singing Mills Brothers quartet.

Moawad, René (1935-Nov. 22), president of Lebanon for just 17 days before he was assassinated.

Mohr, Charles H. (1929-June 16), Pulitzer Prize winning political and military correspondent for *The New York Times.*

Moore, Steve (1960-Oct. 25), starting tackle for football's New England Patriots in 1985 and 1986.

Morial, Ernest N. Dutch (1929-Dec. 24), New Orleans' first black mayor, from 1978 to 1986.

Morris, Richard B. (1904-March 3), historian and expert on the American colonial period.

Deaths

Morrison, Ernie (Frederic Ernest Morrison) (1913?-July 24), actor who played Sunshine Sammy, first black member of the Our Gang comedy team in films.

Morrison, Herbert (1905?-Jan. 10), radio newscaster remembered for his emotional description of the 1937 crash of the airship *Hindenburg*.

Newman, Lionel (1916-Feb. 3), composer and conductor of the music for more than 250 films.

Newton, Huey P. (1942-Aug. 22), cofounder of the Black Panther Party, a radical group that in the 1960's advocated armed self-defense for blacks.

Norris, Clarence (1912-Jan. 23), last surviving defendant of the 1931 Scottsboro rape case, which became a symbol of racial injustice.

Norwood, Ralph (1966-Nov. 24), Atlanta Falcons rookie tackle.

****O'Dell, Scott** (1898-Oct. 15), author of historical novels for children who won the 1961 Newbery Medal for *Island of the Blue Dolphins*.

Ogdon, John (1937-Aug. 1), British pianist known for his virtuoso technique.

O'Hanlon, George (1917-Feb. 11), writer and actor who was the voice of George Jetson on the animated TV series "The Jetsons."

O'Hara, James G. (1925-March 13), Democratic representative from Michigan from 1959 to 1977.

****Olivier, Laurence (Lord Olivier of Brighton)** (1907-July 11), legendary British actor. See **Close-Up.**

Panchen Lama (1937-Jan. 28), Tibet's second most important Buddhist leader, after the Dalai Lama.

Parks, Henry G., Jr. (1916-April 24), founder of the Parks Sausage Company, one of the first black-owned businesses to sell its stock to the public.

Patterson, James T. (1908-Feb. 7), Republican representative from Connecticut from 1947 to 1959.

Patteson, Okey L. (1898-July 3), Democratic governor of West Virginia from 1949 to 1953.

Payne, John (1912-Dec. 6), Hollywood leading man of the 1940's and 1950's who also starred in the TV series "The Restless Gun" (1957-1959).

Pedersen, Charles J. (1904-Oct. 26), industrial chemist, born in Korea of Norwegian and Japanese parents, who shared the 1987 Nobel Prize in chemistry.

Pepper, Claude D. (1900-May 30), oldest member of Congress and a crusader for the elderly; Democratic senator from Florida from 1936 to 1951 and representative from that state from 1963 until his death.

Picott, J. Rupert (1916-Oct. 11), educator and former executive director of the Association for the Study of Afro-American Life and History.

Primeau, Joe (A. Joseph Primeau) (1906-May 15), Canadian hockey star who played forward for the Toronto Maple Leafs from 1928 to 1936 and coached the team from 1950 to 1953; member of the Hockey Hall of Fame.

Pritchard, Sir John (1921-Dec. 5), British-born director of the San Francisco Opera, knighted in 1983.

Quayle, Sir Anthony (1913-Oct. 20), distinguished and versatile British actor.

Radner, Gilda (1946-May 20), comedian who was one of the original stars of TV's "Saturday Night Live."

Roberts, Kenneth A. (1912-May 9), Democratic representative from Alabama from 1951 to 1965.

****Robinson, Ray (Walker Smith, Jr.)** (1921-April 12), five-time world middleweight boxing champion nicknamed "Sugar Ray" after his artistry in the ring inspired one writer to call him "sweet as sugar."

Rusk, Howard A. (1901-Nov. 4), physician who pioneered in the rehabilitation of the physically disabled.

Russell, Charles H. (1903-Sept. 13), Republican representative from Nevada from 1947 to 1949 and governor of that state from 1951 to 1959.

Ruth, Earl Baker (1916-Aug. 15), Republican representative from North Carolina from 1969 to 1975.

Sadler, Barry (1940?-Nov. 5), former staff sergeant with the U.S. Army Special Forces in Vietnam who co-wrote and recorded "The Ballad of the Green Berets" (1966).

****Sakharov, Andrei D.** (1921-Dec. 14), Soviet physicist who won the 1975 Nobel Peace Prize.

Sant'Angelo, Giorgio (1933-Aug. 29), Italian-born fashion designer.

Schaffner, Franklin J. (1920-July 2), motion-picture director who won an Academy Award in 1970 for *Patton*.

Schiff, Dorothy (1903-Aug. 30), former owner and publisher of the *New York Post*.

Scott, Sir Peter (1909-Aug. 29), British conservationist and painter of birds who helped found the World Wildlife Fund; son of polar explorer Robert F. Scott.

Scripps, John P. (1912-March 15), founder and chairman of the board of the John P. Scripps Newspapers division of the Scripps Howard media group.

Sears, Robert R. (1908-May 22), developmental psychologist known for his studies of how childhood discipline affects personality and behavior.

Segrè, Emilio G. (1905-April 22), Italian-born nuclear physicist who shared the 1959 Nobel Prize in physics.

Sewell, Rip (Truett Banks Sewell) (1907-Sept. 3), Pittsburgh Pirates pitcher from 1938 to 1949 who developed a high, arching pitch called the "eephus" or "blooper."

Shaw, Woody Herman (1944-May 9), one of the best bop-influenced jazz trumpeters.

****Shockley, William** (1910-Aug. 12), electrical engineer who shared the 1956 Nobel Prize in physics for discovering the principles that make the transistor possible.

Ferdinand E. Marcos, Philippine president

Alvin Ailey, dancer and choreographer

Andrei D. Sakharov, Soviet physicist

Barbara W. Tuchman, Pulitzer Prize historian

*Simenon, Georges** (1903-Sept. 4), Belgian-born novelist who created the fictional detective Inspector Jules Maigret.

Siri, Giuseppe Cardinal (1906-May 2), Roman Catholic archbishop of Genoa, Italy.

Smith, Larkin I. (1944-Aug. 13), Republican representative from Mississippi since January 1989.

Smith, W. Wallace (1900-Aug. 4), former president of the Reorganized Church of Jesus Christ of Latter Day Saints; grandson of the founder, Joseph Smith, Jr.

Sopwith, Sir Thomas (1888-Jan. 27), British aircraft designer who created the Sopwith Camel, a fighter plane used in World War I (1914-1918).

Stephenson, Sir William (1896-Jan. 31), Canadian-born head of British intelligence whose exploits were recorded in the 1976 best seller *A Man Called Intrepid.*

Stewart, Jay (Jay Fix) (1918?-Sept. 17), booming announcer of TV's "Let's Make a Deal."

Stone, I. F. (Isidor Feinstein) (1907-June 18), gadfly journalist and political commentator.

Stone, Irving (Irving Tennenbaum) (1903-Aug. 26), biographical novelist whose best sellers included *Lust for Life* (1934) and *The Agony and the Ecstasy* (1961).

Syme, Sir Ronald (1903-Sept. 4), British professor of ancient history, born in New Zealand.

Talvela, Martti (1935-July 22), Finnish operatic bass.

Taylor, E. P. (Edward Plunket Taylor) (1901-May 14), Canadian financier and industrialist who founded the Argus Corporation, one of Canada's largest holding companies.

Terry, Bill (William H. Terry) (1898-Jan. 9), first baseman with the New York Giants from 1923 to 1936; member of the National Baseball Hall of Fame.

Thompson, Frank, Jr. (1918-July 22), Democratic representative from New Jersey from 1955 to 1981; convicted of bribery and conspiracy in 1980 as a result of the Abscam investigation.

*Thomson, Virgil** (1896-Sept. 30), composer and music critic.

Tishler, Max (1906-March 18), chemist who developed the processes for mass production of cortisone, penicillin, and several vitamins.

Toran, Stacey (1961-Aug. 5), defensive back for football's Los Angeles Raiders.

Trafford, Lord (Joseph Anthony Porteous Trafford) (1932-Sept. 16), British physician and minister of state for health.

*Tuchman, Barbara Wertheim** (1912-Feb. 6), historian who won two Pulitzer Prizes for nonfiction, in 1963 and 1972.

Twomey, Seamus (1919?-Sept. 12), Irish nationalist leader who helped found the Provisional Irish Republican Army, the more aggressive wing of that underground group.

Van Cleef, Lee (1925-Dec. 16), steely-eyed actor who played villains in *High Noon* (1952) and *The Good, the Bad, and the Ugly* (1966).

Verban, Emil M. (1915-June 8), good-fielding second baseman on four National League teams from 1944 to 1950.

Vogt, Birdie May (1876-July 23), 112-year-old woman listed in the *1989 Guinness Book of World Records* as the "oldest living person for whom there is adequate authentication."

Voorhees, Donald (1903-Jan. 10), conductor and musical director of the "Bell Telephone Hour" on radio from 1940 to 1959 and on TV from 1959 to 1968.

Vreeland, Diana (1903?-Aug. 22), fashion editor of *Harper's Bazaar* from 1937 to 1962 and editor in chief of *Vogue* from 1962 to 1971.

Walker, John T. (1923-Sept. 30), first black Episcopal bishop of Washington, D.C.

Ward, Jay (1920-Oct. 12), TV producer who created Rocky the Flying Squirrel, Bullwinkle Moose, and other characters.

Warner, John Christian (1897-April 12), chemist who supervised plutonium research on the Manhattan Project that developed the first nuclear bomb in 1945.

*Warren, Robert Penn** (1905-Sept. 15), novelist, poet, and literary critic.

Mary McCarthy, versatile woman of letters

Konrad Z. Lorenz, Austrian naturalist

Sugar Ray Robinson, boxing champion

Herbert von Karajan, symphony conductor

Watson, Douglass (Larkin Douglass Watson III) (1921-May 1), actor on the TV soap opera "Another World."

Weaver, Phillip H. (1919-April 16), Republican representative from Nebraska from 1955 to 1963.

Webber, Robert (1924-May 17), versatile character actor who played Cybill Shepherd's father on TV's "Moonlighting."

Weinberg, Arthur (1915-Jan. 28), historian, author, and expert on the American lawyer Clarence Darrow.

Whitley, Keith (1955-May 9), country-music singer who recorded the 1988 hits "Don't Close Your Eyes" and "I'm No Stranger to the Rain."

Wilde, Cornel (Cornelius Louis Wilde) (1915-Oct. 16), swashbuckling film star.

Williams, Guy (Armand Catalano) (1924?-found dead May 6), actor who played Zorro in the 1950's TV series of that name.

*Williams, Roy Lee** (1915-April 28), president of the Teamsters Union from 1981 to 1983.

Wilson, A. W. (1902-Aug. 4), Baptist minister whose church in Montgomery, Ala., was a rallying point for the 1955-1956 bus boycott that launched the civil rights movement.

Wolman, Abel (1892-Feb. 22), sanitary engineer who pioneered the use of chlorine to purify drinking water.

Zemach, Margot (1931-May 21), illustrator and author of children's books who won the Caldecott Medal in 1974 for *Duffy and the Devil.*

Zita (1892-March 14), last Habsburg empress of Austria-Hungary. She and her husband, Emperor Karl I, reigned from 1916 to 1918. Sara Dreyfuss

Delaware. See **State government.**

Democratic Party

Democratic Party. Ronald H. Brown, a lawyer and lobbyist known for his negotiating skills, was elected chairman of the Democratic National Committee (DNC) on Feb. 10, 1989. Brown, who succeeded Paul G. Kirk, Jr., was the first black to become chairman of either major U.S. political party. The 403-member DNC included 81 blacks in 1989; there were no blacks among the 165 elected members of the rival Republican National Committee.

Brown's candidacy for the top DNC post triggered an intense debate in Democratic circles, mostly because of his association with the presidential campaigns of two of the party's most prominent liberals, Jesse L. Jackson and Senator Edward M. Kennedy (D., Mass). Some Democratic moderates expressed the view that Brown might be perceived as leading the party toward a more militant liberalism. Brown's backers contended that he would be the ideal choice to deal with the racial conflicts that developed within the party as a result of Jackson's campaigns for the Democratic presidential nomination in 1984 and 1988.

The prospect of a heated contest for the chairmanship ended on January 25 when Brown's chief rival, Richard N. Wiener, chairman of the Michigan Democratic Party, withdrew and gave his support to Brown, who was born in Washington, D.C., and raised in the Harlem section of New York City. A third candidate, former Oklahoma Representative James R. Jones, later joined Wiener in vacating the field.

Democrat Jim Wright of Texas, accused of ethics violations, announces tearfully on May 31 that he is resigning as Speaker of the House.

Brown rejected suggestions that by remaining a partner in a Washington, D.C., lobbying firm he could have a conflict of interest. Joining a similar firm in the capital was Robert Farmer of Boston, who was elected party treasurer in the February 10 balloting. Farmer, who was chief fund-raiser for Democratic presidential nominee Michael S. Dukakis in his 1988 bid for the White House, was unopposed for the treasurer's post.

As treasurer, Farmer said he would endorse modest revisions in campaign finance laws. He would allow individual donors to give $2,300 a year directly to candidates instead of the existing limit of $1,000. But he said he would take no position on political action committees (PAC's), which raise and distribute campaign funds on behalf of special-interest groups. "So long as PAC's exist, we will encourage them to make a contribution at the DNC level," said Farmer.

Farmer's fund-raising tactics have aroused some controversy. Some nonpartisan groups were critical of his 1988 role in soliciting $100,000 donations to the Dukakis campaign by exploiting loopholes in federal laws that supposedly limited the role of big donors. Ellen Miller, director of the Center for Responsive Politics, a group that seeks tighter campaign finance laws, told *The Wall Street Journal*, "Operating on the fringes . . . is not in the best interests of the national political parties."

Farmer countered, "We ran the most pristine, squeaky-clean campaign in the history of fund-raising for a presidential campaign." He said a committee of lawyers screened every donor of $10,000 or more and that, as a result, he returned four $100,000 checks.

Outspent by the Republicans. On March 26, the Federal Election Commission reported that the Democratic Party raised and spent less than half as much as the Republicans during the 1987-1988 election cycle. The commission said Democrats raised $127.9 million and spent the same amount during the two years, compared with $263.3 million raised and $257 million spent by the Republican Party.

But the gap between the two parties was markedly narrower than in the 1983-1984 campaign, when President Ronald Reagan won reelection. The Republicans then raised a record $297.9 million and spent $300.8-million, while Democrats raised $98.5 million and spent $97.4 million.

Campaign committee in debt. In June, Representative Beryl F. Anthony, Jr., of Arkansas said he would not seek a third two-year term in 1990 as chairman of the Democratic Congressional Campaign Committee, a political support group whose aim is to increase the Democratic membership of the House of Representatives. Anthony blamed the committee's $1.8-million debt on his predecessor as chairman, Representative Tony Coelho of California. *The Washington Post* reported on June 21, however, that Federal Election Commission records showed that the committee had debts and obligations of only $865,911 in 1986, when Anthony succeeded Coelho. But by June,

Coelho had other troubles. He resigned from the House on June 15 rather than undergo an ethics probe into his investment of $100,000 in high-yield "junk" bonds.

Delegate selection. DNC Chairman Brown said in April that he would oppose any effort to change the party's delegate selection rules. Critics of the rules want to scrap a requirement, adopted at the 1988 Democratic National Convention, that all future convention delegates must be chosen under a proportional representation system.

Under that system, if a candidate receives, say, 20 per cent of the votes in a state's primary election, he or she gets 20 per cent of that state's delegates to the national nominating convention. Jesse Jackson had sought the change, considered favorable to him should he again seek the Democratic presidential nomination, and Brown had helped to get the change approved. At a Nashville meeting of the Association of State Democratic Chairs on June 17, Brown's position on the delegate selection rules prevailed.

Staff appointments. Brown made the following top DNC staff appointments in April: Paul R. Tully, director of political operations; Alexis M. Herman, chief of staff; Melissa A. Moss, director of finance; and Michael D. McCurry, director of communications. Jack L. Martin, a moderate Texas Democrat, was appointed "senior adviser." Frank Cormier and Margot Cormier

In *World Book*, see **Democratic Party.**

Denmark, after decades of living with a rising international debt, moved in 1989 to recover its economic equilibrium, mainly by curbing public spending. Denmark is one of the most industrialized states in the world, but it had been falling into the same debt trap that had engulfed many developing nations. Denmark had run a negative balance of payments for 26 years, piling up such a big debt that interest payments were increasing faster than export earnings.

Unless Denmark could turn the debt situation around, it would likely soon find itself applying to the International Monetary Fund (IMF, an agency of the United Nations) for credits. When asked about the IMF option, however, Prime Minister Poul Schlüter said, "Never." Instead, he proposed *austerity* (a cutback in the standard of living) to make more money available to pay the debt.

In a budget submitted on August 31 and adopted in December, the government proposed to cut public spending by 1 per cent after adjustment for inflation. Controversial measures involved a reduction of government reimbursements on some prescription drugs and a shift of some unemployment benefits from the government to private employers. Schlüter said that his long-term plans included tax cuts, further curbs on welfare programs, and a rollback of the public-service sector of the economy. The Federation of Danish Industries, which represents various manufacturing and service industries, had warned that pub-

lic services had "crowded out" the country's free-market economy.

Lukewarm on EC. The industry group said also that more of the nation's wealth needed to be channeled away from government spending and into manufacturing to prepare Denmark for competition in the integrated economy that the European Community (EC or Common Market) plans to launch in 1992. Many Danes expressed a lack of interest in the EC on June 15 by not voting in elections for the European Parliament, the EC's legislative branch. The voter turnout was only 46 per cent, reportedly the lowest in any Danish election during the 1900's.

Other developments. Construction began in June on a bridge-and-tunnel link for automobiles and trucks between the European mainland and the island of Sjælland, on which Copenhagen is located. Plans call for the link to be completed in 1993.

A law passed on May 26 made Denmark the first nation in the EC to recognize civil marriage between homosexuals. The law, however, barred the adoption of children by homosexual couples.

The Danish film *Pelle the Conqueror* in March won a Hollywood Oscar as best foreign film. The movie, the story of an immigrant to Denmark who becomes a rural laborer in the early 1900's, depicts the harsh working conditions of that period. Joseph Fitchett

See also **Europe** (Facts in brief table). In *World Book*, see **Denmark.**

Dentistry. Tests began in 1989 on computerized reconstruction systems that allow dentists to fit patients with crowns in about 15 minutes. (A *crown* is a toothlike cap cemented onto a damaged or decayed tooth.) The University of Alabama School of Dentistry in Birmingham was among the dental schools in the United States developing and evaluating the systems, called *CAD-CAM* (computer-aided design and computer-aided manufacturing).

Before a dentist can fit a patient with a crown, the tooth must be prepared to receive it. The dentist removes the damage or decay and grinds down the outer layers of the tooth until it is a stump. The new permanent crown will eventually be attached to the stump.

The conventional method of fitting a patient with a crown takes several days. The dentist has to make a model of the stump, which is sent to a dental laboratory as a guide for creating the crown. Meanwhile, the dentist fits the patient with a temporary crown. The patient must return to the dentist's office so the temporary crown can be removed and the permanent one put in place.

The CAD-CAM system of making crowns does away with the long wait and the need for a temporary crown. Instead, after the dentist has prepared the tooth, a tiny video camera, small enough to fit inside the patient's mouth, takes a picture of the tooth stump. This picture appears on a television monitor screen as a three-dimensional computer image. Using the monitor, the dentist designs the crown.

When all the necessary dimensions of the crown are correct, the computer directs the operation of a milling machine. The milling machine cuts a ceramic or porcelain block to the exact dimensions needed for the crown in about 15 minutes, while the patient waits. The artificial crown can then be installed.

Hot gums. Dentists in 1989 began using a device that helps them locate severe infections caused by gum disease. The device, developed by the Forsythe Dental Center in Boston, has a probe that measures temperature changes in gum pockets, the spaces that form when inflamed gums separate from teeth. Hot spots in these pockets indicate seriously inflamed areas that need treatment.

Dental exams urged. A panel of health experts on April 19 recommended that cancer patients receive dental and oral examinations before undergoing cancer treatment. The panel, assembled by the National Institutes of Health in Bethesda, Md., said that treatments for head and neck cancer, such as radiation therapy and chemotherapy, can cause tooth decay, gum disease, and other problems. To reduce serious complications, the panel urged dentists to apply fluorides and prescribe antibiotic medications when necessary, as well as treat gum disease before patients undergo cancer therapy.   Kenneth L. Siegel

In *World Book,* see **Dentistry.**

Derwinski, Edward Joseph (1926-   ), was sworn in on March 15, 1989, as the first secretary of the United States Department of Veterans Affairs, formerly the Veterans Administration. As director of the federal government's second-largest department in number of employees, Derwinski took on responsibility for health care and benefits programs for the nation's 27.3 million veterans.

Derwinski was born on Sept. 15, 1926, in Chicago. He entered the U.S. Army as a private in 1945 and served in the Pacific Theater and the occupation of Japan. In 1951, he graduated from Loyola University in Chicago with a bachelor's degree in history. From 1959 to 1983, he represented Illinois's Fourth Congressional District in the U.S. House of Representatives, where he played a major role in passing legislation to reform the Foreign Service, the Postal Service, and the Civil Service.

After 1983, Derwinski served at the Department of State, first as counselor and later as undersecretary of state for security assistance, science, and technology. In that position, he implemented President Ronald Reagan's worldwide security assistance and arms transfer programs, worked to prevent the diversion of U.S. technology to unfriendly nations, and supervised international policy on the environment, oceans, and science.

Derwinski married Bonita Hickey in 1986. He has two children by a previous marriage.   Robin Goldman

Detroit. Mayor Coleman A. Young won a fifth term in office in a Nov. 7, 1989, election, defeating accountant Tom Barrow by 56 per cent to 44 per cent. It was Young's toughest campaign since 1973, when he was elected Detroit's first black mayor.

In the September 12 nonpartisan primary, Young, a Democrat, finished first in a 13-candidate field that included Barrow, also a Democrat; John Conyers, Jr., a well-known Democratic congressman from Detroit; and Erma Henderson, the long-time City Council president. Because Barrow placed second in the primary, he became Young's opponent in the fall election.

Young prevailed despite a revelation that in earlier times might have wrecked his career. In May, a blood test indicated that he is the father of a 6-year-old boy, Joel Loving. The child's mother, Annivory Calvert, a former city employee, filed a paternity suit against Young in January 1989. Young admitted dating the woman but said—until the blood test—that he doubted the boy was his. In October, the mayor agreed to pay $11,700 a year in child support to Calvert and to create a $150,000 trust fund for the boy.

The economy. The 71-year-old mayor ran on his record of attempting to rejuvenate Detroit's sluggish economy, which for 30 years has been hit by the flight of businesses and people to the suburbs and beyond.

On May 31, the mayor joined Chrysler Corporation Chairman Lee A. Iacocca at a groundbreaking ceremony on the city's east side for a $1-billion vehicle assembly plant. The facility, scheduled to begin operation in 1992, will turn out the "ZJ" sport/utility vehicle. Although the plant, which will employ up to 3,000 workers, is expected to give a lift to the Detroit economy, the city had to provide the land for it. Critics noted that the costs of acquiring the land and cleaning it up prior to construction came to $436 million, or more than $145,000 per job—a bill that will be presented to Detroit's taxpayers.

The Chrysler facility will join a nearby General Motors Corporation (GM) assembly plant that opened in 1985. Despite such major investments, the fortunes of Detroit's "Big Three" domestic automakers—GM, Chrysler, and the Ford Motor Company—declined compared with the previous year. Through late 1989, car and truck sales by the Big Three trailed 1988 sales by about 3.5 per cent, with Chrysler hurting the worst. Part of the sales drop-off might have been due to higher prices; sticker prices on many models were as much as 9 per cent higher in 1989 than in 1988.

Smoky trash burner. The city encountered problems during the year with its new $438-million trash incinerator, the most expensive single project in Detroit's 288-year history. In September, the incinerator failed air pollution tests that are required for a state operating permit. Engineers worked to clean up the trash burner's emissions, but by year-end it still had not obtained its state license.

Destruction, construction. During the year, the city speeded up a housing demolition program in re-

On a visit to Hamtramck, Mich., in April, President George Bush—flanked by Detroit's Edmund Cardinal Szoka—greets two girls in ethnic dress.

sponse to protests about more than 13,000 abandoned homes that mar Detroit neighborhoods. Meanwhile, new housing, in the form of riverfront condominiums and apartments, opened at two sites and construction continued at several other locations. In midsummer, tenants began moving into a 28-story office building, the first skyscraper to be built in downtown Detroit in a decade.

Church closings. A bitter controversy over 30 Roman Catholic churches ordered closed by Detroit's Edmund Cardinal Szoka continued in 1989. Protesters picketed Cardinal Szoka's home, filed an unsuccessful lawsuit, and prayed together at church Masses, but the churches were all shut by July. The cardinal ordered the closings because of declining memberships.

New school superintendent. John W. Porter, president of Eastern Michigan University in Ypsilanti, was appointed superintendent of the Detroit public school system on July 1. Swinging into action, he announced a plan aimed at improving school management, tightening finances, and boosting student discipline and academic performance.

Pistons take NBA crown. Crowds flocked to a new sports arena, the Palace of Auburn Hills, in June to cheer on the Detroit Pistons in the National Basketball Association (NBA) finals. The Pistons won their first NBA championship by sweeping the Los Angeles Lakers in four straight games.   Bill McGraw

See also **City.** In *World Book,* see **Detroit.**

Dinkins, David Norman (1927-   ), made history on Nov. 7, 1989, when he was elected the first black mayor of New York City. In the election, Dinkins, president of the borough of Manhattan (a division of New York City) and a Democrat, defeated the Republican candidate, Rudolph W. Giuliani, a former federal prosecutor. Dinkins began his bid for the mayor's office in September by beating three-term Mayor Edward I. Koch in the Democratic primary. Dinkins was sworn into office on Jan. 1, 1990.

The race between Dinkins and Giuliani was marked by bitter debates. Dinkins was able to withstand Giuliani's attempts to tie him to "rotten politics," however, and he won the support of liberal white, black, and Hispanic voters.

Dinkins was born July 10, 1927, in Trenton, N.J. He received a bachelor's degree in mathematics from Howard University in Washington, D.C., in 1950 and a law degree from Brooklyn Law School in 1956.

Dinkins began his political career in 1965, when he was elected a New York state assemblyman. In 1967, he became Democratic district leader, a post he held until 1987. During this period, he also served as counsel, commissioner, and president of the New York City Board of Elections; as city clerk; and as director of the Urban Development Corporation. He became Manhattan borough president in 1986.

In 1953, Dinkins married Joyce Burroughs. They have two children.   Mary A. Krier

Disasters. The worst natural disaster to strike the United States in 1989 was a deadly earthquake that rocked northern California, including Oakland and San Francisco, on October 17. At least 62 people died in the quake, 42 of them in the collapse of a section of Interstate Highway 880 in Oakland. The disaster caused an estimated $7 billion in damage and forced postponement of the World Series between the San Francisco Giants and the Oakland Athletics.

There were several major railroad accidents throughout the world in 1989. Bangladesh suffered its worst train wreck ever on January 15, when an express train carrying pilgrims to a religious festival crashed head-on into a mail train near Dhaka. The collision killed at least 170 people. Disaster struck the Soviet Union's Trans-Siberian Railroad on June 4 when a spark from one of two passing passenger trains set off an explosion in a ruptured liquefied petroleum gas pipeline. An estimated 460 passengers died in the blast, the second-worst train wreck in history, exceeded only by a 1981 crash in India that killed 800 people. A train derailment in Mexico on Aug. 9, 1989, caused at least 112 deaths.

Disasters that resulted in 35 or more deaths in 1989 included the following:

Aircraft crashes
Jan. 8—Kegworth, Great Britain, near Nottingham. A British Midland Airways jetliner developed engine trouble and

Disasters

crashed during an emergency landing, killing 47 of the 79 people aboard.

Feb. 8 — Santa Maria Island, Azores. A U.S. chartered jetliner crashed into a mountain, killing all 144 people aboard.

June 7 — Zanderij, Suriname. A Suriname Airways jetliner trying to land in a dense fog hit a tree and broke apart, causing 177 deaths.

June 21 — Near Tarma, Peru. A Peruvian air force plane hit a mountain in the Andes, killing all 60 people aboard.

July 19 — Sioux City, Iowa. A United Airlines jetliner crashed while trying to make an emergency landing, killing 112 of the 296 people aboard.

July 27 — Tripoli, Libya. A Korean Air Lines jetliner crashed while trying to land in fog, causing as many as 80 deaths, including 6 on the ground.

Sept. 3 — Havana, Cuba. A Cuban jetliner crashed in a thunderstorm, killing all 126 people aboard and at least 25 people on the ground in Cuba's worst-ever air crash.

Sept. 8 — Skagerrak channel, between Denmark and Norway. All 55 people aboard a Norwegian chartered plane died when it crashed in the North Sea in the worst crash in Norway's history.

Oct. 18 — Near Baku, Soviet Union. A Soviet military transport plane caught fire and plunged into the Caspian Sea, killing all 57 people aboard.

Oct. 21 — Las Mesitas, Honduras, near Tegucigalpa. A Honduran jetliner hit a mountain and burst into flames, causing 132 deaths in Central America's worst-ever airline disaster.

Bus and truck crashes

Jan. 17 — Ahungalla, Sri Lanka, near Colombo. At least 51 people, including 35 schoolchildren, died after a train hit their bus.

Jan. 27 — Dajabón, Dominican Republic, near Santo Domingo. A truck carrying sugar cane workers crashed, causing at least 50 deaths.

Jan. 28 — Ivory Coast. A school bus plunged into a water-filled culvert during a thunderstorm, killing 48 schoolchildren.

Oct. 20 — Near Khartoum, Sudan. A bus caught fire after colliding with another bus, and more than 50 passengers burned to death.

Dec. 22 — Near Kempsey, Australia. A head-on collision between two buses killed 35 people in Australia's worst highway accident ever.

Earthquakes

Jan. 23 — Tajikistan, Soviet Union. An earthquake triggered a huge slide of sand, clay, and mud that engulfed three mountain villages and caused about 275 deaths.

Aug. 1 — Irian Jaya, Indonesia. At least 90 people died in an earthquake.

Oct. 17 — Northern California. A powerful earthquake caused 62 deaths.

Mine disasters

Jan. 20 — Near Nazca, Peru. An explosion and cave-in at the Sol de Oro gold mine killed as many as 200 miners.

March 10 — Near Bonthe, Sierra Leone. About 50 miners lost their lives after a diamond mine collapsed.

April 23 — Near Muyinga, Burundi. At least 100 gold prospectors died after the walls of mines they were working collapsed due to heavy rains.

Nov. 17 — Near Aleksina, Yugoslavia. A methane gas explosion and fire in a coal mine killed at least 90 miners.

Shipwrecks

Jan. 1 — Off Puerto Barrios, Guatemala. An overloaded ferry ran out of fuel and sank in Bahía de Amatique, drowning at least 74 people.

Jan. 10 — Near Sahiwal, Pakistan. About 90 people drowned after their boat hit a temporary bridge across the Ravi River, broke into pieces, and sank.

March 8 — South China Sea. A boat carrying Vietnamese refugees capsized and sank, drowning as many as 130 people.

April 7 — Norwegian Sea. A Soviet nuclear-powered submarine caught fire, exploded, and sank, killing 42 sailors.

Aug. 20 — London. A sand dredger rammed a boat carrying more than 100 guests on a pleasure cruise on the River Thames, sinking the boat and drowning 51 of its passengers.

Sept. 10 — Near Galaţi, Romania. A Romanian passenger ship collided with a Bulgarian barge and sank in the Danube River. As many as 161 people died.

Oct. 28 — Near Dedaye, Burma (Myanmar). An estimated 64 people died when a ferry sank in the Andaman Sea.

Storms and floods

Mid-February — Near Tarapoto, Peru. Two rivers burst their banks and flooded several villages in central Peru, leaving 57 people dead and another 50 people missing.

April 20 — Sichuan province, China. A hailstorm killed at least 87 people.

April 26 — Near Manikganj, Bangladesh. More than 1,000 people died in a tornado.

May 26-27 — Eastern India and Bangladesh. A cyclone caused at least 150 deaths and left another 200 people missing.

May 27 — Central Vietnam. Typhoon Cecil left 140 people dead and hundreds more missing.

June 3-6 — Sri Lanka. More than 315 people died in floods and landslides caused by monsoon rains.

July 9-10 — Sichuan province, China. Heavy rains triggered floods and landslides that caused at least 367 deaths.

Mid-July – mid-August — Bangladesh and India. Monsoon rains and floods caused more than 1,600 deaths.

Sept. 17-22 — Caribbean and Southeastern United States. Hurricane Hugo caused at least 71 deaths, 18 of them in South Carolina.

Nov. 2-9 — Thailand and India. Typhoon Gay left more than 365 dead and about 400 missing. Many of the deaths occurred in the Gulf of Thailand, where waves swamped at least eight vessels, including the gas-drilling ship *Seacrest*, which capsized on November 4, drowning 91 crew members.

Train wrecks

Jan. 15 — Pubāil, Bangladesh, near Dhaka. An express train crashed into a mail train, killing at least 170 people.

April 18 — Near Jhansi, India. A high-speed passenger train jumped the tracks, 12 cars tumbling down an embankment and causing at least 67 deaths.

June 4 — Near Ufa, Soviet Union. A spark from two passing passenger trains set off an explosion in a ruptured gas pipeline, killing an estimated 460 passengers.

Aug. 9 — Near Guasava, Mexico. A train's engine and two of its cars plunged into a river after a bridge collapsed under the train's weight. The accident caused at least 112 deaths.

Nov. 1 — Sakaldiha, India. An express train traveling from New Delhi to Calcutta derailed, killing at least 52 people.

Other disasters

Feb. 8 — Mysore, India. Fireworks set off for a wedding scene ignited the set at a television studio, burning 40 film workers to death behind a door locked to keep out spectators.

April 15 — Sheffield, Great Britain. Ninety-five soccer fans suffocated or were crushed to death when they were trapped against a steel fence by a surging crowd trying to push its way into a packed stadium.

Oct. 24 — São Paulo, Brazil. A landslide, possibly triggered by developers excavating on a hill, buried a São Paulo shantytown and killed up to 60 people.   Sara Dreyfuss

Djibouti. See Africa.

The California earthquake

Houses in San Francisco's Marina district lie in ruins, *above,* after an earthquake that jolted northern California on October 17, collapsing a section of the San Francisco-Oakland Bay Bridge, *left.* Fire fighters battle a blaze fueled by a ruptured gas main, *below.*

Dog

Dog. On Feb. 13 and 14, 1989, the Westminster Kennel Club held its 113th annual show at Madison Square Garden in New York City. A female Doberman pinscher, Champion Royal Tudor's Wild As the Wind, was judged Best-in-Show. Nicknamed Indy, the dog is owned by Arthur Korp, Susan Korp, and Beth Wilhite, all of San Jose, and Richard and Carolyn Vida of Sacramento, Calif.

The American Kennel Club (AKC) reported in 1989 that it registered 1,220,500 dogs in 1988. Cocker spaniels led the list of registered breeds for the fifth consecutive year. The second most popular breed was the Labrador retriever, followed by the poodle, golden retriever, German shepherd dog, chow chow, Rottweiler, beagle, dachshund, and miniature schnauzer.

Communities throughout the United States passed or tried to pass laws regulating ownership of specific dog breeds in 1989. The laws, which imply that particular breeds are inherently vicious, are often aimed at dogs commonly called "pit bulls."

The AKC, along with the American Dog Owners Association, the United Kennel Club, and other interest groups, continued to promote laws prohibiting communities from enacting legislation affecting ownership of specific breeds. The groups won passage of laws banning breed-specific ordinances in Minnesota in April and in California in September. Similar legislation was pending in other states.   Roberta Vesley

In *World Book,* see **Dog.**

Dole, Elizabeth Hanford (1936-   ), became United States secretary of labor on Jan. 30, 1989. The post is the latest in a string of high-level executive-branch positions held by Dole.

Elizabeth Hanford was born on July 29, 1936, in Salisbury, N.C. She graduated with honors from Duke University in Durham, N.C., in 1958 and then attended Harvard University in Cambridge, Mass., where she received a master's degree in education and government and a law degree.

After completing her studies, the young lawyer moved to Washington, D.C. In 1968, she was appointed a legislative assistant to President Lyndon B. Johnson's consumer-affairs adviser, and she held other consumer-affairs posts under President Richard M. Nixon. In 1973, Nixon named her a member of the Federal Trade Commission.

Dole switched from the Democratic Party to the Republican Party in the late 1970's. She played a prominent role in the Administration of President Ronald Reagan, including as secretary of transportation. She left that position in 1987 to help with the presidential campaign of her husband, Senator Robert J. Dole (R., Kans.), whom she married in 1975.

In 1988, a national public opinion poll named Elizabeth Dole one of the world's 10 most admired women.   David L. Dreier

Dominican Republic. See **Latin America.**

Drought. See **Water; Weather.**

First lady Barbara Bush and one of her granddaughters pay a visit to the Bushes' dog, Millie, and her new litter of puppies in March.

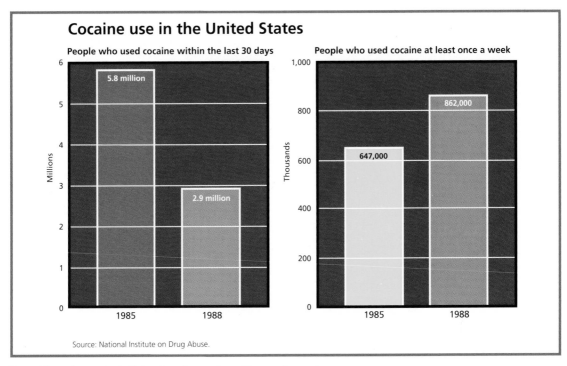

Cocaine use in the United States

People who used cocaine within the last 30 days

- 5.8 million (1985)
- 2.9 million (1988)

(Millions, scale 0–6)

People who used cocaine at least once a week

- 647,000 (1985)
- 862,000 (1988)

(Thousands, scale 0–1,000)

Source: National Institute on Drug Abuse.

"Casual" cocaine use is declining, but the number of frequent users is climbing, according to a federal survey released in July 1989.

Drug abuse. On Sept. 5, 1989, United States President George Bush outlined a $7.9-billion strategy for fighting drug abuse. The plan was drafted by William J. Bennett, who in March became director of national drug control policy, or "drug czar."

The plan called for spending $3.1 billion for law enforcement and $1.6 billion for corrections, along with $2.1 billion for prevention, education, and treatment. Some members of Congress criticized the plan for its focus on enforcement. Congress ended up approving $8.8 billion in antidrug funding—$900 million more than requested. The extra funds were to be used for education, treatment, and research.

Drug use down. Bush's report cited recent findings that overall drug use has declined. The ninth National Institute of Drug Abuse Household Survey, released on July 31, showed a decrease of 37 per cent between 1985 and 1988 in the number of "current" users—people who use an illegal drug at least once a month. Current use of marijuana and cocaine, the two most common illegal drugs, was down 36 and 48 per cent, respectively. But those people who do use cocaine are using it more frequently, the survey reported: The number of people who used cocaine at least once a week jumped 33 per cent.

Public concern over drugs remained high, according to a Gallup Poll released in August 1989. The poll showed that 27 per cent of U.S. adults and 32 per cent of teen-agers consider drugs the nation's greatest problem. Of the teen-agers, 60 per cent rated drug abuse the biggest problem facing people their age, followed by peer pressure—including pressure to use drugs—and alcohol abuse.

"Cocaine babies" emerged in 1989 as another major drug-related problem. Studies show that use of illegal drugs—especially "crack," a cheap, smokable form of cocaine—during pregnancy has contributed to a sharp rise in infant death in the nation's major cities. In addition to facing a higher risk of death, infants exposed to drugs before birth often experience severe physical or developmental problems.

New drug. A particularly dangerous drug emerged in the United States in 1989. Called "crystal meth" or "ice," the drug is a smokable form of the stimulant *methamphetamine*, which is known in powdered form as "speed." Easily manufactured from chemicals, ice arrived in Hawaii from South Korea and Japan. It has appeared in California, Florida, and other states and has become more popular than crack in some areas.

The crystals produce highs lasting for hours—much longer than the 20-minute high from crack. Like crack, ice can cause depression, but long-term effects also include a wide range of severe mental troubles, such as paranoia, hallucinations, delusions, incoherence, and violent behavior. Physical side effects can include irregular heartbeat, convulsions, and fatal lung and kidney disorders.   David C. Lewis

In *World Book,* see **Drug abuse.**

Drugs

Drugs. Concern about the safety and effectiveness of generic drugs in 1989 led the United States Food and Drug Administration (FDA) to order extensive tests of these widely prescribed medications. Generic drugs are less expensive copies of brand-name drugs whose patents have expired. They account for about one-third of all prescription drugs sold each year.

On August 16, the FDA began taking samples of the 30 top-selling generic drugs from manufacturers throughout the country. The products accounted for about 75 per cent of all the generic prescription drugs that are sold in the United States. They included penicillin and other antibiotics; painkillers such as ibuprofen and acetaminophen with codeine; the heart medication nitroglycerin; and the sedative diazepam. Officials at the FDA said they would test the generic medications to make certain that there are no important differences between them and their brand-name counterparts.

The testing program began after revelations of improprieties in the testing and approval of generic drugs. Two generic drug manufacturers said they gave the FDA false information about safety tests on some drugs. In addition, three former FDA employees admitted taking bribes from drug manufacturers in exchange for quicker action in approving drugs.

Baldness "cures" banned. In a crackdown on medical quackery, the FDA on July 7 announced a ban on the sale of nonprescription creams and lotions sold to prevent or treat baldness. The FDA said that none of the products, sold by mail or through barbers or beauticians, are effective. The only treatment proven effective for some forms of baldness is Rogaine (minoxidil), a prescription drug manufactured by The Upjohn Company of Kalamazoo, Mich.

Drug warning. The FDA on March 22 asked prescription drug manufacturers to add a warning to the labels of a group of *nonsteroidal anti-inflammatory drugs* (NSAID's), painkilling medications including ibuprofen. The labels would warn that patients who take NSAID's regularly run the risk of "serious gastrointestinal reactions," such as bleeding ulcers in the stomach and intestines.

Each year, doctors write about 68 million prescriptions for NSAID's, which are used to treat the pain and inflammation of conditions such as arthritis and sprains. The new labels were required on a number of brand-name products, including Anaprox, Dolobid, Feldene, Indocin, Motrin, Nalfon, Naprosyn, Tolectin, and Voltaren. Label changes also were required for generic forms of the drugs ibuprofen, indomethacin, and phenylbutazone.

Elderly concerns. A government study on February 14 reported widespread problems related to the use of prescription drugs among older Americans. The study, conducted by the U.S. Department of Health and Human Services, said that mismedication of the elderly has become a "critical" health care problem in the United States.

The department found, for example, that 51 per cent of the deaths each year from drug side effects occur among people over age 60, though they account for only 17 per cent of the total population. Likewise, about 243,000 older people are hospitalized each year for adverse reactions to drugs. Prescription drugs cause or contribute to mental impairment in thousands of other older people.

Several factors play a role in this problem, the study noted. These include inadequate training of doctors in *geriatrics* (the branch of medicine dealing with old age and its diseases); failure of pharmacists to review patients' records for potentially harmful interactions between drugs; and patients' failure to follow instructions on proper use of prescription drugs.

Heart dangers. On April 25, the FDA advised physicians to stop prescribing two drugs used to treat *arrhythmias* (heartbeat irregularities) in more than 200,000 Americans. The recommendation was based on results of a study conducted by the National Heart, Lung and Blood Institute involving the drugs Tambocor, manufactured by Riker Laboratories in St. Paul, Minn., and Enkaid, made by the Bristol-Myers Company in New York City. The study was to determine how effective the drugs were in preventing death among people who had experienced a previous heart attack.

A heart attack leaves some patients with irregular heartbeats that may increase the risk of death from a subsequent heart attack. Instead of proving that the drugs are useful in treating these irregular heartbeats, the study showed that patients taking the medications were almost twice as likely to die or suffer cardiac arrest as those given a *placebo* (inactive substance). The Food and Drug Administration stressed that patients should consult their physicians before discontinuing the medications.

Help for anemics. On June 1, the FDA approved a new drug that could help thousands of patients with *anemia*, a disorder in which there is a shortage of red cells in the blood. The drug—called *epoetin*—is a form of *erythropoietin*, a hormone that is produced naturally in the kidneys. The hormone acts in the bone marrow, stimulating the manufacture of red blood cells, which carry oxygen throughout the body. Epoetin is a product of genetic engineering, through which new genes were introduced into yeast cells to enable them to manufacture the drug.

FDA Commissioner Frank E. Young called the drug "a big advance." It will be used initially to treat anemia that occurs in patients with kidney failure who require treatment on kidney dialysis machines. Both kidney damage and dialysis decrease a patient's natural erythropoietin production, resulting in a shortage of red blood cells. Later in June, the FDA approved the use of the new drug to treat anemia in patients who have AIDS.   Michael Woods

See also **Drug abuse; Medicine.** In *World Book*, see **Drug.**

Eastern Orthodox Churches. Progress was made in 1989 toward restoring unity between the Eastern Orthodox and the Oriental Orthodox churches. The Eastern Orthodox Church includes the Greek Orthodox and Russian Orthodox churches. The Oriental Orthodox Church includes the Coptic, Armenian, Ethiopian, and Syrian Orthodox churches. The two churches separated about 1,500 years ago due to different beliefs about how the divine and human natures are joined in the person of Christ.

A commission composed of members of both Eastern and Oriental Orthodox churches addressed this difference at a June meeting held at the Anba Bishoy Monastery in Cairo, Egypt. The commission issued a joint theological statement expressing a common faith about the nature of Christ. The document stated, in part, that the commission members "neither separate nor divide the human nature in Christ from His divine nature" nor think that "the former was absorbed in the latter and thus ceased to exist."

Freedom of religion. The lack of religious freedom in the Soviet Union was once again the focus of concern among the Orthodox churches in 1989. During the year, 3 dissident Russian Orthodox priests— Gleb Yakunin, Nikolai Gainov, and Georgy Edelshtein—along with 11 other religious leaders published a widely circulated document criticizing the current state of religious freedom in the Soviet Union. Orthodox Christian leaders were encouraged, however, when the Soviet government issued a proposed law during the year that, if passed, would restore many religious freedoms.

Abortion issue. The Orthodox Church in the United States filed a brief with the Supreme Court of the United States in 1989 prior to the court's July 3 decision upholding the constitutionality of a Missouri law that restricted abortions. The brief stated that the claim made in previous court rulings about the lack of consistent tradition against abortion in the Christian religion is untrue. Antiabortion teachings, according to the brief, can be traced back through the first 1,500 years of Christianity.

Other news. A U.S. district judge on August 8 ordered that four rare mosaics dating from the A.D. 500's be returned to the Greek Orthodox Church of Cyprus. In 1988, an art dealer from Carmel, Ind., purchased the mosaics for $1.2 million from a Turkish dealer in Switzerland. The judge ruled that the Indiana dealer had not gained legal title to the mosaics, which the church and the Cyprus government claimed were stolen from a Cyprus church in the 1970's.

In April 1989, Archbishop Iakovos of the Greek Orthodox Archdiocese of North and South America celebrated 30 years as archbishop. In September, Bishop Methodios was elected president of Hellenic College and Holy Cross Greek Orthodox School of Theology in Brookline, Mass.   Stanley Samuel Harakas

In *World Book,* see **Eastern Orthodox Churches.**

Russian Orthodox clergy in Moscow celebrate Mass in the Kremlin's Uspensky Cathedral on October 13. It was the first Mass there since 1918.

Economics

Economics. The United States economy experienced its seventh consecutive year of growth in 1989. The gross national product (GNP)—the value of all goods and services produced during the year—rose; the rate of inflation remained steady; and more Americans had jobs than ever before. But the economy had its dark spots, especially the trade deficit.

GNP rose at a rate of 2.9 per cent during 1989. By summer, real GNP reached $4.13 trillion in 1982 dollars. (To make year-to-year comparisons easier, economists often measure GNP in the dollars of an earlier fixed year.) But late in 1989, the rate of economic growth slowed as the level of exports fell.

Consumer demand for goods and services rose during the year, spurring U.S. businesses to make greater investments in plants and equipment. Most business investment, however, was devoted to increased inventories. For the first time since 1986, inventories exceeded 1½ months' worth of sales in the third quarter. This led to fears that if sales dropped, businesses would have to severely reduce production to get rid of excess inventory.

The inflation rate in 1989 as measured by the Gross National Product Deflator—also called the Implicit Price Index or Implicit Price Deflator—fell from an annual rate of 4.6 per cent in the spring to 2.9 per cent by summer. But by year-end, this inflation rate stood at 4.2 per cent.

This falling rate of inflation followed two years of

slow growth in the money supply, especially M2. M2 is the broadly defined money supply consisting of money in circulation and in checking accounts as well as in short-term certificates of deposit, money-market deposit accounts, and money-market mutual funds. M2's rate of growth is set by the Federal Reserve Bank, the central bank of the United States.

M2, which grew 4.6 per cent in 1987 and most of 1988, showed almost no growth from December 1988 through May 1989. Some experts complained that the lack of growth could halt the economy's expansion. In response, the Federal Reserve allowed M2 to bounce back to 8.4 per cent by the end of 1989.

Employment. A record number of Americans—more than 119 million—had jobs in 1989. The number of available jobs grew about 2.2 per cent during the year. But though the number of jobs grew, the unemployment rate remained steady at about 5.3 per cent. According to economists, this was because the work force grew at about the same rate as the number of jobs. Some economists believed that after seven years of expansion, the economy had reached its capacity for employment.

Labor productivity. Despite the expanding economy, the productivity of workers in the United States grew slowly. Output per hour rose 1.9 per cent in 1989, the same as in 1988. Hourly wages increased 5.1 per cent. This led to a 4.1 per cent increase in the cost of labor input per physical unit of output.

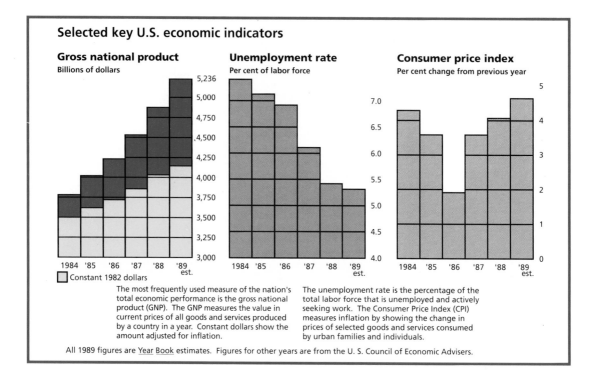

Selected key U.S. economic indicators

Gross national product
Billions of dollars

5,236
5,000
4,750
4,500
4,250
4,000
3,750
3,500
3,250
3,000

1984   '85   '86   '87   '88   '89 est.

☐ Constant 1982 dollars

The most frequently used measure of the nation's total economic performance is the gross national product (GNP). The GNP measures the value in current prices of all goods and services produced by a country in a year. Constant dollars show the amount adjusted for inflation.

Unemployment rate
Per cent of labor force

7.0
6.5
6.0
5.5
5.0
4.5
4.0

1984   '85   '86   '87   '88   '89 est.

The unemployment rate is the percentage of the total labor force that is unemployed and actively seeking work. The Consumer Price Index (CPI) measures inflation by showing the change in prices of selected goods and services consumed by urban families and individuals.

Consumer price index
Per cent change from previous year

5
4
3
2
1
0

1984   '85   '86   '87   '88   '89 est.

All 1989 figures are <u>Year Book</u> estimates. Figures for other years are from the U. S. Council of Economic Advisers.

Leaders of the world's major industrialized nations and the European
Community gathered for an economic summit meeting in Paris in July.

Trade. The growing trade deficit—an excess of imports over exports—continued to worry economists. The deficit remained over $100 billion in the fall of 1989. A deficit is usually financed by selling securities or real assets—such as land or factories—to foreign investors. Investment by foreigners in the United States reached more than $330 billion in 1989.

Stock scare. On October 13, the Dow Jones Industrial Average fell 7 per cent, its biggest drop since the U.S. stock market crash of 1987. But on October 16—the next trading day—the market began to recover, rising 3 per cent.

International scene. The economic picture in other countries was generally good in 1989. Japan's real GNP—adjusted for inflation—rose about 4.8 per cent. Its unemployment rate dropped to 2.3 per cent, and its inflation rate remained steady at 2.6 per cent.

In Great Britain, the growth rate of real GNP rose by 2.4 per cent in 1989. Unemployment fell to 6.1 per cent in 1989 from 8 per cent in 1988. The inflation rate rose from about 6 per cent to 7.6 per cent.

There was some economic growth in most developing nations in 1989, except in Latin America, where economies stagnated. In Argentina and Peru, inflation exceeded 2,500 per cent.   Donald W. Swanton

See also **Bank; International trade; Labor; Manufacturing; Stocks and bonds;** and individual country articles. In *World Book,* see **Economics.**
Ecuador. See **Latin America.**

Education. Many United States leaders sought ways to improve public education in 1989. President George Bush convened an unprecedented "education summit" with the nation's governors on September 27 and 28. The officials met on the campus of the University of Virginia in Charlottesville to discuss topics ranging from teacher recruitment to school reorganization and how to reduce the number of dropouts. They agreed to work together to establish national performance goals for schools and to explore ways to ease federal and state regulations on local school districts. Some observers credited the conference with giving new momentum to a national campaign to upgrade education launched in the early 1980's.

Business backs reform. Earlier in September, several major business groups threw their weight behind the school-reform campaign. Eight national business organizations, including the U.S. Chamber of Commerce and the National Association of Manufacturers, joined together to create the Business Coalition for Education Reform. Also in September, the National Alliance of Business, an organization that works to reduce unemployment among disadvantaged people, published *A Blueprint for Business on Restructuring Education,* which urged businesses to take a range of steps, including supplying experts for school staff training and purchasing computers for schools. That same month, the Business Roundtable, an association of executives at 200 major corporations, urged its

Striking Los Angeles teachers demand increases in salaries and power in May. The teachers accepted a settlement after 10 days.

members to work for education reforms, including an overhaul of vocational education.

Teacher certification. In a major step toward improving the caliber of U.S. teachers, the National Board for Professional Teaching Standards in July published the initial requirements for its new national teaching certificates, the first of which will be awarded in 1993.

The independent, 64-member board announced that a teacher must have a bachelor's degree and three years' teaching experience to apply for a certificate in any of 29 fields. The board will not require candidates to have a degree in education, however. This angered faculties at colleges of education but pleased reformers who want to enlarge the pool of prospective teachers. Advocates of national certification hope that it will raise standards for teachers as well as the profession's level of prestige—and thus make teaching more attractive to the nation's brightest college students.

The troubled condition of many public school systems was highlighted in October 1989 when two states stripped local education officials of their authority. In early October, the New Jersey board of education authorized a take-over of the 28,000-student Jersey City public school system. The board cited "deep and chronic problems" that included corrupt hiring practices and management as well as students' academic failure. The board disbanded the city's school board and fired its superintendent and five other top administrators. Under the take-over, authorized by a 1988 "academic bankruptcy" law, the state will run the city's schools for at least five years. The action made New Jersey the first state to strip authority from local educators under a statewide law.

Also in October, California Governor George Deukmejian signed a law that gives the state broad powers in running Oakland's schools. The 53,000-student school system, California's fifth-largest, had teetered on the brink of financial bankruptcy for months and was the target of a broad corruption investigation that resulted in eight past and present employees being charged with embezzlement, theft, and other crimes. The system's academic programs were in a shambles, and more than 50,000 Oakland residents had signed petitions supporting the take-over bill.

When schools in Chelsea, Mass., opened in September, they had the distinction of belonging to the first privately operated public school system in the United States. Massachusetts Governor Michael S. Dukakis had signed legislation in June granting Boston University control of Chelsea schools for 10 years. The school board in Chelsea, an impoverished town with a population of 25,000, sought the university's help in countering its problems—a shrinking tax base, crumbling school buildings, and a 52 per cent dropout rate.

On January 31, the Educational Testing Service, which conducts tests for the government and other agencies, released a report that pointed to the overall poor performance of U.S. schools. The report revealed the results of a mathematics and science test of 13-year-old students in Canada, Great Britain, Ireland, South Korea, Spain, and the United States. The U.S. students had the worst performance of all the students in math and one of the worst in science.

In the fall, Illinois officials put into effect an unprecedented reform package for Chicago's public schools. The school system, the third-largest in the nation, had been plagued with a 40 per cent dropout rate, low student achievement, and gang-related violence. In an attempt to remedy those problems, state legislators in 1988 passed the Chicago School Reform Act, which transferred considerable power from the Chicago Board of Education to 540 newly created councils consisting of parents, teachers, and community representatives. In October 1989, the board sponsored elections for the local councils and hired a new superintendent of schools.

Financial woes. Two important state court decisions handed down in 1989 addressed a major problem for many school districts: the inability of impoverished communities to raise enough tax revenues to support good schools.

On June 8, the Kentucky Supreme Court struck down not only the state's school-finance laws but also laws governing Kentucky's entire public school system, including those that create school districts, school boards, and the state's department of education. "Kentucky's entire system of common schools is unconstitutional," wrote Chief Justice Robert F. Stephens after hearing a case brought against the state by 66 poor school districts. The districts had charged that deriving school funds from property taxes is unfair because poor districts generate less tax revenue than wealthy ones. The court decision requires Kentucky's legislature to revamp the state's educational system.

Citing "glaring disparities" between rich and poor school districts, the Texas Supreme Court in October ruled that the state's method of funding schools was unconstitutional. About 50 per cent of the funds for Texas schools comes from property taxes. The court's unanimous decision required Texas to narrow the difference between what wealthy districts spend on their students and what impoverished districts spend. The court also implied that the state must demonstrate that students in poor school districts are being adequately educated—a far more rigorous requirement than those that had been placed on states in past funding challenges.

Educational choice. Bush's education summit focused attention on another school-reform issue that took center stage in 1989—educational choice. Some experts have argued that students should have a say in choosing which school they attend instead of being assigned to a neighborhood school. Advocates of educational choice say the policy would compel administrators to improve their schools—or risk losing students and funding. In January, then-President Ronald

Reagan and President-elect Bush championed this approach to school improvement during a White House workshop. In the fall, Secretary of Education Lauro F. Cavazos sponsored six regional meetings to promote educational choice.

Rising college costs. The average cost of a college education continued to escalate in 1989. The College Board, an association of 2,600 schools and colleges that provides college-admissions services, reported in August that tuition increases for the 1989-1990 school year outpaced inflation for the ninth consecutive year. Costs rose by about 9 per cent at private colleges, pushing the price of a bachelor's degree at the most expensive schools to $80,000 or more.

Colleges and universities argued that increases in expenses and the need to raise faculty salaries necessitated the tuition hike. But in August, the U.S. Department of Justice fueled the criticism of skeptics by announcing that it would investigate whether some prominent institutions violated antitrust laws in setting tuition rates and financial aid levels. The investigation includes nearly 30 schools, among them Harvard University in Cambridge, Mass., and the University of Chicago.

The quality of campus life became a major issue at colleges and universities in 1989, as alcohol and drug abuse, racial intolerance, and other problems became increasingly prevalent at many schools.

In September, 27 of the 59 national fraternities in the United States adopted a code of conduct strictly limiting alcohol consumption at fraternity functions. Two fraternities, Tau Kappa Epsilon and Zeta Beta Tau, also ordered their campus affiliates to discontinue pledging among freshmen. The fraternities hoped this would limit the practice of hazing and other disorderly behaviors among their members. Since the late 1970's, at least 44 U.S. college students have died in hazing-related accidents.

Racial problems spurred several universities to take steps in 1989 toward banning statements that are racist or in other ways offensive. Racial unrest at the University of Massachusetts in Amherst prompted school officials to start mounted-police patrols on campus in the fall.

Another important issue in higher education concerned the proper role of intercollegiate sports. The image of college sports was tarnished by scandals at several schools in 1989. Professors at the University of Iowa in Iowa City were charged with improperly aiding underachieving athletes. Athletic recruiters allegedly engaged in questionable recruiting practices at North Carolina State University in Raleigh. And several members of the football team at the University of Oklahoma in Norman were arrested for criminal acts.

In September, a federal study revealed a low graduation rate among basketball players at colleges and universities with major men's basketball programs. At more than 30 per cent of the schools, fewer than 1 in 5 basketball players earned diplomas.

Education

"Politics is weirder than I thought. We learned in
school today that *Garfield* used to be president!"

In October, *U.S. News & World Report* published a
survey of 2,348 college presidents, deans, and admissions officers. Eighty-six per cent of those polled said
that the emphasis on intercollegiate sports has begun
to interfere with schools' primary mission—educating
students.

Enrollments. Notwithstanding spiraling tuition
costs and some campus turmoil, a record proportion
of college-age Americans attended college in the
1988-1989 school year, according to the U.S. Department of Labor. Nearly 60 per cent of the high school
class of 1988 enrolled in college the following fall, up
from 50 per cent in 1978.

Total enrollment in U.S. schools and colleges
reached an estimated 58.7 million in fall 1989, nearly
400,000 higher than the year before. About 45.6 million students attended public and private elementary
and secondary schools, an increase of 150,000 from
the 1988-1989 school year. Total college enrollment
was expected to increase to 13.1 million, up 250,000
from the previous year.

The total education bill in the United States was
estimated at $353 billion for the 1989-1990 school
year, a one-year increase of more than $20 billion.
Spending at the elementary and secondary levels was
estimated at $212 billion, a 6.6 per cent increase.
Higher education expenditures were estimated at
$141 billion, up 7.2 per cent.   Thomas Toch

In *World Book,* see **Education.**

Egypt officially returned to the Arab fold in 1989,
ending 10 years of isolation imposed by other Arab
countries as punishment for Egypt's 1979 decision to
sign a peace treaty with Israel. In May 1989, Egypt was
readmitted to the Arab League and to the Organization of Arab Petroleum Exporting Countries.

Mediation attempt. Egypt's unique relationship
with Israel encouraged President Hosni Mubarak to
attempt to negotiate a peaceful solution to the *intifada,* the Palestinian uprising in the Israeli-occupied
West Bank and Gaza Strip. In August, Mubarak presented a 10-point proposal to Israeli and Palestinian
leaders. The proposal called for internationally supervised elections in the occupied territories and a halt to
the construction of Jewish settlements there. Also under the plan, Israel would agree to trade occupied
land for peace treaties with neighboring Arab countries. See **Israel.**

Taba returned. In March, Egypt formally regained
possession of Taba, a small oceanside resort in the
Sinai Peninsula. In 1988, an international arbitration
panel had awarded Taba to Egypt, ending a nine-year
dispute with Israel. The resort had been the only section of the Sinai not returned to Egypt by Israel under
their 1979 peace treaty.

Relations with the United States were damaged
by two unrelated espionage cases. In June 1989, an
Egyptian-born American rocket expert was sentenced
to prison in the United States for exporting ballistic
missile parts to Egypt illegally. In April, President
Mubarak had reassigned his minister of defense, the
alleged mastermind of the affair. The minister was
also charged with misappropriating government
funds. In July, another Egyptian-American was convicted in Cairo, the capital of Egypt, of passing information on Islamic fundamentalists to the United
States Central Intelligence Agency.

Fundamentalism. In April, Egyptian police arrested 1,500 Islamic fundamentalists after clashes between police and fundamentalist protesters in Al-
Fayyum, southwest of Cairo. Among those arrested
was the spiritual leader of Islamic Jihad, an underground group committed to the violent overthrow of
the government. In August, 41 members of an outlawed Shiite Muslim group were arrested and charged
with plotting to overthrow the government and to
attack U.S., Israeli, and other foreign airlines, embassies, and facilities.

The economy. In April, the United States released
a $230-million cash grant that had been suspended
because of U.S. dissatisfaction with the pace of Egyptian economic reforms. The reversal resulted from
Egypt's improved economic performance and a major
oil find in the Western Desert. Natural gas from new
fields in this region increased the country's production
and provided Egypt with enough fuel to meet 60 per
cent of its electrical needs.   William Spencer

See also **Middle East** (Facts in brief table). In *World
Book,* see **Egypt.**

Elections. Democrats scored big in the two state-wide elections of Nov. 7, 1989, in New Jersey and Virginia. Black candidates recorded historic firsts in Virginia and in mayoral races from New York City to Seattle.

State races. In Virginia, Democratic Lieutenant Governor L. Douglas Wilder became the first black elected governor in United States history. Wilder built his campaign around his prochoice stand on abortion and defeated Republican J. Marshall Coleman by a fraction of 1 per cent of 1.78 million votes cast. See **Wilder, L. Douglas.**

In New Jersey, prochoice Democratic Representative James J. Florio won the governorship over Republican Representative Jim Courter with a decisive 62 per cent of the vote. The win ended eight years of Republican leadership under Governor Thomas H. Kean. Democrats also recaptured control of the New Jersey Assembly, which Republicans had held for four years.

President George Bush campaigned for Coleman and Courter, and the national Republican Party made major efforts in both states. But the Republican platform favors outlawing most abortions, and that stance clearly hurt party candidates.

Mayoral races. Democrat David N. Dinkins, Manhattan borough president, became New York City's first elected black mayor by defeating Republican Rudolph W. Giuliani, a former U.S. Attorney, 51 to 48 per cent. Race was a hidden issue in the election. A *New York Times*/WCBS-TV exit poll indicated that Dinkins won 91 per cent of black votes but only 27 per cent of white votes, and that 63 per cent of Jewish voters abandoned their traditional Democratic allegiance to vote for Giuliani. Earlier, in a September 12 Democratic primary, Dinkins had easily defeated three-term Mayor Edward I. Koch. See **Dinkins, David N.**

Durham, N.C.; New Haven, Conn.; and Seattle also elected black mayors for the first time. In Durham, Chester L. Jenkins defeated J. Nelson Strawbridge, an associate of Senator Jesse Helms (R., N.C.), in a nonpartisan election. In New Haven, State Senator John Daniels, a Democrat, easily defeated Republican Alderwoman Robie Pooley with more than twice as many votes. In Seattle, where only 10 per cent of the voters are black, Democratic City Councilman Norman B. Rice drew 58 per cent of the vote to defeat Republican City Attorney Douglas Jewett.

Mayor Coleman A. Young of Detroit won a fifth term over a challenge by accountant Thomas Barrow, who gave him his stiffest competition ever. Mayor Kathryn J. Whitmire of Houston also won a fifth term, handily defeating former Mayor Fred Hofheinz. In an October election, former Atlanta, Ga., Mayor Maynard H. Jackson was returned to office.

Two blacks competed for the mayor's office in Cleveland in a campaign marked by personal attacks; State Senator Michael R. White defeated City Council President George L. Forbes. Miami's first Cuban-born

L. Douglas Wilder, a Democrat, won election as governor of Virginia on November 7, becoming the first black elected governor in U.S. history.

mayor, Xavier L. Suarez, won a third term, defeating Cuban-born Armando Lacasa. Mayor James D. Griffin of Buffalo, N.Y., won a fourth term.

In St. Paul, Minn., City Council President Jim Scheibel, a Democrat, won a heated contest with independent Bob Fletcher, a police lieutenant, to succeed Democrat George Latimer, who retired after 13 years as mayor. In neighboring Minneapolis, Mayor Donald M. Fraser easily won his bid for a fourth term.

On April 4, Chicago voters elected Richard M. Daley mayor by landslide proportions. Daley—the eldest son of the late Mayor Richard J. Daley—received 56 per cent of the vote over two opponents to serve the final two years of the second term of Mayor Harold Washington, who died in 1987. Daley had easily defeated Washington's successor, Acting Mayor Eugene Sawyer, in the Democratic primary in February 1989 (see **Daley, Richard M.**). And on April 11, Thomas Bradley won a fifth term as mayor of Los Angeles, getting 52 per cent of the vote against two opponents.

May saw several major mayoral races in Texas. On May 6, Mayors Annette G. Strauss of Dallas and Bob Bolen of Fort Worth easily won reelection. Former Mayor Lila Cockrell of San Antonio regained the office, winning 59 per cent of the vote to 31 per cent for insurance executive Carl Mauthe, her closest rival. On May 27, Democrat Suzanne S. Azar scored a landslide in a runoff election victory over Republican Mayor Pro Tem Ed Elsey to become El Paso's first woman mayor.

Congressional elections. Eight special elections during 1989 to fill vacancies in the House of Representatives resulted in a net change of only one seat, with the Democrats gaining the edge.

In Indiana, Democrat Jill Long upset Republican Dan Heath on March 28 to win the Indiana seat left vacant when Dan Coats took over Vice President Dan Quayle's Senate post. On August 29, Republican Ileana Ros-Lehtinen—the first Cuban-American elected to Congress—narrowly defeated Democrat Gerald F. Richman for the Florida seat of the late Claude D. Pepper, a Democrat who had held it since 1962. And on October 17, Democrat Gene Taylor was elected to replace Republican Larkin I. Smith of Mississippi, killed in an August 13 plane crash. Taylor defeated Tom Anderson, veteran aide to Senator Trent Lott (R., Miss.).

On April 4, a Democrat won the Alabama House seat of the late Bill Nichols. A Republican scored an easy victory April 26 to fill the Wyoming seat vacated by Secretary of Defense Richard B. Cheney. On September 12, Democratic candidates won the seats of two resigned Democratic leaders, Speaker James C. Wright, Jr., of Texas, and Party Whip Tony Coelho of California. And on December 9, a Texas Democrat got the seat of Mickey Leland, victim of another plane crash.   Frank Cormier and Margot Cormier

See also **Congress of the United States; Democratic Party; Republican Party; State government.** In *World Book,* see **Election; Election campaign.**

Electric power. See **Energy supply.**

Electronics. For the United States consumer electronics industry, 1989 was a milestone year in more ways than one. Two Japanese video equipment manufacturers entered the business of making motion pictures. The first advanced television signal in the United States was broadcast. And home audio equipment manufacturers and the recording industry reached an agreement to end their long-standing battle over digital audio tape (DAT) machines.

Japanese moviemakers. Although Japanese companies manufacture most videocassette recorders (VCR's) and other home video gear sold in the United States, U.S. studios have produced almost all of the movies sold as video programming. But in April, a Japanese video equipment maker, Victor Company of Japan Limited (JVC), financed its first American feature film, *Mystery Train.* In September, Sony Corporation of Japan reached an agreement to purchase Columbia Pictures Entertainment Incorporated for approximately $3.4 billion. The deal was the first time a foreign company had purchased a U.S. movie studio. Sony chairman Akio Morita, who in 1987 engineered the purchase of CBS Records, indicated that his company wanted to acquire entertainment companies to help it in new enterprises, such as high-definition television (HDTV).

HDTV was at the forefront of industry news in 1989. Currently under development in Japan, the United States, and Europe, HDTV uses a detailed broadcast signal to provide a sharper image than conventional TV. Because of fears that Japanese companies are years ahead of the United States in developing HDTV, industry groups and members of Congress called for government funding of the U.S. effort. None of the proposals were acted upon by year-end.

An advanced television signal—a forerunner to the more detailed signal needed for HDTV—was broadcast for the first time in the United States on April 20. The signal produced a wide-screen, high-definition picture on an experimental TV set at the David Sarnoff Research Center in Princeton, N.J.

DAT agreement. Officials representing recording industries throughout the world met with home audio equipment manufacturers in July in Athens, Greece, to hammer out an agreement over the sale of DAT machines in the United States. Like compact discs (CD's), DAT's digitally reproduce sound with virtually no distortion. Unlike CD players, however, DAT machines are capable of making recordings. Record companies have opposed the introduction of DAT machines because they fear that consumers and record pirates will use the devices to make high-quality unauthorized copies of tapes and CD's. At the Athens meeting, both sides agreed that DAT machines sold in the United States will contain a microchip that limits their ability to duplicate copyrighted material.   Martin Levine

See also **Computer.** In the Special Reports section, see **Television: The Changing Picture.** In *World Book,* see **Electronics; Television.**

El Salvador. Leftist rebels launched one of the largest offensives of El Salvador's 10-year-old civil war on Nov. 11, 1989, with a dramatic assault on San Salvador, the capital. By November 20, government forces had succeeded in routing the guerrillas from most of the positions they held, but the rebels continued to harass government forces with surprise attacks.

At least 1,300 people were killed, and at least 1,300 others were wounded during the fighting. Many were civilians who lived in residential neighborhoods that were bombed and strafed by government troops seeking to dislodge the rebels.

In response, El Salvador's new president, Alfredo Cristiani Burkard, declared a state of siege, and the National Assembly passed legislation curtailing civil liberties. Critics charged that the government used the rebel offensive to intimidate religious groups.

Priests killed. On November 16, a group of uniformed soldiers reportedly entered the grounds of José Simeón Cañas University of Central America on the outskirts of the capital and murdered six Jesuit priests, their housekeeper, and her daughter. The priests were known to be critical of the right wing death squads that have caused many of the nearly 70,000 deaths during El Salvador's civil war.

Government forces raided an Episcopal Church in San Salvador and the home of a representative of Christian Education Seminars, an ecumenical group based in the United States. Two U.S. citizens were arrested in the raids. Leaders of the ruling National Republican Alliance (ARENA) party have often charged that religious groups support the rebels.

The government broke off diplomatic relations with Nicaragua on November 26 after shooting down an airplane carrying antiaircraft missiles. The government charged that the airplane originated from Nicaragua.

Aim unclear. The aim of the rebel offensive was unclear. Some observers said its purpose was to topple the Cristiani government, but others speculated that the rebels sought to induce a change in the government's position in peace negotiations that had begun on October 16 and 17 in San José, Costa Rica. Rebels of the Farabundo Martí National Liberation Front said the offensive was a response to an October 31 bombing—in which 10 people died—of a labor union headquarters, and they broke off the peace talks.

Cristiani had proposed the negotiations following his election on March 19. A wealthy coffee grower, Cristiani sought to project an image of moderation. But critics charged that Cristiani was a figurehead and that the real power in El Salvador was with Roberto D'Aubuisson, the founder of ARENA, who has been implicated in death squad activity.   Nathan A. Haverstock

See also **Cristiani Burkard, Alfredo; Latin America** (Facts in brief table). In *World Book,* see **El Salvador.**
Employment. See Economics; Labor.
Endangered species. See **Conservation.** In the Special Reports section, see **Saving Our Big Birds.**

Presidential candidate Alfredo Cristiani Burkard of El Salvador's right wing ARENA party addresses a campaign rally prior to his electoral victory in March.

Energy supply

Energy supply. There was renewed interest in alternative fuels in the United States during 1989, stemming mainly from concern about environmental pollution caused by burning coal, oil, natural gas, and other fossil fuels.

A national effort to develop automobiles and trucks that burn methanol, natural gas, and other alternative fuels was proposed by U.S. President George Bush on June 12. The alternative-fuels proposal was part of a larger effort by Bush to toughen the federal Clean Air Act by reducing the amount of pollution from motor vehicles.

The proposal called for automobile manufacturers to sell alternative-fuel vehicles in areas of the country with the most severe air pollution problems. The number of such vehicles produced each year would rise from 500,000 in 1995 to 1 million by 1997. Government officials said they expected that most of the alternative-fuel vehicles would burn methanol, or "wood alcohol," fuel that can be produced from natural gas and other materials.

Concerned about the prospect of alternative-fuel vehicles reducing gasoline sales, some oil companies introduced reformulated gasoline and diesel fuel that cause less air pollution.

The Soviet Union on July 14 began the first test flights of an airplane fueled by liquefied natural gas (LNG). The plane was a modified version of the Tu-154, a commercial jetliner used by Aeroflot, the Soviet national airline. The flight tests were designed to determine whether the plane would operate more economically than conventional aircraft that burn aviation kerosene.

Hydrogen fuel. Rapid advances in photovoltaic cells could lead to the use of hydrogen as a practical, low-pollution motor vehicle fuel, according to a report by researchers at Princeton University in New Jersey released on September 27. Photovoltaic, or solar, cells convert sunlight into electricity. The electricity can be used to produce hydrogen from ordinary water in a process called electrolysis.

Hydrogen long has been considered an ideal alternative fuel because it burns so cleanly. But the high cost of the electricity that would be needed to produce adequate amounts of hydrogen has prevented its wide adoption as an alternative to gasoline. The Princeton researchers found, however, that photovoltaic cells could produce electricity cheaply enough by the year 2000 to make hydrogen an economical fuel. They reported that solar cells, installed in sunny desert areas, could produce hydrogen that could be transported by pipeline to urban areas.

Methanol production became a goal of the government of Oman, which decided to build the world's first floating methanol plant, according to the April 10 issue of *Oil & Gas Journal*, an industry publication. The $250-million facility, scheduled for completion in 1991, will convert surplus natural gas into methanol

In China Lake, Calif., a well taps geothermal steam, an experimental power source created when water contacts heated rocks in the earth.

for export to the United States and Europe. Oman, a small country on the Arabian Peninsula, selected a floating design so that the plant can be moved from one offshore gas well to another. It will process gas from the wells that otherwise would be burned off, or "flared," as waste.

Energy use. The U.S. Department of Energy (DOE) on Sept. 25, 1989, reported that Americans consumed 41 quadrillion British thermal units (Btu's) of energy during the first half of 1989, up 1.1 per cent from the first half of 1988. A Btu is the amount of energy needed to raise the temperature of 1 pound (0.45 kilogram) of water 1 degree Fahrenheit (0.56 degree Celsius). The United States produced 33 quadrillion Btu's of energy during the first half of 1989. Coal supplied about 33 per cent, crude oil and natural gas provided about 27 per cent, nuclear power about 8 per cent, and hydroelectric power about 4 per cent. The remaining 1 per cent came from a variety of sources, including geothermal and solar energy.

Americans consumed about 3 per cent more electricity during the first six months of 1989 than during the same period in 1988. Utilities in the United States generated 1.34 trillion kilowatt-hours of electricity during the first half of 1989. The amount generated with coal increased by 2 per cent to 751 billion kilowatt-hours, more than 50 per cent of the total. Nuclear-based generation declined from the record level of 256 billion kilowatt-hours in the first half of 1988 to 239 billion in 1989.

World nuclear safety. Delegates representing owners and operators of more than 400 nuclear power stations throughout the world met in Moscow on May 15 to establish the World Association of Nuclear Operators. The new organization, designed to assure the safety and reliability of nuclear plants, will have a coordinating center in London and regional offices in Moscow, Paris, Tokyo, and Atlanta, Ga. The association will collect and maintain data on the operation of nuclear power plants, notify operators of safety problems at other plants, analyze the causes of equipment failures, and provide other services to plant operators.

Nuclear shut-downs. Citizens of Sacramento County, California, on June 6 voted to shut down the Rancho Seco Nuclear Generating Station, 25 miles (40 kilometers) southeast of Sacramento. Although the referendum was not legally binding, the Sacramento Municipal Utility District, operator of the plant, had agreed to abide by the results. But on June 20, directors of the utility voted to offer the plant for sale, claiming the referendum did not prevent the plant's operation by another utility. Sacramento officials promised to submit any sales agreement for the plant to voter approval.

The Long Island Lighting Company (Lilco) on July 14 began to remove uranium fuel rods from its Shoreham nuclear power station on Long Island, the first step toward possible dismantling of the controversial plant, which had been licensed in April to operate at full power. Lilco agreed to sell the $5.5-billion plant to New York state for $1 and dismantle it to end a long dispute about its safety.

Hundreds of demonstrators were arrested on June 4 during a protest against the first tests of the Seabrook nuclear power station in New Hampshire. The Seabrook site—and especially emergency evacuation plans in case of a nuclear accident—has been a focus of controversy since 1976.

Commercial nuclear fuel. Louisiana Energy Services Company on June 9 announced that it would construct a $750-million plant near Homer, La., to produce enriched uranium fuel for nuclear power plants. When completed in 1996, it would be the first privately owned uranium enrichment facility in the United States. In the past, nuclear power plants have purchased enriched uranium primarily from the United States government. The new plant would be capable of supplying about 15 per cent of the enriched uranium needed by domestic nuclear power plants.

Energy and terrorism. Experts testifying before a United States congressional committee on February 7 warned that the U.S. energy supply system is vulnerable to terrorist attacks. They noted that terrorists have damaged oil pipelines, nuclear reactors, and electric transmission facilities in other countries. It could take weeks or months to repair damages to some facilities, they said, especially large electrical transformers, devices that increase or decrease the voltage of electric current. The nation's long-distance electric power lines depend heavily on about 4,000 large transformers, the witnesses said, and it typically takes one year to build and ship such a transformer.

Shortage concerns. Another Arab oil embargo would not mean an immediate energy crisis for the United States, the National Petroleum Council concluded in a March 17 report. The council, which advises the DOE, said there were 555 million barrels of oil in the Strategic Petroleum Reserve, and this could temporarily compensate for a loss of oil imports. The reserve is an underground storage network in Louisiana and Texas that was created by Congress in 1975, after the Arab oil embargo.

Several years of dry weather in northern Quebec forced Hydro-Québec, the provincial utility, to curtail sales of surplus electricity to other Canadian provinces and to U.S. utilities during 1989. Inadequate rainfall reduced water levels in reservoirs that supply the utility's hydroelectric generating stations. Hydro-Québec officials estimated that the lack of water would cost the utility $255 million (U.S. dollars) in lost sales and other costs during the year.   Michael Woods

See also **Coal; Petroleum and gas.** In the Special Reports section, see **The Coming Energy Squeeze.** In *World Book,* see **Energy supply.**

Engineering. See **Building and construction.**

England. See **Great Britain.**

Environmental pollution

Environmental pollution. Oil spills dominated the environmental news in 1989. Waters near Antarctica were fouled for the first time in history in January. Two months later, an oil tanker ran aground in Alaska's Prince William Sound, causing the worst oil spill ever in United States waters (see **Close-Up**). The year also brought new insight into environmental threats that are even more serious than oil spills.

The "ozone hole." Since the late 1970's, scientists monitoring the atmosphere above Antarctica have detected a seasonal thinning of the earth's protective layer of ozone in the upper atmosphere. The ozone layer shields earth's plants and animals from much of the harmful ultraviolet light emitted by the sun. In October 1989, the thinning reached record levels, an observation that led scientists in the National Aeronautics and Space Administration to conclude that the Antarctic ozone "hole" is growing at a faster rate than had been expected.

Antarctica's ozone hole now lets twice the normal amount of ultraviolet light through to the Antarctic, the National Science Foundation reported in early May. Oceanographers from Texas A&M University in College Station reported in September that their experiments in the Antarctic show that this amount of ultraviolet light can harm—or even kill—tiny floating plants, called phytoplankton, in the surface waters of the Antarctic Ocean, sometimes called the Southern Ocean. Phytoplankton form the basis of a food chain that feeds many animals.

In July, scientists from the University of Wyoming in Laramie reported measuring a wintertime thinning of the ozone layer above the Arctic. This is the first solid evidence to suggest that an ozone hole may eventually form each year above the North Pole as well as the South Pole.

On July 1, the Montreal Protocol, an international treaty, went into effect to limit the production of chemicals called *chlorofluorocarbons* (CFC's). These pollutants—widely used as refrigerants, as aerosol propellants, and in packaging and insulation—are, along with a few other chemicals, responsible for destroying upper atmospheric ozone. The treaty, which was drafted in 1987, originally required ratifying nations to cut their emissions of CFC's in half by 1998. But in May 1989, leaders from 80 nations met in Finland and agreed to revise the treaty so that CFC's are completely banned by the year 2000.

Acid rain effects. Ecologists from the Institute of Ecosystem Studies in Millbrook, N.Y., reported in March that the water in 80 per cent of the lakes in New York's Adirondack Mountains has become acidic, probably because of *acid rain*. Acid rain is a general term used to describe precipitation that contains acids formed from certain pollutants.

The Adirondack Mountain lakes, along with many others in the Northeast, may be suffering severe ecological damage because of acid rain, according to Canadian researchers. They reported in May that many

of the lakes may have lost half or more of their leeches, insects, and clams. Algae have probably suffered also. Where acidification has been severe, whole classes of these plants and animals may have disappeared, threatening the survival of game fish and other prized species.

Forests also suffer from acid rain. As acid rain soaks into the ground, it causes the release of the aluminum present in normal soils. Once freed, the metal makes it difficult for roots to absorb the minerals needed for healthy growth. At the same time, the nitrogen in acid rain acts as a fertilizer, spurring tree growth, according to a May 19 report by ecologist Ernst-Detlef Schulze at the University of Bayreuth in West Germany. Schulze found that the combination of increased aluminum and nitrogen weakens trees, making them especially susceptible to bad weather and attacks by fungi and insects.

New data by other West German researchers indicate that one-third of that nation's trees are weakened or dying because their soils are polluted by acid chemicals. In many areas, all mature trees are dead. American researchers also reported evidence in 1989 that trees at high elevations in the Eastern United States may be suffering the same effects.

Smog. While ozone in the earth's upper atmosphere protects living things, its presence in the air near the earth's surface is part of a potentially serious hazard—photochemical smog. This type of smog is caused by hydrocarbons and nitrogen oxides—pollutants emitted when gasoline and other fossil fuels are burned. These pollutants react in the presence of sunlight to form ozone and other gases. In June, scientists reported that high levels of smog not only slow the breathing rate of human beings but also may cause irreversible lung damage. These findings were revealed at a meeting of the Air and Waste Management Association, based in Pittsburgh, Pa.

Although strong federal regulations limit smog formation, in 1989 almost half the U.S. population lived in areas that violate these ozone standards, according to a July government report. And in August, the U.S. Environmental Protection Agency (EPA) announced that 37 communities were being added to its list of ozone violators for the first time. EPA Administrator William K. Reilly said this dramatic increase proved a need for stronger clean-air regulations.

The 12-member European Community (EC) attacked its smog problem in June by imposing its first standards for automobile emissions. The standards for full-sized cars are the same as United States regulations for large cars.

Benzene pollution. On August 31, the EPA announced new regulations for benzene. The stiff new regulations will lower public exposure to industrial emissions of this cancer-causing chemical. The limits were expected to reduce cases of leukemia linked to industrial-plant emissions of benzene from four per year to no more than one every three years.

Protesters call for the imposition of tougher environmental regulations in a rally on Earth Day, April 22, in New York City.

But an October report by EPA scientist Lance Wallace showed that public exposure to benzene results largely from nonindustrial sources. People are exposed to benzene in and around the home, from such things as cigarette smoke, paint, and solvents. Benzene was also detected in automobile emissions and gasoline fumes. Wallace said this type of exposure causes about 950 cases of leukemia per year. If this estimate is correct, benzene may be the most significant cancer-causing chemical to which the public is exposed.

Food scares. Pesticides on fruits and vegetables pose an unacceptably high cancer risk to U.S. consumers, according to a two-year study released on February 27 by the Natural Resources Defense Council (NRDC), a private organization based in New York City. The group said the lifetime cancer risk posed by these chemicals was 240 times higher than the one-in-a-million risk usually considered acceptable by the EPA. Because children consume more fruits, vegetables, and fruit juices than do adults, exposure occurs primarily in childhood, the study found.

At least 90 per cent of a person's lifetime cancer risk from these sources is linked to a growth regulator called *daminozide*, the NRDC scientists reported. Marketed under the name Alar, the chemical is typically used on apples to promote ripening. Although the EPA has proposed banning daminozide since 1985, the agency said in March 1989 that the NRDC had exaggerated Alar's risks and said it was safe to eat apples.

Nevertheless, some U.S. school districts refused to buy apples that had been treated with Alar. Stores found it difficult to sell apples and apple products. By May, apple growers announced that they would phase out their use of the ripener. One month later, the chemical's only manufacturer announced it would end sales of Alar for use on U.S. food crops.

Trace levels of highly toxic chemicals called *dioxins* and *furans* turned up in almost half the U.S. milk tested for these compounds, the U.S. Food and Drug Administration (FDA) announced in September. This finding confirmed 1988 data indicating that these chemicals can leach out of cardboard cartons into milk. The paper industry argued that the health risks associated with such low levels of contamination are very slight, and the FDA said that changes in milk packaging should eliminate virtually all risk.

Uncertainties about Antarctica. In October, delegates from 39 nations met in Paris to discuss the future of Antarctica. Some delegates advocated opening the continent to limited mineral exploitation, while others favored protecting Antarctica's environment by making it a "wilderness park." The representatives were unable to reach agreement, and they called for more negotiations in 1990. In the Special Reports section, see **The Last Unspoiled Continent.**   Janet Raloff

See also **Conservation.** In *World Book,* see **Environmental pollution.**

Equatorial Guinea. See **Africa.**

1989: The Year of the Oil Spill

An unusual number of major shipping accidents poured oil into waters from Alaska to Antarctica in 1989, raising environmental concerns and causing 1989 to be dubbed "the year of the oil spill."

The first large spill occurred on January 28, when an Argentine ship, the *Bahía Paraíso*, ran aground off the Antarctic Peninsula. The ship capsized, spilling about 200,000 gallons (760,000 liters) of diesel and jet fuel into the previously unspoiled marine environment.

The fuel killed large numbers of *krill*, shrimplike sea creatures that are a major food source for the region's aquatic wildlife. The spill also contaminated thousands of birds, including an entire colony of 30,000 Adélie penguins. Many other penguins may have died at sea, and researchers reported unusually high death rates among sea bird chicks. In the Special Reports section, see **The Last Unspoiled Continent.**

But concerns about this, Antarctica's first oil spill, were overshadowed on March 24, when an oil tanker, the *Exxon Valdez*, ran aground in Alaska's Prince William Sound, a nearly unspoiled area known for its spectacular beauty and wealth of natural resources. The vessel, owned by Exxon Shipping Company, released about 11 million gallons (42 million liters) of crude oil—the largest tanker spill ever in United States waters.

Because there were not enough personnel and equipment on hand to contain the slick, currents carried the oil far south into the Gulf of Alaska. Within weeks, the oil slick had fouled more than 1,000 miles (1,600 kilometers) of shoreline, including beaches in three national parks and five wildlife refuges.

Exxon Corporation undertook a massive and expensive cleanup effort, eventually hiring workers to use steam and towels to remove oil from the rocky shoreline. When the company halted operations for the year on September 15, Exxon officials said that pollution no longer threatened fish and wildlife—though no one claimed the beaches were truly clean. In fact, Alaska officials contended that huge amounts of oil remained in the environment.

Natural processes will break down some of the oil into harmless chemicals, but environmentalists fear that much of the pollution will persist for years. Exxon officials and government experts planned to meet in spring 1990 to decide what additional cleanup efforts are necessary.

Although the impact of the spill is difficult to measure, biologists reported that 33,000 sea birds, 146 eagles, and 980 sea otters had been found dead by the end of the summer. Government experts maintained that these figures represented only 10 to 20 per cent of the actual number of deaths.

No major fish kills were reported, though salmon hatchlings are known to be extremely sensitive to pollutants. The effects of the spill on some salmon species will not be known for several years, when the fish spawned in 1989 should return to the area. Similarly, no one knows what the long-term effects on other animals will be.

Three more large oil spills occurred, coincidentally, within 12 hours on June 23 and 24. Three separate tanker accidents released about 850,000 gallons (3.2 million liters) of petroleum products into the Atlantic Ocean off the coast of Rhode

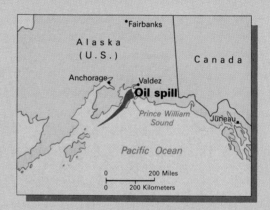

On March 24, the *Exxon Valdez* oil tanker ran aground in Prince William Sound, on the southern coast of Alaska.

A cleanup worker holds a sea bird coated with oil from the *Exxon Valdez* oil spill. By August, the oil had killed thousands of animals.

Island, the Delaware River, and the Houston Ship Channel near Galveston Bay.

In each case, workers removed the oil from the water and shorelines relatively quickly. Because winds pushed the Galveston Bay slick into an artificially created canal with little wildlife, the spill caused only minor damage, federal officials said. They also reported that the Rhode Island and Delaware River accidents had not significantly harmed populations of fish and wildlife. Officials noted some bird deaths, however, and these spills may have long-term effects on shellfish as well as on fish species that were spawning in the areas at the time of the accidents.

All the mishaps—and particularly the *Exxon Valdez* spill—called into question the oil industry's ability to handle shipping accidents. In addition, the attention they focused on the possibility of more such spills hindered the federal government's efforts to open new areas to oil development. The accidents also encouraged federal legislators and oil industry experts to propose new ways to deal with future spills, such as establishing permanent cleanup facilities near areas of heavy oil-shipping traffic.

Other proposals included funding research into better ways of controlling discharges of oil from vessels as well as recovering spilled oil. Improved navigational aids for oil-bearing ships, better training for crews, and more rigorous licensing requirements for crew members and officers were cited as ways to prevent tanker accidents.

Although the large oil spills of 1989 focused attention on this form of pollution, the problem recurs every year. Much of the oil entering the world's rivers, lakes, and oceans comes from smaller but more numerous spills—along with routine tanker operations such as rinsing oil-storage tanks. According to the National Academy of Sciences in Washington, D.C., the earth's waters are annually polluted with about 540 million gallons (2 billion liters) of petroleum products—the equivalent of 50 *Exxon Valdez* accidents every year.   Gerald Karey

Workers use high-pressure water hoses to clean oil off a portion of the hundreds of miles of Alaskan shoreline fouled by the *Exxon Valdez* spill.

Ethiopia. Ethiopia's President Mengistu Haile-Mariam, for the first time since seizing power in 1977, himself faced a coup attempt in 1989. Senior military officers in Addis Ababa and Asmara rebelled on May 16, as Mengistu was making a state visit to East Germany. Returning quickly to Ethiopia, Mengistu threw an elite guard and other loyalists against the mutinous officers and their troops, crushing the uprising. Nine ringleaders and a dozen other senior officers were executed.

The coup leaders had been frustrated by a series of major losses to rebel forces in the regions of Eritrea and Tigre during 1988 and 1989 as well as by political interference in military operations. They were also angered by the regime's decision to call up 100,000 teenage recruits to replace army casualties.

Peace overtures. After two decades, the separate wars in Eritrea and Tigre had resulted in 500,000 deaths and the flight of 625,000 refugees to neighboring countries. Rebel victories, the withdrawal of Cuban support troops, and pressure from the Soviet Union—Mengistu's main military supporter—forced Mengistu to seek a negotiated settlement of the conflicts. On June 5, Mengistu issued a broad call to the rebels to start peace talks.

The Tigrean People's Liberation Front (TPLF), which has been fighting since 1975 for regional self-government and an end to the Mengistu military dictatorship, quickly agreed to talks. The TPLF in March had captured the provincial capital of Mekele and was in virtual control of all Tigre. By the time the peace negotiations began in November in Rome, the TPLF position had been further strengthened by a September victory in which 17,000 government troops were killed or wounded.

The war in Eritrea, which has been going on since 1961, is more complex because the Eritrean People's Liberation Front (EPLF) seeks outright independence. In January 1989, the EPLF rejected Mengistu's plan to divide Eritrea into self-governing Christian and Muslim regions, but the rebel group later accepted a call for peace talks. Meeting in Atlanta, Ga., in September with former United States President Jimmy Carter serving as mediator, representatives of the EPLF and the Ethiopian government hammered out procedures for a second round of negotiations, which took place in Nairobi, Kenya, in November.

Other developments. Mengistu's hostile relations with church and labor leaders were improved by his release of 300 political prisoners in September, but student strikes continued throughout the year. In June and July, the government slightly relaxed its control over the socialist economy by announcing plans to encourage private investment. As always, agricultural production was low, and rainfall in 1989 was less than had been hoped for, raising fears of a major famine in 1990.　　J. Gus Liebenow and Beverly B. Liebenow

See also **Africa** (Facts in brief table). In *World Book,* see **Ethiopia.**

Europe in 1989 experienced its most dramatic changes since World War II (1939-1945) as former Soviet satellite nations tore down the Iron Curtain that had isolated them from the West for 40 years. Eastern Europe's aspirations for political and economic freedom imparted new momentum—and some problems—to Western Europe's already powerful drive toward greater unity. As Europe emerged from the Cold War, Europeans both Western and Eastern began planning for a new era—the "post-postwar" epoch—in which Europe might outrank the United States and Japan economically.

Domino effect. History zoomed into fast-forward in mid-1989 as the Communist system collapsed in Eastern Europe. Regimes installed by Soviet military power after World War II and long deemed impregnable fell like dominoes toppling in a line:

● On May 2, Hungary dismantled the barbed-wire fence on its border with Austria, triggering protests from East Germany, Czechoslovakia, and other members of the Warsaw Pact (the Soviet bloc's military alliance), who feared their citizens might flee to the West via Hungary.

● On June 4 and 18, in Poland's first free elections since 1947, the Communist Party suffered an overwhelming defeat at the hands of Solidarity, a labor union outlawed from 1981 until April 1989.

● On August 9, Poland got its first non-Communist prime minister since the Communist take-over in the late 1940's—Tadeusz Mazowiecki.

● On September 10, Hungary's Communist regime, eager to demonstrate its liberalism for domestic political reasons, lifted border restrictions and tens of thousands of East Germans—supposedly vacationing in Hungary—fled via Austria to West Germany.

● On October 7, Hungary's Communist party repudiated Communism, and on October 18 the Hungarian parliament endorsed multiparty elections.

● On October 18, East German leader Erich Honecker, reputedly the most hard-line, dogmatic Communist leader in Eastern Europe, was ousted.

● On November 9, East Germany, faced with mounting street protests, opened its borders, including the Berlin Wall.

● On November 10, Todor Zhivkov, Communist dictator of Bulgaria for 35 years, lost his job to a reformer.

● On November 17, police in Prague, Czechoslovakia, beat up demonstrators, triggering massive peaceful protests that forced the Communist Party's leadership to resign on November 24.

● On December 7, East Germany's Communist party abandoned power and called for free, multiparty elections in May 1990.

● On December 10, Czechoslovakia formed a government led by a Communist but with a non-Communist majority in the Cabinet. The government promised free elections.

● On December 22, Romania's Communist President Nicolae Ceauşescu fell from power after army troops

East Germans arrive in West Germany on October 5—part of a wave of thousands of refugees who journeyed from Czechoslovakia on special trains.

disobeyed his order to fire on a huge crowd of pro-testers in Bucharest, the capital. Ceauşescu was executed on December 25 after being convicted of crimes against the nation.

The momentous changes in Eastern Europe raised questions among Western Europeans concerning their economic development, led by the European Community (EC or Common Market), and their military security, based on the North Atlantic Treaty Organization (NATO). (The EC nations are Belgium, Denmark, France, Great Britain, Greece, Ireland, Italy, Luxembourg, the Netherlands, Portugal, Spain, and West Germany. The members of NATO are Canada, Iceland, Norway, Turkey, and the United States, plus all the EC nations except Ireland.)

New role for NATO? United States President George Bush met with Soviet Executive President Mikhail S. Gorbachev aboard ship at the Mediterranean island nation of Malta on December 2 and 3. The two leaders discussed a variety of issues, ranging from arms control and economic cooperation to Soviet involvement in Central America.

On December 4, Bush took part in a NATO summit meeting in Brussels, Belgium. Bush reported on his meeting with Gorbachev and then agreed to step up efforts to reach a sweeping accord between NATO and the Warsaw Pact on cuts in conventional forces in Europe. (The members of the Warsaw Pact are the Soviet Union, Bulgaria, Czechoslovakia, East Germany, Hungary, Poland, and Romania.) This agreement

Facts in brief on European countries

Country	Population	Government	Monetary unit*	Foreign trade (million U.S.$) Exports†	Imports†
Albania	3,248,000	Communist Party First Secretary and People's Assembly Presidium Chairman Ramiz Alia; Council of Ministers Chairman Adil Çarçani	lek (6.44 = $1)	428	363
Andorra	49,000	The bishop of Urgel, Spain, and the president of France	French franc & Spanish peseta	no statistics available	
Austria	7,493,000	President Kurt Waldheim; Chancellor Franz Vranitzky	schilling (12.5 = $1)	31,088	36,608
Belgium	9,895,000	King Baudouin I; Prime Minister Wilfried Martens	franc (37.7 = $1)	92,786 (includes Luxembourg)	92,578
Bulgaria	8,985,000	Communist Party General Secretary & State Council Chairman Petur Toshev Mladenov; Council of Ministers Chairman Georgi Ivanov Atanasov	lev (0.83 = $1)	17,223	16,582
Czechoslovakia	15,659,000	Communist Party First Secretary Ladislav Adamec; President Vaclav Havel; Premier Marián Čalfa	koruna (14.7 = $1)	24,946	24,251
Denmark	5,119,000	Queen Margrethe II; Prime Minister Poul Schlüter	krone (6.91 = $1)	27,879	26,514
Finland	4,981,000	President Mauno Koivisto; Prime Minister Harri Holkeri	markka (4.20 = $1)	22,151	21,843
France	56,236,000	President François Mitterrand; Prime Minister Michel Rocard	franc (6.08 = $1)	162,988	177,518
Germany, East	16,645,000	Socialist Unity Party Secretary-General Gregor Gysi; Acting State Council Chairman Manfred Gerlach; Council of Ministers Chairman Hans Modrow	mark (1.78 = $1)	29,870	28,786
Germany, West	60,471,000	President Richard von Weizsäcker; Chancellor Helmut Kohl	mark (1.78 = $1)	322,524	248,880
Great Britain	57,293,000	Queen Elizabeth II; Prime Minister Margaret Thatcher	pound (1.57 = $1)	145,151	189,471
Greece	10,053,000	President Christos Sartzetakis; Prime Minister Xenophon Zolotas	drachma (163 = $1)	6,535	13,056
Hungary	10,545,000	Hungarian Socialist Party President Rezso Nyers; Premier Miklós Németh; President Mátyás Szürös	forint (58.5 = $1)	9,582	9,858
Iceland	250,000	President Vigdis Finnbogadóttir; Prime Minister Steingrimur Hermannsson	krona (62.6 = $1)	1,424	1,574
Ireland	3,637,000	President Patrick J. Hillery; Prime Minister Charles Haughey	pound (punt) (1.48 = $1)	18,739	15,568
Italy	57,380,000	President Francesco Cossiga; Prime Minister Giulio Andreotti	lira (1,310 = $1)	127,114	138,665
Liechtenstein	28,000	Prince Hans Adam; Prime Minister Hans Brunhart	Swiss franc	no statistics available	
Luxembourg	367,000	Grand Duke Jean; Prime Minister Jacques Santer	franc (37.4 = $1)	92,786 (includes Belgium)	92,578
Malta	350,000	President Vincent Tabone; Prime Minister Eddie Fenech Adami	lira (2.89 = $1)	604	1,138
Monaco	29,000	Prince Rainier III	French franc	no statistics available	
Netherlands	14,765,000	Queen Beatrix; Prime Minister Ruud Lubbers	guilder (2.01 = $1)	103,561	99,800
Norway	4,213,000	King Olav V; Prime Minister Jan P. Syse	krone (6.81 = $1)	22,511	23,221
Poland	38,441,000	President Wojciech Jaruzelski; Council of Ministers Chairman Tadeusz Mazowiecki	zloty (3,800 = $1)	12,205	10,595
Portugal	9,903,000	President Mário Alberto Soares; Prime Minister Aníbal Cavaço Silva	escudo (155 = $1)	10,526	15,855
Romania	23,279,000	President Ion Iliescu; Prime Minister Petre Roman	leu (8.55 = $1)	12,543	10,590
San Marino	23,000	2 captains regent appointed by Grand Council every 6 months	Italian lira	no statistics available	
Spain	39,623,000	King Juan Carlos I; Prime Minister Felipe González Márquez	peseta (115 = $1)	40,067	60,576
Sweden	8,346,000	King Carl XVI Gustaf; Prime Minister Ingvar Carlsson	krona (6.38 = $1)	50,010	45,851
Switzerland	6,509,000	President Jean-Pascal Delamuraz‡	franc (1.59 = $1)	50,861	56,630
Turkey	56,549,000	President Turgut Özal; Prime Minister Yildirim Akbulut	lira (2,300 = $1)	10,127	14,149
Union of Soviet Socialist Republics	288,239,000	Communist Party General Secretary & Executive President Mikhail S. Gorbachev; Council of Ministers Chairman Nikolay I. Ryzhkov	ruble (0.62 = $1)	110,559	107,229
Yugoslavia	23,853,000	President Janez Drnovšek; Federal Executive Council President Ante Marković	dinar (77,600 = $1)	12,597	13,154

*Exchange rates as of Dec. 1, 1989, or latest available data. †Latest available data.
‡Delamuraz was to be succeeded on Jan. 1, 1990, by Arnold Koller.

would eliminate the long-standing Soviet superiority in conventional forces, thereby sharply diminishing the threat of a Soviet surprise attack.

With greater East-West military stability, Europe might become more unpredictable politically, however, with old national rivalries reemerging in the wake of Communist rule—and with the Soviet Union remaining by far the strongest power on the European continent. Because of this unpredictability, NATO leaders stressed that NATO should remain intact to guarantee Western security and should become more political—for example, by starting a new East-West dialogue on the verification of arms control.

EC role broadens. As the EC progressed toward the development of a single-market economy in 1992, its international stature grew and it began to assume a special role in Eastern Europe. On July 14, for example, the EC received a special request from the leaders of Canada, France, Great Britain, Italy, Japan, the United States, and West Germany. The heads of these seven countries hold an economic summit meeting each year; the 1989 meeting took place in Paris from July 14 to 16. The seven leaders asked the European Commission—the EC's executive branch—to administer Western aid to Poland and Hungary. The Soviet Union, which had ignored the EC for years, opened trade negotiations with the EC in early 1989.

Amid these marks of recognition, European leaders agreed with France's President François Mitterrand that the success of the EC had transformed the organization into a "magnet," pulling Eastern European nations toward democracy and free-market economies. Mitterrand, EC president during the second half of the year, spoke following a special EC summit meeting that he had convened in Paris on November 18—after the collapse of the Berlin Wall. Mitterrand had called the summit to accelerate the unification of the EC and to prevent West Germany from giving precedence to a new role in Eastern Europe at the expense of its established role in the West.

EC's future debated. Mitterrand strongly backed a plan of Jacques Delors, head of the European Commission, for an economic and political union going beyond the 1992 single-market economy. Delors wants the EC to set up a central bank and to strengthen the power of the European Parliament—the EC's legislative branch.

In 1989, objections to a "deepening" of the EC came from Britain's Prime Minister Margaret Thatcher. She argued that the Soviet empire was collapsing so rapidly that Western European governments should concentrate on "widening" Europe by consolidating democracy in Eastern Europe rather than plunge into potentially divisive activities in the EC. A conservative leader, she resisted faster integration because, she said, the EC bureaucracy would perpetuate welfare-state and other socialist programs that Thatcher's government has rejected. Many West German business leaders shared her objections.

West Germany, eager to dispel doubts of its Western allies, sided with France on these issues at a second EC summit meeting in Strasbourg, France, on December 8 and 9. The EC voted, 11-1, to start negotiations in 1990 on setting up a single currency for the EC countries and forging other institutions to achieve economic and monetary union. Great Britain cast the dissenting vote, but Thatcher agreed that Britain would take part in the 1990 negotiations.

The crucial aspect of the Strasbourg debate was the suddenly increased likelihood that the two Germanys would soon reunite. Although all the allied governments had long supported West Germany's goal of reunification, neighboring European nations were unsettled by the possibility that West Germany, already the leading economic power of the EC, would soon acquire new dimensions by absorbing East Germany.

The German question had emerged dramatically with the demolition of the Berlin Wall, symbolically opening floodgates that had previously made German reunification only a remote possibility. Convinced that some form of reunification was now inevitable, the United States took the lead in urging the NATO allies to support the process. The U.S. motive was to avoid frustrating West Germany, making that country susceptible to a Soviet offer of reunification in exchange for neutrality.

Concentric circles. As Eastern Europe suddenly crowded to the top of Western Europe's agenda, the map of Europe assumed a shape that European Commission chief Delors terms "concentric circles." The 12-nation EC is a stable core. In the next "circle" is the six-nation European Free Trade Association (EFTA), made up of Austria, Finland, Iceland, Norway, Sweden, and Switzerland—all Western industrial states. Iceland and Norway are in NATO, but the remaining four EFTA nations are neutral. In the outer "circle" are seven Eastern countries that had been satellites of the Soviet Union—Bulgaria, Czechoslovakia, East Germany, Hungary, Poland, Romania, and Yugoslavia.

West Germany's Foreign Minister Hans-Dietrich Genscher offered a vision of loose but steadily developing intergovernmental links to create a continentwide association of all 25 of these nations. Most EC leaders, however, said that, before admitting more members, the EC must consolidate its own ties. For example, Greece and Portugal faced difficulties in blending their weak economies with that of West Germany.

Delors called on EFTA to work with the EC in creating a "European economic space" in which goods, services, capital, and people would circulate as freely among the 18 nations as among the 50 states in the United States of America. The combined *gross domestic product* of the EC and EFTA topped $5 trillion, which would make an EC-EFTA combination the world's richest single market. (Gross domestic product is the total value of the goods produced and the services performed within the borders of a nation or a group of nations.)

Chancellor Kohl of West Germany and Great Britain's Prime Minister Thatcher meet in Germany on April 30 to discuss cuts in nuclear missiles.

Because most of its members are neutral, EFTA had no interest in becoming part of the increasingly political EC. And the EC wanted to avoid weakening its own integration to accommodate the EFTA countries' reservations. In mid-December, the two associations met in Brussels for talks that were expected to lead to a treaty in 1990.

Relations with Japan. EC nations increasingly sought to use their prospective unity as a lever to force Japan into greater reciprocity in trade. On December 8, the European Commission asked Japan to apply voluntary restrictions on automobile exports to the EC for three years. Such restrictions would allow European automakers to adjust to open competition after 1992.

Crime threat. As EC countries abolished more barriers, the Royal Institute of International Affairs in London warned in June that "the single European market which is freeing the movement of goods, capital, labor, and services will inevitably increase the scope for criminal activities to be conducted on an EC-wide basis." The opening of borders to the East threatened to make law enforcement even more difficult. These borders had been almost impossible to break through—and suddenly many of them, particularly the border separating the two Germanys, virtually ceased to exist. In late 1989, officials met throughout Western Europe to determine how to check at their borders for illegal immigrants, as well as terror-

ists, drug dealers, and other criminals. The EC leaders discussed this at the Strasbourg summit.

Immigration, already a growing racial issue affecting large communities of "guest workers" in the richer EC countries, became a cause for alarm. Governments of EC nations worried that hordes of Eastern Europeans would pour westward in search of jobs. As a result, most EC countries imposed tighter restrictions on immigration, including new rules for people seeking political asylum.

A particularly sensitive aspect of the immigration issue was West Germany's refusal to screen people arriving from East Germany. Such people could migrate freely via West Germany to the other 11 EC countries—and compete for jobs there.

Leftward shift. Voters throughout the EC went to the polls on June 15 and June 18 to vote for the European Parliament. Socialist parties made the strongest showing. When combined with Communists and members of Green (environmentalist) parties, they commanded a majority, with 260 seats in the 518-seat assembly. In the outgoing Parliament, centrist and rightist parties held 270 seats. The new Parliament is to sit until 1994. Political observers expect its powers to grow.   Joseph Fitchett

See also the various European country articles. In the Special Reports section, see **Opening a Closed Society.** In *World Book,* see **Europe.**

Explosion. See **Disasters.**

Farm and farming. In 1989, a controversy over the possible health risks of a chemical used on apples heightened the debate about the use of pesticides and growth regulators in agriculture and added to consumers' skepticism about the United States government's regulation of food. United States crops recovered from a massive 1988 drought, and American farmers earned a record high income. Agricultural issues were at center stage during international trade-reform negotiations in Geneva, Switzerland.

Alar scare. In February, the Natural Resources Defense Council (NRDC), an environmental organization based in New York City, released a report asserting that American children face an intolerable health risk from the chemicals used on fruit and fruit products. The NRDC charged that the most serious risk came from daminozide, a growth regulator used on apples that was marketed under the trade name Alar.

Federal officials agreed that Alar should be taken off the market. But John A. Moore, acting deputy administrator of the U.S. Environmental Protection Agency (EPA), said the NRDC exaggerated Alar's risks by 100 times and based its conclusions on inaccurate estimates. The NRDC report overshadowed a diet and cancer study issued by the National Research Council (NRC) in Washington, D.C., which reported that increasing consumption of fruits and vegetables lowers the risk of cancer and other diseases—thus greatly outweighing the small potential risk from chemical residues on food.

Nevertheless, the NRDC report caused sales of apples and apple juice to plummet. American apple growers lost millions of dollars, even though most apples were not treated with Alar. On June 2, Uniroyal Chemical Company, the manufacturer of Alar, voluntarily halted sales of the chemical for use on U.S. food crops. On September 1, the EPA announced an official ban, effective May 31, 1991. The controversy spurred President George Bush and members of Congress to propose modernizing food-safety laws to prevent future food scares, but by year-end, no action had been taken.

Alternative agriculture. The debate over chemical use intensified with the September 7 release of another NRC report. Titled *Alternative Agriculture,* the report claimed that the use of chemical fertilizers, pesticides, and antibiotics is not necessary to make farms productive and profitable. According to the report, wider use of nonchemical techniques to improve the yield of croplands could increase profits for farmers and avoid harming the environment. One such technique is crop rotation, in which farmers plant a different crop each year to help maintain soil fertility and to break cycles of disease, weed growth, and infestation.

The report was highly critical of federal agricultural policies that force farmers to plant the same crops year after year in order to collect government subsidies. Members of Congress introduced proposals to increase farmers' flexibility to rotate crops. Some scientists disputed the NRC findings, however.

The same restrictions that discourage crop rotation also discouraged farmers from increasing their cultivation of soybeans in response to demand from other countries. Since the early 1980's, U.S. farmers have cut soybean crops by 10.3 million acres (4.2 million hectares), while competitors, mostly in Brazil and Argentina, have increased their soybean acreage by 23.5 million acres (9.5 million hectares).

At the same time, U.S. farm policy discouraged farmers from responding to the demand for oats created by 1987 research showing that consuming oat bran can lower the level of cholesterol in the blood. American food companies imported oats from Argentina, Canada, Finland, and Sweden in 1989 to add to insufficient domestic supplies.

Booming exports. American farmers were successful at exporting many other crops. United States agricultural exports totaled $39.7 billion in fiscal year 1989, the third consecutive annual increase. Exports were 51 per cent higher than in 1986, the low point of the decade.

The Soviet Union was the second-largest agricultural customer of the United States, after Japan. The Soviet Union bought a record $3.3 billion in agricultural products from the United States. That included a record 21.7 million short tons (19.7 metric tons) of grain under the terms of a grain agreement drafted in 1975.

Robust exports helped raise U.S. farming income to a record high, approximately $49 billion. The Department of Agriculture estimated that about 10 per cent of U.S. commercial farmers were financially troubled but said that a large majority of farmers had improved their finances since the farm crisis of the mid-1980's.

Soybean futures scandals plagued the industry in 1989. (A futures contract is an agreement to buy or sell a commodity for a set price at a future date. Such contracts give farmers, grain merchants, food companies, and investors guides to future prices so that they can successfully market and finance commodities.) On July 11, soybean prices plummeted when the Chicago Board of Trade took the unusual step of intervening in the market. The board ordered traders to liquidate some of their soybean contracts after an Italian trading company refused to voluntarily reduce its contract holdings. The board forced the firm to unload contracts for 23 million bushels of soybeans and accused the company of trying to corner the market.

In an unrelated case, after a two-year undercover investigation, federal prosecutors on August 2 announced the indictment of 46 traders, including 19 who traded soybean futures at the Chicago Board of Trade. The traders were indicted on several charges, including racketeering and fraud.

U.S. harvests rebounded from the severe drought of 1988, but a less widespread drought withered some wheat crops in 1989. The $3.9-billion

Farm and farming

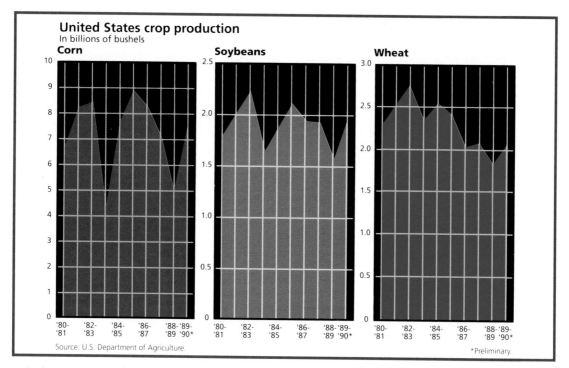

United States crop production
In billions of bushels

Corn

Soybeans

Wheat

'80-'81 '82-'83 '84-'85 '86-'87 '88-'89 '89-'90*

Source: U.S. Department of Agriculture.

*Preliminary.

United States harvests of corn, soybeans, and wheat rebounded in 1989 from the 1988 drought, due to better weather and more land planted.

drought-relief bill passed in 1988 was followed by a $900-million relief law in 1989. The 1989 law provided funds both to drought-stricken regions and to flood-damaged areas, mostly in the South.

Better weather and government programs for returning idled cropland to production helped the U.S. corn harvest rise to 7.59 billion bushels in 1989—up 54 per cent from the disastrous 1988 harvest. The overall wheat harvest increased 13 per cent in 1989. The spring wheat harvest was nearly 250 per cent larger than the 1988 harvest, and crop yields of durum wheat—used to make pasta—increased 107 per cent. But the winter wheat crop, which makes up about 75 per cent of U.S. wheat production, was reduced 7 per cent by a drought in 1989.

Other food crops with increased harvests in 1989 included soybeans, up by 25 per cent; grain sorghum, increasing 9 per cent; oats, up 69 per cent; and peanuts, up 4 per cent. Although most harvests were larger in 1989, the 1988 drought continued to be felt in the form of higher consumer food prices. Prices rose by 6 per cent—the largest increase since 1981.

Notable among the declining harvests were the cotton crop, which dropped 22 per cent in 1989, and the rice crop, which declined 2 per cent. Meat production was uneven, with beef output dropping nearly 3 per cent and pork production dropping more than 1 per cent. Poultry output, on the other hand, increased 6 per cent.

World production. With drought recovery in the United States, the world's corn harvests increased by 17 per cent in 1989. Soybean output rose nearly 14 per cent. World wheat production increased by 6 per cent to set a record. Nonetheless, the world's consumers demanded more wheat than farmers produced for three years, and world supplies fell to their lowest level compared to demand in 30 years. Worldwide cotton production was down 4 per cent, but rice production increased 1 per cent, also setting a record.

Global pork production was stable in 1989, and beef production declined slightly. Broiler chicken output increased by nearly 3 per cent and turkey production by 4 per cent.

Agricultural trade. Representatives from 97 nations struggled to reform the world's heavily subsidized agricultural trading practices in the third of four years of talks in Geneva. Held under the auspices of the General Agreement on Tariffs and Trade (GATT), the talks were the eighth round of trade-liberalization negotiations since GATT was created in 1947. It was the first time that agricultural trade was a top priority at the talks.

In late 1988, negotiators for the United States and the 12-nation European Community reached an impasse, and talks were halted. In April 1989, they broke the impasse with an agreement to keep negotiating and to work toward "substantial and progressive reductions" in government financial support for farmers. They were unable to reach further agreement, however. In May, in a case unrelated to the global talks, a GATT body ruled that U.S. trade quotas limiting sugar imports violated international trading rules.

The U.S. International Trade Commission voted in August that subsidies on Canadian pork products shipped to the United States unfairly hurt U.S. farmers. Canada challenged the finding before a bilateral dispute-settlement panel, a new mechanism created in January by a historic trade agreement between the United States and Canada. The pork case was the first test of how the nations would carry out the agreement.

Genetic engineering. Controversy flared over what was expected to be the first major commercial agricultural product derived from genetic engineering. The product is an artificial version of *bovine somatotropin*, a cow hormone. Dairy cows injected with the genetically engineered hormone produce 10 per cent to 25 per cent more milk. In 1986, the U.S. Food and Drug Administration approved the sale of milk produced with the aid of the hormone while its effects are under study. But, fearful of consumer opposition, some supermarket chains and food processors refused to accept the milk. The nation's largest milk producer assured food processors that none of its milk would contain the hormone.   Sonja Hillgren

See also **Environmental pollution; Food; Weather.** In *World Book,* see **Agriculture; Farm and farming.**

Fashion. The fashion focus in 1989 was on jackets as this staple of most women's wardrobes received new attention from designers. Silk, wool, and linen were the fabrics of choice. Many designers favored smaller shoulder pads and softly tailored silhouettes. Some jackets were short and swingy. Others were long enough to cover the hips and were often worn with stretch pants or tights.

Designers once again created clothes that faithfully followed the lines of the body. Soft, almost transparent fabrics, such as chiffon, further accentuated body shape. The year's popular colors were bright wines, plums, and gold. Animal prints were also popular.

Skirts and dresses could be any length, stopping inches above the knees or descending to the ankles. Coats made of cloth and fake fur received a sales boost thanks to animal-rights activists who urged women to avoid real fur.

European scene. Paris in 1989 strengthened its position as the fashion capital of the world. Early in the year, Italian designers Romeo Gigli, Valentino, and Gianni Versace announced plans to introduce their new collections in Paris—not Milan. Their announcement was a blow to the Italian city, which ranks second to Paris as a fashion center. But fashion retailers applauded the move. With more collections from different countries being unveiled in Paris—including those by Japanese designers—retailers will spend less time traveling and more time at their stores.

Princess Diana inspects the handiwork of designers Graham Fraser and Richard Nott, who took top honors at the 1989 British Fashion Awards.

Fashion

Industry experts predicted that by 1992, fashion designers from Spain, Belgium, and other European countries will choose to introduce their collections in Paris. (The European Community, or Common Market, plans to break down trade barriers between its member countries and form one unified market in 1992.) Paris is the preferred city for most designers because of the wide exposure they receive there. More than 1,000 journalists and about 5,000 retailers attend Paris fashion shows, about twice as many as visit Milan.

London's influence in fashion diminished somewhat in 1989. Retailers found the clothes of British designers either too stodgy or too crazy. An attempt to revive the feel of the swinging London of the 1960's died out as the times—and fashion—became more serious.

Christian Lacroix, who stirred things up in Paris two years ago with bubble skirts, settled down to a more sober style in 1989. He worked to establish ready-to-wear and accessories lines to complement his more flamboyant made-to-order styles.

On the American front. Designers in the United States had a successful year in 1989. Donna Karan's seductive interpretations of American sportswear and her DKNY collection of casual weekend clothes were a hit both in the United States and in Europe. Calvin Klein and Ralph Lauren also began to capture a following abroad.

Bill Blass and Oscar de la Renta continued to hold top place among the designers of evening wear in the United States, while Carolina Herrera and Carolyn Roehm made strong showings. Arnold Scaasi revived interest in custom-made clothes, following the success of the blue evening dress he designed for Barbara Bush, wife of President George Bush, to wear to the inaugural balls in January.

Dior picks Ferré. In May, the house of Christian Dior in Paris chose Italian designer Gianfranco Ferré to design both its couture and ready-to-wear collections. Ferré replaced Marc Bohan, who had been with Dior since 1960. Dior reportedly chose Ferré to revive its failing image. Such a move has proved successful for the house of Chanel, which engaged German-born designer Karl Lagerfeld to bring new life to its designs. Ferré will continue to make ready-to-wear clothes under his own name in Milan.

Going public. To prevent a possible take-over of his company, Yves Saint Laurent in July began offering 11 per cent of his company's stock on the Paris stock exchange. The sale made his the first French design firm to go public.

Fur innovation. During the year, Fendi, the Rome fashion house that is one of the world's leading fur stylists, unveiled reversible coats that could be worn with either the leather side or the fur side out. The coats were made without linings, and their relaxed, unstructured look was expected to have an impact on other fashions in 1990.   Bernadine Morris

In *World Book,* see **Clothing; Fashion.**

Finland. Structural changes in the economies of the Soviet Union and Western Europe gave Finland new opportunities—and new problems—in 1989. Finnish businesses scrambled for new markets to make up for a fall-off in trade with the Soviets, while Finnish diplomats worked to ensure that their country's exports would not get squeezed out of an emerging single-market economy in Western Europe.

Soviet trade drops. Pursuing a policy of *perestroika* (political and economic restructuring), the Soviets continued to open their markets to the West, increasing competition for Finnish exporters. As a result, Finland's sales to the Soviet Union fell below 14 per cent of total exports. By contrast, in the early 1980's, Finland shipped almost one-fourth of its exports to the Soviet Union.

Western markets sought. The drop-off in trade with the Soviets forced Finnish exporters to seek new markets in Western Europe. To help the exporters, the Finnish government pursued closer collaboration between the European Community, or Common Market, and the six-member European Free Trade Association, of which Finland is a member. The other members of the association are Austria, Iceland, Norway, Sweden, and Switzerland.

Caution on Estonia. Finland, like other neutral states in Europe, welcomed signs that Eastern European countries were gaining greater political and diplomatic freedom from the Soviet Union during 1989. And Finland was especially pleased that the Soviet central government had loosened its grip on Estonia, a nearby part of the Soviet Union, because Finns have strong historical and linguistic bonds to Estonians.

Communist Party merges. The decline in Soviet influence was evident in an April decision by the Finnish Communist Party to dissolve itself and merge with its former umbrella organization, the Finnish People's Democratic League. The combined party named itself the Union of the Left.

Technology crime. To protect Finland's access to Western technology, the government successfully prosecuted two Finnish businessmen who illegally sold United States computer technology to the Soviet Union. The men drew prison terms of three years for endangering Finland's relations with a foreign power—the United States.

More troops assigned to UN duty. Finland in 1989 displayed its growing interest in international affairs by expanding its role in United Nations (UN) peacekeeping operations. In March, 900 Finnish troops went on duty in Namibia, raising the number of Finns in UN service to just under 2,000 and making Finland the nation with the largest number of troops under UN command.   Joseph Fitchett.

See also **Europe** (Facts in brief table). In *World Book,* see **Finland.**

Fire. See **Disasters.**

Flood. See **Disasters.**

Florida. See **State government.**

Foley, Thomas Stephen (1929-   ), was elected Speaker of the United States House of Representatives on June 6, 1989. Foley, a Democratic representative from the state of Washington since 1965 and previously the House's majority leader, succeeded Speaker James C. Wright, Jr. (D., Tex.), who resigned after being accused of ethics violations. See **Congress of the United States.**

Foley was born on March 6, 1929, in Spokane, Wash., where his father was a judge on the Superior Court. He graduated from the University of Washington in Seattle in 1951 and earned a law degree there in 1957.

In 1961, after serving briefly as assistant attorney general for the state of Washington, Foley joined the staff of Democratic Senator Henry M. Jackson in Washington, D.C. At Jackson's suggestion, Foley returned home in 1964 to run for Congress against an 11-term Republican incumbent, whom he defeated.

In the House, Foley's political stance has been moderately liberal, and he gained a reputation as a thoughtful lawmaker with a gift for compromise. He was chairman of the Agriculture Committee from 1975 through 1981. From 1981 to 1987, he was House majority whip, the number-three position in the House leadership.

Foley is married to the former Heather Strachan, who serves as his senior adviser. The couple have no children.   David L. Dreier

Food safety became a major concern of the American public in 1989 as several headline-grabbing incidents undermined confidence in a food supply generally considered the safest in the world.

On March 12, United States Food and Drug Administration (FDA) officials in Philadelphia, inspecting fruit imported from Chile, discovered two grapes contaminated with traces of the poison cyanide. The next day, the FDA detained all incoming Chilean fruit and stepped up inspections, and wholesalers and retailers dumped millions of cases of Chilean fruit already in stock. No further tainted fruit was found, and on March 17, the FDA announced that Chilean fruit could return to store shelves. Produce industry officials estimated losses at $240 million.

In February, the Natural Resources Defense Council, an independent environmental group based in New York City, issued a report warning that agricultural chemicals used on foods pose health risks for consumers, especially children. It cited as particularly hazardous the chemical *daminozide*—sold under the trade name Alar—used on apples to regulate growth and ripening. Earlier in February, the Environmental Protection Agency had announced plans to propose a ban on Alar, but the ban would not have taken effect until 1990 or later.

The government and the apple industry pointed out that Alar was used on only 5 per cent of the apple crop and at levels well within government limits. Still,

Tom Meyer, *San Francisco Chronicle;* reprinted by permission of NEA, Inc.

Food

public fears increased, and school systems in such cities as New York City, Los Angeles, Chicago, and San Francisco stopped distributing apple products. Apple growers, faced with an estimated $100 million in losses, announced in May they would stop using Alar. In June, the maker of Alar, Uniroyal Chemical Company of Middlebury, Conn., said it would stop selling Alar in the United States.

The 1988 drought led to unusually high levels of a natural cancer-causing agent, *aflatoxin*, in the corn crop. Aflatoxin is produced by a fungus that thrives in droughts. In February 1989, the FDA announced it had found unacceptable levels of aflatoxin in 6 per cent of the corn tested, though none in finished baked goods. Five states, testing dairy products from corn-fed cows, found—and dumped—aflatoxin-tainted milk. Some nations began requiring tests on corn from the United States, and buyers in other countries rejected some 2 million bushels.

Public confidence in the safety of the food supply declined in the wake of these events, according to the Food Marketing Institute, an industry group based in Washington, D.C. In January, 81 per cent of shoppers surveyed said they were confident that their food was safe. That level dropped to 67 per cent by August.

The FDA warned that the greatest health risk in foods was not chemicals but microbes, such as *salmonella* bacteria. For this reason, legislation was introduced in Congress requiring seafood inspection, and outcry from consumer groups led the Department of Agriculture to abandon plans to change its meat inspection program.

Consumers maintained interest in choosing nutritious foods—especially foods low in cholesterol and saturated fats, substances that have been linked to increased risk of heart disease. Some food manufacturers announced they would stop using highly saturated tropical oils, such as coconut oil, in their products. After declining for several years, the demand for red meat increased slightly, though leaner cuts were preferred. Poultry and fish remained popular.

Food choices expanded to satisfy consumer demand for variety as well as nutrition. Exotic produce (such as passionfruit and Asian pears) and grains (such as quinoa and amaranth) found new buyers.

Food labeling took on new importance as a means of gauging nutritional content. Products labeled "light" or "lean" gained in popularity, despite the lack of government standards for uniform use of these terms. Congress began considering several bills establishing guidelines for health claims on labels and requiring disclosure of amounts of calories, fat, sodium, cholesterol, and nutrients. The food industry indicated it would support such legislation if it led to uniform requirements.

Total food sales rose 4.7 per cent over 1988 levels. In *real terms*—allowing for inflation—sales declined 0.4 per cent. Weekly grocery expenses rose from $71 to $74, but Americans spent only about 14.1 per cent

of their *disposable income* (money left after taxes) on food, almost exactly what they spent in 1988.

Eating out retained its allure. Food service sales rose 6.7 per cent above 1988 to $227.3 billion—a 2.2 per cent rise in real terms. Menu prices increased 4.6 per cent. Consumer demands for nutrition and variety were reflected in expanded menus, emphasis on fresh ingredients, and increased use of low-fat, and low-cholesterol cooking methods. Ethnic dishes remained popular, though regional American dishes began making a comeback.

More restaurants offered take-out service to appeal to time-pressed diners. Pizza remained king of the home-delivery trade, but choices expanded, particularly in Asian foods.

Fast-food establishments continued to grow faster than other segments of the industry, with sales of $65.1 billion in 1989. The rise of 3.6 per cent in real terms over 1988 was slightly less than the previous year's 4.3 per cent rise. The slower but steady growth is expected to continue because fast food chains are opening fewer new units, concentrating instead on overseas markets.

Worldwide crop production was good in 1989. Cereal grain production rose 6 per cent over 1988's poor harvest. World grain reserves, however, fell to their lowest level since 1975.   Bob Gatty

See also **Farm and farming**. In *World Book*, see **Food; Food supply.**

Football. The San Francisco 49ers won the National Football League (NFL) championship by defeating the Denver Broncos, 55-10, in Super Bowl XXIV on Jan. 28, 1990, in New Orleans. The 49ers became the first team to repeat as Super Bowl champions since the Pittsburgh Steelers did it in 1978 and 1979. The University of Miami in Florida became college football's unofficial national champion for the third time since 1983.

Professional football. After the 49ers won Super Bowl XXIII in January 1989, coach Bill Walsh retired to the front office and later left to become a pro-football analyst for NBC television. George Seifert, the defensive coordinator, became head coach, and in the 1989 season he guided the 49ers to a 14-2 record, the best in the league.

The National Conference division winners were the 49ers, the New York Giants (12-4), and the Minnesota Vikings (10-6). They were joined in the play-offs as wild-card teams by the Los Angeles Rams (11-5) and the Philadelphia Eagles (11-5).

The American Conference play-off teams were the Broncos (11-5), the Cleveland Browns (9-6-1), and the Buffalo Bills (9-7) as division champions and the Steelers (9-7) and the Houston Oilers (9-7) as wild-cards.

In the National Conference play-offs, the Rams upset Philadelphia, 21-7, in the wild-card game on December 31 behind quarterback Jim Everett's passing and a creative pass defense. Then, in the conference play-offs on Jan. 7 and 8, 1990, the 49ers easily domi-

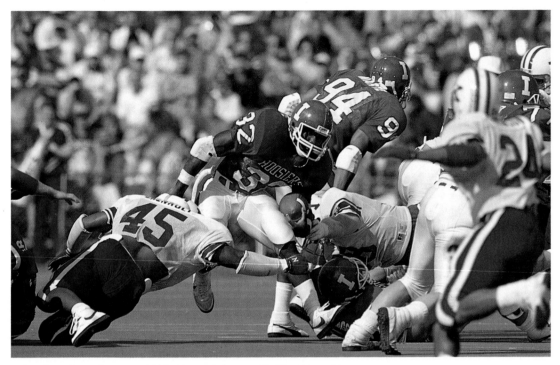

Indiana's Anthony Thompson (32) led in touchdowns with 25 and in rushing, averaging 163 yards per game, and set a single-game record of 377 yards.

nated the Vikings, winning 41-13, and the Rams and the Giants matched up in a defensive struggle until the Rams won, 19-13, in overtime. In the conference title game on January 14, the 49ers defeated the Rams, 30-3, as 49er quarterback Joe Montana completed 26 of 30 passes, including 2 touchdown passes, while the 49er defense stopped Everett, who had 3 interceptions.

In the American Conference, Pittsburgh upset Houston, 26-23, in the wild-card game on Gary Anderson's 50-yard field goal in overtime. In the conference playoffs on January 7 and 8, Cleveland defeated Buffalo, 34-30, and Denver rallied in the fourth quarter to foil an upset bid by Pittsburgh, winning 24-23. In the conference title game on January 14, the Broncos defeated the Browns, 37-21, as quarterback John Elway led the Broncos, completing 20 of 36 passes for 385 yards and 3 touchdowns.

That sent the 49ers and the Broncos into the Super Bowl, where a rout of record proportions occurred. The 49ers set a record for most points scored (55). Montana set one for most touchdown passes (5).

Commissioners. Turmoil marked much of the year in the NFL. Pete Rozelle, the league's commissioner for 29 years, unexpectedly retired on March 22, 1989, but said he would stay until a successor was named.

Rozelle appointed six club owners to a search committee for a new commissioner. The committee recommended Jim Finks, the president and general manager of the New Orleans Saints. Newer owners, upset that they were not represented on the committee, abstained from the voting, thus denying Finks the required two-thirds majority. Rozelle then appointed two more search committees, each including newer owners. The final committee recommended Paul J. Tagliabue, a 48-year-old lawyer from Washington, D.C., who had represented the league for 20 years. On October 26, the owners elected him commissioner.

Cowboys. One of those new owners was Jerry Jones, an oilman from Little Rock, Ark., who bought a 63 per cent interest in the Dallas Cowboys. Then he replaced Tom Landry, the only coach in the team's 29-year history; Texas (Tex) Schramm, the team president and general manager; and other key executives.

The new coach was Jimmy Johnson, Jones's college teammate at Arkansas, who had become a highly successful college coach at the University of Miami. Johnson traded running back Herschel Walker, the Cowboys' best player, to Minnesota for a first-round draft choice in 1992 and a package of five players or six other draft choices. The Cowboys finished the season with a 1-15 record, the worst in the league.

Player relations. The collective-bargaining agreement between the NFL club owners and the players expired in 1987. There was no progress in 1988 toward a new agreement, and the NFL Players Association, the players' union, awaited trial of its federal antitrust suit against the league.

The 1989 college football season

College conference champions

Conference	School
Atlantic Coast	Duke—Virginia (tie)
Big Eight	Colorado
Big Sky	Idaho
Big Ten	Michigan
Big West	Fresno State
Ivy League	Yale—Princeton (tie)
Mid-American	Ball State
Ohio Valley	Middle Tennessee
Pacific Ten	Southern California
Southeastern	Alabama—Tennessee (tie)
Southland	Stephen F. Austin State
Southwest	Arkansas
Southwestern	Grambling
Western Athletic	Brigham Young
Yankee	Connecticut—Maine—Villanova (tie)

Major bowl games

Bowl	Winner	Loser
All-American	Texas Tech 49	Duke 21
Aloha	Michigan State 33	Hawaii 13
Amos Alonzo Stagg (Div. III)	Dayton 17	Union (N.Y.) 7
Blue-Gray	Gray 28	Blue 10
California	Fresno State 27	Ball State 6
Copper	Arizona 17	North Carolina State 10
Cotton	Tennessee 31	Arkansas 27
Fiesta	Florida State 41	Nebraska 17
Florida Citrus	Illinois 31	Virginia 21
Freedom	Washington 34	Florida 7
Gator	Clemson 27	West Virginia 7
Hall of Fame	Auburn 31	Ohio State 14
Holiday	Penn State 50	Brigham Young 39
Hula	West 21	East 13
Independence	Oregon 27	Tulsa 24
Japan	East 24	West 10
John Hancock	Pittsburgh 31	Texas A & M 28
Liberty	Mississippi 42	Air Force 29
Orange	Notre Dame 21	Colorado 6
Palm (Div. II)	Mississippi College 3	Jacksonville State 0
Peach	Syracuse 19	Georgia 18
Rose	Southern California 17	Michigan 10
Senior	North 41	South 0
Sugar	Miami 33	Alabama 25
NCAA Div. I-AA	Georgia Southern 37	Stephen F. Austin State 34
NAIA Div. I	Carson-Newman (Tenn.) 34	Emporia State (Kans.) 20
NAIA Div. II	Westminster (Pa.) 51	Wisconsin-La Crosse 30

All-America team (as picked by AP)

Offense

Quarterback—Andre Ware, Houston
Running backs—Anthony Thompson, Indiana; Emmitt Smith, Florida
Receivers—Clarkston Hines, Duke; Terance Mathis, New Mexico; Emmanuel Hazard, Houston
Center—Michael Tanks, Florida State
Guards—Eric Still, Tennessee; Joe Garten, Colorado
Tackles—Jim Mabry, Arkansas; Bob Kula, Michigan State
Return specialist—Raghib (Rocket) Ismail, Notre Dame
Place kicker—Jason Hanson, Washington State

Defense

Linemen—Chris Zorich, Notre Dame; Greg Mark, Miami (Fla.); Tim Ryan, Southern California; Moe Gardner, Illinois
Linebackers—Percy Snow, Michigan State; Keith McCants, Alabama; James Francis, Baylor
Backs—Todd Lyght, Notre Dame; Mark Carrier, Southern California; Tripp Welborne, Michigan; LeRoy Butler, Florida State
Punter—Tom Rouen, Colorado

Player awards

Heisman Trophy (best player)—Andre Ware, Houston
Lombardi Award (best lineman)—Percy Snow, Michigan State
Outland Award (best interior lineman)—Mohammed Elewonibi, Brigham Young

Instead, the trial was postponed when a federal appeals court ruled on Nov. 1, 1989, that the league was immune from antitrust action over its free agency system. The union was upset by that decision and said it would decertify itself, arguing that this would allow players to become unrestricted free agents, though exposing them to loss of pension and health benefits.

From February 1 to March 1, under the so-called Plan B, the owners had granted temporary free agency to certain fringe players. Each team was allowed to protect 37 players, and all others were made available to other teams without compensation to their previous teams. Of the 619 players eligible, 229 signed with new teams at an average salary of $198,321—up from an average of $141,354 in 1988.

Other leagues. The World League of American Football, an NFL-sponsored spring league, planned to start in 1991 with six teams in the United States, four in Europe, one in Canada, and one in Mexico. The International League of American Football, with eight European teams, planned to start in 1990.

In the eight-team Canadian Football League, the Edmonton Eskimos (16-2) and the Hamilton Tiger-Cats (12-6) won the division titles, and the Saskatchewan Roughriders finished at 9-9. In the Grey Cup championship game on Nov. 26, 1989, in Toronto, Saskatchewan defeated Hamilton, 43-40, on David Ridgway's 35-yard field goal with two seconds left.

Hall of Fame. Quarterback Terry Bradshaw and cornerback Mel Blount of the Steelers, offensive tackle Art Shell of the Oakland and Los Angeles Raiders, and safety Willie Wood of the Green Bay Packers were selected to the Pro Football Hall of Fame in Canton, Ohio. On October 3, the Raiders fired coach Mike Shanahan and promoted Shell, their offensive-line coach, to the job. Shell became the NFL's first black head coach in 64 years.

College. In Division I-A, made up of the major colleges, Colorado (11-0) was the only undefeated team during the regular season. Notre Dame was 11-1, with Miami of Florida, Michigan, Alabama, Nebraska, Arkansas, Tennessee, and Fresno State at 10-1.

Miami lost only to Florida State, 24-10. Miami was coached by Dennis Erickson, who replaced Jimmy Johnson when Johnson took over the Dallas Cowboys. Notre Dame was ranked number one nationally until it lost to Miami, 27-10, on November 25, ending Notre Dame's winning streak of 23 games.

Polls. After the regular season, the Associated Press (AP) board of writers and broadcasters and the United Press International (UPI) board of coaches ranked Colorado first, Miami second, Michigan third, and Notre Dame fourth. That order was shuffled after the bowl games on Jan. 1, 1990.

In the Orange Bowl in Miami, Notre Dame, the 1988 national champion, defeated Colorado, 21-6. In the Sugar Bowl in New Orleans, Miami got by Alabama, 33-25. In the Rose Bowl in Pasadena, Calif., Southern California beat Michigan, 17-10.

National Football League final standings

American Conference

Eastern Division
	W.	L.	T.	Pct.
Buffalo Bills	9	7	0	.563
Indianapolis Colts	8	8	0	.500
Miami Dolphins	8	8	0	.500
New England Patriots	5	11	0	.313
New York Jets	4	12	0	.250

Central Division
	W.	L.	T.	Pct.
Cleveland Browns	9	6	1	.594
Houston Oilers	9	7	0	.563
Pittsburgh Steelers	9	7	0	.563
Cincinnati Bengals	8	8	0	.500

Western Division
	W.	L.	T.	Pct.
Denver Broncos	11	5	0	.688
Kansas City Chiefs	8	7	1	.531
Los Angeles Raiders	8	8	0	.500
Seattle Seahawks	7	9	0	.438
San Diego Chargers	6	10	0	.375

National Conference

Eastern Division
	W.	L.	T.	Pct.
New York Giants	12	4	0	.750
Philadelphia Eagles	11	5	0	.688
Washington Redskins	10	6	0	.625
Phoenix Cardinals	5	11	0	.313
Dallas Cowboys	1	15	0	.063

Central Division
	W.	L.	T.	Pct.
Minnesota Vikings	10	6	0	.625
Green Bay Packers	10	6	0	.625
Detroit Lions	7	9	0	.438
Chicago Bears	6	10	0	.375
Tampa Bay Buccaneers	5	11	0	.313

Western Division
	W.	L.	T.	Pct.
San Francisco 49ers	14	2	0	.875
Los Angeles Rams	11	5	0	.688
New Orleans Saints	9	7	0	.563
Atlanta Falcons	3	13	0	.188

Super Bowl champions—San Francisco 49ers (defeated Denver Broncos, 55-10)

Individual statistics

Leading scorers, touchdowns
	TD's	Rush	Rec.	Ret.	Pts.
Christian Okoye, Kansas City	12	12	0	0	72
Thurman Thomas, Buffalo	12	6	6	0	72
Anthony Miller, San Diego	11	0	10	1	66
Eric Metcalf, Cleveland	10	6	4	0	60
James Brooks, Cincinnati	9	7	2	0	54
Marion Butts, San Diego	9	9	0	0	54
Mark Clayton, Miami	9	0	9	0	54
Mervyn Fernandez, L.A. Raiders	9	0	9	0	54
Rodney Holman, Cincinnati	9	0	9	0	54
Andre Reed, Buffalo	9	0	9	0	54

Leading scorers, kicking
	PAT	FG	Longest	Pts.
David Treadwell, Denver	39-40	27-33	46	120
Scott Norwood, Buffalo	46-47	23-30	48	115
Tony Zendejas, Houston	40-40	25-37	52	115
Nick Lowery, Kansas City	34-35	24-33	50	106
Jeff Jaeger, L.A. Raiders	34-34	23-34	50	103
Pete Stoyanovich, Miami	38-39	19-26	59	95
Dean Biasucci, Indianapolis	31-32	21-27	55	94
Gary Anderson, Pittsburgh	28-28	21-30	49	91

Leading quarterbacks
	Att.	Comp.	Yds.	TD's	Int.
Boomer Esiason, Cincinnati	455	258	3,525	28	11
Warren Moon, Houston	464	280	3,631	23	14
Jim Kelly, Buffalo	391	228	3,130	25	18
Bernie Kosar, Cleveland	513	303	3,533	18	14
Dan Marino, Miami	550	308	3,997	24	22
Steve DeBerg, Kansas City	324	196	2,529	11	16
Dave Krieg, Seattle	499	286	3,309	21	20
Ken O'Brien, New York Jets	477	288	3,346	12	18
John Elway, Denver	416	223	3,051	18	18

Leading receivers
	Number caught	Total yards	Avg. gain	TD's
Andre Reed, Buffalo	88	1,312	14.9	9
Brian Blades, Seattle	77	1,063	13.8	5
Vance Johnson, Denver	76	1,095	14.4	7
John L. Williams, Seattle	76	657	8.6	6
Anthony Miller, San Diego	75	1,252	16.7	10
Drew Hill, Houston	66	938	14.2	8
Webster Slaughter, Cleveland	65	1,236	19.0	6
Tim McGee, Cincinnati	65	1,211	18.6	8
Mark Clayton, Miami	64	1,011	15.8	9
Bill Brooks, Indianapolis	63	919	14.6	4
Al Toon, New York Jets	63	693	11.0	2

Leading rushers
	No.	Yards	Avg.	TD's
Christian Okoye, Kansas City	370	1,480	4.0	12
Eric Dickerson, Indianapolis	314	1,311	4.2	7
Thurman Thomas, Buffalo	298	1,244	4.2	6
James Brooks, Cincinnati	221	1,239	5.6	7
Bobby Humphrey, Denver	294	1,151	3.9	7
Bo Jackson, L.A. Raiders	173	950	5.5	4
John Stephens, New England	244	833	3.4	7
Tim Worley, Pittsburgh	195	770	3.9	5

Leading punters
	No.	Yards	Avg.	Longest
Greg Montgomery, Houston	56	2,422	43.3	63
Rohn Stark, Indianapolis	79	3,392	42.9	64
Reggie Roby, Miami	58	2,458	42.4	58
Harry Newsome, Pittsburgh	82	3,368	41.1	57

Individual statistics

Leading scorers, touchdowns
	TD's	Rush	Rec.	Ret.	Pts.
Dalton Hilliard, New Orleans	18	13	5	0	108
Jerry Rice, San Francisco	17	0	17	0	102
Neal Anderson, Chicago	15	11	4	0	90
Greg Bell, L.A. Rams	15	15	0	0	90
Ottis Anderson, N.Y. Giants	14	14	0	0	84
Barry Sanders, Detroit	14	14	0	0	84
Sterling Sharpe, Green Bay	13	0	12	1	78

Leading scorers, kicking
	PAT	FG	Longest	Pts.
Mike Cofer, San Francisco	49-51	29-36	47	136
Chip Lohmiller, Washington	41-41	29-40	48	128
Rich Karlis, Minnesota	27-28	31-39	51	120
Mike Lansford, L.A. Rams	51-51	23-30	48	120
Chris Jacke, Green Bay	42-42	22-28	52	108
Morten Andersen, New Orleans	44-45	20-29	49	104
Donald Igwebuike, Tampa Bay	33-35	22-28	53	99
Eddie Murray, Detroit	36-36	20-21	53	96

Leading quarterbacks
	Att.	Comp.	Yards	TD's	Int.
Joe Montana, San Francisco	386	271	3,521	26	8
Jim Everett, L.A. Rams	518	304	4,310	29	17
Mark Rypien, Washington	476	280	3,768	22	13
Bobby Hebert, New Orleans	353	222	2,686	15	15
Don Majkowski, Green Bay	599	353	4,318	27	20
Phil Simms, N.Y. Giants	405	228	3,061	14	14
Chris Miller, Atlanta	526	280	3,459	16	10
Randall Cunningham, Philadelphia	532	290	3,400	21	15
Wade Wilson, Minnesota	362	194	2,543	9	12

Leading receivers
	Number caught	Total yards	Avg. gain	TD's
Sterling Sharpe, Green Bay	90	1,423	15.8	12
Mark Carrier, Tampa Bay	86	1,422	16.5	9
Art Monk, Washington	86	1,186	13.8	8
Jerry Rice, San Francisco	82	1,483	18.1	17
Ricky Sanders, Washington	80	1,138	14.2	4
Gary Clark, Washington	79	1,229	15.6	9
Tom Rathman, San Francisco	73	616	8.4	1
Henry Ellard, L.A. Rams	70	1,382	19.7	8
Richard Johnson, Detroit	70	1,091	15.6	8
Eric Martin, New Orleans	68	1,090	16.0	8
Keith Byars, Philadelphia	68	721	10.6	0

Leading rushers
	No.	Yards	Avg.	TD's
Barry Sanders, Detroit	280	1,470	5.3	14
Neal Anderson, Chicago	274	1,275	4.7	11
Dalton Hilliard, New Orleans	344	1,262	3.7	13
Greg Bell, L.A. Rams	272	1,137	4.2	15
Roger Craig, San Francisco	271	1,054	3.9	6
Ottis Anderson, N.Y. Giants	325	1,023	3.1	14
Herschel Walker, Dallas—Minnesota	250	915	3.7	7
Gerald Riggs, Washington	201	834	4.1	4
Brent Fullwood, Green Bay	204	821	4.0	5
John Settle, Atlanta	179	689	3.8	3

Leading punters
	No.	Yards	Avg.	Longest
Rich Camarillo, Phoenix	76	3,298	43.4	58
Jim Arnold, Detroit	82	3,538	43.1	64
Sean Landeta, N.Y. Giants	70	3,019	43.1	71
Ralf Mojsiejenko, Washington	62	2,663	43.0	74

The next day, in the final polls, the AP ranked Miami first, Notre Dame second, Florida State third, Colorado fourth, and Michigan seventh. The UPI poll placed Miami first, Florida State second, Notre Dame third, Colorado fourth, and Michigan eighth.

Honors. Houston led the major colleges in total offense (624.9 yards per game) and passing offense (511.3 yards). On defense, Miami allowed the fewest yards (216.5) and fewest points (9.3) per game.

Anthony Thompson, an Indiana senior, led in rushing (163.0 yards per game) and touchdowns (25), and against Wisconsin he set a single-game rushing record of 377 yards. Andre Ware, a Houston junior, set season passing records of 365 completions and 4,699 yards.

Ware narrowly defeated Thompson in the voting for the Heisman Trophy as the nation's outstanding college player. Thompson won the Maxwell and the Walter Camp awards. Percy Snow of Michigan State won the Vince Lombardi Award as the outstanding lineman and the Dick Butkus Award as the outstanding linebacker.

Coaches. Barry Switzer resigned at Oklahoma and Jackie Sherrill at Texas A&M after the National Collegiate Athletic Association put their teams on probation for recruiting violations. After the season, Glenn (Bo) Schembechler retired at Michigan after a heart attack and two heart operations.   Frank Litsky

In *World Book,* see **Football.**

Foster, Jodie (1962-   ), won the Academy of Motion Picture Arts and Sciences Award for best actress on March 29, 1989, for her role as a gutsy rape victim in *The Accused* (1988). Foster had been nominated for an Oscar for best supporting actress in 1977 for her performance in *Taxi Driver* (1976).

Alicia Christian Foster, nicknamed Jodie, was born on Nov. 19, 1962, in Los Angeles. She graduated from Le Lycée Français, a bilingual academy in Los Angeles, in 1980. In 1985, she received a bachelor's degree in literature from Yale University in New Haven, Conn.

Foster began appearing in commercials at age 3. She made her acting debut in 1969 on the television comedy series "Mayberry, R.F.D.," in which her brother appeared regularly. That role led to parts on other series, including "The Courtship of Eddie's Father," "Bonanza," and "My Three Sons." In 1974, she starred in the short-lived series "Paper Moon."

Foster's motion-picture debut in *Napoleon and Samantha* (1972) was the first of several starring roles in family-oriented movies. That same year, she also tackled her first role in a film for adults—that of a neglected daughter in *Kansas City Bomber.* Her performance as a drug-addicted teen-aged prostitute in *Taxi Driver* won praise for its authenticity and sensitivity.

Foster's other film credits include *Alice Doesn't Live Here Anymore* (1975), *The Little Girl Who Lives Down the Lane* (1977), *The Hotel New Hampshire* (1984), and *Stealing Home* (1988).   Barbara A. Mayes

France. World attention focused on Paris on July 14, 1989, as France celebrated the 200th anniversary of a major event of the French Revolution—the storming of the Bastille, a fortress in Paris and a symbol of royal oppression—and as the city hosted the 15th annual economic summit meeting of the leaders of seven major industrial democracies. Also in Paris were leaders of 25 other countries—invited by France's President François Mitterrand to join in a weeklong celebration of the bicentennial of the revolution.

The bicentennial occurred as a trend toward consensus was building in French domestic politics. "The revolution is over," said historian François Furet, meaning that the revolution's ideals of justice and human rights had won acceptance by all segments of French society and that the French people were ending bitter political divisions inherited from the revolution— between left and right, church and state, and central and local government. Reflecting this change in view, French politicians pursued the more pragmatic politics characteristic of other Western European democracies.

Foreign policy. Mitterrand sought closer ties with West Germany to maintain stability in Western Europe and Western cohesion in dealing with the diplomatic initiatives of Soviet leader Mikhail S. Gorbachev. Eager to keep West Germany solidly anchored in the North Atlantic Treaty Organization (NATO), the major Western military alliance, Mitterrand supported West Germany's opposition to the deployment of new United States short-range nuclear missiles in Europe. At a NATO summit meeting in Brussels, Belgium, in May, however, France backed U.S. President George Bush in rejecting West German pressure for East-West negotiations on withdrawing all U.S. and Soviet nuclear arms from Europe.

France had traditionally been reluctant to enter arms-control talks involving its own forces. With West Germany pressing for across-the-board disarmament accords with the Soviets, however, France in January served as host to an international conference on the elimination of chemical weapons. France also joined a U.S.-led push to reach a quick agreement on ongoing East-West talks in Vienna, Austria, on cutting conventional forces in Europe.

Mitterrand decided in March that France would join a NATO program to build an alliancewide electronic network for air defense. And in May, French officials acknowledged that the United States had secretly helped France with its nuclear weapons program even after France's President Charles de Gaulle withdrew France from NATO's military operations in 1966.

As concern mounted in France about West Germany's growing political and economic influence due to its role in the decomposing Soviet bloc, Mitterrand tried to prevent the development of an independent West German policy in Eastern Europe. He supported moves to speed up the process of integration of the 12-nation European Community (EC or Common Market), backed the EC's coordination of Western efforts to help Eastern European countries seeking to leave the Soviet orbit, and championed attempts to forge a monetary union among the 12 member states. Despite Great Britain's hostility to this approach, Mitterrand's views prevailed at an EC summit meeting held in Strasbourg, France, on Dec. 8 and 9, 1989.

Domestic policy. France's growing political pragmatism, accompanied by a decline in the influence of extremist factions, enabled the Socialists to stay in power throughout 1989 even though they lacked a formal majority in the National Assembly, the more powerful of the two houses of Parliament. Prime Minister Michel Rocard pursued cautious policies of improving France's industrial competitiveness, streamlining government bureaucracies, backing legislation to tailor education more closely to future needs of industry, and modernizing France's legal system. The dwindling Communist faction, while supporting strikes against austerity policies of the Rocard government, refused to join conservative-sponsored votes that would have triggered national elections.

Scandal embarrassed the Socialists during the year. Associates of Mitterrand were indicted on February 16 on charges of insider trading in connection with the take-over in 1988 of a U.S. packaging company, Triangle Industries, Incorporated, by the French state-owned firm Pechiney S.A.

Widespread political corruption came to light in a series of police raids on firms—mainly construction companies—that collected payments for nonexistent goods and services and then handed over the funds to politicians. Although all the political parties were implicated, the Socialists' image suffered most.

The government on June 20, 1989, proposed a bill regulating campaign financing and offering an amnesty for politicians, but public outcry forced the draft legislation to be withdrawn. A revised version depriving members of Parliament of an amnesty passed on December 22.

Immigration policy. Simmering controversy concerning immigrant workers erupted in a debate about whether to permit Muslim girls to wear headscarves in school despite France's tradition of barring religious expression in public schools. The country's supreme constitutional body ruled on November 27 that the education ministry could authorize the wearing of scarves as a mark of piety at certain times and places in secular schools. On December 3, the National Front, a right wing party, won a parliamentary election in Dreux after campaigning against an expansion of immigrants' rights.   Joseph Fitchett

See also **Europe** (Facts in brief table). In *World Book,* see **France.**

Gabon. See **Africa.**

Gambia. See **Africa.**

Games. See **Toys and games.**

Gas and gasoline. See **Energy supply; Petroleum and gas.**

Genetic engineering. See **Biology.**

Fireworks illuminate the Eiffel Tower in Paris on July 14 during the celebration of the 200th anniversary of the French Revolution.

Geology

Geology. An earthquake of magnitude 7.1 on the Richter scale struck a large area in northern California on Oct. 17, 1989. (The Richter scale is a scale for indicating the strength of an earthquake. A quake of 7 or more can cause great damage and kill many people.) The epicenter was located on the San Andreas Fault about 10 miles (16 kilometers) northeast of Santa Cruz. Damage was heavy in that city and surrounding areas, as well as in parts of San Francisco, Oakland, and other cities bordering San Francisco Bay.

Structures built on loose sand and mud suffered the most damage. One of the hardest hit areas was the Marina section of San Francisco, where many houses collapsed.

The *earthquake focus* (place where the faulting began) was 11 miles (18 kilometers) deep on the San Andreas Fault. The fault is part of the boundary between the North American and Pacific plates, 2 of about 20 gigantic plates that make up the earth's crust. A 22-mile (35-kilometer) section of the fault shifted. The western side moved northward about 8 feet (2.5 meters) and upward about 5 feet (1.5 meters) relative to the eastern side. This type of motion is unusual for the San Andreas Fault. Most earthquakes along it involve only horizontal movement of the western side northward past the eastern side.

Another unusual feature of this earthquake was that the fault movement did not reach the surface but was confined to an area of the fault at least 2½ miles (4 kilometers) deep. The section of the fault that moved was in what geologists call a *seismic gap*, an area along plate boundaries where an earthquake has not occurred for many years. Seismologists had warned several years ago that an earthquake there was probable soon.

Earth's oldest rocks. Identification of the world's oldest rocks was reported in October by a team of Canadian, United States, and Australian geologists. The rocks came from an area in Canada's Northwest Territories. The scientists determined that the rocks were 3.96 billion years old, 100 million years older than rocks from western Greenland that up to then had been the oldest known rocks.

The Canadian rocks are granitic rocks with a high proportion of the elements silicon, potassium, sodium, and aluminum. Such rocks are characteristic of continental rather than oceanic regions, and this suggests that at least some continental material had formed before 3.96 billion years ago.

Neptune's strange moon. Triton, the largest moon of Neptune, has a surface that is covered with gigantic fissures, frozen lakes, craters, streaks of dark material, and curious formations that look like the surface of a cantaloupe. All this was revealed in pictures transmitted to earth by the spacecraft *Voyager 2* in August. Scientists suspect that the frozen lakes may represent the frozen states of water, methane, nitrogen, or carbon monoxide. The dark streaks may be caused by volcanic eruptions or geysers of liquid or gaseous nitrogen. Several plumes of dark material rising 5 miles (8 kilometers) high may be giant geysers. Many of the features will need much more study before scientists can understand them.

Fast global warming. Data indicate that the most recent change from a cold glacial climate to a warmer one happened much more quickly than previously thought, according to a report in June by a team of U.S. and Danish geologists. From about 3 million to 11,000 years ago, the earth was in the grip of an ice age, and glaciers covered much of the continents of North America, Antarctica, Eurasia, and southern South America. About 11,000 years ago, the ice began to melt. The huge continental ice sheets mostly disappeared, except for those on Greenland and Antarctica.

The geologists studied cores drilled from the Greenland ice sheet to try to understand how fast the climate changed. By comparing the levels of different *isotopes* (forms) of hydrogen and oxygen from the cores, they determined that the average annual temperature there rose 13 Fahrenheit degrees (7 Celsius degrees) in only 20 years. This suggests that major climatic changes can occur much more rapidly than suspected, and it has important implications for estimates of how present human activities may contribute to global warming. Eldridge M. Moores

See also **Disasters; Space exploration.** In *World Book,* see Geology.

Georgia. See State government.

Germany, East. What may have been the most dramatic political event since World War II (1939-1945) occurred on the night of Nov. 9, 1989, when East Germany suddenly and unexpectedly opened the Berlin Wall. The world was gripped by emotional pictures of East Berliners streaming West—older people reunited with relatives they had not seen for nearly 40 years and young people sightseeing in the well-stocked stores of West Berlin.

Within East Germany, the political pressure that opened the wall also brought down two governments and caused the Socialist Unity Party (SED), the country's Communist party, to change its name. The state even scheduled free, multiparty elections for 1990.

Starting strong—apparently. Early in 1989, SED chief Erich Honecker had been scornfully critical of the liberalization that was taking place in the Soviet Union. East Germany's 40-year effort to build patriotic support for an East German state appeared to have succeeded. The SED, bolstered by an efficient secret police, dominated all aspects of life in East Germany. The development of the highest standard of living in the Soviet bloc apparently had "sold" the East German public on Communism.

Citizens flee. A true picture of the depth of patriotic support for the East German state emerged shortly after Hungary announced on September 2 that it would no longer abide by a commitment to prevent East German citizens from leaving the Soviet bloc. East

312

East Germans stream through Checkpoint Charlie at the Berlin Wall after their country opened its borders with the West on November 9.

Germans started streaming through Hungary and into Austria on their way to West Germany.

Thousands of East Germans sought asylum in the West German Embassy in Prague, Czechoslovakia; about 800, at the embassy in Warsaw, Poland. East Germany announced on September 30 that it had provided special trains to carry these refugees to West Germany but said that it was expelling "irresponsible antisocial traitors and criminals."

Large crowds turned out for prodemocracy demonstrations in Leipzig on September 18 and 25 and on October 2. Peaceful protests, led by small opposition groups with the help of Lutheran churches in East Germany, mounted in several cities in the next few days, resulting in hundreds of arrests.

Gorbachev visits, Honecker fired. The East German regime had been paralyzed all summer, partly because Honecker, 77, had been ill. Honecker recovered enough, however, to welcome Soviet leader Mikhail S. Gorbachev for ceremonies on October 6 and 7 marking the 40th anniversary of the establishment of the East German state. During his visit, Gorbachev said that East Germany was free to choose its own course but added that reform was dangerous only "if you don't react to life." Honecker continued to take a hard line, however, and was forced from power by the Politburo, the SED's policymaking body.

Krenz in, Stoph out. Honecker lost his post on October 18 and was succeeded immediately by Egon Krenz, at 52 years of age the youngest member of the

Germany, East

Politburo. Krenz promised reforms and tried to gain popular support by purging the party's old guard, authorizing free travel, and starting a campaign to reveal the ousted leaders' corruption and inefficiency.

Under unrelenting public pressure for political and economic reform, the entire Council of Ministers—the official government of East Germany—resigned on November 7. On November 8, the Central Committee of the SED nominated Hans Modrow to succeed Willi Stoph as prime minister. Stoph, 75, had held the post since 1964. Modrow, 61, was SED chief in Dresden and was viewed as a reformer.

Wall opened, elections promised. On November 9, East Germany opened its border with West Germany and West Berlin and said that East German citizens would no longer require special permission to take private trips West or even to emigrate. Within hours, thousands of East Germans swarmed across the Berlin Wall. Most returned to East Germany after a few hours of visiting, shopping, or sightseeing in West Berlin.

The SED Central Committee concluded a three-day meeting on November 10 with a promise of "free, democratic, and secret elections," separation of the SED from the state, and a "socialist planned economy oriented to market conditions."

Communist leadership resigns. A wave of popular anger over the corruption of top officials of the SED under Honecker led to the resignation of the entire SED leadership—both the Central Committee and the Politburo, including Krenz—on December 3. A 25-member temporary working group took over the affairs of the SED. On December 5, Honecker was put under house arrest but was later freed.

On December 7, delegations from 12 political groups, including the SED and opposition organizations, held talks in East Berlin. The delegates called for the adoption of a new constitution and recommended that free elections take place by May 6, 1990.

Gysi takes helm. Also on Dec. 7, 1989, the SED held an emergency congress to debate the future of the party. After an all-night session, the delegates elected Gregor Gysi, a 41-year-old lawyer, to the new position of chairman. As 1989 drew to a close, it was unclear whether the revamped Communist organization—or the politically inexperienced opposition groups—would be able to produce a credible leadership in time for the May 1990 elections.

Despite the promise of reform, calls mounted for reunification with West Germany as the shortest path to democracy and greater prosperity. Gysi, like Modrow, rejected reunification but accepted Bonn's offer of aid and closer economic ties.

In December, East German refugees, many of them skilled young workers, arrived in West Germany at the rate of nearly 1,500 a day. The total exodus for the year was about 350,000 people.   Joseph Fitchett

See also **Europe** (Facts in brief table). In *World Book*, see **Germany.**

Germany, West. Long the leading economic power in Europe, emerged in 1989 as the leading European power in both the North Atlantic Treaty Organization (NATO) and the European Community (EC, or Common Market). West Germany was also the most influential Western country—and by far the largest Western economic presence—in Eastern European countries that left the Soviet orbit during the year. And the collapse of Communism in East Germany late in the year triggered debate on the prospect—and the desirability—of an even more powerful German state, created by the reunification of the two Germanys.

Chemical-arms aid admitted. One of the most hectic years in West German politics began on a sour note with United States officials alleging that West German firms had helped Libya build a plant to make poison gas. Bonn initially denied, then affirmed, the allegation.

Missile decision delayed. West Germany objected to a NATO plan to modernize its aging Lance short-range nuclear missiles, most of which are based in West Germany. The United States and Great Britain favored modernization. At a NATO summit meeting in Brussels, Belgium, on May 29 and 30, the United States accepted West Germany's demand to postpone any decision on the Lances and to plan East-West talks on short-range nuclear forces.

Gorbachev visit. Soviet leader Mikhail S. Gorbachev visited West Germany for the first time from June 12 to 15. An enthusiastic public greeted him with chants of "Gorby! Gorby!" and viewed him as the leader most capable of ending decades of confrontation in Europe. A poll released by a German television network on June 11 showed that 90 per cent of West Germans thought they could trust Gorbachev, compared with 50 per cent for Chancellor Helmut Kohl.

East Germans arrive. In August and September, thousands of East Germans crowded into West German embassies throughout Eastern Europe, demanding to be allowed to leave for the West. The Bonn government negotiated with East Germany and the Soviet Union and obtained their release.

On November 9, East German leaders opened the borders and masses of East Germans "voted with their feet" against their government and fled to West Germany. This influx buoyed Kohl's Christian Democratic Party, which had always advocated German reunification, but risked alienating the Republicans, a small right wing party opposed to immigration.

Reunification plan. In a bid to regain the political initiative from the right wing, Kohl on November 28 proposed a 10-point plan to reunify the two Germanys. Kohl called for step-by-step improvement in ties, with no timetable and proceeding on the basis of multiparty elections in East Germany. He did not try to describe the final form of a reunified Germany.

Kohl's plan attracted wide support in West Germany but was rejected by East German leaders, who insisted upon retaining a separate state.

West Germany's allies acknowledged a concern that an extremely rapid reunification might destabilize the process of European disarmament and the relaxation of East-West tension. Speaking at a NATO summit meeting in Brussels on December 4, U.S. President George Bush said that reunification should be gradual, democratic, peaceful, and in keeping with the EC's plan to develop a single market economy. He also said that reunification must not jeopardize NATO or the carrying out of the 1975 Helsinki agreements on European security and cooperation. Bush stressed that the ultimate legal authority to approve a German settlement still belonged to the four allied powers that defeated Nazi Germany in World War II (1939-1945)— France, Great Britain, the Soviet Union, and the United States.

Terrorists murdered one of West Germany's most respected business leaders, Alfred Herrhausen, by blowing up his car in Bad Homburg, a suburb of Frankfurt, on Nov. 30, 1989. Herrhausen, 59, was the chief executive of the Deutsche Bank, the dominant bank in postwar West Germany. He had been instrumental in modernizing West German industry in the 1980's and was a close adviser to Kohl. Herrhausen's killers belonged to the Red Army Faction, a left wing group.   Joseph Fitchett

See also **Europe** (Facts in brief table). In *World Book,* see **Germany**.

Ghana. See **Africa**.

Golf. Tom Kite and Curtis Strange made golf history in 1989. In 1988, Strange won $1,147,644 in prize money, becoming the first professional to earn $1 million in a single year. In 1989, Kite raised the record to $1,395,278. Kite, Strange, and Tom Watson joined Jack Nicklaus as the only golfers to reach $5 million in career earnings. Strange also became the first since Ben Hogan in 1950 and 1951 to win the United States Open championship in consecutive years— 1988 and 1989.

Kite and Strange played on the Professional Golfers' Association (PGA) tour of 44 tournaments with prize money totaling $38 million. Kite and Steve Jones won three tournaments each. In the four grand-slam tournaments, Nick Faldo of England won the Masters, Strange the U.S. Open, Mark Calcavecchia the British Open, and Payne Stewart the PGA.

Men aged 50 and older played on the PGA senior tour of 41 tournaments paying $16 million. The Ladies Professional Golf Association (LPGA) conducted 35 tournaments worth $13 million.

The majors. The first of the four major tournaments for men was the Masters, held from April 6 to 9 in Augusta, Ga. Faldo birdied four of the last six holes for a 65 and tied Scott Hoch with a 72-hole score of 283. Greg Norman of Australia and Ben Crenshaw finished in a tie for third at 284. On the first play-off hole, Hoch missed about a 2-foot (60-centimeter) putt. On the second, in rain, fog, and darkness, Faldo won

with a 25-foot (8-meter) birdie putt. Faldo went on to win the European PGA championship, the British Masters, the French Open, and the world match-play championship.

In the U.S. Open, held from June 15 to 18 in Pittsford, N.Y., Kite led by 3 strokes with 14 holes to play, but then scored a 78 and dropped to ninth place. Strange's 278 beat Ian Woosnam of Wales, Chip Beck, and Mark McCumber by a stroke. An incredible coincidence occurred in the second round of the tournament. During a two-hour span, Nick Price of England, Doug Weaver, Mark Wiebe, and Jerry Pate sank holes-in-one on the 167-yard (153-meter) sixth hole.

In the British Open, held from July 20 to 23 in Troon, Scotland, Calcavecchia sank a 7-foot (2-meter) birdie putt on the 72nd hole and tied Norman and Wayne Grady, also of Australia, at 275, two strokes ahead of Watson. The three leaders then started a four-hole medal-score play-off, which Calcavecchia won with a birdie on the last hole.

In the PGA championship, held from August 10 to 13 in Hawthorn Woods, Ill., Stewart trailed by six strokes with 18 holes to go, five with 9 to go, and three with 3 to go. Stewart rallied with birdies on 4 of the last 5 holes. Stewart's 276 beat Mike Reid, Strange, and Andy Bean by a stroke.

Ryder Cup. In 1985 and 1987, the European pros had upset the Americans in the biennial Ryder Cup matches. In 1989, after match play September 22 to 24 in Sutton Coldfield, England, the teams finished in a 14-14 tie, so the Europeans retained the cup.

On the 18th hole of the final day's singles match play, Calcavecchia and Stewart drove into the water, Fred Couples hit a wide approach, and Ken Green took three putts, and all lost the hole. Had any of the four simply tied his European opponent on that hole, the Americans would have won the cup.

LPGA tour. When Betsy King won the U.S. Open on July 13 to 16 in Lake Orion, Mich., she became the first woman to reach $500,000 in prize money in one year. Then she won the Nestlé World Classic on August 24 to 27 in Buford, Ga., and finished with $654,132.

The 33-year-old King of Limekiln, Pa., won six tournaments during the year and was named the LPGA Player of the Year. Beth Daniel won four tournaments. Nancy Lopez won three, including the LPGA championship. Juli Inkster won the Nabisco Dinah Shore, and Tammie Green won the du Maurier Classic.

Senior tour. In 17 years on the PGA tour, Orville Moody, a former U.S. Army sergeant, won only one tournament—the 1969 U.S. Open. But at age 55, he won regularly on the senior tour. Moody took the Senior Tournament Players Classic on June 11 in Ponte Vedra, Fla., and the U.S. Senior Open on July 2 in Ligonier, Pa. In other major tournaments, Larry Mowry won the PGA Seniors, and Bob Charles of New Zealand won the British Senior Open. Charles won five other tournaments and $725,887.   Frank Litsky

In *World Book,* see **Golf**.

Great Britain. The year 1989 was a difficult one for Prime Minister Margaret Thatcher. Her Conservative government continued to push for controversial tax and health reforms. In public opinion polls, the Conservative Party's popularity dwindled, while support for the opposing Labour Party grew. Many observers wondered if Thatcher, who celebrated her 10th year as prime minister in May, had lost her touch—that is, her ability to gather support for her political agenda.

The root of the Conservative Party's problem was Great Britain's worsening economy. The country's trade deficit continued to grow in 1989, weakening the pound against other currencies. Inflation rose to 8.3 per cent in May, the highest in seven years. To help curb inflation, Chancellor of the Exchequer Nigel Lawson ordered a succession of hikes in interest rates. By October 5, interest rates had reached 15 per cent, the highest level in eight years, and many people began to fear a recession.

The year was also marked by labor unrest. A series of one-day strikes in June and July crippled the country's transportation system as rail, bus, and subway workers walked off the job, demanding higher pay.

Taxes. One of Thatcher's most unpopular reforms—replacing the local property tax with a "community charge"—went into effect in Scotland in 1989. The tax, scheduled to begin in England and Wales in April 1990, is levied on the number of individuals in each household instead of on property val-

ues. It was strongly criticized by the Labour Party, which said that it would hurt the poor.

Anger against the new tax also grew in Conservative rural areas after the government announced that the money generated by the tax would be sent to inner-city areas, most of which are controlled by the Labour Party. At the annual Conservative Party conference in October 1989, party leaders sought to defuse opposition by announcing a 1.3-billion-pound (about U.S. $2 billion) government subsidy to reduce the impact of the tax on the poor.

Going private. Thatcher's Conservative government pressed ahead with plans to transfer utilities owned by the government to private ownership. The Water Act Bill, which would privatize the country's 10 regional water authorities, became law on July 6. For the first time in Great Britain, water meters were installed in homes, and residents braced for a dramatic increase in water bills.

Efforts to privatize the government-owned Central Electricity Generating Board, which supplies electricity to local utilities in England and Wales, encountered problems during the year. On September 29, Energy Secretary John Wakeham announced a six-month delay in the proposed plan because of difficulties in negotiating contracts between local companies that generate and distribute electricity.

Cabinet upheaval. On July 24, Prime Minister Thatcher announced extensive Cabinet changes. Chris-

Late-arriving soccer fans surged into a packed stadium in Sheffield, England, during a match on April 15, crushing and killing 95 people.

topher Patten, minister for overseas development, was promoted to environment secretary, replacing Nicholas Ridley, who was named trade and industry secretary. Ridley had been criticized for his lack of interest in environmental causes. Northern Ireland Secretary Tom King was named defense secretary, replacing George Younger, who retired.

Perhaps the most controversial Cabinet change involved Foreign Secretary Sir Geoffrey Howe. Thatcher replaced Howe with Treasury Secretary John Major. Some political analysts speculated that Howe lost the post because he supported closer economic ties with the European Community (EC or Common Market), a position not shared by Thatcher.

The news media criticized Thatcher for bungling the affair. As Howe fought to keep his position, Thatcher offered him the post of home secretary. In the process, she offended Douglas Hurd, the home secretary, who was not notified of Thatcher's offer to Howe. Howe eventually was named deputy prime minister—a post that is not provided for in the British Constitution—and leader of the House of Commons.

Turmoil continued to plague Thatcher's Cabinet after the July changes. On October 26, Lawson unexpectedly resigned as chancellor of the exchequer because of ongoing disputes with Sir Alan Walters, Thatcher's economic adviser. Hours after Lawson quit, Walters turned in his resignation. Thatcher quickly replaced Lawson with John Major, the newly named foreign secretary. Home Secretary Hurd was named new foreign secretary.

Health-care reform. Britain's 89,000 doctors opposed a government plan proposed on January 31 to overhaul the country's National Health Service (NHS). The NHS provides free medical care to all people in Great Britain.

Under the current NHS program, the government reimburses physicians, hospitals, and other health-care providers for their services. The proposed plan, however, calls for doctors to receive an annual budget to "buy" hospital and other care for their patients. It also would allow NHS hospitals the right to operate without the control of local authorities. The British Medical Association, which represents Britain's physicians, campaigned against the changes, arguing that patients would no longer be able to trust that their doctors were prescribing proper treatment.

Beer bashing. The government also met resistance on March 21, when it sought to break the monopoly of Britain's largest breweries by forcing them to sell off 22,000 of their public houses—or pubs. The action came after a government study found that the breweries were restricting competition, limiting the brands of beer available in pubs, and artificially raising the price of beer. But the breweries are major financial backers of the Conservative Party, and so a compromise was reached. Under the compromise, each of the six major breweries could require 2,000 of the pubs it owned to sell only its products; half of all pubs over

2,000 owned by the six would be free to sell other breweries' products.

EC conflict. During the year, Thatcher found herself once again at odds with the EC, which plans to form one unified European market in 1992. In April, she strongly rejected a report by EC Commission President Jacques Delors proposing the establishment of a single European currency and a central European bank that would set monetary policy for all EC members.

Thatcher also rejected an EC proposal that would standardize the minimum wages and working conditions in all EC countries. Her strident anti-EC tone was believed to have cost the Conservatives many votes in the European Parliament election in June. (The European Parliament is an advisory body of the EC. Its members are elected by voters in member nations.) In the election, the Conservatives lost 13 seats, mostly to the Labour Party.

Labour's strides. Under the leadership of Neil G. Kinnock, the Labour Party replaced many of its unpopular extremist policies with more moderate ones. At its annual conference in October, Labour members voted to abandon their position favoring unilateral nuclear disarmament and to drop their commitment to renationalize the industries that the Conservative government had privatized. The shift to the middle appeared to work. The party gained an 11-point lead over the Conservatives in public opinion polls.

Death threat. On February 14, Iran's leader, Ayatollah Ruhollah Khomeini, called on Muslims around the world to kill Indian-born British author Salman Rushdie for writing a book that Khomeini claimed was blasphemous to Islam. Rushdie, who maintained that the book—*The Satanic Verses*—was not blasphemous, went into hiding.

Despite pressure from the Muslim community, the British government refused to ban the book. On February 20, Britain announced it was withdrawing all its diplomats from Iran. Iran responded on March 7 by breaking all diplomatic relations with Britain. See **Literature (Close-Up)**.

Royal doings. On August 31, Buckingham Palace announced that Princess Anne and her husband, Captain Mark Phillips, were separating. The couple, married in 1973, had been drifting apart for years, but Buckingham Palace said there was no question of a divorce. Earlier in the year, romantic letters written to Princess Anne by an aide were leaked to the press.

Prince Charles in 1989 continued his crusade against modern architecture, much of which he considers ugly and impersonal. His book *A Vision of Britain: A Personal View of Architecture* was published in September. In the spring, the prince announced plans to build four model villages near Dorchester in a style of architecture that he favors (see **Architecture**). The prince also continued to demonstrate his concern for Britain's unemployed youth. In September, he disclosed a plan that would pay 100,000 young people to perform community work.

Traffic comes to a standstill in July on a road to London as one of a series of 24-hour transit strikes forces commuters to drive to work.

On September 12, Buckingham Palace announced that Sarah, the Duchess of York, and her husband, Prince Andrew, the Duke of York, were expecting their second child. Earlier in the year, the British media criticized the royal pair for leaving their first child, Beatrice, alone too much while they traveled.

On April 7, Soviet leader Mikhail S. Gorbachev invited Queen Elizabeth II to visit the Soviet Union. The invitation came at the end of Gorbachev's three-day visit to Britain. If Queen Elizabeth makes the trip, she would be the first reigning British monarch to visit the country since Czar Nicholas II of Russia was killed by Bolshevik revolutionaries in 1918. The czar was a cousin of King George V, the queen's grandfather.

Accidents. Britain's worst sporting disaster occurred on April 15 when 95 spectators were crushed to death during a soccer match at Hillsborough Stadium in Sheffield, England. The tragedy happened when thousands of late-arriving fans surged into the already packed stadium. A preliminary report published on August 4 blamed local police for failing to realize that people were being crushed against the metal fences designed to keep fans off the field.

On August 20, a pleasure boat carrying about 140 people collided with a barge on the River Thames in London. The collision killed 51 people, most of them young bankers and fashion models.   Ian J. Mather

See also **Ireland; Northern Ireland.** In *World Book,* see **Great Britain.**

Greece. The fall in June 1989 of Andreas Papandreou, the controversial and charismatic Socialist prime minister of Greece, confirmed the strength of that country's democracy but left Greece politically unsettled. After eight years in power, the Panhellenic Socialist Movement (PASOK) lost parliamentary elections on June 18 amid a tumult of political and financial scandals engulfing the party and the private life of Papandreou. While the nation sought a new political orientation, crucial decisions were postponed—including the future of United States military bases in Greece. Another election on November 5 left PASOK in a virtual deadlock with its main rival, the conservative New Democracy Party (NDP).

Papandreou loses. In the June elections, PASOK won only 125 seats to 145 for the NDP, leaving both parties short of a majority in the 300-seat Parliament. To break the deadlock, a Communist-led alliance of leftist groups agreed to an unprecedented left-right coalition that would rule only temporarily. The NDP agreed to replace its nominee for prime minister—its campaign leader, Constantine Mitsotakis. Instead, the NDP supported another of its own members, Tzannis Tzannetakis. The new nominee had been a military officer but had actively opposed the military junta that ruled Greece from 1967 to 1974.

Tzannetakis took office on July 1. The temporary government's mandate was to prosecute officials of the previous government who were guilty of corruption before calling new elections.

Papandreou charged. The main allegation against Papandreou involved the Bank of Crete and its owner, George Koskotas. In a *Time* magazine interview published on March 6, 1989, Koskotas said that he had embezzled tens of millions of dollars from his bank for the benefit of Papandreou and PASOK. *Time* interviewed Koskotas in a Salem, Mass., prison, where he was fighting extradition to Greece. Koskotas had fled to the United States in 1988.

Papandreou, 70, was also tarnished by his heavily publicized personal relationship with Dimitra Liani, 35. On June 16, 1989, he was divorced from Margaret, his wife of 38 years. He married Liani on July 13.

In September, the new Parliament charged Papandreou with corruption, abuses of power, bribery, accepting stolen money, and breach of faith. Parliament also charged seven other former officials of the Papandreou government with crimes.

The November election boosted the two major parties' representation in Parliament by 3 seats each, giving PASOK 128 seats to 148 for the NDP—but leaving the NDP still short of a majority. As a result, President Christos Sartzetakis scheduled another election for April 1990. An interim, all-party government headed by Xenophon Zolotas took office on Nov. 23, 1989, to govern until the election.   Joseph Fitchett

See also **Europe** (Facts in brief table). In *World Book,* see **Greece.**

Grenada. See **Latin America.**

Guatemala. Heading toward presidential elections in 1990, Guatemala was troubled in 1989 by political unrest. Many Guatemalans criticized Vinicio Cerezo Arévalo, the country's first civilian president in 20 years, for not taking tough measures to restore order.

On May 9, troops led by rebel air force and army officers marched on the National Palace and the home of General Héctor Gramajo Morales, the defense minister. Bent on ousting Cerezo, the officers were turned back by troops loyal to the president without a shot fired. Credit for aborting the coup was given to Gramajo, an advocate of civilian rule. Thirteen officers were arrested for their role in the coup attempt.

But Cerezo came in for increasing criticism during 1989 as the economy continued to deteriorate. He was also criticized for pushing tax reform and for attempting to open negotiations with leftist rebels who have waged an off-and-on guerrilla war for 30 years.

Within Cerezo's Christian Democrat Party, a split developed in August following the primary election of Alfonso Cabrera as the party's presidential candidate. Some party dissidents began supporting the undeclared candidacy of Efraín Ríos Montt, who ruled as a dictator in 1982 and 1983. Nathan A. Haverstock

See also **Latin America** (Facts in brief table). In *World Book,* see **Guatemala.**

Guinea. See **Africa.**

Guyana. See **Latin America.**

Haiti. See **West Indies.**

Handicapped. A majority of the disabled workers who lost their social security benefits during a review of the disabled rolls by the Administration of President Ronald Reagan were unfairly denied their benefits. That was the conclusion of a study by the General Accounting Office (GAO), the investigative arm of Congress, published in December 1989. Between 1981 and 1984, the Reagan Administration cut 315,910 disabled workers from the social security disability program.

The GAO found that by June 1987, 63 per cent of those cut had won their benefits on appeal. In 1984, Congress ordered the Social Security Administration to continue paying benefits to people appealing their removal from the rolls. According to lawyers representing the disabled workers, the GAO study provides solid evidence that the Reagan Administration's review was seriously flawed.

Losing ground. A smaller percentage of U.S. men with disabilities held full-time jobs in 1988 than in 1981, and the earnings of all workers with disabilities fell even further below those of able-bodied employees, according to a study by the U.S. Bureau of the Census released in August 1989. The bureau reported that only 23.4 per cent of men with disabilities worked full-time in 1988, compared with 29.8 per cent in 1981. The average earnings of such workers during that period dropped from 77 per cent of that earned by able-bodied male workers to 64 per cent.

California Angels starting pitcher Jim Abbott, born without a right hand, finished his rookie season in the major leagues with a 12-12 record.

Harness racing

The proportion of full-time women employees with disabilities rose slightly during that period—from 11.4 per cent to 13.1 per cent. But their average earnings relative to those of able-bodied women workers fell, from 69 per cent to 62 per cent.

Suggested explanations for the employment difficulties faced by workers with disabilities included continuing discrimination in hiring and promotion; a decrease in the number of employees in government, where workers have had antibias protection; and cutbacks in government spending on training and employment programs for people with disabilities.

Educating the severely handicapped. Severely handicapped children are entitled to educational services from public schools even if they may not benefit, according to the Supreme Court of the United States. In November 1989, the court refused to hear an appeal from the Rochester, N.H., school district, which had been ordered by a lower court to provide services for a profoundly retarded boy.

The lower court had based its decision on the All Handicapped Children Act of 1975, which requires public schools to provide handicapped children with "a free appropriate education." The Rochester school district had argued that serving severely handicapped children would divert scarce resources from handicapped children who can learn.   Barbara A. Mayes

In *World Book,* see **Handicapped.**
Harness racing. See **Horse racing.**

Harris, Barbara Clementine (1930-   ), on Feb. 11, 1989, became the first woman ordained a bishop in the Episcopal Church. Her election by the Diocese of Massachusetts renewed debate on the role of women in the Anglican Communion, an international organization of 23 churches including the Episcopal Church.

Although the Episcopal Church has allowed women priests since 1976, many conservative members object to a woman bishop. Others oppose Harris because of her lack of formal seminary training and her liberal opinions. A black civil rights activist, Harris has spoken out against racial and sexual discrimination.

Harris was born June 12, 1930, in Philadelphia. In 1949, she joined Joseph V. Baker Associates, a public relations firm, becoming its president in 1958. In 1968, she joined the Sun Oil Company, where she held a number of management posts. From 1980 to 1983, she was an independent public relations consultant.

Harris participated in the alternative education program for the Diocese of Pennsylvania from 1976 to 1979. She was ordained a priest in 1980. From 1980 to 1984, she was priest-in-charge of St. Augustine of Hippo Church in Norristown, Pa., and in 1988 was named interim rector of the Church of the Advocate in Philadelphia. Harris was elected *suffragan* (assistant bishop) of the Diocese of Massachusetts in 1988. She was executive director of the Episcopal Church Publishing Company from 1984 to 1989.   Mary A. Krier
Hawaii. See **State government.**

Health and disease. Scientists in 1989 reported that they had identified the gene that causes most cases of cystic fibrosis. The discovery, announced August 24 by researchers at the Hospital for Sick Children in Toronto, Canada, and the Howard Hughes Medical Institute at the University of Michigan in Ann Arbor, may eventually lead to a cure for the disease.

Cystic fibrosis is one of the most common inherited diseases in North America, affecting about 1 in every 2,000 white children. An estimated 30,000 people in the United States have the disease, and most will die before their 30th birthday. The disease causes the body to produce large amounts of thick mucus that accumulates in the lungs and pancreas, resulting in respiratory difficulties and recurring infections. It also causes nutritional problems by interfering with the enzymes needed to digest food.

The scientists located the cystic fibrosis gene on one section of the seventh chromosome. Human beings have 23 pairs of chromosomes. These tiny threadlike structures are found in the nucleus of all cells. Chromosomes carry genes, segments of DNA (deoxyribonucleic acid) that contain coded hereditary information. Included in this genetic material are the instructions that can influence a person's vulnerability to a variety of diseases.

Scientists expect the discovery to lead to better treatments for the disease. They also predicted that the achievement would quickly produce a faster, cheaper, and more accurate test for carriers of cystic fibrosis. About 12 million people in the United States are carriers of the disease. They have the genetic defect for cystic fibrosis but show no symptoms of the disorder. If two carriers have a child, there is 1 chance in 4 that the baby will have cystic fibrosis. The existing test is used primarily on expectant parents who have had one child with cystic fibrosis and fear having another. Authorities said that a new test might be inexpensive enough to use on a wider basis.

More breakthroughs. Several groups of scientists in 1989 reported major advances in pinpointing the location of other genes involved in diseases that affect large numbers of people.

On May 25, scientists reported locating a gene that makes some people highly susceptible to developing *malignant melanoma,* a rare but deadly form of skin cancer. Doctors long have suspected that a tendency for malignant melanoma and other, less serious forms of skin cancer is inherited. The discovery of a melanoma gene provided the strongest evidence yet that the disease is at least partly hereditary.

The researchers, with the National Cancer Institute in Bethesda, Md., the Massachusetts Institute of Technology in Cambridge, and the University of Pennsylvania in Philadelphia, tracked the gene in 99 members of six families with a high incidence of malignant melanoma. Estimates indicate that about 10 per cent of the 27,000 new cases of malignant melanoma diagnosed each year occur in such high-risk families.

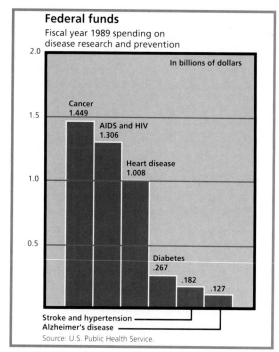

Federal funds

Fiscal year 1989 spending on disease research and prevention

In billions of dollars

Cancer
1.449

AIDS and HIV
1.306

Heart disease
1.008

Diabetes
.267

.182

.127

Stroke and hypertension
Alzheimer's disease

Source: U.S. Public Health Service.

Spending by the U.S. government for AIDS research and prevention exceeds the amount spent to fight heart disease and approaches spending for cancer.

long-term daily use of acetaminophen can increase the risk of developing kidney disease. Acetaminophen is a nonprescription pain medication that is widely used as a substitute for aspirin. It is the active ingredient in a number of popular products, including Tylenol, Anacin-3, Datril, and Panadol.

The study, conducted by researchers at the National Institute for Environmental Health Sciences in Research Triangle Park, N.C., found that people who took acetaminophen daily for at least one year tripled their risk of developing chronic kidney disease. Johnson & Johnson of New Brunswick, N.J., manufacturer of Tylenol, criticized the study and said that acetaminophen products are the safest medicines available for common aches and pains.

Cigarette risk. Smoking brands of cigarettes that are advertised as being lower in nicotine and carbon monoxide does not reduce a woman's risk of a heart attack, researchers reported in June. Their study, conducted at the Boston University School of Medicine, found that women who smoke so-called low-yield cigarettes run the same risk of heart attack as those who smoke regular brands. That risk is four times greater than it is for nonsmokers. Michael Woods

See also **AIDS; Biology; Drugs; Medicine; Public health. In** *World Book,* **see Cell; Cystic fibrosis; Health; Disease.**

Hobbies. See Coin Collecting; Stamp collecting; Toys and games.

Researchers from Houston and Dublin, Ireland, announced on July 17 that they had located a gene that causes one form of *retinitis pigmentosa.* Retinitis pigmentosa is a degenerative eye disease that affects about 100,000 people in the United States, causing gradual loss of vision. Researchers said the finding would make it possible to eventually isolate the gene and perhaps find new treatments for the disease.

Arthritis factor. On June 21, scientists at the National Institutes of Health in Bethesda reported the first biological evidence that a brain defect is involved in rheumatoid arthritis. This type of arthritis occurs when the tissue surrounding the joints becomes inflamed.

The researchers showed that laboratory rats bred to be susceptible to arthritis have a defect in a part of the brain called the *hypothalamus.* The defect affects the ability of the hypothalamus to produce and release a hormone that regulates the body's response to inflammation.

Scientists have long debated the possible factors involved in arthritis. According to Robert L. Wilder, a rheumatologist at the National Institute of Arthritis and Musculoskeletal and Skin Diseases in Bethesda, most physicians had believed that abnormalities inside the affected joint played the most important role in causing arthritis.

Kidney caution. A report in the May 11 issue of *The New England Journal of Medicine* concluded that

Hockey. The Calgary Flames, who achieved the best regular-season record in the National Hockey League (NHL) the previous season, did it again in the 1988-1989 season. This time, they also won the Stanley Cup.

The 21-team NHL had a successful season, with the average attendance rising 2.3 per cent to 14,908 per game. It was a memorable season for Wayne Gretzky and Mario Lemieux, the league's outstanding players. It was memorable, too, because for the first time, players from the Soviet Union joined NHL teams.

Play-offs. In the regular season, each of the 21 teams played 80 games. The division champions were Calgary with 117 points, the Montreal Canadiens with 115, the Washington Capitals with 92, and the Detroit Red Wings with 80. In the 16-team play-offs, Calgary and Montreal reached the final round, though Calgary needed a seventh-game overtime goal to survive its first-round series with the Vancouver Canucks.

In the championship series against Montreal, Calgary won the last three games and the title, four games to two. Al MacInnis of Calgary became the first defenseman to win the Conn Smythe Trophy as the Most Valuable Player in the play-offs.

Honors. After a headline-making trade in August 1988 from the Edmonton Oilers to the Los Angeles Kings, Gretzky played spectacularly for his new team and reawakened hockey interest in Los Angeles. Lemieux, the Pittsburgh Penguins' center, made the fastest scoring start in history with 41 points in the

Hockey

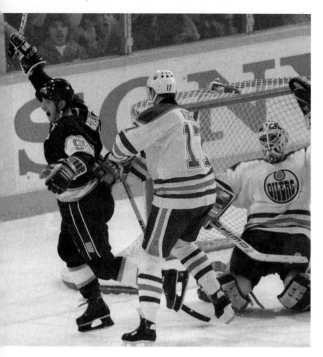

Hockey great Wayne Gretzky of the Los Angeles Kings scores his 1,851st career point, breaking the legendary Gordie Howe's record, in October.

first 12 games. He won the scoring title with 199 points to 168 for Gretzky, the runner-up.

Even so, in voting by writers, Gretzky won his ninth Hart Trophy as the league's Most Valuable Player. Lemieux was second in the voting. Gretzky, averaging $2.5 million a year, and Lemieux, at $2.4 million, were the NHL's highest-paid players ever.

Chris Chelios of Montreal was voted the Norris Trophy as the league's best defenseman, Patrick Roy of Montreal the Vezina Trophy as the best goaltender, Joe Mullen of Calgary the Lady Byng Trophy for sportsmanship, and defenseman Brian Leetch of the New York Rangers the Calder Trophy as the Rookie of the Year. The all-star team comprised Roy in goal, Paul Coffey of Pittsburgh and Chelios on defense, Lemieux at center, and Luc Robitaille of Los Angeles and Mullen on wing.

During and after the season, NHL teams signed Sergei Priakin, Sergei Makarov, Igor Larionov, Vyacheslav Fetisov, Sergei Starikov, Aleksandr Mogilny, and Sergei Mylnikov, all from the Soviet national team. All but Mogilny, who defected in May 1989, had the consent of their national federation.

World hockey. In the eight-nation competition held from April 15 to May 1 in Stockholm, Sweden, the Soviet Union won its 21st World Championship since 1954. Canada took the silver medal and Czechoslovakia the bronze.   Frank Litsky

In **World Book,** see **Hockey.**

National Hockey League standings

Clarence Campbell Conference

James Norris Division

	W.	L.	T.	Pts.
Detroit Red Wings	34	34	12	80
St. Louis Blues	33	35	12	78
Minnesota North Stars	27	37	16	70
Chicago Black Hawks	27	41	12	66
Toronto Maple Leafs	28	46	6	62

Conn Smythe Division

Calgary Flames	54	17	9	117
Los Angeles Kings	42	31	7	91
Edmonton Oilers	38	34	8	84
Vancouver Canucks	33	39	8	74
Winnipeg Jets	26	42	12	64

Prince of Wales Conference

Charles F. Adams Division

Montreal Canadiens	53	18	9	115
Boston Bruins	37	29	14	88
Buffalo Sabres	38	35	7	83
Hartford Whalers	37	38	5	79
Quebec Nordiques	27	46	7	61

Lester Patrick Division

Washington Capitals	41	29	10	92
Pittsburgh Penguins	40	33	7	87
New York Rangers	37	35	8	82
Philadelphia Flyers	36	36	8	80
New Jersey Devils	27	41	12	66
New York Islanders	28	47	5	61

Stanley Cup winner—
Calgary Flames (defeated Montreal Canadiens, 4 games to 2)

Scoring leaders	Games	Goals	Assists	Pts.
Mario Lemieux, Pittsburgh	76	85	114	199
Wayne Gretzky, Los Angeles	78	54	114	168
Steve Yzerman, Detroit	80	65	90	155
Bernie Nicholls, Los Angeles	79	70	80	150
Rob Brown, Pittsburgh	68	49	66	115
Paul Coffey, Pittsburgh	75	30	83	113
Joe Mullen, Calgary	79	51	59	110
Jari Kurri, Edmonton	76	44	58	102
Jimmy Carson, Edmonton	80	49	51	100
Luc Robitaille, Los Angeles	78	46	52	98
Dale Hawerchuk, Winnipeg	75	41	55	96
Dan Quinn, Pittsburgh	79	34	60	94
Mark Messier, Edmonton	72	33	61	94

Leading goalies (25 or more games)	Games	Goals against	Avg.
Patrick Roy, Montreal	48	113	2.47
Mike Vernon, Calgary	52	130	2.65
Pete Peeters, Washington	33	88	2.85
Brian Hayward, Montreal	36	101	2.90
Rick Wamsley, Calgary	35	95	2.96

Awards

Calder Trophy (best rookie)—Brian Leetch, New York Rangers
Hart Trophy (most valuable player)—Wayne Gretzky, Los Angeles
Lady Byng Trophy (sportsmanship)—Joe Mullen, Calgary
Masterton Trophy (perseverance, dedication to hockey)—Tim Kerr, Philadelphia
Norris Trophy (best defenseman)—Chris Chelios, Montreal
Ross Trophy (leading scorer)—Mario Lemieux, Pittsburgh
Selke Trophy (best defensive forward)—Guy Carbonneau, Montreal
Smythe Trophy (most valuable player in Stanley Cup)—Al MacInnis, Calgary
Vezina Trophy (most valuable goalie)—Patrick Roy, Montreal

Hoffman, Dustin (1937-   ), won the Academy of Motion Picture Arts and Sciences Award for best actor on March 29, 1989, for his portrayal of an autistic savant—a retarded person with unusual mental abilities—in *Rain Man*. The award was Hoffman's second Oscar; he was named best actor in 1980 for his 1979 performance in *Kramer vs. Kramer*. And on June 1, 1989, Hoffman made his Shakespearean debut as Shylock in *The Merchant of Venice* at a London theater. He took the role to Broadway in December.

Dustin Lee Hoffman was born on Aug. 8, 1937, in Los Angeles. He studied acting at the Pasadena Playhouse in California for two years. In 1958, he moved to New York City and became a stage actor.

He first gained national recognition for his third movie role, the disillusioned Benjamin in *The Graduate* (1967), which earned him the first of his six Academy Award nominations. Subsequent films—including *Midnight Cowboy* (1969), *Little Big Man* (1970), and *Marathon Man* (1976)—established him as a talented character actor. Hoffman is known for practicing "method" acting, in which an actor prepares for a role by undergoing experiences similar to those of the character to be portrayed. For *Tootsie* (1982), he tried impersonating a woman in real life in order to portray an actor who masquerades as an actress.

Hoffman married Lisa Gottsegan, his second wife, in 1980. He has four children.   Robin Goldman

In *World Book,* see **Hoffman, Dustin**.

Honduras. In presidential elections on Nov. 26, 1989, Rafael Leonardo Callejas of the opposition National Party defeated Carlos Flores of the ruling Liberal Party. Callejas was scheduled to take office for a four-year term on Jan. 27, 1990, the first time in 57 years that an opposition candidate would assume power in a peaceful transition.

In his victory statement, President-elect Callejas said Hondurans had given "a yes to peace and a no to blood." The statement was a reference to Callejas' campaign position that *contra* rebels fighting the Nicaraguan government should leave their bases in Honduras.

The issue of the contra bases loomed large in Honduras during 1989. On January 25, General Gustavo Álvarez Martínez, the former armed forces chief of staff, was assassinated. Álvarez Martínez was the Honduran officer who, in 1981, had given permission to the United States Central Intelligence Agency for the contras to operate from Honduran territory.

The election campaign also raised allegations of profiteering by high-ranking Honduran officers involved in drug trafficking and the resale of equipment and supplies from the United States. Officials of the United States Embassy acknowledged that some Honduran officers were involved in the illicit narcotics trade.   Nathan A. Haverstock

See also **Latin America** (Facts in brief table). In *World Book,* see **Honduras**.

Horse racing. A yearlong rivalry between Sunday Silence and Easy Goer, two 3-year-old colts, highlighted the thoroughbred racing year. The outstanding harness horses were Matt's Scooter, a 4-year-old pacer, and Peace Corps, a 3-year-old filly trotter.

Thoroughbred. In 1978, Affirmed, out of the West, won all three Triple Crown races, and Alydar finished second. In 1989, a similar rivalry involved Sunday Silence from California and Easy Goer, a son of Alydar, from New York. Sunday Silence won two of the three races, plus the $3-million Breeders' Cup Classic on November 4 in Hallandale, Fla.

As a youngster, Sunday Silence overcame a near-fatal bout with colic, and later was shaken up in an accident when the driver of his van suffered a heart attack and the van overturned. Sunday Silence was twice offered at auction and withdrawn after little interest was shown.

In 1989's first two Triple Crown races, Sunday Silence defeated Easy Goer by 2½ lengths in the Kentucky Derby on May 6 in Louisville, Ky., and by a nose after a stirring stretch duel in the Preakness on May 20 in Baltimore. But Easy Goer routed Sunday Silence by eight lengths in the Belmont Stakes on June 10 in Elmont, N.Y.

Easy Goer then won the Whitney Handicap, the Travers Stakes, the Woodward Cup, and the $1-million Jockey Club Gold Cup, but in the Breeders' Cup Classic, Sunday Silence held him off by a neck. In that race,

Major horse races of 1989

Race	Winner	Value to winner
Arlington Million	Steinlen	$600,000
Belmont Stakes	Easy Goer	$413,520
Breeders' Cup Classic	Sunday Silence	$1,350,000
Breeders' Cup Distaff	Bayakoa	$450,000
Breeders' Cup Juvenile	Rhythm	$450,000
Breeders' Cup Juvenile Fillies	Go for Wand	$450,000
Breeders' Cup Mile	Steinlen	$450,000
Breeders' Cup Sprint	Dancing Spree	$450,000
Breeders' Cup Turf	Prized	$900,000
Budweiser International Handicap	Caltech	$450,000
Budweiser Irish Derby (Ireland)	Old Vic	$556,421
Cartier Million (Ireland)	The Caretaker	$743,918
Derby (England)	Nashwan	$593,608
Japan Cup (Japan)	Horlicks	$956,000
Jockey Club Gold Cup Stakes	Easy Goer	$659,400
Kentucky Derby	Sunday Silence	$574,200
Melbourne Cup (Australia)	Tawrrific	$898,492
Molson Export Challenge (Canada)	Prized	$600,000
Pimlico Special	Blushing John	$420,000
Preakness Stakes	Sunday Silence	$438,230
Prix de l'Arc de Triomphe (France)	Carroll House	$828,000
Rothmans International Handicap (Canada)	Hodges Bay	$575,400
Santa Anita Handicap	Martial Law	$550,275
Super Derby	Sunday Silence	$600,000
Travers Stakes	Easy Goer	$653,100
Woodward Handicap	Easy Goer	$485,400

Major U.S. harness races of 1989

Race	Winner	Value to winner
Cane Pace	Dancing Master	$186,363
Hambletonian	Park Avenue Joe*	565,500
Little Brown Jug	Goalie Jeff	151,310
Meadowlands Pace	Dexter Nukes	426,000
Messenger Stakes	Sandman Hanover	192,455
Woodrow Wilson	Sam Francisco Ben	453,500

*Tentative winner. Park Avenue Joe finished in a dead heat with Probe.
Sources: *The Blood-Horse* magazine and United States Trotting Association.

The rebuilt Arlington International Racecourse in Arlington Heights, Ill., opened in June to acclaim for its elegance and many amenities.

Sunday Silence was ridden by Chris McCarron because his regular jockey, Pat Valenzuela, had been suspended after a positive test for cocaine.

Ten days after the Classic, a bone chip was found in Sunday Silence's right knee. He underwent surgery, and Charlie Whittingham, his 76-year-old trainer, said the colt would not race again until the spring of 1990. Easy Goer's handlers said he would also race in 1990.

Among the Breeders' Cup winners were Bayakoa among fillies and mares, Steinlen among sprinters, and Prized among turf horses. Overseas, Nashwan won England's four leading races—the 2,000 Guineas, the Derby, the Eclipse, and the King George VI and Queen Elizabeth Stakes.

Standardbred. Matt's Scooter ended his racing career as the fastest harness horse ever and the second richest, his career earnings of $2,944,591 trailing only Nihilator's $3,225,653. In 61 races over three years, Matt's Scooter recorded 37 victories.

Many harness racing people regarded Peace Corps as the best trotting filly in history. In 1989, she defeated males in the World Trotting Derby, Kentucky Futurity, and season-ending Breeders' Crown. In a three-week span in September, she set a world mile record for filly trotters over a 1-mile track (1 minute 52⅘ seconds) and tied Mack Lobell's world mile record for trotters over a half-mile track (1 minute 56 seconds).   Frank Litsky

In *World Book,* see **Harness racing; Horse racing.**

Hospital. A study by the American Hospital Association (AHA) warned on May 3, 1989, that serious personnel shortages threaten the public's access to hospital care in the United States. The AHA, based in Chicago, said the shortages have forced 25 per cent of American hospitals to cut services. More than 15 per cent have closed *units* (groups of beds occupied by patients with the same disease, such as a coronary care unit), and 13 per cent have been forced to transfer patients to more adequately staffed hospitals.

Shortages are most critical for physical and occupational therapists, the study noted. About 15 per cent of hospital jobs for these workers are unfilled. About 10 per cent of hospital jobs for certified nurse anesthetists are also unfilled. (Nurse anesthetists administer painkilling drugs during surgery.)

Closed down. On September 13, Pentecostal evangelist Oral Roberts announced plans to close his City of Faith Hospital and Medical School in Tulsa, Okla. Roberts said the closing was necessary because of difficulty in raising funds. The hospital was slated to close by Jan. 1, 1990, the medical school in May 1990.

Medical waste. Most U.S. hospitals properly dispose of infectious medical waste, researchers reported September 21 in *The Journal of the American Medical Association.* The study, by William A. Rutala at the University of North Carolina School of Medicine in Chapel Hill, examined waste disposal practices at 441 hospitals in 48 states. It found that 82 per cent of the hospitals use procedures recommended by the U.S. Centers for Disease Control in Atlanta, Ga. According to the study, infectious waste accounts for about 15 per cent of the 6,000 short tons (5,400 metric tons) of waste generated in American hospitals each day.

Health-care overhaul. The government of Great Britain on January 31 proposed the most far-reaching changes in the 40-year history of its National Health Service (NHS). The NHS provides free medical care to all people in Britain.

The plan would permit more than 300 of the biggest and most sophisticated state-operated hospitals to leave the NHS and operate as independent institutions. The independent hospitals would be allowed to sell their services directly to local health authorities, employers, doctors, and other private groups.

Strikes in Canada. On June 14, nurses in British Columbia struck over a wage dispute. The strike affected 80 of the 144 hospitals in the province. The nurses rejected a tentative settlement on June 28. On August 18, a mediator granted the nurses a two-year contract with a wage hike of almost 21 per cent.

Hospital care in Quebec was curtailed on September 5, when about 40,000 nurses at 400 hospitals went on strike. The strike ended on September 13 when the nurses accepted a new contract providing for an 11 per cent pay increase.   Michael Woods

In *World Book,* see **Hospital.**

Housing. See **Building and construction.**

Houston. The economy of Houston showed signs of growth in 1989, continuing an upturn that began in 1988. The unemployment rate fell to 5.5 per cent in September 1989, the lowest since 1982. Construction of new homes and sales of existing homes rose during the year.

Probably the most significant evidence of the city's improving economy occurred on July 12 when the City Council approved a $1.4-billion budget. For the first time in three years, the budget did not require a tax increase or cuts in city services.

Government. On November 7, Kathryn J. Whitmire was reelected mayor for a fifth term. Whitmire captured 63 per cent of the vote to beat Fred Hofheinz, who had been mayor from 1975 to 1979.

On August 7, U.S. Representative Mickey Leland, a Democrat from Houston, died in a plane crash during a tour of refugee camps in Ethiopia. His death triggered a special election for his seat in the 18th Congressional District on December 9. In the election, a contest between two Democrats, State Senator Craig A. Washington beat City Councilman Anthony W. Hall.

Two city officials found themselves in trouble over racial remarks in 1989. On April 12, Don S. Vaughn, head of the Greater Houston Convention and Visitors Bureau, told State Representative Steve Wolens that he hoped minority members of the City Council would not review the bureau's budget because he did not believe they could understand it. Several minority

Boats in Clear Lake near Houston are ablaze with light on the night of July 20 to celebrate the 20th anniversary of the first moon landing.

groups protested the remark, and Vaughn resigned on May 23.

On October 18, during a discussion on whether to rename Houston Intercontinental Airport in honor of Congressman Leland, City Councilman James H. Westmoreland made a racial joke to a reporter. The remark was published in the local papers just weeks before a City Council election. The remark hurt Westmoreland's standing with voters, and on November 7, he was beaten by political newcomer Beverley Clark.

Law enforcement. Controversy arose during the year over the actions of Houston police officers. On July 28, James Cebula, a former officer, was convicted of kidnapping and raping a woman while on duty in 1988. Cebula's file contained 16 prior complaints from citizens. An investigation by *The Houston Post* found at least 28 other active-duty police officers who also had a high number of citizen complaints in their files.

A number of similar incidents occurred in 1989. On October 31, three off-duty police officers driving an unmarked car followed a woman they said cut them off in traffic. When the woman fired a gun at the car, the officers fired back. During the gunfire, the woman was killed and an officer was wounded. On November 15, a police officer killed a security guard during an apparent routine traffic stop. In November and December, three officers were arrested on drug charges.

In response to citizen protests, Police Chief Lee P. Brown noted that a state-mandated arbitration process had returned to the force two-thirds of the officers fired during the past three years. On November 29, the City Council voted to ask the state legislature to remove the arbitration process. On December 18, it was announced that Brown would become police commissioner of New York City in January 1990.

Summit. On December 1, the White House announced that Houston would host the 1990 economic summit. The summit is an annual event that brings together leaders of the major industrialized nations.

Transit. On Aug. 30, 1989, Robert C. Lanier said he would resign as chairman of the Metropolitan Transit Authority (MTA) because he thought it unwise to build a $1-billion rail system for the city. Houston voters had endorsed such a plan in 1988. Business leaders persuaded Lanier to stay on.

On November 20, the MTA's board of directors voted against the rail system. Two days later, Alan F. Kiepper, MTA's general manager and a supporter of the rail system plan, resigned at Lanier's request. On December 11, Lanier resigned again, this time over differences with the mayor on rail proposals from private industry. On Jan. 8, 1990, Kiepper was named president of the New York City Transit Authority.

Education. On July 7, 1989, Houston Independent School District trustees approved a $718-million budget. The budget required a 12 per cent hike in the district's property tax rate, which the trustees approved on November 14.   Charles Reinken

See also **City.** In *World Book,* see **Houston.**

Hungary startled the world in 1989, becoming the first nation in the Soviet bloc to renounce Communism. Hungary also allowed tens of thousands of citizens of another Soviet-bloc state—East Germany—to flee over its soil to the West during the year. Despite these astonishing developments, however, Hungary said it would remain in the Warsaw Pact, the bloc's military alliance—but added that it would support a future agreement to dismantle both the Warsaw Pact and its Western counterpart, the North Atlantic Treaty Organization (NATO).

Hungary entered a new political era on October 7, when the Hungarian Socialist Workers' Party (HSWP), the nation's Communist party, renamed itself the Hungarian Socialist Party. The HSWP had ruled Hungary since the late 1940's. A party congress, meeting from Oct. 6 to 9, 1989, renounced the old party's "crimes, errors, and faulty ideology" and declared that the new party would follow the pattern of traditional Western European and Scandinavian Socialist and Social Democrat parties.

The congress also declared that the new party would replace the single-party state with a multiparty democracy and build a mixed "social market economy" open to all forms of ownership and private enterprise. Hungary's National Assembly on October 18 amended the Constitution to delete the HSWP's "leading role," to change the name of the country from the Hungarian People's Republic to the Republic of Hungary, and to pave the way for open, multiparty elections in early 1990.

Nyers leads new party. The party congress voted at its October 1989 meeting to abolish the former Central Committee, which handled party affairs between congresses. Instead, the party is to be guided by a national committee of about 150 members and by a 24-member Presidium.

Elected president of the new party was Rezso Nyers, a Socialist until the forced merger of his party with the Communist party in 1947. Nyers was a leading author of a reformist plan in 1967. Global recession and antireformist pressure from Moscow during the 1970's had forced him to retire. But in May 1988, Nyers—though already 66—reemerged in a younger, reform-minded leadership. In June 1989, he had become chairman of a four-member collective presidency of the HSWP.

New party loses referendum. On November 26, in the country's first free election since World War II (1939-1945), opposition groups defeated the Hungarian Socialist Party. The Socialists had wanted to hold a presidential election in January 1990, but opponents said this would not give them time to organize. In a *referendum* (direct vote on a question), 50.1 per cent of the voters approved of electing the president after parliamentary elections take place. A new National Assembly is to be chosen by June 1990.

Border opened, Germans flee. On May 2, 1989, Hungary had begun to tear down a barbed-wire fence

Hungary on May 2 becomes the first Communist nation to open a border with the West as guards tear down part of the Iron Curtain between Hungary and Austria.

along its border with Austria, its neutral neighbor to the west. On September 10, Hungary granted permission to East Germans on Hungarian soil to cross the border to Austria without the approval of East Germany. From September 11 to 14, more than 13,000 East Germans traveled from Hungary to Austria on their way to West Germany.

Troop cuts. The Soviet Union began to withdraw troops from Hungary in 1989 in line with Soviet leader Mikhail S. Gorbachev's December 1988 announcement that 50,000 soldiers would be pulled out of Eastern Europe within two years. In September 1989, Hungary disclosed that it had begun its own troop reductions.

Economy. Hungary planned to shift to a free-market economy and over the next three years to inject into the economy $1.5 billion in working capital to boost the country's technological base. The goal of the investment would be to make Hungary's exports competitive in world markets. Hungary also planned to sell off state-owned business enterprises to domestic or foreign private owners and to allow agricultural land to be sold to individual, independent farmers.

Church and state. On June 15, Hungary dissolved the State Office for Church Affairs, through which the Communist regime had controlled religious activity since 1951. Hungary thus became the first Communist state to terminate such an office.   Eric Bourne

See also **Europe** (Facts in brief table). In *World Book*, see **Hungary**.

Ice skating. New rules governing figure skating began to take effect in 1989 and helped Kurt Browning of Edmonton, Canada, and Midori Ito of Japan win the world championships. The interim rules from the International Skating Union reduced the value of the compulsory figures—designs based on the figure eight that skaters must trace on the ice—to 20 per cent from 30 per cent of a skater's score. In July 1990, the compulsory figures will be abolished. The change was designed to make the sport more attractive for the public. It particularly rewarded jumping ability, and Browning and Ito were superb jumpers.

The championships, involving 135 skaters in four events, were held from March 14 to 18, 1989, in Paris. The winners were new because such past champions as Brian Boitano, Brian Orser, Katarina Witt, and Debi Thomas had retired from amateur competition.

Browning completed two triple-axel jumps in his original program and a slightly flawed quadruple toe loop and six triple jumps in his free-skating program. Ito made seven triple jumps, including the first triple axel in a major women's international meet.

Soviet couples won the pairs title with Ekaterina Gordeeva and Sergei Grinkov and the ice dancing with Marina Klimova and Sergei Ponomarenko. The only American medalists were Christopher Bowman of Van Nuys, Calif., who won the silver in men's singles, and Jill Trenary of Colorado Springs, Colo., who took the bronze in women's singles.

Midori Ito of Japan wins the world figure skating championship in March in Paris with an agile and vigorous free-skating program.

Seventeen-year-old Kristi Yamaguchi of Fremont, Calif., became the first American woman since 1954 to qualify for both the women's singles and the pairs. She finished sixth in singles and—with Rudi Galindo of San Jose—fifth in pairs.

In the United States championships held from Feb. 7 to 12, 1989, in Baltimore, the winners were Bowman and Trenary in singles, Yamaguchi and Galindo in pairs, and Susan Wynne of Camillus, N.Y., and Joseph Druar of Amherst, N.Y., in ice dancing.

Speed skating. Bonnie Blair of Champaign, Ill., won a world championship and Eric Flaim of Pembroke, Mass., lost one. In the world sprint championships held on February 25 and 26 in Heerenveen, the Netherlands, the winners were Blair and Igor Zhelezovsky of the Soviet Union.

Leo Visser of the Netherlands won the world overall title for men in events held on February 11 and 12 in Oslo, Norway, and Constanze Moser of East Germany won the women's title in events held on February 4 and 5 in Lake Placid, N.Y. Flaim, the 1988 men's champion, finished fourth this time. Dan Jansen of West Allis, Wis., placed fourth in the men's sprints, and Mary Docter of Madison, Wis., placed fourth in the women's overall.   Frank Litsky

In *World Book,* see **Ice skating.**
Iceland. See **Europe.**
Idaho. See **State government.**
Illinois. See **Chicago; State government.**

Immigration. The 1986 Immigration Reform and Control Act, which aimed at curbing illegal immigration, has succeeded in reducing the flow of illegal immigrants into the United States, according to a study released on July 20, 1989, by the Urban Institute. The nonpartisan private research group said that border patrols operated by the U.S. Immigration and Naturalization Service (INS) arrested 1.3 million illegal immigrants, most from Mexico, in a two-year period ending in September 1988. That figure is 700,000 fewer than would have been found crossing if the 1986 law had not been enacted, according to a computer model that accounted for such factors as Mexican population growth and economic conditions.

The Urban Institute attributed 71 per cent of the decline in border arrests to a provision of the law that placed civil and criminal penalties on U.S. businesses that hire illegal immigrants. The INS initially issued warnings for first offenses but stepped up enforcement ih June 1988. Between then and February 1989, more than 1,200 employers—mostly small businesses—were fined a total of almost $4 million.

Visa lottery. On Feb. 9, 1989, the U.S. Department of State announced that 10,000 extra visas would be issued in both 1989 and 1990 to immigrants from 162 countries—most of them in Europe, Africa, and South America—deemed underrepresented in the usual immigration flow. People from those countries, including aliens living in the United States illegally, were eligible to apply for permanent residency through a special lottery designed to increase geographical diversity within the immigrant pool. Winners of visas would be chosen randomly by computer.

INS audit. On March 3, 1989, *The Washington* (D.C.) *Post* reported that a special Justice Department audit conducted for U.S. Attorney General Richard L. Thornburgh found the INS overwhelmed by sloppy accounting, poor management procedures, and the demands of recent legislation expanding its responsibilities. In eight years, the INS had added 6,000 employees to its payroll while its budget increased by $650 million.

Proposed overhaul. On July 13, the Senate passed an immigration overhaul bill designed to increase immigration by skilled and educated workers, mostly Europeans, who lack close family connections in the United States. Such connections, under present law, favor Latin-American and Asian immigrants.

The bill would set an initial annual immigration ceiling of 630,000, an increase of 136,000. Of the total, 150,000 slots would be reserved for immigrants who have no family connections but who do have skills, education, or other job-related assets. The Senate passed a similar bill in 1988, but it died in the House of Representatives Judiciary Committee. Prospects for House action on the new measure in 1990 were uncertain.   Frank Cormier and Margot Cormier

In *World Book,* see **Immigration.**
Income tax. See **Taxation.**

India held parliamentary elections from Nov. 22 to 26, 1989, and, in general, voters turned against those in office. The election was marked by charges of fraud and by violence in which at least 120 people died. Southern states that were governed by local parties voted overwhelmingly for Prime Minister Rajiv Gandhi's Congress-I Party, but Congress was rejected in the north, its traditional stronghold. Preliminary election results showed that Congress won only 192 of the 525 seats in Parliament's lower house, and, after five years in office, Gandhi resigned on November 29.

Vishwanath Pratap Singh — usually known as V. P. Singh — was sworn in on December 2 as the new prime minister. Singh headed the National Front coalition and was supported by India's two Communist parties and the Hindu conservative Bharatiya Janata Party. Singh, the 58-year-old son of a minor Indian prince, was a former Congress Party minister of commerce, finance, and defense. As finance minister, Singh was credited with having liberalized the economy, leading to India's recent prosperity. Gandhi fired Singh from the Cabinet in 1987, reportedly to keep him from exposing government corruption. During his campaign, Singh accused the Congress government of dishonesty and inefficiency.

The November election defeat capped a year of setbacks for Gandhi and his party. The Congress Party suffered in state elections on January 21 in a southern state, Tamil Nadu. Although Congress won elections at the same time in two small eastern states, Mizoram and Nagaland, the party was left in control of fewer than half of India's politically important states.

Arms scandal. At the heart of the Congress Party's trouble was the Indian army's 1986 purchase of 400 155-millimeter artillery pieces from a Swedish firm, Bofors AB, for $1.4 billion. Sweden's audit office confirmed in 1987 that at least $38 million had been paid in illegal kickbacks, and most people believed that the money had gone to Congress Party officials. India's auditor general reported in March 1989 that "grave irregularities" had occurred. Gandhi tried to suppress the report, and when it became public in July he refused to answer questions about it.

In protest, opposition leaders on July 23 announced the resignation of more than 100 members of the lower house of Parliament, who quit in an unusual show of unity. A loose opposition coalition protesting corruption backed a demand for Gandhi's resignation with a nationwide general strike on August 30. The strike closed businesses and halted transportation, leading to fighting between political factions in which at least 11 people died. Gandhi refused to yield.

General Krishnaswami Sundarji, army chief of staff when the Bofors purchase was made, said in September that he had advised the government to threaten Bofors with cancellation of the contract if the company did not reveal who received the kickbacks but that Gandhi had ignored his advice. This contradicted Gandhi's assertion that he had considered canceling

Victims of a 1984 poison-gas accident in Bhopal protest India's acceptance of a $470-million settlement from Union Carbide in February.

the contract but was opposed by the army. Gandhi's office denied he had blocked an investigation.

Separatist violence took more than 350 lives during 1989 in the northeastern state of Assam. The state had been torn by agitation by ethnic Assamese from 1979 to 1985 against the influx of outside settlers, mostly Muslims from Bangladesh. Their protests were opposed by the Bodo, an ethnic group of about 2 million people. After the Assam People's Party won power in 1986, the Bodo, charging that their interests were ignored, began demanding a separate state. A general strike from Feb. 17 to 21, 1989, led to violence, with Bodo militants using guns, bows and arrows, and homemade bombs. Leaders of the All Bodo Students Union, state officials, and national officials signed a truce on August 28. But Bodo militants refused to accept the agreement, and, within weeks, 70 more people died in separatist violence.

In Punjab — where an effort by militants in the Sikh religious community to win a separate Sikh nation had caused years of bloodshed — more than 900 people died in 1989. Gandhi made proposals on March 3 intended to calm the situation and open the way for compromise. But militants attacked police posts and ambushed paramilitary forces while posting warnings that those who opposed them would die.

In the Indian part of Kashmir, terrorism that began in 1987 increased during 1989. Kashmir, a mountainous area in the north, was divided between India and

India

Pakistan in 1947; since then, the two nations have disputed ownership of the area. Some small groups employing terrorist tactics in Kashmir sought independence. Others wanted all of Kashmir to become part of Pakistan. Indian officials accused Pakistan of training these terrorists.

Bhopal settlement. After lengthy litigation, India's attorney general accepted on February 14 a final settlement for one of the world's worst industrial accidents. More than 2,100 people died in the immediate aftermath of the accident in December 1984, when a cloud of poison gas escaped from a factory in Bhopal. The government estimates that the death toll has since risen to 3,300, with thousands more crippled. The factory was owned by a subsidiary of a United States firm, Union Carbide Corporation. India's Supreme Court suggested that Union Carbide pay $470-million in compensation, and the company agreed. Indian media and voluntary social organizations claimed that the amount was inadequate.

India's weather in 1989 was generally favorable. Although the annual monsoon rains killed more than 600 people in storms and floods in only two days in July, the flooding was not as severe as in 1988. Good harvests helped the economy grow by about 6 per cent. Foreign investment increased, but India's trade deficits remained worrisome.   Henry S. Bradsher

See also **Asia** (Facts in brief table). In *World Book,* see **India.**

Indian, American. American Indian leaders and officials of two leading archaeological collections settled long-standing disputes in 1989 over the skeletal remains of early Native Americans. Museums and universities regard these remains as scientific and historical treasures. Many Indians, however, are offended by the storage and display of their ancestors' bones and argue that whites would not permit such treatment of their own forebears' remains.

In June 1989, officials at Stanford University in California agreed to return the remains of about 525 Indians for reburial by the small Ohlone-Costanoan tribe of California. Some anthropologists criticized the decision as a setback for research. But Indian leaders hailed the move—the first of its kind by a major research institution—as long overdue.

On September 12, Indian leaders signed an agreement with the Smithsonian Institution in Washington, D.C., whose collection of 18,600 Indian bones is the largest in the United States. Smithsonian officials agreed to return, on request, any remains that can be associated with specific tribes. The Indians agreed not to seek return of remains whose origins are unknown.

Indian museum. After years of debate, the Museum of the American Indian, currently located in a deteriorating neighborhood in New York City, agreed in January to transfer its $1-million collection of Native American art and artifacts to the Smithsonian. The Smithsonian will build a new National Museum of

Indians and archaeologists dig a grave near Wounded Knee, S. Dak., in August for prehistoric Indian remains unearthed at a Florida construction site.

the American Indian in Washington, D.C., and will also establish a smaller facility in New York City to display part of the collection.

Navajo leader under fire. Also in January, the U.S. Senate Select Committee on Indian Affairs, investigating corruption in federal programs for Indians, heard testimony on complaints that Navajo tribal chairman Peter MacDonald had accepted bribes on construction contracts and land purchases.

On Feb. 17, 1989, the Navajo Tribal Council, based in Window Rock, Ariz., voted to place MacDonald on paid leave from his duties. MacDonald fought the suspension, and his supporters pressed for his reinstatement. On July 20, 300 supporters turned out in Window Rock for a pro-MacDonald demonstration. The rally turned into a riot, and two men were killed and nine people injured when tribal police opened fire. The police said they shot in self-defense.

In October, the tribe filed complaints in Navajo District Court in Window Rock, charging MacDonald with 107 counts of bribery, fraud, conspiracy, and elections violations. On November 29, MacDonald, who was also still under investigation by a federal grand jury, pleaded not guilty to the tribal court charges.

Casino raids. Since late 1987, some Mohawk Indians have operated gambling casinos on the Akwesasne reservation, which straddles the U.S.–Canada border on the St. Lawrence River. Casino gambling is illegal in both countries, but the Mohawk operators claim independence from those laws. On July 20, 1989, New York State Police troopers and agents from the Federal Bureau of Investigation raided the casinos, arresting 10 people and seizing cash, equipment, and records. In the following months, disputes among Indians—many of whom oppose the casinos—led to more violence, including the burning of one casino.

A judicial inquiry in the Canadian province of Manitoba looked into allegations that Native Americans were being treated unfairly by the justice system. In September 1988, Manitoba province appointed two judges—one white and one Indian—to examine several incidents. One was the March 1988 shooting of an Indian leader by a Winnipeg police constable; testimony in 1989 suggested that police altered accounts of the shooting to shift blame from police. The judges also probed why it took police 14 years to file charges in the 1971 murder of a Cree girl in The Pas, even though many residents of the area knew who her killers were.

The Lubicon Lake Indians, who late in 1988 reached a land-claim agreement with the province of Alberta, failed to settle terms at the federal level early in 1989. In August, the Canadian government further angered the Lubicons by granting official band status to an Indian group that included some Lubicon members. The Lubicons complained that the government was promoting disunity.   Rudy Platiel

In *World Book,* see **Indian, American.**

Indiana. See **State government.**

Indonesia. President Suharto maintained a firm grip on political power during 1989 while alternately stimulating and discouraging speculation about the presidential succession. Suharto, who has led Indonesia with almost no challenge since 1966, began a new five-year term as president in 1988 and will be 72 years old when it ends. In January 1989, several senior officials began talking publicly about the succession process and prospects for political change.

In April, Suharto, normally reluctant to talk about himself, published a 600-page autobiography. The book upset some officials by revealing that the government was behind the killing of about 10,000 people in a crackdown on crime in 1983. At the time, the government blamed the deaths on gang feuds.

Suharto instructed officials and the press on June 5, 1989, to quit speculating about the succession. But Suharto himself stimulated speculation by suggesting in September that he felt under some pressure from the army and possibly other forces and believed he could be replaced by constitutional means.

Military authorities said that on February 7 the army attacked the Sumatra hideout of a Muslim extremist group that had attacked police posts. They said that 27 people were killed in the attack. Although 85 per cent of Indonesia's people are Muslim, the government had tried to keep religion out of politics, and the report raised the specter of renewed religious violence. Officals later changed their story about

During an October visit to Indonesia, Pope John Paul II blesses Javanese dancers in the city of Yogyakarta.

the attack, saying that the army had intervened in a land dispute, and some 100 people were killed. It was the army's worst clash with civilians in five years.

On August 1, the army made a rare admission that it was fighting a separatist movement in Irian Jaya, New Guinea Island's western half, which belongs to Indonesia. Army officials claimed to have captured a leader of the separatist movement. At the same time, the army confirmed that an independence movement had been active in the Moluccas, a group of islands in eastern Indonesia.

Foreign relations. While visiting Tokyo on February 23, Suharto met China's Foreign Minister Qian Qichen to begin restoring relations with China. In September, Suharto became the first Indonesian president to visit Moscow in 25 years, which helped warm Indonesia's frosty relations with the Soviet Union. Indonesia hoped for more trade with both nations.

Economic progress remained slow but steady in 1989, as efforts to diversify the Indonesian economy— once driven by oil and gas exportation—showed success. Exports of wood products, coffee, rubber, and shrimp increased during the year. Indonesia remained dependent on foreign aid, however. Suharto warned domestic pressure groups on August 12 to quit trying to get foreign-aid donors to tie foreign aid to human-rights improvements.   Henry S. Bradsher

See also **Asia** (Facts in brief). In *World Book,* see **Indonesia.**

International trade continued to be vigorous in 1989, rising by about 7 per cent—somewhat slower than the 9 per cent rate of 1988. United States export volume expanded by more than 10 per cent. This was substantially less, however, than the 20 per cent rate of 1988's export "boom."

Trade imbalances. Little progress was made in reducing the massive U.S. trade and payment deficits and the Japanese and West German surpluses, despite warnings that the imbalances might eventually trigger a world recession. The U.S. merchandise trade deficit, though less than in 1988, remained over $100 billion, partly reflecting two factors—a surprisingly strong U.S. dollar and higher prices (and U.S. demand) for oil. By September, the dollar's strength so concerned monetary authorities in the seven largest industrial democracies that they agreed to sell dollars in foreign exchange markets to lower the dollar's value. "A rise in the dollar above current levels could adversely affect prospects for the world economy," the finance ministers of Canada, France, Great Britain, Italy, Japan, West Germany, and the United States announced on Sept. 23, 1989. Their intervention in exchange markets caused a moderate decline in the dollar.

Also of concern was a new deficit in the U.S. services trade, largely because of rising foreign investment in the United States. Much of the services trade includes profit and other remittances foreign investors send back to their home countries. These payments rose

sharply in 1989. By year's end, U.S. foreign debt exceeded $600 billion, by far the biggest debt of any country in history.

Foreign debt remained a major problem in 1989 for many less-developed nations also, especially in Latin America and Africa. Overall, the developing countries' debt rose slightly even though commercial banks reduced their exposure in some debtor countries. By year's end, the debt was about $1.3 trillion.

On March 10, U.S. Treasury Secretary Nicholas F. Brady, in an attempt to ease the debt problem for many developing countries, proposed that the resources of the International Monetary Fund (IMF) and the World Bank—two United Nations agencies—be used for debt reduction. The two agencies, he suggested, should provide collateral for bonds that debtor nations would issue in exchange for their outstanding commercial bank borrowings. The exchange would have the effect of reducing both the principal and the interest owed by debtor nations. In addition, debtor countries could use IMF and World Bank loans to buy back their bank debts at substantial discounts. The IMF and the World Bank, the U.S. Treasury suggested, should each provide $10 billion over the next three years for debt reduction.

Both the IMF and the World Bank approved the Brady proposal by June, and in July the agencies made large loans to Mexico and Venezuela, partly for debt reduction. The IMF also announced similar loans to the Philippines and Costa Rica. Broadening the prospect of debt reduction, Japan said it would provide up to $10 billion over three years to supplement IMF and World Bank assistance.

On July 23, the Mexican government reached an agreement in principle with its commercial creditor banks to reduce its debt by as much as $12 billion by 1992 and to lower its debt interest payments by $1.5-billion a year. The banks, Mexico hoped, also would provide about $2.4 billion in new loans over three years. The Philippines and Costa Rica negotiated other preliminary debt reduction agreements with creditor banks. But by year-end, none of the agreements had been implemented. And the Mexican accord faced a serious problem: banks' reluctance to lend more money. Many economic analysts and bankers said the Brady plan was unlikely to have much impact on the developing countries' debt burden.

In another effort to help the developing nations, Michel Camdessus, the IMF's managing director, urged doubling the IMF's lending resources to $240 billion. The United States, the IMF's largest member, resisted, arguing that the IMF's resources need not be expanded by more than 35 per cent.

The United States, however, agreed to support a World Bank proposal to bolster by $15 billion the resources of the International Development Association, a World Bank affiliate that is the single largest source of low-cost financing for the world's poorest countries. The United States, along with 43 other nations, also agreed to contribute to a $26.4-billion increase in the Inter-American Development Bank's funds, which is expected to double lending to Latin America.

Trade agreements. The United States and more than 90 other nations made further progress toward negotiating a series of trade liberalizing agreements, scheduled to be settled by December 1990. In April 1989, at the General Agreement on Tariffs and Trade talks in Geneva, Switzerland, ministers from the 96 member countries outlined goals for 15 proposed pacts on such topics as patents, agriculture, and trade in insurance, engineering, and other services.

In May, however, the United States upset three of its trading partners—Japan, Brazil, and India—when President George Bush told them that he might retaliate if they did not open their markets wider to U.S. companies. Bush cited Japan's import curbs on forestry products, supercomputers, and satellites; Brazil's import licensing restrictions; and India's foreign investment rules. The President's threat brought no immediate concession from any of the three countries. In response to another U.S. threat of trade reprisals, however, Japan agreed in June to facilitate the sale in Japan of U.S. cellular mobile telephones and two-way radios.

The United States also launched in September an effort to persuade Japan to undertake basic economic reforms that would encourage the sale of U.S. products in Japan. Among the U.S. goals was that Japan modernize its distribution system and toughen its antitrust enforcement. Japanese Prime Minister Toshiki Kaifu said on September 1 that he expected the U.S.-Japan talks to "bear significant fruit," but little progress had been made by the end of 1989.

In October, President Bush and Mexican President Carlos Salinas de Gortari agreed to try to expand U.S.-Mexican trade in textiles, steel, and other products as a step toward an eventual free-trade arrangement.

On July 25, Bush announced he would end U.S. steel import controls by March 1992. The United States subsequently obtained commitments from the 12-nation European Community and six other countries to liberalize their steel-trade policies.

To help advance East European political and economic reform, the U.S. Congress on November 18 authorized the extension of duty-free treatment to Poland on many of its exports. On November 3, President Bush proclaimed permanent "most favored nation" trade treatment for Hungary, which assures Hungarian exporters of the same low tariffs most other nations obtain in the United States. The United States government also said it would insure U.S. investors in Poland and Hungary against political risk. In addition, Congress on November 18 approved a $938-million aid package for the two countries, largely to foster private enterprise.   Richard Lawrence

See also **Economics.** In *World Book,* see **International trade.**

Iowa. See **State government.**

Iran, in February 1989, marked the 10th anniversary of the overthrow of Shah Mohammad Reza Pahlavi and the establishment of an Islamic republic. But the euphoria of the occasion turned to grief in June with the death of the republic's founder and supreme spiritual guide, Ayatollah Ruhollah Khomeini. Khomeini died on June 3 after suffering a heart attack and undergoing surgery for internal bleeding in a Teheran hospital.

His death triggered a frenzy of emotion. On June 5, hundreds of thousands of mourners thronged a hill near Teheran, where Khomeini's body was displayed in a refrigerated coffin. The next day, more than 1 million people marched to the War Martyrs' Cemetery outside Teheran to witness his burial. At the cemetery, the crowd grew so frenzied—spilling Khomeini's body from the coffin and jumping into his grave—that the burial had to be postponed for several hours.

Succession. In his will, Khomeini failed to name anyone to succeed him as supreme spiritual guide. In March, his designated successor, Ayatollah Hussein Ali Montazeri, had resigned at Khomeini's request after publishing an open letter critical of Iran's leadership during the republic's first decade. Montazeri condemned the government's close control of the economy, its treatment of prisoners, and its violation of human rights.

Despite the lack of a designated heir, the succession was resolved with relative ease. On June 4, the Assembly of Experts—a theological body created by Khomeini to appoint a successor—elected Iran's president, Ali Hoseini Khamenei, as the acting supreme spiritual guide. Khamenei, a second-rank theologian, was given the post provisionally, pending a referendum on amendments to the Constitution proposed in February by Khomeini. One of the amendments altered the requirements for the presidency, permitting any theologian, regardless of rank, to hold the office. Under the 1979 Constitution, only a first-rank theologian could serve as president.

Constitutional amendments. Khomeini had initiated the revision of the Constitution in order to provide Iran with a clearer structure of authority. Voters approved the proposed amendments on July 28, 1989.

The most important revisions eliminated the office of prime minister and transferred those powers to the president, previously a largely ceremonial post. The president was given the power to appoint the cabinet—subject to the approval of the Majlis (parliament)—and to direct the day-to-day operations of government. In addition, the president was empowered to resolve disagreements between the Majlis and the Council of Guardians over legislation. The council reviews all new laws to determine if they violate Islamic principles.

New president. In the election for president, also held on July 28, Iranian voters chose between Ali Akbar Hashemi Rafsanjani, the speaker of the Majlis, and Abbas Sheibani, a former minister of agriculture. The

Thousands of mourners in Teheran surround an ornate shrine above the grave of Ayatollah Khomeini, Iran's supreme leader, who died on June 3.

candidacies of 78 others were dismissed by the Council of Guardians, which declared them unqualified for office.

Rafsanjani won handily, as expected, receiving nearly 95 per cent of the more than 14 million votes cast. Iran's new president lost no time in introducing policies intended to expand private investment in the economy and improve ties with other countries.

Rafsanjani won a major political victory on August 29, when the Majlis approved his entire cabinet, which consisted mostly of moderates. Despite opposition from more radical members of parliament, Rafsanjani replaced hard-liners in the previous cabinet, such as Interior Minister Ali Akbar Mohtashemi, reportedly linked to the terrorist Hezbollah (Party of God) militia

in Lebanon that holds a number of American hostages. Rafsanjani's emphasis on moderation in economic and foreign policy won praise from both the Iranian public and the international community.

Rushdie controversy. On February 14, Khomeini triggered an international furor by urging Muslims to kill Salman Rushdie, the author of *The Satanic Verses*, a novel that Khomeini and other Muslims had denounced as blasphemous to Islam. On February 28, the Majlis voted to break diplomatic relations with Great Britain within seven days unless the British government condemned Rushdie and his book. On March 6, Britain, which refused the demand, expelled 20 to 30 Iranians for security reasons. The next day, Iran severed diplomatic ties. See **Literature (Close-Up)**.

U.S. relations. In July, a special claims tribunal at The Hague in the Netherlands awarded Phillips Petroleum $110 million for offshore oil properties nationalized by Iran after the revolution. The payment brought to $1 billion the amount awarded to U.S. companies for claims against Iran. On November 7, the United States, in a good-will gesture, announced that it was freeing $567 million in Iranian assets frozen in U.S. banks after Iranian militants seized the U.S. Embassy in Teheran in 1979. But resumption of diplomatic relations seemed remote.

The economy. In February, Khomeini had approved a five-year, $70-million to $80-million reconstruction plan that would permit Iran to borrow from foreign banks and governments to rebuild its economy, heavily damaged by the war with Iraq. Khomeini's action followed an appeal from moderate Iranian leaders that he intervene personally to deal with such grave economic problems as a 30 per cent unemployment rate, a 50 per cent inflation rate, severe shortages of food and consumer goods, and lagging productivity in most state-run factories.

Some sectors of the economy made progress. The refinery at Abadan on the Persian Gulf, closed for eight years, resumed production. By June, most of Iran's war-damaged petrochemical plants and refineries were back in operation.   William Spencer

See also **Middle East** (Facts in brief table); **Rafsanjani, Ali Akbar Hashemi.** In *World Book,* see **Iran.**

Off to testify in his own defense at his Iran-contra trial, former White House aide Oliver L. North leaves a Washington, D.C., office building on April 6.

Iran-contra affair. The prosecution of key figures in the Iran-contra affair began in 1989 with that of retired Marine Lieutenant Colonel Oliver L. North, a former National Security Council (NSC) aide to President Ronald Reagan. On May 4, North was convicted on three felony counts for his part in the affair. The 1985-1986 undercover operation involved the sale of arms to Iran to obtain the release of hostages and the diversion of arms-sales profits to finance *contra* rebels fighting the Sandinista government of Nicaragua.

Two charges dismissed. On Jan. 13, 1989, U.S. District Judge Gerhard A. Gesell dismissed the two major charges against North—conspiracy to defraud the United States and theft of government property. Gesell dropped those charges because the outgoing Reagan Administration had refused to allow the use of certain classified government documents relating to the Iran-contra operation in North's upcoming trial on charges of attempting to cover up the scandal. The dismissal left 12 other charges pending.

Independent counsel Lawrence E. Walsh, leading the prosecution team, reached an agreement on February 15 with Attorney General Richard L. Thornburgh on the use of other classified information at North's trial. The agreement cleared the way for the trial to begin on February 21.

On May 4, the jury found North guilty on 3 of the 12 counts: obstructing Congress, destroying government documents, and accepting an illegal gift—a

home security system—from an associate. On July 5, Gesell fined North $150,000, gave him a three-year suspended prison sentence, placed him on probation for two years, and ordered him to perform 1,200 hours of community service.

Five plead guilty. One of North's former superiors, Robert C. McFarlane, was fined $20,000 on March 3 and put on two years probation after pleading guilty a year earlier to four misdemeanor counts of misleading Congress about the Iran-contra affair. McFarlane had been Reagan's national security adviser.

Two other North associates, who pleaded guilty in 1987 to charges related to their efforts to raise money for the contras, were sentenced in March 1989 to probation for two years. They were Carl R. Channell, a conservative fund-raiser, and Richard R. Miller, a public relations consultant.

Retired Air Force Major General Richard V. Secord, North's principal nongovernment contact in the Iran-contra operation, pleaded guilty on November 8 to lying to congressional investigators. His partner, Albert A. Hakim, pleaded guilty on November 21 to helping North buy a security fence for his home and covering up the deal. Other charges against both were dropped. They agreed to cooperate in the trial of retired Rear Admiral John M. Poindexter—set to begin in January 1990—on charges of trying to cover up his Iran-contra activities. Poindexter succeeded McFarlane.   Frank Cormier and Margot Cormier

Iraq. Iraq's President Saddam Hussein in 1989 took steps to liberalize the country's political system following the 1988 cease-fire with Iran. Most observers doubted that the changes would significantly loosen Hussein's tight grip on power, however.

In January 1989, a special committee began work on a new constitution to replace the Provisional Constitution adopted in 1970, which in effect established the Arab Baath Socialist Party, Iraq's only legal political party, as the country's most powerful political body. The new constitution would allow Iraqis to form other political parties. The government announced, however, that it would not lift the ban on Iraq's Communist Party because the party had supported Iran during the war. The constitution would also guarantee freedom of the press and make the cabinet responsible to the National Assembly rather than to the Baath Revolutionary Command Council. The Council, which is made up of top Baath Party officials, makes government policy.

Elections. A second liberalization measure involved elections for a new National Assembly. The Assembly's chief task was to endorse the new constitution. The elections took place on April 1, 1989, with 911 approved candidates vying for the 250 seats. In contrast to the previous Assembly election, in 1984, just over 50 per cent of the successful candidates were members of the Baath Party. The rest ran as independents, though some were affiliated with the party.

Relations with Iran. The August 1988 cease-fire halting Iraq's bitter eight-year war with Iran held. But negotiations sponsored by the United Nations to arrive at a peace settlement remained deadlocked. The two former combatants could not even agree on terms for an exchange of prisoners.

Kurdish resettlement. In August 1989, the government completed a two-month program of forced relocation of some 200,000 Kurds from a 20-mile (30-kilometer) area along the border with Iran and Turkey. Iraq said the move was for security reasons. Those relocated were given their choice of residence within Iraq's Kurdish Autonomous Region. In addition, the resettled Kurds were provided with free housing, schools, employment, and social services unavailable in their border zone.

In September, the government held elections for a 50-member legislative council and a 30-member executive council to govern the region. Western countries, including the United States, criticized the relocation of the Kurds, most of whom were livestock herders, to urban areas, where they could not find work.

Child torture. Iraq has imprisoned, tortured, and killed hundreds or even thousands of children, according to a report issued in February by Amnesty International, a human-rights organization based in London. Amnesty International charged President Hussein with "deliberately targeting the children of political opponents." The organization said Iraqi forces tortured the children, most of them Kurds, to obtain information about their parents or to force their parents to confess to illegal acts. In some cases, children were publicly shot to punish villages the regime had accused of supporting Kurdish rebel activities.

Stark compensation. On March 27, the United States agreed to accept $27.3 million in compensation for the families of 37 U.S. sailors killed in an Iraqi missile attack on the frigate U.S.S. *Stark* in 1987. According to Iraq, an Iraqi warplane had mistaken the *Stark*, which was on routine patrol in the Persian Gulf, for an Iranian oil tanker. The United States had demanded $29.6 million in compensation for the deaths.

Iraqi rocket. On December 7, Iraq announced that two days earlier it had launched a rocket into space. According to Iraq, the three-stage rocket carried satellites to be used for scientific research. Such rockets can also carry warheads, including those containing chemical weapons.

The economy. Iraq's postwar reconstruction program moved ahead at full throttle. In July, Japan resumed annual purchases of 500,000 barrels of oil. The expansion of existing oil fields and the reopening of the 30-billion-barrel Majnoon Field, recaptured from Iranian forces during the war, increased Iraq's total oil reserves to 280 billion barrels. Oil refining capacity reached 600,000 barrels per day, half reserved to meet domestic demand.   William Spencer

See also **Middle East** (Facts in brief table). In *World Book,* see **Iraq.**

Ireland. Prime Minister Charles Haughey surprised the country on May 25, 1989, by calling for a general election on June 15, three years before one was due. It was Haughey's fifth attempt to win enough seats in the Dáil (parliament) to give his Fianna Fáil (Soldiers of Destiny) party a majority. Haughey called for the election after his government lost a vote in the Dáil over increasing funds to *hemophiliacs* (people whose blood does not clot properly) infected with AIDS.

But Haughey misjudged the mood of the country. Although public opinion polls showed that Fianna Fáil would capture more than 50 per cent of the vote, his party actually received only 44 per cent in the election. In the end, it lost 4 seats in the Dáil, leaving it with 77, 6 seats short of a majority.

Some political observers speculated that voters resented Haughey for calling an early election. Opinion polls showed that more than 60 per cent of voters thought an election unnecessary because the opposition had usually supported Haughey. He was also hurt by his unpopular cuts in health benefits.

License impact. Fianna Fáil lost some votes because the government had for the first time required anglers to buy a fishing license. Its aim was to raise money to keep lakes and rivers free from pollution, but many of Ireland's 200,000 fishing enthusiasts saw the license as an attempt to take away their rights.

Historic coalition. The June election was followed by a month of intense negotiation, as Haughey tried to create a majority in the Dáil by establishing a coalition between Fianna Fáil and one of the opposition parties. On July 12, Haughey struck a deal with the Progressive Democracy Party (PD), which had split from Fianna Fáil in 1987.

The coalition brought Haughey together with one of his most bitter political opponents, Desmond O'Malley. O'Malley, the PD leader who led the break from Fianna Fáil, and another PD member were given posts in Ireland's 15-member Cabinet. After the coalition was formed, the Dáil elected Haughey to his fourth term as prime minister.

Economy. Ireland's economy continued to respond to Haughey's tough measures. Budget cuts helped boost the *gross national product* (the value of all goods and services produced during the year) by 4 per cent. The trade picture was bright, with exports reaching 14 billion Irish pounds (about $20 billion). Labor relations were also calmer.

But unemployment continued to plague Ireland. By year-end, 17 per cent of the work force was unemployed. The lack of jobs forced thousands of people to leave the country. Government figures published in September revealed that 46,000 people had emigrated from April 1988 through April 1989, the most since 1950.   Ian J. Mather

See also **Northern Ireland.** In *World Book,* see Ireland.

Iron and steel. See Steel industry.

Israel. Israel's Prime Minister Yitzhak Shamir, under international pressure to respond to peace overtures by the Palestine Liberation Organization (PLO), in April 1989 proposed a peace plan for the Israeli-occupied West Bank and Gaza Strip. Under the plan, the 1.7 million Palestinians in the occupied territories would elect representatives to negotiate with Israel for limited self-government for a five-year period. After three years, the representatives and Israel would negotiate the final status of the territories.

Initially, the plan won the support of Israel's Cabinet and Knesset (parliament). But opposition from some members of the right wing Likud bloc—Shamir's own party and the senior partner in Israel's coalition government—forced Shamir to amend the plan to include four hard-line conditions for the elections. The conditions barred the government from giving up territory or agreeing to the establishment of a Palestinian state; excluded the Arab population of East Jerusalem from voting in the elections; and required an end to the violence before elections could be held. In addition, Shamir agreed to continue building Jewish settlements in the West Bank.

Coalition crisis. The changes drew the ire of the Palestinians, the PLO, the United States, and Israel's Labor Party. Labor, the junior partner in the coalition, threatened to withdraw, a move that would have caused the downfall of the government and forced new elections. But strong public sentiment against

A protester wearing a mask of Israeli Prime Minister Shamir decries Shamir's refusal to hold talks with the Palestine Liberation Organization.

calling new elections led Labor and Likud to fashion a compromise. The Knesset voted almost unanimously to endorse Shamir's original proposal, while not requiring Likud to specifically renounce the conditions. As a result, various parties were able to disagree on the interpretation of the plan while keeping the coalition government in place.

Palestinian unrest. The Palestinian uprising in the occupied territories began its third year in December 1989. By November, some 615 Palestinians and 45 Israelis had been killed and 15,000 to 20,000 Palestinians injured in the violence. In June, Amnesty International, a human-rights organization, reported that more than 5,000 Palestinians had been held in detention centers without trial since the uprising began in December 1987.

School closings. In January 1989, Israeli authorities closed all the schools in the West Bank and the universities in the Gaza Strip, charging that they were being used as gathering places for violent demonstrations. In July, following widespread international protests, Israel reopened the elementary and secondary schools in the West Bank. In late November, however, the schools were closed again.

Gaza ID's. The Israeli army in June began issuing computer-coded identification cards to the more than 65,000 Palestinians from the Gaza Strip who work in Israel. The army said the cards were needed to prevent Palestinians considered to be security risks from traveling or working in Israel. In August, when the ID policy went into effect, Gazan workers held a one-day strike. The action delayed enforcement of the policy until summer because the Israeli economy depends on these workers.

Tax revolt. The Israeli army lifted a six-week blockade of the West Bank town of Beit Sahur, near Bethlehem, on October 31. Residents of the largely Christian Arab town had refused to pay their taxes as a gesture of support for the Palestinian uprising. In response, the army sealed off the town, allowing only those residents who had paid their taxes to leave. Israeli tax collectors also seized property worth $1.5 million, an amount in excess of the total owed, and auctioned it to pay the taxes.

Due process for demolition. Israel's High Court of Justice, the country's supreme court, in July restricted the army's practice of demolishing the homes of Palestinians accused of committing crimes. Homes often were demolished within hours of an arrest but before charges were filed. The court ruled that those accused must be allowed to appeal the demolition order through military and civilian courts.

Arab against Arab. The Palestinian uprising was also beset by internal conflict. By December, 150 Arabs accused of collaborating with Israel had been killed.

Who is a Jew? An Israeli High Court ruling in July revived debate over the question: Who is a Jew? The court ruled that the government must register as Jews people who have been converted by Reform or Con-

servative rabbis and who wish to settle in Israel under the Law of Return. This law allows anyone born of a Jewish mother or anyone who converts to Judaism to immigrate to Israel and immediately receive citizenship. (Under Jewish law, the religion of a child is determined by that of the mother.) The ruling was criticized by many Orthodox leaders, who have argued that only conversions by Orthodox rabbis should be recognized.

At the same time, however, the court ruled that Reform or Conservative rabbis cannot conduct marriage ceremonies in Israel. The decision led the Orthodox Chief Rabbinate, the country's highest religious body, to require Orthodox rabbis to obtain proof of conversion by an Orthodox rabbi before conducting marriage ceremonies or burial services for converted Jews.

The economy provided little to cheer about during 1989. Unemployment hovered around 10 per cent, with inflation running at about 23 per cent.

In September, an austerity plan went into effect, cutting government spending in order to reduce inflation and boost Israel's lagging economic growth. The plan included a 13.5 per cent currency devaluation, the dismissal of 10,000 civil service employees, and higher fees for education and health services. The government also raised the prices of subsidized products such as bread and gasoline.   William Spencer

See also **Middle East** (Facts in brief table). In *World Book,* see **Israel.**

Italy continued its politics of revolving-door government in 1989 and made no significant progress in improving public services or curbing a mounting budget deficit. An ineffective public sector remained Italy's major economic problem. Government services such as education were inadequate, state-run business enterprises were unwieldy, and government spending grew steadily.

Industry performed strongly during the year. Fiat continued a remarkable comeback after tying Volkswagen of West Germany for first place in the European car-sales market in 1988. In 1980, the Fiat industrial group, beset by labor problems and poor management, had lost money in its main business of auto manufacturing. But Fiat turned itself into a profit-maker by investing in robot technology, selling nonautomotive businesses, and cutting its work force.

On Feb. 9, 1989, Italy chose the American Telephone and Telegraph Company (AT&T), a United States firm, to be the foreign partner of Italtel S.p.A., the state-owned builder of telecommunications equipment. This selection gave AT&T a strong commercial foothold in the European market. Furthermore, by choosing a company from a country that is not a member of the European Community (EC or Common Market), Italy helped quiet U.S. fears that Europe was becoming industrially inward-looking.

A new government took power on July 23, but Italy continued to be ruled by a coalition of the same five parties that had held power almost continuously since 1981—the Christian Democrats, Socialists, Social Democrats, Liberals, and Republicans. Giulio Andreotti became prime minister of Italy's 12th government in the 1980's. Andreotti, 70, a Christian Democrat who had been foreign minister in successive governments since 1983, replaced Ciriaco De Mita, also a Christian Democrat. De Mita had resigned on May 19, 1989, after attacks on his leadership by Socialist leader Bettino Craxi, Republican chief Giorgio La Malfa, and fellow Christian Democrats.

EC elections. Italy led the European Community in voter turnout in June 18 polling for the European Parliament, the legislative branch of the EC. The turnout in Italy was 81.5 per cent. In the election, the Socialists fell far short of their goal of becoming Italy's leading leftist party, winning less than 14 per cent of the vote compared with the Communists' 27.6 per cent.

Communists move toward center. Although the Italian Communist Party remained the country's second-largest party, behind the Christian Democrats, the Communists moved closer to the political center in a bid to counter their decline in popularity, particularly among Italy's young people. At its annual congress in March, the Communist Party sought new supporters among women and environmentalists and discussed issues such as drug abuse and rights of disabled people.

The party's Central Committee voted on November 24 to change the name of the party and to replace the party symbol, the hammer and sickle. The committee said that it would choose a new name and symbol in 1990.

Mafia power cited. Anti-Mafia High Commissioner Domenico Sica warned throughout 1989 that organized crime, with "incalculable funds from narcotics and centralized management," had taken control of Sicily and the mainland cities of Reggio di Calabria and Naples. He also uncovered Mafia links to terrorist groups in Europe.

Water pollution known as Adriatic slime—a yellow scum of algae caused by river-borne waste and certain weather conditions—affected the northern third of the Adriatic coast in July. The slime cost the vacation industry in the region an estimated 25 per cent of its summer business.

Crash investigated. A panel of scientific experts participating in a reopened investigation into the 1980 crash of an Itavia Airlines jetliner in the Tyrrhenian Sea off Naples found that the aircraft had been hit by a missile. The panel could not identify the source of the missile, however. Amid growing signs of a cover-up by Italian authorities, the attorney representing the families of the 81 victims of the crash said that the missile apparently had been fired at a Libyan military plane.   Joseph Fitchett

See also **Europe** (Facts in brief table). In *World Book,* see **Italy.**

Ivory Coast. See **Africa.**

Jackson, Bo (1962-   ), was named Most Valuable Player in the baseball All-Star Game in 1989, after opening the scoring with a towering 448-foot (137-meter) home run. Already acclaimed as a running back in football, Jackson has accomplished the rare feat of being a star in two major professional sports.

Vincent Edward Jackson was born on Nov. 30, 1962, in Bessemer, Ala., in a single-parent family, the eighth of 10 children. Jackson attended Auburn University in Alabama, where he played both football and baseball. In 1985, Jackson received the Heisman Trophy as the outstanding player in college football.

In 1986, Jackson was the first player picked in the National Football League (NFL) draft and was offered a five-year, $7.4-million contract by the Tampa Bay Buccaneers. But Jackson passed up football to play baseball with the Kansas City Royals, who offered him a guaranteed contract of $200,000.

In July 1987, Jackson announced that he would play both sports professionally and signed with the NFL's Los Angeles Raiders. His best baseball season came in 1989, when he was fourth in the American League in home runs (32) and runs batted in (105). With the Raiders, he has set team records for the longest touchdown run (92 yards) and most yards gained (221) in a single game. He became the first NFL player to make two runs of 90 or more yards from the line of scrimmage.   Rod Such

Jamaica. See **West Indies.**

Japan. Emperor Hirohito died of cancer on Jan. 7, 1989, ending a 62-year reign, the longest in Japanese history. He had been gravely ill for four months.

Hirohito, who became emperor at 25, ruled during one of Japan's most eventful periods. Like the emperors who preceded him, Hirohito was considered a deity for many years. But after Japan surrendered to end World War II (1939-1945), Hirohito renounced claims to divinity for himself and the imperial family.

A private religious funeral ceremony was held at the Imperial Palace, in Tokyo, on February 24. Immediately afterward, Hirohito was given a state funeral in the city's Shinjuku Imperial Garden. Hundreds of thousands of mourners lined the route of the funeral procession from the palace to the garden. Representatives of more than 160 nations attended the state funeral, the largest gathering of foreign dignitaries ever in Japan. After the ceremonies, Hirohito's body was placed in the imperial mausoleum in a Tokyo suburb. In accordance with custom, the Japanese people will henceforth refer to Hirohito as the *Showa Emperor. Showa,* the name he chose for his reign, means *enlightened peace.*

Hirohito's son, Akihito, 55, assumed the throne upon the emperor's death. The Japanese government chose the name *Heisei,* which means *peace and concord,* for the new emperor's reign. In his first official statement, on January 9, Akihito pledged to protect the Japanese Constitution, which establishes the em-

Leaders of Japan's opposition Japan Socialist Party mark the names of their victorious candidates in July parliamentary elections.

peror's role as symbolic of the unity of the people but without political power. See **Akihito.**

Three prime ministers. In the first year of the new Heisei era, the Liberal Democratic Party (LDP) faced the most serious threat to its control of the government since its formation in 1955. Scandals shook voter confidence in the party to such an extent that two successive prime ministers were forced to resign.

Noboru Takeshita, who became prime minister in October 1987, announced his intention to resign on April 25 and did so on June 2. He stepped down because of widespread public resentment over a new 3 per cent sales tax and over the involvement of almost all LDP leaders in an influence-trading scandal.

At the heart of this scandal was the Recruit Company, an aggressive and rapidly expanding firm that deals in real estate transactions and highly specialized information services. Recruit executives sold company stock at low prices to LDP leaders before it was placed on public sale. When it was sold publicly, the price of the stock rose dramatically, enriching its holders. Although such transactions are not illegal, they are considered unethical, especially since influence-peddling has been under fire for years in Japan.

Foreign Minister Sosuke Uno succeeded Takeshita as prime minister on June 2, primarily because he was the only potential candidate not involved in the Recruit scandal. Uno's reputation was soon besmirched by allegations that he had several extramarital affairs

with *geishas*, women who work as paid companions. Such sexual relationships are not uncommon in Japan, but the public was shocked when one of the women spoke out against Uno in magazine and television interviews. Outraged by the sex scandal, voters did not support the LDP in the July 23 parliamentary elections, and one day later, the embattled Uno announced his resignation.

Toshiki Kaifu succeeded Uno on August 9. At 58, he became the second youngest prime minister in Japan's postwar history. Active in national politics since he was 29, Kaifu twice served as education minister. See **Kaifu, Toshiki.**

Kaifu and the LDP made history by appointing two women to his Cabinet. He appointed Mayumi Moriyama director-general of Japan's Environment Agency and Sumiko Takahara director-general of the influential Economic Planning Agency. Kaifu was probably moved to make these appointments to attempt to counterbalance the growing stature of Takako Doi, leader of the Japan Socialist Party and the first woman to head a Japanese political party. When yet another sex scandal forced Kaifu's chief Cabinet secretary to resign in late August, the prime minister gave Moriyama the post, which is roughly equivalent to the U.S. White House chief of staff.

A little more than three weeks after assuming office, Kaifu made a whirlwind, 10-day trip to the United States, Canada, and Mexico. He held talks with U.S. President George Bush and Prime Minister Brian Mulroney of Canada. He also discussed economic and trade relations with Mexico's President Carlos Salinas de Gortari and other Mexican officials.

Election shakeup. In addition to the turmoil in the prime ministership, the LDP suffered its greatest election defeat ever during the July 23 parliamentary elections for half the 252 seats in the House of Councillors, the upper and less powerful house of parliament. The LDP won only 36 seats, giving it a total of 109, well short of the 127 needed for a majority. The Japan Socialist Party won 46 seats, with the remaining 44 going to smaller opposition parties. Although the LDP lost control of the House of Councillors, analysts predicted that only a unified opposition—difficult to achieve given the splits among the opposition parties—could effectively challenge the LDP.

The sex and influence-peddling scandals that caused the rapid turnover in Japan's prime ministers also contributed to the LDP election defeat. Nevertheless, the party still controlled a comfortable majority in the more powerful lower house of parliament, the House of Representatives. The next general election for the lower house, scheduled for 1990, was expected to provide a more accurate reading of the LDP's position with voters.

Relations with the United States continued to be marked by friction over economic issues. The United States criticized Japan for its failure to broaden access to Japanese markets and to stimulate Japanese

Outside the Imperial Palace in Tokyo, Japanese citizens mourn the January 7 death of Hirohito, Japan's emperor for 62 years.

demand for consumer goods, particularly imports. The Japanese, in turn, criticized what they perceived to be shortcomings in the American economy, such as the low savings rate and the huge federal budget deficit. Japanese leaders blamed American businesses for not tailoring their products to foreign markets.

The United States trade deficit with Japan shrank slightly in 1989, reflecting an overall reduction of Japan's world trade surplus. The prospect for a significant reduction in the U.S. trade deficit seemed slight, however, and it was expected to remain at about $50-billion annually.

Long and difficult negotiations over the production of a Japanese fighter plane, the FSX, finally ended in 1989. In November 1988, the United States and Japan had agreed to produce the plane jointly. After the agreement to manufacture the FSX was signed, some U.S. legislators concluded that it was too favorable to Japan, particularly because they thought the Japanese aircraft industry would gain unduly in the exchange of technical information.

The controversy created an unfavorable reaction in Japan because of its anti-Japanese overtones and because it appeared that the United States was trying to withdraw from the agreement. Although Congress passed a bill to place restrictions on the original agreement in June 1989, Bush vetoed it, and on September 13, the Senate failed by one vote to override the veto.

Japan's Sony Corporation purchased Columbia Pictures Entertainment Incorporated for $3.4 billion on September 27, and the Mitsubishi Estate Company of Tokyo on October 30 bought control of the Rockefeller Group—owner of Rockefeller Center and other buildings—for $846 million. But the overall rate of Japanese investment in the United States slowed in 1989. Major Japanese acquisitions of U.S. companies fell from $10.1 billion in 1988 to an estimated $4.8 billion in the first nine months of 1989.

Japan's economy continued to expand. The government estimated that the nation's gross national product—the value of all goods and services produced—would grow by 5 per cent in 1989. This would be the third successive year of rapid expansion. The strong economy resulted in a labor shortage, however, which created a demand for foreign workers. The Labor Ministry estimated that 150,000 illegal aliens—most of them from other Asian countries—were working in Japan in 1989.

Japan's leading financial newspaper reported on August 21 that Japan had become the world's wealthiest nation in 1987. The value of land, production facilities, financial holdings, and other assets in Japan totaled an estimated $43.7 trillion. The total wealth of the United States, ranked second richest, was estimated at $36.2 trillion.   John M. Maki

See also **Asia** (Facts in brief table). In *World Book,* see **Japan.**

Jews and Judaism

Jews and Judaism. Issues of major concern to Jews in the United States in 1989 included the immigration of Soviet Jews to the United States, the flare-up in tension between Jews and Roman Catholics over a Polish convent, and abortion rights.

Soviet Jews. The Soviet Union in 1989 permitted more Jews than ever before to leave the country. During the year, more than 71,000 exit visas were granted. Experts estimated that if the Soviet Union continued its policy of *glasnost* (openness), as many as 100,000 Soviet Jews may be permitted to leave in 1990. For American Jews who have worked for the release of the 200,000 to 400,000 Jews who want to leave the Soviet Union, the news was heartening.

But for the approximately 11,000 *refuseniks*— Jewish activists who have formally applied for visas but have been denied them—glasnost failed to improve their situation. Many refuseniks claimed that anti-Semitism in the Soviet Union increased dramatically in 1989. They reported a rise in physical attacks upon Jews and said that the Soviet government continued to harass those who want to leave the country.

Just as the Soviet Union appeared to ease emigration, however, the United States tightened its immigration policy. On Oct. 1, 1989, the United States announced that all potential Soviet immigrants wishing to enter the United States must have a U.S. visa issued by the American Embassy in Moscow. They also must demonstrate that they suffer a "well-founded fear of persecution." Jewish leaders said the new restrictions could limit the number of Soviet Jews immigrating to the United States.

Convent conflict. A major conflict erupted between Jews and Roman Catholics in 1989 over a convent of Carmelite nuns. The convent was established in 1984 in a building on the grounds of the Nazi concentration camp in Auschwitz (Oświęçim), Poland. During World War II (1939-1945), the building stored poison gas that the Nazis used to kill millions of people, most of them Jews.

In 1987, after some Jewish groups complained that it was inappropriate to locate a Roman Catholic convent in a place where so many Jews were killed, a group of European Catholic cardinals met with Jewish leaders. They signed an agreement that called for the convent to be relocated by February 1989 to new quarters that would be built away from the camp.

When the deadline passed and the convent had not been moved, tension between Jews and Catholics began to build. Many Jews felt hurt and outrage over the continued presence of the convent at Auschwitz. Similar feelings spread among many Catholics after Jewish protesters climbed over the convent fence during a demonstration in July.

On September 19, the Vatican issued a statement encouraging the nuns to move and offering financial aid in building a new convent. Although Jewish leaders applauded the Vatican's move, many believed that

Motorists in Tel Aviv, Israel, observe two minutes of silence on May 2 in memory of Jews who died in the Holocaust during World War II (1939-1945).

the conflict had deeply affected the relationship between the two religions.

In December, a delegation from the American Jewish Congress met with Polish Catholic leaders. They announced that construction of a new building for the nuns would begin in 1990.

Abortion rights. American Jews, who strongly support the U.S. Constitution's guarantee of the free exercise of religion, were concerned about the U.S. Supreme Court's ruling on July 3 that upheld the constitutionality of a Missouri abortion law. The law restricts abortion except in certain cases.

Judaism views abortion as the loss of a potential life and considers all human life sacred. But the religion supports the position that women—not the government—should decide under what conditions to have an abortion. Jewish law allows abortion in cases of physical and emotional pain, especially if the mother's life is in danger.

Law of Return. On July 24, Israel's supreme court ruled that the Law of Return—which grants citizenship to any Jew who chooses to settle in Israel—applies to people converted to Judaism by Reform and Conservative rabbis. Orthodox leaders had argued that only Orthodox conversions should be recognized. The court ruled, however, that only Orthodox rabbis may conduct weddings in Israel.　　Charles S. Levi

See also **Israel; Roman Catholic Church.** In *World Book,* see **Jews; Judaism.**

Jiang Zemin (1926-　　) was named general secretary of China's Communist Party on June 24, 1989. He succeeded Zhao Ziyang, who was ousted following a civil uprising in which students called for democratic reforms. See **China.**

Jiang, formerly Shanghai's Communist Party leader, had dealt harshly with intellectuals in Shanghai who joined the protests—an action that made him unpopular with some citizens but may have earned him the favor of hard-liners in the Communist Party. Observers believed that Jiang had become the chosen political heir to Deng Xiaoping, the 85-year-old leader who had been China's most powerful figure for many years.

Jiang was born in July 1926 in Yangzhou, in the province of Jiangsu. He was educated at Jiaotong University in Shanghai, graduating in 1947 from the electrical machinery department. Jiang worked in Shanghai factories for several years and, in 1955 and 1956, trained at the Stalin Automobile Factory in Moscow.

In 1980, Jiang became a deputy director of commissions on foreign investment and import and export affairs. In 1982, he was appointed to the Ministry of Electronics Industry. Jiang was mayor of Shanghai from 1985 until April 1988, when he became the city's Communist Party leader. Jiang, who is said to speak English fluently, encouraged foreign investment in Shanghai with some success.

Jiang and his wife, Wang Yeping, have one son, a student in the United States.　　Jinger Hoop

Jordan. Riots protesting government austerity measures swept Jordan in April 1989. The violence, which left at least eight people dead, was triggered by price increases of up to 50 per cent on such government-subsidized commodities as gasoline, cooking oil, and cigarettes and by increases in telephone rates and license fees.

The government had imposed the price hikes to comply with demands by the International Monetary Fund (IMF), an agency of the United Nations, that Jordan trim its $240-million budget deficit and reduce its 14 per cent inflation rate. In return, the IMF agreed to reschedule interest payments on some of Jordan's $8-billion foreign debt and to advance new credits of $275 million.

Public discontent. Although the riots were ignited by the price hikes, they were fueled by Jordanians' resentment over a lack of political representation and by anger with government corruption and mismanagement. King Hussein I moved quickly to ease tensions. He dismissed the widely unpopular Prime Minister Zaid Rifa'i and appointed Zayd Bin Shakir, former chief of the armed forces, to the post. He also replaced most of his Cabinet.

New elections. In addition, Hussein called for new elections for the House of Representatives, the lower house of Jordan's National Assembly. The last general elections were in 1967. Hussein had dissolved the House in 1988 just before he severed financial and administrative ties with the Israeli-occupied West Bank in response to the Palestinian uprising there.

Under a new electoral law, only Palestinians living in Jordan—about 60 per cent of the country's population—were allowed to vote. Palestinians in the West Bank, who had previously held 30 House seats, were excluded. The law also increased the number of seats in the House from 60 to 80.

Preelection debate was much freer than expected. And although the government did not lift its ban on political parties, it did not prevent party members from running. Nevertheless, it drew electoral districts and took other steps to help ensure the election of progovernment candidates.

The results of the November election reflected the country's antigovernment mood. At least 17 former high-ranking officials were defeated. In addition, candidates representing or allied with the Muslim Brotherhood, an Islamic fundamentalist party, made an unexpectedly strong showing, especially among Palestinians, winning 32 seats in the House of Representatives. Other opposition candidates won 11 seats. The election setback caused Prime Minister Bin Shakir to resign on December 4. He was succeeded by Mudar Badran, who had held the office twice before. Hussein retained the power to dissolve parliament and declare martial law.　　William Spencer

See also **Middle East** (Facts in brief table). In the World Book Supplement section, see **Jordan.**

Judaism. See **Jews and Judaism.**

Kaifu, Toshiki (1931-   ), became prime minister of Japan, the nation's third in three months, on Aug. 9, 1989. He had been elected president of Japan's ruling Liberal Democratic Party (LDP) the previous day.

Kaifu succeeded Sosuke Uno, who had replaced Noboru Takeshita as prime minister in June. The resignations of both men were spurred in part by citizen outrage over the LDP's involvement in an influence-peddling scandal (see **Japan**). Some observers predicted that Kaifu would also have to step down soon, but the new prime minister declared himself "free from bribe cases or any other scandals."

Kaifu was born on Jan. 2, 1931, in Ichinomiya, near Nagoya. He was educated at Waseda University in Tokyo and received a law degree in 1954.

Kaifu was elected to the Diet, Japan's parliament, at 29, making him the youngest member of parliament at the time. He was reelected to the Diet 10 times and held several posts within the LDP as well as in the Cabinet. In 1966, he was appointed vice minister of labor —again, the youngest person to hold such a post. Later, he served as Japan's minister of education under two prime ministers—Takeo Fukuda in the 1970's and Yasuhiro Nakasone in the 1980's. Kaifu became senior deputy secretary general of the LDP in 1984.

Kaifu and his wife, Sachiyo, are the parents of two children, a daughter and a son.   Jinger Hoop

Kampuchea. See **Cambodia.**

Kansas. See **State government.**

Kemp, Jack French (1935-   ), was sworn in as secretary of housing and urban development on Feb. 13, 1989, after being nominated by President George Bush. Kemp had been a strong supporter of Bush's presidential candidacy, following his own unsuccessful bid for the Republican presidential nomination.

Kemp was born on July 13, 1935, in Los Angeles. His father owned a trucking company, and his mother was a social worker. Kemp attended Occidental College in Los Angeles, where he played football, and graduated in 1957. In 1960, he signed with the Los Angeles Chargers, an American Football League team, to play quarterback. The next year, the Chargers moved to San Diego. Kemp was traded to the Buffalo Bills in 1962 and helped lead the Bills to two league championship titles.

Kemp served as a special assistant to California Governor Ronald Reagan in 1967 and as special assistant to the chairman of the Republican National Committee in 1969. In 1970, Kemp was elected to Congress from a suburban district of Buffalo, N.Y. He was reelected eight times and became nationally prominent as an outspoken conservative. Kemp was also a leading proponent of the supply-side economic theory that low taxes would stimulate growth and lead to higher government revenues.

Kemp is married to the former Joanne Main. The couple have four children.   Rod Such

Kentucky. See **State government.**

Kenya. The Kenyan government announced in 1989 that its family planning efforts had succeeded in lowering Kenya's population growth rate from 4.1 per cent to 3.7 per cent over the preceding 10 years. That rate, however, is still among the world's highest. The need for population control became even more acute during the year as Kenya's unemployment rate approached the 40 per cent mark.

President Daniel T. arap Moi's government continued to be targeted in 1989 by Amnesty International, Africa Watch, and other groups concerned with human rights. Despite the release in June and July of political prisoners being held without trial or formal charges, other human-rights violations allegedly continued. The government banned three Kenyan publications for criticizing the Moi administration's policies and for charging corruption in high places.

The stability of the government was called into question in April as the parliament voted unanimously to censure Vice President Josephat Karanja, accusing him of conspiring with Uganda to undermine President Moi. Karanja resigned on May 1.

Kenya in 1989 took the lead in advocating a worldwide ban on the ivory trade. Poachers have reduced Kenya's elephant herds by nearly three-fourths—from about 65,000 animals to only 17,000—in the last 10 years.   J. Gus Liebenow and Beverly B. Liebenow

See also **Africa** (Facts in brief table). In **World Book,** see **Kenya.**

Korea, North. Normally secretive and closed to almost all foreigners, North Korea opened its doors to 16,000 visitors from July 1 to 8, 1989. The occasion was the 13th World Festival of Youth and Students. Just before the festival, the North Korean government gave a one-month wage bonus to all residents of Pyongyang, the capital, to create the appearance of prosperity. But visitors reported that Pyongyang was a bleak city in which necessities were rationed.

Two American human-rights organizations asserted that between 115,000 and 150,000 North Koreans were imprisoned in labor camps, but North Korean officials denied the charge. The organizations also said that the government classified the population into three groups—an elite class of loyal supporters who were pampered by the government, some 4 million hostile citizens who were treated harshly, and a class whose loyalties were wavering.

The South Korean press reported in July that the United States had evidence that North Korea was developing the capacity to make nuclear weapons. Officials at the United States Department of State declined to comment.

Despite North Korea's continued failure to pay its foreign debt, the government sought to widen economic relations in 1989. It set up more than 100 joint ventures with foreign companies.   Henry S. Bradsher

See also **Asia** (Facts in brief table); **Korea, South.** In **World Book,** see **Korea.**

Korea, South. President Roh Tae Woo announced on March 20, 1989, that he was dropping the idea of an "interim test" of his year-old government through a public referendum. Before winning election in 1987 with only 37 per cent of the popular vote, Roh (pronounced *Noh*) had promised the referendum. But he said in March that the vote would create "concern and anxiety" and worsen his relations with opposition political parties. The cancellation caused little outcry.

Kim Dae Jung, the leader of the main opposition party in the National Assembly, Korea's parliament, supported the cancellation—to the surprise of other opposition leaders. On March 21, Kim told students and workers—whose often-riotous demonstrations against the government he had long supported—not to resort to force. He advocated "solving all problems through dialogues, national consensus, and the electoral process." At the same time, Kim led a campaign to punish the colleagues of former President Chun Doo Hwan, many of whom were serving in Roh's administration.

Contacts with North Korea. Roh tried to make official contacts with North Korea, whose Communist regime is considered a threat to the South, but the nations did not hold significant talks in 1989. Kim Young Sam, leader of the second-largest opposition party, met with a former deputy premier of North Korea in Moscow on June 6. This meeting also failed to break the deadlock in official North-South talks.

Moon Ik Hwan, an elderly Presbyterian minister, made an unauthorized trip to the North for a talk with President Kim Il-sŏng in March. Moon was convicted of treason and sentenced to 10 years in prison.

Kim Dae Jung's party reported to the government on June 28 that one of its Assembly members, So Ky-ong Won, had secretly met Kim Il-sŏng in North Korea in August 1988. The party expelled So, a militant nationalist who was considered eccentric. The government arrested So and three others associated with the party on charges of spying for the North.

Roh fired the head of his intelligence agency on July 19 for failing to know about the illegal visits to the North, and the new intelligence chief involved Kim Dae Jung in the So case. Kim and two fellow Assembly members were indicted on August 25 on charges of knowing about So's illegal trip before it happened but failing to report it. The government also charged Kim with receiving $10,000 North Korean agents had given So. Kim denied the allegations, saying that they were invented to discredit his party.

Unrest among workers and students continued in 1989, though it was not as widespread as in 1986 and 1987. Six riot policemen died in a confrontation with students protesting university policies in Pusan on May 3. Although average wages rose 20 per cent per year in 1987 and 1988, workers staged numerous strikes in 1989, winning pay raises averaging 24 per cent. A newspaper on August 1 reported that more

South Koreans demonstrate against President Roh Tae Woo in early 1989, shortly before Roh decided to cancel a referendum on his administration.

than 780 labor leaders and university students had been arrested in the first seven months of 1989, more than twice the number arrested in previous years.

U.S. relations. United States President George Bush visited Seoul on February 27 and confirmed the American defense commitment to South Korea. On a September 20 visit, U.S. Vice President Dan Quayle said the Bush Administration would oppose any congressional effort to reduce the number of U.S. troops in South Korea unless North Korea also reduced its military forces. Some student demonstrators blamed the United States for the tension with North Korea and South Korea's other problems. On October 13, four days before Roh was to meet with Bush in Washington, D.C., six students invaded the home of U.S. Ambassador Donald P. Gregg, who escaped unhurt.

Disputes over international trade continued to plague South Korea's foreign relations. Several countries, including the United States, accused South Korea of unfairly restricting imports. Foreign food exporters complained in 1989 that Seoul kept too many barriers against food imports. The United States threatened to put South Korea on its list of unfair traders but delayed any action. The growth of South Korean exports slowed, however, cutting the overall national trade surplus.   Henry S. Bradsher

See also **Asia** (Facts in brief table); **Korea, North.** In *World Book,* see **Korea.**

Kuwait. See Middle East.

Labor. After four years of decline, the unemployment rate in the United States remained steady in 1989, leveling off at just above 5 per cent. During the year, an average of 6.5 million people were out of work, putting the unemployment rate close to what it was in the early 1980's.

Businesses in the United States continued to struggle with each other and with companies in other countries for a favorable position in domestic and international markets in 1989. Competition grew fiercer in the high-technology and service industries, where U.S. firms faced new foreign companies both at home and abroad.

Despite tough competition for U.S. businesses, wages and benefits for most employees—excluding federal government workers—rose faster in 1989 than in the previous three years, averaging 5.1 per cent, according to the Employment Cost Index of the U.S. Bureau of Labor Statistics (BLS). Workers in private industry saw their wages and salaries rise 4.7 per cent from September 1988 through September 1989, while state and local government workers experienced an increase of 6.4 per cent.

Organized labor. The proportion of U.S. workers belonging to unions continued to decline in 1989. In the early 1980's, about 1 in 4 workers was represented by organized labor, but by the end of the decade, unions represented only 1 in 6 workers. Labor experts attributed the decline to a number of factors, including the failure of unions to organize professional and service workers, an antiunion stance by the U.S. government, and improved wages and benefits offered by nonunion, foreign-owned firms.

As has been the case since 1984, wages and benefits for union workers rose slower than for nonunion workers in 1989, according to the BLS. During the first nine months of the year, wages and benefits for nonunion workers rose 4.9 per cent. This was almost double union workers' 2.5 per cent increase.

Strikes decline. Work stoppages continued to decline as a weapon in labor-management disputes. According to the BLS, there were 40 stoppages involving 1,000 or more workers in 1988, the last year for which figures are available. This was the lowest number since the bureau began recording strikes in 1947.

Crew cut. The bargaining attitude of railroads and railroad unions appeared to improve in 1989. In January, the United Transportation Union and the CSX Corporation, owner of the nation's third-largest rail system, agreed to cut train crews by one-third. In past negotiations, the size of train crews was a major point of dispute between labor and management.

The agreement called for crews to consist of an engineer, a conductor, and one—instead of two—brakemen. (A brakeman is a person who couples and uncouples train cars and helps brake the train when it is rolling free.) In addition, the deal was sweetened by a $50,000 allowance for employees who have been laid off, a $25,000 allowance for leaves of absence, and a $20,000 allowance for employees who have been relocated.

Auto union setback. At its 1989 convention in June, the United Automobile Workers (UAW) began to map out a strategy to boost its membership, which dropped from 1.5 million in 1979 to about 966,000 in 1989. In addition to membership losses caused by reduced U.S. motor-vehicle production, the union has been unable to organize in any of the Japanese-owned automobile plants in the United States.

Workers at Nissan Motor Manufacturing Corporation USA set back the union's attempts to move into such plants during the year. In an election on July 27, workers at Nissan's assembly plant in Smyrna, Tenn., overwhelmingly defeated the UAW's efforts to organize the plant.

Aviation stalemates. Labor-management disputes continued to plague the aviation industry in 1989. On March 4, the International Association of Machinists and Aerospace Workers went on strike against Eastern Airlines Incorporated. The strike was supported by Eastern pilots and flight attendants, who refused to cross picket lines. The strike had an immediate effect on the airline, shutting down 90 per cent of its operations. On March 9, Eastern filed for bankruptcy.

The strike occurred despite more than a year of negotiations between Eastern and the unions. Bargaining proved difficult because of employees' distrust of Frank Lorenzo, chairman of Texas Air Corporation,

Workers at Nissan Motor's Smyrna, Tenn., plant celebrate on July 27
after employees voted against allowing the plant to be unionized.

Eastern's parent company, because of his cuts in jobs
and wages at Continental Airlines in 1983.

During the stalemate between labor and management, third parties tried to buy the airline. Among the
prospective buyers was a group led by Peter V. Ueberroth, former commissioner of baseball. Although the
three striking unions approved Ueberroth's deal, the
buy-out fell through on April 12.

A few days later, Texas Air announced that it was
taking Eastern off the market and would sell off the
airline's assets. On May 24, a bankruptcy judge approved the sale of Eastern's shuttle service to New
York City tycoon Donald J. Trump. Trump bought the
shuttle, which operates between Boston, New York
City, and Washington, D.C., for a reported $365 mil-
lion. Although pilots and flight attendants returned to
work in November, the machinists remained on strike
at year-end.

UAL and NWA. Attempts by United Air Lines Incorporated and the machinists' union to fend off a
buy-out of the airline weakened in May when a federal court voided the "poisoned purchase" agreement
between United and the union. The agreement was
designed to discourage a buy-out by maintaining or
raising labor costs after the airline was sold. On September 14, the UAL Corporation, parent company of
United, approved a $6.75-billion offer from a group
led by United pilots and management. The deal hit a
snag in October, however, when the buy-out group

announced that it was having trouble getting money
for the purchase.

In July, the machinists' union and the International
Air Line Pilots Association condemned NWA Incorporated, the parent company of Northwest Airlines Incorporated, for agreeing to sell the carrier to a group
of investors. Although it appeared that the sale would
create future trouble between labor and management, NWA was able to reach a new contract with the
machinists' union. It gave employees an $80 to $100
bonus followed by wage increases of 2.7 per cent in
1989 and 3.5 per cent in 1990 and 1991. Republic Airlines employees, who had joined Northwest when the
two carriers merged in 1986, got an additional increase of 7 per cent to bring their salaries up to Northwest levels.

Coal pits. After 14 months of unsuccessful negotiations, the United Mine Workers of America (UMW)
went on strike against the Pittston Company on April
5. The strike initially involved mines in Virginia, West
Virginia, and Kentucky.

The UMW accused Pittston of demanding seven-day
work weeks and eliminating medical benefits for retired and disabled workers and their families. Pittston
argued that it had terminated the benefits only because of the strike and only at those mines where
workers had walked off the job. By June, sympathy
strikes had spread to seven other states and involved
over 40,000 miners. The situation improved at year-

Labor

end, however. On Jan. 1, 1990, Pittston and the UMW reached a tentative agreement.

Broadcasting pact. In April 1989, the American Federation of Television and Radio Artists and the three major commercial broadcasting networks—the American Broadcasting Companies (ABC), the National Broadcasting Company (NBC), and CBS Inc.—agreed to a two-year contract. The contract gave actors with speaking roles wage increases of 3 per cent in November 1989 and November 1990. Other union members received wage increases of 2 per cent over the two-year period.

L.A. law. Police officers in Los Angeles reached a four-year agreement with the city in May 1989. The pact called for a wage increase of 4 per cent retroactive to July 1, 1988, another increase of 4 per cent in 1989 and in 1990, and a boost of 5 per cent in July 1991. The contract made the city's police officers among the highest paid in the United States.

Steel contracts. The United Steelworkers of America (USWA) reached agreements with three major steel companies in 1989 in staggered progression. In the past, the USWA met with the steel companies in a coordinated bargaining session.

On May 5, just three months before the expiration of its contract with Bethlehem Steel Corporation, the USWA and management agreed on a 50-month contract. The pact restored a 1986 pay cut of about 8 per cent. It also provided for a $1-an-hour raise in January

1991, and an average 50-cents-an-hour increase in January 1992. Union members ratified the contract in July 1989. Later in the year, the USWA set up similar agreements with Inland Steel Industries Incorporated, Armco Incorporated, and the National Steel Corporation.

Busy signal. On May 28, the American Telephone & Telegraph Company (AT&T) reached a three-year contract with the Communications Workers of America and the International Brotherhood of Electrical Workers. Not only was it the first time that the two unions joined in contract negotiations, but it also was the first time that AT&T agreed to a contract that called for different pay scales for its manufacturing and nonmanufacturing employees.

Under the contract, manufacturing workers received a lump sum payment equal to 8 per cent of their pay. They also will receive a pay increase of 3.5 per cent in 1990 and an increase of 3 per cent in 1991. Nonmanufacturing employees, such as customer service representatives, will receive wage increases of 2.5 per cent in 1990 and 2.25 per cent in 1991. The contract also provided employees with up to 12 months of unpaid leave to care for family members.

Contract negotiations did not go as smoothly between the two telephone workers' unions and the seven regional telephone companies in 1989. Strike-free settlements were reached at BellSouth Corporation, Southwestern Bell Corporation, and U S West

Machinists, pilots, and flight attendants for Eastern Airlines go on strike on March 4. Days later, the airline declared bankruptcy.

Changes in the United States labor force

	1988	1989
Total labor force	**123,378,000**	**125,554,000**
Armed forces	1,709,000	1,688,000
Civilian labor force	121,669,000	123,866,000
Total employment	116,677,000	119,051,000
Unemployment	6,701,000	6,504,000
Unemployment rate	5.5%	5.3%
Changes in real earnings of production and nonsupervisory workers (private nonfarm sector)*	−0.5%	−0.4%
Change in output per employee hour (private nonfarm sector)†	+1.3%	+0.9%

*Constant (1977) dollars. 1988 change from December 1987 to December 1988; 1989 change from October 1988 to October 1989 (preliminary data).

†Annual rate for 1988; for 1989, change is from third quarter 1988 to third quarter 1989 (preliminary data).

Source: U.S. Bureau of Labor Statistics.

union activities. One person would fill the role of administrator, hearing election disputes and disciplinary cases and having the power to veto spending, appointments, and contracts. Another would hold the post of investigator and would have the ability to file charges and present evidence at hearings. The third person would fill the role of election official and would supervise the 1991 and 1996 elections. On May 31, 1989, three attorneys were named to the posts.

Drugs. The Supreme Court of the United States on March 21 upheld a lower court ruling that permits the Federal Railroad Administration and other federal agencies to test employees for drug use. The court said that drug-testing programs for people directly involved in public health and safety, such as railroad workers and police officers, was not unconstitutional. Although the U.S. Constitution protects against unreasonable searches, the court stated that such tests were reasonable.

Hazard. The U.S. Department of Labor took steps in 1989 to protect health-care workers and other people from exposure to infectious diseases while on the job. On May 23, the department proposed a regulation that would require employers to evaluate procedures that expose workers to body fluids, which could carry diseases such as AIDS, and to take steps to reduce such risks.   Robert W. Fisher

See also **Economics; Manufacturing.** In *World Book,* see **Labor force; Labor movement.**

Incorporated. But at the four other companies— American Information Technologies Corporation (Ameritech), Bell Atlantic Corporation, NYNEX Corporation, and Pacific Telesis Group—strikes idled 200,000 workers in 20 states.

By the end of August, the unions and telephone companies reached separate agreements. The unions won moderate wage increases of between 2 per cent and 4 per cent but received substantially larger boosts in pension benefits. At Bell Atlantic, for example, pensions for future retirees were raised 13 per cent.

Minimum wage. On November 17, President George Bush signed a bill that raised the U.S. minimum wage for the first time since 1981. The bill increased the minimum wage from $3.35 an hour to $3.80 on April 1, 1990, and to $4.25 on April 1, 1991. The bill also provided for a subminimum or "training" wage for new employees. That wage was set at $3.35 for 1990 and $3.61 in 1991.

Teamsters. On March 13, the Teamsters Union and the U.S. Department of Justice reached an agreement in the federal racketeering suit filed against the union in 1988. The agreement allowed Teamsters officials to stay in office but changed election procedures to enable union members to vote directly for future union officers. In the past, officers had been elected by delegates to the union's national convention.

The Teamsters and the Justice Department also agreed to jointly appoint three people to oversee

Laos on March 26, 1989, held its first national election since the Lao People's Revolutionary Party, the national Communist organization, came to power in 1975. Voters had a choice of 121 candidates competing for 79 seats in the Supreme People's Assembly. With no opposition parties allowed, most of the candidates came from the Revolutionary Party, and 65 party members were elected.

At the opening session of the Assembly in late May, members chose Nouhak Phounsavanh as chairman. He was the nation's second-ranked Communist leader, after Kaysone Phomvihan, the party boss and premier.

Efforts to overcome economic stagnation increased opportunities for private enterprise. After years of battling Thailand over border disputes, Laos officials were suspicious of Thai attempts to increase trade. They sought trade and investment from other countries, but prospects were limited.

After conducting four joint searches with the United States since 1985 for the 547 U.S. servicemen listed as missing in Laos during the Vietnam War, Laos temporarily halted the searches in March 1989. Officials were reportedly angry about American criticism of Laos' failure to combat drug trafficking. Representatives from both nations discussed the drug problem and the missing Americans in Washington, D.C., from September 12 to 15.   Henry S. Bradsher

See also **Asia** (Facts in brief table). In *World Book,* see **Laos.**

Latin America

Drugs, debts, armed conflicts in Central America, and a United States invasion of Panama made headlines in Latin America in 1989. Hemisphere leaders met on October 27 and 28 in San José, Costa Rica, for the first time in more than 20 years. Sixteen chief executives, including United States President George Bush, informally discussed future agendas for joint action, particularly against the growing illicit drug trade.

War on drugs. Even before the summit meeting, Colombia's President Virgilio Barco Vargas had declared his own all-out war on drug trafficking. He received a standing ovation at the United Nations (UN) on September 29 when he addressed the issue of joint responsibility for curbing the drug trade. Although Latin America is the chief source of cocaine, most of it is consumed in the United States and Europe. Barco Vargas urged consumer nations to do more to curb the demand for dangerous drugs. "Every tactic and every weapon in the war against narcotics pales in significance compared with the need to reduce demand," he said.

The Colombian leader also called upon the United States and European nations to impose tighter controls on the manufacture and sale of chemicals used in producing cocaine, to guard against sales of arms to drug traffickers, and to put an end to the laundering—that is, disguising the illegal source—of drug profits through the international banking system.

Expressing feelings believed to be widely shared in Latin America, Barco Vargas told the UN General Assembly: "Somehow our sense of justice is warped when a poor farmer who feeds his family by growing coca is seen as the greater villain than the wealthy international banker who illegally transfers millions of dollars of drug money that finances terrorist acts against innocent people."

To many Latin-American leaders, actions by the United States to curb its own drug appetite seemed inadequate. Many resented what they perceived as U.S. government demands that Latin America assume the full brunt of resolving the problem by eradicating the crops, processing facilities, and distribution networks that figure in the supply of narcotics. Bush's antidrug strategy, which he announced on September 5, seemed to many to reflect this imbalance. About 70 per cent of the new funding Bush recommended was for tighter enforcement of existing drug laws, with 30 per cent earmarked for prevention and educational efforts aimed at reducing U.S. drug demand.

Central American conflicts. Five Central American presidents announced an agreement on February 14 under which Nicaragua would hold free elections while U.S.-supported *contra* rebels fighting the country's leftist Sandinista government would be dis-

A GI pauses near a poster of Panama's General Manuel Noriega, *above,* who was ousted by a U.S. invasion in December. American forces secured Panama City, *opposite page, top,* and took many prisoners, *right,* but failed to get Noriega, who surrendered two weeks later to face drug charges.

banded. The United States appeared caught off guard when the same leaders agreed at a meeting in Tela, Honduras, on August 7 to ask the UN and the Organization of American States (OAS) to form a commission that would oversee this course of action. Also at the meeting, Honduras and Nicaragua agreed to seek a UN peacekeeping force to guard their common border. The contras have used Honduras as a base from which to launch attacks inside Nicaragua.

But on November 1, when Nicaragua's President Daniel Ortega unilaterally suspended a cease-fire with the contras, hopes for the carefully elaborated peace plan began to evaporate. Similarly discouraging news came from El Salvador, where peace talks between leftist rebel foes and a newly elected right wing government were suspended, and the rebels launched one of their largest offensives of the 10-year civil war in November.

As a result, a summit meeting of the five Central American presidents opened on December 10 in San José under a cloud of pessimism. The meeting ended, however, with a new agreement that kept peace hopes alive. The new agreement called for the immediate demobilization of the contras and El Salvador's leftist guerrillas. More importantly, it provided a mechanism for ensuring the contras' demobilization by calling for the strengthening of the joint UN-OAS commission formed by the Tela agreement in August to oversee the peace process.

Under the Tela agreement, the contras were to be demobilized and their bases in Honduras dismantled. But as of the December summit, the contras were still based in Honduras and were still carrying out attacks inside Nicaragua. Ortega said he was forced to end the cease-fire because the contra attacks targeted voter registration centers set up for presidential elections scheduled for Feb. 25, 1990.

The new agreement sought to enforce the demobilization by calling for U.S. aid to the contras to be channeled through the UN-OAS commission rather than being sent through Honduras. Presumably, the commission would then have the power to suspend aid to contra units that violated the peace pact.

Also complicating the situation in Central America was the U.S. invasion of Panama on Dec. 20, 1989, to overthrow General Manuel Antonio Noriega Morena. Noriega surrendered to U.S. authorities on Jan. 3, 1990, and was flown to the United States to face drug-trafficking charges. In his place, the United States installed a new government headed by President Guillermo Endara, the apparent winner of a presidential election in May 1989. The invasion and subsequent occupation were condemned by most Latin-American governments. By a vote of 20 to 1, the OAS called for the withdrawal of U.S. forces so Panama could determine its future without "foreign interference." See **Panama**.

Foreign debts. Latin America's leaders were gloomy in assessing the burden of foreign debts on their economies. Speaking in Paris shortly before the July summit of the world's seven major industrial democracies, Brazil's outgoing President José Sarney Costa declared: "If urgent and far-reaching measures are not taken, there will not be any way to contain the social explosion which is approaching."

The economy of Brazil, Latin America's most heavily indebted nation, performed better only to fare worse because of the debt problem. In 1988, due to a successful export promotion drive, Brazil had a $19-billion trade surplus—the third-largest in the world after Japan and West Germany—only to find itself financially worse off in 1989.

The reason was that from 1980 to 1987, Brazil paid out $50.4 billion more in interest and principal repayments on its foreign debt than it received in new loans. As with other oil-short nations, Brazil had been forced to borrow heavily in the late 1970's to finance oil imports that had quadrupled in price. Subsequently, interest rates on those loans skyrocketed, with dire effects on the country's economy. In 1988, Brazil paid out interest on its debt that otherwise might have been used to provide 22 million jobs at the minimum wage, build schoolrooms for 60 million students, and construct low-income housing for 30 million people. Calculating that Brazil had paid out $176 billion in servicing its debt from 1972 to 1988, the country's National Council of Churches concluded that "the current foreign debt [$102 billion] should not be paid, because it already has been paid."

Even so, among Latin-American countries, Brazil could count its blessings because its debt repayments were equal to only about 40 per cent of its annual gross national product. The foreign debt repayments of Argentina and Peru, by contrast, were nearly equal to their total annual national product. In Mexico, they were greater than the gross national product.

Assessing the impact of foreign debt on Latin America, Venezuelan President Carlos Andrés Pérez warned in early October: "If our relations with creditor countries do not improve by next year, there could be unforeseeable consequences in Latin America." In calling for a special summit of rich and poor nations to work out a solution, Pérez noted, "If we do not settle the debt problem, all our sacrifices will be for nothing because of the resources that will have to be spent servicing our debt."

Corruption and nepotism. Television political coverage in several countries vividly brought home the extent of brutality and corruption afflicting Latin America's political life. In Panama, Endara and other candidates opposing Noriega were physically beaten before television cameras—while soldiers looked on —during presidential elections in May. In Haiti, three leaders opposed to the military rule of President Prosper Avril were displayed on live TV in November with their faces bloodied and swollen from beatings they said they received. The three men had tried to organize protests demanding free elections. During

Facts in brief on Latin-American political units

Country	Population	Government	Monetary unit*	Exports†	Foreign trade (million U.S.$) Imports†
Antigua and Barbuda	86,000	Governor General Sir Wilfred Jacobs; Prime Minister Vere C. Bird	dollar (2.7 = $1)	25	199
Argentina	32,361,000	President Carlos Saúl Menem	austral (653 = $1)	9,137	5,322
Bahamas	251,000	Governor General Sir Henry Taylor; Prime Minister Lynden O. Pindling	dollar (1.00 = $1)	2,545	3,233
Barbados	260,000	Governor General Sir Hugh Springer; Prime Minister Lloyd Erskine Sandiford	dollar (2.01 = $1)	176	582
Belize	182,000	Governor General Minita E. Gordon; Prime Minister George C. Price	dollar (2 = $1)	120	178
Bolivia	7,311,000	President Jaime Paz Zamora	boliviano (2.93 = $1)	597	595
Brazil	150,557,000	President José Sarney Costa	cruzado (7.35 = $1)	25,259	10,639
Chile	13,185,000	President Augusto Pinochet Ugarte	peso (278 = $1)	7,048	4,924
Colombia	31,863,000	President Virgilio Barco Vargas	peso (424 = $1)	4,642	3,907
Costa Rica	3,017,000	President Oscar Arias Sánchez	colón (83.6 = $1)	1,184	1,409
Cuba	10,279,000	President Fidel Castro	peso (0.80 = $1)	5,401	7,612
Dominica	98,000	President Clarence Augustus Seignoret; Prime Minister Eugenia Charles	dollar (2.7 = $1)	42	56
Dominican Republic	7,172,000	President Joaquín Balaguer Ricardo	peso (6.79 = $1)	892	1,747
Ecuador	10,782,000	President Rodrigo Borja Cevallos	sucre (667 = $1)	2,165	1,714
El Salvador	5,655,000	President Alfredo Cristiani Burkard	colón (5.0 = $1)	566	1,049
Grenada	96,000	Acting Governor General Sir Hudson Scipio; Prime Minister Ben Jones	dollar (2.7 = $1)	31	88
Guatemala	9,117,000	President Vinicio Cerezo Arévalo	quetzal (2.85 = $1)	419	592
Guyana	868,000	President Hugh Desmond Hoyte; Prime Minister Hamilton Green	dollar (33 = $1)	207	255
Haiti	5,777,000	President Prosper Avril	gourde (5 = $1)	174	442
Honduras	5,144,000	President José Simon Azcona Hoyo	lempira (2 = $1)	782	903
Jamaica	2,520,000	Governor General Florizel Glasspole; Prime Minister Michael Manley	dollar (6.42 = $1)	821	1,433
Mexico	88,560,000	President Carlos Salinas de Gortari	peso (2,654 = $1)	20,658	18,954
Nicaragua	3,606,000	President Daniel Ortega	córdoba (23,500 = $1)	247	770
Panama	2,421,000	President Guillermo Endara	balboa (1 = $1)	280	795
Paraguay	4,278,000	President Andrés Rodríguez Pedotti	guaraní (1,200 = $1)	379	590
Peru	22,330,000	President Alan García Pérez; Prime Minister Luis Alberto Sánchez Sánchez	inti (4,700 = $1)	2,672	2,556
Puerto Rico	3,282,000	Governor Rafael Hernández Colón	U.S. dollar	11,600	10,100
St. Christopher and Nevis	48,000	Governor General Clement Athelston Arrindell; Prime Minister Kennedy Alphonse Simmonds	dollar (2.7 = $1)	34	63
St. Lucia	143,000	Governor General Sir Stanislaus James; Prime Minister John Compton	dollar (2.7 = $1)	83	155
St. Vincent and the Grenadines	117,000	Acting Governor General Henry Harvey Williams; Prime Minister James F. Mitchell	dollar (2.7 = $1)	68	87
Suriname	408,000	Commander of the National Army Désiré D. Bouterse; President Ramsewak Shankar	guilder (1.79 = $1)	241	244
Trinidad and Tobago	1,283,000	President Noor Hassanali; Prime Minister Arthur Napoleon Raymond Robinson	dollar (4.25 = $1)	1,405	1,123
Uruguay	3,130,000	President Julio María Sanguinetti	peso (763 = $1)	1,405	1,177
Venezuela	19,744,000	President Carlos Andrés Pérez	bolívar (44.3 = $1)	9,629	11,461

*Exchange rates as of Dec. 1, 1989, or latest available data. †Latest available data.

the government broadcast announcing the cancellation of the protests, the cameras panned to the three opposition leaders in a display apparently meant to intimidate Haitians.

In Brazil, television played a major role in that country's first direct presidential election in more than 25 years, with the winning candidate, Fernando Collor de Mello, receiving generous coverage from Brazil's most important TV network. Collor's principal campaign theme—attacking government corruption and nepotism—also dovetailed nicely with a hit TV series that fictionalized the corrupt lives of politicians in Brazil's Congress. Nightly newscasts chronicled a survey revealing that more than 200 Brazilian congressmen had placed relatives on the 13,000-strong congressional staff.

In Argentina, a television talk-show host in Buenos Aires equated that country with a train on which everybody is trying to ride free. Stung by the criticism, Argentina's newly appointed treasury secretary investigated and found that 40 per cent of all passengers on Argentina's national railway system were riding free with passes that had been issued as a form of political patronage.

According to another story circulating in Buenos Aires, a pilot on an Argentine airline, shortly after take-off, expressed his special thanks to the three passengers on his crowded Boeing 737 who had paid for their tickets. Checking it out, the country's interior minister discovered that his own department was issuing tickets for free air travel at the rate of nearly 15,000 per month. Regulations permit free air travel to representatives of 31 political parties, though some parties are so small they have no elected representatives in Congress.

The interior minister estimated that in the four years since Argentina's Congress approved the regulations, the government had lost at least $100 million in airline revenues. A former cabinet member put the total cost of Argentine government giveaways, including preferential rates for electricity, water, and gas enjoyed by many industries, at $3 billion annually.

Coffee woes. The failure to extend the International Coffee Agreement, whereby producing and consuming nations had jointly regulated trade in the commodity since 1962, led to a collapse in earnings for several Latin-American countries. Latin America produces 70 per cent of the world's coffee. Brazil and Colombia were among the hardest hit by a 40 per cent drop in prices in the two months following the agreement's suspension in July 1989.

Hope for the Amazon. Photographs taken from U.S. space satellites in 1989 provided encouraging evidence that the number of fires set in the ecologically important Amazon rain forest was lower than in 1988. By June, there were 37 per cent fewer blazes, compared with the previous year. Although the principal reason for this was abnormally wet conditions during what is usually the dry season, the Brazilian government also played an important role by ending subsidies to ranchers in the Amazon region who clear land by burning, and by levying fines against those who start fires.

Hispanic power. On October 11, the U.S. Bureau of the Census announced that the number of Hispanics legally residing in the United States had passed the 20 million mark, up 39 per cent since 1980. Even before the figures were released, Hispanic Americans were gearing up for a drive to ensure that census takers in 1990 include in their count the number of Hispanics who illegally reside in the United States. According to estimates by U.S. immigration officials, the number of illegal Hispanic immigrants has continued to swell by more than 2 million per year despite the Immigration Reform and Control Act of 1986, designed to stem the tide of illegal immigration.

Peruvian discoveries. During 1989, archaeologists yielded new insights into the beginnings of civilization in the Americas. Working at sites in more than 50 narrow river valleys of Peru during the 1980's, archaeologists found monumental architecture and planned urban developments dating back 3,500 to 5,000 years, roughly contemporary with Egypt's pyramids.

Discoveries in Peru include tall pyramids and U-shaped temples and plazas flanked by residential dwellings indicating a complex societal organization. The largest pyramid excavated so far is more than 10 stories high.

The Andean structures predate those of the Maya by nearly 2,000 years and those of the Aztecs by 3,000. Assessing the Peruvian discoveries, Yale archaeologist Richard Burger noted, "This idea of the Old World being ahead of the New World has to be put on hold."

Rediscovering ancient crops. In 1989, scientists continued to rediscover nutritious and delicious crops grown by the Aztecs and Incas long before the arrival of the Spanish conquistadors. The U.S. National Research Council, the research arm of the National Academy of Sciences, which advises the U.S. government on scientific matters, reported on several Incan foods that may have a bright future at U.S. supermarkets. They include *arracacha*, a carrotlike root whose delicate flavor is a blend of cabbage, celery, and roasted chestnuts; and *ulluco*, a potatolike root that has a nutty taste and is particularly rich in vitamin C.

In California, a health-food distributor began marketing Amaranth Flakes, made from *amaranth*, a grain rich in vitamins, minerals, and fiber. The box in which it comes advertises amaranth as "the grain the Aztecs were willing to die for"—a reference to the use of the plant's flowers in ancient rituals involving human sacrifice. 　　Nathan A. Haverstock

See also articles on the various Latin-American nations. In the World Book Supplement section, see **Hispanic Americans.** In *World Book,* see **Latin America** and articles on the individual countries.

Law. See **Civil rights; Courts; Crime; Supreme Court of the United States.**

Residents of Beirut arrive in Israeli-controlled southern Lebanon after fleeing ferocious artillery duels that pulverized the city in late summer.

Lebanon in 1989 was racked by one of the most destructive episodes in its 14-year civil war. The violence killed at least 900 people and nearly destroyed Beirut. Lebanon's civil strife also left the country's newly elected president dead and imperiled a political accord that enjoyed widespread support and offered some hope of ending the bloodshed.

The persistent conflict between Lebanon's Muslims and Christians escalated in March when General Michel Awn, the commander of the Christian units in the Lebanese army, declared a "war of liberation" against the 40,000 Syrian troops in Lebanon. He also imposed a blockade on seaports controlled by Muslim militias allied with Syria. The militias had been collecting $200,000 a month in customs fees that Awn said should belong to him as the legitimate authority in Lebanon.

In response to Awn's blockade, Syrian and Muslim forces began shelling Christian ports. That led to ferocious artillery duels that pulverized Beirut.

Awn has considered himself Lebanon's leader since September 1988, when factional strife prevented the election of a new president to succeed Amine Gemayel, whose term had expired. Gemayel then named Awn as the head of an interim military government to serve until a new president could be elected. This was opposed by the existing civilian government headed by Salim al-Huss, Gemayel's Muslim prime minister. When al-Huss, who had never resigned, declared himself the legitimate authority in Lebanon, the country was left with two governments.

Negotiations. In early April 1989, a special committee of the Arab League began an intense effort to negotiate a cease-fire. A truce that began on May 11 lasted until late July, when the murderous artillery bombardments resumed. The shellfire drove more than three-fourths of Beirut's 1.5 million residents from the city. Despite appeals by the Arab League and the United Nations (UN), among others, the shelling continued until early September.

During the summer, the Arab League committee attempted to arrange a political settlement to the conflict. But on August 1, the mediators announced they were abandoning their efforts, laying most of the blame for their failure on Syria. On August 13, Syria and its allies launched a large-scale ground attack on Awn's position in the hills above Beirut.

On September 16, the Arab League committee announced it was resuming its mediation efforts and issued a new peace proposal. It called for a cease-fire, a lifting of seaport blockades, and an embargo on Syria's arms shipments to its Muslim allies and on Iraq's provision of supplies for Awn's forces. Awn reluctantly agreed to the cease-fire after Syria, Iraq, and various Lebanese factions announced their support.

Charter debate. On September 30, 63 of the 73 surviving members of the Chamber of Deputies, Lebanon's parliament, met in Taif, Saudi Arabia, to debate

A bride and her father venture from their fortified home in Beirut during a lull in artillery bombardments in April.

a "charter of national reconciliation" drafted by Arab League negotiators. The charter, adopted on October 24, shifted significant political power from Lebanon's once-dominant Christian community, which had controlled the reins of power, to the country's Muslims, now the more populous group. The Lebanese lawmakers agreed to increase the number of seats in parliament from 99 to 108 and divide them equally between Christians and Muslims. The delegates also agreed to transfer some power from the president, who has traditionally been a Maronite Christian, to the Cabinet, which would also have an equal number of Christians and Muslims.

In addition, the delegates agreed to allow Syrian troops to maintain their position in Lebanon for up to two years while the new government was being formed. The Syrians would then withdraw to eastern Lebanon. Controversy over the Syrian pullout had threatened to derail the talks. But Christian delegates finally dropped their insistence on a firm timetable for the Syrian withdrawal.

New president. On November 5, the Lebanese parliament met in a remote mountain village in northern Lebanon to approve the accord. They were prevented from meeting in Beirut by Awn, who vehemently opposed the new charter because it did not guarantee the withdrawal of Syrian forces. On November 4, Awn had announced that, using his powers as chief of state, he was dissolving parliament. Never-

theless, the Lebanese lawmakers ratified the accord the next day and elected René Moawad, a Maronite Christian moderate who had the backing of Syria, as president. Awn declared the election "null and void."

Less than three weeks later, on November 22, Moawad was assassinated along with 23 others by a remote-control bomb. Two days later, the parliament elected another moderate, Elias Hrawi, to succeed him.

Late in November, Syria began pouring tanks and troops into Lebanon, apparently in preparation for an assault on Awn's stronghold. Hrawi threatened to resign if the deadlock between his government and Awn continued.

Hostages. The United States failed to make any progress in 1989 in securing the release of American hostages held in Lebanon. On July 28, Israeli troops abducted a pro-Iranian Shiite religious leader, Sheik Abdul-Karim Obeid, from southern Lebanon. The Israelis apparently planned to use him to win the freedom of Israeli soldiers held by the Shiites. Hezbollah (Party of God), the pro-Iranian group holding most of the hostages, threatened to kill U.S. Marine Colonel William R. Higgins unless Obeid was released. Higgins had been kidnapped in 1988 while serving with UN peacekeeping troops in Lebanon. On July 31, a videotape of a hanged man believed to be Higgins was sent to news agencies in Beirut.   William Spencer

See also **Middle East** (Facts in brief table). In *World Book*, see **Lebanon**.

Lee, Spike (1957-   ), emerged as one of the hottest filmmakers in the United States in 1989 with the release of *Do the Right Thing*, a movie about racial tensions in a New York City neighborhood. Although the motion picture received considerable acclaim, some film critics denounced its apparent acceptance of violence as a response to racial discrimination. The mixed reviews notwithstanding, *Do the Right Thing* established Lee as one of the most prominent black spokesmen and artists in the nation.

Lee was born on March 20, 1957, in Atlanta, Ga., and grew up in the Brooklyn section of New York City. After graduating from Morehouse College in Atlanta in 1979, he studied filmmaking at New York University. His final film-school project, *Joe's Bed-Stuy Barbershop: We Cut Heads*, a movie about a barber who engages in petty crime, won a student Oscar from the Academy of Motion Picture Arts and Sciences.

In 1986, Lee made his professional debut with *She's Gotta Have It*, about the sexual relationships of a young black woman. The movie won the award for best new director at the Cannes Film Festival in France. Lee's next effort, *School Daze*, a musical about black college life, became Columbia Pictures' most profitable film of 1988.

Lee has his own production company, 40 Acres and a Mule Filmworks, in Brooklyn. He writes, directs, and co-stars in all of his movies.   David L. Dreier

Lesotho. See **Africa**.

Liberia. President Samuel K. Doe continued his tight personal control over all aspects of Liberian government and business in 1989. Doe decides how more than 40 per cent of the government's revenues will be spent each year, without supervision by the National Assembly.

Two human-rights organizations—Amnesty International and Africa Watch—reported during the year that Doe has continued to harass leaders of the political opposition and that his government is riddled with corruption and guilty of frequent human-rights violations. In June, Doe ordered the closing of a Roman Catholic radio station, ELCM, because its reporting of a riot at a soccer match was embarrassing to the government. Two independent newspapers, the *Sun-Times* and *Footprints Today*, which had been banned in 1988, were not allowed to reopen in 1989.

The economy. The July closing of LAMCO—the Liberian-American-Swedish Minerals Corporation—caused the loss of more than 15,000 jobs in the iron mining area in Nimba County. The Nimba Mining Company, a new joint enterprise of the Liberian government and foreign interests, planned to acquire the LAMCO assets and start production in 1992.

World prices for rubber, Liberia's second-largest export after iron, improved by 12 per cent over 1988 prices, bringing Liberia's 1988-1989 export earnings to more than $89.5 million.

Foreign debt. Liberia's foreign debt mounted to $1.3 billion in 1989, and back interest payments came to more than $550 million. The International Monetary Fund, an agency of the United Nations that consults on debt problems, set new economic restrictions on further loans to the Doe government. In April, the United States government announced that Liberia, which is the largest per-capita recipient of U.S. aid in sub-Saharan Africa, must repay $7 million of its $183-million debt to the United States or it would be ineligible for additional assistance. To meet that demand, the Doe government took the novel approach of requesting the Liberian people to contribute to a special debt-repayment fund.

Ritual murder. During much of the year, public attention was focused on the ritual murder of a police officer whose decapitated body was discovered in March. In August, Major General Gray D. Allison, Liberia's minister of defense and the number-two man in the Doe government, was found guilty of the crime and sentenced to death. Allison reportedly performed the ritual murder as part of a witchcraft rite designed to bring about the overthrow of the Doe regime.

Coup attempt. Thousands of Liberians fled to Ivory Coast to escape fighting caused by a failed coup attempt in late December. Rebels reportedly entered Liberia from Ivory Coast, and fighting between them and the Liberian army devastated several towns. J. Gus Liebenow and Beverly B. Liebenow

See also **Africa** (Facts in brief table). In *World Book,* see **Liberia.**

Actor William Hurt poses with a popular book by Dr. Seuss in a poster promoting reading and libraries for the American Library Association.

Library. Children and young adults received special attention from United States libraries in 1989, officially designated by Congress as "The Year of the Young Reader." Sponsored by the Library of Congress's Center for the Book, a privately funded organization that promotes reading, the celebration emphasized the joys and value of books for children and young adults. Librarians also used the congressional proclamation as a focus for publicity and special events highlighting the importance of family literacy.

Private action. The increased attention to libraries and literacy also inspired action from the private sector. In July, the Bell Atlantic Foundation, a nonprofit organization funded by Bell Atlantic Corporation, announced a $300,000 literacy grant to the American Library Association (ALA). The grant was to help 25 public libraries develop programs to improve parents' reading skills so they could help teach their children to read.

The California Raisin Advisory Board in September launched a nationwide reading club in the 15,000 U.S. public libraries for more than 2.5 million children aged 5 through 10. The California Raisin Reading Club will "send a message to kids that reading is cool, fun, and rewarding," according to the board.

Censorship. Libraries and bookstores throughout the United States in September sponsored programs, displays, and other events to publicize the dangers of censorship during Banned Books Week '89—Celebrating the Freedom to Read. It was the eighth annual commemoration of the First Amendment to the United States Constitution, which specifies that Congress shall make no law abridging freedom of speech or of the press.

Reports of attempts to limit access to books and other materials considered offensive by some people were at record highs in 1989. More than 500 incidents of attempted censorship were reported to the ALA's Office for Intellectual Freedom in 1988. Most of the censorship complaints focused on books considered too sexually explicit or books allegedly promoting worship of Satan.

School libraries continued to be the main battleground for more than three-fourths of all censorship challenges. The Office for Intellectual Freedom reported that people calling for censorship are more likely to be part of a national organized effort and more likely to be successful than in previous years.

Freedom award. The ALA won the 1989 "Open Book" award from the American Society of Journalists and Authors for its "courageous stand in upholding freedom to read by exposing and opposing" the Library Awareness Program. That program was set up by the Federal Bureau of Investigation (FBI) in the mid-1970's to monitor the use of U.S. libraries by suspected spies.

The library community learned of the program in June 1987 when FBI agents asked a New York City librarian for circulation records of scientific journals. The FBI also asked librarians to report on "suspicious" activities of foreigners or people with accents or "foreign-sounding names." Librarians refused to cooperate, and the ALA filed suit seeking bureau records on the program. In 1988, the FBI announced that participation in the program was strictly voluntary.

In November 1989, the National Security Archive, a nonprofit research group in Washington, D.C., released FBI documents revealing that earlier in the year the bureau had investigated librarians protesting the awareness program. The documents indicated that the FBI had conducted checks to determine if the librarians were part of a Soviet-backed effort to discredit the program.

ALA news. Thomas J. Galvin resigned as executive director of the 50,000-member ALA, effective in October. Linda F. Crismond, director of the Los Angeles County Public Library, was named to the post. She is the first woman to serve as ALA executive director.

F. William Summers, dean of the School of Library and Information Studies at Florida State University in Tallahassee and ALA president, presided over the organization's 108th annual conference attended by 17,408 participants in Dallas June 24 to 29. At the end of the meeting, Patricia Wilson Berger, director of information resources and services at the National Institute of Standards and Technology, took over as president.   Peggy Barber

In *World Book,* see **Library.**

Libya in September 1989 celebrated with parades, speeches, and gymnastic displays the 20th anniversary of the military coup that brought Leader of the Revolution Muammar Muhammad al-Qadhafi to power. Libya held the festivities in an atmosphere of reconciliation with its neighbors. On August 31, the eve of the celebration, Libya signed a peace treaty with Chad that ended a 16-year conflict over the Aozou Strip, a 43,000-square-mile (111,000-square-kilometer) border area claimed by both countries. Under the treaty, Libya promised to withdraw its troops from the region, and the two countries agreed to resolve the ownership question within a year by peaceful means. If they failed to do so, the question would be referred to the International Court of Justice, an organ of the United Nations, for binding arbitration.

Arab common market. In February, the General People's Congress, Libya's legislative body, ratified the treaty forming the Arab Maghreb Union, a North African common market made up of Libya, Tunisia, Algeria, Morocco, and Mauritania. Among the provisions was a noninterference clause, under which the five countries promised not to intervene in one another's internal affairs. Some observers suggested that including Libya in the union was an attempt by the four other countries to check Qadhafi's inclination for regional meddling.

Relations with the United States in 1989 continued to be stormy. On January 4, two U.S. Navy F-14 fighters shot down two Libyan MIG-23's over international waters of the Mediterranean Sea about 70 miles (110 kilometers) off Libya's coast. According to the United States, the Libyan jets clearly displayed "hostile intent" toward the U.S. fighters, which were on routine patrol. The United States also said the F-14's fired only after repeatedly taking evasive action to avoid a confrontation. Libya claimed that its planes were unarmed reconnaissance craft shot down in a "premeditated attack." The United States however, released a videotape made by one of the F-14's during the clash that the Navy said showed four missiles under the wings of one of the MIG's.

Chemical plant uproar. The downing of the jets occurred at a time of already heightened tensions between Libya and the United States over charges that a Libyan chemical plant was being built to manufacture chemical weapons. Libya insisted that the plant, located about 40 miles (65 kilometers) southwest of Tripoli—Libya's capital—was a pharmaceutical factory. Although the plant was in production at year's end, Libya had moved what Western analysts considered chemical-weapons supplies to other sites.

Ban reversed. In January, the Administration of President Ronald Reagan rescinded a 1986 ban on U.S. oil company operations in Libya. The ban was part of an order severing economic ties with Libya as punishment for that country's involvement in terrorism. But the oil companies had complained that the Libyans were operating the oil fields and keeping the income.

Image polishing. During 1989, Qadhafi worked to play down his image as a chief sponsor of international terrorism. In July, he intervened to secure the release of a Belgian physician taken hostage in Lebanon. In August, he announced that Libya would no longer fund terrorist organizations or movements.

Internal changes. In March, the General People's Congress enlarged the General Secretariat, a cabinet-like body, at Qadhafi's urging. Among the new appointees to the Secretariat was Libya's first woman member. She was named secretary of education.

The economy. With oil revenues continuing to decline, the government adopted a 1989 budget that set strict controls on spending. Workers were to receive incentive pay and bonuses to boost productivity.

The discovery of an important offshore oil field at Bouri, near Tobruk, early in 1989 promised to increase Libyan oil production significantly. A refinery at Tobruk, opened in 1988, reached capacity production of 220,000 barrels per day in 1989.

The Great Man-Made River, Qadhafi's mammoth project to use water from underground reservoirs in the Sahara to irrigate coastal farmlands, continued on schedule. By January, the first 500 miles (800 kilometers) of the 2,500-mile (4,000-kilometer) pipeline had been completed.　　William Spencer

See also **Africa** (Facts in brief table). In *World Book,* see **Libya.**

Liechtenstein. See **Europe.**

Literature. Fiction published in the United States during 1989 included some notable works, but in general the offerings of established novelists and short-story writers were unremarkable. Saving the year from total mediocrity was a trio of superb novels whose achievement was significant enough to give many readers hope that American fiction would be able to hold its own with other national literatures in vigor and originality.

Each of these three novels presented a point of view not often heard in American literature. Amy Tan's *The Joy Luck Club,* about the lives of four Chinese immigrant women and their American-born daughters in California, was easily the year's most impressive debut. Not far behind was Allan Gurganus' massive first novel, *Oldest Living Confederate Widow Tells All,* in which an aged woman recollects a panorama of Southern family history from her rest-home rocking chair. Oscar Hijuelos' second novel, *The Mambo Kings Play Songs of Love,* brilliantly followed a Cuban family's fortunes in the United States in terms of several generations of Latin music.

Other highly promising first novels included Jerome Badanes' *The Final Opus of Leon Solomon,* Susan Chace's *Intimacy,* and Maxine Hong Kingston's *Tripmaster Monkey: His Fake Book.*

Three established novelists brought out able work on unusual subjects. Brad Leithauser set *Hence,* his inventive novel about computer chess, in the very

John le Carré impressed both readers and critics with his best-selling espionage novel about reduced East-West tensions, *The Russia House.*

near future. John Casey's *Spartina*, a lyric novel with a remarkably mythic quality set in a Narragansett Bay fishing town, won the National Book Award for fiction. And in *John Dollar*, Marianne Wiggins ably explored a theme that William Golding had introduced in his 1954 classic *Lord of the Flies*, which described the moral decay among a group of boys stranded on a desert island. Wiggins came close to matching Golding's achievement by telling a similar story with a largely female cast.

Some seasoned writers turned out creditable new novels. *Billy Bathgate*, by E. L. Doctorow, was an amusing and stylish tale about a 15-year-old boy who falls in with gangsters. *Jack Gance*, by Ward Just, explored moral dilemmas in the political worlds of Chicago and Washington, D.C. And with *Buffalo Afternoon*, Susan Fromberg Schaeffer produced a convincing Vietnam novel, complete with vivid scenes of combat from a male point of view.

In a striking departure from common practice, Nobel laureate Saul Bellow had two new short novels published as inexpensive paperbacks, rather than hardbacks. *A Theft* and *The Bellarosa Connection* were well received both by critics and by readers.

Other competent novels came from Paul Auster, Russell Banks, Madison Smartt Bell, Thomas Berger, Anne Bernays, Joan Chase, Jim Crace, Anita Desai, Charles Dickinson, Mary Gordon, John Irving, Joyce Johnson, David Leavitt, David Lodge, Thomas McGuane, Cynthia Ozick, Thomas Sanchez, Jane Smiley, and Alice Walker.

Important short-story collections were Rick Bass's *The Watch;* T. Coraghessan Boyle's *If the River Was Whiskey;* Frederick Busch's *Absent Friends;* Barbara Kingsolver's *Homeland;* Bobbie Ann Mason's *Love Life;* Peter Matthiessen's *On the River Styx;* Susan Minot's *Lust and Other Stories;* and Bob Shacochis' *The Next New World.*

Fiction from other countries. Salman Rushdie's controversial *The Satanic Verses*, received favorably by American critics, was blasted by many Muslim readers, some of whom threatened the writer's life. Rushdie, an Indian-born author living in London, went into hiding. See **Close-Up.**

Other significant work in English from abroad included Anita Brookner's *Latecomers*, Anthony Burgess' *Any Old Iron*, Margaret Drabble's *A Natural Curiosity*, and Fay Weldon's *Leader of the Band*, all from England; Margaret Atwood's *Cat's Eye* and Bharati Mukherjee's *Jasmine*, both from Canada; Australian writer Thomas Keneally's *To Asmara;* and Irish writer Desmond Hogan's volume of short stories, *A Link with the River.*

Important novels in translation from Spanish were Mexican writer Carlos Fuentes' *Christopher Unborn* and Peruvian writer Mario Vargas Llosa's *The Storyteller.* A. B. Yehoshua's *Five Seasons* and David Grossman's *See Under: Love* were translated from Hebrew. Translated from Italian was Umberto Eco's *Foucault's*

Pendulum, which—like Eco's first novel, *The Name of the Rose*—was a best seller in the United States despite its immense length and highly intellectual subject matter.

Autobiography. An unusual number of excellent autobiographies appeared in 1989. The most elegant was *Sketches from a Life*, a collection of bittersweet and stylish snippets from the diaries of the eminent diplomat-scholar George F. Kennan.

Young novelist Tobias Wolff's *This Boy's Life*, a creative memoir of growing up with a monstrous alcoholic parent, broke new ground by employing the techniques of fiction in the genre of autobiography. *The Good Times*, the second volume of Russell Baker's endearing memoirs, took his career to his ascendancy as a columnist for *The New York Times.*

From other noted writers came *Self-Consciousness: Memoirs*, a fragmentary yet elegant sampling of novelist John Updike's distinguished life in letters; *Loyalties*, former *Washington Post* reporter Carl Bernstein's story of life with parents who had Communist connections; *Harp*, novelist John Gregory Dunne's often caustic, always entertaining memoir of life as an Irish Roman Catholic in the United States; and *The Broken Cord*, Native American novelist Michael Dorris' heartbreaking story of the effect of fetal alcohol syndrome on his adopted son and the Indian community.

And the Walls Came Tumbling Down, by civil rights leader Ralph David Abernathy, won critical respect but stirred considerable controversy over a few pages discussing the alleged extramarital activities of Martin Luther King, Jr., Abernathy's colleague in the civil rights movement. In *The Most Beautiful House in the World*, architectural philosopher Witold Rybczynski described the intellectual experience of building his own house.

Working Days, edited by Robert DeMott, was a revealing collection of John Steinbeck's journals written 50 years ago as he was working on *The Grapes of Wrath*. In *When Heaven and Earth Changed Places*, Vietnamese immigrant Le Ly Hayslip told of growing up in the shadow of war. And in *Miles*, jazz musician Miles Davis recounted his egocentric but fascinating life.

Biography. Two particularly significant show-business biographies were published in 1989. In *Paul Robeson*, Martin Bauml Duberman restored dignity to the tragic story of the black singer who fought racism but was brought down by his own socialist political views. *Goldwyn*, A. Scott Berg's life of film producer Samuel Goldwyn, also offered a broad and deep history of Hollywood.

Important political biographies included *Let Them Call Me Rebel: Saul Alinsky—His Life and Legacy*, by Sanford Horwitt; *Goering*, by David Irving; *Unseasonable Truths: The Life of Robert Maynard Hutchins*, by Harry S. Ashmore; *Harold Macmillan: Politician 1894-1956*, by Alistair Horne; *Richard Milhous Nixon: The Rise of an American Politician*, by Roger Morris; *Nixon,*

Veteran novelist E. L. Doctorow chronicled a boy's education among gangsters in New York City in the 1930's in his novel *Billy Bathgate.*

Volume Two: The Triumph of a Politician, 1962-1972, by Stephen E. Ambrose; and *Adlai Stevenson: His Life and Legacy,* by Porter McKeever.

Among the better literary biographies were Frederick R. Karl's *William Faulkner;* Herbert Lottman's *Flaubert;* Barry Miles's *Ginsberg,* about the poet Allen Ginsberg; Norman Sherry's *The Life of Graham Greene, Volume One: 1904-1939;* Ian Gibson's *Federico Garcia Lorca: A Life;* Anne Stevenson's *Bitter Fame: A Life of Sylvia Plath;* Michael Shnayerson's *Irwin Shaw;* and Michael Holroyd's *Bernard Shaw: Volume Two, 1898-1918: The Pursuit of Power.*

Criticism. Two books of literary criticism stood out in 1989. *Safe at Last in the Middle Years* was Margaret Morganroth Gullette's engrossing study of the life-affirming works written in middle age by Saul Bellow, Margaret Drabble, Anne Tyler, and John Updike. In *The Company We Keep: An Ethics of Fiction,* Wayne C. Booth considered the presence and lack of morals and ethics in modern novels.

Contemporary affairs. Thomas L. Friedman's *From Beirut to Jerusalem* revealed how its author, a Pulitzer Prize-winning *New York Times* correspondent with a Jewish background, became sympathetic to the Arab and Palestinian cause as well as that of Israel. Rigorously honest as well as astute, Friedman concluded that all sides in the Middle East deserve a great deal of criticism. The book won the National Book Award for nonfiction.

In *A Turn in the South,* V. S. Naipaul offered a sampling of life in several Southern states. In *Profscam: Professors and the Demise of Higher Education,* Charles J. Sykes presented a polemical view of what he considered underworked and overpaid professors in the contemporary university, with an emphasis on their lack of teaching. Jonathan Schell's *Observing the Nixon Years* was a collection of his *New Yorker* magazine essays discussing the Vietnam War and the Watergate crisis.

Tracy Kidder's *Among Schoolchildren* told of a dedicated schoolteacher's struggle to cope with fifth-grade life and crises in industrial Holyoke, Mass. Oliver Sacks's *Seeing Voices: A Journey into the World of the Deaf* provided a fascinating personal exploration of the natural sign language of the deaf-born. And Richard Rhodes's *Farm* gave a surprisingly optimistic chronicle of a year in the life of an American farmer.

History. Of the many books both celebrating and lamenting the bicentennial of the French Revolution, Simon Schama's *Citizens* was the most original. It maintained that far from being decrepit and reactionary, the French nobility of the time was vigorous and far-seeing, and its downfall to the Paris mob was a true historical tragedy.

Several important books marked the 50th anniversary of the start of World War II. Donald Cameron Watt's *How War Came* was a superb study of the failure of diplomats to avert the bloody events of 1939.

A Book Ignites a Firestorm

A novel denounced as blasphemous to Islam and championed as a symbol of freedom of expression created an international furor in 1989. *The Satanic Verses* (1988) by British writer Salman Rushdie provoked death threats, government bans, bookstore bombings, and protests that left scores of people dead.

Rushdie, born to Muslim parents in India, has said that the book is about people, like himself, who are a product of two cultures but truly belong to neither. One of the many stories in the book, however, concerns a charismatic Arab named Mahound (an Arabic name for the Devil). A businessman turned prophet and religious leader, Mahound is a thinly disguised representation of the prophet Muhammad, the founder of Islam, whose writings are accepted by Muslims as the word of God.

Rushdie's irreverent portrayal of Mahound as an ordinary person outraged many Muslims. They also condemned a passage in the book in which Mahound's writings are twisted by an unfaithful scribe. In demanding that the book be banned, Muslims contended that freedom of expression did not extend to attacks on their religion.

Actions against the novel, which included public book burnings and bans by India and a number of other countries, turned bloody on February 12 when police fired into a crowd marching on the United States cultural center in Islamabad, Pakistan. At least six of the protesters, who were denouncing U.S. publication of the book, died. More protesters died in later demonstrations in Pakistan and India.

Muslims in Bradford, England, in February burn a copy of Salman Rushdie's novel *The Satanic Verses,* denounced as blasphemous to Islam.

The controversy escalated on February 14 when Iran's supreme leader, Ayatollah Ruhollah Khomeini, condemned *The Satanic Verses* as blasphemous and urged Muslims to kill Rushdie. Rushdie and his wife, American novelist Marianne Wiggins, immediately went into hiding in England.

Khomeini's action had an immediate and chilling effect. A number of European publishing companies dropped plans to publish the book, though some later reversed that decision. Several bookstore chains in the United States, including Waldenbooks Incorporated, the largest U.S. bookseller, at least temporarily removed copies of the novel from their shelves, citing concerns over employee safety. Canada banned the book after protests from that country's Muslims.

Viking Penguin, Rushdie's publisher, temporarily evacuated its New York City offices after numerous bomb threats so security could be improved. Two bookstores in Berkeley, Calif., selling Viking Penguin books were firebombed in February, as were a number of British bookstores later in the year. In August, a man building a bomb in a London hotel room was blown up while—an Iranian terrorist group claimed—preparing an attack on Rushdie.

Although some writers accused Rushdie of deliberately being provocative to boost sales of the book, others rallied to his support, holding a public reading of the book on February 22. Rushdie's supporters—and Rushdie himself—also pointed out that few of the book's critics had actually read the novel and that many of the reports circulating about it were wrong.

In February, the European Community (EC or Common Market) withdrew its top diplomats from Iran for about a month to protest what the EC called Khomeini's "incitement to murder." Canada, which lifted its ban on the book, followed suit, as did Sweden and Norway.

The Rushdie affair also divided Muslims, sometimes with deadly effect. The leader of Belgium's Muslim community, a moderate who had criticized Khomeini's death threat, was gunned down in March. Also that month, the Organization of the Islamic Conference, a group of 46 Muslim nations and political organizations, refused to endorse Khomeini's action, though the delegates harshly censured Rushdie.

The affair created turmoil even in Iran. Some observers speculated that Khomeini had, in fact, issued the death threat to give radicals in the government leverage in their ongoing power struggle with moderates.

At year's end, Rushdie remained in hiding. Separated from his wife in August, he was reportedly working on a children's book.　　Barbara A. Mayes

Paul Fussell's controversial *Wartime* was a splendidly imaginative if eccentric attempt to plumb Allied military and civilian attitudes and behavior during the conflict. In *Why Did the Heavens Not Darken?*, Arno J. Mayer attempted, largely successfully, to interpret the Holocaust of World War II in a historical context so that humanity could better understand how Nazi Germany could attempt to exterminate the Jews.

Even as the Cold War seemed to be winding down in 1989, three books about Soviet espionage in Great Britain were published: Robert Cecil's *A Divided Life: A Personal Portrait of the Spy Donald Maclean*, Phillip Knightley's *The Master Spy: The Story of Kim Philby*, and Nigel West's *Molehunt: Searching for Soviet Spies in MI5*.

An important exploration of U.S. diplomatic history was Stanley Karnow's *In Our Image: America's Empire in the Philippines*. Elizabeth Fox-Genovese's *Within the Plantation Household*, which investigated the lives of the last generation of both white and black women in the South during the days of slavery, contributed significantly to women's and Southern history.

Science. One of the year's most charming books in this category was *An Old Man's Toy: Gravity at Work and Play in Einstein's Universe*, in which A. Zee investigated recent theories about gravity, often with startling humor. John McPhee's *The Control of Nature*, another collection of his superb essays in *The New Yorker*, explored some notable attempts of humanity to subject the earth to its wishes. Stephen Jay Gould's *Wonderful Life* illuminated ideas about evolution, notably that it may be more a product of random accident than of orderly development.

Reference. The long-awaited second edition of *The Oxford English Dictionary*—all 20 volumes and 21,728 pages—made a splash among word lovers as well as language and literature scholars. The comprehensive set defines more than 500,000 words, illustrating them with nearly 2.5 million quotations culled from centuries of writing. Another new reference—this one American—was *The Encyclopedia of Southern Culture*. Edited by Charles Reagan Wilson and William L. Ferris, the book is a paragon of regional scholarship.

Best sellers. Popular novels of high literary quality that enjoyed long runs on hardcover best-seller lists in 1989 included John le Carré's *The Russia House*, an up-to-date espionage novel that reflected reduced East-West tensions, and Martin Cruz Smith's *Polar Star*, a police thriller set on a Soviet fishing boat.

Two notable nonfiction best sellers were by the same author of inspirational literature, the Unitarian minister Robert Fulghum: *All I Really Need to Know I Learned in Kindergarten*, published in 1988, and *It Was on Fire When I Lay Down on It*, new in 1989. The first Fulghum book ranked high on the paperback best-seller list as well. Henry Kisor

See also **Awards and prizes** (Literature awards); **Canadian literature; Literature for children; Poetry**. In *World Book,* see **Literature**.

Literature for children. Children's books published in 1989 included many imaginative picture books for young readers. There were fewer fantasies for older readers but a continued flow of informational books and a pleasing selection of poetry. Much humorous fiction offset the more serious novels.

Outstanding books of 1989 included the following:

Picture books. *Baba* by Tanya Shpakow (Knopf). Haunting illustrations capture a little girl's belief that her grandma knows magic. Ages 4 to 7.

Charlie Drives the Stage by Eric A. Kimmel, illustrated by Glen Rounds (Holiday House). Charlie takes a senator on a memorable ride to the train. Ages 6 to 9.

CitySounds by Rebecca Emberley (Little, Brown). Brightly colored collages illustrate sounds ranging from toasters to shoes to buses. Ages 3 to 6.

Dinosaurs Dinosaurs by Byron Barton (Crowell). Simple descriptions, brilliant colors, and endpapers with names and pronunciations make this a fine introduction for young children. Ages 3 to 6.

Dove Isabeau by Jane Yolen, illustrated by Dennis Nolan (Harcourt Brace Jovanovich). Her wicked stepmother turns Dove into a dragon, and only a rescuer willing to die can save her. Ages 8 to 12.

Dylan's Day Out by Peter Catalanotto (Orchard Bks.). A Dalmatian escapes from the house and has an unusual day. Clever use of black and white within color paintings. Ages 3 to 6.

Heron Street by Ann Turner, illustrated by Lisa Desimini (Harper & Row). Superb paintings illustrate a poetic tale of a patch of land and swamp and the changes it undergoes through the years. Ages 6 to 9.

Hershel and the Hanukkah Goblins by Eric A. Kimmel, illustrated by Trina Schart Hyman (Holiday House). Hershel tricks the goblins so that he can light the holiday candles. Ages 5 to 8.

In Search of the Last Dodo by Anne and Reg Cartwright, illustrated by Reg Cartwright (Joy St.). King Glut wants to eat the last dodo egg, but something unexpected happens. Ages 4 to 7.

Jack and the Beanstalk retold and illustrated by John Howe (Little, Brown). Dramatic paintings make this retelling unforgettable. Ages 5 to 8.

Lon Po Po translated and illustrated by Ed Young (Philomel Bks.). Haunting paintings accompany a Chinese tale similar to the fable of Red Riding Hood, in which the wolf visits three children and pretends to be their grandmother. Ages 5 to 9.

Nettie Jo's Friends by Patricia McKissack, illustrated by Scott Cook (Knopf). Wonderful oil paintings illustrate Nettie's search for a needle. Ages 4 to 8.

Nicholas Cricket by Joyce Maxner, illustrated by William Joyce (Harper & Row). Imaginative paintings highlight the song about creatures dancing in the moonlight to the Crickets' band. Ages 5 to 8.

Night Cars by Teddy Jam, illustrated by Eric Beddows (Orchard Bks.). A toddler sees and dreams of all kinds of cars and night scenes as his father holds him. Ages 3 to 6.

Literature for children

Joyful Noise, a poetry book by Paul Fleischman, won the American Library Association's Newbery Medal for best children's book of 1989.

Night Noises by Mem Fox, illustrated by Terry Denton (Gulliver Bks.). Old Lily Laceby dreams on despite sounds from outside that agitate her dog. Ages 3 to 7.

The Pied Piper of Hamelin by Robert Browning, retold by Sara and Stephen Corrin, illustrated by Errol Le Cain (Harcourt Brace Jovanovich). A highly dramatic retelling features detailed paintings and a historical note. Ages 4 to 10.

Ragtime Tumpie by Alan Schroeder, illustrated by Bernie Fuchs (Joy St.). Tumpie's love for dance and rhythm glows in wonderful paintings. Ages 5 to 9.

The Sand Horse by Ann Turnbull, illustrated by Michael Foreman (Atheneum Pubs.). An artist sculpts a horse in the sand, with surprising results. Ages 5 to 8.

Tom Thumb retold by Richard Jesse Watson (Harcourt Brace Jovanovich). Detailed paintings add to a fine retelling of the tale of the tiny boy. Ages 4 to 8.

When Bluebell Sang by Lisa Campbell Ernst (Bradbury Press). An unscrupulous agent keeps talented Bluebell the cow from returning to the farm, but her cleverness saves the day. Ages 4 to 8.

Fiction. *Afternoon of the Elves* by Janet Taylor Lisle (Orchard Bks.). Hillary finds out about Sara-Kate and her strange home life. Ages 8 to 10.

Alice in Rapture, Sort Of by Phyllis Reynolds Naylor (Atheneum Pubs.). Alice has her first boyfriend, and she is beset with worries. Ages 8 to 12.

And One for All by Theresa Nelson (Orchard Bks.). When Geraldine's brother enlists, she and her broth-er's best friend struggle with conflicts over the Vietnam War. Ages 11 to 13.

Flight of the Albatross by Deborah Savage (Houghton Mifflin). A New Zealand tale describes the cultural clashes when Sara and Mako fall in love. Ages 12 and up.

Heartbeats and Other Stories by Peter D. Sieruta (Harper & Row). Nine stories about teen-agers focus on feelings, friendship, love, and motivations. Ages 12 and up.

A Map of Nowhere by Gillian Cross (Holiday House). Nick becomes involved in a "Dungeons and Dragons"-type game with real-life choices. Ages 12 and up.

My Brother Stealing Second by Jim Naughton (Harper & Row). A grieving boy learns the truth about his brother's fatal automobile accident. Ages 12 and up.

My War with Goggle-Eyes by Anne Fine (Joy St.). Kitty tells Helen about her difficulty adjusting to her mom's boyfriend. Ages 9 to 12.

Red Rover, Red Rover by George Ella Lyon (Orchard Bks.). Sumi must come to terms with death and growing up. Ages 12 and up.

Silver Days by Sonia Levitin (Atheneum Pubs.). A Jewish family escapes from Nazi Germany to the United States and finds life hard but promising. Ages 10 and up.

So Much to Tell You by John Marsden (Joy St.). A disfigured, silent girl finds gradual healing through her journal and her friends. Ages 12 and up.

The Voyage of the Frog by Gary Paulsen (Orchard Bks.). David finds himself lost in the Pacific Ocean on a sailboat. Ages 11 to 13.

Fantasy. *Anno's Aesop* by Mitsumasa Anno (Orchard Bks.). Mr. Fox adds stories of his own to Aesop's traditional fables. Ages 4 to 7.

The Blood-and-Thunder Adventure on Hurricane Peak by Margaret Mahy, illustrated by Wendy Smith (Margaret K. McElderry Bks.). Talking cats, a hurricane, and magic enliven this zany tale of the Unexpected School and its inhabitants. Ages 9 to 12.

The Faery Flag: Stories and Poems of Fantasy and the Supernatural by Jane Yolen (Orchard Bks.). Fantasies in prose and verse span the old and the modern. Ages 10 and up.

Ghost Abbey by Robert Westall (Scholastic). When Maggi's family moves into an old abbey, she discovers its dark powers. Ages 12 and up.

The Jedera Adventure by Lloyd Alexander (Dutton). Vesper Holly and her guardian have a frightening time returning an overdue book to a library in Africa. Ages 11 to 13.

Jump On Over! by Joel Chandler Harris, adapted by Van Dyke Parks, illustrated by Barry Moser (Harcourt Brace Jovanovich). Brer Rabbit outwits Brer Fox and others in five tales accompanied by wonderful paintings. All ages.

Melisande by E. Nesbit, illustrated by Patrick Lynch (Harcourt Brace Jovanovich). Modern reasoning livens

He spins and jumps into the air. Touching the stage again, he kneels with his arms spread out, and the silk top hat and gold-tipped cane lie side by side at his feet. His shoes are still, and the show is over.

Stephen Gammell's illustrations for *Song and Dance Man,* by Karen Ackerman, won the 1989 Caldecott Medal for children's picture books.

traditional elements in this now-classic tale of the bald princess. Lavish paintings. Ages 5 to 8.

Rootabaga Stories: Part Two by Carl Sandburg, illustrated by Michael Hague (Harcourt Brace Jovanovich). Exuberant, imaginative tales feature characters with zany names and fine water-color paintings. All ages.

Swan Lake by Mark Helprin, illustrated by Chris Van Allsburg (Houghton Mifflin). Deep, beautiful color paintings enrich this tale of romance and intrigue in a European court. Ages 10 and up.

The Third Magic by Welwyn Wilton Katz (Margaret K. McElderry Bks.). Morgan goes back in time for a magical adventure involving King Arthur. Ages 12 and up.

Poetry. *Eric Carle's Animals Animals* selected by Laura Whipple, illustrated by Eric Carle (Philomel Bks.). Animal poems from many times and cultures accompany illustrations in collage and water color. All ages.

Best Witches: Poems for Halloween by Jane Yolen, illustrated by Elise Primavera (Putnam). The collection, with humorous full-page illustrations, is perfect for the holiday or any other time. Ages 5 to 9.

Chocolate Dreams by Arnold Adoff, illustrated by Turi MacCombie (Lothrop, Lee & Shepard). Chocolate poem treats and paintings will have readers heading for the kitchen. All ages.

Dancing Teepees: Poems of American Indian Youth edited by Virginia Driving Hawk Sneve, illustrated by Stephen Gammell (Holiday House). Poems and water colors describe ceremonies, lullabies, life, and creation. All ages.

Ghastlies, Goops and Pincushions by X. J. Kennedy, illustrated by Ron Barrett (Margaret K. McElderry Bks.). Zany poems tell about ridiculous situations. Ages 9 and up.

Hey World, Here I Am by Jean Little, illustrated by Sue Truesdell (Harper & Row). Poetry and prose combined describe Kate's antics, feelings, and thoughts. Ages 8 to 11.

hist whist by e. e. cummings, illustrated by Deborah Kogan Ray (Crown). Paintings give a dramatic treatment to a fine Halloween poem. All ages.

The Hopeful Trout and Other Limericks by John Ciardi, illustrated by Susan Meddaugh (Houghton Mifflin). Ciardi pokes fun at people, creatures, and the reader. Ages 7 to 10.

Nonstop Nonsense by Margaret Mahy, illustrated by Quentin Blake (Margaret K. McElderry Bks.). Nonsense poems and stories have equally wacky drawings. Ages 7 to 11.

Peacock Pie by Walter de la Mare, illustrated by Louise Brierley (Holt & Co.). This reissue of a classic collection attracts the reader with eerie sketches and color illustrations. Ages 8 and up.

Poems for Fathers selected by Myra Cohn Livingston, illustrated by Robert Casilla (Holiday House). Eighteen poems by various poets capture a range of emotions. Ages 5 to 8.

Literature for children

Spooky Poems collected by Jill Bennett, illustrated by Mary Rees (Joy St.). Funny poems and paintings are right for Halloween or anytime. Ages 5 to 9.

Still As a Star: A Book of Nighttime Poems selected by Lee Bennett Hopkins, illustrated by Karen Milone (Little, Brown). Luminous, imaginative illustrations accompany 14 poems for bedtime reading. Ages 3 to 8.

Animals, people, places, and things. *Anno's Math Games II* by Mitsumasa Anno (Philomel Bks.). Anno teaches mathematical concepts by raising questions and making the reader look closely. Ages 5 to 9.

Before the Sun Dies: The Story of Evolution by Roy A. Gallant (Macmillan). Beginning with the big bang, Gallant explores life, matter, future possibilities, and outer space. Ages 10 and up.

Bill Peet: An Autobiography by Bill Peet (Houghton Mifflin). A popular author-artist and former Disney illustrator tells of his life. Ages 8 to 12.

Fire Fighters by Robert Maas (Scholastic). A clear text and bright color photographs reveal the fire fighter's many roles. Ages 5 to 8.

If You Made a Million by David M. Schwartz, illustrated by Steven Kellogg (Lothrop, Lee & Shepard). Readers learn about money matters, including checks, interest, and taxes. All ages.

The Lincoln Brigade: A Picture History by William Loren Katz and Marc Crawford (Atheneum Pubs.). Numerous photos and a clear explanation tell of the United States volunteers who fought in the Spanish Civil War (1936-1939). Ages 10 and up.

The Magic School Bus Inside the Human Body by Joanna Cole, illustrated by Bruce Degen (Scholastic). The bus shrinks and Arnold swallows it, and the rest of the class gets a tour of his insides. Ages 6 to 9.

Nuclear Energy: Troubled Past Uncertain Future by Laurence Pringle (Macmillan). An incisive analysis— with many photographs, a glossary, and an index— helps clarify the controversy over nuclear energy. Ages 12 and up.

Panama Canal: Gateway to the World by Judith St. George (Putnam). A truthful, detailed account, accompanied by historical photographs, tells of the hazards, the personalities, and the cost in lives and money involved in this enormous undertaking. Ages 10 and up.

The Skeleton Inside You by Philip Balestrino, illustrated by True Kelley (Crowell). Bright, humorous illustrations enrich a clear, interesting discussion of the skeleton. Ages 5 to 8.

Awards in 1989. The Newbery Medal for the best American children's book was awarded to Paul Fleischman for *Joyful Noise: Poems for Two Voices*. The Caldecott Medal for "the most distinguished American picture book for children" went to Stephen Gammell, the illustrator of *Song and Dance Man* by Karen Ackerman. The Mildred L. Batchelder Award cited Lothrop, Lee & Shepard Books for its publication of *Crutches* by Peter Hartling.   Marilyn Fain Apseloff

In *World Book,* see **Caldecott Medal; Literature for children; Newbery Medal.**

Los Angeles. Mayor Thomas Bradley won an unprecedented fifth term in office on April 11, 1989, in a close nonpartisan election, but it also was a year of political troubles for Bradley as federal and city investigators probed his personal finances. City Attorney James K. Hahn released a 1,165-page report on September 13 concluding that there was "damaging" evidence that a local bank had benefited financially from the mayor's influence. Bradley was paid $18,000 in 1988 as a consultant to the Far East National Bank, which obtained $3 million in city deposits in 1988 and 1989. The mayor later returned the money.

Although Hahn said there were insufficient grounds for criminal charges, he did file a civil lawsuit against Bradley. The suit charged the mayor with violating a financial-disclosure law for officials by failing to reveal several large investments made between 1986 and 1988. On December 28, Bradley agreed to pay $20,000 to settle the suit. On November 28, Mike Gage, Bradley's chief of staff, announced his resignation. He said it was not connected with Bradley's troubles and that a job offer from industry was too good to turn down.

On November 20, a special commission proposed a tough new ethics code for Los Angeles' city government. The code would require elected officials, high-ranking civil servants, and office seekers to fully disclose all investments.

Traffic ban. The Los Angeles City Council on November 14 approved a plan to reduce traffic congestion and air pollution in the metropolitan area by banning 70 per cent of large trucks from city streets during rush hours. The ban, thought to be the first in the United States, affects between 100,000 and 500,000 heavy-duty trucks that regularly use Los Angeles streets.

School strike settled. The Los Angeles Unified School District and 13,000 striking teachers ratified a new three-year contract on May 25 and the teachers returned to class the next day, ending a strike that disrupted the nation's second-largest school system for 10 days. The settlement, which is retroactive to 1988, will boost teacher salaries by 24 per cent by July 1990 and give instructors a greater say in school policy matters.

City and county budgets. The Los Angeles City Council on June 13 overrode only 2 of Mayor Bradley's 16 vetoes in adopting a record $3.25-billion city budget. The budget included $35 million in new programs and established a Department of Environmental Affairs. The council also agreed to the mayor's request for money to hire pollution experts to begin work on a city smog-reduction policy.

In Los Angeles County, the board of supervisors adopted a $9.6-billion budget on July 20 after removing cost-of-living increases for welfare recipients and using the money to avert the threatened closure of five mental health clinics. The county also provided funds for four new probation camps for juvenile law-breakers, another jail facility for the sheriff's department, and additional municipal court and superior court judges.

Fruit fly infestation. Los Angeles County was plagued with the worst infestation of Mediterranean fruit flies (Medflies) in its history in 1989. Medflies pose a threat to the state's multimillion-dollar agricultural industry because the female flies lay their eggs in fruits and vegetables, making them unsalable.

After the first Medfly was found on July 20, state and local officials began aerial spraying of the pesticide Malathion and released millions of sterile Medflies—which mate with the wild Medflies—to control the outbreak. But the infestation persisted into the fall, making it necessary to step up aerial spraying.

Culture. The *Los Angeles Herald Examiner*, once the largest afternoon daily newspaper in the United States, folded on November 1. The 238,000-circulation daily closed out a 118-year history ailing from declining readership and shrinking revenues.

The Los Angeles Philharmonic orchestra got a new music director on August 14. Esa-Pekka Salonen, a Finnish composer and conductor, was named to replace André Previn, who resigned in April after five years as head of the Philharmonic.   Victor Merina

See also **City.** In *World Book,* see **Los Angeles; Previn, André.**

Louisiana. See **State government.**

Lujan, Manuel, Jr. (1928-   ), was sworn in as United States secretary of the interior on Feb. 3, 1989. He had been a member of the House of Representatives representing New Mexico from 1969 until 1989. Lujan (pronounced *LOO hahn*) was the first Hispanic Republican elected to the House. In 1988, he declined to run again. He had undergone triple bypass heart surgery in 1986 but said that he was not retiring from the House because of his health.

Since 1969, Lujan had served on the House Interior and Insular Affairs Committee. He gave up the position of ranking Republican on that committee in 1985 and assumed the same post on the Science, Space, and Technology Committee.

Lujan's nomination for the Cabinet post drew criticism from environmentalist organizations, due largely to his prodevelopment voting record. But Charles J. DiBona, president of the American Petroleum Institute, cited Lujan's "understanding of the . . . responsible, balanced use of federal lands."

Lujan was born on May 12, 1928, in San Ildefonso, N. Mex. He was raised in Santa Fe, where his father served three terms as mayor. Lujan entered his family's insurance business in 1948. In 1950, he received a bachelor's degree from the College of Santa Fe.

Lujan married Jean Kay Couchman in 1948. They have two sons and two daughters.   Jay Myers

Luxembourg. See **Europe.**

Madagascar. See **Africa.**

Magazine. The world's biggest media and entertainment company was created in July 1989 by the merger of Time Incorporated and Warner Communications Incorporated. Annual revenue of Time Warner Incorporated will likely top $10 billion.

New magazines appearing in 1989 included *First for Women*, published by West Germany's The Bauer Group. Bauer placed 7 million copies of the magazine on newsstands in January 1989—backed by a network television advertising campaign that cost more than $1 million.

Murdoch Magazines, a division of News America Publishing, Incorporated, introduced *Mirabella*, a monthly life-style magazine for women who are 30 to 50 years old. News America is owned by Australian-born media magnate Rupert Murdoch. *Sports Travel*, another Murdoch publication introduced in 1989, is aimed at college and university managers, athletic directors, coaches, promoters, and media people.

Other sports magazines introduced during the year were *Pro Athlete* and *Spring Training*. New magazines aimed at minorities were *Emerge*, for upwardly mobile blacks; and *Que Pasa* and *Imagen* for Hispanics.

Magazines for students. Several publishers launched magazines for college students in 1989. Stamats Communications, Incorporated, of Cedar Rapids, Iowa, introduced *Campus Scene*, which is tailored to each campus where it is distributed. Whittle Communications Incorporated of Knoxville, Tenn., launched *In*

Mirabella strides into the crowded field of women's magazines in mid-1989 directed by Grace Mirabella, former editor of *Vogue.*

View, a magazine for college women. *Career Vision*, published by InterVision of New York City, covers the life styles and careers of college students.

Spin-offs. Several magazines introduced spin-offs. *Elle Decor* first appeared on newsstands in October, in a direct challenge to *Architectural Digest. Elle Decor's* publisher is Diamandis Communications, a U.S. subsidiary of Paris-based publishing giant Hachette S.A. *Elle Decor* is a spin-off of the popular fashion magazine *Elle. Sports Illustrated* unveiled *Sports Illustrated for Kids*. And *Entrepreneur,* a fast-growing business magazine, introduced *Entrepreneurial Woman*, for women who own businesses.

Awards. The Magazine Publishers of America (MPA) named John Mack Carter, who is director of magazine development at Hearst Magazines and editor in chief of *Good Housekeeping* in New York City, to receive the 1989 Henry Johnson Fisher Award, the magazine publishing industry's most prestigious honor. The Stephen E. Kelly Award and the accompanying prize of $100,000, granted for outstanding advertising in magazines, went to TBWA of New York City, for that agency's campaign for Absolut Vodka.

The American Society of Magazine Editors presented its National Magazine Awards for editorial excellence in April. Winners were *Good Housekeeping* for personal service; *Condé Nast Traveler* for special interests; *The New Yorker* for news reporting and fiction; *Esquire* for feature writing; *California* for public interest journalism; *Rolling Stone* for design; *Hippocrates* for single-topic issue; *National Geographic Magazine* for photography; and *Harper's* for essays and criticism. In the category of general excellence, which is presented in four groups according to circulation size, the winners were *The Sciences* (less than 100,000); *American Heritage* (100,000 to 400,000); *Vanity Fair* (400,000 to 1,000,000); and *Sports Illustrated* (more than 1 million).

Magazine advertising revenues in the United States increased during the first 11 months of 1989 by 11.7 per cent over the same period in 1988, reaching $6.1 billion. The number of advertising pages also rose during the first 11 months of 1989, totaling nearly 162,000, an increase of 4 per cent.

The combined circulation per issue of all consumer magazines surveyed by the Audit Bureau of Circulations (ABC) in the United States climbed to 363.1 million during the first six months of 1989, up 4.7 per cent over the same period in 1988. (The ABC is an independent company that issues circulation figures, verified by auditors, for magazines.)

An annual survey conducted by the MPA and the accounting firm of Price Waterhouse indicated that the surveyed magazines showed a pretax operating profit of 12.4 per cent in 1988, compared with 13.5 per cent in 1987.　Sharon Roccaforte

In *World Book,* see **Magazine.**
Maine. See **State government.**
Malawi. See **Africa.**

Malaysia. On March 2, 1989, the nine hereditary rulers of state governments in Malaysia elected Azlan Muhibbuddin Shah ibni Sultan Yusof Izzudin to be the nation's king. Azlan succeeded Mahmood Iskandar on April 26. Malaysia's office of head of state is rotated among the hereditary rulers every five years.

The election was unusually political, even though the government is run by a prime minister chosen by an elected Parliament and the king has only the power of constitutional oversight. Azlan headed Malaysia's Supreme Court from 1982 to 1984. In that job, he came into conflict with Prime Minister Mahathir bin Mohamad. Observers believed that Mahathir wanted another ruler elected king.

UMNO Baru comeback. Mahathir underwent a quintuple-bypass heart operation at the age of 63 on January 24. As he recovered, his political party, the New United Malays National Organization, known as UMNO Baru (new UMNO), also recovered from a year of political turmoil. The party's candidate won a January 28 election for a seat in Parliament against a candidate from a party led by Prince Razaleigh Hamzah. Following other special parliamentary elections, the National Front coalition, led by UMNO Baru, had by September won 5 out of 7 contests against Razaleigh and his political allies.

On January 31, Musa Hitam returned to UMNO Baru. Musa, Mahathir's deputy prime minister and presumed political heir from 1981 to 1986, had resigned in 1986 because of "irreconcilable differences" with Mahathir. Musa had cooperated for a time with Razaleigh, who led an unsuccessful challenge to Mahathir's control of UMNO. On Aug. 23, 1989, Mahathir made Musa a special envoy to the United Nations—a step toward Musa's political comeback.

With a general election for Parliament due by August 1991, Mahathir consulted his colleagues about calling an early vote to capitalize on his advantages. These included the successful hosting of the Southeast Asia Games in August and of an October meeting of Commonwealth representatives.

Prosperity also helped Mahathir's position. World prices for such Malaysian exports as tin, timber, and petroleum were high; the demand for rubber gloves—another Malaysian export—soared; and manufacturing increased by 15 per cent. The nation's economic growth rate appeared likely to match 1988's rate, 8 per cent. Mahathir said in mid-July 1989 that Malaysia did not intend to become a newly industrialized country—a term applied to countries with recently booming economies—because that would bring political and economic pressures from industrial nations. But economists said that Malaysia might become one anyway.　Henry S. Bradsher

See also **Asia** (Facts in brief table). In *World Book,* see **Malaysia.**
Maldives. See **Asia.**
Mali. See **Africa.**
Malta. See **Europe.**

Manitoba. Summer 1989 brought the worst fires to the forests of northern Manitoba in the 80 years that records have been kept. A state of emergency was declared July 20, as more than 200 fires burned over rugged territory. Twenty-three mining towns, Indian reserves, and settlements were wholly or partly evacuated, and 23,000 people were moved to secure locations elsewhere in the province. The fires ravaged 18,000 square kilometers (7,000 square miles) of land with an estimated 360 million trees. Unusually high temperatures and tornado activity contributed to the fires, most of which were caused by lightning strikes.

Police forces faced charges of racism during a judicial inquiry into the administration of justice for native peoples. The inquiry, which began in September 1988, was set up to investigate several incidents, including the March 1988 death of an Indian leader during a police search. The officer who had investigated the shooting killed himself on Sept. 20, 1989, hours before he was to testify at the inquiry.

Premier Gary A. Filmon's Progressive Conservative government announced on June 5 that it would pass up the chance to balance the province's budget. Instead, the new budget reduced personal income taxes by $61 million Canadian (about $50 million United States) and set aside $150 million (about $125 million United States) in a fund designed to head off future tax increases.   David M. L. Farr

See also **Canada.** In *World Book*, see **Manitoba.**

Manufacturing. In December 1989, the United States entered an eighth consecutive year of peacetime economic expansion. But, after two high-growth years in 1987 and 1988, 1989 was sluggish for U.S. manufacturing and for the U.S. economy as a whole.

Higher interest rates resulted in reduced demand for housing, automobiles, and other big-ticket items. A stronger U.S. dollar slowed the growth of U.S. exports. The dollar rose 11.4 per cent in value against other major currencies in 1989.

Brisk consumer spending and dramatically increased exports had fueled the growth in manufacturing in the late 1980's. But consumers cut back on spending in 1989, especially on automobiles. Incentives on 1989 models kept sales strong for the first half of the year, but there was little response to the fully priced 1990 models introduced in late September. Sales dropped to an anemic annual rate of 5.6 million in November. As a result of this weakness, the ailing auto industry dragged much of manufacturing down with it in 1989.

Not all transportation companies suffered. Sales of civilian aircraft were strong as airlines sought to upgrade aging fleets. Such producers as the Boeing Company and the McDonnell Douglas Corporation were the leading gainers as Delta Air Lines placed a $10-billion order for 519 airplanes. American Airlines ordered 552 planes; United Airlines, 486; and Northwest Airlines, 227. In 1989, Boeing alone accepted orders for 878 planes valued at $46.1 billion.

Despite a stronger dollar, making U.S. manufactured goods more expensive overseas, the value of U.S. exports rose from $157.6 billion in the first half of 1988 to $182.7 billion in the first half of 1989. But this was a smaller rate of increase than in 1987 and 1988, according to the International Monetary Fund, an agency of the United Nations. With the value of the dollar almost 30 per cent lower since mid-1985, U.S. exports of manufactured goods had increased from $254 billion in 1987 to $322 billion in 1988.

Factory output. When consumers cut spending in 1989, manufacturers trimmed overall output levels. Output at U.S. factories, mines, and utilities dropped 0.7 per cent in October, according to the Department of Commerce. Automobile production in the fourth quarter of 1989 was the weakest since 1982. And with fewer houses being built, production of home appliances fell 4.2 per cent in October 1989. As a result of declining output, American factories ran at only 82.8 per cent of capacity in October, having peaked for the year at 84.7 per cent in January.

Factory orders, affected by a decline in defense spending, dropped 0.2 per cent in October to $233.9-billion. This came on top of a 0.1 per cent decline in September. Orders for *durable goods*—machinery and home appliances expected to last at least three years—fell 0.6 per cent in October to $124.59 billion, after a 1.1 per cent drop in September. There were declines in primary metals, machinery, military equipment, and nonelectrical machinery, including computers. Transportation equipment and nondefense capital goods were the only gainers, led by civilian aircraft.

The last time there was similar weakness in durable goods orders was 1986, when U.S. manufacturers faced heavy competition from imports and had weak sales overseas. Manufacturers rebounded in 1987 and 1988 when the dollar declined in value, making American goods less expensive overseas.

Durable-goods producers operated at only 80.9 per cent of capacity in October 1989, while producers of *nondurable goods*—goods expected to last less than three years—ran their factories at 85.5 per cent of capacity. One category of durable-goods orders that had been consistently strong from the late 1970's until late in 1989 was military goods. Orders for defense-related equipment were up a whopping 33.9 per cent in September, marking the end of the fiscal year, but similar orders were down 12.4 per cent in October.

Defense orders had averaged an annual 5.8 per cent gain from 1980 until peaking in the third quarter of 1987 and averaging a 2.3 per cent annual decline since then. Secretary of Defense Richard B. Cheney's November 1989 announcement of large cuts planned for the defense budget over the next five years indicated this trend of reduced military orders would continue. Nondurable goods orders, meanwhile, led by food and chemicals, were up 1.1 per cent in October.

Inventories. One reason for slower factory output was that business inventories grew faster than sales.

Manufacturing

West German Chancellor Helmut Kohl, center, presses a button to start a
4-megabit chip production line at an IBM plant in Sindelfingen, West Germany.

This was especially true for domestic car sales, which were substantially less than the number of cars produced, resulting in bloated inventories and cutbacks in output. Manufacturers' inventories decreased slightly to $371.16 billion in September, but manufacturers' sales also dropped 1.6 per cent to $234.4 billion.

Employment. The overall unemployment rate in the United States rose to 5.3 per cent in November. It had been as low as 5.0 per cent earlier in the year. But it was a different story in American factories, as employment dropped for the eighth consecutive month in October. The factory jobless rate rose above the overall unemployment rate for the first time in nearly three years. Manufacturing wages rose only 2.6 per cent in 1989, to an average hourly wage in November of $10.57 per hour.

As manufacturers saw profits erode due to reduced overseas demand and increased competition, more than 133,000 factory workers were laid off from January through October. More than 101,000 jobs were cut in September and October alone. Overall factory employment—about 19.5 million jobs—was no higher than in 1988. Much of the employment loss occurred in the two weakest sectors of the economy—automotive and housing. Automakers cut 50,000 jobs between January and October 1989. Computer companies also laid off thousands of workers in 1989. International Business Machines Corporation (IBM) in December announced a reduction of 10,000 jobs.

Productivity. Growth in factory wages and benefits continued to outpace productivity gains in U.S. factories in 1989. Compensation, which includes wages and benefits, rose an average of 4.5 per cent, while overall productivity increased by only 2.4 per cent, down from gains of 2.9 per cent and 3.8 per cent in 1988 and 1987, respectively, according to the Department of Labor. The United States factory worker in 1989 was the world's best paid but by only a small margin over a worker in West Germany. The U.S. output per employed person was the world's highest in 1989, but productivity was growing faster in other countries.

Capital spending. American manufacturers have had to modernize plants and invest in technology to remain competitive at home and overseas. Overall *capital spending*—that is, spending on new plants and equipment—rose 10.1 per cent in 1988 and 8.5 per cent in 1989 to an estimated $467.15 billion, according to the Commerce Department.

Machine tool orders. The machine tool industry was a good indicator of capital spending plans and the overall health of the U.S. economy. These tools, such as lathes, presses, and other equipment, are used to make machinery. The weaker dollar of 1987 and 1988 enabled U.S. manufacturers to compete better overseas. Investments in capital spending to modernize plants in the United States also created an improving domestic market. But weakness in tool orders in

1989 reflected the slower growth of the United States economy.

Machine tool orders fell sharply in October 1989 to $205 million, down 22 per cent from October 1988's $262.3 million, according to the National Machine Tool Builders Association. And the October 1989 orders were down 32 per cent from September's levels. Overall, orders in 1989 averaged $241.7 million per month, compared with $299.2 million per month in 1988. And orders from other countries for machine tools through October 1989 rose 33 per cent to $712.8-million from $536.5 million a year earlier. Orders from other countries account for 12 per cent of all machine tool orders in the United States.

The biggest reason for the slump in machine tool orders was the auto industry, which accounts for about 9.5 per cent of all machine tool orders and 17.5 per cent of all orders for durable goods. When the auto industry slumps, it also directly impacts industries that supply automakers, such as producers of glass, metal, and plastics.

While overall machine tool orders were down, orders for modern systems featuring computer-controlled machine tools were healthy. The overall industry backlog of $2.11 billion in orders in October 1989 declined only 3.8 per cent from 1988. Also generating some optimism was the prospect of potential demand from manufacturers in liberalized Eastern Europe and Soviet Union, who will need help modernizing their factories.

Technology. New technology for the shop floor continued to help manufacturers compete more effectively. CAD/CAM (computer-aided design and computer-aided manufacturing) systems, designed to streamline production and improve plant productivity, continued to grow in 1989.

Small companies—such as 3D Systems Incorporated of Valencia, Calif.—developed computer-aided systems to enable designers to make plastic prototypes of parts of products at their desks. The prototypes can be produced in hours rather than days, as required with conventional industrial-design technology.

Another manufacturing technique gaining acceptance in 1989 as a means of saving time and enhancing productivity was *flexible manufacturing*. A flexible manufacturing system can be programmed to produce different types of products on the same assembly line, with little downtime during product changes. According to a study by the Harvard University Graduate School of Business Administration in Cambridge, Mass., United States companies turn out an average of 25 different products per machine, while Japanese companies produce an average of 240.   Ronald Kolgraf

In *World Book,* see **Manufacturing.**

Marine Corps, U.S. See Armed forces.
Maryland. See State government.
Massachusetts. See State government.
Mauritania. See Africa.
Mauritius. See Africa.

Mazowiecki, Tadeusz (1927-   ), was confirmed as prime minister of Poland on Aug. 24, 1989, becoming that country's first non-Communist prime minister since the Communist Party came to power at the end of World War II in 1945. He succeeded Czesław Kiszczak. Tadeusz Mazowiecki—pronounced *tah DAY oosh mah zoh VYEHT skee*—is a leading Roman Catholic intellectual who was editor in chief of the weekly newspaper of the independent labor union Solidarity. See **Poland.**

Mazowiecki was born on April 18, 1927, in Plock, a city in central Poland. He studied law at Warsaw University, then began a career in journalism. In 1958, he helped found a liberal Catholic monthly journal, *Wiez* (Polish for *Link*), and became its editor—a position he held until 1981.

In 1980, he became an adviser to Solidarity. The next year, he was named editor in chief of the Solidarity newspaper.

The regime arrested Mazowiecki in December 1981, when it declared martial law and suppressed Solidarity. He was released a year later. Mazowiecki was one of the initiators of round-table talks that began on Feb. 6, 1989, between the government and opposition groups. After Solidarity was legalized on April 17, Mazowiecki resumed his editorial post with the Solidarity newspaper.

Mazowiecki is a widower with three grown sons and four grandchildren.   Jay Myers

McLachlin, Beverley Mary (1943-   ), was appointed to the Supreme Court of Canada on March 30, 1989. McLachlin became the court's third woman member and, at age 45, one of the youngest Supreme Court justices ever. She was Prime Minister Brian Mulroney's sixth appointment to the nine-member court.

McLachlin was born Beverley Mary Gietz on Sept. 7, 1943, in Pincher Creek, Alta. She attended the University of Alberta, receiving a bachelor's degree in 1964 and her master's and law degrees in 1969. Between 1969 and 1975, she practiced law in Edmonton, Alta.; Fort St. John, B.C.; and Vancouver, B.C.

From 1974 to 1978, she served on the faculty of the University of British Columbia, where she attained the rank of professor with tenure. Her background is in civil law, rather than criminal or constitutional law. Among her many publications is a prominent reference text on civil procedure in British Columbia.

McLachlin began her judicial career in April 1981 as a county court judge in Vancouver. Five months later, she was elevated to the Supreme Court of British Columbia, and in 1985, she became the first woman appointed to the province's Court of Appeal. In September 1988, she was appointed chief justice of British Columbia's Supreme Court, serving six months before her appointment to Canada's highest court.

She married Roderick McLachlin in 1967, while she was a law student. He died in 1988. Justice McLachlin lives with her son in Ottawa.   Robin Goldman

Medicine

Medicine. A United States government study concluded on July 7, 1989, that more than one-third of American adults—about 64 million people—have dangerously high blood cholesterol levels. The study recommended that these people obtain medical help, such as special diets or cholesterol-lowering drugs, to reduce their risk of a heart attack. Doctors previously believed that about 40 million Americans aged 20 and above had high blood cholesterol.

The study, reported in *The Journal of the American Medical Association*, was the first attempt to estimate the extent of high blood cholesterol based upon new criteria adopted by health officials for defining this condition. It was conducted by researchers at the U.S. Centers for Disease Control in Atlanta, Ga.

In the past, many health experts believed that only people with more than 240 milligrams of cholesterol per deciliter of blood should see a doctor about adopting a low-cholesterol diet or taking cholesterol-lowering drugs. The new criteria indicate that people with readings as low as 200 milligrams of cholesterol also should see a doctor if they have two or more risk factors for a heart attack. The risk factors include being a male, smoking cigarettes, having high blood pressure, being obese, or having a family history of heart disease at an early age.

Consensus on mammograms. A dozen medical organizations on June 27 announced new guidelines to help end confusion about the use of mammograms to detect breast cancer. A mammogram is an X ray of the breast that can detect cancer before a lump or other symptom is apparent to the patient. This is the earliest, most curable stage of the disease.

The groups, which included the American Cancer Society, recommended that women between the ages of 40 and 49 who have no symptoms should have a mammogram every one or two years. In the past, the medical groups agreed that all women aged 50 and older should have an annual mammogram. But they disagreed about how often younger women should have a mammogram. It is among this group that about one-third of all breast cancers occur.

Health experts estimate that about 142,000 cases of breast cancer were detected in the United States in 1989. The disease was expected to claim about 43,000 lives during the year, making it second to lung cancer as a leading cause of cancer death in American women. Experts said mammograms could reduce the toll. But only 15 per cent of women who should have a mammogram take the test.

Hope for Parkinson's patients. Medical researchers on August 3 reported that a new medication can slow the progress of Parkinson's disease, a crippling brain disorder that affects about 400,000 people in the United States. Preliminary tests conducted at 26 medical centers by scientists from the University of Rochester in New York found that the drug deprenyl slowed the rate of the disease by 40 to 80 per cent in Parkinson's patients.

Authorities said it was the first time that any drug appeared to be effective in delaying a neurological disease. Existing treatments for Parkinson's disease and other nerve disorders merely treat symptoms. But deprenyl is believed to actually prevent the progressive death of brain cells that causes the tremors, muscle stiffness, and rigidity among Parkinson's patients.

Concern over contact lenses. The U.S. Food and Drug Administration (FDA) on May 30 asked makers of disposable and extended-wear soft contact lenses to relabel the products so consumers would not wear them for more than seven days. Existing labeling allowed for up to 30 days of continuous use.

The FDA based its decision in part on a study sponsored by the Contact Lens Institute, an organization of contact-lens manufacturers. The study was conducted by researchers at the Harvard University Medical School's Massachusetts Eye and Ear Infirmary in Boston, and Abt Associates, Incorporated, in Cambridge, Mass. The FDA said that people who wear contacts longer than seven days face an unacceptably high risk of developing ulcerative keratitis—a disease in which ulcers form on the cornea, the transparent dome over the front of the eye.

Wearers of extended-wear soft contact lenses received another warning from the Contact Lens Institute study. On September 21, the Boston researchers reported that people who wear extended-wear contacts while they sleep are 10 to 15 times more likely to

HERMAN®

Jim Unger; © 1989 Universal Press Syndicate

All your tests were negative
. . . which is positive.

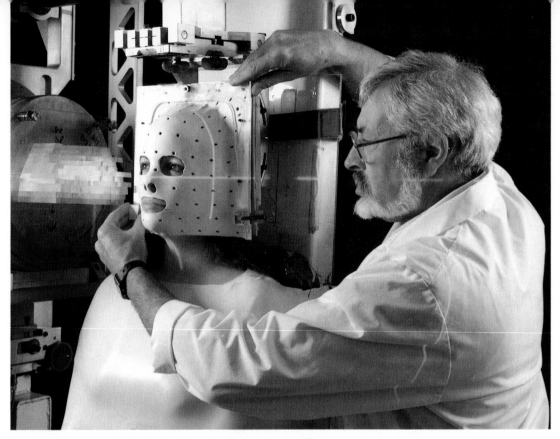

A technician adjusts a device that holds a patient's head steady while a particle accelerator emits a high-energy beam to destroy cancer cells.

develop ulcerative keratitis than people who remove their lenses at night. The scientists also found that sleeping while wearing ordinary soft lenses just twice a month results in a ninefold increase in a person's risk of developing the disease.

Labels for sunglasses. On May 15, the FDA announced a new labeling program to inform consumers about the effectiveness of sunglasses in protecting the eyes from damaging ultraviolet light. Ultraviolet light from the sun can increase the risk of *cataracts* (a clouding of the eye's natural lens).

In the past, information on the amount of ultraviolet light transmitted through sunglasses was not generally available. The new labels will furnish such information as well as list the recommended times when sunglasses should be worn, based on the amount of protection that the glasses provide.

Transplant firsts. On November 27, surgeons at the University of Chicago Medical Center became the first in the United States to perform a liver transplant using a liver from a living donor. The surgeons removed part of the liver from Teresa Smith and transplanted it into her 21-month-old daughter Alyssa, who was dying from a rare liver disease. The procedure is expected to save the lives of hundreds of babies who die each year because there are not enough livers available for transplants from *cadavers* (corpses).

On December 4, doctors at Presbyterian-University Hospital in Pittsburgh, Pa., performed the world's first triple organ transplant on a 26-year-old woman. She received a new heart, liver, and kidney.

Bone treatment. On January 12, Texas researchers announced that they had developed the first effective treatment for spinal osteoporosis, a bone disorder that can affect millions of women following *menopause* (the time in a woman's life when menstruation stops). Women with spinal osteoporosis suffer from a series of small fractures that cause their spinal column to collapse. The result is a back deformity called *dowager's hump*. The new treatment is a slow-release form of the mineral sodium fluoride.

The researchers, working at the University of Texas Southwestern Medical Center in Dallas, treated 65 patients who had spinal osteoporosis with sodium fluoride over an average of 3½ years. They found that the treatment not only reduced the number of fractures but also stimulated the growth of new bone. According to the researchers, 65 patients treated at the Dallas hospital gained an average of 3 to 6 per cent new spinal bone per year. Tests performed on the new bone indicated that it was as strong as normal bone.

Previous studies had linked sodium fluoride with gastrointestinal problems. But such complications were not reported with the slow-release form of the mineral, which appears to pass through the stomach before it can cause any adverse side effects.

Cancer therapy. The National Cancer Institute (NCI) in Bethesda, Md., announced on Oct. 2, 1989, that a combination of two drugs can decrease the risk of death in patients with advanced colon cancer. Cancer of the colon, a part of the large intestine, kills more than 53,000 Americans each year—more than any other cancer except cancer of the lung.

The two drugs—levamisole and 5-fluorouracil—were tested in a national study involving 1,300 patients. The patients had been treated with surgery, but their cancer had spread to their *lymph nodes* (glandlike bodies that filter harmful matter from body fluids). The study found that the two drugs reduced the risk of death from a cancer recurrence by about one-third. According to Samuel Broder, director of the NCI, the drugs represent the first significant advance to help prevent recurrences in patients with advanced colon cancer.

Many patients with advanced colon cancer die because cancer cells spread from the colon to form tumors in other parts of the body. Scientists said that levamisole and 5-fluorouracil, administered three to five weeks after surgery, apparently stimulate the body's immune system to destroy cancer cells that have spread. The NCI said the treatment had not yet been proved effective in patients with early colon cancer, or in those who underwent colon cancer surgery some time ago.   Michael Woods

See also **AIDS; Biology; Drug abuse; Drugs; Health and disease; Public health.** In *World Book,* see **Cholesterol; Medicine.**

Menem, Carlos Saúl (1930-   ), the candidate of the Justicialist Party—also called the Peronist Party—was elected president of Argentina on May 14, 1989. Menem, the political heir of former dictator Juan Perón, defeated Eduardo C. Angeloz of the Radical Civic Union party, and returned the Peronists to power after a 13-year hiatus.

Born on July 2, 1930, in Anillaco in La Rioja province, Menem was the son of Syrian immigrants. He graduated from the National University of Córdoba with a law degree and then began his political career. In 1963, Menem headed the Justicialist Party in La Rioja province and in 1973, he was elected provincial governor.

In the aftermath of the 1976 military coup that ousted President Isabel Perón, Menem was arrested and jailed for five years. In October 1983, he was re-elected governor of La Rioja province.

Menem is married to Zulema Yoma de Menem, and the couple have two teen-aged children. Menem and his wife were separated for long periods in the 1980's when she charged that her husband had converted from the Islamic faith of his parents to Roman Catholicism solely because of his presidential aspirations. The Argentine Constitution requires that the president be a Catholic.

Menem enjoys tennis and soccer. He also drives race cars and flies planes.   Rod Such

See also **Argentina.**

Mental illness. At least 7.5 million children in the United States suffer from a diagnosable mental disorder, a major study concluded on June 7, 1989. But the study noted that of these children, only 2.5 million receive any treatment.

The study was conducted for the National Institute of Mental Health (NIMH) by a panel of authorities organized by the Institute of Medicine, an agency of the National Academy of Sciences. The NIMH is an agency of the U.S. Department of Health and Human Services.

Children with mental disorders may suffer from a variety of conditions, ranging from intense anxiety or depression to behavioral problems. The study estimated that the costs of childhood mental illness, which include medical care, special schools, and juvenile court cases, total billions of dollars per year. It also noted that mental illness does not always cease when the child grows up. Rather, children with mental disorders often grow into disturbed adults.

The future for these children, however, is not always bleak. The study found that the chances of successfully diagnosing, treating, and even preventing childhood mental disorders are much greater today than 20 years ago. To continue this progress, the study recommended a new national program on childhood mental illness that would increase funding from $52-million per year to $199 million.

Help for schizophrenics. The U.S. Food and Drug Administration (FDA) on October 3 approved a new drug that could help people with severe schizophrenia. Schizophrenia is a mental disorder characterized by delusions, hallucinations, and disorientation. The agency estimated that 200,000 people in the United States may benefit from the drug.

The FDA cautioned, however, that the drug, clozapine, has severe side effects and should be used only on patients who fail to respond to conventional therapy. The agency said the drug can cause seizures and a potentially fatal blood disorder.

Homeless problem. Most homeless people suffer from psychiatric illness or substance abuse, a study concluded in September 1989. The study, conducted by researchers at Johns Hopkins University in Baltimore, found that 91 per cent of homeless men and 80 per cent of homeless women had at least one form of psychiatric illness, such as schizophrenia and phobias. In addition, about 68 per cent of the men and 32 per cent of the women were alcoholic, and about half of the subjects used some illicit drug.

The researchers said their results emphasized the need for including mental health care among the community services provided for homeless people. They noted that such services may prevent some people from becoming homeless and help many who are already homeless. In the Special Reports section, see **No Place to Call Home.**

Court ruling. The Supreme Court of the United States in June ruled that mentally retarded people convicted of murder can be sentenced to death so long as judges and juries have determined to their satisfaction that such defendants are aware that their criminal actions are wrong. The decision came in the case of a mentally retarded Texas man convicted of rape and murder. Attorneys argued that the Constitution prohibits execution of retarded people because of their impaired reasoning abilities. But the court said that not all mentally retarded people lack the mental capabilities and life experiences needed to distinguish right from wrong.

Nursing home problems. On August 8, representatives of two mental health groups told Congress that mentally ill people in nursing homes often receive improper care because of the lack of sufficient federal funds and adequately trained staff. Estimates indicate that mental disorders affect 50 to 90 per cent of the 1.5 million residents of nursing homes.

Experts from the National Association for Mental Health and the American Psychiatric Association said that government policies discourage nursing homes from diagnosing patients as mentally ill. They noted that nursing homes with a high percentage of mentally ill patients could be reclassified as mental institutions, making them ineligible for certain government funding. Likewise, they said that government reimbursement rates are too low to encourage psychiatrists to treat nursing home patients.   Michael Woods

See also **Psychology**. In *World Book,* see **Mental illness.**

Mexico. In 1989, his first full year in office, Mexican President Carlos Salinas de Gortari won praise at home and abroad for toughness in confronting Mexico's economic and political problems. He began the year with several bold moves.

On January 10, Salinas ordered Mexican troops to arrest Joaquín Hernández Galicia, the powerful head of Mexico's 210,000-member oil workers' union, on charges of corruption, gangsterism, and arms smuggling. The labor leader's arrest demonstrated the new president's resolve to reform Mexico's state-run oil monopoly, which allegedly has been bled for years by union corruption.

Then, in February, Salinas sought to defuse complaints about human-rights violations by pardoning more than 800 political prisoners, some of whom had languished in jail for more than 10 years. Such bold actions heightened Salinas' popularity and demonstrated that the former budget and planning minister, though he had not previously held elective office, was an effective political leader.

Debt issues. In March, thousands of peasants cheered Salinas during his carefully orchestrated visit to the state of Tamaulipas. In a demonstration organized with government backing, peasants waved banners promising their support should Salinas declare a moratorium on Mexico's $102-billion foreign debt.

In preparing for negotiations to reduce that debt, Mexico took several steps to improve its political standing with its principal creditor, the United States. To stem the flow of drugs, Mexico began construction of a $40-million radar screen along its southern border to detect aircraft that might be engaged in illicit drug trafficking from cocaine-producing Latin-American nations. Salinas also called for the formation of a 1,200-member task force under the attorney general to root out drug-related corruption in the Mexican government.

Economic reforms. On May 15, the Mexican government announced sweeping economic reforms that allow foreign investors to have majority ownership of Mexican-based enterprises.

Also during 1989, majority stakes in several deficit-ridden, government-owned companies were put up for sale. Among the companies were the national airline Mexicana de Aviación; the Cananea Mining Company, which declared bankruptcy in August; and Teléfonos de México, the widely disliked utility responsible for letting Mexico's telephone service deteriorate badly. In announcing the privatization of the telephone company, President Salinas noted, "Today, 8 out of every 10 homes in our country don't have telephone service, and there are more than 1.5 million requests for new installations that Teléfonos de México has not been able to satisfy."

Apparently satisfied that Mexico was taking the necessary steps to meet its problems, U.S. Secretary of the Treasury Nicholas F. Brady announced on July 23 a restructuring of Mexico's foreign debt. Under the plan, worked out jointly by the United States government and U.S. banks, Mexico received about $2 billion to $3 billion in debt relief.

Whether this was enough relief was a matter of debate. From 1982 to 1988, Mexico spent $56 billion more to repay its debt than it received in new loans, resulting in an annual drain of about 6 per cent of the country's total production. The debt burden has fallen most heavily on the average worker, who had to work 3½ hours to buy 1 pound (0.45 kilogram) of chicken in 1989, compared with 1982 when it took 45 minutes to earn that much.

Political defeat. On July 2, 1989, Mexican voters handed the ruling Institutional Revolutionary Party—established in 1929—its first defeat in a governor's election. Ernesto Ruffo Appel of the right wing National Action Party triumphed decisively in the state of Baja California Norte.

Trade agreement. On October 3, U.S. President George Bush and President Salinas signed an agreement at the White House in Washington, D.C., to encourage reciprocal trade and investment. Under the accord, Mexico will receive preferential access to the U.S. market for some of its textile, steel, and farm crops, whose production employs a large proportion of Mexico's workers.   Nathan A. Haverstock

See also **Latin America** (Facts in brief table). In *World Book,* see **Mexico.**

Michigan. See **Detroit; State government.**

Middle East

Much of the Middle East remained in a holding pattern in 1989. The armed conflicts that had kept the region in turmoil for more than a decade still simmered in some areas, but the warring parties submitted to arbitration by outside forces.

Permanent solutions to the Middle East's three major conflicts—the Iran-Iraq War, Morocco's struggle with the Saharan nationalist movement Polisario for control of Western Sahara, and Israel's occupation of the West Bank and Gaza Strip—continued to elude negotiators. Still, the fact that those conflicts were under serious discussion imparted a certain stability.

The holding pattern that prevailed enabled a number of Middle Eastern states to concentrate on economic development, while others initiated political reforms intended to introduce representative government. Leaders in Algeria, Jordan, Tunisia, and even hard-line Iraq responded to popular pressures for liberalization of their political systems.

Palestinian-Israeli conflict. Intensive international mediation efforts produced only slight progress in the stubborn conflict between the Israelis and the Palestinians in the occupied West Bank and Gaza Strip. The December 1988 statements by Palestine Liberation

ued to refuse to negotiate with the PLO or Palestinians affiliated with the organization.

In April, Israel's Prime Minister Yitzhak Shamir, under heavy U.S. pressure, issued his government's peace plan for the occupied territories. Omitting any references to the PLO, the plan called for elections in the West Bank and Gaza Strip for a Palestinian delegation empowered to negotiate with Israel for limited self-government over a three-year period. At the end of that period, the delegates and Israel would negotiate the final status of the territories. Israel's Knesset (parliament) approved Shamir's plan on May 14, but restrictions attached later by the right wing Likud bloc, the dominant party in Israel's coalition government, rendered the plan unacceptable both to the PLO and to the United States.

In September, the stalled peace process was given a boost when Egypt's President Hosni Mubarak, the leader of the only Arab state with diplomatic relations with Israel, submitted a 10-point plan for elections in the occupied territories. Under Mubarak's plan, Palestinians in East Jerusalem would be included in the voting, which would be held under international supervision. The construction and expansion of Israeli settlements in the West Bank would be temporarily frozen, and Israel would agree to negotiate an exchange of land for a peace settlement. Egypt also offered to host, in Cairo, preliminary talks about the election between the Israelis and Palestinian delegates.

Although Mubarak's plan was acceptable to the United States, the Shamir government rejected it, mainly because of the points on West Bank settlements and giving up territory. The PLO neither endorsed nor rejected the plan, which did not specifically call for the creation of a Palestinian state or a role for the PLO in peace talks.

In October, the United States presented yet another peace plan, a five-point proposal prepared by Secretary of State James A. Baker III. The Baker plan proposed talks between Israel and Egypt's foreign ministers to be held in Washington, D.C., to determine the makeup of the Palestinian delegation to meet with the Israelis in Cairo.

Prospects for the elections improved slightly in November. After Israel's Labor Party, the junior partner in Israel's ruling coalition, threatened to withdraw from the government, the Cabinet gave a "qualified acceptance" to the Baker plan. In December, Egypt also endorsed Baker's plan with some conditions.

Palestinian uprising. Palestinians in the occupied territories in November marked the first anniversary of the PLO proclamation of an independent Palestinian state in the West Bank, the Gaza Strip, and East Jerusalem. The Palestinian state was recognized by a number of countries both inside and outside the Arab bloc during 1989.

The anniversary coincided with the 23rd month of the *intifada* (uprising) in the territories. During that

Organization (PLO) leader Yasir Arafat recognizing Israel's right to exist as a state and renouncing terrorism were viewed by most other countries, notably the United States, as a significant concession. United States diplomats began meeting with PLO representatives early in 1989 at neutral sites to lay the groundwork for an international conference at which Israel, the PLO, and Palestinians in the occupied territories would negotiate a peace settlement under United Nations (UN) sponsorship.

But early optimism that PLO concessions had at last opened the way toward a solution to the Middle East's most difficult long-term political problem proved unfounded. A bitterly divided Israeli government, reflecting the fragmented Israeli public, contin-

Country	Population	Government	Monetary unit*	Exports†	Foreign trade (million U.S.$) Imports†
Bahrain	516,000	Amir Isa bin Sulman Al-Khalifa; Prime Minister Khalifa bin Salman Al-Khalifa	dinar (0.38 = $1)	2,384	2,717
Cyprus	701,000	President George Vassiliou (Turkish Republic of Northern Cyprus: Acting President Rauf R. Denktaş)	pound (2.03 = $1)	731	1,859
Egypt	53,522,000	President Hosni Mubarak; Prime Minister Atef Sedky	pound (1.10 = $1)	4,352	16,226
Iran	56,800,000	Leader of the Islamic Revolution Ayatollah Ali Hoseini Khamenei; President Ali Akbar Hashemi Rafsanjani	rial (71.6 = $1)	20,247	18,296
Iraq	18,048,000	President Saddam Hussein	dinar (0.32 = $1)	9,785	6,636
Israel	4,585,000	President Chaim Herzog; Prime Minister Yitzhak Shamir	shekel (1.96 = $1)	9,145	12,506
Jordan	3,065,000	King Hussein I; Prime Minister Mudar Badran	dinar (0.64 = $1)	734	2,703
Kuwait	2,096,000	Amir Jabir al-Ahmad al-Jabir Al-Sabah; Prime Minister & Crown Prince Sad al-Abdallah al-Salim Al-Sabah	dinar (0.30 = $1)	8,357	5,299
Lebanon	2,947,000	Acting Prime Minister Michel Awn; Acting Prime Minister Salim al-Huss; President Elias Hrawi‡	pound (443 = $1)	500	2,200
Oman	1,469,000	Sultan Qaboos bin Said Al-Said	rial (0.39 = $1)	3,776	1,823
Qatar	369,000	Amir and Prime Minister Khalifa bin Hamad Al-Thani	riyal (3.64 = $1)	3,541	1,139
Saudi Arabia	12,939,000	King & Prime Minister Fahd bin Abd al-Aziz Al-Saud	riyal (3.75 = $1)	20,085	19,113
Sudan	23,797,000	National Revolutionary Council Chairman Umar Hasan Ahmad al-Bashir	pound (4.5 = $1)	333	961
Syria	12,471,000	President Hafiz al-Assad; Prime Minister Mahmud Zubi	pound (21 = $1)	1,345	2,231
Turkey	56,549,000	President Turgut Özal; Prime Minister Yildirim Akbulut	lira (2,300= $1)	10,127	14,149
United Arab Emirates	1,731,000	President Zayid bin Sultan Al-Nuhayyan; Prime Minister Rashid bin Said Al-Maktum	dirham (3.67 = $1)	15,837	5,838
Yemen (Aden)	2,486,000	Supreme People's Council Presidium Chairman Haydar Abu Bakr al-Attas; Council of Ministers Chairman Yasin Said Numan	dinar (0.34 = $1)	29	483
Yemen (Sana)	7,993,000	President Ali Abdallah Salih; Prime Minister Abd al-Aziz Abd al-Ghani	rial (9.75 = $1)	8	1,123

*Exchange rates as of Dec. 1, 1989, or latest available data. †Latest available data.
‡Al-Huss and Hrawi have the support of Lebanon's parliament, many Lebanese Muslims, and most other nations. Awn, who refuses to recognize Hrawi, has the support of Christian units of Lebanon's army and many Lebanese Christians.

period, 600 Palestinians had been killed and 7,000 seriously injured. Thousands more were held in detention or were serving long jail terms. A number of Palestinian leaders had been deported from the territories in violation of international law.

In February, the United States, in its annual report on human rights throughout the world, accused Israel of substantial human-rights violations in the West Bank and the Gaza Strip. Israeli officials termed the report "harsh" and unbalanced. Human-rights organizations—such as Amnesty International, based in London; the Lawyers' Committee for Human Rights, headquartered in New York City; and B'Tselem, an Israeli human-rights monitoring group—criticized Israel for ignoring the civil rights of the Palestinians.

Condemned were such tactics as demolishing the houses of Palestinians accused of committing crimes, indefinitely detaining suspects without trial, levying collective fines on villages, and closing Palestinian schools. In October, the U.S. Conference of Catholic Bishops issued a statement denouncing the occupation as an injustice and a denial of fundamental human rights for the Palestinians.

Crisis in Lebanon. A determined effort by General Michel Awn, the commander of Christian units in the Lebanese army and head of one of two interim governments, to expel Syrian troops in Lebanon set off one of the fiercest rounds of fighting in that country's 14-year civil war. Artillery duels between Syrian forces and their Lebanese Muslim allies and Christian forces lasted for most of the spring and summer. Hundreds of people died in the shelling, which destroyed much of what was left of Beirut.

The Arab League arranged several cease-fires, including one in September that significantly reduced—but did not totally stop—the artillery duels. In October, members of Lebanon's parliament met with Arab League mediators in Taif, Saudi Arabia, and approved a peace accord. Under the plan, Christians, who had formerly dominated the government, allowed Muslims equal representation in parliament. The accord also shifted some power from Lebanon's president, who has traditionally been a Christian, to the Cabinet, which would also be equally divided between Christians and Muslims.

In November, parliament formally endorsed the plan and elected René Moawad, a Christian lawyer, as the new president of a "government of national reconciliation." Awn, however, refused to accept the appointment, saying he would remain as head of state until Syrian troops were withdrawn. Moawad was murdered in a car-bomb attack on November 22. Two days later, parliament elected Elias Hrawi, also a Christian, to succeed Moawad.

Hrawi lost no time in ordering Awn's dismissal from the army and the dissolution of his interim government. To oversee the power-sharing plan, the new president also formed a national unity Cabinet, which included representatives of the seven major Lebanese

sects, under Muslim Prime Minister Salim al-Huss. But Awn refused to accept either the dismissal order or the new government and peace accord, insisting he would not be bound by any pact that did not set a specific timetable for Syrian withdrawal.

Hostage death. The abduction by Israeli commandos on July 28 of Sheik Abdul-Karim Obeid, a key religious leader in a Shiite Muslim group, from southern Lebanon focused international concern on the plight of Americans and other hostages held in Lebanon. Israel had hoped to use Obeid as a bargaining chip for release of Israeli soldiers held by Hezbollah (Party of God), a pro-Iranian terrorist group in Lebanon believed to hold most of the American hostages. Obeid's group has links with Hezbollah.

But Hezbollah threatened to kill U.S. Marine Lieutenant Colonel William R. Higgins unless Obeid was released. Higgins had been seized in 1988 while on a UN observer mission in Lebanon. On July 31, news agencies in Beirut received a videotape of a hanged man believed to be Higgins. Hezbollah had also threatened to kill other hostages. None apparently were killed, possibly because of the influence of Ali Akbar Hashemi Rafsanjani, Iran's new president. Rafsanjani, elected in July after the death of Ayatollah Ruhollah Khomeini, was widely considered a moderate who wishes to expand contacts with the West.

Political changes. In November, Jordan held its first parliamentary elections since 1967. With political

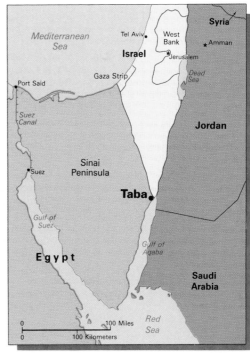

Egyptian army officers raise the flag, *left,* over Taba, a resort on the Mediterranean Sea that Egypt regained from Israel in March 1989.

parties officially banned, candidates for the 80-seat National Assembly ran as independents. In a surprising outcome, candidates belonging to or allied with the Muslim Brotherhood, a Muslim fundamentalist organization that advocates greater adherence to Islamic law, won more than 30 seats.

Tunisia, which has been a single-party state since winning independence from France in 1956, took a tentative step toward a multiparty system by allowing opposition parties to register and compete in parliamentary elections held in April 1989. The winner-take-all electoral system, however, favored the ruling Democratic Constitutional Assembly, which won all seats. But members of the Islamic fundamentalist group Ennahda (Renaissance), who ran as independents, captured 14.5 per cent of the overall popular vote—30 per cent in urban areas. The group had been denied approval as a political party because its platform advocating strict application of Islamic law in Tunisia violates a constitutional ban on religious parties.

Iraq, another one-party state, experienced some political liberalization in April when independent candidates won nearly half the 250 seats in the National Assembly, Iraq's parliament. The remaining seats were won by members of the ruling Ba'ath Party. The government of President Saddam Hussein also appointed a special committee to draft a new constitution that would allow Iraqis to form other political parties.

Perhaps the most significant political reforms in the Middle East took place in Algeria. In 1988, Algeria's President Chadli Bendjedid, in response to popular demands, began transforming the country from a one-party socialist state to a multiparty democracy. In February 1989, voters overwhelmingly approved a new Constitution in a national referendum. Although the new Constitution did not formally establish a multiparty system, it did grant Algerians the right to form associations of "a political nature." As a result, five opposition parties competed with the ruling National Liberation Front in local elections in December.

Regional blocs. A sign of growing cooperation in the Middle East was the formation in February of two regional associations. Five North African states— Algeria, Libya, Mauritania, Morocco, and Tunisia— formed the Arab Maghreb Union (AMU) to promote regional economic development and political cooperation. The creation of the AMU contributed significantly to the winding down of the war in Western Sahara between Morocco and the Polisario Front, which is fighting for the independence of the region. Algeria withdrew its support for the Polisario guerrillas in the interests of good relations with Morocco.

Also in February, Jordan, Egypt, Iraq, and the Yemen Arab Republic—also known as Northern Yemen or Yemen (Sana)—formed a regional bloc called the Arab Cooperation Council. The council would create an integrated industrial and banking system for some 80 million people whose countries have a combined gross national product (GNP) of $100 billion, exports of $15 billion, and imports of $30 billion. The four countries also reportedly agreed to a joint defense pact. Jordan, Egypt, and Yemen had supported Iraq in the Iran-Iraq War.

In December, Syria and Egypt agreed to restore diplomatic relations for the first time since 1977. Sixteen other Arab nations had severed relations with Egypt after it signed a peace treaty with Israel in 1979. By 1989, all except Libya had restored ties.

Negotiation stalemate. In November, more than a year after a cease-fire halted fighting in the Iran-Iraq War, the two former combatants offered rival plans for a peace settlement. Iran offered a simultaneous release of its Iraqi war prisoners if Iraq would withdraw from 1,000 square miles (2,600 square kilometers) of Iranian border territory. Previously, the Iranians had insisted on Iraqi withdrawal before prisoners were exchanged or any other settlement issues were discussed. Iraq insisted on a prisoner exchange and the reopening of the Shatt al Arab waterway, which both countries claim, as the first steps toward a permanent settlement. Iraq also demanded that the border between the two countries be redrawn to give it permanent control over the waterway. In December, Iran rejected the Iraqi proposal, insisting on mutual control based on a 1975 treaty.   William Spencer

See also articles on the various Middle Eastern countries. In *World Book,* see **Middle East** and individual Middle Eastern country articles.

Mining. Ten coal miners died and three were injured in an explosion and fire in the William Station Mine northeast of Paducah, Ky., on Sept. 13, 1989. It was the worst United States mine disaster since 1984, when 27 people died in a fire in a mine near Huntington, Utah. Mine safety officials said the explosion probably occurred when sparks from a piece of mining equipment ignited methane gas, a major component of natural gas that is commonly found in coal mines.

Pittston strike. A strike by the United Mine Workers of America against the Pittston Company dragged on until the end of 1989. The walkout, which began in Virginia and West Virginia in April, triggered sympathy strikes that involved more than 40,000 miners in 10 states. See **Labor.**

Soviet strikes. Thousands of miners in the Soviet Union struck during 1989 to protest low pay and poor living conditions. One of the largest strikes in Soviet history began on July 10 in Siberia's Kuznetsky Basin, the country's second-richest coal-mining region. About 300,000 miners from Siberia, the Ukraine, and other areas eventually joined the work stoppage, sharply reducing coal production. The miners ended their strike later in the month, when the government agreed to their demands. In October, however, about 16,000 miners walked off the job again, charging the government with failing to fulfill its promises. The walkouts left the Soviet Union with dangerously low supplies of coal as winter began.

Members of the United Mine Workers in St. Paul, Va., rally in support of their strike against the Pittston Coal Group, which began in April.

Polish walkout. From February 6 to 9, about 5,000 Polish coal miners at Belchatow, about 90 miles (140 kilometers) southwest of Warsaw, staged a wildcat strike to demand higher wages. (A wildcat strike is a strike not authorized by the union leadership.) Many of the miners belonged to Solidarity, the independent labor union. The strikers returned to work at the urging of Solidarity officials after the mine's management agreed to some of their demands.

Mexican protest. Mexico in August used army troops to close a copper mine in Cananea, about 25 miles (40 kilometers) south of the Arizona border. About 4,000 workers at the mine had struck to protest the government's plan to sell many state-owned mines to private industry. Mexican officials said the mine's new management would include private investors.

Australian gold. Australia's government on June 9 reported that gold mines in that country had produced a record 152 metric tons (168 short tons) of gold in 1988, surpassing the previous record of 119 metric tons (131 short tons) set in 1903. Australian mining companies were trying to produce as much gold as possible before 1991, when the government was to resume taxing profits on gold mining for the first time since 1925.   Michael Woods

In *World Book,* see **Mining.**

Minnesota. See **State government.**
Mississippi. See **State government.**
Missouri. See **State government.**

Mitchell, George John (1933-   ), a Democratic senator from Maine, took his place as Senate majority leader on Jan. 3, 1989. He was elected to that post in November 1988, succeeding Senator Robert C. Byrd (D., W. Va.), who stepped down to become chairman of the Appropriations Committee.

Mitchell was born on Aug. 20, 1933, in Waterville, Me. His family had to struggle; his father was a janitor, and his mother worked nights in a textile mill. Nevertheless, Mitchell was able to attend Bowdoin College in Brunswick, Me., from which he graduated in 1954. From 1954 to 1956, he served as an officer in the U.S. Army.

Mitchell earned a law degree at Georgetown University in Washington, D.C., in 1960. He later practiced law in Maine, where he became active in the state's Democratic Party.

In 1977, Mitchell was named the U.S. attorney for Maine. Two years later, he was appointed a U.S. district court judge, but he resigned in 1980 to complete the unexpired term of Senator Edmund S. Muskie of Maine, who had become secretary of state. Mitchell was returned to the Senate in 1982 and 1988.

Mitchell is a strong supporter of nuclear-arms control and environmental protection.

Mitchell is divorced. He has one child, a daughter, from his marriage.   David L. Dreier

Mongolia. See **Asia.**
Montana. See **State government.**

Montreal reeled in shock after a lone gunman walked into the engineering school of the University of Montreal on Dec. 6, 1989, and murdered 14 women. The gunman wounded 13 other people before killing himself.

The man, later identified as 25-year-old Marc Lepine, moved through the classrooms and hallways, separating men from women and shooting down the women with a high-powered hunting rifle. A letter he was carrying stated that he intended to attack feminists, whom he blamed for ruining his life.

The victims, mostly engineering students, ranged in age from 21 to 31. Funeral ceremonies were attended by every major political figure in Canada, including Prime Minister Brian Mulroney, and by more than 10,000 other citizens.

The event was the worst mass murder in Canada's history. The last mass murder in Quebec was in 1984, when three people were shot to death in the National Assembly in Quebec City. The December deaths brought to 95 the already high 1989 murder toll for the Montreal metropolitan area, which has a population of about 3 million. At the same point in 1988, only 58 homicides had been reported.

MCM woes. The city's ruling party, the Montreal Citizen's Movement (MCM), continued to disintegrate in 1989. Elected in 1986, the party was a coalition of many political viewpoints gathered under left wing Mayor Jean Doré. Left wingers, however, subsequently

Montreal

became disenchanted. In October 1989, City Council member Pierre Bastien became the fifth member to quit the party and sit as an independent. He and four other council members, who left the party late in 1988, were expected to join to form a new left wing party in time for a 1990 election.

Linguistic tensions increased in the wake of a language law, passed in December 1988 by the province of Quebec, that restricted the use of English on commercial signs. In a provincial election on Sept. 25, 1989, Montreal's English-speaking minority struck back by electing four members of the new Equality Party (EP) to the provincial National Assembly. A one-issue party devoted to rights for the 35 per cent of Montrealers whose chief language is English, the EP took four districts away from the ruling Liberals and unseated one important provincial cabinet minister. In October, Quebec Premier Robert Bourassa reduced the number of English speakers in his cabinet.

Economy. A planned downtown complex—backed by Bell Canada, the privately owned telephone utility, and Lavalin International Incorporated, a prominent engineering company—was put on hold because of financial problems. At year-end, some work was proceeding slowly on the complex, which would occupy 500,000 square feet (46,000 square meters).

Vacancy rates for apartments rose to the highest level of any major Canadian city, at times reaching 6 per cent. Rental rates for prime office space held steady at about 20 per cent less than in Toronto.

Soaring real estate prices showed signs of cracking after several boom years. Prices for homes, including condominiums, softened; they dropped by about 20 per cent at midyear and climbed slightly thereafter. Some analysts predicted further declines in housing prices, based on demographic projections that show Montreal's population has not grown appreciably in the 1980's and may decline slightly in the 1990's.

More than 200 retail outlets in Montreal's central shopping area went bankrupt in the first half of 1989. The failures were attributed to oversaturation of the market; more than 600 new shops were added in 1989, all within an area of five city blocks.

Unemployment hovered around the 10 per cent mark in Montreal for 1989, down slightly from 1988. This was far below the 40 per cent levels reported by some outlying areas not far from the city, but still a marked contrast to Toronto, where labor shortages were reported in the fall.

Municipal spending during 1990, according to figures available in September 1989, will increase by 5.9 per cent to about $911 million Canadian ($765 million U.S.). The largest expenditures scheduled are for public security (40.2 per cent of the budget) and transit (33 per cent of the budget). Administrative costs will increase by 8.6 per cent to $23.9 million Canadian (about $20 million U.S.). Montreal's administrators are the highest paid in Canada.   Kendal Windeyer

See also **Canada.** In *World Book,* see **Montreal.**

Morocco. King Hassan II of Morocco played a highly visible role in Arab affairs in 1989, being instrumental in the formation of the Arab Maghreb Union (AMU), a North African common market (see **Algeria**). In May, Morocco hosted an "emergency" summit conference of the Arab League, seeking a settlement to the crisis in Lebanon. The king also took the lead in coordinating Arab support for the Palestinian uprising in the Israeli-occupied West Bank and Gaza Strip.

Relations with Algeria. Morocco's relations with Algeria improved significantly as a result of the formation of the AMU and good personal relations between Hassan and Algeria's President Chadli Bendjedid. In March, the Chamber of Representatives, Morocco's parliament, ratified a 1972 treaty that settled a long-standing dispute between Algeria and Morocco over a section of their common border. Morocco had refused to sign the treaty in protest against Algerian support of the Polisario Front guerrillas. The rebels have been fighting for independence for Western Sahara, which is controlled by Morocco. In August 1989, the two countries signed a cooperation agreement that allows free movement of people and property across their common border.

Western Sahara. Despite improved relations between Morocco and Algeria, there was little progress toward a political settlement in Western Sahara. On January 4, Hassan and Polisario leaders held their first direct talks. Hassan said he would recognize their movement as a legitimate political movement rather than an outlawed rebel group. But Morocco indefinitely postponed the second round of talks scheduled for February.

At year-end, a *referendum* (direct vote) to decide the future of Western Sahara still had not been held. Although the rebels had agreed to the referendum in principle as part of a United Nations-sponsored peace plan in 1988, they insisted that Morocco withdraw from the territory before the vote is held. Morocco refused.

Economic strategy. In the long run, Morocco's economic development of Western Sahara seemed more likely to yield dividends than did its political program. Investment of nearly $1 billion in the territory has encouraged the migration there of several hundred thousand Moroccans, especially from the country's depressed southeastern regions. The changing makeup of the territory makes a vote for integration with Morocco more likely than a vote for independence.

The economy. Good harvests in 1989 gave Morocco the first recorded agricultural surplus in its history, and inflation was held to a record low of 2.5 per cent. But exports of phosphates, Morocco's main mineral resource, dropped due to growing concerns over the environmental effects of phosphate-based fertilizers.   William Spencer

See also **Middle East** (Facts in brief table). In *World Book,* see **Morocco.**

Mosbacher, Robert Adam (1927-), became United States secretary of commerce on Feb. 3, 1989. He had been a director of the New York Life Insurance Company of New York City and of Texas Commerce Bancshares, Incorporated, a bank holding company in Houston.

Mosbacher has been a friend and political ally of President George Bush since the 1960's. Like Bush, Mosbacher was the son of a wealthy Wall Street investor, was raised in the East, and prospered in the oil business in Texas.

Mosbacher was born on March 11, 1927, in Mount Vernon, N.Y. In 1947, he received a bachelor's degree in business administration at Washington and Lee University in Lexington, Va. After spending a year working for his father, he moved to Texas.

Mosbacher raised money for Bush's unsuccessful campaigns for the Senate in 1964 and 1970 and for Bush's successful bid for the House of Representatives in 1966. Mosbacher was finance cochairman for the Republican Party in 1976, finance chairman for Bush's attempt to win the presidential nomination in 1980, and chief fund-raiser for the Bush presidential campaign of 1988.

In 1985, Mosbacher married Georgette Paulsin, who heads a cosmetics company. He has three daughters and a son by his first wife, Jane Pennybacker, who died in 1970. A second marriage ended in divorce in 1982.   Jay Myers

Motion pictures. Motion-picture box-office receipts in the United States attained a new high in 1989, even though some feature films reached video racks only six months after their release to theaters. The year-end total for 1989 topped $5 billion. Each of the summer's three biggest hits—*Batman*, *Indiana Jones and the Last Crusade*, and *Lethal Weapon 2*— grossed more than the major success of the 1988 summer, *Who Framed Roger Rabbit*. The week ending July 6, 1989, set a single-week record of $197 million, surpassing the earlier record of $158 million set for the week ending Dec. 31, 1987.

Weekend box-office records were broken by single films on a regular basis. The mark set by Steven Spielberg's *Indiana Jones and the Last Crusade* in May was surpassed in June by Ivan Reitman's *Ghostbusters II* and later that month by Tim Burton's *Batman*. Record-breaking fall openings were achieved by *Sea of Love*, *Look Who's Talking*, and *Harlem Nights*, and a phenomenal Thanksgiving weekend record was attained by *Back to the Future, Part II*.

Batmania swept the United States in 1989, inspired by the blockbuster success of *Batman*. Michael Keaton starred in the title role, with Jack Nicholson as Batman's nemesis, The Joker. Director Burton opted for a return to the dark, *film noir* tones of the original comic book rather than the campy, light-hearted approach of the 1960's television series. (*Film noir* is a term first used by French film critics to describe certain U.S. movies of the 1940's and 1950's, marked by a brooding atmosphere and many nighttime scenes.) Not all critics embraced the movie, but the public flocked to see it in huge numbers.

Batman inevitably proved a merchandising bonanza. Lunch boxes, sunglasses, T-shirts, mugs, models of the Batmobile, and other items—all boasting the image of the caped crime fighter or his yellow-and-black logo—reached unprecedented sales.

At a final domestic gross of more than $250 million, *Batman* fell $100 million short of the record set by *E.T.: The Extra-Terrestrial* in 1982. Burton's gloomy tale failed to earn the repeat trade that Spielberg's more warm-hearted fantasy had enjoyed seven years previously. Moreover, Warner Brothers surprised the film industry by releasing *Batman* to home video on Nov. 15, 1989, less than five months after its June 23 opening in theaters. The movie continued to play in some theaters even after its video release.

Other hits contributing solidly to 1989's record-breaking box office included *Parenthood*, a genial comedy about contemporary family problems in which Steve Martin headed a large, strong cast; *Dead Poets Society*, with Robin Williams as an unorthodox teacher at a tradition-bound boys' school; and *When Harry Met Sally . . .*, in which Meg Ryan and Billy Crystal endured the rigors of friendship and romance.

Honey, I Shrunk the Kids, a Walt Disney fantasy, proved a bonanza with vacationing youngsters. The

In *Steel Magnolias*, Julia Roberts plays a newly married woman who decides to have a baby despite warnings that pregnancy will ruin her health.

Motion pictures

Disney Studio also released *The Little Mermaid*, its most warmly received animated feature in years, based on a Hans Christian Andersen fairy tale about a mermaid who falls in love with a human prince. *Steel Magnolias* featured a star-studded cast—including Sally Field, Shirley MacLaine, and Dolly Parton—in a drama about women's friendship.

Driving Miss Daisy, starring Jessica Tandy as a Southern matriarch and Morgan Freeman as her chauffeur, drew year-end raves. Also winning favorable reviews was *Glory*, with Matthew Broderick as the commander of the first black fighting unit in the Civil War (1861-1865). *The War of the Roses*, a bitter comedy about divorce, was a box-office success.

Fine smaller films. Although 1989 was clearly the year of the blockbuster, there still was room for smaller films. Steven Soderberg's *sex, lies, and videotape*, detailing a quartet of mismatched men and women in Baton Rouge, La., was one of the year's hits on the art-house circuit. Gus Van Sant's *Drugstore Cowboy*, in which former teen-age idol Matt Dillon gave a poignant performance as a drug addict, won favor with audiences and critics. *The Fabulous Baker Boys*, written and directed by Steve Kloves, featured outstanding performances by real-life brothers Jeff Bridges and Beau Bridges as a Seattle lounge act, while Michelle Pfeiffer gave a star-making performance as the vocalist who comes between them.

Woody Allen's *Crimes and Misdemeanors* proved his biggest success since *Hannah and Her Sisters* in 1986. It featured an outstanding performance by Martin Landau as a respected physician who arranges the murder of his mistress.

Michael Moore's documentary *Roger & Me*, about the effects of the closing of a General Motors plant on the community of Flint, Mich., was a hit at the New York Film Festival in October. The film was expected to be widely shown throughout the United States and Canada in 1990.

Spike Lee's *Do the Right Thing* was one of 1989's major critical triumphs. Its tale of mushrooming racial violence on a hot summer day in New York City was interpreted by some as a call to arms. Others saw it as an honest statement of how violence can erupt from even the most trivial incident. See **Lee, Spike.**

Father-son themes were in vogue during 1989. The well-regarded *Field of Dreams*, in which Kevin Costner reinforced his status as one of the film industry's hottest stars, dealt with father-son reconciliation, as did *Dad, Indiana Jones, Parenthood*, and, to a lesser degree, even *Star Trek V: The Final Frontier*.

Steven Spielberg had a successful year in 1989. In addition to *Indiana Jones*, he brought out the romantic fantasy *Always*, a long-planned remake of 1943's *A Guy Named Joe*. The film, starring Richard Dreyfuss and Holly Hunter, promised to be one of the holiday season's brightest adornments.

Spielberg said, however, that all 1989 releases were dwarfed by the restoration and reissue of David Lean's 1962 Academy Award winner, *Lawrence of Arabia*. Both Spielberg and Martin Scorsese had lobbied for restoration of the epic, and Columbia Pictures spent $600,000 restoring it to its director's vision. Thirty-one minutes had been cut from the film by producer Sam Spiegel. These were restored, and director Lean helped reassemble some of the footage.

Other revivals. The 50th anniversary of what many critics call Hollywood's Golden Year, 1939, saw the successful reissues of *Wuthering Heights* and *The Wizard of Oz*, as well as a fresh, color-corrected print of *Gone with the Wind*, which added an additional $3-million to its take during 1989.

A 209-minute reconstructed version of film pioneer D. W. Griffith's 1916 epic *Intolerance* earned a five-minute standing ovation upon its Oct. 2, 1989, presentation at the New York Film Festival. The reconstruction, sponsored by the Library of Congress and the Museum of Modern Art, cost $120,000. The project included the shooting of new footage using original frames of the film that Griffith had deposited with the U.S. Copyright Office in June 1916. The film is expected to be shown worldwide at other film festivals.

Film treasures. *Intolerance* was one of the first 25 films chosen for the National Film Registry, Librarian of Congress James H. Billington announced in September. Congress set up the registry after extensive lobbying by the film community to protect filmmakers' "moral rights" in decisions regarding the alterations of their works. The 13-member National Film Board—composed of directors, producers, writers, and historians—will select 25 films each year for three years to be designated "national treasures," worthy of preservation without alterations, such as colorization.

The other 24 films chosen in 1989 were *The Best Years of Our Lives* (1946), *Casablanca* (1943), *Citizen Kane* (1941), *The Crowd* (1928), *Dr. Strangelove* (1964), *The General* (1927), *Gone with the Wind* (1939), *The Grapes of Wrath* (1940), *High Noon* (1952), *The Learning Tree* (1969), *The Maltese Falcon* (1941), *Mr. Smith Goes to Washington* (1939), *Modern Times* (1936), *Nanook of the North* (1922), *On the Waterfront* (1954), *The Searchers* (1956), *Singin' in the Rain* (1952), *Snow White and the Seven Dwarfs* (1937), *Some Like It Hot* (1959), *Star Wars* (1977), *Sunrise* (1927), *Sunset Boulevard* (1950), *Vertigo* (1958), and *The Wizard of Oz* (1939).

The British film industry. *Licence to Kill*, the second in the James Bond series to star Timothy Dalton, was a major disappointment in the United States but did well in Great Britain, surpassing the first film with Dalton as Bond, *The Living Daylights*. Ironically, Sean Connery, the original Agent 007, had one of his most successful years in 1989 since leaving the series. He won strong notices as Harrison Ford's cantankerous father in *Indiana Jones* as well as Dustin Hoffman's roguish parent in *Family Business*. Connery also starred in the movie version of Tom Clancy's thriller *The Hunt for Red October*, to be released in the spring

"That's all, folks."

There was a time—the late 1930's through the 1950's—remembered as the golden age of animation. During that era, studios made hundreds of 6½-minute cartoons as short features for movie theaters. The characters in those cartoons were really, well, *characters*. They had distinctive personalities, owing in no small part to their voices. Often the voice alone, such as the good-natured stuttering of Porky Pig or the wild-eyed squawks of Donald Duck, was enough to get a laugh.

Cartoon characters are indestructible, but sadly the people who give them life are not. By 1989, many of the great cartoon voices had passed from the scene, and there were few new ones to take their place.

The first to go was Clarence Nash, who died in 1985 at the age of 80. For 51 years, Nash was the man at the microphone for all of Walt Disney Productions' Donald Duck cartoons. When Disney introduced the short-tempered duck in the 1934 cartoon *The Wise Little Hen*, he knew he had a character that might rival Mickey Mouse in popularity. But the duck—soon named Donald—had to have a memorable voice. Disney spoke for Mickey at that time (and for about 10 years thereafter), but neither he nor anyone else at the studio could come up with a convincing voice for their new creation.

One day, Disney was listening to a local radio program as a young California schoolteacher named Clarence Nash did an impression of a duck reciting "Mary Had a Little Lamb." Before you could say quack, Nash had been hired by Disney

SPEECHLESS.

MEL BLANC
1908-1989

In a memorial ad, some of Warner Brothers' most famous characters are rendered "speechless" by the loss of Mel Blanc, the man who made them talk.

studios to dub Donald's voice in a cartoon entitled *The Orphan's Benefit*. Donald Duck became a huge hit, and Nash found himself with a new career and a nickname. From then on, he was known as "Ducky."

Jim Backus was already an established actor in the late 1940's when he was asked by United Producers of America (UPA) if he would be interested in doing the voice of a character then in development, the near-sighted Mr. Magoo. Backus said yes and worked up a voice based on a know-it-all character called The Man in the Club Car, whom he had played on the New York City stage.

The squinting, cane-wielding Magoo debuted in a 1949 cartoon, *Ragtime Bear*. UPA produced Mr. Magoo cartoons for another 10 years, always with Backus doing the voice. Backus also played many roles on camera, including that of millionaire Thurston Howell III on television's "Gilligan's Island." He died on July 3, 1989, at age 76.

The industry lost its most versatile voice artist just a week later, on July 10, with the death of Mel Blanc at age 81. Blanc spoke for a fun house full of characters, including Porky Pig, Bugs Bunny, Daffy Duck, and some 500 others. During his long career, he dubbed more than 3,000 cartoons. He was the original voice of Woody Woodpecker for Walter Lantz studios, and in the 1960's he played the part of Barney Rubble in the animated TV series "The Flintstones." But it was with Warner Brothers that Blanc's name was most closely linked.

Blanc, a former musician and bandleader, got his first dubbing job at Warner in the mid-1930's. His assignment was to come up with a voice for a drunken bull. The producers were so delighted with Blanc's impression that they soon had him creating voices for every new character the studio developed. At the same time, Blanc became a regular on several national radio shows, including the Jack Benny program. He stayed with the Benny troupe when it moved to TV.

In 1961, Blanc was in an automobile accident that broke nearly every bone in his body and left him in a coma. Day after day, a brain specialist stopped by Blanc's bedside but could get no response from him. Finally, the doctor decided to try a novel approach. "Hey, Bugs Bunny," he said, "how are you?" In Bugs's voice came the reply, "Just fine, doc. How are *you*?" Recounting the incident years later, Blanc mused, "I guess Mel Blanc was dead, but the characters were still alive."

There's an epitaph in there somewhere, not just for Blanc but for all the great dubbing artists of animation's glory days. May the voices of these masters, and the characters they made so real, live forever.   David L. Dreier

Jack Nicholson as The Joker (on the video screens) taunts Michael Keaton as Batman
in 1989's blockbuster *Batman*, which shattered many box-office records.

of 1990, and in late 1989 was shooting the film of John le Carré's spy novel *The Russia House*.

Kenneth Branagh, a 28-year-old Irish filmmaker, wrote, directed, and starred in an earthy version of William Shakespeare's *Henry V*. The film made the conquering hero seem like an ordinary mortal plagued by doubts and faults, and it won praise from both critics and the public. Coincidentally, Branagh's film came out the same year as the death of legendary British actor Laurence Olivier, whose more idealistic vision of *Henry V* had been a morale booster for war-time audiences in 1944 (see **Deaths [Close-Up]**). The 1989 film was financed by a group of British investors and the Bank of Boston. Its supporting cast included Paul Scofield, Judi Dench, Ian Holm, and Derek Jacobi.

The British film industry scored another success with *My Left Foot*, featuring a memorable performance by Daniel Day-Lewis as a cerebral palsy victim. *Scandal* revisited the government-shaking 1963 sex scandal in which Secretary for War John D. Profumo resigned after confessing to a sexual relationship with Christine Keeler. *High Hopes* presented the comic plight of a group of individualists amid the conformity and materialism of modern England.

Serious political themes continued to be ignored by most movie customers. *A Dry White Season*, a searing antiapartheid drama, drew only modest attendance despite critical endorsement. The film starred Donald Sutherland and featured Marlon Brando's first

appearance since *The Formula* in 1980. Two Vietnam dramas—*In Country* and *Welcome Home*—had only short runs in theaters. Brian DePalma's disturbing *Casualties of War*, starring Michael J. Fox and Sean Penn, got good reviews but also faded quickly. At year's end, Universal Studios hoped that Oliver Stone's *Born on the Fourth of July*, starring Tom Cruise as a bitter Vietnam veteran, would help alleviate public indifference to the theme.

Glasnost in films. *Little Vera*, one of the first films produced under the Soviet Union's policy of *glasnost* (openness in the flow of information), was an international hit. The film, which told of a young working-class woman's sexual awakening, was noticeably critical of life in a barren Soviet industrial town. Much interest was provoked when the film's young star, Natalya Negoda, posed for a photographic display in *Playboy* magazine.

The effects of glasnost were apparent at the 16th annual International Moscow Film Festival, held in July. Capacity audiences greeted with cheers Philip Kaufman's 1988 film *The Unbearable Lightness of Being*, set during the 1968 Soviet invasion of Czechoslovakia. The film was based on a novel by Czechoslovak author Milan Kundera that had been banned in the Soviet Union.   Philip Wuntch

See also **Awards and prizes** (Arts awards); **Foster, Jodie; Hoffman, Dustin.** In *World Book,* see **Motion picture.**

Mozambique. For the first time in the 14 years of civil strife in Mozambique, peace negotiations were begun in August 1989 between representatives of Mozambique's government and the Mozambique National Resistance (Renamo), a large rebel group. The meetings, held in Nairobi, Kenya, were preceded by months of behind-the-scenes diplomatic contacts involving South Africa, the United States, the Soviet Union, Great Britain, and a number of African nations.

The Nairobi meetings were mediated by Kenya's President Daniel T. arap Moi and President Robert Mugabe of Zimbabwe. The Mozambican government of President Joaquím Alberto Chissano was represented by members of the 17-denomination Mozambique Christian Council. The chief Renamo representative was Afonso Dhaklama, who presented a short agenda calling for free elections, government tolerance of traditional religions and customs, and a share of power for Renamo.

Years of violence. Renamo has conducted a reign of terror in Mozambique, destroying bridges, hospitals, dams, and other facilities. An estimated 700,000 people have been killed, or have died from war-related famine, and 1.5 million others have fled to neighboring countries. Zimbabwe and Malawi have provided 12,000 troops to protect the rail link to the Mozambican port of Beira.

The August discussions in Nairobi set the stage for future direct talks between Renamo and the Chissano government. Since 1987, the government has extended an offer of amnesty to individual Renamo members; some 3,000 rebel troops had accepted the offer by late 1989.

The economy. Once considered the most Marxist-oriented nation in Africa, Mozambique in 1989 continued to move toward a free-market economy and private enterprise. On July 30, the fifth congress of Mozambique's ruling party, the Front for the Liberation of Mozambique (Frelimo), dropped all references to Marxism, and party membership was opened to owners of private property and members of the business community. Also during the year, the government continued to phase out communal state farms.

Although the economy improved during the year, growing at an annual rate of 4 per cent, the country was still in desperate straits. The per capita income of Mozambicans was just $150 a year—one of the world's lowest—and 85 per cent of the country's food was imported or provided in famine relief.

In April, an international donor conference in Maputo, Mozambique's capital, pledged about $325-million in emergency relief for Mozambique. In addition, South Africa, Sweden, Britain, and several other countries, together with private investors, were helping Mozambique develop hydroelectric dams, rebuild ports and railroads, and increase agricultural production.   J. Gus Liebenow and Beverly B. Liebenow

See also **Africa** (Facts in brief table). In *World Book,* see **Mozambique.**

Mulroney, Brian (1939-   ) traveled extensively in 1989, the first year of his second term as Canada's 17th prime minister. In March, Mulroney went to England and then to the Netherlands for an international conference on the environment. In May, he joined President François Mitterrand of France in Dakar, Senegal, for the third summit of French-speaking countries. (Canada has two official languages, English and French.) An economic summit of the seven major industrial countries took Mulroney to Paris in July. In October, he met in Kuala Lumpur, Malaysia, with heads of other Commonwealth nations.

Late in November, Mulroney visited the Soviet Union to meet with President Mikhail S. Gorbachev. Then, in early December, Mulroney met in Brussels, Belgium, with leaders of other North Atlantic Treaty Organization nations. He also found four occasions to meet privately with United States President George Bush during 1989.

Hurt by unpopular measures such as a planned new federal sales tax and reductions in social programs, Mulroney's Progressive Conservative Party saw its support fall from 48 per cent of decided voters in January to 27 per cent in October, according to public opinion polls.   David M. L. Farr

See also **Canada.** In *World Book,* see **Mulroney, Brian.**

Music. See Classical music; Popular music.

Myanmar. See Burma.

Namibia. The November 1989 electoral victory of the South West Africa People's Organization (SWAPO), a large rebel organization that had battled South African troops for 23 years, brought independence one step closer for Namibia, Africa's last colony. South Africa had held onto Namibia—formerly called South West Africa—which it seized from Germany in 1916, despite a 1978 United Nations (UN) Security Council resolution censuring it for doing so. A UN timetable for Namibian independence became possible in December 1988 with the signing of a peace pact between South Africa, Angola, and Cuba. That agreement linked Namibian freedom with the withdrawal of Cuban and South African troops from Angola.

During 1989, a UN Transition Assistance Group (UNTAG) monitored the independence process. Martti Ahtisaari of Finland headed the 25-nation UNTAG peacekeeping force as well as 1,500 police supervisors and 1,000 civilian election supervisors.

Shaky peace. An April 1 cease-fire—the first stage of the independence timetable—was immediately violated by some 1,200 heavily armed SWAPO fighters who infiltrated Namibia from bases in Angola at the end of March. The guerrillas were pursued by South African troops near the Angolan border, and nearly 350 of the rebels were killed during the first week of April. Under pressure from many quarters, SWAPO dismantled all of its Namibian bases and withdrew about 100 miles (160 kilometers) into Angola. In June,

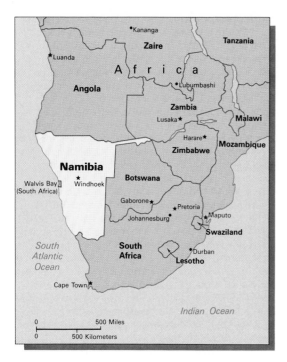

Namibia, ruled by South Africa since 1916, held
United Nations-monitored elections in November
1989 and was slated to gain independence in 1990.

South Africa reduced its military presence in Namibia
to 1,500 troops, who were confined to barracks.

The elections in November created an assembly to
draft a new constitution. Prior to the vote, some
65,000 Namibian exiles returned to Namibia, many of
them airlifted home on UN-chartered airplanes.
Among the returnees was SWAPO President Sam Nujoma, who had spent some 30 years in exile. Nujoma
made a triumphal homecoming in Windhoek, Namibia's capital, on September 14.

The elections gave SWAPO a 57.3 per cent majority.
By winning only 41 of the 72 assembly seats, however,
it came up short of the two-thirds majority needed to
dictate the terms of the constitution. SWAPO will thus
have to cooperate with the Democratic Turnhalle Alliance, a broad coalition of racial and ethnic parties
that won 28.6 per cent of the vote and 21 seats in the
assembly. Smaller parties won the remaining 10 seats.

Even before the election, SWAPO dropped its call
for a Marxist one-party state. It did so in an effort to
appeal to black ethnic groups other than the Ovambo,
its main base of support—as well as to white and
mixed-race Namibians. Nujoma pledged multiparty
democracy, with a bill of rights and an independent
judiciary.   J. Gus Liebenow and Beverly B. Liebenow

See also **Africa** (Facts in brief table). In *World Book,*
see **Namibia.**

Navy. See Armed forces.

Nebraska. See State government.

Netherlands shifted slightly to the political left in
1989. Prime Minister Ruud Lubbers led his centrist
Christian Democrat Party to victory in parliamentary
elections on September 6. Lubbers' Party remained the
biggest single party in the States-General (parliament)
but did not gain a majority. Instead of maintaining his
governing coalition with the Liberals—who in Holland are a conservative party—he formed an alliance
with the Labor Party. Lubbers, 50, marked his eighth
year and third successive term in office, making him
the longest-serving Dutch leader in three decades.

Lubbers turned to the Labor Party to help him make
good on a campaign pledge to spend part of the
Netherlands' new wealth—the result of an improved
economy—on social welfare and environmental recovery. The main issue during the campaign was the
environment.

Lubbers' previous government had been toppled in
May when the Liberals rebelled against a plan to finance a program to cut pollution by 70 per cent by
the year 2010. The program would have doubled anti-
pollution spending to $7.5 billion per year by 1994.
The Liberals objected to a provision that Lubbers
deemed critical in his approach to environmental
cleanup: the cancellation of income-tax deductions
currently granted to Dutch taxpayers who drive cars to
work. The new center-left coalition took office on
Nov. 7, 1989.

Left wing parties gain. In the September voting,
the Christian Democrats retained their 54 seats in the
150-member lower house of the States-General. The
Liberals, who had been in coalition with Lubbers since
1982, lost 5 of their 27 seats.

Labor lost 3 of its 52 seats. Two small, left wing parties registered gains. The Democrats '66, a group close
to Labor, advanced from 9 seats to 12. The Green Left,
an alliance of environmentalists and pacifists, picked
up 2 seats for a total of 7.

Private TV station flops. An attempt to break the
government's virtual monopoly on television broadcasting fell apart when a planned commercial station,
TV10, was declared illegal by a Dutch court. A commercial station may use a transmitter located outside
the country to broadcast signals into the Netherlands,
provided that station is essentially foreign-owned.
Plans for TV10, announced in May, included offshore
broadcasting facilities and some foreign ownership,
together with strong financing designed to lure star
performers and fund attractive programs.

In October, shortly before TV10 was to go on the
air, the court ruled that the station was essentially
Dutch-owned. On November 13, TV10 collapsed under
a burden of debt. Dutch courts have allowed a smaller
commercial station to broadcast into the country from
Luxembourg because Dutch investors own only a minor percentage of that station.   Joseph Fitchett

See also **Europe** (Facts in brief table). In *World Book,*
see **Netherlands.**

Nevada. See State government.

New Brunswick. Long one of the disadvantaged provinces of Canada, New Brunswick attempted to improve its image in May 1989 by publishing an ambitious economic plan, *Toward 2000*. The 58-page prospectus outlined prospects for small business ventures in the province. The government promised to reduce red tape for small businesses and to set up a small-business directorate, aided by a mobile unit that would tour the province offering advice to founders of new firms.

The government's scope for action was limited by a tight financial position. About 40 per cent of New Brunswick's revenue comes from the federal government, yet the province's residents are among the most heavily taxed in Canada, paying an 11 per cent sales tax and income taxes amounting to 60 per cent of the basic federal tax. Still, the provincial budget, released on March 30, was optimistic. No increases in personal or corporate income taxes were announced, though taxes on cigarettes and gasoline were raised slightly. A surplus of $3.1 million Canadian (about $2.6 million U.S.) in the daily operations budget was predicted, but plans for capital projects led to a 6.9 per cent increase in expenditures overall.   David M. L. Farr

World Book, see **New Brunswick.**

New Hampshire. See **State government.**

New Jersey. See **State government.**

New Mexico. See **State government.**

New York. See **New York City; State government.**

New York City. David N. Dinkins, the 62-year-old Democratic president of Manhattan—one of New York City's five boroughs, or political subdivisions—was elected the city's first black mayor on Nov. 7, 1989. In a bitter and close election, Dinkins defeated Republican Rudolph W. Giuliani, a former United States prosecutor, by just 47,080 votes out of 1.9 million. Dinkins took office on Jan. 1, 1990.

In the Sept. 12, 1989, Democratic primary, Dinkins defeated incumbent Mayor Edward I. Koch and two other Democrats—City Controller Harrison J. Goldin and businessman Richard Ravitch. Koch, in office since January 1978, presided over the city's robust economic rebound from a financial crisis in the mid-1970's and won reelection by lopsided margins in 1981 and 1985. But a series of municipal scandals that surfaced in his third term, a slowdown in the city's economy, and Dinkins' campaign promises of unity after several racial incidents all figured in Koch's loss.

City power structure revised. Voters also approved a city charter revision that eliminated the city's Board of Estimate. Since 1898, the board had exercised power over the city's budgets, land use, and municipal contracts. But the Supreme Court of the United States ruled unanimously on March 22, 1989, that the board was unconstitutional because it equalized powers between the boroughs of Brooklyn, with more than 2 million residents, and Staten Island, which has fewer than 400,000. Under the charter revision, the

Democrat David N. Dinkins gives a "thumbs up" gesture after learning that he has been elected New York City's first black mayor on November 7.

board's powers will be transferred to the City Council and the City Planning Commission. The U.S. Department of Justice approved the charter on December 13.

In response to Staten Island's loss of power, the borough's leaders initiated a campaign to secede from New York City. Governor Mario M. Cuomo on December 15 signed a bill permitting Staten Islanders to vote on secession in November 1990.

New schools chief. New Yorkers were stunned on May 10, 1989, by the death of public schools Chancellor Richard R. Green, 52, from an asthma attack. Green, who became chancellor in March 1988, was just beginning an overhaul of the city's school system. On Sept. 20, 1989, the Board of Education appointed Joseph A. Fernandez, the superintendent of the Dade County, Florida, school system, as Green's successor.

New police chief. On December 18, Mayor-elect Dinkins named Lee P. Brown, police chief of Houston, as New York City police commissioner. Brown succeeds Benjamin Ward, who retired.

Congressman convicted. United States Representative Robert Garcia, a Democratic congressman from the borough of the Bronx, was convicted on October 20, together with his wife, Jane Lee Garcia, on charges of extorting payments from executives of the Wedtech Corporation. Investigations of Wedtech, a military contractor in the South Bronx, had uncovered evidence of payoffs, extortion, and official corruption. Garcia resigned from Congress on Jan. 7, 1990.

Crime. Two crimes had a strong impact on New York City and the rest of the nation in 1989. On April 19, a 28-year-old woman investment banker running in Central Park was gang raped and beaten almost to death by a band of youths. The woman, whose name was withheld by the media, made what doctors called a miraculous recovery, though she had no recollection of the attack. At year-end, eight youths, arrested soon after the crime, were awaiting trial.

Yusuf Hawkins, 16, a black honor student, was attacked and killed in the Bensonhurst section of Brooklyn on August 23 by a group of white youths who reportedly mistook him for another youth. The incident, and a protest march by about 7,500 blacks a week later, brought racial tensions in the city to a head and figured prominently in the Democratic primary. At year-end, six white teen-aged boys were awaiting trial for the murder.

Japanese buy Rockefeller Center. The Rockefeller Group, a company owned by the Rockefeller family, announced on October 30 that it had sold controlling interest in the company to Japan's Mitsubishi Estate Company for $846 million. The company's holdings include Rockefeller Center—the symbolic center of midtown Manhattan for a half-century and home of the famed Radio City Music Hall and the studios of the National Broadcasting Company.   Owen Moritz

See also **City; Dinkins, David N.** In *World Book,* see **New York City.**

New Zealand was stunned on Aug. 7, 1989, when Prime Minister David R. Lange announced that he was resigning. He said that it had long been his intention to step down before the 1990 general election and that the timing had been determined by his Labour Party's improved showing in opinion polls. The news media suggested that ill health had led to his decision.

But some political watchers speculated that Lange's action may have been spurred by the Labour Party's vote on August 3 to reinstate former Finance Minister Roger O. Douglas to the Cabinet. Lange had dismissed Douglas in 1988 over a clash on economic policy.

Lange's announcement left those interested in succeeding him little time to rally Labour support. On August 8, Deputy Prime Minister Geoffrey Palmer was elected prime minister.

After the election, Health and Housing Minister Helen Clark was named deputy prime minister, the first woman in New Zealand history to hold the post. Lange agreed to become attorney general.

Foreign affairs. Relations with the United States, cool since New Zealand began banning nuclear-powered and nuclear-armed ships from its ports in 1985, showed signs of improving in 1989. Prime Minister Palmer seemed to favor resuming dialogue with the United States. He said, however, that he would continue to support the ban on nuclear ships.

New Zealand's other diplomatic initiatives in 1989 involved environmental issues. The country played a prominent role in an environmental summit in London in March by urging faster action to limit chlorofluorocarbons (CFC's). CFC's, synthetic chemicals used as refrigerants and as propellants in aerosol sprays, are suspected of depleting the ozone layer, a part of the atmosphere that shields the earth from ultraviolet radiation. New Zealand banned the import of CFC's, beginning in July 1990.

New Zealand also worked to outlaw drift-net fishing, which is depleting fish stocks in the Pacific Ocean. (A drift net is a large net set in the water in a line.)

Naval agreement. On August 29, New Zealand and Australia agreed on the purchase of warships. Australia will build 12 frigates, and New Zealand will buy 2 of them, with an option to buy 2 more.

Economy. New Zealand's economy continued to show steady improvement in 1989. In June, the country's balance of payments (the value of goods exported compared to the value of goods imported) showed a surplus of $NZ 48 million (about $80 million U.S.). The balance later returned to a deficit.

In September, inflation hit an 18-month high of 7.2 per cent. Economists attributed the increase to a 25 per cent hike in the general consumer tax and to higher food prices caused by poor growing conditions in the country. Earlier in the year, inflation had been holding steady at about 4 per cent.   Gavin Ellis

See also **Asia** (Facts in brief table); **Australia.** In *World Book,* see **New Zealand.**

Newfoundland. Liberal Party leader Clyde K. Wells was sworn in as Newfoundland's fifth premier on May 5, 1989, ending 17 years of rule by the Progressive Conservatives (PC's). Wells's predecessor, Thomas Rideout, had served as premier only since March 22, when A. Brian Peckford stepped down after 10 years as PC leader and premier.

The Liberals won 31 seats in the election on April 20. The other 21 seats went to the PC's. Wells himself was narrowly defeated, but he achieved a place in the Legislative Assembly in May when a Liberal member resigned to free a seat for the new premier.

Newfoundland's chief industry, fishing, suffered in 1989. A decline in stocks of cod was blamed on overfishing by foreign fleets. To conserve fish, the federal government in February tightened limits on the amount of cod to be taken from northern waters in 1989. Worried plant workers in the province's two giant fish companies went on strike early in the year; settlements in March and April boosted wages and created a pension fund. But on March 31, in negotiations over fishing rights with France, the federal government further angered Newfoundland when it granted France a 70 per cent increase in its cod catch over the next three years in exchange for France's agreement to turn water ownership disputes over to an international tribunal.   David M. L. Farr

See also **Canada; Wells, Clyde Kirby.** In *World Book,* see **Newfoundland.**

Newsmakers of 1989 included the following:

The beat goes on. On March 23, Dick Clark, emcee of the television dance show "American Bandstand," announced that he was calling it quits after 33 years. Clark, a youthful looking 59-year-old who has been dubbed "the world's oldest teen-ager," introduced thousands of musical guests during his reign over the Bandstand dance floor, including Buddy Holly, the Beach Boys, Stevie Wonder, the Jackson Five, and Madonna. Taking over as new host on April 8 was a 33-year-old actor named David Hirsch.

Love among politicians. John R. McKernan, Jr., the governor of Maine, and Olympia J. Snowe, one of Maine's two U.S. representatives, were married on February 24 in Lewiston, Me. It may be the first marriage between a governor and member of Congress while both were in office.

Polar dispute cools. On February 15, astronomer Dennis Rawlins, who in 1988 announced that Admiral Robert E. Peary had faked his 1909 discovery of the North Pole, acknowledged that the National Geographic Society had cast doubt on his evidence. Rawlins had found a copy of Peary's notes seeming to show that the explorer knew he was about 120 miles (190 kilometers) away from the North Pole on April 6, 1909, the day he claimed to have reached the pole.

After a yearlong investigation, the National Geographic Society reported that Peary did discover the pole just when he said he did. The documents Rawlins

found had been mislabeled and were really from a 1906 expedition. Navigational experts said that the numbers Rawlins had interpreted as compass readings were actually serial numbers found on watches Peary carried with him.

Grandpa Elvis. Lisa Marie Presley, the 21-year-old daughter of rock legend Elvis Presley, gave birth to a daughter—Danielle—on May 29, in Los Angeles. Her husband is musician Danny Keough.

A royal invention. In February, King Hassan II of Morocco became the first monarch to receive a patent from the U.S. Patent and Trademark Office. The king invented a system that uses a video camera and an *electrocardiogram* (a printed record of a heart's electrical impulses) to monitor the heart during exercise.

A millionaire with a heart. Sheelah Ryan, a real estate broker from Winter Springs, Fla., who won the largest lottery prize ever awarded to one person in North America in 1988, is putting her $55.16 million to good use. On Jan. 5, 1989, Ryan announced the formation of the Ryan Foundation, a nonprofit organization that will help the homeless, the poor, the elderly, and abused women and children. "It's a dream I want to live on long after I'm gone," Ryan said.

Cave lady. As part of a scientific experiment to see how people may be affected by long periods of solitude in space, Stefania Follini, a 27-year-old Italian interior decorator, spent 130 days alone in an underground cave near Carlsbad, N. Mex. When she

Walt Disney Chairman Michael Eisner and Muppet creator Jim Henson (with beard) celebrate Disney's purchase of the Muppet characters in August.

Gretchen Polhemus waves to the crowd on February 28 after becoming the fifth Miss Texas in a row to be crowned Miss USA.

guests. The talk of the evening was, of course, the accomplishments of the guest of honor. Never one to limit herself, Barbie has been a ballerina, a nurse, an astronaut, an Olympic athlete, a doctor, an aerobics coach, a rock star, and an executive. To that list one could also add clothes addict. Over the past 30 years, Mattel has sold about 250 million Barbie outfits and 1.2 million pairs of shoes.

Earhart mystery solved? In February, Roy Nesbit, a British aviation historian, reported that there is really no mystery behind the 1937 disappearance of American aviator Amelia Earhart—she probably just ran out of gas. The world last heard of Earhart as she was flying over the Pacific Ocean during an attempt to be the first person to fly around the world by following the equator. No trace of her or her navigator, Fred Noonan, was ever found.

Many people have speculated on what could have happened. Earhart disappeared on the leg of the journey that was to take her from New Guinea to Howland Island. One theory is that she and Noonan landed on one of the Marshall Islands, then under Japanese control, and were put in prison, where they died. But after examining documents at the Public Records Office in London, Nesbit says that it is more likely that Earhart's plane, carrying just enough fuel for the trip, ran out of gas because of bad weather and because poor navigational equipment took her off course. He believes she and Noonan died when their plane crashed into the sea.

Bookish crime. On January 4, Gustav Hasford was sentenced in Los Angeles Court to six months in jail for possessing 748 books stolen from libraries in the United States and Great Britain. Hasford, a novelist and screenwriter who adapted his own Vietnam War novel into the 1987 movie *Full Metal Jacket*, was also fined $1,100 and ordered to return the books.

Don't cry over spilt wine. "I did something terrible . . . I committed murder." So said New York City wine merchant William Sokolin on the night of April 24 after he accidentally broke a bottle of red wine valued at more than $500,000. The victim was a 1787 Chateau Margaux reportedly owned by Thomas Jefferson. The "murder" occurred at the Four Seasons restaurant in New York City during a gathering of wine experts. According to reports, the wine lovers watched in horror as the beverage flowed down Sokolin's pants. Luckily for Sokolin, the bottle was insured.

Spelling whiz. On June 1, 14-year-old Scott Isaacs of Littleton, Colo., correctly spelled the word *spoliator* (a spoiler) to win the 62nd Scripps-Howard National Spelling Bee in Washington, D.C. This was Isaacs' third try for the national title. He said he prepared by studying 104 words a day for six months.

Gymnast defects. Nadia Comaneci, the gymnast who made history in 1976 by earning the first perfect scores in Olympic gymnastics, defected from Romania on November 29. When she landed in New York City days later, she told reporters that though she knows

emerged from the cave on May 23, she had set the women's record for living underground.

To pass the time, Follini played her guitar, read, exercised, decorated the plastic hut in which she lived, and became friends with the mice, frogs, and grasshoppers in the cave. Researchers believe that while the isolation improved her concentration, the lack of human contact and sunlight lowered the level of calcium in her bones and slowed down the activity of her body's disease-fighting immune system.

White House birth. President George Bush couldn't believe that he and his wife, Barbara, would ". . . go through something like this again after the 6 kids and 11 grandchildren," but on March 17 they did. Millie, the Bushes' English springer spaniel, gave birth to six puppies, making the President and his wife feel like grandparents again.

Glasnost beauty. She is a student and an aerobics fan who plans a career in advertising and who values freedom. And on May 21, 17-year-old Yulia Sukhanova won the first Miss U.S.S.R. beauty pageant. Sukhanova was selected by judges at the Moscow pageant and by home viewers watching a live telecast of the event who phoned in their vote.

What a doll. Although she doesn't look a day over 20, Barbie, Mattel Incorporated's best-selling doll, turned 30 on February 13. With her characteristic good taste, Barbie marked the occasion—her "pink jubilee"—with a formal gala in New York City for 700

living in the United States will be different, she "wanted to have a free life."

TV tiff. Bryant Gumbel, cohost of NBC's "Today" show, probably was not too popular with his co-workers in February. That month, a confidential 1988 memo he wrote to NBC executives about the show's drop in ratings was leaked to the press. In the memo, Gumbel made some not-too-kind remarks about Willard Scott, the show's folksy weatherman, who gives birthday greetings to people turning 100. Gumbel wrote that Scott was "killing the show" with his "whims, wishes, birthdays, and bad taste."

On March 6, Gumbel tried to put things right by telling viewers that the "Today" family is "intact and still smiling." On a later show, Scott showed that he was not outwardly holding a grudge when he gave Gumbel a kiss on the cheek.

No welcome for UFO's. Southern hospitality turned unfriendly on May 16 when the city council of Nashville, Tenn., voted not to build a landing pad in the city to welcome unidentified flying objects (UFO's). Councilman George Darden, who made the proposal, said that he came up with the idea after many people told him that they have seen UFO's. The council did try to compromise on the proposal. One member suggested that a landing pad be allowed only in Darden's district. But another objected because the area has "too much traffic already."

Who needs a landing pad? For the town of Voronezh in the Soviet Union, a landing pad does not seem to be necessary to attract UFO's. In October, the Soviet news agency Tass reported that a banana-shaped UFO landed in a park in Voronezh carrying a tall alien with three eyes. Scientists and reporters in the United States and other countries pooh-poohed the sighting, but Tass insisted that Soviet scientists had confirmed it. To most observers, however, the report only suggested that Tass, once devoted to somber political news, had decided to try a little sensationalism.

Climbing feat. On July 26, Mark Wellman became the first paraplegic to climb 3,600 feet (1,100 meters) to the summit of El Capitan in Yosemite National Park in California. (A paraplegic is a person whose legs and lower body are paralyzed.) He did it by using his arms to pull himself up the peak's sheer granite wall 6 inches (15 centimeters) at a time. Battling strong winds and high temperatures, Wellman and fellow climber Mike Corbett completed their ascent in nine days. Wellman was paralyzed in a 1982 fall from another Yosemite peak.

Playboy weds playmate. Hugh M. Hefner, 63-year-old founder of Playboy Enterprises in Chicago, married Kimberley Conrad, a 26-year-old Canadian model, on July 1 at his mansion in Los Angeles.

Disney doings. Things were hopping at the Magic Kingdom in 1989. On May 1, the Walt Disney Company unveiled its Disney-MGM Studios Theme Park at Walt Disney World near Orlando, Fla. In its salute to the movie industry, the park offers visitors a ride

Big Bird, Maria, and Luis welcome a new "Sesame Street" character, baby Gabriela, whose birth was depicted on May 11.

through re-created scenes from classic movies and the chance to tour a working movie and television studio. Disney made news again on August 28, when the company announced that Kermit the Frog and the entire Muppet gang had become part of the Disney family. Muppets creator Jim Henson sold his characters to Disney for an undisclosed sum.

Free at last. Prosecutors in Dallas and Chicago in 1989 dropped criminal charges against two men who collectively had spent almost 20 years in prison. On March 23, the Dallas district attorney's office said it was dropping murder charges against Randall Dale Adams. In 1977, Adams was convicted of killing a Dallas police officer and sentenced to death. He spent nearly 13 years in prison before a 1988 documentary film called *The Thin Blue Line* drew national attention to his case by raising questions about the methods used by the police and prosecutors in the trial. When Adams flew home to Columbus, Ohio, he was greeted by 100 supporters, including the documentary's maker, Errol Morris.

The highly publicized case of Gary E. Dotson reached a similar ending on August 14. Chicago prosecutors dropped charges against Dotson 10 years after he was convicted of kidnapping and raping Cathleen Crowell Webb. In 1985, Webb announced that she had lied in 1977 when she had accused Dotson of raping her, and Illinois Governor James R. Thompson commuted Dotson's sentence from 25 years to the 6 years

Newsmakers of 1989

Hugh Hefner, founder of Playboy Enterprises, exchanges wedding vows with Kimberley Conrad at his Playboy mansion in Los Angeles on July 1.

he had already served. Dotson's lawyers had requested a retrial in 1988 after genetic tests indicated Dotson's innocence.

Too many winners spoil the contest. Just ask Kraft USA in Glenview, Ill. In June, the food company ran newspaper ads for a contest called "Ready to Roll." To win the first prize, a Dodge Caravan, a person had to match the game piece in the ad with the game piece in specially marked packages of Kraft Singles cheese slices. The chances of winning the van? One in more than 15 million, according to Kraft.

Imagine Kraft's surprise when hundreds of people called to say that they had won the first prize. And they had, thanks to Kraft's printer, who accidentally ran off more than 2 million winning pieces and only a few losing pieces. Kraft declared the contest void, but the would-be winners would have none of that. After nearly 1,000 of them filed two lawsuits against Kraft, the company announced on June 15 that it would award cash amounts to those who matched pieces for the van and other prizes.

It's a girl. The 20th anniversary season of "Sesame Street" ended on May 11 with the birth of Gabriela to characters Maria and Luis, played by actors Sonia Manzano and Emilio Delgado. Maria's pregnancy during the season enabled the program to show preschoolers how a baby develops.

Oh Dahling. Life was not easy for entertainer Zsa Zsa Gabor in 1989. First, she and her two dogs were kicked off a Delta Air Lines flight in January. Then, in June, she was arrested in Beverly Hills, Calif. She was charged with slapping a policeman, driving an unregistered car—it was a Rolls-Royce—with an invalid driver's license, and having an open liquor bottle in the vehicle.

Things got worse on September 29, when a California jury convicted her of battery for slapping the officer. "I think Russia can't be worse than this," said Gabor. On October 24, she was sentenced to 72 hours in jail and ordered to pay more than $12,000 in fines and penalties and to perform 120 hours of community service. She appealed the conviction.

An officer and a lady. In August, the United States Military Academy at West Point, N.Y., selected Kristin M. Baker as brigade commander and first captain of the Corps of Cadets. Baker, a 20-year-old philosophy major and the daughter of an Army colonel, was the first woman chosen for the post in West Point history. Her post called for her to oversee all aspects of life for the academy's more than 4,000 cadets—90 per cent of whom are men.

Good-by, Secretariat. Suffering from an incurable hoof disease, Secretariat, one of the greatest horses in racing history, was given a lethal injection on October 4 at Claiborne Farm in Paris, Ky. The stallion in 1973 became the first horse since 1948 to win the Triple Crown—the Kentucky Derby, the Preakness, and the Belmont Stakes.   Mary A. Krier

Newspaper competition in the United States suffered in 1989 as the number of cities with two papers continued to shrink. In two cities, the competing newspapers asked the permission of the federal government to form joint operating agreements (JOA's) under the Newspaper Preservation Act, which is designed to help keep unprofitable newspapers in business. In a JOA, newspapers combine business operations such as delivery and advertising sales and split their profits or losses. The newspapers maintain separate newsrooms, however, and compete on stories.

The *Las Vegas Sun* on August 8 asked the United States Department of Justice to let it join with the *Las Vegas Review-Journal*. In York, Pa., the smallest U.S. city supporting two independent daily newspapers, the *York Daily Record* said in February that it needed a JOA with the 48,000-circulation *York Dispatch*.

High court allows JOA. The United States Supreme Court on November 13 let stand an unusual JOA between the *Detroit Free Press* and *The Detroit News*. The agreement allows the two papers to remain separate five days a week but to publish a joint paper on Saturday and Sunday.

Losses and gains. Kansas City, Mo., learned on October 5 that it would soon be dropped from the ranks of two-newspaper cities. ABC/Capital Cities Communications, Incorporated, announced that it would merge *The Kansas City Star*, an afternoon paper, with *The Kansas City Times*, published in the morning.

The *Los Angeles Herald Examiner* ceased publishing on November 2 after 118 years in business. On November 3, the afternoon *Raleigh* (N.C.) *Times* was shut down by its owners, who continued to publish the morning *Raleigh News & Observer*.

Competition got a boost on September 25, however, when the first edition of the tabloid *St. Louis* (Mo.) *Sun* hit the streets. The *Sun* gave the *St. Louis Post-Dispatch* its first daily competition since the *St. Louis Globe-Democrat* folded in 1986.

Libel judgment upheld. The U.S. Supreme Court in July 1989 let stand the largest libel award ever upheld against a newspaper. The $2.8-million libel judgment against the *Pittsburgh* (Pa.) *Post-Gazette* was for a story published in 1979 suggesting that a state judge conspired to alter a will while practicing as a private attorney.

Picture delivered in 40 seconds. The Associated Press (AP) on Jan. 20, 1989, demonstrated a dramatic advance in newspaper photography. The AP snapped a picture of President George Bush taking the oath of office, then began delivering the photo to more than 1,000 newspapers in 40 seconds. The AP used a new electronic photography technique called *still video*. In this technique, a filmless camera captures images on a magnetic disk, which is then used to transmit the pictures over telephone lines.   Mark Fitzgerald

See also **Awards and prizes** (Journalism awards). In *World Book,* see **Newspaper.**

The first issue of the *St. Louis Sun* appears on September 25 to challenge what had been St. Louis' only major daily, the *Post-Dispatch.*

Nicaragua. Nicaraguan President Daniel Ortega shocked world opinion on Oct. 27, 1989, by threatening to end a 19-month cease-fire with United States-backed *contra* rebels. The threat was made in San José, Costa Rica, as 16 hemisphere chiefs of state, including U.S. President George Bush, were gathering to begin a two-day summit.

On November 1, Ortega followed through on his threat, sending troops into a large-scale military operation against contras operating in the remote mountains of northern Nicaragua. Ortega said his actions were in response to increased attacks by the contras, including an October 21 ambush in which 19 army reservists were killed. Ortega said the contras' attacks were designed to disrupt presidential elections scheduled for Feb. 25, 1990.

Election campaign. Officials of the United Nations and the Organization of American States were in Nicaragua at the government's invitation to oversee the conduct of the election campaign. The leading opposition candidate was Violeta Barrios de Chamorro, widow of well-known newspaper publisher Pedro Joaquín Chamorro Cardenal, who was assassinated in 1978 during the dictatorship of Anastasio Somoza Debayle. The publisher's murder touched off widespread domestic and international support for the Sandinista revolution.

Chamorro, 59, succeeded her husband as publisher of *La Prensa,* Nicaragua's largest independent daily newspaper, which had been shut down by the Sandinista government from June 1986 to October 1987. She was selected on Sept. 2, 1989, as the candidate of the National Opposition Union, a coalition of five opposition parties formed in 1988. Chamorro had been a member of the ruling Sandinista junta after the revolution of 1979, but she became disillusioned and resigned a year later. Selected as her running mate was Virgilio Godoy Reyes, 55, of the center-left Independent Liberal Party, who had served as the Sandinista regime's labor minister from 1979 to 1984.

To no one's surprise, President Ortega announced on Sept. 24, 1989, that he would be the candidate of the Sandinista National Liberation Front, with Vice President Sergio Ramírez Mercado as his running mate.

Economic woes. Going into the campaign, there seemed little to celebrate when Nicaraguans marked the 10th anniversary of the Sandinista triumph in July. An authoritative report, financed by the Swedish government, showed that since 1980, Nicaragua's per capita output had fallen by 25 per cent and the Nicaraguans' standard of living by 60 per cent. The economy had declined every year since 1983, so that 1988 production figures were below those for 1979—the final year of the Somoza dictatorship.

Among the reasons for the economic woes were a trade embargo imposed by the United States in 1985, heavy outlays for national defense to counter the U.S.-supported contra insurgency, and U.S. resistance to new loans for Nicaragua from international financial agencies. With economic troubles of its own, the Soviet Union let Nicaragua know in 1989 that it could not continue making up the country's nearly $600-million-a-year deficit through loans that accounted for one-third of Nicaragua's total income.

Money sent to friends and relatives back home by an estimated 100,000 Nicaraguan refugees in the United States helped prop up the economy. To evade the trade embargo, Nicaraguans in the United States increasingly shopped for relatives and friends in their homeland by ordering from catalogs that ship their products to Nicaragua via Panama, Mexico, or Guatemala. To bring in needed foreign exchange, the Sandinista regime permitted the creation of special "diplomatic stores" where people can spend U.S. dollars sent from relatives abroad to purchase scarce goods such as mirrors and toilet paper.

Contra aid. In March, the United States Congress and the Bush Administration reached agreement on providing the contras with about $4.5 million a month in nonmilitary aid until the elections in 1990. Even with Ortega's termination of the cease-fire, there were no indications, either in the White House or Congress, of an effort to renew military assistance to the contras.　　Nathan A. Haverstock

See also **Latin America** (Facts in brief table). In *World Book,* see **Nicaragua.**

Niger. See **Africa.**

Nigeria. Riots erupted in Nigeria in 1989 as growing dissatisfaction with President Ibrahim Babangida's economic austerity program, begun in 1986, reached the boiling point. The first signs of unrest came early in the year, when many Nigerians complained about food prices, rising unemployment, and other hardships. In May, a student-led protest in Lagos, the capital city, escalated into rioting, burning, and looting. The violence quickly spread to other major cities. More than 50 people died in clashes with the police. The military regime imposed a dusk-to-dawn curfew, banned public meetings, and ordered six state universities closed for one year.

In June, the government modified its economic program by relaxing its ban on imported cars and trucks, raising civil-service salaries, and creating 62,000 new government jobs.

Despite the unpopularity of the austerity program, it has had its favorable side. The stern measures have curbed inflation, stimulated economic growth, and reduced the trade deficit.

Return to civilian rule. On April 5, the Constituent Assembly presented Babangida with its draft of a new national constitution for the reestablishment of civilian government, scheduled for 1992. The Assembly proposed a continuation of a strong central government with a powerful presidency. The proposed constitution left two important issues to be decided by the military rulers: whether the courts would continue to be based on Islamic law and what role the military would play in civilian politics.

In anticipation of state and local elections in 1990 and presidential elections in 1992, the military in May 1989 lifted a five-year ban on political activity. By mid-July, the number of national parties had been reduced from more than 30 to 13, and a National Electoral Commission had been charged with consolidating those 13 into 2 broad-based parties.

Social policy. In an attempt to lower Nigeria's population-growth rate—at more than 3 per cent a year, one of the world's highest—the Babangida government in May launched a voluntary educational program to limit family size. The government also announced that same month that by 1992 Nigerians from the age of 6 onward will be guaranteed nine years of free education. School attendance will be compulsory.

Foreign relations. In January 1989, President Babangida paid a state visit to Ghana in an effort to end hostility that has existed for several years between the two countries. The meeting resulted in a pledge to expand trade between Nigeria and Ghana and to engage in joint development projects.

In September, Joseph Nanven Garba, a former major general in the Nigerian armed forces, was elected president of the United Nations General Assembly for the next session.　　J. Gus Liebenow and Beverly B. Liebenow

See also **Africa** (Facts in brief table). In *World Book,* see **Nigeria.**

Nobel Prizes in peace, literature, economics, and the sciences were awarded in 1989 by the Norwegian Storting (parliament) in Oslo and by the Royal Academy of Science, the Caroline Institute, and the Swedish Academy of Literature in Stockholm, Sweden.

The peace prize was awarded to the Dalai Lama, the spiritual and political leader of Tibetan Buddhists, who has been exiled in India since 1959. The award recognized the Dalai Lama's nonviolent campaign to end Chinese domination of Tibet and his efforts to "preserve the historical and cultural heritage of his people."

The Dalai Lama was born Tenzin Gyatso in Tibet and was chosen as the 14th Dalai Lama at the age of 5. In 1989, the Dalai Lama proposed a compromise solution for Tibet, under which China could determine Tibet's foreign policy and keep troops on its soil, though Tibet would become a "self-governing, democratic political entity" in association with China.

The literature prize was given to Camilo José Cela, 73, of Spain, a novelist and short-story writer. Cela's 1942 novel, *The Family of Pascual Duarte*, is considered the most widely read novel in Spanish literature after Miguel de Cervantes' *Don Quixote*. Cela has written 10 novels and is regarded as an experimental and provocative writer.

The Spanish Civil War (1936-1939) plays an important role in much of Cela's work. As a young man, Cela fought on the side of fascist forces led by General Francisco Franco. Cela's recognized masterpiece is *The Hive*, published in 1951, which describes three days in the life of Madrid following the end of the civil war.

The economics prize was awarded to Trygve Haavelmo, 77, of Norway, a professor emeritus at the University of Oslo, who pioneered in the use of statistics and probability theory to forecast economic developments. Haavelmo's work laid the foundations for the science of econometrics, which uses mathematical models to study the behavior of an economy.

Much of Haavelmo's pathbreaking work was done while he was living in the United States, first as a researcher at the University of Chicago and later with the Norwegian Trade Ministry in New York City. In 1947, Haavelmo returned to Norway, where he became an economics professor.

The physics prize was divided between Norman F. Ramsey, Jr., 74, of Harvard University in Cambridge, Mass., who won half of the $470,000 prize, and Hans G. Dehmelt, 67, of the University of Washington in Seattle and Wolfgang Paul, 76, of the University of Bonn in West Germany, who shared the other half. The three physicists were recognized as brilliant experimentalists who devised techniques for making precise measurements at the tiny scales of the atom.

Ramsey was recognized for inventing a method of measuring the minute movements, or oscillations, of atomic nuclei, which spin like tops inside a magnetic field. This technique led to the development of the atomic clock, the world's most accurate timepiece, in which cesium nuclei oscillate at a rate of 9,192,631.770 times per second. Atomic clocks have had important uses in navigation and communication systems and in astronomy and geology.

Dehmelt, a naturalized United States citizen who was born in Germany, and Paul, also German-born, developed methods for isolating *ions* (electrically charged atoms) and electrons so they could be studied in greater detail. The physicists' methods also involved illuminating ions in laser beams.

The chemistry prize was shared by Thomas R. Cech, 41, of the University of Colorado in Boulder and Canadian-born Sidney Altman, 50, of Yale University in New Haven, Conn. The two molecular biologists independently discovered that *RNA (ribonucleic acid)*, a type of nucleic acid involved in heredity, can also act as an enzyme, aiding a chemical reaction without being changed or consumed. Previously, scientists thought that all enzymes were proteins.

Cech also found that RNA can duplicate itself, indicating that it may have existed before another unit of heredity known as *DNA (deoxyribonucleic acid)* and therefore could have been the key molecule in the origin of life billions of years ago.

The physiology or medicine prize was shared by cancer researchers J. Michael Bishop, 53, and Harold E. Varmus, 49, of the University of California at San Francisco for work that opened up a new era in cancer research. The two virologists discovered that normal genes that control cell growth can go awry and cause cancer.

Previously, scientists had speculated that cancer-causing viruses inserted their own genes into normal cells, turning them cancerous. But in studying a virus called the *Rous sarcoma virus*, which causes cancer in chickens, the two scientists discovered that the virus's cancer-causing gene is actually an evolutionary hitchhiker. It is a gene found in the cells of many animals—and in human cells as well—that got picked up by that kind of virus millions of years ago and passed on to all of its "descendants." Within our cells, these *oncogenes* can cause cancer, without the presence of the virus, if disrupted by mutations or inappropriately activated by *carcinogens* (cancer-causing substances, such as certain chemicals). A number of other oncogenes have been found.

1988 winners of Nobel Prizes were the United Nations peacekeeping forces for peace; Egyptian novelist Naguib Mahfouz for literature; Maurice Allais of France for economics; U.S. physicists Leon M. Lederman, Melvin Schwartz, and Jack Steinberger for physics; West German scientists Johann Deisenhofer, Robert Huber, and Hartmut Michel for chemistry; and U.S. biochemists Gertrude B. Elion and George H. Hitchings and British pharmacologist Sir James Black for physiology or medicine.   Rod Such

In *World Book,* see **Nobel Prizes.**

North Carolina. See State government.

North Dakota. See State government.

Northern Ireland. The outlawed Irish Republican Army (IRA) extended its campaign of violence outside Northern Ireland in 1989. On July 2, an IRA car bomb killed a British Army corporal in Hannover, West Germany. Following the attack, the British Army ordered that the distinctive army license plates on cars driven by British troops be replaced by civilian plates.

But British soldiers and their families continued to be easy targets in West Germany because their cars had steering wheels on the right side. Other European cars have steering wheels on the left side. On September 1, two British soldiers were shot and injured in Münster. On September 7, the West German wife of a British soldier was shot and killed near Dortmund.

The IRA launched attacks in England as well. On September 22, 10 Marine bandsmen were killed by an IRA bomb that exploded inside the Royal Marines School of Music in Deal in southern England.

Security leaks. Accusations that British security forces were cooperating with Protestant terrorist groups in Northern Ireland made headlines in 1989. On August 29, the British Broadcasting Corporation (BBC) reported that the Ulster Freedom Fighters, one such terrorist group, used confidential British security files to locate and kill a Roman Catholic man in Northern Ireland on August 25. The man, Loughlin Maginn, was identified in the files as an IRA member.

Following the BBC report, a number of other secret documents surfaced. The British government responded on September 15 by launching an investigation. Hugh Annesley, chief constable of the Royal Ulster Constabulary, followed suit on October 2 by ordering an investigation to discover if members of his own force had conspired to murder IRA suspects.

Security was at the top of the agenda when Peter Brooke, secretary of state for Northern Ireland, and Gerard Collins, the foreign minister of Ireland, met on October 5. No progress was made on the Irish demand that the mainly Protestant Ulster Defense Regiment, which carries out most army duties in Northern Ireland, be restricted to non-Catholic areas.

Convictions overturned. Four people who had been serving life prison sentences for bombing a pub in Guildford, England, in 1974 were released on Oct. 19, 1989. A British appeals court in London threw out the convictions after Allan Gree, Britain's director of prosecutions, announced on October 7 that new evidence showed that British police had withheld and tampered with evidence. One of the four was immediately arrested on an unrelated murder charge.

Since their conviction in 1975, the four had maintained their innocence. But even though IRA members later confessed to the bombing, a British court in 1977 upheld the convictions. Following their release, the British government launched a judicial inquiry into police conduct.   Ian J. Mather

See also **Ireland.** In *World Book,* see **Northern Ireland.**

A truck burns after an outbreak of violence in Belfast on August 14, the 20th anniversary of the arrival of British troops in Northern Ireland.

Northwest Territories. The territorial government of the Northwest Territories gained three new departments in 1989: safety and public services (to enforce safety regulations at work sites); transportation; and energy, mines, and petroleum resources (to manage the energy accord signed in September 1988 with Canadian Prime Minister Brian Mulroney). The departments are managed by ministers chosen from the 24-member nonpartisan territorial assembly. These cabinet members operate under the supervision of a federally appointed administrator.

Dry weather and above-normal temperatures in August—usually a rainy month—brought one of the worst seasons for forest fires ever recorded in the Northwest Territories. In the last week of August, a massive fire burned out of control over more than 133,000 acres (54,000 hectares) of spruce-covered hills in the northern part of the Mackenzie River Valley. By the end of August, 579 fires were recorded—about twice the summer-season average of 286.

In December, federal negotiators and Inuit (Eskimo) leaders reached an agreement-in-principle on a massive land claim. If ratified by all parties, the deal would give the Inuit surface rights to about 225,000 square kilometers (87,000 square miles) in the Northwest Territories and $580 million Canadian (about $490 million U.S.) over 14 years.   David M. L. Farr

See also **Canada.** In *World Book,* see **Northwest Territories.**

Norway struggled in 1989 to recover from a 1986 collapse in the price of oil that plunged the nation into a deep recession. Voters rebelled on Sept. 10 and 11, 1989, against three years of *austerity* (a cutback in the standard of living to fuel the economy) imposed by the minority Labor government of Prime Minister Gro Harlem Brundtland. As a result, Norway's two mainstream parties—Labor and the Conservatives—lost ground to more radical groups on both the left and right, and Brundtland's government was replaced by a fragile alliance of conservative parties.

In the election, Labor won 34.3 per cent of the votes to lead all parties, but this was the lowest percentage for Labor in any election since 1930. Labor lost 7 seats, finishing with 63 of the 165 seats in the Storting (parliament). The more radical Left Socialists, who had often helped Brundtland pass legislation during her three years at the helm, climbed from 6 to 17 seats. Non-Socialist parties emerged with 84 seats. The Conservatives dropped from 50 seats to 37, but, in the most surprising result, the Progress Party soared from 2 seats to 22.

Led by the brash, charismatic Carl I. Hagen, 45, the Progress Party attacked Norway's welfare-state practices. He called for less government bureaucracy, lower taxes, and a larger role for private business in providing services. Hagen also echoed resentment among some Norwegians toward immigrants from the Middle East and Central America.

A new government took office on October 16, led by Prime Minister Jan P. Syse, a Conservative, and with the participation of two small center-right parties. The coalition controlled only 62 seats.

Syse faced major economic problems. Commercial banks continued to report large losses, a result of making heavy loans when oil prices were high. In addition, the unemployment rate had climbed to 4.8 per cent, roughly double the average since World War II (1939-1945).

Military affairs. Norway continued to increase its military cooperation with the North Atlantic Treaty Organization (NATO) in 1989. For decades, Norway had played down its security ties with the West in keeping with a Scandinavian tradition of neutrality, and had attempted to avoid antagonizing its neighbor the Soviet Union. Norway prepared to sign an accord allowing United States aircraft carrier task forces to use Norwegian port facilities. And construction proceeded on improving the nation's military airfields so that they could handle large U.S. reinforcements in a crisis.

Two Soviet nuclear-powered submarines suffered accidents in the Norwegian Sea in 1989. One submarine caught fire and sank on April 7, and on June 26 another had to shut down its reactors but managed to limp back to a Soviet port.   Joseph Fitchett

See also **Europe** (Facts in brief table). In *World Book,* see **Norway.**

Nova Scotia. A seesaw contest for a legislative seat on Cape Breton Island reflected the narrowly divided state of Nova Scotia party politics in 1989. A by-election (a special election to fill a vacancy) on Aug. 22, 1989, resulted in a victory for the Progressive Conservative (PC) candidate by seven votes. A month later, a judicial recount turned the seat over to the Liberals by three votes. The PC's demanded another recount, which was expected to be completed in early 1990. At year-end, the Conservatives held 28 seats in the 52-seat legislature, the Liberals held 21, the New Democratic Party held 2, and an independent member held the remaining seat.

Premier John Buchanan, whose government had suffered from frequent political scandals, announced in February the creation of a public ethics council to lay down standards of behavior for members of the legislature. A legislative committee was to review the fitness of all senior public service appointments.

The budget, presented on May 5, ended the retail sales tax exemption for the 14,000 Indians of Nova Scotia on goods purchased outside reserves. Goods would be tax-exempt only if they were delivered to the reserve. Earlier, complaints had surfaced about Indians buying cigarettes tax-free and selling them to non-Indians at a profit.   David M. L. Farr

See also **Canada.** In *World Book,* see **Nova Scotia.**
Nuclear energy. See Energy supply.
Nutrition. See Food.

Ocean

Ocean. Scientists with the Ocean Drilling Program reported in July 1989 that they were able to record the geologic history of the Izu and Bonin islands near Japan. On board the research vessel *JOIDES Resolution*, the oceanographers took sample cores from the sea floor near this arc-shaped island chain.

The cores revealed a fascinating history that began when part of the Pacific Ocean floor broke apart millions of years ago and was pushed under what is now the floor of the Philippine Sea. According to the widely accepted theory of plate tectonics, the earth's crust is made of huge plates that slowly move about on a layer of partially molten rock called the mantle. When two ocean plates converge, as they did in this region, one is forced beneath the other. Partial melting of the lower plate leads to volcanic eruptions, which can eventually form islands such as these.

During the last 31 million years, the island chain stretched and pulled apart in several places. Lava from volcanic eruptions at these locations is of a type never seen before and has the frothy appearance of chocolate mousse. Piles of volcanic ash hundreds of yards thick were deposited on top of the volcanic rubble. They provide evidence that volcanic eruptions occurred in two stages. The first began 31 million years ago and ended 27 million years ago; the second stage began 13 million years ago and continues today.

Sunken treasure. In September, treasure hunters from Columbus, Ohio, began retrieving gold from what may be the most valuable shipwreck in United States history. The group used a remote-controlled submersible to haul up gold coins and bars—many in mint condition—from a shipwreck in international waters off the coast of South Carolina.

The ship, the *Central America*, sank in a hurricane on Sept. 12, 1857, during the California gold rush. A paddle-wheel steamer, the *Central America* belonged to a class of ships known as "Panama packets" because they ferried passengers between the United States and Panama. Before the Panama Canal was built, many people who wanted to travel between California and New York took a ship to Panama, crossed Panama by rail, then took another ship to their destination in the United States. The *Central America*'s last sail was from Panama to New York; the ship was loaded with passengers and gold from California. Thomas Thompson, a project director for the salvage operation, said that the ship's cargo could be worth as much as $1 billion.

Oil spill disaster. The largest oil tanker spill ever in U.S. waters turned Alaska's Prince William Sound into a disaster area. On March 24, the fully loaded oil tanker *Exxon Valdez* struck a reef shortly after leaving the Alaska pipeline terminal in Valdez, spilling about 11 million gallons (42 million liters) of oil. Despite a $1.28-billion cleanup effort mounted by the Exxon Corporation, hundreds of miles of coastline remained fouled. See **Environmental pollution (Close-Up).**

Gold from an 1857 shipwreck rests on the ocean floor 200 miles (320 kilometers) off South Carolina. Treasure hunters began retrieving it in 1989.

Soviet seagoing mishaps. A Soviet nuclear submarine caught fire and sank on April 7, killing 42 of the 69 crew members on board. The disaster occurred in international waters in the Norwegian Sea between Bear Island and the coast of Norway. The submarine, launched in 1984, was powered by two nuclear reactors. The Soviet Union reported that sailors shut down the reactors before the ship sank, indicating that the radioactive fuel elements are now entombed in a solid mass of metal. If so, radiation from the reactors will be released at a slow and relatively safe rate. Tests of the air near the scene of the disaster indicated that radiation was not leaking from the vessel.

On June 20, the Soviet cruise liner *Maxim Gorky* struck an iceberg in the Greenland Sea. More than 900 passengers and crew were aboard. A quick and masterful rescue operation helped avert catastrophe, however, and all the people aboard were safely evacuated.

Another Soviet nuclear submarine suffered a disabling accident in Norwegian waters on June 26. This sub was seen billowing smoke as it slowly made its way toward home port in the Arctic. According to a Soviet official, no lives were lost and the submarine's reactors were shut down.   Arthur G. Alexiou

In the World Book Supplement section, see **Ocean.**

Ohio. See State government.

Oklahoma. See State government.

Old age. See Social security.

Olympic Games. The International Olympic Committee (IOC), which expelled South Africa in 1970 because of that nation's restrictive racial policies, further isolated South Africa in 1989. The IOC voted that any athlete who competed there after August 31, the day the resolution was passed, would be barred from future Olympics.

The IOC sold United States television rights to the 1994 Winter Olympics in Lillehammer, Norway, to CBS Inc. for $300 million. Earlier, CBS paid $243 million for similar rights to the 1992 Winter Olympics in Albertville, France. Later, CBS sold 50 hours of its 1992 and 1994 Winter Olympic programming to the Turner Network Television cable system for $50 million.

In Olympic-type competition, the United States and the Soviet Union won major events in the World University Games in August in Duisburg, West Germany. When São Paulo, Brazil, withdrew as host city because of financial problems, Duisburg became the host, though the planned 10-sport program was trimmed to 4 sports.

The Winter World University Games in March in Sofia, Bulgaria, were dominated by the Soviet Union. The Maccabiah Games in July in Tel Aviv, Israel, were dominated by Israel and the United States. Indonesia led the Southeast Asian Games in August in Kuala Lumpur, Malaysia.   Frank Litsky

In *World Book,* see **Olympic Games.**

Oman. See Middle East.

Ontario. Public opinion polls showed that most voters continued to support Premier David Peterson's Liberal government despite embarrassments it faced in 1989. Most troubling were allegations of financial ties between government officials, party fund-raisers, certain charitable agencies, and a large development corporation. The affair prompted a judicial inquiry beginning in September 1989.

The trouble began in June when Patricia Starr, the head of a charitable foundation set up by the Toronto branch of the National Council of Jewish Women, was accused of making illegal political contributions. Peterson shuffled his cabinet on August 2, dropping eight ministers and naming six new ones. Among those dropped were three who had received donations from Starr's fund, one who had been accused of permitting too close a tie between the housing ministry and Starr, and one who had questionable business dealings with Starr's agency. Earlier, one of Peterson's top aides resigned because of the scandal.

Legislation. On February 7, the legislature passed two bills concerning Sunday shopping. One bill allowed municipalities to determine what types of stores may operate on Sundays; the other protected retail employees from being forced to work on Sundays. The bills had been bitterly fought by the opposition parties and church and labor groups.

A new workers' compensation bill, passed on July 24, established a two-point system of payment: a lump sum for pain and suffering and a continuing allowance for lost earning power until retirement age. This replaced a system under which disabled workers received a pension according to their physical impairment, with the possibility of wage-loss supplements in some cases. The New Democratic Party mounted a 17-hour filibuster over the bill.

To combat skyrocketing automobile insurance costs, the government proposed a no-fault automobile insurance plan on September 15. Under the plan, only people seriously injured in auto accidents—or the estates of those killed—would be allowed to sue for pain, suffering, and economic loss. In return for giving up the right to sue, drivers would be entitled to claim a weekly allowance for lost income and a lump sum for medical care and rehabilitation. With these changes, the government expected that auto insurance premiums would rise no more than 8 per cent in urban areas in 1990—and not at all in rural areas.

The budget, presented by Treasurer Robert Nixon on May 17, 1989, imposed many new taxes to pay for record provincial spending and to reduce the deficit. The budget forecast expenditures of $41.3 billion Canadian (about $34.7 billion U.S.). The resulting deficit of $577 million (about $485 million U.S.) would be the lowest in 15 years.   David M. L. Farr

See also **Canada; Toronto.** In *World Book,* see **Ontario.**

Opera. See Classical music.

Oregon. See State government.

Pacific Islands. A rebellion on the island of Bougainville created serious problems for Papua New Guinea in 1989. It was the worst threat to national unity since Papua New Guinea attained independence in 1975.

The trouble began in 1988, when a group of militants called the Bougainville Revolutionary Army ordered Papua New Guinea to close a copper mine operated by Bougainville Copper Limited and to pay Bougainville residents about $12 billion for environmental damage caused by the mine. They also demanded independence from Papua New Guinea.

When their demands were ignored, the militants began a series of attacks against Bougainville Copper installations and its employees. As civil unrest grew during 1989, the island's main airport terminal was gutted by fire and riots broke out in some towns.

The violence forced the closing of the copper mine on May 15. On June 26, Papua New Guinea declared a state of emergency in Bougainville. By the end of October, more than 30 civilians and security personnel had been killed. Among them was Bougainville's Commerce Minister John Bika.

The closing of the copper mine substantially reduced Papua New Guinea's income. The country owns 19.1 per cent of the mine, which is a subsidiary of CRA Limited, an Australian firm. The mine accounts for almost 20 per cent of Papua New Guinea's government revenue and 45 per cent of its export income.

New Caledonia. The Matignon Accord, a 1988 agreement that halted the threat of civil war in New Caledonia, was severely tested in 1989. The agreement had been worked out between ethnic French residents (people of French descent), called *loyalists,* who want the territory to remain a part of France, and *Kanaks,* descendants of the original Melanesian inhabitants, who favor independence. The pact called for dividing the territory into three self-governing provinces and for a referendum in 1998 to determine the territory's political future.

On May 4, 1989, a month before the first provincial elections were to be held, Kanak leader Jean-Marie Tjibaou, who negotiated the Matignon Accord, was assassinated on Ouvea, one of the territory's Loyalty Islands. Apparently he was killed by militant Kanaks who opposed the agreement.

Tjibaou had dominated New Caledonia politics for more than 10 years. His moderate views helped unite Kanak political factions into a proindependence coalition called the Kanak Socialist National Liberation Front. While Tjibaou's death renewed fear of a return to widespread violence, many Kanaks and loyalists reaffirmed his belief in the need for good will and conciliation between the two groups.

The provincial elections went ahead as planned on June 11. The loyalists won a majority in the south province, which includes the capital city of Nouméa. The Kanak coalition, however, gained control of the

Facts in brief on Pacific Island countries

Country	Population	Government	Monetary unit*	Exports†	Foreign trade (million U.S.$) Imports†
Australia	16,365,000	Governor General Bill Hayden; Prime Minister Robert Hawke	dollar (1.28 = $1)	32,734	33,245
Fiji	772,000	President Ratu Sir Penaia Ganilau; Interim Prime Minister Ratu Sir Kamisese Mara	dollar (1.52 = $1)	343	454
Kiribati	69,000	President Ieremia Tabai	Australian dollar	1	12
Nauru	9,000	President Bernard Dowiyogo	Australian dollar	93	73
New Zealand	3,402,000	Governor General Sir Paul Reeves; Prime Minister Geoffrey Palmer	dollar (1.69 = $1)	8,806	7,305
Papua New Guinea	3,824,000	Governor General (vacant); Prime Minister Rabbie Namaliu	kina (0.86 = $1)	1,399	1,200
Solomon Islands	329,000	Governor General Sir George Lepping; Prime Minister Solomon Mamaloni	dollar (2.38 = $1)	64	79
Tonga	101,000	King Taufa'ahau Tupou IV; Prime Minister Prince Fatafehi Tu'ipelehake	pa'anga (1.28 = $1)	7	48
Tuvalu	8,000	Governor General Tupua Leupena; Prime Minister Bikenibeu Paeniu	Australian dollar	1	3
Vanuatu	164,000	President Fred Timakata; Prime Minister Walter Lini	vatu (121 = $1)	18	70
Western Samoa	170,000	Head of State Malietoa Tanumafili II; Prime Minister Tofilau Eti	tala (2.30 = $1)	15	75

*Exchange rates as of Dec. 1, 1989, or latest available data. †Latest available data.

remaining two provinces—the north and the Loyalty Islands. The 54 elected members met in a territorial congress in Nouméa on June 26. The provinces were formally established on July 14.

Fiji. The interim government established after two military coups in 1987 continued to control the island in 1989. The coups attempted to return control of the government to ethnic Fijians by ousting the elected government of Timoci Bavadra. Although Bavadra was an ethnic Fijian, the majority in his coalition and nearly half of his Cabinet were ethnic Indians. On November 3, Bavadra died. On December 16, his widow, Adi Kuini Bavadra, was appointed leader of Fiji's coalition parties in his place.

Clashes between Ratu Sir Kamisese Mara, the interim prime minister, and Major General Sitiveni Rabuka, Fiji's army commander and minister of home affairs, intensified during the year. In September, Mara issued an ultimatum to Rabuka, demanding he either step down from the Cabinet or relinquish his military command. Rabuka agreed to give up his Cabinet post. Mara, who had planned to retire, said he would continue as interim prime minister.

Nauru. President Hammer DeRoburt received a vote of no-confidence in Nauru's Parliament on August 17. (A vote of confidence is usually called when a parliament votes on a bill introduced by the government. If the parliament votes no, the prime minister and cabinet are forced to resign.) Parliament elected Kenas Aroi, chairman of the Nauru Phosphate Corporation and former finance minister, as the country's new president. Following general elections in December, Aroi was replaced by Bernard Dowiyogo, who had been president from 1976 to 1978.

In May, the republic of Nauru filed a claim against Australia in the International Court of Justice. The claim sought damages for the destruction of a large part of the island's land by phosphate mining that occurred before Nauru won independence in 1968.

Phosphates are phosphorous-containing compounds used to make fertilizers. Since phosphate mining began on Nauru in 1907, much of the island has been stripped of its topsoil. According to the claim, one-third of the island was damaged before Nauru gained control of the mining operation in July 1967.

Vanuatu. On March 7, Ati George Sokomanu, Vanuatu's former president, and three other men were sentenced to jail after they were convicted of inciting mutiny within the country's security forces. In 1988, the four unsuccessfully attempted to oust Prime Minister Walter Lini. Among the group was Barak Sope, secretary-general of Lini's Vanua'aku Party.

On April 14, however, an appeals court acquitted all four men because of insufficient evidence. In January, Vanuatu's Electoral College had removed Sokomanu from office and elected Fred Timakata as the country's new president.   Stuart Inder

In *World Book,* see **Pacific Islands.**
Painting. See Art.

Pakistan. Prime Minister Benazir Bhutto struggled during 1989 to maintain control of her politically divided nation. On January 28, Bhutto's government had its first electoral test since she became prime minister in late 1988. In this by-election to fill vacancies in the national and provincial assemblies, Bhutto's Pakistan People's Party won several seats. The opposition Islamic Democratic Alliance was victorious in the Punjab, where 54 per cent of all Pakistanis live. The Alliance, which challenged Bhutto by saying she was weak and indecisive, was dominated by supporters of former President M. Zia-ul-Haq. Zia died in a mysterious 1988 plane crash.

On Nov. 1, 1989, an opposition coalition in the National Assembly tried to oust Bhutto by a vote of no confidence but failed to win enough votes. With further challenges likely, Bhutto promised to make changes in her Cabinet and policy agenda.

Bhutto tried to assert her authority over the armed forces, which had dominated Pakistan for many of the years since the nation won its independence in 1947. In late May 1989, she dismissed the head of the powerful military intelligence service, Lieutenant General Hamid Gul. In August, Bhutto sought to replace the chairman of the joint chiefs of staff, Admiral Iftikhar Ahmad Sirohey, but President Ghulam Ishaq Khan blocked the move. Army chief General Mirza Aslam Beg in September reiterated the military's support for democracy.

Bhutto also began efforts to break the ties between politics and organized crime, especially the annual export of an estimated $7 billion worth of heroin and other narcotics. In addition to the export problem, almost 1 million Pakistanis were believed to be narcotics addicts.

Law and order deteriorated in the Sind, Bhutto's home province. Ethnic conflict smoldered among the Sindhi majority, Muslim Indian immigrants, Afghan refugees, and other ethnic groups. Political competition, the availability of modern weapons from the civil war in nearby Afghanistan, and increasing narcotics trading worsened the conflict. Armed gangs operated almost unrestrained in some parts of the Sind, and gun battles broke out in towns. Drivers were forced to form protective convoys on some highways.

Other news. Pakistan rejoined the Commonwealth, a group of countries with ties to Great Britain, at the association's meeting in Malaysia on October 18. Bhutto's late father, Prime Minister Zulfikar Ali Bhutto, had taken Pakistan out of the Commonwealth in 1972, when the association recognized Bangladesh, which had been East Pakistan before seceding in 1971.

The economy improved slowly as 1989 brought generally good weather for agriculture. Bhutto, whose father had nationalized many of Pakistan's industries, joined the international trend toward returning industries to private control.   Henry S. Bradsher

See also **Asia** (Facts in brief table). In *World Book,* see **Pakistan.**

Paleontology

Paleontology. What may be one of the biggest scandals in the history of paleontology erupted in April 1989. Paleontologist John A. Talent of Macquarie University in Sydney, Australia, accused paleontologist Viswa Jit Gupta of Panjab University in Chandigarh, India, of falsifying fossil data that serve as the foundation for much of scientists' understanding of the natural history of the Asian mountain range called the Himalaya. For example, Talent, who is a specialist in fossil *ammonoids* (chambered shells of ancient squidlike animals), charged that distinctive ammonoids that Gupta reported finding in India were actually from Morocco.

During the past 25 years, Gupta has been one of the few paleontologists working in the Himalaya. If the charges are true, scientists would have to reevaluate not only hundreds of Gupta's articles but also many reports by other researchers based on his work.

Gupta denied all accusations of fraud. By year-end, however, he had not answered his critics with a detailed defense of his work.

Tyrannosaurus find. The discovery of the most complete fossil skeleton of a *Tyrannosaurus rex* ever found was reported in October. The 65-million-year-old fossil was unearthed in Montana by a team of scientists from the Museum of the Rockies in Bozeman. The fossil is the first *Tyrannosaurus rex* skeleton found with its lower arm bones. Paleontologists hope the fossilized bones will provide clues about how the dinosaur used its short arms.

Ancient arachnids. New research reported in 1989 shed important light on the evolutionary history of two major groups of arachnids: pseudoscorpions and spiders. Arachnids constitute one of the groups of *arthropods* (invertebrate animals with segmented bodies and hollow, jointed legs). In October, biologist William A. Shear of the American Museum of Natural History in New York City and two colleagues reported finding well-preserved fossils of pseudoscorpions, a relatively little known but diverse and abundant group of tiny scorpionlike animals. These fossils came from Devonian rocks nearly 380 million years old from upstate New York. Previously, the oldest known pseudoscorpions were 35-million-year-old fossils in amber from the Baltic Sea region. The new discovery indicates that land-dwelling arthropods existed far earlier than scientists had believed.

The discovery of fossils of the oldest known web-forming spiders was reported in August by paleontologist Paul A. Sendon of the University of Manchester in England. The well-preserved fossils, found in 120-million-year-old beds of limestone from the Cretaceous Period in northeastern Spain, preserve details of *spinnerets* (silk-forming organs) and specialized features on the legs that are used in weaving webs. The fossils represent the oldest known evidence of the spinning of webs for capturing prey animals, such as insects.   Carlton E. Brett

In *World Book,* see **Paleontology.**

Panama. A powerful United States military force invaded Panama on Dec. 20, 1989, and overthrew the dictatorship of General Manuel Antonio Noriega Morena. More than 20,000 troops participated in the action, which was the largest U.S. military operation since the war in Vietnam (1957-1975). It was the 13th U.S. intervention in Panamanian affairs in the 1900's and was preceded by the swearing in of a new Panamanian president.

Justifying the invasion, dubbed "Operation Just Cause," U.S. President George Bush said, "Noriega's reckless threats and attacks upon Americans in Panama created an imminent danger to the 35,000 Americans" who live there. Bush also cited U.S. obligations to defend the Panama Canal, warlike statements by Noriega, and the December 16 killing of a U.S. marine by Panamanian soldiers.

The invasion began at midnight, and by 2 a.m., U.S. forces had destroyed the headquarters of the Panamanian Defense Forces. But U.S. troops failed to apprehend Noriega, whose capture and extradition to the United States to stand trial on drug-trafficking charges was a major U.S. objective.

Noriega eluded U.S. forces and on December 24 entered the Vatican embassy in Panama City, where he sought asylum. Noriega finally surrendered to United States authorities outside the embassy on Jan. 3, 1990. He was put aboard a C-130 military transport plane and flown to Miami, Fla., for trial.

In the first days of fighting, the U.S. Department of Defense said, 23 soldiers and 3 U.S. civilians were killed and more than 320 soldiers were wounded. Estimates of Panamanian military and civilians killed ranged from 60 to the hundreds.

International reaction to the invasion was mixed. The Soviet Union criticized the United States for "gunboat diplomacy." Most Latin-American governments denounced the action, and, by a vote of 20 to 1, the Organization of American States called for an immediate U.S. withdrawal. Great Britain's Prime Minister Margaret Thatcher unequivocally supported Bush's decision to invade, calling it "courageous."

Initial U.S. reaction to the invasion was overwhelmingly supportive, including bipartisan appeals for national unity on Capitol Hill. Representative Don Edwards (D., Calif.) was something of a lone voice in calling the invasion unconstitutional and declaring, "There was no danger to our national security from this weak, small country, nor was the Panama Canal in real peril."

Other critics charged that in invading Panama the Bush Administration was seeking to make up for its handling of an abortive coup by members of the Panamanian Defense Forces on Oct. 3, 1989. On that occasion, dissidents led by Major Moisés Giroldi Vega briefly held Noriega after a gun battle. Noriega, who rose to power as a paid informant for the U.S. Central Intelligence Agency, was brutal in meting out punishment. At his order, Major Giroldi Vega and some 70

A member of a paramilitary unit beats opposition vice presidential candidate Guillermo Ford in Panama City after elections in May.

other officers and men were executed in the aftermath of the coup attempt. Bush Administration officials later conceded that poor handling of "crisis management" procedures on the part of the United States contributed to the coup's failure.

New government. Immediately following the invasion, the U.S. government hurried to aid the new Panamanian president, Guillermo Endara. Bush lifted economic sanctions that had been imposed to weaken Panama's economy and force Noriega's resignation, and made available to Endara's new government $400 million in frozen Panamanian assets on deposit at U.S. banks. With the fighting over, the U.S. government also assisted in caring for the thousands of Panamanians made homeless by the U.S. military action.

Endara had been the apparent winner of presidential elections held on May 7. Unofficial tallies by independent election observers, including former U.S. Presidents Jimmy Carter and Gerald R. Ford, had given him a 3 to 1 edge over Noriega's hand-picked candidate. Official results of the vote were never announced, and on May 10, Noriega nullified the election, charging foreign interference. The day following the election, Endara and one of his running mates, Guillermo Ford, were beaten by paramilitary squads organized by Noriega.   Nathan A. Haverstock

See also **Latin America** (Facts in brief table). In *World Book,* see **Panama.**

Papua New Guinea. See **Pacific Islands.**

Paraguay. The 34-year reign of Paraguay's President Alfredo Stroessner—the longest dictatorship in Latin America—ended in a military coup on Feb. 3, 1989. The coup was led by General Andrés Rodríguez Pedotti, who had been Stroessner's second-in-command.

Stroessner, who seized control in a 1954 coup, had used his police and his military powers as commander in chief of the armed forces to assure his reelection eight times. Political opponents were jailed or sent into exile. But following the February 1989 coup, it was Stroessner who went into exile in Brazil.

Rodríguez ended press censorship, freed political prisoners, welcomed home political exiles, and scheduled presidential and congressional elections for May 1. Riding on a wave of popularity resulting from those moves, Rodríguez won the presidential election with 74 per cent of the vote. Although an international group of observers invited to witness the elections reported some "irregularities," the observers said they were not widespread enough to change the outcome of the vote. Rodríguez' closest opponent received 20 per cent of the vote. Rodríguez ran as the candidate of the ruling Colorado Party.

At his inauguration on May 15, Rodríguez pledged a program of economic revival for Paraguay. He announced plans to sell ailing, state-owned companies to the private sector.   Nathan A. Haverstock

In *World Book,* see **Paraguay.**

Pennsylvania. See **Philadelphia; State government.**

Peru. A Maoist guerrilla movement known as Shining Path, which has been in armed rebellion for nine years, in 1989 provided evidence of its ability to disrupt Peru's political life. In the first 10 months of 1989, the rebels, who number an estimated 4,000, assassinated 123 mayors and other local officials and threw Peru's tottering economy into a state of near anarchy.

In mid-May, about 1 million Peruvian workers obeyed the guerrilla movement's call for a three-day strike in the highlands. The strike cut off the coastal capital city of Lima from food and electric power and from minerals mined in three Andean states on which the national economy depends.

Drug involvement. To finance terrorist activities, Shining Path has reportedly struck a deal with traffickers in coca, the raw material of the drug cocaine. In return for "protection," guerrillas reportedly receive a share of the profits from the illicit trade, which amounts to anywhere from $30 million to $500 million a year, according to United States and Peruvian government estimates.

During 1989, the Peruvian government conceded that Shining Path was in virtual control of the departments (states) of Huánuco, Pasco, and Junín, plus the Upper Huallaga Valley, source of much of the cocaine consumed in the United States. From January through October, more than 1,000 civilians and nearly 300 soldiers were killed by rebel bullets and bombs.

Virtually no area of Peru seemed beyond Shining Path's reach. Half of Peru's people lived in emergency zones, where the Peruvian army had broad powers to combat the rebellion. Terrorist acts in Lima became commonplace in 1989, but a threat to disrupt municipal elections on November 12 failed to materialize.

Inflation. Peru's economy, which had declined by 20 per cent in 1988, was further battered by an inflation rate of about 2,775 per cent in 1989. Support for Peru's once popular President Alan García Pérez fell drastically. He dared make only a few appearances outside of Lima. During a trip in June to Huancayo, a provincial capital, García Pérez was greeted by sparse and sullen crowds; at night his sleep was interrupted by explosions of dynamite and gunfire.

Presidential campaign. As Peru approached the April 1990 presidential election, public opinion polls gave a comfortable margin to the candidacy of famed novelist Mario Vargas Llosa of the center-right Democratic Front coalition. The coalition consisted of the Popular Action Party led by former President Fernando Belaúnde Terry, and the Popular Christian Party, led by Luis Bedoya, a former mayor of Lima. As the campaign heated up, Vargas Llosa toured Europe and the United States to win international support. He repeatedly called for more government protection for candidates from "those who want to destroy our democratic system."   Nathan A. Haverstock

See also **Latin America** (Facts in brief table). In *World Book,* see **Peru.**

Pet. See **Cat; Dog.**

Petroleum and gas. Decreased production of domestic crude oil and higher demand for gasoline and other petroleum products made the United States increasingly dependent on imported petroleum during 1989. On August 16, the American Petroleum Institute (API), an oil and natural gas association, reported that during July imported crude oil accounted for more than half of all petroleum used in the United States. It was the first time since 1977—and only the fourth month in history—in which the United States had relied on imports to that extent. The three other months were in 1977.

During July 1989, Americans used about 17 million barrels of oil per day (bpd), 1.7 per cent more than in 1988. Imports averaged 8.6 million bpd, up 17.9 per cent from 1988. Domestic production averaged 7.5 million bpd, down 7.1 per cent from July 1988.

Oil spill. The oil tanker *Exxon Valdez* hit a submerged reef in Alaska's Prince William Sound on March 24, 1989, spilling some 240,000 barrels of crude oil. The spill, largest in U.S. history, caused extensive environmental damage (see **Environmental pollution [Close-Up]**). In August, the state of Alaska sued the Exxon Corporation and six other oil firms for negligence in the accident. Alaska did not specify the amount of damages it hoped to recover, but state officials said the figure could total billions of dollars.

In the wake of strong public criticism of the oil industry following the accident, the industry on June 20 announced a new program to prevent, contain, and clean up major oil spills. The program, expected to cost more than $250 million during the first five years, would establish 5 regional emergency "response centers" and 15 "staging areas" for the storage of cleanup equipment. The program also was to include efforts to improve tanker safety and navigation and extensive new research on ways to control oil spills.

Oil prices. The U.S. Department of Energy (DOE) on September 25 reported that prices of crude oil rose by 13 per cent during the first half of 1989. The increase contributed to a financial recovery for U.S. oil and natural gas companies, which had reported reduced profits in 1988. The DOE said that the net income of 41 independent oil companies more than tripled, rising from $90.4 million for the first six months of 1988 to $294.1 million for the same period in 1989. The net income of the major petroleum companies rose by 8 per cent, from $10.3 billion for the first half of 1988 to $11.1 billion for the same period in 1989.

OPEC quotas. On November 28, the Organization of Petroleum Exporting Countries (OPEC), the 13-member oil cartel, said it would raise its official production ceiling to 22 million bpd from the previous 20.5 million bpd. Oil industry analysts said the increase would have little effect on world oil prices because OPEC members already were violating existing quotas by producing more than 23 million bpd.

Reserves. The DOE on September 12 reported that U.S. proven reserves of domestic crude oil in 1988 declined by 1.6 per cent, or about 431 million barrels. Reserves at the end of 1988 totaled 26.8 billion barrels, compared with 27.3 billion barrels at the end of 1987. The DOE said that U.S. oil reserves have declined by an average of 2 per cent per year since 1976. With low oil prices discouraging exploration for new oil fields, U.S. drillers discovered only 513 million barrels of new crude oil in 1988, 20 per cent less than in 1987.

Reserve sale. On October 2, USX Company, a steel and energy company, said it would sell about $1 billion in oil and natural gas reserves owned by the Texas Oil and Gas Company, which USX bought in 1986. The reserves include 28 million barrels of oil and 1.2 trillion cubic feet (34 billion cubic meters) of natural gas.

Oil find. The Atlantic Richfield Company (ARCO) in August announced the discovery of a major new oil field on the North Slope of Alaska. The field, believed to contain about 300 million barrels of oil, is located at Point McIntyre, about 2.5 miles (4 kilometers) north of the Prudhoe Bay oil field. ARCO said it was one of the largest oil strikes in the last 10 years.

Production. The API reported on Jan. 18, 1989, that U.S. oil production declined for the third straight year in 1988, reaching the lowest level since 1964. On Feb. 1, 1989, Spears & Associates, a research firm in Tulsa, Okla., reported that exploration for new oil and gas wells in the United States declined in 1988 to the lowest point since 1948.

Cleaner gasoline. Government efforts to toughen air pollution regulations led major oil companies to introduce cleaner-burning fuel for motor vehicles in 1989. ARCO on September 1 began replacing the leaded gasoline sold at its service stations in Southern California with a new low-pollution fuel. Southern California has the strictest air-pollution regulations in the United States. The reformulated gasoline, named Environmental Control-1 (EC-1), can cut by 15 per cent the pollution emitted by cars manufactured prior to 1975. These older cars, which were designed to run on leaded gasoline, do not have sophisticated emission control systems to reduce the amount of pollution released. Older cars are believed to cause about one-third of all air pollution in Southern California.

The Sun Refining and Marketing Company on September 27 announced that it would begin limited marketing of a low-pollution diesel fuel. Sun said the fuel was the first stage of a plan to develop a variety of reformulated fuels, including low-pollution gasolines.

South Africa pullout. The Mobil Corporation on April 28 announced that it was ending all operations in South Africa. Mobil, the second-largest U.S. oil company, said the withdrawal was the result of U.S. tax laws intended to discourage American investment in South Africa because of that country's policy of *apartheid* (racial separation). Mobil was the largest United States company still doing business in South Africa. It had assets of $400 million and about 3,000 employees there.

A driver in British Columbia, Canada, fills her car's fuel tank with compressed natural gas, being tested as an alternative to gasoline.

Gas controls lifted. United States President George Bush on July 26 signed legislation that ended all remaining government price controls on natural gas. In 1978, the government eliminated price controls on newly discovered gas. The new law affects natural gas discovered before that date that is still under contract. Under the new law, producers will be allowed to set their own prices as of Jan. 1, 1993. The legislation was intended to encourage exploration for new sources of domestic gas that could reduce dependence on foreign energy supplies.

Gas reserves. The DOE on Sept. 12, 1989, reported that proven reserves of natural gas declined by about 10 per cent, or 19.2 trillion cubic feet (544 million cubic meters), in 1988. Proven reserves totaled 168.0 trillion cubic feet (4.8 billion cubic meters) at the end of 1988, compared with 187.2 trillion cubic feet (5.3 trillion cubic meters) at the end of 1987. The decline resulted chiefly from a revision in the amount of natural gas the government believes can be recovered from Alaska's North Slope. Proven reserves in the continental United States increased in 1988, the DOE said.

Natural gas production during the first six months of 1989 totaled 8.4 trillion cubic feet (238 million cubic meters), about the same as in the first half of 1988. Consumption during the same period increased slightly, totaling 10.1 trillion cubic feet (286 million cubic meters), compared with 10.0 trillion cubic feet (283 million cubic meters) in 1988.

Petroleum and gas

Crude oil trails from the *Exxon Valdez,* which spilled an estimated 240,000 barrels of oil into Alaska's Prince William Sound in March.

Canadian exports. Canada's National Energy Board in October approved a project allowing three Canadian companies to export 9.2 trillion cubic feet (260 million cubic meters) of natural gas worth $11-billion Canadian (about $9.4 billion U.S.) to the United States. The exports would begin in 1996 and continue for 20 years. *Oil & Gas Journal*, an industry publication, reported on March 27, 1989, that Canadian exports account for about 7 per cent of the U.S. natural gas supply.

North Sea supply. Great Britain will remain self-sufficient in oil and natural gas over the next 25 years, according to a study released in September by the U.K. Offshore Operators Association. The study said that output from Britain's North Sea wells will decline, but at a rate slower than previously believed. The report predicted that over the next 25 years hundreds of new offshore wells will be developed and that these wells will be able to fill all the country's needs and provide for continued exports.

Saudi oil. The Arabian American Oil Company (Aramco) on January 9 said that Saudi Arabia has about 252 billion barrels of recoverable oil reserves, 50 per cent more than the previous estimate of 167 billion barrels. Aramco also said Saudi Arabia has about 25 per cent of all known oil reserves.   Michael Woods

In the Special Reports section, see **The Coming Energy Squeeze.** In *World Book,* see **Gas; Gasoline; Petroleum.**

Philadelphia. Major national developers who have taken an interest in Philadelphia since the mid-1980's began to transform the city's skyline in 1989, particularly in Center City, the downtown district. The developers have been attracted to Philadelphia because its land prices are low, compared with those in other large East Coast cities, and because a number of large lots have been available in Center City.

At least seven new multistory buildings opened or were being built or planned during the year. Until the 1980's, none of them could have been constructed because of an unwritten agreement that no Philadelphia building would rise higher than the statue of William Penn, the founder of Pennsylvania, atop City Hall. Penn's hat is 548 feet (167 meters) above the ground—not tall by this century's building standards. The City Council canceled the agreement in the mid-1980's, allowing developers to build higher than the summit of City Hall in a restricted downtown area.

The City Hall tower, undergoing restoration of the huge cast-iron plates that cover it, was visible in 1989 for the first time in four years as crews began to dismantle the scaffolding around the structure. The project, scheduled for completion in 1990, will cost about $18.5 million.

Another major construction project, the rebuilding of the Schuylkill Expressway, one of the two major arteries to and from the city, was completed on September 13, five days ahead of schedule. The following morning, drivers from throughout the Philadelphia area converged on the expressway, but traffic moved smoothly.

Construction start-up of a new $500-million convention center and an adjacent hotel was put on hold during the year. Although several blocks of buildings had been razed to make way for the project, city officials were still negotiating for the title to eight properties on the site.

Stadium closed. The 63-year-old John F. Kennedy Stadium, site of the annual Army-Navy football game and of such events as the Live Aid concert in 1985 and the 1988 Amnesty International Human Rights Now concert, was closed by Mayor W. Wilson Goode on July 13. The stadium, which can seat 102,000 people, had been deteriorating for years. The mayor said the stadium would probably be razed.

New sports arena? Even before it was confirmed that Kennedy Stadium would close, the owners of the Philadelphia Flyers hockey team and the Philadelphia 76ers basketball team had asked the city to build a new athletic arena on the stadium site. In late 1989, those owners were negotiating with city officials on the question of whether to keep their teams in Philadelphia. At the same time, the state of New Jersey was attempting to lure them across the Delaware River to Camden, N.J. Presumably, the construction of a new sports arena on the Kennedy Stadium site would settle the issue in favor of Philadelphia.

Crime. Expanding a program begun in 1988 to combat the influx of *crack*—a concentrated, smokable form of cocaine—the city in 1989 mounted a media campaign called "Join the Resistance." That call to action touched a responsive chord in the community; during the year, a coalition of neighborhood antidrug groups formed and grew. Nonetheless, the crack problem continued to escalate. At least a dozen people in the city were slain and nearly as many wounded in drug-related violence in 1989. Among the dead and wounded were passers-by who had by chance been nearby when gunfights broke out between rival drug dealers. The police said they traced much of the violence to a group called the Junior Black Mafia, which is reportedly conducting a multimillion-dollar narcotics trade in the Philadelphia area.

In October, a masked gunman shot and seriously wounded Nicodemo Scarfo, Jr., the son of Nicodemo (Little Nicky) Scarfo. The senior Scarfo, the reputed leader of organized crime in Philadelphia, is serving a life term in prison for murder.

Homeless funds cut. Faced with severe budget problems, the city in 1989 made deep cuts in many social programs, including a 50 per cent funding reduction in programs for the homeless. The city also closed 12 shelters for the homeless and evicted about 300 people from shelters for violating rules intended to help homeless individuals become more self-sufficient. 　Howard S. Shapiro

See also **City.** In *World Book,* see **Philadelphia.**

Philippines. President Corazon C. Aquino's government in December 1989 put down the fifth military uprising since she took office in 1986. An estimated 1,000 rebels seized several military bases and a government television station at about 1:30 a.m. on December 1. Rebel planes bombed the presidential palace and loyalist military bases. Aquino asked United States President George Bush for air support, which he authorized, and American warplanes stationed at Clark Air Base flew cover for loyalist planes that attacked rebel bases. Some rebels held buildings in Manila's financial district until surrendering on December 7, and rebels holding an air base in the central Philippines gave up two days later. At least 95 people died during the fighting.

The coup attempt was believed to have been led by Colonel Gregorio Honasan. He had been imprisoned for leading an unsuccessful coup in 1987 but escaped detention. Honasan had accused Aquino of failing to deal adequately with corruption, a Communist insurgency, and discontent within the armed forces. Vice President Salvador H. Laurel and former Defense Minister Juan Ponce Enrile, who earlier had united in opposition to Aquino, expressed sympathy for the rebels.

Aquino said on October 19 that she would not seek reelection; her present term ends in 1992. Aquino is a popular figure who has improved economic and political conditions since she replaced President Ferdinand E. Marcos in 1986. But she has been unable to eliminate the nation's social problems, such as unemployment, injustice, and corruption. Large landholders dominate the Congress, squabbling among themselves rather than addressing major problems. In 1989, for example, they weakened a land-reform program that might have limited the appeal of Communism.

Communist rebels. The government made limited gains in 1989 against the insurgency of the Communist Party of the Philippines and its guerrilla force, the New People's Army. A witch hunt for government informers and dissidents within the Communist Party left the guerrillas weakened by executions and defections. Mass graves containing Communists murdered by their comrades were discovered throughout the nation. Observers accused the guerrillas of terrorizing those who did not support them, in one case on June 25 killing 39 people in a rural church. Communist recruitment apparently declined as Aquino's efforts to reform the government reduced the appeal of rebellion, but the guerrillas continued to dominate several areas in the provinces.

The Philippine army stepped up its campaign against the rebels by increasing its patrols and its rural development work. But human-rights organizations said the army acted illegally against people suspected of being Communist supporters.

The Communists, who denounced the United States for its support of Aquino, targeted Americans in 1989. They tried unsuccessfully on April 6 to blow up a bus carrying 30 U.S. servicemen near Clark Air Base. On

Imelda Marcos views the body of her late husband, former Philippine President Ferdinand E. Marcos, who died in Hawaii on September 28.

April 21, the guerrillas killed Colonel James N. Rowe, head of the U.S. Military Assistance Group's Army division in Manila. Gunmen killed two Americans working for the U.S. military on September 26, two hours before U.S. Vice President Dan Quayle arrived to discuss the American desire to continue using military bases in the Philippines.

Marcos died at age 72 in Hawaii on September 28 of a kidney disorder and other ailments. He had been in exile since a 1986 popular uprising against his administration, which in the course of 20 years had become increasingly dictatorial. At the time of his death, Marcos was under U.S. indictment, charged with stealing millions of dollars from the Philippines while president. Aquino refused to allow Marcos' body to be buried in the Philippines. The Supreme Court supported her decision on October 27, ruling that even in death Marcos was a threat to the nation's security. Marcos was buried on October 15 in Honolulu.

Economy. The economic growth rate in 1989 was more than 5 per cent for the third year in a row, but with the population increasing at 2.7 per cent per year, average incomes made little recovery from earlier setbacks. Despite continuing economic difficulties, foreign confidence in the Philippines remained strong. Investment flowed into the islands, and foreign-aid donors promised continuing help.   Henry S. Bradsher

See also **Asia** (Facts in brief table). In *World Book,* see **Philippines.**

Physics. The world's two newest particle accelerators produced evidence in 1989 that all matter is composed of only three generations, or families, of elementary particles. The discovery of a few simple particles that serve as building blocks for all matter has been a major goal of modern physics. Eleven such particles have been found, and it now appears that only one may remain to be discovered.

The matter in most of the universe is constructed of only four building blocks. One is the familiar *electron,* with one unit of negative electric charge. Another is the *electron-neutrino,* which resembles the electron but has zero electric charge. Neutrinos are not present in atoms but are emitted in some nuclear reactions, including those that power the sun. The other two building blocks are the *u-quark* and the *d-quark,* of which protons and neutrons are made. The u has two-thirds of a unit of positive electric charge; the d, one-third of a unit of negative charge.

In addition to these building blocks, there are several other particles called *bosons* that serve as the "glue" that holds them together. And each particle has its *antiparticle,* which is opposite to the particle in electric charge and other properties.

Three generations. The pattern of four building blocks seems to be repeated twice. Each successive set of four particles is called a *generation.* In the second and third generations, the three electrically charged particles are much heavier than their first-generation counterparts. Their extra mass makes these particles unstable. They break up into first-generation particles. Neutrinos show no sign of having any mass at all.

No known law of nature "requires" that the heavy particles exist. Inside a nucleus, they occasionally pop into existence, only to be immediately reabsorbed. A few are produced when radiation from outer space strikes the earth's atmosphere. And in certain rare, violent processes such as supernova explosions, heavy particles appear in large numbers.

Discovering the particles. Physicists discovered most of the heavy particles with the help of powerful machines called *particle accelerators,* which generate beams of swift-moving particles that belong to the first generation. When particles collide with one another, their energy can be converted to mass, creating second- and third-generation particles.

The missing piece in the puzzle—the undetected 12th particle—is the third-generation equivalent of the u. It has already been christened the *t-quark.* Physicists presume that the t has not yet been observed because it is too heavy to produce in present-day accelerators.

The two new machines produced data strongly suggesting that there is no fourth generation of particles. The new accelerators are the Stanford Linear Collider (SLC), near Palo Alto, Calif., and the Large Electron-Positron Collider (LEP), which straddles the French-Swiss border near Geneva, Switzerland. Each produces two beams—one of electrons and the other of their antimatter equivalents, positrons—moving in opposite directions. Where the beams meet, some of the particles collide.

Both accelerators were designed to produce large numbers of one kind of boson, the Z^0. This is the heaviest known particle. Physicists have calculated that the rate at which the Z^0 is produced and the speed with which it breaks up are influenced by how many kinds of neutrinos there are.

The SLC produced its first Z^0 in April 1989, and LEP followed in August. By October, both accelerators had produced data consistent with there being only three generations of neutrinos. If there were a fourth-generation neutrino, the lifetime of the Z^0 would be about 7 per cent shorter, and its production rate 13 per cent less, than observed at the two accelerators.

SSC construction approved. The future of particle research in the United States received a boost in September 1989 when Congress approved the start of construction of a huge particle accelerator called the Superconducting Super Collider (SSC). This machine is to circulate two opposing proton beams within a gigantic ring and direct the beams to collide head-on, creating a shower of particles. Plans call for housing the SSC in a tunnel 53 miles (85 kilometers) in diameter, which is to be bored in the ground surrounding Waxahachie, Tex. The SSC would be the most powerful accelerator ever built.   Robert H. March

In *World Book,* see **Particle accelerator; Physics.**

Poetry. The most authoritative survey of the year's poetry was the 1989 edition of *The Best American Poetry.* The annual series, inaugurated in 1988 under general editor David Lehman, features poems chosen by a prominent poet serving as guest editor. For the 1989 collection, Donald Hall selected 75 works, chiefly from magazines spanning every critical, scholarly, and poetical hue.

Collections. Outstanding retrospective collections of the year included a new edition of *Opus Posthumous,* an anthology of poetic fragments, plays, essays, and notebook entries by Wallace Stevens. The revision, edited by Milton J. Bates, contains 25 per cent more material than the 1957 version. Nearly as important was John Berryman's *Collected Poems: 1937-1971,* which includes all of Berryman's published volumes of poetry except his best-known work, "The Dream Songs."

Two established poets combined retrospective collections with new work. Frederick Seidel's *Poems: 1959-1979* appeared at the same time as *These Days,* a volume of new poems; the combination allows a full reading of a poet whose eloquent, formal work has been rarely available. And Tom Disch's *Yes, Let's* includes selections from five earlier volumes as well as many new poems. Disch, noted as a scholar and science-fiction writer as well as a poet, enjoys playing with formal limitations; his style is readable, humorous, and often satirical.

New work. Notable new books of 1989 included Richard Howard's elegant and witty *No Traveller.* In his verse monologues, Howard often impersonates real or imagined Victorian minor poets or forgotten scholars. One poem, a verse letter called "Even in Paris," builds on the pretext of Wallace Stevens in Paris. *The Farther Shore* by Paul Kane displayed poems of great variety, with a preference for dramatic monologue. Especially notable was the long poem "Mr. Emerson Assisted on His Walk." And in *The Year of the Olive Oil,* Charles North offered, among other fine pieces, a wonderful parody of Stevens.

Maxine Kumin's *Nurture* focused on animals and nature, typically with a critical edge or social comment. Mary Jo Salter's *Unfinished Painting* reflected with wit and warmth on her mother, the death of a friend, and her marriage to poet Brad Leithauser.

Prose poems—poems whose form incorporates stylized, highly cadenced sentences and paragraphs—enjoyed a small revival. Charles Simic's *The World Doesn't End* showed this master of the prose poem at his most whimsical and fantastic. Robert Hass's *Human Wishes* included some moving prose poems in which he tells brief stories, examining such topics as childhood, passion, or life in California with equal vividness. In a contrasting style, William Bronk, another California poet, compressed his visions about death, work, and fathers and sons into three- and four-line haiku-like verses in *Death Is the Place.*

Metaphysical wit marks *Transparent Gestures* by Rodney Jones; one poem opens by describing "a mechanic who reads Nietzsche." April Bernard's *Blackbird Bye Bye* also offered quick wit, frequently directed at the pretensions of contemporary poets and artists; one poem begins, "When the anthology arrives with your name in it . . ." *Balance as Belief* displayed Wyatt Prunty's skill in such poems as "Learning the Bicycle," which describes a father teaching his daughter to ride and, in the process, learning to let go.

Also notable were Alan Ansen's *Contact Highs,* Killarney Clary's *Who Whispered Near Me,* Peter Davison's *The Great Ledge,* Deborah Digges' *Late in the Millenium,* Gregory Djanikian's *Falling Deeply into America,* Rita Dove's *Grace Notes,* Edward Hirsch's *The Night Parade,* Herbert Morris' *The Little Voices of the Pears,* Michael Ryan's *God Hunger,* Elizabeth Spires' *Annonciade,* and Nancy Willard's *Water Walker.*

Criticism. The outstanding book of contemporary poetry criticism of 1989 was J. D. McClatchy's *White Paper,* marked by fine close readings and far-ranging taste. Also of interest was the late David Kalstone's gossipy *Becoming a Poet: Elizabeth Bishop with Marianne Moore and Robert Lowell,* a mixture of interpretation and memoir. Anne Stevenson's *Bitter Fame: A Life of Sylvia Plath* stood to become the standard biography of Plath, though controversy arose from the book's frank view of the poet as a demanding wife and difficult woman.   Michael Dirda

In *World Book,* see **Poetry.**

Poland

Poland saw a transformation of its domestic political scene in 1989, ending four decades of totalitarian Communist rule with the emergence of the independent labor union Solidarity as a political powerhouse. The August 24 confirmation of Solidarity adviser Tadeusz Mazowiecki as Poland's first non-Communist prime minister since 1945 was an unprecedented event that challenged the entire Communist world. Almost as striking as Mazowiecki's election was Soviet leader Mikhail S. Gorbachev's privately conveyed advice to Poland's Communist Party that the party should work with the Mazowiecki administration. See **Mazowiecki, Tadeusz.**

As Mazowiecki presented his cabinet to Poland's Sejm (the lower house of parliament) on September 12, he proclaimed that his government's policy was to create "a normal market economy" and full democracy. The government announced on October 12 that it would transform Poland's centrally controlled economy into a free-market system by the beginning of 1992. Communists retained the critical defense and interior posts in the cabinet.

How change came. By the beginning of 1989, it had become apparent that the Communist regime would have to share power with Solidarity to relieve the tremendous political and social stresses that had built up throughout the country. Poland's economy—controlled by the central government in Warsaw—was in a shambles, with consumer goods sorely lack-

ing. Polish workers, with no opportunity to make their demands heard in the Sejm, had resorted to strikes to pressure the regime to reform the economy. In mid-September 1988, with Poland racked with strikes, the government had proposed to hold talks with all opposition groups.

Poland's political transformation began in February 1989, when the Communists and a Solidarity-led opposition met to hammer out an agreement on constitutional and political changes. On March 9, the two sides agreed to a host of new measures, including an end to the Communist Party's monopoly on political power; the creation of a second house of parliament, the Senate; the choosing of senators by the Polish people in free elections; and the election of a president by parliament. On April 7, the Sejm passed six laws incorporating the changes.

Solidarity was relegalized on April 17 and three days later so was Rural Solidarity, a union of independent farmers. The government had banned both organizations in 1982. The first free elections in Poland since 1947 took place on June 4 and 18, 1989. They resulted in the eclipse of the Communist Party and almost all its leading figures. On July 19, parliament elected Communist Party leader Wojciech Jaruzelski president—but by the narrowest possible margin, and that thanks to the tactful support of Solidarity.

At a meeting with Solidarity leader Lech Walesa on July 25, Jaruzelski proposed that Solidarity and the Communists form a coalition government, but Walesa turned him down. Jaruzelski resigned as leader of the Communist Party on July 29, honoring a preelection promise. Mieczysław Rakowski, then prime minister, succeeded him.

On July 31, the Communist leadership selected Interior Minister Czesław Kiszczak to succeed Rakowski as prime minister, but he was unable to form a cabinet. On August 19, Jaruzelski nominated Mazowiecki, who assembled a coalition cabinet made up of 11 members of Solidarity, 4 Communists, 4 from the United Peasants' Party, 3 Democrats, and 1 independent.

Economic help needed. The new government needed immediate help to salvage Poland's ruined economy. Visiting Washington, D.C., on September 27, Finance Minister Leszek Balierowicz said that Poland needed $500 million from the West to import food and other necessities during the remainder of 1989. Poland also pressed for a rescheduling of its huge foreign debt.

Church and state. The Sejm in May 1989 granted the Roman Catholic Church legal standing in Poland for the first time since 1945. The 1989 law guarantees the church's right to govern its own affairs, including appointments to clerical offices. The Vatican announced on July 17 that it had reestablished full diplomatic relations with Poland. Eric Bourne

See also **Europe** (Facts in brief table). In *World Book,* see **Poland.**

Pollution. See **Environmental pollution.**

Tadeusz Mazowiecki greets well-wishers on August 24 after his election as Poland's first non-Communist prime minister in four decades.

Popular music. Vinyl album sales continued their decline in 1989 as the compact disc (CD) format grew in popularity. Vinyl singles edged closer to extinction, as record stores shifted to the cassette single format, and the WEA record label family announced that in 1990 it would no longer accept record-store returns of new singles. Meanwhile, the Personics custom taping system was introduced at record stores, enabling customers to electronically compile their choice of songs on cassette tapes.

Reunions and comebacks led the 1989 music scene. The Who reunited for a hugely successful summer tour capped in August by a pay-per-view cable television performance of the rock opera *Tommy*. After years of infighting, the Rolling Stones returned in September with a new studio album (*Steel Wheels*), a multi-album set of classic singles, and the group's first United States tour since 1981. The most successful lineup of former members of Yes regrouped under their own names as Anderson, Bruford, Wakeman, Howe. Other legendary groups that reunited included the Jefferson Airplane, Poco, the Doobie Brothers, the Allman Brothers, and Ten Years After.

In November, Paul McCartney started his first U.S. tour since 1976. This followed a summer tour by former Beatles bandmate Ringo Starr and an all-star band. The Bee Gees overcame a long-running disco stigma with a tour and the single "One," their first song since 1979 to reach the top 10 on *Billboard* magazine's chart of top singles. (The *Billboard* charts, an industry standard, rank records according to sales and radio airplay.) Pop-chart exiles Donny Osmond and Donna Summer enjoyed comebacks. Other solo artists who reemerged after lengthy absences were Alice Cooper, Carole King, Kate Bush, and Rickie Lee Jones.

Controversy. Madonna's "Like a Prayer" single made history by debuting in March in a Pepsi commercial. But the video that followed a week later caused such an uproar with its religious imagery that Pepsi eventually pulled the multimillion-dollar ad campaign.

In June, the provocative rap group Public Enemy, who topped the *Village Voice* critics' poll for 1988, came under fire when group member Professor Griff made anti-Semitic statements in a newspaper interview. Leader Chuck D first dismissed Griff and then announced the band's total breakup. But by August, Public Enemy—whose rap "Fight the Power" was central to Spike Lee's controversial film *Do the Right Thing*—was back together.

Other rap artists—including Slick Rick, 2 Live Crew, and N.W.A.—were criticized for sexism in their lyrics. Hard rock group Guns N' Roses, which continued its 1988 success with release of its album *G N' R Lies*, was rejected from an AIDS benefit because of antigay sentiments in the song "One in a Million." The Washington, D.C.-based watchdog group Parents' Music Resource Center continued its campaign to have warning labels placed on albums it deemed offensive.

Rock band Bon Jovi maintained its popularity in 1989 with "I'll Be There for You," the second number-one single from the group's *New Jersey* album.

Paula Abdul triumphed in 1989 with two number-one singles—"Straight Up" and "Forever Your Girl"—and four MTV video awards.

Causes and benefits. Environmental concerns brought together 31 acts for the *Rainbow Warriors* album benefiting Greenpeace, an activist environmental organization. Sting and Madonna were among those calling for preservation of the tropical rain forests, while Paul McCartney linked his tour with the environmental group Friends of the Earth.

Closer to home, Living Colour performed to benefit the homeless. And such rap stars as Public Enemy, KRS-1, and Kool Moe Dee joined a "Stop the Violence" movement for the National Urban League's fight against black-against-black crime and illiteracy.

Soviet rock. Dylanesque rock-poet Boris Grebenshikov and his English-language album *Radio Silence* led an influx of rock from the Soviet Union. Other Soviet groups with American releases were the theatrical band Zvuki Mu and the pop-metal band Gorky Park.

Mainstream rock. Top albums of 1989 included Richard Marx's *Repeat Offender*, Billy Joel's *Stormfront*, and Prince's *Batman* soundtrack, which became the singer's biggest success since the soundtrack to his 1984 movie, *Purple Rain*. Lou Reed, Bonnie Raitt, and Bob Dylan released their best-received albums in years, while Stevie Nicks and Tom Petty returned with solo albums. David Bowie—whose long-awaited CD reissue series began with the 46-song *Sound + Vision* set—formed a new band, Tin Machine.

Veteran women artists with 1989 albums included Linda Ronstadt, Cher, and Gloria Estefan, while Tracy

Chapman and Melissa Etheridge solidified the successes of their 1988 debut albums with strong follow-ups. Don Henley and Phil Collins were big among male artists. Returning duos included Tears for Fears, the Thompson Twins, and Eurythmics.

Teen acts were led by New Kids on the Block, the first teen group to top the singles chart since the Osmonds in 1971. The group's *Hangin' Tough* album and its title track were number one simultaneously on the album and singles charts in September, when frenzy for the group reminded music industry veterans of the Beatlemania of the 1960's. In January, 19-year-old Bobby Brown's *Don't Be Cruel* made him the youngest male vocalist with a number-one album since 13-year-old Stevie Wonder in 1963. In March, Debbie Gibson, age 18, became the youngest female singer to have a top album and a top single at the same time.

Alternative artists broke into mainstream radio in surprising numbers. Fine Young Cannibals' "She Drives Me Crazy" was a number-one single, and Love and Rockets, R.E.M., Was (Not Was), and the Cure earned top-10 hits as well. Other alternative groups with breakthroughs included Cowboy Junkies, the Pixies, and the acoustic duo Indigo Girls. Meanwhile, Talking Heads leader David Byrne spearheaded growing interest in Latin music with two compilations of Brazilian pop music and a Latin-influenced solo album.

Heavy metal groups Metallica and Queensryche used video to increase their fan base, as did less-heavy rock acts Winger and Warrant. New releases by Aerosmith and Mötley Crüe earned strong support.

Rap acts continued to increase their album sales and prestige. Paving the way was Tone-Lōc, whose *Lōc-ed After Dark* was the first rap album with two top-10 singles. De La Soul further expanded the boundaries of the genre with an album, *3 Feet High and Rising*, that was hailed for its creative diversity. Other top rappers were Slick Rick, Kool Moe Dee, L. L. Cool J, EPMD, and the Beastie Boys.

Black musicians prominent in 1989—besides the mainstream stars, teens, and rappers—included Janet Jackson, who released the hugely successful *Rhythm Nation 1814*. Tina Turner returned with a new album, while such younger artists as Guy, Karyn White, and Surface gained recognition on the black-music charts. Living Colour, the first black rock band with a top-10 album since the early 1970's, earned an opening slot on the Stones tour.

Dance music acquired several bright new faces. Paula Abdul's "Straight Up" and "Forever Your Girl" topped the singles charts and helped her earn four MTV video awards. Neneh Cherry, Martika, and the duo Milli Vanilli also made striking debuts.

Country music saw the return of Dolly Parton and Ronnie Milsap to traditional country records. Clint Black rocketed to stardom with his debut "A Better Man," while Rodney Crowell became the first country musician to have five straight number-one hits from the same album. Buck Owens rerecorded his 1963 classic "Act Naturally" with Ringo Starr, who had sung it with the Beatles in 1965. The Nitty Gritty Dirt Band released a highly acclaimed rock-country album, *Will the Circle Be Unbroken, Vol. II*, 17 years after its landmark predecessor.

Jazz was represented by contemporary artists such as the Rippingtons, Hiroshima, and Tuck & Patti, as well as Harry Connick, Jr., a young New Orleans piano player in the traditional mode. The legendary Blue Note jazz label celebrated its 50th anniversary with a boxed set featuring its greatest artists.

Video highlights included "There's a Tear in My Beer," in which Hank Williams, Jr., created a "duet" with his late father by joining new and old tape footage. In an ironic twist, Neil Young's "This Note's for You," banned on MTV in 1988 because it prominently featured commercial products, was named Video of the Year in the 1989 MTV awards. Kenny Rogers may have set a record for extravagance; his 5½-minute "Planet Texas" reportedly cost $600,000.

Long-format music videos came of age in 1989. Michael Jackson's *Moonwalker* swiftly became the best-selling music videocassette ever. Other hits included *Bruce Springsteen: Video Anthology—1978-1988*, U2's *Rattle and Hum*, and Pink Floyd's *The Delicate Sound of Thunder*.   Jim Bessman

See also **Awards and prizes** (Arts awards). In *World Book,* see **Country music; Jazz; Popular music; Rock music.**

Population. The world's population reached approximately 5.2 billion in 1989, according to the United Nations (UN) Population Fund. The overall population growth rate remained at 1.7 per cent—0.1 percentage point higher than the UN had predicted in the late 1970's. At this growth rate, the world's population will reach 10 billion by 2025 and 14 billion by 2099.

The UN had predicted that widespread adoption of birth control practices would cause the world's population to level off at about 10 billion sometime before 2100. This projection was based on the assumption that 71 per cent of all women of childbearing age would use birth control, but currently only 45 per cent use some means of family planning. In the United States, about 65 per cent of women of reproductive age use birth control. The percentage is higher in China and some European nations but much lower in some developing countries.

Life expectancy. According to a report on worldwide life expectancy by the U.S. Bureau of the Census, life expectancies in developing nations are improving. For example, children born in the African nation of Malawi in 1989 will live an average of 48 years; in 1983, the average life expectancy there was only 43. In general, however, life expectancy in developing nations is significantly lower than in industrialized nations. The overall life expectancy for Africans is 53 years. For Asians, it is 61 years, and for Latin Ameri-

cans it is 67 years. By contrast, life expectancy in developed countries is about 75 years.

U.S. statistics. The U.S. population—which reached 247 million at the beginning of 1989—was expected to climb to 249 million by the end of the year, according to the Census Bureau. Although the rate of immigration remains high, the overall growth rate—estimated at 0.8 per cent for 1989—has gradually declined since 1964. The increased use of birth control and the aging of the population are responsible for the decrease. These factors have made the birth rate grow more slowly than the death rate.

The Census Bureau also reported that regional population growth in the 1980's was greatest in the West and South and least in the Northeast and Midwest. Alaska, Arizona, Florida, and Nevada all had population increases of more than 20 per cent from 1980 to 1988. By contrast, the populations of Iowa; Michigan; Washington, D.C.; and West Virginia decreased during the 1980's.

In January 1989, the Census Bureau predicted for the first time that the U.S. population will eventually decrease as the number of women of childbearing age declines. The bureau projected that the annual growth rate will remain at 0.8 per cent until 1995, when it will drop. The population should reach a peak of about 302 million by 2038 and then begin to decrease slowly.   Jinger Hoop

In *World Book,* see **Life expectancy; Population.**

Portugal struggled with domestic economic problems in 1989 as it tried to adjust to its membership in the European Community (EC or Common Market), which it joined on Jan. 1, 1986. The EC plans to develop into a single-market economy in 1992. Portugal's Prime Minister Aníbal Cavaço Silva had determined that, to compete effectively in this new setting, Portugal must inject a large dose of private enterprise into its economy.

Before Portugal could privatize extensively, however, it needed to amend its Constitution, which had been written after a left wing revolution. In 1974, a group of military officers overthrew a dictatorship that had ruled Portugal since 1926. Once in control, the officers nationalized certain industries and farms and wrote a Constitution prohibiting the government from selling them.

Constitutional changes. On June 1, 1989, Parliament removed from the Constitution a prohibition on the privatization of industries in which the government possessed a majority holding. These industries are to be transferred to private owners through a public sale of shares.

The constitutional changes had the overwhelming support of the ruling Social Democratic Party, which controls 51 per cent of the seats in Parliament, and of the Socialists, with 34 per cent of the seats. Opposing the changes were the Communists and some independents and Greens.

Postal Service, United States

Protests against privatization. Earlier in the year, the Social Democrats had pledged to privatize certain specific industries such as television broadcasting, to sell government-owned farms, and to increase competition in the medical profession. Most physicians in Portugal worked for fees that were set by the government. With privatization, doctors who wanted to open a private practice would set their own fees, while government pay would be increased for doctors who continued working for the public health service. Disputes over this privatization plan led to a doctors' strike from February 8 to 10—and to government reconsideration of the plan.

In addition, many employees of state-owned firms such as public transportation companies feared that they might lose their jobs if the firms were privatized. A series of strikes in various industries boiled over in a general strike on June 13 and 14, idling about 15 per cent of the country's work force.

EC election. The general strike hurt the Social Democrats in June 13 voting for the European Parliament, the EC's legislative branch. The Social Democrats won 33 per cent of the vote, down 3 percentage points from the previous election in 1987. The Socialists and a leftist coalition led by Communists and Greens gained slightly. Voter turnout was only 51 per cent.   Joseph Fitchett

See also **Europe** (Facts in brief table). In *World Book,* see **Portugal.**

Postal Service, United States. Postmaster General Anthony M. Frank said on Aug. 28, 1989, that the United States Postal Service will seek an increase in mailing rates in 1991. Frank said the increase would boost the price of a first-class stamp, now 25 cents, by 3 to 7 cents. For all categories of mail, he said, the increase would most likely range from 20 to 25 per cent and would take effect in January 1991.

Barely a month after Frank took over as postmaster general in March 1988, the Postal Service adopted long-planned rate increases averaging 16.4 per cent. The cost of a first-class stamp was increased to 25 cents from 22 cents. Nonetheless, the service was again losing money in 1989. Ralph Stewart, a Postal Service spokesman, said the agency expected to run a deficit of $100 million in the 1989 fiscal year, which ended September 30.

Cost-cutting moves. The Postal Service has spent more than $1 billion in recent years to automate mail handling, but savings realized as a result have been offset by higher outlays elsewhere, such as for employee health insurance. Seeking to reduce operating costs, the service announced in August that it would eliminate about 1,000 administrative jobs and cut back 39 facilities in order to save $30 million or more a year. Postal officials insisted that mail service would not suffer as a result of those actions.

Speaking at a meeting in Washington, D.C., on Jan. 6, 1989, Frank said the service would try to contract out more of its work, even though that would likely draw fire from postal unions. He said a proposal to have outsiders maintain postal vehicles had been considered and rejected.

Post offices at stores. As a model for what it hoped would be a nationwide cost-saving effort, the Postal Service in 1988 persuaded Sears, Roebuck and Company, as a one-year experiment, to open small post offices in 11 of its Midwestern stores. Although the offices were staffed by store employees, the service assured postal unions that the move would not cost any postal workers' jobs. Nonetheless, the 365,000-member American Postal Workers Union was opposed to the venture, so on June 30, 1989, several months before the experiment was to end, Sears announced it would close the post offices. The Postal Service said it would continue the program by contracting with individual merchants in large shopping malls.

In another effort to improve service and gain new sources of revenue, the Postal Service announced in November that it would install credit-card-operated fax machines in selected post offices. In a one-year test program, 54 post offices in Boston, New York City, and Providence, R.I., will have the machines, which transmit replicas of drawn or written pages over telephone lines.   Frank Cormier and Margot Cormier

In *World Book,* see **Post office; Postal Service, United States.**

Powell, Colin Luther (1937-   ), a general in the United States Army, on Oct. 1, 1989, became chairman of the Joint Chiefs of Staff, the top military post in the United States. Since April 1989, he had been head of the Army Forces Command, which is responsible for the combat readiness of forces in the United States, Puerto Rico, and the Virgin Islands. Powell, named to the post by President George Bush, became the first black chairman of the Joint Chiefs. He brought to the position a wealth of experience in military command and involvement in the highest levels of politics.

Powell was born on April 5, 1937, in New York City. His parents were immigrants from Jamaica. He received a bachelor's degree in geology at the City College of New York in 1958 and joined the Army upon graduation. He served in Vietnam in the 1960's and was wounded twice. In 1971, he obtained a master's degree in business administration at George Washington University in Washington, D.C.

Powell then held a succession of command and administrative positions. In January 1987, he became deputy to the national security adviser, Frank J. Carlucci. In November 1987, Carlucci became secretary of defense and Powell succeeded him as national security adviser.

Powell married Alma Vivian Johnson in 1962. The Powells have two daughters and one son.   Jay Myers

President of the United States. See **Bush, George H.W.; United States, Government of the.**

Prince Edward Island. A proposal for a fixed link with mainland Canada was postponed indefinitely in January 1989 when the Canadian government decided to hold further hearings on the project's environmental impact. Federal officials remained committed to a proposed 9-mile (14-kilometer) bridge linking the island with New Brunswick.

The Liberal government's new budget, brought out on March 7, 1989, prompted rumors of an imminent election. The budget promised no new taxes, no tax increases, and increased spending on such popular items as health care and highways. Premier Joseph A. Ghiz called the election for May 29.

One campaign issue was the federal government's decision to close the Canadian Forces base at Summerside. The closure, and the loss of 1,300 jobs, represented a serious blow to the province, whose unemployment rate was more than 14 per cent. Ghiz pledged to fight the closing at the national level. The Liberals won a resounding victory, taking 30 of the 32 seats in the legislature and 61 per cent of the popular vote—the highest proportion for any party in the province's history. The Progressive Conservative Party won the 2 remaining seats.

On July 12, 1989, the island lost its rail service when CN (Canadian National) Rail abandoned seven freight lines and a rail link leading to the mainland ferry. Passenger rail service ended in 1969.   David M. L. Farr

In *World Book,* see **Prince Edward Island.**

Party leaders Joseph Ghiz and Melbourne Gass open Canada Fitweek in May, three days before they face off in Prince Edward Island's election.

Prison. Crowding problems in United States prisons and jails reached record proportions in 1989, fueled in part by an increase in drug-related convictions. In the first six months of 1989, the number of inmates in state and federal prisons rose 7.3 per cent, from 627,561 to 673,565, according to the Department of Justice's Bureau of Justice Statistics. This six-month leap of 46,004 prisoners not only broke the record for half-year increases but also was higher than any annual increase since the government began recording inmate populations in 1886.

Most of the increase was in state prison systems, which grew by 41,214 inmates, or 7.1 per cent. The smaller federal prison population rose by 4,790 inmates, or 9.6 per cent. The number of women in prison continued to grow faster than the number of men—13 per cent and 7 per cent, respectively. In all, the rise reflected a need for 1,800 more beds per week.

Boot camps. Military-style *shock incarceration* programs, known to many as "boot camps," gained public popularity in 1989. These programs use military recruit-training exercises to instill discipline in participants. In October, North Carolina became the latest state to incorporate this type of program into its corrections system, bringing the number of states that use shock incarceration to 12. Although the use of these programs has increased, their cost-effectiveness and rehabilitative value have not yet been determined through any conclusive studies.

Furloughs. Following up on the strong opposition to prison furloughs he expressed in his 1988 campaign, President George Bush took steps during his first year in office to curb the use of furloughs within the federal system. In July 1989, U.S. Attorney General Richard L. Thornburgh outlined plans to exclude certain inmates from furlough consideration. These included serious drug offenders, inmates convicted of violent crimes against people, and offenders with histories of weapon use in crimes.

Executions. The Jan. 24, 1989, execution of serial killer Ted Bundy was widely publicized throughout the United States, as were the demonstrations that took place outside his Florida prison. Angry citizens carried signs with such messages as "Burn, Bundy, Burn!" Bundy was convicted in 1979 and 1980 of three 1978 sex-related murders. In his final days on death row, he confessed to 16 other killings.

In all, 16 offenders were executed in the United States in 1989, bringing the number of executions to 120 since the death penalty was reinstated in 1977. In June 1989, the Supreme Court of the United States upheld the use of the death penalty for murderers who are mentally retarded as well as for juveniles as young as 16 years old when they committed murder. As of December 31, some 2,300 people were on death row in state and federal prisons.   Linda R. Acorn

In *World Book,* see **Prison.**

Prizes. See **Awards and prizes; Nobel Prizes.**

Protestantism

Protestantism. Protestants continued to seek improved relations with the Roman Catholic Church in 1989. Robert A. K. Runcie, the archbishop of Canterbury and head of the Anglican Communion, an international organization of 23 Episcopal churches, met with Pope John Paul II at the Vatican in the fall. Their meeting was only the fourth between an archbishop of Canterbury and a pope since Protestants broke from the Roman Catholic Church in the 1500's.

During their meeting, the two leaders discussed the differences that separate the two churches. A major stumbling block is the Anglican position on the role of women in the clergy. Since 1976, many churches in the Anglican Communion, which includes the Episcopal Church in the United States, have permitted the ordination of women. The Roman Catholic Church, however, has taken a firm stand against ordaining women as priests. In a joint statement issued on October 2, the two leaders stated that the difference "prevents reconciliation between us even where there is otherwise progress."

Role of women. Debate over the role of women in the clergy escalated among Episcopalians in 1989. On February 11, Barbara C. Harris, an Episcopalian priest, became the first woman to be ordained a bishop in the Episcopal Church. See **Harris, Barbara C.**

Although the Episcopal Church has long allowed women priests, conservative members strongly objected to a woman bishop. On June 2 in Fort Worth, Tex., a group of conservative Episcopalian bishops announced the creation of the Episcopal Synod of America, an association for Episcopalians who do not agree with the liberal theology of the church. The synod opposes such policies as the ordination of women, tolerance of homosexuality, and revisions of liturgical texts to eliminate gender references.

To prevent a possible split among its members, the Episcopal Church's House of Bishops on September 28 reaffirmed the church's decision to ordain women. They did, however, recognize opposition to such ordinations as a legitimate theological position within the church. In November, the Church of England supported the policy of ordaining women.

Issue of homosexuality. The United Church of Canada, which includes Methodist, Congregational, and Presbyterian churches in Canada, was also torn by a controversy involving the clergy. During the year, the church's General Council received more than 1,000 petitions from member churches asking it to reverse the policy permitting the ordination of homosexuals. The council had approved the new policy in August 1988. Community of Concern, a group that claimed to have the support of one-fourth of the United Church clergy, worked during 1989 to have the policy revoked.

Protestants and Communism. The Chinese government's crackdown on prodemocracy demonstrators in Beijing in June left the country's Protestant

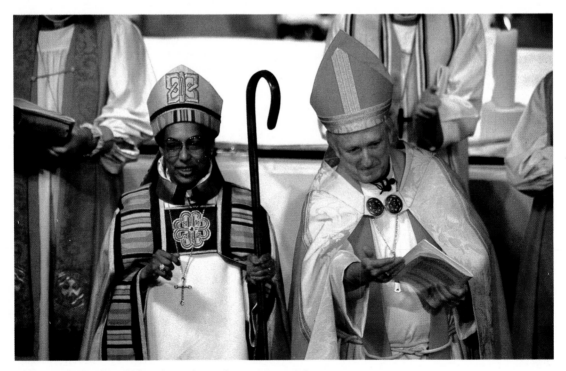

Barbara C. Harris acknowledges the applause of supporters on February 11 after being ordained the first woman bishop in the Episcopal Church.

churches confused about their future. In May, Bishop K. H. Ding of the China Christian Council issued a statement that "wholeheartedly affirmed" the demonstrations. But after the government crushed the movement, the council supported the repressions.

Many observers predicted that some church leaders would suffer for supporting the demonstrations. But there were signs that the church intended to find ways to coexist with the Communist government and—when possible—protest against restrictive government policies.

In the Soviet Union, Protestants took advantage of the increasingly open political climate to become more public about their faith. The same was true in other Communist countries. The government of Hungary permitted more open *evangelism* (the preaching of the Gospel) and Christian education. Evangelist Billy Graham in July attracted 90,000 people to a religious rally in Budapest.

In East Germany, Protestant churches—most of them Lutheran—turned their buildings over to demonstrators protesting government repression during the year. Protestant leaders also provided public leadership. In September, church leaders issued a statement urging citizens not to leave East Germany and promised to support those people who would stay to work for better conditions.

Converts. The work of conservative evangelists and *pentecostals* (fundamentalist Protestants who stress the personal inspiration of the Holy Spirit) to convert Roman Catholics in Latin America strained relations between Protestants and Catholics. Roman Catholic leaders in Latin America accused Protestant leaders in Guatemala of beguiling prospective converts and disrupting the spiritual life of that nation.

Evangelical conversion efforts were also beginning to be felt among Hispanics in the United States. Religious observers estimated in 1989 that about 4 million of the 20 million Hispanics in the United States had left the Roman Catholic Church to join evangelical and pentecostal Protestant groups. Archbishop Pio Laghi, the Vatican's representative in the United States, called the number of converts "disturbingly high."

Jewish relations. A shadow was cast over relations between evangelicals and Jews in 1989. At a meeting of the World Evangelical Fellowship in Bermuda, a group of theologians issued a statement urging continued efforts to convert Jews. Members of the Jewish community, who had been working to foster a relationship with evangelicals, expressed disappointment over the statement, which said that to be saved Jews must accept Jesus Christ as their savior.

Council feud. The National Council of Churches (NCC), an organization of more than 30 Protestant and Orthodox church denominations, experienced internal battles during the year. In May, the council's governing board attempted to remove Arie R. Brouwer, its general secretary. Brouwer, who held the post for 4½ years, had ongoing quarrels with leaders of a

number of NCC agencies, including the Church World Service, which provides disaster relief and other aid. Brouwer, accusing some NCC leaders of "lust for retribution" and "character assassination," resigned in June. His action left the NCC fumbling to define its future and to attract new leaders.

Abortion battles. Protestants were visible in the controversy over abortion in 1989. On July 3, the Supreme Court of the United States upheld the constitutionality of a Missouri abortion law limiting the procedure, a move that encouraged conservative Protestants to press for more restrictive abortion laws.

One of the most controversial Protestant antiabortion groups during the year was Operation Rescue, a militant nondenominational group. Randall Terry, the group's national director, called on people to obstruct abortion clinics despite the risk of arrest. He and his followers were arrested in Atlanta, Ga., and other cities during demonstrations at clinics. Many antiabortion evangelicals criticized Terry's approach, saying that it was counterproductive.

While some Protestant churches in 1989 made bolder attempts to support a woman's right to abortion, most avoided taking a clear position on the issue during the year. The decision to remain neutral reflected the division among their members over the abortion issue.

Televangelist traumas. It was another difficult year for television evangelists. In September, a jury in Charlotte, N.C., convicted Jim Bakker on 24 counts of fraud and conspiracy. Bakker, leader of the evangelistic and entertainment organization called PTL (Praise the Lord or People That Love), was found to have misled his followers by selling products and programs he could not deliver. In October, a federal district judge sentenced him to 45 years in prison and fined him $500,000.

Bakker's trial, which began in August, was marked by high drama. The day after a witness collapsed while giving testimony, Bakker suffered a panic attack and had to undergo psychiatric testing.

In September, Pentecostal evangelist Oral Roberts announced that he was closing his City of Faith Hospital and Medical School in Tulsa, Okla., and selling some of his houses because of a $25-million debt. Evangelist Robert Schuller saw some financial setbacks in 1989, even though he had one of the largest television ministries in the United States.

On June 10, Baptist evangelist Jerry Falwell announced that he was folding his two conservative political organizations—the Moral Majority and the Liberty Federation—because they had achieved his purpose. Falwell created the Moral Majority in 1979 and the Liberty Federation in 1986 to influence lawmakers and to encourage religious conservatives to become politically active.   Martin E. Marty

See also **Eastern Orthodox Churches; Jews and Judaism; Religion; Roman Catholic Church.** In *World Book,* see **Protestantism.**

Psychology

Psychology. Scientists in 1989 shed new light on why men tend to have better mathematical skills while women seem to have better verbal skills. Despite evidence that some of these differences result from social and environmental causes, such as boys being encouraged more than girls to study math and science, new evidence suggests that other variations may be due to subtle differences in the brain structures of men and women.

At a meeting of the New York Academy of Sciences in New York City in March, two *neuropsychologists* (scientists who study the psychological functions of the nervous system) reported evidence of gender differences between male and female brains. Neuropsychologist Sandra F. Witelson of McMaster University in Hamilton, Canada, conducted post-mortem examinations of the brains of 15 men and 35 women who had undergone neuropsychological testing before they died. She found that an area of the *corpus callosum*, the bundle of nerve fibers that connects the brain's left and right hemispheres, is larger in women than in men. That area, called the *isthmus*, is located near the *splenium*, the rear part of the corpus callosum that previous research suggested may also be larger in women than men.

Because the isthmus and the splenium are located in an area of the corpus callosum that connects the parts of the brain that control speech, their enlargement in women could account for their greater verbal ability.

Neuropsychologist Melissa Hines of the University of California at Los Angeles presented evidence at the March meeting supporting this theory. She used *magnetic resonance imaging* (a technique in which magnetic energy and radio waves create images of internal parts of the body) to examine the brains of 29 women. The women who had the largest spleniums did best on tests of verbal ability.

Education and experience can erase whatever differences there may be in mental abilities, even if the brains of men and women are slightly different. This was reported at a January 1989 meeting in San Francisco of the American Association for the Advancement of Science by psychologists Marcia C. Linn of the University of California at Berkeley and Janet S. Hyde of the University of Wisconsin in Madison.

After evaluating hundreds of studies, Linn and Hyde concluded that the differences in verbal and mathematical abilities between men and women have declined almost to zero since 1974. Among the possible reasons they cited for this were changes in sex roles as well as in the educational experiences and expectations of both men and women. With more experience at writing, for example, men are enhancing their verbal abilities, while increased experience at math is helping women to improve in that area, Linn said.

Small-family advantage. Family size may influence the verbal abilities of children, according to sociologist Judith Blake of the University of California at

Bill Hoest, ©1989; reprinted courtesy Hoest and *Parade* magazine

"But what if you get me back to reality and I don't *like* it?"

Los Angeles. After reviewing verbal test results and family information on more than 100,000 children and adults, she reported in July that children born into large families tend to have poorer verbal skills and receive less education than do children from small families. One reason for this, she explained, is that children from small families likely spend more time talking to their parents than children from large families. Youngsters with many brothers and sisters spend more time conversing with them and must share their parents' time. By interacting more with their parents, children from small families tend to develop greater verbal abilities. Such abilities best predict future academic success.

Blake predicted that verbal abilities and educational achievement in children will continue to increase because the number of children being born to families in the United States is decreasing. For the first time in history, she noted, as many as 75 per cent of all children are being reared in families that have three or fewer children.

Depression and cancer. Researchers at the National Institute on Aging in Baltimore reported in September that depression does not seem to increase the risk of cancer. After studying more than 6,000 people for 10 years, the researchers found no higher incidence of cancer among people with symptoms of depression than among those without.   Robert J. Trotter

In *World Book,* see **Psychology.**

Public health. A major dietary study concluded on March 1, 1989, that people in the United States could substantially reduce their risk of heart disease, cancer, and many other chronic diseases by changing their eating habits. The study, conducted by the National Research Council, was the most comprehensive scientific analysis ever made of the potential health benefits associated with diet. The council is an agency of the National Academy of Sciences, an organization that advises the federal government on science and technology.

The study recommended that people eat five or more ½-cup (110-gram) servings of vegetables and fruits daily and six or more servings of bread, cereals, and *legumes* (vegetables in the pea family, such as kidney beans). Adults should eat a moderate amount of protein, at most about 6 ounces (170 grams) per day. The study also advised people to reduce their consumption of *cholesterol,* a fatty substance, and *saturated fat,* the fat found in animal products.

Fruit scare. Supermarkets in the United States began removing grapes and other fresh fruit from their shelves after the U.S. Food and Drug Administration (FDA) detected traces of cyanide in two grapes imported from Chile in March.

The FDA put a quarantine on imports of Chilean fruit on March 13, but lifted the ban on March 17 after extensive testing of Chilean fruit showed no further contamination. The FDA said all Chilean fruit was safe to eat, but it advised consumers to examine fresh fruit for discolorations and punctures.

Apples and Alar. A controversy over the safety of apples treated with a chemical called Alar arose early in 1989. Some apple growers in the United States had been using Alar to regulate the growth and ripening of the fruit. In February, a consumer group claimed that children eating apples treated with Alar faced an increased risk of cancer. But on March 16, the FDA, the U.S. Department of Agriculture, and the U.S. Environmental Protection Agency (EPA) reassured consumers that it was safe to eat apples. In response to public concern, however, Alar's manufacturer halted U.S. sales of the chemical in June.

Antidrinking campaign. Surgeon General of the United States C. Everett Koop on May 31 recommended a national campaign against drunken driving, which causes 25,000 deaths each year in the United States. The program called for a major increase in taxes on alcoholic beverages and voluntary controls on the advertising of beer, wine, and hard liquor. Koop also urged tougher laws that would make bars and restaurants legally responsible for traffic accidents caused by customers who drank too much. Koop, whose term as surgeon general ended on September 30, said the program could save up to 11,000 lives each year.

On November 1, President George Bush nominated Antonia C. Novello, a pediatrician with the National Institutes of Health in Bethesda, Md., to succeed Koop as surgeon general, the nation's chief public-health officer.

Measles precaution. In the face of growing outbreaks of measles in the United States, the American Academy of Pediatrics on July 17 recommended that all children receive an additional measles vaccination when they are about 12 years old. Health experts had recommended that children receive a single measles shot when they are about 15 months old. The academy said the extra vaccination is needed because a single vaccination has not wiped out the disease. As a result, there have been outbreaks of measles among older children and adults.

Physicians said children still should get their first vaccine for measles at 15 months of age. The second dose should be administered when a child is between the ages of 10 and 13.

In mid-December, the U.S. Centers for Disease Control in Atlanta, Ga., said that more cases of measles had been reported in 1989 than in any year since 1980. The total—14,714 cases—was more than five times higher than the 2,876 cases reported during the same period in 1988.

Asbestos ban. The EPA on July 6 said it would ban almost all products containing asbestos by 1996. Asbestos, a heat-resistant mineral once widely used as insulation, can cause cancer.   Michael Woods

See also **AIDS; Food; Health and disease; Medicine.** In *World Book,* see **Public health.**

Puerto Rico. In 1989, Puerto Ricans prepared for a possible plebiscite—a direct vote of the people—in 1991 to determine whether Puerto Rico will become the 51st state, an independent nation, or continue as a United States commonwealth but with more self-government. Under the current commonwealth status, Puerto Ricans have U.S. citizenship but they do not have to pay federal income taxes and cannot vote in presidential elections.

The adoption of commonwealth status in 1952 was credited with spurring the island's industrialization, partly because of special tax concessions for U.S. companies setting up operations there. But in the 1980's, the island's economy has stagnated. The per capita income in Puerto Rico in 1988 was $5,157, less than half that in the United States. Unemployment on the island in 1988 stood at 15 per cent, almost three times the U.S. level.

In mid-June 1989, some 80,000 Puerto Ricans expressed their feelings at a rally in favor of independence in the capital city of San Juan. In November, the Administration of President George Bush endorsed a bill in the U.S. Senate that would enable Puerto Ricans to vote in 1991 on the future status of their island. The bill was expected to reach the Senate floor early in 1990.   Nathan A. Haverstock

See also **Latin America** (Facts in brief table). In *World Book,* see **Puerto Rico.**

Pulitzer Prizes. See **Awards and prizes.**

Quayle, Dan (1947-   ), took the oath of office as the 44th Vice President of the United States on Jan. 20, 1989. During the year, he maintained a relatively low profile in Washington, D.C., perhaps because of 1988 campaign controversy over his qualifications for the post. But Quayle kept a busy schedule of overseas travel, much as President George Bush did when he was Vice President. In October, Bush said he would want Quayle as his running mate again in 1992.

After less than two weeks in office, Quayle flew to Caracas, Venezuela, on February 1 for the inauguration of that country's newly elected president, Carlos Andrés Pérez. Quayle also visited El Salvador in Central America. In June, he returned to Central America for a three-day tour of Guatemala, Honduras, Costa Rica, and El Salvador.

From April 24 to May 5, the Vice President and his wife, Marilyn, visited the South Pacific region and Asia, making stops in American Samoa, Australia, Indonesia, Singapore, and Thailand. Quayle returned to Asia in September, making a nine-day trip to Japan, the Philippines, and South Korea.

On October 18, the day after an earthquake hit California, Quayle toured the area by helicopter.

On April 12, the Quayles reported that they paid $24,314 in federal income taxes on a 1988 income of $156,546. They were penalized $254 for underwithholding.   Frank Cormier and Margot Cormier

In *World Book,* see **Quayle, Dan.**

Quebec. The Liberal government of Premier Robert Bourassa was reelected on Sept. 25, 1989, despite an uproar caused by massive strikes in the public sector and popular demonstrations against the dumping of toxic wastes. The Liberals won 92 seats in the 125-seat provincial legislature, called the National Assembly, taking almost 50 per cent of the popular vote. The election victory solidly confirmed Bourassa's hold on power, achieved when he ousted the secessionist Parti Québécois (PQ) government of René Lévesque in 1985.

The PQ campaigned under a new leader, Jacques Parizeau, who frankly emphasized independence for Quebec as the party's chief goal. By electing 29 members and gaining 40 per cent of the popular vote, the party showed itself still a strong movement in Quebec politics, with the ability to compel Bourassa to adopt a more nationalist stance in relations with the federal government.

A new party, the Equality Party, won four seats in English-speaking districts in Montreal. The appearance of the new party showed the strong dissatisfaction of English-speaking Quebeckers with the Bourassa government's new language law, which bans the use of any language but French on exterior commercial signs.

Widespread strikes during the campaign arose from Quebec's unique structure of labor-management relations, in which the three-year contracts of most public service employees are negotiated at the same time. The arrangement allows the unions to pool their strength in bargaining and lets the government carry out orderly economic planning.

On Sept. 5, 1989, 40,000 nurses began a weeklong strike, defying laws requiring them to maintain 90 per cent of their regular staffing levels during a walkout. Strikes by other health-care workers, teachers, and public servants followed; at the height of the labor unrest in mid-September, more than 225,000 public sector workers were on strike. The nurses agreed to a contract in time for the September 25 election, and public servants settled in November. Health-care workers and teachers continued negotiations through December, but all were back at work.

Environmental protests stemmed from an attempt to dispose of wastes contaminated by polychlorinated biphenyls (PCB's) left from a fire at St.-Basile-le-Grande in August 1988. The government arranged with a private disposal company to ship the contaminated material to Wales for destruction, but two freighters carrying the wastes were turned back at British ports in August 1989. One of the vessels returned to Canada and unloaded its cargo at Baie-Comeau, Que., on August 24, despite local protests and a temporary injunction issued by a Quebec court. The injunction was later lifted, and the second ship unloaded without disruption on August 30. The wastes were trucked to a nearby hydroelectric plant for temporary storage.   David M. L. Farr

See also **Montreal; Canada.** In *World Book,* see **Quebec.**

Rafsanjani, Ali Akbar Hashemi (1934?-   ), was elected president of Iran on July 28, 1989. He succeeded Ali Hoseini Khamenei, who became Iran's supreme spiritual leader following the death of Ayatollah Ruhollah Khomeini on June 3. Rafsanjani has the reputation of being a moderate who favors increased contact with Western countries. See **Iran.**

Rafsanjani was born in 1934 or 1935 in a village near Kerman in western Iran. In the late 1940's, he went to Qom, Iran's holiest city, to study theology and there became a follower of Khomeini. In the 1960's, he participated in a campaign organized by Iran's clergy against the government of Shah Mohammad Reza Pahlavi and was jailed several times. Rafsanjani continued his political activity in the 1970's while operating a small trucking company in Teheran, Iran's capital, and was jailed again.

After the fall of the shah in 1979, Rafsanjani was appointed by Khomeini to the Revolutionary Council, which governed Iran until 1980, when parliamentary elections were held. Elected to the Majlis (parliament), Rafsanjani was also chosen speaker. He was reelected to that post in 1984 and 1988. Khomeini also appointed him to several important government committees, and in 1988 named him acting commander in chief of Iran's armed forces.

Rafsanjani is married and has five children. His wife reportedly saved his life in 1979 by shielding him from an assassin's bullets.   Barbara A. Mayes

Railroad. The year 1989 started out as a busy one for railroads in the United States. But the amount of rail shipments dropped in the fall, reflecting a slowdown in the automobile and steel industries and an ongoing miners' strike against the Pittston Company.

Even so, railroads posted 745.2 billion ton miles for the first nine months of 1989, just slightly below the record 746.4 billion ton miles posted for the same months in 1988. (A ton mile is one ton of freight carried a distance of one mile.)

Accidents. Although the number of train accidents in the United States rose slightly for the first half of 1989, the number of injuries and deaths declined. In the first six months of 1989, 11 people were killed and 195 injured, according to the Association of American Railroads. For the same period in 1988, 15 people were killed and 365 injured. The statistics exclude accidents at railroad crossings.

Safety. Congress continued to show concern over rail-safety issues in 1989. On November 14, the House of Representatives Subcommittee on Transportation and Hazardous Materials approved legislation prohibiting rail cars and trucks used to carry hazardous materials and garbage from hauling food, drugs, cosmetics, and other items intended for human use.

On July 31, the House passed legislation requiring that railroad workers be tested for alcohol and drug use on a random basis as well as after train accidents, on reasonable suspicion, and before employment. But

A gas pipeline explosion near the Trans-Siberian Railroad in the Soviet Union on June 4 wrecked two trains and killed about 460 people.

Reagan, Ronald Wilson

the Senate's testing bill, which was also passed in 1989, included airline pilots and truckdrivers as well as railroad workers. Some senators said the House bill was not tough or comprehensive enough. The two chambers were unable to work out their differences, dooming both bills for 1989.

The U.S. Department of Transportation (DOT), meanwhile, issued new rules ordering transportation workers in several industries, including railroad, to undergo drug tests beginning in late 1989 and early 1990. The rules do not cover alcohol use. Advocates of drug testing legislation said the DOT's order does not replace the need for a drug testing law since the order can be repealed by a future DOT secretary.

Sale. On June 6, 1989, the CNW Corporation, a railroad holding company, agreed to be acquired by Blackstone Capital Partners Limited Partnership, an investor group. The sale price was $950 million.

Cutback. The Canadian government announced on October 4 that it would cut passenger service on Via Rail Canada by about 50 per cent. The action, which was to go into effect in January 1990, would leave some provinces with no passenger rail service.

New record. On Dec. 5, 1989, France's TGV, a high-speed passenger train, set a new world speed record. During a trip between the cities of Courtalain and Tours, the train averaged 299 miles (481 kilometers) per hour.   Laurie McGinley

In *World Book,* see **Railroad.**

Departing office, Reagan gives a farewell salute before joining his wife, Nancy, aboard the helicopter that will take them from the White House.

Reagan, Ronald Wilson (1911-   ), 40th President of the United States, turned over his office to President George Bush on Jan. 20, 1989. Immediately after Bush took the oath of office and gave his inaugural address, Reagan flew with his wife, Nancy, to California, where they took occupancy of their three-bedroom retirement home in Bel Air.

Antidrug campaign. Nancy Reagan continued her antidrug efforts in California, making headlines on April 6 when she joined Los Angeles police in a drug raid. Fourteen people were arrested on suspicion of selling drugs. Mrs. Reagan also sponsored a celebrity tennis tournament in October at Pacific Palisades, Calif., which raised $450,000 for the Nancy Reagan Foundation, an antidrug organization.

Honors abroad. Reagan was knighted by Queen Elizabeth II of Great Britain in London on June 14. The former President was the 58th American to receive an honorary knighthood. Reagan cannot use the title "Sir" because he is not a British subject, but the honor does allow him to sit closer to the queen at dinner parties. A day later, in Paris, he was installed as an associate member of the Institut de France (Institute of France), a group of five learned societies supported by the French government.

Brain surgery. While vacationing on a friend's ranch in Mexico, Reagan, 78, was thrown from a bucking horse on July 4 and was hospitalized briefly at an Army base near Tucson, Ariz. He was released after

treatment for cuts and bruises, and he provided an inning of commentary at major league baseball's televised All-Star Game a week later, on July 11. On September 8, Reagan underwent successful surgery at the Mayo Clinic in Rochester, Minn., to remove fluid that had accumulated on the right side of his brain as a result of the riding accident.

Reagan had undergone surgery earlier in 1989. Before leaving office, he had minor surgery on January 7 to correct a curvature of a finger on his left hand.

Hefty earnings. The Reagans' spokesman, Mark Weinberg, said on May 11 that—because of pensions, book earnings, and speaking fees—the couple had not applied for the social security benefits to which they were entitled. Both Reagans signed contracts, with hefty advances, to write their White House memoirs. Mrs. Reagan's book, *My Turn,* written with William Novak, appeared in October. On June 1, Mrs. Reagan was elected to a paid seat on the board of the Revlon group, a cosmetics firm.

In October, the Reagans also made a lucrative nine-day visit to Japan, which was financed by Fujisankei Communications Group, a television and newspaper conglomerate. The group paid Reagan about $2 million for two 20-minute speeches. Emperor Akihito presented Reagan with Japan's highest imperial honor, the Grand Cordon of the Supreme Order of the Chrysanthemum.   Frank Cormier and Margot Cormier

In *World Book,* see **Reagan, Ronald Wilson.**

Religion. A heated dispute arose in 1989 between some members of the Roman Catholic Church and the Jewish community over a convent located at the site of a Nazi concentration camp in Poland. The dispute cooled relations between the two religions. See **Jews and Judaism; Roman Catholic Church.**

More giving. In July 1989, the American Association of Fund-Raising Counsel said contributions to religious groups and other organizations is on the rise in the United States. According to the association, which represents firms that plan fund-raising campaigns for nonprofit institutions, Americans gave $104.3 billion in 1988, up 6.7 per cent from 1987.

The most popular recipients are religious groups. The association said that religious contributions reached $48.2 billion in 1988, an increase of 8.2 per cent. It noted, however, that religious groups donate nearly half of what they receive to outside hospitals, schools, and social services.

Religion and the law. A number of decisions made by U.S. courts in 1989 involved religious beliefs. One of the most publicized occurred on July 3 when the Supreme Court of the United States upheld Missouri's restrictive abortion law. The law forbids public employees to perform—or to assist in—abortions unless the mother's life is in danger. The state law also bars the use of public buildings for performing abortions and requires doctors, before doing abortions on women who have been pregnant for 20 weeks or longer, to conduct tests to see if the fetus could live outside the womb. (A separate law forbids doctors to abort a viable fetus.)

On March 29, the Supreme Court ruled that the Constitution of the United States protects the religious beliefs of not just organized religion but also of the individual. The case involved an Illinois man who refused to work on Sunday. He said his refusal was not dictated by his church, but because " . . . as a Christian, I feel it's wrong." The Supreme Court's decision overturned the ruling of an Illinois court, which said that to receive constitutional protection the man's refusal to work Sunday must be based on a "tenet or dogma of an established religious sect."

A jury in Sarasota, Fla., convicted a Christian Scientist couple of third-degree murder and child abuse in the 1986 death of their 7-year-old daughter. The couple had refused to seek medical care for their daughter, who had diabetes, because of their religious beliefs. (Christian Scientists believe in spiritual healing rather than conventional medical treatment.) It was the first time in 22 years that Christian Scientists in the United States had been held criminally responsible for the death of a child after relying on prayer as a treatment.

Religious persecution remained a reality around the world in 1989. In its report on religious freedom, the United Nations Human Rights Commission on February 6 said that violations of religious rights are still common in many countries.

U.S. membership reported for religious groups with 150,000 or more members*

African Methodist Episcopal Church	2,210,000
African Methodist Episcopal Zion Church	1,220,260
American Baptist Association	250,000
American Baptist Churches in the U.S.A.	1,549,563
Antiochian Orthodox Christian Archdiocese of North America	300,000
Armenian Church of America, Diocese of the	450,000
Assemblies of God	2,147,041
Baptist Bible Fellowship, International	1,405,900
Baptist Missionary Association of America	227,897
Christian and Missionary Alliance	259,612
Christian Church (Disciples of Christ)	1,073,119
Christian Churches and Churches of Christ	1,070,616
Christian Methodist Episcopal Church	718,992
Christian Reformed Church in North America	222,408
Church of God (Anderson, Ind.)	198,842
Church of God (Cleveland, Tenn.)	582,203
Church of God in Christ	3,709,661
Church of God in Christ, International	200,000
Church of Jesus Christ of Latter-day Saints	4,000,000
Church of the Brethren	151,169
Church of the Nazarene	552,264
Churches of Christ	1,626,000
Conservative Baptist Association of America	204,496
Episcopal Church	2,455,422
Evangelical Lutheran Church in America	5,251,534
Free Will Baptists	204,382
General Association of Regular Baptist Churches	260,000
Greek Orthodox Archdiocese of North and South America	1,950,000
International Church of the Foursquare Gospel	198,715
International Council of Community Churches	250,000
Jehovah's Witnesses	804,639
Jews	5,935,000
Liberty Baptist Fellowship	200,000
Lutheran Church—Missouri Synod	2,604,278
National Baptist Convention of America	2,668,799
National Baptist Convention, U.S.A., Inc.	5,500,000
National Primitive Baptist Convention	250,000
Orthodox Church in America	1,000,000
Polish National Catholic Church	282,411
Presbyterian Church in America	190,960
Presbyterian Church (U.S.A.)	2,929,608
Progressive National Baptist Convention, Inc.	521,692
Reformed Church in America	333,798
Reorganized Church of Jesus Christ of Latter Day Saints	190,950
Roman Catholic Church	54,918,949
Salvation Army	433,443
Seventh-day Adventist Church	687,200
Southern Baptist Convention	14,812,844
Unitarian Universalist Association	178,623
United Church of Christ	1,644,787
United Methodist Church	9,124,575
United Pentecostal Church, International	500,000
Wisconsin Evangelical Lutheran Synod	418,691

*A majority of the figures are for the years 1988 and 1989.
Source: National Council of the Churches of Christ in the U.S.A., *Yearbook of American and Canadian Churches* for 1990.

Workers pour water on Jews demonstrating in July against the presence of a Roman Catholic convent at the former Nazi death camp at Auschwitz, Poland.

The United Nations report noted that Iran continued to harass members of the Bahá'í faith (a religion founded in what is now Iraq) and that Iraq closed the mosques and schools of the Shiites (people who follow the Shiah divison of Islam). The report accused Romania of suppressing Roman Catholic worship among the country's minority population of Hungarian ancestry and said that in Albania, people who prayed or kept religious symbols in their home were being imprisoned.

The United Nations report did cite countries where religious freedom improved. These included the Soviet Union and Czechoslovakia, where Pope John Paul II was permitted to appoint new bishops, and Mozambique, which granted religious liberty to its citizens.

Other news. On October 5, the Dalai Lama, the exiled religious and political leader of Tibet, received the 1989 Nobel Peace Prize. It recognized his nonviolent campaign to end China's control over Tibet.

During the year, the National Council of Churches of Christ U.S.A. completed its update of the Revised Standard Version of the Bible, to be called the New Revised Standard Version. The new version, to be released in early 1990, eliminates the use of masculine words to describe people of both sexes.   Owen F. Campion

See also **Eastern Orthodox Churches; Jews and Judaism; Protestantism; Roman Catholic Church.** In *World Book,* see **Religion.**

Republican Party. Lee Atwater, campaign manager for President George Bush's successful 1988 presidential race, was elected chairman of the Republican National Committee (RNC) on Jan. 18, 1989. He succeeded Frank J. Fahrenkopf, Jr.

As if to belie his reputation as a harsh, aggressive campaigner, Atwater, 37, gave a low-key acceptance speech in which he declared that reviving black support for the Republican Party (GOP) was "a moral imperative" as well as "a political necessity." Promising redoubled efforts to reach out to black, Hispanic, Asian, and disabled Americans, he said, "Our party, like an old and towering tree, cannot flourish if its leaves are green but its roots are weak."

The Democratic Party had won the allegiance of most blacks during the Administration of President Franklin D. Roosevelt and solidified this support with its strong support of civil rights legislation under President Lyndon B. Johnson. The Republican Party in 1964 nominated Senator Barry Goldwater of Arizona, an opponent of the landmark Civil Rights Act of 1964, as its nominee to oppose Johnson. Since then, blacks have supported Democratic candidates by margins often exceeding 10 to 1.

Atwater later said his goal, shared with Bush, was to win 20 per cent of the black vote in the 1992 presidential election and 40 per cent of the Hispanic vote. In 1988, Bush gained about 10 per cent of black votes and 30 per cent of Hispanic votes.

Of the 165 elected members of the RNC, not one was black. The Democratic National Committee had 81 blacks among its 403 members and in February 1989 elected a black, Ronald H. Brown, as its chairman.

Howard University protest. In January, Atwater was elected to the board of trustees of Howard University, a federally supported, predominantly black university in Washington, D.C. Howard University President James E. Cheek, who has close ties to Republican leaders, invited Atwater to join the board. On March 3, a convocation marking Howard's 122nd anniversary was disrupted when hundreds of students occupied the stage to protest Atwater's election. The students said they were angered at what they considered racist undertones in Bush's presidential campaign and blamed Atwater. About 2,000 students later in the day staged a sit-in at Howard's administration building.

On March 7, more than 100 District of Columbia police officers, some in full riot gear, moved toward the administration building with the objective of arresting hundreds of students who remained barricaded there. They withdrew after Washington, D.C., Mayor Marion S. Barry, Jr., arrived to negotiate with the protesters. Atwater himself defused the situation by resigning his trusteeship that same day.

Flap over Foley memo. Atwater became a central figure in another controversy in June after Democrat Thomas S. Foley of Washington state was elected Speaker of the House of Representatives. At issue was an RNC memorandum to party leaders headed, "Tom

President George Bush and Republican National Committee Chairman Lee
Atwater, with guitars, clown it up at a Washington, D.C., concert in January.

Foley: Out of the Liberal Closet.'' The memo compared Foley's voting record to that of Representative
Barney Frank (D., Mass.), an admitted homosexual.
The phrase, ''out of the closet,'' has come to refer to a
public avowal of homosexuality. The memo was
widely viewed as an innuendo about the personal life
of Foley, who has many friends among congressional
Republicans as well as Democrats.

On June 6, Atwater refused to disavow the memo,
defending it as ''factually accurate.'' Declaring it was
''no big deal,'' he said any effort by the news media to
suggest it was a smear would be ''irresponsible.'' But
the GOP chairman phoned Foley to apologize later in
the day, having been told by fellow Republicans that
the memo had been a serious mistake. Republican
Senate leader Robert J. Dole of Kansas praised Foley in
a Senate speech and said of the memo: ''This is not
politics. This is garbage. And we are disgusted by it.''
Democratic Chairman Brown called on Bush to remove
Atwater and to ''stop this madness by telling operatives to stop peddling rumors, stop spreading dirt, and
put away the negative campaign playbook.''

On June 7, Bush told Atwater the memo was ''dis-
gusting'' and that such tactics should not be repeated.
Atwater reported, ''I told him it wouldn't happen
again and that I would tighten up on what goes out
of the committee.'' Foley had lunch with Bush and
said, ''I think the issue is closed; it's closed.'' Earlier he
had termed the innuendo ''totally false.''

The RNC communications director, Mark Goodin,
accepted responsibility for the memo and resigned on
June 7. Atwater said Goodin ''made a serious mistake
in judgment'' and ''paid the price by resigning.'' The
GOP chairman insisted, ''I did not know about it [the
memo] beforehand and, had I known, I would not
have put it out.''

White House Press Secretary Marlin Fitzwater reported Bush retained ''full confidence'' in Atwater
and said, ''He has been with the President a long time
and has proven his value.''

On June 16, the RNC gave Atwater a formal vote of
confidence. Said Arizona national committeeman Jack
Londen: ''Why do you think the Democrats want to
get rid of him? Because he has the courage . . . to do
what all of us need to do.''

Excessive campaign contributions. On January
31, the Federal Election Commission levied a $20,000
civil penalty against the National Republican Senato-
rial Committee for making $545,249 in excessive con-
tributions to 12 Republican Senate candidates during
the 1986 campaign. Common Cause, a self-described
citizens' lobby, had contended the committee used an
illegal technique to skirt legal limits on the amount of
financial assistance a political party may provide for its
candidates.   Frank Cormier and Margot Cormier

See also **Democratic Party.** In *World Book,* see **Republican Party.**

Rhode Island. See **State government.**

Roman Catholic Church

Roman Catholic Church. A convent of Carmelite nuns was the focus of an intense dispute between Roman Catholics and Jews in 1989. The convent was located in a building that overlooks the Nazi concentration camp in Auschwitz (Oświęcim) in Poland. During World War II (1939-1945), the Nazis killed millions of people at Auschwitz, most of them Jews.

The dispute began soon after the convent was established in 1984. Some Jewish groups complained that it was inappropriate to locate a Roman Catholic convent in a place where so many Jews were killed. So, in 1987, four European Catholic cardinals, including Franciszek Cardinal Macharski of Kraków, Poland, agreed to move the convent to an interfaith prayer center that would be built away from the camp by February 1989.

The building, however, was never built. After the February deadline passed, Jewish groups held a number of demonstrations in front of the convent. In one incident on July 14, Polish workers assaulted seven Jews who climbed over the convent's fence.

On August 10, Cardinal Macharski called the protests "aggressive" and said that the church would not honor the 1987 agreement. His position was supported by Jozef Cardinal Glemp, Poland's Roman Catholic primate and archbishop of Warsaw, who insisted that the 1987 accord be revoked. Glemp's comments angered many people, who viewed them as harsh and anti-Semitic. In the United States, John Cardinal O'Connor of New York City disassociated himself from Cardinal Glemp's statement. He joined Archbishop Roger P. Mahony of Los Angeles and three other U.S. cardinals in an appeal to the nuns to move.

On September 19, the Vatican released a statement encouraging the nuns to move to another site and pledging financial help in building a new convent. According to Johannes Cardinal Willebrands, head of the Vatican's Commission for Religious Relations with Judaism, the pope approved the statement and also endorsed the idea of an interfaith center near Auschwitz. Jewish leaders applauded the Vatican's statement, and the World Jewish Council said it would urge its members to resume contact with the Vatican.

Church split. The first *schism* (split) in the Roman Catholic Church in the United States in 85 years occurred in 1989. On June 21, George A. Stallings, a black pastor of a church in Washington, D.C., announced plans to establish a separate African-American Catholic Church.

In meetings with James Cardinal Hickey, archbishop of Washington, D.C., Stallings said the Roman Catholic Church in the United States was unresponsive to the cultural, social, and spiritual needs of blacks. Hickey advised Stallings that if he went ahead with his plan he would face disciplinary action. He also warned black Catholics that the new church would not be a Roman Catholic parish.

Despite the warning, Stallings established the new church—the African-American Catholic Congregation, or Imani Temple—on July 2. He celebrated the church's first Mass before more than 2,000 people at a high school in Maryland on July 4. Hickey immediately suspended Stallings from his duties as priest, and forbade him from offering Mass. Stallings ignored the order and continued to celebrate Mass.

Several black Catholic bishops in the United States expressed concern at Stallings' suspension, but they supported Hickey's action. On July 12, the bishops appealed for an end to the dispute.

Gains in Poland. Almost 40 years of religious suppression in Poland ended on May 1 when the country's Sejm (parliament) legally recognized the Roman Catholic Church. The action established freedom of worship, restored church property seized by the government, and recognized the church's right to build churches, teach religion, and operate schools. It also granted the church the right to broadcast religious programs, and publish books and periodicals.

In a joint announcement on July 17, the Vatican and the Polish government said they had reestablished diplomatic relations for the first time since 1939.

Soviet relations. Tensions continued to ease between the Vatican and the Soviet Union in 1989. On December 1, Soviet leader Mikhail S. Gorbachev visited Pope John Paul II at the Vatican. Their meeting was the first in history between a pope and a general secretary of the Soviet Communist Party.

During the meeting, Gorbachev pledged to reestablish diplomatic ties with the Vatican, which were broken off in 1917 during the Russian Revolution. He also vowed to establish greater freedom of religion in the Soviet Union. Appealing for an end to religious persecution under Communism, the pope made a special plea for the Ukrainian Catholic Church. The church was suppressed in 1914 because of its support for Ukrainian nationalism, and in 1946 it was forced to merge with the Russian Orthodox Church. On the day that the pope and Gorbachev met, the Ukrainian government announced that it had restored legal status to the Ukrainian church.

On July 25, Pope John Paul II had named Tadeusz Kondrusiewicz the Catholic bishop of Minsk in the Soviet republic of Byelorussia. Kondrusiewicz became the first bishop in Byelorussia in more than 60 years. Following his appointment, the Vatican issued a statement that hailed the "new spirit" guiding the Soviet government's policy on the church.

The Communist governments of other countries loosened restrictions on Catholics in 1989. The government of Czechoslovakia, which rigidly restricted church activities, permitted the pope to appoint three bishops in July. In Hungary, on March 31, the government revealed plans to reopen the trial of Joseph Cardinal Mindszenty, who was convicted of treason in 1949 and died in exile in 1975.

Pope criticized. On January 25, 163 European Catholic theologians meeting in Cologne, West Germany, issued a statement strongly criticizing what

Pope John Paul II and bishops from the United States meet in Rome in March to help ease tensions between U.S. Catholics and the Vatican.

they called Pope John Paul II's authoritarian style of leadership and his conservative interpretation of church teachings. In particular, the theologians complained about the pope's decision to overrule local opinion in the naming of bishops, his firm support of the church's stance against artificial birth control, and his silencing of theologians who disagree with the church's conservative teachings. In a related essay, German theologian Bernard Haring asked the pope to reopen discussion about birth control and called upon bishops, theologians, and *laity* (people who are not members of the clergy) to study the question.

Church in the United States. The District of Columbia Supreme Court on February 28 ruled that the Catholic University of America in Washington, D.C., acted within its rights when it removed priest and theologian Charles E. Curran from its faculty in 1987. The university took the action following a 1986 Vatican decision to ban Curran from teaching in any Catholic college or university because his position on moral issues went against traditional Catholic teachings. Curran had filed suit in 1987 claiming that the university had denied him his rights as a tenured professor.

From March 8 to 11, 1989, 35 U.S. bishops met with Pope John Paul II and high Vatican officials to discuss the differences between the Vatican's orthodox interpretations of the church's teachings and the more liberal interpretation favored by many American Catholics. Of the meetings, the pope said on March 22, "Our

task as pastors is to speak always the truth of Jesus Christ entrusted to the Church—the truth which gives life and which alone can set us free."

Abortion. Catholic groups that oppose abortion applauded the U.S. Supreme Court on July 3 for upholding the constitutionality of a Missouri law that restricts abortions except in certain cases. Catholic antiabortionists vowed to work for similar legislation in other states and to encourage the Supreme Court to reverse its 1973 decision in the case of *Roe v. Wade*. That decision prevents states from banning abortions during the first three months of pregnancy.

Racism condemned. On Feb. 10, 1989, the Vatican's Pontifical Council for Justice and Peace issued a major document against racism. The document, which had the approval of Pope John Paul II, asserted that the belief that "God is at the origin of humankind" establishes "the most radical affirmation of the equal dignity of all persons." Affronting that dignity in today's world, the document said, are institutionalized racism, such as *apartheid* (racial segregation), and anti-Semitism.

Pope goes north. Pope John Paul II on June 1 began a 10-day visit to the predominantly Protestant nations of Norway, Iceland, Finland, Denmark, and Sweden. It was the first time a pope had visited Scandinavia.   Owen F. Campion

See also **Jews and Judaism; Protestantism; Religion.** In *World Book,* see **Roman Catholic Church.**

Romania

Romania was torn in December 1989 by a revolution that toppled the hard-line Communist regime of President Nicolae Ceauşescu and left thousands of Romanians dead—including Ceauşescu himself. Since 1965, Ceauşescu had ruled Romania as a dictator, operating through a small group of powerful officials personally loyal to him. His wife, Elena, served as his second-in-command. The Securitate, Romania's security police, functioned as Ceauşescu's private militia.

Poverty and persecution. The ruling group lived in luxury while many ordinary citizens suffered from malnutrition and poverty because of harsh economic policies. Furthermore, the government persecuted dissidents—in 1989, particularly writers and former high officials of the Communist Party. And the regime continued a forced resettlement program that it had launched in 1988. The plan called for the demolition of about 6,500 villages—many of them populated by people of Hungarian ancestry. Residents were to be relocated to 548 new, agricultural-industrial centers.

Demonstrations. Beginning in mid-1989, a wave of reform toppled Eastern European regimes that were much less repressive than Ceauşescu's. Nevertheless, Ceauşescu seemed to be firmly at the helm as late as November 24, when he was elected to another five-year term as Communist Party chief.

The event that brought the revolution to Romania was a decision in mid-December 1989 to deport Laszlo Toekes, a Hungarian-born dissident Protestant minister in Timişoara, a city in the western part of the country. By December 17, thousands of people had gathered in Timişoara to protect him. Riots broke out and, on that day and the next, dozens—some estimates said hundreds or thousands—of demonstrators were killed by the Securitate. Protests spread to other major cities, including Bucharest, the capital.

Downfall. By this time, it was apparent that Ceauşescu could no longer govern. Army units joined demonstrators and dissident Communists to form a National Salvation Front, which removed Ceauşescu from office on December 22. Army troops battled the Securitate, and thousands were killed. After a secret trial, a firing squad executed Nicolae and Elena Cesuşescu on December 25. With them dead, members of the Securitate began to lay down their arms.

On December 26, the National Salvation Front named Ion Iliescu president. Iliescu had once been a high official in the Communist Party, but Ceauşescu had demoted him for advocating reform.

The new government halted the forced resettlement program, ended food rationing, and repealed several repressive laws. It also promised to hold free elections in April 1990.   Eric Bourne

See also **Europe** (Facts in brief table). In *World Book,* see **Romania**.

Rowing. See Sports.

Russia. See **Union of Soviet Socialist Republics.**

Rwanda. See **Africa.**

Romanian soldiers display a flag from which a Communist emblem has been cut, symbolizing the toppling of President Nicolae Ceauşescu in December.

Safety in the air was a major concern during 1989. The concern centered on potential defects in aircraft parts and the possibility of structural failure due to metal fatigue in aging airliners.

A defective part may have caused the crash of a United Airlines DC-10 on July 19, 1989. The plane, en route from Denver to Chicago, crashed while attempting an emergency landing at Sioux City, Iowa. Of the 296 persons aboard, 112 were killed and 184 survived.

The problem began when the jet's tail-mounted engine exploded at 37,000 feet (11,300 meters). Blades from the engine severed the jet's hydraulic lines that operate movable parts of the tail and wings, which are essential to controlling the plane during flight. By alternately accelerating and slowing the two wing-mounted engines, the pilot and the cockpit crew managed to maneuver the plane on a twisting, 42-minute descent to the airport at Sioux City. Just as the plane was touching down, however, a wing tip dipped and caught on the ground. The plane cartwheeled, its fuselage broke apart, and its 5,200 gallons (19,700 liters) of jet fuel burst into flames.

Almost three months later, on October 10, a woman harvesting corn on her farm near Alta, Iowa, discovered a fan assembly from the engine, which investigators had considered crucial to their analysis of what had caused the mishap. Subsequent analysis showed a crack on a fan disk that spins 38 blades in the engine. Aviation experts theorized that this contributed to the events that resulted in the crash.

Structural failure. Nine people were swept to their deaths through a hole measuring 11 by 20 feet (3.4 by 6 meters) that tore open in the fuselage of a United Airlines 747 jumbo jet flying from Honolulu to New Zealand on February 24. The plane returned to Honolulu International Airport and landed safely. About 33 of the 345 survivors were injured. Investigators found that the forward cargo door also had been ripped away. They then concentrated on looking for signs of metal fatigue in the 18-year-old plane.

Neither mechanical nor structural failure appeared to be involved in the crash of a USAir Boeing 737 at New York's La Guardia Airport on September 20. The plane, bound for Charlotte, N.C., had been rolling down the runway when the pilot decided to abort the take-off. The plane skidded off the runway and broke up across an East River pier. Many of the 61 survivors were rescued from the water; 2 of the 63 persons aboard the plane died.

New bomb detector. The U.S. Federal Aviation Adminstration (FAA) in September ruled that U.S. airlines must install a new type of bomb detector at more than 40 of the busiest airports in the United States and abroad. These machines, called Thermal Neutron Analysis (TNA) devices, can detect all types of bombs, including plastic explosives, in checked luggage. The devices use neutron radiation to detect the presence of nitrogen, an element found in all types of explosives. The first TNA device was installed in Au-

	1987-1988*		1988-1989*	
	Number	Rate†	Number	Rate†
Motor vehicle	49,020	20.0	48,410	19.6
Public	17,300	7.1	17,900	7.2
Home	21,300	8.7	23,900	9.7
Work	10,900	4.5	10,700	4.3
Total‡	**94,100**	**38.4**	**96,700**	**39.1**

Accidental deaths in the United States

*For 12-month period ending June 30.

†Deaths per 100,000 U.S. population.

‡The total does not equal the sum of the four classes because *Motor vehicle* includes some deaths listed under *Work* and *Home.*

Source: National Safety Council estimates.

gust at New York City's John F. Kennedy International Airport.

Critics of the FAA ruling questioned whether TNA is sensitive enough to detect small quantities of plastic explosives hidden in luggage. They also objected to the size and cost of the machines, which are about as large as a small car and cost $750,000.

The need for new security measures was demonstrated by the December 1988 sabotage of a Pan American World Airways jet, which exploded over Lockerbie, Scotland, killing 270 people in the air and on the ground. British investigators concluded that plastic explosives hidden inside a radio-cassette player in a forward luggage compartment blew up the London-to-New York City Pan Am Flight 103.

The FAA concluded, in a report issued on Sept. 20, 1989, that Pan Am failed to follow proper security screening procedures for some passengers who boarded at London's Heathrow Airport and at Frankfurt, West Germany. The FAA proposed a fine of $630,000 against Pan Am, the largest ever sought for airport security violations.

Motor-vehicle accidents in 1988 caused 46,730 deaths, according to a report released by the National Transportation Safety Board (NTSB) on May 19, 1989. This was the highest toll since 1981, when 49,301 people died. Experts blamed drugs, alcohol, and higher speed limits for the increase in deaths.

A report released on Oct. 23, 1989, by the National

Highway Traffic Safety Administration (NHTSA) said that the two-year-old federal policy of allowing states to raise the speed limit to 65 miles per hour (mph)—105 kilometers per hour (kph)—on rural interstate highways had resulted in a 21 per cent increase in traffic deaths on those roads between 1986 and 1988. No rise was seen in states that kept the 55 mph (89 kph) speed limit for all roads.

As of Sept. 1, 1989, the NHTSA required that all new cars sold in the United States be equipped with a front-seat airbag or automatic safety belts. Because about 22,000 people are killed each year in the front seats of passenger cars and 300,000 suffer serious injury, the new rule is expected to save lives and reduce injuries.

Approximately 4.9 million cars equipped with automatic belts were produced in 1989. Automatic safety belts cost as little as $45. A driver-side-only airbag costs about $270, and the NHTSA expects up to 1 million cars to have airbags by 1993.

Nuclear-weapons plant safety. In June 1989, the U.S. Department of Energy announced a "fundamental change of priorities" at the nation's 17 nuclear-weapons plants, in which serious safety problems were uncovered during 1988. Secretary of Energy James D. Watkins said that a "culture of mismanagement and ineptitude" would have to be overcome in his department before those plants could be brought into compliance with safety, environmental, and public health laws. On Aug. 1, 1989, he announced a compliance plan that would cost $17.2 billion over the next five years. On December 1, Watkins said that plutonium operations would be halted indefinitely at the Rocky Flats nuclear weapons plant near Boulder, Colo., until safety concerns were resolved.

Food safety. The use of Alar, a chemical that helps maintain color and freshness in apples, caused a furor during the year after the public learned that Alar breaks down into a chemical suspected of causing cancer. The extensive publicity surrounding the issue led the apple industry to announce on May 14 that U.S. growers would voluntarily stop using Alar. See **Environmental pollution.**

In March, the U.S. government received anonymous warnings that shipments of Chilean fruit had been poisoned. Government inspectors checked more than 1 million cases of fruit from Chile but found traces of poisonous cyanide in only two grapes. See **Chile; Food.**

Occupational safety. On March 1, new exposure limits for nearly 400 hazardous materials, set by the Occupational Safety and Health Administration of the Department of Labor, took effect. This represented the first overhaul of the exposure standards since passage of the Occupational Safety and Health Act 17 years earlier.   Odom Fanning

See also **Aviation; Consumerism; Farm and farming.** In *World Book,* see **Safety.**

Sailing. See **Boating.**

Saskatchewan. Premier Grant Devine's Progressive Conservative (PC) government announced early in 1989 that it planned to turn three province-owned corporations into private companies. Bitter debate met the announcement that the government would sell a potash mining company, a natural gas utility, and an insurance company. On April 21, the New Democratic Party began a 17-day walkout from the legislature to protest the privatization measures. The lawmakers resumed business after the PC's agreed to hold public hearings before calling a vote.

A bill transferring the Potash Corporation—the Western world's largest producer of potash, used to make fertilizer—to private ownership was passed on August 14, after the government cut off debate. The corporation, with assets of $1.2 billion Canadian (about $1 billion U.S.), would be sold to the public as market conditions permitted. The other privatization plans were put on hold.

The $125-million ($105-million U.S.) Rafferty-Alameda dams project on the Souris River in south Saskatchewan, halted by a federal court order in April, was allowed to proceed on August 31 after an environmental review. The federal government attached 22 strict conditions to the new license. Saskatchewan, the builder of the two dams, must replace lost habitats for waterfowl and fish and meet international water quality standards.   David M. L. Farr

See also **Canada.** In *World Book,* see **Saskatchewan.**

Saudi Arabia in 1989 took the lead in granting diplomatic recognition to an independent Palestinian state proclaimed in 1988 by the Palestine Liberation Organization (PLO). According to the PLO, the state would include the Israeli-occupied West Bank and Gaza Strip and the Arab sector of Jerusalem. In January, the Saudi government allowed the PLO to open an Embassy of Palestine in Riyadh, the Saudi capital. The government of King and Prime Minister Fahd bin Abd al-Aziz Al-Saud was also first to recognize the Provisional Government of Afghanistan. This body was formed by the leaders of the seven main Afghan guerrilla groups after the withdrawal of Soviet forces from that country in February 1989. It would take power if the Afghan government collapsed.

Relations with Iran remained hostile. In 1989, for the second year, Iran rejected the Saudi quota limiting the number of Iranian pilgrims permitted to attend the annual *hajj* (pilgrimage) to Mecca, Islam's holiest city. Iran refused to send any pilgrims. The Saudis had established the quota in 1988 after failing to obtain assurances from Iran that Iranian pilgrims would not hold political demonstrations. More than 400 people died in clashes between Iranian pilgrims and Saudi police in Mecca in 1987.

In September 1989, Saudi Arabia executed 16 citizens of Kuwait for acts of terrorism, including two bombings in Mecca during the hajj in July. The Saudi government said Iranian diplomats in Kuwait had pro-

Saudi Arabia's King Fahd, at right, reviews an honor guard with Egypt's President Hosni Mubarak at a March meeting in Egypt.

Sauvé, Jeanne Mathilde (1922-   ), who as governor general of Canada represents head of state Queen Elizabeth II, spent 1989—her final year in the post—undertaking an extensive round of official duties. The governor general led the Canadian delegation to the funeral of Emperor Hirohito of Japan on February 24 and also paid state visits to Brazil and Uruguay.

She entertained such foreign visitors as President Chaim Herzog of Israel, King Hussein I of Jordan, and Prime Minister Toshiki Kaifu of Japan. British royal visitors to Canada included Elizabeth the Queen Mother and Prince Andrew and Sarah, the Duke and Duchess of York.

Sauvé traveled throughout Canada in 1989 to officiate at ceremonies and commemorative occasions. A highlight was the opening on June 29 of the Canadian Museum of Civilization, located in Hull, across the Ottawa River from the national capital, Ottawa. Designed by Douglas Cardinal, an Alberta architect, the museum is Canada's largest, at 39,000 square meters (420,000 square feet).

Sauvé's five-year term as governor general ends in January 1990. On Oct. 6, 1989, Prime Minister Brian Mulroney nominated as Sauvé's successor Ramon J. Hnatyshyn, former minister of justice and leader of the House of Commons.   David M. L. Farr

In *World Book,* see **Sauvé, Jeanne Mathilde.**

School. See **Education.**

vided the explosives and trained the terrorists, who were of Saudi or Iranian origin, in their use.

The economy. Increased oil reserves and higher prices for Saudi oil exports spurred an upturn in the country's economic position. In January, the Arabian American Oil Company reported that Saudi Arabia had about 252 billion barrels of recoverable crude oil reserves, 50 per cent more than previously believed. Those reserves represent 25 per cent of all known reserves and the highest share for any country. The 1989 budget, approved by the Council of Ministers in January, cut expenditures in order to reduce the deficit from $9 billion in 1988 to $6.7 billion.

Saudi agriculture continued its remarkable success story, aided by large-scale government financing, subsidies to farmers, and sophisticated technology. The wheat harvest set a new record of 3.3 million short tons (3 million metric tons). In 1989, Saudi Arabia became self-sufficient in barley, vegetables, eggs, poultry, and dairy products.

But this agricultural windfall carried environmental risks, especially to water resources. Depletion of ground water in some areas reached critical levels in summer. A new desalination plant, opened at Shwaiba on the Red Sea, eased the strain on freshwater resources by supplying 40 million gallons (150 million liters) per day to the Mecca area.   William Spencer

See also **Middle East** (Facts in brief table). In *World Book,* see **Saudi Arabia.**

Senegal. A minor incident on April 9, 1989, between Senegalese farmers and Mauritanian herders in a disputed border area escalated into widespread violence and destruction throughout the two countries. Over a five-month period, more than 400 people were killed and several thousand were injured.

In the wake of the violence, the two nations expelled tens of thousands of each other's citizens. Many of the people forced out of Mauritania, however, were reportedly black Mauritanians, who have long been discriminated against by the lighter-skinned Arabs who govern the country. Efforts by President Moussa Traoré of Mali and the Organization of African Unity to mediate the conflict failed, and diplomatic links were broken in mid-August.

Senegal's relations with Guinea-Bissau, its neighbor to the south, also deteriorated during the year. The bad feelings arose in August, when Guinea-Bissau refused to accept the decision of an international arbitration commission to award Senegal possession of a mineral-rich area on their mutual border.

To reverse an economic decline, the government in March relaxed rules regulating private investment in Senegal.   J. Gus Liebenow and Beverly B. Liebenow

See also **Africa** (Facts in brief table). In *World Book,* see **Senegal.**

Sierra Leone. See **Africa.**

Singapore. See **Asia.**

Skating. See **Hockey; Ice skating; Sports.**

Skiing

Skiing. Vreni Schneider of Switzerland and Austrian-born Marc Girardelli of Luxembourg won world championships and the World Cup overall titles during the 1988-1989 Alpine skiing season. Tamara McKinney of Olympic Valley, Calif., won a gold and a bronze medal in the world championships.

World. The Swiss, as expected, dominated the biennial championships held from Jan. 29 to Feb. 12, 1989, in Vail, Colo. Of the 30 medals, Switzerland won 11.

Rudolf Nierlich, a 22-year-old Austrian carpenter, was the only double winner, taking the men's slalom and giant slalom. The other men's champions were Martin Hangl of Switzerland in the supergiant slalom, Hansjörg Tauscher of West Germany in downhill, and Girardelli in the combined.

The best women's competition came in the slalom, where Mateja Svet of Yugoslavia finished first, Schneider second, and McKinney third. Schneider won the women's giant slalom, Ulrike Maier of Austria the supergiant slalom, Maria Walliser of Switzerland the downhill, and McKinney the combined, which incorporated a special slalom and a special downhill. McKinney had missed most of the previous season because of a broken ankle, and in October 1989 she broke her left leg and missed the 1989-1990 season.

McKinney was the only American medalist in the world championships. The best finish by an American man was ninth in the giant slalom by Kyle Wieche of Farmington, Conn.

World Cup. The World Cup series ran from November 1988 to March 1989 in Europe, the United States, Canada, and Japan. Swiss men and women won 31 of the 59 races, and the three women's overall leaders —Schneider, Walliser, and Michela Figini—were from Switzerland.

Schneider won 14 events—7 slalom, 6 giant slalom, and 1 combined. She broke the one-season record of 13 victories set by Ingemar Stenmark of Sweden in 1979. When the season ended, Stenmark, almost 33 years old, retired with a record 86 victories in 270 races in 16 seasons. He had almost three times as many victories as Girardelli, his nearest rival.

Other. Gunde Svan of Sweden won three gold medals in the world Nordic championships and his fifth World Cup overall title in six years. Marjo Matikänen of Finland took medals in all five women's cross-country races in the world championships.

In freestyle ballet competition, Jan Bucher of Salt Lake City, Utah, won the world championship and her eighth World Cup title in 11 years. Nelson Carmichael of Steamboat Springs, Colo., gained his second consecutive World Cup mogul title.

Phil and Steve Mahre of Yakima, Wash., ended a five-year retirement and joined the U.S. professional tour. Phil finished second to Jorgen Sundqvist of Sweden in the world overall championships, then won the World Cup overall title.   Frank Litsky

In *World Book*, see **Skiing.**

Vreni Schneider of Switzerland leans into a gate during the World Alpine Championships in February in Vail, Colo., on her way to the World Cup title.

Skinner, Samuel Knox (1938-   ), was sworn in as United States secretary of transportation on Feb. 1, 1989. Skinner had been chairman of the Regional Transportation Authority (RTA) of Northeastern Illinois, one of the largest mass transportation systems in the United States.

Skinner was born in Chicago on June 10, 1938. In 1960, he graduated with a degree in accounting from the University of Illinois in Urbana-Champaign. He received a law degree in 1966 from DePaul University College of Law in Chicago.

From 1961 to 1968, Skinner worked in various positions at International Business Machines Corporation (IBM). He was named assistant U.S. attorney for the northern district of Illinois in 1968. He became U.S. attorney in 1975.

While U.S. attorney, Skinner was a member of the Department of Justice's White-Collar Crime Committee. He left the post of U.S. attorney in 1977 and joined the Chicago law firm of Sidley & Austin as a senior partner. In 1983, he was appointed to the President's Commission on Organized Crime.

Skinner was named RTA chairman in 1984. He encouraged the use of mass transit by establishing new bus links between Chicago and its suburbs and by building park-and-ride lots along train lines.

Skinner married Mary Margaret Jacobs in August 1989. He has three children from a marriage that ended in divorce earlier in the year.   Mary A. Krier

Soccer. The United States national team qualified in 1989 for the 1990 World Cup, the first time since 1950 that the United States had won a place in this prestigious championship. The accomplishment was especially important because the United States will host the competition, held every four years, in 1994. Had the United States failed to qualify, its team would not have played in a major competition until the 1992 Summer Olympics and U.S. interest in the 1994 World Cup probably would have been dampened.

World Cup. In 1988, in the qualifying round from the North America, Central America, and Caribbean region, the United States received a first-round bye and eliminated Jamaica in the second round. That sent the United States into a 1989 double-round-robin series with Costa Rica, Trinidad and Tobago, Guatemala, and El Salvador. Two of those five teams would qualify for the 1990 World Cup in Italy.

The final World Cup berth from the region was decided on Nov. 19, 1989, in Port-of-Spain, Trinidad. The United States had to defeat Trinidad and Tobago to qualify, and it won, 1-0, on a goal by Paul Caliguiri. Because of injuries, Caliguiri had played a total of only 75 minutes in the 7 previous qualifying matches. He had scored only one other goal in his 24 international matches.

During the year, 22 nations qualified in regional eliminations for the World Cup and joined two automatic qualifiers—Italy as the host nation and Argen-

tina as the defender of the cup title. On December 9, the U.S. team drew top-seeded Italy—as well as Czechoslovakia and Austria—as the teams it must play in a single-round-robin series beginning on June 8, 1990, in Rome and Florence, Italy. The U.S. team was not expected to get beyond this round.

Of the 24 World Cup qualifiers, 14 were from Europe, including Belgium, England, the Netherlands, Romania, Scotland, the Soviet Union, Spain, Sweden, West Germany, and Yugoslavia. Ireland qualified for the first time. The other teams that qualified from the Americas were Brazil, Colombia, Costa Rica, and Uruguay. South Korea and the United Arab Emirates qualified from Asia, Egypt and Cameroon from Africa.

Europe. On April 15, 1989, thousands of late-arriving fans surged into a stadium in Sheffield, England, for an English Football Association Cup match. They pushed against fans in a standing-room-only terrace, crushing them against a fence, and 95 people were killed. Three months later, the Fédération Internationale de Football Association—soccer's world governing body—ruled that no standing room could be used for games for the 1994 World Cup, starting with the qualifying games in 1992.

In competition, Italian teams won the European Cup (A. C. Milan) and the UEFA Cup (Naples). Liverpool gained the English Football Association Cup but lost the English League title to Arsenal.   Frank Litsky

In *World Book,* see **Soccer.**

Social security. The tax rates that 130 million American workers pay to finance the United States social security system were to increase on Jan. 1, 1990. Under a 1977 law, the payroll tax rate paid by both employers and employees was to rise to 7.65 per cent, from 7.51 per cent in 1989. For self-employed workers, the rate was to be boosted to 15.3 per cent from 13.02 per cent, but half of the tax was to be deductible as a business expense.

The *wage base* (the maximum taxable amount of earnings) for social security payroll taxes also was to increase in 1990, to $51,300 from $48,000, in line with an increase in average wages paid during 1989. As a result of the higher wage base and the higher tax rates, the maximum per-worker tax was to rise to $3,924.45 from $3,604.80 in 1989.

Also to take effect on Jan. 1, 1990, was a 4.7 per cent increase in the social security benefits paid to 38.9 million Americans. Payments are hiked annually under the cost-of-living adjustment (COLA) program. The Social Security Administration estimates that payments rise by $2 billion for each percentage point of inflation.

In 1990, a social security recipient aged 65 to 69 will be able to earn up to $9,360 a year from employment without reduction of benefits, up from $8,800 in 1989. Those under 65 will be able to earn $6,840 without losing benefits, up from $6,480 in 1989. There is no limit on earnings of those 70 and older.

Somalia

"Catastrophic" changes. Citizens' protests over a threat of higher taxes for middle- and upper-income Medicare recipients moved Congress to repeal a "catastrophic" health insurance law enacted in 1988. Effective Jan. 1, 1989, the law increased hospital benefits to a full year from 60 days. To finance these new benefits and others, an income tax surtax of as much as $1,600 per couple was to have been imposed, starting with 1989 income taxes due in 1990.

In October 1989, the House of Representatives voted to repeal the entire 1988 law, while the Senate voted simply to pare benefits and scrap the surtax. On November 22, Congress agreed to kill the program. The action affected premiums paid by older and disabled Americans participating in Part B of the Medicare program, which covers doctor bills, laboratory fees, and outpatient hospital services. Repeal of new benefits meant that these people's monthly premiums were to decrease to $29.00 from $31.90 effective Jan. 1, 1990. Because of computer programming difficulties, higher premiums were to be collected at the start of 1990 and repaid retroactively in the spring.

New director. Gwendolyn S. King, a former aide to President Ronald Reagan, became the director of the Social Security Administration in August 1989. She was President George Bush's choice to replace Dorcas R. Hardy.   Frank Cormier and Margot Cormier

In *World Book,* see **Social security.**
Somalia. See Africa.

South Africa. The African National Congress (ANC), the main black opposition group in South Africa, came closer in 1989 to receiving official recognition. Despite warnings from the government, a steady stream of white politicians, business people, lawyers, writers, and other influential South Africans visited ANC President Oliver Tambo during the year at his headquarters in exile in Lusaka, Zambia.

Startling evidence of the ANC's newly elevated status came in July when State President Pieter W. Botha invited long-time ANC leader Nelson R. Mandela, who has been in jail for 27 years on charges of sabotage and attempting to overthrow the government, to a meeting at the presidential residence in Cape Town. Although Mandela was afterward returned to jail, he concurred with Botha that both sought "support for peaceful development in South Africa."

Botha was persuaded to resign in August because of ill health. His successor, Frederick Willem de Klerk, encouraged the ANC to renounce violence and join talks aimed at giving South Africa's black majority a share of political power.

Following de Klerk's election, the police ceased taking repressive action at demonstrations against *apartheid* (racial segregation). On October 15, de Klerk released eight long-term political prisoners, seven of whom were ANC leaders.

De Klerk pledged to establish a "nation without [white] domination." In addition to restraining police

tactics, de Klerk in November opened South African beaches to all races and promised that libraries, parks, and other facilities would soon be desegregated. Four urban districts were permitted to integrate. On December 13, de Klerk met with Mandela at the president's official Cape Town residence to discuss "obstacles in the way of meaningful dialogue."

On the other hand, some things remained the same. Emergency decrees were still in effect, harassment of the *New Nation* and other antiapartheid newspapers continued, and no hint was given regarding voting rights for blacks.

The National Party (NP), which has governed South Africa since 1948, and of which both Botha and de Klerk are members, held elections to all three houses of Parliament in September. The party called the elections largely in an effort to strengthen its hold on the white chamber so as to have a free hand to continue its promised reform of apartheid. The NP was challenged on the right by the Conservative Party (CP), which wants to continue racial segregation. To the left was the liberal Democratic Party (DP)—formed in April through the fusion of the Progressive Federal Party, the Independent Party, and the National Democratic Movement. The DP favors a government with universal adult voting privileges combined with constitutional protections for minority rights.

The CP increased its seats in the 178-seat all-white House of Assembly from 22 to 39 in the September

Blacks and whites ride together on a Johannesburg bus in September after South Africa's largest city ended many long-standing forms of racial segregation.

A police van at a September antigovernment demonstration in Cape Town, South Africa, sprays purple dye at protesters to mark them for later identification.

balloting. Receiving 47 per cent of the vote, the NP hung on to a narrow majority of 93 seats, down from 123. Rather than dwelling on the NP's losses, however, de Klerk chose to regard the increased showing of the DP—up from 20 seats to 33—as an endorsement by the electorate for the reform of apartheid.

New economic sanctions against South Africa, for the purpose of hastening the end of apartheid, were proposed in October by the Commonwealth countries—Great Britain and its former colonies. Sanctions, plus depressed gold prices on the world market—South Africa is a leading producer of gold—caused the rand, South Africa's currency, to fall to new lows against the United States dollar. More than 550 foreign firms had left South Africa by the end of 1989.

Peace for southern Africa seemed possible in 1989. Armed conflict in Angola and Namibia appeared to be ending, due largely to a peace accord in 1988 between South Africa, Angola, and Cuba. South Africa dispatched trade missions during 1989 to Gabon, Ivory Coast, Zaire, and several other countries.

J. Gus Liebenow and Beverly B. Liebenow

See also **Africa** (Facts in brief table); **De Klerk, Frederick W.** In *World Book,* see **South Africa.**

South America. See **Latin America** and articles on Latin-American countries.

South Carolina. See **State government.**

South Dakota. See **State government.**

Space exploration. The United States space probe *Voyager 2* sent back dramatic photographs from Neptune in 1989, and astronauts launched spacecraft from Earth orbit to Venus and Jupiter. A Soviet probe paid a brief visit to Mars in March, and Soviet cosmonauts closed down, then reopened, the *Mir* space station during the year.

Neptune mission. *Voyager 2* flew about 3,000 miles (4,800 kilometers) above the cloud tops of Neptune on August 24. About four hours later, it passed within 24,000 miles (38,600 kilometers) of Triton, the planet's largest moon. Instruments aboard the craft detected six new moons and four rings orbiting the pale-blue planet, located 2.8 billion miles (4.5 billion kilometers) from Earth. See **Astronomy.**

Shuttle launches. As *Voyager 2* flew toward and beyond Neptune, the National Aeronautics and Space Administration (NASA) launched manned missions into Earth orbit. The shuttle *Discovery* lifted off from Cape Canaveral, Fla., on March 13 with 5 astronauts, 4 rats, and 32 chicken embryos. The animals were involved in biomedical experiments designed by high school students.

Discovery launched the third of a network of three satellites designed to improve communications between orbiting spacecraft and ground stations. The shuttle landed safely at Edwards Air Force Base in California on March 18.

On May 4, the shuttle *Atlantis* blasted off, carrying

437

Space exploration

A McDonnell Douglas Delta booster on August 27 became the first privately owned rocket to put a satellite into orbit around Earth.

the *Magellan* planetary probe in its cargo bay. *Magellan*'s launch from orbit that same day marked the first successful deployment of a probe from a shuttle and the first new U.S. planetary mission since 1978. The probe is scheduled to arrive at Venus in 1990. *Atlantis* returned to Earth on May 8.

In its first flight since January 1986, the shuttle *Columbia* carried an all-military crew and two secret satellites into orbit on August 8. *Columbia* landed without incident on August 13.

Atlantis rocketed back into orbit on October 18, carrying the *Galileo* spacecraft. On the shuttle's fifth orbit, its crew launched *Galileo* on a complex trajectory calculated to reach Jupiter in 1995. *Atlantis'* five-person crew, which included two women, conducted various experiments, and the shuttle landed safely on Oct. 23, 1989.

Discovery returned to orbit on November 22 on a secret military mission—reportedly, to put a spy satellite into orbit. Mission commander was Frederick Gregory, an Air Force colonel. With this flight, Gregory became the first black to command a shuttle mission. High winds forced NASA to postpone the landing scheduled for November 26, but *Discovery* landed safely the next day.

A brief view of Mars. July 20 was the 20th anniversary of the first U.S. manned landing on the moon, and President George Bush marked the occasion by calling for an increased effort in space exploration. Bush said that the United States should establish a permanent base on the moon and send a manned mission to Mars.

Earlier in the year, an effort by the Soviet Union to explore Mars and its moon Phobos with an unmanned probe went awry when Soviet flight controllers lost contact with the probe. The mission had begun successfully, with the probe, named *Phobos 2*, going into orbit around Mars on January 29. The mission plan called for the probe to make a close approach to the moon Phobos and drop two landing craft on its surface. On March 27, however, the Soviet controllers lost contact. During its short life in orbit, the probe sent to Earth the first temperature map of the Martian surface and data revealing that Mars has little or no magnetic field.

Space station closed, reopened. Less than a month after the loss of contact with *Phobos 2*, the three cosmonauts aboard *Mir* were ordered to begin shutting down the space station. Sergei Krikalev, Valery Polyakov, and Alexander Volkov did so, then returned to Earth on April 27, leaving the station unoccupied for the first time in more than two years.

An unmanned space tanker carried fuel and supplies to the station in August. On September 5, Alexander Viktorenko and Alexander Serebrov blasted off for what the Soviet press reported was a six-month mission to reactivate and enlarge *Mir*.

Satellite plunges out of orbit. The *Solar Maximum Mission* (*Solar Max*) research satellite, launched in February 1980, fell out of orbit and burned in the atmosphere on Dec. 2, 1989. A small number of fragments may have fallen into the Indian Ocean, but no debris was sighted.

During its years of operation, the satellite radioed to Earth information concerning the sun, especially solar flares, which emit high-energy particles that cause magnetic storms in the terrestrial atmosphere. The craft was the first satellite ever repaired in orbit by astronauts. In April 1984, the crew of the space shuttle *Challenger* hoisted *Solar Max* into the cargo bay, replaced some parts, and then returned the satellite into orbit.

A space-age era ended on Sept. 25, 1989, when NASA launched its last unmanned rocket from Cape Canaveral. An Atlas-Centaur boosted a military communications satellite into orbit, marking the 448th launch by NASA in 31 years. The last NASA-owned unmanned rocket lofted a scientific satellite from Vandenberg Air Force Base in California on November 18.

Following the 1986 explosion of the *Challenger* shuttle, President Ronald Reagan directed NASA to stop launching commercial payloads. NASA is now responsible for manned flight and scientific probes, the Air Force for unmanned military payloads, and private corporations for commercial satellites.

Following this plan, the Air Force on June 14, 1989, had launched the nation's newest, most powerful unmanned rocket, a Titan 4, from Cape Canaveral. In its long-delayed maiden flight, the rocket put into orbit a satellite designed to provide early warning of a missile attack.

The first U.S. launch by a private commercial rocket also succeeded. On August 27, a Delta 187 booster put a British commercial satellite, *Marcopolo 1*, into orbit. The $30-million rocket was built by McDonnell Douglas Corporation.

Ariane. NASA's exit from the commercial-launch business promises more flights for the European company Arianespace. That company completed its second successful mission on March 6 when an Ariane 3 rocket placed into orbit a U.S.-made Japanese telecommunications satellite and a European weather satellite. On July 11, the last Ariane 3 rocket built put a 5,710-pound (2,590-kilogram) European communications satellite called *Olympus* into orbit.

On August 8, the more powerful Ariane 4 carried into space a $300-million *Hipparcos* astronomy satellite built by the 13-nation European Space Agency. The satellite did not reach its intended orbit 22,300 miles (35,890 kilometers) above Earth, however, and repeated attempts to get it out of a lower orbit failed.

In another international mission, the Soviets launched the *Cosmos '89* biosatellite on September 15. Nearly 3,000 biological samples taken into space were returned to U.S. laboratories for analysis after completion of the 14-day mission.   William J. Cromie

See also **Astronomy.** In *World Book,* see **Communications satellite; Space travel.**

Spain held a national election on Oct. 29, 1989, its fifth since the death in 1975 of Francisco Franco, who ruled as dictator for 39 years. The Socialist Party of Prime Minister Felipe González Márquez appeared at first to have retained its majority in the Cortes (parliament), but by the narrowest of margins—176 seats for the Socialists to 174 for other parties. An election committee in the province of Murcia ruled, however, that a seat initially awarded to the Socialists actually belonged to the United Left, a Communist-led alliance. The Socialists appealed the ruling, and 1989 drew to a close with the seat—and the Socialists' majority—still in dispute.

In spite of the Socialists' decline—they held 184 seats in the previous Cortes—the election assured González of a third term because minority parties and independent members of the Cortes voted regularly to support him. The Socialists had only one significant challenger—the conservative Popular Party, which won 106 seats, a gain of 1.

Election reflects social unrest. During seven years in power, the González government had pursued policies that gave Spain the fastest-growing economy in Europe—an annual gain of 4 to 5 per cent. A growing number of Spaniards, however, including lower-paid workers, many retired people, and the unemployed, felt left out of the improving economic picture.

With Spain's unemployment rate near 20 per cent in 1989, labor union leaders and some of González' followers in the Socialist Party complained that the government pursued probusiness policies and too little of Spain's new wealth trickled down to the less well off. After prolonged strikes, the General Union of Workers, the Socialists' labor affiliate, withdrew its support from the party.

Austerity ahead? The government appeared likely to apply austerity measures to hold down inflation so Spain could remain competitive with its neighbors in the European Community (EC or Common Market), which Spain had joined in 1986. Spain's ability to compete was becoming more important because the EC planned to complete the development of a single-market economy in 1992.

Deaths. Dolores Ibarruri Gómez, 93, better known as "La Pasionaria (The Passionflower)," died on Nov. 12, 1989. Ibarruri was a Communist heroine of the Spanish Civil War (1936-1939). She gave the leftist Republicans the battle cry for their struggle against the fascists when she said in a broadcast at the outbreak of the Civil War, "No pasarán," meaning "They shall not pass."

Salvador Dali, 85, a flamboyant modern artist, died on Jan. 23, 1989. A talented master of classical painting techniques, Dali triumphed as a member of various modern movements—especially surrealism—then abandoned each in turn.   Joseph Fitchett

See also **Europe** (Facts in brief table). In *World Book,* see **Spain.**

Sports

Sports. Controversy continued in 1989 over academic standards and regulations for American college athletes. The rules are established and enforced by the National Collegiate Athletic Association (NCAA), whose members include all of the major colleges and many smaller ones. In January, at the NCAA's annual convention, the colleges voted to deny any type of financial aid to incoming freshmen who fail to meet minimum academic standards set by the NCAA. The new regulations—known as Proposition 42—would amend a regulation in effect since 1986 known as Proposition 48 and would take effect in the fall of 1990.

Many predominantly black colleges and athletic directors and coaches at other colleges objected to the new restrictions. They said Proposition 42 would prevent minority and poor students from attending universities. Basketball coach John Thompson of Georgetown University in Washington, D.C., boycotted two games in protest. He returned after the presidents of the NCAA and the NCAA Presidents' Commission said they would recommend postponing enforcement of the new rule.

In October 1989, the Presidents' Commission said it would recommend to the NCAA's 1990 convention a one-year delay in enforcing the new rule. It also said the rule should be amended so that certain athletes otherwise ineligible for aid could receive nonathletic financial aid based on need.

The commission also proposed restrictions on football and basketball, the two major revenue sports. The restrictions were designed to limit the amount of time athletes must spend on their sports, which keeps them away from the classroom. The commission proposed that, starting in 1990, the basketball season begin on December 20, one month later than usual, and that the 28-game ceiling be lowered to 25 games, not including the NCAA post-season tournament. It also wanted to limit spring football practice to 10 days from the present 20 and eliminate the part of those practices that involves physical contact.

Many coaches and athletic directors objected to the commission's recommendations. The dissenters said the presidents did not understand the situation. They said the changes would hurt rather than help the athletes. And they said the decreased revenue from a shorter basketball season would force colleges to eliminate some nonrevenue sports.

Illegal payments. The NCAA's enforcement branch continued to punish colleges that broke the rules. It placed Oklahoma State on four-year probation for giving money to football players, Kentucky on three-year probation for recruiting and academic violations involving basketball players, and North Carolina State on two-year probation because basketball players sold complimentary tickets and sneakers provided by the university. Eddie Sutton resigned as Florida football coach, admitting he had made illegal payments to assistant coaches and a player. Norm Sloan negotiated

retirement as Florida basketball coach amid charges by the university of NCAA infractions.

In April 1989, a federal court jury in Chicago found two sports agents guilty of racketeering, conspiracy, and fraud for signing and paying thousands of dollars to athletes who had college eligibility remaining. The agents were Norby Walters of Chicago and Lloyd Bloom of New York City. Walters was sentenced to five years in prison and Bloom to three years. There were no indictments of the 43 players who signed with them and then helped the federal government prepare its case.

Awards. The Amateur Athletic Union presented the James E. Sullivan Memorial Award as the leading amateur athlete in the United States in 1988 to Florence Griffith Joyner. In 1988, Griffith Joyner won three gold medals and one silver in the Summer Olympics in Seoul, South Korea, and she broke the women's world records for the 100- and 200-meter dashes.

Among the winners in 1989 were the following:

Cycling. Greg LeMond of Wayzata, Minn., won the closest Tour de France in history, beating Laurent Fignon of France by 8 seconds on July 23 in Paris. Five weeks later, LeMond won the world road-racing championship. Jeannie Longo of France won the women's Tour de France and three world titles. John Tomac of Chatsworth, Calif., won the American and European versions of the world mountain-bike championship.

Diving. China won four of the six events in the World Cup championships held from May 3 to 7 in Indianapolis. Mark Lenzi of Fredericksburg, Va., won the men's 1-meter and Wendy Lian Williams of Bridgeton, Mo., the women's 3-meter. Lenzi later became the first diver to do 4¹/₂ somersaults in competition.

Fencing. The Soviet Union won 4 of the 10 titles, and West Germany took 2 in the world championships held from July 5 to 15 in Denver.

Gymnastics. The Soviet Union won the men's and women's team titles, both all-around titles, and 5 of the 10 apparatus titles in the world championships held from October 22 to 24 in Stuttgart, West Germany. The all-around champions were Igor Korobchinsky among the men and Svetlana Bogunskaya among the women.

Rowing. Kris Karlson of Weston, Conn., won gold medals in women's lightweight single and double sculls in the world championships from September 3 to 10 in Bled, Yugoslavia. Of the 22 gold medals, East Germany won 7, West Germany 3, and Romania 3. The best collegiate eight-oared crews were the Harvard men and the Cornell women.

Wrestling. John Smith (137 pounds) and Kenneth Monday (163 pounds), both from Stillwater, Okla., won freestyle titles in the world championships, held from August 18 to September 4 in Martigny, Switzerland. The United States also won 4 silver medals in freestyle and 1 in Greco-Roman. Soviets won 4 of the 10 titles in freestyle and 5 of the 10 in Greco-Roman.

Other champions

Archery, world champions: men, Stanislav Zabrodsky, Soviet Union; women, Kim Soo Nyung, South Korea.

Badminton, world champions: men, Yang Yang, China; women, Li Lingwei, China.

Biathlon, world champions: men's 20-kilometer, Eirik Kvalfoss, Norway; women's 15-kilometer, Petra Schaaf, West Germany.

Billiards, world three-cushion champion: Torbjorn Blomdahl, Sweden.

Bobsledding, world champions: two-man, Wolfgang Hoppe, East Germany; four-man, Gustav Weder, Switzerland.

Canoeing, world slalom canoe champion: Jon Lugbill, Bethesda, Md.

Court tennis, world champion: Wayne Davies, New York City.

Cross-country, world champions: men, John Ngugi, Kenya; women, Annette Sergent, France.

Curling, world champions: men, Pat Ryan, Kelowna, Canada; women, Heather Houston, Thunder Bay, Canada.

Darts, U.S. champion: Dan Valletto, Cape May, N.J.

Equestrian, World Cup champions: jumping, Ian Millar, Perth, Canada; dressage, Margit Otto Crepin, France.

Field hockey, Champions Trophy: men, Australia; women, South Korea.

Frisbee, U.S. overall champions: men, Rick LeBeau, San Diego; women, Amy Bekken, San Diego.

Handball, U.S. four-wall champions: men, Poncho Monreal, El Paso, Tex.; women, Anna Engele, St. Paul, Minn.

Horseshoe pitching, world champions: men, Alan Francis, Blytheville, Mo.; women, Phyllis Negaard, St. Joseph, Minn.

Judo, World open champions: men, Noya Ogawa, Japan; women, Estella Rodriguez, Cuba.

Lacrosse, U.S. college champion: Syracuse University.

Luge, world champions: men, Georg Hackl, West Germany; women, Susi Erdmann, East Germany.

Marathon, World Cup champions: men, Keleke Metaferia, Ethiopia; women, Sue Marchiano, Henderson, Nev.

Modern pentathlon, world champions: men, Laszlo Fabian, Hungary; women, Lori Norwood, Bryan, Tex.

Motorcycle racing, world 500-cc champion: Eddie Lawson, Upland, Calif.

Paddle tennis, U.S. champions: men, Javier Sartorius, Spain; women, Denise Yogi, Glendale, Calif.

Parachute jumping, world paraski champions: men, Alexander Struber, Austria; women, Marina Kucher, Austria.

Platform tennis, U.S. doubles champions: Rich Maier, Scarsdale, N.Y., and Steve Baird, Harrison, N.Y.

Racquetball, U.S. champions: men, Mike Ray, Marietta, Ohio; women, Caryn McKinney, Atlanta, Ga.

Racquets, U.S. open champion: James Male, Great Britain.

Rhythmic gymnastics, world all-around champion: Blanka Panova, Bulgaria.

Rodeo, U.S. all-around champion: Ty Murray, Odessa, Tex.

Roller skating, world champions: men's freestyle, Scott Cohen, North Brunswick, N.J.; women's freestyle, Rafaella Del Vinaccio, Italy; men's speed, Antony Muse, West Des Moines, Iowa; women's speed, Deanna Parker, West Des Moines, Iowa.

Shooting, small-bore rifle three-position champions: U.S., Thomas Tamas, Columbus, Ga.; U.S. International, Glenn Dubis, Fort Benning, Ga.

Softball, U.S. fast-pitch champions: men, Penn Corporation, Sioux City, Iowa; women, Whittier (Calif.) Raiders.

Surfing, OP pro champions: men, Richie Collins, Costa Mesa, Calif.; women, Frieda Zamba, Flagler Beach, Fla.

Synchronized swimming, World Cup champion: Tracy Long, Walnut Creek, Calif.

Table tennis, world champions: men, Jan-Ove Waldner, Sweden; women, Qiao Hong, China.

Tae kwon do, world heavyweight champions: men, Amr Khairy Mahmoud, Egypt; women, Wan Sook Jung, S. Korea.

Team handball, U.S. champions: men, Garden City, N.Y.; women, University of Minnesota.

Triathlon, world champions: men, Mark Allen, Cardiff, Calif.; women, Erin Baker, New Zealand.

Volleyball, U.S. open champions: men, Kenneth Allen Volleyball Club, Chicago; women, Burmy, Long Beach, Calif.

Water polo, World Cup champions: men, Yugoslavia; women, Netherlands.

Water skiing, world overall champions: men, Patrice Martin, France; women, Deena Brush Mapple, Windermere, Fla.

Weightlifting, world superheavyweight champion: Aleksandr Kurlovich, Soviet Union.   Frank Litsky

See also articles on the various sports. In *World Book,* see articles on the sports.

Greg LeMond of the United States races along the Champs Élysées in Paris en route to an 8-second win, closest finish ever in the Tour de France.

Sri Lanka

Sri Lanka slipped into virtual civil war in 1989. In the island nation's central and southern regions, where most of the Sinhalese ethnic majority live, the Marxist People's Liberation Front tried to destroy the government through terrorism, but in November the Front's leaders were killed. In the north and east, the Liberation Tigers of Tamil Eelam, who claim to speak for the Tamil ethnic minority, continued their guerrilla campaign for a separate Tamil state.

Indian army troops—who entered Sri Lanka in 1987 by government agreement to try to control the Tigers—became the source of increasing controversy. Ranasinghe Premadasa, who became president on Jan. 2, 1989, demanded in June that the 45,000 Indian troops in Sri Lanka leave by July 29. Although about 2,000 Tiger guerrillas still threatened the survival of a Tamil provincial council set up to erode support for the Tigers, Premadasa hoped to work out a settlement. He also believed that the troops' departure would eliminate one of the grievances of the People's Liberation Front. But after Sri Lanka's leading Tamil politician was assassinated on July 13, moderate Tamils feared the prospect of facing the Tigers without the help of the Indian army.

On June 14, India's Prime Minister Rajiv Gandhi rejected Premadasa's demand for a pullout. After negotiations, Sri Lanka and India on September 18 agreed with some qualifications to a troop withdrawal by the year's end. On December 28, however, India announced that the pullout would not be completed until March 31, 1990.

Campaign of terror. Meanwhile, the People's Liberation Front conducted a campaign of mass intimidation. In the first seven months of Premadasa's term, the terrorists killed about 1,000 members of the president's United National Party (UNP), including some senior officials. The Front also targeted journalists and other citizens and used terror to enforce its call for general strikes. In retaliation, death squads—which some critics said operated with the secret support of the police—killed hundreds of young men suspected of being Front activists or supporters. Observers estimated the death toll on both sides to be 700 to 1,000 per month. Piles of burning corpses became a common sight around Colombo, the capital, and Sri Lanka's rivers carried bullet-ridden bodies to the sea.

On Nov. 12, 1989, the Front's leader, Rohana Wijeweera, was captured by the police, who said he then died in a shoot-out while seeking documents from another Front official. Acting on information received from Wijeweera, the police killed his deputy and captured other Front officials.

After a brief but bloody campaign, elections for the 225-seat Parliament were held on February 15. The UNP won 125 seats, and the opposition Sri Lanka Freedom Party won 67. In March, Premadasa named D. B. Wijetunge prime minister.　　Henry S. Bradsher

See also **Asia** (Facts in brief table). In *World Book,* see **Sri Lanka.**

Stamp collecting. The United States Postal Service in 1989 issued 25-cent commemorative stamps celebrating the 100th statehood anniversaries of Montana, North Dakota, South Dakota, and Washington and the 200th anniversary of North Carolina. Baseball player Lou Gehrig, author Ernest Hemingway, and orchestra conductor Arturo Toscanini were also honored on 25-cent stamps.

The Postal Service commemorated the 1889 Oklahoma land run with a 15-cent postal card. The card's striking design, based on a detail of the painting *Opening of the Cherokee Strip*, portrays homesteaders rushing to make land claims.

The 200th anniversary of the French Revolution was commemorated with a 45-cent airmail stamp issued on Bastille Day, July 14. The design incorporated the same French allegorical figures for Liberty, Equality, and Fraternity that appeared on a series of three 2.20-franc stamps issued on the same day in Paris.

Other new U.S. stamps in 1989 included a block of four 25-cent dinosaur stamps issued on October 1 to honor Stamp Collecting Month and a large $2.40 priority-mail stamp featuring two astronauts placing an American flag on the surface of the moon. The latter stamp, issued on July 20, commemorated the first moon landing on the same date in 1969. The stamp was designed by artist Chris Calle. He is the son of artist Paul Calle, who designed the 1969 10-cent stamp honoring the moon landing. The $2.40 priority-mail rate provides first-class service for items weighing from 12 ounces to 2 pounds (340 to 900 grams).

Polls conducted during the year by *Linn's Stamp News* and *Stamp Collector* selected a block of four 25-cent carrousel animal stamps as the most popular stamp issue of 1988. Runner-up was a booklet of five stamps with classic-car designs.

The 20th Universal Postal Union Congress was held in Washington, D.C., in November 1989. About 1,700 delegates from 170 member nations attended the congress, which meets periodically to update regulations for international mail service. To commemorate the event, the U.S. Postal Service issued 11 new items. Among them were two souvenir sheets—each with blocks of four different stamps—showing past and predicted future modes of transporting the mail.

British, Chinese stamps. On August 22, the British Post Office issued its first two *nondenominated stamps* (stamps with no price indicated on them) to help simplify postal rate changes. The stamps, with the profile of Queen Elizabeth II, are inscribed "first" or "second"—first-class or second-class postage. The price of the stamps will be determined by first- and second-class mailing rates prevailing at the time of purchase. Stamps bought prior to a postal rate hike will continue to be valid for full postage after the rate increase.

China issued an 8-fen stamp on May 4 honoring the 70th anniversary of a student demonstration against the Versailles Peace Conference after World War I

(1914-1917). The demonstration, known as the May Fourth Movement, was organized to protest the conference's decision to allow Japan to keep control of parts of China that it seized during the war. Ironically, just one month after issuing the stamp in 1989, the Chinese government crushed another student demonstration calling for democratic reforms.

Auctions. On April 19, the Harmer's gallery of New York City held the first of a final series of auctions of the Dale-Lichtenstein collection. The collection, which many experts considered the finest private stamp collection in the world, was built by Alfred F. Lichtenstein, a wealthy businessman, and his daughter, Louise Boyd Dale. A pair of stamps in the collection—fine specimens of the so-called St. Louis Bear provisional stamps, issued in 1845-1846 by the postmaster of St. Louis, Mo.—sold for a combined price of $46,750.

Another famous group of stamps that went on the auction block in 1989 was the stock of Raymond and Roger Weill, stamp dealers in New Orleans since 1932. The Weill stamps were to be sold off in a series of auctions in various cities. At the first auction, held in October at Christie's Robson Lowe galleries in New York City, a block of four 1918 U.S. 24-cent stamps printed with an upside-down picture of a Jenny biplane sold for a record $1.1 million. That price was more than twice the previous record for a United States postal item.   Paul A. Larsen

In *World Book,* see **Stamp collecting.**

State government. Headline-making issues on the national scene—drugs, gun control, abortion, and education—were also prominent in state legislative debate in 1989. Many states tried various combinations of spending cuts and tax hikes to balance their budgets. And California's Supreme Court ruled on a far-reaching measure to reform that state's insurance industry.

Tough antidrug laws were passed in several states. Maryland made a prison term of 25 years with no chance of parole mandatory for top drug dealers. New York and Virginia began to require fines of up to $100,000 for drug crimes. An Indiana law imposed fines of up to $400 on drug offenders.

By the end of 1989, drug users could be fined or could lose their driver's licenses in 21 states. A new law in Rhode Island required a $400 fine for drugged drivers.

To keep drugs away from schools, 29 states enacted versions of the federal schoolyard drug law, with mandatory penalties for selling drugs within 1,000 feet (300 meters) of a school. One of the toughest laws was Virginia's measure, which made selling drugs in a school zone punishable by five years in prison and a $100,000 fine.

Drug education and prevention efforts were underway in 37 states by the end of the year. California in 1989 approved $16.7 million in new funds for drug education in grades four through seven. Pennsylvania

Wagoners join a celebration of the 100th anniversary of South Dakota's statehood. North Dakota, Montana, and Washington also turned 100 in 1989.

Selected statistics on state governments

State	Resident population*	Governor†	Legislature† House (D)	House (R)	Senate (D)	Senate (R)	State tax revenue‡	Tax revenue per capita‡	Public school expenditures per pupil§
Alabama	4,118,000	Guy Hunt (R)	83	22	28	7	$ 3,374,000,000	$ 820	$2,750
Alaska	527,000	Steve Cowper (D)	24	16	8	12	1,251,000,000	2,440	7,040
Arizona	3,556,000	Rose Mofford (D)	26	34	13	17	3,722,000,000	1,070	3,450
Arkansas	2,406,000	Bill Clinton (D)	88	11#	31	4	2,021,000,000	830	2,620
California	29,063,000	George Deukmejian (R)	47	33	24	15#	36,075,000,000	1,280	3,920
Colorado	3,317,000	Roy Romer (D)	26	39	11	24	2,726,000,000	830	4,380
Connecticut	3,239,000	William A. O'Neill (D)	88	63	23	13	4,376,000,000	1,350	6,400
Delaware	673,000	Michael N. Castle (R)	18	23	13	8	1,018,000,000	1,540	5,140
Florida	12,671,000	Bob Martinez (R)	73	47	23	17	11,460,000,000	930	4,350
Georgia	6,436,000	Joe Frank Harris (D)	144	36	45	11	5,783,000,000	900	3,720
Hawaii	1,112,000	John D. Waihee III (D)	45	6	22	3	2,039,000,000	1,870	3,860
Idaho	1,014,000	Cecil D. Andrus (D)	20	64	19	23	894,000,000	890	2,780
Illinois	11,658,000	James R. Thompson (R)	67	51	31	28	11,079,000,000	960	4,290
Indiana	5,593,000	Evan Bayh (D)	50	50	24	26	5,312,000,000	950	3,620
Iowa	2,840,000	Terry E. Branstad (R)	61	39	30	20	2,842,000,000	1,000	4,160
Kansas	2,513,000	Mike Hayden (R)	57	68	18	22	2,445,000,000	980	4,270
Kentucky	3,727,000	Wallace G. Wilkinson (D)	71	29	29	9	3,664,000,000	980	3,440
Louisiana	4,382,000	Charles E. (Buddy) Roemer III (D)	86	18#	33	6	3,774,000,000	850	3,150
Maine	1,222,000	John R. McKernan, Jr. (R)	98	53	20	15	1,506,000,000	1,250	4,430
Maryland	4,694,000	William D. Schaefer (D)	125	16	40	7	5,807,000,000	1,250	4,900
Massachusetts	5,913,000	Michael S. Dukakis (D)	128	32	32	8	8,521,000,000	1,450	5,470
Michigan	9,273,000	James J. Blanchard (D)	61	49	18	20	10,515,000,000	1,130	4,310
Minnesota	4,353,000	Rudolph G. Perpich (D)	80	54	44	23	6,144,000,000	1,430	4,390
Mississippi	2,621,000	Ray Mabus (D)	109	13	43	9	2,126,000,000	810	2,720
Missouri	5,159,000	John Ashcroft (R)	104	59	22	12	4,406,000,000	860	3,640
Montana	806,000	Stan Stephens (R)	52	48	23	27	715,000,000	890	4,060
Nebraska	1,611,000	Kay A. Orr (R)	(unicameral) 49 nonpartisan				1,343,000,000	840	3,600
Nevada	1,111,000	Robert J. Miller (D)	30	12	8	13	1,186,000,000	1,120	3,800
New Hampshire	1,107,000	Judd Gregg (R)	119	281	8	16	583,000,000	530	4,150
New Jersey	7,736,000	James J. Florio (D)	45	35	24	16	9,762,000,000	1,260	6,930
New Mexico	1,528,000	Garrey E. Carruthers (R)	45	25	26	16	1,793,000,000	1,190	3,880
New York	17,950,000	Mario M. Cuomo (D)	92	58	27	34	26,172,000,000	1,460	6,890
North Carolina	6,571,000	James G. Martin (R)	74	46	37	13	6,923,000,000	1,060	3,640
North Dakota	660,000	George A. Sinner (D)	46	60	32	21	633,000,000	960	3,390
Ohio	10,907,000	Richard F. Celeste (D)	59	40	14	19	9,991,000,000	920	3,850
Oklahoma	3,224,000	Henry Bellmon (R)	69	32	33	15	3,150,000,000	970	3,130
Oregon	2,820,000	Neil Goldschmidt (D)	32	28	19	11	2,111,000,000	770	4,570
Pennsylvania	12,040,000	Robert P. Casey (D)	104	99	24	26	11,825,000,000	980	5,100
Rhode Island	998,000	Edward D. DiPrete (R)	83	17	41	9	1,121,000,000	1,130	5,380
South Carolina	3,512,000	Carroll A. Campbell, Jr. (R)	87	37	34	12	3,438,000,000	980	3,340
South Dakota	715,000	George S. Mickelson (R)	24	46	15	20	476,000,000	670	3,170
Tennessee	4,940,000	Ned Ray McWherter (D)	58	41	22	11	3,855,000,000	780	3,090
Texas	16,991,000	William P. Clements, Jr. (R)	90	60	23	8	13,426,000,000	800	3,720
Utah	1,707,000	Norman H. Bangerter (R)	27	48	7	22	1,602,000,000	950	2,630
Vermont	567,000	Madeleine M. Kunin (D)	74	76	16	14	617,000,000	1,110	4,790
Virginia	6,098,000	L. Douglas Wilder (D)	59	39**	30	10	6,137,000,000	1,020	4,440
Washington	4,761,000	Booth Gardner (D)	63	35	24	25	5,995,000,000	1,300	4,020
West Virginia	1,857,000	Gaston Caperton (D)	80	20	30	4	1,744,000,000	930	3,690
Wisconsin	4,867,000	Tommy G. Thompson (R)	56	43	20	13	6,006,000,000	1,240	4,950
Wyoming	475,000	Michael Sullivan (D)	23	41	11	19	573,000,000	1,220	5,500

*1989 estimates (source: U.S. Bureau of the Census).
†As of January 1990 (source: state government officials).
‡1988 figures (source: U.S. Bureau of the Census).

§1987-1988 figures for elementary and secondary students in average daily attendance (source: National Education Association).
#One independent.
**Two independents.

mandated drug education from kindergarten through the 12th grade as part of a $250-million package of education, treatment, and enforcement measures.

Gun laws. California in May became the first state to ban military-type assault weapons. On January 17, an assailant had used such a weapon and two pistols to kill 5 children and wound 29 others and a teacher in a Stockton, Calif., schoolyard. The ban, which was to take effect on Jan. 1, 1990, applies to 50 different semiautomatic weapons.

More than a dozen other states considered similar measures, but all failed. Watered-down laws requiring waiting periods for sales of assault guns passed in Maryland and Virginia. Oregon restricted access to rifles, shotguns, and assault weapons. Florida mandated a prison sentence and a fine for any gun owner whose weapon is used by a person under age 17 in a fatal or extremely injurious shooting.

Abortion restrictions. The Supreme Court of the United States on July 3 upheld a Missouri law restricting abortion in various ways. Two days later, Governor Bob Martinez of Florida called a special session of that state's legislature for October 10 to consider measures to restrict abortion. On October 5, however, the Florida Supreme Court struck down a 1988 law requiring a minor to obtain parental consent for an abortion.

The legislature met as scheduled, but Martinez did not even have enough support to get his measures out of committee. The session adjourned the next day.

Pennsylvania enacted one of the country's most restrictive abortion laws in November. The new law includes measures banning abortions after 24 weeks of pregnancy, except when the woman faces death or "irreversible" physical damage; requiring married women to inform their husbands before having an abortion; and providing criminal penalties for violations. Governor Robert P. Casey signed the law on November 17.

Abortion was a major campaign issue in the year's only two governor's races; both elections were held on November 7. In Virginia, Lieutenant Governor L. Douglas Wilder narrowly defeated Republican J. Marshall Coleman, a former state attorney general with a strong record against abortion. Wilder thus became the first black to be elected governor of a state. See **Wilder, L. Douglas.**

In New Jersey's governor's race, Democratic Congressman James J. Florio handily defeated Republican Congressman James Courter, who was also seen as antiabortion.

Education. School financing systems were voided by state supreme courts in Montana in February, Kentucky in June, and Texas in October. The Montana court ordered the state to provide more equitable funding. As a result, Montana enacted a 5 per cent individual income tax surtax to raise more money for needy schools. Kentucky and Texas scheduled action for their 1990 legislative sessions.

New Jersey in October 1989 became the first state to take control of a local school district for educational, rather than financial, reasons. The Jersey City school system had failed to meet minimum educational standards, so the state board of education disbanded the local board and appointed a state official to run the system for at least five years.

Five states joined Minnesota in allowing parents to pick the public school their children attend. School-choice laws were enacted in Arkansas, Arizona, Iowa, Nebraska, and Ohio. Arkansas also raised the minimum salary for teachers to $16,000. The Florida, Oklahoma, and Texas legislatures joined West Virginia in passing laws to deny driver's licenses to 16- and 17-year-olds who drop out of school.

Money matters. Northeastern states experienced the nation's most severe financial problems because of their slowing economies. By midyear, 12 states—most of them in the Northeast—had cut their budgets by a total of $923 million to avoid deficits.

Massachusetts Governor Michael S. Dukakis witnessed the disappearance of an earlier economic recovery called the "Massachusetts Miracle." The state's economy faded with a downturn in computer manufacturing and other high-technology industries. As a result, Dukakis faced a deficit as high as $700 million for fiscal year 1990, which began on July 1, 1989. To balance the budget, the governor ordered massive cuts in spending and slashed the government payroll. The legislature raised the personal income tax rate from 5 per cent to 5.75 per cent as of July 1, 1989, but was unable to agree with the governor on a comprehensive cure for the state's budget ills.

Connecticut Governor William A. O'Neill signed $247 million in new taxes. New York cut spending and passed laws to hike taxes and fees by $1 billion.

In Louisiana, however, not even threats of a deficit and massive spending cuts could persuade voters to adopt Governor Charles E. (Buddy) Roemer's plan to hike income taxes, cut business and sales taxes, and revise property taxes. In a *referendum* (direct vote) on April 28, the electorate rejected the plan by a margin of 55 per cent to 45 per cent. On December 5, North Dakota voters turned down increases in gasoline, income, and sales taxes.

West Virginia's Governor Gaston Caperton pushed through taxes on groceries and gasoline to deal with a $230-million deficit and some $280 million in state pension fund investment losses. The governor also ordered $50 million in spending cuts and reduced the number of state departments from 150 to 7.

Personal income tax rates rose in Connecticut, Illinois, Massachusetts, Montana, North Dakota, and Vermont but fell in Hawaii, Kansas, Maine, and North Carolina. Corporate income or franchise taxes rose in 8 states, sales and use taxes in 5 states, motor-fuel taxes in 18 states, taxes on cigarettes in 13, and taxes on alcoholic beverages in 9. Property tax rates fell in Maine, Minnesota, Nebraska, and Wisconsin.

Steel industry

Lotteries. Kentucky started its new lottery on April 4. In May, that state awarded its first $1-million prize based on the winner of the Kentucky Derby. Kentucky also planned to expand into lottery betting on other sports in October, but racing interests pressured the state to drop this plan. One result of this change was that Oregon's lottery based on National Football League (NFL) games, started on September 6, remained the only state-run lottery on NFL contests.

Insurance. The California Supreme Court on May 4 upheld Proposition 103, an insurance-reform measure approved by voters in November 1988. Proposition 103 called for rollbacks in premiums for property and casualty insurance. The court, however, voided a provision that would exempt from rollbacks only insurers on the brink of insolvency. The court allowed an exemption to any insurer who showed that the new rates were too low to provide a "fair and reasonable profit."

State Insurance Commissioner Roxanne Gillespie said on May 11, 1989, that she would apply a "fair return" standard to each kind of insurance. Supporters of Proposition 103 filed suit in September, however, to force Gillespie to order price rollbacks for automobile insurance. The commission held hearings in December to establish fair rates of return. Gillespie said the goal was to determine rollbacks, if any, by March 1990.   Elaine S. Knapp

In *World Book,* see **State government** and articles on the individual states.

Steel industry. The United States steel industry continued in 1989 to rebound from years of heavy financial losses. During the first half of 1989, steel production increased by 1.8 per cent, reaching 51.3 million short tons (46.5 million metric tons), compared with 50.4 million short tons (45.7 million metric tons) for the same period in 1988. Sales totaled $16.5 billion, compared with $16.4 billion for the first half of 1988. In addition, U.S. steel mills ran at about the same capacity as they did in 1988.

Turning point. The American Iron and Steel Institute (AISI), the chief association of U.S. steel producers, reported on May 1, 1989, that the years 1987 and 1988 represented a turning point for the domestic steel industry, which had lost $12 billion between 1982 and 1986. According to the AISI, sales of U.S. steel in 1988 increased to $32.3 billion, up from $26.9-billion in 1987. Profits during 1988 more than doubled, reaching $2.3 billion, compared with $1.1 billion in 1987. The figures were based on reports from 24 steel firms that together produce about 76 per cent of all the steel manufactured in the United States.

Steel imports declined sharply during the first half of 1989, totaling 8.7 million short tons (7.9 million metric tons), the AISI reported on August 28. About 11 million short tons (10 million metric tons) were imported during the same period in 1988.

U.S.-Japanese ventures. United States and Japanese steelmakers continued to negotiate cooperative production agreements in 1989. On February 14, USX Corporation, the largest U.S. steel producer, announced that it would operate its big steel mill in Lorain, Ohio, jointly with Japan's Kobe Steel Limited. Under the terms of the partnership, USX will supply rust-resistant galvanized steel to Japanese automobile manufacturing plants in the United States. In March, Armco Incorporated, the fifth-largest U.S. steel firm, agreed to sell 40 per cent of its steelmaking operations to the Kawasaki Steel Corporation of Japan.

Five other U.S. and Asian steel firms have announced joint ventures since 1983. The ventures give Asian companies access to U.S. markets and give U.S. firms access to Asian technology and capital.

Quotas extended. United States President George Bush on July 25, 1989, announced a 30-month extension of government quotas limiting the amount of steel imported into the United States. The quotas, which apply to 40 types of steel imported from 29 countries, were scheduled to expire in September. The United States imposed the restrictions in 1984 to protect its steel industry from financial losses due to sales of less expensive foreign steel.

The 30-month extension disappointed U.S. steelmakers, who had lobbied for a five-year continuation. But companies that use steel applauded the decision. They had argued that the quotas raised the prices of domestic steel products and contributed to shortages of some types of steel.

Bush also announced that while the restrictions were in effect, the United States would attempt to negotiate an end to unfair trade practices in the international steel market. But, he said, the quotas would "permanently" expire in 1992, even if the negotiations failed. The United States subsequently obtained commitments from all 29 countries to liberalize their steel-trade policies.

One-step steelmaking. The U.S. Department of Energy on May 24 approved funding for research aimed at developing the technology to produce steel directly from iron ore. The $30-million project, cofunded by the steel industry, will last for three years and involve both laboratory research and construction of a pilot plant near Pittsburgh, Pa.

Currently, steelmaking is a four-stage operation requiring a number of ovens and furnaces. Coal, used as fuel, must first be converted to coke, a hard substance from which the gases have been removed. The iron ore used to produce steel must be made into pellets, then combined with limestone to produce pig iron.

In the one-step process, called melting reduction, coal and iron ore are mixed in a single vessel containing molten iron. As in the traditional process, oxygen is then injected into the mixture to convert the iron to steel. If successful, the new process would eliminate the need to convert coal into coke. In addition, it would enable steelmakers to produce steel continuously, rather than in batches.   Michael Woods

In *World Book,* see **Iron and steel.**

Stocks and bonds. The year 1989 was generally a good one for investors in the United States but not for professionals in the securities business. The volume of trading and of new financing in both bond and stock markets was unusually low during 1989, causing lay-offs among brokers and dealers. Newly issued stocks and bonds in 1989 totaled only about $233 billion, down from $409 billion in 1988.

Stock prices rose to new heights on October 9 and remained high for the rest of the year. The average return for all stocks traded on the New York Stock Exchange (NYSE) was 31.4 per cent for the year, including about 4 per cent dividends. The average return on all stocks is usually about 12 per cent per year.

On the international scene, the Nikkei average in Japan gained 30.9 per cent and the Financial Times Ordinary Index of London stocks gained 33.2 per cent. Worldwide gains were generally at least 20 per cent.

The Dow Jones Industrial Average (the Dow), the best-known index of stock prices, tracks the prices of 30 long-established corporations and ignores dividends paid to stockholders. It closed on Dec. 31, 1988, at 2,168.57 and hit the new year's low on the first trading day, Jan. 3, 1989, at 2,144.64. It immediately started to rise, breaking through the post-1987-crash high of 2,439.70 on May 22, to close at 2,502.02. It hit a new record high of 2,734.64 on August 24.

On October 9, it reached an all-time high of 2,791.41, but the good cheer was short lived. On Fri-

day, October 13, the Dow lost 190 points, falling to under 2,570. Anxiety over the default of several so-called junk bond issues was blamed for the drop. The world waited to see whether the great crash of October 1987 was going to be repeated, but by the end of the week the Dow was back up in the 2,680 range. It closed the year at 2,753.20 and hit another new high, 2,810.15, on the first trading day of 1990. Expected lower interest rates and the easing of East-West tensions were credited for the rally.

The Standard & Poor's Composite Index (the S&P 500), which tracks prices of a much broader collection of stocks on the NYSE, behaved much the same as the Dow. It began 1989 at 277.72 and reached a record high on October 9 of 359.80—before losing 22 points on October 13. In November, it climbed back through the 330's, and it finished December at 353.40.

Price swings. A major concern in the wake of the October 1989 price crash centered on the increased volatility of stock prices. Market analysts feared that the large rises and falls in stock prices might scare off small investors. The price swings were often blamed on "program trading," in which a computer automatically buys or sells large blocks of stock according to some previously programmed scheme, usually based on the relationship of the stock price to the prices of options. In November, the NYSE asked big traders to halt program trading until the role of such trading in creating volatile prices could be studied. Studies by

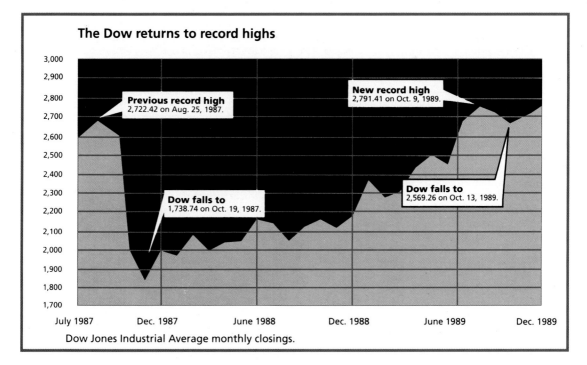

The Dow returns to record highs

Previous record high
2,722.42 on Aug. 25, 1987.

New record high
2,791.41 on Oct. 9, 1989.

Dow falls to
1,738.74 on Oct. 19, 1987.

Dow falls to
2,569.26 on Oct. 13, 1989.

July 1987 — Dec. 1987 — June 1988 — Dec. 1988 — June 1989 — Dec. 1989

Dow Jones Industrial Average monthly closings.

Stock prices rose steadily for most of 1989, and the market recovered fully from the crash of 1987 in spite of a plunge on October 13.

Sudan

academic economists, however, showed that volatility in 1989 was not unusually high by historical standards. Furthermore, program trading dropped sharply in October, when price changes were the greatest.

Bond activity. Long-term, low-risk bonds were fairly stable in 1989. The five-year Treasury bond interest rate rose to the year's high of 9.8 per cent in the first week in March but began to fall in May, dropping below 8.5 per cent at the end of November. It ended the year at 7.8 per cent.

Much of the action in the bond markets was in junk bonds, used to finance take-overs or to enable a corporation to buy back its stock. Such bonds are unusually risky and so must promise interest rates that are much higher than those for low-risk (AAA-rated) corporate bonds. The interest-rate spread between junk and low-risk bonds was less than 4 percentage points at the beginning of the year, but rose sharply to more than 4.5 percentage points in the third week of April. This followed the March 29 indictment of Drexel Burnham Lambert Incorporated's junk-bond manager Michael R. Milken. Milken, known as the "father of the junk bond," and two other Drexel employees were charged with racketeering, fraud, and insider trading. Bills were introduced in Congress to curb the issue of new junk bonds and make corporate take-overs more difficult.   Donald W. Swanton

In *World Book,* see **Bond; Investment; Stock, Capital.**

Sudan. The armed forces of Sudan seized control of the government in a bloodless coup on June 30, 1989. Army leaders acted after food shortages and soaring inflation led to riots in Khartoum, Sudan's capital, and in other cities. But the officers were equally disturbed by the failure of the civilian government of Prime Minister Al-Sadiq Al-Mahdi to end Sudan's civil war.

Since 1956, Sudanese in the South, most of whom are Christian or practice local religions, have resisted domination by the Muslim North. The conflict escalated in 1983, when the government attempted to impose Islamic law on the entire country.

Ultimatum. In February 1989, Sudan's military leaders had issued an ultimatum to the government demanding that Al-Mahdi either negotiate a peace settlement with the rebel Sudanese People's Liberation Army (SPLA) or give the army the resources to win a military victory. The army also demanded that Al-Mahdi form a government more broadly based than the coalition then in place, whose main partners were Al-Mahdi's Umma Party and the National Islamic Front, an Islamic fundamentalist party.

Al-Mahdi's new government, formed in March, included members from labor unions and a number of parties, including the Democratic Unionist Party (DUP). The DUP had quit the government in December 1988, after the National Assembly, Sudan's parliament, rejected a peace settlement signed by the DUP and the SPLA. The Islamic Front boycotted the new coalition, saying it would oppose any peace pact that does not require nationwide enforcement of Islamic law.

Taking control. The leader of the coup, Lieutenant General Umar Hasan Ahmad al-Bashir, formed a 15-member revolutionary council as an interim government. Al-Bashir suspended the Constitution and banned political parties, labor unions, and other associations. He also banned all newspapers except the army's publication. In July, al-Bashir formed a new cabinet that was mostly civilian.

Civil conflict. A series of cease-fires proclaimed by both the government and the SPLA kept the civil war at a simmer during 1989. The new government seemed as unwilling or unable as Al-Mahdi's government to settle the conflict. Talks between the government and the SPLA broke down in early December over the issue of Islamic law. In December, the government executed two civilian opponents despite pleas by various countries and human-rights organizations.

Famine averted. The strife-torn southern Sudan escaped another famine like the one that killed an estimated 250,000 people in 1988. In November 1989, the government halted shipments of food and medical supplies to the South, accusing international relief agencies of delivering weapons to the SPLA. The government also bombed several southern towns where relief workers were stationed.   William Spencer

See also **Africa** (Facts in brief table). In *World Book,* see **Sudan.**

Sullivan, Louis Wade (1933-   ), president of the Morehouse School of Medicine in Atlanta, Ga., was sworn in as United States secretary of health and human services on March 10, 1989. His nomination by President-elect George Bush had been criticized after Sullivan was quoted in the press as supporting abortion. Sullivan assured antiabortion groups that he is opposed to abortion except in certain cases. The Senate confirmed his nomination by a 98-1 vote.

Sullivan was born Nov. 3, 1933, in Atlanta. He received a bachelor's degree from Morehouse College in 1954 and a medical degree from Boston University in 1958.

In 1966, Sullivan was named codirector of *hematology* (the branch of medicine involving disorders of the blood) at Boston University Medical Center. He held a number of positions there, including that of professor of medicine. From 1972 to 1975, Sullivan was also director of hematology at Boston City Hospital and was co-project director of the Boston Sickle Cell Center. (Sickle cell—or sickle cell disease—is a blood disorder that occurs mainly among blacks.)

In 1975, Sullivan returned to Morehouse College as professor of biology and medicine. That year, he helped found the college's medical education program. The Morehouse School of Medicine became an independent school in 1981.

Sullivan and his wife, Ginger, have three children. They live in Alexandria, Va.   Mary A. Krier

Supreme Court of the United States. At its last public session of the 1988-1989 term, the Supreme Court of the United States on July 3, 1989, upheld a woman's constitutional right to an abortion but gave states new authority to restrict the procedure. The decision, in a Missouri case known as *Webster v. Reproductive Health Services*, marked the first time the court had significantly limited the effect of its 1973 ruling in *Roe v. Wade*. The 1973 ruling established the right to an abortion free from state interference during the first three months of pregnancy, with regulations to protect the mother's health allowable in the next three months.

The 5 to 4 *Webster* ruling, written by Chief Justice William H. Rehnquist, upheld a Missouri law requiring physicians to determine whether the fetus is *viable* (able to survive outside the womb) if a woman seeking an abortion was believed to be at least 20 weeks pregnant. Also upheld was the state's ban on the services of public employees and the use of public facilities for abortions.

Rehnquist expressed doubts about the regulatory scheme created by *Roe v. Wade*. Speaking for the court, however, the chief justice stopped short of overruling that decision. Joining his opinion were Justices Byron R. White and Anthony M. Kennedy. Two other justices—Sandra Day O'Connor and Antonin Scalia—agreed that the Missouri abortion regulations were valid but declined to join Rehnquist's opinion.

The abortion case dominated the term despite an array of cases involving such controversial issues as civil rights, freedom of expression, the death penalty, and drug testing. With few exceptions, Rehnquist and the new conservative bloc—created by President Ronald Reagan's appointments of O'Connor, Scalia, and Kennedy to the court—controlled the major cases.

A furor over the flag. One of the exceptions was a 5 to 4 decision on June 21 that burning the American flag as an expression of political discontent is protected by the First Amendment's free-speech guarantee. The opinion was written by Justice William J. Brennan, Jr., who was joined by two other liberal justices—Harry A. Blackmun and Thurgood Marshall—and by conservatives Scalia and Kennedy. The ruling provoked sharp dissents from other members of the court and demands from many members of Congress and President George Bush for a constitutional amendment protecting the flag.

At issue in the case, *Texas v. Johnson*, was a state criminal statute forbidding "the desecration of a venerated object." Texas had turned to the Supreme Court after the state's Court of Criminal Appeals overturned the conviction of Gregory L. Johnson. Johnson had received a one-year prison term and a $2,000 fine for burning an American flag outside the 1984 Republican National Convention in Dallas.

Limiting affirmative action. The court's conservative direction was apparent, however, in a series of decisions that subjected affirmative-action programs

An estimated 300,000 prochoice demonstrators march in Washington, D.C., in April to urge the Supreme Court not to restrict access to abortion.

to new challenges and established new rules for proving job discrimination claims.

On January 23, the court ruled, 6 to 3, that a Richmond, Va., "set aside" program, which earmarked 30 per cent of the city's construction funds for minority subcontractors, violated the equal-protection clause of the 14th Amendment. The court's opinion, written by Justice O'Connor, asserted that the United States Constitution bars cities and states from adopting affirmative-action plans, which give preferential treatment to minorities and women, except in well-documented cases of discrimination by government bodies or private parties.

The court dealt another blow to affirmative action on June 12. In a case originating in Birmingham, Ala., the court held, 5 to 4, that a group of white fire fighters could challenge a court-approved arrangement between the city and a group of black fire fighters that gave promotion advantages to blacks. The court said the white fire fighters, who did not participate in that 1974 agreement, were entitled to file a *reverse-discrimination suit* (a lawsuit contending that the agreement discriminates against whites).

In one of the term's most closely watched cases, the court on June 15 unanimously reaffirmed that a landmark 1866 civil rights law prohibits private as well as state-sanctioned acts of racial discrimination. The court divided 5-4, however, in holding that with regard to treatment by private employers, the 1866 law

Antiabortion advocates converge on the Supreme Court Building in January, calling for the court to uphold state laws restricting abortion.

covers only the initial hiring and terms of employment. The court refused to extend the law's protection to harassment on the job or other discriminatory working conditions.

Family violence. In a 6 to 3 ruling handed down on February 22, the court held that state and local governments have no constitutional duty to safeguard people from child abuse or other private acts of violence unless the individuals are in protective custody. The decision rejected claims brought against a county social services agency in Wisconsin by the mother of Joshua DeShaney, a 9-year-old boy institutionalized since 1984 because of brain damage resulting from a beating by his father. The mother charged that the county, by failing to respond to reports and repeated evidence of child abuse, had deprived Joshua of his rights under the 14th Amendment.

Capital punishment. On the recurring question of the death penalty, the court in a June 26 ruling held, 5 to 4, that the execution of convicted murderers who were 16 or 17 years old when they committed their crimes does not violate the Constitution's bar against "cruel and unusual punishments." Also on June 26, the court held in another 5 to 4 decision that the Constitution does not prevent the execution of a mentally retarded killer.

Drug and alcohol testing. The court for the first time addressed the issue of testing employees for drug and alcohol use. In two opinions handed down

on March 21, the court ruled that the Constitution does not require a search warrant or some suspicion of wrongdoing before certain categories of employees can be forced to provide a urine, blood, or breath sample.

In a case involving railroad personnel, the court said that the government's interest in public safety justified a departure from the traditional warrant and probable-cause requirements of the Fourth Amendment, which forbids "unreasonable searches and seizures." The justices split 5 to 4 in a case affecting employees of the U.S. Customs Service. The majority asserted that the government must ensure that customs agents do not use drugs because a drug habit raises the risk of bribery and blackmail.

Religious displays. In a 5 to 4 ruling on July 3 in a Pittsburgh, Pa., case, the court found that the display of a Nativity scene at the county courthouse was an unconstitutional endorsement of the Christian religion. By a vote of 6 to 3 in a companion case, however, the court upheld the display of a Hanukkah menorah, or Jewish candelabrum, just outside the city-county building next to a Christmas tree, a secular symbol of the holiday season.   Glen R. Elsasser

See also **Courts.** In *World Book,* see **Supreme Court of the United States.**

Surgery. See Medicine.

Suriname. See Latin America.

Swaziland. See Africa.

Sweden received several doses of bad news in 1989: It became unlikely that the police would ever find the individual who assassinated Prime Minister Olof Palme in 1986, a scandal involving sales of Swedish arms erupted, a popular biotechnology executive was convicted of financial misconduct, and the only prototype of a military aircraft crashed.

There was good news, however, for Swedish taxpayers. The government proposed to lower the nation's income taxes.

Assassination conviction overturned. A Swedish court on July 27, 1989, convicted Carl Gustav Christer Pettersson, 42, who had a long criminal record and history of drug and alcohol abuse, of assassinating Palme. On October 12, however, an appeals court overturned this verdict. The prosecution had relied heavily on testimony by Palme's widow, Lisbet, who said that she recognized Pettersson as the man who killed her husband and wounded her at point-blank range. Some other witnesses for the prosecution, however, retracted their initial statements placing Pettersson near the scene of the crime.

Pettersson's release reinforced the view of many Swedes that the riddle of who killed Palme might never be solved. Police bungling had blurred the killer's trail. An investigation that cost millions of dollars had produced widely different theories, including one holding that Palme had been killed because he had tried to block the sale of Swedish arms to Iran during the Iran-Iraq War (1980-1988).

Arms scandal. A newspaper in New Delhi, India, on Oct. 9, 1989, published excerpts from a secret report of the Swedish government confirming that a Swedish weapons manufacturer had acknowledged the payment of bribes to Indian officials. According to the report, Bofors AB admitted paying out more than $100 million in 1986 to win a $1.4-billion contract for artillery. India's Prime Minister Rajiv Gandhi denied that the officials had been bribed.

Executive convicted. In Sweden's biggest business scandal of the 1980's, a panel of judges on July 19, 1989, convicted Refaat al-Sayed of financial misconduct in connection with the management of Fermaenta AB, a biotechnology company. Al-Sayed, 44, was an Egyptian immigrant who became a popular hero as a rags-to-riches entrepreneur.

Plane crash. The crash on February 1 of the only prototype of the JAS 39 Gripen fighter-bomber jeopardized the future of the Swedish Air Force's $4-billion program to develop a new aircraft. Officials blamed the crash on a defect in the plane's electronic flight-control system.

Tax reform. The government in November submitted a bill to reduce the nation's income taxes. By 1991, Swedes would pay no more than 50 per cent of their income in tax. Sweden's top rate on earned income in 1989 was 72 per cent.   Joseph Fitchett

See also **Europe** (Facts in brief table). In *World Book,* see **Sweden.**

Swimming. World records were broken in 1989 in only 6 of swimming's 34 standard events, compared with 15 of 34 in 1988. Americans broke 4 of those 6 records on Aug. 20, 1989, in the Pan Pacific Championships in Tokyo, the first time four Americans had achieved that on the same day.

The four Americans included 17-year-old Janet Evans of Placentia, Calif. She was the only woman to break a world record during the year. Her time of 8 minutes 16.22 seconds in the 800-meter freestyle lowered her 1988 record of 8:17.12. Evans also swam the year's fastest times in the 400-meter freestyle (4 minutes 4.53 seconds) and the 400-meter individual medley (4 minutes 39.36 seconds).

The other world record breakers in the Pan Pacific meet were Tom Jager of Topanga, Calif., in the 50-meter freestyle (22.12 seconds); David Wharton of Warminster, Pa., in the 200-meter individual medley (2 minutes 0.11 second), and Mike Barrowman of Rockville, Md., in the 200-meter breaststroke (2 minutes 12.89 seconds). Evans was a freshman-to-be at Stanford University in California, Jager a University of California at Los Angeles graduate, Wharton a Southern California sophomore, and Barrowman a University of Michigan sophomore.

It was a good year for the Americans, who had not lived up to their expectations in the 1988 Summer Olympics. This time, they won 25 of the 36 Pan Pacific events and defeated the Soviet Union, 201-136, in the Alamo Cup competition held from Aug. 24 to 26, 1989, in Atlanta, Ga.

The only world records set by non-Americans came on August 15 in the European championships in Bonn, West Germany. They were set by Giorgio Lamberti of Italy in the 200-meter freestyle (1 minute 46.69 seconds) and Adrian Moorhouse of Great Britain in the 100-meter breaststroke (1 minute 1.49 seconds). In that meet, Italy won 4 of the 16 gold medals for men, and East Germany won 14 of the 16 for women.

Old heroes. In the 1988 Olympics, Kristin Otto of East Germany won six gold medals in six events, Evans won three in three events, and Matt Biondi of Moraga, Calif., won five gold, one silver, and one bronze in seven events. In 1989, Otto won both backstroke titles in the East German championships. She also took one gold medal and one bronze in backstroke in the European championships.

In beating Jager in the 50-meter freestyle in the 1988 Olympics, Biondi lowered the world record—previously held by Jager—to 22.14 seconds. Biondi and Jager had been leapfrogging each other in setting world records in the 50-meter freestyle for almost four years. Both qualified for the final in the United States long-course championships held from July 31 to Aug. 4, 1989, in Los Angeles. Biondi won. Jager was charged with a false start and disqualified, a decision that stunned him and led to loud and angry protests by Jager and spectators.   Frank Litsky

In *World Book,* see **Swimming.**

Switzerland

Switzerland began to curtail the almost legendary strict secrecy of its banks in 1989, in a move caused by scandals implicating Swiss banks in the handling of money that was illegally obtained by depositors. Such funds included tremendous sums deposited by international drug dealers for *laundering* (the transfer of money to conceal its illegal source).

The Lebanese connection. The Swiss government on May 10 proposed a law making it a crime to conceal criminal funds. The draft bill followed an April report by the national banking commission saying that Swiss banks had laundered $1.3 billion—apparently drug-smuggling profits—for Lebanese brothers Barkev and Jean Magharian. A grand jury in California had indicted the brothers on March 3 in a drug case.

The Lebanese connection had already forced from office Elisabeth Kopp, justice minister and the first woman in the Swiss cabinet, after she admitted tipping off her husband about an impending investigation into his connections with the Magharian brothers. Kopp resigned on January 12.

Public backs army. The Swiss on November 26 overwhelmingly defeated a move to abolish the country's army. In a *referendum* (direct vote) on an abolition proposal, 64 per cent of the Swiss who cast ballots voted against the measure.　Joseph Fitchett

See also **Europe** (Facts in brief table). In *World Book,* see **Switzerland.**

Syria. Syria's persistent involvement in Lebanon's escalating civil war drew international criticism in 1989 and left Syria virtually without allies in the Arab world. In March and again in August, Syria and its Lebanese Muslim allies engaged in ferocious artillery battles with Christian forces. The fighting left Beirut, Lebanon's capital, devastated and at least 800 people dead. In August, Pope John Paul II called Syria's bombardment of Christian positions "genocide."

Rivalry with Iraq. Also in August, a three-member committee from the Arab League charged with negotiating a settlement to the Lebanese conflict suspended its activities, accusing Syria of blocking its efforts. One major obstacle to any Lebanese settlement was the bitter hatred between Syria and its archenemy Iraq. In Lebanon, Iraq has backed the Christian units of the Lebanese army led by General Michel Awn, who in March began a campaign to drive Syria's estimated 40,000-member force out of Lebanon.

Power broker. Another stumbling block to a peace plan was the determination of Syria's President Hafiz al-Assad to play power broker in any Lebanese political agreement. In November, Syria approved a plan negotiated by the Arab League. In its first stage, the Lebanese parliament elected a Syrian-backed Christian as president. When Lebanon's new president was assassinated less than three weeks after taking office, another candidate acceptable to Syria was elected to the post.

The agreement also preserved Syria's position as a major player in Lebanese politics. It called for only gradual withdrawal of Syrian forces from parts of Lebanon.

PLO relations. In June, President Assad released 140 members of Al Fatah, a major guerrilla group within the Palestine Liberation Organization (PLO), as a gesture of support for the Palestinian uprising in Israeli-occupied territories. But Assad continued to back hard-line factions in the PLO that were opposed to PLO leader Yasir Arafat, whom Assad expelled from Syria in 1983.

The economy. President Assad's economic reform program introduced in 1988 to spur development and loosen government control over the Syrian economy began to show results in 1989. New marketing and export rules for agriculture, which were issued in February, raised prices paid to growers of grain and cotton, Syria's major export crops. Cotton production rose to 176,000 short tons (160,000 metric tons), a 25 per cent increase.

Expanded oil production from the new fields in the Dayr az Zawr area in western Syria also boosted Syria's economic prospects. Production in 1989 averaged 340,000 barrels per day (bpd), a 70,000-bpd increase over 1988. But inefficiency in state-run industries continued to hamper development.　William Spencer

See also **Middle East** (Facts in brief table). In *World Book,* see **Syria.**

Taiwan. Elections on Dec. 2, 1989, set back Taiwan's ruling party, the Kuomintang (KMT), which won only 53 per cent of the popular vote. In Taiwan's previous general election, in November 1986, the KMT won 70 per cent of the vote.

The elections were the first since opposition political parties were made legal in January 1989. At stake were local offices and seats in the provincial Assembly and in the legislative *yuan* (council), Taiwan's parliament. Popular vote filled 78 seats in the 294-member legislative yuan, and special-interest groups chose 52. The remaining seats continued to be held by KMT members elected for life in 1947 in mainland China.

The main opposition to the KMT was the Democratic Progressive Party (DPP), which won 21 seats with 38 per cent of the vote. It also won six city and county posts. The DPP charged the KMT with vote fraud, and some newspapers backed the claim.

The DPP wanted all parliamentary seats to be filled by popular vote and supported a bill passed in January 1989 calling for the voluntary retirement of hundreds of aged lawmakers. The party opposed a provision of the law granting $136,000 in severance pay for each elderly member, few of whom wanted to retire.

Relations with China. Finance Minister Shirley Kuo led a Taiwanese delegation to a meeting of the Asian Development Bank that began on May 4 in Beijing. It was the first time senior officials from Taiwan had visited the mainland. (The government of Taiwan has claimed to represent China since the Communists came to power there in 1949.) The visit was overshadowed by student demonstrations for democracy in Beijing. In a show of support for the demonstrators in China, about 1 million Taiwanese joined hands to form a human chain stretching across the island.

New prime minister. President Li Teng-hui on May 21 accepted the resignation of Prime Minister Yu Kuo-hwa, a conservative member of the KMT's old guard. He was succeeded by Li Huan, a 72-year-old moderate who was secretary general of the KMT.

Economic diplomacy. Li Teng-hui went abroad in March on the first state trip by a president of Taiwan in 12 years. As part of his "flexible diplomacy" policy, he visited Singapore even though it does not formally recognize Taiwan. A wealthy international trader, Taiwan in 1989 began using its influence as a potential aid donor to gain diplomatic recognition. When Liberia recognized Taiwan on October 9—in expectation of $150 million in Taiwanese aid—China angrily broke off its relations with Liberia and accused Taiwan of buying friends. Even as Taiwan's booming economy attracted foreign investment, the island emerged as Asia's fastest-growing investor in other Asian nations, including China.   Henry S. Bradsher

See also **Asia** (Facts in brief table); **China.** In *World Book,* see **Taiwan.**

Tanzania. See **Africa.** In the World Book Supplement section, see **Tanzania.**

Taxation. United States President George Bush and Republicans in Congress failed in 1989 to cut taxes on *capital gains* (profit from the sale of property or securities). Bush had promised such a cut during the 1988 presidential campaign. To the surprise of many, the proposal was approved by the heavily Democratic House of Representatives. But Senate Democrats stymied the measure, calling it a tax break for the rich. An estimated 80 per cent of the benefits from the House-approved cut would have gone to individuals earning more than $100,000 a year.

The Bush plan would have marked a significant departure from the philosophy of the massive Tax Reform Act of 1986, that all types of income be treated alike. The 1986 law fixed the top tax rate on capital gains at 33 per cent. The House-approved cut would have reduced this ceiling to 19.6 per cent on most capital gains for 2½ years. After that, the rate would have risen to 28 per cent and gains on assets acquired after Dec. 31, 1991, would have been indexed for inflation. Bush had sought a permanent rate reduction.

The House approval followed a key vote on September 28 that rejected, 239-190, an effort to kill the bill. The House also defeated a rival proposal by the Democratic leadership to increase the taxes of the wealthiest Americans and expand the deduction for individual retirement accounts (IRA's).

The capital gains provisions were part of a 1,935-page bill aimed at reducing the federal budget deficit.

Drawing by Baloo, *Good Housekeeping* magazine; reprinted with permission of Rex F. May

"We'll have one long form, one short form, and one just-right form."

Television

The bill also included health-care and child-care initiatives and dozens of special-interest items. On October 13, the Senate voted to limit the measure to deficit-reducing moves. This came after Republicans acknowledged they could not muster enough votes to retain the capital gains cut, whose addition to the bill was blocked by procedural requirements imposed by the Democratic majority.

On November 2, Bush reluctantly abandoned the Administration's hope of attaching capital gains cuts to either the deficit-reduction bill or separate legislation to raise the national debt limit. His announcement ended the capital gains battle for 1989.

Congress did approve some tax provisions as part of the deficit-reduction bill, which passed on November 22. Most of the new items, which would boost revenues by about $5.6 billion, affected only businesses; the largest mandated faster payroll tax collection.

Citizen protests over a threat of higher taxes for middle- and upper-income Medicare recipients prompted Congress to repeal a 1988 "catastrophic" health insurance law. See **Social security.**

State tax revenues increased by 7 per cent to $264 billion in the fiscal year ending June 30, 1988, up from $246 billion the previous year, the Commerce Department said in August 1989. The largest gains— 20 per cent each—were in Hawaii, Montana, and Oklahoma.   Frank Cormier and Margot Cormier

In *World Book,* see **Taxation.**

Television. Despite thousands of hours of entertainment programming, an earthquake in California and political upheaval in Eastern Europe provided the most memorable hours of television in the United States in 1989. On October 17, just moments after the American Broadcasting Companies (ABC) began live coverage of the third game of major league baseball's World Series from San Francisco's Candlestick Park, an earthquake occurred. Although the quake knocked out electric power, ABC was able to restore its broadcast signal about 40 minutes later. Al Michaels, one of the network's sportscasters, took on the role of news reporter as he covered the disaster from the park.

CBS Inc. and the National Broadcasting Company (NBC), along with Turner Broadcasting's Cable News Network (CNN), also provided viewers with special coverage of the disaster. But it was the local TV stations in San Francisco that gave viewers around the country the best look at the immediate effects of the quake. All three networks aired live broadcasts from their San Francisco affiliates. In the days that followed, the network's top anchormen—ABC's Peter Jennings, NBC's Tom Brokaw, and CBS's Dan Rather— originated broadcasts from the quake-damaged city.

Berlin Wall. Television cameras were ready to record history on November 9 after East German officials announced an end to travel restrictions. The action allowed East Germans to freely cross the Berlin Wall into West Germany for the first time. American viewers witnessed the emotional event, much of it in live broadcasts showing joyous East and West Germans reuniting after 28 years of separation. In the weeks that followed, newscasts and news specials focused on the continuing civil unrest in East Germany and in Czechoslovakia, Hungary, and Romania.

"Today" tiffs. In February, a confidential memo written by Bryant Gumbel, co-host of NBC's "Today" show, was leaked to the press. In the memo, Gumbel criticized a few of his "Today" co-workers, including Willard Scott, the show's folksy weatherman. After a few weeks of tense broadcasts, Gumbel and Scott had an on-air reconciliation in March.

But just a few months later, "Today" was hit with another personality crisis. Rumors surfaced that NBC was trying to force Jane Pauley, the other host of "Today," off the show to make room for Deborah Norville, an NBC anchorwoman. On October 27, Pauley said she was leaving the show to host a new NBC program and that Norville would replace her. Although the press hinted that Norville had been involved in a plot to get rid of Pauley, both women denied it and said there was no feud between them. Pauley's last "Today" appearance was on December 29.

Controversies. On September 27, the *New York Post* charged that the "CBS Evening News with Dan Rather" used faked battle footage in its coverage of the war in Afghanistan. CBS denied that the footage, purchased from a free-lance cameraman, was staged.

Top-rated U.S. television series

The following were the most-watched network television series for the 31-week regular season— Sept. 18, 1988, through April 16, 1989—as determined by the A. C. Nielsen Company.

1. "The Cosby Show" (NBC)
2. "Roseanne" (ABC)
3. "A Different World" (NBC)
4. "Cheers" (NBC)
5. "60 Minutes" (CBS)
6. "The Golden Girls" (NBC)
7. "Who's the Boss?" (ABC)
8. "Murder, She Wrote" (CBS)
9. "Empty Nest" (NBC)
10. "Anything but Love" (ABC)
11. "Dear John" (NBC)
12. "Growing Pains" (ABC)
13. (tie) "ALF" (NBC)
           "L.A. Law" (NBC)
15. "Matlock" (NBC)
16. (tie) "Hunter" (NBC)
           "Unsolved Mysteries" (NBC)
18. "In the Heat of the Night" (NBC)
19. "Head of the Class" (ABC)
20. "NFL Monday Night Football" (ABC)
21. "Night Court" (NBC)
22. "NBC Monday Night Movies" (NBC)
23. (tie) "The Hogan Family" (NBC)
           "The Wonder Years" (ABC)
25. "One of the Boys" (NBC)

The World Loved Lucy

Lucille Ball was the great red-haired clown known as Lucy to millions of television viewers throughout the world. After she died on April 26, 1989, former President Ronald Reagan and his wife, Nancy, said, "Her red hair, her antics on the screen, her timing, and her zest for life made her an American institution."

As the star of the slapstick situation comedy "I Love Lucy" on the CBS television network, Ball played Lucy Ricardo, the scatterbrained, conniving wife of a Cuban-born bandleader, Ricky—played by her first husband, Desi Arnaz—whose perpetual exasperation with her antics was expressed in broken English. "I Love Lucy" debuted on Oct. 15, 1951, and for six years was a Monday night habit of 30 million viewers. It is still in syndication and, in 1989, was viewed in more than 80 countries.

Part of the show's success lay in the supporting roles of Vivian Vance and William Frawley, veteran actors who played Ethel and Fred Mertz, the Ricardos' best friends and landlords. The show's plot followed a simple formula. Each week, Lucy got into trouble. When her back was against the wall, she confessed to Ricky, who rescued her. Fred was Ricky's ally; Ethel was Lucy's co-conspirator.

"I Love Lucy" shaped the future of network television programming by shifting production from New York City to Hollywood film studios where better quality for rebroadcast could be assured. The Arnazes formed Desilu Productions, Incorporated, and used three film cameras to shoot close-ups and diverse angles simulta-neously, permitting motion-picture-type editing. Before then, nearly all TV shows were one-camera local broadcasts shown live in New York City. These shows were distributed elsewhere as kinescopes, which were made by using a film camera to take crude pictures of a studio's television monitor, resulting in a low-quality print. "Lucy's" uniformly high-quality picture created the potential for reruns and off-network syndication. "Lucy" was also the first television program to be filmed before a live audience.

By 1957, Desilu Productions was producing other hit shows, such as "Whirlybirds," "The Ann Sothern Show," and "The Sheriff of Cochise." That year, the Arnazes sold their rights to the 179 episodes of "I Love Lucy" to CBS Inc. for $5 million and used the money to buy the Hollywood film studio RKO Pictures to produce more TV hits, including "The Danny Thomas Show" and "My Three Sons."

In 1960, Lucy and Desi ended their television show collaboration and divorced. In 1961, Lucy married comedian Gary Morton and bought Desi's share of Desilu for $2.5 million, becoming the first woman to head a major Hollywood production company. She continued to perform, beginning a new television series, "The Lucy Show," in 1962. In that series, she played Lucy Carlyle, secretary to an overstuffed bank president portrayed by Gale Gordon, who reacted to her antics with explosions of indignation. The series had 156 episodes and lasted until 1968.

In 1967, Lucy sold her share of Desilu to Gulf & Western, Incorporated, for $10 million. She formed Lucille Ball Productions and presented yet another Lucy to television in "Here's Lucy," which had 144 episodes from 1968 to 1974. This character, Lucy Carter, worked for an employment agency owned by her brother-in-law, played by Gordon. Her TV children were her real children, Lucie Arnaz and Desi Arnaz, Jr.

Born on Aug. 6, 1911, to Henry and Désirée Ball, in Jamestown, N.Y., Lucille Ball scarcely knew her father, who died when she was 3. Her mother, a concert pianist, enrolled Lucy at age 15 in John Murray Anderson's dramatic school in New York City, where her instructor reacted to her first reading by closing his eyes in disbelief at the way she garbled her lines.

In the late 1920's, Ball had become a successful model when an automobile accident felled her for three and a half years. In 1933, modeling again, she landed a bit part in the motion picture *Roman Scandals*. In dozens of movies over the next 20 years, usually playing comic relief, Lucille Ball never became a first-magnitude star but began to locate the talents she assembled into the Lucy character that television audiences came to love.   Clarence G. Petersen

Co-conspirators in mischief, actresses Vivian Vance, left, and Lucille Ball tackle a household problem in an episode of "I Love Lucy."

Robert Duvall, left, and Tommy Lee Jones starred in CBS's *Lonesome Dove.*
The miniseries, which aired in February, drew 40 million viewers.

During 1989, the three major networks were criticized for using "re-created" or "simulated" news footage on some of their news programs. These so-called *news re-creations* featured reenactments of real news events. Such simulated footage was broadcast on ABC's "World News Tonight" and was a prominent feature of CBS's "Saturday Night with Connie Chung" and NBC's "Yesterday, Today & Tomorrow."

Supporters of news re-creations said the technique did not mislead viewers because such footage was identified as a simulation. Critics, however, maintained that reenactments blurred the distinction between news and entertainment. In response to the criticism, CBS announced in October that it would scale back its use of the technique on "Saturday Night with Connie Chung." In November, NBC said it was discontinuing the practice altogether and pulled "Yesterday, Today & Tomorrow" off the air.

Early in 1989, Terry Rakolta, a Bloomfield, Mich., homemaker, launched a one-woman campaign against the Fox Broadcasting Company's comedy "Married . . . With Children." Rakolta wrote letters to the show's advertisers complaining that the program promoted antifamily attitudes. Her campaign, aided by a front-page story in *The New York Times*, persuaded such companies as Coca-Cola and Procter & Gamble to withdraw commercials from the program.

Prime time. According to the A. C. Nielsen Company, the three major networks' share of the audience during prime time—the hours between 8 and 11 p.m., Eastern Standard Time—continued to drop in 1989. The networks had only a 64 per cent share of the prime-time audience, down from 69 per cent in 1988.

Industry watchers attributed the decline to increased competition from videocassettes and cable television. The major networks also felt the impact of the newest network, Fox, which had a popular line-up of programs on Saturday and Sunday nights.

At the start of the 1989-1990 season, the most popular show on television continued to be NBC's "The Cosby Show." But by October, Nielsen ratings showed that "The Cosby Show" had lost its place as the most-watched television series to ABC's "Roseanne."

Despite the toppling of "The Cosby Show," NBC remained the top-rated network in prime time for the fifth consecutive season. ABC placed second, followed by CBS. CBS's lack of success—emphasized by the lowest November ratings in its history—resulted in the resignation of Earl H. (Kim) LeMasters III, president of CBS's Entertainment Division, on November 30.

New programs unveiled in the fall offered a few new faces but no big hits. ABC's family drama "Life Goes On" made television history by giving a starring role to an actor with *Down's syndrome* (a genetic disorder that causes mental retardation). The actor, Christopher Burke, played the role of Corky Thatcher.

Among the season's new comedies was ABC's "Chicken Soup," starring comedian Jackie Mason. The show was canceled before year-end. A similar fate befell NBC's "Nutt House," a comedy produced by Mel Brooks and starring Harvey Korman and Cloris Leachman.

So long. At the end of the 1988-1989 season, several long-running television series came to an end. Among them were NBC's "Family Ties" and "Miami Vice" and ABC's "Moonlighting" and "Dynasty."

Miniseries. During the year, ABC aired the last 11½ hours of the miniseries *War and Remembrance*. The first 18 hours were broadcast in 1988. The miniseries, based on Herman Wouk's 1978 novel of the same title, was the longest in television history.

CBS's eight-hour miniseries *Lonesome Dove* was a surprise hit in 1989, earning critical and popular acclaim. The saga, based on Larry McMurtry's Pulitzer Prize-winning book of the same name, drew 40 million viewers, making it one of the highest rated miniseries of the 1980's. Among its all-star cast were Robert Duvall, Tommy Lee Jones, and Anjelica Huston.

On October 29, ABC presented *The Final Days*, a made-for-television film based on the book written by Bob Woodward and Carl Bernstein, *The Washington Post* reporters who covered the Watergate scandal in 1972. The drama takes place in 1974 and tells the story of President Richard M. Nixon's last days in the White House. The film upset former President Nixon, who wrote a note to the movie's sponsor complaining that it was a "smear" on his reputation.

Late night. In January, CBS unveiled two new talk shows to compete with NBC's "Tonight Show Starring Johnny Carson" and "Late Night with David Letterman." Going up against Carson was "The Pat Sajak Show," featuring the host of the popular game show "Wheel of Fortune." Poor ratings forced the network in October to trim the show from 90 minutes to an hour.

CBS had more success with "The Arsenio Hall Show," which competed with Letterman for late-night viewers. Hall's offbeat show became a national hit.

Public television. The noncommercial Public Broadcasting Service (PBS) premiered "America's Century" in 1989, a program that looked at the foreign policy of the United States in the 1900's. Journalist Bill Moyers returned to PBS with two new series, "The Public Mind" and "The Power of the Word." "Masterpiece Theatre" presented an adaptation of Charles Dickens' *A Tale of Two Cities*.

Cable. Two new cable channels appeared in 1989, but neither attracted large audiences. In April, NBC and Cablevision System Corporation began an all-business channel called Consumer News and Business Channel (CNBC). In November, Home Box Office started The Comedy Channel.   P. J. Bednarski

See also **Awards and prizes; Barr, Roseanne.** In the Special Reports section, see **Television: The Changing Picture.** In *World Book,* see **Television.**

Tennessee. See **State government.**

Tennis. Twenty-year-old Steffi Graf and 21-year-old Boris Becker, childhood friends in West Germany, were named world champions in 1989 by the International Tennis Federation.

Becker won his third Wimbledon championship in four years and then his first United States Open. Graf, who swept the four grand-slam tournaments in 1988, won three in 1989, losing her French Open title to 17-year-old Arantxa Sánchez Vicario of Spain. Graf finished the year with an 85-2 record.

Graf, Becker, and Ivan Lendl earned more than $2-million each on the court and millions more for endorsements. Lendl became the first man to surpass $14 million in career prize money.

Chris Evert lost to Zina Garrison in the U.S. Open quarterfinals and then, at age 34, retired from the circuit. A crowd favorite since she was 16, Evert left with a career record of 1,304-145, a record total of 157 singles titles—including 18 grand-slam singles championships—and almost $9 million in prize money.

Men. The grand slams started with the Australian Open on January 16 to 29 in Melbourne. Lendl, a Czechoslovak awaiting U.S. citizenship, routed Miloslav Mecir of Czechoslovakia, 6-2, 6-2, 6-2, in the final. Lendl thus regained the number-one position in the Association of Tennis Professionals (ATP) computer rankings, which Mats Wilander of Sweden had held for 20 weeks. After winning three grand-slam titles in 1988, Wilander played poorly in 1989.

Christopher Burke, left, became the first person with Down's syndrome to star in a TV series in "Life Goes On," which premiered on ABC in 1989.

Still a crowd favorite, Chris Evert waves to well-wishers at the U.S. Open as she retires from tennis in September at age 34.

The most successful young male of the year was 17-year-old Michael Chang, a patient, defensive player from Placentia, Calif. In the French Open, held on clay from May 29 to June 10 in Paris, he upset Lendl, 4-6, 4-6, 6-3, 6-3, 6-3, to reach the quarterfinals. In the final, he defeated Stefan Edberg of Sweden, 6-1, 3-6, 4-6, 6-4, 6-2, and became the first American to win this title since Tony Trabert in 1955. He also became the youngest male grand-slam champion ever.

The next major tournament was the Wimbledon championships on grass, held from June 26 to July 9 in Wimbledon, England. Becker beat Lendl, 7-5, 6-7, 2-6, 6-4, 6-3, in the semifinals and defeated Edberg, the defender, 6-0, 7-6, 6-4, in the final.

The last grand-slam tournament was the U.S. Open on August 29 to September 10 in Flushing Meadow, N.Y. Becker defeated Lendl in the final, 7-6, 1-6, 6-3, 7-6, with 11 aces and 23 service winners. It was Lendl's eighth consecutive final in the Open, tying Bill Tilden's record (1918-1925). Chang lost in the fourth round to Tim Mayotte, as he did at Wimbledon.

Women. Graf won the Australian Open final from Helena Sukova of Czechoslovakia, 6-4, 6-4, on a day so hot that the temperature at the court surface reached 144°F. (62°C). In the French Open final, Graf suffered stomach cramps and dissipated a 5-3 lead in the last set as the patient Sánchez won, 7-6, 3-6, 7-5.

At Wimbledon, Graf defeated Evert, 6-2, 6-1, in the semifinals and 32-year-old Martina Navratilova of Dallas, 6-2, 6-7, 6-1, in the final. In the U.S. Open final, Graf trailed Navratilova by one set and 4-2 in the second set before winning, 3-6, 7-5, 6-1.

Davis Cup. The United States, which had been shunted to regional eliminations, returned to the main draw and defeated Paraguay and France, both by 5-0. But in the semifinals, with John McEnroe sidelined by an ailing shoulder, Becker led West Germany to a 3-2 victory over the Americans. That sent West Germany, the defending champion, into the final against Sweden on December 15 to 17 in West Germany. West Germany won, 3 matches to 2.

Tours. The ATP completed plans to start its own worldwide men's tour in 1990. The schedule listed 77 tournaments in 28 nations, including the Soviet Union and China, with prize money exceeding $35 million. The players would be free to compete in the grand-slam tournaments, which are not part of the tour. Since 1981, the tour had been run by the Men's Tennis Council, and the players were dissatisfied because they held only three of the nine seats on the council.

The Women's International Professional Tennis Council signed a five-year, $30-million contract with Kraft General Foods as its worldwide sponsor, starting in 1990. Virginia Slims, the previous sponsor, agreed to continue to stage 14 tournaments. The 1990 schedule will comprise 64 tournaments in 19 nations with $23 million in prize money.   Frank Litsky

In *World Book,* see **Tennis.**

Texas. See **Houston; State government.**

Thailand continued its impressive economic growth in 1989. The International Monetary Fund put Thailand on its list of nations that have progressed from being poor countries preoccupied with growing food to being manufacturers and exporters. Thailand's volume of exports almost doubled in the 1980's, with computer chips and other high-technology goods joining such traditional exports as rice, textiles, and clothing. As foreign investment poured in to build factories to take advantage of Thailand's cheap labor and politically stable environment, export levels were expected to continue to rise rapidly—as was prosperity.

The average annual per capita income reached $1,000, more than twice the level in most other Asian countries. With an economic growth rate of 9 per cent or more per year, Thailand expected average personal incomes to double in eight years. Economists predicted that Thailand would join the ranks of such Asian economic miracles as South Korea and Taiwan.

The economic boom centered on Bangkok, the capital. The city became increasingly polluted and crowded as new factories rose from surrounding rice fields. The government encouraged industry to spread out across the country, but most rural areas lacked roads and other facilities to support factories. Good harvests and higher crop prices helped rural areas during 1989, though about 25 per cent of the people there lived below the official poverty level.

Other developments. On August 3, General Chaovalit Yongchaiyut, the commander of Thailand's politically powerful army, spoke out against corruption, particularly in the government of Prime Minister Chatchai Chunhawan (sometimes spelled Chatichai Choonhavan). One of Chatchai's chief advisers responded by saying that those accusing the government of corruption should "put their own house in order," and that the army should be more professional and less political. About 1,000 army officers met to protest the adviser's statement. The adviser was forced to resign on August 8.

Chatchai, who advocated turning Southeast Asia "from a battleground to a marketplace," also differed with the army—as well as with Foreign Minister Sitthi Sawetsila (sometimes spelled Siddhi Savetsila)—over Thailand's policy toward its war-torn neighbor, Cambodia (formerly Kampuchea). In January, Chatchai began friendly contacts with Cambodia's Vietnamese-installed prime minister, Hun Sen. Sitthi, on the other hand, worked with other Southeast Asian nations to replace Hun Sen's regime with an opposition coalition. The Thai army channeled Chinese military aid to opposition guerrillas in camps along the Thailand-Cambodia border. See **Cambodia.**

The worst typhoon to hit the southern part of Thailand in more than 30 years killed at least 300 people on November 4. Hundreds of thousands were left homeless.   Henry S. Bradsher

See also **Asia** (Facts in brief table). In *World Book,* see **Thailand.**

Theater. Stars shone on Broadway and throughout the United States in 1989. The willingness of well-known artists in other fields—ballet, music, and motion pictures—to appear onstage enabled Broadway producers to present plays that would otherwise not reach a popular audience.

Ballet's biggest superstar, Mikhail Baryshnikov, played the leading role in *Metamorphosis,* an adaptation by British playwright and director Steven Berkoff of Czech writer Franz Kafka's story about a man transformed into an insect. The rock star Sting took the leading role of Macheath, the suave gangleader, in a revival of *The Threepenny Opera* (1928) by German playwright Bertolt Brecht and composer Kurt Weill. Although Sting's fans initially filled the theater, bad reviews led to shrinking audiences, and the play folded after a few months. And Dustin Hoffman—who won an Academy Award for best actor in 1989 for *Rain Man* (1988)—appeared on Broadway as Shylock in William Shakespeare's *The Merchant of Venice* after a sold-out run in London. At $55 each for the best seats, this production set a new record for ticket prices for nonmusical plays on Broadway.

Broadway musicals, however, looked not to the stars but to the past. The most successful musical of 1989 was *Jerome Robbins' Broadway,* an anthology of the director-choreographer's most beloved dance numbers from a dozen hit shows, including *High Button Shoes* (1947), *West Side Story* (1957), and *Fiddler on the Roof* (1964). With this show, the ticket price for Broadway musicals hit $60.

Gypsy, the 1959 musical show business saga of stripper Gypsy Rose Lee and her mother, Rose, had a successful second major revival, this time with television star Tyne Daly in the leading role. *Sweeney Todd,* composer Stephen Sondheim's 1979 operatic musical about a murderous barber, returned to the stage in an off-off-Broadway production that moved to Broadway for an extended run.

Two new Broadway musicals brought beloved movie classics to the stage—with less than perfect results. Reviewers called the atmosphere artificial and the acting insipid in *Meet Me in St. Louis,* based on the 1944 movie starring Judy Garland. The staging of *Grand Hotel,* set, like the 1932 movie, in Berlin in 1928, was spectacular. But critics found fault with the score by George Forrest and Robert Wright.

A revue called *Black and Blue,* conceived and directed by Argentine theatrical designers Claudio Segovia and Héctor Orezzoli, arrived on Broadway after successful productions in Europe. Blues singers Ruth Brown, Linda Hopkins, and Carrie Smith belted out classic blues and vaudeville songs, while a large company of young and old jazz- and tap-dancers presented numbers by such fine black choreographers as Cholly Atkins and Henry LeTang.

Issues on stage. Amid star vehicles and musical throwbacks, Broadway found a place for plays with some social significance. Vanessa Redgrave appeared

459

in a revival of Tennessee Williams' *Orpheus Descending* (1957). The production, which first opened in London, won Redgrave much praise for her performance as an unhappily married Italian woman in the American South who falls in love with a musician.

Wendy Wasserstein's rueful comedy *The Heidi Chronicles* surveyed the women's movement over the last 20 years. Larry Gelbart's *Mastergate* satirized Washington politics by sending up the murky language of the Iran-contra hearings. Like many other productions, these two plays were first developed in not-for-profit theaters before entering the commercial arena. *Heidi* premiered at the Seattle Repertory Theater and then at Playwrights Horizons in New York City. *Mastergate* moved to Broadway from the American Repertory Theatre in Boston.

Aaron Sorkin's *A Few Good Men* was the only new American play produced directly for Broadway in 1989. It was a military courtroom drama featuring stirring performances by Tom Hulce and Stephen Lang.

Other productions. The oddest play to appear on Broadway in 1989 had no words. *Largely New York*, starring dancer and clown Bill Irwin, combined slapstick with modern dance and street dancing.

Two British imports also reached Broadway. Willy Russell's *Shirley Valentine*, starring Pauline Collins, was a one-woman show about an unhappy British housewife who finds happiness by running away. *Lend Me a Tenor*, a farce about a Midwestern clerk who achieves stardom as a last-minute substitute for an ailing opera singer, was written by American lawyer Ken Ludwig but premiered in London.

Off-Broadway. Not-for-profit theaters generated several long-running off-Broadway shows. Terrence McNally's *The Lisbon Traviata* was part show business comedy, part romantic tragedy. Brian Friel's *Aristocrats* was the saga of an Irish family on the verge of collapse. Both these plays were produced by Manhattan Theatre Club.

In Jerry Sterner's *Other People's Money*, a ruthless entrepreneur determined to take over a failing New England family business encounters a feisty young woman lawyer who struggles to save the company. A comic primer on the vocabulary and tactics of Wall Street traders, the play drew a large, appreciative audience from Manhattan's financial district. Charles Busch, a comic writer and performer who specializes in female roles, had his third off-Broadway hit with *The Lady in Question*, an affectionate spoof of 1940's anti-Nazi movies.

Production sharing. The high cost of producing theater has forced producers to devise new methods of bringing shows to the stage economically. One increasingly popular trend is known as "production sharing," in which two or more theaters share the cost of mounting a show.

In 1989, the La Jolla Playhouse near San Diego experimented with three different forms of production

News of an ailing opera star starts the action in *Lend Me a Tenor,* a farce about a Midwestern clerk's chance to win stardom.

Peter Pan soars above the cast of *Jerome Robbins' Broadway,* an anthology of the choreographer's most beloved dance numbers from numerous hit musicals.

sharing. Its season opened with Frank Galati's adaptation of John Steinbeck's novel *The Grapes of Wrath* (1939), a production created by the Steppenwolf Theatre in Chicago. After considerable revision in La Jolla, the production traveled to the Royal National Theatre of Great Britain for a brief run and was scheduled to open on Broadway in 1990.

The La Jolla also presented a new adaptation of French dramatist Molière's 1666 classic *The Misanthrope,* set in contemporary Hollywood, that subsequently played at the Goodman Theatre in Chicago. In addition, the La Jolla was one of several theaters that collaborated in developing a musical called *Dangerous Games.* Directed and choreographed by Graciela Daniele with music by Argentine composer Astor Piazzolla, *Dangerous Games* finally opened on Broadway to bad reviews and closed after a brief run.

Also beyond New York. The Guthrie Theater in Minneapolis, Minn., offered its audiences two unusual large-scale productions. One was the U.S. premiere of *Pravda,* David Hare and Howard Brenton's sprawling exposé of contemporary journalism. The Guthrie also presented a rare staging of French playwright Jean Genet's last play, *The Screens* (1961), a five-hour epic set during the French-Algerian war of the 1950's and early 1960's. The production, directed by JoAnne Akalaitis, featured a cast of 50 and a new score composed by Philip Glass and Foday Musa Suso.

In Los Angeles, renowned British actor Derek Jacobi played the English poet Lord Byron in a show called *Byron—Mad, Bad, and Dangerous to Know.* At the Ahmanson Theatre in Los Angeles, playwright Edward Albee directed a revival of his 1962 play *Who's Afraid of Virginia Woolf?* starring Glenda Jackson and John Lithgow.

Festivals. The Soviet Union's policy of *glasnost* (openness in the flow of information) had its effect on the U.S. theater festival circuit. In its 10th and final year, the PepsiCo Summerfare in Purchase, N.Y., offered Soviet director Anatoly Vasiliev's staging of Italian writer Luigi Pirandello's *Six Characters in Search of an Author* (1921). The Pushkin Theater in Leningrad was represented by a brutal adaptation of the Anton Chekhov short story "Ward Six" (1892). The San Diego Arts Festival presented the U.S. premiere of a five-hour Soviet play called *Brothers and Sisters* at the Old Globe Theater.

The American Music Theater Festival in Philadelphia mounted the premiere of *Betsey Brown.* It is based on American writer Ntozake Shange's 1985 novel about a black family in St. Louis, Mo.

The first National Black Theater Festival kicked off in August in Winston-Salem, N.C. More than 125 U.S. black theater companies sent representatives to the festival, which featured workshops, conferences, and productions by 17 companies.   Don Shewey

In *World Book,* see **Theater.**

Togo. See Africa.

Toronto. Enthusiasm for "megaprojects," including a new sports stadium and bids for a world's fair and the 1996 Summer Olympic Games, were major themes during 1989 in the public life of Toronto, capital of Ontario, Canada's richest province. At the same time, there was a growing public concern about the city's hectic pace of growth.

A new sports stadium, the 60,000-seat SkyDome, opened in June. The multipurpose sports stadium has a three-part retractable roof that can be opened or closed in 20 minutes.

A private consortium owns the SkyDome, but it was built with the help of government funding. The regional Metropolitan Toronto government and the province of Ontario each contributed $30 million Canadian (about $25 million U.S.) and the provincial government, in addition, guaranteed construction loans.

The final cost of about $550 million ($460 million U.S.) was more than double the original estimate of $241 million (about $200 million U.S.). The design of the stadium—originally intended simply as an all-weather home for the Blue Jays baseball team and the Argonauts football team—was expanded to include a hotel, restaurants, a discothèque, and a health club.

Critics said the SkyDome would lose money and its downtown location would cause horrendous traffic jams. The waterfront site of the stadium is only five blocks from the soaring, crowded office towers of Toronto's financial district. But the SkyDome proved popular with the public, and the traffic jams never happened. Crowds were content to leave cars at home and rely on the subway and commuter rail lines.

The Blue Jays marked the first year in their new home by winning the American League East, though they lost the pennant to the Oakland Athletics.

Olympic and world's fair bids. The success of the dome inspired Toronto Mayor Arthur Eggleton and the Toronto Olympic Organizing Committee to press ahead with a bid for Toronto to host the Summer Olympics in 1996. Meanwhile, a group of business leaders and architects put in a bid to hold a world's fair in Toronto in the year 2000.

Supporters claimed that these international events would bring Toronto great benefits, including tourist dollars, stadiums, and housing projects. Their claims sounded so convincing that in September 1989 the Toronto City Council, though dominated by a coalition of protect-our-neighborhood reformers, voted 14 to 1 to support the Olympic bid. But other groups in the city formed a coalition to protest the projects and demand that more money be spent on the needy.

Success stress. In 1989, Toronto continued to feel the strains of success, mainly in the housing area. The city's unemployment rate fell to 3.5 per cent, the lowest among Canada's major cities, and the welfare rolls decreased by 2,000 clients—a drop of almost 10 per cent. But the city's prosperity pushed housing prices up from a median price of $219,464 ($184,350 U.S.) in 1988 to $236,000 ($198,240 U.S.) in 1989. Renting was also a problem because only 3 out of every 1,000 apartments were vacant.

To ease the housing shortage, the province of Ontario and the city of Toronto in 1988 had joined in a project to build housing for 12,000 people on 70 acres (28 hectares) of downtown industrial land. But in 1989, the developers discovered that the soil had been badly polluted by wastes from earlier manufacturing operations, and the cleanup is expected to be costly and time consuming.

New skyscrapers continued to enlarge Toronto's spectacular downtown skyline. Work was completed during the year on the 68-story Scotia Plaza Tower, and construction was underway on BCE Place, a 53-story tower. The City Council gave final approval for construction of the 57-story Bay Adelaide project, across the street from the Scotia Plaza Tower.

When projects under construction or in the approval process during 1989 are added to the buildings already up, Toronto will have more than 75 million square feet (7 million square meters) of office space. City planners believe this is the point at which the city should consider building major new downtown transit facilities. In deference to public concern about the growth of downtown, Toronto's reform-minded council set tight new limits on the deals the city can make with office developers.   David Lewis Stein

See also **Ontario.** In *World Book,* see **Ontario; Toronto.**

Toys and games. Retail toy sales in the United States in 1989 increased about 5 per cent over 1988 sales. Toy industry analysts attributed the gain to the popularity of video games and to the increased profitability of medium-sized toy companies that offer more than one or two product lines.

Video games were the industry's hottest items during the year, with sales reaching more than $3 billion. But many toy industry analysts predicted that the video-game craze—which started in the early 1980's, faded out in the middle of the decade, and then made a comeback—may have reached its peak.

To try to hold on to consumer interest, video-game manufacturers in 1989 introduced game systems with expanded play capabilities, better graphics, and more sophisticated accessories. Nintendo of America, Incorporated, of Redmond, Wash., brought out Game Boy, the first handheld, battery-operated portable video-game system. Game Boy has a 2-inch (5-centimeter) screen and a set of headphones. Sega Enterprises Limited of San Francisco rolled out Genesis, a video-game system with more realistic images.

Holy bat craze! "Batmania" swept the toy industry in 1989, thanks to the hit motion picture *Batman.* The movie, based on the adventures of the popular comic book hero, inspired such merchandise as action figures, Halloween costumes, and a battery-powered Batmobile for children to ride. By the end of the year, however, interest in Batman items appeared to fade.

Power Pad, introduced by Nintendo of America in 1989, lets players control the action of a video game by jumping on a vinyl mat.

Muppets join Mickey. On August 28, the Walt Disney Company of Burbank, Calif., purchased the Muppet characters from their creator, Jim Henson. The sale gives Disney the right to use Kermit the Frog, Miss Piggy, and any future characters created by Henson & Associates of New York City.

Baby doll boom. There was a rebirth in the baby doll market in 1989. Tyco Toys, Incorporated, of Mount Laurel, N.J., reintroduced two classic dolls from the 1960's—Betsy Wetsy, who wets her pants when she drinks, and Tiny Tears, who cries when she drinks. Tyco Toys also had a hit with a doll called Oopsie Daisy, who crawls, falls, cries, and then gets back up to start crawling again. Mattel Incorporated of Hawthorne, Calif., unveiled the P. J. Sparkles doll. The doll has tiny lights on her heart-shaped pendant, bracelet, earrings, and hairbow. The lights twinkle when her back is squeezed.

A special Barbie. Mattel's fashion doll, Barbie, celebrated her 30th birthday in 1989. In honor of this milestone, and to celebrate the 30th anniversary of the United Nations Declaration of the Rights of the Child, Mattel introduced a Special Edition Barbie. The white, black, Asian, and Hispanic Special Edition Barbies came with a United Nations Children's Fund (UNICEF) poster. A percentage of the profit from every sale was donated to UNICEF.

Newest fad? Superfast race cars, one of the best-selling toys in Japan, hit the United States in late 1989.

The battery-powered racers, also called *hypercars*, are 6 inches (15 centimeters) long and can reach speeds of up to 30 miles per hour (mph), or 48 kilometers per hour (kph). This is the equivalent of a real car traveling more than 300 mph (480 kph). In Japan, where they made their debut in 1987, almost 40 million racers have been sold.

More than 10 different hypercar lines were introduced into stores in the United States during the year. These included Record Breakers from Hasbro Incorporated of Pawtucket, R.I.; Hyper Drivers from the Tonka Corporation of Minnetonka, Minn.; and Superfast Machines from Matchbox Toys (U.S.A.) Limited of Moonachie, N.J.

Kid restaurant. In 1989, Fisher-Price Toys of East Aurora, N.Y., introduced McDonald's Restaurant Center, a child-sized, portable restaurant. The center has a kitchen where the grill and fryer make sizzling sounds, a drive-through counter, and a cash register. Parents can buy play food that looks just like the fast food sold at McDonald's restaurants.

Food fight. Mattel introduced a new line of action figures during the year called Food Fighters. The line pits the good Kitchen Commandos—Burgerdier General, Major Munch, Lieutenant Legg, and Private Pizza—against the evil Refrigerator Rejects—Mean Weener, Fat Frenchy, Taco Terror, Short Stack, and Chip-The-Ripper.   Diane P. Cardinale

In *World Book,* see **Doll; Game; Toy.**

Track and field

Track and field. Javier Sotomayor of Cuba, Said Aouita of Morocco, and Roger Kingdom of Pittsburgh, Pa., capped a 1989 season with world records. Carl Lewis gained a world record in the 100-meter dash when the International Amateur Athletic Federation (IAAF), which governs track and field worldwide, stripped Canada's Ben Johnson of his previous record because of Johnson's admitted use of steroids.

In the 1988 Summer Olympics in Seoul, South Korea, Johnson won the 100-meter dash in 9.79 seconds, a world record. Lewis finished second in 9.92 seconds. Three days later, the International Olympic Committee said Johnson's postrace urine test showed the presence of anabolic steroids, artificial male sex hormones banned because they give users an unfair advantage and because of dangerous side effects.

Johnson was disqualified and his time was thrown out, so his 9.83 in 1987 remained the world record in the 100-meter dash. But on June 12, 1989, in a Canadian government hearing into drug use in sports, Johnson admitted that he had used banned drugs since 1981. Although he had passed a drug test after he had set his 1987 world record, Johnson confessed that he had used steroids in training for that race. The IAAF ruled on Sept. 5, 1989, that the world record in the 100-meter dash was the 9.92 seconds run by Lewis at the 1988 Summer Olympics.

Other records. The 21-year-old Sotomayor became the first to clear 8 feet (2.44 meters) in the high jump.

He raised the world indoor record to 7 feet 11½ inches (2.43 meters) on March 4, 1989, in the world indoor championships in Budapest, Hungary. His outdoor breakthrough came on July 29 in the Central America and Caribbean Championships in San Juan, Puerto Rico.

The 29-year-old Aouita was the outstanding distance runner of the 1980's. On Aug. 20, 1989, in Cologne, West Germany, he lowered the world record for 3,000 meters by more than 2½ seconds, winning in 7 minutes 29.45 seconds. Aouita also held the world records for 1,500, 2,000, and 5,000 meters.

For the second consecutive year, Aouita and Paula Ivan of Romania won the overall titles in the season-long World Cup series. Ivan was the only female runner to break a world record on the track. On July 10 in Nice, France, she ran the mile in 4 minutes 15.61 seconds, breaking Mary Decker Slaney's record.

In 1978, Henry Rono of Kenya set four world records. One of them fell to Aouita in the 3,000 meters in August 1989. Another one, in the 3,000-meter steeplechase, was broken on July 3 in Stockholm, Sweden, when Peter Koech of Kenya ran it in 8 minutes 5.35 seconds.

In 1981 in Zurich, Switzerland, Renaldo Nehemiah set the world record of 12.93 seconds for the 110-meter hurdles. On Aug. 16, 1989, on the same track, Kingdom improved the record to 12.92 seconds as Nehemiah watched from the stands.

World outdoor track and field records established in 1989

Men

Event	Holder	Country	Where set	Date	Record
100 meters	Carl Lewis	U.S.A.	Seoul, South Korea	Sept. 24, 1988*	0:09.92
3,000 meters	Said Aouita	Morocco	Cologne, West Germany	Aug. 20, 1989	7:29.45
10,000 meters	Arturo Barrios	Mexico	West Berlin, West Germany	Aug. 18	27:08.23
110-meter hurdles	Roger Kingdom	U.S.A.	Zurich, Switzerland	Aug. 16	0:12.92
3,000-meter steeplechase	Peter Koech	Kenya	Stockholm, Sweden	July 3	8:05.35
4 × 200 meter relay	Danny Everett, LeRoy Burrell, Floyd Heard, and Carl Lewis	U.S.A.	Koblenz, West Germany	Aug. 23	1:19.38
High jump	Javier Sotomayor	Cuba	San Juan, Puerto Rico	July 29	8 ft. (2.44 m)

Women

Event	Holder	Country	Where set	Date	Record
Mile	Paula Ivan	Romania	Nice, France	July 10	4:15.61
Triple jump	Galina Chistyakova	Soviet Union	Stockholm, Sweden	July 3	47 ft. 7¾ in. (14.52 m)†

m = meters
*The International Amateur Athletic Federation in 1989 stripped the 1987 world record of 9.83 seconds from Ben Johnson of Canada after Johnson admitted under oath that he had violated the rules by using anabolic steroids in training for that race. The record was then given to Lewis, who had the fastest time of anyone who had passed a drug test.
†Unofficial record.

Javier Sotomayor of Cuba clears the bar in the high jump, setting a world record of 8 feet (2.44 meters) at a meet in San Juan, Puerto Rico, in July.

Major meets. The World Cup, which was held from September 8 to 10 in Barcelona, Spain, matched the best national teams against continental all-star teams. The team winners were the men from the United States and the women from East Germany.

Kingdom won the 110-meter hurdles in 12.87 seconds, the fastest ever, but a slightly excessive tail wind ruled it out as a record. Ana Quirot of Cuba won the women's 400 and 800 meters and ended the year undefeated in those races. Abdi Bile of Somalia won the men's 1,500 meters and was the year's fastest in the 1,500 and the mile.

David Patrick of Austin, Tex., won the men's 400-meter hurdles, and Sandra Farmer-Patrick won the women's 400-meter hurdles. They became the first husband and wife to win the same running event in a major international championship.

In the world indoor championships held from March 3 to 5, the leaders in total medals were the Soviet Union (13) and the United States (11), each nation with 4 gold metals. There were world indoor records by Sotomayor, Paul Ereng of Kenya in the men's 800 meters (1 minute 44.84 seconds), and Elly Van Hulst of the Netherlands in the women's 3,000 meters (8 minutes 33.92 seconds). Among the defending champions who repeated were three Americans—Larry Myricks in the long jump, Mike Conley in the triple jump, and Antonio McKay in the 400 meters.   Frank Litsky

In *World Book,* see **Track and field.**

Transit. The year 1989 brought a mix of good and bad news to transit systems in the United States. Overall, the industry carried approximately 9 billion riders, about the same as in 1988. New York City subways, however, had ridership gains of about 2 per cent monthly, and served more than 3.8 million patrons daily. In Washington, D.C., rail ridership rose to more than 520,000 people per day. With this increase, Washington's rapid transit system replaced Chicago's as the second-largest in the United States in daily riders. (Chicago ridership fell below 500,000 passengers, apparently due mainly to a series of violent assaults and a murder on the system early in the year.) In Boston, commuter rail ridership grew to more than 60,000 people per day, a 100 per cent increase since 1983.

Graffiti cleanup. The New York City Transit Authority concluded a five-year effort to clean graffiti from subway cars in the spring of 1989, when the last graffiti-covered train was removed from service. At year's end, the agency was fulfilling its pledge to keep subway trains graffiti-free.

Out West. The Seattle trolley bus tunnel opened for testing on March 15. (Both trolley buses and trolley cars draw power from an overhead electric wire. Trolley buses, however, can maneuver in traffic, whereas trolley cars run on a track.) Bus number 5001 made the first 1.3-mile (2-kilometer) trip under the city's downtown area. Sixty articulated trolley buses, which have two sections linked by a flexible joint, are

465

Work crews remove graffiti from subway cars in San Francisco, one of several cities with special programs in 1989 to keep trains graffiti-free.

to operate in each direction in the tunnel each hour starting in mid-1990.

In San Diego, work began on April 26 on the city's new Bayside Trolley Line. The 1-mile (1.6-kilometer) line, scheduled to be completed in mid-1990, will run between downtown stops and the Convention and Performing Arts Center. On June 24, San Diego opened the 11-mile (18-kilometer) East Trolley Line, which serves the suburban community of El Cajon. About 12,000 people are expected to use the new trolley line each day.

Ridership on the 18-mile (29-kilometer) light rail line in Sacramento, Calif., reached 18,000 daily passengers in 1989, forcing the city to order 10 more cars to add to its 26-car fleet. (Light rail systems, like trolleys, use electrically powered cars that run on a track.) By the end of the year, 11 miles of the line had been expanded from a single track to a double track, permitting cars to run continuously in both directions.

Baltimore boom. On May 15, the State of Maryland Mass Transit Administration (MTA) began construction on the Hunt Valley to Glen Burnie Central Light Rail Line. The 27.5-mile (44-kilometer) line, which will serve Baltimore's outlying suburbs as well as downtown, is slated to open in 1993 at a cost of $290 million. On July 27, the MTA broke ground on a 1.5-mile (2.4-kilometer) extension of the city's subway system. The extension, to cost $326 million, will link Charles Center with Johns Hopkins Hospital.

Federal policy. The growth of the country's transit systems in 1989 was accomplished despite tight federal funding. President George Bush's Administration proposed $3.2 billion in fiscal 1990 for the Urban Mass Transportation Administration (UMTA), which makes federal grants to cities for their mass transportation systems. This amount was almost identical to the funding allocated to UMTA in 1988 and about 20 per cent below the more than $4 billion UMTA received in fiscal 1981.

Bus woes. Uncertainty faced manufacturers of transit buses in 1989. As a result of a new federal requirement that went into effect October 1, all new bus models must be tested for safety and performance at the manufacturer's expense at a test facility in Altoona, Pa. Bus companies were concerned about the cost of the testing and the possible leaking of manufacturing secrets to competitors at the facility.

Serving the disabled. On February 13, a U.S. circuit court of appeals in Philadelphia supported the 1988 ruling of a federal judge that wheelchair-accessible bus service must be provided in all communities with a transit system. But on July 24, a federal appeals court ruled that not all buses need be accessible, and that other means may be used to move disabled passengers.   George M. Smerk

In *World Book,* see **Bus; Electric railroad; Subway; Transportation.**

Trinidad and Tobago. See **Latin America.**

Trump, Donald John (1946-), a real estate developer and casino-hotel operator, entered the aviation business in June 1989, buying Eastern Airlines' Eastern Shuttle. He promptly renamed the shuttle—a passenger service linking New York City with Boston and Washington, D.C.—calling it the Trump Shuttle. Trump is president of the New York City-based Trump Organization, which was founded by his father, Fred C. Trump.

The shuttle deal was just one of many events that have kept Donald Trump in the limelight since the mid-1980's. In 1985, for example, he proposed to erect a 150-floor skyscraper, which would be the world's tallest building, in New York City. In 1988, he bought the Plaza Hotel in New York City for $410 million but was outbid for control of the casino company Resorts International by entertainer Merv Griffin. And in October 1989, Trump bid $7.54 billion for AMR Corporation, the parent company of American Airlines, but withdrew the offer later that month.

Trump's autobiography, *Trump: The Art of the Deal* (1987), was a best seller. In May 1989, the Milton Bradley Company introduced Trump—The Game.

Trump was born in New York City on June 14, 1946. In 1968, he received a bachelor's degree in economics from Wharton School of Finance at the University of Pennsylvania in Philadelphia.

Trump married Ivana Winkelmayr in 1977. The Trumps have three children.　　Jay Myers

Tunisia, on April 2, 1989, held its first elections since winning its independence from France in 1956 in which parties opposed to the government were allowed to participate. Five opposition parties vied with the ruling Democratic Constitutional Assembly (RCD) for seats in the National Assembly, Tunisia's parliament. The government enlarged the Assembly to 141 seats to encourage broader political participation. But the winner-take-all voting system set up in 1988 enabled RCD candidates to win all 141 seats because none of the opposition parties gained more than 3 per cent of the popular vote. In the elections, President Zine El-Abidine Ben Ali also won a five-year term as president, gathering 99.3 per cent of the popular vote.

The strongest opposition showing was by candidates belonging to Ennahda (Renaissance), an illegal Islamic fundamentalist party. They were required to run as independents because the government denied the party legal recognition on grounds that its platform was based on religion, a violation of Tunisia's Constitution. Even so, Ennahda candidates won 14.5 per cent of the overall popular vote. In urban areas, they captured 30 per cent.

The elections were considered by many observers to be a test of Ben Ali's continued efforts, begun when he seized power from Habib Bourguiba in 1987, to liberalize Tunisia's political system. Most observers agreed that, in general, the elections were fair. The

government was criticized, however, for deliberately discouraging young first-time voters from registering, apparently because such voters were expected to support orthodox Islamic candidates.

Shakeup. In September 1989, Ben Ali dismissed Prime Minister Hedi Baccouche, the only Cabinet holdover from the Bourguiba regime. Baccouche, who reportedly had become increasingly opposed to Ben Ali's reforms, was replaced by Justice Minister Hamed Karoui.

Regional relations. In March, Tunisia joined the Arab Maghreb Union, a North African common market (see **Algeria**). Relations with Libya continued to improve in 1989. Libyan tourists spent some $600 million in Tunisia during the year, mainly to buy consumer goods.

The economy. Ben Ali pushed economic reform along with political liberalization. In April, the National Assembly approved a measure loosening government controls on the economy. Tunisia's currency was devalued by 22 per cent, and special incentives were established to entice foreign investors. The measure also transferred the ownership of 300 state enterprises into private hands. To reduce Tunisia's trade deficit, the government in August cut state subsidies for such imported commodities as flour, sugar, and cooking oil.　　William Spencer

See also **Middle East** (Facts in brief table). In *World Book,* see **Tunisia.**

Turkey. Turkish Prime Minister Turgut Özal's ruling Motherland Party (ANAP) suffered a major defeat in local and municipal elections on March 26, 1989. The centrist ANAP came in third, receiving only about 22 per cent of the popular vote. It trailed both the liberal Social Democratic Populist Party and former Prime Minister Süleyman Demirel's conservative True Path Party, which got 28 and 26 per cent, respectively.

The results reflected widespread public dissatisfaction with the government's failure to bring the country's 72 per cent inflation rate under control or to reduce its 15 per cent unemployment rate. Özal's opponents also attacked him for placing family members and relatives in policymaking positions.

From prime minister to president. Despite the ANAP's dismal showing in the elections, Özal initially insisted that he would remain in office until 1992, when his term would expire. But in September 1989, he announced he would run for president to succeed Kenan Evren, whose term ended in November and who could not succeed himself. The president, whose duties are largely ceremonial, is elected to a seven-year term by parliament. After twice failing to win the required number of votes in parliament, Özal finally was elected president on October 31.

Bulgarian refugees. In May, the government launched a diplomatic offensive to call attention to Bulgaria's persecution of its ethnic Turkish population—Bulgarian citizens of Turkish ancestry. Under a

467

Bulgarian assimilation campaign launched in late 1984, ethnic Turks were forbidden to speak Turkish in public or use Turkish names. After riots broke out in May 1989 in several of eastern Bulgaria's largely Turkish provinces, Bulgaria began to expel ethnic Turks or encourage them to leave the country.

By mid-August, an estimated 320,000 ethnic Turks had fled across the border into Turkey. On August 22, however, Turkey closed its border with Bulgaria amid concerns that the government would be unable to support or provide jobs for the refugees.

EC bid rejected. On December 18, the European Community (EC or Common Market) rejected Turkey's application for membership. The 12-member EC said that Turkey could improve its chances for acceptance if it continued to reduce its reliance on agriculture and diversify its economy, bettered its performance on human rights, and improved relations with its longtime enemy Greece.

Kurdish guerrillas fighting for a separate state in eastern Turkey stepped up their attacks on Turkish army posts there. In response, the government increased troop strength in the area to 110,000. But it also eased restrictions on use of the Kurdish language in court trials and lifted a ban on giving children Kurdish names.   William Spencer

See also **Middle East** (Facts in brief table). In *World Book,* see **Turkey.**

Uganda. See **Africa.**

Union of Soviet Socialist Republics

(U.S.S.R.). Communist Party General Secretary and Executive President Mikhail S. Gorbachev's reform policies underwent severe testing in 1989 as his "revolution from above" was overtaken—and in many ways surpassed—by a "revolution from below." Gorbachev's international standing remained high as he completed the withdrawal of the Soviet army from Afghanistan, proposed drastic cuts in nuclear arms and conventional forces, and encouraged Soviet satellite states in Eastern Europe to undertake political and economic reforms. Gorbachev pledged that the Soviets would not interfere with the reform process, and he stuck to this pledge even as those countries nullified their Communist parties' monopoly on political power. See **Bulgaria; Czechoslovakia; Germany, East; Hungary; Poland; Romania.**

At home, Gorbachev's policy of *glasnost* (openness in the flow of information) further vitalized news media—and triggered strong public reactions to worsening defects of society. Gorbachev's policy of *perestroika* (political and economic restructuring) produced tremendous results in the voting booth but minimal results in the marketplace as the first cautious reforms met fierce resistance from conservatives in the leadership and an entrenched bureaucracy.

Political change began on March 26 with a stunning rejection of Communist candidates in the Soviet Union's first truly contested national elections. Soviet voters went to the polls to elect 1,500 members of a new 2,250-seat Congress of People's Deputies designed to replace the old rubber-stamp Supreme Soviet with a new one that would function like a genuine parliament. The remaining 750 seats were reserved for deputies selected by the Communist Party and labor, youth, and social organizations. Voting for the 1,500 contested seats was by district. In about 75 per cent of the districts, more than one candidate ran for the seat.

In the election, more than 20 senior Communist leaders lost. In the three Baltic republics—the Estonian, Latvian, and Lithuanian Soviet Socialist Republics (S.S.R.'s)—nationalist-reform tickets won.

Gorbachev elected. The new Congress on May 25 elected Gorbachev to the just-created post of executive president. He had held a similar position under the old Supreme Soviet, but the new post carried much broader powers. The election gave Gorbachev official responsibility for foreign policy, defense, and social and economic programs.

With his election, Gorbachev became the top official in the Soviet government. Under the old system, the chairman of the Council of Ministers—presently, Nikolay I. Ryzhkov—had that distinction. Under the new system, the council takes instructions from the executive president and a new, 542-member Supreme Soviet.

Supreme Soviet chosen. On May 26, the Congress of People's Deputies elected by secret ballot members of the new Supreme Soviet, which was given powers somewhat like those of legislatures in Western democracies. These powers were without precedent in the Communist world, and the Supreme Soviet increasingly asserted them. On June 26, for example, the Supreme Soviet rejected three of Chairman Ryzhkov's choices for the Council of Ministers.

Coal miners walk out. The Supreme Soviet's example fueled a new spirit of dissent in broad segments of the population—including Soviet labor. Siberian coal miners struck in early July. By mid-month, about 300,000 miners had stopped work in the two main Soviet coal fields, the Kuznetsk Basin in western Siberia and the Donetsk Basin in the eastern Ukraine.

The miners' initial grievances included unsafe working conditions, low pay and pensions, and shortages of food and such consumer items as soap. Demands soon became political, however, with calls for unions that would be independent of Moscow.

Miners rejected pleas from Gorbachev and other leaders for a return to work pending an inquiry into the grievances. They returned to work in late July, however, when the regime promised to raise their pay, pledged that a government commission would negotiate further with them, and said that the strike committees could monitor the carrying out of reforms.

On October 9, the Supreme Soviet banned strikes in vital industries such as coal mining and set up conciliation and arbitration systems similar to those in Western nations. On October 25, however, thousands of miners walked off the job in the region of Vorkuta, in the northeast corner of the European part of the Soviet Union. The miners demanded higher wages and pensions and sought constitutional changes that would eliminate the Communist Party's assurance of a "leading role" in public life and would call for the election of the executive president by a direct vote of the people.

Ethnic unrest. Through the spring and summer of 1989, a crescendo of popular agitation over local self-government, language, and religion spread across several parts of the Soviet Union inhabited mostly by non-Russian peoples. These areas included the Kazakh and Tajik S.S.R.'s in central Asia, the Georgian S.S.R. in the Caucasus Mountains, and the Moldavian S.S.R. on the Soviet border with Romania.

Meanwhile, a bloody conflict continued to rage between the Azerbaijan and Armenian S.S.R.'s, which lie next to each other on the Soviet border with Turkey and Iran. The conflict concerned the status of the Nagorno-Karabakh Autonomous Region of the Azerbaijan S.S.R. About 75 per cent of the residents of the region are ethnic Armenians (people of Armenian ancestry), and they want the Soviet central government to transfer the region to the Armenian S.S.R.

The region came under Moscow's direct rule in January, but to little avail. Beginning in early August, an Azerbaijani blockade of rail supply routes brought life

in the disputed area to a virtual standstill. By October, when the quarrel was 20 months old, ethnic clashes had already claimed more than 100 lives—despite the presence of a large force of Soviet troops. On November 28, Moscow returned control of the region to the Azerbaijan S.S.R. but left the troops in place.

Popular front movements in the Estonian, Latvian, and Lithuanian S.S.R.'s stepped up demands for self-rule and the invalidation of Soviet laws incorporating the Baltic republics into the Soviet Union under secret clauses of a 1939 pact between the Soviet Union and Nazi Germany. On July 27, 1989, the Supreme Soviet supported plans by Estonia and Lithuania to develop free-market economies. On August 23, as many as 1 million Estonians, Latvians, and Lithuanians linked hands to form a human chain across the three republics to protest the 50th anniversary of the 1939 pact. On December 7, Lithuania's legislature removed from that republic's constitution a clause guaranteeing the Communist Party the "leading role" in politics and society—thereby paving the way for the multiparty elections. Latvia's legislature did the same on December 28.

Economic problems. Bad news was abundant on Oct. 20, 1989, when Soviet ministers met to review reports on the national economy for the first nine months of the year. Industrial output had increased by only 2.2 per cent, compared with a planned hike of 7 per cent. Soviet farmers had produced slightly more

A human chain links Estonia, Latvia, and Lithuania in August to protest a 1939 Russian-German pact that led to Soviet rule of those lands.

Siberian miners strike in July during walkouts that idled about 300,000 workers at Soviet coal fields and cost $60 million in lost production.

grain than in the first nine months of 1988, but big imports would again be necessary.

At the beginning of 1989, Gorbachev had warned that "without price reform, economic reform can make no progress." Yet, the regime postponed effective pricing measures because of the political risk of large hikes in prices and the increased unemployment.

Disarmament. Gorbachev, already pledged to big unilateral reductions of Soviet tanks and troops in Eastern Europe, presented new disarmament proposals in 1989. During a May visit to Moscow by United States Secretary of State James A. Baker III, Gorbachev offered an early withdrawal of 500 short-range nuclear missiles from Eastern Europe. Gorbachev apparently intended to draw the United States into talks on the elimination of such weapons throughout Europe. The United States and its allies in the North Atlantic Treaty Organization (NATO), however, wanted to see bigger cuts in the Soviet Union's conventional forces.

In talks with Baker in Wyoming on September 22 and 23, Soviet Foreign Minister Eduard A. Shevardnadze offered concessions on U.S. space defense research and agreed to abandon a long-controversial radar station at Krasnoyarsk in Siberia—viewed by the United States as a breach of the Antiballistic Missile Treaty of 1972. Shevardnadze and Baker also arranged for Gorbachev and President George Bush to hold a summit meeting in early 1990. Even before that formal summit, however, the two leaders met for in-

formal talks on Dec. 2 and 3, 1989, alternating between U.S. and Soviet vessels at Malta in the Mediterranean Sea.

Pullout from Afghanistan. The Soviet Union announced on February 15 that it had withdrawn the last of its troops from Afghanistan, ending more than nine years of intervention in a civil war between Afghanistan's Communist government and various rebel factions. Many political observers in the West said that, without Soviet military support, the Afghan regime would crumble. At year-end, however, the Communist government was still in control—though the rebellion continued to rage. See **Afghanistan.**

Relations with China. After three decades of diplomatic estrangement, the leaders of the Soviet Union and China met in Beijing in mid-May. Ironically, the meeting proved to be a prelude to a fresh chill. Student demonstrators in Beijing hailed the Soviet leader's presence in a show of esteem for his reforms as an example for their own prodemocracy movement. In a joint communiqué, the two powers agreed to resume contacts between their Communist parties, to discuss demilitarization along their common border, and to negotiate border disputes.

Throughout his stay, Gorbachev studiously refrained from commenting on the student turmoil. At a news conference shortly before his departure, however, Gorbachev said that reforms might be "painful, but are a necessary process" that could not be reversed.

Moscow remained silent on the June 3 and 4 massacre in Beijing's Tiananmen Square and on the subsequent crackdown on student leaders and Communists who sympathized with the demonstrators. In October, however, the Soviets sent only a low-level delegation to China's celebration of its 40th anniversary of Communist rule. This diplomatic signal set back China's hopes that the Soviet Union would boost its trade with China and provide more technological assistance. See **China.**

Church and state. The government eased restrictions on the practice of religion during the year. In April, the State Council of Religious Affairs lifted bans on church activities ranging from charity work to bell ringing. It also registered 1,611 new churches and mosques, compared with 104 in 1988. Members of the Russian Orthodox Church celebrated the 400th anniversary of the establishment of the Patriarchate (church district) of Moscow in mid-October 1989—the first such service allowed since 1918.

On Dec. 1, 1989, Gorbachev met with Pope John Paul II at the Vatican. Gorbachev pledged greater religious freedom for Soviet citizens and a renewal of diplomatic ties between the Soviet Union and the Vatican.   Eric Bourne

See also **Europe** (Facts in brief table). In the Special Reports section, see **Opening a Closed Society.** In *World Book,* see **Russia; Union of Soviet Socialist Republics.**

United Nations (UN) continued to work for world peace in 1989. A UN peacekeeping force went to Namibia (South West Africa) to oversee that land's transformation into an independent country—a venture that UN Secretary-General Javier Pérez de Cuéllar considered to be the world organization's greatest success. Another UN peacemaking effort, however, was not so successful—Pérez de Cuéllar's attempts throughout the year to reconcile Iran and Iraq, who fought a war from 1980 to 1988.

Namibia. A UN peace force of more than 7,000 soldiers and civilians began arriving in Namibia on April 1, 1989, to organize and supervise elections to a Constituent Assembly that would write a constitution for an independent Namibia. UN Special Representative Martti Ahtisaari of Finland led this force, known as the United Nations Transition Assistance Group (UN-TAG). Ahtisaari worked with the administrator general for Namibia, Louis A. Pienaar, who had been appointed by South Africa. Namibia has been under the control of South Africa since 1916.

The UN plan for Namibia's independence began to take effect on April 1, 1989, with a cease-fire between guerrillas of the South West Africa People's Organization (SWAPO) and South African forces. The plan was suspended briefly after SWAPO guerrillas left their bases in Angola and crossed into Namibia. Fighting broke out, and in the first week of April more than 300 guerrillas and South African soldiers were killed.

Alarmed by the war's threat to the independence process, a joint commission of representatives from South Africa, Angola, and Cuba and observers from the United States and the Soviet Union settled the shaky situation and put the UN plan back on track.

Twenty-seven countries contributed troops to UN-TAG. To pay for the peacekeeping operation, the UN set up a fund of $450 million, which was to be spent during a one-year period beginning April 1.

Namibia held elections November 7 to 11. SWAPO won 41 of the 72 seats in the Constituent Assembly, thereby assuming the leadership in that body.

The Constituent Assembly held its first meeting on November 21 to begin drafting a constitution. SWAPO's President Sam Nujoma, majority leader in the Assembly, promised to cooperate with Pienaar, much to the relief of Namibia's other political parties. Under the UN plan, Pienaar was to remain sole ruler until independence day in April 1990.

Iran-Iraq negotiations. In 1987, Iraq had accepted UN Security Council Resolution 598, calling for a cease-fire and peace negotiations. Iran accepted the resolution in July 1988, and a cease-fire went into effect the next month. Peace talks made little progress in 1988, however, and 1989 was no better.

From Feb. 8 to 11, 1989, Foreign Minister Ali Akbar Velayati of Iran and his Iraqi counterpart, Tariq Aziz, met with Pérez de Cuéllar at UN Headquarters in New York City to continue negotiations on troop withdrawals, the release of prisoners of war, and other problems such as navigation in the Persian Gulf. The foreign ministers met with Pérez de Cuéllar again from April 20 to 23 in Geneva, Switzerland, but apparently made no progress.

The secretary-general sent his special representative, Sweden's Ambassador to the UN Jan Eliasson, to Iran and Iraq in late October to try to persuade the two governments to negotiate more flexibly. Eliasson spent 17 days shuttling between the two countries. Although there was little progress in negotiations, the cease-fire was holding well due to the cooperation of Iran and Iraq and the effectiveness of 300 UN military officers who were monitoring the cease-fire along the border between Iran and Iraq.

General Assembly. The 44th session of the UN General Assembly opened on September 19. Nigeria's Ambassador Joseph Nanven Garba was elected president for the session. In the first three weeks of the session, 16 presidents, 5 prime ministers, and 105 foreign ministers delivered speeches covering a variety of topics ranging from the war in Cambodia (formerly Kampuchea) to nuclear disarmament. The speakers focused their remarks on the fight against drug abuse and drug trafficking, environmental pollution, and economic problems of developing countries.

United States President George Bush on September 25 made his first address to the General Assembly, proposing to destroy immediately more than 80 per cent of U.S. chemical weapons if the Soviet Union car-

Country singer Roy Clark celebrates with a song in March after being named an ambassador for UNICEF—the United Nations Children's Fund.

ried out a similar action. Soviet Foreign Minister Eduard A. Shevardnadze on September 26 replied to Bush that the two superpowers should go further, and he urged immediate elimination of their chemical-weapons stockpiles and a ban on production of more.

Representatives of the two countries held their first joint press conference at the UN on November 3. United States Assistant Secretary of State John R. Bolton and Soviet Deputy Foreign Minister Vladimir Petrovsky said at the conference that they supported a UN resolution calling on UN members to improve the UN's effectiveness in maintaining peace and security.

Invasion of Panama. The General Assembly on December 29 approved a resolution "strongly deploring" a U.S. invasion of Panama. United States troops entered Panama on December 20 and overthrew the dictatorship of General Manuel Antonio Noriega Morena. See **Panama.**

Children's rights. The General Assembly on November 20 adopted a Convention on the Rights of the Child, a document climaxing 10 years of work. The document was due to be signed by UN members in January 1990. When at least 20 nations ratify the convention, it is to become binding on those nations.

The convention defines a child as a person under 18 who should enjoy certain fundamental rights, such as health care, education, and protection from exploitation and abuse. It also says that a child has a right to freedom of thought, conscience, and religion.

Refugees. Pérez de Cuéllar on November 20 appointed Norway's former Foreign Minister Thorvald Stoltenberg as high commissioner for refugees. Stoltenberg replaced Jean-Pierre Hocké of Switzerland, who had resigned on October 25 amid charges that he had misused funds donated for refugee education.

The Geneva-based office of the UN High Commissioner for Refugees assists more than 14 million refugees throughout the world. Funds for this agency come from voluntary contributions of member countries, which currently are giving less than in past years. This decline in donations comes at a time of a great surge in the number of people leaving their countries for political reasons. The largest group of refugees, about 5 million Afghans, have been living in Pakistan and Iran since 1980. They fled when Soviet troops invaded their country to support the Communist government in Kabul.

The UN coordinator for humanitarian aid and reconstruction in Afghanistan, Prince Saddrudin Aga Khan of Iran, said on Nov. 20, 1989, that the UN has collected only half the $1 billion pledged by governments to assist the Afghan people. Aga Khan said that continued fighting between U.S.-armed rebels and the Soviet-backed Afghan government has prevented the UN from carrying out its humanitarian mission.

PLO applications frozen. The World Health Organization (WHO), a specialized organization of the UN, voted on May 12 to delay for one year a decision on

472

an application for full membership submitted by the Palestine Liberation Organization (PLO). In 1974, the UN recognized the PLO as the representative of the Palestinian Arabs and granted the PLO *observer status* (the right to attend sessions of the General Assembly but not to take part). The PLO has been seeking to participate in UN affairs by obtaining membership in specialized agencies such as the WHO. The United States has strongly opposed these attempts.

Another agency, the UN Educational, Scientific, and Cultural Organization (UNESCO), on October 11 delayed action on a PLO application for membership. The UNESCO delay was for two years.

The PLO also had applied to a third UN agency, the Food and Agriculture Organization (FAO), for technical assistance. In spite of U.S. objections, the FAO on November 29 ordered a fact-finding mission to the West Bank and the Gaza Strip—areas occupied by Israel—to find out what kind of aid Palestinians living there need.

The United States had warned the UN on November 27 that it would cut its payments of UN dues if the General Assembly upgraded the designation of the PLO to the "State of Palestine." The United States formerly provided 25 per cent of the UN's annual funding. Beginning in 1986, however, the U.S. Congress reduced payments. At the end of 1989, the United States owed the UN $450 million. On November 28, U.S. Secretary of Agriculture Clayton K. Yeutter said that the United States might withdraw from the FAO if that organization upgraded the status of the PLO.

U.S. veto. The United States on June 9 vetoed a Security Council resolution condemning Israel's activities in the occupied territories. The other 14 members of the Council voted for the resolution, which was drafted by Algeria, Colombia, Ethiopia, Malaysia, Nepal, Senegal, and Yugoslavia. (Those nations and Brazil, Canada, and Finland were the nonpermanent members of the Security Council. The permanent members are China, France, Great Britain, the Soviet Union, and the United States.) Thomas R. Pickering, the U.S. ambassador to the UN and Security Council president for June, said that the United States cast the veto because of an "unbalanced" condemnation of Israel "without any reference to any of the serious acts of violence by the other side."

UNICEF, the United Nations Children's Fund, on April 1 launched a massive campaign to save from starvation tens of thousands of people who are caught in a civil war in southern Sudan. The United Nations raised more than $120 million for the operation, called "Operation Lifeline Sudan." UNICEF's Director General James P. Grant, who directed the program, obtained a cease-fire agreement so that convoys carrying more than 100,000 tons of food and medical supplies could travel safely to remote areas in the country. By late summer, it was clear that the campaign was succeeding.   J. Tuyet Nguyen

In *World Book,* see **United Nations.**

United States, Government of the.

The Democratic-controlled Congress, after reaching a surprise April agreement with President George Bush on ways to shrink the ever-troublesome federal budget deficit, wrestled until the final hour of its 1989 session, on November 22, to transform the accord into legislation. In theory, the annual budget reconciliation bill will reduce the deficit for the 1990 fiscal year, which began on Oct. 1, 1989, to about $103 billion, well within the $110-billion target fixed by the 1985 Gramm-Rudman budget-balancing law. But the fiscal 1989 deficit was estimated at $161.4 billion, compared with a target of $136 billion.

Bush and Congress were supposed to agree on a budget bill by October 15. When they failed to do so, automatic across-the-board spending cuts went into effect under the Gramm-Rudman law. In finally reaching agreement, the President and Congress decided to keep those cuts in effect until the first week of February 1990, achieving an estimated savings of $4.6 billion out of a total deficit-reduction figure of about $14.7 billion. The balance was to come from a combination of spending cuts, revenue increases, and accounting gimmicks, such as excluding $1.8 billion in Postal Service losses from the deficit calculation.

Tower nomination rejected. The early months of Bush's presidency were soured by a heated battle over his nomination of former Senator John G. Tower (R., Tex.) for secretary of defense. After one of the bitterest Senate debates of modern times, the nomination was rejected 53 to 47 on March 9, with only 1 Republican voting against Tower and just 3 Democrats voting for him. For Bush, it was a major defeat after less than two months in office. Never before had a new President been denied an initial choice for his Cabinet.

A day later, Bush named Representative Richard B. Cheney of Wyoming, the Republican whip in the House of Representatives, as his replacement nominee. Senators from both parties welcomed his choice, and a week later Cheney was confirmed unanimously.

Another failed nomination. The Tower nomination was not alone in being killed in the Senate. On a 7-7 tie vote, the Senate Judiciary Committee on August 1 rejected Bush's nomination of William C. Lucas to head the Justice Department's Civil Rights Division. Lucas, a black who had been sheriff and county executive of Wayne County, Michigan, was opposed by all but one Democrat on the committee as "lacking in experience and qualifications." On August 13, Attorney General Richard L. Thornburgh appointed Lucas to a lower-level Justice Department post that did not require Senate confirmation.

Two other nominations faced little opposition. In October, Bush nominated Antonia C. Novello, a pediatrician, to be the first woman surgeon general, succeeding C. Everett Koop, who resigned in July. Novello, who was still awaiting confirmation at year-end, had been deputy director of the National Institute of Child Health and Human Development. In August,

Bush nominated Army General Colin L. Powell, former national security adviser to President Ronald Reagan, to replace Admiral William J. Crowe, Jr., as chairman of the Joint Chiefs of Staff. Powell was the youngest man, and the first black, ever named to head the Joint Chiefs. He was confirmed on September 21.

Military spending. On November 21, Bush signed a $286-billion military spending bill that cut $1.1 billion from his $4.9-billion request for the Strategic Defense Initiative—the "Star Wars" missile defense system. It was the first cut for the six-year-old program.

That small cutback was just the first of many larger ones likely to come. With the Cold War between the United States and the Soviet Union apparently at an end, many in Washington foresaw greatly reduced military expenditures in the 1990's. In November, Cheney asked the armed forces to draw up plans for cutting their budgets by a total of $180 billion for the fiscal years 1992 through 1994.

Military experts predicted that in coming years, the armed forces' role will be largely restricted to regional interventions and the protection of sea lanes. Such operations in recent years have included the invasion of Grenada in 1983, the patrolling of the Persian Gulf in the late 1980's, and—in the closing days of 1989—the overthrow of Panama's dictatorial ruler, General Manuel Antonio Noriega Morena. See **Panama.**

As Pentagon boss, Cheney inherited major problems from the Reagan Administration: radioactive contamination at the 17 nuclear-weapons plants operated by the Department of Energy (DOE) and a continuing scandal in defense contracting.

In January, the DOE estimated it would cost $91 billion to $128 billion over 20 years to clean up its contaminated facilities. On June 16, it announced a "fundamental change of priorities" at the nuclear-arms plants, putting greater emphasis on "environmental safety and health" than on weapons production.

By mid-July, about a year after the announcement of a major investigation into Pentagon contracting procedures, two big defense contractors—Hazeltine Corporation and Teledyne Industries, Incorporated—had pleaded guilty to conspiracy and other charges and paid more than $6 million in penalties. Three government employees and 16 corporate executives and consultants also pleaded guilty or were convicted. One Teledyne employee was acquitted.

On March 17, a former Hazeltine vice president, Charles A. Furciniti, was the first person given a prison sentence in the scandal. He was sentenced to three months in prison and fined $20,000 for obtaining inside information about Pentagon buying plans and competitors' contract bids, allegedly from Navy employee Stuart E. Berlin. On June 2, Berlin and William L. Parkin, a private defense consultant, were each sentenced to 26 months in prison and fined $25,000 on their guilty pleas.

On July 14, the investigative net widened when a former Navy engineer, Garland L. Tomlin, Jr., admitted receiving $475,000 in bribes from two military contractors. Tomlin admitted providing confidential information about a Navy computer maintenance contract to Honeywell Incorporated and the Sperry Corporation, now a part of the Unisys Corporation. He was sentenced on October 27 to 18 months in prison.

On November 13, the Boeing Company pleaded guilty to charges of illegally obtaining hundreds of secret Pentagon documents and using them to gain an advantage in bidding for contracts. Boeing agreed to pay more than $5 million in fines.

The Navy also had problems of a different sort. On November 14, it ordered a 48-hour suspension of all routine air, sea, and land operations—an unprecedented move—to review "basic safety procedures" following a seven-month string of serious accidents. The mishaps began on April 19 with the explosion of a gun turret on the battleship U.S.S. *Iowa*, killing 47 men. The Navy later attributed the explosion to a suicidal seaman, but that conclusion was being strongly contested at year-end.

With regard to the other incidents—which included the collision of a destroyer with a merchant ship and the accidental dropping of a bomb on a guided-missile cruiser—the chief of naval operations, Admiral Carlisle A. H. Trost, on December 17 laid the blame on inadequate supervision of personnel, lax attention to safety procedures, and general complacency.

HUD scandal. The Department of Housing and Urban Development (HUD) and its new secretary, former U.S. Representative Jack F. Kemp (R., N.Y.), were confronted with another inherited scandal. Investigations by several committees in the House of Representatives revealed that under Reagan's HUD secretary, Samuel R. Pierce, Jr., the department was a center of influence peddling, favoritism toward influential Republicans, mismanagement, and, quite possibly, fraud. Millions, if not billions, of dollars were squandered.

Called twice before a House Government Operations subcommittee, in September and October, Pierce refused to testify, invoking his Fifth Amendment right against self-incrimination. His chief aide, Deborah Gore Dean, also declined to answer questions. On November 2, 19 of the 20 Democrats on the House Judiciary Committee asked the Justice Department to appoint a special prosecutor to investigate the "serious possibility of criminal conduct" by Pierce. Attorney General Thornburgh said the department already was "aggressively pursuing allegations of misconduct within HUD" and accused organizers of the Judiciary Committee letter of injecting "partisan politics" into the matter.

On October 3, Kemp announced financial and management changes to end HUD abuses and said, "It is a tragedy that . . . programs designed to help poor people and low-income communities were riddled with systemic flaws that allowed them to be corrupted by greedy individuals who used political influence to gain unfair access to HUD's resources. . . . "

Selected agencies and bureaus of the U.S. government*

Executive Office of the President

President, George Bush
  Vice President, Dan Quayle
  White House Chief of Staff, John H. Sununu
  Presidential Press Secretary, Marlin Fitzwater
  Assistant to the President for National Security Affairs, Brent Scowcroft
  Assistant to the President for Science and Technology, D. Allan Bromley
  Council of Economic Advisers—Michael J. Boskin, Chairman
  Office of Management and Budget—Richard G. Darman, Director
  Office of National Drug Control Policy—William J. Bennett, Director
  U.S. Trade Representative, Carla A. Hills

Department of Agriculture

Secretary of Agriculture, Clayton K. Yeutter

Department of Commerce

Secretary of Commerce, Robert A. Mosbacher
  Bureau of Economic Analysis—Allan H. Young, Director
  Bureau of the Census—John G. Keane, Director

Department of Defense

Secretary of Defense, Richard B. Cheney
  Secretary of the Air Force, Donald B. Rice
  Secretary of the Army, Michael P. W. Stone
  Secretary of the Navy, H. Lawrence Garrett III
  Joint Chiefs of Staff—
    General Colin L. Powell, Chairman
    General Larry D. Welch, Chief of Staff, Air Force
    General Carl E. Vuono, Chief of Staff, Army
    Admiral Carlisle A. H. Trost, Chief of Naval Operations
    General Alfred M. Gray, Jr., Commandant, Marine Corps

Department of Education

Secretary of Education, Lauro F. Cavazos

Department of Energy

Secretary of Energy, James D. Watkins

Department of Health and Human Services

Secretary of Health and Human Services, Louis W. Sullivan
  Public Health Service—James O. Mason, Assistant Secretary
  Centers for Disease Control—Walter R. Dowdle, Acting Director
  Food and Drug Administration—James S. Benson, Acting Commissioner
  National Institutes of Health—William F. Raub, Acting Director
  Surgeon General of the United States, Antonia C. Novello†
  Social Security Administration—Gwendolyn S. King, Commissioner

Department of Housing and Urban Development

Secretary of Housing and Urban Development, Jack F. Kemp

Department of the Interior

Secretary of the Interior, Manuel Lujan, Jr.

Department of Justice

Attorney General, Richard L. Thornburgh
  Bureau of Prisons—J. Michael Quinlan, Director
  Drug Enforcement Administration—John C. Lawn, Administrator
  Federal Bureau of Investigation—William S. Sessions, Director
  Immigration and Naturalization Service—Gene McNary, Commissioner
  Solicitor General, Kenneth W. Starr

Department of Labor

Secretary of Labor, Elizabeth H. Dole

Department of State

Secretary of State, James A. Baker III
  U.S. Representative to the United Nations, Thomas R. Pickering

Department of Transportation

Secretary of Transportation, Samuel K. Skinner
  Federal Aviation Administration—James B. Busey IV, Administrator
  U.S. Coast Guard—Admiral Paul A. Yost, Jr., Commandant

*As of Jan. 2, 1990. †Nominated but not yet confirmed.

Department of the Treasury

Secretary of the Treasury, Nicholas F. Brady
  Internal Revenue Service—Fred T. Goldberg, Jr., Commissioner
  Treasurer of the United States, Catalina Vasquez Villalpando,
  U.S. Secret Service—John R. Simpson, Director
  Office of Thrift Supervision—M. Danny Wall, Director

Department of Veterans Affairs

Secretary of Veterans Affairs, Edward J. Derwinski

Supreme Court of the United States

Chief Justice of the United States, William H. Rehnquist
  Associate Justices
    William J. Brennan, Jr.   John Paul Stevens
    Byron R. White   Sandra Day O'Connor
    Thurgood Marshall   Antonin Scalia
    Harry A. Blackmun   Anthony M. Kennedy

Congressional officials

President of the Senate pro tempore, Robert C. Byrd
  Senate Majority Leader, George J. Mitchell
  Senate Minority Leader, Robert J. Dole
  Speaker of the House, Thomas S. Foley
  House Majority Leader, Richard A. Gephardt
  House Minority Leader, Robert H. Michel
  Congressional Budget Office—Robert D. Reischauer, Director
  General Accounting Office—Charles A. Bowsher, Comptroller General of the United States
  Library of Congress—James H. Billington, Librarian of Congress
  Office of Technology Assessment—John H. Gibbons, Director

Independent agencies

ACTION—Jane A. Kenny, Director
Agency for International Development—Mark L. Edelman, Acting Administrator
Central Intelligence Agency—William H. Webster, Director
Commission on Civil Rights—Murray Friedman, Acting Chairman
Commission of Fine Arts—J. Carter Brown, Chairman
Consumer Product Safety Commission—Jacqueline Smith-Jones, Chairman
Environmental Protection Agency—William K. Reilly, Administrator
Equal Employment Opportunity Commission—Clarence Thomas, Chairman
Federal Communications Commission—Alfred C. Sikes, Chairman
Federal Deposit Insurance Corporation—L. William Seidman, Chairman
Federal Election Commission—Danny L. McDonald, Chairman
Federal Emergency Management Agency—Robert H. Morris, Acting Director
Federal Reserve System Board of Governors—Alan Greenspan, Chairman
Federal Trade Commission—Janet D. Steiger, Chairman
General Services Administration—Richard G. Austin†, Administrator
Interstate Commerce Commission—Heather J. Gradison, Chairman
National Aeronautics and Space Administration—Richard H. Truly, Administrator
National Endowment for the Arts—John E. Frohnmayer, Chairman
National Endowment for the Humanities—Lynne V. Cheney, Chairman
National Labor Relations Board—James M. Stephens, Chairman
National Railroad Passenger Corporation (Amtrak)—W. Graham Claytor, Jr., Chairman
National Science Foundation—Erich Bloch, Director
National Transportation Safety Board—James L. Kolstad, Acting Chairman
Nuclear Regulatory Commission—Kenneth M. Carr, Chairman
Peace Corps—Paul D. Coverdell, Director
Securities and Exchange Commission—Richard C. Breeden, Chairman
Selective Service System—Samuel K. Lessey, Jr., Director
Small Business Administration—Susan S. Engeleiter, Administrator
Smithsonian Institution—Robert McC. Adams, Secretary
U.S. Arms Control and Disarmament Agency—Ronald F. Lehman II, Director
U.S. Information Agency—Bruce S. Gelb, Director
U.S. Postal Service—Anthony M. Frank, Postmaster General

Federal spending

United States budget for fiscal 1989*

	Billions of dollars
National defense	303.6
International affairs	9.6
General science, space, technology	12.9
Energy	3.7
Natural resources and environment	16.1
Agriculture	16.9
Commerce and housing credit	27.8
Transportation	27.6
Community and regional development	5.8
Education, training, employment, and social services	35.7
Health	48.4
Social security	232.5
Medicare	85.0
Income security	136.8
Veterans' benefits and services	30.1
Administration of justice	9.4
General government	8.9
Interest	169.3
Undistributed offsetting receipts	-37.2
Total budget outlays	**1,142.9**

*Oct. 1, 1988, to Sept. 30, 1989.

Source: U.S. Department of the Treasury.

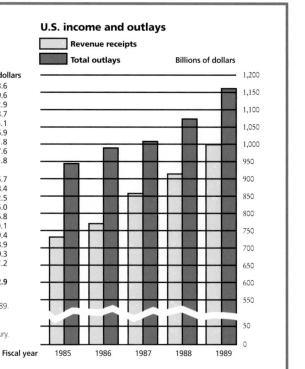

U.S. income and outlays

Revenue receipts

Total outlays

Billions of dollars

Fiscal year 1985 1986 1987 1988 1989

The federal judiciary also was hit by scandal as the Senate voted to convict two U.S. District Court judges on impeachment charges brought by the House, removing them from office. On October 20, the Senate voted to convict Judge Alcee L. Hastings of Florida of taking part in a "corrupt conspiracy" to extort a $150,000 bribe. On November 3, Judge Walter L. Nixon, Jr., of Mississippi was convicted of twice lying under oath to a federal grand jury that was looking into his handling of a drug-smuggling case. In the nation's history, only seven federal officials, all judges, have been removed from office by the Senate for high crimes and misdemeanors.

Lyn Nofziger, a onetime aide to President Reagan, fared better in 1989. Nofziger was convicted in 1988 of illegal lobbying on behalf of three clients after leaving government. But on June 27, 1989, a federal appeals court in Washington, D.C., ruled that the ethics law under which he was tried was ambiguous, and it reversed the verdict.

Meese lambasted. On January 17, before Bush took office, the Justice Department's Office of Professional Responsibility issued a scathing report on the ethics of former Attorney General Edwin Meese III, accusing him of "conduct which should not be tolerated of any government employee, especially not the attorney general." The report cited in particular Meese's dealings with a friend, E. Robert Wallach, who subsequently was convicted of racketeering.

Crackdown on wheeler-dealers. The government in 1989 continued its criminal investigation of the "junk bond" financing of corporate take-overs by Drexel Burnham Lambert, Incorporated. On March 29, Michael R. Milken, the key bond marketer at the firm, was indicted on 98 counts of fraud, insider trading, racketeering, stock price manipulation, and other violations. On August 2, as the result of a separate investigation, 46 commodity traders and brokers at the Chicago Board of Trade and the Chicago Mercantile Exchange were indicted on charges of cheating customers, dodging taxes, and manipulating prices.

Third World debt. On March 10, Treasury Secretary Nicholas F. Brady unveiled a proposal for dealing with the debt burdens of Third World countries, notably in Latin America. Under one provision of the Brady Plan, as it soon came to be called, banks would be encouraged to forgive a portion of debts owed by Third World nations in return for guarantees by the World Bank and International Monetary Fund—agencies of the United Nations—that the remaining debts would be honored. The plan marked a departure from earlier U.S. policy of providing debtors with new loans on top of old. On July 23, Mexico became the first country to reach agreement with lenders on a package of debt reduction and lower interest rates.

Assault rifles. One of the nation's most successful pressure groups, the National Rifle Association (NRA), suffered a minor setback on March 14 when Bush, a

476

lifetime member of the organization, imposed a temporary ban on the imports of several kinds of semiautomatic assault weapons, which law-enforcement officials say have greatly increased the firepower of drug gangs. Such weapons have also been used in a number of mass slayings. The President's action followed a schoolyard massacre on January 17 in Stockton, Calif., in which a man with a semiautomatic rifle killed 5 children and wounded 29 others and a teacher.

On April 5, Bush expanded the import ban to include 24 additional types of assault rifles, and on July 7 he made the ban permanent. United States gun manufacturers, however, were not included in the ruling, so American-made semiautomatic weapons will still be readily available to buyers.

Disaster relief. The Bush Administration came in for criticism after Hurricane Hugo struck the Carolinas on September 21 and 22, as complaints mounted that the Federal Emergency Management Agency (FEMA) was ineffective in aiding victims of the storm. Then the agency admitted to being hard-pressed in responding to the California earthquake of October 17. Congressional Democrats took Bush to task for not filling a single top FEMA job during his first nine months in office.   Frank Cormier and Margot Cormier

See also **Bush, George H. W.; Cabinet, United States; Congress of the United States; Supreme Court of the United States.** In *World Book,* see **United States, Government of the.**

Uruguay. On Nov. 26, 1989, Uruguayans elected Luis Alberto Lacalle of the centrist National Party to a five-year term as president. Lacalle pledged to work in harmony with Tabaré Vásquez, a doctor and a leftist, who was elected mayor of Montevideo, Uruguay's capital and home to half the country's population.

Vásquez' victory was made possible by the votes of the Broad Front, a Marxist coalition including Communists, Socialists, and former Tupamaro guerrillas, which won a surprising majority of Montevideo's city council seats. Symbolic of the split personality demonstrated by Uruguayan voters, supporters of the leftist Broad Front took over one section of Montevideo's main avenue to celebrate, while those of the rural-based National Party reveled in another section.

Departing President Julio María Sanguinetti and his Colorado Party left Uruguay with a stagnant economy. More and more young Uruguayans have had to seek employment outside the country, and poorly run state enterprises have driven up government deficits.

Lacalle's election marked the second visit to the polls by Uruguayans in 1989. On April 16, voters approved by more than 50 per cent a controversial 1986 law that provides amnesty for those accused of human-rights violations during 12 years of military rule from 1973 to 1985.   Nathan A. Haverstock

See also **Latin America** (Facts in brief table). In *World Book,* see **Uruguay.**

Utah. See **State government.**

Venezuela. On Feb. 2, 1989, Carlos Andrés Pérez was sworn in as president of Venezuela for the second time. Attending his inauguration were Vice President of the United States Dan Quayle and 21 heads of state, including Cuban President Fidel Castro.

In his inaugural address, Pérez stressed the need for economic reform. Venezuela's economy had been crippled by a $33-billion foreign debt and by a reduction in oil profits. This was in sharp contrast to Pérez' first term in office, from 1974 to 1979, when Venezuela enjoyed windfall profits from oil exports.

Foreign debt. After his inauguration, Pérez quickly positioned himself as a spokesman for Latin America on the problem of foreign debt. On February 4, he called on the United States and other developed countries to cut Latin America's $420-billion foreign debt in half to help safeguard democracy in the region.

Pérez lost little time in moving toward other goals as well. Early in the year, he helped reestablish dialogue between the Organization of Petroleum Exporting Countries (OPEC), of which Venezuela is a founding member, and non-OPEC members. He also worked toward an end to the conflicts in Central America.

Austerity program. On February 16, Pérez announced that the government was initiating an austerity program to satisfy the country's foreign creditors. As part of the program, the government raised the price of gasoline by 90 per cent and transportation fares by more than 30 per cent.

But the increases, coupled with food shortages, spurred civil unrest throughout the country. From February 27 to March 1, more than a dozen cities were rocked by riots that left an estimated 300 people dead. Pérez attributed the violence directly to Venezuela's foreign debt. To reduce the impact of the austerity program, Pérez announced wage increases for most workers in the private sector on March 1.

Discontent continued during the year, however. On May 18, the powerful Confederation of Venezuelan Workers mounted its first national strike in 30 years in protest over Pérez' austerity measures.

Import investigation. Pérez' administration sent mixed signals to foreign investors in 1989. While the country relaxed investment laws to attract new foreign investment, it also mounted an investigation of import practices that some investors labeled a "witch hunt."

The target of the investigation was a government agency no longer in operation. The agency, set up in 1983, provided dollars at half the official exchange rate to importers of essential items, such as food and medicine. But according to investigators, importers of nonessential items allegedly bribed agency officials to give them the same rate. High on the list of suspects were Venezuelan subsidiaries of U.S. and European corporations.   Nathan A. Haverstock

See also **Latin America** (Facts in brief table). In *World Book,* see **Venezuela.**

Vermont. See **State government.**

Veterans. A new United States Department of Veterans Affairs came into existence on March 15, 1989. Congress had voted in 1988 to transform the old Veterans Administration into the $30-billion Cabinet-level department, on the theory that its enhanced status would give the nation's 27.3 million veterans a stronger voice in government. President George Bush nominated, and the Senate confirmed, former Congressman Edward J. Derwinski as the first secretary of veterans affairs. See **Derwinski, Edward Joseph.**

Even before the new department began operating, Derwinski warned veterans not to expect too much from it. In a February 27 speech to American Legion officials, Derwinski said that in an era of tight federal budgets, veterans would not be a top priority for the Bush Administration. In May, Derwinski made clear that he wanted the agency to take a fresh look at its practices when he announced that he had invited the General Accounting Office, an arm of Congress, to study the department's management.

Agent Orange turnaround. On May 3, 1989, a U.S. district court in San Francisco ruled that the government had used too severe a standard in determining whether veterans who served in the Vietnam War (1957-1975) had been harmed by exposure to the chemical Agent Orange. The military used Agent Orange to clear jungle foliage in Vietnam during the war.

The government maintained that only one disease—a nonfatal skin ailment—could be attributed to contact with Agent Orange. Based on that rule, it granted direct benefits to only 5 of the first 33,272 veterans who claimed they were harmed by the chemical. Veterans groups, which have sought Agent Orange benefits for their members since 1979, argued that it caused cancer, miscarriages, birth defects, and other serious health problems.

On May 11, 1989, Derwinski sharply reversed the government's position, announcing that the Department of Veterans Affairs would not appeal the ruling and would reconsider the claims of more than 31,000 veterans. The department proceeded to develop new regulations for reviewing Agent Orange claims under broader criteria.

Death rates at veterans hospitals. In June, a Veterans Department study found overall mortality rates excessively high at 12 of the 172 hospitals it operates. Another 32 of the veterans hospitals showed "significantly elevated" death rates in particular disease categories, based on evaluation of 1,771 patient deaths in 1986. A panel of doctors who were asked to review 123 of those cases in more detail found that 90 of them—more than 5 per cent of all the patients studied—had received inappropriate care in the hospitals.   Frank Cormier and Margot Cormier

In *World Book,* see **Veterans Administration; Veterans' organizations.**

Vice President of the United States. See Quayle, Dan.

Vietnam. Officials struggled over political control and economic policy in 1989 as Vietnam withdrew its troops from Cambodia (formerly Kampuchea). Vietnam hoped that ending its 11-year military occupation of Cambodia—which had been internationally denounced—would open the way for foreign aid and investment, but there was no immediate benefit.

Officials of Vietnam's ruling Communist Party reacted harshly to the news of political and economic liberalization in the Soviet Union and Eastern Europe. Communist Party General Secretary Nguyen Van Linh, Vietnam's top official, said on March 29 that the party would remain dominant in Vietnam; multiparty democracy would not be permitted; and the number of private businesses would be limited. At a meeting from August 15 through 24 of the party's Central Committee, its main policymaking body, Linh charged that "insidious schemes and tricks of imperialism" by the United States were being used to try to drive Communist nations to capitalism.

Leaders diverge. Linh also said that a handful of party members and officials had developed "deviant ideological viewpoints," a reference to disputes between Linh and a retired leader, Le Duc Tho, over economic policies. Linh wanted to cut back government subsidies to failing state businesses and permit more free enterprise. A leader of party conservatives, Tho feared that economic liberalization would endanger the party's control, and he encouraged officials to resist reforms. As the factions struggled, intellectuals and journalists who had sought more freedom to debate policy were reined in sharply.

Foreign aid. Justice Minister Phan Hien announced on February 27 that the preamble to Vietnam's Constitution had been changed to delete charges that the United States, China, France, and Japan had been imperialistic aggressors against Vietnam. Vietnam hoped for trade and aid from these countries.

But the volatile political situation that developed in Cambodia after the reported Vietnamese military withdrawal left foreigners skeptical about the region's stability. The United States maintained its trade embargo against Vietnam, which influenced Japan and other potential investors to limit their roles to funding small businesses. Foreign aid remained sparse.

The inflation rate dropped from a runaway rate of about 700 per cent in 1988 to a manageable level in 1989. The black market in foreign currency virtually disappeared as confidence in Vietnam's money grew. The price of rice, Vietnam's basic food, dropped. After years of shortages, the nation began its first significant exports of rice in almost three decades. Economic gains did not stem the flood of "boat people" trying to escape, however.   Henry S. Bradsher

See also **Asia** (Facts in brief table); **Cambodia.** In *World Book,* see **Vietnam.**

Virginia. See State government.

Vital statistics. See Population.

Washington. See State government.

First lady Barbara Bush cuts a cake at a celebration of the 100th birthday of the National Zoo in Washington, D.C., in March.

Washington, D.C. Throughout 1989, federal investigators intensified their probe of alleged drug use by Mayor Marion S. Barry, Jr. Although Barry continued to deny he had ever used drugs, he was contradicted by Charles Lewis, an admitted drug dealer. In November, Lewis, who once worked in the city's personnel office, pleaded guilty in United States District Court to conspiring to provide cocaine to Barry and various other people.

Lewis said in court that Barry gave him money on three occasions to buy crack—a smokable form of cocaine. The federal investigation began after disclosures that Barry was visiting Lewis' room at the Ramada Inn in downtown Washington on Dec. 22, 1988, when police detectives arrived to check out a report that Lewis had offered cocaine to a housekeeper. At year-end, federal prosecutors had not indicted Barry.

Mayoral campaign. Despite his mounting troubles, Barry announced in August that he will run for his fourth term as mayor in the 1990 elections, when he likely will face a number of opponents. Those announcing that they would challenge Barry for the Democratic nomination for mayor included City Council Chairman David A. Clarke; council members John Ray and Charlene Drew Jarvis; and Sharon Pratt Dixon, a Democratic Party activist and former power-company executive.

Another possible candidate is Jesse L. Jackson, a prominent figure in national politics, who ran for the Democratic presidential nomination in 1988. Jackson indicated that he was considering a run for mayor, and in September he moved his family and political organization to Washington.

Maurice T. Turner, Jr., who stepped down as the city's police chief at the end of July 1989, said he would seek the Republican nomination for mayor, and the leadership of the District of Columbia Republican Party endorsed his candidacy in October. Turner switched his party affiliation from Democrat to Republican at a White House ceremony in July after a visit with President George Bush, a Republican.

Drugs and death. For the second year in a row in 1989, Washington had a record number of homicides. By early November, the city had exceeded the 1988 total of 369 murders, and at the end of the year the death toll stood at 438. The police attributed most of the murders to drug-related violence.

National drug-control director William J. Bennett announced shortly after taking office in March that he would name Washington a "high-intensity drug trafficking area" and use the city as the federal government's first "test case" in efforts to stem drug abuse and violence. In April, Bennett outlined an antidrug plan for the city that included building two federal prisons in the Washington area, evicting drug dealers from public housing projects, creating a narcotics task force with both federal agents and district police officers, and adding U.S. prosecutors and drug agents to

Water

the city's antidrug resources. The program is expected to cost $70 million to $80 million.

Budget veto. In October, President Bush vetoed the city's fiscal 1990 budget—part of a federal appropriations bill—because it contained abortion provisions that he considered unacceptable. Those provisions would have restored the city's authority to use its own funds to pay for abortions for poor women and would have allowed federal funds to be used for abortions for rape and incest victims.

The city's budget must be approved each year by Congress and signed by the President. In November, Congress amended the bill, allowing the use of federal funds for abortions in the district only to save the life of the woman and prohibiting the use of local funds for abortions. Bush signed the bill on November 21. The $3.4-billion spending plan also contains a $32-million package of federally funded antidrug measures, including money to hire 700 more police.

Recycling. The first phase of a new recycling program, the most sweeping in the east-central United States, was launched in Washington in October to much public confusion. The plan required district residents to separate newspapers and yard waste from the rest of their trash. Beginning in 1990, glass and metal products were also to be separated out. In addition, city businesses must now sort out different types of office paper for recycling.   Sandra Evans

See also **City.** In *World Book,* see **Washington, D.C.**

Water. Los Angeles approved two agreements in September 1989 that may end the city's decade-long disputes over using water from Owens Valley and Mono Lake. The pacts—hailed as a turning point from confrontation to negotiation—will limit the amount of water tapped by the Los Angeles Aqueduct.

The aqueduct extends 220 miles (350 kilometers) north of Los Angeles to Inyo County, where it taps streams and ground water in Owens Valley. The bitter struggle over the valley's water—which was dramatized in the 1974 movie *Chinatown*—began in the early 1900's. City agents purchased water rights in Inyo County before the city revealed its plans to build the aqueduct and take the water, which had been used to irrigate the county's orchards and crops.

Although people opposed to the aqueduct's construction dynamited it several times, Los Angeles eventually took much of the valley's water, which led to the depopulation of Inyo County. In recent years, controversy has centered on the effects of declining ground water levels in the valley. As ground water has been depleted, trees and other vegetation have died, and the area is now swept with ferocious dust storms.

The new agreement between Los Angeles and Inyo County requires the city to stop pumping ground water into the aqueduct if doing so will harm the valley's vegetation. Los Angeles also agreed to pay Inyo County $2 million per year to be used for parks and recreation.

The aqueduct also extends another 60 miles (100 kilometers) north to reach streams feeding Mono Lake, an ancient saltwater lake known for its castlelike limestone formations and for its role as a resting and breeding area for millions of migratory shore birds. As water from those streams has been diverted to the city, the lake levels have dropped. The lake has also become so salty that it threatens the area's plant and animal life. The second agreement, between Los Angeles and the state of California, provides $65 million to help Los Angeles find other water sources so that Mono Lake can recover.

"Colonias" water supply. On May 28, the Texas legislature passed a law to provide clean water and sewers for makeshift subdivisions called *colonias* that house thousands of poor Hispanic Americans living in the Rio Grande Valley. Most colonias have inadequate water supplies. In the colonias near El Paso, for example, an estimated 30,000 people have no safe drinking water, and 53,000 lack sewers.

Residents of the colonias suffer severely from dysentery, hepatitis, and other diseases transmitted by the use of unsanitary water. Children in particular are afflicted at rates more typically found in Third World nations. The new law provides $30 million for construction of drinking-water and sewer systems and allows the sale of bonds exceeding $100 million to help pay for the projects.   Iris Priestaf

In *World Book,* see **Water.**

Watkins, James David (1927-   ), was sworn in as United States secretary of energy on March 1, 1989. Watkins, known for his technical background in nuclear energy and his strong administrative skills, inherited a department facing controversy over nuclear weapons production and nuclear waste disposal.

Watkins was born on March 7, 1927, in Alhambra, Calif. He graduated from the U.S. Naval Academy at Annapolis, Md., in 1949 and received a master's degree in mechanical engineering in 1958 from the Naval Postgraduate School. He entered the Navy's nuclear submarine program in 1959, eventually commanding a nuclear submarine and the world's first nuclear cruiser. His posts included commander of the Sixth Fleet, vice chief of naval operations, and commander in chief of the Pacific Fleet. His naval career culminated with his 1982 appointment to the Navy's highest office, chief of naval operations.

After retiring from the Navy in 1986, Watkins devoted his time to youth and educational issues. From October 1987 to June 1988, he headed President Ronald Reagan's Commission on the Human Immunodeficiency Virus Epidemic. In that post, he recommended broad federal efforts to protect and treat AIDS victims, surprising observers who had predicted he would support a conservative strategy for containing AIDS.

Watkins married Sheila Jo McKinney in 1950; they have six children and eight grandchildren. The couple live in Pasadena, Calif.   Robin Goldman

Weather. After a period of spectacular extremes—drought and record-breaking hot and cold spells—the weather over the United States had settled down by mid-1989 into a more normal pattern of rainfall and temperatures. Nevertheless, there were many unusual weather events late in the year, including deadly Hurricane Hugo in September and a killer tornado in Huntsville, Ala., in November.

Hurricane Hugo, the worst storm to hit the United States since Hurricane Camille in 1969, made its appearance in early September 1989 in the eastern Atlantic Ocean. Gaining strength as it slowly moved across the water, it passed over Guadeloupe, St. Croix, Puerto Rico, and other Caribbean islands on September 17 and 18.

The storm then continued northwest and hit Charleston, S.C., on September 21 with winds of 135 miles per hour (mph)—or 220 kilometers per hour (kph). These winds, together with a storm surge of water 17 feet (5 meters) high, wrecked buildings and marinas along more than 100 miles (160 kilometers) of coastline. Away from the coast, high winds and several tornadoes damaged buildings and downed trees and power lines. Damage estimates exceeded $8 billion, and several thousand people were left homeless. At least 71 people were killed in the Caribbean and the United States, but timely warnings and evacuation were credited with saving many lives.

The storm continued inland through central Ohio with moderating winds and heavy rain. In its wake came an unusually severe cold outbreak with snow and ice pellets in western Pennsylvania on September 23 and the earliest freezes ever in southern Missouri and northern Arkansas on September 24 and 25.

A much smaller hurricane named Jerry formed in the Gulf of Mexico on Friday, October 13, and struck Galveston, Tex., two days later. Winds gusted up to 100 mph (160 kph), and rainfall was between 4 and 8 inches (10 and 20 centimeters) in some areas. Three people driving along the coast of the Gulf of Mexico were swept away by the high waves.

A rare weather event occurred on June 23, when a storm system in the Pacific Ocean named Hurricane Cosme crossed over Mexico and entered the Gulf of Mexico. It was then renamed Tropical Storm Allison. It brought 17 inches (43 centimeters) of rain to Houston suburbs on June 28 and 29 and caused heavy rains across Louisiana and neighboring states. New monthly rainfall records were set at Birmingham, Ala.; Shreveport, La.; and Winnfield, La.

The rain returns. The drought that had plagued much of the Midwestern United States during 1988 was broken in 1989. Although April, as a whole, was dry, March and May both averaged near normal rainfall. There were, however, some lingering drought problems in parts of Iowa, Kansas, and Nebraska; southern California; the Texas coast; and portions of Wyoming, Montana, and Washington. For the period from October 1988 to May 1989, Nebraska had its smallest rainfall on record—4.5 inches (11.4 centimeters). The dry conditions in Nebraska and Kansas finally came to an end in late August.

Several Eastern cities had their wettest May on record: Pittsburgh, Pa., had more than double its normal 3.1 inches (7.9 centimeters), and Hartford, Conn., had 12.0 inches (30.5 centimeters) instead of its usual 3.3 inches (8.4 centimeters). The heavy rains ended fears that Northeastern reservoirs might dry up because of an unusually dry winter. Abundant precipitation in the East continued through June and July.

Tornadoes. The dry conditions in the Midwest and humid conditions in the East were particularly favorable for severe spring thunderstorms and tornadoes. From March through May, 457 tornadoes were reported in the eastern half of the United States, compared with an average of 321 for this period. Nearly 400 more were recorded in the next three months, most of them in June. Preliminary figures indicated that 1989 had the second highest total number of tornadoes in history.

The year's worst tornado struck on November 15, tearing a path of destruction 10 miles (16 kilometers) long and ½ mile (0.8 kilometer) wide through Huntsville. With winds up to 250 mph (400 kph), the tornado destroyed or damaged more than 200 homes, stores, schools, churches, and other buildings and left 18 people dead and hundreds injured.

The same storm system that spawned Huntsville's killer tornado continued northeastward, causing damage to homes in New Jersey and skyscrapers in Philadelphia. On November 16, the storm's high winds caused a wall of a school near Newburgh, N.Y., to collapse, killing nine children.

Alaska's bitter winter. A bitterly cold air mass accumulated over Alaska during January. Mean temperatures for the state were 35 to 45 Fahrenheit degrees (19 to 25 Celsius degrees) below normal. At Tanana, the temperature plunged to −76°F. (−60°C). Nome's temperature of −54°F. (−48°C) on January 28—as well as the city's average temperature for the month—were the coldest since record keeping began in 1906.

Meanwhile, much of Canada and the continental, or lower 48, states were experiencing their second warmest January in 35 years. Then, a massive high pressure system propelled the cold air southward from Alaska on January 30 and 31. Meteorologists at Northway Airport, near the Alaskan border, on January 31 observed the highest barometric pressure ever recorded in North America—31.85 inches (808.99 millimeters) of mercury.

The high pressure rapidly advanced the cold air's leading edge, bringing the lengthy January thaw to an abrupt end. At Lethbridge, Canada, the temperature dropped from 54°F. (12°C) to 16°F. (−9°C) in a single hour; and at Russell, Kans., the temperature fell from 84°F. (29°C) on January 31 to 12°F. (−11°C) the next morning.

In September, Hurricane Hugo killed more than 70 people as it blasted coastal areas in South Carolina, *above left*, and the Caribbean.

Within 24 hours, the cold air had reached as far south as northern Texas. High winds and blizzard conditions accompanied the frigid air. As the cold air advanced, Brownsville, the southernmost city in Texas, experienced 28 consecutive hours of below-freezing temperatures, and Amarillo, Tex., recorded a low of −4°F. (−20°C).

The cold air then flooded into southern California, setting several low temperature records and bringing snow to portions of Los Angeles. Meanwhile, Alaska returned to above average temperatures.

The cold persisted in the Western United States for the rest of February, making it the coldest winter on record for Oregon, Washington, and Idaho. Along the Atlantic and Gulf coasts, however, warmth returned and February temperatures averaged above normal. In between, the boundary of the cold air set in along the lower Mississippi and Tennessee valleys, giving rise to a sequence of heavy rain- and snow-producing storms during late February. Severe flooding occurred in the Tennessee and lower Mississippi valleys, and there were snowfalls of up to 18 inches (46 centimeters) in North Carolina and southern Virginia.

Other notable weather events. The Poconos, Catskills, and Berkshires in the Northeast, mountainous centers of the Eastern ski industry, experienced their greatest lack of snow this century with a total of only 2 to 5 inches (5.1 to 12.7 centimeters) from November 1988 to February 1989. But snow was plentiful elsewhere. A snowstorm at Fargo, N. Dak., from January 5 to 8 left a record 30 inches (76 centimeters) of snow on the ground. A late winter storm struck the Pacific Northwest on March 1 and 2, dropping 6 inches (15 centimeters) of snow in Seattle and 12 to 14 inches (30.5 to 35.6 centimeters) in the suburbs. The same storm brought heavy rain to northern California, and later, as it reached the Gulf states, it spawned the formation of 22 tornadoes.

A heat wave surged into the central United States from March 10 to 12, and extreme heat prevailed in the Western states during April. Thermometers in Los Angeles on April 6 recorded temperatures up to 106°F. (41°C). Between April 4 and 8, San Francisco temperatures reached record highs of 90°F. (32°C). Phoenix temperatures broke records on six consecutive days, and Tucson, Ariz., had record high temperatures on 21 days between March 4 and April 10.

In October, the United States again had record-setting highs and lows. There were record highs of about 90°F. in Nebraska, while record-breaking cold hit the Great Lakes, South, and Gulf Coast. On November 23, a storm blanketed much of the Northeastern United States with a record Thanksgiving Day snowfall. The storm set the stage for one of the coldest Decembers ever recorded in the Eastern and Central states.　　Alfred K. Blackadar and Paul G. Knight

In *World Book,* see **Weather.**

Weightlifting. See Sports.

Welfare. The poverty rate in the United States inched downward in 1988 for the fifth straight year, according to figures released by the U.S. Bureau of the Census on Oct. 18, 1989. But the decline was so slight that family and household incomes essentially were unchanged from 1987, Census Bureau officials said.

In 1988, a family of four was considered poor if its cash income was below $12,092. According to the Census Bureau, 31.9 million Americans, or 13.1 per cent of the population, fell below the poverty line. This marked a drop from 13.4 per cent in 1987.

The official poverty line, which reflects the amount of money needed for a minimum adequate diet and other needs, is raised each year to account for inflation. The measure determines eligibility for a variety of welfare benefits.

The proportion of Americans living in poverty dropped to a low of 11.1 per cent in 1973. It then moved upward to 15.2 per cent in 1983 before starting a gradual decline. But the slowness of that decline indicates that poverty remains stubbornly persistent even as the economy has prospered.

Median income for family households, which account for 71 per cent of all households, fell for the first time since 1982, dropping 0.2 per cent to $32,191. But median household income, which includes people living alone or in unrelated groups as well as families, rose 0.3 per cent to $27,225.

Tight budgets. With President George Bush holding to his "no new taxes" edict, social welfare programs shared in an overall restraint on federal spending. The National League of Cities, a federation of municipal governments based in Washington, D.C., reported on July 11, 1989, that local governments were hard pressed to cope with a growing list of "crisis issues or unfunded mandates" that the federal government was neglecting. The league reported that in 1988, 69 per cent of cities raised fees and charges for municipal services, 41 per cent raised property taxes, 36 per cent imposed new fees and charges, and 10 per cent instituted new taxes.

In May 1989, a Ford Foundation study called for a $29-billion increase in federal spending for welfare, education, and health care, to be financed by taxing most social security benefits. The three-year study was prepared by a panel of business, civic, education, labor, and civil rights leaders headed by Irving S. Shapiro, former chief executive of the Du Pont Company.

Shapiro called the current social welfare system "out of date" with "severe gaps in protection and opportunity." The study recommended a broad range of improvements, including a nationwide standard for welfare benefits, universal health-care coverage, and expansion of the Head Start program of educational and social services for impoverished children and the Women, Infants, and Children supplemental food program.   Frank Cormier and Margot Cormier

In the Special Reports section, see **No Place to Call Home.** In *World Book,* see **Welfare.**

Wells, Clyde Kirby (1937-   ), was sworn in as Newfoundland's fifth premier on May 5, 1989. He replaced Thomas Rideout, who served briefly as premier after the resignation of A. Brian Peckford in March. Wells's Liberal Party defeated Rideout's Progressive Conservatives by taking 31 of the province's 52 House of Assembly seats in an April 20 election. Wells immediately vowed to reduce the province's 16 per cent unemployment rate. See **Newfoundland.**

Wells was born on Nov. 9, 1937, in Buchans Junction, Nfld. He earned a bachelor's degree in 1959 from Memorial University of Newfoundland and a law degree in 1962 from Dalhousie University in Halifax, N.S. After serving in the Canadian Army's legal branch from 1962 to 1964, he entered private law practice.

Wells was elected to the provincial Assembly in 1966, serving as minister of labor for his first two years. In 1971, he returned to full-time practice of corporate law, eventually as senior partner of his own legal firm.

In 1987, he reentered public life as leader of the Liberal Party of Newfoundland and Labrador and was elected to the Assembly later that year. Wells failed to win a seat for himself in the April 1989 election that gave him the premier's post but was acclaimed as the member for the Bay of Islands district on May 25.

Wells married Eleanor Bishop in 1962; they have three grown children and two grandchildren. The couple live in St. John's.   Robin Goldman

West Indies. With winds clocked at 140 miles (225 kilometers) per hour, Hurricane Hugo battered the West Indies beginning Sept. 17, 1989, knocking out electric, water, and telephone service and leaving about 50,000 people homeless. Worst hit was tiny Montserrat, where Hugo's destruction was nearly total, returning the British dependency "to the kerosene age," according to Governor Christopher J. Turner.

Hugo then veered across the United States Virgin Islands. The destruction it caused touched off looting severe enough that President George Bush sent in troops to preserve order. The hurricane also caused widespread damage in the northeast corner of Puerto Rico and its offshore islands, even defoliating a tropical forest with the fury of its winds.

Improved communications and hurricane forecasting were credited for a relatively low loss of life, with about 40 deaths occurring throughout the Caribbean. The affected islands rushed to restore vital utilities and repair the damage in preparation for the winter tourism season.

Jamaica. On February 9, Jamaicans gave a landslide victory to Michael Manley of the People's National Party. Manley was elected prime minister, and his party won 45 of 60 seats in Parliament. At his inaugural on February 13, Manley pledged his administration to "national unity." In office, Manley sought to steer a more moderate course than when he previously served as prime minister from 1972 to 1980. Then, he

Supporters of rebel troops burn tires in Port-au-Prince, Haiti's capital, in April, but the rebellion was quashed by the government.

soured relations with the United States by pushing for close ties with Cuba's Communist President Fidel Castro and by promoting an ideology that seemed to worsen class divisions among Jamaicans:

Elsewhere in the Caribbean, there was continuity. Prime Minister Vere C. Bird, Sr., and the Antigua Labor Party handily won reelection in March 1989 in the twin-island nation of Antigua and Barbuda. Bird, 79, has dominated the nation's politics since long before it achieved independence in 1981; two of his sons hold Cabinet rank.

Also in March 1989, Prime Minister Kennedy Alphonse Simmonds and the People's Action Movement won their third straight victory at the polls in another twin-island nation, St. Christopher (St. Kitts) and Nevis. Simmonds pledged his administration to a program aimed at producing "a higher standard of living, full employment, good education."

In the Caribbean nation of Belize on the Central American mainland, Prime Minister George C. Price and the People's United Party were returned to power in a narrow electoral victory on September 4. Price, 70, had ruled the country for 30 years before being ousted at the polls in 1984. Price oversaw Belize's transformation from a British colony to an independent nation in 1981.   Nathan A. Haverstock

See also **Latin America** (Facts in brief table). In *World Book,* see **West Indies.**
West Virginia. See **State government.**

White, Bill (1934-   ), was named president of baseball's National League in February 1989, becoming the highest-ranking black executive in professional sports. White succeeded A. Bartlett Giamatti, who became commissioner of baseball. (Giamatti died on September 1.)

William DeKova White was born in Lakewood, Fla., and educated at Hiram College in Hiram, Ohio. He interrupted his studies to become a professional baseball player and was called up to the major leagues in 1956 with the New York (now San Francisco) Giants.

In 1959, the Giants traded White to the St. Louis Cardinals. He remained with the Cardinals through 1965, winning seven consecutive Gold Glove Awards as a first baseman and playing on the 1964 world championship team. He was traded to the Philadelphia Phillies in 1966 and spent his final season with the Cardinals in 1969. A left-handed hitter, White had 1,706 hits, 202 home runs, 870 runs batted in, and a lifetime .286 batting average during his 13-year career. He played on six All-Star squads, hit over .300 four times, and had 20 or more home runs seven times.

At the end of his baseball career, White became a sports broadcaster—first for St. Louis, then for Philadelphia, and from 1971 until 1989 for the New York Yankees.

White, who is divorced, has five children and lives in Upper Black Eddy, Pa.   Rod Such

Wilder, L. Douglas (1931-   ), became the first black elected governor in United States history when he won election as the chief executive of Virginia on Nov. 7, 1989. Wilder, a Democrat, defeated Republican J. Marshall Coleman 50.2 per cent to 49.8 per cent in one of the closest elections in Virginia history. Many observers credited prochoice voters with giving the victory to Wilder, who campaigned as a strong supporter of abortion rights.

Lawrence Douglas Wilder was born on Jan. 17, 1931, in Richmond, Va., the seventh of eight children. His grandparents had been born into slavery. His father sold insurance door-to-door, and his mother worked as a maid.

Wilder received a bachelor's degree from Virginia Union University in Richmond in 1951. Soon afterward, he was drafted into the Army and won a Bronze Star for bravery in the Korean War (1950-1953). Using his veteran's benefits, Wilder enrolled in Howard University School of Law in Washington, D.C. After graduating in 1959, he returned to Richmond and became a successful trial lawyer.

Wilder entered politics in 1969, winning a seat in the Virginia state Senate. He was elected lieutenant governor in 1985. Wilder is divorced and has three grown children.   Sara Dreyfuss
Wisconsin. See **State government.**
Wyoming. See **State government.**
Yemen (Aden or **Sana).** See **Middle East.**

Yeutter, Clayton Keith (1930-   ), was sworn in as secretary of the United States Department of Agriculture (USDA) on Feb. 16, 1989. Yeutter, who had served as U.S. trade representative under President Ronald Reagan, is a strong advocate of free trade and has worked to lower barriers to U.S. food exports.

Yeutter was born on Dec. 10, 1930, in Eustis, Nebr. He earned a bachelor's degree in 1952 and a law degree in 1963 from the University of Nebraska in Lincoln. He was awarded a doctorate in agricultural economics from that institution in 1966.

After getting his bachelor's degree, Yeutter served five years in the U.S. Air Force. He then operated a farm and ranch in central Nebraska for several years. In 1960, he joined the University of Nebraska faculty and from 1968 to 1979 directed the university's agricultural assistance program in Colombia. In 1970, Yeutter went to work at the USDA, where he held a variety of posts over the next five years. In 1975, he became deputy U.S. trade representative.

Yeutter left public service in 1977, first joining a law firm in Nebraska and then, the following year, becoming the president and chief executive officer of the Chicago Mercantile Exchange, one of the world's biggest commodities markets. He held that post until 1985, when Reagan appointed him U.S. trade representative.

Yeutter is married to the former Jeanne Vierk. They have four children.   Barbara A. Mayes

Yugoslavia, for decades the Communist world's front-runner in economic and political reform, lagged far behind Poland, Hungary, East Germany, and Czechoslovakia in that respect in 1989. Yugoslav leaders endlessly debated a turn to a free market economy but did little to create one. Ethnic conflict continued during the year, fueling a power struggle among the six republics that make up Yugoslavia.

The main opponents in this struggle were the biggest republic, Serbia, and one of the smallest, Slovenia. Serbia, which has 40 per cent of Yugoslavia's population, wanted the country ruled by a strong central government that would favor Serbia and enable it to dominate Yugoslavia as it had between the two world wars, from 1918 to 1939.

By contrast, Slovenia, with only 8 per cent of Yugoslavia's people, opposed strong central government and favored radical economic and political reform. On Sept. 27, 1989, Slovenia's legislature defied objections from the federal authorities in Belgrade, the capital, and amended the republic's constitution to make explicit a general right to secede from Yugoslavia. This legislation was referred to Yugoslavia's Constitutional Court. As 1989 ended, political observers saw Serbia as swimming against a rising tide of change in Yugoslavia—an increasing acceptance of the opinion that the central authorities and governments of other republics must follow Slovenia's example in liberalization and party pluralism.

Kosovo, a province of Serbia, faced a second year of occupation by federal police after Serbia put into force constitutional amendments ending local self-rule by the province's largest ethnic group—individuals of Albanian ancestry. Yugoslavia poured more police into Kosovo in 1989. In February and March, the police arrested thousands of protesters in the province, mostly young people. Serbian authorities forced scores of ethnic Albanian officials to resign or purged them.

Among the purged was the regional party leader, Azem Vlasi. The authorities charged Vlasi with subversion and put him on trial October 30.

The Serbian authorities' disregard of human rights, including the forced "isolation" and silencing in May of 240 ethnic Albanian intellectuals who resisted Serbian controls, drew sharp criticism from the West. The Serbian Writers' Union, which had favored a stronger role for Serbia in the Yugoslav federation, also criticized the rights abuse.

Economic plan. Federal Executive Council President (prime minister) Ante Marković on October 12 presented an anti-inflation plan that included the closing of unprofitable businesses — even though closures would increase unemployment. He also advocated a shift to a fully open market and closer links with the West.   Eric Bourne

See also **Europe** (Facts in brief table). In *World Book*, see **Yugoslavia.**

Yukon Territory reelected Canada's only Socialist government on Feb. 20, 1989, when it returned the New Democratic Party (NDP) to power. Party leader Antony Penikett, a former mine union organizer who has been in power since 1985, named a five-member cabinet with himself as government leader (a post corresponding to that of premier in the provinces).

The NDP captured 9 of the 16 seats in the Legislative Assembly, winning 45 per cent of the popular vote. The Progressive Conservative Party took the remaining 7 seats, attracting 43 per cent of the vote. More than three-fourths of the Yukon's 15,100 voters went to the polls.

The NDP, known for its action on human-rights legislation and Indian land claims, drew much of the vote of the territory's 5,500 Indians. The four Indians elected to the Assembly were NDP members.

The closing of three silver mines in January 1989 at Elsa demonstrated once again the boom-and-bust economy of Yukon. Low silver prices and high costs were blamed for the closures. With silver prices averaging $5.80 Canadian ($4.90 U.S.) a troy ounce (31 grams) in the early part of 1989 and production costs totaling more than $9 ($7.50 U.S.) an ounce in 1988, the mines faced an impossible future.   David M. L. Farr

In *World Book*, see **Yukon Territory.**

Zaire. See **Africa.**

Zambia. See **Africa.**

Zimbabwe. See **Africa.**

Zoology

Zoology. Zoologist Brian Barnes of the University of Alaska in Fairbanks reported in June that hibernating Arctic ground squirrels can survive in their dens with air temperatures well below freezing. Previously, it was thought that hibernating squirrels must warm up or die under such temperatures because they could not survive if ice crystals formed in their tissues.

Barnes was interested in these animals because they hibernate in soil temperatures that reach $-0.4°F$. ($-18°C$) in the Brooks Mountain Range of Alaska. To test their hibernating ability, Barnes placed ground squirrels in an environmentally controlled chamber that gradually decreased in temperature to 24.3°F. ($-4.3°C$) over a month. The squirrels' deep body temperatures dropped as low as 26.8°F. ($-2.9°C$).

It was not clear how the ground squirrels managed to avoid freezing. Separate studies of their blood suggest that freezing should have occurred at about 30.9°F. ($-0.6°C$). The squirrels do not seem to form antifreeze compounds, such as those made by Arctic fish, which keep those fish from freezing in icy waters. Instead, the animals appear to be in a supercooled state in which the temperature of liquids in their tissues is below the normal freezing point but the liquids do not solidify. Other mammals survive such temperatures for less than an hour before solid ice crystals form in their body tissues and they die. Arctic ground squirrels, however, were able to survive subfreezing body temperatures for more than three weeks.

Mantis shrimp eyes. Many mammals, such as dogs and cats, cannot see color. Monkeys and birds, however, have excellent color vision due to special pigments in their eyes that absorb light of different wavelengths corresponding to different colors. Human beings have three types of color-vision cells, each with a different pigment. Certain flies and fishes have five pigments, and up until 1989, these animals held the record for the number of different color-vision cells. In May 1989, however, biologists Thomas W. Cronin of the University of Maryland at Catonsville and N. Justin Marshall of the University of Sussex in England reported in *Nature* magazine that the mantis shrimp has 10 visual pigments, a new record.

The eyes of insects and shrimp are subdivided into many subunits or facets called *ommatidia*. Most of the color-vision cells of the mantis shrimp seem confined to a narrow band of ommatidia running across the center of each eye. Colored filters occur over certain cells to screen out certain wavelengths, while allowing others in to strike the retina. This itself would not be newsworthy, because birds and reptiles have tiny oil droplets in retinal cells that perform the same function. What is notable is the unprecedented number of colored pigments that mantis shrimp use, which give this species excellent color vision. The investigators speculated that color vision may enable the shrimps to recognize one another and communicate by means of visual signals.   Clyde Freeman Herreid

In *World Book*, see **Zoology**.

Zoos and aquariums in the United States blended art, science, and advanced technology to create a broad variety of new exhibits in 1989. The St. Louis (Mo.) Zoo's Living World, which opened June 1, shows visitors how life evolved on earth and what can happen when people try to alter the natural world. In addition to more than 150 species of animals and their habitats—among them a colony of 10,000 leaf-cutter ants and a cave inhabited by bats—the display includes 30 computer terminals, 32 large video screens, and 10 educational video games. There is even an animated figure of Charles Darwin, the British naturalist known for his theories of evolution.

Technology took an aquatic turn in Brooklyn, a borough of New York City, at The New York Aquarium's Discovery Cove, which opened July 6. Mechanically generated surf demonstrates how beaches are formed. Visitors can stand waist-deep in vegetation to get a bird's-eye view of a salt marsh. They can also sense the crash of a wave dumping 400 gallons (1,500 liters) of water into a tidal pool as they stand beneath the wave, protected by a clear acrylic panel.

The largest habitats at Discovery Cove duplicate water ecosystems, such as an underwater *kelp* (seaweed) "forest" and a coral reef. (An ecosystem is a group of plants and animals living in an environment, together with nonliving features of the environment, such as soil and water.) Groups of themed exhibits demonstrate ways in which aquatic animals survive and adapt to their environment.

Children's zoo. On May 5, the Los Angeles Zoo opened Adventure Island, a complex of five exhibits spotlighting animals of the Southwest. In one exhibit, children can explore a cave inhabited by bats, owls, and raccoonlike ringtails. They can also visit replicas of a meadow, a coastline, a desert, and a Spanish *hacienda* (ranch), where they can pet domestic animals.

Elephant exhibits. The Woodland Park Zoo in Seattle brought together more than 12,000 trees and plants, a winding stream, a waterfall, and a large pond to create a new tropical Asian forest for its elephants. The exhibit, which opened in May, has a replica of a logging camp in Thailand.

New York City's Bronx Zoo completed modernizing its 81-year-old elephant house and opened the new facility on July 19. Realistic Asian habitats display elephants, Malayan tapirs (bulky, long-nosed relatives of horses), and Indian rhinoceroses.

Little bears. On June 30, the San Diego Zoo unveiled Sun Bear Forest, a replica of an Asian woodland. Sun bears, also called Malayan bears, are the smallest of all bear species, measuring only 3 to 4 feet (90 to 120 centimeters) long. An artificial fig tree provides heated limbs where the bears can nap, and releases honey several times a day as a treat. Also in the exhibit are a colony of large monkeys called *liontailed macaques* and a variety of colorful birds.

Chimp habitat. The Detroit Zoo opened the world's largest exhibit for chimpanzees on October 19.

An elephant at Zoo Atlanta in Georgia receives stainless steel crowns in February to protect the tips of her tusks.

The 11 resident chimps can explore nearly 4 acres (1.6 hectares) of realistic habitat that features a variety of natural touches, such as a replica of a termite mound. Using twigs, they can poke the mound for termites, a chimp delicacy.

The habitat is the only exhibit in the United States where people can interact with chimps. For example, visitors can "communicate" with them by pounding on a fiberglass tree trunk. The chimps can answer back by pounding on their own tree. Visitors can also ride a barge along a "river" that separates them from the apes and can explore a replica of a fossil dig that reveals the similarities between human beings and these close primate relatives.

Reptiles on view. The Louisville (Ky.) Zoo's Herpaquarium opened May 27 with 62 exhibits featuring 700 reptiles, amphibians, and fish. Mammals, birds, and *invertebrates* (animals without backbones) share the exhibits, which are devoted to aquatic, forest, and arid environments.

Wetland birds. To bring attention to the birds that live in wetland environments, such as marshes and swamps, the National Zoological Park in Washington, D.C., opened its Wetlands Habitat on May 3. It displays 42 species of ducks, geese, swans, and wading birds as well as frogs and other wetland animals.

High-tech breeding. An unusual event occurred at the Cincinnati (Ohio) Zoo on February 7, when a domestic cat gave birth to a rare wild desert cat. The kit-ten was a product of two techniques—*in vitro* (test-tube) fertilization and embryo transfer. Sperm and eggs from a pair of desert cats were combined in an artificial medium, and a resulting *embryo* (fertilized egg) was implanted in the domestic cat. The birth was part of a long-range research program designed to improve reproduction of endangered species.

Rare births. The Cincinnati Zoo was the site of another rare birth in May when a banded linsang gave birth to two cubs. The catlike linsang comes from Southeast Asia. Cincinnati is the only zoo in North America to display the species.

The San Diego Zoo made history in 1989 when a male Sichuan takin calf was born on June 17 and another on July 1. Takins are shaggy hoofed mammals with curving helmetlike horns. They live in mountain forests of central Asia but are rarely exhibited in zoos. The San Diego Zoo is the only one in the United States to exhibit the animals, which somewhat resemble the musk ox, their closest relative. These are the first zoo births of the species outside China.

Panda disappointment. The National Zoo's staff had high hopes when the giant panda Ling-Ling gave birth on September 1. The tiny, 4-ounce (110-gram) cub did not live long, however, dying three days later of a bacterial infection. It was Ling-Ling's fifth cub; not one has survived.   Eugene J. Walter, Jr.

In the Special Reports section, see **Saving Our Big Birds.** In *World Book*, see **Zoo.**

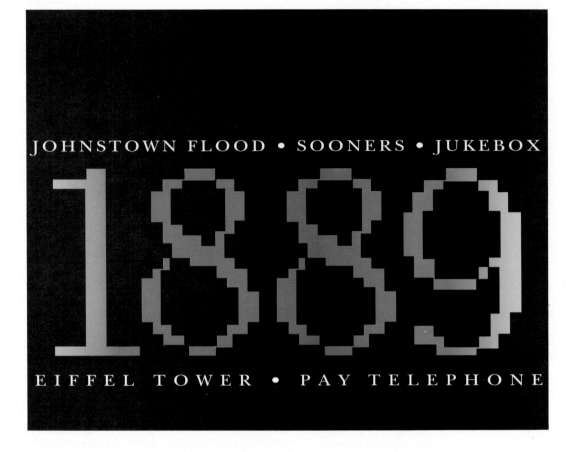

JOHNSTOWN FLOOD • SOONERS • JUKEBOX

1889

EIFFEL TOWER • PAY TELEPHONE

A Year in Perspective

From the perspective of 1989, *The World Book Year Book* looks at some of the political developments and popular culture of 100 years ago and, in a special section, casts a backward glance at events of 50 years ago as reported in *The World Book Encyclopedia Annual for 1939.*

See page 495 ▶

By Sara Dreyfuss

1889: A Year in Perspective

The Johnstown flood killed thousands, and the Eiffel Tower was erected for a huge world's fair in Paris.

The people of Johnstown heard the water coming before they saw it. The sound began as a low rumble and quickly swelled to a thunderous roar. There were many shouted warnings—"Run for your lives! The dam has broke!"—but the noise nearly drowned them out. Days of heavy rain had weakened an earthen dam about 12 miles (19 kilometers) upriver from the city, a thriving iron and steel center in southwestern Pennsylvania. On the afternoon of May 31, 1889, the dam collapsed. The South Fork Reservoir, a summer resort for such millionaires as Andrew Carnegie and Andrew Mellon, emptied in minutes. A wall of water more than 35 feet (11 meters) high crashed down the Conemaugh River Valley, carrying away steel mills, trees, houses, livestock, and people. In just 10 minutes, the floodwaters drowned more than 2,000 people and reduced Johnstown to a sea of muck and rubble.

Reporters rushed to Johnstown to cover the tragedy but found themselves groping for words to describe it. "The human mind is incapable of comprehending the awful extent of the Johnstown calamity," declared *Frank Leslie's Illustrated Newspaper.* "Every detail that comes over the broken and patched wires is burdened with agony and tears." *Harper's Weekly* magazine commented, "No one has adequately described this appalling disaster; no one can possibly tell the tale."

Help pours in

The dramatic accounts of the Johnstown flood set off the greatest outpouring of charity the United States had ever seen. Within days, concerned citizens donated more than $3 million in cash and trainloads of food, clothing, blankets, and building materials. Clara Barton, head of the newly organized American Red Cross, took charge of the relief efforts. "If there is a bright spot in all the awful affair," said *Leslie's* newspaper, it is "the generosity with which the American people have responded to the demands of the hour."

The founding of Hull House

The desire to help others that motivated Clara Barton and the flood-relief donors also inspired two Chicago social workers, Jane Addams and Ellen G. Starr, who founded Hull House, one of the first settlement houses in the United States. It opened on Sept. 14, 1889, in a dilapidated mansion donated by businessman Charles J. Hull in a poor neighborhood crowded with immigrants from Greece, Italy, Russia, and other lands. Hull House grew rapidly to include a day-care center, a medical clinic, and a boarding house for working girls.

The author: Sara Dreyfuss is Associate Editor of *The World Book Year Book.*

Addams and Starr founded Hull House not only to help immigrant families but also to give privileged young people an understanding of the problems of the poor and an opportunity to help. Settlement work, Starr wrote, "is more for the benefit of the people who do it than for the other class . . . one gets as much as she gives." Today, the Hull House Association operates about 25 community centers in the Chicago area.

The Mayerling mystery

One of the most famous mysteries of all time occurred in 1889 in the snow-covered Vienna Woods near an Austrian village called Mayerling, where the royal family had a hunting lodge. There, on the morning of January 30, the Archduke Rudolph, 31-year-old crown prince of Austria-Hungary and heir to the throne of Emperor Francis Joseph, was found shot to death with his 17-year-old lover, Baroness Marie Vetsera. The deaths at Mayerling have inspired books, films, plays, and a ballet, but no one knows what actually happened. Most historians believe the prince killed his lover and then himself in a suicide pact.

A new U.S. President

Shortly after Austria-Hungary lost the heir to its throne, the United States acquired a new President. Republican Benjamin Harrison, the grandson of former President William Henry Harrison, took the oath of office as the 23rd President on March 4, 1889. Relentless rain had drenched Washington, D.C., for several days, and it continued during the inauguration. A huge crowd gathered under a sea of umbrellas to watch the inaugural parade. Units of infantry, artillery, and cavalry marched through a curtain of rain. Buffalo Bill Cody, the famous frontiersman, rode a silver-gray stallion in the parade.

The inaugural ball took place that night in the interior courtyard of the U.S. Pension Office, transformed into a festive ballroom by fresh flowers and potted plants. The guests danced to the music of the U.S. Marine Band directed by the dapper John

Girls gather in front of Hull House in Chicago, one of the first settlement houses in the United States, founded in 1889.

493

Mysterious deaths at Mayerling
Archduke Rudolph, *top,* crown prince of Austria-Hungary, was found dead in his lodge at Mayerling in 1889. His lover, Baroness Marie Vetsera, *above,* died with him. Historians think the two had a suicide pact.

Philip Sousa, who wrote two of his best-known marches, "Thunderer" and "The Washington Post," that year.

The Pension Office was an appropriate setting for Harrison's inaugural ball because veterans' pensions had been a key campaign issue that helped him win the election. Harrison's Democratic opponent, then-President Grover Cleveland, had become unpopular by vetoing many pension bills and taking a firm stand against pension fraud. Harrison inherited a surplus of about $105 million from the tight-fisted Cleveland Administration. James Tanner, Harrison's commissioner of pensions, promised to raise pension payments across the board, "though I may wring from the hearts of some the prayer, 'God help the surplus!' "

The American frontier closes

The United States in 1889 was largely agricultural. Farming employed about twice as many workers as did manufacturing. To serve the needs of farmers, the Department of Agriculture became a Cabinet-level agency that year. But the nation was rapidly becoming industrialized as the result of a business boom that began in the 1870's. Industrial growth had brought wealth to many Americans, including Carnegie, Mellon, and oil millionaire John D. Rockefeller. The Amoco Corporation, now one of the world's largest petroleum and chemical companies, was founded by Rockefeller in 1889 as the Standard Oil Company of Indiana. To meet the growing demand for business information, *The Wall Street Journal,* today a leading financial newspaper, began publication on July 8 that year as a four-page daily selling for 2 cents.

By 1889, the growth of agriculture and industry signaled the end of the American frontier. The farmers' and ranchers' hunger for land had all but swallowed up the vast reaches of open space in the West. Four states that had been wilderness just 30 years earlier joined the Union. North and South Dakota were admitted simultaneously on November 2. Harrison shuffled the states' admission papers before signing them so neither state could claim to have been admitted before the other. Montana entered the Union as the 41st state on November 8, and Washington as the 42nd on November 11. The first railroad service

The Oklahoma land rush

Settlers race to stake their claims, *left,* after central Oklahoma is opened for settlement at noon on April 22, 1889. Present-day Guthrie, Okla., an open prairie that afternoon, *below,* is a bustling city of 10,000 people five days later, *bottom.*

linking the East with California started that same month. "The hunting-ground of the Indian is now the home of the white settler," reported *Leslie's* newspaper. "The wilderness of yesterday is a populated territory." In 1890, the U.S. Bureau of the Census officially recognized the end of the frontier era, noting that, "There can hardly be said to be a frontier line."

The Oklahoma land rush

One area of land had escaped the westward surge of white settlement. The rolling prairie of the Indian Territory, in what is now Oklahoma, was deeded to several Indian tribes by treaty with the U.S. government. Eager homesteaders urged the government to open the region for white settlement. Good farmland had become scarce, and, as *Harper's Weekly* commented, "The Oklahoma territory is a beautiful stretch of country, well watered by springs, brooks, and rivers." Yielding to the pressure, the government bought much of central Oklahoma from the Creek and Seminole tribes. President Harrison declared that nearly 1.9 million acres (769,000 hectares) would be opened for settlement at noon on April 22, 1889. As much as a quarter section—160 acres (65 hectares)—of land would go free to the first person who legally staked out a claim to it.

More than 40,000 settlers gathered at the Oklahoma border to await the opening. The Army held them back until a pistol shot signaled the opening. Horses, carriages, wagons, bicycles, and even runners on foot then burst across the line in clouds of dust, beginning a wild stampede dubbed "Harrison's Hoss Race." The Santa Fe Railroad ran five special trains into the region. Many riders jumped off the moving trains without waiting for them to stop and began pounding in the stakes they had brought along to claim the best farms and town lots. One drunken man was said to have fallen from his train and lain down to sleep on the prairie. An hour or two later, he was awakened by a man who shook his shoulder and offered $500 for his claim.

By nightfall, every last acre had been claimed. Guthrie and Oklahoma City had sprung into existence and become cities of 10,000 people or more. In a single afternoon, *Harper's Weekly* said, "Streets had been laid out, town lots staked off, and steps taken toward formation of a municipal government. At twilight, the camp-fires of ten thousand people gleamed . . . where, the night before, the coyote, the gray wolf, and the deer had roamed undisturbed."

Some settlers had sneaked across the line before the opening to claim the best land, hiding in trees or gullies to avoid detection. Their premature arrival earned them the nickname *Sooners*. Disputes over Sooner claims clogged the courts for years, but except for those conflicts, *Leslie's* newspaper commented, "The grand rush was accomplished with surprisingly little strife and disorder." The Sooners nickname soon lost its association with cheating and came to be used for all Oklahomans.

The first all-Americans

College football had become an increasingly popular sport by 1889, when professional football did not yet exist. That year, Yale football coach Walter Camp and *Harper's Weekly* sportswriter Caspar Whitney began the tradition of picking an annual all-American team to honor the nation's best college football players. The first all-Americans included Yale's W. Walter (Pudge) Heffelfinger and Amos Alonzo Stagg (later one of the top coaches in the history of college football).

The last bare-knuckle championship

The biggest sports story of 1889 was a boxing match that became legendary. Heavyweight champion John L. Sullivan, known as "the great John L.," defended his crown against challenger Jake Kilrain in the last important prizefight fought with bare knuckles. Since then, all title bouts have been fought under the Queensberry Rules, which require boxing gloves to be used.

It was amazing that the Sullivan-Kilrain match took place at all. Sullivan, at the age of 31, had begun to show damage from

A bare-knuckle battle

Heavyweight boxing champion John L. Sullivan, *inset top,* successfully defends his title against Jake Kilrain, *inset above,* in Richburg, Miss., in July 1889. The fight lasted 75 rounds and was the last bare-knuckle championship bout.

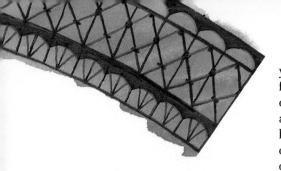

years of heavy drinking. He had been sick in bed from August to November of 1888, suffering from cirrhosis of the liver and delirium tremens, an alcohol-linked disorder marked by trembling and hallucinations. Sullivan recovered enough to sign a contract on Jan. 1, 1889, agreeing to fight Kilrain on July 8 for the heavyweight championship and $10,000.

The site was unnamed because prizefighting was illegal in every state of the Union. The promoters made secret arrangements to hold the match on the estate of a lumberman in Richburg, Miss., about 100 miles (160 kilometers) north of New Orleans.

The day before the fight, the promoters announced that special trains would leave the New Orleans depot at about midnight for the still-secret site of the bout. Hundreds of boxing fans jammed the trains, including some 200 sports-writers and Bat Masterson, the former sheriff of Dodge City, Kans. The attorney general of Louisiana rode along to make sure the train did not stop in his state—then stayed to see the fight.

An epic bout

The bout began at 10:10 a.m. The temperature at ringside was 104°F. (40°C). By the 34th round, both men dripped sweat and blood. Sullivan had a black eye and Kilrain a broken nose. The champion, who sipped tea laced with brandy between rounds, stopped in the 45th round to vomit. A ringside observer commented, "John L. got rid of the tea, but I bet he kept the brandy down." Kilrain offered to call the fight a draw, but Sullivan refused and knocked him down with a straight right. After the 75th round, Kilrain's trainer threw in the sponge to admit defeat. The epic struggle had lasted 2 hours and 16 minutes.

Both fighters were arrested a few days later and were fined and briefly held in jail. *Leslie's* deplored what it called "the spectacle of two bruised and battered ruffians dodging about the country, to escape the officers of the law," but *Life* magazine commented, "The idea of suffering such a penalty for behavior which was the pride and admiration of many thousands of his fellow-citizens must strike the big slugger [Sullivan] as the very abomination of tyranny."

Sullivan remained heavyweight champion until 1892. In 1905, the former champ unexpectedly vowed that he would never take another drink—and he never did. Sullivan became a temperance lecturer and lived quietly on a farm in Massachusetts.

Paris holds a fair

Paris hosted a world's fair called the Universal Exposition of 1889 to mark the centennial of the French Revolution. *Scientific American* described the fair as "the greatest and most imposing manifestation of human industry that has ever been carried out." Fairgoers marveled at the latest technological wonders in the blocklong Hall of Machines, thrilled to Buffalo Bill Cody's Wild West show, and ogled exotic dancers from France's African and Asian colonies.

Dominating the U.S. exhibit was a display of the creations of the great inventor Thomas A. Edison, including a model of his electric light bulb 40 feet (12 meters) high and his new phonograph. People crowded around the phonograph for a turn at one of the four sets of earphones.

The awful Eiffel Tower?

The centerpiece of the fair was the new Eiffel Tower, the world's tallest building at that time, soaring 300 meters (984 feet) above the fairgrounds. The directors of the Universal Exposition had commissioned a bridge engineer named Alexandre Gustave Eiffel to design a structure that would symbolize the event, a practice followed by world's fairs ever since.

Eiffel's design for a lacy wrought-iron structure stirred controversy. About 300 French artists and intellectuals, including the composer Charles Gounod and the novelist Alexandre Dumas the younger, signed a petition opposing "this monstrous and useless Eiffel Tower." The writer Guy de Maupassant urged Parisians to "smash this tall, lanky pyramid, this assemblage of iron ladders." In later years, de Maupassant frequently dined at a restaurant in the building because, he said, it was the only place in Paris where he did not have to look at the Eiffel Tower while eating.

Despite such criticism, some 2 million fairgoers visited the tower in the first year, and the Eiffel Tower soon became the most famous and beloved symbol of Paris. Said *Scientific American*, "Its early detractors are mute, and the approbation of engineers and artists is unanimous. . . . We can now no longer deny that the gigantic work is absolutely beautiful." *The Illustrated London News* found something else to recommend the tower. "It has been proved," said the *News*, "that the air at the summit will be absolutely pure and free from microbes, so the visitors who decide to make the entire skyward journey of 1000 feet will be rewarded by the freshest breath of air they have ever enjoyed."

To help people reach the pure air at the top of the Eiffel Tower, the soaring landmark was equipped with hydraulic eleva-

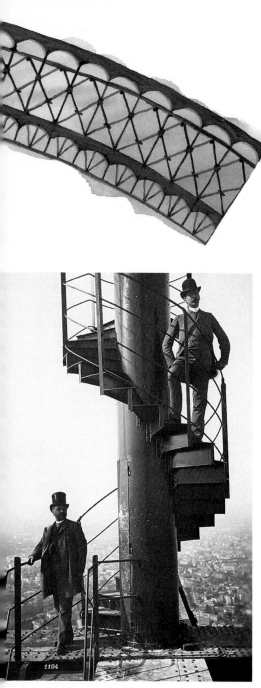

tors manufactured by the New York City firm of Otis Brothers and Company. *Scientific American* crowed, "It is no small tribute to American ingenuity and enterprise that a leading French engineer should appeal to America when confronted with a new problem."

The Auditorium Theatre

Another architectural landmark that opened in 1889 was the Chicago Auditorium Building, a combination hotel, office building, and theater. The building was probably the first original design by Louis Sullivan, who became one of the greatest U.S. architects. *Harper's Weekly* called it "probably the most complete and perfect building of its kind on the Western Continent." President Harrison presided over a gala opening on Dec. 9, 1889, which also featured the reigning queen of opera, a Spanish-born soprano named Adelina Patti. The Auditorium Theatre, still in use, remains famous for its fine acoustics and sightlines.

Household firsts

While Paris fairgoers marveled at the many new inventions on display, busy inventors devised even more wonders. Many new inventions were intended for household use. The Singer Manufacturing Company (now the Singer Company) made the first electric sewing machine in 1889 at its factory in Elizabethport (now Elizabeth), N.J. A million of the electric machines were sold the first year.

A Philadelphia farm equipment maker named Samuel Leeds Allen patented a sled called the Flexible Flyer, with runners of flexible steel instead of the rigid runners on other sleds. The Flexible Flyer has remained popular with children ever since it went on the market.

A milling company in St. Joseph, Mo., marketed the first ready-mix convenience food, originally called simply "self-rising pancake flour."

Paris gains a landmark

French engineer Alexandre Gustave Eiffel and his son-in-law pause on the spiral staircase of the Eiffel Tower, which he designed as the centerpiece of the Universal Exposition of 1889 in Paris. The tower is shown under construction below.

The pancake mix acquired a name after one of the owners, Chris L. Rutt, attended a minstrel show where entertainers in blackface performed a dance called the Aunt Jemima. Rutt invented the character of Aunt Jemima, a symbol of good cooking and Southern hospitality, to represent the pancake mix. A popular brand of breakfast foods is still sold under the Aunt Jemima trademark.

Bathrooms and elevators

Much of the new technology of 1889 increased the comfort of everyday life. One of the first hotels to have private baths was London's Savoy Hotel, which opened on August 6. It boasted 70 private bathrooms. The hotel's owner, British theatrical producer Richard D'Oyly Carte, was better known for bringing to the stage the operettas of Sir William Gilbert and Sir Arthur Sullivan, including 1889's *The Gondoliers. The Illustrated London News* predicted, "The provision of private bath-rooms . . . is a new idea, and one that will no doubt be appreciated." Under the management of Swiss-born hotelier César Ritz, the Savoy became one of the world's leading luxury hotels. Ritz later opened his own hotels in London, Paris, and New York City, and from his name came the word *ritzy*, meaning *classy* or *luxurious.*

Otis Brothers and Company, who had provided the hydraulic elevators for the Eiffel Tower, installed the first practical electric elevators in 1889, in the Demarest Building in New York City. The use of elevators revolutionized architecture. Until that time, the height of buildings had been limited by the number of stairs people would be willing or able to climb. Few buildings were more than five stories tall. Now, reported *The Illustrated London News*, "The development of

Visitors to the Paris exposition listen to Thomas A. Edison's new phonograph through its four sets of earphones.

The World Book Encyclopedia Annual 50 Years Ago

The foreword to *The World Book Encyclopedia Annual for 1939* says, "The story of 1939 is dominated by the outbreak of what has sometimes been called the Second World War, but which we record as the European War." Excerpts from the annual are printed here in boldface type. The words in lightface type did not appear in the annual but are included here to help identify or explain the events described.

AUTOMOBILES. For several years most of the automobile builders have been working on some type of automatic transmission. This year, Oldsmobile announced one as optional equipment on all of their cars. It is fully automatic in the forward gears, so that the car may be started and driven forward by means of the accelerator pedal alone. It is called the hydramatic drive. No clutch pedal is provided or needed.

CELEBRATIONS. Baseball Centennial. On June 12, the 100th anniversary of America's national game was observed at Cooperstown, N.Y., where the sport was originated by Abner Doubleday. The Cavalcade of Baseball portrayed its history and the Baseball Museum and Hall of Fame was dedicated. Historians now believe that Doubleday had little, if anything, to do with inventing baseball.

CHILDREN'S BOOKS. There were some books of funny pictures planned to amuse both children and adults. *Madeline* by Ludwig Bemelmans is the amusing story in rhyme of a little French girl who lost her appendix. . . . *Mike Mulligan and His Steam Shovel* by Virginia Lee Burton is about a hard-working steam shovel of character.

CZECHO-SLOVAKIA. After a "third-degree" conversation which lasted five hours, at 4:30 A.M. on March 15, [Czechoslovak President Emil] **Hacha signed an agreement consenting to placing "the destiny of the Czech people and lands trustfully in the hands of the Fuehrer." A few hours later the German army and police, as though after a successful war of conquest, entered to occupy the country. Hitler himself proceeded to Prague to take over control. On the following day, a decree was issued adding the Protectorate of Bohemia and Moravia to the Greater German Reich.** Czechoslovakia did not regain its independence until 1945.

EUROPEAN WAR. The mighty German military machine struck the Poles so quickly and suddenly that the three Polish armies never had a chance to carry out fully their mobilization and concentration plans. . . . The far larger and stronger German air forces swept over Poland, destroying Polish planes and air bases, bombing railroads and bridges, and cutting telephone and telegraph wires. . . . Warsaw finally gave up its heroic but hopeless struggle on September 27. Germany's invasion of Poland started World War II (1939-1945), the most destructive war in history. In that war, the United States, Great Britain, the Soviet Union, and their allies defeated Germany, Italy, Japan, and their allies.

LITERATURE. The outstanding success of the year, however, has been a novel not of the past but of the present. *The Grapes of Wrath* by John Steinbeck depicts the lives of the migrant laborers of Oklahoma, Kansas, and Texas who seek homes and work in southern California. It is a flaming social document as well as a moving story, told with unsparing frankness, in language which frequently is vulgar in the extreme but which accurately reflects the idiom of the people. This book has persistently held the top of the best seller lists. . . . *The Grapes of Wrath* won the 1940 Pulitzer Prize for fiction, and in 1962, Steinbeck received the Nobel Prize for literature.

MOTION PICTURES. The biggest and most widely heralded event was the presentation of the mammoth screen version of *Gone with the Wind*. . . . Its sheer length of four hours' running time, some spectacular tech-

nicolor recreations of the Civil War, and the fine acting of Vivien Leigh and Clark Gable, insured vast popularity for the film. . . . The outstanding films of 1939 ranged from *Stagecoach*, the fine Western directed by John Ford, to the imaginative screen version of James Hilton's *Goodbye, Mr. Chips*. . . . *Wuthering Heights* was another literary work brought to the screen with skill and taste. *Gone with the Wind* received the 1939 Academy Award for best picture. So many fine films were made that year—including *Beau Geste, Dark Victory, The Hunchback of Notre Dame, Mr. Smith Goes to Washington, Ninotchka, The Wizard of Oz,* and *The Women*—that numerous critics consider it the best year in Hollywood history.

NEW YORK WORLD'S FAIR, THE. The Fair opened on April 30 and closed at 2 A.M., November 1. In all, 25,817,265 persons paid their way to see the wonders of science and industry, the glamor of faraway lands and the glittering amusements included in the Fair's 1,216½ acres. . . . The theme centers, a 700-foot, three-sided obelisk, and a 200-foot sphere—the Trylon and the Perisphere— housed "Democracity" where the City of Tomorrow was displayed inside the huge sphere. Visitors saw dawn break, day progress, and night fall on this ideal city in which factories formed the outer rim of structures, gardens and dwellings the inner circle, and office buildings and retail establishments the nucleus.

SPAIN. The longest and bloodiest civil war in modern Spanish history ended in an Insurgent victory in the last days of March, 1939. . . . With an overwhelming superiority in armaments and aircraft, thanks to his Fascist allies, General [Francisco] **Franco finally succeeded in crushing Spanish democracy.** Franco ruled Spain as a dictator from 1939 until his death in 1975, when Spain again became a democracy.

TELEVISION. April 30, 1939, marked the beginning of scheduled television service in the United States. Field tests of transmitters and receivers . . . had resulted in technical improvements in equipment that enabled the National Broadcasting Company to offer entertaining programs on a reliable service basis. First schedules included two hours of broadcasting per week, but by the end of 1939 this had been increased to fifteen hours, comprising two programs daily, five times per week.   [S.D.]

Preparing for enemy attack, Parisians gather in a shelter during a 1939 air-raid drill.

the system [of elevators] has gone so far that office buildings are erected in New York ten storeys in height; and the upper floors not only let [rent] for as much as those lower, but even more."

Literature and music

New technology also figured in one of the year's most popular novels, Mark Twain's *A Connecticut Yankee in King Arthur's Court*. This book tells the story of a factory superintendent from Hartford, Conn., who finds himself magically transported back to England in the A.D. 500's. He tries to reform that society by introducing the intellectual and technological benefits of the late 1880's. Another popular book of the year was *The Master of Ballantrae*, by British author Robert Louis Stevenson. The novel, which some critics consider Stevenson's best, tells the story of hatred between two brothers during Scotland's revolt against England in the 1740's.

The great composer Peter I. Tchaikovsky of Russia completed his classic ballet *Sleeping Beauty* in 1889, and France's César Franck finished his most frequently performed work, the Symphony in D minor. Popular songs of the year included "Oh! Promise Me," a romantic ballad by songwriter Reginald De-Koven that has been a standard feature at weddings ever since. The biggest hit of the year, however, was a comic song called "Down Went McGinty" by Joseph Flynn, which describes various mishaps suffered by a man named Dan McGinty "Dress'd in his best suit of clothes."

The first jukebox in history, one of many devices that would bring popular songs to millions of listeners, was installed at the Palais Royal Saloon in San Francisco on Nov. 23, 1889. It consisted of an electrically operated Edison phonograph with four listening tubes, each controlled by a separate nickel-in-the slot mechanism.

People paid twice as much to use the first coin-operated telephone, installed at a bank in Hartford, Conn., by the Southern New England Telephone Company in 1889. The phone was a bulky wooden box, which the caller cranked to send a signal to the operator. After the operator reached the other party, the caller deposited 10 cents.

Looking forward

New inventions came so rapidly in 1889, exulted *Scientific American*, "in such a magnificent procession, with results so marvellous, that doubt exists in many minds as to the possibility of maintaining this pace through coming centuries." The magazine dismissed such doubt, predicting that the people of 1989 would be "as far ahead of us in science and its applications as we are superior in that respect to our ancestors of 1789." Said *The Illustrated London News*, "The living age is one of hope, and therefore of splendid possibilities." Future historians may judge whether such optimism was justified.

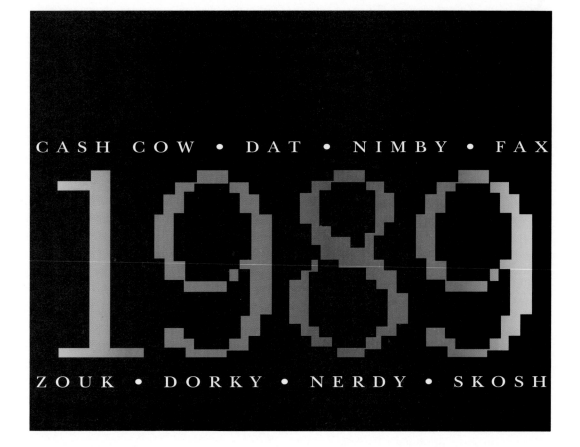

Dictionary Supplement

An informative essay on how words get added to our living language leads off this section. It is followed by a listing of important words from the 1990 edition of *The World Book Dictionary.* This dictionary, first published in 1963, keeps abreast of our changing language with a program of continuous editorial revision. The following supplement was prepared under the direction of the editors of *The World Book Encyclopedia* and Clarence L. Barnhart and Robert K. Barnhart, editors of *The World Book Dictionary.*

New words are interesting clues to what is happening in a society or what interests it. For example, the women's movement brought us *consciousness-raising, networking, sexism,* and many other terms. Dramatic changes in the Soviet Union introduced two Russian words—*glasnost* (openness) and *perestroika* (a restructuring)—into our language. *Bioengineering, black hole, compatibility, multitasking,* and *parallel processing* use old words in new ways to describe the frontiers of science. And *couch potato, crackhead, gridlock, pinstriper,* and *urban guerrilla* have come into general use from a variety of soources.

New words usually arise in the everyday language of a particular group. And while our speech is always active, it is often a bit careless in communicating exactly what we mean. So dictionary editors tend to read what others write—newspapers, magazines, and books. They begin by making files of possible new entries.

Obviously, many more words are collected than can or should be added to the dictionary in any given year. And so the editors wait and watch until enough evidence has been accumulated to indicate that the word or phrase will be encountered by more than a handful of people. Then the word should go into the dictionary, and that is the process that led to selecting the words for inclusion in the 1990 edition of *The World Book Dictionary.*

But there are many, many words and expressions that were not yet deemed important enough to add to the dictionary, either because they were rarely found in the sources being read or were being used only by specialists in a particular field. Here are some of the words that the editors of *The World Book Dictionary* are currently monitoring:

açordas, *n.* a Portuguese soup thickened with bread.

Arabbish, *n.* a blend of Arabic and English.

buppie, *n.* a slang term for a young urban professional (yuppie) who is black.

grazing, *n.* 1) having a meal that consists of small portions of many items from the menu of a restaurant. 2) tuning in on many TV programs for a short time, watching several at once, or casually seeing what is playing on TV.

malling, *n.* gathering in or cruising a shopping mall, for social entertainment or casual shopping.

mall rat or **mallie,** *n.* a person who goes to a shopping mall for social entertainment or casual shopping.

Of these words, *malling, mall rat* or *mallie,* and *grazing* might become popular enough to become dictionary entries; all are regular formations in English and are very descriptive. *Açordas* and *Arabbish* are unfamiliar in form, but such words sometimes become part of our language. For example, the Portuguese soup *açordas* might take its place in the English language alongside the French *crepes,* the Italian *pizza,* and the Japanese *sushi.*

As the language mavins argue back and forth about the state of English, the language itself keeps flowing on. The dictionary maker just watches and records.   *Robert K. Barnhart*

A a

abortion pill, a tablet of synthetic steroid taken to abort a pregnancy by blocking progesterone so that the fertilized egg does not become implanted in the uterus: *The revolutionary new abortion pill, RU 486, is . . . considered by the medical profession to be a far better means of abortion than surgical procedures* (New York Times).

access speed, = access time (def. 1): *Matsushita's 4-megabit DRAM chip . . . provides an access speed of 60 billionth of a second* (Japan Times).

affinity card, a credit card issued at special rates to members of an affinity group: *The affinity card . . . is a Visa or MasterCard that a university, union, club, or some other group issues to its members* (Washington Post).

Af|ri|can-A|mer|i|can (af′rə kən ə mer′ə kən), *adj., n.* = Afro-American: *. . . the movement the Rev. Jesse Jackson is spearheading to officially declare us African-Americans* (Washington Post).

a|lit|er|ate (ā lit′ər it), *n., adj. —n.* a person who shows no interest in reading or literature: *These are the "aliterates," people who know how to read but just don't bother* (Newsday). *—adj.* showing no interest in reading or literature: *an aliterate society.* [< a-⁴ + (il)*literate*]

arb (ärb), *n. U.S. Informal.* an arbitrager: *The arbs sometimes play a role in a defensive restructuring when the company wants to get its share price up* (Economist).

a|vi|a|pho|bi|a (ā′vē ə fō′bē ə), *n.* = aviophobia: *The spate of recent air accidents . . . has grounded those who suffer from aviaphobia* (Washington Post).

a|vi|o|pho|bi|a (ā′vē ə fō′bē ə), *n.* fear of flying in an aircraft: *Aviophobia . . . is believed to cost the airline industry up to $1.5 billion a year* (Robert L. DuPont). [< *aviaphobia* < *avia*(tion) + *phobia*]

B b

bi|o|chip (bī′ō chip′), *n.* a microcircuit whose components consist of organic molecules instead of electronic circuits: *Some molecules that could be used are so small that a three-dimensional biochip occupying 1 cubic centimeter (0.06 cubic inch) could be crowded with an astonishing million billion molecular switches* (Arthur Fisher).

bioelectronics, *n.* 2 the application of the biological sciences to the study and development of electronic systems or processes, as in the creation of biochips: *Bioelectronics incorporates the development of functional neuronal interfaces which permit contiguity between neural tissue and . . . computing technology* (Christopher R. Lowe).

C c

CAD (no periods) 2 coronary artery disease: *CAD is the most common cause of death in the United States* (Joanne Silberner).

car|ce|plex (kär′sə pleks), *n.* a molecular complex consisting of a large molecule in which a smaller molecule has been chemically trapped: *A carceplex consists of . . . a hollow "prison" molecule and a "guest" molecule trapped inside. These guest molecules . . . exist in a state of matter different from the familiar states represented by solids, liquids, gases and electrically charged plasmas* (New York Times). [< Latin *carcer* prison + English (com)*plex*]

cash cow, *U.S. Finance.* a regular and reliable source of income or profit: *Karin Lissakers of the Carnegie Endowment quotes a banker in . . . an unguarded moment: "That (unmentioned country) is a cash cow for us. We hope they never repay!"* (Washington Post).

ce|leb|u|tante (sə leb′yə tänt, -tant), *n.* a young woman who becomes a celebrity on her first appearance in society or in the arts: *. . . the Hollywood celebutante Brigitte Neilsen* (Melody Maker). *"Being a celebutante means you're famous for not really doing anything," the 20-year-old says* (Maureen Dowd). [< *celeb*(rity) + (deb)*utante*]

channel, *n.* 11 a person through whom invisible beings, spirits, or forces supposedly communicate: *. . . J.Z. Knight, the "channel" for Ramtha* (Atlanta Journal/Constitution). *—v.t.* 4 to supposedly communicate with (invisible beings, spirits, or forces): *Not all the channeled voices are from outer space* (Time).

chan|nel|ing (chan′ə ling), *n.* the act or process of supposedly communicating with invisible beings, spirits, or forces: *The extraterrestrials who turn up in the course of channeling . . . appear almost unfailingly wise and benevolent* (Time).

circuit breaker 2 *U.S. Economics.* a rebate on property tax or income tax granted by a state to certain taxpayers, such as persons over 65, whenever the tax exceeds a specified percentage of income: *Measures already in use in about 30 states, known as circuit breakers, accomplish this* (Today's Education).

core melt, the melting of the core of a nuclear reactor; meltdown: *The likelihood of a core melt in any one reactor is only once every 20,000 years* (U.S. News & World Report).

corporate raider, a person or company that makes a tender offer or starts a proxy fight to gain forcible control of a corporation: *Steinberg used to be a corporate raider, and Kravis is a leveraged buyout impresario* (New York Times Magazine).

crash¹, *v.i.* 7 (of a computer) to become inoperative because of a malfunction in the hardware or software: *Viruses . . . can modify a program's operation, causing computers to malfunction or crash* (Yonkers Herald Statesman).

crisis management, the expert handling of a crisis or emergency so as to reduce or eliminate danger, damage, or the like, especially in government, law enforcement, and industry: *The President's Commission also concluded that the N.R.C. [Nuclear Regulatory Commission] itself, when it was called to provide crisis management, performed with marked ineptitude* (New Yorker). **—crisis manager.**

crown jewel, 2 *Figurative.* the most valuable asset of a country, company, or the like: *The archipelago had been the crown jewel of the Dutch Empire for almost 350 years* (Arnold C. Brackman). *The Hughes Tool Co., crown jewel of* the Howard Hughes financial empire (Time).

cygnet, *n.* 2 a highly energetic and penetrating form of radiation detected underground and believed to come from the constellation Cygnus and certain other celestial sources: *These cygnets have become the ugly ducklings of underground astronomy* (Science News).

D d

damage control, any means used to minimize or reduce the damage caused by an accident, crime, financial loss, adverse publicity, or other calamity.

DAT (no periods), digital audiotape: *Unlike CDs, which cannot be used to copy live music or other recorded tapes, the DAT is . . . able to rerecord and play back sounds* (B.A. Leerburger).

de|con|struc|tiv|ism (dē′kən struk′tə viz əm), *n.* a movement in modern architecture that seeks to change conventional ways of perceiving form and space by producing buildings of sharp, clashing angles, skewed shapes, and incomplete forms: *Deconstructivism is highly theoretical; . . . its proponents want to change our fundamental perceptions of buildings. They do not accept the conventions of architectural culture—floors, walls, windows, doors, and ornamentation* (Paul Goldberger).

DNA fingerprint, a distinctive pattern of bands formed by repeating sequences of base pairs of satellite DNA, used as a means of personal identification because of its unique quality to one individual; genetic fingerprint: *Except for identical twins, even close relatives can be distinguished by these DNA fingerprints* (J.A. Miller).

DNA fingerprinting, the technique of analyzing satellite DNA in a specimen of body tissue or fluid to reveal a person's DNA fingerprint; genetic fingerprinting: *It is envisaged that DNA fingerprinting will revolutionize forensic biology particularly with regard to the identification of rape suspects* (Science News).

dork|y (dôr′kē), *adj.*, **dork|i|er, dork|i|est.** *Slang.* dull, stupid, or ineffectual: *She asked Kate what she thought of Cle. "He's dorky," Kate responded. She said she didn't like his glasses* (Chicago Tribune).

dram|e|dy (dram′ə dē), *n., pl.* **-dies.** *U.S.* a situation comedy containing elements of realistic drama: *The so-called dramedy . . . didn't punch the viewer with a joke every 30 seconds, used one-camera film instead of videotape, and was shot indoors and out* (Delia Ephron). [< *dram*(a) + (com)*edy*]

dumb down, *U.S. Informal.* to make less intelligent; lower the intellectual level of: *Are we dumbing down texts and minds?* (Knoxville Journal). *They are generally blamed . . . as having been a major force in dumbing down textbooks nationwide* (Atlanta Constitution). *There are jobs that will be dumbed down . . . simply because of the retraining costs* (Harrison Sunday Patriot-News).

F f

fax, *n., v. —n.* 1 = fax machine: *Today's faxes are as user-friendly as a toaster*

507

(Money). **2** a copy of graphic material sent or received by a fax machine: *Even more aggravating, unsolicited faxes use your electricity and your facsimile paper* (New York Times).
—*v.t.* to send by a fax machine.
fax machine, an electronic device that transmits and receives facsimiles of graphic material over telephone lines; facsimile machine: *Corporate high-rollers fire off memos from the rear of limousines, using portable fax machines* (New York Times).
fitness center, a gymnasium: *Metropolitan Tower was graced by a '24 hour concierge,'' a ''state of the art security system,'' a ''24 hour catering kitchen,'' a ''private fitness center''* (New York Monthly).
FORTH or **Forth** (fôrth, fōrth), *n.* a computer language that uses common English words, used especially for computer games and real-time applications involving control of machinery: *Whereas most high-level languages are somewhat abstract—dealing with variables, relations, formulas—FORTH feels very direct* (Whole Earth Software Catalog).

G g

gene therapy, the treatment of a genetic disorder by replacing a defective gene on a chromosome with a normal one: *Other strategies of gene therapy . . . would be to implant normal cells (cells with the right genes and chromosomes) in developing embryos* (Joseph Fletcher).
genetic fingerprint, = DNA fingerprint: *No two people have the same genetic fingerprint, unless they are identical twins* (Peter Gill).
gluino (glü ē′nō), *n., pl.* **-nos.** a hypothetical nuclear particle that is a weakly interacting form of the gluon: *A scenario with supersymmetry: gluinos from within a proton and an antiproton collide, and make supersymmetric gluinos, each of which decays into two quarks and one photon* (Discovery).

H h

heptathlon (hep tath′lon), *n.* a two-day competition for women in the Olympic Games, consisting of seven events that include the 100-meter hurdles, high jump, shot-put, and 200-meter run on the first day, and the long jump, javelin throw, and 800-meter run on the second day: *Jackie Joyner-Kersee won gold medals in the . . . heptathlon, in which she broke her previous world record with 7,291 points* (Frank Litsky). [< Greek *heptá* seven + *âthlon* exercise of skill; patterned on *pentathlon*]
high-temperature superconductor (hī′tem′pər ə chər, -chùr; -prə-), any one of a class of ceramic compounds that can conduct electric current with no resistance at temperatures above 77 degrees Kelvin (the boiling point of liquid nitrogen): *The new high-temperature superconductors . . . may revolutionize various technologies by allowing electricity to flow without losses and without much cooling—making magnetically levitated trains feasible, for example* (Science News).
homeboy (hōm′boi′), *n. U.S.* a boy or man from one's own hometown, region, or community: *''I don't know how to read or write 'cause I was always out with the homeboys''* (People Weekly).
honeymouthed (hun′ē moutht′, -moutнd′), *adj.* sweet-talking; sweet-sounding; glib.

I i

insider trading, the buying and selling of stock on the basis of information obtained from persons with secret knowledge of a company's action that is likely to change its stock price on the market. Insider trading is now illegal in the United States. —**insider trader.**
intifada or **intifadeh** (in′tə fä′də), *n.* a popular uprising of Palestinian Arabs against Israeli occupation of the West Bank and Gaza Strip, begun in 1988: *The intifada became a focal point of political and social change among the Palestinian Arab community in the territories* (Don Peretz). *And in a poorer quarter, Sabha Mubarak . . . said, ''The intifadeh has held our heads high''* (New York Times). [< Arabic *intifāda* uprising]

J j

J curve, *Economics.* a curve showing that after devaluation of a country's currency, its trade deficit normally worsens before it improves, reflecting the higher import prices resulting from the devaluation: *In the case of the United States, the J curve appeared to be immobilized at the bottom of the ''J,'' and experts searched for the reasons* (William Neikirk).

K k

kinetic-energy weapon (ki net′ik en′ər jē), a missile that uses a laser beam to track its target and kinetic energy to produce its destructive effect: *Kinetic-energy weapons move at more or less ordinary rocket speeds and deliver explosive charges to their targets* (Science News).

L l

leveraged buyout (lev′ər ijd, lē′vər-; lev′rijd), *U.S. Finance.* the purchase of a company with borrowed money to be paid back largely from the profits obtained from the purchase: *Maxwell Communications acquired Macmillan Publishing in a $2.62 billion leveraged buyout* (Stewart M. Lee).
low-rent (lō′rent′), *adj. U.S. Slang.* shoddy; sleazy: *Penn and Teller play two low-rent types living off the land of show business* (New York Times Magazine). *The Italian publisher Longanesi brought out a low-rent docunovel . . . about sex, drugs, models, the Mafia and death* (New York Monthly).

M m

mesclun (mes klυɴ′, -klùn′; mes′klun), *n.* a salad of a mixture of tender young lettuces, spicy wild green herbs, and sometimes edible flowers: *Clearly mesclun gives a whole new sparkle to the green salad* (Linda Wells). [< French

(originally dialectal) *mesclun* < Old French *mescler* to mix < Medieval Latin *misculare* to mix thoroughly < Latin *miscēre* to mix]
mid-rise (mid′rīz′), *adj.* midway between low-rise and high-rise; not excessively tall: *The biggest newsmakers in architecture . . . were arguably not these high-profile urban public buildings but their lowly suburban counterpart—the mid-rise office building* (Daralice D. Boles).

N n

nerdy (nèr′dē), *adj.,* **nerdier, nerdiest.** *U.S. Slang.* clumsy, foolish, or ineffectual: *Playing with numbers is no longer a nerdy accountant's game* (James M. Glassman).
New Age or **new age,** **1** a popular cultural movement concerned with mysticism, metaphysics, astrology, spiritualism, holism, and occultism: *Many elements of the New Age, like faith healing, fortunetelling, and transmigration of souls, go back for centuries* (Time). **2** having to do with or designating a form of popular music influenced by jazz and characterized by soft, restrained playing on such instruments as the piano, flute, harp, and synthesizer: *George Winton's pastoral piano is the essence of New Age music—serene, introspective and quietly inventive* (Washington Post).
Nimby (nim′bē), *n. Slang.* opposition by a community or a group within a community to the establishment of a public facility which it regards as undesirable in its local area, such as a prison, a waste dump, a shelter for the homeless, or the like: *Because of the Nimby syndrome, the garbage chain is becoming so tortuous that the solid-waste industry is considering shipping our household garbage to third world countries* (New York Times). [< acronym for *N*ot *i*n *m*y *b*ack *y*ard]
Nimbyism (nim′bē iz′əm), *n.* = Nimby: *Leading Tory opponents of the Channel tunnel link were still threatened a rough ride for the scheme through Parliament, despite winning a partial victory for Nimbyism* (London Independent).
nuke, *v.t.* **3** *U.S. Slang.* to microwave: *Nothing that can't be set to rights by nuking a little frozen za* (Fairfax Journal).

O o

oil patch, *U.S. Informal.* **1** the petroleum industry: *Gulf is known in the oil patch for being cautious* (Christian Science Monitor). **2** a petroleum-producing region: *Satellite dishes now bloom . . . throughout the oil patch like giant flowers* (TV Guide).
orature (ôr′ə chùr, -chər), *n.* the oral poems and narratives of a preliterate people or nation: *The Greeks had vast and complex oral heritages that might*

Pronunciation Key: hat, āge, cãre, fär; let, ēqual, tèrm; it, īce; hot, ōpen, ôrder; oil, out; cup, pùt, rüle; child; long; thin; тнen; zh, measure; ə represents a in about, e in taken, i in pencil, o in lemon, u in circus.

more accurately be called their orature (Tom McArthur). [< ora(l) (litera)ture]

P p

Pac-Man defense (pak′man′), U.S. Finance. a way of protecting a company from acquisition by another company in which the company seeking to protect itself retaliates by trying to acquire the company making the unwanted takeover: There was a vague feeling of distaste for . . . the Pac-Man defense in which . . . the target company bids to acquire the would-be acquirer (New York Times). [< Pac-Man, trademark of a video game in which attackers are sometimes swallowed up by their intended victims]

paper trail, a record compiled from letters, notes, and other written sources: Under this law the Government can not "monitor the paper trail" to track down bribers (New Scientist).

pent|ur|bi|a (pen tėr′bē ə), n. U.S. small cities or towns that attract new residents because of their simple way of life, cheap land and housing, and often job or business opportunities: Long-run growth will be greater in penturbia than anywhere else in the nation (Jack Lessinger). [< pent- five + (sub)urbia (because it supposedly represents the fifth major social migration in American history)]

people meter, a remote-control device that measures television ratings by requiring participating viewers to punch a series of buttons each time they watch television: People meters . . . have logged prime-time network viewership at nearly 10 percent below previous ratings, which were based on the diary system (Atlantic).

photo op, U.S. Informal. = photo opportunity: They operate in the slick new tradition of political handlers, whose job is to reduce a campaign to photo ops and sound bites (Times).

power, adj. 4 U.S. Informal. **a** involving powerful individuals: a power breakfast. I was at a power lunch with network executives (Valerie Harper). **b** expressive of power; dynamic: Yellow ties are on their way out, . . . with pink and red the new power colors (Wall Street Journal).

R r

re|flag (rē flag′), v.t., -flagged, -flagging. to register under another flag: . . . the confusion and controversy that surround the unexceptional White House plan to reflag 11 Kuwaiti oil tankers with the Stars and Stripes (Washington Post).

reverse vending machine, a machine that dispenses money or credit coupons in exchange for items, such as empty bottles or other used containers, deposited in it: Rockware Reclamation supplies a reverse vending machine that buys used aluminum cans and packs them off to the smelters (New Scientist).

S s

seasonal affective disorder, a mild form of depression occurring at certain seasons of the year, especially in winter, characterized by loss of energy and sexual drive: Research shows that among some patients suffering from seasonal affective disorder . . . melatonin levels rise and fall at odd hours (Newsweek). Abbr: SAD (no periods).

semi|am|a|teur (sem′ē am′ə chủr, -chər, -tyủr, -tủr, -tər), adj., n. —**adj.** 1 not playing a sport for money but supported in part by a sponsor: He returned to play for the Maccabi Tel Aviv team, a semiamateur team sponsored by a chocolate company (Washington Post). 2 partly amateur: The Chelsea Opera Group performance . . . is a substantial undertaking for a semiamateur group of this kind (Financial Times). —**n.** a semiamateur athlete: People are realizing that these yachtsmen are athletes . . . They're even semiamateurs (New York Times).

sequencer, n. 2 a woman who combines a career and motherhood through sequencing: Some experts are . . . warning that the sequencer is just another doomed variation of women trying to do it all (Sara Rimer).

se|quenc|ing (sē′kwən sing), n. the practice by a professional woman of leaving her career to bring up children and resuming professional work several years later: Sequencing, she argues, "combines the best of modern feminism with the best of traditional mothering" (New York Times).

shark repellent 2 U.S. Finance. any means used by a company to prevent a corporate raider from acquiring it: There are other strategies as well—those designed as "shark repellent" ploys to ward off unwelcome suitors (Maclean's).

skosh (skōsh), n. U.S. Slang. a small amount; little: A new line of Levi's for men is constructed with "a skosh more room where I need it" (Detroit Free Press). [< Japanese sukoshi a little]

sound bite, a small piece of film or videotape that captures the highlight of a speech, scene, or event: Shot and edited on video . . . the nightly news reduces speakers to pithy sound bites (Vanity Fair). Print journalists . . . like to sneer at television coverage as a collection of inconsequential, sensationalistic, sloganeering sound bites (William Safire).

spin doctor, U.S. Slang. a press agent hired to interpret news events for public presentation: The spin doctors came out after Reykjavik; the spin doctors came out after the "Iranian connection" (Bernard Kalb). You have just been massaged . . . —and maybe had—by some savvy movie publicists, the spin doctors of the entertainment industry (Time).

street, adj. 7 associated with or used by people excluded from the customary fabric of society or people who have rejected the traditional values of society: street drugs.

suitor, n. 4 U.S. Finance. a person or group that seeks to acquire a company through a tender offer. A suitor may be friendly or hostile. Once an offer has been made, the odds of eluding a suitor are about 1 to 4 (Lydia Chavez).

T t

tissue plasminogen activator, a protein substance in the cells that cata-lyzes the conversion of plasminogen to plasmin, produced through biotechnology as a drug capable of rapidly dissolving blood clots in the arteries: Tissue plasminogen activator . . . acts only at clots, whereas streptokinase acts throughout the bloodstream and can cause excess bleeding (Science News). Abbr: t-PA or TPA (no periods).

t-PA or **TPA** (no periods), tissue plasminogen activator: Called t-PA, it reduces the damage caused by a heart attack by dissolving harmful blood clots (Michael Woods).

triple witching hour, U.S. Finance. the final hour of trading on a stock market on four specified Fridays of the year when contracts on stock options, futures, and options on futures expire simultaneously: That 60-minute period has become known as "the triple witching hour" because . . . traders are frantically buying or selling stocks in the final hour to offset expiring futures or options (Business Week).

V v

vaccination program, a computer program that aids in detecting computer viruses and prevents them from destroying or altering data: At least 14 vaccination programs designed to protect computer disks . . . are now available (Philadelphia Inquirer).

virus, n. 6 = computer virus: Because of a design error the virus reproduced itself at an extraordinary rate within individual computers, causing them to jam (Richard Sandza).

W w

wilding, n. 4b Slang. A violent group attack on strangers, for the sake of violence: The random, apparently motiveless rampage . . . the suspects in the case call wilding (New York Times).

World Beat, popular dance music combining traditional African rhythms with elements of jazz and rock: The proliferation of radio programs offering World Beat indicates that a growing minority of listeners wants to hear something exotic (Arizona Republic).

Z z

za (zä), n. U.S. Slang. pizza: Nothing that can't be set to rights by nuking a little frozen za, of course (Fairfax Journal).

zi|do|vu|dine (zī′də vủ dēn′), n. = azidothymidine: Recently renamed zidovudine, AZT slows viral replication and currently is the only federally approved AIDS treatment (Science News).

zouk (zủk), n. a lively form of Caribbean music with a strong beat, which originated in Guadeloupe and Martinique and combines elements of highlife, soca, salsa, funk, and disco music, played with a synthesizer and other electronic instruments: What's missing from zouk is much verbal content . . . But zouk, like Nigerian juju and the best reggae, tells a story through music itself (New York Times). [< West Indies Creole zouk, probably < English juke]

509

JORDAN • OCEAN • TANZANIA

1989

HISPANIC AMERICANS • OCEAN

World Book Supplement

To help **World Book** owners keep their
encyclopedias up to date, the following
articles are reprinted from the 1990 edition of the encyclopedia.

See page 518 ▶

Jordan is an Arab kingdom on the East Bank of the River Jordan in the heart of the Middle East. The country is bordered by Syria; Iraq; Saudi Arabia; Israel; and the West Bank, a territory west of the River Jordan. Amman is Jordan's capital and largest city.

Much of Jordan's modern history has been shaped by events in an area often called Palestine. Today, Israel, the West Bank, and the tiny Gaza Strip cover this region. Jordan was once called *Transjordan* because it lay across the River Jordan from Palestine.

In 1950, Jordan annexed the West Bank. Jordan lost the West Bank during the Arab-Israeli war of 1967, and Israel has occupied the territory since then. In 1974, Jordan officially gave up political responsibility for the West Bank. King Hussein of Jordan and other Arab leaders gave the Palestine Liberation Organization (PLO) responsibility for any West Bank territory from which Israel might withdraw (see **Palestine Liberation Organization**). But Jordan continued to play important roles in the administration and financial support of the West Bank. In July 1988, King Hussein broke Jordan's ties with the West Bank. He called for the PLO to take over the functions Jordan had handled.

Jordan has a rapidly growing population. About 60 per cent of the people are native Jordanians. Most of the others are Palestinians. About 95 per cent of the people are Muslims. Christians make up a small minority group.

Jordan's varied terrain includes deserts, mountains, deep valleys, and rolling plains. The country has a warm, pleasant climate, but receives little rain.

Jordan has few natural resources. It mines phosphates and potash but lacks the petroleum deposits of its Arab neighbors. Service industries, such as government and commerce, employ the largest number of workers.

Ruins from various periods of Jordan's history still stand. They include those of the Nabataean capital of Petra from about 400 B.C., the Greek and Roman cities of Jarash and Philadelphia, and several churches built around A.D. 500 during Byzantine rule. Jordan also has a 900-year-old castle built by crusaders at Al Karak.

Government

National government. Jordan is a constitutional monarchy. The king of Jordan has widespread powers.

Facts in brief

Capital: Amman.
Official language: Arabic.
Official name: Al-Mamlakah Al-Urdiniyah Al-Hashimiyah (Hashemite Kingdom of Jordan).
Area: 35,475 sq. mi. (91,880 km²).
Elevation: *Highest*—Jabal Ramm, 5,755 ft. (1,754 m) above sea level. *Lowest*—shore of the Dead Sea, about 1,310 ft. (399 m) below sea level.
Population: *Estimated 1990 population*—3,065,000; density, 86 persons per sq. mi. (33 persons per km²); distribution, 68 per cent urban, 32 per cent rural. *1979 census*—2,132,997. *Estimated 1995 population*—3,656,000.
Chief products: *Agriculture*—barley, cabbages, citrus fruits, cucumbers, eggplants, goats, grapes, melons, olives and olive oil, poultry, sheep, tomatoes, wheat. *Manufacturing*—batteries, cement, ceramics, detergents, fertilizer, petroleum products, pharmaceutical products, shoes, textiles. *Mining*—phosphate, potash.
National anthem: "Al-Salam Al-Malaki" ("The Royal Salute").
Money: *Basic unit*—dinar. See **Money** (table).

He appoints a prime minister to head the government, as well as members of the Council of Ministers, or cabinet. The king also appoints members of Jordan's Senate to four-year terms. The Senate is one house of the National Assembly, Jordan's legislature. The other house is the Chamber of Deputies. Its members are elected by the people to four-year terms. King Hussein dismissed the National Assembly in 1974, recalled it in 1984, and dismissed it again in 1988. In 1989, the government announced that it would hold elections for a new Chamber of Deputies later that year.

Local government. Jordan is divided into eight districts called *governorates*. A governor appointed by the king heads each district.

Courts. Jordan's judicial system consists of civil, religious, and special courts. Civil courts handle most commercial, criminal, and civil cases. Muslims and various Christian groups each have their own religious courts. These courts rule on personal and family matters, such as marriages, divorces, guardianship, inheritances, and wills. Special courts deal with technical legal matters. The king appoints all judges.

Armed forces. The Jordan Arab Army consists of an army of more than 70,000 men, an air force with about 10,000 members, and a small navy. The military employs a high percentage of Jordan's work force, thereby placing a burden on the economy. But Jordan has fought several wars with its neighbor Israel and has also faced rebellions by its own Palestinian population. Because of these external and internal security threats, the government maintains large armed forces despite the cost.

People

Population and ancestry. Jordan has about 3 million people. Most Jordanians live in the fertile highlands of the northwest. About two-thirds of the people live in towns and cities with populations of 5,000 or more. Amman has nearly 1 million people. Other cities with more than 100,000 people are Az Zarqa and Irbid.

Native Jordanian Arabs account for about 60 per cent of the population. The remaining population of Jordan consists mainly of Palestinian Arabs, most of whom came to the country as refugees as a result of the Arab-Israeli wars of 1948 and 1967. Other Palestinians moved from the West Bank to Amman between the wars, when the West Bank was part of Jordan. Ethnic minorities in Jordan include small numbers of Armenian Christians and Circassian Muslims.

Languages. Arabic is the official language of Jordan. English is also widely taught and spoken. The government prints many documents in Arabic and English. Ethnic minorities often speak their own language.

Way of life. In urban areas, almost all homes and apartments have electricity and running water. Some urban neighborhoods are densely populated. But in general, living conditions are better than in many other developing countries.

About 10 per cent of Jordan's population lives in crowded Palestinian refugee camps set up by the United Nations. The refugees live in simple, two-room shelters made of concrete.

Most rural Jordanians live in villages and have homes built of stone and mud, or of concrete. Many villagers grow crops and raise goats and chickens. Others work

© C. Ferrare, Imapress from NSP

© C. Ferrare, Imapress from NSP ·

Jordan presents a sharp contrast between its up-to-date cities and its ancient ruins. Jordan's capital and largest city, Amman, *left,* features modern office buildings and apartment houses. The treasury at Petra, *right,* was carved into the cliffs of this historic trading center during the 100's A.D.

in construction and mining. Bedouin nomads make up under 5 per cent of the people. They live in tents and move from place to place with their camels and sheep in search of water and pasture. Since the mid-1900's, many Bedouins have settled in towns and villages.

Most Jordanian men and women wear Western-style clothing. The men may cover their head with a cloth called a *kaffiyeh.* Some women wear long, loose-fitting dresses. Some rural Jordanians, including Bedouin men and women, wear traditional flowing robes.

Food and drink. Jordanians eat a variety of foods, including cheese, cracked wheat, flat bread, rice, vegetables, and yogurt. Chicken and lamb are popular meats. A traditional Jordanian dish called *mansef* features lamb cooked in yogurt and served on a large tray of rice. Popular beverages include coffee, fruit juices, mineral water, soft drinks, and tea.

Recreation. Jordanians enjoy watching and playing various sports, particularly basketball, camel racing, horse racing, martial arts, and soccer. Jordanians are very social. Large families frequently gather for a meal or for a picnic in the country. Folk dances, such as the *debke,* are popular at family events.

Religion. Islam is the official religion of Jordan. About 95 per cent of Jordan's people are Muslims. Almost all of them follow the *Sunni* or orthodox branch of Islam. Most other Jordanians are Christians.

Islam deeply affects the lives of many Jordanians. Devout Muslims pray five times a day, attend a *mosque* (an Islamic house of worship), fast, give money or goods to the poor, and make a pilgrimage to Mecca, Saudi Arabia, the sacred city of Islam.

Most Jordanian Christians belong to the Eastern Orthodox Church. Jordan has various other Christian groups, including Roman Catholics and Protestants.

Education. Jordan requires children to attend school

through the ninth grade. Most children go to government schools. A United Nations agency operates schools for Palestinian refugees. More than 70 per cent of the adult population can read and write.

Jordan has many community colleges, vocational schools, and technical institutions. More than 28,000 students attend Jordan's four universities. An even larger number of Jordanians attend universities in other Arab countries, Europe, and the United States.

Jordan is a country in the Middle East. It is bordered by Iraq, Israel, Saudi Arabia, Syria, and the West Bank—a territory Israel has occupied since 1967.

WORLD BOOK map

Flag Research Center

Jordan's flag was adopted in 1928. It features a seven-pointed star. The points of the star stand for the first seven verses of the Koran, the holy book of Islam.

The coat of arms displays the shield, helmet, and eagle of Saladin, a Muslim warrior. The inscription, written in Arabic, is the king's prayer for aid and success.

The arts. Jordanian craftworkers make a variety of decorative and useful objects, including jewelry, coffeepots, daggers, and Islamic prayer beads. Many mosques and other buildings feature delicate geometric designs called *arabesques*. Other art forms include elaborate cross-stitch embroidery and beautiful Arabic *calligraphy* (fine handwriting).

Land and climate

Jordan has three main land regions: (1) the Jordan River Valley, (2) the Transjordan Plateau, and (3) the Syrian Desert.

The Jordan River Valley is a deep, narrow valley that extends, in Jordan, from just south of the Sea of Galilee to the Dead Sea. The River Jordan flows through the center of the valley and ends in the Dead Sea. Summer temperatures in this region regularly exceed 100° F. (38° C). The valley receives little rain. But since the 1960's, Jordan has developed an irrigation system that allows extensive cultivation of fruits and vegetables. The Jordan River Valley is part of the *Great Rift Valley,* a deep cut in the earth's surface. Another part of the Great Rift Valley extends from the Dead Sea to Al Aqabah (see **Great Rift Valley**).

© Don Smetzer, TSW Click/Chicago

Muslim men read the Koran and use prayer beads in the courtyard of a *mosque* (Islamic house of worship) in Amman. Islam is the religion of more than 90 per cent of Jordan's people.

Jordan map index

Cities

Ajlun	6,280	B	1
Al Aqabah	40,275	F	1
Al Fuhays*	7,400	C	1
Al Karak	16,930	D	1
Al Mafraq	30,100	B	2
Al Mazar ash Shamaliyah*	9,105	B	2
Al Mushayrifah*	15,940	D	2
Amman	900,000	C	2
Anjarah*	10,435	B	1
An Nu'ayyimah*	8,060	B	2
Ar Ramtha	38,110	B	2
Ar Rusayfah*	70,085	C	2
Ash Shajarah*	6,920	B	2
Ash Shunah ash Shamaliyah*	11,095	B	1
As Salt	45,900	B	1
As Safiyah	8,690	D	1
At Tafila	17,355	D	1
Aydun*	6,115	B	2
Ayy*	6,065	D	1
Az Zarqa	306,500	B	2
Hawwarah*	7,025	B	2
Husn	11,530	B	2
Irbid	161,690	B	2
Jarash	13,980	B	2
Kufrinjah*	11,870	B	1
Ma'an	15,815	E	1
Madaba	38,700	C	2
Na'ur*	7,410	C	2
Sahab*	16,290	C	2
Sakhrah*	7,145	B	2
Suwaylih*	33,900	B	2
Wadi as Sir*	34,630	G	2
Wadi Musa	7,410	E	1

*Does not appear on map; key shows general location.
Source: 1988 official estimates.

Physical features

Dead Sea	C	1
East Ghor Canal	B	1
Gulf of Aqaba	F	1
Jabal al Ashaqif (mountains)	B	4
Jabal Ramm (mountain)	F	1
Jabash Ruins	B	1
Mediterranean Sea	A	1
Mount Nebo	G	2
Petra Ruins	E	1
River Jordan	B	1
Sea of Galilee	A	1
Syrian Desert	A	4
West Bank	B	1
Yarmuk (river)	B	2
Zarqa (river)	B	2

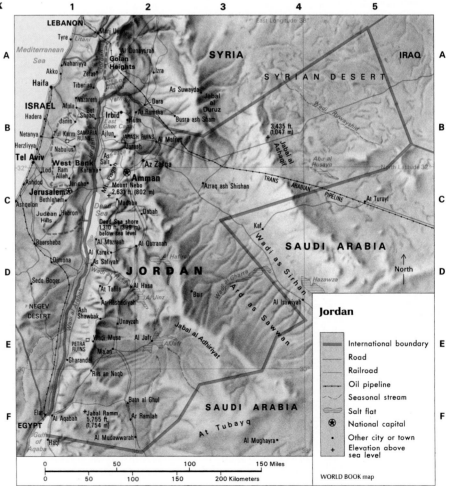

Jordan

▬▬	International boundary
──	Road
┼─┼─	Railroad
─•─•─	Oil pipeline
∿	Seasonal stream
⬭	Salt flat
⊛	National capital
•	Other city or town
+	Elevation above sea level

WORLD BOOK map

The Transjordan Plateau rises steeply from the Jordan River Valley and the Dead Sea. The plateau covers a wedge-shaped area that begins at the Syrian border and narrows as it extends southward to the region around Ma'an. It consists of broad, rolling plains that have an average elevation of about 3,000 feet (900 meters) above sea level. Steep *wadis* (valleys) cut the plateau.

The plateau includes Jordan's largest cities and most of its farmland. Annual rainfall averages about 25 inches (64 centimeters) in the north. Rainfall on the southern plateau is less dependable and averages between 10 and 15 inches (25 and 38 centimeters) a year—barely enough to grow wheat. Average temperatures range between 64° and 86° F. (18° and 30° C) in the summer and between 40° and 52° F. (4° and 11° C) in the winter.

The Syrian Desert, also called the northern Arabian Desert, is a vast wasteland to the east and south of the plateau. The desert receives less than 5 inches (13 centimeters) of rain annually. Summer temperatures sometimes reach 120° F. (49° C).

Economy

Jordan has a developing economy based on free enterprise. Service industries make up the largest part of the economy. The economy depends on foreign aid and on the larger economy of the Middle East. Many Jordanians work abroad, in the service industries of wealthy, oil-producing Arab countries. These workers send money to their families in Jordan.

Service industries employ about 70 per cent of Jordan's workers and account for more than 65 per cent of the total value of economic production. The government and military employ many Jordanians. Others work in education, trade, and transportation. Tourism helps support many businesses, including hotels and restaurants. Other important service industries include banking and insurance.

Manufacturing and mining employ about 12 per cent of Jordan's workers and account for about 20 per cent of the total value of economic production. Large plants include a petroleum refinery and fertilizer and cement factories. Smaller industries manufacture batteries, ceramics, cigarettes, detergents, food products, pharmaceutical products, shoes and textiles. Most of Jordan's

small factories are located near Amman. Mining operations produce phosphates and potash, which are used in the production of fertilizer.

Agriculture. Because Jordan is mostly desert, only 3 per cent of the land is cultivated. Chief crops of the Jordan River Valley include citrus fruits and such vegetables as cabbages, cucumbers, eggplants, melons, and tomatoes. On the Transjordan Plateau, farmers cultivate such grains as barley and wheat; grapes, olives, and other fruits; vegetables; and nuts. Modern farming methods have become increasingly widespread, especially in the Jordan River Valley.

Foreign trade. Jordan's main exports are phosphates, chemicals, potash, fruits and vegetables, and manufactured products. Imports include machinery, petroleum, grain, and meat. Jordan's chief trading partners are Saudi Arabia, the United States, Iraq, Italy, Japan, Great Britain, West Germany, and India.

Transportation and communication. Jordan has a well-developed transportation system. Paved highways link Jordan with all its neighbors. Al Aqabah, Jordan's only port has been extensively developed to handle cargo shipped through the Red Sea. Amman has a major international airport.

Four daily newspapers—three in Arabic and one in English—are published in Jordan. The government owns and operates the country's radio and television stations. An average of about 1 out of 5 Jordanians owns a radio and about 1 out of 8 owns a TV set. Although the government closely controls communications, there is more freedom of expression in Jordan than in many other Arab countries in the Middle East.

Energy. Except for one dam that produces electricity, Jordan depends on imported oil to generate electricity. Electric power is available throughout most of Jordan.

History

Early days. Written history first mentions what is now Jordan in about 2000 B.C., when Semitic nomads entered the region. By about 1200 B.C., four Semitic peoples—the Ammonites, Amorites, Edomites, and Moabites—farmed and traded in lands east of the River Jordan. During the 900's B.C., the Israelites under Kings David and Solomon conquered and ruled the region.

Rami G. Khouri

The Jordan River Valley is Jordan's major agricultural region. This hot, dry area was once largely unsuitable for farming. Today, irrigation and the use of plastic-covered hothouses, *lower left,* allow farmers to grow a variety of fruits, vegetables, and other crops. The land rises, *background,* toward the Transjordan Plateau east of the valley.

Rami G. Khouri

Production of leather goods is an important industry in Jordan. The factory workers shown above are sewing leather pieces to make boots.

But Moabites led by King Mesha regained control about 850 B.C. Later, the Egyptians, Assyrians, Chaldeans, and Persians invaded and controlled the area. The Nabataeans, a trading people who spoke Arabic, came to power in the 400's B.C. The Nabataeans ruled from their unique capital city carved out of the rose-colored stone cliffs of Petra. Their architecture and art were strongly influenced by the Greeks after about 331 B.C., when Alexander the Great conquered the area. After his death, the Seleucids ruled the northern part of present-day Jordan, and the Nabataeans continued to control the southern part.

In the 60's B.C., the Romans took control of Jordan. They built vast trading centers at Philadelphia (now Amman) and Gerasa (now Jarash). When the Roman Empire split in the late 300's A.D., Jordan became part of the Byzantine Empire, also called the East Roman Empire.

Arab and Ottoman rule. In 636, Arab Muslims from the Arabian Peninsula defeated Byzantine armies in the northern Jordan region. The conquering Arabs established their language and religion among the people who lived in the region. They developed an important route through Jordan for Islamic pilgrimages to Mecca.

At the close of the 1000's, Christian crusaders from Europe conquered the eastern Mediterranean coast, including Jerusalem and parts of Jordan. The region had great religious significance for both Christians and Muslims. In 1187, the Muslim leader Saladin drove out the crusaders. His successors were overthrown by Egyptian Mamelukes in 1250.

In 1517, Ottoman Turks easily defeated the Mamelukes, and most of Jordan became part of the Ottoman Empire. During Ottoman rule, the region's only attraction for outsiders was the pilgrimage route. Bedouins and peasant farmers inhabited the region. The Ottomans did not govern Jordan directly until the late 1800's, when they brought Circassian families to settle in and near Amman. In 1908, a railway was completed along the pilgrimage route, stimulating Jordan's economy.

Independence. During World War I (1914-1918), Sherif Hussein of Mecca in Saudi Arabia led an Arab revolt

against Ottoman rule. With the help of Great Britain, the revolt led to the defeat of the Ottomans in the Middle East and the establishment of several Arab states.

After the war, the League of Nations appointed Britain to administer lands east and west of the River Jordan as the mandate of Palestine (see **Mandated territory**). In 1921, the British gave the territory east of the Jordan partial self-government by making it an emirate called Transjordan. Abdullah, a son of Hussein, ruled Transjordan as *emir* (prince) under British supervision. In 1922, Transjordan became a mandate separate from Palestine.

Abdullah made Amman the capital of Transjordan and established his authority with considerable help from Great Britain. In 1923, Britain declared that Transjordan should become an independent state. But the British kept control of the state's defenses, finances, and foreign affairs. Transjordan gained complete independence in 1946 and was renamed Jordan. But Jordan still depended on Britain for economic aid, and British officers commanded the Arab Legion, Jordan's army.

The Palestinian conflict. In 1917, Britain issued the Balfour Declaration. This document supported the establishment of a Jewish homeland in Palestine without violating the civil and religious rights of the non-Jewish population. At that time, thousands of Jews had immigrated to Palestine, and after World War I, tens of thousands more came. Many came from Europe during the 1930's and 1940's because of German persecution. The Jewish immigration led to fighting between Jews and Palestinian Arabs for control of the land.

Jordan became involved in the Palestinian conflict in 1948. That year, the British mandate of Palestine ended, and the Jews established the state of Israel. Jordan and other Arab countries at once went to war with Israel. When the war ended in January 1949, Israel occupied much of Palestine. Jordan held the West Bank, and Jerusalem was divided between Israel and Jordan. In 1950, Jordan officially annexed the West Bank.

Jordan's population of about 400,000 more than tripled as a result of the war. It gained about 400,000 Palestinian residents of the West Bank and about 450,000 Palestinian refugees from Israel. The Palestinian population caused political and economic tensions. Some Palestinians competed for power with East Bank Jordanians who controlled the government. The refugees burdened Jordan's economy because of the food, shelter, and services they required. But some brought valuable skills and savings to Jordan and set up businesses.

By the mid-1950's, Jordan began to develop petroleum-refining, cement, and phosphate industries. Other parts of the Jordanian economy, including agriculture, manufacturing, and tourism, also began a period of steady growth.

In 1951, Palestinians assassinated Abdullah. His son, Talal, succeeded him. But Talal was removed from the throne in 1952 because of mental illness. Talal's son, 17-year-old Hussein, succeeded him but did not officially take up the duties of king until he turned 18 in 1953.

During the 1950's, Jordan remained unstable. Arab countries competed for political power in the Middle East, and the United States and the Soviet Union each sought to extend influence in the region. In 1956, King Hussein replaced the British officers in the Arab Legion with Jordanians and renamed it the Jordan Arab Army.

The army helped put down a plot to overthrow Hussein in 1957. In the late 1950's, the United States became Jordan's chief source of financial and military support in the West.

Tensions between Israel and Arab nations, including Jordan, increased during the early 1960's. Arabs and Israelis disagreed over rights to the waters of the River Jordan. Continuing problems of the Palestinian refugees led to the creation of the Palestine Liberation Organization in 1964. The PLO organized raids into Israel from Jordan and Lebanon, and Israel responded with raids into Arab territory. Also in 1964, Jordan and other Arab nations united their armies under one command.

The 1967 war. In June 1967, Israel attacked and defeated Jordan, Egypt, and Syria in a six-day war. Jordan lost east Jerusalem and all of the West Bank to Israeli occupation. About 300,000 Palestinians—both refugees and permanent residents—who had been living in the West Bank fled east. Jordan's economy suffered from the loss of the farmlands and tourist attractions on the West Bank.

Civil war. After the 1967 war, many Palestinian refugees joined guerrilla groups to fight Israel and regain their homeland. By early 1970, these forces represented an unofficial second government within Jordan and threatened to overthrow the monarchy.

On Sept. 17, 1970, the Jordanian army attacked the Palestinian guerrillas. Syrian tanks and troops entered Jordan to support the Palestinians, but they later withdrew. Jordan's army defeated the Palestinians within a month. But fighting between the army and isolated guerrilla groups continued into 1971 and beyond. Drained by these ongoing battles, Jordan played only a minor role in the 1973 Arab-Israeli war.

Relations with the West Bank. At a meeting of Arab leaders in 1974, King Hussein lost influence in Palestinian affairs when the PLO was declared the only representative of the Palestinian people. Hussein and other Arab leaders agreed that the West Bank should become part of an independent Palestinian state in the event of an Israeli withdrawal. They gave the PLO responsibility for any West Bank territory from which Israel might withdraw. However, Jordan continued to play important roles in the West Bank. For example, the Jordanian government paid the salaries of many West Bank public service workers, including doctors, teachers, and government employees.

Recent developments. Disagreements between Jordan and the PLO over Palestinian policy led to a major break in 1986. King Hussein tried to set up new leadership for the Palestinians. But the next year, the Palestinians demonstrated their loyalty to the PLO in an uprising against Israel's occupying forces in the West Bank. In 1988, Hussein broke Jordan's political and administrative ties to the West Bank. He called for the PLO to take over the financial support and other functions that Jordan had handled. Later that year, the PLO declared the existence of an independent Palestinian nation in the West Bank and the Gaza Strip. But Israel still occupies both regions.

During the mid-1980's, Jordan's economy struggled to maintain growth because of a decline in petroleum earnings in the Middle East. In 1989, Jordan, Egypt, Iraq, and Yemen (Sana) established the Arab Cooperation Council. The council reduced or eliminated trade tariffs

© Sautereau, Photo Researchers

Palestinian refugee camps in Jordan swelled after the 1967 war between Arab nations and Israel. Many Palestinians fled to these camps after Israel occupied their homes in the West Bank.

between member countries.   Peter Gubser

Related articles in *World Book* include:

Amman	Jordan, River
Arab League	Middle East
Arabs	Mount Pisgah
Dead Sea	Palestine
Dead Sea Scrolls	Petra
Hussein I	Samaria
Israel (History)	West Bank
Jerusalem	

Outline

I. Government
A. National government	C. Courts
B. Local government	D. Armed forces

II. People
A. Population and ancestry	E. Recreation
	F. Religion
B. Languages	G. Education
C. Way of life	H. The arts
D. Food and drink	

III. Land and climate
   A. The Jordan River Valley
   B. The Transjordan Plateau
   C. The Syrian Desert

IV. Economy
A. Service industries	D. Foreign trade
B. Manufacturing and mining	E. Transportation and communication
C. Agriculture	F. Energy

V. History

Questions

What role has Great Britain had in Jordan's history?
What are Jordan's land regions?
What types of clothing do Jordanian men and women wear?
When did Jordan gain control of the West Bank? How did Jordan lose the territory?
What powers belong to the king of Jordan?
How has irrigation helped agriculture in Jordan?
What role does Islam play in Jordanian life?
Why was Jordan once called *Transjordan*?
What are Jordan's chief manufactured products?
What is Jordan's capital and largest city?

Additional resources

Fodor's Jordan and the Holy Land. Fodor's. Revised frequently.
Gubser, Peter. *Jordan: Crossroads of Middle Eastern Events.* Westview, 1983.
Whitehead, Susan. *Jordan.* Chelsea House, 1988. For younger readers.

© Harvey Lloyd, The Stock Market
© Alan Gurney, The Stock Market

© Barry E. Parker, Bruce Coleman Inc.

The vast ocean covers more than 70 per cent of the earth's surface, from the ice-choked seas of the polar regions, *lower left,* to the warm waters of the tropics, *above.* Its waters move constantly, whether crashing against a rocky coast, *upper left,* or gently rising and falling with the tide.

Ocean

Ocean is the great body of water that covers more than 70 per cent of the earth's surface. People also call it the *sea.* The ocean contains 97 per cent of all the water on the earth.

The ocean provides us with many things. It is far more than a place for swimming, boating, and other recreation. The ocean serves as a source of food, energy, and minerals. Ships use the ocean to carry cargo between continents. But above all else, the sea helps keep the earth's climate healthful by regulating the air temperature and by supplying the moisture for rainfall. If there were no ocean, life could not exist on our planet.

The bottom of the ocean has features as varied as those on land. Huge plains spread out across the ocean floor, and long mountain chains rise toward the surface. Volcanoes erupt from the ocean bottom, and deep valleys gash the floor.

Arnold L. Gordon, the contributor of this article, is Professor of Oceanography at Columbia University and Head of the Physical Oceanography Section at Lamont-Doherty Geological Observatory of Columbia University.

The ocean is a fascinating place that we have only begun to understand. Scientists called *oceanographers* work to discover the secrets of the sea. They study how the ocean moves and how it affects the atmosphere. They investigate how organisms live in the sea and how various forces shape the sea floor. Such modern tools as satellites and computers have greatly increased scientists' understanding of the ocean.

The world ocean

The waters of the ocean form one great connected body often called the *world ocean* or the *global ocean.* However, the continents divide the world ocean into three major parts. They are, in order of size, the Pacific Ocean, the Atlantic Ocean, and the Indian Ocean. Each ocean includes smaller bodies of water called *seas, gulfs,* or *bays,* which lie along the ocean margins. For example, the Caribbean Sea and the Mediterranean Sea are part of the Atlantic, and the Bering Sea and the South China Sea are part of the Pacific. The word *sea* also means the ocean in general. See **Pacific Ocean; Atlantic Ocean; Indian Ocean.**

A small fourth ocean, known as the Arctic Ocean, lies north of Asia, Europe, and North America. Many geographers consider it part of the Atlantic rather than a separate ocean, and they refer to it as the Arctic Sea. See **Arctic Ocean.**

At the southern end of the earth, the Pacific, Atlantic, and Indian oceans meet around the continent of Antarctica. Some people call the waters surrounding Antarctica the Antarctic Ocean or the Southern Ocean. But many geographers say the waters are simply the southern parts of the three major oceans and do not form another ocean. See **Antarctic Ocean.**

The world ocean contains about 97 per cent of all the water on the earth. Most of the remaining water is frozen in glaciers and icecaps. The rest is in lakes and rivers, underground, and in the air.

Area. The world ocean covers about 70 per cent of the earth's surface. Most of the ocean lies in the Southern Hemisphere—that is, south of the equator. The Southern Hemisphere consists of about 80 per cent ocean, and the Northern Hemisphere about 60 per cent.

The Pacific Ocean is the largest ocean by far. It covers about 70 million square miles (181 million square kilometers)—nearly a third of the earth's surface. The Pacific contains about half the water in the world ocean and could hold all the continents. Near the equator, the Pacific stretches about 15,000 miles (24,000 kilometers), almost halfway around the globe. North and South America border the Pacific on the east, and Asia and Australia lie to the west. To the north, the Bering Strait links the Pacific with Arctic waters.

The Atlantic Ocean covers about 36 million square miles (94 million square kilometers), not including the waters of the Arctic. Europe and Africa lie east of the Atlantic, and North and South America lie west.

The Indian Ocean has an area of about 29 million square miles (74 million square kilometers). Africa lies to the west. Australia and Indonesia lie to the east. Asia borders the Indian Ocean on the north.

Depth. The world ocean has an average depth of 12,200 feet (3,730 meters), but parts of the ocean plunge much deeper. The deepest areas occur in *trenches*— long, narrow valleys on the sea floor. The deepest known spot is in the Mariana Trench in the western Pacific Ocean, near the island of Guam. It lies 36,198 feet (11,033 meters) below sea level. If the world's highest mountain, 29,028-foot (8,848-meter) Mount Everest, were placed in that spot, more than 1 mile (1.6 kilometers) of water would cover the mountaintop.

The Pacific is the deepest ocean, with an average depth of 12,900 feet (3,940 meters). The Atlantic is the shallowest ocean, averaging 11,700 feet (3,580 meters) deep. Its deepest known point, 28,374 feet (8,648 meters) below the surface, lies in the Puerto Rico Trench. The Indian Ocean averages 12,600 feet (3,840 meters) deep. Its deepest known spot plunges 25,344 feet (7,725 meters) below sea level in the Java Trench.

Temperature. The surface temperature of the ocean varies from about 28° F. (−2° C) near the North and South poles to about 86° F. (30° C) near the equator. In the polar regions, the surface seawater freezes. The western tropical Pacific has the warmest surface water. Ocean currents affect the surface temperature. As the currents move about in the ocean, they carry warm trop-

Interesting facts about the ocean

WORLD BOOK illustrations by John F. Eggert

Life began in the ocean according to most scientists. Fossils of one type of sea worm, *right,* show that this organism has remained unchanged for over 500 million years.

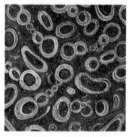

There is a bit of "ocean" inside us. The body of an adult male contains about 19 quarts (72 liters) of salt water. The composition of this fluid is similar to seawater.

The ocean floor is in constant motion. The floor of the Atlantic spreads about 1 inch (2.5 centimeters) every year, widening the ocean basin. The Pacific floor spreads even faster, about 5 inches (13 centimeters) every year. But its basin does not widen because the edges of its floor sink under the continents.

Giant kelp, a large brown seaweed, may grow up to 200 feet (161 meters) long, forming great underwater forests in the ocean.

A *tsunami*—a powerful wave caused by an earthquake—can reach a speed of 600 miles (970 kilometers) per hour and travel across an entire ocean.

The world ocean would rise about 200 feet (60 meters) if the Greenland and Antarctic icecaps should suddenly melt. New York City would be submerged, with only the tops of the tallest buildings above water.

ical water toward the poles. Other ocean movements bring colder, deeper water up to the surface and so lower the surface water temperature.

Ocean temperature also varies with depth. In general, the temperature falls as the depth increases. The warm surface waters extend to depths of about 500 feet (150 meters) in the tropics, and about 1,000 feet (300 meters) in the subtropics. Below the surface waters, the temperature drops rapidly, forming a layer called the *thermocline.* The thermocline varies in thickness, from about 1,000 feet (300 meters) to 3,000 feet (910 meters). Below the thermocline, the water cools more slowly. Close to the deep-sea floor, the temperature of the ocean ranges between 34° and 39° F. (1° and 4° C).

Composition. Every natural element can be found in the waters of the ocean. But the ocean is especially known for its salts. Seawater contains, on the average, about $3\frac{1}{2}$ per cent salts. Six elements account for 99 per cent of the ocean's *salinity* (saltiness). They are, in order

of amount, chloride, sodium, sulfur (as sulfate), magnesium, calcium, and potassium. Most of the salty material in the sea consists of the compound sodium chloride, or ordinary table salt.

Many salts in the ocean come chiefly from the wearing away of rocks on land. As rocks break down, rivers carry the salts and other material the rocks consist of to the ocean. Material released by volcanoes and undersea

The world ocean

This map shows the world ocean, which includes the Atlantic, Indian, and Pacific oceans. It also shows the ocean's major surface currents.

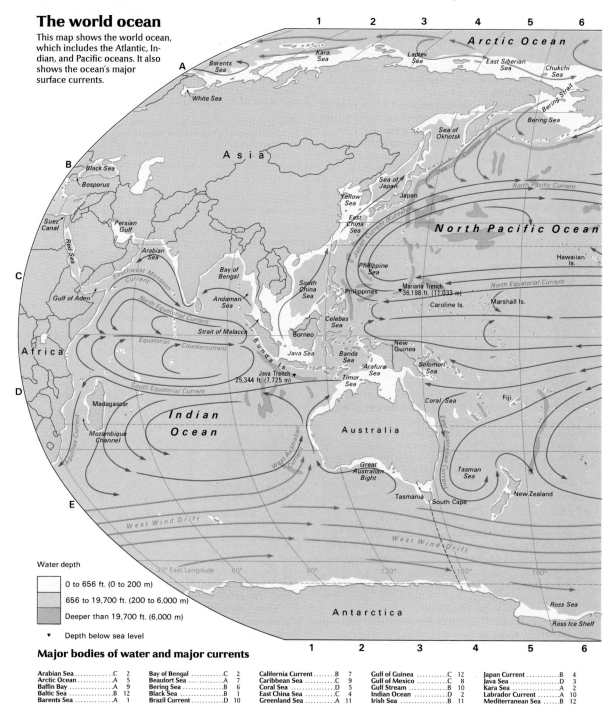

Water depth

	0 to 656 ft. (0 to 200 m)
	656 to 19,700 ft. (200 to 6,000 m)
	Deeper than 19,700 ft. (6,000 m)

▼ Depth below sea level

Major bodies of water and major currents

Arabian Sea	C	2	Bay of Bengal	C	2	California Current	B	7	Gulf of Guinea	C	12
Arctic Ocean	A	5	Beaufort Sea	A	7	Caribbean Sea	C	9	Gulf of Mexico	C	8
Baffin Bay	A	9	Bering Sea	B	6	Coral Sea	D	5	Gulf Stream	B	10
Baltic Sea	B	12	Black Sea	B	1	East China Sea	C	4	Indian Ocean	D	2
Barents Sea	A	1	Brazil Current	D	10	Greenland Sea	A	11	Irish Sea	B	11

Japan Current	B	4			
Java Sea	D	3			
Kara Sea	A	2			
Labrador Current	A	10			
Mediterranean Sea	B	12			

springs also contributes salts to the ocean. Evaporation and precipitation further affect the ocean's salinity. Evaporation removes fresh water from the ocean surface, leaving behind the salts. Evaporation is high in subtropical areas, and so the surface waters are especially salty in those areas. Precipitation returns fresh water to the ocean. Precipitation is greater than evaporation near the equator, making surface waters less salty there. Rivers also bring fresh water to the ocean, which lowers the salinity of seawater near river mouths.

The importance of the ocean

As a wealth of resources. The ocean provides—or can provide—many major resources. They include (1) food, (2) energy, (3) minerals, and (4) medicines.

Food from the ocean consists mainly of fish and shell-

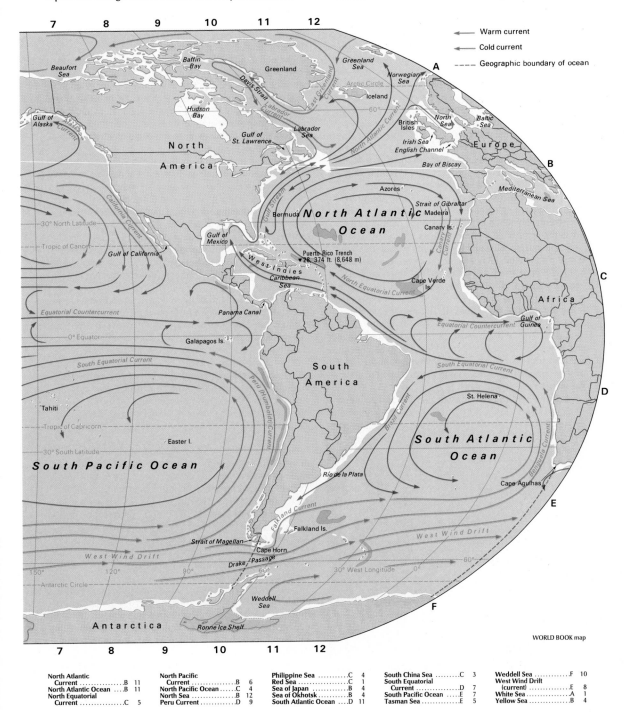

WORLD BOOK map

North Atlantic			North Pacific			Philippine Sea	C	4	South China Sea	C	3	Weddell Sea	F	10
Current	B	11	Current	B	6	Red Sea	C	1	South Equatorial			West Wind Drift		
North Atlantic Ocean	B	11	North Pacific Ocean	C	4	Sea of Japan	B	4	Current	D	7	(current)	E	8
North Equatorial			North Sea	B	12	Sea of Okhotsk	B	4	South Pacific Ocean	E	7	White Sea	A	1
Current	C	5	Peru Current	D	9	South Atlantic Ocean	D	11	Tasman Sea	E	5	Yellow Sea	B	4

fish. The worldwide commercial fish and shellfish catch from the ocean totals about 200 billion pounds (90 billion kilograms) annually. Most of the catch comes from coastal waters. People eat about 60 per cent of the fish and shellfish directly. Processors use the rest of the catch to make such products as fish oil and fish meal, which is added to livestock feed and pet food.

The world's fishing fleets harvest many kinds of fish and shellfish. The chief kinds include anchovies, cod, haddock, herring, lobsters, mackerel, oysters, sardines, shrimp, and tuna. The fishing industry also is harvesting unfamiliar types of seafood and developing new products and markets for the catch. For example, *krill,* a small shrimplike animal found in cold ocean waters, already provides high-protein food for people. *Surimi,* a fish product developed in Japan, can be made into imitation crab, lobster, scallop, and shrimp. Processors use hake and some other types of fish not traditionally eaten as food to make a protein powder. In addition, the market for such animals as squids is growing.

Seaweeds also serve as a source of food, in addition to having industrial uses. *Kelp,* a large, brown variety, is one of the most important seaweeds. Kelp contains many vitamins and such minerals as iodine and potassium. However, its chief value is as a source of *algin,* a thickening substance used in making ice cream, salad dressing, cosmetics, and many other products.

People are increasingly farming the ocean much as they farm the land. Fish farming, also called *aquaculture* or *mariculture,* has been practiced for thousands of years in China and some other Asian countries. Its use has been growing in Western countries since the 1960's. Fish farmers raise fish, shellfish, and seaweeds near ocean shores as well as in ponds. They use special methods to make the animals and seaweeds grow faster and larger than they would in the wild. Fish hatcheries, a related industry, produce healthy young salmon and other young fish for release into the ocean. See **Aquaculture.**

Energy from the ocean has several forms. Petroleum

Terry Domico, Earth Images

An abundance of fish and other animals makes the ocean a major food source. Most fish are caught in coastal waters.

and natural gas are the ocean's most valuable energy resources. Offshore wells tap deposits of oil and gas beneath the sea floor. In the late 1980's, offshore wells produced about 25 per cent of the world's oil and about 20 per cent of the world's gas. Scientists estimate that 3 trillion barrels of oil lie undiscovered beneath the ocean. Equally huge amounts of untapped gas accompany the oil. As gas and oil reserves on land are used up or become too difficult and expensive to obtain, finding and recovering undersea deposits will become increasingly important. See **Gas** (Producing gas); **Petroleum** (Offshore drilling).

The ocean tides also provide energy. Tidal power facilities use the energy in the rise and fall of the tides to produce electricity. The first tidal power plant opened in 1966 on the Rance River near St.-Malo, France. Plants on a bay near the city of Murmansk in the Soviet Union and on the Annapolis River in the Canadian province of Nova Scotia also use tidal power to generate electricity. See **Energy supply** (Tidal energy).

Minerals recovered from the ocean include sand and gravel mined from the sea floor and used to make construction materials. Some sands also have value because they are rich in phosphorite and other chemicals. Seawater itself contains such important minerals as bromide, manganese, and salt. The minerals can be removed by letting the seawater evaporate in large shallow basins under sunlight. The evaporation leaves the minerals behind. Other methods to remove minerals from seawater include chemical and electrochemical processes.

The mineral wealth of the ocean extends to the deep-sea floor. Deposits near undersea hot springs contain copper, iron, and zinc. But mining the ores would be expensive and difficult, and the techniques must still be developed. Manganese deposits lie on the ocean bottom in lumps called *nodules.* The nodules also contain cobalt, copper, and nickel. Scientists are trying to develop ways to gather the nodules and bring them to the surface. Possible gathering techniques include using buckets that run on conveyor belts between a ship and the sea floor and operating a device that works like a giant vacuum cleaner.

Medicines have been produced from many forms of marine life. For example, plantlike organisms called *red algae* provide an *anticoagulant,* a drug that keeps blood from clotting. A species of marine snail produces a substance that relaxes muscles. Sea life has also been valuable in medical research. The blood of horseshoe crabs contains a substance used to test for various infections. The substance can also be used to determine the purity of many drugs. Researchers study giant nerve cells from lobsters, squids, and marine worms to learn more about nerve functions in people.

Other products from the ocean include coral, pearls, and shells used in jewelry. Sponges from the ocean bottom have higher quality than synthetic sponges. In many dry areas near seacoasts, people *desalinate* (remove the salt from) seawater to produce fresh water (see **Water** [Fresh water from the sea]).

As an influence on climate. The ocean helps keep the earth's environment healthful. The ocean's great size and the slowness of water to change temperature have a steadying influence on the temperature of the atmosphere. In summer, the ocean stores excess heat from the sun. In winter, when the sunlight is weaker, the ocean releases the stored heat into the air. Circulation of the ocean waters also affects air temperatures. Currents carry excess heat of tropical waters toward the poles, thereby cooling the tropics and warming the polar regions.

The ocean is the source of most of the precipitation that falls to the earth. The sun's heat evaporates water from the ocean surface. The water rises as invisible vapor and forms clouds as it cools. It then falls back to the earth as rain, sleet, snow, or some other form of precipitation.

As a vast highway. The ocean has been a highway for trade since people built the first ships thousands of years ago. Today, transportation—especially of heavy and bulky products—remains an important use of the ocean. See **Ship; Transportation.**

Life in the ocean

An incredible variety of living things reside in the ocean. Marine life ranges from microscopic one-celled organisms to the largest animal that has ever lived—the blue whale, which may measure up to 100 feet (30 meters) long. Ocean plants and plantlike organisms use sunlight and the minerals in the water to grow. Sea animals eat these organisms and one another. Marine plants and plantlike organisms can live only in the sunlit surface waters of the ocean, which is called the *photic zone.* The photic zone extends only about 330 feet (100 meters) below the surface. Beyond that point, the light is insufficient to support plants and plant-like organisms in the sea. Animals, however, live throughout the ocean, from the surface waters to the greatest depths.

All ocean life can be divided into three groups. These groups are (1) the plankton, (2) the nekton, and (3) the benthos.

The plankton consists of plantlike organisms and animals that drift with the ocean currents. They have very little ability to move through the water on their own. Most of them cannot be seen without a microscope. The plantlike organisms of the plankton form the *phytoplankton,* and include such simple organisms as diatoms and other algae. The animals of the plankton form the *zooplankton.* Some minute types of bacteria are included in the plankton.

The phytoplankton consists of several kinds of plantlike organisms. Most have only one cell. The phytoplankton floats in the photic zone, where the organisms obtain sunlight and nutrients. Although the organisms generally drift about, some kinds have long, whiplike parts called *flagella* that enable them to swim. The phytoplankton serves as food for the zooplankton and for some larger marine animals.

The most numerous members of the phytoplankton are diatoms and dinoflagellates. A diatom consists of one cell enclosed in a hard, glasslike shell made of opal. Diatoms live mainly in the colder regions of the ocean. Some even live within sea ice. Most dinoflagellates also are one-celled organisms. They generally live in more tropical regions. A dinoflagellate has two flagella it can use to move in a swirling motion. Some species of dinoflagellates produce powerful poisons. When such species become plentiful, they may discolor the water and

Plankton

Plankton consists of small marine organisms that drift with the ocean currents. The plantlike organisms are called *phytoplankton.* Planktonic animals are known as *zooplankton.*

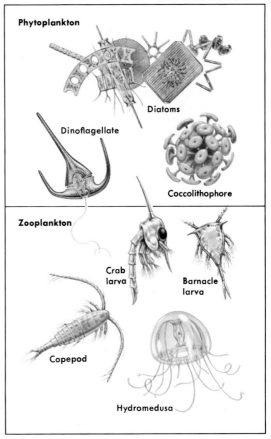

create a *red tide* that kills sea animals (see **Red tide**). Other kinds of phytoplankton include coccolithophores and silicoflagellates.

The zooplankton consists of many kinds of animals, ranging from one-celled organisms to jellyfish up to 6 feet (1.8 meters) wide. The animals live in surface and deep waters of the ocean. Some planktonic animals float about freely throughout their lives. The rest spend only the early part of their lives as plankton. As adults, some become strong swimmers and join the nekton. Others settle to the sea floor or attach themselves to it and become part of the benthos.

Crustaceans make up about 70 per cent of all planktonic animals. A crustacean has jointed legs, and a shell called an *exoskeleton* covers its body. Copepods are the most numerous crustaceans. Krill, which are also crustaceans, serve as food for fish, sea birds, seals, squids, and whales in the waters surrounding Antarctica. Other animals of the plankton include arrowworms and sea snails.

The nekton consists of animals that can swim freely in the sea. They are strong swimmers and include fish, squids, and marine mammals. Most species of nektonic

Nekton

Nekton is made up of fish and other animals that have the ability to swim freely in water without the help of currents. Most nektonic creatures live in the upper layer of the ocean.

Benthos

Benthos consists of marine organisms that live on the ocean bottom. Some members of the benthos are attached to the bottom in one position throughout their lives.

WORLD BOOK illustrations by Alex Ebel

Anchovies

Loggerhead turtle

Common squid

Sea lion

Butterfly fish

Angelfish

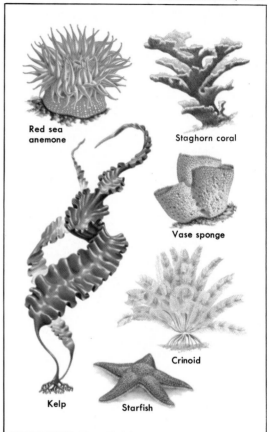

Red sea anemone

Staghorn coral

Vase sponge

Crinoid

Kelp

Starfish

animals live near the sea surface, where food is plentiful. But many other animals of the nekton live in the deep ocean.

Fish are the most important animals of the nekton. About 13,300 kinds of fish live in the ocean. They differ greatly in size and shape. The smallest fish, the pygmy goby, grows less than $\frac{1}{2}$ inch (13 millimeters) long. The largest fish, the whale shark, measures up to 60 feet (18 meters) long. Such fish as the tuna and the mackerel have streamlined bodies that enable them to move rapidly through the water in search of food. Other fish, such as cod and flounder, have burrowing whiskers or flat bodies that help them feed along the ocean bottom. Many fish of the deeper parts of the ocean have light-producing organs that may help attract prey. Such fish include deep-sea anglers and lanternfish.

Squids are free-swimming *mollusks* (animals with soft, boneless bodies) that have 10 arms. Related animals include octopuses and cuttlefish. Squids live in surface and deep waters. The animals may measure from less than 1 foot (0.3 meter) to as much as 60 feet (18 meters) long, including the arms. A squid moves backward through the water in a jetlike action by forcing water

through a tube that lies beneath its head.

Nektonic mammals include dugongs, manatees, porpoises, and whales, all of which remain in the ocean for their entire lives. Other marine mammals, such as sea lions, sea otters, seals, and walruses, spend time on land.

The benthos is made up of marine organisms that live on or near the sea floor. Animals of the benthos may burrow in the ocean floor, attach themselves to the bottom, or crawl or swim about within the bottom waters. Where sunlight can reach the sea floor, the benthos includes plants and plantlike organisms, such as kelp and sea grass, which become anchored to the bottom. Among the common animals that live on the sea floor are clams, crabs, lobsters, starfish, and several types of worms. Some fish have features specially suited for life on the ocean floor. For example, halibut and sole, which lie flat on the bottom, have both eyes on the side of the head facing up.

Most bottom-dwelling creatures are part of the plankton and drift with the currents during the early stages of their development. They then sink to the sea floor where, as adults, they become part of the benthos. Such

Animals of the ocean

The creatures shown below represent only a small part of the great variety of animal life found in the ocean.

WORLD BOOK illustrations by Tom Dolan and James Teason

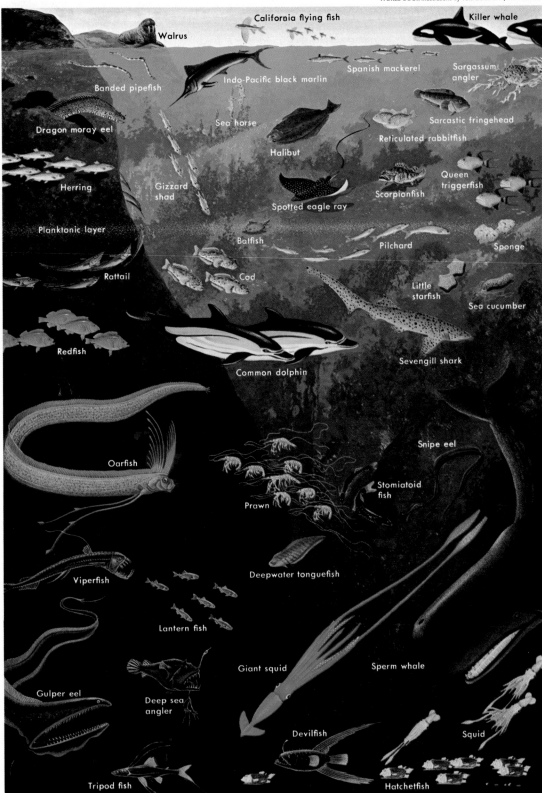

Walrus
California flying fish
Killer whale
Indo-Pacific black marlin
Spanish mackerel
Sargassum angler
Banded pipefish
Sea horse
Sarcastic fringehead
Dragon moray eel
Halibut
Reticulated rabbitfish
Herring
Gizzard shad
Scorpionfish
Queen triggerfish
Spotted eagle ray
Planktonic layer
Batfish
Pilchard
Sponge
Rattail
Cod
Little starfish
Sea cucumber
Redfish
Common dolphin
Sevengill shark
Oarfish
Snipe eel
Stomiatoid fish
Prawn
Deepwater tonguefish
Viperfish
Lantern fish
Giant squid
Sperm whale
Gulper eel
Deep sea angler
Devilfish
Squid
Tripod fish
Hatchetfish

animals include barnacles, clams, corals, oysters, and various snails and worms.

The food cycle in the sea begins with the phytoplankton. In a process called *photosynthesis,* the organisms of the phytoplankton use sunlight, carbon dioxide, water, and nutrients in the water to produce food (see **Photosynthesis**). Certain animals of the zooplankton eat the phytoplankton. Those animals, in turn, become food for other members of the zooplankton or for fish and other animals of the nekton.

After ocean animals die, they begin to sink. Before most dead animals sink very far, they are eaten by creatures dwelling at lower depths. Animals begin to decay as soon as they die. In addition, animals give off waste products. The waste products—and dead animals that are not eaten—are broken down into mineral salts by bacteria. Rising currents carry the minerals to the surface, where the phytoplankton use them to make food, thus completing the food cycle.

In the late 1970's, oceanographers discovered vents in the deep-sea floor from which hot water flows. The scientists learned that the vents support thriving communities of marine life. However, the food cycle in the vent communities is not based on phytoplankton. Instead, certain forms of bacteria serve as the food base. In a process called *chemosynthesis,* the bacteria use chemicals in the hot water to grow and reproduce. Other organisms then feed on the bacteria. The section *Exploring the ocean* discusses hot vents more fully.

How the ocean moves

The waters of the ocean move constantly. Ocean currents course through the sea like giant rivers. Winds and earthquakes create waves across the surface of the ocean. Even the gravitational pull of the moon and sun causes movement, producing the daily rise and fall of the tides.

Currents. Two types of circulation create the currents in the ocean. They are (1) wind-driven circulation and (2) thermohaline circulation.

Wind-driven circulation results from the wind blowing on the ocean surface. The wind sets the surface waters into motion as currents. The currents generally flow horizontally—that is, parallel to the earth's surface. The wind mainly affects only the upper 330 to 660 feet (100 to 200 meters) of water. However, the flow of wind-driven currents may extend to depths of 3,300 feet (1,000 meters) or more.

Wind-driven currents move in enormous circular patterns called *gyres.* The gyres flow clockwise in the subtropics of the Northern Hemisphere and counterclockwise in the subtropics of the Southern Hemisphere. Several conditions influence the direction of wind-driven currents and make them form the gyres. The earth's wind systems drive the currents in an easterly or westerly direction (see **Wind**). On the other hand, the continents direct the flow toward the north or south. The earth's rotation further causes the currents' circular paths. Major wind-driven currents include the North and South Equatorial currents, the California Current, the Canary Current, the Gulf Stream, the Japan Current, the Labrador Current, and the Peru Current. The Antarctic Circumpolar Current, also called the West Wind Drift, is the strongest current in the ocean and the only one that circles the earth. See the map in the section *The world ocean* for the location of the major currents.

Ocean currents result from two forces: (1) the action of the wind on surface waters, and (2) the differences in temperature and salt content of surface and deeper waters. The earth's general wind circulation produces the major currents—great streams that carry the ocean's surface waters in roughly circular patterns. Wind also causes *upwelling,* which occurs when coastal waters are blown offshore and replaced by colder, deeper waters. *Thermohaline circulation* takes place because colder, saltier water sinks. This action produces great vertical currents in the ocean.

WORLD BOOK illustration by Sarah Woodward

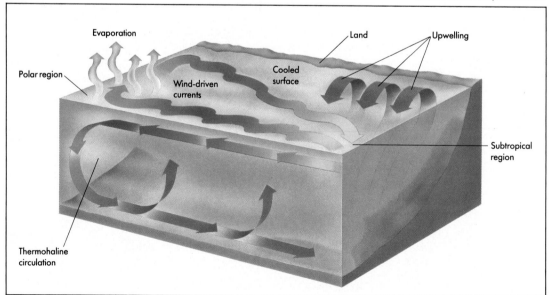

In some areas, *upwelling* occurs when winds cause surface waters near the coast to move offshore. Colder, deeper waters, which are rich in nutrients, then rise to the surface near the coast. The upwelling of deeper waters provides nutrients for the growth of tiny plantlike organisms, which fish and other sea animals eat. Upwelling areas have great numbers of fish and, in fact, yield half the world's fish catch. Chief upwelling regions include the coasts of Peru and northwestern Africa. Other upwelling areas occur along the equator and around Antarctica. Winds may also cause a *downwelling,* or sinking, of surface waters. Downwelling areas lack nutrients and support little marine life.

Thermohaline circulation produces great vertical currents that flow from the surface to the ocean bottom and back. The currents largely result from differences in water temperature and salinity. The currents move sluggishly from the polar regions, along the sea floor, and back to the surface. In the polar regions, the surface waters become colder and saltier. Being colder and saltier makes these waters heavier, and they sink toward the ocean bottom. The cold bottom waters then spread out slowly toward the equator. They gradually flow back toward the surface and replace the surface waters that sink.

Waves. In an ocean wave, water moves up and down. No forward motion of water occurs as the wave goes through the water. The action resembles the waves you can make in a rope tied to a tree. When you shake the free end of the rope, waves run along it. But the rope itself does not move forward. When an ocean wave reaches land, however, it starts to drag on the bottom. Then the water also moves. See **Waves.**

The wind causes most ocean waves, from small ripples to giant hurricane waves more than 100 feet (30 meters) high. It makes the familiar lapping waves seen at the beach or from a ship. The size of such waves depends on wind speed, on how long the wind blows, and on how far it blows over the ocean. As the wind continues to blow out at sea, the waves grow to their greatest size and then break. The breaking waves are called *whitecaps.* After the wind stops, the waves continue to move over the ocean surface and can travel great distances from where they originated. They become smoother and longer. Finally, the waves reach the shoreline, where they break and form the surf.

The action of ocean waves changes the shoreline. Waves cut away sloping land and leave steep cliffs. They break up exposed rocks and form beaches. The movement of the waves and currents shapes beaches and builds up sand bars along the shore. Waves also carry beach sand away, particularly during storms when the waves are high and choppy.

Another type of wave results from sudden movements of the sea floor caused by earthquakes. The waves are often called *tidal waves,* though the tide does not cause them. Scientists call such waves *tsunamis.* On the surface of the open ocean, tsunamis can barely be seen. The waves measure only about 1 inch (2.5 centimeters) high. But they can travel as fast as 600 miles (970 kilometers) per hour. As they approach a coast, they slow down and may pile up to a tremendous height, causing great damage along the coast. Tsunamis have destroyed large towns and drowned hundreds of people. Most

tsunamis strike land areas in or bordering the Pacific Ocean. Fortunately, scientists can predict how fast a tsunami is moving and warn people in its path. See **Tidal wave.**

Tides are the rhythmic rise and fall of the ocean waters. Every day, the water slowly rises along the shoreline for about six hours. Then it slowly falls back for about six hours. Tides are caused chiefly by the gravitational pull of the moon on the earth. The pull is strongest on the side of the earth facing the moon. The moon's gravity pulls up the water directly below it, forming a high tide at that point. A high tide also occurs on the opposite side of the earth because the moon pulls the solid earth there away from the water. In addition, the earth's rotation, which tends to make water fly away from the earth's surface, causes water to pile up slightly on the side opposite the moon. At any one time, the moon's gravity therefore produces two bulges, or high tide areas, on the ocean.

The sun's gravitational pull also affects the ocean. But the distance between the sun and the earth is much greater than that between the moon and the earth. As a result, the sun causes tides only about half as high as those caused by the moon. The gravitational pull of the moon and sun combine during the full moon and new moon. At such times, the sun, moon, and earth are in a straight line. The tides then rise higher and fall lower than usual. They are called *spring tides.* When the moon is in its first and third quarters, the sun and moon are at right angles to each other. The resulting tides do not rise or fall as much as usual. They are called *neap tides.* See **Tide.**

The land at the bottom of the sea

The ocean floor is a region of spectacular contrasts. Beneath the sea, broad plains cover huge distances, towering mountain chains circle the earth, undersea volcanoes rise toward the surface, and deep trenches and valleys cut through the bottom.

The continental margin forms the part of the seabed that borders the continents. It consists of (1) the continental shelf, (2) the continental slope, and (3) the continental rise.

The continental shelf is the submerged land at the edge of the continents. It begins at the shoreline and gently slopes underwater to an average depth of about 430 feet (130 meters). The width of the continental shelf averages 47 miles (75 kilometers). In certain areas, such as parts of the Arctic region, the shelf extends as far as 750 miles (1,200 kilometers). In some other areas, particularly those bordering much of the Pacific, it measures only 1 mile (1.6 kilometers) or less. Valleys of varying depths cut through the shelf. The shelf collects much of the *sediment* (deposits of sand and mud) carried into the ocean by rivers.

The continental slope begins at the outer edge of the shelf. The slope is much steeper than the shelf and plunges to depths of $2\frac{1}{4}$ miles (3.6 kilometers). The slope forms, in effect, the sides of the continents. Its width ranges from 12 to 60 miles (20 to 100 kilometers). In many places, deep underwater canyons gash the slope. Some canyons rival the gigantic Grand Canyon of North America in size. Most such underwater canyons lie offshore from large rivers, and former rivers may have

The land beneath the oceans has varied features. It consists of huge mountain ranges; broad basins and plains; and long, narrow valleys. The map below shows the major landforms of the world's ocean floor. The map index on the page following this map indicates their locations.

WORLD BOOK map

carved them. The movement of sediment along the ocean bottom also may form some canyons.

The continental rise consists of sediment from the continental shelf and slope that accumulates at the bottom of the slope. The thick sediment deposits of the continental rise extend up to about 600 miles (1,000 kilometers) from the slope.

Deep-sea peaks, valleys, and plains lie beyond the continental margin in the ocean basin. The *midocean ridges* form a chief feature of the basin. The ridges consist of a chain of mountains that runs about 37,000 miles (60,000 kilometers) through the three major oceans. Scientists discovered the mountain chain independently in each ocean and gave it different names, including Mid-Atlantic Ridge, East Pacific Rise, and Mid-Indian Ridge. Most mountains of the midocean ridges stand about 5,000 feet (1,500 meters) above the sea floor. Some peaks rise above the surface and form islands, such as the Azores and Iceland in the Atlantic Ocean. Deep valleys cut across the ridges in many places, producing a rugged, fractured surface. Some midocean ridges have valleys that slice down through the center of them. Frequent volcanic activity occurs along such central valleys.

The sides of the midocean ridges slope down into vast regions called *abyssal plains.* The accumulation of sediment buries most features of the ocean floor along the abyssal plains, which are flat as a result. The two chief sources of deep-sea sediment are the land itself and marine life. The breaking down and wearing away of rock produces land sediment, which rivers carry to the ocean. Wind also carries land sediment—mostly from deserts—to the ocean. In addition, volcanic eruptions spread large amounts of sediment over the ocean. Marine life sediment consists mainly of tiny shells and the remains of dead organisms of the plankton. When such matter makes up a large part of a sediment, scientists call it an *ooze* (see **Ooze**).

Other features of the deep-sea basin include the long, narrow trenches and isolated underwater mountains called *seamounts.* Trenches form the deepest parts of the ocean. Volcanic eruptions produce seamounts. The mountains have steep sides and may rise as high as 13,000 feet (4,000 meters) above the sea floor.

How the sea floor was formed. Since the late 1800's, scientists have developed several theories of how the sea floor was formed. The theory of continental drift first received wide attention during the early 1900's. According to this theory, the continents originally consisted of a single great land mass surrounded by one ocean. The mass broke up into continents, which slowly drifted apart. The theory explains why the shape of the eastern coast of the Americas and that of the western coast of Africa seem to fit together like pieces of a jig-saw puzzle. New oceans, including the Atlantic and the Indian oceans, resulted from the drift of the continents. See **Continental drift.**

At first, many scientists rejected the continental drift theory because no one could explain what forces might move continents. Then in the early 1960's, a theory called *sea-floor spreading* provided some explanation. According to the theory, the sea floor itself moves, carrying the continents along. Circulating movements deep within the earth's *mantle*—that is, the thick layer of hot melted rock beneath the earth's crust—make the sea floor move. The circulating movements carry melted rock up to the midocean ridges and force it into the central valleys of the ridges. As the melted rock cools and hardens, it forms new sea floor and pushes the old floor and the continents away from the ridges.

Another theory, called *plate tectonics,* combines and expands on the ideas of sea-floor spreading and continental drift. According to plate tectonics, the earth's outer shell consists of huge rigid plates that move continuously. As the plates move, they carry the ocean floor and the continents with them. The plates move about $\frac{1}{2}$ to 8 inches (1.3 to 20 centimeters) a year. Different movements of the plates have different effects on the ocean bottom and the continents. Sea-floor spreading—and the formation of new sea floor—occurs where plates move apart. The midocean ridges mark such areas.

As plates move away from one another in one place, they must move toward one another elsewhere. When two plates collide, one plate may pile up against the other, forming mountains. Or one plate may be drawn down into the mantle under the other plate. Such action produces trenches and volcanoes. Earthquakes occur at the boundaries of plates that slide past one another. The Atlantic Ocean is slowly growing wider and the Pacific smaller because of plate tectonics. See **Earth** (illustration: The earth's plates); **Tectonics.**

The oceanic crust forms the ocean floor. It consists of hard rock called *basalt.* The continents lie on the continental crust, which consists mainly of granite. Granite is lighter than basalt, and so the continental crust basically "floats" on the mantle, above the oceanic crust. The ocean basins, as sunken areas, thus collect water. Scientists have several theories to explain how the ocean basins originally filled with water. But most scientists believe that the water came from the earth's interior and was released as water vapor through volcanoes. As the earth cooled, the vapor condensed to water and fell as rain, filling the ocean basins.

Exploring the ocean

Why explore the ocean? As we have seen, the ocean serves as a source of food, energy, minerals, and

Features of the ocean floor

This index lists the main features shown on the map on the preceding two pages.

medicines. It is important for transportation and trade. It provides recreation in the form of boating, fishing, swimming, and other activities. The action of the ocean and the atmosphere on each other affects the weather and the climate. We depend on the ocean in so many ways that we should find out all we can about it. By exploring and understanding the ocean, we can learn to manage its resources wisely.

Tools of exploration. To understand the ocean better, scientists must gather information about its behavior. The tools that oceanographers use in their efforts to explore the sea include (1) research ships, (2) research submarines called *submersibles*, (3) satellites, and (4) computers.

Research ships typically measure about 100 to 300 feet (30 to 90 meters) long and include laboratory space where scientists can work while at sea. Oceanographers travel on research vessels to make observations and take measurements. They may stay at sea for weeks or months at a time. They often work in rough seas and in distant locations.

Oceanographers use several types of instruments on research ships. They operate underwater cameras to photograph the sea floor. Electronic devices send out sound waves and record the echoes from the ocean floor. The records of the echoes provide information about the depth of the sea. The most powerful of such instruments records echoes from deep within the earth's crust. Scientists analyze the records to learn about the structure of the crust. Oceanographers also use special devices to collect samples of seawater from various depths and then measure the temperature, salinity, and other characteristics of the seawater samples. Nets towed behind research ships gather samples of marine life for study.

Oceanographers also use a number of floating devices. For example, a *mooring* consists of an anchor and a float connected by a cable. The float may be placed on the ocean surface or at a determined depth. Scientists attach various instruments to the cable section of a mooring. Some instruments measure the speed and direction of ocean currents at different depths. Other devices record the temperature and salinity of the water. A mooring may remain out at sea several years before the research ship picks up the device and the data it has collected.

Other floating devices include *buoys,* which drift with the ocean's surface currents. Buoys chiefly provide information about ocean circulation. However, they may also record air pressure or surface water temperature. Buoys relay data to scientists through orbiting space satellites. Certain buoys can drift with currents below the ocean surface.

Oceanographers use specialized ships that have equipment to drill into the ocean bottom. The equipment removes *cores* (samples) of sediment and hard rock from beneath the sea floor. The cores provide scientists with information about the age, composition, and development of the ocean floor. See **Ocean Drilling Program.**

Submersibles can descend to the depths of the ocean. They enable scientists to observe features on the sea floor that may be missed by instruments lowered from research ships on the surface. *Manned submers-*

ibles, such as the U.S. *Alvin* and *Turtle,* carry a human crew. The crew members take photographs and, using a mechanical arm outside the vessel, gather samples and set out instruments. *Unmanned submersibles* carry no crew. They have television cameras that scientists operate from a surface ship. In 1985, two unmanned

Woods Hole Oceanographic Institution

The submersible *Alvin* can carry a crew of scientists to the ocean floor, where they take photographs and gather samples.

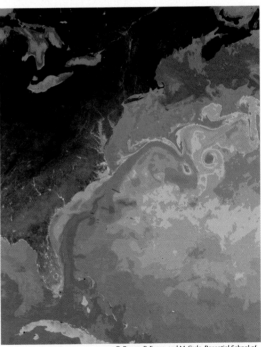

O. Brown, R. Evans, and M. Carle, Rosentiel School of Marine and Atmospheric Science, University of Miami

Satellite photographs can provide data on surface water temperatures and current patterns in the ocean. In the satellite picture above, red and orange indicate the warmest temperatures, and blue and purple represent the coldest. The Gulf Stream is visible as a red "river" off the coast of North America, *left.*

submersibles—the U.S. *Argo* and the French *Sar*—found and explored the wreckage of the *Titanic,* a British passenger ship that sank in the Atlantic in 1912. Submersibles can also carry divers to the ocean depths, where they leave the vehicles to study the ocean environment directly. See **Diving, Underwater.**

Satellites transmit data from buoys and other instruments at sea to oceanographers on shore. They also provide views of vast expanses of the sea as they sweep around the earth. Satellite photographs can show the distribution of sea ice, the extent of surface oil slicks, and the cloud formations over the ocean. Satellites can also be used to map the temperature and color of the ocean surface, enabling scientists to study daily variations in the routes and patterns of ocean currents. Oceanographers rely increasingly on satellites, which supply a greater range of information more quickly than do research ships.

Computers enable oceanographers to collect and analyze the enormous amounts of data obtained every day from satellites and from instruments on research ships. Scientists also use computers to create *models* (mathematical representations) of the ocean's movement and structure. They study the models to understand and predict the ocean's behavior and its effect on the environment.

Discoveries. Oceanographers constantly discover new and interesting facts about the sea. One of the most exciting discoveries occurred in 1977, when they detected a hot vent on the sea floor near the Galapagos Islands in the eastern Pacific Ocean. Discoveries of similar vents followed, chiefly in the eastern Pacific. Hot vents occur along the midocean ridges, where the sea floor is expanding, at depths of about 8,200 to 10,000 feet (2,500 to 3,000 meters). Water containing such minerals as copper, iron, and zinc flows from the vents. As the hot water comes into contact with the colder seawater, the minerals settle out and form deposits around the vents. The deposits take the shape of "chimneys" through which the water shoots out. The presence of iron darkens the water, and so black "smoke" appears to be flowing from the chimneys. For that reason, hot vents are often called *black smokers.*

The hot vents support large communities of strange marine life. Certain forms of bacteria use chemicals in the hot water to grow and reproduce. The bacteria serve as the base of the food chain of the vent communities. Other forms of life found near hot vents include clams up to 1 foot (30 centimeters) long and giant, bright red tubeworms measuring up to 8 feet (2.5 meters) long. Scientists have further discovered various species of crabs, fish, shrimp, and other animals in the vent communities. Most of the animals were previously unknown species of marine life.

Oceanographers also make discoveries as they apply new tools and techniques to familiar subjects of research. For example, the use of satellites and computers has increased their understanding of El Niño, a marine *phenomenon* (event) that occurs about every two to seven years. During an El Niño, a warm current flows southward along the west coast of South America, warming the normally cold coastal waters of Ecuador and Peru. The term El Niño also refers to the current itself. The warming of the ocean waters kills many fish

and sea birds, damaging the economy of Ecuador and Peru.

For many years, El Niño was considered only a local phenomenon. In the late 1960's, however, scientists observed a connection between El Niño and a change in the wind pattern over the entire tropical Pacific Ocean. Scientists used the information to predict an El Niño for the first time in 1975. In 1982 and 1983, the shift in wind pattern over the tropical Pacific led to a particularly powerful El Niño that affected rainfall in several parts of the world. For example, droughts occurred in Australia and Indonesia, while floods drenched parts of South America. Oceanographers continue to study El Niño closely. Improvements in their ability to predict the phenomenon would benefit countries in many parts of the world. See **El Niño.**

Ocean problems

Ocean pollution. *Pollutants* (substances that cause pollution) enter the ocean through accidents, carelessness, and the deliberate dumping of wastes. The ocean can absorb some types of pollutants in certain quantities because of its great size and the natural chemical processes that occur within it. But people continue to introduce more and more pollutants into the sea. The ocean will not be able to absorb it all. The ocean provides us with many necessities—and it helps keep our environment healthful. It is therefore extremely important that we work to control ocean pollution.

Oil is a major source of ocean pollution. Most oil pollution enters the ocean from oil spills on land or in rivers used to transport petroleum. Oil also seeps into the ocean naturally from cracks in the sea floor. Oil tanker

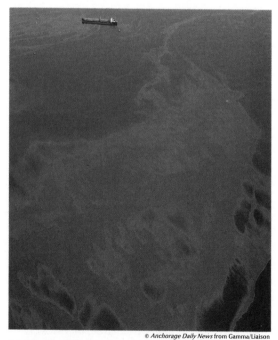

© *Anchorage Daily News* from Gamma/Liaison

An oil spill—in this case the result of an oil tanker accident—is a well-known example of ocean pollution. Such spills foul the water and coastlines, killing both sea and land organisms.

and oil well accidents at sea account for only a small portion of ocean oil pollution, but their effects may be disastrous. The world's largest oil spill occurred in June 1979, when an oil well blew out off the east coast of Mexico and spilled about 130 million gallons (490 million liters) of oil. The world's worst tanker oil spill occurred in March 1978, when a tanker ran aground off the coast of France, spilling 68 million gallons (257 million liters). The worst oil spill in the United States occurred in March 1989, when a tanker ran aground off Alaska and leaked more than 10 million gallons (38 million liters). In water, much of the oil forms tarlike lumps, which litter beaches and other coastal areas. Oil also coats fish, birds, and marine mammals, killing many of them.

Scientists and engineers have devised several methods to clean up oil spills. One method involves placing a ring of floating devices around the spill to prevent it from spreading. Pumps or skimming devices then collect the oil, which floats on the surface of the water. Oil may also be recovered by placing sheets or particles of floating, oil-absorbing material on the ocean surface. Burning the oil cleans a spill, but it produces air pollution. Detergents help break up spills, but they may cause additional harm to marine life.

Ocean dumping. The deliberate dumping of waste products into the sea is another major source of ocean pollution. Such products include industrial wastes and sewage. Industries dump chemicals, animal and plant matter, and other pollutants. Sewerage systems carry human wastes, ground-up garbage, and water used for bathing and laundering to the sea. Waste treatment plants remove some of the most poisonous wastes from sewage, but most treated sewage still contains material harmful to the ocean. By the late 1980's, the United States was dumping millions of tons of waste products into the ocean every year. But in 1988, President Ronald Reagan signed a law banning all ocean dumping by the United States by 1992.

Plastics dumped into the ocean form an especially damaging group of pollutants because they do not break down easily. Sea birds, turtles, seals, whales, and other marine animals eat or become entangled in plastic nets, bags, and packing material. Animals that mistake plastic items for food die of starvation if the plastic blocks the digestive system. Animals entangled in plastic may drown or die because they cannot obtain food. Tiny plastic pellets also litter the ocean. These pellets tend to float on the ocean surface, where they disrupt the environment of microscopic, surface-dwelling organisms.

By the late 1980's, an estimated 16 billion pounds (6.4 billion kilograms) of plastic was being dumped into the ocean annually. The figure includes plastic trash discarded from ships and fishing vessels. In December 1988, an international treaty banning the dumping of plastics from ships and other vessels went into effect. Great Britain, the Soviet Union, the United States, and several other countries have ratified the treaty.

Who owns the ocean? This question has become increasingly important as countries have learned that fish and other ocean resources can be used up and that valuable minerals lie on and under the sea floor. Various United Nations committees have worked to develop an agreement on ownership of the sea. Their efforts resulted in the Law of the Sea Treaty, drafted in 1982. The treaty calls for a system to protect the economic and environmental interests of coastal nations, while allowing the free passage of other countries' ships.

Under the treaty, the laws of a coastal nation would apply throughout its *territorial sea,* which extends 12 nautical miles (22 kilometers) from the nation's shoreline. An *exclusive economic zone* (EEZ) would extend, in most cases, 200 nautical miles (370 kilometers) beyond the nation's territorial sea. Each coastal nation, even if it is an island, would have total control over resources and research within its EEZ. The remaining ocean area is defined as the *high seas,* where no nation may make a territorial claim. But even on the high seas, various international agreements govern fishing.

Although many nations already follow the treaty's provisions, the Law of the Sea does not officially take effect until 60 countries have ratified it. By late 1989, 40 countries had ratified the treaty. The United States has not signed it, believing that it does not adequately protect private industries involved in mining operations in the deep sea. However, the United States supports exclusive economic zones. In 1983, President Reagan proclaimed a 200-nautical-mile EEZ for the United States.

Careers in oceanography

The ocean can be studied in many ways, and the science of oceanography includes many specialties. *Physical oceanographers* study waves, tides, currents, and the action of the ocean and the atmosphere on each other. *Chemical oceanographers* deal with the chemicals in seawater and the chemical reactions that occur in the ocean. *Marine geologists* and *marine geophysicists* analyze the form and composition of the sea floor, as well as the forces that shape the ocean floor. Marine geologists mainly study the sediments and surface features of the ocean bottom. Marine geophysicists deal with the deeper oceanic crust. *Biological oceanographers* and *marine biologists* study marine life, from microscopic bacteria to large marine mammals. *Ocean engineers* design oceanographic research tools and develop methods for obtaining minerals and other resources from the sea.

To become an oceanographer, a person needs a background in science and mathematics. Solid knowledge of at least one basic science, such as biology, chemistry, geology, or physics, is required. In college, oceanography courses help an undergraduate student learn how the basic sciences apply to the study of the ocean. However, most future oceanographers acquire detailed knowledge about the ocean through graduate training.

An oceanographer may choose from several types of careers after completing training. Research jobs are available at colleges and universities, at oceanographic institutions, in the government, and in industry laboratories. Colleges and universities also provide teaching opportunities. Some oceanographers go on lengthy research expeditions or make deep-sea dives. Others formulate theories or interpret scientific observations. Oceanographers may also work with computers in an attempt to re-create, analyze, and predict ocean behavior.   Arnold L. Gordon

Dar es Salaam, Tanzania's capital and largest city, has modern buildings and large parks. The city's harbor, *background,* has helped it become an important trading center.

Tanzania

Tanzania, *TAN zuh NEE uh* or *tan ZAN ee uh,* is a large country in eastern Africa that borders the Indian Ocean. Most of Tanzania lies on the mainland of Africa. Several nearby islands make up the rest of the country. Dar es Salaam is Tanzania's capital and largest city. A new capital is under construction at Dodoma, in central Tanzania. The country's official name is the United Republic of Tanzania.

Tanzania's population consists mainly of black Africans. The rest are people of Asian or European descent. Tanzania is one of the world's poorest countries. About 85 per cent of its people live in rural areas and farm for a living. The government has tried to develop industries, but the economy still depends heavily on agricultural production and imported goods.

Tanzania's fascinating wildlife and spectacular scenery are world famous. Elephants, giraffes, lions, zebras, and many other wild animals roam across the vast Serengeti National Park, Selous Game Reserve, and other areas where hunting is banned or limited. Africa's highest mountain, the majestic, snow-capped Kilimanjaro, rises 19,340 feet (5,895 meters) in northern Tanzania. Lake Tanganyika, the longest freshwater lake in the world, extends 420 miles (680 kilometers) along the country's western border. Part of Lake Victoria, which is the largest lake in Africa, lies within northern Tanzania. The lake covers an area of 26,828 square miles (69,484 square kilometers).

During the 1800's, Germany established a colony on the mainland of what is now Tanzania. Great Britain ruled a group of nearby islands, known as Zanzibar. The mainland area became the British colony of Tanganyika during the early 1900's. Both Tanganyika and Zanzibar

gained independence during the early 1960's. In 1964, they united to form Tanzania.

Government

Tanzania is a one-party state. The only legal political party, the Chama Cha Mapinduzi (CCM) or Revolutionary Party, establishes government policies.

National government. A president heads Tanzania's national government. The Chama Cha Mapinduzi nominates the president, whom the people elect to a five-year term. The president appoints a first vice president and a second vice president. One vice president serves as prime minister and the other is president of Zanzibar. If the president is from the mainland, the first vice president is from Zanzibar, and vice versa.

The National Assembly is the nation's lawmaking body. It has 244 members who serve five-year terms. Most members are elected by the people. Others are elected by government bodies, are appointed by the president, or hold membership as government officials.

Facts in brief

Capital: Dar es Salaam.
Official languages: English and Swahili.
Area: 364,900 sq. mi. (945,087 km²).
Population: *Estimated 1990 population*—25,955,000; density, 71 persons per sq. mi. (27 persons per km²); distribution, 85 per cent rural, 15 per cent urban. *1978 census*—17,512,611. *Estimated 1995 population*—30,618,000.
Chief products: *Agriculture*—bananas, beef, cashews, cassava, cloves, coconuts, coffee, corn, cotton, milk, millet, rice, sisal, sorghum, sugar cane, tea, tobacco, wheat. *Manufacturing*—fertilizer, food products, textiles.
National anthem: "Mungo Ibariki Africa" ("God the Almighty Bless Africa").
Money: *Basic unit*—shilling. See **Money** (table).

In general, the Assembly makes CCM policies into law.

Regional and local government. Tanzania is divided into 25 regions for administrative purposes. Local government has special responsibility in the areas of agriculture, education, and health care.

Politics. The Chama Cha Mapinduzi approves all candidates for election to the National Assembly. All candidates for elective posts must be CCM members.

Courts. The Tanzania Court of Appeals is the country's highest court. Lower courts include district courts and local primary courts.

Armed forces. Tanzania has an army of more than 38,000 members. The country also has a small navy and air force. Military service is voluntary.

People

Population and ancestry. Tanzania has about 26 million people. It ranks among Africa's least urbanized nations. Only about 15 per cent of Tanzania's people live in cities. Dar es Salaam has a population of about 820,000. Other cities include Zanzibar on Zanzibar Island and Mbeya, Mwanza, and Tanga on the mainland.

More than two-thirds of Tanzania's rural population live in the northern third of the country. Areas near mountains in the north and lakes in the west have especially dense populations.

About 98 per cent of Tanzania's people are black Africans. Most of the rest are people descended from Arabs, Europeans, and Asians from India and Pakistan.

The black Africans belong to about 120 ethnic groups, including the Sukuma, Chagga, Makonde, and Nyamwezi peoples. No single group is large enough to control the country, and Tanzania has not suffered the ethnic violence that has troubled other African nations. Tanzania's ethnic balance has helped the government develop a sense of national unity.

Way of life. Most rural Tanzanians farm for a living. Some raise livestock, such as chickens, goats, and sheep. Raising cattle is the chief activity of the Masai and other peoples in the interior of Tanzania. Cows' milk is an important part of their diet. Fishing is an important activity for people who live along the Indian Ocean coast, on the nearby islands, and near inland lakes.

Many city dwellers work for the national government. Many others work in trade, tourism, and other service industries.

Under Tanzanian law, women have the same rights as men. In practice, however, women still have lesser

© Bernard Pierre Wolff, Photo Researchers

Farmers harvest rice, *above,* near a lake in central Tanzania. Rice ranks among the country's chief food crops. Agriculture employs about 85 per cent of Tanzania's workers.

rights in such areas as education, marriage, and ownership of property. Women are largely responsible for homemaking and raising children. In rural areas, they often perform more farm work than men.

Languages. Swahili and English are the official languages of Tanzania. Swahili, a blend of Arab and African languages, is more commonly used in everyday speech and serves as the national language. Most blacks also speak at least one tribal language. Almost all the tribal

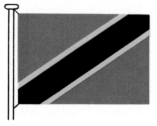

The Flag Research Center

WORLD BOOK map

Tanzania's flag was adopted in 1964. The green represents agriculture; the black, the nation's people; the blue, the Indian Ocean; and the gold, mineral resources.

The coat of arms was adopted in 1964. The flaming torch represents freedom and knowledge, and the ax and the hoe stand for agricultural development.

Tanzania is a large country in eastern Africa. It includes Zanzibar and Pemba islands in the Indian Ocean.

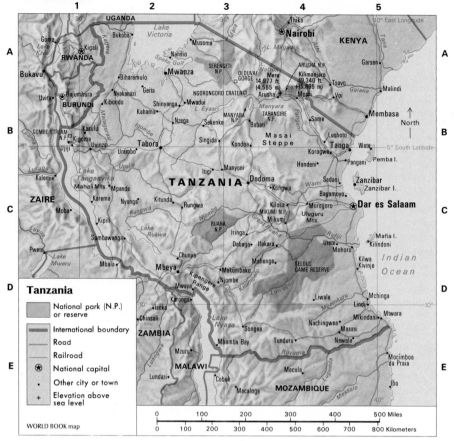

Tanzania map index

Cities

Arusha ....55,281..B 4
Dar es Salaam ..870,020..C 5
Dodoma ....45,703..C 3
Iringa ....57,182..C 3
Kigoma ....50,044..B 1
Mbeya ....76,606..D 2
Morogoro ......61,890..C 4
Moshi ....52,000..B 4
Mtwara ....48,510..D 5
Mwanza ....110,611..A 2
Tabora ....67,392..B 2
Tanga ....103,409..B 5
Zanzibar ....110,669..C 5
Source: 1978 census.

Physical features

Arusha
  National Park ....A 4
Gombe Stream
  National Park ....B 1
Great Ruaha River ....C 4
Indian Ocean ....D 5
Kilimanjaro (mountain) ..A 4
Kipengere Range ....D 3
Lake Eyasi ....B 3
Lake Manyara ....B 3
Lake Natron ....A 3
Lake Nyasa ....D 3
Lake Rukwa ....C 2
Lake Tanganyika ....C 1
Lake Victoria ....A 2
Mahali Mountains ....C 1
Manyara
  National Park ....B 3
Masai Steppe ....B 4
Mikumi
  National Park ....C 4
Mount Meru ....A 4
Olduvai Gorge ....A 3
Pangani River ....B 4
Pemba Island ....B 5
Ruaha
  National Park ....C 3
Rufiji River ....C 4
Ruvuma River ....E 4
Selous
  Game Reserve ....D 4
Serengeti
  National Park ....A 3
Tarangire
  National Park ....B 4
Uluguru Mountains ......C 4
Wami River ....C 4
Zanzibar Island ....C 5

Tanzania

Legend:
- National park (N.P.) or reserve
- International boundary
- Road
- Railroad
- ⊛ National capital
- • Other city or town
- + Elevation above sea level

WORLD BOOK map

languages belong to the Bantu language family.

Housing. Most homes are made of wooden frames plastered with mud and include a garden area nearby. Some homes are round with thatched roofs. Others are rectangular with flat mud roofs. Some homes have metal roofs. In urban areas, some homes are made of cement blocks or baked clay bricks.

Clothing in Tanzania is similar to that worn in other parts of eastern Africa. Traditional clothing among the black Africans includes a colorful, wrap-style garment for women, called the *kanga,* and the *kikoi wrap* for men. Many Muslim men wear a flowing white robe called the *kanzu.* Since about 1960, Western-style pants and shirts for men have become increasingly popular.

Food and drink. Tanzanians prepare a variety of dishes with corn, sorghum, and other grains. One of the most popular meals, called *ugali,* is a porridge made with corn. Fish is an important part of the diet of Tanzanians who live on the islands and along the coast. Bottled beers and soft drinks are popular. The Chagga people produce a well-known beer called *mbege.*

Recreation. The most common forms of recreation in Tanzania include dancing and singing. Many Tanzanians also enjoy playing or watching soccer. A number of Tanzanians have become world-class long-distance runners.

Religion. About 35 per cent of the population are *Muslims* (followers of Islam). Many of Tanzania's Mus-

lims live on Zanzibar and along the coast. Christians make up about 30 per cent of the population. Most other Tanzanians practice traditional African religions.

Education. Tanzania has one of the highest literacy rates in Africa. About 80 per cent of the adult population of Tanzania can read and write. Although Tanzanian law requires seven years of elementary education, only about half of the children go to elementary school. Only about 3 per cent attend high school. Many children who do not attend school come from poor families and are needed to work on family farm plots. Since the early 1980's, economic problems have caused a shortage of basic school supplies.

The University of Dar es Salaam is Tanzania's chief university. It has about 3,500 students. Many adults attend technical and vocational schools.

The arts. Tanzania's most common artistic expressions include traditional African music and dance. These art forms often tell stories of tribal heroes and local gods. Other notable art forms are associated with various ethnic groups, such as carved figures and masks of the Makonde, carved animal figures of the Zaramo, and leather shields of the Masai.

Land and climate

Tanzania covers 364,900 square miles (945,087 square kilometers). Many mountains and Lakes Tanganyika and Nyasa in Tanzania are part of the Great Rift Valley. This valley, which runs north and south through eastern Africa, consists of a series of cracks in the earth that form deep, steep-sided valleys. The valley has branches that extend through central Tanzania and along the country's western border. Tanzania's land regions include (1) the coastal lowlands and islands, (2) the plateaus, and (3) the highlands.

The coastal lowlands and islands. The mainland borders the Indian Ocean along a 500-mile (800-kilometer) coast. The coastal strip has many mangrove swamps and coconut palm groves. The northern and southern lowlands extend inland between 10 to 40 miles (16 to 64 kilometers). The central lowlands extend farther into the country.

Zanzibar, the largest coral island off the African coast, covers 640 square miles (1,658 square kilometers). Another Tanzanian island, Pemba Island, lies 25 miles (40 kilometers) northeast of Zanzibar Island. Pemba covers 380 square miles (984 square kilometers).

The coastal lowlands and islands make up the hottest and wettest part of Tanzania. High temperatures average 85° F. (29° C). year around. Annual rainfall totals between about 31 and 55 inches (80 to 140 centimeters) on the lowlands and exceeds 40 inches (100 centimeters) on the islands.

The plateaus rise gradually from the coastal lowlands. They include a vast grassland in northeastern Tanzania, called the Masai Steppe, and a grassy central plateau that covers more than a third of the country. The Masai Steppe rises to about 3,500 feet (1,100 meters) above sea level. It is home to the Masai people, who graze cattle there. West of the steppe, the central plateau reaches about 4,000 feet (1,200 meters) above sea level. The central section is usually drier than the coastal lowlands or highlands. It is mostly covered by grasses or barren land, with patches of trees and shrubs. Parts of this region receive less than 20 inches (50 centimeters)

of rain annually. The plateaus have average daytime highs of 84° F. (29° C) and cool nights.

The highlands. Northern Tanzania has some of the country's highest mountain ranges, which include Kilimanjaro. Several other highlands rise in the central and southern regions. Temperatures in the highlands average about 75° F. (24° C). Highland regions often receive more than 40 inches (100 centimeters) of rain each year.

Rivers and lakes. The Rufiji is Tanzania's chief river. It flows from the southern highlands and drains much of southern Tanzania. Other major rivers include the Pangani, the Ruvuma, and the Wami. Lake Victoria lies in northern Tanzania and forms part of its border with Kenya and Uganda. Lakes Tanganyika and Nyasa lie along the country's western border.

Animal life. Tanzania is famous for its millions of large, wild animals that thrive in vast parklands. In northern Tanzania, Serengeti National Park covers about 5,600 square miles (14,500 square kilometers) and is noted for its lions and huge herds of antelopes and zebras. In the south, the Selous Game Reserve—the world's largest animal reserve—covers about 21,000 square miles (54,000 square kilometers). It has about 50,000 elephants—one of the largest populations in Africa. Other animals common to Tanzania include baboons, buffaloes, hippopotamuses, giraffes, monkeys, and rhinoceroses. The government allows limited hunting in some areas. But *poachers* (people who hunt illegally) remain a problem.

Economy

Tanzania has a developing economy based on agriculture. The country follows a socialist economic system, under which the government controls the nation's banks, major industries, and large farms. Some small businesses are privately owned. Although the government has encouraged industrial development, most industries are small and unprofitable. Tanzania depends

E. R. Degginger

Zebras and gnus roam across Tarangire National Park, *left,* in northern Tanzania. These animals and other wildlife are protected in Tanzania's many national parks. The country also has many game reserves, where hunting is limited. These parklands cover large areas of Tanzania and include Serengeti National Park, Ngorongoro Crater, and Selous Game Reserve.

on hydroelectric plants and imported petroleum to generate electricity.

Agriculture. Although only about 5 per cent of Tanzania's land area is used for farming, agriculture accounts for more than a third of the country's economic production. The richest soil lies in the northern and southern highlands and around Lake Victoria.

Most farming is done by hand with hoes and long-bladed knives. Many farmers can grow only enough food to feed themselves and their families. Chief food crops include bananas, cassava, corn, millet, rice, sorghum, wheat, and vegetables. The Masai and some other peoples raise cattle.

Large, government-operated farms produce many of the crops that Tanzania exports. Most of these farms were private plantations under British rule. The major export crops include coffee, cotton, tea, and tobacco. About two-thirds of Tanzania's export earnings come from these crops. Other important crops produced for foreign trade include cashew nuts, cloves, coconuts, *sisal* (a plant used in making rope), and sugar cane.

Service industries, taken together, account for about half the total value of Tanzania's economic production. Government and trade are the leading service industries. Other service industries include banking, education, health care, insurance, and tourism.

The government administers many service industries, including banking, education, insurance, and health care. Most of Tanzania's wholesale and retail trade involves the sale of farm products. Tourism benefits many types of establishments, including hotels, national parks, and restaurants. The chief tourist attractions are the wildlife in the national parks. Many tourists also enjoy the palm-shaded coastal beaches.

Manufacturing contributes about 5 per cent of the country's economic production. Food processing is Tanzania's chief industry. Other important industries produce fertilizer, textiles, and petroleum products. Tanzania also has factories that produce aluminum, cement, paper, sugar, and steel.

Mining accounts for less than 1 per cent of the economic production of Tanzania. Mining operations produce diamonds and other gemstones, coal, and gold.

Tanzanians sell bananas at an open-air market on the island of Zanzibar, *above.* Selling farm products is an important economic activity in Tanzania's cities and towns.

Foreign trade. Coffee, cotton, tea, and tobacco are Tanzania's main exports. Zanzibar's primary export is cloves. The chief imports include chemicals, construction materials, food, machinery, petroleum and petroleum products, and transportation equipment. Tanzania's main trading partners are Great Britain, Italy, Japan, and West Germany.

Transportation and communication. Tanzania's large area and poor economic conditions have made development of transportation and communication services difficult. The country has about 50,000 miles (80,000 kilometers) of roads. But few roads are paved, and most are poorly maintained. Less than 1 per cent of all Tanzanians own an automobile. Tanzania's main railway links Dar es Salaam with Zambia on the west. Dar es Salaam, which has a fine harbor, is Tanzania's chief port. It handles trade from Burundi, Malawi, Rwanda, Uganda, Zaire, and Zambia. International airports operate at Dar es Salaam, near Arusha, and on Zanzibar.

Three daily newspapers are published in Tanzania—two in Swahili and one in English. The country has two radio stations and an average of 1 radio for every 12 people. Television service is available only on Zanzibar.

History

In Tanzania, scientists have found remains of some of the earliest-known human settlements. Anthropologist Louis Leakey and other members of the Leakey family discovered bones, tools, and other signs of early human life in the Olduvai Gorge area of northern Tanzania. Some remains date back more than 1 million years.

The prehistoric human beings who lived in what is now Tanzania were hunters and gatherers. They lived in small groups, catching animals and collecting wild plants for food. By about A.D. 500, people who spoke Bantu languages migrated from the north and from central Africa to eastern Africa.

The development of trade. Arab traders from the Middle East began to settle along the coast of eastern Africa during the 1100's. These traders often married African women. These Arab-African families and their settlements produced the Swahili culture. Major trading centers developed on Zanzibar and other islands.

In the early 1500's, Portuguese traders gained control of Africa's east coast. Local rebellions helped push out the Portuguese in the late 1600's. In 1698, Arabs from Oman, a country on the Arabian Peninsula, took control of Zanzibar and developed trade on the mainland. By this time, the Nyamwezi and Yao ethnic groups had become active in long-distance trade. Their caravans brought gold, ivory, and slaves from the interior to the coast, where they exchanged them for such items as cloth, glassware, and ceramics from Asia.

The Arabs also developed the slave trade. From the mid-1700's to the late 1800's, the Arabs sold thousands of black Africans from the mainland into slavery. Zanzibar was a major slave market. The slave trade caused much conflict and broke up many African communities.

German and British rule. During the 1800's, explorers and Christian missionaries from Europe traveled deep into the mainland of what is now Tanzania. European nations increasingly competed for control of African territory. In the 1880's, Germany took control of the present-day mainland of Tanzania. The Germans forced many Africans to work on plantations. This action contributed to a major uprising in 1905 called the Maji Maji rebellion. German forces killed many thousands of Africans before putting down the revolt.

Great Britain made Zanzibar and Pemba islands a British protectorate in 1890. The British gradually took over the powers of the Omani sultans in local affairs. After Germany's defeat in World War I (1914-1918), Britain gained control over the mainland and named it Tanganyika. During this period, people from other parts of the British Empire and Europe began to settle in Tanganyika. These immigrants included thousands of Indians who worked as merchants and traders.

Independence. In 1946, Tanganyika became a United Nations trust territory. Britain had the responsibility of preparing it for independence.

In Tanganyika, Britain sought to create a political system with equal representation of Europeans, Asians, and Africans. The Africans argued that such a system denied them their rights as the vast majority. In 1954, the Africans formed the Tanganyika African National Union (TANU). Led by Julius Nyerere and others, TANU won independence with majority rule for Tanganyika in 1961. The next year, Nyerere was elected president. Britain granted Zanzibar independence in 1963.

The united republic. Tanganyika and Zanzibar joined together in April 1964 and adopted the name of the United Republic of Tanzania in October. Nyerere became the country's first president. Under his direction, Tanzania adopted a socialist economic system. Nyerere based the system on *ujamaa,* a Swahili word for traditional African cooperation and self-reliance. The government took control of many privately owned businesses. It also encouraged farmers to move from small, widely scattered village sites to larger *ujamaa villages.* These villages were supposed to increase agricultural production and make it easier for the government to provide health and educational services.

At first, families moved voluntarily to ujamaa villages. But during the mid-1970's, police and military forces forced about 5 million others to move. Many farmers disliked the ujamaa villages, which were far from the farmers' plots of land in their former villages.

In foreign affairs, Nyerere worked to increase regional cooperation. In 1967, Tanzania, Kenya, and Uganda formed the East African Community. This organization promoted trade and coordinated economic development between the countries. In 1977, however, the East African Community fell apart. The collapse occurred largely because of Kenya's emphasis on private enterprise and Tanzania's commitment to socialism. In addition, Uganda was ruled by a brutal dictator, Idi Amin Dada. Amin's government, which killed thousands of Ugandans, sent troops that invaded Tanzania in 1978. Tanzanian forces soon beat back the invaders and helped Ugandan rebels overthrow Amin. The war was a moral and military triumph for Tanzania. But it cost over $500 million at a time when the country's economy was suffering from the high price of imported oil.

Recent developments. During the 1980's, growing trade deficits and debt contributed to an economic collapse. The economic hard times forced Tanzania to alter its socialist system. The government decreased its control of the economy and opened more areas for private businesses. This program included the firing of thousands of government employees and the reduction of state-owned operations. Some improvements occurred, but the economy still faced serious difficulties.

In 1985, Nyerere retired as president. But he remained a major influence in Tanzania as chairman of the CCM. His recommended successor, Ali Hassan Mwinyi, the president of Zanzibar, became president of Tanzania. Mwinyi continued to work for less state control of the economy.   Stephen K. Commins

Related articles in *World Book* include:

Dodoma	Lake Victoria	Races, Human
Kilimanjaro	Leakey family	(picture: African)
Lake Tanganyika	Nyerere, Julius K.	Zanzibar

Outline

I. Government
   A. National government
   B. Regional and local
      government
   C. Politics
   D. Courts
   E. Armed forces

II. People
   A. Population
      and
      ancestry
   B. Way of life
   C. Languages
   D. Housing
   E. Clothing
   F. Food and drink
   G. Recreation
   H. Religion
   I. Education
   J. The arts

III. Land and climate
   A. The coastal lowlands
      and islands
   B. The plateaus
   C. The highlands
   D. Rivers and lakes
   E. Animal life

IV. Economy
   A. Agriculture
   B. Service industries
   C. Manufacturing
   D. Mining
   E. Foreign trade
   F. Transportation and
      communication

V. History

Questions

What two former British colonies united in 1964 to form Tanzania?
What are some powers of Tanzania's only political party?
What are Tanzania's chief exports?
What led to the collapse of the East African Community in 1977?
Who was the first president of Tanzania?
What are Tanzania's *ujamaa villages?*
Where is most of Tanzania's fertile land?
Which European countries ruled what is now Tanzania during the late 1800's and early 1900's?
How did the slave trade affect Tanzanian communities?
What is the national language of Tanzania?

Kim Naylor, Aspect Picture Library Ltd.
The Palace of Wonders on Zanzibar, *above,* was home to many Arab *sultans* (rulers). The Arabs developed Zanzibar into a trading center in the 1700's and governed the island until 1964.

© Randy Taylor, Sygma

© Joseph Rodriguez, Black Star

© Chuck Fishman, Woodfin Camp, Inc.

Hispanic Americans represent several different cultures. In the pictures above, Mexican-American men play chess in a park, *left;* a Puerto Rican shop owner greets a customer, *top right;* and Cuban-American dancers and musicians perform in a parade, *bottom right.*

Hispanic Americans

Hispanic Americans are Americans of Spanish-speaking descent. Many Hispanic Americans are the descendants of Mexican people who lived in the Southwest when it became part of the United States. Almost all other Hispanic Americans or their ancestors migrated to the United States from Latin America. The three largest Hispanic groups in the United States are Mexican Americans, Puerto Ricans, and Cuban Americans. As a group, Hispanic Americans represent a mixture of several racial and cultural backgrounds, including European, American Indian, and African.

Today, more than 20 million people of Hispanic descent live in the United States. They make up the second largest minority group in the country. Black Americans are the largest U.S. minority group. Hispanics are also the fastest growing minority in the United States, as a result of a high birth rate and continuing immigration.

Even though a majority of Hispanic Americans speak English, most continue to use Spanish as well. As Spanish-speakers, they form the largest *language minority* in the United States. In addition to their language,

Manuel P. Galvan, the contributor of this article, is a member of the editorial board of the Chicago Tribune *and a former president of the National Association of Hispanic Journalists.*

Hispanic Americans have preserved many other traditions of their homelands. The foods, music, clothing styles, and architecture of these countries have greatly influenced American culture.

Hispanic Americans are also called *Latinos,* because most are of Latin-American origin. Many Hispanic people in the United States describe themselves simply as Americans. Others, however, identify themselves with their cultural or national background and refer to themselves as Mexican Americans, Puerto Ricans, Cuban Americans, and so on. Members of some groups use special names to describe themselves. For example, some Mexican Americans call themselves *Chicanos,* and some Puerto Ricans who live in New York City refer to themselves as *Nuyoricans.*

Like other minorities, Hispanic Americans have suffered from discrimination in jobs, housing, and education. Many new Hispanic immigrants are also hampered by not being able to speak or understand English. Discrimination and poor English skills have contributed to a high rate of unemployment—and, consequently, a high rate of poverty—among Hispanics. Although millions of Hispanic Americans have overcome these obstacles, many others remain in poverty.

This article focuses on Mexican Americans, Puerto Ricans, and Cuban Americans. It discusses the cultural backgrounds of these groups, the history of their immigration to the United States, and the issues that face them today.

Who are the Hispanic Americans?

In the late 1980's, the number of Hispanics living in the United States was estimated at more than 20 million. This figure includes an estimated 4 million undocumented aliens—immigrants who have entered the country illegally. Hispanic Americans represent about 8 per cent of the total U.S. population. Nearly 63 per cent of all Hispanics in the United States are Mexican Americans. Puerto Ricans make up about 12 per cent of the Hispanic population, and Cuban Americans account for about 5 per cent. People from Central America, South America, and Spain together make up about 20 per cent of the U.S. Hispanic population.

The various Hispanic groups in the United States have tended to maintain their separate identities over the years. Since the 1970's, however, efforts to unite Mexican Americans, Puerto Ricans, Cuban Americans, and other groups have gained increasing support. Such efforts often emphasize cultural similarities that date back hundreds of years.

The Spanish language and the Roman Catholic religion are among the oldest and most important cultural bonds that unite Hispanics. During Spain's colonial period, which lasted from the 1500's to the 1800's, Spanish missionaries and landowners spread their language and religion throughout the areas they controlled. As a result, nearly all Hispanic Americans can speak Spanish, and a large majority are Roman Catholics.

Hispanics in the United States today speak a variety of Spanish dialects, depending on their country or region

Ethnic background of Hispanic Americans

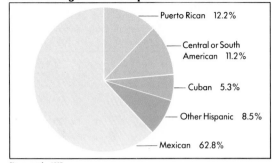

Figures are for 1987.
Source: Current Population Reports, U.S. Bureau of the Census.

of origin. But the speakers of one dialect can usually understand the speakers of another with no difficulty. Although some Hispanic Americans do not use Spanish at all, most continue to speak Spanish in their homes and teach the language to their children. Many adult immigrants have difficulty learning English, but their children usually grow up speaking both Spanish and English.

Another unifying element is the recognition of common problems. Those Hispanics who are not fluent in English face obstacles in schooling and employment. Moreover, some white, English-speaking Americans regard all Hispanics as one group—a group whose racial, linguistic, and social background is different from their own. Such perceptions have led to discrimination in housing and employment that affect all Hispanic-American groups and foster unity among them.

Within the Hispanic American minority, there are people of different national and racial origins. Physical appearances vary widely and often show the blending of European, American Indian, and African features that has occurred over many generations. Most Mexican Americans are *mestizos*—that is, they are of white and American Indian ancestry. Their white ancestors were mostly Spaniards who colonized what are now Mexico and the American Southwest. Their Indian ancestors were living in these regions when the Spaniards arrived. Many Puerto Ricans are of mixed Spanish and African descent, with their African ancestors having been brought over by the Spaniards to work as slaves. Other Puerto Ricans have some American Indian ancestry as well. Most Cuban Americans are of Spanish descent, though some blacks and *mulattoes* (people of mixed European and African ancestry) also emigrated from Cuba.

Where Hispanics live

About 90 per cent of Hispanic Americans live in urban areas, particularly in New York City, Los Angeles, Chicago, Miami, and numerous cities in the Southwest. About half of all Puerto Ricans living on the mainland live in New York City. The New York City area is also home to large groups of Hispanics from Colombia, Cuba, the Dominican Republic, and Ecuador. Chicago has large Mexican-American, Puerto Rican, and Cuban-American populations. Colombians and other South American groups have also settled in Chicago. Mexican Americans form the largest Hispanic group in most Southwestern cities, including Los Angeles and San Antonio. Los Angeles also has small Cuban, Guatemalan,

© Lee Foster, Bruce Coleman, Inc.

Spanish missions shaped colonial cultures by passing on the Spanish language and Roman Catholicism. San Diego de Alcala, *above,* the first mission in California, was established in 1769.

Where Hispanic Americans live

This map shows the state-by-state distribution of the U.S. Hispanic population according to the 1980 Census. Numbers on the map indicate the percentage of Hispanics in the total population of each state. The cities on the map have more than 100,000 Hispanic residents.

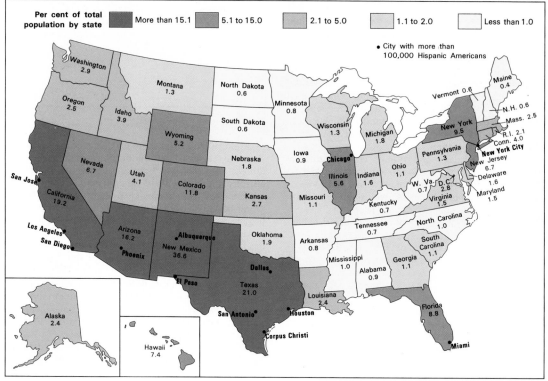

WORLD BOOK map; source: U.S. Bureau of the Census.

and Puerto Rican communities. Miami has the largest Cuban-American population of any U.S. city. Large numbers of Nicaraguan immigrants have also settled in Miami and other cities in southern Florida. Because of the overcrowded conditions and high unemployment many immigrants face in large cities, some recent Hispanic immigrants have settled in smaller cities, such as Boise, Idaho, and Yakima, Wash.

Cultural backgrounds

In Puerto Rico and Cuba, early Spanish settlers came into close contact with the Arawak Indians. At first, the Spaniards and the Arawaks enjoyed friendly relations. But as more Spaniards settled Puerto Rico and Cuba in the early 1500's, they took land from the Arawaks and forced the Indians to work for them. The Arawaks rebelled against this treatment, but their stone weapons were no match for the Spaniards' guns. Fighting, physical abuse, and disease began to take a heavy toll among the Indians. By the mid-1500's, almost all of the Arawaks in Puerto Rico and Cuba had died. See also **Arawak Indians.**

Soon after the first Spanish settlers arrived in the West Indies, they began to import black Africans to replace the rapidly dwindling Indian labor force. Although the hundreds of thousands of enslaved blacks brought to the Spanish colonies far outnumbered the Spaniards,

the conditions of slavery limited contact between Spaniards and Africans for many years. The blacks were able to maintain much of their own culture, including religions, folklore, and music. The Spanish colonists, meanwhile, carried on a fairly traditional way of life. Cities in Puerto Rico and Cuba resembled European cities in appearance. Spanish musicians performed the music of Spanish composers in concert halls and churches. The few artists working in the colonies also tended to imitate the European styles of the day.

Eventually, the Spanish and African influences began to blend in Puerto Rico and Cuba. The Spanish influences dominated in language, religion, and architecture. But although many blacks had been baptized as Christians, they combined Christian religious observances with their traditional ceremonies. They also identified some Christian saints with certain African deities.

Other aspects of African culture had a wider influence in Puerto Rico and Cuba. The music and dancing of the Africans became probably their best-known contribution to Latin-American culture. In addition, the blacks told traditional African tales that became part of the folklore of the islands.

Probably the most obvious aspect of cultural blending in the West Indies was the intermingling of the races. Many of the Spanish men took African mistresses or wives. Today, most Puerto Ricans have both Spanish

African influences helped create the distinctive sounds of Latin music. Many songs feature African rhythms, played on drums like the timbales, *center of photograph,* and the congas, *right of photograph.* Like the musicians shown at the left, many Latin music groups perform at festivals throughout the United States.

and African ancestry. Many Cubans also have a mixed racial ancestry.

In Mexico, the empire of the Aztec Indians covered large areas of central and southern Mexico by the early 1500's. The Aztec capital was Tenochtitlán, one of the most important centers of trade and religion in the Americas. With an estimated population of more than 100,000, Tenochtitlán was also one of the largest cities in the world at that time. See also **Aztec.**

Religion and war were the focal points of Aztec society. Much of the Aztec's art, music, and poetry was intended to glorify their many gods. To remain in favor with their gods, the Aztec practiced human sacrifice. They waged war almost constantly to obtain prisoners to be used as sacrifices.

A complex, highly organized society grew up around the Aztec's religion and military activities. A large government was needed to administer the empire. Laws were strictly enforced by a system of courts, and criminals were often punished harshly for even small crimes. The Aztec encouraged their children to develop a sense of social responsibility from an early age. All children were required to attend school, where they prepared to become priests, warriors, craftsmen, or householders.

Following the Spanish conquest of Mexico in 1521, the Spanish government moved quickly to establish political control of the new territory. It was the Roman Catholic clergy, however, that most effectively introduced Spanish culture among the Indians. Spanish priests and friars started missions where they instructed the Indians in Spanish, Roman Catholicism, and various practical crafts. The missions did not succeed in molding the Indians to live and work in a European society. But they did help start the process of *mestizaje,* the blending of Spanish and Indian cultures.

As in the West Indies, the language and religion of the Spaniards came to dominate. But like the Africans in Cuba and Puerto Rico, the Mexican Indians transformed many Spanish religious ceremonies. For example, Spanish priests used Christmas carols called *villancicos* and solemn pageants called *posadas* to teach the Indians about the events surrounding the birth of Jesus Christ. Over the years, Indian composers wrote many villancicos about nonreligious subjects. The Indians also turned the posadas into festive processions that took place in people's homes rather than in church.

In the arts, the talents of Indian sculptors, craftsmen, and musicians were recognized by the Spaniards. Indian wood and stone carvings decorated many buildings that otherwise were of traditional Spanish design. New kinds of music were produced by musicians who combined

Indian influences can be seen in the foods of Mexican Americans. These women are making *tortillas,* thin flour or corn meal pancakes used in many traditional dishes.

the sounds of European and Indian instruments.

The Spaniards brought many technological improvements to Mexico. European farming methods and equipment generally brought better harvests than did Indian methods. But in some cases—the cultivation of corn, for example—the Spaniards adopted Indian techniques.

Racial intermixing took place in Mexico, as it did in the West Indies. But in Mexico, the intermingling occurred mainly among Spanish men and Indian women. The children of Spanish and Indian parentage became the mestizos, who today are the largest racial group among Mexicans and Mexican Americans.

Hispanic influences on American culture

Hispanics in the United States share many of the traditional values claimed by most Americans. They place high value on their families and on success through hard work. They are also proud of their Latin-American heritage. Many Hispanic Americans feel that they should not lose contact with their cultures or their language. Instead, they seek to be bicultural and bilingual. Many hope that their cultures will someday be accepted as being part of American culture.

Although many people consider them a single group, Hispanic Americans represent a rich variety of cultures. A single, common Hispanic culture does not exist. There are, however, important similarities among Hispanic groups, who together strongly influence U.S. culture.

Food is one area in which Hispanic influences are readily apparent in the United States. Mexican foods have become especially popular. The *taco,* a folded tortilla filled with meat, cheese, and other ingredients, is as common in some areas as hamburgers and hot dogs. Other Mexican dishes, such as *enchiladas, tamales,* and *tostadas,* are also served in restaurants throughout the United States.

Entertainment and arts. Since the 1940's, the music and dances of Latin America have also "crossed over" into American culture. Mexican mariachi bands—small ensembles usually consisting of violins, guitars, and trumpets—have long enjoyed popularity in the United States. Dances and dance music from the Caribbean islands, especially Cuba, were first performed in American ballrooms in the late 1800's. Some popular Cuban dances have included the bomba, the cha-cha, the conga, the mambo, the rumba, and salsa. Much of the music and dancing was derived from the culture of African slaves who worked on West Indian sugar plantations from the early 1500's to the 1800's. The music has strong, *syncopated* (irregularly accented) rhythms. It features instruments of African and American Indian origin, including conga drums, claves, güiros, maracas, and marimbas.

Latin-American music has long been an important influence on the popular music of the United States. Since the 1950's, a number of Hispanic-American rock music performers have gained widespread popularity, including Richie Valens, Carlos Santana, Gloria Estefan, and the group Los Lobos. Traditional Latin music has also attracted a large audience in the United States. One of the most popular performers of traditional Latin music is Celia Cruz. Known as *la Reina de la Salsa* (the Queen of Salsa), Cruz has performed for more than 40 years in both Cuba and the United States.

A number of painters and writers have sought to capture the Hispanic American experience. Important Hispanic artists include John Valadez, Martin Ramirez, Frank Romero, and Arnaldo Roche. Tomas Rivera, Luis Valdez, and Heberto Padilla rank among the many Hispanic writers who have won distinction. Other major Hispanic American figures in the arts include architect Bernardo Fort-Brescia and fashion designers Adolfo and Oscar de la Renta.

Like other minority groups, Hispanic Americans have often been portrayed as stereotypes on radio and television and in movies and advertisements. Since the 1960's, however, TV shows, movies, and plays that dealt more realistically with Hispanic characters have appealed to both Hispanic and non-Hispanic audiences. Hispanic-American actors are now able to play roles that previously would have been reserved for *Anglo* (English-speaking) actors. Successful Hispanic-American actors and actresses include José Ferrer, Raul Julia, Rita Moreno, and Anthony Quinn.

Chris Gulker

Roosters, a play by Milcha Sanchez-Scott, combines realism and fantasy in its portrayal of the life of a Hispanic farmworker. Like many plays written by Hispanic Americans, *Roosters* deals with problems that confront the Hispanic community.

Here are your

1990 *Year Book*
Cross-Reference Tabs

For insertion in your *World Book*

Each year, *The World Book Year Book* adds a valuable dimension to your *World Book* set. The Cross-Reference Tab System is designed especially to help youngsters and parents alike link *The Year Book*'s new and revised *World Book* articles, its Special Reports, and its Close-Ups to the related *World Book* articles they update.

How to use these Tabs

First, remove this page from *The Year Book*. The top Tab on this page is ANTARCTICA. Turn to the A volume of your *World Book* and find the page with the ANTARCTICA article on it. Affix the ANTARCTICA Tab to that page. Note that the HISPANIC AMERICANS Tab should go on a *World Book* page where there is no such article, but only a one-line dummy entry. Put this Tab on that page.

Put all of your Tabs in your *World Book* volumes, and your new *Year Book* will be linked to your encyclopedia set.

© John Running, After Image

Cinco de Mayo (May 5) is a national holiday in Mexico. Many Mexican Americans, like these dancers, take part in colorful Cinco de Mayo festivals, especially in the Southwest.

Sports. Many Hispanics share in the American enthusiasm for sports, and a number of Hispanic athletes have become professional sports stars. Well-known Hispanic-American athletes include baseball greats Roberto Clemente, Jose Canseco, and Fernando Valenzuela; golfers Nancy Lopez and Lee Trevino; and jockeys Angel Cordero and Jorge Velasquez.

Holidays. Many Hispanic Americans observe the major holidays of their homelands in addition to U.S. holidays. Mexican Americans celebrate the anniversary of Mexico's independence from Spain on September 16. Cinco de Mayo, which commemorates Mexico's victory over an invading French army on May 5, 1862, is also a day of celebration among Mexican Americans. Puerto Ricans observe Constitution Day on July 25, the date on which Puerto Rico's constitution became effective in 1952. Cuban Americans celebrate Cuban Independence

© Herbert Eisenberg, Shostal

The annual Puerto Rican Day parade in New York City features music and dancing as well as performers in traditional costumes of Puerto Rico and the countries of Latin America.

© Joe Viesti

Las posadas (the inns), a Mexican Christmas festival, is celebrated in San Antonio, *left,* and other U.S. cities with large Mexican-American populations. Each night from December 16 through Christmas Eve, people take part in processions that represent Mary and Joseph's search for lodgings in Bethlehem on the first Christmas Eve. The people carry candles or lanterns and sing special posada songs.

Day on May 20, the date Cuba gained its independence from Spain in 1898.

The United States observes National Hispanic Heritage Month each year from September 15 to October 15, when many Latin-American countries celebrate their independence. Besides Mexico, these countries include Costa Rica, El Salvador, Guatemala, Honduras, and Nicaragua.

Some cities with large Hispanic communities hold annual festivals featuring the arts and crafts, food, and music and dancing of Latin America. These festivals include Miami's nine-day Calle Ocho, held in March of each year, and the Fiesta de la Primavera, held in San Diego in May. Other Hispanic festivals are held at Christmas and Easter and on other religious holidays. One of the largest of these festivals is the nine-day Mexican Christmas festival of *las posadas,* which features songs and processions commemorating Mary and Joseph's search for an inn in Bethlehem.

The history of Hispanic-American immigration

Exploration and settlement. The Hispanic presence in what is now the United States actually began before the country existed. Spanish explorers established colonies in what would become the Southeast and Southwest regions of the United States.

In the Southeast. In 1513, the explorer Juan Ponce de León sailed from Puerto Rico to the east coast of Florida. He claimed the peninsula, which he thought was an island, for Spain, thus becoming one of the first explorers to stake a Spanish claim in North America.

In 1526, a colonizing force under the leadership of Lucas Vásquez de Ayllón, a Spanish nobleman, founded a settlement at the mouth of the Waccamaw River in South Carolina. This colony, named San Miguel de Gualdape, was the first European settlement in the present-day United States. Before the end of the year, malaria and other diseases killed about two-thirds of the original population of 600, including Ayllón. The remaining settlers returned to the West Indies in early 1527.

The Spaniards did not establish a permanent settle-

ment in the Southeast until 1565. In that year, the Spanish explorer Pedro Menéndez de Avilés founded St. Augustine in Florida. This was the first permanent European settlement in what would become the United States. It predated Jamestown—the first permanent British settlement in North America—by more than 40 years. St. Augustine served as Spain's military headquarters in North America during the 1500's.

Florida remained under Spanish control until 1763, at which time Spain was forced to give the territory to Britain. Spain regained Florida in 1783, but problems soon broke out between the Spanish colony and the new United States. American settlers moved into Florida, and the U.S. government sought to purchase the territory from Spain. In 1821, Florida came under United States control, and thousands of Americans poured into the territory. Soon the Spanish presence in Florida was overwhelmed by the tide of English-speaking settlers.

In the Southwest. To the west, the desire for wealth and fame led the Spaniards to expand their claims in Mexico. In 1540, the explorer Francisco Vásquez de Coronado set out to conquer the legendary Seven Cities of Cibola, which were said to lie north of Mexico. Coronado and his men explored areas of present-day New Mexico, Arizona, Texas, Oklahoma, and Kansas in the hope of finding the great riches they had heard described. The expedition returned to Mexico in 1542. No gold had been found, but Coronado had claimed a vast area of the North American continent for Spain. The area was given the name New Mexico. See also **Cibola, Seven Cities of; Coronado, Francisco Vásquez de.**

In 1598, the first Spanish settlers arrived in New Mexico to begin missionary work among the Pueblo Indians. The settlers established Santa Fe, the capital of New Mexico, in 1609 or 1610. The Spaniards treated the Indians harshly, and in 1680 the Pueblos revolted. The Indians killed about 400 Spaniards and captured Santa Fe. The Spaniards did not retake Santa Fe until 1692.

The Spanish settlement of Texas began in 1682, when two missions were built by Franciscan friars. By 1731, the Spaniards had established missions throughout cen-

University of South Florida Archives

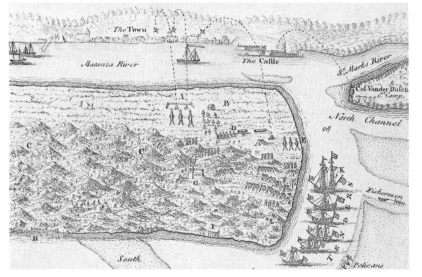

St. Augustine was the first permanent European settlement in the United States. It was founded in 1565 to secure Spanish claims in Florida. This engraving shows the town and its fortress, *top,* under attack by British forces encamped on Anastasia Island, *center.* The engraving dates from 1740, 23 years before the British gained control of Florida. The region became a U.S. territory in 1821.

The Mexican War resulted from disputes between Mexico and the United States over control of Mexico's northern territories. In one of the final battles of the war, attacking American troops, *above,* defeated a much larger Mexican force at Churubusco, near Mexico City, on Aug. 20, 1847. On Sept. 14, 1847, Mexico surrendered. During the peace negotiations following the war, the United States acquired the vast territories that now include California, Nevada, Utah, and parts of four other states.

Culver

tral, east, and southwest Texas. But Spanish colonization of Texas proceeded slowly. By 1793, the territory had only about 7,000 white settlers.

California also was part of the Spanish Empire in the New World. First settled by the Spaniards in 1769, California remained sparsely populated for many years. By the 1820's, Franciscan friars had established 21 missions in California. The Spanish governors had also built a number of *presidios* (forts) in California.

During the early 1800's, the westward expansion of the United States alarmed the Spanish colonial governors. These officials restricted trade between the United States and the northern colonial provinces of New Mexico, Texas, and California. By so doing, they hoped to avoid a heavy flow of American settlers into the sparsely populated colonies.

In 1821, Mexico gained its independence from Spain. The new nation included the northern provinces as well as present-day Mexico. Soon, free trade with the United States was established in New Mexico. The government of the Republic of Mexico tried to regulate U.S. trade in New Mexico, which led to increasing resistance among the New Mexicans, many of whom did not feel especially loyal to Mexico.

Mexicans living in California, called *Californios,* also opened free trade with the United States and other countries. The Mexican government broke up the missions and gave or sold huge tracts of ranch lands to private individuals. As a result, a small group of several hundred Mexican landowners became very wealthy. But most Californios, like the majority of settlers throughout Mexico's northern territories, remained poor.

The abundant resources of California attracted many American settlers in the 1830's and 1840's. The United States was already considering ways of acquiring California as a territory. The Californios enjoyed the benefits of their trade with the United States and saw advantages to becoming a U.S. territory. The Mexican government neglected its northern territories, and many Californios

resented the interference of government officials from Mexico City.

Texas had by far the smallest population of any of the northern Mexican territories, and the Mexican government's hold on Texas was weak. In January 1821, American merchant Moses Austin received permission from Spanish authorities in Mexico to settle 300 Americans in Texas. The project eventually passed into the hands of Austin's son, Stephen Fuller Austin. Instead of being limited to 300 settlers, however, the American settlement of Texas swelled to thousands of people. In 1836, Texas won its independence from Mexico and became a republic. See **Texas** (History).

Conflict. In 1845, the United States annexed Texas. In response, the Mexican government broke off relations with the United States. Texas claimed territory as far south as the Rio Grande, but Mexico disputed the claim, saying that Texas' southwest border was the Nueces River. These and other events led to the Mexican War (1846-1848) between the United States and Mexico. The United States won the war. The Treaty of Guadalupe Hidalgo, which ended the war, awarded the United States the territory that now makes up the states of California, Nevada, Utah, most of New Mexico and Arizona, and part of Colorado and Wyoming. This vast area was home to approximately 80,000 Mexicans, most of whom were granted U.S. citizenship. See also **Mexican War.**

The original draft of the Treaty of Guadalupe Hidalgo stated that the United States would honor any land grants that had been made by the government of Mexico. However, this provision was deleted in the U.S. government's revision of the treaty. Mexican officials protested this change. At the signing of the treaty, the U.S. representatives also signed the Protocol of Querétaro, which stated that the U.S. government's changes in the original treaty did not invalidate the civil, political, and religious guarantees that the treaty had extended to Mexican residents of the new U.S. territories. The U.S. government, however, did not ratify the Protocol of

Querétaro, claiming that its representatives at the treaty signing did not have the authority to sign the protocol. Mexico's government also failed to ratify the protocol.

Many of the new Hispanic Americans were living on land that had been granted to them by the Mexican government. For many years after the war, Mexican-American landowners in the Southwest were able to maintain their claims. But as more and more Anglo settlers came in search of land on which to raise crops and livestock, the demand for land soared. Mexican-American landowners had to legally confirm their claims. The process was so lengthy and expensive that many were forced to take out large loans to pay court costs. They often sold large tracts of their land in order to pay off their loans. Many Mexican Americans were unable to communicate with the English-speaking judges and did not understand the U.S. court system. As a result, they were often cheated out of their legitimate claims to the land.

By the late 1800's, most Mexican Americans had become tenants or workers on land that belonged to Anglo Americans. The two groups lived apart in towns and cities, and each had its own schools, stores, and places of entertainment. The Mexican Americans called their sections *barrios,* the Spanish word for *neighborhoods.*

During this period, the immigration of Mexicans to the United States was relatively small. Jobs on large cattle, sheep, cotton, and vegetable farms attracted some Mexicans to Texas. But the great period of Mexican-American immigration was yet to come.

The early 1900's. In 1900, the total Mexican-American population was estimated to be between 380,000 and 560,000. The early 1900's saw a sharp increase in the number of Mexican immigrants as economic conditions in Mexico worsened. In 1910, the Mexican Revolution broke out. This conflict plummeted Mexico into years of political and economic chaos. The revolution also sparked a tremendous wave of immigration that continued until the 1930's.

Between 1910 and 1930, more than 680,000 Mexicans came to live in the United States. During the 1920's, Mexicans accounted for more than 10 per cent of all immigration to the United States. Most Mexicans fleeing the Mexican Revolution settled in the Southwest, where they took jobs in factories and mines or on railroads, farms, and ranches.

In 1917, the United States entered World War I (1914-1918), and thousands of Mexican Americans volunteered for service in the U.S. armed forces. The wartime economy also provided new opportunities for Mexican Americans. Some were able to move into better-paying, skilled occupations in construction and in the war industries.

Despite these gains, Mexican Americans continued to suffer discrimination in jobs, wages, and housing. To fight these conditions, they organized labor unions and took part in strikes to obtain higher wages and better working conditions. Mexican Americans also formed civic groups to deal with their problems. In 1929, the major groups merged to form the League of United Latin American Citizens (LULAC).

Immigration restrictions and growing discrimination. In 1917, the United States passed a law requiring all adult immigrants to be able to read and write at least one language. In 1924, the U.S. Bureau of Immigration established the Border Patrol to control illegal immigration across the Mexican-U.S. border. Strict enforcement of the 1917 adult literacy law led to a decline in Mexican immigration in the late 1920's. This decline continued through the Great Depression—the economic hard times of the 1930's—when only about 33,000 Mexicans entered the United States.

The 1930's brought heightened discrimination against Mexican Americans. Many people viewed them as a drain on the American economy because they held many low-paying jobs while other, "true" Americans went unemployed. In response to such angry views, the U.S. and Mexican governments cosponsored a *repatriation program* that returned thousands of Mexican immigrants to Mexico.

The program was intended to encourage people to return voluntarily to Mexico, but thousands were deported against their wishes. Many of these immigrants had lived in the United States for more than 10 years. Their American-born children were U.S. citizens. In some cases, adults who were deported were U.S. citizens who were mistakenly or intentionally forced to leave their country. In California especially, many Mexican Americans were placed in detention camps, where they were mistreated by government officials. Of the approximately 3 million people of Mexican descent living in the United States in 1930, about 500,000 had been repatriated by 1939. The repatriation program created much anger and resentment among Mexican Americans. Family relationships were often strained because young people who had been born in the United States did not want to go to Mexico.

In addition to the humiliation of repatriation, Mexican Americans suffered other forms of discrimination. Many restaurants refused to serve Mexican Americans. Public swimming pools, rest rooms, drinking fountains, and theaters were often segregated. Mexican-American schoolchildren were often forbidden to speak Spanish in schools and were sometimes punished severely for doing so.

Effects of World War II. During World War II (1939-1945), more than 300,000 Mexican Americans served in the U.S. armed forces. Their courage and determination helped them earn proportionally more military honors than any other ethnic group. Many Mexican-American veterans returned from the war with new-found skills. Unwilling to go back to living with the pressures and barriers of discrimination, they formed a number of social, political, and service organizations, including the Mexican American Political Association (MAPA) and the American G.I. Forum. Such organizations have helped Mexican Americans fight poverty, lack of education, and discrimination.

World War II had renewed the demand for immigrant labor. In 1942, the U.S. and Mexican governments developed the bracero program. Under the program, Mexican *braceros* (day laborers) could enter the United States legally for seasonal agricultural work and for work on U.S. railroads. Bracero programs were in effect from 1942 to 1947 and from 1951 to 1964. The programs provided almost 5 million Mexicans with temporary work in the United States. The braceros often worked under harsh conditions for unsympathetic employers, but they took the work because they were unable to find jobs in Mexico.

Growing numbers of newcomers. The mid-1900's saw a great influx of Hispanic people into the United States. These new arrivals included not only Mexicans, but large numbers of Puerto Ricans and Cubans, too.

Mexican immigration to the United States—both legal and illegal—climbed steeply during the 1950's. The U.S. government developed a program to curb illegal immigration. The program was highly publicized in order to encourage undocumented immigrants to leave voluntarily. It resulted in the deportation of a total of 3.8 million undocumented immigrants. It did little, however, to control illegal immigration, which continued to increase from the 1960's through the 1980's.

Puerto Rican migration. The mid-1900's also brought the first great wave of people from Puerto Rico. This island had been a U.S. possession since 1898, and its people had been U.S. citizens since 1917. As citizens, Puerto Ricans may enter the United States without restriction. Between 1940 and 1960, more than 545,000 Puerto Ricans came to the U.S. mainland to look for jobs. By 1960, almost 70 per cent of Puerto Ricans living on the mainland had settled in East Harlem in New York City. New York City has continued to have the largest Puerto Rican population of any mainland U.S. city, with about half of all Puerto Ricans on the mainland living in the city.

For many years, Puerto Ricans have remained one of the poorest groups in the United States. Unemployment among Puerto Ricans is about 50 per cent higher than it is among the general population. The poverty rate among Puerto Ricans is almost four times that of the general population.

Cuban immigration to the United States picked up sharply during the late 1950's, as a result of increasing political turmoil in Cuba. Until the mid-1950's, only a few thousand Cubans came to the United States each year. But during the late 1950's and early 1960's, the number of Cuban immigrants increased dramatically. In 1959, Cuban revolutionary Fidel Castro came to power. He announced the restructuring of Cuban society. Many

Photoworld from FPG

Hundreds of thousands of Puerto Ricans, such as this family, came to the U.S. mainland between 1940 and 1960 to find jobs.

middle- and upper-class Cubans found Castro's plans threatening to their way of life. Between 1959 and late 1962, about 200,000 anti-Castro Cubans immigrated to the United States.

In October 1962, commercial air flights between Cuba and the United States were suspended. Nonetheless, about 50,000 Cubans entered the United States between late 1962 and 1965. Many sailed secretly from Cuba in small boats, some of which were apprehended by the Cuban navy before they reached the United States. In 1965, the U.S and Cuban governments agreed to set up an airlift between Cuba and Miami. The airlift brought about 250,000 Cubans into the United States between 1966 and 1973.

Up through the early 1970's, the United States wel-

UPI/Bettmann Newsphotos

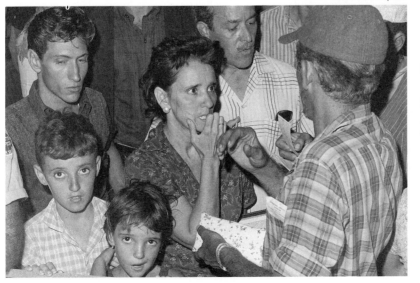

Many Cubans fled to the United States following the 1959 take-over of the Cuban government by Fidel Castro. This anxious Cuban family is shown on arrival in Miami in August 1963—hours after they had escaped capture by a Cuban navy patrol in the Bahamas.

comed Cuban immigrants as victims of an oppressive regime. Many of the first Cubans to flee Castro's dictatorship in the early 1960's were from wealthy families and were well educated. The U.S. government granted asylum to these people and offered federal help to qualified applicants in finding homes and in making job contacts. Most later Cuban immigrants were relatives of the first group or were poor people looking for work.

The last major influx of Cuban immigrants was the arrival in 1980 of the *Marielitos*. Numbering about 125,000, the Marielitos were a large group that the Cuban government wanted out of Cuba. They included many unskilled workers, criminals, and mentally ill people. These people were put aboard boats at the Cuban port of Mariel and sent to Miami. The U.S. government allowed the Marielitos to enter the United States, though U.S. officials had not expected such large numbers of people and were at first unaware of the presence of criminals on board the boats. Some of the criminals were placed in U.S. prisons. Many of them were rehabilitated and released. A few were returned to Cuba.

Miami has the largest Cuban-American population of any U.S. city. Large numbers of Cuban Americans also live in suburban towns outside Miami and in Tampa, on Florida's west coast. About 80 per cent of all Hispanics in southern Florida are Cubans. Although the Little Havana section of Miami remains the center of the Cuban-American population, many Cubans have now moved into the city's more affluent neighborhoods. Some of Miami's most successful businesses are owned and operated by Cuban Americans. In addition to Miami and other Flor-

ida cities, there are significant Cuban populations in New York City; Jersey City and Newark, N.J.; Los Angeles; and Chicago.

Cuban Americans face many of the same problems that trouble other minority groups, though to a lesser degree. In the 1980's, the level of educational achievement among Cuban Americans matched the national average. Their unemployment rate and poverty rate are much lower than those of other Hispanic groups.

Recent Hispanic immigrants. People from Latin-American countries continue to immigrate in large numbers to the United States. In the 1980's alone, Hispanics accounted for more than a third of all legal immigration to the United States. For many, the United States represents opportunities unavailable in their homelands. Most desire to work hard in order to improve the lives of their families.

Since the 1970's, large numbers of Hispanic immigrants have come from war-torn countries in Central America, including El Salvador and Nicaragua. Many of these immigrants are children and teen-agers whose parents have been killed or have disappeared. Some U.S. citizens feel that Central Americans fleeing military conflict should be granted political asylum in the United States. However, the U.S. government has maintained that most of these immigrants are motivated by economic, not political, concerns. Therefore, they are not entitled to the special treatment given political refugees under U.S. immigration law. Many of the immigrants from Central America have been placed in large detention camps until they can be relocated or returned to their homelands.

Hispanic Americans today

The fastest-growing minority. A high rate of immigration and a high birth rate have combined to make Hispanic Americans the fastest-growing minority group in the United States. Between 1980 and 1990, the Hispanic population of the United States increased five times faster than the total population. Many experts predict that Hispanics will be the nation's largest minority group by the mid-2020's.

As a group, Hispanic Americans are generally younger than non-Hispanics. In the late 1980's, a large percentage of the Hispanic population was just entering the childbearing years. During the 1980's, Hispanics accounted for more than 10 per cent of all births in the United States, even though they made up only about 8 per cent of the total U.S. population.

Some non-Hispanics in the United States fear that the country's rapidly growing Hispanic population will not adopt the language, customs, and viewpoint of the dominant, English-speaking culture. Some of these people fear that their way of life will be replaced by the "foreign ways" of Hispanic Americans. Others worry that a large Spanish-speaking minority will become a permanent underclass, locked out of economic advancement by a lack of fluency in English. Many historians and sociologists discount such fears. They point to the many immigrant groups that have become part of American culture. They also note that except for recent immigrants, most Hispanic Americans can speak English.

© Bill Gentile, Picture Group

Military conflicts in Central America have caused many people to seek refuge in the United States. In Nicaragua, fighting between rebel *contras, above,* and government troops in the 1980's resulted in thousands of deaths and left many homeless.

Nevertheless, language has become an increasingly controversial issue in some states with large Spanish-

© Eric Carle, Bruce Coleman, Inc.

Signs in Spanish and English are common in areas with large Hispanic-American populations. Bilingual public signs and documents have become controversial in some places, and several states have passed laws making English their official language.

speaking populations. In 1988, the state legislatures of Arizona, Colorado, and Florida passed laws making English the states' official language. Fourteen other states already had similar laws. Some people support the passage of an amendment to the U.S. Constitution that would make English the official language of the United States.

An increased demand among Hispanic Americans for Spanish-language media led to the development of two national Spanish-language television networks. In addition, more than 200 U.S. radio stations broadcast in Spanish in the 1980's—almost four times the number of Spanish-language stations in operation during the 1960's. The number of Hispanic newspapers, magazines, and journals published in the United States also increased dramatically.

Political developments. Although Hispanic Americans are the fastest-growing minority group in the country, their political influence has increased at a much slower pace. Until the 1960's, discrimination at the polls discouraged many Hispanics from registering to vote. Some states required the payment of a *poll tax* before a person was allowed to vote. The tax was intended to keep Hispanics, blacks, and other minorities—many of whom were too poor to afford the tax—from voting. In areas with large Hispanic populations, voting district boundaries were often drawn to scatter the Hispanic voters over several districts. This practice, called *gerrymandering,* held down the percentage of Hispanic voters within any one district.

Expanding influence. During the 1960's, four Mexican Americans won election to Congress and became champions of civil rights. They were Senator Joseph Montoya of New Mexico and Representatives Eligio de la Garza and Henry B. Gonzalez of Texas and Edward R. Roybal of California. In 1965, Congress enacted the Voting Rights Act, which outlawed the poll tax.

President Lyndon B. Johnson appointed several Hispanics to high government posts in the 1960's. For example, Vicente T. Ximenes became chairman of the President's Cabinet Committee on Mexican-American Affairs. Johnson made Hector P. García a member of the U.S. delegation to the United Nations and appointed Raul H. Castro U.S. ambassador to El Salvador.

The Chicano movement. In spite of the success of a growing number of Hispanic Americans, many others became increasingly resentful about their unsolved problems. Among Mexican Americans in particular, such feelings found expression in the Chicano, or "brown power," movement. In Mexico, *Chicano* is a mocking slang expression for a clumsy person. Mexican Americans used the term in jest during the 1950's when referring to one another. But in the 1960's, many young Mexican Americans gave the term a positive meaning that suggested racial and cultural pride.

Mural by Wayne Healy; Ramona Housing Projects, Los Angeles (photograph © Danny Lehman, After Image)

Ghosts of the Barrio, a mural on a building in East Los Angeles, honors the heritage of Mexican Americans by including historical figures in a modern scene. An Indian warrior and a Spanish conquistador appear in the right of the mural, and a Mexican revolutionary stands at the left. Murals that celebrate Hispanic-American ethnic pride, cultural history, and individual achievement are common in East Los Angeles.

Labor leader Cesar Chavez has worked to improve the lot of his fellow Mexican Americans since the early 1960's. He is shown here receiving Communion after ending a hunger strike in the summer of 1988. Chavez had gone on the hunger strike to protest the use of suspected cancer-causing pesticides by California table grape growers. The chemicals posed a potential danger to migrant farmworkers—most of whom are Mexican Americans.

© Jim Caccavo, Picture Group

One of the foremost Hispanic Americans to reflect this new ethnic pride was Cesar Chavez, a labor leader who began to organize California grape pickers in 1962. In 1963, Reies López Tijerina founded the Alianza Federal de Mercedes (Federal Alliance of Land Grants) in New Mexico. This group fought to win compensation for descendants of families whose lands had been seized illegally. Another leader was Rodolfo Gonzales, who founded the Crusade for Justice in Denver in 1965. This group worked to provide social services and to develop job opportunities for Mexican Americans. In 1970, José Angel Gutiérrez helped establish La Raza Unida, a political party based in Texas. He later became school board president in Crystal City, Tex.

Despite these events, many Hispanics still felt excluded from the political process. Voter registration continued to lag because of the widespread belief among Hispanics that voting could not effectively change their lives.

During the 1980's, Hispanic attitudes toward politics began to change. Voter registration drives added hundreds of thousands of Hispanics to the rolls. Political activists challenged gerrymandering in a number of lawsuits. The federal courts agreed that voting district boundaries had been purposely drawn to split up Hispanic communities. The courts ordered that the district lines be redrawn to better represent established communities. With the new boundaries in place, more candidates supported by Hispanics were elected to office.

In 1980, there were only six Hispanic Americans serving in the U.S. Congress. By 1990, the number of Hispanics in Congress had doubled. The 1980's also saw the election of hundreds of Hispanic Americans as state officials, mayors, county and municipal officials, and school board members. These officials included former Miami mayor Maurice Ferre, of Puerto Rican descent, the first Hispanic mayor of a large U.S. city; former mayor of San Antonio Henry G. Cisneros, the first Mexican-American mayor of a major U.S. city; Xavier Suarez, Miami's first Cuban-born mayor; Mayor Federico Pena of Denver; and Governor Bob Martinez of Florida. Despite these gains, however, Hispanic Americans still accounted for less than 1 per cent of U.S. elected officials in the late 1980's.

In 1988, Lauro Cavazos became the first Hispanic Cabinet member when President Ronald Reagan appointed him secretary of education. Reagan's successor, President George Bush, kept Cavazos in this post. Other presidential appointments during the 1980's included Katherine Ortega, U.S. treasurer under Reagan; Catalina Villapando, U.S. treasurer under Bush; and Manuel Lujan, secretary of the interior under Bush.

Education. For many years, the educational achievements of most Hispanic-American students have not equaled those of non-Hispanic students. During the 1980's, Hispanic Americans made slight gains in education. In 1980, only 45 per cent of Hispanics age 25 and older were high school graduates. By 1989, 51 per cent of Hispanics age 25 and older had graduated from high school. Despite this modest increase, the dropout rate among Hispanic students remained almost double that of non-Hispanic students.

The number of Hispanic Americans age 25 and older who completed four or more years of college also rose

© Levenson, Gamma/Liaison

Increased voter participation among Hispanic Americans has helped them make important political gains. This man is casting his ballot in an election in California.

UPI/Bettmann Newsphotos

Lauro Cavazos, at the left, became secretary of education—and the first Hispanic Cabinet member—in 1988.

© José Azel, Contact/Woodfin Camp, Inc.

Katherine Ortega, shown here addressing the 1984 Republican National Convention, became U.S. treasurer in 1983.

slightly in the 1980's. Still, fewer than 10 per cent of Hispanic Americans are college graduates, compared with more than 20 per cent of other Americans. With more and more jobs requiring a college degree, Hispanic business and education leaders are especially concerned about high dropout rates and low college attendance among Hispanic young people.

According to several studies, discrimination continued to plague many Hispanic-American students in the 1980's. Studies showed that Hispanic students were often assigned to classes for low achievers, forced to repeat grades, or classified as mentally handicapped because they did not speak English well or because of other cultural differences. Segregation of Hispanic students became more common, with more Hispanic students attending segregated schools in the late 1980's than in the late 1960's.

One of the earliest programs designed to improve public education for Hispanic students was bilingual education. Since 1968, the U.S. government has funded bilingual programs for students who do not speak English

as their first language. In most bilingual programs serving Hispanics, students are taught in Spanish in such basic subjects as mathematics and science. Meanwhile, they study English as a second language. When they are ready, they transfer to classes taught only in English. The goal is to prevent students from falling behind in basic subjects while they master English.

Since it began, bilingual education has been highly controversial. Critics voice concern that bilingual programs do not help students learn English thoroughly, or that the programs encourage students to rely too much on Spanish. Studies of the effectiveness of bilingual education have reported conflicting results.

Hispanic leaders support the hiring of more Hispanic teachers for Spanish-speaking students. Such teachers tend to be more sensitive to the linguistic and cultural background of Hispanic students. Leaders also call for improvements in English-language courses and counseling services for Hispanic students. Some schools have developed dropout prevention programs, career guidance programs, and multicultural education pro-

© Bob Roha, Jr., Gamma/Liaison

Bilingual education programs are designed to help students who speak little or no English keep up in other subjects while they learn the language. In the bilingual class at the left, Hispanic students are taught math and science in Spanish, and they study English as a second language. When the students can readily speak and understand English, they transfer to all English-speaking classes.

grams aimed at providing better educational opportunities for Hispanic students.

Many educators believe that more funding for school loans and more flexible college admissions requirements are needed to raise college attendance levels among Hispanics. College scholarships are offered by several Hispanic-American organizations, including the American G.I. Forum, the League of United Latin American Citizens, the Mexican American Legal Defense and Education Fund, and the National Council of La Raza.

Employment. Low education levels, poor English skills, discrimination, and the continued immigration of unskilled workers have contributed to high unemployment among Hispanic Americans. Since the early 1970's, the unemployment rate among Hispanics has been about 50 per cent higher than among non-Hispanics. The median income of Hispanics has also been consistently lower than that of non-Hispanics.

Throughout the 1980's, 25 per cent of Hispanic families lived in poverty, while 10 per cent of non-Hispanic families were impoverished. Public funding to help the poor find jobs was cut during the 1980's, worsening employment problems in the Hispanic community.

Although Hispanic Americans experienced many economic problems in the 1980's, the number of Hispanic-owned businesses increased during the period. By the end of the decade, Hispanic-owned companies represented about 2 per cent of all U.S. firms.

Immigration. Immigration rates among Hispanic groups in the United States have varied widely. Emigration from Mexico has remained steady since the 1950's. In the 1980's, Mexicans continued to form the largest group of legal immigrants to the United States. Unknown thousands of Mexicans also enter the United States illegally each year. An estimated 4 million undocumented Mexican immigrants were living illegally in the United States in the late 1980's.

© Stephanie Maze, Woodfin Camp, Inc.

Extreme poverty in some areas of Mexico, including these slums outside Mexico City, has led many Mexicans to continue to seek employment opportunities in the United States.

The migration from Puerto Rico reached its height in the 1940's and 1950's. Still many Puerto Ricans come to the U.S. mainland each year to look for jobs or to settle near relatives.

Cuban immigration has dropped dramatically from the levels of the 1960's and 1970's. In 1986, President Reagan announced that only long-term political prisoners in Cuba and close relatives of Cuban Americans would be allowed to enter the United States. He also stated that U.S. visas would no longer be granted to Cubans seeking to enter the United States from other countries.

During the 1980's, Congress struggled to find a way to stop the flow of thousands of people who enter the country illegally each year. After years of study and debate, Congress finally passed the Immigration Reform and Control Act of 1986, which became effective in 1987. The act was one of the most sweeping efforts to halt illegal immigration in U.S. history.

Unlike the repatriation programs of the 1930's and 1950's, the new law did not call for mass deportations. Instead, it offered legal status to undocumented immigrants who had lived continuously in the United States since before Jan. 1, 1982. The law enabled 3.1 million previously illegal immigrants—most of them Hispanics—to obtain legal status. It also allowed temporary agricultural workers to enter the United States during harvest season. The law also imposed penalties on employers who knowingly hired undocumented immigrants. Several studies have shown, however, that many employers find the law difficult to understand and even harder to apply. Some people questioned the effectiveness of the act, pointing out that it even may have encouraged the unlawful entry of relatives of those who obtained legal status.   Manuel P. Galvan

Related articles in *World Book* include:

Biographies

Baca, Elfego	Gonzales, Rodolfo
Bañuelos, Ramona Acosta	Gutiérrez, José Angel
Castro, Raul Hector	Hidalgo y Costilla, Miguel
Cavazos, Lauro	Kino, Eusebio
Chavez, Cesar E.	Montezuma
Cisneros, Henry G.	Murieta, Joaquín
Clemente, Roberto	Ponce de León, Juan
Cortés, Hernando	Popé
Cortina, Juan Nepomuceno	Sánchez, George Isidore
Cuauhtémoc	Serra, Junípero
Galarza, Ernesto	Trevino, Lee
Gamio, Manuel	

History

Gadsden Purchase	Mexican War
Guadalupe Hidalgo, Treaty of	Mission life in America
Indian wars (The Pueblo Revolt, 1680-1692)	Spanish-American War

Organizations

American G.I. Forum
League of United Latin American Citizens

Other related articles

Chicago (Ethnic groups)	Minority group
Immigration	New York City (Ethnic groups)
Los Angeles (Ethnic groups; picture)	San Antonio
	Texas Rangers

Index

How to use the index

This index covers the contents of the 1988, 1989, and 1990 editions of *The World Book Year Book.*

There are two basic kinds of index entries. One kind of entry is followed immediately by an edition year and a page number, as:

Hungary, 90-326

This means that an article on Hungary begins on page 326 of the 1990 *Year Book.*

The other kind of entry has a key word or words between it and the edition year, as:

Iowa, **U.S.S.:** armed forces, 90-175

This means that information about the ship U.S.S. *Iowa* can be found on page 175 of the **Armed forces** article in the 1990 *Year Book.*

The "See" and "See also" cross-references are to other entries within the index, as:

U.S.S.R. See **Union of Soviet Socialist Republics.**

Clue words or phrases are used when two or more references to the same subject appear in the same edition of *The Year Book,* as:

Brain: health and disease, 90-321; psychology, 90-420

The indication "il." means that the reference is to an illustration only, as:

Eiffel Tower: il., 90-311

An index entry followed by "WBE" refers to a new or revised *World Book Encyclopedia* article in the supplement section, as:

Hispanic Americans: WBE, 90-540

Index

Index

558

Index

Index

Index

Acknowledgments

The publishers acknowledge the following sources for illustrations. Credits read from top to bottom, left to right, on their respective pages. An asterisk (*) denotes illustrations and photographs that are the exclusive property of *The Year Book*. All maps, charts, and diagrams were prepared by *The Year Book* staff unless otherwise noted.

4   © Al Grillo, Picture Group; © Shooting Star; © Gilles Peress, Magnum
5   LaJet Energy Company; © Scott Manchester, Sipa Press; © John Running, After-Image
9   © Robert Wallis, Sipa Press
10   © Chesnot, Sipa Press
11   © J. Leighton, Reflex; © DPA from Photoreporters
12   © McNamee, Sipa Press
13   AP/Wide World; © Brad Markel, Gamma/Liaison
14   © Paul O'Driscoll, Gamma/Liaison; © Charlie Cole, Picture Group
16   © Al Grillo, Picture Group
17   © MGM from Shooting Star
18   Syndication International Ltd.
20   Agence France-Presse
21   AP/Wide World
22   Moradabadi/Reflex from Picture Group
23   © J. Langevin, Sygma; AP/Wide World
24   © Daniel Simon, Gamma/Liaison
25   © Laski, Sipa Press
26   Jet Propulsion Laboratory
27   © Vlastimir Shone, Gamma/Liaison
28   © Roger W. Yargo, *Los Angeles Daily News* from Sygma
29   © Witt, Sipa Press; © Bob McNeely, Sipa Press
30   © Paul Scott, Sygma
31   Focus on Sports
32   © Trippett, Sipa Press
33   © Scott Andrews, Sipa Press; © DPA from Photoreporters
34   © Sipa Press; © Andy Hernandez, Sipa Press
35   © Sygma
37   © Cass Germany
38   © Bob Armstrong, Animals Animals
41   © Cass Germany; Allison Leete, Los Angeles Zoo
44-45   © Wendy Shattil and Bob Rozinski
46   © Carl Koford, NAS from Photo Researchers; © Tom Mangelsen
47   Johnny Johnson, DRK Photo
50   National Park Service; © Wendy Shattil and Bob Rozinski; © Ron Garrison, Zoological Society of San Diego
52   © Bates Littlehales, Animals Animals; Jeff Foott
55   AP/Wide World
57   © Sygma; © Zoja Pictures from Gamma/Liaison
61   © Joe Traver, Gamma/Liaison; © David Burnett, Contact
62   © Chris Niedenthal, *Time* Magazine; © David Burnett, Contact
65   © Laski, Sipa Press
66   © George Merillon, Gamma/Liaison
68   © Peter Turnley, Black Star
70   Roberta Polfus*; Culver
71   © Shooting Star
72   Roberta Polfus*; *World Book* photo
75   RCA
77   FPG; Photofest; Culver; Photofest
78   © Shooting Star; UPI/Bettmann Newsphotos; Photofest; NASA
79   Group W Cable
80   © Warner Brothers, Inc. All Rights Reserved; © Al Tielemans, Duomo; Ken Regan, Camera 5; Photofest
81   © Lawrence Migdale
82   © Enrico Ferorelli
83   Trudy Rogers*
87   Roberta Polfus*
88   Gamma/Liaison; © Robin Laurance
92   Roberta Polfus*
93   © Jay Brousseau
94   © Hank Morgan; © Chuck O'Rear, Westlight
96   © Gilles Peress, Magnum
99   © Eugene Richards, Magnum; Shepard Sherbell, Picture Group
100   © Yvonne Hemsley, Gamma/Liaison; © Eli Reed, Magnum
103   © Tony Savino, Sipa Press; © Ricki Rosen, Picture Group
104   © Rob Nelson; © Eli Reed, Magnum
109   © Al Francekevich, The Stock Market
113   Greg Steele*
114   © Juan-Pablo Lira, The Image Bank; © Grafton M. Smith, The Image Bank; Greg Steele*; Donna Bise, Photo Researchers
115   Greg Steele*; © Joe Sterling, Click/Chicago
116   Tom Jelen Photography from Nawrocki Stock Photo; Greg Steele*; Greg Steele*
117   Department of Energy
119   LaJet Energy Company; Greg Steele*
120   Greg Steele*; Lawrence Livermore National Laboratory; University of Utah

124   © Keith-Nels Swenson, Greenpeace
126   © Brian Storey
127   © Wolfe, Allstock from Picture Group
128   © NRSC/NOAA
131-132   © Keith-Nels Swenson, Greenpeace
133   © Ian Dalziel, Institute for Geophysics, University of Texas
134   © Keith-Nels Swenson, Greenpeace; © Russ Kinne, National Science Foundation; © Mark Muller, National Science Foundation
137   © Keith-Nels Swenson, Greenpeace; © Pat Morrow
138   © Ian Dalziel, Institute for Geophysics, University of Texas
140-141   © Scott McKiernan
143   Roberta Polfus*
144   © Enrico Ferorelli
148   © Thomas Bouchard, Minnesota Center for Twin and Adoption Research
150   Bettmann Archive
151   © Tardy-Perrin, Gamma/Liaison; AP/Wide World; Bettmann Archive
155   AP/Wide World
156   Quality Inns International, Inc.
158   AP/Wide World
163   © Betty Press
164   © Michael Grecco, Picture Group
167   © Patrick Aventurier, Gamma/Liaison
168   © 1989; Reprinted courtesy Hoest and *Parade* magazine
169   AP/Wide World
170   Jonathan Player
172   © N'Diaye, Imapress; © Nathaniel Lieberman
174   Bill Sikes, Sygma
175   AP/Wide World
176   U.S. Air Force
178   Phil Greer, *Chicago Tribune*; © Copyrighted, Chicago Tribune Company, all rights reserved, used with permission
179   AP/Wide World
180   © Novosti from Sygma
183   © Anderson, Gamma/Liaison
184   Jet Propulsion Laboratory
186   Peter O'Halloran
187   © Sichov, Sipa Press
190   AP/Wide World
191   Luc Novovitch, Gamma/Liaison
192   AP/Wide World
194   © Alan Davidson, LGI
196   © Fox Broadcasting Company
198   © Miladinovic, Sipa
199   From *The Wall Street Journal*—permission, Cartoon Features Syndicate
202   © Ed Calwell, Duomo
204   © John McDonough, *Sports Illustrated*
207   Lawrence Berkeley Laboratory
209   © David R. Frazier Photolibrary
211   Reuters/Bettmann Newsphotos
213   © Lenscape Incorporated
215   © Trippett, Sipa Press
216-217   AP/Wide World
218   © J. Langevin, Sygma
219   Canapress
220   Greg Steele*
221   Canapress
226   AP/Wide World
228   © Copyrighted, Chicago Tribune Company, all rights reserved, used with permission
229-231   AP/Wide World
232   © J. Langevin, Sygma
233   AP/Wide World
234   Ray Fairall, Photoreporters
238   © Alan Weiner, Gamma/Liaison
240   © Beatriz Schiller
243   © Timothy Ross, Picture Group
244   Greg Steele*
245   © 1989; Reprinted courtesy of Hoest and *Parade* magazine
246-251   AP/Wide World
252   Raul De Molina, Shooting Star
254   Steve Jackson, *Time* Magazine
256   AP/Wide World
258   © S. Record, Sipa Press
261   © Tajo, Sipa Press
262-264   © Jack Vartoogian
265   © T. Matsumoto, Sygma; AP/Wide World; AP/Wide World; Canapress
266   AP/Wide World; AP/Wide World; UPI/Bettmann Newsphotos; Bettmann Archive

267 A.S.P. from Tom Stack & Assoc.; AP/Wide World; UPI/
    Bettmann Newsphotos; AP/Wide World
268 Bettmann Archive
269 AP/Wide World; © J. Andanson, Sygma; AP/Wide World;
    UPI/Bettmann Newsphotos
270 © Andy Hernandez, Sygma; Yelena Bonner, Gamma/Liaison;
    AP/Wide World; UPI/Bettmann Newsphotos
271 Jerry Bauer; AP/Wide World; UPI/Bettmann Newsphotos;
    © François Guenet, Gamma/Liaison
272 AP/Wide World
273 © Sipa Press
275 AP/Wide World
277 © Scott Manchester, Sipa Press; © Scott Manchester, Sipa
    Press; © Lysaght, Gamma/Liaison
278 © Valdez, Sipa Press
279 Greg Steele*
281 © Vlastimir Shone, Gamma/Liaison
282 Greg Steele*
283 © Dirck Halstead, Gamma/Liaison
284 AP/Wide World
286 From The Wall Street Journal— permission, Cartoon Features
    Syndicate
287 © Cynthia Johnson, Gamma/Liaison
289 © P. F. Bentley, Photoreporters
290 California Energy Company
293 © Jim Lukoski, JB Pictures
294 © Randy Brandon, Sipa Press
295 © Michael Baytoff, Black Star
297-300 AP/Wide World
302 Greg Steele*
303 AP/Wide World
305 Reprinted by permission of NEA, Inc.
307 © Rick Stewart, Allsport
311 AP/Wide World
313 Reuters/Bettmann Newsphotos
316 Syndication International Ltd.
318 AP/Wide World
319 Focus on Sports
321 Greg Steele*
322 Steve Simon, The Edmonton Journal
324 © Copyrighted, Chicago Tribune Company, all rights re-
    served, used with permission
325 Gaylon Wampler
327 Eric Bouvet, Gamma/Liaison
328 © Vandystadt, Allsport
329 Reuters/Bettmann Newsphotos
330 Karen Zimmerman, University of South Dakota
331 Reuters/Bettmann Newsphotos
334-335 AP/Wide World
337 © Brian Hendler, Picture Group
340 AP/Wide World
341 © Shigeo Kogure, Time Magazine
342 © S. Mackstrand, AFP
345 © C. K. Kim
347-348 AP/Wide World
350 Reuters/Bettmånn Newsphotos
351 © Carlos Angel, Gamma/Liaison; UPI/Bettmann Newsphotos
355 AP/Wide World
356 Reuters/Bettmann Newsphotos
357 American Library Association
359 © Terry O'Neill, Sygma
361 © Jacques Chenet, Woodfin Camp, Inc.
362 R. Maiman, Sygma
364 Ralph Brunke*
365 From Song and Dance Man by Karen Ackerman, illustrated
    by Stephen Gammell. Copyright © 1988 by Karen Ackerman.
    Reprinted by permission of Alfred A. Knopf, Inc.
367 Reprinted from September 1989 MIRABELLA, © 1989 Mur-
    doch Magazines, All Rights Reserved. (Cover photo by Guz-
    man)
370 IBM Europe
372 HERMAN Copyright 1989 Universal Press Syndicate. Re-
    printed with permission. All rights reserved.
373 Lawrence Berkeley Laboratory, University of California
376 Sygma
379 Reuters/Bettmann Newsphotos
381 William Cambell, Sygma
383 © 1989 Tri-Star Pictures
385 © Warner Bros. Inc.
386 Gamma/Liaison
389 AP/Wide World
391 Copyright 1989 Disney
392 AP/Wide World
393 © Richard Termine, Children's Television Network
394 © David Kennerly, Gamma/Liaison
395 © Karen A. McCormack
398 AP/Wide World
400 © 1989 Columbus-America Discovery Group, Inc.
405 Agence France-Presse
407 Bill Staley*
408 Ron Levy, Gamma/Liaison
410 Agence France-Presse
412 AP/Wide World
413 © Todd Kaplan, Star File
414 © Charles Martin, Star File
417 Canapress
418 Ira Wyman, Sygma
420 © 1989; Reprinted courtesy Hoest and Parade magazine
423 Blanche, Gamma/Liaison
424 Steve Liss, Gamma/Liaison
426 © Druszczz, Agence France-Presse
427-429 AP/Wide World
430 © Sicnoy, Sipa Press
433-436 AP/Wide World
437 Time Magazine
438 McDonnell Douglas
441 © Darcy Kiefel
443 South Dakota Centennial Commission
447 Greg Steele*
449 © Dennis Brack, Black Star
450 Sygma
453 Reprinted with permission of Rex F. May
455 Freelance Photographers Guild
456 Tony Esparza, Columbia Broadcasting System
457 © 1989 Warner Bros. Inc. All Rights Reserved
458 AP/Wide World
460 © Martha Swope
461 © 1989 Martha Swope
463 © Chad Slattery
465 © Gary Williams, Gamma/Liaison
466 © James D. Wilson, Newsweek from Woodfin Camp, Inc.
469 AP/Wide World
470 Reuters/Bettmann Newsphotos
472 AP/Wide World
476 Greg Steele*
479 Jessie Cohen, National Zoological Park, Smithsonian
    Institution
482 Nina Berman, © Sipa Press
484 © Steve Winter, Gamma/Liaison
487 © Rich Addicks, Atlanta Journal and Constitution
489 Archives and Manuscripts Division, Oklahoma Historical
    Society (L. Michael Smith)
490 Penn Central Railroad Collection, Pennsylvania State
    Archives
493 Jane Addams Memorial Collection, Special Collections Li-
    brary, University of Illinois at Chicago; Donna Kae Nelson*
494 Bild-Archiv der Osterreichischen Nationalbibliothek, Wien;
    Austrian National Tourist Office
495 Archives and Manuscripts Division, Oklahoma Historical
    Society (L. Michael Smith); Archives and Manuscripts
    Division, Oklahoma Historical Society; Western History
    Collection, University of Oklahoma Library
496 Donna Kae Nelson*
497 Brown Bros.; Bettmann Archive; Brown Bros.
498-499 Donna Kae Nelson*
500 Donna Kae Nelson*; © ND-Viollet; © Roger-Viollet;
    © Roger-Viollet
501 © Roger-Viollet; The Newberry Library; AP/Wide World
502 World Book photo
503 AP/Wide World
504 Donna Kae Nelson*

Family milestones of 1989

In the preceding pages, *The World Book Year Book* reported the major events and trends of 1989. Use these two pages to record the developments that made the year memorable for *your* family.

Family members (names)	Ages	Family pets
_____	_____	_____
_____	_____	_____
_____	_____	_____
_____	_____	_____
_____	_____	_____
_____	_____	_____
_____	_____	_____

Births (name)	Date	Where born	Weight	Height
_____	_____	_____	_____	_____
_____	_____	_____	_____	_____
_____	_____	_____	_____	_____

Weddings (names)	Date	Where held
_____	_____	_____
_____	_____	_____
_____	_____	_____

Religious events _____ _____
_____ _____

Graduations _____ _____
_____ _____

Anniversaries _____ _____
_____ _____

In memoriam
Awards, honors,
and prizes _____ _____
_____ _____
_____ _____
_____ _____

Sports and club
achievements _____ _____
_____ _____

Vacations
and trips _____ _____
_____ _____

Most enjoyable books

_____
_____
_____
_____
_____

Most-played recordings and tapes

_____
_____
_____
_____
_____

Most unforgettable motion pictures

_____
_____
_____
_____
_____

Most-watched television programs

_____
_____
_____
_____
_____

Paste a favorite family photograph
or snapshot here.

Date

_____

Location

_____

Occasion

_____
_____

World Book Encyclopedia, Inc., provides high-quality educational and reference products for the family and school. They include Science Year, which presents information about developments in science and technology; The World Book Medical Encyclopedia, a 1,040-page, fully illustrated family health reference; the Student Information Finder and How to Study Video, a fast-paced video presentation of key study skills, with information students need to succeed in school; and Put Your Best Foot Forward With the Alphabet Pals™, a book, audio tape, and activity-based program designed to help young children develop good behavior and proper manners. For further information, write to World Book Encyclopedia, Inc., P.O. Box 3074, Evanston, IL 60204-3074.